3rd Edition

파고다교육그룹 언어교육연구소 | 저

PAGODA TOEFL

80+ Listening

PAGODA Books

목차

이 책의 구성과 특징

>> New TOEFL 변경사항 및 최신 출제 유형 완벽 반영!

2023년 7월부터 변경된 새로운 토플 시험을 반영, iBT TOEFL® 80점 이상을 목표로 하는 학습자를 위해 최근 iBT TOEFL®의 출제 경향을 완벽하게 반영한 문제와 주제를 골고루 다루고 있습니다.

>> 배경 지식을 통한 Lecture 내용 파악!

각 Lecture 단원의 Lesson에 등장하는 지문 주제들의 주요 배경 지식과 어휘 등을 정리하여 Lecture의 이해도를 높일 수 있도록 구성하였습니다.

>> 전체 미국인 버전과 미국인+영국인 버전 두 가지 음원 QR코드&온라인 다운로드로 제공!

iBT TOEFL® Listening 영역 듣기에서는 주로 미국인 성우들이 등장하지만, 때에 따라서는 영국인 성우가 일부 등장하는 경우가 있습니다. 이에 따라 학습자들의 학습 편의와 효과적인 시험 대비를 위해 본 교재에서는 2가지 유형의 듣기 음원을 제공하고 있습니다.

- 전체 미국인 성우 버전 음원: 보다 익숙한 발음으로 듣기 연습을 하고 싶은 학습자분들을 위해 모든 내용을 미국인 성우가 녹음한 버전입니다.
- 미국인 + 영국인 버전: 실제 Listening 시험에서의 미국인과 영국인 음성 비중을 반영하여, 미국인 성우와 함께 영국인 성우가 일부 포함된 버전입니다.

모든 음원은 모바일/태블릿에서 다운로드 없이 바로 듣기 가능한 QR 코드(교재 내 해당 유닛 페이지 수록) 인증 방식과, PC를 사용하여 온라인 홈페이지를 통한 MP3 파일 다운로드 방식으로 제공됩니다. 파고다북스 홈페이지를 통해 MP3 파일을 다운로드 받으실 경우, 전체 내용을 하나의 파일로 묶은 통파일, 원활한 복습을 위해 문제별로 나뉜 분할 음원 파일을 제공합니다.

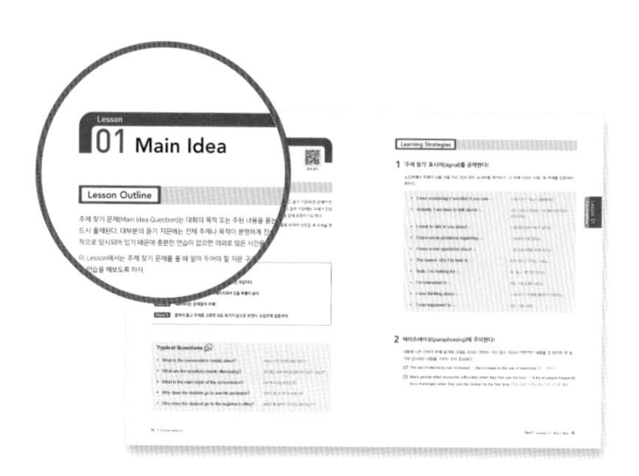

Lesson Outline & Learning Strategies

각각의 문제 유형을 살펴보고, iBT TOEFL® 전문 연구원이 제안하는 효과적인 문제풀이 전략과 예시 문제 학습을 통해 정답을 찾는 능력을 배양합니다.

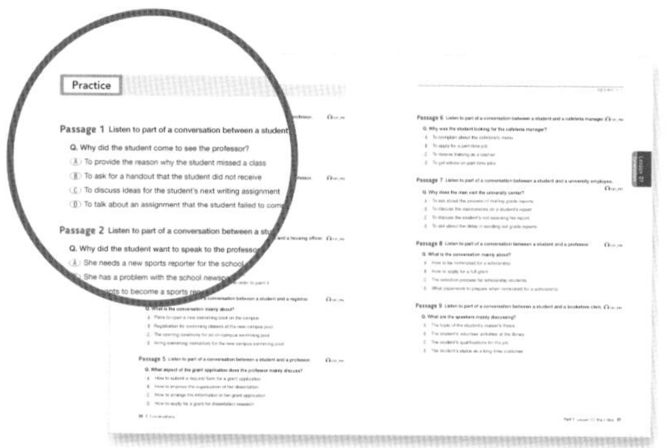

Practice

앞에서 배운 Lesson별 문제풀이 전략을 적용하여, 점진적으로 난이도가 높아지는 연습문제를 풀어보며 해당 문제 유형을 집중 공략합니다.

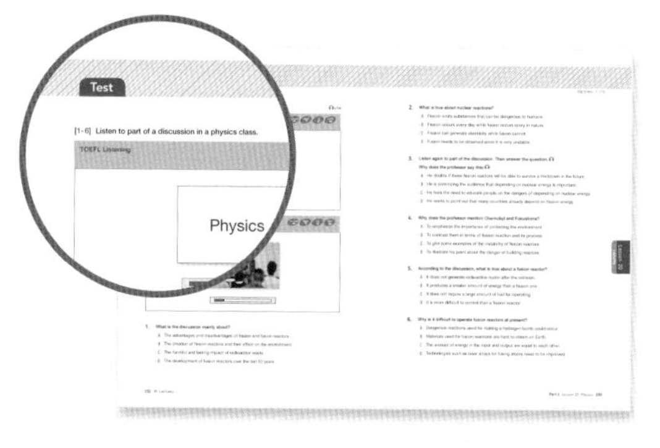

Test

실전과 유사한 유형과 난이도로 구성된 연습문제를 풀며 iBT TOEFL® 실전 감각을 익힙니다.

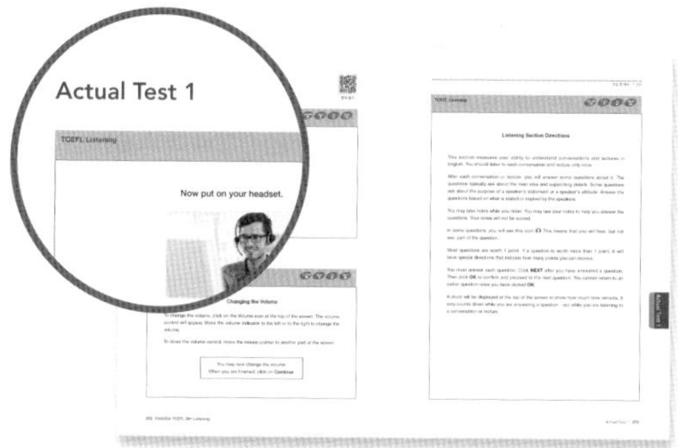

Actual Test

실제 시험과 동일하게 구성된 3회분의 Actual Test를 통해 실전에 대비합니다.

6주 완성 학습 플랜

DAY 1	DAY 2	DAY 3	DAY 4	DAY 5
Diagnostic Test	Conversations | Part 1. Conversation Question Types			
	Introduction & Tips Lesson 01 Main Idea	Lesson 02 Details	Lesson 03 Function & Attitude	Lesson 04 Connecting Contents
DAY 6	**DAY 7**	**DAY 8**	**DAY 9**	**DAY 10**
	Conversations | Part 2. Conversation Topic Types			
Lesson 05 Inference	Lesson 01 Office Hours	Lesson 02 Service-Related	Section Review • 지문 다시 듣기 • 어휘 재정리 하기	Introduction & Tips Lesson 01 Main Idea
DAY 11	**DAY 12**	**DAY 13**	**DAY 14**	**DAY 15**
Lectures | Part 1. Lecture Question Types				
Lesson 02 Details	Lesson 03 Function & Attitude	Lesson 04 Connecting Contents	Lesson 05 Inference	Lesson 01 Anthropology Lesson 02 Archaeology
DAY 16	**DAY 17**	**DAY 18**	**DAY 19**	**DAY 20**
Lectures | Part 2. Lecture Topic Types				
Lesson 03 Architecture Lesson 04 Art	Lesson 05 Astronomy Lesson 06 Biology	Lesson 07 Chemistry Lesson 08 Communications	Lesson 09 Economics Lesson 10 Engineering	Lesson 11 Environmental Science Lesson 12 Film Studies
DAY 21	**DAY 22**	**DAY 23**	**DAY 24**	**DAY 25**
Lectures | Part 2. Lecture Topic Types				
Lesson 13 Geology Lesson 14 History	Lesson 15 Linguistics Lesson 16 Literature	Lesson 17 Music Lesson 18 Paleontology	Lesson 19 Photography Lesson 20 Physics	Lesson 21 Physiology Lesson 22 Psychology Lesson 23 Sociology
DAY 26	**DAY 27**	**DAY 28**	**DAY 29**	**DAY 30**
	Actual Test			
Section Review • 배경 지식 읽기 • 어휘 재정리 하기	Actual Test 1 & Test Review • 틀린 문제 확인하기 • 어휘 재정리 하기	Actual Test 2 & Test Review • 틀린 문제 확인하기 • 어휘 재정리 하기	Actual Test 3 & Test Review • 틀린 문제 확인하기 • 어휘 재정리 하기	Actual Test 1~3 Test Review • 틀린 문제 확인하기 • 어휘 재정리 하기

iBT TOEFL® 개요

1. iBT TOEFL® 이란?

TOEFL은 영어 사용 국가로 유학을 가고자 하는 외국인들의 영어 능력을 평가하기 위해 개발된 시험이다. TOEFL 시험 출제 기관인 ETS는 이러한 TOEFL 본연의 목적에 맞게 문제의 변별력을 더욱 높이고자 PBT(Paper-Based Test), CBT(Computer-Based Test)에 이어 차세대 시험인 인터넷 기반의 iBT(Internet-Based Test)를 2005년 9월부터 시행하고 있다. ETS에서 연간 30~40회 정도로 지정한 날짜에 등록함으로써 치르게 되는 이 시험은 Reading, Listening, Speaking, Writing 총 4개 영역으로 구성되며 총 시험 시간은 약 2시간이다. 각 영역별 점수는 30점으로 총점 120점을 만점으로 하며 성적은 시험 시행 약 4~8일 후에 온라인에서 확인할 수 있다.

2. iBT TOEFL®의 특징

1) 영어 사용 국가로 유학 시 필요한 언어 능력을 평가한다.

각 시험 영역은 실제 학업이나 캠퍼스 생활에 반드시 필요한 언어 능력을 측정한다. 평가되는 언어 능력에는 자신의 의견 및 선호도 전달하기, 강의 요약하기, 에세이 작성하기, 학술적인 주제의 글을 읽고 내용 이해하기 등이 포함되며, 각 영역에 걸쳐 고르게 평가된다.

2) Reading, Listening, Speaking, Writing 전 영역의 통합적인 영어 능력(Integrated Skill)을 평가한다.

시험이 4개 영역으로 분류되어 있기는 하지만 Speaking과 Writing 영역에서는 [Listening + Speaking], [Reading + Listening + Speaking], [Reading + Listening + Writing]과 같은 형태로 학습자가 둘 또는 세 개의 언어 영역을 통합해서 사용할 수 있는지를 평가한다.

3) Reading 지문 및 Listening 스크립트가 길다.

Reading 지문은 700단어 내외로 A4용지 약 1.5장 분량이며, Listening은 3~4분 가량의 대화와 6~8분 가량의 강의로 구성된다.

4) 전 영역에서 노트 필기(Note-taking)를 할 수 있다.

긴 지문을 읽거나 강의를 들으면서 핵심 사항을 간략하게 적어두었다가 문제를 풀 때 참고할 수 있다. 노트 필기한 종이는 시험 후 수거 및 폐기된다.

5) 선형적(Linear) 방식으로 평가된다.

응시자가 시험을 보는 과정에서 실력에 따라 문제의 난이도가 조정되어 출제되는 CAT(Computer Adaptive Test) 방식이 아니라, 정해진 문제가 모든 응시자에게 동일하게 제시되는 선형적인 방식으로 평가된다.

6) 시험 응시일이 제한된다.

시험은 주로 토요일과 일요일에만 시행되며, 시험에 재응시할 경우, 시험 응시일 3일 후부터 재응시 가능하다.

7) Performance Feedback이 주어진다.

온라인 및 우편으로 발송된 성적표에는 수치화된 점수뿐 아니라 각 영역별로 수험자의 과제 수행 정도를 나타내는 표도 제공된다.

3. iBT TOEFL®의 구성

시험 영역	Reading, Listening, Speaking, Writing
시험 시간	약 2시간
시험 횟수	연 30~40회(날짜는 ETS에서 지정)
총점	0~120점
영역별 점수	각 영역별 30점
성적 확인	응시일로부터 4~8일 후 온라인에서 성적 확인 가능

시험 영역	문제 구성	시간
Reading	• 독해 지문 2개, 총 20문제가 출제된다. • 각 지문 길이 700단어 내외, 지문당 10개 문제	36분
Listening	• 대화(Conversation) 2개(각 5문제씩)와 강의(Lecture) 3개(각 6문제씩)가 출제된다.	36분
Break		10분
Speaking	• 독립형 과제(Independent Task) 1개, 통합형 과제(Integrated Task) 3개 총 4개 문제가 출제된다.	17분
Writing	• 통합형 과제(Integrated Task) 1개(20분) • 수업 토론형 과제 (Writing for Academic Discussion) 1개(9분)	30분

4. iBT TOEFL®의 점수

1) 영역별 점수

Reading	0~30	Listening	0~30
Speaking	0~30	Writing	0~30

2) iBT, CBT, PBT 간 점수 비교

기존에 있던 CBT, PBT 시험은 폐지되었으며, 마지막으로 시행된 CBT, PBT 시험 이후 2년 이상이 경과되어 과거 응시자의 시험 성적 또한 유효하지 않다.

5. 시험 등록 및 응시 절차

1) 시험 등록

온라인과 전화로 시험 응시일과 각 지역의 시험장을 확인하여 신청할 수 있으며, 일반 접수는 시험 희망 응시일 7일 전까지 가능하다.

❶ 온라인 등록

ETS 토플 등록 사이트(https://www.ets.org/mytoefl)에 들어가 화면 지시에 따라 등록한다. 비용은 신용카드로 지불하게 되므로 American Express, Master Card, VISA 등 국제적으로 통용되는 신용카드를 미리 준비해 둔다. 시험을 등록하기 위해서는 회원 가입이 선행되어야 한다.

❷ 전화 등록

한국 프로메트릭 콜센터(00-7981-4203-0248)에 09:00~17:00 사이에 전화를 걸어 등록한다.

2) 추가 등록

시험 희망 응시일 3일(공휴일을 제외한 업무일 기준) 전까지 US $60의 추가 비용으로 등록 가능하다.

3) 등록 비용

2023년 현재 US $220(가격 변동이 있을 수 있음)

4) 시험 취소와 변경

ETS 토플 등록 사이트나 한국 프로메트릭(00-7981-4203-0248)으로 전화해서 시험을 취소하거나 응시 날짜를 변경할 수 있다. 등록 취소와 날짜 변경은 시험 날짜 4일 전까지 해야 한다. 날짜를 변경하려면 등록 번호와 등록 시 사용했던 성명이 필요하며 비용은 US $60이다.

5) 시험 당일 소지품

❶ 사진이 포함된 신분증(주민등록증, 운전면허증, 여권 중 하나)

❷ 시험 등록 번호(Registration Number)

6) 시험 절차

❶ 사무실에서 신분증과 등록 번호를 통해 등록을 확인한다.

❷ 기밀 서약서(Confidentiality Statement)를 작성한 후 서명한다.

❸ 소지품 검사, 사진 촬영, 음성 녹음 및 최종 신분 확인을 하고 연필과 연습장(Scratch Paper)을 제공받는다.

❹ 감독관의 지시에 따라 시험실에 입실하여 지정된 개인 부스로 이동하여 시험을 시작한다.

❺ Reading과 Listening 영역이 끝난 후 10분간의 휴식이 주어진다.

❻ 시험 진행에 문제가 있을 경우 손을 들어 감독관의 지시에 따르도록 한다.

❼ Writing 영역 답안 작성까지 모두 마치면 화면 종료 메시지를 확인한 후에 신분증을 챙겨 퇴실한다.

7) 성적 확인

응시일로부터 약 4~8일 후부터 온라인으로 점수 확인이 가능하며, 시험 전에 종이 사본 수령을 신청했을 경우 약 11-15일 후 우편으로 성적표를 받을 수 있다.

6. 실제 시험 화면 구성

TOEFL

CONTINUE

General Test Information

This test measures you ability to use English in an academic context. There are 4 sections.

In the Reading section, you will answer questions to 2 reading passages.

In the Listening section, you will answer questions about 2 conversations and 3 lectures.

In the Speaking section, you will answer 4 questions. One of the questions asks you to speak about familiar topics. Other questions ask you to speak about lectures, conversations, and reading passages.

In the Writing section, you will answer 2 questions. The first question asks you to write about the relationship between a lecture you will hear and a passage you will read. The second questions asks you to write a response to an academic discussion topic.

There will be directions for each section which explain how to answer the question in that section.

Click Continue to go on.

전체 Direction

시험 전체에 대한 구성 설명

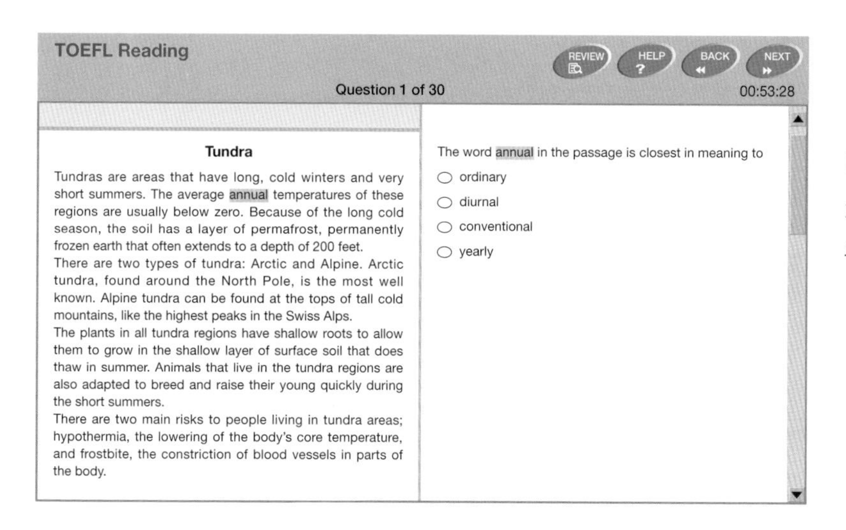

Reading 영역 화면

지문은 왼쪽에, 문제는 오른쪽에 제시

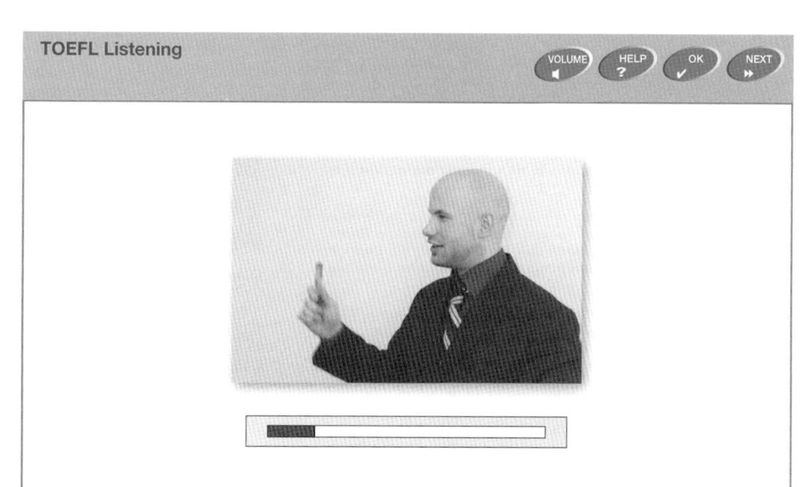

Listening 영역 화면

수험자가 대화나 강의를 듣는 동안 사진이 제시됨

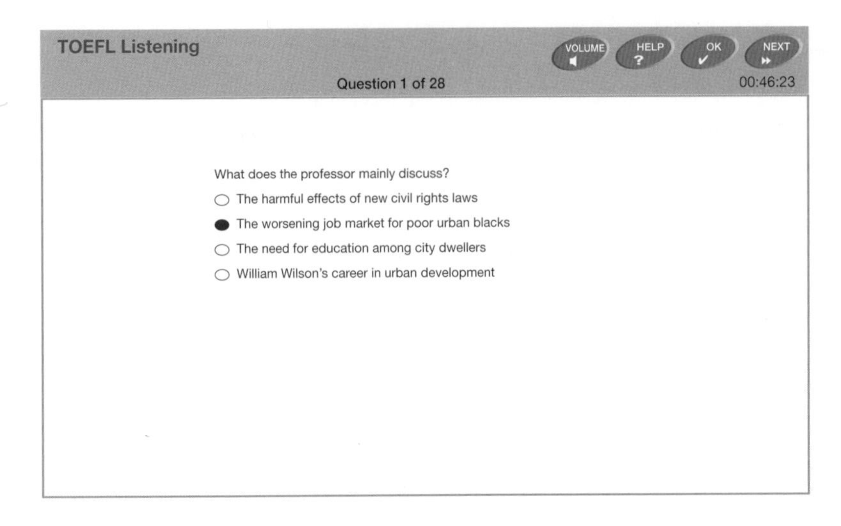

Listening 영역 화면

듣기가 끝난 후 문제 화면이 등장

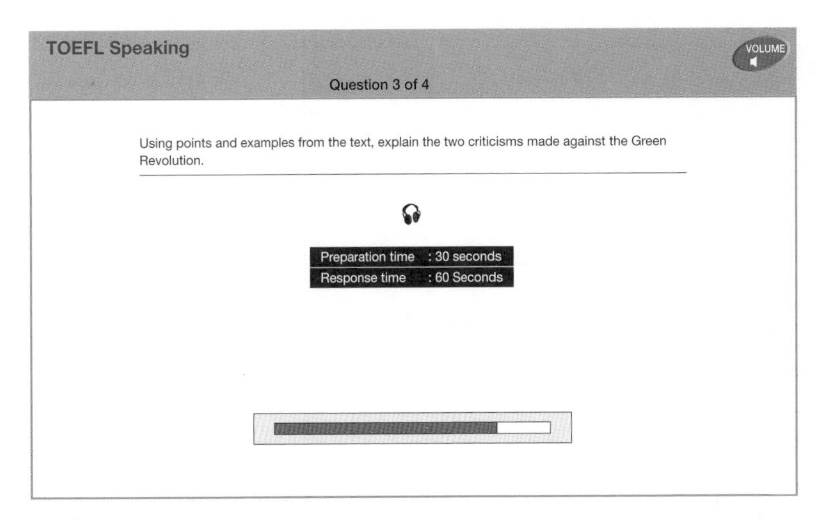

Speaking 영역 화면

문제가 주어진 후, 답변을 준비하는 시간과 말하는 시간을 알려줌

TOEFL Writing

VOLUME HELP NEXT

Question 1 of 2

In the late 14th century, an unknown poet from the Midlands composed four poems titled *Pearl*, *Sir Gawain and the Green Knight*, *Patience*, and *Cleanness*. This collection of poems is referred to as Cotton Nero A.x and the author is often referred to as the Pearl Poet. Up to this day, there have been many theories regarding the identity of this poet, and these are three of the most popular ones.

The first theory is that the author's name was Hugh, and it is based on the *Chronicle of Andrew of Wyntoun*. In the chronicle, an author called Hucheon (little Hugh) is credited with writing three poems, one of which is about the adventures of Gawain. Not only that, but all three poems are written in alliterative verse, as are all four of the poems in *Cotton Nero A.x*. Since they are written in the same style and one poem from each set concerns Gawain, some people contend that all of the *Cotton Nero A.x* poems were written by Hugh.

The second theory is that John Massey was the poet, and it is supported by another poem called *St. Erkenwald* and penmanship. Although the actual authorship of *St. Erkenwald* is unknown, John Massey was a poet who lived in the correct area and time for scholars to attribute it to him. This manuscript was written in very similar handwriting to that of the Pearl Poet, which indicates that one person is likely the author of all five of the poems.

The third theory is that the poems were actually written by different authors from the same region of England. This comes from the fact that there is little linking the poems to each other. Two are concerned with the Arthur legends, but the only link connecting the other two is that they describe the same area of the countryside. They also seem to be written in the same dialect. Taken together, these facts indicate that they were written in the same region, but they probably were not written by the same person.

Writing 영역 화면

왼쪽에 문제가 주어지고 오른쪽에 답을 직접 타이핑할 수 있는 공간이 주어짐

복사(Copy), 자르기(Cut), 붙여넣기(Paste) 버튼이 위쪽에 위치함

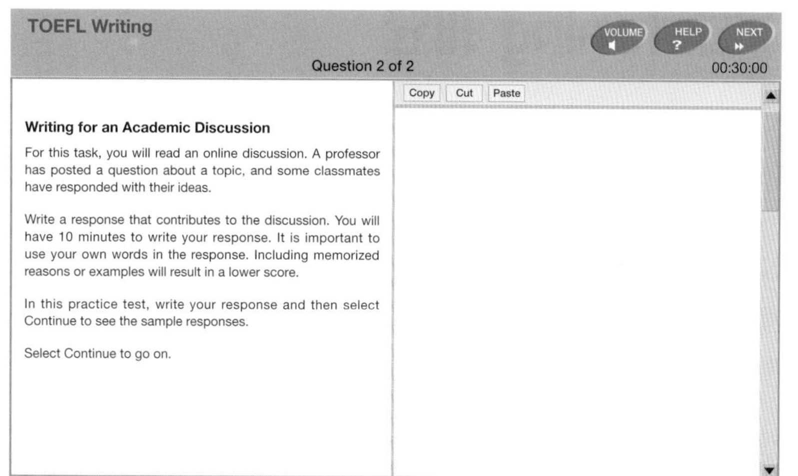

Writing 영역 화면

왼쪽에 문제가 주어지고 오른쪽에 답을 직접 타이핑할 수 있는 공간이 주어짐

복사(Copy), 자르기(Cut), 붙여넣기(Paste) 버튼이 위쪽에 위치함

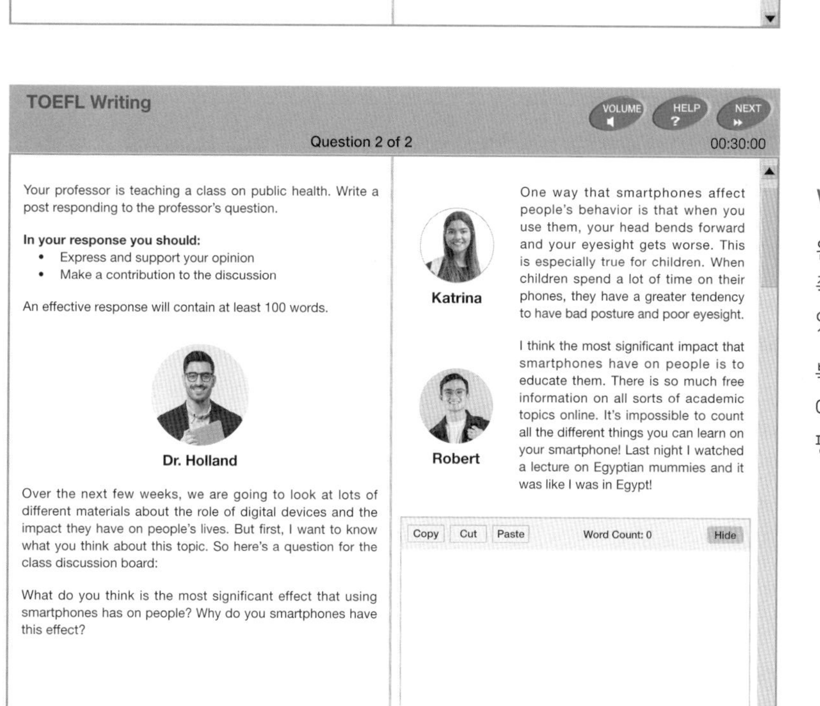

Writing 영역 화면

왼쪽에 문제가 주어지고 오른쪽에 답을 직접 타이핑할 수 있는 공간이 주어짐

복사(Copy), 자르기(Cut), 붙여넣기(Paste) 버튼이 타이핑하는 곳 위쪽에 위치함

iBT TOEFL® Listening 개요

1. Listening 영역의 구성

Listening 영역은 약 2개의 파트로 구분되며, 각 파트에는 대화(Conversation), 강의(Lecture) 및 토론(Discussion)의 청취 지문이 등장한다. 대화 지문은 2개가 출제되며, 강의 지문은 3개가 출제된다.

* Conversation 지문 2개, 지문당 각 5문제 출제

* Lecture 지문 3개, 지문당 각 6문제 출제

2. Listening 영역의 특징 및 학습 방법

1) 반드시 노트 필기를 한다.

iBT TOEFL®에서는 청취 지문을 듣는 동안 주어진 필기 용지(Scratch Paper)에 들은 내용을 필기할 수 있다. 따라서 강의나 토론과 같은 긴 지문을 들을 때, 기억력에 의존하기보다는 강의의 중요한 내용과 예측 가능한 문제의 답을 미리 노트 필기하면 문제의 정답을 좀 더 쉽게 찾을 수 있다.

2) 다양한 대화와 주제에 익숙해지자.

iBT TOEFL®은 실제 영어 사용 국가에서 학업을 할 수 있는 능력을 평가하는 TOEFL 본래의 목적에 충실하도록 변화한 만큼, 시험의 내용 또한 실제와 흡사하게 변화했다고 볼 수 있다. 대화의 내용이 좀 더 캠퍼스 상황으로 한정되었고, 대화와 강의의 길이가 길어졌으며, 주저하며 말하거나 대화 중간에 끼어든다거나 하는 자연스러운 청취 지문이 제시되고 있다. 발음에 있어서는 미국식 발음 외에 영국이나 호주식 발음도 가끔 청취 지문에 등장하여 다양한 언어가 사용되는 학업 상황을 좀 더 현실적으로 보여주고 있다.

3) 전체 내용을 이해한다.

iBT TOEFL®에서는 지문 전반의 내용을 이해하여 전체 주제를 찾거나(Main Idea Question) 또는 특정 정보의 상호 관계를 파악하는 문제(Connecting Content Question)가 많이 등장한다.

4) 억양이나 톤에 주의한다.

iBT TOEFL®에서 특히 눈에 띄는 문제 유형은 지문의 일부분을 다시 듣고 화자의 억양, 목소리 톤, 문맥상 전후 관계를 통해 정보에 대한 화자의 태도나 목적을 파악하는 문제 유형이다. 태도 파악 문제(Attitude Question)와 의도 파악 문제(Function Question)라고 불리는 이 문제 유형들은 지문의 의미 그 자체만으로 정답을 찾기보다는 특정 부분의 문맥상 의미를 파악하여 선택지에서 올바른 답을 골라야 한다.

3. Listening 영역의 문제 유형

iBT Listening 영역에서는 크게 5개의 문제 유형이 출제된다. 아래의 표는 Listening 영역의 문제를 유형별로 나누어 각 유형별 특징과 출제 문항 수를 표시해 놓은 것이다.

< iBT Listening 영역의 5가지 문제 유형>

주제 찾기 문제 Main Idea Question	강의나 대화의 목적 또는 전반적인 흐름을 묻는 문제 예) What is the conversation mainly about? 대화는 주로 무엇에 관한 것인가?
세부 사항 찾기 문제 Details Question	강의나 대화의 주요한 정보들에 관해 묻는 문제 예) What are the characteristics of ~? ~의 특징은 무엇인가?
의도 및 태도 파악 문제 Function & Attitude Question	화자가 특정 문장을 언급한 의도나 문장에 담긴 화자의 태도나 관점을 묻는 문제 예) Listen again to part of the conversation. Then answer the question. Why does the student say this: 대화의 일부를 다시 듣고 질문에 답하시오. 학생은 왜 이렇게 말하는가:
관계 파악 문제 Connecting Contents Question	강의나 대화에 주어진 정보들 간의 유기적 관계를 묻는 문제 (e.g. 인과, 비교, 추론하기, 결과 예측하기, 일반화하기) 예) Why does the professor say ~? 교수는 왜 ~라고 말하는가? In the conversation, the speakers discuss ~. Indicate in the table below ~. 대화에서 화자들은 ~에 대해 논의한다. ~인지 아래 표에 표시하시오.
추론 문제 Inference Question	강의나 대화를 통해 유추할 수 있는 것을 묻는 문제 예) What is the student most likely to do next? 학생이 다음에 무엇을 할 것 같은가?

4. 기존 시험과 개정 시험 간 Listening 영역 비교

	기존 iBT (2023년 7월 전)	개정 후 iBT (2023년 7월 이후)
지문 개수	대화 2~3개 강의 3~5개	대화 2개 강의 3개
지문당 문제 수	대화 각 5문제 강의 각 6문제	대화 각 5문제 강의 각 6문제
전체 시험 시간	41~57분	36분

• 지문 및 질문 유형은 기존과 동일하다.

Diagnostic Test

실제 TOEFL Listening 시험 구성과 유사한 진단 테스트를 풀어보면서 현재 내 실력이 얼마나 되는지, 내가 어려워하는 문제유형이 어떤 것인지 점검해 보자.

Diagnostic Test

TOEFL Listening

Now put on your headset.

Click on **Continue** to go on.

TOEFL Listening

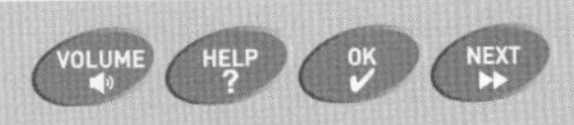

Changing the Volume

To change the volume, click on the Volume icon at the top of the screen. The volume control will appear. Move the volume indicator to the left or to the right to change the volume.

To close the volume control, move the mouse pointer to another part of the screen.

You may now change the volume.
When you are finished, click on **Continue**.

TOEFL Listening

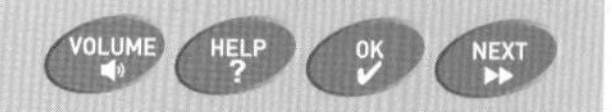

Listening Section Directions

This section measures your ability to understand conversations and lectures in English. You should listen to each conversation and lecture only once.

After each conversation or lecture, you will answer some questions about it. The questions typically ask about the main idea and supporting details. Some questions ask about the purpose of a speaker's statement or a speaker's attitude. Answer the questions based on what is stated or implied by the speakers.

You may take notes while you listen. You may use your notes to help you answer the questions. Your notes will not be scored.

In some questions, you will see this icon: 🎧 This means that you will hear, but not see, part of the question.

Most questions are worth 1 point. If a question is worth more than 1 point, it will have special directions that indicate how many points you can receive.

You must answer each question. Click **NEXT** after you have answered a question. Then click **OK** to confirm and proceed to the next question. You cannot return to an earlier question once you have clicked **OK**.

A clock will be displayed at the top of the screen to show how much time remains. It only counts down while you are answering a question - not while you are listening to a conversation or lecture.

Conversation 1

[1-5] Listen to part of a conversation between two students in their first class of the term. DT_01

1. What are the speakers mainly talking about?

Ⓐ 300 level courses that are good for taking as an elective

Ⓑ Required classes for a meteorology major

Ⓒ What they have planned for their future and career goals

Ⓓ Various career options for meteorology majors

2. Why does the woman say this: 🎧

Ⓐ She knows the man is doing something suspicious in the class.

Ⓑ She thinks that the man does not have to take an ecology course.

Ⓒ She believes that the class would be too hard for the man.

Ⓓ She feels glad to see the man in the class that she is taking.

3. Why is the man taking this course?

Ⓐ It is an elective course for a meteorology major.

Ⓑ It is a required course for an ecology minor.

Ⓒ It is important to him because he needs more credits.

Ⓓ It is enjoyable since he cares about the environment.

4. Why did the woman decide to major in meteorology?

Ⓐ She was inspired by a relative to become a weather forecaster.

Ⓑ She was heavily influenced by extreme weather conditions.

Ⓒ She wants to share information about it with other people.

Ⓓ She wanted a major that could provide her various job options.

5. What will the woman do next?

Ⓐ Consider what kind of field she wants to work in

Ⓑ Search for any kind of available jobs online

Ⓒ Go and see an advisor to talk about changing her major

Ⓓ Try to find an internship position that is related to her major

Lecture 1

[6-11] Listen to part of a discussion in an art class.

DT_02

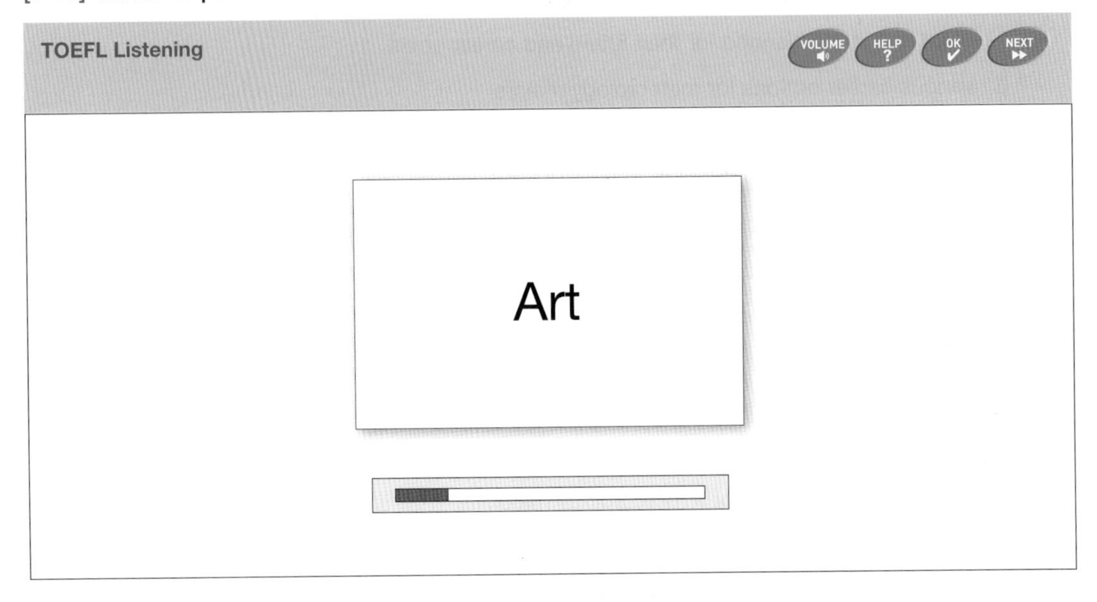

6. **What is the discussion mainly about?**

Ⓐ The origin of written languages in some regions

Ⓑ The characteristics and importance of petroglyphs

Ⓒ The study of petroglyphs and petrographs

Ⓓ The methods used for creating petroglyphs

7. **According to the discussion, what is one of the common motifs for petroglyphs?**

Ⓐ People who are planting and harvesting

Ⓑ Methods for gathering fruits and vegetables

Ⓒ Different stories regarding myths and history

Ⓓ Various tools that were used for hunting

8. **Listen again to part of the discussion. Then answer the question.**

Why does the student say this:

Ⓐ He thinks the professor is underestimating the societies of well-developed cultures.

Ⓑ He is not sure whether he is allowed to call their cultures primitive or not.

Ⓒ He is emphasizing that calling other cultures primitive could be insulting to them.

Ⓓ He wants to distinguish some prehistoric societies and cultures as primitive ones.

9. **According to the discussion, what is the difference between petroglyphs and petrographs?**
Choose 2 answers.

Ⓐ Harder material was used for petroglyphs.

Ⓑ Petroglyphs were more colorful than petrographs.

Ⓒ Petrographs are destroyed more easily.

Ⓓ Petroglyphs were more common than petrographs.

10. **Why does the professor mention chalk?**

Ⓐ To give an example of a common tool that ancient people used

Ⓑ To illustrate that it was helpful for adding finer details to images

Ⓒ To introduce a medium the people used for creating petroglyphs

Ⓓ To explain one of the older methods for recording petroglyphs

11. **According to the professor, what can be inferred about rock art?**

Ⓐ It represents people's highly developed skills in stone masonry.

Ⓑ It was found mostly in caves, which were located in remote regions.

Ⓒ It was usually very long, extending more than 2 meters.

Ⓓ It provides more information than bones do when studying prehistoric people.

Lecture 2

[12-17] Listen to part of a discussion in a biology class. DT_03

12. What is the main topic of the discussion?

Ⓐ How complex the theories regarding intelligent animals are

Ⓑ How humanity's perspective on intelligent species can have flaws

Ⓒ How five intelligent species are smarter than sheep

Ⓓ How scientists proved the intelligence of different animals

13. Why does the professor mention the top five intelligent animals?

Ⓐ To explain how they are related to the topic of the lecture

Ⓑ To continue the discussion regarding them from the last class

Ⓒ To check if the students finished their reading assignment

Ⓓ To describe how the lecture topic is influenced by them

14. According to the professor, what is the problem with human evaluation of animal intelligence?

Ⓐ Not enough animals were evaluated by scientists.

Ⓑ There are some traits that both humans and animals share.

Ⓒ The technology that mankind possess right now still needs improvement.

Ⓓ Humans have not evaluated animal behavior objectively.

15. What does the professor try to convey through the example of woodpeckers?

Ⓐ Observing animals in the wild can bring unexpected discoveries.

Ⓑ Holding on to one's belief regarding animal behavior can be difficult.

Ⓒ Trusting one's instinct is vital when it comes to examining animal intelligence.

Ⓓ Just because something is not visible, that doesn't mean it is not there.

16. Why does the professor say this: 🎧

Ⓐ He thinks people should reevaluate their own beliefs regarding dogs.

Ⓑ He feels sorry that dogs' wild cousins are not very intelligent.

Ⓒ He wants to know if the students really view any of these animals as smart.

Ⓓ He believes that dogs often show some resemblance to their cousins.

17. What can be inferred about sheep?

Ⓐ Their learning ability is far superior to that of dogs.

Ⓑ They showed startling behavior when exposed to unfamiliar surroundings.

Ⓒ Their evaluation as not-intelligent animals should be reconsidered.

Ⓓ They graze and move together in a disorganized fashion on purpose.

PAGODA TOEFL 80+ Listening

TOEFL Listening

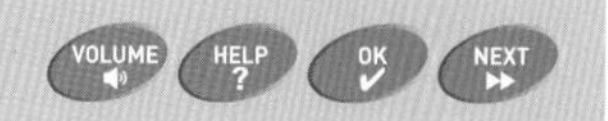

Listening Directions

You will now begin the next part of the Listening Section.

You must answer each question. After you answer, click on **NEXT**. Then click on **OK** to confirm your answer and go on to the next question. After you click on **OK**, you cannot return to previous questions.

Click on **CONTINUE** to go on.

Conversation 2

[1-5] Listen to part of a conversation between a student and a professor. DT_04

1. **Why does the student go to see the professor?**

Ⓐ To analyze the language development of his nephew

Ⓑ To propose a topic for a class paper

Ⓒ To share information about his fall break

Ⓓ To talk about a supplementary reading

2. **Why is the professor disappointed that the student couldn't read the reading?**

Ⓐ It was a required reading for the class.

Ⓑ It would have been greatly helpful to the student's paper topic.

Ⓒ It would have been useful for the student.

Ⓓ There will be no time to read it during the semester.

3. **Which of the following is true about the student's nephew? Choose 2 answers.**

Ⓐ He is currently towards the end of the second stage of language development.

Ⓑ He is mostly speaking in single-word utterances.

Ⓒ He understands his parents better than other speakers.

Ⓓ He will speak in very simple sentences for the next few months.

4. **Listen again to part of the lecture. Then answer the question.**

Why does the professor say this:

Ⓐ She cannot reduce the student's workload.

Ⓑ The student's interest and diligence is misplaced.

Ⓒ She expects the student's notes are not going to be very detailed.

Ⓓ She does not find his research proposal sufficient.

5. **What will the student most likely do next?**

Ⓐ He will look for secondary data to use in his paper.

Ⓑ He will go over his notes on his nephew.

Ⓒ He will reconsider his choice of topic.

Ⓓ He will make an outline for his paper that meets his professor's demands.

Lecture 3

[6-11] Listen to part of a lecture in a film class.

DT_05

6. What does the professor mainly talk about?

Ⓐ Some of romantic comedy's landmark feature films

Ⓑ Characteristics and types of romantic comedy

Ⓒ The roots and history of romantic comedy as a genre

Ⓓ The influence of various rom com sub genres on subsequent movements

7. **What is the professor's opinion on romantic comedies?**

Ⓐ She is relieved to see a few people enjoy the genre.

Ⓑ She believes that romantic comedies have been on the decline in recent years.

Ⓒ The genre doesn't suit her taste as much as other genres.

Ⓓ The genre receives more attention than it deserves.

8. **According to the lecture, how does romantic comedy find its roots in Shakespeare?**

Ⓐ Shakespeare worked with the interplay of romance and comedy in some of his plays.

Ⓑ *Much Ado About Nothing* provided the formula for modern romantic comedy films.

Ⓒ Shakespeare used comedy to make love stories less boring.

Ⓓ Shakespeare added physical humor, wordplay, and witty banter to some of his plays' tense moments.

9. **According to the lecture, which of the following is true of comedies of manners?**

Choose 2 answers.

Ⓐ Films from this genre lacked dialogue.

Ⓑ The films often dealt with issues of economic disparity.

Ⓒ They were among the first so-called "talkies" of the film industry.

Ⓓ The genre became popular around the time of the American Depression.

10. **According to the lecture, why were films such as *Bringing Up Baby* labeled as screwball comedies?**

Ⓐ The plots of these films can be compared to a certain type of baseball pitch.

Ⓑ Their films often featured an absurd blend of many comedy types.

Ⓒ Katharine Hepburn used the term in one of her most iconic films.

Ⓓ The characters in these films were often very unusual.

11. **What will the class most likely do next?**

Ⓐ The teacher will turn on a few more lights for the class.

Ⓑ They will learn about the neoclassical romantic comedies of the 90s.

Ⓒ They will read part of the script of *Lover Come Back*.

Ⓓ They will watch a clip from a romantic comedy the professor just mentioned.

I
Conversations

Introduction & Tips

Part 1. Conversation Question Types

Part 2. Conversation Topic Types

Conversations

Introduction

iBT TOEFL Listening Conversations

TOEFL Listening에서 대화(Conversation) 유형은 총 2~3개 출제된다. 보통 교수와 학생, 또는 대학교 직원과 학생의 대화를 다룬다. 보통 1 지문당 450~550단어의 길이로 이루어져 있으며(약 3분), 대화를 듣고 1~5번 문제를 풀게 된다. 필기용 종이가 제공되기 때문에 대화를 들으면서 노트 필기와 요약이 가능하다.

Conversation Question Types

대화 하나당 다섯 문제를 풀게 되며 문제 유형은 아래와 같이 총 다섯 가지이다.

1. **주제 찾기(Main Idea):** 대화의 주제·목적 찾기
2. **세부 사항 찾기(Details):** 대화를 들으며 알 수 있는 세부 내용 찾기
3. **의도 및 태도 파악(Function & Attitude):** 듣기 지문의 일부를 다시 듣고 화자가 어떠한 말을 한 이유 또는 무언가에 대한 화자의 태도 파악하기
4. **관계 파악(Connecting Contents):** 대화가 연결된 방식 또는 무언가가 언급된 이유 파악하기
5. **추론(Inference):** 대화를 통해 유추할 수 있는 내용 찾기

Conversation Topic Types

대화 주제는 크게 두 가지로 분류할 수 있다.

1. **집무 시간(Office Hours):** 교수·지도교수의 집무 시간에 교수 연구실에서 이루어지는 대화로, 주로 학생이 교수에게 성적과 과제, 전공·진로 상담, 인턴십, 취업 등에 관해 다양하게 묻는 내용이다. 때로는 교수가 학생을 불러 학업이나 과제와 관련해 묻는 대화도 있다.

2. **교내 서비스 관련(Service-Related):** 캠퍼스 내 모든 곳에서 이루어지는 대화로, 학생과 대학교 직원 간의 대화로 구성된다. 주로 도서관, 구내 식당, 기숙사 관련 내용이 많으며 교내 주차 문제부터 책 대출, 등록금 납부까지 다양한 문의 사항이 나온다.

Tips

이 대화의 주제·중심 내용이 무엇인가?

대화의 주제가 무엇인지 파악하지 못한다면 결코 그 대화를 잘 이해했다고 볼 수 없다. 대화의 주제와 중심 내용은 보통 대화가 시작되고 나서 거의 바로 확인할 수 있다. 학생이나 교수, 직원의 말을 통해 왜 이 대화가 이루어지고 있는지, 학생이 왜 찾아왔는지에 집중하자. 주제·중심 내용을 묻는 문제는 반드시 한 문제씩 출제되며 가장 기본적인 사항이므로 절대 놓치지 말자.

세부 정보를 파악하라!

주제·중심 내용을 알면 그에 맞춰 세부 정보를 파악할 수 있다. 세부 정보 문제 역시 대화 하나당 1~2개의 문제가 반드시 출제되므로 대화의 처음부터 끝까지 긴장을 놓지 말고 듣자. 세부 정보 문제로 많이 나오는 내용은 흔히 다음과 같다.

❶ 화자(주로 학생)의 문제

❷ 그 문제·상황이 발생한 원인과 이유

❸ 그 문제·상황을 해결하기 위한 방법·수단(주로 교수나 직원이 제안)

❹ 대화에서 등장한 예시·설명

❺ 그 외의 세부 정보

화자의 말투와 대화 분위기는 어떤가?

의도 및 태도 파악 문제(Function & Attitude Question)에서는 특히 화자의 말투와 대화의 분위기 등을 파악하는 내용이 많이 나온다. 대화를 듣고 있으면 문제점이나 고민 사항, 불만 내용 등을 알 수 있으며 그에 따라 화자의 어투와 분위기 역시 달라진다. 화자가 불만을 갖고 비꼬아서 말할 수도 있고, 화를 내거나 아쉬워하는 등 다양한 상황이 등장하므로 오가는 대화 속의 명확한 의미를 파악할 수 있도록 하자.

정답은 정직하게 출제되지 않는다!

대화에서 나온 단어가 문제 보기에 그대로 출제되는 경우는 거의 없다. 같은 내용이지만 다른 말로 약간 변화를 주며, 이 때문에 혼란이 올 수 있지만 단어 자체를 보지 말고 내용과 뜻에 집중하자. 이렇게 같은 의미를 다른 말로 바꿔 표현하는 것을 패러프레이징(paraphrasing)이라고 하며 Listening뿐만 아니라 Reading과 Writing, Speaking 영역에서도 흔히 나타난다. 수험자가 방심하도록 일부러 대화에서 등장한 단어와 똑같은 단어를 문제 보기에 출제할 때도 있다는 점을 명심하자.

Conversation Question Types

- Lesson 01 Main Idea
- Lesson 02 Details
- Lesson 03 Function & Attitude
- Lesson 04 Connecting Contents
- Lesson 05 Inference

Lesson

01 Main Idea

문제 듣기

Lesson Outline

주제 찾기 문제(Main Idea Question)는 대화의 목적 또는 주된 내용을 묻는 문제로, 모든 듣기 지문에 한 문제씩 반드시 출제된다. 대부분의 듣기 지문에는 전체 주제나 목적이 분명하게 진술되어 있으나 일부 지문에는 주제가 간접적으로 암시되어 있기 때문에 충분한 연습이 없으면 의외로 많은 시간을 소비하기 쉬운 문제 유형이기도 하다.

이 Lesson에서는 주제 찾기 문제를 풀 때 알아 두어야 할 지문 구조와, 답이 다른 말로 바뀌어 쓰였을 때 주제를 찾는 연습을 해보도록 하자.

Lesson Point

Point 1 도입부 + 표시어(signal) = 주제!

Point 2 너무 일반적이거나 너무 구체적인 보기는 오답이다.

Point 3 보기에서 키워드가 패러프레이즈되어 있을 확률이 높다.

Point 4 대화에서는 문제점이 주제!

Point 5 끝까지 듣고 주제를 고르면 모든 보기가 답으로 보인다. 도입부에 집중하자.

Typical Questions 

- What is the conversation mainly about? 대화는 주로 무엇에 관한 것인가?
- What are the speakers mainly discussing? 화자들은 주로 무엇에 관해 이야기하고 있는가?
- What is the main topic of the conversation? 대화의 주제는 무엇인가?
- Why does the student go to see his professor? 학생은 왜 교수를 찾아가는가?
- Why does the student go to the registrar's office? 학생은 왜 학적부 사무실을 찾아가는가?

Learning Strategies

1 '주제 찾기' 표시어(signal)를 공략한다!

도입부에서 주제가 나올 것을 미리 알려 주는 표시어를 파악하고, 그 뒤에 나오는 내용, 즉 주제를 집중해서 듣는다.

- I was wondering (I wonder) if you can ~. — ~해 주실 수 있는지 궁금해서요.
- Actually, I am here to talk about ~. — 사실, 제가 온 이유는 ~에 대해 이야기하기 위해서예요.
- I want to talk to you about ~. — ~에 대해 말씀 드리고 싶어요.
- I have some problems regarding ~. — ~에 문제가 좀 있어요.
- I have some questions about ~. — ~에 관해 여쭤볼 게 좀 있어요.
- The reason why I'm here is ~. — 제가 여기 온 이유는 ~예요.
- Yeah, I'm looking for ~. — 네, 저는 ~를 찾고 있어요.
- I'm interested in ~. — 저는 ~에 관심이 있어요.
- I was thinking about ~. — ~하려고/~에 대해 생각하고 있었어요.
- I was supposed to ~. — 저는 ~해야 해요.

2 패러프레이징(paraphrasing)에 주의한다!

대화에 나온 단어가 문제 보기에 그대로 쓰이는 경우는 거의 없다. 따라서 전반적인 내용을 잘 파악한 뒤 보기와 일치하는 내용을 고르는 것이 중요하다.

Ex The use of electricity has increased → the increase in the use of electricity [절 → 명사구]

Ex Many people often encounter difficulties when they first use the tool. → A lot of people frequently face challenges when they use the device for the first time. [동사/형용사/명사 등을 다른 단어로 대체]

Example

Woman: Professor | Man: Student

C01_EX

Listen to a conversation between a student and a professor.

W Hello, Joel, I'm glad you could find time to meet me.

M Of course, Professor. Is something wrong?

W Well, I sincerely hope not. You are aware that you were supposed to arrange a meeting with me to discuss your term paper, aren't you?

M Yes, but I don't remember when the deadline for scheduling the meeting was...

W It is tomorrow. So you can see why I was concerned. Have you made any progress on your paper?

M Oh! I'm so sorry! I thought I still had a week or so. But, yes, I have chosen my topic, and I have gotten started on my research.

W That is very good to hear. What have you selected as a topic to write about?

M Well, you said that we should write about the history of our neighborhoods. I grew up near a hat factory in Concord—maybe you are familiar with it?

W I think so, after all Concord is not far from here. Are you referring to Massachusetts Millinery?

M Yes, I am.

W That is a very good choice. That company has been around for a long time.

M Yes. It was founded nearly 150 years ago, in 1867.

W That is going to be a lot of history for you to cover. Have you decided on what type of focus to take to narrow down your perspective?

M Yes. Growing up in the shadow of the landmark has always made it feel like a part of my home. I want to focus more on the history of the owners' families than the business side of the factory, so I have been approaching it from a genealogical angle.

Q. Why did the professor want to see the student?

Ⓐ The student forgot the due date of his term paper and turned it in late.

Ⓑ She was worried that the student was still confused about the topic.

Ⓒ The student had not contacted her to discuss the progress of his paper.

Ⓓ She wanted to explain why she is not going to give the student extra time for the paper.

학생과 교수의 대화를 들으시오.

여 안녕, 조엘. 나와 만날 시간이 있다니 다행이네요.

남 그럼요, 교수님. 무슨 문제가 있나요?

여 음, 진심으로 없기를 바라요. 학생의 학기말 리포트를 논의하기 위해 나와 회의할 시간을 잡았어야 한다는 걸 알고 있죠, 그렇죠?

남 네, 하지만 회의 날짜를 정하기로 한 기한이 언제였는지 기억이 안 나네요...

여 내일이에요. 내가 왜 걱정했는지 알겠죠. 리포트에 어떤 진척이라도 있나요?

남 아! 정말 죄송해요! 아직 한 주 정도 더 시간이 있다고 생각했어요. 하지만, 네, 주제를 정했고 리서치를 시작했어요.

여 다행이네요. 무엇을 주제로 정해서 쓰기로 했나요?

남 음, 우리 근처 이웃의 역사에 대해 써야 한다고 말씀하셨죠. 저는 콩코드의 모자 공장 근처에서 자랐어요. 아마 교수님도 아실지 모르겠네요.

여 그런 것 같아요. 어쨌든 콩코드는 여기에서 멀지 않으니까요. 매사추세츠 여성용 모자 제작 공장에 대해 말하고 있는 건가요?

남 네, 맞아요.

여 매우 좋은 선택이네요. 그 회사는 꽤 오래된 곳이니까요.

남 네, 거의 150년 전인 1867년에 세워졌어요.

여 학생이 다루기에는 역사의 범위가 너무 넓을 텐데요. 관점을 좀 더 좁히기 위해 어디에 집중할지 결정했나요?

남 네, 이 역사적인 건물 근처에서 자랐다는 것이 이곳을 제가 저희 집의 일부처럼 느끼도록 만들었어요. 공장쪽 사업보다 공장 주인 가족들의 역사에 집중하고 싶고, 그래서 계보의 각도에서 접근했어요.

Q. 교수는 왜 학생을 보고자 했는가?

Ⓐ 학생이 학기말 리포트의 마감 기한을 잊어 제출을 늦게 했다.

Ⓑ 학생이 여전히 주제에 대해 헷갈려 했기에 걱정했다.

Ⓒ 학생이 리포트의 진척에 대해 논의하기 위한 연락을 하지 않았다.

Ⓓ 왜 학생에게 리포트 기한 연장을 해줄 수 없는지를 설명하고자 했다.

Lesson 01 Conversations

정답 (C)

해설 학생이 교수에게 무슨 문제가 있냐고 묻자 교수가 리포트를 논의할 회의 시간을 잡았어야 하는데 학생이 연락을 하지 않았다고 대화 도입부에 밝히고 있다. 따라서 정답은 (C)이다. 한편, (A)가 교묘하게 패러프레이즈되었다는 점을 발견할 수 있다. 학생이 리포트 자체를 제출하는 것이 아니라 리포트 논의를 위한 회의 시간을 잡는 것이 대화의 목적인데, '리포트 마감 기한'으로 내용이 살짝 바뀌어 출제되었다. 문제 보기들은 패러프레이징을 통해 본문에 쓰인 단어에서 살짝 바뀌어서 출제된다는 점을 항상 기억하고 보기를 주의 깊게 읽도록 하자.

어휘 sincerely adv 진심으로 | arrange v 마련하다, 주선하다 | discuss v 논의하다 | term paper 학기말 리포트 | deadline n 마감일 | concerned adj 염려하는 | progress n 진전, 진척 | millinery n 여성 모자 제작업/판매업 | narrow down 좁히다, 줄이다 | genealogical adj 족보의, 계보의

Practice

Passage 1 Listen to part of a conversation between a student and a professor.

C01_P01

Q. Why did the student come to see the professor?

Ⓐ To provide the reason why the student missed a class

Ⓑ To ask for a handout that the student did not receive

Ⓒ To discuss ideas for the student's next writing assignment

Ⓓ To talk about an assignment that the student failed to complete

Passage 2 Listen to part of a conversation between a student and a professor.

C01_P02

Q. Why did the student want to speak to the professor?

Ⓐ She needs a new sports reporter for the school newspaper.

Ⓑ She has a problem with the school newspaper's sports reporter.

Ⓒ She wants to become a sports reporter for the school newspaper.

Ⓓ She wants to create a sports section in the school newspaper.

Passage 3 Listen to part of a conversation between a student and a housing officer.

C01_P03

Q. What are the speakers discussing?

Ⓐ Hiring workmen to repaint the school dormitories

Ⓑ Problems with a painting in a dormitory room

Ⓒ Applying to have a dormitory room repainted

Ⓓ Organizing access to a student's room in order to paint it

Passage 4 Listen to part of a conversation between a student and a registrar.

C01_P04

Q. What is the conversation mainly about?

Ⓐ Plans to open a new swimming pool on the campus

Ⓑ Registration for swimming classes at the new campus pool

Ⓒ The opening ceremony for an on-campus swimming pool

Ⓓ Hiring swimming instructors for the new campus swimming pool

Passage 5 Listen to part of a conversation between a student and a professor.

C01_P05

Q. What aspect of the grant application does the professor mainly discuss?

Ⓐ How to submit a request form for a grant application

Ⓑ How to improve the organization of her dissertation

Ⓒ How to arrange the information in her grant application

Ⓓ How to apply for a grant for dissertation research

Passage 6 Listen to part of a conversation between a student and a cafeteria manager. C01_P06

Q. Why was the student looking for the cafeteria manager?

(A) To complain about the cafeteria's menu

(B) To apply for a part-time job

(C) To receive training as a cashier

(D) To get advice on part-time jobs

Passage 7 Listen to part of a conversation between a student and a university employee. C01_P07

Q. Why does the man visit the university center?

(A) To ask about the process of mailing grade reports

(B) To discuss the inaccuracies on a student's report

(C) To discuss the student's not receiving his report

(D) To ask about the delay in sending out grade reports

Passage 8 Listen to part of a conversation between a student and a professor. C01_P08

Q. What is the conversation mainly about?

(A) How to be nominated for a scholarship

(B) How to apply for a full grant

(C) The selection process for scholarship students

(D) What paperwork to prepare when nominated for a scholarship

Passage 9 Listen to part of a conversation between a student and a bookstore clerk. C01_P09

Q. What are the speakers mainly discussing?

(A) The topic of the student's master's thesis

(B) The student's volunteer activities at the library

(C) The student's qualifications for the job

(D) The student's status as a long-time customer

Test

Passage 1

[1-5] Listen to part of a conversation between a student and a registrar. 

정답 및 해석 | P. 24

1. **What is the conversation mainly about?**

   Ⓐ Applying to attend summer school
   Ⓑ Applying to change universities
   Ⓒ Applying for financial aid
   Ⓓ Applying to extra classes

2. **What made the student apply to a different university?**

   Ⓐ It offers more varied classes.
   Ⓑ It has better professors.
   Ⓒ It is near his parents' house.
   Ⓓ It has classes his school doesn't offer.

3. **What documents will the student submit the next day?**

   Ⓐ A letter of reference and a transcript
   Ⓑ An application form and an SOP
   Ⓒ A transcript and the tuition fees
   Ⓓ An application form and a transcript

4. **What is the student's attitude toward his studies?**

   Ⓐ He enjoys studying and wants to stay in school for as long as possible.
   Ⓑ He hates school but studies to please his parents.
   Ⓒ He is a motivated student who wants to take classes in advance.
   Ⓓ He is a lazy student and tries to avoid studying.

5. **Why does the registrar say this:** 🎧

   Ⓐ To warn the student his desired classes are popular
   Ⓑ To warn the student he might not be accepted
   Ⓒ To warn the student the classes might be cancelled
   Ⓓ To warn the student the classes will be big

Passage 2

[1-5] Listen to part of a conversation between a student and a housing officer. 

Lesson 01 Conversations

1. **Why did the student come to see the housing officer?**

Ⓐ To inquire if there are any empty rooms available in other dormitories

Ⓑ To get her advice on dealing with roommates who are always very noisy

Ⓒ To see if he could convince the officer to remove a fine from his account

Ⓓ To find a way to get his housing deposit back earlier than the original date

2. **What is true about the room inspection? Choose 2 answers.**

Ⓐ It usually takes place after the final exam period.

Ⓑ Students can schedule the date at the beginning of a new term.

Ⓒ If repair work is required, residents have to pay for it.

Ⓓ All residents should be present during the room inspection.

3. **Why is the student moving out of the dormitory?**

Ⓐ If he lives with his friend, he doesn't have to pay rent for three months.

Ⓑ He was having some trouble with his current roommates.

Ⓒ Living off-campus is cheaper than living in the dormitory.

Ⓓ His friend, who is living off-campus, needs a new roommate.

4. **Why does the woman say this:** 🎧

Ⓐ To ask the student to clean his room thoroughly and make necessary repairs

Ⓑ To emphasize that moving out of a dormitory in the middle of the term is usually forbidden

Ⓒ To tell the student that there are some official guidelines for this process

Ⓓ To point out the fact that she is doing something that she is not allowed to do

5. **What will the student most likely do?**

Ⓐ Fill out the required paperwork and give them to his residence assistant

Ⓑ Visit his residence assistant with his current roommates

Ⓒ Go and find another housing officer to make a repair appointment

Ⓓ Discuss with his roommates who is going to pay for repair work

Lesson

02 Details

문제 듣기

Lesson Outline

세부 사항 찾기 문제(Details Question)는 TOEFL Listening 문제에서 가장 빈도수가 높은 문제 유형으로, 지문의 세부 사항에 대해 질문한다. 세부 사항 찾기 문제는 주로 대화에서 다루는 문제점과 연관된 자세한 사항, 화자가 강조하거나 반복해서 말하고 있는 사항, 주제를 뒷받침하는 예나 특징으로 사용된 것 등을 묻고, 2개의 답을 선택해야 하는 경우도 있기 때문에 정확도가 중요하다.

이 문제 해결의 관건은 전반적인 내용 파악을 바탕으로 한 정확한 노트 필기(note-taking)이다. 전체 내용의 흐름을 이해한다고 해도 자칫 세부적인 질문에 대해서는 답이 기억 나지 않을 수 있기 때문에 노트 필기를 활용하여 정확도를 높여야 한다. 자신만의 노트 필기 방법을 연습하고 그 안에서 답을 찾는 연습을 해 보자.

Lesson Point

Point 1 세부 사항 찾기 = 최고 빈출 문제 유형!

Point 2 문제점과 해결책에 주목한다.

Point 3 노트 필기(note-taking) 실력 없이는 고득점으로 갈 수 없다.

Point 4 표시어(signal)를 바탕으로 한 정확하고 간결한 노트 필기를 연습한다.

Typical Questions

- What does the professor offer to do? 교수는 무엇을 해주겠다고 제시하는가?
- What are two kcy features of ~? ~의 두 가지 주요 특징은 무엇인가?
- What are the characteristics of ~? ~의 특징들은 무엇인가?
- What is the reason that ~? ~하는 이유는 무엇인가?
- According to the student, what is ~? 학생에 의하면, ~은 무엇인가?
- What does the [student/professor] say about ~? [학생은/교수는] ~에 관해 무엇이라고 말하는가?

Learning Strategies

1 '세부 사항 찾기' 표시어(signal)를 공략한다!

세부 사항 표시어를 바탕으로 한 정확한 노트 필기를 통해 강조 또는 반복되는 내용을 정리한다. 표시어를 들으면 다음에 어떤 내용이 나올지 짐작이 가능하다. 특히 아래와 같은 표시어가 나오면 화자가 무언가에 관해 예를 들 거라는 점을 미리 예측할 수 있고, 이러한 예시는 세부 사항 문제로 출제될 가능성이 높다.

- such as ~ 예를 들면, ~와 같은
- things like ~ ~와 같은 것들
- for instance, 예를 들어,
- in this case, 이 경우에 있어서,
- referred to as ~ 보통 ~로 불리는/~라 하는

위의 표시어를 바탕으로 노트 필기(note-taking)를 한다. 언급된 내용이 너무 길면 자신이 알아볼 수 있는 줄임말과 축약형을 사용해 간단하고 빠르게 적도록 하자.

2 패러프레이징(paraphrasing) 역시 잊지 말자!

세부 사항 문제에서도 화자가 했던 말을 그대로 문제에 쓰기보다는 내용은 같지만 쓰이는 단어는 다른 것으로 바꾸는 패러프레이징이 보기에 등장한다. 그 점에 유의하며 보기를 하나씩 잘 살펴보고, 같은 단어를 포함한 보기가 아니라 지문의 내용에 부합하는 보기를 고르도록 하자.

Ex Read it **carefully** → careful reading is **required** [부사 → 형용사]

Ex A person should never **make** an important decision alone. → An important decision should not be **made** alone. [능동태 → 수동태]

Example

Man: Professor | Woman: Student

C02_EX

Listen to part of a conversation between a student and a professor.

W Excuse me, professor. Maria told me you wanted to speak with me?

M Paola, yes, I do. Please have a seat. I'm not interfering with your schedule today, am I?

W What? Oh, no. No, I'm not busy today. My next class doesn't start for two more hours.

M Good. Is that true of your schedule in general? What I mean to say is do you usually have much free time? Do you have a job this semester?

W Uh, I'm not sure where you are going with this.... No, I do not have a job this semester. I am ahead of schedule with my major courses, so I am taking some electives to fill up my schedule. Only three of my remaining mandatory courses were available this semester, so this semester my schedule is pretty light. [1] May I ask why you are so interested in my schedule?

M [1] Of course, are you familiar with our night math program?

W Kind of. I know that it exists. [2] I also took part in one when I was in high school.

M Oh really? What did you think of it?

W Well, it was at a community college. My parents enrolled me in it. Not because I was bad at math or anything.

M Of course, you wouldn't be pursuing a doctorate in physics if you were.

W Exactly. But, to answer your question, I wasn't very impressed by it. They thought it would be like an advanced class, but I found it was far too easy for me. I dropped out after just a few sessions.

M That doesn't surprise me. [2] That program was probably very similar to ours, which is a remedial math program. It is aimed at adults who find their math skills to be lacking, and not intended for advanced students.

1. Why did the professor want to see the student?

Ⓐ To discuss her class schedule for the upcoming semester

Ⓑ To tell her to work harder to become a math teacher

Ⓒ To persuade her to become a volunteer at a math teaching center

Ⓓ To encourage her to take more elective courses next year

2. According to the conversation, what is true about the school's night math program?

Ⓐ It usually takes place at national universities.

Ⓑ It teaches math to high school students and adults.

Ⓒ It accepts students who usually excel at math.

Ⓓ It is an introductory math course for freshmen.

W Yeah, most of the students were much older than me. But the class level was beneath me, so I quit.

M And rightly so. [1] But tell me, would you be interested in teaching such a program?

학생과 교수의 대화를 들으시오.

여 실례합니다 교수님, 마리아가 교수님께서 절 보길 원하셨다고 했는데요?

남 파올라, 맞아요. 자리에 앉아요. 오늘 학생의 일정을 내가 방해하고 있는 건 아니죠, 그렇죠?

여 네? 아, 아니에요. 오늘은 바쁘지 않거든요. 다음 수업이 시작하기까지는 2시간이 남았어요.

남 좋아요. 학생의 시간표 전반적으로 그런 식인가요? 내 말은, 남는 시간이 많나요? 이번 학기에 하는 일이라도 있어요?

여 음, 무슨 말씀을 하려고 하시는지 잘 모르겠어요.... 아니요. 이번 학기에는 일을 하지 않아요. 제 전공 과목 수업들은 앞서 있어서 스케줄을 채우기 위해 선택 과목을 몇 개 듣고 있어요. 남아 있는 필수 과목들 중에서 이번 학기에 세 개밖에 열리지 않아서 시간표가 꽤 한가한 편이에요. [1] 왜 제 스케줄에 대해 궁금해하시는지 여쭤봐도 되나요?

남 [1] 물론이죠. 우리 학교의 야간 수학 프로그램에 대해 알고 있나요?

여 약간은요. 있다는 건 알아요. [2] 제가 고등학교 때 들었던 적이 있거든요.

남 정말인가요? 그 프로그램을 어떻게 생각했죠?

여 음, 전문 대학에서 들은 거였어요. 부모님이 저를 등록시키셨죠. 제가 수학을 못해서라거나 그런 건 아니었어요.

남 그럼요. 만약 그랬다면 물리학 박사 학위를 목표로 하고 있지 않겠죠.

여 맞아요. 하지만 교수님의 질문에 답하자면, 그다지 깊은 인상을 받지 못했어요. 부모님은 이 프로그램이 고급반 수업 같을 거라고 생각하셨지만, 저에겐 너무 쉬웠어요. 몇 번 듣고 그만두었죠.

남 놀랍지는 않네요. [2] 그 프로그램은 아마 우리가 가진 프로그램과 매우 비슷한 거였을 거예요. 수학 보충 프로그램 같은 거죠. 고급반 학생들을 위한 것이 아니라, 수학 능력이 부족하다고 느끼는 성인들을 위해 만들어진 프로그램이니까요.

여 네, 대부분의 학생들이 저보다 나이가 훨씬 많았지만, 수업의 레벨이 제 실력보다 낮았기에 그만뒀어요.

남 그만두기를 잘한 거죠. [1] 하지만 말해줄 수 있어요? 혹시 그런 프로그램을 가르치는 데 관심이 있나요?

1. 교수는 왜 학생을 보고자 했는가?

Ⓐ 학생의 다음 학기 스케줄을 논의하기 위해
Ⓑ 수학 교사가 되기 위해 더 열심히 공부하라고 말하기 위해
Ⓒ 수학 교육 센터에서 자원 봉사자로 일하라고 설득하기 위해
Ⓓ 내년에 더 많은 선택 과목을 들으라고 학생을 장려하기 위해

2. 대화에 의하면, 학교의 야간 수학 프로그램에 대해 옳은 것은 무엇인가?

Ⓐ 보통 국립 대학에서 진행된다.
Ⓑ 고등학생들과 성인들에게 수학을 가르친다.
Ⓒ 수학을 매우 잘 하는 학생들을 받아들인다.
Ⓓ 1학년생들을 위한 수학 입문 수업이다.

1.

정답 (C)

해설 학생이 교수가 왜 자신의 스케줄에 관해 궁금해 하는지를 묻자 교수가 '물론이죠'라고 대답하며 야간 수학 프로그램 이야기를 꺼낸다. 그리고 대화 마지막 부분에도 학생에게 직접 가르치는 일에 관심이 있는지 물었으므로 정답은 (C)이다. 한편, 'volunteer'라는 단어를 사용하여 수학 프로그램을 가르치는 일을 패러프레이즈했다는 점을 눈여겨보자.

2.

정답 (B)

해설 학생이 먼저 '고등학교 때 들었다'고 밝혔고, 뒤에 교수가 '수학 능력이 부족하다고 느끼는 성인들을 위해 만들어진 프로그램'이라고 설명했으므로, 정답은 (B)이다. 교수가 야간 수학 프로그램에 관해 설명하기 시작할 때부터 이 프로그램의 특징을 노트 필기해 두는 것이 큰 도움이 된다.

어휘 **interfere** v 방해하다, 간섭하다 | **ahead of** ~앞에, ~보다 빨리 | **elective** n 선택 과목, 교양 과목 | **mandatory** adj 필수의 | **familiar** adj 익숙한, 친숙한 | **take part in** ~에 참가하다 | **enroll** v 등록하다, 명부에 올리다 | **pursue** v 추구하다 | **doctorate** n 박사 학위 | **physics** n 물리학 | **impress** v 깊은 인상을 주다 | **advanced** adj 고급의, 상급의 | **drop out** 중도 하차하다 | **remedial** adj 보충하는, 개선하는 | **aim** v ~을 목표로 하다 | **intend** v 의도하다, 생각하다 | **rightly** adv 당연히, 마땅히

Practice

정답 및 해석 | P. 29

Passage 1 Listen to part of a conversation between a student and a professor. C02_P01

Q. What will the woman do a presentation on?

Ⓐ Reasons that the war was fought

Ⓑ The beginning of the American Civil War

Ⓒ Why poor Southerners opposed the war

Ⓓ The experiences of African American soldiers

Passage 2 Listen to part of a conversation between a student and a professor. C02_P02

Q. What document does the man need to get?

Ⓐ A copy of his transcript

Ⓑ A letter of recommendation

Ⓒ A certificate of his language ability

Ⓓ An essay written in French

Passage 3 Listen to part of a conversation between a student and a university employee. C02_P03

Q. What does the woman want to do?

Ⓐ Get a refund for a course

Ⓑ Drop a class she cannot handle

Ⓒ Add a class to her schedule

Ⓓ Look up her grade point average

Passage 4 Listen to part of a conversation between a student and a professor.

Q. What does the man need to do first?

Ⓐ Visit an art exhibition

Ⓑ Write a report

Ⓒ Locate a partner to work with

Ⓓ Select a destination

Passage 5 Listen to part of a conversation between a student and a professor. C02_P05

Q. What is the student's essay about?

Ⓐ The evolution of a type of photography

Ⓑ Constraints that a medium places on artists

Ⓒ How limitations can create great artworks

Ⓓ Why artists replicate the work of others

Passage 6 Listen to part of a conversation between a student and a housing officer. C02_P06

Q. According to the student, what are the problems with the room he was assigned? Choose 2 answers.

Ⓐ It is not in the building he wanted.

Ⓑ It has no remaining openings.

Ⓒ It requires him to have many roommates.

Ⓓ It is the wrong kind of room.

Passage 7 Listen to part of a conversation between a student and a bookstore clerk. C02_P07

Q. What is the problem that the student has with asking her professor for the book?

Ⓐ She is afraid of her professor's reaction.

Ⓑ She knows her professor does not have it.

Ⓒ She has already tried that and failed.

Ⓓ She is not doing a good job in her class.

Passage 8 Listen to part of a conversation between a student and a professor. C02_P08

Q. Why didn't the professor believe that the student couldn't find resources?

Ⓐ She knew there were many books and articles on the subject.

Ⓑ She has published an article on the subject every six months.

Ⓒ She had made sure the library had relevant resources.

Ⓓ She had created a reading list on the subject for the students.

Passage 9 Listen to part of a conversation between a student and a store employee. C02_P09

Q. What is the problem with fixing the computer?

Ⓐ It is a discontinued model, so they can't find parts for it.

Ⓑ It is an obscure brand, so parts are hard to find.

Ⓒ It is a limited edition model, so parts need to be made for it.

Ⓓ The suppliers are sold out of parts for that particular model.

Passage 10 Listen to part of a conversation between a student and a professor.

C02_P10

Q. How was the professor's experience in choosing a major similar to the student's?

Ⓐ He wanted to major in something that he was interested in but lacked talent to do so.

Ⓑ He also wanted to be an English literature major but was good at science.

Ⓒ He studied science before doing graduate study in literature.

Ⓓ He decided to major in science and humanities at the same time.

Passage 11 Listen to part of a conversation between a student and a librarian.

C02_P11

1. With what is the conversation mainly concerned?

Ⓐ Finding the University Center

Ⓑ Getting a student ID card

Ⓒ Learning about Student Support Center

Ⓓ Checking out books without a student ID card

2. Which of the following is an option according to the librarian?

Ⓐ Use the books in the library and make photocopies

Ⓑ Complain to the head librarian about the policy

Ⓒ Check out the books using a temporary library card

Ⓓ Borrow a friend's ID card and check out the books

3. Where should the student check to get his ID card?

Ⓐ In the library

Ⓑ At the 1st floor of the University Center

Ⓒ At Student Services

Ⓓ At the Student Center

Passage 12 Listen to part of a conversation between a student and a professor. C02_P12

1. Why did the student miss class on Monday?

Ⓐ She overslept.

Ⓑ She missed the bus.

Ⓒ She misunderstood when the class was scheduled.

Ⓓ She had car trouble.

2. What does the professor tell the student?

Ⓐ The student must attend every remaining class.

Ⓑ The student must write a make-up essay.

Ⓒ The student will have points deducted from her final grade due to her absence.

Ⓓ The student should read the section on long-term investments again.

3. What did the student do with the help of the professor? Choose 2 answers.

Ⓐ She got a copy of the test from last semester.

Ⓑ She got her car fixed.

Ⓒ She got the materials that she requested.

Ⓓ She found out what would be covered on the test.

Test

Passage 1

[1-5] Listen to part of a conversation between a student and a university housing officer. C02_T01

정답 및 해석 | P. 40

1. What are the speakers mainly discussing?

Ⓐ How to apply for off-campus housing

Ⓑ The difficulties of living with roommates

Ⓒ Housing options for senior students

Ⓓ Getting assigned to a dormitory room

2. What problem does the student discuss with the housing officer?

Ⓐ He wanted to apply for a double room.

Ⓑ He didn't want to have roommates.

Ⓒ He wanted to live in a dormitory where smoking was allowed.

Ⓓ He had an argument with his roommate and wanted to move.

3. Why is it difficult for the student to get the type of room that he wants? Choose 2 answers.

Ⓐ He is not a senior, and private rooms are usually reserved for seniors.

Ⓑ Some senior students haven't yet been assigned to private rooms.

Ⓒ There is a housing shortage on campus.

Ⓓ All private rooms were booked on a first-come, first-served basis.

4. What is the student's concern with the double room?

Ⓐ He may not like his roommate.

Ⓑ It will probably be quite distracting.

Ⓒ It is a room where smoking is allowed.

Ⓓ There is no private bathroom.

5. How does the housing officer solve the student's problem? Choose 2 answers.

Ⓐ She gives him a private room as per his request.

Ⓑ She offers him an off-campus apartment on a temporary basis.

Ⓒ She reserves a double occupancy room for him.

Ⓓ She will contact him if there is a single room available.

Passage 2

[1-5] Listen to part of a conversation between a student and a student advisor. 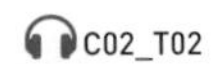 C02_T02

1. **What is the purpose of the student's visit to the advisor?**

Ⓐ Submitting some paperwork related to a trip to Lebanon

Ⓑ Asking questions regarding declaring a double major

Ⓒ Getting help to change her major to a different subject

Ⓓ Explaining the unavoidable situation of changing universities

2. **Why does the student want to change her major?**

Ⓐ She thinks that majoring in biology will lead to better job options.

Ⓑ She realized that she wanted to work with nature and animals.

Ⓒ She does not find math interesting anymore and prefers science courses.

Ⓓ She wants to have a lighter class load than she currently does.

3. **What will the student have to do to graduate on time? Choose 2 answers.**

Ⓐ She needs to transfer to Dayton Community College.

Ⓑ She should start looking for some internship positions.

Ⓒ She should register for some introductory level courses during the summer.

Ⓓ She needs to gain some experience by participating in research projects.

4. **What is the advisor's opinion about changing one's major?**

Ⓐ He thinks it is not unusual since people often change their mind.

Ⓑ He doubts it is wise to change it during a person's junior or senior year.

Ⓒ He believes that many people do not know what they want to do.

Ⓓ He finds it interesting that so many people are confused about their career.

5. **Why does the advisor say this:** 🎧

Ⓐ He is not interested in helping students who are changing their majors.

Ⓑ He cannot help the student since he is not in the same department.

Ⓒ He is convinced that the student is making a serious mistake.

Ⓓ He does not know how to help the student with the necessary paperwork.

Lesson

03 Function & Attitude

문제 듣기

Lesson Outline

의도 및 태도 파악 문제(Function & Attitude Question)는 화자의 말이나 표현에 집중해야 한다. 의도 파악(Function) 문제의 경우 화자가 어떤 말을 한 목적과 그 말 속에 내재된 숨은 의도를 파악해야 하며, 주로 짧은 구간을 다시 들려주고 문제를 푸는 방식으로 출제된다. 태도 파악(Attitude) 문제는 화자의 태도와 감정, 또는 확신하는 정도를 파악하는 문제가 출제된다.

Lesson Point

Point 1 직역보다는 지문의 문맥이나 화자의 말투 또는 억양을 통해 파악한다.

Point 2 다시 들려줄 때도 있지만 기억력에 의존해 풀어야 하는 경우가 많으니 주의하자!

Point 3 다시 들었던 표현이 선택지에 그대로 나오는 경우 오답일 확률이 높다.

Point 4 생소한 표현은 반드시 정리 및 숙지한다.

Point 5 노트 필기보다는 글의 흐름과 이야기하는 사람들의 분위기, 그리고 속뜻을 파악하는 것이 중요하다.

Typical Questions

의도 파악(Function)

- Listen again to part of the conversation. Then answer the question. Why does the student say this:
  대화의 일부를 다시 듣고 질문에 답하시오. 학생은 왜 이렇게 말하는가:
- Listen again to part of the conversation. Then answer the question. What does the student mean when he/she says this:
  대화의 일부를 다시 듣고 질문에 답하시오. 학생은 다음과 같이 말하며 무엇을 의미하는가:

태도 파악(Attitude)

- What is the man's attitude toward ~?
  ~에 관한 남자의 태도는 어떠한가?
- What is the student's opinion about ~?
  ~에 관한 학생의 의견은 무엇인가?

Learning Strategies

의도 및 태도 파악 빈출 표현

의도·태도 파악 문제와 관련하여 대화에 자주 등장하는 표현들을 알아두자.

'동의함' 관련 표현

• You can say that again!	정말 그래요! (=전적으로 동의해요)
• You can't be more right about that.	정말 맞는 말이에요. (=이보다 더 맞는 말을 할 수는 없을 거예요.)
• You are on the right track.	잘하고 있어요. (=옳은 방향으로 나아가고 있어요.)
• You hit the nail on the head.	정곡을 찔렀네요.
• Let me elaborate on that a little.	거기에 대해서 내가 좀 더 자세히 설명할게요.

'동의하지 않음' 관련 표현

• You've got to be kidding me.	농담하시는 거죠?
• I doubt that ~.	~할/~일 것 같지 않아요.
• That may be true, but ~.	그게 사실일 수도 있는데요, 그런데 ~

'혼란스러움' 관련 표현

• I'm not sure I understand the problem.	제가 그 문제에 대해 제대로 이해한 건지 모르겠네요.
• I didn't know such a thing even existed!	그런 게 있는지도 몰랐어요!
• It just doesn't make sense.	이건 그냥 말이 안 돼요.

'불확실함' 관련 표현

• I'm not so sure about that.	거기에 대해서는 잘 모르겠어요. (=확신할 수 없어요.)
• You can't be serious.	그럴 리가요. (=정말 진심은 아니겠지.)
• Are you sure?	확실해요?

Example

Man: Professor | Woman: Student

C03_EX

Listen to part of a conversation between a student and a professor.

W Hello, Professor Buelle.

M Good morning, Lucy. Have a seat. I just wanted to know how you are doing with preparations for your performance coming along?

W Pretty well, I guess. I didn't realize how hard it can be to choreograph a ten-minute performance alone.

M [1] Yes, it can be a lot of work. It takes commitment—a lot of commitment in terms of time and effort. Which dancer are you basing your performance on, if you don't mind my asking?

W [1] I don't mind. Um, I am creating a performance in the style of Isadora Duncan.

M Oh really? Then I think I can see why you are having a difficult time with it. Duncan was a pioneer of dance. Some even call her the creator of modern dance.

W Yes, she has a unique style that is definitely true. With ballet, the movements are so rigid and precise, but her dancing flowed. The movements were so much more natural.

M Indeed, that was an important part of her philosophy of dance. She took much of her inspiration from ancient Greece and combined it with her sense of freedom. Some critics referred to it as her "American love of freedom," but her work was not very well received in America. Most of her fame came in Europe, which is also where she established her schools.

W Right, and her love of Greece made the costume at least easy. She usually wore a tunic reminiscent of ancient Greek clothing. It is fairly easy to make, and it allows for so much more range of movement than a corseted ballet outfit.

1. Listen again to part of the conversation. Then answer the question.

Why does the student say this:

Ⓐ She does not know what to say about the professor's previous comment.

Ⓑ She is okay with the professor checking the progress of her project.

Ⓒ She is annoyed by the fact that the professor is pressuring her.

Ⓓ She still has not decided what to do with her performance theme.

2. What is the professor's opinion about understanding an artist?

Ⓐ He sees that it will allow the student to achieve better grades on her performance.

Ⓑ He feels that it can explain how the artist came up with such choreography.

Ⓒ He thinks it helps one to imitate the artist's style and performance better.

Ⓓ He believes that it inspires one to create more radical and innovative styles.

M Yes, her style of dress had many benefits. [2] Have you done any research about Isadora's life? It is important to understand an artist's experiences and motivation if you want to accurately emulate their style.

Lesson 03 Conversations

학생과 교수의 대화를 들으시오.

여 안녕하세요, 뷰엘 교수님.

남 안녕하세요, 루시. 자리에 앉아요. 공연 준비는 어떻게 되고 있는지 알고 싶어서요.

여 잘 되고 있는 것 같아요. 10분짜리 공연의 안무를 혼자 짠다는 것이 얼마나 어려운 건지 깨닫지 못했어요.

남 [1] 그래요, 매우 할 일이 많죠. 헌신이 필요해요. 시간과 정성 면에서 말이죠. 물어봐도 괜찮다면, 어떤 무용수에 기반을 두고 공연을 작업하고 있나요?

여 [1] 물어보셔도 괜찮습니다. 음, 이사도라 던컨의 스타일로 공연을 만들고 있어요.

남 오, 그래요? 그러면 왜 학생이 어려워하고 있는지 알 것 같네요. 던컨은 춤의 선구자였어요. 어떤 이들은 심지어 그녀를 현대 무용의 선구자라고 부르기도 하죠.

여 맞아요, 그녀는 분명히 진정하고 참신한 스타일을 갖고 있어요. 발레의 경우 움직임이 뻣뻣하고 정확하지만 그녀의 춤은 흐르는 듯했어요. 움직임이 훨씬 더 자연스러웠죠.

남 정말 그래요. 그녀가 가진 춤에 대한 철학의 중요한 부분이었죠. 던컨은 고대 그리스에서 많은 영감을 받았고 그것을 자유에 대한 그녀의 감각과 결합시켰어요. 어떤 비평가들은 그것을 그녀의 "자유에 대한 미국식 사랑"이라고 불렀지만 그녀의 작품은 미국에서 큰 호응을 얻지 못했어요. 명성의 대부분은 유럽에서 얻었는데, 이곳에 그녀는 학교들도 세웠죠.

여 네, 그리고 그리스에 대한 그녀의 사랑은 의상을 적어도 편하게 만들었어요. 그녀는 보통 고대 그리스의 옷을 연상시키는 튜닉을 입었죠. 꽤 만들기 쉬울 뿐 아니라 코르셋을 입어야 하는 발레 의상보다 훨씬 더 넓은 범위의 움직임을 가능하게 했어요.

남 네, 그녀의 드레스 스타일은 많은 이점이 있었죠. [2] 이사도라의 삶에 대해서도 조사해 봤나요? 예술가들의 스타일을 정확히 모방하고 싶다면 그들의 경험과 동기 부여를 이해하는 것이 중요해요.

1. 대화의 일부를 다시 듣고 질문에 답하시오.

남 그래요, 매우 할 일이 많죠. 헌신이 필요해요. 시간과 정성 면에서 말이죠. 물어봐도 괜찮다면, 어떤 무용수에 기반을 두고 공연을 작업하고 있나요?

여 물어보셔도 괜찮습니다.

학생은 왜 이렇게 말하는가:

여 물어보셔도 괜찮습니다.

Ⓐ 교수가 방금 말한 것에 대해 어떻게 대답해야 할지 모른다.

Ⓑ 교수가 그녀의 프로젝트가 어떻게 진행되고 있는지 확인하는 것이 괜찮다.

Ⓒ 교수가 그녀를 재촉한다는 사실에 짜증이 났다.

Ⓓ 공연의 주제를 어떻게 해야 할지 여전히 결정하지 못했다.

2. 예술가를 이해하는 것에 대한 교수의 의견은 어떠한가?

Ⓐ 학생이 그녀의 공연에서 더 좋은 성적을 내도록 도와줄 것이라고 본다.

Ⓑ 어떻게 예술가가 이러한 안무를 창조해냈는지 설명해줄 수 있다고 느낀다.

Ⓒ 예술가의 스타일과 공연을 더 잘 모방하도록 도와준다고 생각한다.

Ⓓ 더 극단적이고 혁신적인 스타일을 창조하도록 영감을 준다고 믿는다.

1.

정답 (B)

해설 학생이 왜 이 말을 했는지에 대한 이유를 묻는 의도 파악 문제이므로 대화의 맥락을 파악해야 한다. 교수가 학생에게 공연 준비에 대해 물으며 어떤 무용수에 기반을 두고 작업하고 있는지 '물어봐도 괜찮으냐(if you don't mind ~?)'고 했고, 학생은 '신경 쓰지 않습니다(=괜찮습니다)', 즉 물어봐도 괜찮다고 대답한 것이므로 학생은 교수가 자신의 프로젝트 진행 상황을 확인해도 신경 쓰지 않음을 알 수 있다. 정답은 (B)이다.

2.

정답 (C)

해설 상황이나 문제에 대한 화자의 의견·태도를 파악하는 태도 파악 문제이므로 화자가 대상에 관해 어떤 태도와 관점을 가졌는지 알아야 한다. 대화의 맨 마지막 부분을 보면 교수가 학생에게 '예술가의 스타일을 정확히 모방하고 싶다면 그의 경험과 동기 부여를 이해하는 것이 중요합니다'라고 했으므로 예술가를 이해하는 것이 스타일을 모방하는 데 도움을 준다고 생각하고 있음을 알 수 있다. 즉 교수는 예술가를 이해하면 스타일과 공연을 더 잘 따라 할 수 있다고 보고 있으므로 정답은 (C)이다.

어휘 **preparation** n 준비 | **performance** n 공연 | **choreograph** v 안무를 하다 | **commitment** n 헌신, 전념 | **in terms of** ~면에서 | **pioneer** n 선구자, 개척자 | **definitely** adv 분명히, 틀림없이 | **rigid** adj 뻣뻣한 | **precise** adj 정확한 | **flow** v 흐르다 | **natural** adj 자연스러운 | **philosophy** n 철학 | **inspiration** n 영감 | **ancient** adj 고대의 | **combine** v 결합하다 | **freedom** n 자유 | **refer to** ~를 나타내다, 지칭하다 | **fame** n 명성 | **establish** v 설립하다, 수립하다 | **tunic** n 튜닉(고대 그리스나 로마인들이 입던 헐렁한 웃옷) | **reminiscent** adj 연상시키는 | **range** n 폭, 범위 | **corseted** adj 코르셋을 입은 | **motivation** n 동기 부여, 자극 | **accurately** adv 정확히 | **emulate** v 모방하다, 따라 하다

Practice

정답 및 해석 I P. 44

Passage 1 Listen to part of a conversation between a student and a librarian. C03_P01

Q. What does the woman mean when she says this:

Ⓐ The librarian should not bother the student.

Ⓑ The student still has much information to find.

Ⓒ Certain materials cannot be removed from the library.

Ⓓ The copier may damage the books if she uses it.

Passage 2 Listen to part of a conversation between a student and a professor. C03_P02

Q. What is the woman's opinion of the exam?

Ⓐ She thinks the student is already well prepared.

Ⓑ She believes that it will be very difficult.

Ⓒ She wishes that she was allowed to write it.

Ⓓ She feels that the student is wasting time.

Passage 3 Listen to part of a conversation between a student and a professor. C03_P03

Q. Why does the professor say this:

Ⓐ To indicate that the student should change her topic

Ⓑ To emphasize the importance of regular attendance

Ⓒ To suggest that the student wrote her paper incorrectly

Ⓓ To express concern about the student's performance

Passage 4 Listen to part of a conversation between a student and a university employee. C03_P04

Q. Why does the student say this:

Ⓐ He has not had time to meet his advisor.

Ⓑ He does not know about university procedures.

Ⓒ He forgot that he needed to have permission.

Ⓓ He thinks that he should be allowed to register anyway.

Passage 5 Listen to part of a conversation between a student and a professor. C03_P05

Q. What is the woman's attitude toward the professor's suggestion?

Ⓐ She is not satisfied with the advice that he gave her.

Ⓑ She believes that it will be simple to do what he said.

Ⓒ She feels that he doesn't understand her situation.

Ⓓ She thinks that the deadline is too soon.

Passage 6 Listen to part of a conversation between a student and a professor.

C03_P06

Q. What does the professor mean when she says this:

Ⓐ The student comes to class fairly regularly.

Ⓑ The student's course load is not unusual.

Ⓒ The course normally has many students.

Ⓓ The class is not a high-level course.

Passage 7 Listen to part of a conversation between a student and a housing officer.

C03_P07

Q. What does the woman mean when she says this:

Ⓐ The student should have known the university code.

Ⓑ The student should have arranged to be at his room.

Ⓒ The student should have known about the inspections.

Ⓓ The student should have posted a notice on the board.

Passage 8 Listen to part of a conversation between a student and a librarian.

C03_P08

Q. What is the attitude of the librarian towards orientation?

Ⓐ She thinks orientation should be made mandatory for all new students.

Ⓑ She thinks orientation information can be learned in other ways.

Ⓒ She thinks orientation provides no important information and is unnecessary.

Ⓓ She thinks orientation is important for new students to attend.

Passage 9 Listen to part of a conversation between a student and a university employee.

C03_P09

Q. What does the woman mean when she says this:

Ⓐ The student must have missed his appointment.

Ⓑ The student should go to a different department.

Ⓒ The student needs to pay an additional fee.

Ⓓ The student has to make a new reservation.

Passage 10 Listen to part of a conversation between a student DJ and a radio director.

C03_P10

Q. What is the woman's attitude about her responsibilities?

Ⓐ She thinks that some tasks are tedious.

Ⓑ She wants the rules to be made clearer.

Ⓒ She is ignoring the man's suggestions.

Ⓓ She feels the changes are unnecessary.

Passage 11 Listen to part of a conversation between a student and a professor. C03_P11

Q. What does the man mean when he says this:

Ⓐ The student is trying to impress him.
Ⓑ The student needs to edit her work carefully.
Ⓒ The student should listen to criticism.
Ⓓ The student seems overconfident.

Passage 12 Listen to part of a conversation between a student and a manager. C03_P12

Q. What is the woman's opinion of the man's request?

Ⓐ She thinks that it is completely unreasonable.
Ⓑ She wants to help him, but the rules do not allow it.
Ⓒ She believes that she may be able to accommodate him.
Ⓓ She feels that he should be more considerate of other students.

Passage 13 Listen to part of a conversation between a student and a registrar. C03_P13

1. Why does the man say this:

Ⓐ He is wondering why the student has come to see him.
Ⓑ He wants to know why the professor ignores his students.
Ⓒ He thinks it is common for that professor to change his schedule.
Ⓓ He is implying that the student should have expected what happened.

2. What is the man's opinion of the professor?

Ⓐ He thinks that he is an unrivaled expert on his subject.
Ⓑ He was not impressed by him when he was a student.
Ⓒ He believes students give the professor too much credit.
Ⓓ He feels that he should teach more classes than he does.

Passage 14 Listen to part of a conversation between a student and a postal worker. C03_P14

1. What does the man mean when he says this:

Ⓐ His employer has changed its official policies.
Ⓑ His employer has replaced problematic employees.
Ⓒ His employer has lost items it should have delivered.
Ⓓ His employer does not work with students anymore.

2. What is the student's attitude toward a temporary change of address?

Ⓐ She thinks forwarding the mail is a good idea.
Ⓑ She does not think that it sounds very reliable.
Ⓒ She is surprised that few people choose that option.
Ⓓ She would prefer that only some of the mail be forwarded.

Test

Passage 1

[1-5] Listen to part of a conversation between a student and a lab proctor. 

정답 및 해석 | P. 55

1. What topic are the speakers discussing?

Ⓐ The proper way to do a lab assignment
Ⓑ How to register for the chemistry class
Ⓒ How the student can gain access to the lab
Ⓓ Bringing guests into the labs on campus

2. What made the student come to the lab?

Ⓐ The student registered late and needs to catch up on work.
Ⓑ The professor ordered the student to begin lab work.
Ⓒ The student is meeting a friend at the lab.
Ⓓ The student wants to start his coursework early.

3. What is the lab proctor's attitude toward the student?

Ⓐ She is irritated by the student's stubbornness.
Ⓑ She seems indifferent toward the student.
Ⓒ She feels sympathy toward the student.
Ⓓ She has a firm attitude toward the student.

4. What does the lab proctor do for the student?

Ⓐ She gives the student access to the lab on another day.
Ⓑ She tells the student another way to get into the lab.
Ⓒ She provides the student keys to another lab on campus.
Ⓓ She opens the door of the chemistry lab for the student.

5. Why does the lab proctor say this: 🎧

Ⓐ She is directing the student to read the rules.
Ⓑ She is emphasizing the severity of the policy.
Ⓒ She is encouraging the student to register for class.
Ⓓ She is indicating that she is taking a risk for him.

Passage 2

[1-5] Listen to part of a conversation between a student and a student advisor.

1. Listen again to part of the conversation. Then answer the question.

Why does the professor say this:

(A) She doubts if the student knows what she is saying.

(B) She wants to apologize to the student for being offensive.

(C) She noticed that what she said could have been misleading.

(D) She feels bad for telling such sad news to the student.

2. Why did the student come to see the professor?

(A) To get some advice about watching an opera he is interested in

(B) To ask her how the former professor is doing at his new school

(C) To pay for his tickets for the opera the class is going to watch

(D) To get her permission to volunteer as an usher for the opera

3. What are the reasons that the professor cannot let the student attend this year's opera performance? Choose 2 answers.

(A) The student already took the same course last semester.

(B) The tickets are sold out since the opera is so popular.

(C) The student came too late to register for the class.

(D) All students in the class already purchased their tickets.

4. Why does the professor mention the Variant Opera House?

(A) To inform the student about a part-time position they offer

(B) To explain the capacity of the opera house to the student

(C) To tell the student that the opera house has a long history

(D) To suggest the student go there to meet the manager

5. What is the professor's opinion of the options she suggests to the student?

(A) She thinks that purchasing one's own ticket is best.

(B) She believes they cannot ensure that the student will see the performance.

(C) She feels working as an usher is good because the student can earn some money.

(D) She knows they require the permission of the manager of the opera house.

Lesson

04 Connecting Contents

문제 듣기

Lesson Outline

관계 파악 문제(Connecting Contents Question)는 지문의 정보가 서로 어떻게 관련되었는지 묻는 문제이다. 대화에서 아예 나오지 않을 때도 있으나 보통 1개가 출제된다. 주로 어떤 내용이 왜 언급되었는지 묻는 문제가 많이 나오지만, 짝이나 순서 맞추기 문제가 출제되기도 한다.

Lesson Point

Point 1 전체 흐름을 통해 전반적인 구조를 파악하는 문제 유형

Ex How is the conversation organized?

···› 초반부와 중반부의 구조를 파악한다!

Point 2 특정 정보를 강조한 후, 그 정보의 역할을 묻는 문제 유형

Ex Why does the professor mention ~?

···› 해당 특정 정보의 구조적 성격을 파악한다!

Typical Questions 

언급 이유

- Why does the professor say ~? 교수는 왜 ~라고 말하는가?
- Why does the student mention ~? 학생은 왜 ~를 언급하는가?

짝 맞추기

- In the conversation, the speakers discuss ~. Indicate in the table below ~.

  대화에서 화자들은 ~에 대해 논의한다. ~인지 아래 표에 표시하시오.

	Category A	Category B
Characteristic 1		
Characteristic 2		
Characteristic 3		

순서 맞추기

- Put the following steps in order. 다음 단계들을 순서에 맞게 배열하시오.

Step 1	
Step 2	
Step 3	

Learning Strategies

1 내용의 흐름을 파악한다.

대화에서 지문의 요점은 다음과 같은 방식으로 전개된다.

- ▶ **유형 1** ① 문제 제기 ···› ② 문제 세부 설명 ···› ③ 해결책 제시
- ▶ **유형 2** ① 불만 제기 ···› ② 불만 세부 설명 ···› ③ 관련 인물의 사과 또는 해결책 제시
- ▶ **유형 3** ① 건의 사항 제시 ···› ② 세부 설명 ···› ③ 관련 인물의 동의 또는 거절
- ▶ **유형 4** ① 학생이 교수에게 질문 제시 ···› ② 수업 관련 내용 언급 ···› ③ 교수의 답변
- ▶ **유형 5** ① 교수가 학생을 부름 ···› ② 수업 관련 내용 언급 ···› ③ 함께 과제나 그 외의 해결책 논의

2 특정 정보를 사용한 의도를 파악한다.

특정 문장이나 내용의 역할을 파악할 때 주로 등장하는 표시어를 알아두면 도움이 된다.

주제 소개

- I came here to discuss ~. ~에 대해 논의하러 왔어요.
- I have a question about ~. ~에 대해 질문이 있어요.
- I'm having a problem with ~. ~에 문제가 있어요.
- The reason why I came here is because ~. 제가 여기 온 이유는 ~이에요.

예시

- Let's imagine ~. ~라고 상상해 봐요.
- Let's look at it this way: 이렇게 생각해 보세요.
- Let's suppose ~. ~라고 가정해 봐요.
- I can give you an example about ~. ~에 대한 예시를 드릴 수 있어요.

여담

- Incidentally, 그건 그렇고,
- As far as I remember, 제가 기억하기로는,
- That reminds me of ~. 그건 ~를 떠올리게 하네요.
- By the way, I have experienced ~. 그나저나, 저는 ~를 경험했어요.

결론

- Thank you, I will go there right now. 고맙습니다, 지금 바로 거기로 갈게요.
- Let me [get/print] this material for you. 제가 이 자료를 [갖다 드릴게요/출력해 드릴게요].
- Can I get his/her contact information? 그 사람의 연락처를 알 수 있을까요?
- I really appreciate your help. 도와주셔서 정말 고마워요.

Example

Man: Professor | **Woman:** Student

C04_EX

Listen to part of a conversation between a student and a professor.

W Hello, Professor Carter. I came to see you because of the article you assigned for us to read about Francis Bacon. A few questions came into my mind while I was reading it. You referred to him as the "father of the scientific method," didn't you?

M Actually, I was quoting Voltaire. Bacon is widely regarded as the creator of the modern approach to science, though. He did not formulate the scientific method as we know it today, but he placed great importance on inductive reasoning. He argued that knowledge must be based upon our observations of the natural world.

W Scientists didn't observe things before him?

M Of course they did, but the fundamental basis for their knowledge and reasoning was flawed. They believed that the senses and the human mind were imperfect, which made them unreliable. He agreed with them on that basic point, but he also realized that our flawed senses were our only tools with which to make any sense of the world. So, he said that we must doubt everything until we can prove it is true. [1] We should never assume that something is true.

W [1] That sounds logical. How did people arrive at conclusions before that?

M [1] Largely by deductive reasoning—what is referred to as syllogism. They also relied upon classical texts, like those of Aristotle and the other ancient Greek philosophers.

W [1] Wait, what is syllogism? That sounds familiar....

1. Why does the professor mention syllogisms?

Ⓐ To give an example of the modern decision-making method

Ⓑ To criticize the student for missing too many class sessions recently

Ⓒ To explain the method people used in the past to arrive at conclusions

Ⓓ To suggest the student use it as well when she conducts her own experiment

M [1] I should hope so. It was mentioned in class before, after all. A syllogism is a logical argument that is based upon two or more statements that are generally agreed to be correct. As in Aristotle's classic example: "All men are mortal. Socrates is a man. Therefore, Socrates is mortal."

W Yes, I remember that. But, that isn't necessarily true, right? I mean, that statement is, but other such arguments may not be.

M Correct. So, [2] Bacon did not like this type of deductive reasoning. Logical proof was not enough, and observation was key. So, he said that you must observe, and then experiment. He insisted that scientists must manipulate nature in order to test their hypothesis, but not to prove themselves right. Their goal should be to prove their ideas wrong. They must always doubt what they think they know.

W Can you give me an example?

M People had no idea where diseases really came from. So, Bacon advised scientists to expose healthy people to all of the outside influences that they thought might cause disease: cold, dampness, smells, etc. If one of these got someone sick, then they should repeat the experiment again and again, until it was established that this was a likely cause. When enough scientists reached the same conclusion independently, then it could be considered a truth.

W That sounds like a lot to understand. Anyways, thank you for your help, professor. I'll go and read the article more thoroughly.

2. In the conversation, the speakers discuss Francis Bacon and his theories. Indicate in the table below whether each of the following is one of his theories.

Click in the correct box for each sentence.

	Yes	No
Ⓐ Experiment is more important than observation.		
Ⓑ Proving a hypothesis is deeply related to nature.		
Ⓒ Observation is required for deductive reasoning.		
Ⓓ A person needs to doubt even proved hypothesis.		

학생과 교수의 대화를 들으시오.

여 안녕하세요, 카터 교수님. 프랜시스 베이컨에 대해 읽으라고 정리해주신 자료 때문에 왔습니다. 읽다가 몇 가지 질문이 생겼거든요. 교수님께서는 베이컨을 '과학적 방법의 아버지'라고 하셨어요. 그렇죠?

남 사실, 나는 볼테르가 한 말을 인용한 겁니다. 베이컨은 과학에 대한 현대적 접근법의 창시자로 널리 인정받고 있어요. 오늘날 우리가 아는 과학적 방법을 만든 것은 아니지만, 그는 귀납적 추리에 큰 중요성을 두었어요. 그는 지식이 우리의 자연 세계 관찰에 기반을 두어야 한다고 주장했죠.

여 베이컨 이전의 과학자들은 사물을 관찰하지 않았나요?

남 물론 했지만, 그들의 지식과 추리의 근본적 기반에 결함이 있었어요. 그들은 감각과 인간의 생각이 불완전하다고 믿었기 때문에 그것을 신뢰할 수 없었어요. 베이컨은 그들의 그러한 기본적 요점에는 동의했지만 세계를 어떻게든 이해하기 위해서는 우리의 불완전한 감각이 우리가 사용할 수 있는 유일한 도구라는 것을 깨달았습니다. 그래서 그는 어떠한 것을 사실이라고 증명할 수 있을 때까지 모든 것을 의심해야 한다고 주장했죠. [1] 무언가가 진실이라고 가정해서는 절대 안 된다는 겁니다.

여 [1] 논리적으로 들리네요. 그 전에는 사람들이 어떻게 결론을 내렸나요?

남 [1] 대개 연역적 추리로요. 삼단 논법이라고 불리죠. 그리고 아리스토텔레스나 다른 고대 그리스 철학자들의 고문서에 의지하기도 했어요.

여 [1] 잠깐만요, 삼단 논법이 무엇인가요? 들어본 것 같은데요....

남 [1] 그랬기를 바라요. 전에 수업에서 언급한 것이니까요. 삼단 논법은 일반적으로 옳다고 동의한 두 개 이상의 주장에 기반한 하나의 논리적인 주장입니다. 아리스토텔레스의 고전적 예시를 들면, "모든 인간은 죽는다. 소크라테스는 인간이다. 그러므로 소크라테스 역시 죽는다."

여 네, 기억해요. 하지만 그게 진짜로 맞지는 않잖아요, 그렇죠? 제 말은, 방금 이야기하신 건 맞지만, 다른 주장들은 맞지 않을 수도 있어요.

남 그렇습니다. 그래서 [2] 베이컨은 이러한 연역적 추리를 좋아하지 않았어요. 논리적 증명은 충분하지 않았으며 관찰이 열쇠였습니다. 그래서 그는 우리가 관찰을 하고 난 뒤에 실험해야 한다고 말했죠. 과학자들은 자신이 옳다는 것을 증명하기 위해서가 아니라, 가설을 시험하기 위해 자연을 조종해야 한다고 주장했습니다. 과학자들의 목표는 그들의 생각이 틀렸다는 것을 증명하는 것이어야 한다는 거죠. 그들이 안다고 생각하는 것을 항상 의심해야 했습니다.

여 예시를 들어주실 수 있나요?

남 사람들은 질병이 어디에서 오는 것인지 전혀 알지 못했습니나. 그래서 베이컨은 과학자들에게 그들이 생각하는 '병을 초래할 수 있는 외적 영향'에 건강한 사람들을 노출시키도록 조언했죠. 추위, 습기, 냄새 등등 말이에요. 만약 이들 중 하나가 누군가를 아프게 만들었다면 그 실험을 몇 번이고 다시 반복했습니다. 이것이 가능한 원인일 수도 있다는 것이 정립될 때까지요. 충분한 수의 과학자들이 독립적으로 같은 결론에 이르렀을 때 이것은 사실로 여겨질 수 있는 겁니다.

1. 교수는 왜 삼단 논법을 언급하는가?

Ⓐ 현대의 의사 결정 방법의 한 예시를 들기 위해

Ⓑ 최근 학생이 수업에 너무 많이 빠진 것을 지적하기 위해

Ⓒ 결론에 도달하기 위해 과거의 사람들이 사용했던 방법을 설명하기 위해

Ⓓ 학생이 실험을 할 때에도 삼단 논법을 써 보도록 제안하기 위해

2. 대화에서 화자들은 프랜시스 베이컨과 그의 이론들을 논의한다. 다음 각 사항이 그의 이론인지 아닌지를 아래 표에 표시하시오.

각 문장에 대해 맞는 칸에 표시하시오.

	Yes	No
Ⓐ 실험이 관찰보다 더 중요하다.		✓
Ⓑ 가설을 증명하는 것은 자연과 깊이 관련되어 있다.	✓	
Ⓒ 관찰은 연역적 추리에 반드시 필요하다.		✓
Ⓓ 사람은 심지어 증명된 가설도 의심해봐야 한다.		✓

여 이해할 것이 참 많은 것 같네요. 어쨌든 도와주셔서 감사합니다, 교수님. 가서 그 자료를 더 철저히 읽어볼게요.

1.

정답 (C)

해설 교수가 무언가를 언급한 이유를 묻는 문제이므로 앞뒤 맥락을 살펴보자. 학생이 "그 전에는 사람들이 어떻게 결론을 내렸나요?"라고 묻자 교수가 "대개 연역적 추리로요. 삼단 논법이라고 불리죠."라고 대답한다. 과거의 사람들이 이용한 방법을 물은 것이기 때문에 (C)가 정답이다.

2.

정답 Yes - (B) / No - (A), (C), (D)

해설 교수가 프랜시스 베이컨에 관해 설명하고, 그 설명이 옳은 내용인지를 가려내는 문제이다. 두 번째 주장을 보면 베이컨이 "가설을 시험하기 위해 자연을 조종해야 한다고 주장했다"는 교수의 설명과 부합하므로 Yes이다. 나머지 주장은 교수의 설명과 일치하지 않으므로 모두 No다.

어휘 assign v 맡기다, 배정하다 | scientific adj 과학의, 과학적인 | method n 방법 | approach n 접근법, 접근 | formulate v 만들어내다; 표현하다 | inductive reasoning 귀납적 추리 | argue v 주장하다 | observation n 관찰 | fundamental adj 근본적인 | flawed adj 결함이 있는 | imperfect adj 불완전한 | unreliable adj 신뢰할 수 없는 | prove v 증명하다, 입증하다 | logical adj 논리적인 | conclusion n 결론, 판단 | deductive reasoning 연역적 추리 | syllogism n 삼단 논법 | classical text 고문서 | philosopher n 철학자 | familiar adj 익숙한 | argument n 주장 | statement n 진술, 의견(주장) | generally adv 일반적으로 | mortal adj 유한한 생명의, 언젠가는 반드시 죽는 | proof n 증거 | experiment v 실험하다 | insist v 주장하다, 고집하다 | manipulate v 조종하다, 조작하다 | hypothesis n 가설, 추정 | doubt v 의심하다 | disease n 질병 | expose v 노출시키다 | influence n 영향 | dampness n 습기, 눅눅함 | establish v 정립하다, 수립하다 | independently adv 독립적으로 | thoroughly adv 철저히

Practice

Passage 1 Listen to part of a conversation between a student and a librarian. C04_P01

Q. In the conversation, the speakers discuss the requirements for watching foreign language videos. Indicate in the table below whether each of the following is one of those requirements. Click in the correct box for each sentence.

	Yes	No
(A) Video rooms can be reserved in two-hour blocks.		
(B) Students must present their student ID card.		
(C) Rooms must be reserved on the day or the day before they will be used.		
(D) Students must reserve rooms at least a few days in advance to watch videos.		
(E) Students may check out the videos for up to one week.		

Passage 2 Listen to part of a conversation between a student and an academic counselor. C04_P02

Q. In the conversation, the speakers discuss the advantages of two internships. Indicate in the table below which internship has each advantage. Click in the correct box for each phrase.

	Internship 1	Internship 2
(A) Not much competition for the position		
(B) The pay is fairly high for an internship		
(C) The position is at an international company		
(D) Offers experience in marketing		

Passage 3 Listen to part of a conversation between a student and a professor.

C04_P03

1. In the conversation, the speakers discuss the requirements of a research paper. Indicate in the table below which of the requirements apply to the student's assignment.

Click in the correct box for each phrase.

	Yes	No
Ⓐ Conduct research at the library on Childhood Behavioral Development		
Ⓑ Make predictions about behavioral patterns that may arise		
Ⓒ Locate children to participate in the behavioral study		
Ⓓ Observe the test subjects to see if their behavior corresponds with research		

2. Why does the professor mention the assistant in the psychology department?

Ⓐ To express how annoyed he is by the student's attitude
Ⓑ To direct the student to someone else who can provide help
Ⓒ To show the student the first step for starting her assignment
Ⓓ To tell the student that he needs to help someone else right now

Passage 4 Listen to part of a conversation between a student and a university employee.

C04_P04

1. In the conversation, the speakers discuss the process by which documents may be obtained. Indicate in the table below whether each of the following is indicated about that process. Click in the correct box for each sentence.

	Yes	No
Ⓐ The person must come to the university in person.		
Ⓑ There is a limit to the number of documents that can be obtained.		
Ⓒ The person must present a valid identification card.		
Ⓓ The transcripts take a week to process.		
Ⓔ The person may access the documents on the university website.		

2. Why does the man mention a fellow alumnus?

Ⓐ To tell the woman that she misunderstood him
Ⓑ To show the woman has wrong information
Ⓒ To ask the woman to make an exception
Ⓓ To persuade the woman that she could be wrong

Test

Passage 1

[1-5] Listen to part of a conversation between a student and a professor. In the conversation, the professor and his student are discussing a well-made play, which is a genre of play and not an opinion of quality. C04_T01

정답 및 해석 | P. 66

1. **Why did the professor want to see the student?**

Ⓐ To explain the concept of a well-made play to the student

Ⓑ To clarify the information the student included in her paper

Ⓒ To see if the student was doing okay with her assignment

Ⓓ To discuss certain characteristics of *A Doll's House*

2. **What is the professor's opinion of the information that the student provided?**

Ⓐ He considers historical background not necessary for the student's paper.

Ⓑ He finds some of it to be excessive for the readers.

Ⓒ He thinks the student should revise some controversial issues.

Ⓓ He believes that the information supports the student's view well.

3. **In the conversation, the speakers discuss the characteristics of a well-made play. Indicate in the table below whether each of the following is one of those characteristics.**

Click in the correct box for each sentence.

	Yes	No
Ⓐ Most of the action has already taken place before the play begins.		
Ⓑ The play is set in a public space with many people watching.		
Ⓒ The protagonist meets a sudden and surprising end.		
Ⓓ Its story develops as the characters leave the play one by one.		
Ⓔ There is a pivotal piece of information that some characters lack.		

4. **What can be inferred about *A Doll's House*?**

Ⓐ It introduced ideas that were not dealt with at that time.

Ⓑ It was controversial due to its influence on society.

Ⓒ It ended up emphasizing the immoral nature of man.

Ⓓ It received both positive and negative reviews from critics.

5. **How was *A Doll's House* different from traditional well-made plays?**

Ⓐ It introduced more than one ending for each theater.

Ⓑ It embraced the theme of marriage and concentrated heavily on it.

Ⓒ It developed its story around a woman's life, which was not popular at the time.

Ⓓ It focused on themes that people viewed as uncomfortable and taboo.

Passage 2

[1-5] Listen to part of a conversation between a student and a professor. 

1. What are the speakers mainly discussing?

Ⓐ The differences between the two candidates who applied for a teaching position

Ⓑ The teaching styles of two teaching assistants during a film studies class

Ⓒ The evaluation of two people who applied to become teaching assistants

Ⓓ The topics of the sample lessons that two different professors taught

2. Why does the student prefer the female professor to the male professor?

Ⓐ He did not like the male professor's usage of technical terms.

Ⓑ He thinks the female professor's explanation was more direct.

Ⓒ He likes the female professor since she is an expert in Shakespeare.

Ⓓ He felt bored during the male professor's lecture and did not learn anything.

3. Why does the professor mention Baltimore?

Ⓐ To explain why the male professor is a better candidate

Ⓑ To provide more background information of the male professor

Ⓒ To show another difference between the two professors

Ⓓ To confirm that the student's assumption is correct

4. What is the professor's opinion of the female professor?

Ⓐ Her ability to explain complex concepts will be very helpful in the future.

Ⓑ She showed excellent skill for making students participate in a class discussion.

Ⓒ She is good at what she does, but she might not be the best candidate.

Ⓓ Her accent would be somewhat problematic when she teaches students.

5. Listen again to part of the conversation. Then answer the question.

Why does the woman say this:

Ⓐ To illustrate the importance of Shakespeare and cinematic history in the class

Ⓑ To emphasize the contribution the male professor makes to the lecture's overall quality

Ⓒ To convince the student that the male professor is a better teacher than the woman

Ⓓ To express her opinion regarding the competition between the two professors

Lesson 05 Inference

문제 듣기

Lesson Outline

추론 문제(Inference Question)는 하나의 정보를 토대로 답을 찾는 것이 아니라, 지문에서 주어진 여러 정보 간의 관계에 대해 답하거나 그 정보를 기반으로 추론하는 문제이다. 대화에서 따로 언급되지는 않았지만 대화의 내용과 맥락을 통해 유추·추론할 수 있는 사실을 묻는다.

Lesson Point

Point 1 5개 문제 유형 중 최고난도의 문제 유형!

Point 2 문제에 imply, infer, next, result, cause, conclude 등의 단어가 있으면 추론 문제!

Point 3 들은 것 또는 노트 필기한 것을 바탕으로 제시된 정보의 특징을 추론 또는 유추한다.

Point 4 보기에서 키워드가 패러프레이징 된 것을 찾으면 정답!

Typical Questions 

• What is the student most likely to do next?	학생이 다음에 무엇을 할 것 같은가?
• What does the student imply about ~?	학생은 ~에 관해 무엇을 암시하는가?
• What can be inferred about the woman?	여자에 대해 무엇을 추론할 수 있는가?
• What can be inferred from the student's situation?	학생의 상황으로부터 무엇을 추론할 수 있는가?
• What can be concluded about ~?	~에 관해 어떤 결론을 내릴 수 있는가?

Learning Strategies

대화 주제의 특징을 나타내는 표시어(signal)를 공략한다!

주제의 주요 특징 및 예시에 관해 유추·추론하는 문제가 나오므로, 주제의 특징과 관련된 원인, 문제, 해결책 등을 나타내는 표시어를 중심으로 노트 필기하며 듣는다.

원인

- It all started with ~. 모든 일은 ~로부터 시작되었어요.
- It happened because ~. ~때문에/~해서 생긴 일이에요.
- I did X and Y happened ~. 제가 X했는데 Y가 되었어요(발생했어요).
- I had to do X because ~. ~때문에/~해서 제가 X해야만 했어요.

문제

- I have a problem with X, so I came to ~. X로 인한 문제가 있어서, ~하러 왔어요.
- I could not do X, so ~. X할 수가 없어서 ~해요.
- I am concerned because ~. ~때문에/~해서 걱정이 돼요.
- The thing is, I ~. 사실, 저는 ~.
- I have to tell you that ~. ~라는 것을 말씀드려야겠네요.
- It seems that ~ is a problem. ~가 문제인 것 같아요.

해결책

- What about ~? ~는/~하는 건 어떨까요?
- Why don't you ~? ~하는 게 어때요?
- If I were you, I would ~. 제가 당신이라면, ~하겠어요.
- I had the same problem, I did ~. 저도 똑같은 문제를 겪었는데, 저는 ~했어요.
- I want to suggest doing ~. ~해 보시라고 말씀 드리고 싶어요.

Example

Man: Student | Woman: Professor

C05_EX

Listen to part of a conversation between a student and a professor.

M Excuse me, Professor Zhang. Can I bother you for a minute?

W Come in, Joel. Of course you can. What can I help you with? I'm sure it's no bother.

M [1] Well, the council has decided that they want to invite a band to play at our fall festival.

W [1] That sounds like a good idea to me. In fact, don't they usually have some musical entertainment?

M [1] Yes, they do. But, it's usually local bands—student bands actually—that play at the festival. But, the vice president's cousin is in a band whose career is just starting to take off, so we decided to invite them to play.

W Again, that sounds like a good idea. Is there a problem?

M Unfortunately, there is. They are eager to play here, and they are going to be on a break during their tour at the time. But, they would need us to pay their expenses. The treasurer said that we would have to have a fundraiser to earn the money.

W Do you have any ideas as to what kind of fundraiser you want to organize?

M So far, the best solution we have been able to come up with is a carwash. People always have cars that need to be washed.

W That is true, but it isn't going to raise much money. You cannot charge much, and there are only so many cars that you can wash in one day. How about you hold an auction? You can publicize your event and make money at the same time.

M An auction? What could we auction off?

1. What can be inferred about the university's fall festival?

Ⓐ It features some kind of music performance every year.

Ⓑ It has many different types of entertainment including auctions.

Ⓒ It helped a few local bands to gain popularity.

Ⓓ It holds an annual auction to raise money for the musicians.

2. What will the student most likely do next?

Ⓐ Call local stores and museums to ask for their help

Ⓑ Fill out an application form to participate in the auction event

Ⓒ Meet Professor Singh to persuade her to become his advisor

Ⓓ Contact Professor Zhang's friend to ask detailed questions

W Well, anything really. You can go around to local businesses and ask them for products to auction. You can also go to libraries and museums. As long as you endorse them during the auction—you know, say which company donated the item and praise them—most businesses will happily donate something. It's a very inexpensive form of advertising for them. Since people will be trying to outbid each other, you should be able to make money fairly quickly.

M That sounds like a great idea, but where would we host such an event?

W You just need an empty lecture hall. Those rooms can hold quite a few people, and they already have AV systems installed.

M You seem to know a lot about this. Have you ever organized an auction before?

W No, [2] not personally, but a colleague of mine organized one at Crichton College last year. They were able to raise enough money to fund two events.

M [2] OK, I will propose this at the next council meeting, which is tonight. Could you put me in touch with your colleague?

W [2] Certainly. Her name is Professor Rhona Singh. She is a tenured professor at Crichton. I have one of her business cards right here.

M Thank you for all of your help, Professor Zhang.

학생과 교수의 대화를 들으시오.

남 실례합니다, 장 교수님, 잠시 시간을 내주실 수 있으세요?

여 들어와요, 조엘, 물론 가능하죠. 어떻게 도와줄까요? 귀찮은 일이 아닐 거라고 확신해요.

남 [1] 음, 위원회에서는 우리 학교의 가을 축제에 공연해줄 밴드를 초청하기로 결정했어요.

여 [1] 좋은 생각 같네요. 사실 항상 음악 공연이 있지 않나요?

남 [1] 네, 맞아요. 하지만 축제에서 공연했던 건 보통 지역 밴드, 사실 학생 밴드였어요. 그렇지만 부회장의 사촌이 이제 막 잘 나가기 시작한 밴드의 멤버여서 그 밴드를 초대하기로 결정했어요.

여 다시 말하지만 좋은 생각이에요. 문제가 있나요?

남 불행히도 있습니다. 그 밴드 역시 우리 학교 축제에서 공연하고 싶어 하고, 그 시기에 공연 투어를 잠시 쉬거든요. 그렇지만 비용을 우리가 내주길 원해요. 회계 담당자분이 그 돈을 벌기 위해 저희가 모금 행사를 해야 할 거라고 말하더군요.

여 어떤 종류의 모금 행사를 조직할지 생각한 게 있나요?

남 저희가 지금까지 생각해낸 것들 중 가장 좋은 해결책은 세차였어요. 사람들은 항상 세차를 필요로 하니까요.

여 맞아요. 하지만 많은 돈을 벌진 못할 거예요. 세차에 많은 비용을 청구할 수도 없고, 그리고 하루에 세차를 할 수 있는 차 역시 한정되어 있으니까요. 경매를 개최하는 건 어때요? 학교 축제를 알리고 동시에 돈도 벌 수 있잖아요.

남 경매요? 저희가 경매에 무엇을 내놓을 수 있을까요?

여 음, 사실 아무 거나요. 지역의 사업체들을 돌아다니면서 경매에 내놓을 물건을 요청할 수 있어요. 도서관이나 박물관에 갈 수도 있죠. 학생이 경매 중간에 이 사업체들을 홍보해주기만 한다면, 즉 어떤 회사에서 이 물건을 내놓았는지 말하고 그 회사를 칭찬한다면, 대부분의 사업체들에서 기쁘게 무언가를 기부할 거예요. 그들에게 있어 매우 값싼 방식의 광고니까요. 사람들이 서로를 이기려고 금액을 부를 테니, 돈을 꽤 빨리 벌 수 있죠.

남 정말 좋은 생각이네요. 하지만 이런 행사를 어디서 열 수 있나요?

여 그저 빈 강당만 하나 있으면 돼요. 그런 강당은 꽤 많은 수의 사람을 수용할 수 있고, 이미 시청각 시스템이 설치되어 있으니까요.

남 경매에 대해 아시는 게 많은 것 같네요. 전에도 경매를 주관해 본 적이 있으세요?

여 아니에요, [2] 개인적으로 해 본 적은 없지만 동료 교수가 작년에 크라이튼 대학에서 경매를 주관했어요. 두 개의 행사에 자금을 댈 수 있을 정도로 충분한 돈을 모았죠.

남 [2] 알겠습니다. 오늘 밤에 있는 위원회 회의에서 경매를 제안해 볼게요. 동료분의 연락처를 가르쳐주실 수 있으신가요?

1. 대학의 가을 축제에 관해 무엇을 추론할 수 있는가?

Ⓐ 매년 어떠한 종류의 음악 공연이 있는 것이 특징이다.

Ⓑ 경매를 포함해 많은 다양한 여흥 거리가 있다.

Ⓒ 몇몇 지역 밴드들이 인기를 얻는 것을 도왔다.

Ⓓ 음악가들을 위한 기금을 모으려고 매년 경매를 연다.

2. 학생이 무엇을 할 것 같은가?

Ⓐ 지역의 가게와 박물관들에 전화를 걸어 도움을 요청한다

Ⓑ 경매 행사에 참석하기 위해 지원서를 작성한다

Ⓒ 싱 교수를 만나 지도 교수가 되어 달라고 설득한다

Ⓓ 장 교수의 친구에게 연락하여 더 자세한 질문들을 물어본다

여 ² 물론이죠. 로나 싱 교수예요. 크라이튼 대학의 종신 재직 교수죠. 여기 명함 한 장이 있어요.

남 도와주셔서 감사합니다, 장 교수님.

1.

정답 (A)

해설 학생이 가을 축제에 밴드를 초대하겠다고 하자 교수가 늘 음악 공연이 있지 않느냐고 물었고, 학생이 그렇다고 대답했으므로 가을 축제에 항상 어떠한 종류의 음악 공연이 있었다는 점을 유추할 수 있다. 정답은 (A)이다.

2.

정답 (D)

해설 학생이 경매 행사를 조직하는 데 관심을 보이자 교수가 자신의 동료가 경험이 있다고 했고, 학생이 그 동료와 연락할 수 있게 해 달라고 부탁한다. 교수가 승낙하며 동료의 명함을 주었으므로 학생이 조만간 교수의 동료에게 연락해 조언을 구할 것이라는 점을 알 수 있다. 정답은 (D)이다.

어휘 bother n 성가신 일 | council n 위원회, 의회 | entertainment n 오락, 여흥 | vice president 부회장 | take off 도약하다 | unfortunately adv 불행히도 | eager adj 간절히 바라는, 열렬한 | expense n 비용 | treasurer n 회계 담당자 | fundraiser n 모금 행사 | earn v 벌다 | organize v 조직하다, 준비하다 | solution n 해결책 | carwash n 세차 | auction n 경매 | publicize v 알리다, 홍보하다 | product n 제품 | endorse v 홍보하다, 지지하다 | donate v 기부하다 | praise v 칭찬하다 | inexpensive adj 비싸지 않은 | advertising n 광고 | outbid v 더 비싼 값을 부르다 | host v 주최하다 | empty adj 비어 있는 | install v 설치하다 | personally adv 개인적으로 | colleague n 동료 | fund v 자금을 대다 | tenured professor 종신 재직 교수

Practice

Passage 1 Listen to part of a conversation between a student and a university employee.

C05_P01

Q. What can be inferred about the man?

(A) He has experience as a tutor.

(B) He is not very good at math.

(C) He does not think the woman is qualified.

(D) He is not interested in hiring the woman.

Passage 2 Listen to part of a conversation between a student and a professor.

C05_P02

Q. What can be inferred about the professor?

(A) He works on the campus literary magazine.

(B) He often submits stories to the magazine.

(C) He does not think the woman is qualified.

(D) He is a well-known and popular author.

Passage 3 Listen to part of a conversation between a student and a registrar.

C05_P03

Q. What can be inferred about the student's situation?

(A) His academic advisor didn't tell him he should take the course.

(B) The class always fills up very quickly every semester.

(C) He was not sure if the class was required to graduate.

(D) He already had a full schedule in his freshman year.

Passage 4 Listen to part of a conversation between a student and a housing officer.

C05_P04

Q. What is implied about the school housing policy?

(A) The school housing policy allows some exceptions.

(B) All the freshmen must live in the dormitories.

(C) The school housing policy does not allow any exceptions.

(D) Seniors must leave the dorm immediately after school finishes.

Passage 5 Listen to part of a conversation between a student and a technician. C05_P05

Q. What can be inferred about the woman?

Ⓐ She has decided to major in computer science.

Ⓑ She will probably want to get a refund on her purchase.

Ⓒ She has never owned a notebook computer before.

Ⓓ She will attend a class about computers on Monday.

Passage 6 Listen to part of a conversation between a student and an administrator. C05_P06

Q. What does the administrator imply about the Asian Studies class?

Ⓐ It is not likely that the student will get into the class.

Ⓑ The class is not very useful to students with his major.

Ⓒ There are not many people interested in taking it.

Ⓓ The class is usually held in the evening.

Passage 7 Listen to part of a conversation between a student and a university employee.

C05_P07

Q. What is implied about the payroll office?

Ⓐ Its computer system was taken down by a virus.

Ⓑ It has recently updated its operating software.

Ⓒ Its computers operate without human assistance.

Ⓓ It does not communicate well with other departments.

Passage 8 Listen to part of a conversation between a student and a professor.

C05_P08

1. What does the professor imply about the student?

Ⓐ He should not be asking the professor for favors.

Ⓑ He has no chance of passing the interview.

Ⓒ He cannot afford to miss the final examination.

Ⓓ He deserves to receive special treatment.

2. What will the student most likely do on Wednesday?

Ⓐ He will take his final exam.

Ⓑ He will fly to New York.

Ⓒ He will refuse the job offer.

Ⓓ He will visit the professor's office.

3. What will the professor most likely do next?

Ⓐ Write a new test for the student to take

Ⓑ Help the student study for his exam

Ⓒ Discuss the company the student may work at

Ⓓ Make travel arrangements for the student

Passage 9 Listen to part of a conversation between a student and a professor. C05_P09

1. What can be inferred about the professor?

   (A) He would not have allowed the student to turn in her assignment late.
   (B) He does not think that the student had a good reason to miss class.
   (C) He has also had to replace his corrective lenses unexpectedly.
   (D) He does not accept homework that is not done in the workbook.

2. What is implied about the other instructor?

   (A) He did not order enough books for the extra students.
   (B) He normally does not teach this level of classes.
   (C) He has to inform other teachers about his schedule.
   (D) He will not be able to help the student with her problem.

3. What will the professor most likely do next?

   (A) He will find out who is teaching the extra class.
   (B) He will give the student a copy of the book.
   (C) He will contact the campus bookstore.
   (D) He will call the head of his department.

Test

Passage 1

[1-5] Listen to part of a conversation between a student and a professor.

정답 및 해석 | P. 82

1. What is the main topic of the conversation?

Ⓐ The student wants a higher grade.
Ⓑ The student is debating changing majors.
Ⓒ The student is considering the Honors Program.
Ⓓ The student is failing the professor's class.

2. What does the professor imply about the Honors Program?

Ⓐ The Honors Program is only for Continental Philosophy.
Ⓑ The student is not eligible for the Honors Program.
Ⓒ The Honors Program is worth the extra work.
Ⓓ There are a limited number of spaces in the Honors Program.

3. What are two key features of the Honors Program? Choose 2 answers.

Ⓐ Doing lots of presentations
Ⓑ Writing a thesis
Ⓒ Taking an oral exam
Ⓓ Taking a long written exam

4. What is the student most likely to do next?

Ⓐ He will meet the professor to develop his thesis.
Ⓑ He will apply to the university for funding.
Ⓒ He will apply to enter the Honors Program.
Ⓓ He will read some work by previous graduates.

5. What does the professor offer to do for the student?

Ⓐ To write a letter of recommendation
Ⓑ To become the student's advisor
Ⓒ To get the student into the program
Ⓓ To help the student with the thesis

Passage 2

[1-5] Listen to part of a conversation between a student and an academic advisor.

1. **Why did the student come to see the academic advisor?**

Ⓐ To enquire about the requirements for the class he wants to take

Ⓑ To get help regarding a class that he could not register for

Ⓒ To ask some questions about his chemistry assignment

Ⓓ To decide what classes he should take for his career

2. **Why is the student unable to take the class that is on Tuesday and Thursday?**

Ⓐ He wants to reserve some time for doing his assignments.

Ⓑ He usually has laboratory sessions during that time.

Ⓒ He has a part-time job on Tuesdays and Thursdays.

Ⓓ He already has another class that coincides with the class.

3. **Why does the advisor mention an online course?**

Ⓐ To point out the fact that the university offers many online lectures

Ⓑ To explain that the student can still take the class he wants

Ⓒ To persuade the student to start taking more of them in the future

Ⓓ To emphasize that some chemistry classes are only offered online

4. **According to the advisor, what is the disadvantage of taking an online course?**

Ⓐ The student is going to miss laboratory sessions.

Ⓑ The student will lose 10% of his final grade.

Ⓒ The student is not allowed to attend study sessions.

Ⓓ The student will not be able to take pop quizzes.

5. **What will the student most likely do next?**

Ⓐ Go back to his room and find another available biology course

Ⓑ Visit another building to pay for his class tuition

Ⓒ Go to see Professor Stepanov to get her signature

Ⓓ Call Professor Stepanov to ask for further instructions

Conversation Topic Types

대화 주제는 크게 아래 두 가지로 나눌 수 있다. 앞에서 학습한 문제 유형별 전략을 바탕으로, 각 유형별로 준비된 5~6개의 대화를 듣고 문제를 풀어보면서 다양한 대화 주제와 상황에 대응하는 연습을 해 보자.

Lesson

01 Office Hours

Lesson Outline

집무 시간(Office Hours)과 관련된 대화는 주로 교수의 사무실에 학생이 찾아가거나, 교수가 학생에게 물을 것이 있어 부른 뒤 대화가 시작된다. 대화의 주제는 시험, 과제나 성적 관련이 많으며 진로 상담이나 학교 규정에 관한 내용도 찾아볼 수 있다. 시험, 과제와 관련된 대화의 경우 짤막하게 학술적 내용이 등장할 때가 많다. 예를 들어, 학생이 특정 작가에 관한 에세이를 쓸 경우, 해당 작가의 생애나 작품에 관해 교수와 구체적인 이야기를 나누는 식이다.

Conversation Flow

일반적으로 대화가 진행되는 방식을 정리하면 다음과 같다.

1 인사

교수와 학생이 서로에게 인사한다. 교수가 '무슨 일로 날 찾아왔나요?'라고 묻거나 학생이 '무슨 일로 저를 부르셨어요?'라고 한다.

2 이유 설명

교수나 학생이 대화를 하고 싶어한 이유를 설명한다. 이 이유가 주제 찾기 문제(Main Idea Question)의 답인 경우가 대부분이다.

3 상황이나 문제 논의

교수와 학생이 문제점이나 상황을 놓고 이야기한다. 학술적 내용은 주로 이때 나온다. 세부 사항 찾기 문제(Details Question)가 이 학술적 내용에서 자주 출제되므로 긴장을 놓지 말고 듣자.

4 상황이나 문제에 관한 해결책·대응 방안 제시

문제가 무엇인지 파악한 뒤 교수나 학생이 '그러면 이러이러한 방법은 어떨까요?' 혹은 '이렇게 해주실 수 있나요?'라고 제안한다.

5 대화 마무리

학생이 교수의 제안에 대해 감사 인사를 할 때가 많다. 혹은 교수가 학생의 자신감을 북돋워주거나 도움이 되어 기쁘다고 마무리하기도 한다.

Key Signals

1 인사

▶ 교수가 학생을 부른 경우: 교수의 말에서 상황/문제점이 제시된다.

Hello, Kevin. I'm glad you could make it. 안녕하세요, 케빈 학생. 올 수 있어서 다행이에요.

You wanted to see[speak] to me, professor? 저를 찾으셨다고요, 교수님?

▶ 학생이 교수를 찾아간 경우: 학생의 말에서 상황/문제점이 제시된다.

What brings you to my office today? 무슨 일로 오늘 제 연구실에 온 건가요?

May I talk to you for a moment, professor? 잠깐 이야기 좀 할 수 있을까요, 교수님?

2 이유 설명

- I just wanted to check ~. ~에 대해 확인하고 싶었을 뿐이에요.
- You said you wanted to discuss my ~? 제 ~에 관해 논의하고 싶다고 하셨다면서요?
- I need your help with my ~. 제 ~와 관련해서 도움이 필요해요.
- I need your advice about ~. ~에 대한 교수님의 조언이 필요해요.
- I am having some trouble with ~. ~로 문제를 좀 겪고 있어서요.

3 상황이나 문제 논의

- What seems to be the problem? 무슨 문제가 있나요?
- What is your situation? 어떤 상황인가요?
- I have to submit this form for ~. ~를 위해 이 양식을 제출해야 해요.
- Is there someone who can help me ~? 제가 ~하는 걸 도와줄 사람이 있을까요?
- How do I go about ~? ~하려면 어떻게 해야 할까요?

4 상황이나 문제에 관한 해결책·대응 방안 제시

- Have you considered ~? ~를 고려해 봤나요?
- First, you need to ~. 먼저, ~해야 해요.
- I'll make arrangements to ~. ~할 수 있도록 준비할게요.
- I will tell ~ about the situation. ~에게 이 상황에 대해 말할게요.
- That depends upon ~. 그건 ~에 따라 달라요.

5 대화 마무리

- That would work quite well. 그렇게 하면 상당히 괜찮겠네요.
- I'll go and do that immediately. 지금 바로 가서 그렇게 할게요.
- That will solve a lot of problems for me. 그걸로 많은 문제가 해결될 것 같아요.

Test

Passage 1

[1-5] Listen to part of a conversation between a student and a professor.

정답 및 해석 | P. 87

1. What are the speakers mainly discussing?

Ⓐ The effects of eating various bitter vegetables

Ⓑ The reason why some people do not like vegetables

Ⓒ The student's research for a class presentation

Ⓓ The reasons for not being able to do a presentation on time

2. Why does the student ask the professor whether or not she likes broccoli?

Ⓐ To introduce the topic of the research he has been working on

Ⓑ To find out if she dislikes vegetables like he does

Ⓒ To ask why she does not like bitter vegetables

Ⓓ To make a point about the bitter-tasting foods

3. According to the student's research, why are some people not affected by the bitterness of vegetables?

Ⓐ They have become used to the taste.

Ⓑ They suffered a childhood trauma.

Ⓒ They only eat them with sauces.

Ⓓ They have a genetic predisposition.

4. What can be inferred about the student?

Ⓐ He would do anything to avoid eating bitter things.

Ⓑ He is not sure if his topic would be good for the presentation.

Ⓒ He has prepared a lot for his class presentation.

Ⓓ He has a mutation in his DNA related to taste.

5. What does the man mean when he says this: 🎧

Ⓐ He doesn't know if the chemicals are legal to purchase.

Ⓑ He is hoping to get inspiration by going shopping.

Ⓒ He thinks that the grocery pharmacy may have the chemicals he needs.

Ⓓ He believes he will be able to find certain ingredients from the store.

Passage 2

[1-5] Listen to part of a conversation between a student and a professor.  C01_T02

1. **Why did the professor want to see the student?**

Ⓐ To question the credibility of the references the student used

Ⓑ To cast doubt on the student's ability to cite references

Ⓒ To ask the student to add information regarding wind turbines

Ⓓ To explain the difference between tidal and wind turbines

2. **What is the biggest problem of using company websites as resources?**

Ⓐ It creates conflict between the student's ideas and reality.

Ⓑ It cannot provide enough information for the paper.

Ⓒ It might lead the writer to use wrong information and data.

Ⓓ It can provide the writer with information from a biased perspective.

3. **According to the professor, what is true about tidal turbines? Choose 2 answers.**

Ⓐ Utilizing them eventually brings negative effects on the environment.

Ⓑ They cannot be made of common metals since they are vulnerable to seawater.

Ⓒ They depend on weather conditions too much, thus limiting their usage.

Ⓓ Using tidal turbines is more dependable than utilizing solar panels.

4. **Listen again to part of the conversation. Then answer the question.**

Why does the professor say this:

Ⓐ He is surprised by the student's insight into environmental problems.

Ⓑ He thought the student would ask other questions related to tidal turbines.

Ⓒ He thinks the student already knows much about her research topic.

Ⓓ He wants to tell the student that there are indeed some drawbacks.

5. **Why does the professor mention New York City, Norway, and England?**

Ⓐ To give examples of the places that have constructed tidal turbines

Ⓑ To show how these places affected the development of tidal turbines

Ⓒ To provide more references that could be useful for the student's paper

Ⓓ To tell the student to do more research regarding these important locations

Passage 3

[1-5] Listen to part of a conversation between a student and a professor.  C01_T03

1. **Why did the student come to see her professor?**

Ⓐ To get his opinion regarding the theme of her final paper

Ⓑ To get the email address of Doctor Kandaris from him

Ⓒ To ask a question that she was not able to ask during the class

Ⓓ To explain why she was not able to understand the class material

2. **What can be inferred about animals' sleep?**

Ⓐ There is a high chance that they dream like humans do.

Ⓑ They often exhibit different sleeping patterns from humans'.

Ⓒ The evidence of animal dreaming was found about 10 years ago.

Ⓓ Their dreaming does not take place during REM sleep.

3. **What do the student and the professor say about observing animals in their sleep? Choose 2 answers.**

Ⓐ They show some possible signs of dreaming like twitching or barking.

Ⓑ The brain activity of animals in sleep is dramatically different from humans'.

Ⓒ Tracking devices were used when animals were observed in a laboratory setting.

Ⓓ Observing them in the wild is difficult and needs further technical development.

4. **Listen again to part of the conversation. Then answer the question.**

Why does the professor say this:

Ⓐ He does not want the student to waste her time.

Ⓑ He is encouraging the student to take an opportunity now.

Ⓒ He is telling the student to be patient because there will be other opportunities.

Ⓓ He does not understand why the student is reluctant to participate.

5. **What is the student's attitude toward Doctor Kandaris' research project?**

Ⓐ She enjoyed being part of the project and wants to participate again.

Ⓑ She is unable to make a decision because she feels confused.

Ⓒ She sees it as a great opportunity and she is interested in it.

Ⓓ She wants to join the project but is too busy with her class schedule.

Passage 4

[1-5] Listen to part of a conversation between a student and a professor. 

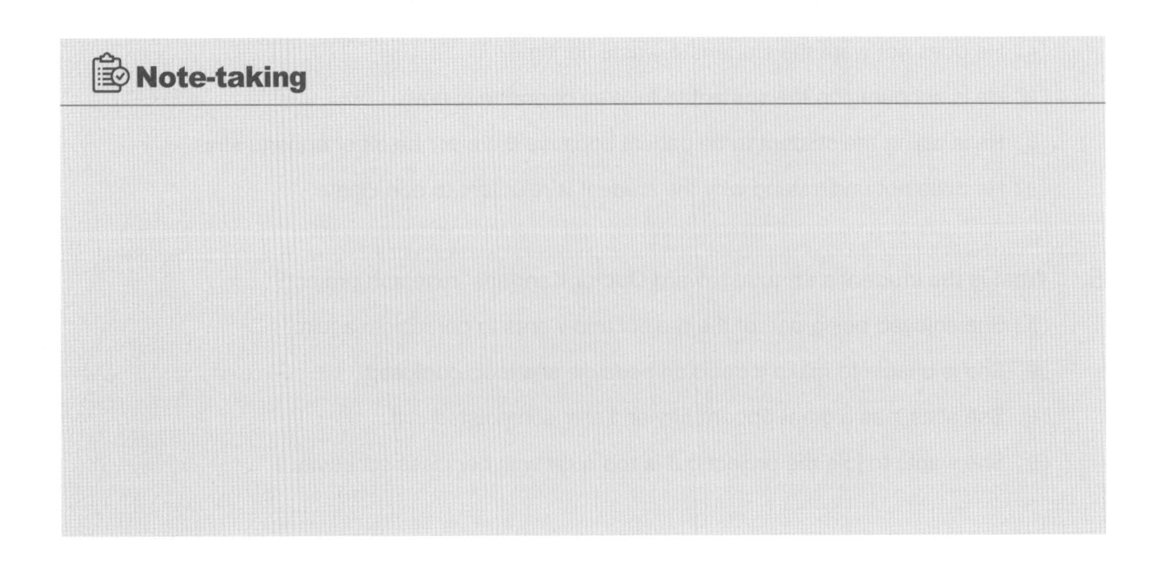

1. **Why did the student come to see her professor?**

Ⓐ To see if she is doing well with her class presentation

Ⓑ To ask questions about a teacher's assistant position

Ⓒ To discuss the topic of her thesis paper with the professor

Ⓓ To reschedule her working shift as a teacher's assistant

2. **What was mentioned about Margaret Cavendish?**

Ⓐ She dressed outrageously since she liked showing off.

Ⓑ She was a philosopher who expressed some radical ideas.

Ⓒ She tried to convince other philosophers with her theories.

Ⓓ She shared her ideas with the public and gained support.

3. **Listen again to part of a conversation. Then answer the question.**

Why does the professor say this:

Ⓐ To suggest the student apply for the position quickly

Ⓑ To make sure that the information he has is up-do-date

Ⓒ To tell the student that she is too advanced for the position

Ⓓ To imply that she may be ineligible for the position

4. **Why does the professor mention Jeremy Bentham?**

Ⓐ To tell the student who she needs to know about for a tutoring session

Ⓑ To introduce the topic of the next discussion in her class

Ⓒ To ask the student to study more about him for her term paper

Ⓓ To emphasize the influence he had on Lady Cavendish

5. **What can be inferred about the student?**

Ⓐ She will start working as a philosophy tutor soon.

Ⓑ She is going to change her schedule to work as a tutor.

Ⓒ She is taking small-credit classes this semester.

Ⓓ She will teach only on Tuesdays and Wednesdays.

Passage 5

[1-5] Listen to part of a conversation between a student and a professor.

1. What are the speakers mainly discussing?

(A) The benefits of buying art supplies that cause no harm to the environment
(B) Using and purchasing green art supplies in the art department
(C) Finding a green art supply company to be the university's partner
(D) Getting advice regarding how to write an official petition

2. What makes using environmentally friendly art supplies difficult?

(A) They are usually too expensive to fit in the art department budget.
(B) The school only accepts items manufactured by the university's partners.
(C) The university would not purchase them because they are made overseas.
(D) The green art supply companies are not certified by the government.

3. What does the professor suggest the student do?

(A) Submit a proposal to the university regarding the use of green art supplies
(B) Collect art major students' signatures to increase the department budget
(C) Purchase and use environmentally friendly art supplies himself
(D) Continue his research on the advantages of using green art supplies

4. Listen to part of the conversation. Then answer the question:
Why does the professor say this:

(A) To compare the quality and price of those two types of art supplies
(B) To ask him about the benefits of using supplies made of recycled materials
(C) To inquire about the student's opinion of some green art supplies
(D) To decide whether or not to write a customer review about them

5. Why does the professor mention a business arrangement?

(A) To explain that the board of directors prefer having business partners
(B) To tell the student about the process of writing an official petition
(C) To illustrate a way of buying green art supplies at reduced prices
(D) To show the necessity of one when it comes to big department budgets

Passage 6

[1-5] Listen to part of a conversation between a student and a professor.  C01_T06

1. What is the purpose of the student's visit? **Choose 2 answers.**

Ⓐ To get the professor's help with writing effective essays

Ⓑ To ask for the professor's advice regarding her internship opportunity

Ⓒ To see if the professor would be willing to provide a reference letter

Ⓓ To acquire information on using personal anecdotes in an essay

2. What is the student's opinion about business writing?

Ⓐ She does not feel confident doing it since she did not do well in the class.

Ⓑ She thinks it is confusing since it is quite similar to academic writing.

Ⓒ She believes she can manage since she is good at writing research papers.

Ⓓ She sees it as quite challenging since she does not have much business experience.

3. What are the differences between business and essay writing? **Choose 2 answers.**

Ⓐ Business writing usually starts with the purpose of writing.

Ⓑ Business writing tends to use much more indirect language.

Ⓒ People tend to make more mistakes in business writing.

Ⓓ Essay writing is often more creative than business writing.

4. Why does the professor mention 20-dollar words?

Ⓐ To show an example of why people make mistakes with their word choices

Ⓑ To name one of the mistakes that people often make when they do business writing

Ⓒ To emphasize that business writing should not be longer than research papers

Ⓓ To give another example of things that make business writing less restrictive

5. What makes the professor think the student's anecdote is perfect for the intern position?

Ⓐ It shows that the student is aware of how to organize a team to win a competition.

Ⓑ It shows that the student knows how to manage production costs and deal with a small budget.

Ⓒ It shows that the student was able to overcome difficult situations even though she was new.

Ⓓ It shows that the student already has some experience in coordinating music-related events.

Lesson

02 Service-Related

문제 듣기

Lesson Outline

교내 서비스 관련(Service-Related) 대화는 대학 캠퍼스의 다양한 곳에서 일어날 수 있는 상황을 다루고 있다. 기숙사, 구내 식당, 대학 서점, 행정 사무실이나 학생회관 등에서 학생이 담당자 또는 학교 직원과 이야기하는 방식으로 구성되어 있다. 학생이 문제를 해결하기 위해 질문하거나 도움을 요청하는 경우가 대부분이다.

Conversation Flow

일반적으로 대화가 진행되는 방식을 정리하면 다음과 같다.

1 인사

직원과 학생이 서로 인사한다.

2 이유 설명

직원이 '어떻게 도와드릴까요?'라고 묻거나 학생이 '이러저러한 문제 때문에 왔어요'라고 설명한다. 이 이유가 주제 찾기 문제(Main Idea Question)의 답인 경우가 대부분이다.

3 상황이나 문제 논의

직원과 학생이 문제점이나 상황을 놓고 이야기한다.

4 상황이나 문제에 관한 해결책·정보 제시

문제가 무엇인지 파악한 뒤 직원이 학생을 돕기 위한 해결책이나 정보를 제시한다.

5 대화 마무리

학생이 직원의 제안에 대해 감사 인사를 할 때가 많다. 혹은 직원이 학생에게 필요한 자료나 서류를 제공하며 끝날 때도 있다.

Key Signals

1 인사·이유 설명

도입부에서 대화가 이루어지는 장소와 상황·문제 파악 관련 정보가 주어지는 경우가 많다.

- Hello, is this ~? 안녕하세요, 여기가 ~인가요?
- I came to check if ~. ~인지 확인하러 왔어요.
- I came here to ~. ~하려고 여기 왔어요.
- I'm looking for some information on ~. ~에 대한 정보를 찾고 있어요.
- Can I sign up for ~ here? 여기서 ~를 등록할 수 있나요?

2 상황이나 문제 논의

- What is troubling you? 무슨 문제를 겪고 계신가요?
- I have an issue with ~. ~에 문제가 있어요.
- We have to inspect ~. ~를 조사해 봐야 되겠어요.
- Let me check ~ to see what's happened. 어떻게 된 일인지 ~를 확인해 볼게요.

3 상황이나 문제에 관한 해결책·정보 제시

- Actually, we have had a bit of a problem ~. 사실, 저희가 ~에 문제가 좀 있었어요.
- You could also look for other ~. 다른 ~를 찾아보실 수도 있어요.
- You need to check ~. ~를 확인하세요.
- First, you need to ~. 먼저, ~해야 해요.
- Your ~ will be sufficient. 학생의 ~면 충분해요.
- Once you ~, it should take about + 기간. 일단 ~하고 나면, (기간) 정도 걸릴 거예요.
- Today is the deadline for ~. 오늘이 ~의 마감일이에요.

4 대화 마무리

대화가 끝난 후 이어질 행동에 대한 정보가 나올 수 있으므로 끝까지 주의해서 듣는다.

- Thanks. I'll go over to ~ right now. 감사합니다. ~로 바로 가 볼게요.
- I think we can work something out. 어떻게든 해 볼 수 있을 거예요.
- You can get X at the ~. ~에서 X를 얻을 수 있어요.
- I will let X know ~. X에게 ~라고/~를 알려 놓을게요.

Test

Passage 1

[1-5] Listen to part of a conversation between a student and a university employee. C02_T01

정답 및 해석 | P. 104

1. **What is the student's problem?**

Ⓐ She has too many papers to make copies of.

Ⓑ She noticed that the copy machine is not taking coins.

Ⓒ She cannot get the copy machine to print her flyers.

Ⓓ She needs change to run the copy machine.

2. **What is the purpose of the fundraising event the student is organizing?**

Ⓐ Paying for her graduate school tuition to continue her research

Ⓑ Providing playthings for little children who need help

Ⓒ Purchasing sandboxes for some preschools to do research

Ⓓ Making sandboxes and board games for child participants

3. **What can be inferred about the fundraising event?**

Ⓐ The student will give out a book that is worth 15 dollars.

Ⓑ Professor Marat is in charge of organizing the event.

Ⓒ The state government is also supporting the event.

Ⓓ The attendees will be receiving Professor Marat's book.

4. **What is the employee's opinion about the fundraising event?**

Ⓐ He thinks many people would be willing to pay 15 dollars.

Ⓑ He thinks the students did an excellent job of planning it.

Ⓒ He believes that the event will be a huge success.

Ⓓ He feels that the event needs more promotion in the school.

5. **What does the employee suggest the student do?**

Ⓐ Get some help from the technician to fix the copy machine

Ⓑ Get enough coins to print 500 flyers in the library

Ⓒ Use another copy machine on another floor

Ⓓ Find someone to help her making copies of the flyers

Passage 2

[1-5] Listen to part of a conversation between a student and a dining services director. C02_T02

1. **What is the purpose of the student's visit to the dining service director?**

Ⓐ Persuading the director to give him a refund for his left-over meals

Ⓑ Explaining the reason why he could not use the whole meal plan

Ⓒ Obtaining information to fill out a petition form about meal plans

Ⓓ Asking questions regarding his meal plan since he has some left over

2. **What is the reason why the student thinks he will be unable to spend the rest of his meal plan?**

Ⓐ The current semester will end in just a few weeks.

Ⓑ He skips meals often as he is busy with school activities.

Ⓒ He is unable to share his meal plan with a friend.

Ⓓ Students cannot spend more than three meals per day.

3. **What can be inferred about the student's opinion about the meal plan with 195 meals?**

Ⓐ He thinks it is more cost-effective than the 150-meal plan.

Ⓑ He still doubts if he will be able to use the entire plan.

Ⓒ He wonders if he could purchase that option next semester.

Ⓓ He feels that 195 meals would not be enough for him.

4. **Listen again to part of the conversation. Then answer the question.**

Why does the woman say this:

Ⓐ To show that they are strict rules that were established by the university

Ⓑ To clarify that his parents should pay attention when purchasing meal plans

Ⓒ To explain that they do not limit the decisions of students and parents

Ⓓ To emphasize the importance of purchasing a meal plan in advance

5. **What will the student do next?**

Ⓐ Fill out the registration form for the next semester's meal plan

Ⓑ Pick up a form to file a petition regarding meal plans

Ⓒ Visit the Student Hall in the next building to obtain a document

Ⓓ Look for people who would be willing to support his idea

Passage 3

[1-5] Listen to part of a conversation between a student and a housing officer.  C02_T03

1. **What is the purpose of the student's return to the university office?**

(A) To see if he can make a change to his current situation

(B) To ask for details about the process of the room selection system

(C) To inquire whether it is possible to swap rooms with one of his friends

(D) To obtain some information regarding choosing his roommates

2. **What is the employee's concern at the beginning of the conversation?**

(A) She feels bad for the student since she did not grant him permission.

(B) She finds the student's situation to be easy since he should already know the answer.

(C) She thinks the student will be dissatisfied since she will not be of much help.

(D) She believes the student has a complicated problem since he has returned.

3. **What can be inferred about the student's situation based on the lottery number he drew?**

(A) He needs to find someone to change numbers with as soon as possible.

(B) His new room might be very similar to the one that he has now.

(C) He has a very low chance of getting the room that he wants to have.

(D) Students who drew numbers above 1,000 are placed in Harris Hall.

4. **In the conversation, the speakers discuss the regulations regarding room selection. Indicate in the table below whether each of the following is one of those regulations.**

Click in the correct box for each sentence.

	Yes	No
(A) Rooms are selected in alphabetical order for each class.		
(B) Upperclassmen are given the first choice of accommodations.		
(C) Rooms are selected using a lottery system to make it fairer.		
(D) Students are not allowed to exchange their lottery numbers.		

5. **What suggestion does the employee make?**

(A) To look for some of his friends who were already assigned their room

(B) To find people who have a good room number but do not have roommates yet

(C) To search for a smaller single room that was declined by other students

(D) To become a roommate of a second year student who has a higher chance

Passage 4

[1-5] Listen to part of a conversation between a student and a library employee. 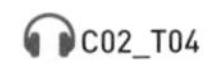 C02_T04

1. **Why did the student come to see the library employee?**

Ⓐ To receive recently updated information from the library

Ⓑ To inquire how to gain access to a certain floor of the library

Ⓒ To get his advice on finding online articles in the library

Ⓓ To find out if she can check out books at a late hour

2. **Why was the student not notified about the renovation of the third floor?**

Ⓐ Her thesis advisor was away in another country for research.

Ⓑ She was so busy that she forgot to check her email.

Ⓒ She was unable to visit the library for quite a while.

Ⓓ The university only sent notification to the library staff.

3. **Listen again to part of the conversation. Then answer the question.**

Why does the man say this:

Ⓐ To explain that the school often does unexpected things

Ⓑ To apologize for the fact that the student has to wait for a week

Ⓒ To say that the library was not prepared for the renovation either

Ⓓ To show how surprised he is that the renovation is occurring

4. **What does the library employee suggest the student do?**

Ⓐ Sign her name on the waiting list to read the books at Ratchet Hall

Ⓑ Go and check out the necessary books from the library basement

Ⓒ Wait until next Monday when the renovation will be completed

Ⓓ Visit another building to find the materials needed for her thesis paper

5. **In the conversation, the student states reasons that keeping documents in the basement of Ratchet Hall is inconvenient. Indicate in the table below whether each of the following is one of those reasons. Click in the correct box for each sentence.**

	Yes	No
Ⓐ Ratchet Hall is too far away from the student's dormitory.		
Ⓑ It is prohibited to check out any of the books that are there.		
Ⓒ Students cannot have access there after 5 p.m.		
Ⓓ The place is too small to keep such a large amount of books.		
Ⓔ Ratchet Hall is currently being renovated to update its collection.		

Passage 5

[1-5] Listen to part of a conversation between a student and an employee of the campus management department.

C02_T05

1. What is the purpose of the student's visit?

Ⓐ To ask questions about two lecture halls in different buildings
Ⓑ To inquire about the confirmation of his reservation
Ⓒ To repair a program for the campus management
Ⓓ To reserve another lecture hall for a guest speaker

2. What is the reason why the student wanted to change the lecture hall?

Ⓐ He always preferred room 1025 to room 1245.
Ⓑ He was confused about what would be the best location.
Ⓒ He failed to predict that the audience would be so large.
Ⓓ He was not able to book a room due to a system failure.

3. What is the biggest problem with the department's new program?

Ⓐ It will not show students the changes they have made.
Ⓑ It continues to stop and freeze, canceling reservations.
Ⓒ It stopped updating the requests that were submitted.
Ⓓ It only allows automated changes to show up on the program.

4. What can be inferred about the student's new reservation?

Ⓐ The student has to notify attendees about the change of location.
Ⓑ The student has to book the lecture hall in Carter Hall himself.
Ⓒ Students cannot make new reservations currently.
Ⓓ The student has to come back again to make a new reservation.

5. What is the woman's attitude toward the student's suggestion?

Ⓐ She is interested to see how he is going to repair the computer program.
Ⓑ She feels sorry because she has to get the manager's permission first.
Ⓒ She is somewhat hesitant about the student's ability to fix the program.
Ⓓ She gladly accepts his offer since the department needs assistance.

Passage 6

[1-5] Listen to part of a conversation between a student and a scholarship administrator. C02_T06

1. **Why did the student come to see the administrator?**

Ⓐ He came to check the result of applying for a curator position.

Ⓑ He wanted to ask some questions about the museum's scholarship.

Ⓒ He was trying to find someone who can help him with his job search.

Ⓓ He does not know where to go to see the museum's art exhibition.

2. **Why does the woman mention the student's résumé?**

Ⓐ It shows how good of a candidate the student is for the position.

Ⓑ It is necessary for all students who want to work at the museum.

Ⓒ She wants to see if he has sufficient experience to hire him.

Ⓓ She thought he came to apply to become a curator.

3. **What is true about the scholarship? Choose 2 answers.**

Ⓐ The scholarship amount was included on the flyer.

Ⓑ The due date for applications is coming soon.

Ⓒ It requires students to turn in their portfolios.

Ⓓ All applicants need to submit the appropriate form.

4. **What is the woman's attitude toward the student's work?**

Ⓐ She feels that the man needs to work more on his skills in interior design.

Ⓑ She doubts if the man could get the scholarship, but she wants to be polite.

Ⓒ She thinks it is good since she encourages him to apply for the scholarship.

Ⓓ She does not really know what to say since she is not an expert on sculpture.

5. **Listen again to part of the conversation. Then answer the question.**

Why does the woman say this:

Ⓐ She is telling the student not to miss this good opportunity.

Ⓑ She is urging him to apply as soon as possible for the scholarship.

Ⓒ She is being indirect about telling the student his evaluation result.

Ⓓ She is worried about the fact that the student does not seem eager.

II
Lectures

Introduction & Tips

Part 1. Lecture Question Types

Part 2. Lecture Topics Types

Lectures

Introduction

iBT TOEFL Listening Lectures

TOEFL Listening에서 강의(Lecture) 유형은 총 3~5개 출제된다. 교수 혼자 강의하는 유형과 교수가 강의하는 도중 학생이 한두 마디 질문을 하는 유형이 있다. 보통 1 지문당 550~850단어의 길이로 이루어져 있으며(약 4~5분), 강의를 듣고 1~6번 문제를 풀게 된다. 대화와 마찬가지로 필기용 종이가 제공되기 때문에 강의를 들으면서 노트 필기와 요약이 가능하다.

Lecture Question Types

강의 하나당 여섯 문제를 풀게 되며 문제 유형은 아래와 같이 총 다섯 가지이다.

1. **주제 찾기(Main Idea):** 강의의 주제·목적 찾기
2. **세부 사항 찾기(Details):** 강의를 들으며 알 수 있는 주제 관련 세부 내용 찾기
3. **의도 및 태도 파악(Function & Attitude):** 교수나 학생이 어떠한 말을 한 이유 또는 무언가에 대한 화자의 태도 파악하기
4. **관계 파악(Connecting Contents):** 강의가 연결된 방식 또는 무언가가 언급된 이유 파악하기
5. **추론(Inference):** 강의를 통해 유추할 수 있는 내용 찾기

Lecture Topic Types

강의 주제는 크게 두 가지로 분류할 수 있으며, 각각의 대분류 아래에 다음과 같은 주제들이 주로 등장한다.

1. **과학(Science)**

   건축(Architecture), 천문학(Astronomy), 생물학(Biology), 화학(Chemistry), 공학(Engineering), 환경 과학(Environmental Science), 지질학(Geology), 기상학(Meteorology), 고생물학(Paleontology), 물리학(Physics), 생리학(Physiology)

2. **인문학(Humanities)**

   인류학(Anthropology), 고고학(Archaeology), 미술(Art), 경영학(Business Management), 경제학(Economics), 영화 연구(Film Studies), 역사(History), 언어학(Linguistics), 문학(Literature), 음악(Music), 사진술(Photography), 심리학(Psychology)

Tips

이 강의의 주제·중심 내용이 무엇인가?

대화와 마찬가지로 강의의 주제와 중심 내용은 일반적으로 강의가 시작되고 나서 거의 바로 파악할 수 있다. 교수의 도입부 설명을 통해 이 강의가 무엇에 관한 강의인지 알 수 있다. 강의의 주제·중심 내용을 묻는 문제는 반드시 한 문제씩 출제되며 강의 전체의 맥락을 잡는 데 있어서 가장 기본적인 사항이므로 주의해서 듣도록 하자.

세부 정보를 파악하라!

강의의 주제와 중심 내용을 알면 그에 맞춰 세부 정보를 파악할 수 있다. 세부 정보 역시 강의 하나당 1~2개의 문제가 반드시 출제되므로 처음부터 끝까지 긴장을 놓지 말고 듣자.

화자의 말투와 대화 분위기는 어떤가?

의도 및 태도 파악 문제(Function & Attitude Question)는 강의에서도 찾아볼 수 있다. 대화와 마찬가지로 강의 맥락 속에서 화자의 의견과 태도를 파악해야 하는 문제가 나온다. 교수가 특정 주제를 비꼬아서 말할 수도 있고, 주제에 관해 찬성하거나 반대하는 등 다양한 형식이 등장하므로 상황 속의 명확한 의미를 파악할 수 있도록 하자.

강의에서도 노트 필기를 놓치지 말자!

강의는 대화에 비해 더 길며, 어렵거나 익숙하지 않은 주제가 나오면 듣는 도중에 집중력이 흐트러지기 쉽다. 노트 필기를 하며 강의 주제의 요점과 특징을 알아보기 쉽도록 간단히 정리하는 법을 익혀보자.

정답은 정직하게 출제되지 않는다!

대화와 마찬가지로 강의 또한 교수나 학생이 말한 단어가 문제 보기에 그대로 출제되는 경우는 거의 없다. 특정 단어에만 너무 초점을 맞추지 말고 전반적인 내용과 뜻에 집중하도록 하자. 내용을 먼저 이해한 후 같은 단어가 아니라 다른 단어를 사용했더라도 같은 의미를 나타내는 패러프레이징된 표현을 골라낼 수 있어야 한다.

주제에 대한 친밀감을 높이자!

강의 지문의 경우 대학교 전공 수업 수준의 내용이 등장하다 보니, 조금 생소한 주제와 단어가 나오면 내용 자체를 따라잡는 데 어려움을 겪고 당황하는 경우가 많다. 다양한 강의 주제에 익숙해질 수 있도록 자주 등장하는 주제에 대한 배경지식과 핵심 어휘를 꼭 익혀두자.

Lecture Question Types

Lesson

01 Main Idea

문제 듣기

Lesson Outline

주제 찾기 문제(Main Idea Question)는 강의나 토론을 듣고 주제를 찾는 문제로, 지문마다 한 문제씩 반드시 출제된다. 대부분의 경우 교수가 강의 주제를 직접 말하므로 크게 어렵지 않지만, 가끔 너무 세부적인 내용에 집중하게 되면 강의 내용 전체를 포함하지 않는 선택지를 고르게 되므로 주의해서 전체를 보아야 한다.

Lesson Point

Point 1 도입부 + 교수가 말하는 표시어(signal) = 강의의 주제!

Point 2 너무 세부적인 내용을 다루는 보기는 오답이다.

Point 3 보기에서 키워드가 패러프레이징 되어 있을 확률이 높다.

Point 4 강의에서는 주제가 곧 Main Idea!

Point 5 끝까지 듣고 주제를 고르면 모든 보기가 답으로 보인다. 도입부에서 교수가 하는 말에 집중하자.

Typical Questions

- What is the [lecture/discussion/talk] mainly about? [강의/토론/담화]는 주로 무엇에 관한 것인가?
- What is the professor mainly discussing? 교수는 주로 무엇을 논의하고 있는가?
- What is the main idea of the lecture? 강의의 요지는 무엇인가?
- What is the main purpose of the lecture? 강의의 주요 목적은 무엇인가?
- What is the speaker talking about? 화자는 무엇에 관해 이야기하고 있는가?

Learning Strategies

'주제 찾기' 표시어(signal)를 공략한다!

대화와 마찬가지로 강의/토론의 도입부에서 교수가 하는 말 중 주제가 나올 것을 미리 알리는 표시어를 파악하고, 그 뒤에 나오는 주제를 집중해서 듣는다.

- Today, we're going to talk about ~. — 오늘 우리는 ~에 대해서 이야기할 겁니다.
- Okay, let's start with ~. — 좋아요, ~부터 시작합시다.
- I'd like to focus on ~ today. — 오늘은 ~에 초점을 맞춰 보고자 합니다.
- What I'd like to talk about today is ~. — 제가 오늘 하려는 이야기는 ~입니다.
- Today, I want to take a look at ~. — 오늘은 ~에 대해 살펴보고자 합니다.
- Our discussion for today is going to be ~. — 오늘 우리가 토론할 것은 ~입니다.
- Today, I would like to turn our attention to ~. — 오늘은 ~로 관심을 돌려 볼 겁니다.
- The topic we're going to focus on today is ~. — 오늘 우리가 초점을 두고자 하는 주제는 ~입니다.
- Last time, we talked about ~, and we're going to continue ~. — 지난 시간에는 ~에 대해 이야기했었는데요, 계속해서 ~해 보겠습니다.

Example

Man: Professor

Listen to part of a lecture in an art history class.

M Pablo Picasso is an artist who tried his hand at just about every medium imaginable and was successful at pretty much everything he attempted. He was a painter, printmaker, sculptor, ceramicist, poet, playwright, and stage designer who is known as a co-founder of the Cubist movement, collage, and the invention of constructed sculpture, and for developing and exploring a diverse array of other artistic styles. Along with Marcel Duchamp and Henri Matisse, Picasso is viewed as one of the chief artists who embodied the revolutionary artistic movements in visual arts at the beginning of the 20th century. Picasso was extraordinarily prolific throughout his life, and he achieved worldwide fame and amassed great personal wealth for his artistic accomplishments. From a very early age, Picasso displayed immense artistic talent, and although he began painting in a very realistic manner, his style shifted as he experimented with other techniques and theories of art. For this reason, critics and historians typically categorize his works into different periods defined by their stylistic, technical, and thematic content.

After World War I, he and many other artists returned to a more neoclassical style of art, and he painted some realistic portraits, like those of his wife Olga Khokhlova. He entered into an exclusive contract with art dealer Paul Rosenberg, and he began to become wealthy. He half-heartedly entered the Surrealist movement for a time, but after the Spanish Civil War, he seems to have fully embraced Cubism as his predominant style. After the German bombing of Guernica, Spain, he produced his most famous cubist painting, *Guernica*, which depicted the horrors of war and its effects on humanity.

Q. What is the lecture mainly about?

(A) Characteristics of cubism and its influence

(B) A pioneer who worked with the natural environment

(C) An artist's struggles to become famous

(D) A famous artist's life and artistic styles

미술사 강의의 일부를 들으시오.

남 파블로 피카소는 상상할 수 있는 모든 표현 수단을 시도했었고, 그가 시도했던 거의 모든 것들에 성공을 거두었던 예술가입니다. 그는 화가, 판화 제작자, 조각가, 도예가, 시인, 극작가, 그리고 무대 디자이너였으며 입체파 운동의 공동 창설자, 콜라주, 건축 조형물 발명으로 알려져 있고, 다른 여러 다양한 예술 양식을 발전시키고 탐구한 것으로도 잘 알려져 있습니다. 마르셀 뒤샹과 앙리 마티스와 함께 파카소는 20세기 초에 혁명적 예술 운동을 시각 예술에 구현했던 가장 주요한 예술가 중의 한 명으로 여겨집니다. 그는 전 생애에 걸쳐 엄청나게 다작을 했으며 세계적인 명성을 얻었고 그의 예술적 성취로 굉장한 개인적 부를 축적했습니다. 파카소는 어렸을 때부터 월등한 예술적 재능을 보였으며 처음 그림을 시작했을 때는 매우 현실적인 방식으로 작품 활동을 했으나 예술의 다른 기법과 이론들을 가지고 실험하면서 화풍이 바뀌었습니다. 이러한 이유로 비평가들과 역사학자들은 일반적으로 그의 작품들을 화풍, 기법, 그리고 주제에 기반해 서로 다른 시대들로 분류합니다.

1차 세계 대전 뒤, 그와 다른 많은 예술가들은 좀 더 신고전주의적인 화풍으로 돌아왔는데, 파카소는 그의 아내 올가 코클로바의 것과 같은 몇 점의 현실적인 초상화들을 그렸습니다. 그는 폴 로젠버그라는 미술상과 독점 계약을 맺었고 부유해지기 시작했죠. 그는 건성으로 초현실주의 운동에 잠시 동참하기도 했지만, 스페인 내전 후 그는 입체주의를 자신의 가장 두드러진 화풍으로 받아들인 것처럼 보입니다. 스페인의 게르니카가 독일에게 폭격을 당한 뒤 그는 그의 가장 유명한 입체파 작품인 〈게르니카〉를 그렸는데, 이 작품은 전쟁의 공포와 전쟁이 인류에 미치는 영향을 묘사했습니다.

Q. 강의는 주로 무엇에 관한 것인가?

Ⓐ 입체주의의 특징과 그 영향
Ⓑ 자연 환경으로 작품 활동을 한 선구자
Ⓒ 유명해지기 위한 한 예술가의 분투
Ⓓ 유명한 예술가의 삶과 화풍

정답 (D)

해설 교수가 강의 초반부터 파블로 피카소라는 주제를 언급하며 그의 삶과 화풍에 관해 계속 설명하고 있으므로 정답은 (D)이다. 강의의 전반적인 내용을 포괄할 수 있는 선택지를 골라야 한다는 점을 잊지 말자. 강의에서 언급된 내용이더라도 주제가 아닌 세부 내용일 경우는 주제 찾기 문제에서는 오답이므로 주의해야 한다.

어휘 medium n 수단 | imaginable adj 상상할 수 있는 | successful adj 성공한 | attempt v 시도하다 | printmaker n 판화 제작자 | sculptor n 조각가 | ceramicist n 도예가 | playwright n 극작가 | co-founder n 공동 창시자/창업자 | collage n 콜라주 | invention n 발명 | construct v 건설하다, 구성하다 | sculpture n 조형물, 조각품, 조각 | explore v 탐구하다 | diverse adj 다양한 | array n 모음, 무리 | embody v 구현하다, 상징하다 | revolutionary adj 혁명적인 | visual art 시각 예술 | extraordinarily adv 엄청나게 | prolific adj 다작하는 | worldwide adj 전 세계적인 | amass v 축적하다, 모으다 | accomplishment n 성취 | immense v 엄청난, 어마어마한 | realistic adj 현실적인 | shift v 이동하다 | typically adv 일반적으로 | categorize v 분류하다 | thematic adj 주제의 | neoclassical adj 신고전주의의 | portrait n 초상화 | exclusive contract 독점 계약 | half-heartedly adv 건성으로 | surrealist n 초현실주의자 | embrace v 받아들이다, 안다 | predominant adj 두드러진, 우세한, 뚜렷한 | humanity n 인류

Practice

Passage 1 Listen to part of a lecture in a science class.

L01_P01

Q. What is the lecture mainly about?

Ⓐ The importance of alternative fuels

Ⓑ The difficulty of finding an energy source to replace oil

Ⓒ The different types of alternative fuels

Ⓓ Environmental safety

Passage 2 Listen to part of a lecture in a psychology class.

L01_P02

Q. What is the lecture mainly about?

Ⓐ The eating habits of dogs

Ⓑ Pavlov's experiments on animal learning

Ⓒ Trial-and-error learning

Ⓓ Animal abuse in the 19th century

Passage 3 Listen to part of a lecture in an engineering class.

L01_P03

Q. What is the lecture mainly about?

Ⓐ The pros and cons of automation

Ⓑ The ways that automation has helped society

Ⓒ The importance of computers to our lives

Ⓓ The increase of product quality throughout the world

Passage 4 Listen to part of a lecture in a history class.

L01_P04

Q. What is the main idea of the lecture?

Ⓐ How aggression forced the Pueblo to move to a new type of housing

Ⓑ The interest of modern scholars in the Utah cliff dwellings

Ⓒ What cliff dwellings are and why they were helpful to the Pueblo people

Ⓓ Rain and its impact on the Pueblo people's cliff dwellings

Passage 5 Listen to part of a lecture in a sociology class.

L01_P05

Q. What is the lecture mostly about?

Ⓐ Good impressions that people try to make

Ⓑ The pressure people feel during job interviews

Ⓒ How society forces people to conform to its ideals

Ⓓ Public figures and their struggles with identity

Passage 6 Listen to part of a discussion in a literature class.

L01_P06

Q. What is the discussion mainly about?

Ⓐ An American author's discontent with his society in the 1920s

Ⓑ The American Jazz Age

Ⓒ The theme and main characters in *The Great Gatsby*

Ⓓ The life of F. Scott Fitzgerald

Passage 7 Listen to part of a lecture in a biology class.

L01_P07

Q. What is the main idea of the lecture?

Ⓐ Tetrastigma and how it sustains the Rafflesia

Ⓑ Photosynthesis and how plants rely on it to survive

Ⓒ Rafflesia and how it differs from most plants

Ⓓ Rafflesia's strong odor and unusual size

Passage 8 Listen to part of a discussion in a geology class.

L01_P08

Q. What aspect of plate tectonics does the professor mainly discuss?

Ⓐ The formation of tectonic plates

Ⓑ How tectonic plates move

Ⓒ The different types of tectonic plates

Ⓓ How plates are destroyed

Passage 9 Listen to part of a lecture in an American history class.

L01_P09

Q. What is the lecture mainly about?

Ⓐ The family history of Wright Brothers

Ⓑ The importance of Kitty Hawk to the history of the airplane

Ⓒ The technique and efforts that Wright Brothers used to make gliders fly

Ⓓ The Wright Brothers' motivation for building gliders and airplanes

Test

[1-6] Listen to part of a discussion in an astronomy class.

L01_T01

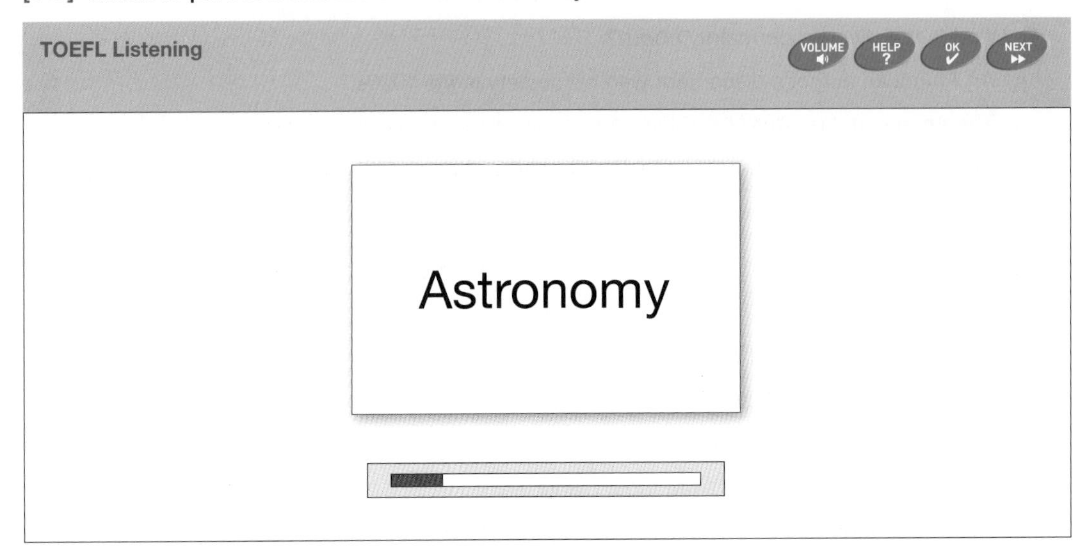

1. What is the main idea of the discussion?

Ⓐ Possible methods of isolating and collecting oxygen molecules

Ⓑ Setting up a colony in space, specifically on the Moon

Ⓒ A way to generate oxygen to sustain a colony on the Moon

Ⓓ Using pyrolysis to separate oxygen from metallic compounds

2. **According to the discussion, what characteristics does the Moon have? Choose 2 answers.**

Ⓐ Its soil contains a very low amount of oxygen and hydrogen.

Ⓑ It is composed of iron, hydrogen oxide, and other metals.

Ⓒ It has a thin atmosphere, which makes extracting oxygen easier.

Ⓓ Its atmosphere has a lower amount of oxygen than the Earth's.

Ⓔ It has an abundance of ilmenite, which contains oxygen.

3. **How is pyrolysis helpful in building a colony on the Moon?**

Ⓐ It requires less ilmenite, which is necessary to supply oxygen.

Ⓑ Any material on the Moon can be reduced to atoms to generate oxygen.

Ⓒ It reduces the amount of material that needs to be brought to the Moon.

Ⓓ The raw resources on the Moon can be directly used to extract oxygen.

4. **What is the professor's opinion about pyrolysis?**

Ⓐ It is theoretically perfect, but the actual situation is much more challenging.

Ⓑ It is too dangerous and difficult to be fully utilized on the Moon.

Ⓒ It is as simple as it sounds if there is enough ilmenite.

Ⓓ It takes too much time to implement a practical solution on Earth.

5. **Why does the professor mention Moon dust?**

Ⓐ It got into machines currently operating on the Moon.

Ⓑ It requires a high temperature to separate compounds into atoms, making pyrolysis difficult.

Ⓒ It causes one of the problems that interferes with building pyrolysis machines on the Moon.

Ⓓ It is abrasive and can even damage spacecraft in orbit around the Moon.

6. **What can be inferred about the method of pyrolysis mentioned using a lens?**

Ⓐ It generates some metallic materials that are exposed to radiation.

Ⓑ It provides other leftover oxygen products that can be used for other purposes.

Ⓒ It does not require a man-made energy source to carry out the process.

Ⓓ It made it possible to establish more pyrolysis machines on the Moon.

Lesson
02 Details

Lesson Outline

세부 사항 찾기 문제(Details Question)는 TOEFL Listening 문제에서 가장 빈도수가 높은 문제 유형이며, 강의에서는 한 개에서 세 개까지 출제된다. 대화와 마찬가지로 지문의 세부 사항에 대해 묻는데, 강의 주제에 관한 자세한 내용, 교수가 강조하거나 반복해서 말하는 사항, 또는 주제를 뒷받침하는 예나 특징으로 사용된 것을 묻는다.

하나 이상의 답을 선택해야 하는 경우도 있기 때문에 문제를 풀 때 정확도가 중요하며, 정확한 노트 필기가 생명이다. 특히 강의 지문 특성상 기억해야 할 세부 내용이 많고 어려운 용어도 많아서 전체 강의의 흐름을 이해했다 하더라도 세부적인 내용은 잘 기억이 나지 않을 수 있기 때문에 노트 필기를 최대한 활용해야 한다. 모르는 단어를 포함해서 빠르게 노트 필기하는 방법을 꾸준히 연습하고 그 필기한 내용을 재구성해 답을 찾는 연습을 해 보자.

Lesson Point

Point 1 강의 지문 최고 빈출 문제 유형!

Point 2 특징(characteristic)과 예시(example)에 주목한다.

Point 3 빠른 노트 필기 연습이 고득점으로 가는 관건이다.

Point 4 표시어(signal)를 바탕으로 한 정확하고 재구성하기 쉬운 노트 필기를 연습한다.

Typical Questions 

- What [is/are] the characteristic(s) of ~? ~의 특징(들)은 무엇인가?
- What does the professor talk about ~? 교수는 ~에 관해 뭐라고 말하는가?
- What does ~ [show/demonstrate]? ~는 무엇을 [나타내는가/보여주는가]?
- According to the professor, [why/what] is ~? 교수에 의하면, [왜/무엇]인가?
- What [is/are] the reason(s) for ~? ~의 이유(들)는 무엇인가?
- What point does the professor make by ~? 교수가 ~함으로써 주장하고자 하는 것은 무엇인가?

Learning Strategies

'세부 사항 찾기' 표시어(signal)를 공략한다!

세부 사항 표시어를 바탕으로 한 정확한 노트 필기를 통해 강조·반복되는 내용을 정리한다.

정의

- X means ~. X는 ~를 의미합니다.
- X is called ~. X는 ~라고 불립니다.
- X is referred to as ~. X는 ~를 나타냅니다.

서술 및 나열

- Some X, but others Y. 일부는 X하지만 나머지는 Y합니다.
- Not only X, but also Y. X뿐만 아니라, Y이기도 합니다.
- In other words 다시 말해서
- The reason why ~ ~의 이유는

강조

- You should remember that ~. ~를 기억해야 합니다.
- We need to make sure ~. ~를 확실히 해 둘 필요가 있습니다.
- It's interesting to note that ~. ~는 매우 흥미로운 사실입니다.
- It is quite a surprise ~. ~라니 참으로 놀라운 일입니다.
- This could actually mean ~. 이것은 사실 ~임을 의미합니다.
- In fact 사실은, 실은

예시

- For example 예를 들어
- Let's take ~ for example. ~를 예로 들어 봅시다.
- To illustrate this 이것을 설명하기 위해서

비유

- Similarly 비슷하게, 유사하게
- Likewise 똑같이, 비슷하게
- In the same manner 마찬가지로

반전

- But/Yet/However 그렇지만, 그러나
- While/Whereas ~인 데 반해, 반면
- Contrary to ~ ~와는 반대로
- In contrast to ~ ~와 대조적으로
- On the other hand 다른 한편으로는
- On the contrary 그와는 반대로
- Although X, Y. 비록 X이긴 하지만, Y입니다.
- The problem is ~. 문제는 ~입니다.

Example

Woman: Professor

L02_EX

Listen to part of a lecture in a marine biology class.

W In our last class, we discussed Darwin's journey on the Beagle and the concept of evolution that he developed after observing the finches of the Galapagos Islands. Beginning as one species, those birds adapted to the unique environment of their particular islands and their morphology changed. These adaptations led to the development of new species. As you know, this phenomenon is not limited to those islands or to birds. Indeed all animals have undergone this process to some degree, including fish. Some types of fish have remained fairly static for millions of years, like sharks, while others have continued to change. The fish in the suborder Notothenioidei, which live in the Southern Ocean, fit into this category. Because they make their home in the frigid waters surrounding Antarctica, they have adapted in many ways to survive.

Many millions of years ago, the globe looked very different. There was a single supercontinent called Pangaea, and the rest of the planet's surface was ocean. The seas around this supercontinent were fairly warm, and they supported a wide variety of species of fish—much like the Caribbean today. [1] Due to plate tectonics, the supercontinent split apart, and the pieces drifted on their plates to form the current continents. As the landmass that would become Antarctica moved south, many of the fish species abandoned the area because the water around it was getting colder. However, the Notothenioidei stayed.

The South Pole does not receive much sunlight, and it is even darker in the water, especially at over 1,000 meters down! [2] So, some of these species have developed large eyes to allow them to see in very low light conditions. Unfortunately, large eyes contain a lot of fluid, which would freeze in such

1. According to the professor, what happened to the fish species after the split of the supercontinent?

Ⓐ Many species moved to regions with milder climates.

Ⓑ Most of them migrated from the south to the north.

Ⓒ They quickly adapted to survive without the interconnected land.

Ⓓ Many species ended up going extinct afterward.

2. Which characteristic allowed the Notothenioidei to survive in the Antarctic?

Ⓐ Protective eyelids

Ⓑ Thick proteins

Ⓒ More bone mass

Ⓓ Being cold-blooded

cold water. So, the fish have developed a special transparent eyelid that allows them to see without allowing the eye to freeze. They also have an extremely low amount of red blood cells. The extremely cold and stable temperature allows there to be a higher concentration of oxygen in the water than there would be in warmer regions. So, the fish don't need many red blood cells to transport oxygen throughout their bodies. As a result, their blood is only 1 percent hemoglobin, compared to the 45 percent found in other fish.

해양 생물학 강의의 일부를 들으시오.

W 지난 시간에 우리는 비글에서의 다윈의 여행과 갈라파고스 제도의 되새들을 관찰한 뒤 그가 발전시킨 진화의 개념에 대해 이야기했습니다. 하나의 종으로 시작된 이 새들은 특별한 제도의 독특한 환경에 적응했고, 이들의 형태는 변화되었습니다. 이러한 적응은 새로운 종의 발생으로 이어졌습니다. 여러분도 알다시피 이 현상은 그 제도에만 국한된 것이 아니며, 새들에게만 국한된 것도 아닙니다. 실제로 모든 동물들이 어느 정도 이 과정을 거쳤는데, 물고기도 포함됩니다. 상어와 같은 몇몇 종류의 물고기는 수백만 년 동안 꽤나 변화 없이 남아 있었던 반면, 다른 종들은 계속해서 변화했죠. 남쪽 바다에 서식하는 남극암치아목이라는 아목에 속하는 물고기가 이 분류에 속합니다. 이들은 남극 대륙을 둘러싼 매우 차가운 물에서 서식하기 때문에 생존하기 위해 많은 방법으로 적응했습니다.

수백만 년 전, 지구는 매우 다른 모습을 갖고 있었습니다. 판게아라고 불리는 하나의 초대륙이 있었고 지구 표면의 나머지 부분은 바다였습니다. 이 초대륙을 둘러싼 바다는 꽤 따뜻했으며 매우 다양한 물고기 종들이 살고 있었습니다. 오늘날의 카리브해와 매우 비슷했죠. [1] 판구조론에 의해 이 초대륙은 분열되었고 조각난 땅들은 흘러가서 현재의 대륙이 되었습니다. 후에 남극 대륙이 될 땅덩어리가 남쪽으로 이동할 때 많은 종의 물고기들이 그 지역을 떠났는데, 이는 주변의 물이 점점 차가워졌기 때문이었죠. 그러나 남극암치아목 물고기들은 남았습니다.

남극은 햇빛을 그다지 많이 받지 않고, 물 속은 한층 더 어두운데, 특히 1,000미터가 넘는 수심에서는 훨씬 그렇겠죠! [2] 그래서 이들 중 몇몇 종은 매우 어두운 환경에서도 볼 수 있도록 커다란 눈으로 발달되었습니다. 불행하게도 커다란 눈에는 액체가 많이 포함되어 있는데 이렇게 차가운 물에서는 얼어붙고 말죠. 그래서 이 물고기들은 눈이 얼어붙지 않으면서 볼 수 있도록 특별한 투명 눈꺼풀을 발생시켰습니다. 그리고 이들은 극도록 적은 양의 적혈구를 가지고 있습니다. 그 매우 차갑고 안정적인 수온은 따뜻한 지역에 비해 물 속 산소 농도를 더 높게 만듭니다. 그래서 이 물고기들은 몸을 통해 산소를 운반해줄 적혈구들이 그다지 많이 필요하지 않습니다. 그 결과, 다른 물고기들의 피는 45%가 헤모글로빈인 반면 이들의 피에는 헤모글로빈이 단 1%입니다.

1. 교수에 의하면, 초대륙의 분열 뒤 물고기 종들에게 무슨 일이 일어났는가?

Ⓐ 많은 종들이 더 온화한 기후의 지역으로 옮겨갔다.
Ⓑ 대부분의 종들이 남쪽에서 북쪽으로 이주했다.
Ⓒ 서로 연결된 대륙 없이도 빠르게 생존에 적응했다.
Ⓓ 많은 종들이 그 뒤 멸종에 이르렀다.

2. 어떠한 특징이 남극암치아목 물고기들이 남극에서 살아남을 수 있도록 했는가?

Ⓐ 보호용 눈꺼풀
Ⓑ 두꺼운 단백질
Ⓒ 더 높은 골밀도
Ⓓ 냉혈성

Lesson 02 Lectures

1

정답 (A)

해설 강의에서 초대륙이 분열된 뒤 남극 대륙이 될 땅덩어리가 남쪽으로 이동할 때 많은 종류의 물고기가 그 지역을 떠났는데, 물이 점점 차가워졌기 때문이었다는 내용이 나오므로 정답은 (A)이다. 한편, 물이 점점 차가워져서 옮겼다는 말이 '더 온화한 기후로 이동했다'라는 의미로 살짝 바꿔 패러프레이즈되었다는 점을 눈여겨보자.

2

정답 (A)

해설 교수가 이 물고기 중 몇몇 종은 환경에 적응하기 위해 커다란 눈으로 발달되었고, 나아가 눈이 얼어붙지 않게 하려고 투명 눈꺼풀까지 발생시켰다고 설명했으므로 정답은 (A)이다. 투명 눈꺼풀(transparent eyelid)이 보호용 눈꺼풀(protective eyelid)로 패러프레이즈되었다.

어휘 **concept** n 개념 | **evolution** n 진화 | **finch** n 되새 | **adapt** v 적응하다 | **particular** adj 특정한, 특별한 | **morphology** n 형태, 형태학 | **adaptation** n 적응, 순응 | **phenomenon** n 현상 | **undergo** v 겪다, 받다 | **static** adj 변화가 없는, 정지 상태의 | **suborder** n 아목 | **Notothenioidei** n 남극암치아목 | **frigid** adj 몹시 추운 | **Antarctica** n 남극 대륙 | **globe** n 지구, 세계 | **supercontinent** n 초대륙(수억 년 전 존재했던 거대 대륙) | **surface** n 표면 | **plate tectonics** 판구조론 | **continent** n 대륙 | **landmass** n 땅덩어리, 대륙 | **abandon** v 떠나다, 버리다 | **South Pole** n 남극 | **transparent** adj 투명한 | **eyelid** n 눈꺼풀 | **red blood cell** 적혈구 | **stable** adj 안정적인 | **concentration** n 농도 | **transport** v 운반하다, 수송하다 | **hemoglobin** n 헤모글로빈, 혈색소

Practice

정답 및 해석 | P. 133

Passage 1 Listen to part of a lecture in an architecture class.

L02_P01

Q. According to the professor, what advantage did adobe bricks have over adobe balls in the rain?

Ⓐ They could let rain sit on top of the bricks.

Ⓑ They were flat, which kept the water from soaking in.

Ⓒ They were slanted, which allowed the rain to run off.

Ⓓ They wouldn't roll as much as the adobe balls did.

Passage 2 Listen to part of a discussion in a psychology class.

L02_P02

Q. How does the professor reward her daughter for reading?

Ⓐ By giving her extra free time

Ⓑ By buying her more books

Ⓒ By giving her drawing supplies

Ⓓ By buying her music

Passage 3 Listen to part of a lecture in a biology class.

L02_P03

Q. According to the professor, what provides most of the energy needed in the water cycle?

Ⓐ Wind

Ⓑ The Sun

Ⓒ Heat from the Earth's core

Ⓓ Energy released when water evaporates

Passage 4 Listen to part of a lecture in an astronomy class.

Q. When does a new lunar month start?

Ⓐ When the Moon reaches its fullest point

Ⓑ On the 15th of each month of the Gregorian solar calendar

Ⓒ When the Moon is in its new phase

Ⓓ Approximately half a day before the start of each solar month

Passage 5 Listen to part of a lecture in an art history class.

L02_P05

Q. What is the key characteristic of Impressionism?

Ⓐ Refined brush strokes

Ⓑ Colors mixed on the canvas

Ⓒ Heavy use of dark colors

Ⓓ A rough quality focusing on overall look

Passage 6 Listen to part of a discussion in a biology class.

L02_P06

Q. According to the discussion, which of the following are reasons that bears aren't true hibernators? Choose 2 answers.

Ⓐ Their body temperatures do not drop enough in the winter.

Ⓑ They don't show enough activity in the winter.

Ⓒ Their heart rates are too fast in the winter.

Ⓓ They are easily awoken in the winter.

Passage 7 Listen to part of a lecture in a geology class.

L02_P07

1. What features below are true of tectonic plate movement? Choose 2 answers.

Ⓐ Collisions can create mountain formations by pushing land upwards.

Ⓑ Over many years, it has caused the decomposition of soft rock.

Ⓒ It helped separate the Earth's landmasses into continents.

Ⓓ The plates' lack of density caused molten rock to protrude through the Earth's surface.

2. Which mountain or group of mountains was formed by erosion?

Ⓐ The Appalachian Mountains

Ⓑ Mt. Rainier

Ⓒ The Ozark Mountains

Ⓓ Mt. St. Helens

3. Which of the following was NOT mentioned as a process of mountain formation?

Ⓐ Hard rock remains standing after soft rock gradually wears away.

Ⓑ Crust plates run into each other and form waves of solid rock.

Ⓒ Molten rock is pushed to the Earth's surface due to density and pressure.

Ⓓ Ice sheets remove softer layers of rock leaving behind low, broad mountains.

Passage 8 Listen to part of a lecture in a sociology class.

L02_P08

1. **What does the professor indicate about social influence?**

Ⓐ Conforming to a group is detrimental to society.

Ⓑ It is an inevitable part of living in social groups.

Ⓒ Peer pressure can cause people to change their beliefs.

Ⓓ It can make people do things that they would not normally do.

2. **What does the professor say about peer pressure?**

Ⓐ It usually has negative effects on society.

Ⓑ It seems more influential in certain countries.

Ⓒ It occurs when the majority makes others conform.

Ⓓ It proves why the majority opinion is dominant in society.

3. **What did Solomon Asch's experiment on conformity show? Choose 2 answers.**

Ⓐ The rate of conformity was drastically reduced by a single supporter.

Ⓑ The cards could result in many different answers.

Ⓒ Only one of the test participants didn't know what was going on.

Ⓓ About a third of subjects conformed to the majority.

Test

정답 및 해석 | P. 142

[1-6] Listen to part of a discussion in an art history class.

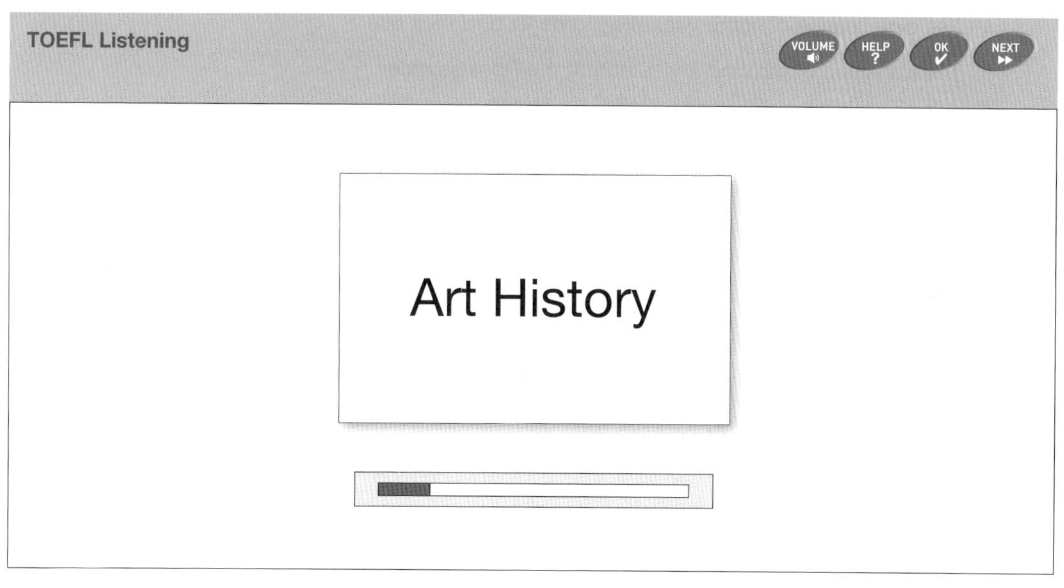

1. **What is the main idea of the discussion?**

Ⓐ The significance of some valuable pigments and their use

Ⓑ The transition of painting styles during the Renaissance

Ⓒ The change that occurred in the way people view artists

Ⓓ The shift in the relationship between patrons and artists

2. **According to the discussion, how was the concept of an artist in the past different from that of today?**

Ⓐ Artists decided the painting styles and subject matter for all of their works.

Ⓑ Patrons financially supported artists in order to receive high-quality paintings.

Ⓒ Artists continuously tried to resist their patrons' control over their works.

Ⓓ Artists often had less control over their artworks because of their patrons.

3. **What can be inferred from the artwork contracts that were discovered?**

Ⓐ Gold and ultramarine were the most popular and widely used colors at that time.

Ⓑ Patrons provided expensive art supplies such as gold pigments to their artists.

Ⓒ There were strict guidelines that artists needed to follow when they painted.

Ⓓ Ultramarine pigment was used more frequently in Europe than it was in Asia.

4. **Why does the professor mention the Virgin Mary?**

Ⓐ To explain that ultramarine was used for the most important subject of the painting

Ⓑ To suggest that she was the most popular painting subject of the Renaissance era

Ⓒ To describe how nobles used her image to boast about their wealth and reputation

Ⓓ To emphasize that she and ultramarine were inseparable in the eyes of the rich

5. **What changed the concept of an artist at the end of the 15th century?**

Ⓐ The price of expensive art supplies was significantly reduced.

Ⓑ People came to regard boasting of wealth as vulgar.

Ⓒ The way of displaying wealth changed from fashion to art.

Ⓓ The number of talented artists had increased from the past.

6. **What does the phrase "reversal in status" mean at the end of the discussion?**

Ⓐ People focused more on the quality of a painting than the material that was used.

Ⓑ People began to view artists as being in a higher position than the patrons who bought their art.

Ⓒ People stopped revealing their wealth to others to show that they were humble.

Ⓓ People eagerly tried to find high-quality art due to the influence of the Renaissance.

Lesson

03 Function & Attitude

문제 듣기

Lesson Outline

의도 및 태도 파악 문제(Function & Attitude Question)는 화자의 말이나 표현에 집중해야 한다. 의도 파악(Function) 문제의 경우 화자, 특히 교수가 강의 중 어떠한 말을 한 목적과 그 말 속에 내재된 의도를 파악해야 한다. 학생이 교수에게 질문한 내용에 관해 출제될 때도 있다. 주로 '짧은 구간을 다시 들려주고 풀기' 방식으로 출제되며, 태도 파악(Attitude) 문제는 강의 중의 특정 내용에 대한 화자의 태도와 감정, 또는 확신 정도를 파악하는 문제가 주로 출제된다.

Lesson Point

Point 1 앞뒤 문맥과 화자의 말투를 종합해서 들리는 그대로가 아닌 숨겨진 뜻을 파악한다.

Point 2 말을 번복 또는 수정하거나 여담처럼 말하는 부분에 주의해서 듣는다.

Point 3 개인적인 의견을 말하는 부분이 태도 파악(Attitude) 문제로 나오는 경우가 많으니 주의!

Point 4 다시 들었던 표현이 선택지에 그대로 나오는 경우 오답일 확률이 높다.

Point 5 노트 필기보다는 감각을 사용해서 화자의 말투를 파악한다.

Typical Questions

의도 파악(Function)

- Listen again to part of the lecture. Then answer the question. Why does the professor say this:
  강의의 일부를 다시 듣고 질문에 답하시오. 교수는 왜 이렇게 말하는가:
- What does the professor mean when he/she says this:
  교수는 다음과 같이 말하며 무엇을 의미하는가:

태도 파악(Attitude)

- What is the professor's attitude toward ~?
  ~에 대한 교수의 태도는 어떠한가?
- What does the professor feel by saying ~?
  ~라고 말할 때 교수는 어떤 감정을 느끼고 있는가?
- What is the professor's opinion about ~?
  ~에 대한 교수의 의견은 무엇인가?

Learning Strategies

의도 및 태도 파악 빈출 표현

의도·태도 파악 문제와 관련하여 강의에 자주 등장하는 표현들을 알아두자.

'확신' 관련 표현

• As you can see,	보시다시피,
• I'm sure you all know that ~.	~라는 건 다들 아실 겁니다.
• You all remember this, right?	다들 이 내용 기억하시죠, 그렇죠?
• I guarantee that ~.	~라는 걸 보장합니다.

'동의하지 않음' 관련 표현

• I have some other opinions for ~.	~에 대해서 저는 좀 다른 의견을 갖고 있어요.
• I doubt that ~.	(제 생각에는) ~할 것 같지 않아요.
• That may be true, but ~.	그게 사실일 수도 있겠지만, 그러나 ~.
• Contrary to that, the evidence suggests ~.	그와 반대로, 그 증거는 ~임을 보여줍니다.
• This is different from what we know ~.	이건 우리가 ~에 대해 알고 있는 것과는 다릅니다.
• However, now we know that ~.	그러나, 이제 우리는 ~라는 걸 압니다.

'혼란스러움' 관련 표현

• I'm not sure if I understand your question.	제가 질문을 제대로 이해했는지 모르겠군요.
• Can you elaborate on that again?	그것에 대해 다시 자세히 설명해 주실 수 있을까요?
• I don't think that makes sense.	이해가 안 돼요.
• I know that it is confusing, but ~.	헷갈리는 내용이라는 건 알아요, 하지만 ~.

'불확실함' 관련 표현

• We can't be certain that ~.	~라고 확신할 수는 없습니다.
• It is not safe to say ~.	~라고 말하는 건 위험한 발언이죠.
• Are we sure about this?	여기에 대해서 다들 확신하나요?
• Hmm...	흠...

Example

Man: Professor

Listen to part of a lecture in an Earth science class.

M Today, we will be talking about the benefits and limitations of wind energy. As you know, the majority of energy that is utilized by human beings is generated by the combustion of fossil fuels, but their supply is finite, so alternatives must be found. Nuclear reactors generate vast amounts of electricity, but their fuel is also limited, and they produce toxic waste far more dangerous than the pollution created by burning coal, oil, and gas. Many areas rely upon hydroelectric plants to generate electricity, which is renewable, but dependent upon many factors including location and average rainfall. There are two other options that are gaining popularity, which are wind and solar power, but these also have their limitations. Now, as I said earlier, let's start with wind energy.

Harnessing wind energy is hardly a new concept, and it dates back well into prehistoric time. The first use for wind energy was most likely the sails on ships, and people have used windmills for over 2,000 years to pump water and grind grain. The first time a windmill was built with the express purpose of generating electricity was in Scotland in 1887, and it was quickly replicated in the United States. Since then, wind generators have been a common solution to providing power to buildings located in remote or isolated areas.

The ability to provide power in areas where conventional power plants are impractical is only one of the advantages of wind power. The most important is that it is an infinite resource. As long as the Earth possesses an atmosphere, there will be wind. In addition, it generates no pollution once the installation of the wind turbines for a wind farm has been completed. True, they incorporate synthetic materials that are made from oil, and the pieces must be

Q. Why does the professor mention synthetic materials?

Ⓐ To show some harmful effects of wind farms on the environment

Ⓑ To name the substances needed for constructing wind turbines

Ⓒ To explain how they influence the performance of wind plants

Ⓓ To describe the process of generating electricity from wind energy

transported to site, but they compensate for this via the energy they produce in the first few months. The farms also use only a fraction of the land that conventional plants require. A wind farm may cover a large area, but the foundations of the turbines and their attendant structures only use a small portion of the surface, leaving the rest open for agriculture or other purposes. To name some limitations of wind power, well, wind is not stable. It constantly fluctuates in strength, and some days may have no wind at all.

지구 과학 강의의 일부를 들으시오.

남 오늘 우리는 풍력의 이점과 한계에 대해 이야기할 겁니다. 여러분도 알고 있듯이, 인간이 사용하는 에너지의 대다수는 화석 연료의 연소로 만들어지지만, 화석 연료의 공급은 유한하기에 대체 연료를 반드시 찾아야만 하죠. 원자로가 막대한 양의 전기를 생산하지만 이들의 연료 역시 제한되어 있을 뿐만 아니라, 석탄, 석유, 가스를 태움으로써 만들어지는 오염 물질보다 훨씬 위험한 독성 폐기물을 만들어 냅니다. 많은 분야에서 수력 발전 시설이 만드는 전기에 의존하고 있는데, 이는 재생 가능하지만 장소와 평균 강우량에 따라 달라집니다. 인기를 얻고 있는 다른 두 가지 방법이 있는데, 이는 풍력과 태양열입니다. 그러나 이 둘에도 한계가 있어요. 이제 아까 말했던 대로 풍력에 대해 먼저 시작해 봅시다.

풍력 에너지를 이용하는 것은 새로운 개념이 아니며 선사 시대까지 거슬러 올라가 찾아볼 수 있습니다. 최초의 풍력 에너지 이용은 아마도 배에 달린 돛이었을 가능성이 가장 크고, 사람들은 2,000년이 넘게 물을 끌어올리고 곡식을 빻는 데 풍차를 사용해 왔죠. 전기 발전을 위한 분명한 목적으로 풍차가 지어진 최초의 시기는 1887년의 스코틀랜드에서였습니다. 그리고 미국에서도 빠르게 풍차를 도입했죠. 그 뒤로 풍력 발전소는 외지거나 외딴곳에 있는 건물들에 전력을 공급하는 일반적인 해결책이 되어 왔습니다.

전통적인 발전소를 세울 수 없는 지역에 전력을 공급할 수 있는 능력은 풍력이 가진 이점들 중 겨우 하나일 뿐입니다. 가장 중요한 것은 무한한 자원이라는 것이죠. 지구에 대기가 존재하는 이상 바람은 존재할 테니까요. 그리고 일단 풍력 발전 단지에 터빈이 설치되고 나면 전혀 오염을 만들어내지 않습니다. 사실, 터빈에 석유로 만들어진 합성 물질들이 포함되어 있으며 터빈 부품들이 현장으로 운송되어야 하지만, 이는 풍력 발전소가 세워지고 처음 몇 달 동안 생산하는 에너지로 보상받을 수 있습니다. 풍력 발전 단지들은 또한 전통적인 발전소들이 필요로 했던 많은 토지의 극히 일부만 사용합니다. 풍력 발전 단지가 넓은 지역에 걸쳐 세워질 수도 있지만 터빈의 기초와 보조 구조물들은 표면의 작은 부문만을 사용하기에 남은 부분의 땅을 농업이나 다른 목적에 사용할 수 있게 됩니다. 풍력의 한계 몇 가지를 들자면, 음, 바람은 안정적인 것이 아닙니다. 그 세기가 계속해서 변하며 어떤 날에는 바람이 아예 안 불 수도 있죠.

Q. 교수는 왜 합성 물질을 언급하는가?

Ⓐ 풍력 발전 단지가 환경에 끼치는 몇몇 해로운 영향을 보여주려고

Ⓑ 풍력 터빈 건설에 필요한 물질을 말하려고

Ⓒ 합성 물질이 풍력 발전소의 성능에 어떻게 영향을 주는지 설명하려고

Ⓓ 풍력으로 전기를 발생시키는 과정을 묘사하려고

정답 (B)

해설 터빈의 설치와 관련된 이야기를 하는 부분에서 이 터빈에 석유로 만들어진 합성 물질이 포함되어 있다고 했으므로 정답은 (B)이다. 합성 물질(synthetic materials)이 물질(substances)로 대체되었다는 점을 눈여겨보자.

어휘 benefit n 이점 | limitation n 한계, 제한 | wind energy 풍력 | majority n 대다수 | utilize v 사용하다 | generate v 만들어 내다 | combustion n 연소, 불에 탐 | fossil fuel 화석 연료 | supply n 공급 | finite adj 유한한 | alternative n 대안 | nuclear reactor 원자로 | vast adj 막대한 | electricity n 전기 | produce v 생산하다 | toxic adj 독성의 | waste n 폐기물 | pollution n 오염 | coal n 석탄 | hydroelectric adj 수력 전기의 | plant n 공장 | renewable adj 재생 가능한 | dependent adj 의존하는 | average adj 평균의 | rainfall n 강우량 | popularity n 인기 | harness v 이용하다, 활용하다 | prehistoric adj 선사 시대의 | sail n 돛 | windmill n 풍차 | pump v (물을) 펌프로 퍼 올리다 | grind v 갈다 | express adj 분명한 | replicate v 복제하다 | remote adj 외진 | isolated adj 외떨어진 | conventional adj 전통적인, 관습적인 | impractical adj 비현실적인 | infinite adj 무한한 | installation n 설치 | turbine n 터빈 | incorporate v 포함하다 | synthetic material 합성 물질 | transport v 운송하다 | compensate v 보상하다 | fraction n 부분, 일부 | attendant adj 수반되는 | agriculture n 농업 | stable adj 안정적인 | constantly adv 끊임없이 | fluctuate v 변동하다

Practice

정답 및 해석 | P. 145

Passage 1 Listen to part of a lecture in a genetics class.

L03_P01

Q. Listen again to part of the lecture. Then answer the question.
Why does the professor say this:

Ⓐ To imply that people's ideas about the animals may be incorrect
Ⓑ To show that people are mistaking a dog breed for a hybrid
Ⓒ To indicate that coywolf is an inaccurate name for the species
Ⓓ To state that she does not think that it is a new organism at all

Passage 2 Listen to part of a lecture in a biology class.

L03_P02

Q. Listen again to part of the lecture. Then answer the question.
What does the professor imply by saying this:

Ⓐ The expedition found the only organisms that existed.
Ⓑ The surveyors were not well educated about marine biology.
Ⓒ The techniques that the scientists were using were primitive.
Ⓓ The scientists were using the best technology available to them.

Passage 3 Listen to part of a lecture in an environmentology class.

L03_P03

Q. Listen again to part of the lecture. Then answer the question.
Why does the professor say this:

Ⓐ To imply that humans may be ignoring a serious health threat
Ⓑ To express his skepticism that humans need to be concerned
Ⓒ To point out that only people who often eat seafood are affected
Ⓓ To indicate that only people living near the poles need to worry

Passage 4 Listen to part of a discussion in a nutritional science class.

L03_P04

Q. What is the professor's attitude about the organic food industry?

Ⓐ It protects its consumers.

Ⓑ It is full of corruption.

Ⓒ It is not very reliable.

Ⓓ It is not very profitable.

Passage 5 Listen to part of a lecture in a marketing class.

L03_P05

Q. What is the professor's attitude toward product-driven companies?

Ⓐ She feels that their focus is too limited.

Ⓑ She thinks that they should do more internal research.

Ⓒ She believes that they are more successful.

Ⓓ She advises against working for them.

Passage 6 Listen to part of a lecture in a psychology class.

L03_P06

Q. Listen again to part of the lecture. Then answer the question.
Why does the professor say this:

Ⓐ To point out a contradiction in approaches to happiness

Ⓑ To express her dissatisfaction with positive psychology

Ⓒ To illustrate the difficulty she has had with losing weight

Ⓓ To explain why money does not really make people happy

Passage 7 Listen to part of a lecture in a biology class.

L03_P07

Q. Listen again to part of the lecture. Then answer the question.
Why does the professor say this:

Ⓐ To indicate that climate change threatens keystone species

Ⓑ To imply that global warming should be a familiar explanation

Ⓒ To show how tired he is of discussing that particular concept

Ⓓ To state that he has already talked about it in the lecture

Passage 8 Listen to part of a lecture in a geography class.

L03_P08

Q. Listen again to part of the lecture. Then answer the question.
What does the professor imply by saying this:

Ⓐ The decision had essentially been made before the meeting.

Ⓑ The British Empire was the most powerful nation so it won.

Ⓒ The Greenwich meridian was chosen because it was already popular.

Ⓓ The Royal Observatory was ideally situated, so it was selected.

Passage 9 Listen to part of a lecture in a biology class.

L03_P09

Q. What is the professor's opinion about Antonie van Leeuwenhoek?

Ⓐ He feels that he brought the Age of Enlightenment in the Netherlands.

Ⓑ He believes that he is given too much credit in the scientific community.

Ⓒ He thinks that his innovations were integral to the discovery of cells.

Ⓓ He regards him as the first scientist to ever view organic cells.

Passage 10 Listen to part of a lecture in a psychology class.

L03_P10

Q. Listen again to part of the lecture. Then answer the question.

Why does the professor say this:

(A) To introduce an example of a species with little mental capacity

(B) To show how houseflies display a basic level of inhibition

(C) To indicate that houseflies are well known for their inhibition

(D) To state people underestimate the insect's cognitive abilities

Passage 11 Listen to part of a discussion in an astronomy class.

L03_P11

Q. What is the professor's opinion about Halley's comet?

(A) She feels that scientists spend too much time studying it.

(B) She believes that the comet will not pass the Earth again.

(C) She thinks that the comet is unique because it returns so often.

(D) She does not understand why the students do not know about it.

Passage 12 Listen to part of a lecture in an art class.

L03_P12

Q. What is the professor's attitude toward the creation of Mount Rushmore?

(A) He thinks that the location of the monument was poorly chosen.

(B) He believes that it is inferior to the sculptures of ancient Egypt.

(C) He feels that they should have been able to finish more quickly.

(D) He is impressed by how safe the workers were using such techniques.

Passage 13 Listen to part of a lecture in a health science class.

L03_P13

Q. Listen again to part of the lecture. Then answer the question.
Why does the professor say this:

(A) To illustrate the effects of certain drugs in an amusing way

(B) To show how surprising the effects of some chemicals are

(C) To indicate how some chemical causes operate in the body

(D) To state that many people are unaware of the causes of insomnia

Passage 14 Listen to part of a lecture in an economics class.

L03_P14

Q. Listen again to part of the lecture. Then answer the question.
Why does the professor say this:

(A) To show that the effects of the economic downturn are often exaggerated

(B) To illustrate the importance of the stock market crash on a global scale

(C) To indicate that people do not understand how important the event was

(D) To state that the common name for a period in history is poorly chosen

Passage 15 Listen to part of a lecture in a botany class.

L03_P15

1. Listen again to part of the lecture. Then answer the question.

   Why does the professor say this:

   (A) To state that the rain forest is not as easy to live in as people think

   (B) To indicate that any organism would have difficulty finding enough water

   (C) To question how well cacti actually are adapted to their environment

   (D) To illustrate how impressive the adaptations of cacti are

2. What is the professor's opinion of the saguaro cactus?

   (A) She thinks its ability to retract itself underground is amazing.

   (B) She is impressed by the large diameter of its root system.

   (C) She is surprised at how quickly the cactus is able to grow.

   (D) She believes that it holds the most water of any cactus species.

3. Listen again to part of the lecture. Then answer the question.

   Why does the professor say this:

   (A) To point out that cacti adaptations could have negative results as well

   (B) To illustrate the effectiveness of cacti's defensive adaptations

   (C) To encourage the students to imagine what caused adaptations

   (D) To indicate that the students should know what she is discussing

Passage 16 Listen to part of a lecture in a biology class.

L03_P16

1. **Listen again to part of the lecture. Then answer the question.**

Why does the professor say this:

Ⓐ To introduce the topic of the lecture he is going to give

Ⓑ To question whether people know where jewelry comes from

Ⓒ To indicate that some organisms create beautiful shells

Ⓓ To illustrate how different cultures value different things

2. **What is the professor's attitude toward pearl farming?**

Ⓐ He thinks it requires the lives of too many mollusks.

Ⓑ He believes that it is much more efficient than catching them.

Ⓒ He feels that is driven purely by human greed and fashion.

Ⓓ He questions whether it actually helps wild mollusks.

3. **Listen again to part of the lecture. Then answer the question.**

Why does the professor say this:

Ⓐ To state that farmed pearls are not genuine pearls

Ⓑ To indicate that human-made copies are worthless

Ⓒ To explain how farmed pearls affected sales of real pearls

Ⓓ To illustrate how humans have learned to farm pearls

Test

[1-6] Listen to part of a lecture in a health science class. L03_T01

1. What is the speaker mainly discussing?

Ⓐ Wernicke's aphasics and the challenges they face in life

Ⓑ The brain and two common language disorders

Ⓒ Why Broca's aphasics can understand spoken language

Ⓓ How people suffer from language disorders

정답 및 해석 | P. 169

2. **Listen again to part of the lecture. Then answer the question.**

What does the professor imply by stating this:

Ⓐ He thinks that the students should already know what he is going to explain.

Ⓑ He understands that the students want to move on to more interesting topics.

Ⓒ He knows that there is a wealth of information on the subject that needs to be covered.

Ⓓ He wants to provide a basic background before the main topic of the class.

3. **What does the professor say about the brain?**

Ⓐ It is very difficult for the brain to organize information sequentially.

Ⓑ The right hemisphere is central to the production of language.

Ⓒ Language disorders can sometimes result in disease.

Ⓓ The left hemisphere is the center of using language.

4. **What is the result of Broca's aphasia?**

Ⓐ There is a decrease in speaking and reading ability with few effects on listening ability.

Ⓑ Listening skills decrease with moderately-affected speaking ability.

Ⓒ Listening skills decrease with speech remaining fluent but nonsensical.

Ⓓ There is a significant decrease in only speaking ability.

5. **What is the professor's attitude toward people with Wernicke's aphasia?**

Ⓐ He thinks it's impressive that Wernicke's aphasics can even survive.

Ⓑ He understands the difficulties that come from having a listening disorder.

Ⓒ He feels pity for Wernicke's aphasics as they suffer from several problems.

Ⓓ He wants people to speak more clearly when interacting with stroke victims.

6. **What will the professor most likely discuss in the next lecture?**

Ⓐ He will discuss Wernicke's aphasia in more detail.

Ⓑ He will explore how the language centers function.

Ⓒ He will address a question raised during the class.

Ⓓ He will introduce some other language disorders.

Lesson
04 Connecting Contents

Lesson Outline

관계 파악 문제(Connecting Contents Question)는 지문의 정보가 서로 어떻게 관련되었는지 묻는 문제로, 강의에서 나올 경우 보통 1개가 출제된다. 강의에서 어떤 내용이 언급되었는지 묻는 문제가 많이 나오며 짝이나 순서 맞추기 문제가 출제되기도 한다.

Lesson Point

Point 1 전체 흐름을 통해 전반적인 구조를 파악하는 문제 유형:

Ex How is the lecture organized?

⋯→ 강의에서 언급되는 정보들 간의 전체적인 상관관계를 파악하며 듣는다!

⋯→ 노트 필기 시 간단한 구조도를 그려가며 정리하는 것도 도움이 된다.

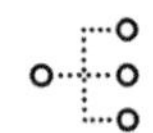

Point 2 특정 정보와 관련된 화자의 의도/정보의 역할을 묻는 문제 유형:

Ex Why does the professor mention ~?

⋯→ 해당 정보의 구조적 성격을 파악한다!

⋯→ 주제와 상관 없어 보이는 특정 정보가 갑자기 등장하는 경우, 주제 강조 목적의 예시나 비유로 쓰이는 경우가 많다.

Typical Questions

언급 이유

- Why does the professor say ~? 교수는 왜 ~라고 말하는가?
- Why does the student mention ~? 학생은 왜 ~를 언급하는가?
- How is the lecture organized? 강의는 어떻게 구성되어 있는가?

짝 맞추기

- In the lecture, the professor listed ~. Indicate which of the following features are mentioned in the lecture. 강의에서 교수는 ~를 열거한다. 다음 중 어느 특징이 강의에서 언급되었는지 표시하시오.

	Category A	Category B
Characteristic 1		
Characteristic 2		
Characteristic 3		

순서 맞추기

- Put the following steps in order. 다음 단계들을 순서에 맞게 배열하시오.

Step 1	
Step 2	
Step 3	

Learning Strategies

1 내용의 흐름을 파악한다.

강의에서 지문의 요점은 다음과 같은 방식으로 전개된다.

- ▶ **유형 1** ① 주제 ···› ② 정의/설명 ···› ③ 예시 ···› ④ 영향
- ▶ **유형 2** ① 주제 ···› ② 원인 ···› ③ 결과
- ▶ **유형 3** ① 주제 ···› ② 과정 1, 2, 3
- ▶ **유형 4** ① 주제 ···› ② 설명 ···› ③ 찬성 vs. 반대 ···› ④ 결론
- ▶ **유형 5** ① 주제 ···› ② 비교 ···› ③ 대조
- ▶ **유형 6** ① 주제 ···› ② 특징 1, 2, 3

2 특정 정보를 사용한 의도를 파악한다.

특정 문장이나 내용의 역할을 파악할 때 주로 등장하는 표시어를 알아두면 도움이 된다.

주제 소개

- Let's move on to ~. — ~로 넘어가겠습니다.
- The next topic of discussion is ~. — 다음으로 논의할 주제는 ~입니다.
- What we're going to cover in the remainder of the lecture is ~. — 남은 강의 시간에 다룰 내용은 ~입니다.
- We've looked at X, and now I'd like to mention Y. — X를 들여다봤으니, 이제 Y에 대해 이야기하고 싶군요.

예시

- Let's imagine that X is Y. — X가 Y라고 상상해 봅시다.
- Let's look at an example of ~. — ~의 예를 한 번 봅시다.
- Let's suppose ~. — ~라고 가정해 봅시다.
- One example of X is ~. — X의 한 예는 ~입니다.

여담

- Incidentally, — 그건 그렇고,
- I have a personal anecdote concerning ~. — ~에 대한 개인적인 일화가 있습니다.
- That reminds me of ~. — 그건 ~를 떠올리게 하는군요.
- One time, I had a chance of ~. — 한번은, ~할 기회가 있었습니다.

결론

- I'd like to end with ~. — ~로 끝내고 싶습니다.
- Let me just run over X again. — X를 다시 한번 간략하게 훑어봅시다.
- So far we've seen that ~. — 지금까지 우리는 ~에 대해 알아보았습니다.
- So, just to quickly recap, ~. — 그럼, 빠르게 요약해 보면, ~.

Example

Woman: Professor | Man: Student

L04_EX

Listen to part of a discussion in an engineering class.

W As we continue our discussion of electromagnetic radiation today, we will be focusing on light generation. Before humans harnessed electricity, we relied upon the light generated by the Sun and from combustion. This severely limited the tasks that we could perform at night or in rooms without windows. Many scientists attempted to develop artificial means of generating light, and the first successful electric lamp was created by Humphry Davy in 1802. Davy had created a powerful battery, and he passed the current from that battery through a thin strip of platinum, which he chose because it has an extremely high melting point. It did not generate a bright light, nor did it last long enough to be usable, but it did prove the principle of incandescence and provide the precedent for future experimenters.

M Professor, didn't Thomas Edison invent the first light bulb?

W No, actually, he did not. Some historians list as many as 22 inventors who developed incandescent lamps before Edison, including Joseph Swan, who actually created the first practical lamp. Edison and Swan did not work together, but the companies that produced their products eventually merged. (C) The reason that Edison receives so much credit is because his version of the bulb incorporated the best aspects of others. (B) It had an effective material for the filament based on Swan's work, (A) a better vacuum inside the bulb using Herman Sprengel's magnificent vacuum pump, and high resistance that allowed it to operate using his centralized power distribution system. He is remembered while other equally qualified scientists have been forgotten because he created not only components, but also an integrated system of lighting that included his generators and power distribution system.

Q. The professor explains the characteristics of Edison's light bulb, which incorporated elements of other inventors' work. Match each of the following to the inventor.

	Swan	Sprengel	Edison
(A) An efficient vacuum pump to remove the air			
(B) A filament made of a practical substance			
(C) A comprehensive power distribution system			

공학 수업 중 토론의 일부를 들으시오.

여 오늘 전자기 방사선에 대한 이야기를 계속하면서 빛 생성에 집중해 보도록 하겠습니다. 인류가 전기를 활용하기 전 우리는 태양과 연소에서 생성되는 빛에 의존했어요. 이는 밤이나 창문이 없는 방에서 우리가 할 수 있는 업무를 심각하게 제한했습니다. 많은 과학자들이 빛을 생성시키는 인공적인 수단을 발전시키려고 시도했고, 1802년에 험프리 데이비가 첫 번째의 성공적인 전등을 만들어 냈습니다. 그는 강력한 건전지를 만들었고 얇은 백금 조각을 통해 이 건전지로부터 전류를 통하게 했습니다. 백금은 매우 높은 용해점을 가지고 있기에 이것을 선택한 것이었죠. 이 전등은 밝은 빛을 만들어내지 않았고 사용 가능할 만큼 길게 지속된 것도 아니었지만, 백열의 원리를 증명했으며 미래의 실험자들을 위한 선례가 되었습니다.

남 교수님, 토마스 에디슨이 최초의 전구를 발명하지 않았나요?

여 아니오, 사실 아닙니다. 어떤 역사가들은 에디슨 전에 백열전등을 만든 발명가를 많게는 22명까지 열거할 수 있는데, 이는 최초의 실용적인 전등을 만든 조셉 스완을 포함합니다. 에디슨과 스완은 함께 일한 것은 아니었지만 이들의 제품을 생산한 회사들은 결국 합병했죠. (C) 에디슨이 그렇게 많은 인정을 받는 이유는 그의 전구가 다른 이들의 가장 뛰어난 점을 포함했기 때문입니다. (B) 스완의 제품에 기반한 필라멘트를 위한 효율적인 재료와 (A) 헤르만 스프렝겔의 멋진 진공 펌프를 사용한 전구 안의 더 성능 좋은 진공, 그리고 그의 집중 전력 시스템을 이용하여 작동하게 한 높은 저항값이 그것이죠. 동일하게 자격을 갖춘 다른 과학자들이 잊혀진 반면 에디슨이 기억된 이유는 그가 부품들만 만든 것이 아니라 그의 발전기와 배전 시스템을 포함한 조명의 통합 시스템을 발명했기 때문입니다.

Q. 교수는 다른 발명가들의 작업 요소를 포함한 에디슨의 전구가 가진 특징들을 설명한다. 다음 각 사항을 발명가와 연결하시오.

	스완	스프렝겔	에디슨
Ⓐ 공기를 제거하기 위한 효율적인 진공 펌프		✓	
Ⓑ 실용적인 물질로 만들어진 필라멘트	✓		
Ⓒ 포괄적인 배전 시스템			✓

정답 Swan - B, Sprengel - A, Edison - C

해설 강의에서 '스완의 제품에 기반한 필라멘트를 위한 효율적인 재료', '스프렝겔의 멋진 진공 펌프를 사용한 전구 안의 더 성능 좋은 진공', '그(에디슨)의 집중 전력 시스템을 이용하여 작동하게 한 높은 저항값'이라고 말한 데서 정답을 찾을 수 있다.
어떻게 보면 제품의 세부 정보를 묻는 '세부 사항 찾기 문제'와 비슷하다고 할 수 있다. 세부적인 내용, 특히 여러 인물과 특성이 나올 경우 반드시 노트 필기를 하도록 하자.

어휘 electromagnetic radiation 전자기 방사선 | light generation 빛 생성 | harness v 이용하다, 활용하다 | electricity n 전기, 전력 | rely v 의존하다, 기대다 | combustion n 연소 | severely adv 심하게, 엄격하게 | task n 일, 과업 | perform v 행하다, 실시하다 | artificial adj 인공의 | electric lamp 전등 | current n 전류 | strip n 가느다란 조각 | platinum n 백금 | melting point 용해점 | usable adj 사용할 수 있는, 쓸모 있는 | principle n 원리, 원칙 | incandescence n 백열 | precedent n 전례 | historian n 역사가 | inventor n 발명가 | incandescent adj 백열의 | practical adj 실용적인 | merge v 합병하다, 합치다 | incorporate v 포함하다 | aspect n 측면, 양상 | effective adj 효과적인 | filament n 필라멘트 | vacuum n 진공 | magnificent adj 멋진, 훌륭한 | resistance n 저항 | operate v 작동하다 | centralized adj 집중된 | power distribution 배전 | equally adv 동일하게 | qualified adj 자격이 있는 | component n 부품 | integrated adj 통합된 | generator n 발전기

Practice

Passage 1 Listen to part of a lecture in an art history class.

L04_P01

Q. Why does the professor mention Dadaism in the lecture?

Ⓐ To contrast it with Surrealism as an art form

Ⓑ To illustrate why one movement was more popular

Ⓒ To explain what influenced the creation of surrealism

Ⓓ To compare the techniques that the artists used

Passage 2 Listen to part of a lecture in an ecology class.

L04_P02

Q. Why does the professor mention Venus in the lecture?

Ⓐ To introduce the concept of the greenhouse effect

Ⓑ To tell the students how the greenhouse effect can be positive

Ⓒ To explain what could possibly happen to the Earth

Ⓓ To indicate how the planet is similar to our own

Passage 3 Listen to part of a lecture in a biology class.

L04_P03

Q. Why does the professor mention the hummingbirds in her backyard?

Ⓐ To introduce the interesting way that hummingbirds fly

Ⓑ To inform the students about the hummingbird's habitat

Ⓒ To tell the students where they can go to study hummingbirds

Ⓓ To describe some of the reasons why the hummingbird is important

Passage 4 Listen to part of a lecture in a paleontology class.

L04_P04

Q. Why does the professor mention chisels and power tools in the lecture?

Ⓐ To explain how fossils are often damaged

Ⓑ To illustrate how fossils were studied in the past

Ⓒ To show how fossil skeletons are reconstructed

Ⓓ To give an example of tools used by archaeologists

Passage 5 Listen to part of a lecture in an ecology class.

L04_P05

Q. Why does the professor talk about the different oil clean-up methods?

Ⓐ To classify them into traditional and non-traditional methods

Ⓑ To indicate the scale of the environmental catastrophe

Ⓒ To examine why some were more effective than others

Ⓓ To emphasize the difficulty of cleaning up the Exxon Valdez oil spill

정답 및 해석 | P. 173

Passage 6 Listen to part of a discussion in an art class.

L04_P06

Q. How does the professor proceed with her discussion of environment art?

Ⓐ She explains a concept and then provides examples of it.

Ⓑ She describes an artwork then explains the concepts behind it.

Ⓒ She gives the history of an artistic movement and talks about its important artists.

Ⓓ She examines an artist's works then discusses her personal history.

Passage 7 Listen to part of a lecture in an American history class.

L04_P07

Q. The professor described some of the events that occurred during the life of Chief Tecumseh in the lecture. Put those events in the correct order. Drag each answer choice to the space where it belongs. One of the answer choices will not be used.

Ⓐ The Shawnee and other tribes sided with the British in the War of 1812.

Ⓑ Tecumseh tried to rally other Native American Tribes to form a confederacy.

Ⓒ The United States purchased the Louisiana Territory from France.

Ⓓ The Indian Removal Act was passed by the United States government.

Ⓔ Tecumseh became the chief of his tribe, the Shawnee.

1	
2	
3	
4	

Passage 8 Listen to part of a lecture in an astronomy class.

L04_P08

Q. In the lecture, the professor listed many features of the planet Uranus. Indicate which of the following features are mentioned in the lecture.

Click in the correct box for each sentence.

	Yes	No
Ⓐ The planet rotates on a horizontal axis.		
Ⓑ Its orbit lies between Jupiter and Saturn.		
Ⓒ Its temperature is the lowest in the solar system.		
Ⓓ The planet looks blue because of its atmosphere.		
Ⓔ Its atmosphere is composed mostly of methane.		

Passage 9 Listen to part of a lecture in a zoology class.

L04_P09

Q. In the lecture, the professor described how a blue whale feeds. Put the steps in the correct order. Drag each answer choice to the space where it belongs. One of the answer choices will not be used.

Ⓐ It takes a huge mouthful of sea water.

Ⓑ It forces the water out through its blow hole.

Ⓒ The whale swallows its prey after expelling the water.

Ⓓ The baleen plates trap small organisms in its mouth.

Ⓔ The whale locates a large group of its preferred prey.

1	
2	
3	
4	

Passage 10 Listen to part of a lecture in an ecology class.

L04_P10

Q. In the lecture, the professor describes how a knife is made. Put the steps in the correct order. Drag each answer choice to the space where it belongs. One of the answer choices will not be used.

Ⓐ The crafter shatters the stone to reduce its size.

Ⓑ The crafter fashions a handle and tie it with a blade.

Ⓒ The crafter locates a big piece of rock to work on.

Ⓓ The crafter uses sinew to sharpen the edge.

Ⓔ The crafter shapes the stone by slowly removing its flakes.

1	
2	
3	
4	

Passage 11 Listen to part of a lecture in a history class.

L04_P11

Q. In the lecture, the professor listed many developments that contributed to the Harlem Renaissance. Indicate which of the following developments are mentioned in the lecture. Click in the correct box for each sentence.

	Yes	No
Ⓐ The creation of black-authored literature that was critical of society		
Ⓑ The birth of jazz music		
Ⓒ An increase in immigration from African countries		
Ⓓ The beginnings of black theater		
Ⓔ African Americans served in the military in World War I		

Passage 12 Listen to part of a discussion in a meteorology class.

L04_P12

1. In the discussion, the professor described the series of events that take place when a tornado forms. Put those events in the correct order. Drag each answer choice to the space where it belongs. One of the answer choices will not be used.

Ⓐ Strong winds cause the rising air to rotate.

Ⓑ A tornado watch is declared by the National Weather Service.

Ⓒ Warm moist air meets cool dry air forming a supercell.

Ⓓ Warm air rises up through the storm clouds.

Ⓔ The storm extends down to the ground.

1	
2	
3	
4	

2. Why does the professor mention Kansas during the discussion?

Ⓐ To explain the area covered by the region called Tornado Alley

Ⓑ To provide a story about his own experience with a tornado warning

Ⓒ To state a statistic about the occurrence of tornadoes

Ⓓ To illustrate the amount of damage that a single tornado can cause

Passage 13 Listen to part of a lecture in a physics class.

L04_P13

1. How does the professor proceed with her explanation of color?

Ⓐ She identifies the steps in a process and explains how they are connected.

Ⓑ She describes and explains the reasons for a change.

Ⓒ She identifies and explains parts of a phenomenon.

Ⓓ She defines and analyzes mathematical formulas.

2. In the lecture, the professor lists the factors that influence how we perceive color. Indicate which of the following factors are mentioned in the lecture.

Click in the correct box for each phrase.

	Yes	No
Ⓐ The distance between the crests of waves		
Ⓑ The amount of light that is present		
Ⓒ The distribution of light across wavelengths		
Ⓓ The angle at which the light is being reflected		
Ⓔ The movement of the object being observed		

Passage 14 Listen to part of a discussion in an American history class.

L04_P14

1. In the discussion, the professor described the series of events that led up to the Boston Tea Party. Put those events in the correct order. Drag each answer choice to the space where it belongs. One of the answer choices will not be used.

Ⓐ The governor forbade ships from departing without unloading their cargo.

Ⓑ The British Empire imposed the Townshend Acts.

Ⓒ The colonists refused to allow ships to unload their cargo.

Ⓓ Colonists in disguise boarded the ship and threw the tea overboard.

Ⓔ The parliament passed the laws known as the Intolerable Acts.

1	
2	
3	
4	

2. Why does the professor talk about the Intolerable Acts?

Ⓐ To give an example of why the colonists were outraged and motivated to strive for independence

Ⓑ To give the students more background about why the colonists rebelled in 1773

Ⓒ To explain why the U.S. Constitution took the form that it did

Ⓓ To explain how the Townshend Acts were related to future acts by Britain

Test

정답 및 해석 | P. 191

[1-6] Listen to part of a discussion in an architecture class.

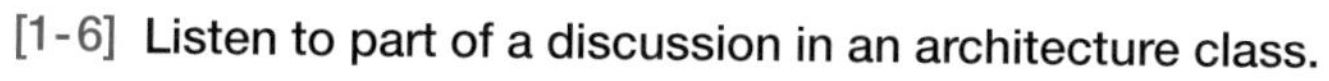

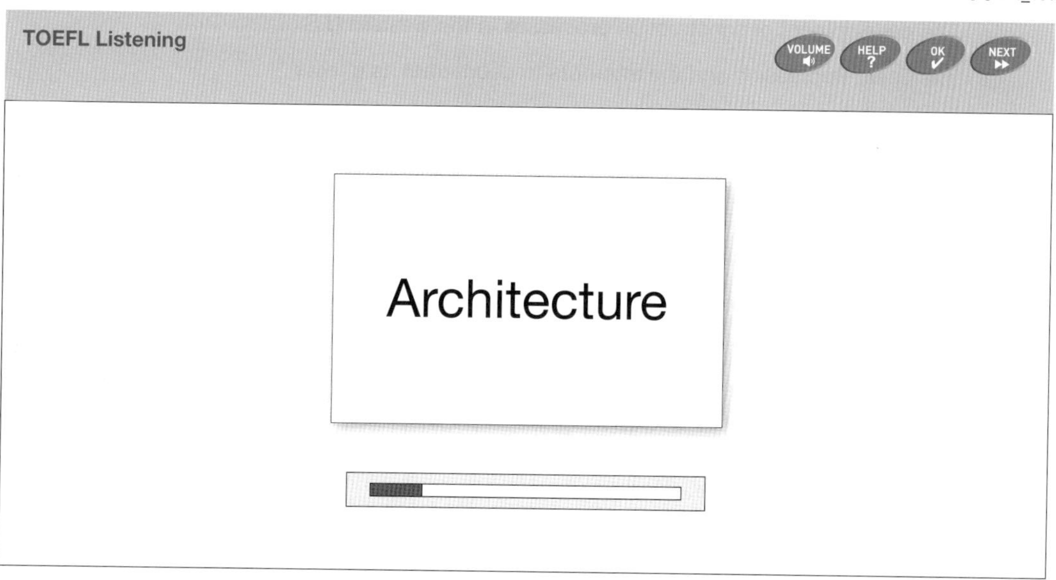

1. **What is the discussion mainly about?**

Ⓐ The development of construction processes in the western U.S.

Ⓑ The Great Depression and the attempts to counteract its effects

Ⓒ The Hoover Dam's importance and how it was built

Ⓓ The Colorado River's impact on American construction projects

2. **Why does the professor mention the students' taking trips to Las Vegas?**

Ⓐ To use their personal experiences as an introduction to the lecture's topic

Ⓑ To begin talking about how the Hoover Dam has helped improve Las Vegas

Ⓒ To give an example of how the Hoover Dam has increased tourism in Nevada

Ⓓ To compare the two places and how they are both interesting tourist attractions

3. **According to the professor, how did the construction of the Hoover Dam affect the American public?**

Ⓐ It resulted in increased spending that pushed Americans even further into debt.

Ⓑ It gave Americans hope that they could overcome the difficulties facing them.

Ⓒ It caused Americans to move to the western states in search of economic opportunities.

Ⓓ It diverted Americans' water supply and forced them to find alternative sources of water.

4. Listen again to part of the discussion. Then answer the question.

What does the professor imply when she says:

Ⓐ The dam actually had an overall negative effect on the economy.

Ⓑ The dam was unable to generate as much electricity as planned.

Ⓒ The dam was beneficial for some people but not the entire country.

Ⓓ The dam discouraged people from moving to the Las Vegas area.

5. According to the professor, which of the following are reasons that people opposed the building of the dam? Choose 2 answers.

Ⓐ Water pollution

Ⓑ Earthquakes

Ⓒ Flooding

Ⓓ Landslides

Ⓔ Air pollution

6. In the discussion, the professor described the process of constructing the Hoover Dam. Put the steps in the correct order. Drag each answer choice to the space where it belongs. One of the answer choices will not be used.

Ⓐ The pipes were removed and concrete was poured into the holes.

Ⓑ The government had roads and housing constructed for the workers.

Ⓒ Water was run through pipes to keep the concrete from heating up.

Ⓓ The Colorado River was diverted from its usual course.

Ⓔ Pipes were set in the framework before concrete was poured.

1	
2	
3	
4	

Lesson

05 Inference

문제 듣기

Lesson Outline

추론 문제(Inference Question)는 지문에서 주어진 여러 정보 간의 관계에 대해 답하거나 그 정보를 기반으로 추론해서 답을 찾는 문제이다. 강의에서 따로 언급되지는 않았지만 강의 전체의 내용과 맥락을 통해 추론·유추할 수 있는 사실을 묻는다.

Lesson Point

Point 1 5개 문제 유형 중 최고난도의 문제 유형!

Point 2 문제에 imply, infer, next, result, cause, conclude 등의 단어가 있으면 추론 문제!

Point 3 들은 것(노트 필기한 것)을 바탕으로 제시된 정보의 특징을 유추, 추론한다.

Point 4 너무 깊게 생각하여 강의 내용을 벗어난 추론을 하지 않도록 주의!
추론의 근거는 어디까지나 화자가 한 말 안에 있어야 한다.

Typical Questions

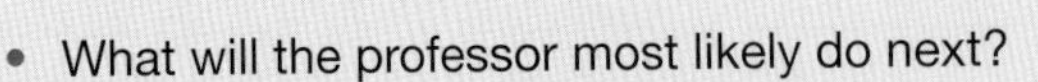

- What will the professor most likely do next? 교수는 다음에 무엇을 할 것 같은가?
- What does the professor imply about ~? 교수는 ~에 관해 무엇을 암시하는가?
- What can be inferred about ~? ~에 대해 무엇을 추론할 수 있는가?
- What can be inferred from the professor's explanation about ~? 교수의 ~에 대한 설명으로부터 무엇을 추론할 수 있는가?
- What will the professor discuss next? 교수는 다음에 무엇에 대해 이야기하겠는가?
- What can be concluded about ~? ~에 관해 어떤 결론을 내릴 수 있는가?

Learning Strategies

주제의 특징을 나타내는 표시어(signal)를 공략한다!

주제의 주요 특징 및 예시에 관해 유추 · 추론하는 문제가 나오므로, 주제의 특징과 관련된 원인, 결과, 비교, 대조 등을 나타내는 표시어를 중심으로 노트 필기하며 듣는다.

원인

• The reason why it happened was ~.	그 일이 발생한 이유는 ~였습니다.
• This is due to ~.	이것은 ~때문입니다.
• This is caused by ~.	이것은 ~에 의해 야기되었습니다.
• What happened was ~.	무슨 일이 일어났는가 하면 ~.
• How did it happen? Well, ~.	어떻게 그 일이 일어났을까요? 자, ~.

결과

• As a result	그 결과로
• This results in ~.	이는 결과적으로 ~가/~하게 됩니다.
• X comes as a result of Y.	Y의 결과로 X가 되게 됩니다.
• This led to ~.	이는 ~로 이어졌습니다.
• Consequently	그 결과, 따라서

비교

• Both X and Y	X와 Y 모두
• Similarly	비슷하게, 유사하게
• Likewise	똑같이, 비슷하게
• In the same way	같은 방법으로
• In a similar fashion	유사한 방식으로

대조

• Whilst/While/Whereas X, Y.	X인데 반해, Y입니다.
• On the contrary	그와는 반대로
• In contrast	그에 반해서
• On the other hand	다른 한편으로는
• However/But	그렇지만, 그러나

Example

Woman: Professor

L05_EX

Listen to part of a lecture in a biology class.

W Over the last fifty years, anthropogenic global warming has been causing the polar ice caps to steadily shrink, which is reducing the polar bears' natural habitat. As you know, the majority of a polar bear's diet consists of seals, which they use the ice to capture. Seals must surface to refill their lungs before diving again to hunt their own prey, so they often emerge from holes in the ice to breathe. Polar bears lurk by such holes, patiently waiting for a seal to breach the surface, at which point the bear will seize the defenseless creature in its jaws and wrest it from its aquatic home. The vitamin and nutrient dense meat and blubber of the seals satisfy all of the bears' dietary needs. They do most of their hunting in the spring and summer, when they pack on needed weight for the long polar winter. But, with increasingly less ice to stage their ambushes from, these giants are unable to gorge themselves. Like all organisms, the bears must prioritize their energy usage, so if they cannot feed enough, they are less likely to reproduce. Even if they do mate, there is less chance that their offspring will survive long enough to learn to hunt. In 2004, archaeologists discovered a polar bear jawbone that has been dated to 110,000 to 130,000 years old, which provided some interesting information through its DNA. By analyzing the mitochondrial DNA of ancient and modern polar bears and comparing it with that of other ancient and modern bear species, they have concretely proven that polar bears are actually a highly specialized form of brown bear. This relationship has been further proven by the confirmation of polar bear-grizzly bear hybrids. Dubbed "grolar bears," these animals may point to the future of the species. If they continue to interbreed, that could hasten the disappearance of polar bears, but their DNA would live on in their descendants. So, when the conditions once again become more favorable, the traits that define polar bears may emerge again, allowing the rebirth of the species.

Q. What can be inferred from the professor's explanation about "grolar bears"?

(A) Grolar bears can be a future solution for the survival of polar bears.

(B) The method to interbreed polar bears and grizzly bears has yet to be discovered.

(C) Grolar bears can survive extreme weather conditions that polar bears cannot.

(D) The advance of science will be able to lengthen the survival of grolar bears.

생물학 강의의 일부를 들으시오.

여 지난 50년간 인류로 인해 야기된 지구 온난화가 극지방의 만년설을 지속적으로 줄어들게 만들고 있는데, 이는 북극곰들의 자연 서식지를 감소시키고 있어요. 여러분도 알겠지만 북극곰의 대부분의 음식 섭취는 바다표범으로 이루어지는데, 이들을 잡기 위해 얼음을 이용합니다. 바다표범들은 먹이를 사냥하러 물에 다시 들어가기 전에 물 밖으로 나와 폐에 숨을 채워야만 하는데, 숨을 쉬기 위해 종종 얼음에 난 구멍을 통해 올라옵니다. 북극곰들은 이들 구멍 주변에 숨어서 참을성 있게 바다표범이 수면 위로 올라오길 기다리는데, 올라오는 순간 무방비 상태의 바다표범을 턱으로 물어 물 속의 집으로부터 끄집어내서 잡습니다. 바다표범 고기와 지방에 잔뜩 함유된 비타민과 영양분은 북극곰의 음식으로 필요한 영양소들을 모두 만족시켜주죠. 사냥의 대부분을 봄과 여름에 해서 긴 극지방의 겨울에 대비해 필요한 무게를 늘립니다. 그러나 몰래 숨어있다가 기습하는 데 필요한 얼음이 점점 녹고 있기에 이 거대한 곰들은 배를 불리지 못하고 있어요. 모든 생물들과 마찬가지로 이 곰들은 에너지 사용에 우선 순위를 매겨야만 하는데, 그래서 충분히 먹이를 섭취하지 못하면 번식을 할 가능성이 줄어듭니다. 그리고 짝짓기를 한다 해도 이들의 새끼가 사냥을 배울 때까지 생존할 가능성은 적습니다. 2004년에 고고학자들은 약 11만 년에서 13만 년 전으로 추정되는 북극곰의 턱뼈를 발견했는데, 이 뼈의 DNA를 통해 흥미로운 정보를 제공했습니다. 고대와 현대의 북극곰들의 미토콘드리아 DNA를 분석하고 고대와 현대의 곰 종들의 DNA를 비교했을 때 이는 북극곰들이 사실 매우 전문화된 불곰의 한 종류라는 것을 명확하게 증명했어요. 이 관계는 북극곰과 회색곰 잡종에 대한 확인을 통해 더 증명되었습니다. '그롤라곰'이라고 별명 붙여진 이 곰들은 종의 미래에 중요한 핵심이 될 수도 있습니다. 이들이 계속해서 이종 교배를 한다면 이는 북극곰이 더 빨리 사라지도록 만들 가능성이 있지만, 이들의 DNA는 후손들을 통해 전해질 겁니다. 그래서 환경이 좀 더 좋아진다면 북극곰을 정의하는 이 특징들이 다시 나타나서 북극곰 종의 부활로 이어질 수도 있죠.

Q. '그롤라곰'에 대한 교수의 설명에서 무엇을 유추할 수 있는가?

Ⓐ 그롤라곰들은 북극곰의 생존에 있어 미래의 해결책이 될 수 있다.

Ⓑ 북극곰과 회색곰을 이종 교배시키는 방법은 아직 발견되지 않았다.

Ⓒ 그롤라곰들은 북극곰들이 생존할 수 없는 극단적인 기후에서도 생존할 수 있다.

Ⓓ 과학의 발전은 그롤라곰의 생존을 더 연장할 수 있을 것이다.

정답 (A)

해설 북극곰의 턱뼈를 통해 과학자들은 북극곰이 아주 전문화된 불곰의 한 종류라는 점을 밝혀냈으며 북극곰과 회색곰 잡종, 즉 '그롤라곰'을 통해 이것을 확인했다고 강의에서 나온다. 이 점을 이용해 두 종이 계속해서 이종 교배를 하게 하여 북극곰의 DNA를 계속 남길 수 있다고 했으므로 북극곰의 미래 생존 가능성을 염두에 두고 있다는 점을 알 수 있다.

어휘 anthropogenic adj 인류 발생의(인류로부터 만들어진) | global warming 지구 온난화 | steadily adv 꾸준히, 착실하게 | shrink v 줄어들다, 오그라들다 | reduce v 줄이다, 축소하다 | habitat n 서식지 | majority n 다수, 가장 많은 수 | consist v 이루어져 있다 | seal n 바다표범 | capture v 잡다, 포획하다 | surface v 수면으로 올라오다 | refill v 다시 채우다 | lung n 폐 | emerge v 나오다, 모습을 드러내다 | lurk v 숨어 있다, 도사리다 | patiently adv 참을성 있게 | breach v 구멍을 뚫다 | seize v 붙잡다, 움켜잡다 | defenseless adj 무방비의, 방어할 수 없는 | jaw n 턱 | wrest v 비틀다 | aquatic adj 물속에서 자라는 | blubber n 해양 동물의 지방 | satisfy v 만족시키다 | dietary adj 음식물의 | pack v 싸다, 꾸리다 | ambush n 매복 | gorge v 실컷 먹다 | prioritize v 우선 순위를 매기다 | reproduce v 복사하다, 복제하다 | mate v 짝짓기를 하다 | offspring n 새끼, 자식 | analyze v 분석하다 | mitochondrial adj 미토콘드리아의 | concretely adv 구체적으로, 명확하게 | specialized adj 전문화된 | confirmation n 확인, 확정 | hybrid n 잡종 | dub v 별명을 붙이다 | interbreed v 이종 교배하다 | hasten v 재촉하다 | descendant n 자손, 후손 | define v 정의하다, 규정하다 | rebirth n 부활

Practice

Passage 1 Listen to part of a lecture in an American history class. L05_P01

Q. What can be inferred about the whaling industry in the United States?

(A) It exported oil products around the world.

(B) It was the largest contributor to the nation's export.

(C) It contributed greatly to the country's economy.

(D) It supported the industrialization of the nation.

Passage 2 Listen to part of a lecture in a biology class. L05_P02

Q. What is implied about blood plasma?

(A) It is the main component in blood.

(B) It allows wounds to heal more quickly.

(C) It defends the body against illnesses.

(D) It is a watery yellow fluid produced by the body.

Passage 3 Listen to part of a lecture in a linguistics class. L05_P03

Q. In the lecture, what is implied about a pre-existing knowledge of grammatical structures?

(A) It would cause a child to do better than others in school.

(B) It would cause children to learn language quickly.

(C) It would cause simplified learning to be unnecessary.

(D) It would cause children to repeat things to adults.

Passage 4 Listen to part of a lecture in an architecture class. L05_P04

Q. What can be inferred about Inuit people from the professor's comments?

(A) Inuit people stay in their igloos until the structures melt.

(B) Inuit people generally live in structures other than igloos.

(C) Inuit people have small families that do not require much space.

(D) Inuit people think that the interiors of igloos are too cold.

정답 및 해석 | P. 194

Passage 5 Listen to part of a lecture in a psychology class.

L05_P05

Q. What generalization can be made from the professor's lecture?

(A) Students should never study the same information for over five minutes.

(B) Students who perform well often study a lot the day before a test.

(C) Flashcards are the best way for students to learn geographical facts.

(D) Learning something over time is better than learning it quickly.

Passage 6 Listen to part of a lecture in an environmentology class.

L05_P06

Q. What can be deduced about El Niño from the lecture?

(A) It results in increased rainfall throughout the world.

(B) It contributes to a sharp increase in boating accidents.

(C) It causes natural disasters around the world.

(D) It brings about problems on the Atlantic side of South America.

Passage 7 Listen to part of a discussion in a biology class.

L05_P07

Q. What does the professor imply about the lateral line?

(A) It allows the shark to perceive its prey in the dark.

(B) It allows the shark to sense a human being moving in the water.

(C) It allows the shark to breathe through its gills.

(D) It allows a shark to swim in a circular pattern all day.

Passage 8 Listen to part of a lecture in an ecology class.

L05_P08

Q. What does the professor imply about current agricultural practices?

(A) Raising large herds of animals compacts the soil.

(B) Too much salt is building up in the soil.

(C) Fertilizers accumulate in the ground water.

(D) Farmers are using up the land that can be farmed.

Passage 9 Listen to part of a lecture in a history class.

L05_P09

1. What can be inferred about the Sumerian culture?

(A) Their writing system is the basis for Western languages.
(B) They were responsible for many innovations.
(C) They had very early legal and judicial systems.
(D) They practiced an organized form of religion.

2. What can be concluded about salt from the lecture?

(A) Salt from the soil was seeping into rivers that Sumerians drank from.
(B) When vegetables absorb too much salt, it can be harmful to humans.
(C) An abundance of salt in the ground prevents crop growth.
(D) Salt encourages the growth of certain plants but not others.

3. What does the professor imply about Sumerian leaders?

(A) They supported the farmers' recommendations.
(B) They were not effective at governing their people.
(C) They organized the projects that tamed the rivers.
(D) They were not knowledgeable about agriculture.

Passage 10 Listen to part of a discussion in a sociology class.

L05_P10

1. What is implied about Malthus' overpopulation theory?

(A) It was proven to be an interesting but groundless theory.
(B) It was based on a small study with an insufficient sample size.
(C) It was very controversial among social scientists.
(D) It was the basis for economics in the Western world today.

2. What can be inferred about China's one child policy?

(A) It had little to no practical effect on population growth.
(B) It was a poorly conceived policy that did more harm than good.
(C) It was designed by people who believed Malthus' predictions.
(D) It may have helped to slow down overall population growth.

3. What does the professor imply about Malthus' predictions?

(A) They may still prove correct.
(B) They were a product of his time.
(C) They should be disregarded.
(D) They were partially accurate.

Test

Passage 1

[1-6] Listen to part of a lecture in an English literature class. L05_T01

1. What is the lecture mainly about?

Ⓐ The difference between Defoe's work and his contemporaries

Ⓑ The characteristics and the influence of a famous novel

Ⓒ The development of first person narrative novels

Ⓓ The history of the travelogue and its development over time

정답 및 해석 | P. 206

2. **According to the lecture, what is true about a novel? Choose 2 answers.**

Ⓐ It is often short or medium in length.

Ⓑ It takes the form of prose.

Ⓒ It describes events that happen simultaneously.

Ⓓ It talks about fictional events.

3. **Why does the professor mention a general merchant?**

Ⓐ To illustrate how Defoe was financially unstable during his lifetime

Ⓑ To compare the salary of a merchant to that of an author

Ⓒ To explain that Defoe did not begin his career as a writer

Ⓓ To show how being a merchant influenced *Robinson Crusoe*

4. **What is the professor's attitude toward novels with long titles?**

Ⓐ He doubts whether having a long title for novels was really necessary.

Ⓑ He thinks that popularity of a novel did not depend on its title.

Ⓒ He knows that novels that had long titles tended to become more popular.

Ⓓ He believes that it was not an unusual thing during Defoe's time.

5. **What is indicated about *Robinson Crusoe*? Choose 2 answers.**

Ⓐ Defoe pretended that the protagonist of the novel was the writer of the story.

Ⓑ It instantly became popular because people were interested in the life of a castaway.

Ⓒ Defoe wrote the novel based on the experiences of some other travelers.

Ⓓ Robinson Crusoe, the protagonist of the novel, was a castaway for four years.

6. **What can be inferred from the professor's explanation about *Robinson Crusoe*?**

Ⓐ Its unusual narrative style is what made Defoe receive a positive critical response.

Ⓑ It influenced the general style of travelogues in many European countries.

Ⓒ The readers could not see through everything that was happening in the novel.

Ⓓ The novel switches back and forth from a first person narrative to a third person one.

Passage 2

[1-6] Listen to part of a lecture in a biology class. L05_T02

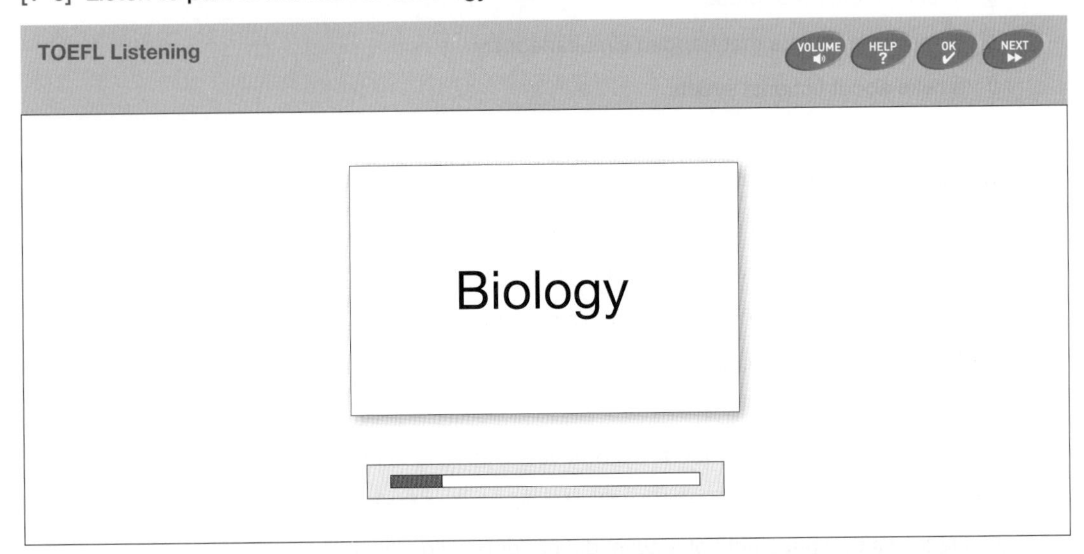

1. What is the lecture mainly about?

Ⓐ How bird species behave differently during the winter

Ⓑ How birds migrate and find their way as winter approaches

Ⓒ How birds' bodies are deeply sensitive to outside changes

Ⓓ How birds use their instincts to determine how they should act

2. Why does the professor mention birds on the university campus?

Ⓐ To use something familiar to introduce the lecture's topic

Ⓑ To give the students an example of how birds know to migrate

Ⓒ To clarify a previous point about bird flight patterns during winter

Ⓓ To explain why the topic of the lecture is important to everyone

3. What can be inferred about ducks from the lecture?

Ⓐ They eat things that are found in or under water.

Ⓑ They do not have thick plumage to protect them from snow.

Ⓒ They do not migrate in the same direction as other birds.

Ⓓ They do not fly very well when the air is cold.

4. According to the lecture, what do hormones do to birds' bodies as winter approaches?

Ⓐ Muscle is built up in their wings and chests.

Ⓑ Their brains signal them to store food.

Ⓒ Their bodies develop more fat under their feathers.

Ⓓ Their noses become more sensitive to change.

5. What is the professor's attitude toward the idea the birds use land structures to navigate?

Ⓐ She believes that it is probably the best-supported theory.

Ⓑ She believes that some of the evidence supporting it is not reliable.

Ⓒ She believes that birds rely more heavily on other forms of navigation.

Ⓓ She believes that the scientists studying the phenomenon are mistaken.

6. What is implied about bird migration?

Ⓐ Temperature is not the only factor birds depend on when migrating.

Ⓑ Birds are able to find their groups using the Earth's magnetic field.

Ⓒ Some bird species do not migrate so they store food for the winter.

Ⓓ All species of birds fly south when they migrate for the winter.

Lecture Topics Types

TOEFL 강의 영역에서 자주 등장하는 주제로는 아래와 같은 것들이 있다. 각 주제별로 시험에 나올 가능성이 큰 배경지식들을 숙지하고 문제를 풀어보면서 다양한 강의 주제에 대응하는 연습을 해 보자.

Lesson

01 Anthropology

문제 듣기

History of human migration 인류 이주의 역사

이주(migration)는 사람들이 새로운 장소를 찾아 일시적으로, 또는 영구적으로 떠나는 것이다. 초기 인류의 경우, 이들이 새로 옮겨간 곳에는 사람이 이미 살고 있는 경우가 드물었기에 그냥 정착할 수 있었지만 신석기 시대에 이르자 이주는 전쟁과 비슷해졌다. 남의 땅에 쳐들어가 영토(territory)를 빼앗는 행위나 마찬가지였기 때문이다. 최초의 이주는 아프리카에 있던 호모 에렉투스가 약 175만 년 전 유라시아 대륙으로 흩어진 때로 본다.

배경 지식 관련 어휘 migration n 이주 | temporary adj 일시적인 | permanent adj 영구적인 | Neolithic adj 신석기의 | territory n 영토 | Homo Erectus 호모 에렉투스(홍적세 초기에서 중기까지 생존한 직립한 사람을 가르킴) | Eurasia n 유라시아

Ancient writing system 고대 문자 체계

고대의 문자 체계는 당연히 나라와 지역마다 달랐으며, 어떤 곳에서는 돌에 그림과 기호(symbol)를 그려 문자 체계를 표현한 반면, 다른 곳에서는 자신들이 만든 도구를 사용해 의미와 뜻을 표현했다. 적어도 세 곳에서 문자 체계가 처음으로 시작되었을 것으로 보는데, 그 세 곳은 메소포타미아, 중국과 중앙아메리카이다. 또한, 이집트와 인더스강 유역에서는 메소포타미아와 별개로 문자가 발명되었을 가능성이 높다고 한다.

배경 지식 관련 어휘 region n 지역 | symbol n 기호 | Mesopotamia n 메소포타미아(서아시아 티그리스강과 유프라테스강 사이의 지역 일대를 가리키는 명칭으로, 메소포타미아 문명은 인류가 발달하면서 사회 생활을 위한 기술과 제도가 발전된 문명 상태를 뜻함) | Mesoamerica n 중앙아메리카 | invent v 발명하다

Test

정답 및 해석 | P. 212

[1-6] Listen to part of a discussion in an anthropology class.

1. What is the discussion mainly about?

Ⓐ The life of North American tribes, especially the way they obtained their food

Ⓑ A distinctive custom that was once widely shared by some North American tribes

Ⓒ The social structure of Native American tribes and its development

Ⓓ The different food distributing ceremonies of Native American tribes

2. **According to the discussion, what is a potlatch?**

Ⓐ A celebration of a new season

Ⓑ A gathering for sharing food

Ⓒ A ritual for gift distribution

Ⓓ An annual social gathering

3. **What was the purpose of the potlatch ceremony? Choose 2 answers.**

Ⓐ Showing others how wealthy the host is

Ⓑ Sharing the hunting methods of each tribe

Ⓒ Resolving conflicts between the tribes

Ⓓ Collecting a communal food supply

4. **What can be inferred about a potlatch?**

Ⓐ Ordinary people were not allowed to receive gifts.

Ⓑ It was heavily influenced by English explorers.

Ⓒ It is still celebrated these days by a wide variety of tribes.

Ⓓ Poor people were simply not able to afford one.

5. **According to the professor, what are some gifts that were usually given in a potlatch?**

Ⓐ Kitchen supplies made of wood

Ⓑ Various animals for farming

Ⓒ Weapons that were made of copper

Ⓓ Carpets and fabrics that were woven

6. **Why does the professor mention the Great Dying?**

Ⓐ To explain the influence of the Spanish explorers on the English settlers

Ⓑ To give an example of a religious ritual that was widely spread during the time

Ⓒ To illustrate the harsh living conditions of the Native Americans in the U.S.

Ⓓ To introduce an event that brought changes to a traditional custom

Lesson

02 Archaeology

문제 듣기

Mayan civilization 고대 마야 문명의 발견

마야 문명의 급작스러운 증발은 언제나 미스터리로 여겨져 왔다. 고고학자 윌리엄 새터노(William Saturno)는 우연히 마야 문명 발굴지 주변 동굴에서 마야인들이 그려 놓은 벽화(Mayan murals)를 발견하였고, 이어 더 많은 동굴 및 유적을 찾고자 하였다. 이에 NASA로부터 적외선 사진(infrared picture)을 지원받아 본격적 탐색에 나섰는데, 그 사진을 통해 사진 속 나무들의 색깔이 다른 것을 발견하게 되었다. 조사 결과 이 나무 색의 차이는 유적지의 부식(decay)으로 인한 미소 서식 환경(microenvironment) 때문인 것으로 밝혀졌다. 즉, 회반죽(lime plaster)으로 만들어진 유적지들이 부식되면서 탄산칼슘(calcium carbonate)들이 나뭇잎 속으로 스며들어가 적외선 사진 속에서 노란색을 띄었던 것이다. 이 사진들을 통해 마야 문명의 위치 및 범위를 파악할 수 있게 되었고 문명 증발의 원인도 곧 밝혀질 것이라 기대되고 있다.

배경 지식 관련 어휘 chamber n 방, 동굴 | mural n 벽화 | infrared adj 적외선의 | hue n 빛깔, 색조 | microenvironment n 미소 서식 환경 | ruin n 폐허, 유적, 잔해 | lime plaster 회반죽 | calcium carbonate 탄산칼슘

Lesson 02 Lectures

Underwater archaeology 수중 고고학

수중 고고학(Underwater archaeology)은 해적선 등이 잃어버린 보물뿐만 아니라 해수면이 증가하면서 물로 덮여 버린 인간 거주지의 발굴(excavation)에 대해서도 다루는 학문이다. 수중 고고학에 있어 가장 중요한 발굴은 바사(Vasa)호라고 불리는 침몰선이다. 바사호는 스웨덴 해안가 앞에서 출항 후 얼마 되지 않아 전복된 배로, 당시 많은 장식과 대포(cannon) 및 그 당시 선원들의 일상을 알 수 있는 다양한 유물들이 발굴되었다. 난파의 주된 원인은 배에 있던 대포가 풀려 굴러다니면서 배가 균형을 잃은 것으로 추정된다. 배는 보존 상태가 우수했는데 그 이유는 배가 매우 차가운 물 속에 잠겨 있어서 목재를 부식시키는 나무좀조개(shipworm)들의 활동이 억제됐기 때문이다. 그러나 선박이 물에서 인양되었을 때부터 물이 증발하기 시작해 선박을 보존하는 것이 까다로운 일이 되었고, 연구자들은 PEG를 뿌려 배를 코팅하고 보호하였으나 PEG의 장기간 남용으로 나무가 깨지기 쉬운 불안정한 상태가 되었다. 따라서 바사호 보존은 아직도 진행 중이다.

배경 지식 관련 어휘 excavation n 발굴 | tip over 뒤집히다, 기울다 | shipwreck n 난파선 | water-logged adj 침수된, 물에 흠뻑 젖은 | brittle adj 약한, 깨지기 쉬운

Test

[1-6] Listen to part of a discussion in an archaeology class.

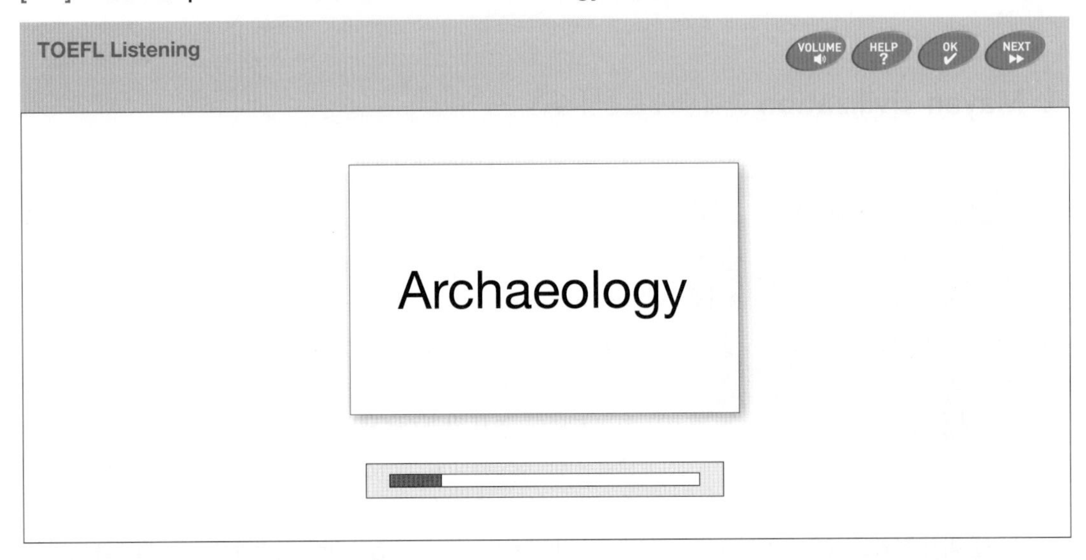

1. What is the discussion mainly about?

Ⓐ Tracing back the history of human inhabitance of England

Ⓑ Observing different theories regarding the existence of modern humans

Ⓒ Discussing the startling discovery made at Norfolk in 2010

Ⓓ Finding various patterns of early human migration in Europe

정답 및 해석 | P. 215

2. Listen again to part of the discussion. Then answer the question.

Why does the professor say this:

Ⓐ She wants the student to realize that he made a keen observation.

Ⓑ She is aware of the fact that she must introduce today's topic.

Ⓒ She wants to thank the student for providing a transition.

Ⓓ She appreciates the man participating so eagerly in the discussion.

3. What is true about the earliest modern humans? Choose 2 answers.

Ⓐ There is still debate regarding whether they are really the earliest ones.

Ⓑ Homo erectus, who did not make it to England, was the earliest modern humans.

Ⓒ They used to reside on the African continent before they started migrating.

Ⓓ They appeared in England around 14,000 BCE, when the ice sheets withdrew.

4. What can be inferred about the earliest human presence in Britain?

Ⓐ Many shinbones of Neanderthals prove that they were moving from place to place.

Ⓑ Homo sapiens dominated the region until the climate suddenly became harsh.

Ⓒ The estimated period was established with evidence of their impact, not their remains.

Ⓓ The discovery of Homo heidelbergensis revealed that they were the first inhabitants.

5. What does the professor explain about Homo antecessor?

Ⓐ Their presence eventually decreased the animal population in the forest.

Ⓑ They are considered to be the earliest ancestor of modern humans.

Ⓒ To prepare for natural disasters, they built shelters underground

Ⓓ They had the ability to cope with tough, cold weather conditions.

6. Why does the professor mention the Thames River?

Ⓐ To describe how it influenced the weather conditions of the region

Ⓑ To point out the main water source of Homo antecessors to students

Ⓒ To show the environmental obstructions the Homo antecessors faced

Ⓓ To support the evolutionary theory that was provided by scientists

Lesson

03 Architecture

문제 듣기

Design of public space 공공장소의 디자인

공공장소의 건설 계획과 디자인에는 매우 뚜렷한 두 가지 방법이 있다. 첫 번째는 유럽의 부르주아 층이 주로 사용한 방법으로, 자연에 대한 인간의 지배(man's mastery over nature)를 나타내며 잘 다듬어서 가지런히 정돈된(straight and neat) 식물이 건물을 보완하는 방식이다. 두 번째는 인공적인 아름다움을 강조한 유럽과 달리 자연 그대로의 미를 반영한 공공장소가 있는데 그 대표적인 예로 뉴욕의 센트럴 파크(Central Park)가 있다. 센트럴 파크를 건설한 건축가 프레드릭 옴스테드(Frederick Olmsted)는 부와 계급에 상관없이 모든 사람들이 즐길 수 있도록 공원을 건축하였으며 공공장소의 친근함과 편안함을 강조하였다. 그리하여 센트럴 파크는 모든 사람들이 편히 휴식을 취하는 미국의 대표적인 공공장소로 자리매김했다.

배경 지식 관련 어휘 bourgeois n 부르주아(14-15세기 봉건적 체제가 흔들리고 농노 해방이 이뤄지던 16세기에 경제적 실권을 쥐게 된 상인 또는 지주 계층) | mastery n 지배, 숙달, 통달 | trim v 다듬다, 손질하다 | neat adj 정돈된 | complement v 보완하다 | artificial adj 인공의, 인위적인 | hierarchy n (사회나 조직 내의) 계급, 계층

Post World War II housing development 제2차 세계대전 이후의 주택 개발

제2차 세계대전 이후, 경제가 어려워지고 실용주의(pragmatism) 경향이 강해지면서 사람들은 합리적이고 저렴한 집을 선호하게 되었고 이에 따라 저렴한 목조 주택인 케이프 코드 주택(Caps Cod House)이 생겨났다. 이 주택은 별다른 장식이 없고 지붕과 외벽을 널빤지(shingle)를 이용하여 만든 단층 구조로, 보통 확장 가능한 다락방(expansion attic)이 딸려 있었으며, 집의 중앙에 현관문(front door)이 위치해 있었다. 그러나 이러한 건축 구조는 너무 단순한 모양을 하고 있어서 금세 그 인기가 미 서부 목장 주택의 형태에서 고안된 랜치 주택(Ranch House)으로 옮겨갔다. 랜치 주택은 케이프 코드 주택과 비슷한 단순한 단층 형태였지만, 더 커다란 창문과 집 뒤편의 파티오(patio)로 통하는 유리 미닫이 문 등을 특징으로 갖고 있었다.

배경 지식 관련 어휘 pragmatism n 실용주의(미국 19세기 말과 20세기 초에 시작된 현대철학의 사조로 행동과 실천을 중시하며 생활에 있어서 유용성에 따라 사물의 가치를 결정하려는 사상) | reasonable adj 합리적인 | shingle n 널빤지 | expansion attic 필요할 때에 언제든지 손을 보아서 살 수 있게 만든 지붕 밑 공간

Test

정답 및 해석 | P. 219

[1-6] Listen to part of a discussion in an architecture class.

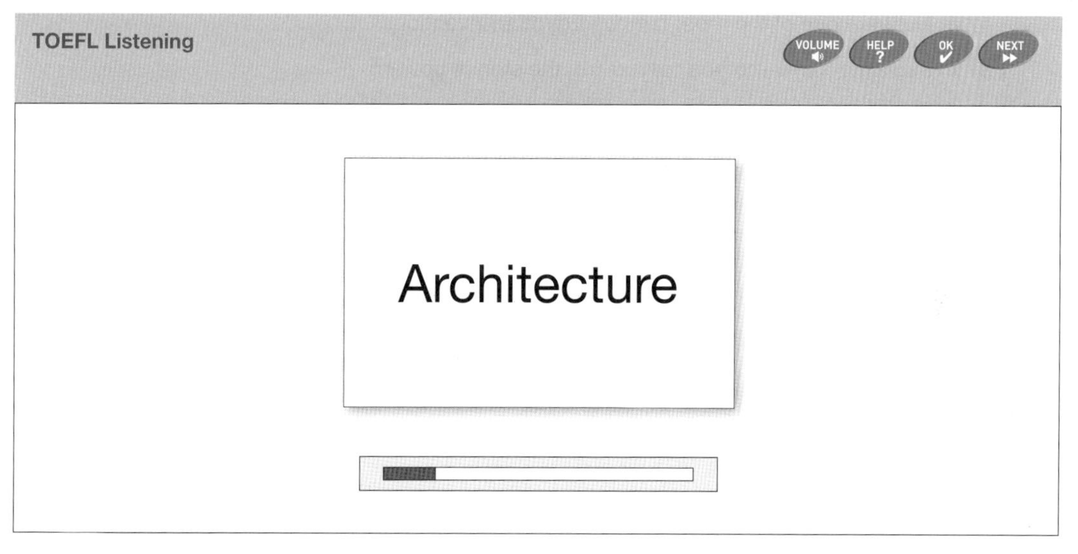

Lesson 03
Lectures

1. What is the discussion mainly about?

Ⓐ The possible explanations about the construction of the Pyramid of Giza

Ⓑ The mystery behind the actual purpose of the Pyramid of Giza

Ⓒ The information regarding the working conditions of Hebrew slaves

Ⓓ The French architect who proposed the accurate construction method

2. **Why does the professor mention a copper chisel?**

Ⓐ To illustrate one of the most famous Egyptian inventions

Ⓑ To explain another method for moving the stones upward

Ⓒ To give an example of a simple tool that was used for cutting limestone

Ⓓ To show that the Egyptians derived their idea from little objects

3. **What was the main problem with the first theory mentioned in the discussion?**

Ⓐ Using cranes for construction was still in development.

Ⓑ There would have been no room to place the cranes.

Ⓒ It was unable to explain how the stones were transported.

Ⓓ It is difficult to use wood crane since it is too weak for stones.

4. **According to the professor, what happens if a single straight ramp has an 8 degree grade?**

Ⓐ It brings the fastest results for transporting limestone.

Ⓑ The empty space inside the pyramid could collapse.

Ⓒ The ramp becomes far too long to be used.

Ⓓ It won't be able to support itself and will break apart soon.

5. **According to the professor, how did the microgravimetry device give possible evidence to support Houdin's theory?**

Ⓐ It revealed traces of the wooden cranes used in construction.

Ⓑ It found that there was empty space inside the pyramid.

Ⓒ It discovered a spiral figure resembling an internal ramp.

Ⓓ It made calculations about where the ramps had been placed.

6. **What can be inferred about the three methods presented by the professor?**

Ⓐ The wooden crane theory can explain how Egyptians transported the limestone.

Ⓑ Evidence shows that all of three were used to build the Great Pyramid of Giza.

Ⓒ The existence of a spiral ramp made the construction rather more time-consuming.

Ⓓ Houdin's method still needs more supporting evidence to be proven accurate.

Lesson

04 Art

문제 듣기

Dadaism 다다이즘

다다이즘(Dadaism)은 기존 예술에 대한 반박으로 1916년 스위스에서 시작된 예술 사조이다. 이는 제1차 세계대전 후의 혼란(chaos) 속에서 기존 예술이 추구하던 논리(logic), 이성(reason), 미(beauty)의 의미를 찾지 못한 예술가들이 새로운 예술 사조를 형성한 것으로 두 가지 특징을 띠고 있다. 첫 번째는 고전 예술(classical art)이 추구하던 모든 관습적인 개념에 반박한다는 것이며, 두 번째는 예술에 있어서 논리(logic), 순서(order) 등을 무시하고 임의성(randomness)을 중시하는 데 있다. 다다이즘을 보여준 최초의 예술은 카바레 볼테르(Cabaret Voltaire)의 쇼였는데, 이 쇼는 자유 형식 무용(free-form dance)부터 무의미시(nonsense verse)에 이르기까지 다양한 장르가 뒤섞인, 줄거리(plot)나 순서, 연기자(performer)와 관객(audience)의 구분이 없는 형태의 행위예술이었다.

배경 지식 관련 어휘 Dadaism n 다다이즘(유럽과 미국에서 일어난 프랑스, 독일, 스위스의 전위적인 미술가와 작가들이 본능이나 자발성, 불합리성을 강조하며 기존 체계와 관습적인 예술에 반발한 예술 운동) | convention n 관습 | randomness n 임의, 무작위 | free-form adj 자유로운 형식의 | nonsense n 허튼 소리, 아무 의미가 없는 말 | performance art 행위예술

Art conservation 예술 보존

예술 보존이란 예술품뿐만 아니라 문화적으로 중요성을 띠는 물건을 보존하는 것을 의미한다. 그 예로 아르키메데스의 덧씌워진 고대 문서(Archimedes Palimpsest)를 들 수 있는데, 수학적 공식을 설명한 이 문서는 그 당시로서는 혁명적인 내용을 담고 있었다. 그러나 이 문서가 보관되어 있던 도서관의 서기(scribe)가 양피지(parchment)를 아끼기 위해서 문서의 글씨를 전부 지우고 다른 내용을 적어 버렸고, 여기에 더해 20세기의 한 위조범(forger)이 문서의 가치를 높이려는 목적으로 그 위에 고전적인 양식의 그림을 덧그려 놓았다. 현대에 와서 과학자들이 자외선(ultraviolet)까지 이용하며 이 문서를 해독하기 위해 노력을 기울였으나 위조범이 그려 넣은 그림 아래의 글자를 복원하는 데에는 실패하였는데, 이후 아르키메데스가 사용했던 잉크에 철이 함유되어 있던 것이 밝혀지면서 X선을 이용해 해당 부분의 내용을 복구하는 데 성공하였다. 이와 같이 예술 보존은 많은 노력을 필요로 하는 작업으로, 다양한 분야 간의 협업이 있어야 더욱 수월하게 이루어질 수 있다.

배경 지식 관련 어휘 conservation n 보존 | palimpsest n 원래의 글 일부 또는 전체를 지우고 다시 쓴 고대 문서 | equation n 공식 | parchment n 양피지 | scratch off 긁어 내다 | forger n 위조범 | ultraviolet adj 자외선의

Test

[1-6] Listen to part of a lecture in an art history class. LT04

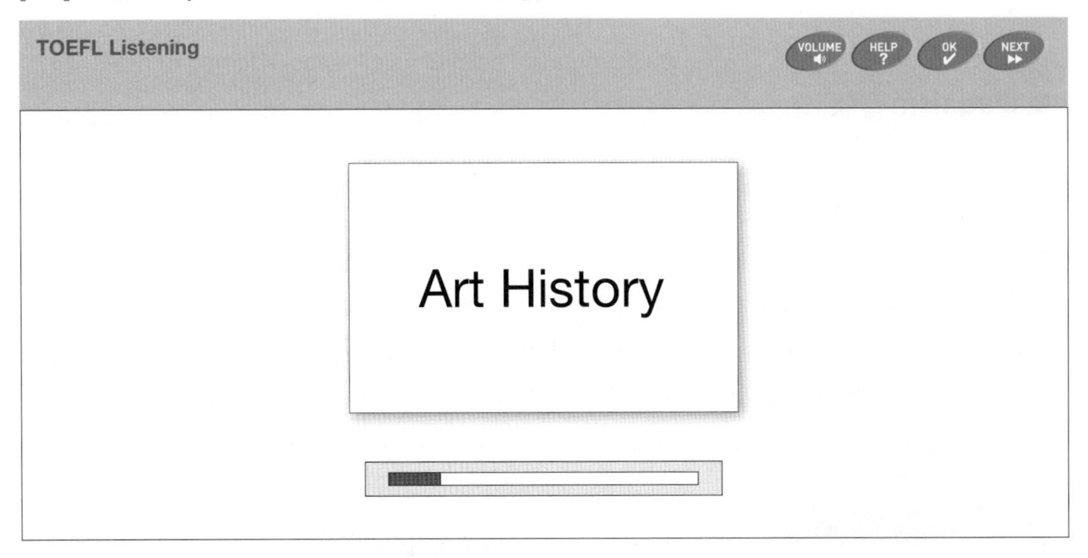

1. What is the main idea of the lecture?

Ⓐ The influence of Rembrandt on his students and the chiaroscuro techniques they shared

Ⓑ Some advanced tools that were used recently to prove a painter's works authentic

Ⓒ A painter's most well-known artwork and the reasons why it became so popular

Ⓓ The art techniques of a certain painter and the method used for proving his works genuine

정답 및 해석 | P. 223

2. **Why did Rembrandt use chiaroscuro technique in his works?**

Ⓐ To emphasize particular parts of the object or person in the painting

Ⓑ To show the importance of background and foreground when it comes to portraits

Ⓒ To guide the viewers' perspectives to the center of the artwork effectively

Ⓓ To highlight his heavy focus on detail, especially a person's jewelry and clothing

3. **What are the characteristics of Rembrandt's painting style? Choose 2 answers.**

Ⓐ He painted the whole canvas in transparent shades of gray first.

Ⓑ He avoided using a wide spectrum of colors for his works.

Ⓒ He enjoyed applying an excessive amount of paint.

Ⓓ He often used many layers to make the subject more real.

4. **Why does the professor mention forgery?**

Ⓐ To introduce another problem authenticating a genuine Rembrandt painting

Ⓑ To explain the process of making a forgery of the works of a famous painter

Ⓒ To emphasize the fact that Rembrandt's paintings were often forged

Ⓓ To illustrate that Rembrandt's painting style was hard to reproduce

5. **What can be inferred about autoradiography?**

Ⓐ It has a function similar to the conventional X-radiography scanner.

Ⓑ It can only detect red and white colors, which contain lead and mercury.

Ⓒ It shows where pigments were used by determining the elements in them.

Ⓓ It is able to distinguish between the brushstroke styles of different painters.

6. **Which of the following is true about *Old Man with Beard*?**

Ⓐ Rembrandt ran out of some paint colors before he finished the second layer.

Ⓑ Its second layer was eventually left unfinished by Rembrandt.

Ⓒ The use of autoradiography revealed that it was a genuine Rembrandt.

Ⓓ The top layer and the bottom layer both used a large amount of copper.

Lesson

05 Astronomy

문제 듣기

Halley's comet 핼리 혜성

핼리 혜성(Halley's comet)은 약 75년마다 지구로 접근하는 주기 궤도(periodic orbit)를 갖고 있는 혜성으로, 일반적인 태양계 내의 천체들과 달리 역방향(retrograde) 공전을 하며, 긴 타원형(elliptical)의 궤도를 갖고 있어 태양을 벗어나면서부터 빠른 속도로 태양과 멀어지는 특징을 지닌다. 궤도가 지구 등 다른 행성과 교차하기도 하는데, 이 때문에 한때 지구와 충돌할 것이라는 설이 나돌며 많은 사람들을 공포에 빠뜨리기도 하였다.

혜성은 기본적으로 얼음덩어리로 되어 있는데, 이는 이산화탄소, 메탄, 암모니아, 먼지 등이 뒤섞인 얼음이다. 혜성이 태양에 가까워지면 태양의 강한 중력(gravitational force)으로 인해 회전 속도가 증가하면서 중심부의 먼지와 얼음이 기화되어 밤하늘에 보이는 긴 꼬리를 형성하게 된다.

배경 지식 관련 어휘 periodic adj 정기적인, 일정한 | orbit n 궤도 | retrograde adj 역행하는, 역순의 | elliptical adj 타원형의 | gravitational adj 중력의 | evaporate v 기화하다

Hooker telescope 후커 망원경

후커 망원경(Hooker telescope)은 1917년 완공된 후 1949년 헤일(Hale) 망원경이 등장하기 전까지 세계에서 가장 큰 망원경이었다. 후커 망원경의 발명을 통해 드디어 은하계(Milky Way)를 관측할 수 있게 되었으며, 우리 은하계 외부에 존재하는 셀 수 없이 많은 은하계들의 실체 또한 밝힐 수 있게 되었다. 이를 통해 과학자들은 우주 창조에 대한 여러 이론을 생각하게 되었으며 마침내 혁명을 일으킨 빅뱅 이론(Big Bang Theory)이 제시되었다.

이후 기술이 더 발전하면서 6개의 망원경을 연결하여 만든 간섭 관측기(interferometer)가 발명되었으며, 이는 각 망원경에 맺히는 상을 바로 컴퓨터로 전송하여 하나의 합쳐진(synchronized) 사진을 만들어 냄으로써 전보다 훨씬 더 해상도가 높은 사진을 현상할 수 있게 만들었다. 이처럼 천체 망원경의 발달에 따라 더 많은 행성을 발견할 수 있게 되었으며, 더 나아가 지구 외에 생명체가 살 수 있는 행성도 찾을 수 있게 될 것이다.

배경 지식 관련 어휘 Milky Way 은하(수), 은하계 | galaxy n 은하계 | Big Bang Theory 빅뱅 이론(태초의 대폭발로 우주가 시작되었다는 이론) | interferometer n 간섭 관측기 | pipe v 보내다, 수송하다 | synchronize v 동시에 일어나다, 동기화시키다 | resolution n 해상도

Test

정답 및 해석 | P. 226

[1-6] Listen to part of a discussion in an astronomy class.

1. What is the discussion mainly about?

Ⓐ One of the most well-known examples of an asterism and its characteristics

Ⓑ The characteristics of the relationship between Ursa Major and Ursa Minor

Ⓒ Interesting features of ancient Greek astronomy and its influence

Ⓓ The difference between past and modern ways of naming the stars

2. **According to the discussion, what are asterisms?**

Ⓐ Clusters of stars that are physically close to each other

Ⓑ Groupings of stars that are not considered constellations

Ⓒ The classification of stars that have many different names

Ⓓ The stars that are visible in the night sky from Earth

3. **Why does the professor mention cave paintings?**

Ⓐ To show how astronomy has changed throughout history

Ⓑ To indicate their influence on naming constellations and asterisms

Ⓒ To point out that grouping and naming stars have been done for a long time

Ⓓ To tell the students that ancient astronomy still remains a mystery

4. **According to the discussion, which of the following are true about asterisms?**
Choose 2 answers.

Ⓐ They can be located inside a constellation.

Ⓑ Most of them were named by the ancient Greeks.

Ⓒ Their shapes do not always follow their names.

Ⓓ The official list of asterisms was compiled by the IAU.

5. **According to the discussion, which of the following are true about the Big Dipper?**
Choose 2 answers.

Ⓐ Its relationship with the Little Dipper has yet to be discovered.

Ⓑ Many cultures have referred to it with different names.

Ⓒ Its resemblance to a bear has been internationally agreed upon.

Ⓓ It can be found inside of a constellation named Ursa Major.

6. **What can be inferred from the professor's explanation regarding arbitrariness?**

Ⓐ When stars move away from each other, they are no longer part of an asterism.

Ⓑ Constellations are bound to change someday since all stars fade eventually.

Ⓒ Stars that shine constantly were called variable stars by astronomers.

Ⓓ The arrangement of stars changes depending on one's location in the universe.

Lesson

06 Biology

문제 듣기

Natural selection 자연 선택

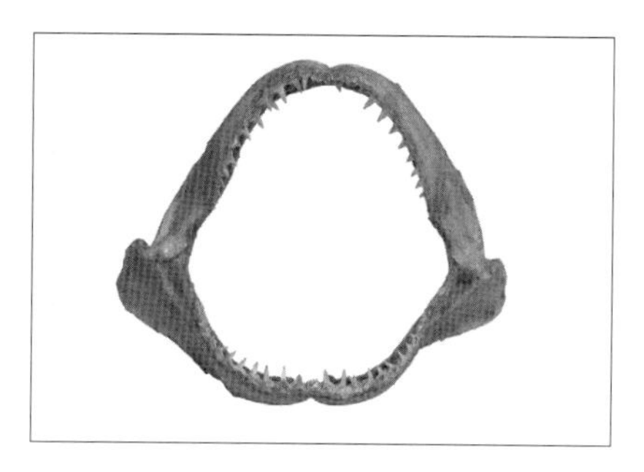

생물이 자손에게 유전적 데이터를 물려줄 때 항상 정확한 유전자 복제(genetic copy)가 이루어지는 것은 아니며, 돌연변이(mutation), 즉 DNA를 무작위로 복제하는 데 실수가 발생할 수도 있다. 하지만 이러한 돌연변이는 때때로 특정 환경에서 살아남을 수 있는 장점이 될 수 있다. 예를 들어, 오늘날 상어의 턱 구조는 돌연변이의 산물인데, 과거 물고기의 아가미 뼈(gill bar)가 발달해서 지금의 상어의 턱(jaw)이 된 것이다. 또한, 상어의 이빨은 상어의 피부를 감싸고 있던 작은 이빨처럼 생긴 구조물(denticle)이 점점 자라서 턱 안으로 들어가 이빨 기능을 하게 된 것이며 이는 고대 상어의 화석을 통해 알 수 있다.

배경 지식 관련 어휘 natural selection 자연 선택(자연계 생활 조건에 적응하면 생존 가능하나 그렇지 않는 생물은 자연스레 도태되어 사라진다는 설) | genetic adj 유전자의 | mutation n 돌연변이 | gill n 아가미 | denticle n 작은 이, 이 모양의 돌기 | fossil n 화석

Fishing 어획

어획(Fishing)은 바다에 인접한 국가 경제에 큰 영향을 미친다. 그 예로 1970년대 앤초비(anchovies)의 급격한 어획량 감소로 페루는 국가 경제에 막대한 손실을 입었다. 이와 같이 과도한 어획으로 어획량이 감소하면서 물고기 개체 수 유지의 중요성이 대두되자, 각국은 어획량 확보를 위해 경쟁함과 동시에 어획량 유지를 위한 어획 제한(fishing limits) 제도를 실행하고 있지만 여전히 어획량 감소는 심각한 문제로 남아 있다. 유엔 식량농업기구(FAO)에 따르면 현재 지구상에 존재하는 수산자원(fishery resources) 중 31%가 이미 남획 상태로 생물학적으로 지속 가능하지 않은 수준(biologically unsustainable level)이며, 58%의 수산자원은 최대 수준으로 어획되고(fully fished) 있어 수산자원 보전을 위한 국제적인 노력이 필요한 상황이다.

배경 지식 관련 어휘 anchovies n 멸치류 | secure v 확보하다, 어렵게 얻어내다 | limit n 제한, 허용치 v 제한하다 | fishery n (물고기가 대량으로 잡히는) 어장 | overfishing n (물고기의) 남획 | biologically adv 생물학적으로 | unsustainable adj 지속 불가능한

Bird migration 철새 이동

철새(migratory birds)들이 이동하는 이유로 기후 변화(climate change)와 먹이의 부족(scarcity of food)을 들 수 있다. 번식하기 좋고 먹이도 풍부한 살기 좋은 환경으로 이동하려는 본능은 인간이나 새나 마찬가지다. 철새는 봄과 가을에 제각기 일정한 곳으로 날아갔다가 다시 일정한 곳으로 돌아오는 귀소(homing) 본능을 갖고 있으며, 길을 찾는 방법에는 여러 가지가 있는 것으로 추측된다. 먼저, 새는 인간보다 수십 배나 좋은 시력(eyesight)을 갖고 있기 때문에 산과 건물 등 특정 이정표(landmark)를 따라 길을 되짚어 갈(retrace) 수 있다. 또한 특별한 지형 지물이 없을 경우, 낮에는 태양을 기준으로, 밤에는 별자리(constellation)를 보면서 방향을 잡는다. 게다가 철새의 부리 위에 있는 콧구멍에는 지구의 자기장(magnetic field)을 감지할 수 있는 일종의 나침반(magnetic compass)이 있어 이동을 돕는다.

배경 지식 관련 어휘 scarcity n 부족, 결핍 | homing adj 귀소성이 있는 | retrace v (왔던 길을) 되짚어 가다 | constellation n 별자리 | internal adj 내부의 | magnetic adj 자성의 | compass n 나침반

Degeneration of coral reef 산호초의 퇴화

산호초는 산호의 군락이 만든 탄산 칼슘이 쌓여 만들어진 것으로, 물고기 등 해양 생물들에게 서식처를 제공하고 해안 지역의 침식을 막아주는 등 생태계에 미치는 영향이 매우 크다. 그런데 최근 들어 이 산호초가 산호들의 외골격이 하얗게 변색되고 결국 죽게 되는 백화(coral bleaching) 현상으로 인해 파괴되는 양상이 가속화되면서 전 세계적인 우려를 낳고 있다. 여기에는 다양한 원인이 있을 수 있는데, 지구 온난화(global warming)로 인한 수온 변화, 어류 남획(overfishing)으로 인해 동물성 플랑크톤(zooplankton)이 급증하면서 겪게 되는 산소 부족(oxygen starvation) 현상, 해양 속 미생물(microorganism) 감염, 해수욕하는 사람들이 많이 쓰는 자외선 차단제(sunscreen) 성분들로 인한 해양 오염 등이 원인으로 지목되고 있다.

배경 지식 관련 어휘 coral n 산호 | habitat n 서식지 | bleaching n 표백 | zooplankton n 동물성 플랑크톤 | oxygen n 산소 | starvation n 기아, 굶주림, 결핍 | microorganism n 미생물 | marine pollution 해양 오염

Test

정답 및 해석 | P. 230

[1-6] Listen to part of a discussion in a biology class.

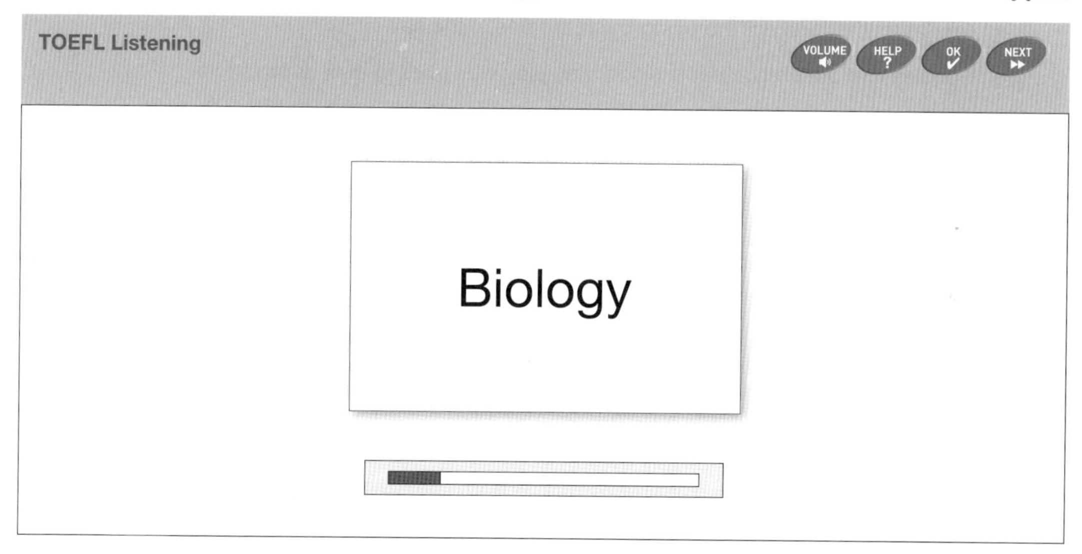

1. What is the discussion mainly about?

   Ⓐ Some species' roles and their ecological impact

   Ⓑ The importance of keystone species in the ocean

   Ⓒ The relationship between sea otters and sea urchins

   Ⓓ Robert T. Paine's radical experiment in the 1960s

2. **According to the discussion, what are keystone species?**

(A) Predators that prevent the overgrowth of trees in the savannah

(B) Species that are irreplaceable since they play vital roles in their ecosystems

(C) Plant eaters who influence the growth of grass and other plant species

(D) A few species that are near extinction and in need of conservation

3. **What can be inferred about a mountain lion?**

(A) It revealed that predators can survive without prey for quite a long time.

(B) It can deplete its resources faster than any other predators in the region.

(C) Even though it is a solitary predator, it can have a huge effect on its surroundings.

(D) Because of its wide territorial range, its influence is often overestimated.

4. **Listen again to part of the discussion. Then answer the question.**

Why does the professor say this:

(A) To talk about Paine's innovative nature and the consequences it brought

(B) To show how much scientists have to worry about keeping their financers happy

(C) To emphasize the scale and the difficulty of Paine's experiment

(D) To tell her students that Paine's experiment was a controversial one

5. **What is true about the sea otters of the Pacific Northwest? Choose 2 answers.**

(A) They are responsible for maintaining the population size of kelp plants.

(B) It was reported that about 2,000 of them are living in the region in these days.

(C) Their population increased after hunting was banned by the government.

(D) They maintain symbiotic relationships with sea urchins and kelp plants.

6. **Why does the professor mention prairie dogs and elephants?**

(A) To name some animals that influence keystone species

(B) To give some herbivore examples of keystone species

(C) To compare their roles as keystone species in their ecosystems

(D) To introduce the topics of the next lecture to the students

Lesson

07 Chemistry

문제 듣기

Properties of water 물의 특성

일반적인 액체(liquid)는 얼어서 고체(solid)가 되면 액체일 때보다 밀도(density)가 증가한다. 그러나 물의 경우는 다르다. 물은 다른 액체와 달리 온도가 낮아져 0℃에 가까워질수록 밀도가 떨어지며 부피가 팽창하게 된다. 즉, 물 분자(molecule) 사이의 간격이 멀어지는 것인데, 이처럼 얼음은 액체 상태의 물보다 밀도가 낮아서 물 위에 뜨게 된다. 물은 우주에도 존재할 정도로 굉장히 보편적이지만, 지구상에서 인간의 생존에 중요한 역할을 하는 액체 상태의 물의 희소성은 갈수록 높아지고 있다.

배경 지식 관련 어휘 property n 특성, 특징 | density n 밀도 | volume n 부피 | molecule n 분자 | universal adj 보편적인 | scarcity n 희소성

Trace metals 미량 금속

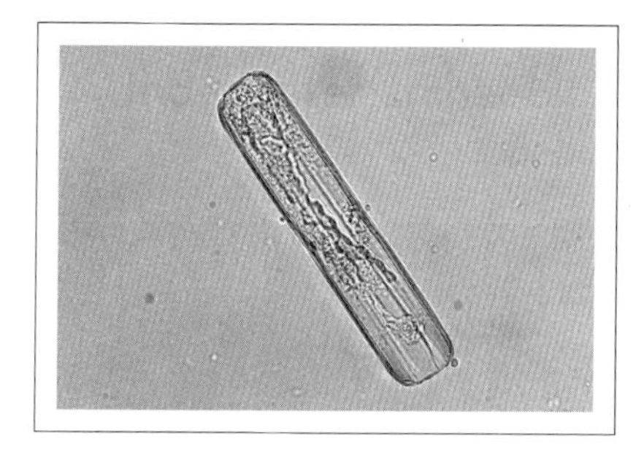

미량 금속(trace metal)은 동식물의 세포 내에 소량으로 존재하는 금속으로 효소(enzyme) 역할을 하며 아연(zinc)이 그 대표적인 예이다. 아연은 탄소(carbon) 순환을 촉진시켜 독성인 이산화탄소를 탄산(carbon acid)으로 바꾼 뒤 폐에 도달하여 다시 탄산을 이산화탄소로 바꾸어 체내에서 안전하게 배출시키는 역할을 한다. 반면 규조(diatom)라는 식물은 아연이 없는 물속에서 살기 때문에 아연 대신 카드뮴(cadmium)을 이용하여 체내 탄소 순환을 촉진시킨다. 이렇게 이산화탄소를 흡수하여 탄산으로 바꾸는 미량 금속에 대해 더 많은 연구가 진행된다면 지구의 이산화탄소 발생을 줄여 궁극적으로는 지구 온난화 해결에도 기여할 수 있을 것이라 기대된다.

배경 지식 관련 어휘 trace metal 미량 금속 | enzyme n 효소 | zinc n 아연 | carbon acid 탄산 | diatom n 규조, 돌말(바다 식물의 일종) | catalyze v 촉진시키다

Test

[1-6] Listen to part of a lecture in a chemistry class.

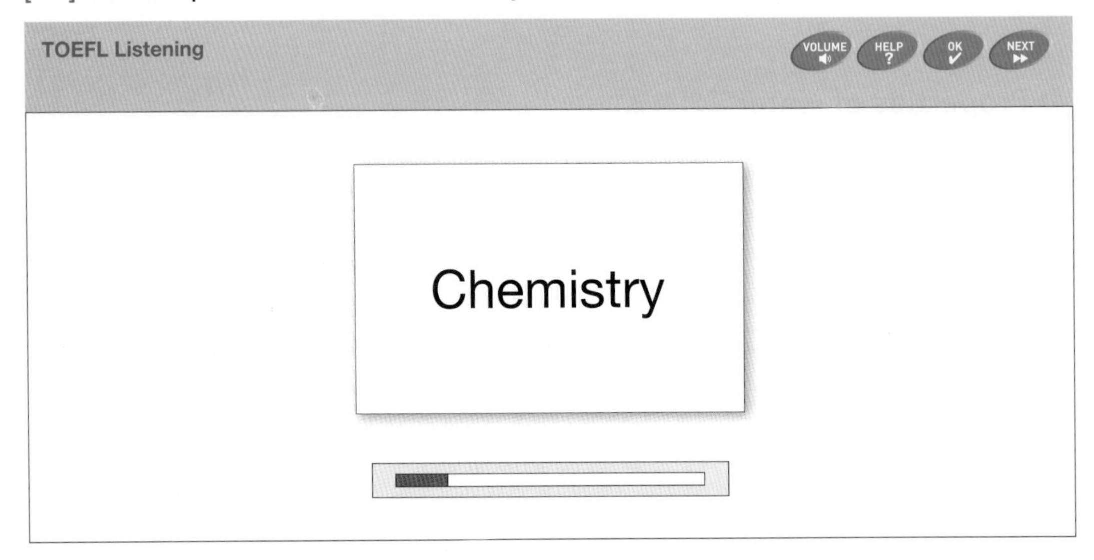

1. What is the main topic of the lecture?

Ⓐ Hydrogen concentration in rainwater in recent years

Ⓑ Radioactive decay and the half-lives of certain isotopes

Ⓒ Different properties of stable and unstable isotopes

Ⓓ Various uses of stable isotopes in law enforcement

정답 및 해석 | P. 233

2. According to the lecture, what are the characteristics of isotopes? **Choose 2 answers.**

Ⓐ They have the same number of neutrons as their normal atomic element.

Ⓑ They have a different mass number than their normal atomic element.

Ⓒ When they are separated, they produce radioactive waste.

Ⓓ When they are unstable, they discard extra neutrons.

3. What is the professor's opinion about stable isotopes?

Ⓐ He thinks they are important, especially in the field of law enforcement.

Ⓑ He knows that their use should be developed further in the future.

Ⓒ He believes that they should be treated carefully because of their nature.

Ⓓ He feels that their use is limited to just a few applications.

4. Why does the professor mention hydrogen?

Ⓐ To illustrate the difference between hydrogen and deuterium

Ⓑ To introduce a widely used type of isotope and its applications

Ⓒ To explain how it is the most easily found element on the Earth

Ⓓ To describe the role it plays in predicting criminal acts

5. Why is deuterium important in the area of forensic science?

Ⓐ It is most commonly found in lakes, rivers, and oceans.

Ⓑ It can provide a person's current whereabouts.

Ⓒ Its concentration differs depending on the location of the water source.

Ⓓ Its abundance in rainwater can provide environmental information.

6. What can be inferred about counterfeited items?

Ⓐ Stable isotopes can identify if they are real or fake.

Ⓑ Stable isotopes are used to produce counterfeited money.

Ⓒ Most of them contain stable isotopes in their signature.

Ⓓ Their location can make stable isotopes unstable.

Lesson

08 Communications

문제 듣기

Old Media 올드 미디어

올드 미디어(Old Media)는 전통 미디어라고도 불리며 정보화 시대(Information Age) 이전의 매스미디어를 뜻한다. 올드 미디어에는 인쇄물, 영화, 음악, 광고, 라디오 방송과 TV가 있으며 이것들은 지금도 우리와 밀접한 관계를 맺고 있다. 올드 미디어의 특징은 일방통행이라는 점인데, 한 매체에서 광범위한 대중에게 메시지를 전달하고 소통하는 방식이기 때문이다. 올드 미디어는 뉴 미디어가 등장하면서 점차 밀려나는 추세이지만, 아예 사라질지는 미지수이다.

배경 지식 관련 어휘 traditional adj 전통의 | Information Age 정보화 시대(물질적인 가치가 중시된 공업화 사회에 이어 도래한 사회로 물질의 가치에 비해 정보의 가치와 정보가 갖는 의미가 더 중요한 사회) | mass media 대중 매체 | advertisement n 광고 | one-way 일방통행의 | communicate v 소통하다 | disappear v 사라지다

New Media 뉴 미디어

뉴 미디어(New Media)는 컴퓨터와 컴퓨터 연산(computer operation)에 기반한 형태의 새로운 미디어이며 기존의 올드 미디어를 대체하고 있다. 뉴 미디어의 예시는 전화기, 컴퓨터, 웹사이트 게임, 컴퓨터 애니메이션, 인간-컴퓨터 인터페이스(interface), 소셜 미디어(social media) 등이다. 우리가 매일같이 즐겨 사용하는 페이스북과 유튜브 등이 여기에 포함된다. 뉴 미디어의 또 다른 특징은 정보 제공이다. 사람들은 신문(올드 미디어)을 읽는 대신 페이스북이나 트위터(뉴 미디어)를 통해 정보를 얻기 시작했다. 물론 이 때문에 정보 편향이라는 위험에 노출되기 쉽다.

배경 지식 관련 어휘 replace v 대체하다 | interface n 인터페이스 | social media 소셜 미디어 | bias n 편향 | risk n 위험

Test

정답 및 해석 | P. 237

[1-6] Listen to part of a lecture in a communications class.

Lesson 08
Lectures

1. What is the lecture mainly about?

Ⓐ The changes in people's perception of radio

Ⓑ The development of radio as a medium

Ⓒ The influence of radio on forms of communication

Ⓓ The relationship between radio and politics

2. **According to the lecture, why was radio more useful than the telegraph?**

Ⓐ Its operation was much simpler than that of the telegraph.

Ⓑ It did not have to be linked to the message source by wire.

Ⓒ It was able to receive and send messages through wire.

Ⓓ It used hardware that was much more inexpensive.

3. **What made radio in the U.S. different from that of other countries?**

Ⓐ It charged companies higher costs for advertising their products.

Ⓑ Most U.S. radio stations were owned by private companies.

Ⓒ Companies that were promoted on air financed U.S. radio.

Ⓓ It was supported mostly by taxes and was owned by the government.

4. **Why does the professor mention "fireside chats"?**

Ⓐ To illustrate the relationship between radio and wars

Ⓑ To show the strong influence of radio on U.S. history

Ⓒ To examine the first time radio was used for politics

Ⓓ To provide an example of what boosted radio's popularity

5. **What can be inferred about the change in radio after the development of television?**

Ⓐ It put more emphasis on music and eventually influenced the music industry.

Ⓑ It started to prefer news programs over other programs.

Ⓒ It moved from having a few channels to more than a hundred of them.

Ⓓ It gave birth to disc jockeys, who played live music on radio shows.

6. **According to the lecture, what is true about radio today?**

Ⓐ There are fewer disc jockeys compared to the past.

Ⓑ Most people prefer watching television to listening to radio.

Ⓒ Its accessibility and use have improved from before.

Ⓓ Radio programs expanded beyond the area of music.

Lesson

09 Economics

문제 듣기

Accounting 회계

회계는 예측(forecast) 가능하며 정확(precise)해야 한다. 이러한 회계의 결과물인 회사의 재무제표(accounting report)는 회사 경영과 관련된 미래의 결정을 예상할 수 있게 해주며 영업팀의 효율성(effectiveness)을 측정하여 직원들의 실적(performance)과 보너스(bonus) 등을 알 수 있게 해준다. 하지만 실적 감소가 발생했을 경우 재무제표만으로는 세부 사항이 설명되어 있지 않아 그 원인이 직원들의 사기(morale) 저하인지 혹은 단순한 업무 효율성 저하인지 알 수 없으므로 평가자의 입장에서는 주의해야 한다.

배경 지식 관련 어휘 forecast v 예측하다 | accounting report 재무제표 | management n 경영 | decline v 감소하다, 줄어들다 | low morale 사기 저하 | efficiency n 효율(성), 능률

Competitors in a business sector 사업 부분에서의 경쟁자들

사업을 시작할 때 경쟁자들(competitors)에 대한 경영 전략(management strategy)을 세우고 진행하는 것은 매우 중요하다. 그 중 가장 먼저 이해해야 할 것은 상대 회사의 경영 전략을 추측하는 것이며, 이는 과거 실적(past performance)과 지도 체제(leadership structure)를 통해 알아낼 수 있다. 과거 실적을 알게 되면 회사의 미래 전략을 알 수 있고, 지도 체제를 통해서는 회사를 이끄는 사람들의 배경을 알 수 있다. 따라서 이를 통해 상대 회사의 향후 전략을 알아낸다면 그 기업보다 더 나은 제품을 더 싼 가격에 제공할 수 있고, 결국 경쟁에서 우위를 차지할 수 있다.

배경 지식 관련 어휘 enterprise n 사업, 기업 | strategy n 전략 | assumption n 추측 | leadership n 대표(직), (회사 등의) 지도부 | provide v 제공하다, 공급하다 | dominant adj 우세한, 지배적인

Test

[1-6] Listen to part of a discussion in an economics class. LT09

1. What is the discussion mainly about?

Ⓐ Varying types of crises and how they influence people's lives

Ⓑ Different ways to deal with a crisis that a company encountered

Ⓒ People's opinion on a company's credibility in times of crisis

Ⓓ Examples of some companies that dealt with crises wisely

정답 및 해석 | P. 240

2. **When there is a crisis, why is it important to make a quick statement to the public?**

Ⓐ The public wants to know every detail about the crisis since they are curious.

Ⓑ If the crisis is a serious one, it is directly related to saving people's lives.

Ⓒ Failure to do so could result in even bigger threats to the entire nation.

Ⓓ It is required by the United States Constitution since the beginning of the 20th century.

3. **What can be inferred about misinformation?**

Ⓐ It will get out of control and governmental interference would be required.

Ⓑ It has a high chance of preventing the damage done to a company.

Ⓒ It often results from a company's delayed response regarding a crisis.

Ⓓ It can teach people the significance of dealing with different crises.

4. **According to the discussion, what is required of a company's carefully selected spokesperson? Choose 2 answers.**

Ⓐ Conveying information to people by using words that are easy to understand

Ⓑ Acting confidently by making eye contact and not making distracting gestures

Ⓒ Providing detailed information to the press, Internet, and broadcasters

Ⓓ Cooperating with government authorities regardless of the size of the crisis

5. **Why does the professor mention carmakers?**

Ⓐ To tell the students that carmakers have dealt with some crises recently

Ⓑ To give an example of a good way to take responsibility in times of crisis

Ⓒ To describe the hardships and results they face when a crisis occurs

Ⓓ To point out the significance of a company taking responsibility for a crisis

6. **Listen again to part of the discussion. Then answer the question.**

Why does the professor say this:

Ⓐ She is explaining why companies try to blame the customers for the problem.

Ⓑ She is saying that many companies often fail to acknowledge their mistakes.

Ⓒ She is showing why companies should accept responsibility even if they are unsure.

Ⓓ She is emphasizing that customers want to know who the guilty party is.

Lesson

10 Engineering

문제 듣기

Computational fluid dynamics 전산 유체 역학

전산 유체 역학(Computational fluid dynamics)은 유체 흐름에 관련된 일을 처리하기 위해 수치를 분석하고 자료 구조를 활용한다. 엄청나게 많은 양의 데이터, 그리고 무엇보다 복잡한 데이터를 이용해야 하므로 슈퍼컴퓨터(super computer)를 이용해 정보를 처리하는 경우가 많다. 전산 유체 역학이 쓰이는 분야(field)는 매우 다양하며, 여기에는 공기 역학, 항공 우주, 날씨 예측은 물론 엔진 설계도 포함된다.

배경 지식 관련 어휘 fluid flow 유체 흐름 | analyze v 분석하다 | aerodynamics n 공기 역학 | aerospace n 항공 우주

Aerospace engineering 항공 우주 공학

항공 우주 공학(Aerospace engineering)은 비행기(aircraft), 우주선(spacecraft) 개발과 관련된 공학 분야이다. 항공 우주 공학이라고는 하지만 비행기와 우주선에 매우 다양한 분야가 요구되기 때문에 여러 분야의 전문가들이 서로 팀을 이뤄 함께 일하는 모습을 볼 수 있다. 수학, 유체 역학, 재료 과학, 소프트웨어, 추진 등 그 수가 엄청나게 많다. 항공 우주 공학이라고 했을 때 사람들이 보통 떠올리는 기관은 미국 항공 우주국인 나사(National Aeronautics and Space Administration)이다. 나사의 리더인 국장은 미국 대통령이 상원의 승인 하에 임명하며, 대통령에게 항공 과학 고문으로서 직접 보고한다. 본사는 워싱턴 D.C.에 있다.

배경 지식 관련 어휘 aircraft n 비행기 | spacecraft n 우주선 | expert n 전문가 | hydrodynamics n 유체 역학 | materials science 재료 과학 | propulsion n 추진 | administrator n 국장 | U.S. Senate 미국 상원 | approval n 승인 | advisor n 고문 | report v 보고하다 | headquarters n 본사

Test

정답 및 해석 | P. 244

[1-6] Listen to part of a discussion in an engineering class.

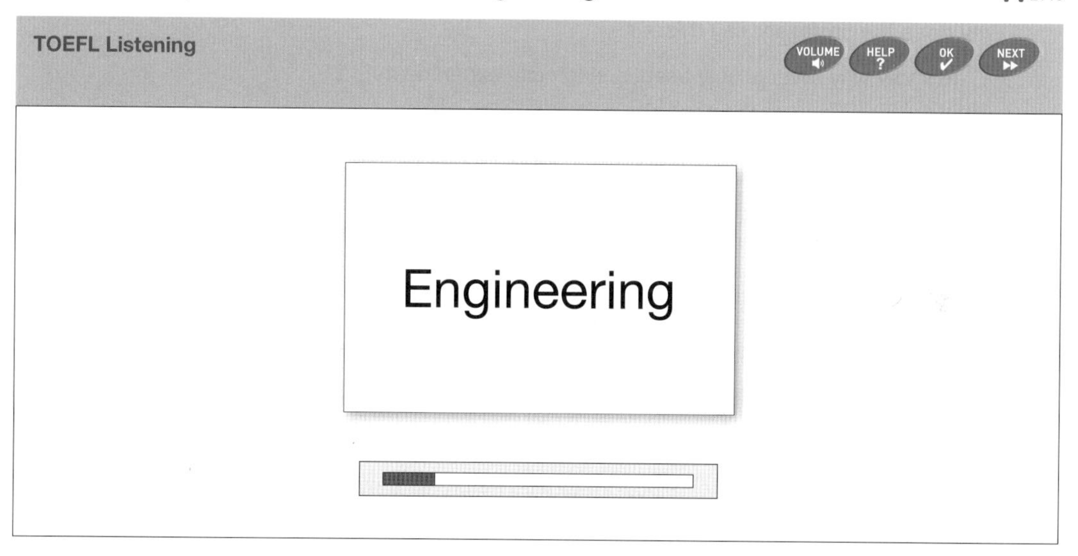

Lesson 10
Lectures

1. What is the discussion mainly about?

Ⓐ Some drawbacks that occur when using superconductors

Ⓑ The characteristics of materials named superconductors

Ⓒ The frequent use of superconductors in the medical field

Ⓓ Comparing the properties of copper and other metals

2. Listen again to part of the discussion. Then answer the question.

Why does the professor say this:

(A) To show why silver is only used in electricity experiments

(B) To state that silver is actually the best metal for wiring

(C) To question why copper is generally used to transmit electricity

(D) To indicate why silver is not suitable for electrical wiring

3. According to the discussion, what are superconductors?

(A) Materials that have zero electrical resistance when put into a proper state

(B) Materials that are resistant to extreme temperatures as low as zero degrees Kelvin

(C) Materials that can maintain heat longer than other non-precious metals

(D) Materials that change their electromagnetic nature as they lose energy

4. What is true of superconductors? Choose 2 answers.

(A) They need to be at their critical temperature to achieve superconductivity.

(B) Liquid helium and liquid nitrogen can be used for temperature control.

(C) Their superconductivity gradually increases when the temperature is high.

(D) Heike K. Onnes discovered the ideal temperatures for all superconductors.

5. Why does the professor mention liquid nitrogen?

(A) To show how it can possibly turn copper and silver into superconductors

(B) To give an example of another superconductor that is used in the industry

(C) To name a substance that can be used to reach critical temperatures

(D) To illustrate the process of cooling superconductors to 23 degrees Kelvin

6. What can be inferred about the use of superconductors?

(A) They are rarely useful for X-ray imaging and MRI systems in hospitals.

(B) Scientists are trying to replace liquid nitrogen with other materials for better performance.

(C) For now, their use is limited to certain settings because of their cooling system.

(D) It is potentially dangerous to people's health because of their radioactive nature.

Lesson

11 Environmental Science

문제 듣기

Biofuel 바이오 연료

바이오 연료(Biofuel)에는 여러 종류가 있지만 가장 많이 언급되는 것 중에는 에탄올과 바이오 디젤 두 가지가 있다. 우선 에탄올은 화석 연료(fossil fuel)의 2/3밖에 에너지를 내지 못하여 에너지 효율성이 낮으나, 석유와 같은 방식의 연료로 사용될 수 있어 유럽에서는 사용도가 높고 개발 가치가 있다고 평가된다. 반면에 바이오 디젤은 식물과 씨앗에서 추출하는 연료인데, 여러 씨앗들 중에서 유채씨(rapeseed)는 효율성이 떨어지며 야자유(oil palm tree)는 자연 환경 훼손의 문제가 있는 반면, 해조류(algae)에서 추출되는 바이오 디젤은 해조류의 빠른 성장으로 인해 공급이 용이하다는 특징을 갖고 있다. 해조류에서 추출한 바이오 디젤은 자동차 배기 가스 배출량을 감소시키는 장점 또한 지닌 것으로 밝혀졌다. 이 기술은 앞으로 매우 유망하지만, 개발 비용이 높아 아직까지는 비용 효율적이지 못해 실제 사용으로 이어지기까지는 시간이 걸릴 것이라 판단된다.

배경 지식 관련 어휘 fossil fuel 화석 연료 | energy efficiency 에너지 효율성 | supply n 공급, 제공 v 공급하다, 제공하다 | exhaust fumes 배기 가스 | emission n 배출 | cost-effective adj 비용 효율이 높은

Lesson 11 Lectures

New speciation in Amazon 아마존의 새로운 종의 탄생

생물종의 분배(species allocation)란 한 종이 지역적 장벽으로 인해 다른 두 그룹으로 나뉘어지는 것을 의미하며, 이렇게 나누어진 두 그룹이 더 이상 번식을 할 수 없는 곳에서 긴 시간 동안 각각 진화할 때 새로운 종의 형성(speciation)이 이루어진다고 본다. 종의 형성은 긴 시간과 매우 넓은 지역적 장벽이 있을 때 가능한데, 이에 적절한 조건을 갖춘 곳으로 아마존이 있다. 아마존에는 매우 다양한 생물종이 서식하고 있는데, 아마존 지역의 많은 작은 강들이 지역적 장벽의 역할을 함으로써 다양한 종의 형성을 가능하게 했다고 여겨진다.

배경 지식 관련 어휘 speciation n 종 형성, 종 분화 | species n (생물의) 종 | allocation n 할당, 배분 | evolutionary adj 진화의 | barrier n 장벽, 장애물 | biodiversity n 생물의 다양성

Helium-3 헬륨3

화석 연료(fossil fuel) 고갈에 따른 대체 에너지(alternative energy)의 필요성이 대두됨에 따라 헬륨3(helium-3)가 잠재적 대체 에너지가 될 가능성이 높아지고 있다. 헬륨3는 헬륨의 동위 원소로, 양성자 2개와 중성자 2개를 지닌 일반적인 헬륨 원자와 달리 원자가 양성자 2개와 중성자 1개로 이루어져 있다. 헬륨3는 중수소와의 핵융합을 통해 엄청난 양의 에너지를 발생시킬 수 있는데, 이는 핵분열(nuclear fission)보다 안전하고 환경 오염의 위험이 없는 것으로 알려져 있다. 문제는 지구에는 헬륨3가 거의 없다는 점인데, 반면 달(moon)에는 많은 양이 있어 여러 국가들에서 이를 채취하는 방법을 다방면으로 연구 중이다.

배경 지식 관련 어휘 helium **n** 헬륨 I isotope **n** 동위 원소 I proton **n** 양성자 I neutron **n** 중성자 I deuterium **n** 듀테륨, 중수소 I nuclear fusion reaction 핵융합 반응 I fission **n** 분열

Gause's law 가우스 이론

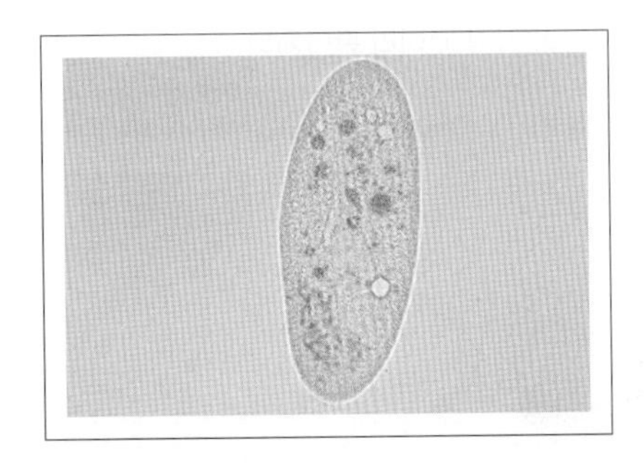

가우스의 경쟁 배타 원리(competitive exclusion principle)에 따르면, 같은 서식지에 생활 양식이 서로 비슷한 두 종의 생물체들이 공존하고 있을 경우, 먹이나 서식지를 가지고 경쟁해 두 종 중 더 약한 쪽이 도태되게 된다. 가우스는 짚신벌레(paramecium)를 이용한 실험에서 이를 증명하였다. 짚신벌레 두 종을 따로 키웠을 때, 각 종의 개체군은 예상대로 환경수용력 한계에 도달할 때까지 S자 모양의 빠른 개체군 생장 곡선을 보였다. 그러나 두 종을 같이 키웠을 때, 처음에는 두 종 모두가 S자 모양의 생장 곡선을 보이며 자라나다가 시간이 지나자 한 종은 생존하고 다른 종은 멸종되었다. 이런 결과들에 기초하여 가우스는 "제한된 자원을 공동으로 이용하는 두 종은 공존할 수 없다"는 경쟁 배타 원리를 제안하였다. 하지만 반대자들은 해당 실험이 자연 상태의 모든 조건을 만족하지 못했다고 주장하며 가우스 이론을 인정하지 않고 있다. 그들의 연구에 따르면 휘파람새(warbler)들은 먹이를 공유할 때 먹이에 대한 경쟁을 피하기 위해 서로 다른 영역에서 먹이사냥을 하며, 경쟁을 줄이기 위해 서로 다른 시기에 새끼를 낳는데 이는 가우스 이론에 위배되는 결과이다.

배경 지식 관련 어휘 competitive exclusion principle 경쟁 배타 원리(생태학의 원리 중 하나로 동일한 생태적 지위를 가지는 두 종은 공존할 수 없다는 원리) I habitat **n** 서식지 I coexist **v** 공존하다 I paramecium **n** 짚신벌레 I environmental carrying capacity 환경수용력 I growth curve 생장/성장 곡선 I extinction **n** 멸종, 절멸, 소멸 I warbler **n** 휘파람새, 울새

Test

정답 및 해석 | P. 247

[1-6] Listen to part of a discussion in an environmental science class. LT11

1. What is the main idea of the discussion?

   (A) Ways to develop thermal depolymerization to use it for other recycled products

   (B) The process of breaking down carbon chains with thermal depolymerization

   (C) Various methods of utilizing thermal depolymerization in a safer environment

   (D) The advantages of using thermal depolymerization for recycling various products

2. **According to the discussion, what are the downsides of traditional plastic recycling? Choose 2 answers.**

Ⓐ It only depends on combustion.

Ⓑ Harmful chemicals are often generated by it.

Ⓒ Other kinds of products cannot be recycled together.

Ⓓ It changes most products into solid matter.

3. **The professor describes the process of recycling plastics by thermal depolymerization. Put the steps below in order.**

Ⓐ The mixture is heated to an extremely high temperature.

Ⓑ The matter is subjected to about 500 degrees Celsius.

Ⓒ The mixture is exposed to high pressure for 15 minutes.

Ⓓ The plastic is reduced to small pieces and is put into water.

Step 1	
Step 2	
Step 3	
Step 4	

4. **What is true about thermal depolymerization?**

Ⓐ Its effect on the environment is questionable because it produces methane.

Ⓑ It can help recycle many different kinds of products that are carbon-based.

Ⓒ Its performance heavily depends on the content of the material it recycles.

Ⓓ It breaks down carbon molecules and creates new chemicals.

5. **What is the professor's opinion of thermal depolymerization?**

Ⓐ He thinks it requires too much energy input compared to the output.

Ⓑ He considers it to be efficient and quite safe for the environment.

Ⓒ He sees it as the perfect solution for recycling plastics.

Ⓓ He believes it actually has a negative impact on the environment.

6. **What can be inferred about the future of thermal depolymerization?**

Ⓐ It has great potential since it can help reduce a massive amount of waste and garbage.

Ⓑ It will be developed further to solve the problem of removing greenhouse gases.

Ⓒ It can be used in a variety of ways, though it still has some limitations regarding transportation.

Ⓓ It will get support from the public since it can reduce gas prices in the long run.

Lesson

12 Film Studies

문제 듣기

Alfred Hitchcock 알프레드 히치콕

1899년에 태어나 1980년에 사망한 알프레드 조셉 히치콕(Alfred Joseph Hitchcock)은 영국과 미국을 오가며 활동한 영화감독이자 프로듀서였으며, 영화사에 히치콕이 끼친 영향은 엄청나다. 히치콕에게 영향을 받은 감독은 셀 수 없을 정도이며, 촬영 기법과 스타일, 모티프, 제작 등 모든 면에서 영향력을 발휘했다. 특히 서스펜스 영화의 거장으로 잘 알려져 있으며 <현기증(Vertigo; 1958)>, <사이코(Psycho; 1960)>, <새(The Birds; 1963)> 등의 작품이 세계적으로 잘 알려져 있다.

배경 지식 관련 어휘 film director 영화감독 | producer n 프로듀서 | impact n 영향 | suspense n 서스펜스, 긴장감 | vertigo n 현기증 | psycho n 사이코, (이상하게 폭력적인) 정신병자 | worldwide adv 전 세계적으로

Cameo role 카메오 배역

카메오 배역, 혹은 그냥 '카메오(cameo)'는 연예인이나 영화감독, 운동선수와 정치인 등 유명 인물이 공연 예술에 잠시 출연하는 것을 의미한다. 보통 눈에 띄지 않는 작은 역할을 맡으며, 말을 하지 않고 쓱 지나가거나 화면에 아주 잠깐 비춰질 때도 많다. 알프레드 히치콕 감독은 자신이 만든 영화 대부분에 카메오로 출연하는 것으로 유명했으며, 쿠엔틴 타란티노(Quentin Tarantino) 감독 또한 자기 작품의 다수에서 카메오로 나왔다.

배경 지식 관련 어휘 cameo n 카메오(영화나 방송에서 연기자가 아닌 유명인사가 예기치 않은 장면에 잠깐 출연하여 단역을 잠시 맡는 것 또는 그 역할) | celebrity n 유명 인사, 연예인 | athlete n 운동선수 | politician n 정치인 | well-known adj 유명한

Test

[1-6] Listen to part of a lecture in a film studies class.

LT12

1. What is the main topic of the lecture?

Ⓐ The requirements of stage acting

Ⓑ The development of method acting

Ⓒ The comparison of classical and method acting

Ⓓ The changes that film brought to acting

정답 및 해석 | P. 251

2. According to the professor, what are some characteristics of stage performances? Choose 3 answers.

(A) The use of exaggerated body language

(B) Expressing emotion through facial expressions

(C) Heavy reliance upon the lines of the play

(D) Narration to explain what is happening

(E) Sudden changes in an actor's voice

3. According to the professor, what made performing Shakespeare's plays so difficult?

(A) They take hours to perform.

(B) They required the actors to use accents.

(C) The actors had to speak loudly.

(D) The lines were difficult to pronounce.

4. What defines the difference between classical and method acting most clearly?

(A) The kind of vocal training the actor goes through

(B) The way in which the performance is filmed

(C) The director's treatment of the film cast

(D) The actor's relationship with the character

5. What can be inferred about method acting?

(A) Actors must take drastic measures to become the characters they play.

(B) Staying in character can affect an actor's personal life.

(C) Preparing for roles can require actors to study intensely.

(D) Actors may never fully return to their normal selves.

6. How does the professor conclude the lecture?

(A) By giving the listeners an assignment for the next session

(B) By inviting his audience to provide him with examples

(C) By telling an anecdote that illustrates his point

(D) By providing a summary of the lecture as a whole

Lesson

13 Geology

문제 듣기

Channeled scabland 수로가 있는 화산 용암지

워싱턴주 남동쪽에 위치한 여러 개의 수로(channel)가 형성된 화산 용암지(channeled scabland)는 오랫동안 미스터리로 여겨져 왔다. 그러다가 1922년 지질학자 J. 할런 브레츠(J. Harlen Bretz)의 조사를 통해서 이 물길들은 갑작스러운 홍수로 인해 몇 시간 만에 생긴 것이라는 주장이 나왔다. 하지만 그 후 지질학자 조셉 파디(Joseph Pardee)의 계속된 분석 끝에 이 수로는 화산 주변의 호수와 관계가 있다는 사실이 밝혀졌다. 파디에 따르면, 빙하기가 끝나면서 화산 용암지 동쪽에 있는 미줄라(Missoula) 호수에서 많은 양의 물이 쏟아졌었고, 그로 인해 홍수와 같은 현상이 일어나서 오늘날과 같은 수로를 형성하게 되었다고 한다.

배경 지식 관련 어휘 channel n 수로 | scabland n 화산 용암지 | flood n 홍수 | Ice Age 빙하기 | gush v 쏟아지다, 솟구치다 | surge v 급증하다

Sand dune 모래 언덕(사구)

사구(Sand dune)는 모래가 바람에 의해 운반, 퇴적되어 생긴 언덕으로, 주로 건조한 지역이나 해안 등지에서 찾아볼 수 있다. 형성 장소에 따라서 사막과 같이 건조한 내륙에서 만들어지는 내륙 사구(inland dune), 해안가의 모래에 의해 만들어지는 해안 사구(coastal sand dune), 거대한 호숫가나 강가의 모래에 의해 만들어지는 호반 사구와 하반 사구로 나뉜다. 또한 모래의 공급량이나 풍속, 풍향의 변화, 주변 지형 등에 따라 사구의 모양도 다양하다. 모래의 공급량이 적으면 타원형의 순상 사구(shield sand dune)가 형성되고, 바람받이 쪽(바람이 불어오는 쪽) 사면은 완경사, 바람그늘 쪽(바람이 가려지는 쪽)은 급경사가 되며, 양쪽 끝이 돌출하여 초승달처럼 생긴 바르한(barchan)이 된다. 이것이 이동하여 옆으로 이어지면 풍향에 대해서 직각으로 배열되는 횡사구가 형성되며, 풍속이 셀 경우에는 바람그늘 쪽으로 열려진 V자형이나 포물선형 사구가 형성되며 이것이 이어지면 풍향과 평행하는 종사구가 형성된다.

배경 지식 관련 어휘 sedimentation n 퇴적(작용) | windward adj 바람이 불어오는 쪽의, 바람을 받는 쪽의 | leeward adj 바람이 가려지는 쪽의, 바람이 불어가는 쪽의 | crescentic adj 초승달 모양의 | barchan n 바르한(초승달 모양의 사구) | perpendicular adj 직각의, 수직적인

Test

정답 및 해석 | P. 254

[1-6] Listen to part of a discussion in a geology class.

1. What is the discussion mainly about?

Ⓐ The formation and the characteristics of a mysterious geological structure

Ⓑ The reason behind the color variation of stones in Bryce Canyon

Ⓒ The influence that hoodoos had to the inhabitants in the region

Ⓓ The geographical advantages that hoodoos have for their formation

2. What can be inferred about hoodoos?

Ⓐ They usually require many years to form.

Ⓑ Their outer surface is flat and smooth in general.

Ⓒ They were used as material for totem poles in the past.

Ⓓ They can only be found in Utah and Arizona.

3. Listen again to part of the discussion. Then answer the question.

Why does the professor say this:

Ⓐ He is explaining that geology is a discipline that was developed fairly recently.

Ⓑ He is telling the students that mysterious things did happen in the past.

Ⓒ He is trying to convince his students to have a better appreciation of geology.

Ⓓ He is saying that the name of hoodoos came from people's uncertainty.

4. What are the two weathering processes that form hoodoos? Choose 2 answers.

Ⓐ Windstorms in the winter

Ⓑ Solar radiation during summer

Ⓒ Expansion of water during winter

Ⓓ Acidic rainwater in the summer

5. According to the discussion, why do rocks in this area erode at different rates?

Ⓐ The weather in the area is continuously becoming hotter and more arid.

Ⓑ Since they are all located in different places, some erode more quickly than others.

Ⓒ Limestone is more affected by acidic rain than sandstone and mudstone are.

Ⓓ Some stones are less frequently exposed to rain than other stones.

6. Why does the professor mention the Cappadocia region of Turkey?

Ⓐ To recommend students another good region to study and see hoodoos

Ⓑ To give an example to students of how people in the past used these formations

Ⓒ To illustrate the well-preserved condition of the hoodoos in this area

Ⓓ To compare the hoodoos in Bryce Canyon and the ones in the Cappadocia region

Lesson
14 History

문제 듣기

American Revolutionary War 미국 독립전쟁(1775-1783)

18세기 중엽 식민지(colony) 확장 사업으로 자금난을 겪고 있던 영국 정부는 톤젠드 조례(Townshend Acts), 차법(Tea Act) 등을 통해 미국 식민지 주민들로부터 높은 세금을 착취하였다. 이에 맞서 1773년 한 무리의 시민들이 모여 보스턴항에 정박한 영국 선박에 실려 있던 342개의 차 상자를 모조리 바다에 던져버리는 보스턴 차 사건(Boston Tea Party)이 일어났는데, 이로부터 영국 정부에 대한 미국인들의 본격적인 저항이 시작되게 된다. 더욱이 이 사건으로 영국 의회가 1774년 영국군을 일반 미국 가정에 주둔시킬 수 있게 하는 등의 내용을 담은 참을 수 없는 법(Intolerable Acts)을 통과시킴에 따라 영국 정부에 대한 불만이 최고조에 이르러, 결국 미국 독립을 위한 전쟁으로 확장되었다. 이후 1783년 파리 조약에서 영국 정부가 미국의 독립을 공식적으로 인정함으로써 미국은 독립국이 되었고, 각 식민지는 주(state)로 명명되고 이들이 연합하여 미합중국(the United States of America)을 이루게 되었다.

배경 지식 관련 어휘 Townshend Acts 톤젠드 조례(영국 재무상인 톤젠드가 북아메리카 13개 식민지에 종이, 차, 유리 등에 세금을 새로 부과한 법령) | Intolerable Acts 참을 수 없는 법(영국 의회가 아메리카 식민지를 통제하기 위해 제정한 네 가지 법) | colony n 식민지 | expansion n 확장 | resident n 주민 | tax n 세금 | resistance n 저항 | independence n 독립

World War II 제2차 세계 대전(1939-1945)

제2차 세계 대전은 '세계' 대전이라는 이름답게 유럽의 다수 국가와 아시아, 북아프리카, 미국 등 가장 많은 나라들이 참전하여 벌어진 전쟁으로, 인류 역사상 최악의 피해를 불러왔으며 각 국가에게 돌이킬 수 없는 영향을 미쳤다. 또한 이 전쟁으로 세계의 힘의 중심이 유럽에서 미국과 러시아로 옮겨갔으며, 이 두 나라는 제2차 세계 대전이 끝난 뒤에도 냉전(Cold War)에 들어가 힘겨루기를 하게 된다. 이 전쟁에서 가장 부각된 인물들이 있다면 독일의 아돌프 히틀러(Adolf Hitler)와 소련(러시아)의 이오시프 스탈린(Joseph Stalin)이다. 이 전쟁으로 약 2,500만 명의 군인이 희생되었으며 민간인 희생자도 약 3,000만 명에 달했다. 또한 이 전쟁에서 최초로 핵무기가 도입되었다.

배경 지식 관련 어휘 influence n 영향 | hegemony n 헤게모니, 패권, 주도권 | Cold War 냉전 | casualty n 사상자, 피해자 | civilian n 민간인 | nuclear weapon 핵무기

Test

[1-6] Listen to part of a discussion in a U.S. history class. LT14

1. What is the discussion mainly about?

Ⓐ The influence of Christopher Columbus on the United States

Ⓑ How Washington D.C. became the capital of the United States

Ⓒ The early structure of the U.S. government and its development

Ⓓ What contributed to the outbreak of the Revolutionary War

정답 및 해석 | P. 258

2. **According to the discussion, what was the reason behind the soldiers' rebellion?**

Ⓐ Despite their service during the Revolutionary War, they were not paid.

Ⓑ They wanted the capital to be moved to the southern region of the U.S.

Ⓒ After they were discharged from the army, they had nowhere else to go.

Ⓓ They wanted to sell the munitions and weapons to a foreign country.

3. **Why does the professor mention Article One, Section 8 of the United States Constitution?**

Ⓐ To provide an explanation regarding the treatment of the United States soldiers

Ⓑ To show the students the past process of repaying debt to other countries

Ⓒ To emphasize how the federal government lacked power to protect itself

Ⓓ To point out its importance in every aspect of U.S. society and culture

4. **According to the professor, what is true about the capital? Choose 2 answers.**

Ⓐ The Continental Congress had no official capital.

Ⓑ Finding the location for it was an easy task.

Ⓒ Princeton was the capital for a short period.

Ⓓ People had to vote to select the location of the capital.

5. **What can be inferred about the debt the U.S. had back then?**

Ⓐ Southern states had to pay back the full debt.

Ⓑ Most of it was owed to Great Britain and France.

Ⓒ Domestic creditors did not get their money back.

Ⓓ It eventually influenced the location of the capital.

6. **Listen again to part of the discussion. Then answer the question.**

Why does the professor say this?

Ⓐ To explain how large the capital was compared to those of other countries

Ⓑ To show the students how the name of the capital has changed

Ⓒ To illustrate the history of the District of Columbia as the capital

Ⓓ To ask the students to focus on some other interesting points

Lesson
15 Linguistics

문제 듣기

Syntax 통사론

통사론(Syntax)은 문장의 형식, 즉 문장과 구, 절 등의 구조를 연구하는 언어학의 한 분야이다. 통사론은 단어가 모여 문장을 이루는 방법에 대해 다루는 학문으로, 문장을 이루는 요소들 하나하나가 서로 어떻게 결합하고 영향을 주는지, 이들의 순서와 중요도에 대해서도 연구한다. 따라서 어느 언어에서든 문법 연구에 있어서 빠질 수 없는 역할을 하며, 음운론(phonology)과 함께 현대 언어학에서 중요한 부분을 차지하고 있다.

배경 지식 관련 어휘 phrase n 구 | clause n 절 | structure n 구조 | sentence n 문장 | element n 요소 | combine v 결합하다 | influence v 영향을 주다 | order n 순서 | importance n 중요성 | grammar n 문법 | phonology n 음운학(언어학의 한 분야로 추상적이고 심리적인 말소리인 음운을 대상으로 음운 체계를 밝히고, 그 역사적 변천을 연구하는 학문)

Noam Chomsky 노엄 촘스키

현존하는 가장 위대한 언어학자 중 한 사람으로 여겨지는 노엄 촘스키(Noam Chomsky)는 1928년 미국 필라델피아주에서 태어났다. 그는 언어학자일 뿐 아니라 철학자이고, 정치 활동가로도 활약하고 있다. 그는 언어가 인간이 가진 고유한 특성이라고 주장했으며 우리의 뇌에 언어 습득 장치(Language acquisition device)가 있어 언어를 학습하게 된다고 믿었다. 자신이 세운 연구와 가설에 기반해 다양한 이론과 문법을 주장했고, 계속해서 연구하며 이를 수정하고 있다. 언어학과 관련하여 촘스키의 영향을 받지 않은 학자는 없다고 보아도 무방할 정도이다. 현재 90세가 넘었지만 MIT에 이어 애리조나 대학교에서 계속 교수로 일하고 있다.

배경 지식 관련 어휘 linguist n 언어학자 | philosopher n 철학자 | political activist 정치 활동가 | language acquisition 언어 습득 | hypothesis n 가설 | theory n 이론 | revise v 수정하다

Test

정답 및 해석 | P. 261

[1-6] Listen to part of a discussion in a linguistics class. LT15

Lesson 15
Lectures

1. What is the main topic of the discussion?

Ⓐ Active communication between different animal species

Ⓑ The advantage of tail-flagging and tail heating for squirrels

Ⓒ The effective communication of animals inside a laboratory

Ⓓ The general relationship between predator and prey in nature

2. Listen to part of the discussion and answer the question.

Why does the professor say this:

Ⓐ He believes that the class should go on a field trip someday.

Ⓑ He thinks that the student did not comprehend his question.

Ⓒ He feels sorry for students since their ideas are always so predictable.

Ⓓ He wants an example that was not influenced by human actions.

3. According to the discussion, how do animals of different species communicate with each other?

Ⓐ They display a variety of body language to make one another nervous.

Ⓑ Predators show aggressive behavior toward their prey when they are near.

Ⓒ They use chemical signals to each other at a close distance.

Ⓓ Prey organisms utilize warning coloration to make their predators give up.

4. What role do the pit organs of rattlesnakes play?

Ⓐ They make the snake produce more energy.

Ⓑ They help the snake to sense prey's body heat.

Ⓒ They increase the snake's speed for a moment.

Ⓓ They allow the snake to process its food faster.

5. Why does the professor mention tail-flagging?

Ⓐ To give an example of one of the ways that squirrels communicate

Ⓑ To explain the importance of how squirrels consume their food

Ⓒ To point out another advantage that squirrels have when fighting

Ⓓ To illustrate how it can help squirrels by scaring away their predators

6. What can be inferred about the scientists' experiment with robotic squirrels?

Ⓐ Robotic squirrels failed to confuse snakes since they were made by humans.

Ⓑ Snakes were able to distinguish the robotic squirrels from real ones.

Ⓒ Squirrels' ability to flag their heated tails is quite useful for avoiding snakes.

Ⓓ Tail heating ability scared away the snakes and helped the squirrels survive.

Lesson

16 Literature

문제 듣기

Gertrude Stein 거트루드 스타인

거트루드 스타인(Gertrude Stein)의 문학 작품은 동일어가 계속해서 반복(repetition)되는 실험적이고 추상적(abstract)인 작품이라 평가받는다. 스타인은 피카소같이 추상적인 그림을 그리는 입체파(cubism)의 작품을 선호하였으며 반복을 통해 자신의 문학 작품들이 입체파처럼 보이길 원하였다. 이러한 추상적인 특징으로 인해 그녀의 작품들은 대다수의 비평가들에게 비난을 받았지만 점점 그 독특함을 인정받았고 결국 미국 내 가장 영향력 있는 작가 중 한 명으로 자리매김했다.

배경 지식 관련 어휘 literary adj 문학의 | repetition n (말·행동의) 반복, 되풀이 | experimental adj 실험적인 | cubism n 입체파(20세기 초기에 프랑스에서 일어난 회화운동을 지칭하며 대상을 원뿔, 원통, 구 따위의 기하학적 형태로 분해하고 주관에 따라 재구성하여 입체적으로 여러 방향에서 본 상태를 평면적으로 한 화면에 구성하여 표현함) | critic n 비평가, 평론가 | prominent adj 중요한, 유명한

Lesson 16 Lectures

William Wordsworth 윌리엄 워즈워스

윌리엄 워즈워스(William Wordsworth)는 영국 낭만주의(Romanticism)의 대표적인 시인으로, 이성과 논리 및 형식을 중시하던 신고전주의(Neo-classicism)에서 벗어나 감정(emotion)과 자연에 대한 동경을 추구하는 새로운 문학 사조를 창시하였다. 워즈워스의 작품 중 <서정 민요집(Lyrical Ballads)>은 일상 생활 및 자연을 평이하고 일상적인 언어로 표현하여 당대의 비판을 샀으나, 후에 발표한 <서곡(The Prelude)>은 좋은 평가를 받으며 그의 대표작이 되었다.

배경 지식 관련 어휘 romanticism n 낭만주의(신고전주의와 대립되는 사상으로 창작자 자신의 감정을 드러내고 정신적 자세나 지적 동향 그리고 자유로운 공상 세계를 동경하는 사조) | verse n 운문 | reason n 이성, 사고력 | longing n 갈망, 열망, 동경 | lyrical adj 서정적인

Test

[1-6] Listen to part of a discussion in an English literature class. LT16

1. What is the main topic of the discussion?

Ⓐ The life of a prominent author and what her works show

Ⓑ The successful career of an author and her legacy

Ⓒ The typical family life of the 19th century England

Ⓓ The notion of women and marriage during the 19th century

2. **According to the discussion, what is true about Jane Austen? Choose 2 answers.**

Ⓐ She usually wrote novels with fantasy and mythical themes.

Ⓑ She achieved international success when her second novel was published.

Ⓒ She did not publish her first novel under her real name.

Ⓓ She was not able to make a fortune with her novels.

3. **What are the characteristics of Jane Austen's novels? Choose 2 answers.**

Ⓐ Overcoming physical and psychological hardships

Ⓑ Reflecting the author's own life through the protagonists' lives

Ⓒ Criticizing political and cultural issues using sarcasm

Ⓓ Representing the author's views on society

4. **Why does the professor mention Elizabeth, the protagonist of *Pride and Prejudice*?**

Ⓐ To further explain the psychological development in the novel

Ⓑ To show some similarities between Elizabeth and Jane Austen

Ⓒ To describe how Jane Austen portrayed a typical English woman

Ⓓ To point out that Elizabeth's character was based on Austen's sister

5. **Listen again to part of the discussion. Then answer the question.**
Why does the student say this:

Ⓐ Jane Austen actually thought that marriage is not a necessary thing.

Ⓑ *Pride and Prejudice* was able to point out the irony of marriage.

Ⓒ The story of *Pride and Prejudice* is the opposite of the quote.

Ⓓ In *Pride and Prejudice*, most of the male characters do not get married.

6. **What can be inferred about *Pride and Prejudice*?**

Ⓐ It emphasizes the importance of marriage as a financial benefit.

Ⓑ It tried to describe young women who are in financial trouble.

Ⓒ It shows that marrying someone of higher rank was almost impossible.

Ⓓ It displays the rise of the middle class and minor aristocracy.

Lesson
17 Music

문제 듣기

Synthesizer and its sound 신디사이저와 그 소리

신디사이저(Synthesizer)는 작곡가와 음악가들이 음파(sound wave)를 조작함으로써 소리의 형태를 변형할 수 있게 해주는 기계이다. 또한 한 음이 발생해서 사라질 때까지 그 파형의 끝을 연결하여 그래프로 나타낸 사운드 엔빌로프(sound envelope)를 가능하게 해주어 소리의 형태를 시각적으로 보여준다. 사운드 엔빌로프는 ADSR(Attack, Decay, Sustain, and Release)의 4단계로 구성되며 이는 소리의 세기(intensity)에 따라 나눠진다.

배경 지식 관련 어휘 synthesizer n (음향) 합성기 | manipulate v 조작하다, 처리하다 | sound wave 음파 | visual adj 시각의, 눈으로 보는 | decay v 쇠퇴하다, 퇴락하다 | sustain v 지속시키다, 지탱하다 | release v 발산하다, 방출하다 | intensity n 세기, 강도

Rap 랩

랩(Rap)은 원시 시대의 전승 시인인 그리오(griot)에서부터 유래되었다는 설이 있지만 현대 랩의 시작은 자메이카의 토스팅(toasting)으로 볼 수 있다. 자메이카의 파티나 클럽에서 DJ들은 음반을 틀어놓고 그 음악 위에 잡담(toasting)을 얹어가며 청중들과 호흡을 맞춤으로써 파티 분위기를 고조시켰다. 또한 DJ들은 음반을 틀 때 곡 중에서 리듬과 비트가 강한 부분을 집중적으로 틀었으며 그 위에 갖가지 구호나 은어를 외침으로써 최초의 랩을 선보였다. 이는 처음에 음악 사이의 휴식 시간(break)에만 적용되다가 인기가 많아짐에 따라 그 분량도 점차 길어졌다. 또한, DJ들은 두 개의 턴테이블에 같은 음반을 한 장씩 올려놓고 오디오 믹서를 사용하여 두 개의 음반 사이를 왔다 갔다 하며 원하는 부분만을 계속 이어냄으로써 랩에 맞는 비트를 만들게 되었다. 자메이카의 DJ들이 미국에서 명성을 떨치게 되자 턴테이블을 돌리는 사람과 따로 랩을 담당할 MC들이 영입되었고 이로 인해 전문 랩퍼(rapper)들이 탄생하게 되었다.

배경 지식 관련 어휘 griot n 그리오(서아프리카 지역 등에서 과거에 구전 설화를 이야기나 노래로 들려주던 사람) | forerunner n 선구자 | toast n 흑인 문화에서 구전으로 공유되는 즉흥시 형식 | turntable n (음반을 돌리는) 턴테이블(회전반)

Test

정답 및 해석 | P. 268

[1-6] Listen to part of a discussion in a music history class.  LT17

Lesson 17
Lectures

1. What is the discussion mainly about?

Ⓐ A music composer who had a lasting impact on jazz

Ⓑ The important characteristics of a certain genre of music

Ⓒ Three events that led to the revival of ragtime

Ⓓ Famous musicians who experimented with various genres

2. According to the discussion, what is true about ragtime? Choose 2 answers.

Ⓐ John Philip Sousa is credited as the first innovator of ragtime.

Ⓑ It included some features of marching music and classical music.

Ⓒ The name came from its unexpected and irregular rhythm.

Ⓓ It first appeared in New York City and gained popularity there.

3. Why does the professor mention Scott Joplin?

Ⓐ To introduce a fundamental figure of ragtime music

Ⓑ To show his influence on classical musicians

Ⓒ To emphasize his achievements in marching music

Ⓓ To bring up another topic regarding the history of jazz

4. What is the relationship between ragtime and jazz?

Ⓐ Jazz actually preceded ragtime music.

Ⓑ They both evolved around the same time.

Ⓒ Ragtime music heavily influenced jazz.

Ⓓ They had a huge impact on marching music.

5. Listen again to part of the discussion. Then answer the question.

Why does the professor say this:

Ⓐ To ask the students to do some more research

Ⓑ To show that he is not sure why ragtime originated in nightclubs

Ⓒ To explain the concept of ragtime during the 1970s

Ⓓ To emphasize that the music was intended to make people dance

6. What can be inferred about Scott Joplin?

Ⓐ He worked with Joshua Rifkin and received a Grammy Award.

Ⓑ He became famous for his opera, rather than ragtime music.

Ⓒ He brought about the revival of ragtime during the 1970s.

Ⓓ He helped ragtime to gain widespread appeal with the public.

Lesson

18 Paleontology

문제 듣기

Fossil 화석

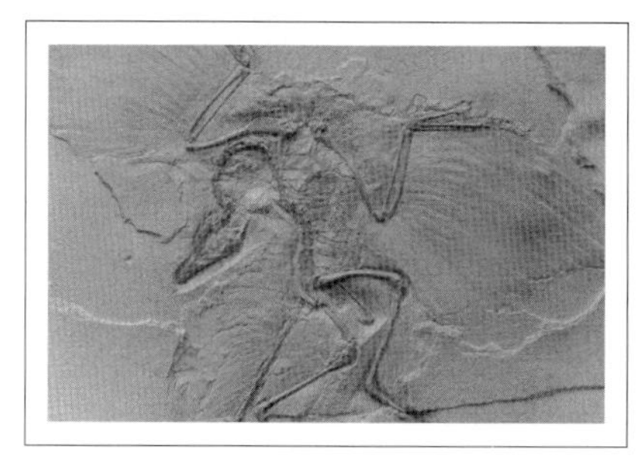

화석(fossil)은 고생물학에 없어서는 안 될 존재이다. 화석은 생물의 신체 부위나 발자국 등의 흔적이 퇴적물(sediment)에 그대로 남은 채 보존되어 돌이 된 것이며, 가끔 엄청나게 보존 상태가 좋은 화석이 발굴되기도 한다. 화석으로 흔히 남는 부분은 뼈나 껍질 등의 단단한 조직이지만 그런 부위라 해도 이렇게 화석이 되는 경우는 극히 드물다. 화석은 지구에 인류를 제외한 어떤 생명체가 존재했으며 어떤 삶을 살았고, 어떻게 진화했는지 보여주는 증거이기도 하다.

배경 지식 관련 어휘 body part 신체 부위 | footprint n 발자국 | sediment n 퇴적물 | preserve v 보존하다 | bone n 뼈 | skin n 껍질 | rare adj 드문 | organism n 생물, 생명체 | evolve v 진화하다

Missing link 잃어버린 고리, 중간 화석

잃어버린 고리(missing link)는 생물의 진화(evolution) 과정을 보여주는 것으로 추정되는 생물이지만 화석으로 발견되지 않은 존재를 가리키며, 그래서 둘의 사이를 이어주는 잃어버린 고리라고 불린다. 진화 단계의 중간에 해당하는 것으로 추정되지만 발견되지 않아서 많은 고생물학자들을 혼란스럽게 만들기도 하는데, 진화론(evolution theory)을 믿지 않는 창조론(creationism) 지지자들은 이 잃어버린 고리를 예로 들며 진화론을 비판하기도 한다. 다른 한편으로는 진화라는 것은 일직선으로 이어지는 과정이 아니라 한 줄기에서 여러 갈래로 가지를 쳐 나가는 과정에 가깝기 때문에, 어떤 두 생물의 사이를 잇는 중간 생물이 존재한다고 가정하는 것이 과연 옳은가 하는 주장도 있다.

배경 지식 관련 어휘 organism n 생물 | evolution n 진화 | suppose v 추정하다 | fossil n 화석 | discover v 발견하다 | confuse v 혼란스럽게 하다 | evolution theory 진화론 | creationism n 창조론 | criticize v 비판하다 | distinction n 구분 | vague adj 모호한 | connect v 연결하다, 잇다

Lesson 18 Lectures

Test

[1-6] Listen to part of a lecture in a paleontology class.  LT18

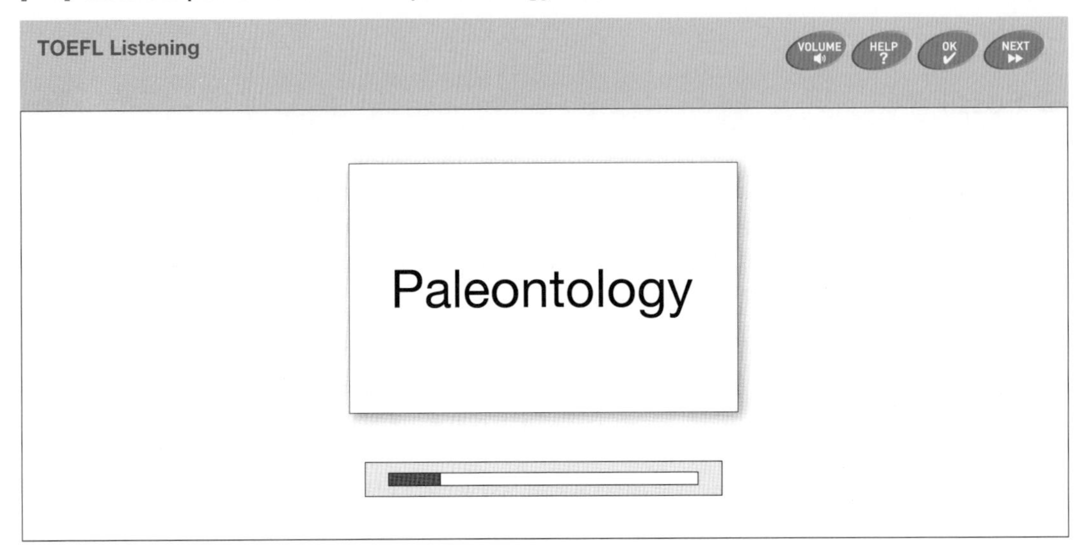

1. What is the main topic of the lecture?

Ⓐ How fish evolved to become land organisms

Ⓑ The characteristics of a possible missing link organism

Ⓒ Common species from the Devonian period

Ⓓ The process by which gills developed into lungs

정답 및 해석 | P. 272

2. What are the characteristics of Tiktaalik that fish lack? Choose 2 answers.

Ⓐ It could move its head separately from its body.

Ⓑ It had bony plates located on the sides of its neck.

Ⓒ It breathed air into its lungs.

Ⓓ Its body was covered with scales.

3. How were Tiktaalik's front limbs different from modern tetrapods?

Ⓐ They had mobile wrist joints.

Ⓑ They had attachment points for large muscles.

Ⓒ They had large shoulder blades.

Ⓓ They had fins at the ends of them.

4. According to the professor, why would Tiktaalik leave the water?

Ⓐ To avoid infectious bacteria

Ⓑ To be able to get more oxygen

Ⓒ To have access to a food source

Ⓓ To escape from predators

5. Why does the professor mention a whale?

Ⓐ To name an animal that made a similar transition

Ⓑ To emphasize that many aquatic species breathe air

Ⓒ To suggest what an organism may have evolved into

Ⓓ To provide an example of a similar body structure

6. What can be inferred about missing links?

Ⓐ People often assume that animals with similar traits must share the same ancestor.

Ⓑ Transitional organisms are now easy to find due to the completeness of the fossil record.

Ⓒ Many fossils of missing links were discovered during the 19th century.

Ⓓ Missing link organisms always show the transitions between different habitats.

Lesson

19 Photography

문제 듣기

Henri Cartier-Bresson 앙리 카르티에-브레송

1908년 프랑스에서 태어나 2004년 사망한 앙리 카르티에-브레송(Henri Cartier-Bresson)은 20세기 사진계의 대가라 일컬어지던 사진작가이다. '찰나'를 강조하는 그의 사진은 세계 여러 곳에서 전시회를 통해 대중에게 잘 알려져 있다. 사진작가들의 권리를 지키기 위해 1947년 자유 보도사진작가 그룹인 매그넘 포토스(Magnum Photos)를 설립하였으며, 유럽과 미국의 세계적인 사진작가들이 이 단체에 속해 있다. 브레송 없이는 현대 포토저널리즘(photojournalism)을 논할 수 없다는 말이 있을 정도로 큰 영향을 끼쳤으며, 사람들의 일상에 주목하는 사진과 찰나를 포착하는 캔디드 포토(candid photo)로 유명하며 라이카(Leica) 카메라로 잘 알려져 있다.

배경 지식 관련 어휘 moment n 찰나 | emphasize v 강조하다 | exhibition n 전시회 | public n 대중 | right n 권리 | establish v 설립하다 | organization n 단체, 조직 | photojournalism n 포토저널리즘(사진에 중점을 둔 보도 및 출판물을 통칭하는 말) | influence n 영향 | capture v 포착하다

Camera obscura 카메라 옵스큐라, 암상자

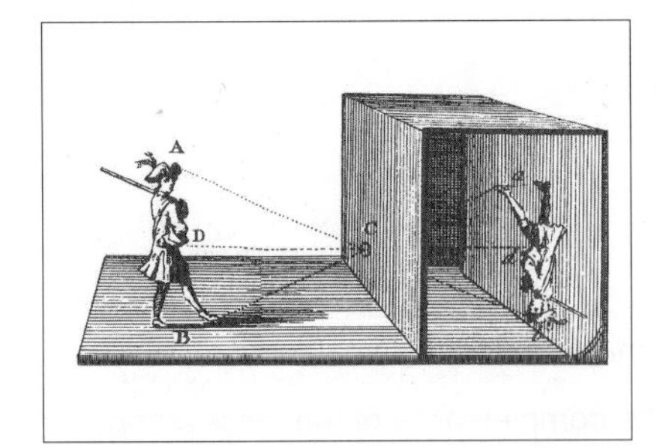

사진에 관해 잘 모르는 사람들도 '카메라 옵스큐라(camera obscura)'라는 단어는 들어봤을 만큼 유명한 용어인데, 오늘날의 카메라가 바로 이 카메라 옵스큐라에 기반하여 만들어졌기 때문이다. 다른 말로 하면 현대 카메라의 시초라고 할 수 있다. 라틴어로 카메라 옵스쿠라는 '어두운 방'을 의미하며, 그 이름 그대로 내부를 어둡게 한 상자 또는 방에 구멍을 뚫은 뒤, 밖에서 어두운 쪽으로 투과되는 빛으로 상을 맺히게 했다. 따라서 상이 굴절되어(refracted) 보인다. 일찍부터 고대 그리스인들은 이미 카메라 옵스큐라의 원리를 알고 있었다고 하며, 화가들은 이 장치를 이용해 그림을 그리는 데 도움을 받기도 했다.

배경 지식 관련 어휘 based on ~에 기반한 | produce v 제작하다, 생산하다 | beginning n 시초 | darken v 어둡게 하다 | hole n 구멍 | penetrate v 투과하다 | image n 상 | refracted adj 굴절된 | fundamental n 원리, 핵심 | device n 장치

Test

정답 및 해석 | P. 275

[1-6] Listen to part of a lecture in a photography class.

LT19

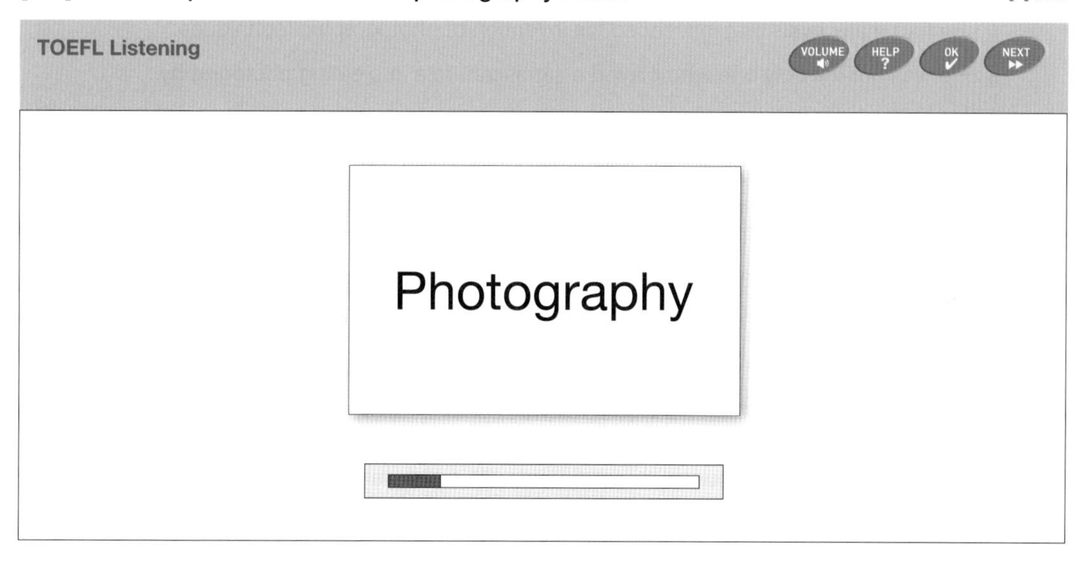

1. What is the lecture mainly about?

Ⓐ The inventors that led the development of photography

Ⓑ The creation of the first diorama and camera obscura

Ⓒ The difference between daguerreotypes and calotypes

Ⓓ The influence that Niépce had on Daguerre

2. What does the professor say about Louis Daguerre?

Ⓐ He had many rivals that influenced his invention of photographic techniques.

Ⓑ He was not the only one who played a significant role in creating photography.

Ⓒ He spent more than 10 years on developing his daguerreotype process.

Ⓓ He did not receive credit for the invention of the diorama while he was alive.

3. What can be inferred about Nicéphore Niépce?

Ⓐ He had a hard time importing bitumen from Judea.

Ⓑ He had conflicts with Daguerre, which caused their separation.

Ⓒ He was able to invent the camera obscura after a few years of research.

Ⓓ He ended up not finishing his experiment with silver salts.

4. The professor explains Daguerre's experiment with silver salts for creating images. Put the steps below in order.

Ⓐ Expose copper to iodine vapor.

Ⓑ Cover copper sheet with silver.

Ⓒ Expose silver iodide in the camera.

Ⓓ Silver iodide is produced.

Step 1	
Step 2	
Step 3	
Step 4	

5. According to the lecture, which of the following is true about William Henry Fox Talbot?

Ⓐ He sold his invention to a French company.

Ⓑ He mostly experimented with negative images.

Ⓒ He was also a colleague of Daguerre, studying silver salt.

Ⓓ He did not know about the work of Daguerre.

6. Listen again to part of the lecture. Then answer the question. 🎧

Why does the professor say this: 🎧

Ⓐ She is trying to convince her students to do more research about photographers.

Ⓑ She forgot to mention other photographers who had influenced Louis Daguerre.

Ⓒ She wants to say that other people also contributed to the development of photography.

Ⓓ She is emphasizing the importance of photography and its history to her students.

Lesson

20 Physics

문제 듣기

Isaac Newton 아이작 뉴턴

뉴턴(Newton)은 1642년 영국에서 태어나 1727년 사망했으며 기사 작위를 받은 최초의 과학자이다. 그만큼 과학계는 물론 인류 자체에 엄청난 영향을 미친 인물로 평가 받고 있다. 직업도 다수여서 물리학자였을 뿐 아니라 수학자, 천문학자, 철학자, 신학자는 물론 연금술 연구까지 했다. 고전 물리학(classical physics)을 정립했고, 반사 망원경을 제작했으며 미분법(differentiation)을 발명하는 등 오늘날 우리가 자연스럽게 알고 있는 다수의 지식을 정립한 인물이라고 해도 좋을 것이다. 과학자로 유명하지만 사실 신학 연구를 더 많이 했다고 한다.

배경 지식 관련 어휘 knight n 기사 | physicist n 물리학자 | mathematician n 수학자 | astronomer n 천문학자 | philosopher n 철학자 | theologian n 신학자 | alchemy n 연금술 | classical physics 고전 물리학 | establish v 정립하다 | reflecting telescope 반사 망원경 | differentiation n 미분법 | invent v 발명하다 | knowledge n 지식 | theology n 신학

Lesson 20 Lectures

Albert Einstein 알버트 아인슈타인

아인슈타인(Einstein)은 1879년 독일에서 태어났으나 1955년 미국에서 사망했다. 천재 하면 사람들이 으레 아인슈타인을 떠올릴 정도로 위대한 과학자였으며, 특히 현대 물리학 발전에 지대한 영향을 끼쳤다. 어렸을 때부터 천재성을 발휘하였으며 열두 살의 나이에 이미 자신만의 방식으로 피타고라스의 정리(Pythagorean Theorem)를 이해했고 몇 년 뒤에는 자기장(magnetic field)에 관련된 논문을 발표하기도 했다. 유대인을 탄압하는 나치당 때문에 1933년 미국으로 망명하여 그 뒤로는 계속 미국에서 살며 프린스턴 대학의 교수로 일했고 수많은 업적을 남겼다. 가장 잘 알려진 업적이자 이론으로는 상대성 이론(theory of relativity)과 중력파(gravitational wave)에 대한 예측이 있으며 노벨 물리학상을 수상했다.

배경 지식 관련 어휘 genius n 천재, 천재성 | scientist n 과학자 | influence v 영향을 끼치다 | Pythagorean Theorem 피타고라스의 정리(직각삼각형의 빗변을 한 변으로 하는 정사각형의 넓이는 나머지 두 변을 각각 한 변으로 하는 정사각형 두 개의 넓이의 합과 같다는 정리) | magnetic field 자기장 | thesis n 논문 | Jew n 유대인 | the Nazis 나치당 | achievement n 업적 | theory n 이론

Test

[1-6] Listen to part of a discussion in a physics class.

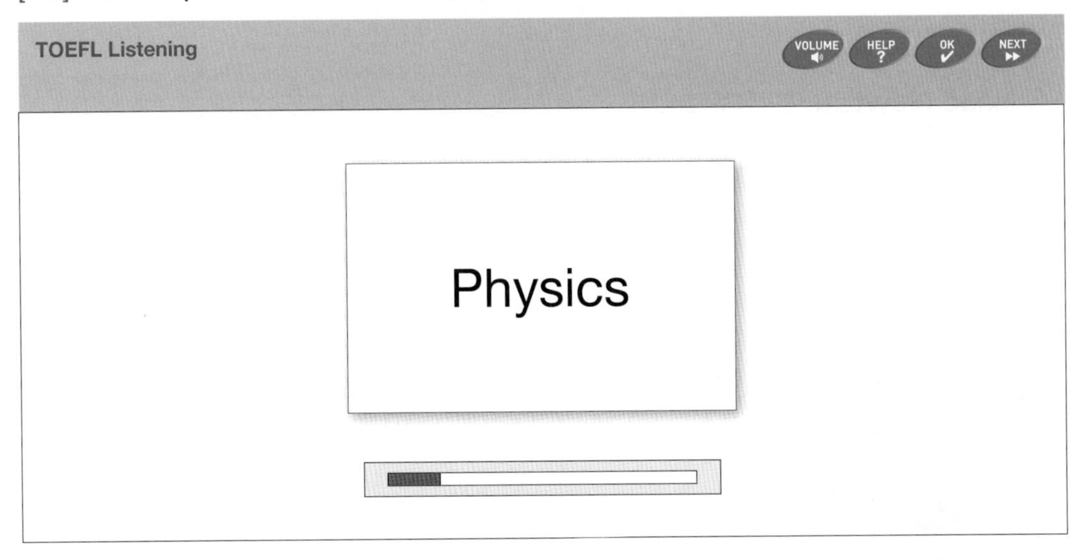

1. What is the discussion mainly about?

Ⓐ The advantages and disadvantages of fission and fusion reactors

Ⓑ The creation of fission reactors and their effect on the environment

Ⓒ The harmful and lasting impact of radioactive waste

Ⓓ The development of fusion reactors over the last 50 years

정답 및 해석 | P. 279

2. **What is true about nuclear reactions?**

Ⓐ Fission emits substances that can be dangerous to humans.

Ⓑ Fission occurs every day while fusion occurs rarely in nature.

Ⓒ Fission can generate electricity while fusion cannot.

Ⓓ Fusion needs to be observed since it is very unstable.

3. **Listen again to part of the discussion. Then answer the question.**

Why does the professor say this:

Ⓐ He doubts if these fission reactors will be able to survive a meltdown in the future.

Ⓑ He is convincing the audience that depending on nuclear energy is important.

Ⓒ He feels the need to educate people on the dangers of depending on nuclear energy.

Ⓓ He wants to point out that many countries already depend on fission energy.

4. **Why does the professor mention Chernobyl and Fukushima?**

Ⓐ To emphasize the importance of protecting the environment

Ⓑ To contrast them in terms of fission reaction and its process

Ⓒ To give some examples of the instability of fission reactors

Ⓓ To illustrate his point about the danger of building reactors

5. **According to the discussion, what is true about a fusion reactor?**

Ⓐ It does not generate radioactive nuclei after the collision.

Ⓑ It produces a smaller amount of energy than a fission one.

Ⓒ It does not require a large amount of fuel for operating.

Ⓓ It is more difficult to control than a fission reactor.

6. **Why is it difficult to operate fusion reactors at present?**

Ⓐ Dangerous reactions used for making a hydrogen bomb could occur.

Ⓑ Materials used for fusion reactions are hard to obtain on Earth.

Ⓒ The amount of energy in the input and output are equal to each other.

Ⓓ Technologies such as laser arrays for fusing atoms need to be improved.

Lesson

21 Physiology

문제 듣기

Physiology 생리학

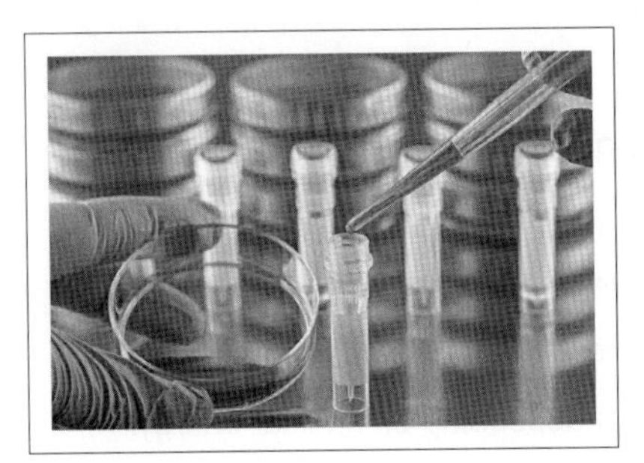

생리학(Physiology)은 생물학(Biology)과 혼동될 때도 있으며 겹치는 부분이 실제로 있는 학문이다. 생물의 구조, 기능, 원인을 연구하는 학문으로 여겨지며 세포 생리학(cytophysiology), 미생물 생리학(microbial physiology), 인체 생리학(human physiology), 식물·동물 생리학 등 매우 다양한 하위 분야가 있다. 생물의 구조와 기능을 연구하다 보니 의학과도 많은 부분에서 겹치며, 오늘날에도 의학의 한 분야로 취급되고 있다. 현대적인 학문처럼 보이지만 사실 고대 그리스 시대부터 연구가 진행되었다고 한다.

배경 지식 관련 어휘 biology n 생물학 | confuse v 혼동하다, 혼동시키다 | overlap v 겹치다 | discipline n 학문 분야 | structure n 구조 | function n 기능 | cause n 원인 | subfield n 하위 분야 | plant physiology 식물 생리학 | animal physiology 동물 생리학 | medical science 의학 | modern adj 현대적인 | ancient adj 고대의

Neuroscience 신경 과학

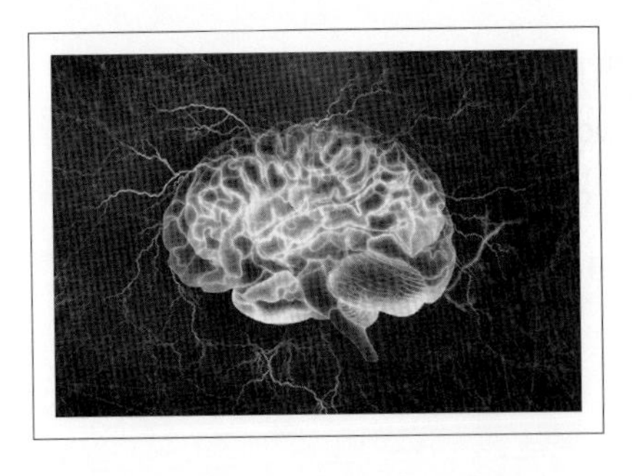

생리학(Physiology)과 생물학(Biology)의 하위 학문으로 신경(계)에 관해 연구하는 학문이며, 보통 인간을 포함한 동물을 주로 연구하지만 인공 신경망(artificial neural network)이나 컴퓨터 과학 또한 다루기도 한다. 신경을 연구하기 때문에 뇌와 떼려야 뗄 수 없는 관계를 가지며 우리나라에서는 뇌 과학(brain science)이라고 부르기도 하지만 정확히 말하면 신경 과학이 뇌 과학을 포함한다. 현대에는 신경 경제학(neuroeconomics), 사회 신경 과학(social neuroscience), 신경 사회학(neurosociology), 신경 윤리학(neuroethics), 신경 미학(neuroaesthetics) 등 다양한 분야와 합쳐져 연구되는 모습도 보인다.

배경 지식 관련 어휘 physiology n 생리학 | biology n 생물학 | subdiscipline 하위 학문 분야 | nervous system 신경계 | artificial neural network 인공 신경망 | computer science 컴퓨터 과학 | brain n 뇌 | relationship n 관계

Test

정답 및 해석 | P. 282

[1-6] Listen to part of a lecture in a physiology class.  LT21

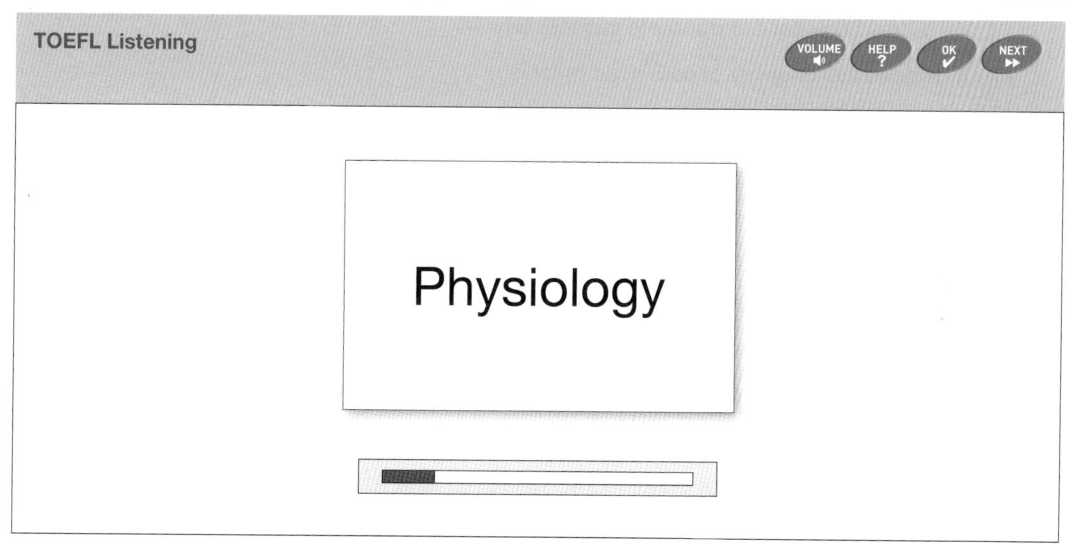

1. What is the lecture mainly about?

Ⓐ Reasons behind the aging of cells and related research

Ⓑ Observing imperfect cells and their effect on the human body

Ⓒ Discoveries regarding free radical theory and their legacy

Ⓓ Different theories about cell aging and how to prevent it

2. According to the professor, what are the roles of the internal clock? **Choose 2 answers.**

Ⓐ It enables body cells to duplicate successfully.

Ⓑ It decides the longevity of cells in an organism.

Ⓒ It can regulate the amount of cell reproduction.

Ⓓ It determines the limitation of imperfect cells.

3. What are the characteristics of oxygen? **Choose 3 answers.**

Ⓐ Most oxygen molecules have the potential of becoming free radicals.

Ⓑ Oxygen molecules that bring negative effects are called free radicals.

Ⓒ It breaks down some chemical compounds through combustion.

Ⓓ Oxygen becomes free radicals when an organism is under too much stress.

Ⓔ Some free radicals do not bring harmful results to organisms.

Ⓕ Inflammation and injuries are the main causes of harmful oxygen molecules.

4. Why does the professor mention the domino effect?

Ⓐ To give an example of the effects free radicals could bring

Ⓑ To illustrate how free radicals destroy DNA and cells

Ⓒ To emphasize the importance of oxygen for organisms

Ⓓ To explain the chemical processes that create free radicals

5. What is true about superoxide dismutases(SODs)?

Ⓐ Experiments show that they could possibly cause damage to DNA.

Ⓑ They are the result of the free radical chemical chain reaction.

Ⓒ They are a type of antioxidant that fights against oxygen molecules.

Ⓓ Some researchers believe that they contribute to healthier cells.

6. What can be inferred about the free radical theory?

Ⓐ It is actually the reason behind prolonged cell life in organisms.

Ⓑ It reminded scientists of the role of antioxidants in the human body.

Ⓒ It cannot yet prove that free radicals are one of the causes of cell aging.

Ⓓ It approaches the cell aging process in a very indirect way.

Lesson

22 Psychology

문제 듣기

Brain anatomy and behavior 뇌의 해부와 행동

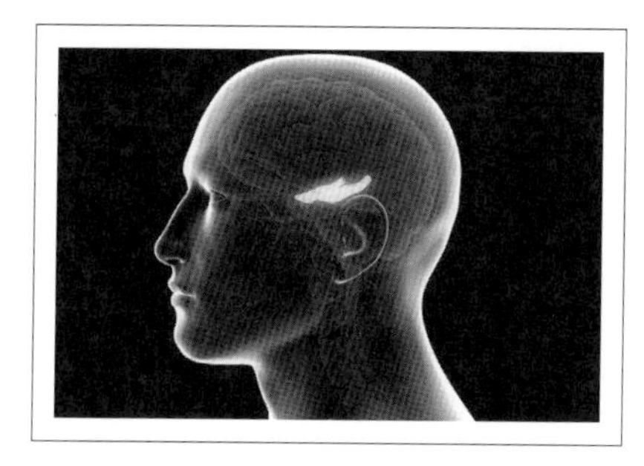

기억 형성(memory formation)을 담당하는 뇌의 주요 기관인 해마(hippocampus)는 동물과 사람의 공간 기억(spatial memory)에 중대한 영향을 끼치는데, 특히 최근 까마귀와 개를 대상으로 한 실험을 통해 해마의 크기가 동물의 공간 기억에 영향을 준다는 사실이 밝혀졌다. 또한 일반인보다 공간 기억을 많이 해야 하는 택시 기사들의 해마 크기가 일반인에 비해 더 큰 것으로 밝혀짐에 따라 해마의 크기와 공간 기억 능력 간의 상관관계는 인간에게도 적용된다는 사실이 입증되었다.

배경 지식 관련 어휘 memory formation 기억 형성 | hippocampus n (대뇌 측두엽의) 해마 | spatial adj 공간적인 | correlate v 연관성이 있다, 상관관계가 있다 | prove v 입증하다, 증명하다

Variables in decision making 의사 결정 속의 변수

사람들이 하는 두 가지 결정에는 단순한 결정과 복잡한 결정이 있고 이는 고려되어야 할 변수들(variables)의 차이에 따라 구분되는데, 단순한 결정에는 의식적 생각(conscious mind)이 도움을 주지만, 복잡한 결정에는 무의식적 생각(unconscious mind)이 더 도움을 준다는 사실이 밝혀졌다. 연구에 따르면, 의식적인 생각을 한 참가자들은 단순한 결정에서는 더 나은 선택을 했지만 복잡한 결정에서는 어려움을 겪었다. 이와는 달리 놀랍게도 복잡한 결정에 있어서는 무의식적으로 생각을 한 사람들이 가장 나은 선택을 더 자주 이끌어냈다. 왜냐하면 무의식적인 사고는 겉으로 드러나지는 않지만 수많은 변수와 가능성을 동시에 재빨리 따져보는 작업을 수행할 수 있기 때문이다. 반면 의식적인 사고는 그 중 극히 일부 변수의 경우만을 판단해볼 수 있을 뿐이다. 따라서 변수가 많은 복잡한 결정일수록 판단을 무의식에 맡겨야 한다는 주장이 제기된다.

배경 지식 관련 어휘 variable n 변수 | conscious adj 의식적인, 의도적인 | probability n 확률, 개연성

Test

[1-6] Listen to part of a discussion in a psychology class. LT22

1. What is the discussion mainly about?

   (A) Ways to analyze fMRI data with questionnaires

   (B) Observing emotion through brain activity using fMRI

   (C) Differences between fMRI and a basic MRI scanning

   (D) Interpreting neuron signals to control emotion

정답 및 해석 I P. 286

2. **What is the difference between the fMRI and MRI?**

Ⓐ The fMRI enables people to control neuron activity.

Ⓑ MRI scanning uses a powerful magnetic field for imaging.

Ⓒ The fMRI detects changes in the oxygen supply inside the brain.

Ⓓ MRI does not show the full internal structure of the human body.

3. **What can be inferred about neurons?**

Ⓐ They depend upon more oxygen as their activity increases.

Ⓑ They show a decrease in their use of hydrogen over time.

Ⓒ Their activity can be observed through black and white images.

Ⓓ Their behavior changed when the fMRI experiment began.

4. **What is true about the experiments conducted using fMRI?**

Ⓐ Participant groups consisted of people varying in age from their 20s to 50s.

Ⓑ Researchers could observe areas with increased and decreased activity.

Ⓒ Participants were asked to describe different images displayed in front of them.

Ⓓ Scientists were able to distinguish participants' emotions with various colors.

5. **What is the professor's opinion toward questionnaires?**

Ⓐ He thinks they will not be used when fMRIs are more developed.

Ⓑ He believes students will be able to realize their importance someday.

Ⓒ He knows that they are helpful even though they seem old-fashioned.

Ⓓ He doubts if they are necessary in a long-term perspective.

6. **What can be inferred about using questionnaires after the experiment?**

Ⓐ Some participants try to manipulate the test result during questionnaires.

Ⓑ The longer the questionnaires are, the better the results of the experiment.

Ⓒ Using questionnaires eventually provides less information about the participant.

Ⓓ It is necessary to prevent any alteration of the results from occurring.

Lesson

23 Sociology

문제 듣기

Newspaper – USA Today 미국 신문 〈USA Today〉

미국의 종합 일간지 중 유일하게 전국에 발간되는 <USA Today>의 성공은 기존 신문과는 다른 차별성을 보였다는 점에서 기인한다. <USA Today>가 창간되었을 당시인 1980년대에는 사회 전반적으로 신문에 대한 흥미가 저조했다. 이에 변화를 추구한 <USA Today>는 독자의 관심을 끌기 위해 긴 기사 대신 짧은 기사로 대체하고, 컬러 사진(color photos)과 도표(graphics), 스포츠 경기 결과(sports scores), 연예가 소식(entertainment stories) 등을 추가함으로써 젊은 독자층을 끌어들였다. 하지만 초기에는 대중들로부터 짧은 기사에 대해 단순하다고 비웃음을 샀고, 어느 지역에서나 볼 수 있는 전국적인 신문 즉, 소위 'McPaper'라 불리며 비난받았다. 그러나 <USA Today>는 인공위성(satellite)까지 사용하며 최신 기사(latest news)를 속보로 전달함으로써 독자에게 호응을 얻기 시작하였고 그 결과 지금의 인기를 누리게 되었다.

배경 지식 관련 어휘 daily newspaper 일간지 | distribute v 유통시키다, 분포시키다 | publication n 출판, 발행 | dumb down 지나치게 단순화하다

History of road paving 도로 포장의 역사

19세기 최초로 포장된 도로는 일명 '머캐덤 도로(Macadam road)'라 불렸으며 이는 배수 시설을 용이하게 하기 위해 작은 모난 자갈(angular gravel)로 건설된 도로였으나 먼지가 잘 날리는 심각한 문제점을 지니고 있었다. 이 단점을 보완하기 위해 머캐덤 도로에 콜타르(tar)와 모래(sand)가 합쳐진 도로가 개발되었으며, 얼마 후, 콜타르에 광석에서 금속을 빼고 남은 찌꺼기(slag)를 더한 타맥(tarmac; tar-penetration macadam) 포장재가 탄생해 기존보다 더욱 안전한 도로 포장재로 인기를 끌었다. 이후 미국에서 석유 찌꺼기인 아스팔트(asphalt)로 포장한 도로가 등장해 타맥보다 인기를 얻게 되면서 이것이 현재 포장 도로의 전형이 되었다.

배경 지식 관련 어휘 paving n 포장된 표면, 포장재 | angular adj 각이 진, 모난 | tar n (석탄을 건류할 때 생기는) 콜타르, 타르 | slag n 광재, 용재 | asphalt n 아스팔트

Test

정답 및 해석 | P. 289

[1-6] Listen to part of a lecture in a sociology class.

Lesson 23 Lectures

1. What is the lecture mainly about?

Ⓐ The characteristics of utilitarianism and opposing perspectives

Ⓑ Different concepts of famous philosophers including Mill and Sartre

Ⓒ The influence of utilitarianism in the 21st century in Europe

Ⓓ The concept of utilitarianism and philosophers' views about it

2. **What is true about the consequentialist theory?**

(A) It was misused by criminals who wanted to justify their actions.

(B) It states that the process has the biggest influence on the result.

(C) It views a positive outcome as the most important thing.

(D) It is one of the many branches of the utilitarianist theory.

3. **Why does the professor mention Jeremy Bentham?**

(A) To explain how his early view on utilitarianism influenced others

(B) To express the chief concept of utilitarianism in a precise way

(C) To point out the philosopher who had the greatest influence on utilitarianism

(D) To illustrate the ideas regarding utilitarianism during the 1940s

4. **According to the lecture, why were there conflicts among philosophers regarding utilitarianism? Choose 2 answers.**

(A) The definition of utility can easily vary from person to person.

(B) Pleasure always depends on the balance of both quality and quantity.

(C) Pleasure is not something that can be described by only quantity.

(D) People have different views regarding what is good and profitable.

5. **What can be inferred about the professor's example of people obtaining resources and goods?**

(A) People can limit their desires for the advantages of a larger group.

(B) People will learn how to take advantage of others over time.

(C) People sometimes choose to leave a group rather than compromise.

(D) People will always try to satisfy themselves by taking as many goods as possible.

6. **In the lecture, what does Jean-Paul Sartre's moral dilemma example signify?**

(A) All actions and decisions people face have positive and negative sides.

(B) Providing maximum happiness to the largest number of people should be prioritized.

(C) In wars, people always experience dilemmas due to life and death situations.

(D) People often encounter a conflict between the duties to society and family.

PAGODA TOEFL 80+ Listening

Actual Test

Actual Test 1

Actual Test 2

Actual Test 3

Actual Test 1

문제 듣기

TOEFL Listening

Now put on your headset.

Click on **Continue** to go on.

TOEFL Listening

Changing the Volume

To change the volume, click on the Volume icon at the top of the screen. The volume control will appear. Move the volume indicator to the left or to the right to change the volume.

To close the volume control, move the mouse pointer to another part of the screen.

You may now change the volume.
When you are finished, click on **Continue**.

정답 및 해석 | P. 293

TOEFL Listening

Listening Section Directions

This section measures your ability to understand conversations and lectures in English. You should listen to each conversation and lecture only once.

After each conversation or lecture, you will answer some questions about it. The questions typically ask about the main idea and supporting details. Some questions ask about the purpose of a speaker's statement or a speaker's attitude. Answer the questions based on what is stated or implied by the speakers.

You may take notes while you listen. You may use your notes to help you answer the questions. Your notes will not be scored.

In some questions, you will see this icon: 🎧 This means that you will hear, but not see, part of the question.

Most questions are worth 1 point. If a question is worth more than 1 point, it will have special directions that indicate how many points you can receive.

You must answer each question. Click **NEXT** after you have answered a question. Then click **OK** to confirm and proceed to the next question. You cannot return to an earlier question once you have clicked **OK**.

A clock will be displayed at the top of the screen to show how much time remains. It only counts down while you are answering a question - not while you are listening to a conversation or lecture.

Conversation 1

[1-5] Listen to part of a conversation between a student and a librarian. AT1_01

정답 및 해석 | P. 293

1. **Why does the student go to the library?**

Ⓐ To check out some materials for a paper he is writing

Ⓑ To find out why he is receiving notices from the library

Ⓒ To inquire about obtaining notes for a psychology lecture

Ⓓ To request a timeline for picking up reserve materials

2. **What is a key feature of the library's checkout policy?**

Ⓐ Seniors are permitted to keep books out without a time limit.

Ⓑ Seniors are permitted to keep books out longer with some restrictions.

Ⓒ All underclassmen must return books as soon as seniors request them.

Ⓓ Seniors and underclassmen have the same library privileges.

3. **Listen again to part of the conversation. Then answer the question.**

What does the student imply when he says this:

Ⓐ He does not comprehend the rules of the book return policy.

Ⓑ He is irritated about the ineffective book return policy.

Ⓒ He thinks the policy regarding a senior extension is unfair.

Ⓓ He believes that the library should lengthen the policy time.

4. **What is true about the return request?**

Ⓐ It is something that does not happen that often.

Ⓑ It guarantees a semester-long checkout for seniors.

Ⓒ It requires students to fill out a form.

Ⓓ It has to be fulfilled within a week.

5. **What is the likely outcome of the conversation?**

Ⓐ The student will be allowed to keep the book until the completion of his project.

Ⓑ The student will no longer be able to check books out from the library.

Ⓒ The student will return the book but receive it back sooner than thought.

Ⓓ The student will not utilize the services of the library any longer.

Lecture 1

[6-11] Listen to part of a lecture in an astronomy class. AT1_02

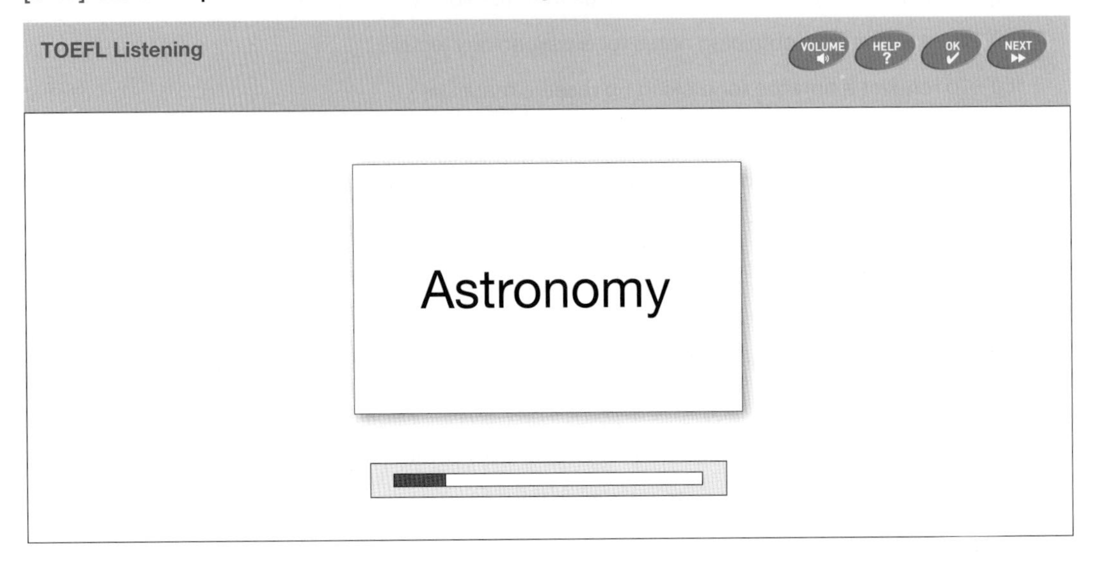

6. What is the topic of this lecture?

(A) Pluto and its constantly-changing position in the solar system

(B) Pluto and the space agencies that are fighting to reach it first

(C) The characteristics of Pluto and the ongoing process of learning about it

(D) Pluto and the type of spacecrafts that have explored there

7. What does the professor imply about the discovery of Pluto?

Ⓐ The mistake was not very important to the discovery of Pluto.

Ⓑ Pluto exists only as a mathematical possibility.

Ⓒ Pluto was only discovered because of a mistake.

Ⓓ We know about Pluto only because of its influence on Neptune's orbit.

8. How does the professor account for the fact that so little is known about Pluto?

Ⓐ Pluto cannot be seen clearly even with our best telescope.

Ⓑ Pluto is large and is located very far from Earth.

Ⓒ Pluto has only been observed from other planets.

Ⓓ Pluto has a circular orbit, which makes it invisible for long periods.

9. What does the professor say are the characteristics of Pluto's atmosphere? Choose 2 answers.

Ⓐ It is not affected by Pluto's orbit.

Ⓑ It is composed of methane, carbon monoxide, and nitrogen.

Ⓒ It is very stable.

Ⓓ It stays frozen for hundreds of years at a time.

Ⓔ The snow and ice covering Pluto melt spontaneously.

10. Listen again to part of the lecture. Then answer the question.

Why does the professor say this:

Ⓐ He thinks that the students can understand based on what he has already said.

Ⓑ He thinks that the students couldn't possibly understand why it is important.

Ⓒ He thinks that the students already knew why the probe is important.

Ⓓ He thinks the students will find this boring because they already know a lot about it.

11. What will the professor probably talk about next?

Ⓐ He will go on to discuss the New Horizons mission in more detail.

Ⓑ He will move to a discussion about Mars and the Hubble telescope.

Ⓒ He will talk about the possibility of humans living on Pluto.

Ⓓ He will discuss the costs and benefits of space exploration.

PAGODA TOEFL 80+ Listening

TOEFL Listening

Listening Directions

You will now begin the next part of the Listening Section.

You must answer each question. After you answer, click on **NEXT**. Then click on **OK** to confirm your answer and go on to the next question. After you click on **OK**, you cannot return to previous questions.

Click on **CONTINUE** to go on.

Conversation 2

[1-5] Listen to part of a conversation between a student and a cafeteria manager. AT1_03

1. **Why does the student go to see the cafeteria manager?**

Ⓐ To make a complaint about the quality of the food

Ⓑ To apply for a vacant work position at the cafeteria

Ⓒ To ask about information involving a baking class

Ⓓ To substitute a working shift for a sick friend

2. **What is the man's attitude at the beginning of the conversation?**

Ⓐ He is trying to show that he is too busy to talk at the moment.

Ⓑ He is implying that the student is not qualified for the job.

Ⓒ He is stating that the cooking class has filled up.

Ⓓ He is wondering if the woman filled the lunch order.

3. **What made the student want to register for the cooking class?**

Ⓐ She wants to improve her cooking skills because she lives alone.

Ⓑ She wants to learn to bake a cake to cheer up her injured friend.

Ⓒ She is trying to impress her parents, who are coming to visit.

Ⓓ She is considering changing her major to the culinary arts.

4. **Listen again to part of the conversation. Then answer the question.**

Why does the student say this:

Ⓐ She is excited that she got a job working at the cafeteria.

Ⓑ She is angry because she thinks the manager overcharged her.

Ⓒ She is very happy because the class will be beneficial to her.

Ⓓ She is upset at the man because he gave away her spot in the class.

5. **What are two items that the student needs to bring to the cooking class?**
Choose 2 answers.

Ⓐ Spatula

Ⓑ Apron

Ⓒ Beater

Ⓓ Old clothes

Lecture 2

[6-11] Listen to part of a discussion in a marine biology class. AT1_04

6. What is the discussion mainly about?

Ⓐ The life cycle of the fiddler crab

Ⓑ The role of the fiddler crab in its local ecosystem

Ⓒ The fiddler crab's features and patterns of behavior

Ⓓ The dating rituals of the fiddler crab

7. What are the main characteristics of fiddler crabs mentioned by the professor? Choose 3 answers.

Ⓐ They filter their food from mud.
Ⓑ They are most active during high tide.
Ⓒ They live in networks of small tunnels.
Ⓓ They breathe air.
Ⓔ Their main food is small birds and fish.

8. According to the professor, how can male and female crabs be differentiated?

Ⓐ Female fiddler crabs' claws are both the same size, whereas the males' aren't.
Ⓑ Female fiddler crabs remain in their burrows more than males do.
Ⓒ Female fiddler crabs look for food in the intertidal region, while males don't.
Ⓓ Both male and female fiddler crabs wave their claws during dating.

9. What does the professor infer when she talks about goliath beetles and walruses?

Ⓐ Male fiddler crabs have the same body parts as these creatures.
Ⓑ Male fiddler crabs have structures that look very similar to the structure of these organisms.
Ⓒ The behavior of male fiddler crabs is similar to these creatures.
Ⓓ The enlarged claw of male fiddler crabs has a function similar to body parts of these creatures.

10. Put the following words in the same order as the professor used when talking about the characteristics of the crabs.

Ⓐ Mating Behavior
Ⓑ Habitat
Ⓒ Body Structure
Ⓓ Feeding Behavior

1	
2	
3	
4	

11. Listen again to part of the discussion. Then answer the question.

Why does the professor say this:

Ⓐ To help students understand that crabs mate very often during their lifetime
Ⓑ To demonstrate ways that females behave and ways that males try to get their attention
Ⓒ To add humor and interest and give students a vivid image that they will more easily remember
Ⓓ To help students see that crabs behave strangely during breeding season

Lecture 3

[12-17] Listen to part of a lecture in a psychology class. AT1_05

12. What is the lecture mainly about?

Ⓐ Using cooking to learn about other things

Ⓑ John Dewey's personal life

Ⓒ Reforms in rote-learning techniques

Ⓓ A revolutionary development in education

13. What does the professor say about memorization?

Ⓐ It's a critical part of student-centered learning.

Ⓑ It's not a useful indicator of practical intelligence.

Ⓒ It can be used in any classroom situation.

Ⓓ It cannot be influenced by repetition.

14. How is the lecture organized?

Ⓐ The spokesperson gives a biographical account of a prominent figure in 20th-century education.

Ⓑ The professor shows students feedback received from a class that used a learner-centered style.

Ⓒ The teacher introduces an alternative form of education followed by its pros and cons.

Ⓓ The instructor discusses a traditional teaching method before presenting John Dewey's alternative.

15. According to the professor, what does her son do to learn about geometry?

Ⓐ He uses toys to construct different things.

Ⓑ He breaks his toys into pieces.

Ⓒ He attends a public school taught by Dewey.

Ⓓ He practices making buildings outside in nature.

16. What is the professor's attitude toward her son's playing with wooden blocks?

Ⓐ She is disappointed that he has to use toys to learn a subject taught in schools.

Ⓑ She likes the structures he creates with the wooden toy blocks.

Ⓒ She feels that his public school should use this type of learning in its classrooms.

Ⓓ She is happy he is enjoying himself while naturally learning about geometry.

17. Listen again to part of the lecture. Then answer the question.

Why does the professor say this:

Ⓐ Since the students are already cooperating with each other, the professor doesn't want to do any lecturing in the next class.

Ⓑ Since she lectures during the class, the students will be listening to her rather than cooperatively working toward their goals together.

Ⓒ Since each student is already in charge of achieving his or her goals, the professor feels it is unnecessary to do any lecturing.

Ⓓ Since listening isn't necessary in a learner-centered class, the professor feels it doesn't need to be practiced in the next class.

Actual Test 2

문제 듣기

TOEFL Listening

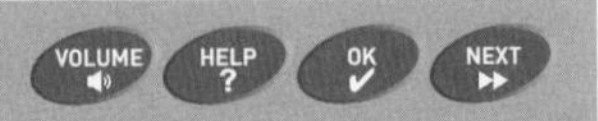

Now put on your headset.

Click on **Continue** to go on.

TOEFL Listening

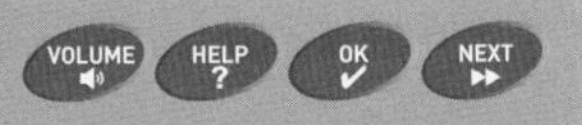

Changing the Volume

To change the volume, click on the Volume icon at the top of the screen. The volume control will appear. Move the volume indicator to the left or to the right to change the volume.

To close the volume control, move the mouse pointer to another part of the screen.

You may now change the volume.
When you are finished, click on **Continue**.

TOEFL Listening

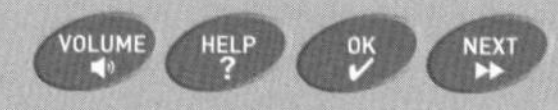

Listening Section Directions

This section measures your ability to understand conversations and lectures in English. You should listen to each conversation and lecture only once.

After each conversation or lecture, you will answer some questions about it. The questions typically ask about the main idea and supporting details. Some questions ask about the purpose of a speaker's statement or a speaker's attitude. Answer the questions based on what is stated or implied by the speakers.

You may take notes while you listen. You may use your notes to help you answer the questions. Your notes will not be scored.

In some questions, you will see this icon: 🎧 This means that you will hear, but not see, part of the question.

Most questions are worth 1 point. If a question is worth more than 1 point, it will have special directions that indicate how many points you can receive.

You must answer each question. Click **NEXT** after you have answered a question. Then click **OK** to confirm and proceed to the next question. You cannot return to an earlier question once you have clicked **OK**.

A clock will be displayed at the top of the screen to show how much time remains. It only counts down while you are answering a question - not while you are listening to a conversation or lecture.

Conversation 1

[1-5] Listen to part of a conversation between a student and a resident assistant. AT2_01

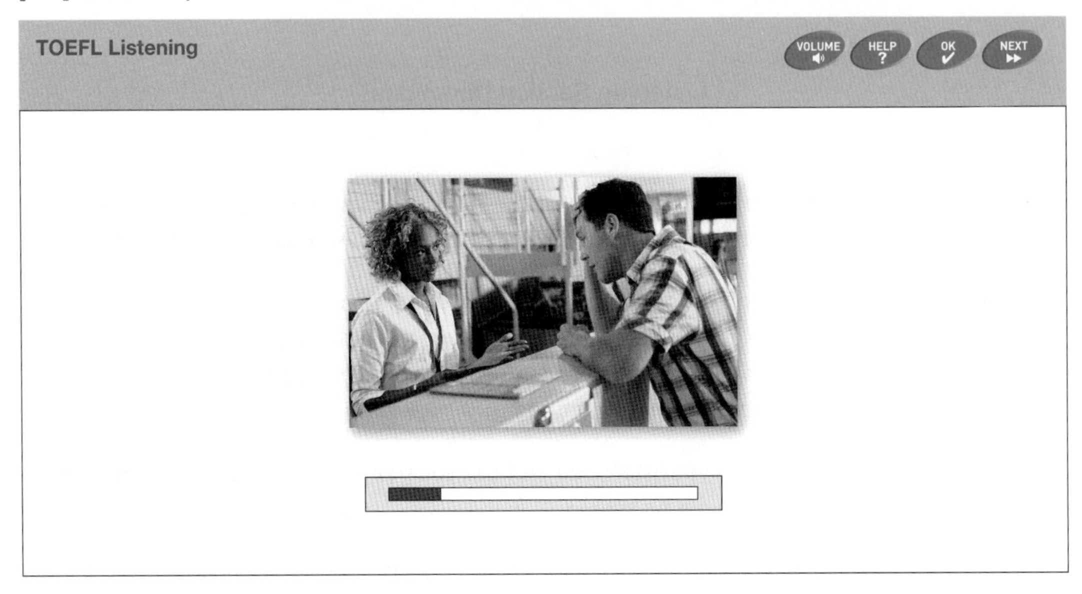

정답 및 해석 | P. 309

1. **What is the conversation mainly about?**

Ⓐ The speakers are discussing a problem with the dormitory lease.

Ⓑ The speakers are debating the benefits of living in the dorm.

Ⓒ The speakers are wondering where a late student is.

Ⓓ The speakers are trying to resolve a roommate issue.

2. **What is implied about the school's policy toward student problems in the dorms?**

Ⓐ The school has very strict regulations regarding students' behavior.

Ⓑ The school would prefer that students solve problems on their own.

Ⓒ The school never permits students to change rooms in mid-semester.

Ⓓ The school allows students to change rooms at any point in the year.

3. **What does the housing officer tell the student to do?**

Ⓐ She insists that the student solve the problem on his own with the roommate.

Ⓑ She directs the student to take up the problem with the Dean of Students.

Ⓒ She suggests that the student gather the signatures needed to change rooms.

Ⓓ She advises the student to coordinate schedules with the roommate.

4. **What does the student say about the R.A.'s second suggestion?**

Ⓐ He is concerned about his new roommate's current roommate.

Ⓑ He believes it will be effective since he already got their signatures.

Ⓒ He is worried since he needs to persuade a few people.

Ⓓ He thinks it can work out very well since he already knows what to do.

5. **Listen again to part of the conversation. Then answer the question.**

What does the student mean when he says this:

Ⓐ The student would like the R.A. to repeat the instructions.

Ⓑ The student is upset he has to do the appropriate paperwork.

Ⓒ The student understands the signatures are most important.

Ⓓ The student doubts that he will be able to get all the signatures.

Lecture 1

[6-11] Listen to part of a discussion in a history class. AT2_02

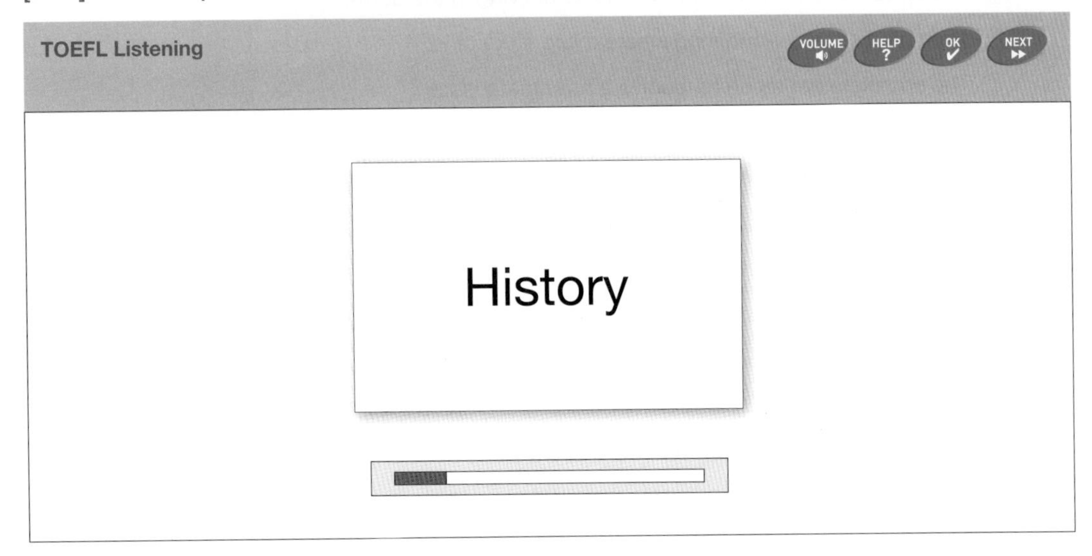

6. What is the discussion mainly about?

Ⓐ The time-consuming process of excavating the Nebra sky disk

Ⓑ The interesting discovery that was made in Germany

Ⓒ The lives of people who lived during the Neolithic period

Ⓓ The astrological observances made with an ancient calendar

7. **What is true about the Nebra sky disk?**

Ⓐ It was invented for ritual purposes.

Ⓑ Its age has yet to be discovered.

Ⓒ It was made of gold, bronze, and silver.

Ⓓ Its diameter is about one meter.

8. **Why did scientists assume that the Nebra sky disk was some form of calendar? Choose 2 answers.**

Ⓐ The area that it was found is deeply related with astrology.

Ⓑ The numbers carved on the disk showed similarities with today's calendar.

Ⓒ There are some celestial bodies portrayed on the surface of the disk.

Ⓓ People during the Neolithic period had already been using calendars.

9. **What can be inferred about the Nebra sky disk and other artifacts?**

Ⓐ Their original burial site cannot solely prove their authenticity.

Ⓑ There are various ways to prove that they were forged.

Ⓒ They were almost sold to another country by the hunters.

Ⓓ Their existence proved the widespread use of iron in the region.

10. **Why does the professor mention a piece of birch bark?**

Ⓐ To show the interesting use of trees during the Neolithic period

Ⓑ To emphasize the importance of small objects for a burial ritual

Ⓒ To introduce another important discovery from the Bronze Age

Ⓓ To explain how scientists discovered the burial date of the artifacts

11. **Why does the professor say this:** 🎧

Ⓐ He is telling the students that many things still need to be revealed.

Ⓑ He sees the difficulty of determining whether the disk is authentic or not.

Ⓒ He finds it interesting to see the earliest trade route of mankind.

Ⓓ He is excited that the authenticity of the disk was finally made certain.

PAGODA TOEFL 80+ Listening

TOEFL Listening

Listening Directions

You will now begin the next part of the Listening Section.

You must answer each question. After you answer, click on **NEXT**. Then click on **OK** to confirm your answer and go on to the next question. After you click on **OK**, you cannot return to previous questions.

Click on **CONTINUE** to go on.

Conversation 2

[1-5] Listen to part of a conversation between a student and a registrar. AT2_03

1. **Why does the student go to the registrar's office?**

Ⓐ She wants to check an error on her tuition bill.

Ⓑ She needs to pay a political seminar fee.

Ⓒ She wants to sign up for a required class.

Ⓓ She has signed up for the wrong class.

2. **What is the man's attitude toward the student at the beginning of the conversation?**

Ⓐ He is annoyed by the fact that the student could not register the class herself.

Ⓑ He is puzzled why the student took so long to register for the class.

Ⓒ He is irritated that the student is taking so long to complete the registration.

Ⓓ He is not sure if the class is really important for the student.

3. **What suggestions does the registrar give to the student? Choose 2 answers.**

Ⓐ He suggests that the student make up the course in the summer.

Ⓑ He suggests that the student get an override from the professor.

Ⓒ He suggests that the student try to audit the class and wait.

Ⓓ He suggests that the student take the class at a different university.

4. **Listen again to part of the conversation. Then answer the question.**

What does the student mean when she says this:

Ⓐ She thinks the idea doesn't sound necessary.

Ⓑ She does not understand why there are so many people on the list.

Ⓒ She thinks she will get into the course soon in the semester.

Ⓓ She thinks that she will not be admitted into the class this semester.

5. **What will the student most likely do?**

Ⓐ Find an open spot to audit the required course

Ⓑ Visit City Hall to sign up for the political seminar

Ⓒ Go and see Professor Peterson regarding her grade

Ⓓ Visit Professor Peterson's office to ask for help

Lecture 2

[6-11] Listen to part of a lecture in a biology class.

AT2_04

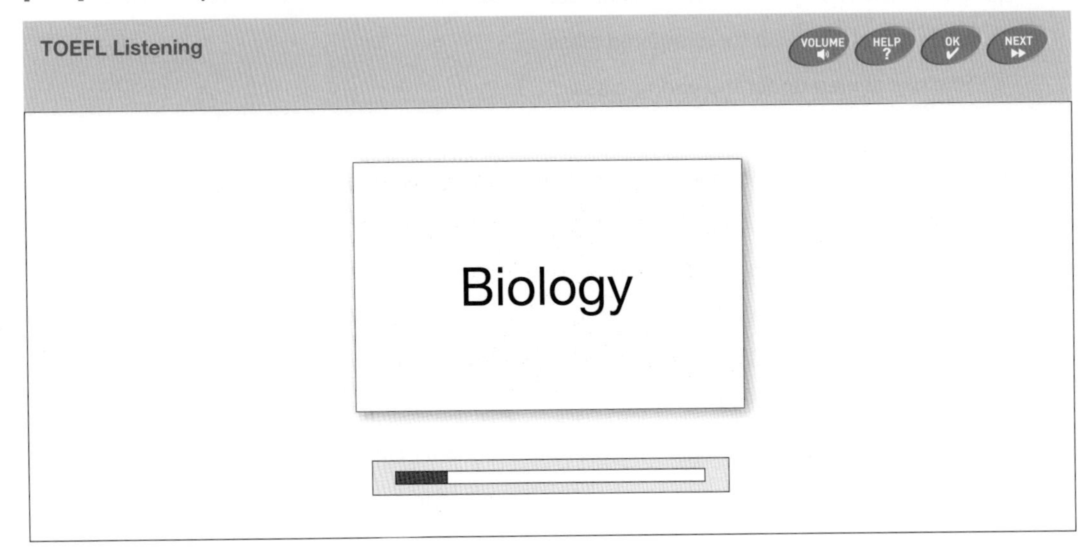

6. What is the topic of the lecture?

Ⓐ Self-pollination and how plants do it

Ⓑ The way farmers can make more money

Ⓒ The different ways plants create new plants

Ⓓ Cross-pollination and what makes it happen

7. What does the professor say about pollen?

Ⓐ It is commonly seen in the springtime.

Ⓑ It makes all flowers yellow in color.

Ⓒ It is helpful for protecting flowers.

Ⓓ It is the male portion of a plant.

8. What is the professor's attitude toward wind as a pollinator of large areas?

Ⓐ He feels the wind is the best for them.

Ⓑ He thinks the wind is better for flowers.

Ⓒ He wants more information.

Ⓓ He isn't sure the wind is strong enough to be effective.

9. How can honeybees be compared to the bees native to the area?

Ⓐ They are less expensive than native bees.

Ⓑ They are larger than native bees.

Ⓒ They aren't as efficient at pollinating as native bees.

Ⓓ They pollinate plants faster than native bees.

10. Listen again to part of the lecture. Then answer the question.

Why does the professor say this:

Ⓐ To develop ideas for discussion in the next class

Ⓑ To talk about how pollination fertilizes plants

Ⓒ To inform students what they will be reading about for homework

Ⓓ To describe the process that creates new plants

11. How does the professor conclude the lecture?

Ⓐ By assigning homework and reviewing the lecture

Ⓑ By answering questions about pollination

Ⓒ By telling students to read about vegetables

Ⓓ By giving a homework assignment and asking a question

Lecture 3

[12-17] Listen to part of a discussion in a business class. AT2_05

12. What aspects of advertising is the professor mainly discussing?

Ⓐ The costs and benefits of advertising

Ⓑ The types of messages that companies try to send through advertisements

Ⓒ The main elements companies must consider when planning advertisements

Ⓓ The four types of advertising media

13. Listen again to part of the discussion. Then answer the question.

Why does the professor say this:

Ⓐ She does not think the students need another definition.

Ⓑ She wants to give a definition that is a little easier to understand.

Ⓒ She feels like the students should be able to understand the first definition.

Ⓓ She's trying to say that the first definition is not confusing.

14. What is the market in the 4 M's of advertising?

Ⓐ The method used to show the advertisements

Ⓑ Who will buy the product and how much they need it

Ⓒ The number of people who will see the TV commercial

Ⓓ The style the company uses to make the ad

15. According to the professor, how is market related to media?

Ⓐ Market and target consumers are more important than the media form.

Ⓑ The media that is chosen is more important than the market.

Ⓒ The target customer must be established before determining which form of media to use.

Ⓓ The media message should be chosen first, then companies can decide whom to target.

16. Why is time important in terms of the third M, 'money'?

Ⓐ It gets the most viewership and maximizes the number of potential consumers.

Ⓑ It reminds existing consumers of a certain product again to purchase.

Ⓒ It can estimate the number of people who watch the Super Bowl.

Ⓓ It attracts different groups of people who can affect a company's sales.

17. How does the professor conclude the discussion?

Ⓐ By repeating the main topic of the lecture

Ⓑ By giving several examples of the main topic

Ⓒ By asking the students if they can remember something

Ⓓ By reminding the students the most important example of the lecture

Actual Test 3

문제 듣기

TOEFL Listening

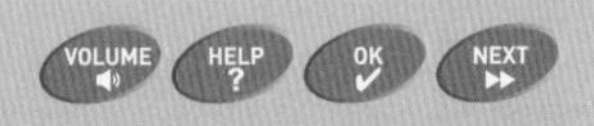

Now put on your headset.

Click on **Continue** to go on.

TOEFL Listening

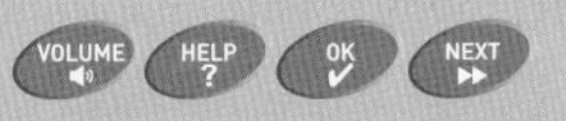

Changing the Volume

To change the volume, click on the Volume icon at the top of the screen. The volume control will appear. Move the volume indicator to the left or to the right to change the volume.

To close the volume control, move the mouse pointer to another part of the screen.

You may now change the volume.
When you are finished, click on **Continue**.

TOEFL Listening

Listening Section Directions

This section measures your ability to understand conversations and lectures in English. You should listen to each conversation and lecture only once.

After each conversation or lecture, you will answer some questions about it. The questions typically ask about the main idea and supporting details. Some questions ask about the purpose of a speaker's statement or a speaker's attitude. Answer the questions based on what is stated or implied by the speakers.

You may take notes while you listen. You may use your notes to help you answer the questions. Your notes will not be scored.

In some questions, you will see this icon: 🎧 This means that you will hear, but not see, part of the question.

Most questions are worth 1 point. If a question is worth more than 1 point, it will have special directions that indicate how many points you can receive.

You must answer each question. Click **NEXT** after you have answered a question. Then click **OK** to confirm and proceed to the next question. You cannot return to an earlier question once you have clicked **OK**.

A clock will be displayed at the top of the screen to show how much time remains. It only counts down while you are answering a question - not while you are listening to a conversation or lecture.

Conversation 1

[1-5] Listen to part of a conversation between a student and an employee of a university art gallery. AT3_01

1. What is the purpose of the student's visit to the university art gallery?

Ⓐ She wanted to change the date of her scheduled guided tour.
Ⓑ She was not sure if her application form was properly submitted.
Ⓒ She wanted to see if she is the right candidate for a position.
Ⓓ She was interested in working in the art gallery's souvenir shop.

2. Why does the student want to work at the university art gallery?

Ⓐ She is interested in getting the extra credit that her professor offered.
Ⓑ She is majoring in art history and volunteer activity is required for all such students.
Ⓒ She is making up for some tests she missed with volunteer activity.
Ⓓ She is trying to earn some money by working as an art tour guide.

3. Why does the student say this: 🎧

Ⓐ The other students had more experience than the student did.
Ⓑ The other students were faster at applying for those positions.
Ⓒ The other students had an advantage that the student did not have.
Ⓓ The other students were better at finding open positions.

4. Why can't the student become a tour guide?

Ⓐ She is not very good at researching art history and related reference books.
Ⓑ She did not have a meeting with the chief manager to discuss the tour schedule.
Ⓒ She is unable to take two training sessions from a professional tour guide.
Ⓓ She is not majoring in art history even though she is taking Professor Campbell's class.

5. What will the student most likely do next?

Ⓐ Go to see Professor Campbell tomorrow
Ⓑ Visit the gallery again tomorrow for a meeting
Ⓒ Change her appointment time to Tuesday
Ⓓ Fill out the offline application form and submit it

Lecture 1

[6-11] Listen to part of a discussion in an archaeology class.  AT3_02

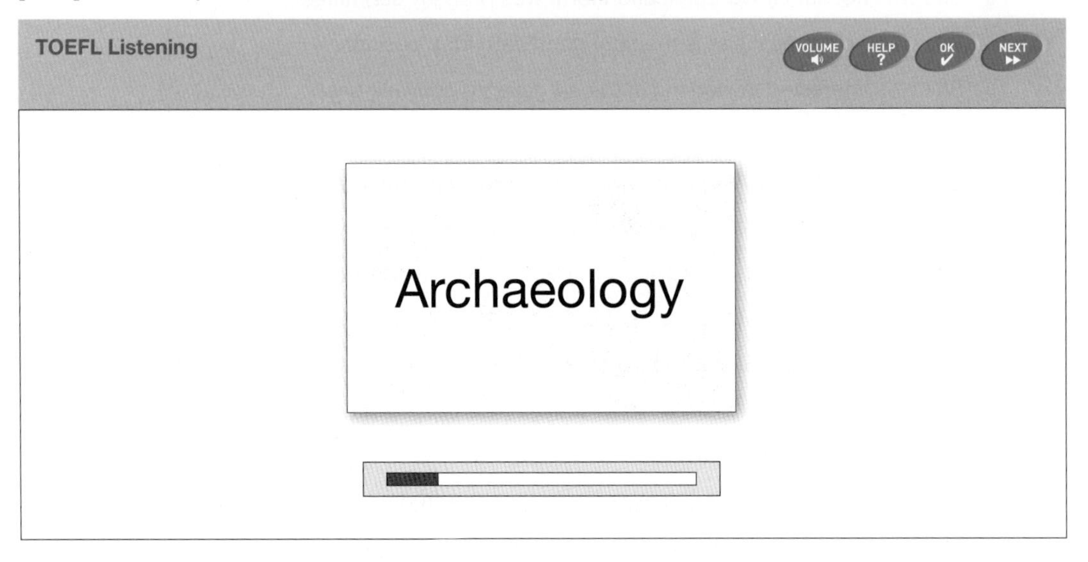

6. What is the main idea of the discussion?

Ⓐ Four classifications that make Mayan pottery different from other cultures'

Ⓑ Important classifications that could help when analyzing ancient pottery

Ⓒ Some classifications that were established to study ancient and modern pottery

Ⓓ Four classifications that the Mayans organized to spread their pottery

7. **What does the professor say about the shape of a vessel?**

Ⓐ It plainly shows the purpose of the vessel to the viewers.

Ⓑ It is the least important factor out of the four classifications.

Ⓒ It was revealed that its shape and purpose did not always match.

Ⓓ It shows that most pottery from that period was used for drinking purposes.

8. **Why does the professor mention a shard?**

Ⓐ It shows the development of style in Mayan ceramics.

Ⓑ It could help archaeologists to discover the usage of the pottery.

Ⓒ It was recently discovered at an ancient Mayan settlement.

Ⓓ It can be valuable when finding out the paste type of the pottery.

9. **According to the discussion, which of the following are true about the four classifications? Choose 2 answers.**

Ⓐ The Mayans used varying types of materials when glazing their pottery.

Ⓑ Dry clay was used to remove any residue remaining on the surface of pottery.

Ⓒ Types of pastes and surface work were also included in the decoration category.

Ⓓ Decorations and the theme the artist chose often depicted his culture.

10. **Listen again to part of the discussion. Then answer the question.**

Why does the student say this:

Ⓐ To highlight the importance of the technique the Mayans utilized

Ⓑ To show that the method the Mayans used did not change that much

Ⓒ To convince the professor that the Mayans' technique has a long history

Ⓓ To explain how the Mayans formed their pottery into a desired shape

11. **What can be inferred about the pottery produced during the Late Preclassic period?**

Ⓐ It showed serpent figures, which is the proof of their belief in the afterlife.

Ⓑ It always represented certain kinds of animals, especially birds.

Ⓒ It started to have shapes that were more complex and human-like.

Ⓓ It had carvings of significant events that occurred in history.

PAGODA TOEFL 80+ Listening

TOEFL Listening

Listening Directions

You will now begin the next part of the Listening Section.

You must answer each question. After you answer, click on **NEXT**. Then click on **OK** to confirm your answer and go on to the next question. After you click on **OK**, you cannot return to previous questions.

Click on **CONTINUE** to go on.

Conversation 2

[1-5] Listen to part of a conversation between a student and a university library employee. AT3_03

정답 및 해석 | P. 331

1. **Why did the student meet with the employee?**

Ⓐ To inquire about an article

Ⓑ To ask for directions to the satellite campus

Ⓒ To learn how to understand library codes

Ⓓ To register for a journal website

2. **Why can't the student access a physical copy of the journal right away? Choose 2 answers.**

Ⓐ It is only available as an electronic copy.

Ⓑ The journal is held in a different library.

Ⓒ The student's roommate is away.

Ⓓ The journal is being used by another student.

3. **What can be inferred about students at the university?**

Ⓐ Many students are unhappy about the size of the campus.

Ⓑ Most students have to write papers during finals week.

Ⓒ Many students procrastinate on their final papers.

Ⓓ Not many students have cars.

4. **Why does the student have to register with the publisher's website?**

Ⓐ The publisher only provides an electronic copy.

Ⓑ The publisher has no agreement to share material with the university.

Ⓒ The publisher wants to protect the material's copyrights.

Ⓓ The publisher wants to increase access to the material.

5. **Why does the student need to input her course code?**

Ⓐ To restrict access to only film majors

Ⓑ To limit the number of times a student can access the journal

Ⓒ To ensure that the student is enrolled in the right course

Ⓓ For the sake of the publisher's record keeping

Lecture 2

[6-11] Listen to part of a lecture in a biology class. AT3_04

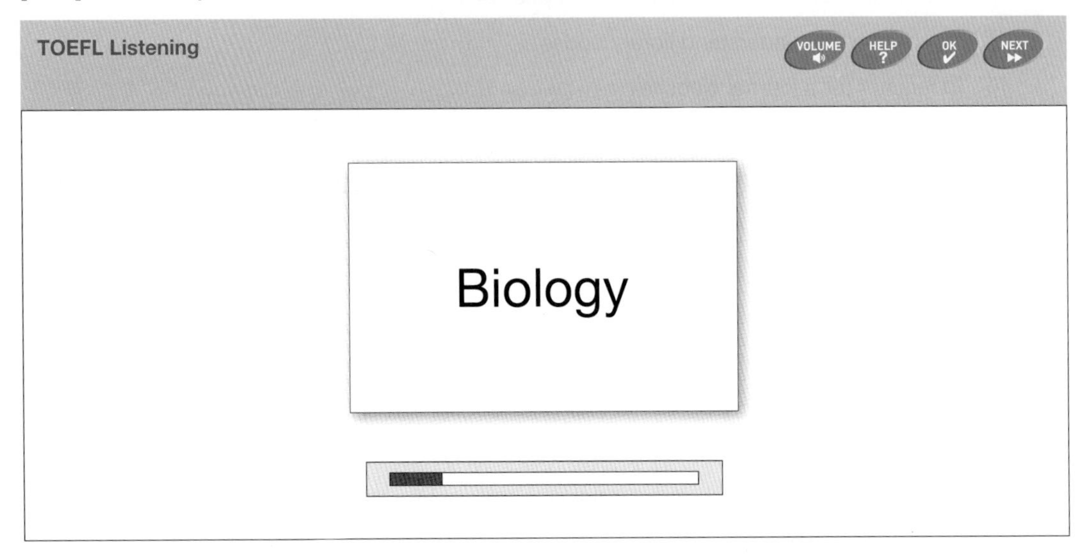

6. What is the main topic of the lecture?

(A) The state of Seychellois endemic species

(B) The contributions of Darwin's Galapagos Island expeditions to our understanding of evolution

(C) The effects of environment on evolution

(D) The evolution and adaptations of island species

7. **According to the lecture, which of the following are examples of adaptation among animals on the Galapagos Islands? Choose 2 answers.**

Ⓐ Iguanas feeding on algae

Ⓑ Iguanas eating fish

Ⓒ Iguanas filtering out salt from saltwater

Ⓓ Varying shapes of finches' tails

8. **Listen again to part of the lecture. Then answer the question.**

Why does the professor say this:

Ⓐ The professor is making a witty reference to the hot weather of the tropics.

Ⓑ The student's second answer was more correct than the first.

Ⓒ The student's first answer was on the right track.

Ⓓ The professor is acknowledging that the student may be embarrassed.

9. **According to the lecture, why do islands have more unique plant and animal species?**

Ⓐ Many islands broke off from larger continents.

Ⓑ Volcanic activity altered the habitats of many island species.

Ⓒ The climate on islands is typically more inhospitable.

Ⓓ Many species were forced to adapt quickly to a new environment.

10. **Why does the professor mention Seychelles?**

Ⓐ To introduce a particular species that exhibits island evolution

Ⓑ To provide statistics on endemic species on islands

Ⓒ To illustrate the distinct qualities of evolution on islands

Ⓓ To discuss endemic and endangered island bird species

11. **What will the class most likely do next?**

Ⓐ They will learn about the urgency of endemic species protection through a case study.

Ⓑ They will discuss the state of several endangered species on the Seychelles islands.

Ⓒ They will discuss some of the unique adaptations of the Seychelles Warbler.

Ⓓ They will compare continental endangered species with those on islands.

Lecture 3

[12-17] Listen to part of a lecture in an archaeology class.

AT3_05

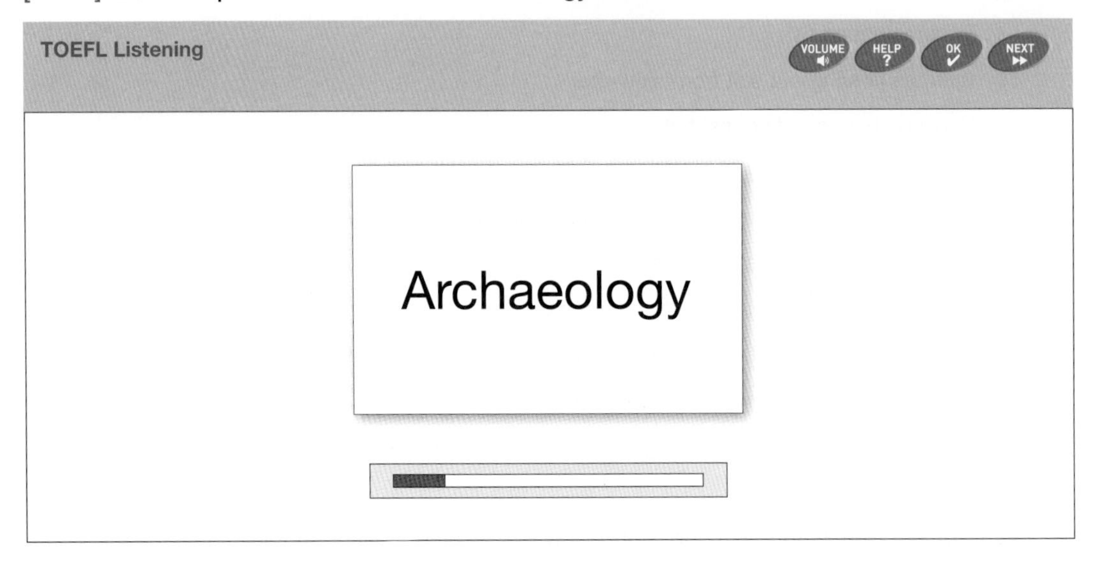

12. What does the professor mainly talk about?

Ⓐ A summary of the Frontier Thesis

Ⓑ Criticisms of the Frontier Thesis

Ⓒ Manifest Destiny and its related theories

Ⓓ An analysis of American exceptionalism

13. **According to the lecture, which of the following is NOT true of Manifest Destiny?**
Choose 2 answers.

Ⓐ It was the most important predecessor to the Frontier Thesis.
Ⓑ It taught that Americans had a mission to expand and transform.
Ⓒ It gave Americans meaning in their expansionary activities.
Ⓓ It emphasized the exceptional nature of American family and societal values.

14. **According to the lecture, how is westward expansion related to the Frontier Thesis?**

Ⓐ The East represented the old, while the West represented a departure from the old.
Ⓑ The American ideals of liberty, equality, and democracy were founded by societies to the West.
Ⓒ Westward expansion cemented once and for all the departure from the old societies of Europe.
Ⓓ Land in the West was free for anyone to grab, making it the perfect breeding ground for other American ideals to grow.

15. **Why does the professor mention Chicago?**

Ⓐ To give an example of a city that urbanized without becoming agrarian
Ⓑ To cast doubt on the idea of an exceptional American spirit
Ⓒ To point out the importance of capitalism in frontier expansion
Ⓓ To further the idea that Americanism ultimately led to urbanization

16. **Listen again to part of the lecture. Then answer the question.** 🎧
Why does the professor say this: 🎧

Ⓐ The professor wants the students to ask themselves if any of them are shy or timid.
Ⓑ The professor is pushing for the celebration of diversity in the American entrepreneurial experience.
Ⓒ The professor is implying that it would be very easy to cast doubt on Turner's idea.
Ⓓ The professor is arguing that quieter, more thoughtful personalities contributed more to American expansion.

17. **What will the class most likely do next?**

Ⓐ The class will discuss further criticisms of the thesis.
Ⓑ The professor will talk about the role of Indigenous people in the frontier experience.
Ⓒ The professor will hear some of the students' opinions on the thesis.
Ⓓ The class will debate on what precisely was behind the American expansion.

PAGODA TOEFL 80+ Listening

PAGODA TOEFL 80+ Listening

PAGODA TOEFL 80+ Listening

3rd Edition

파고다교육그룹 언어교육연구소 | 저

PAGODA TOEFL

80+ Listening

해설서

PAGODA Books

Diagnostic Test

Conversation 1
1. C 2. B 3. B 4. B 5. D

Lecture 1
6. B 7. C 8. A 9. A, C 10. D 11. D

Lecture 2
12. B 13. A 14. D 15. D 16. A 17. C

Conversation 2
1. B 2. C 3. C, D 4. D 5. C

Lecture 3
6. C 7. C 8. A 9. B, D 10. A 11. D

Conversation 1

본서 | P. 22

Man: Student | Woman: Student

[1-5] Listen to part of a conversation between two students in their first class of the term.

W Well, hello, Mikhail.

M Oh hi, Alice!

W 2 Wait, aren't you a business major? What are you doing in an ecology course?

M Yes, business administration. Are business majors forbidden to take ecology courses for some reason?

W No, no. I'm just surprised. Especially since this is a 300 level course. Usually, non-major students don't go above 100 level, introductory courses.

M Yes, I know. 3 The thing is, I've decided to make ecology my minor and it makes this course a requirement.

W Why is that? I mean, that's great, but why?

M Well, I really want to work for a company that cares about the environment... a green company. There are so many companies that pollute and contribute to global warming, so I want to study ecology as well as administration.

W That makes sense. 1 It's good that you are thinking about your future after school. Many of my friends don't really know what they want to do after they graduate. Me included, I guess.

M 1 You don't have future plans? Aren't you going to be a scientist... an ecologist?

W A scientist, yes, but not an ecologist. I actually want to

남자: 학생 | 여자: 학생

학기 첫 수업 시간에 두 학생이 나누는 대화를 들으시오.

여 안녕, 미카엘.

남 어 안녕, 앨리스!

여 2 잠깐, 너 경영 전공 아니었어? 생태학 수업엔 웬 일이니?

남 응, 경영학 전공 맞아. 혹시 어떤 이유로 경영 전공자들은 생태학 수업을 들으면 안되는 거야?

여 아니, 아니야. 그냥 놀라서 그래. 특히 이건 300레벨 수업이니까. 보통, 비전공자들이 100레벨의 입문 수업 이상으론 잘 듣지 않잖아.

남 아, 나도 알아. 3 사실, 난 부전공으로 생태학을 하기로 결정했고, 그래서 이 수업이 필수 과목이야.

여 왜? 내 말은, 멋지긴 하지만, 왜 그런 결정을 했니?

남 음, 난 환경을 생각하는 회사에서 일하고 싶어... 친환경 회사. 환경을 오염시키고 지구 온난화에 기여하는 회사들이 많잖아, 그래서 난 경영뿐 아니라 생태학도 공부하고 싶어.

여 일리 있는 말이야. 1 졸업 후 자신의 미래에 대해서 생각한다는 것은 좋은 것 같아. 내 친구들 중에는 졸업한 후에 자신이 하고 싶은 것이 뭔지 모르는 애들이 많아. 나를 포함해서 말이야.

남 1 넌 미래 계획이 없어? 과학자... 생태학자가 될 거 아니야?

여 과학자는 맞지만, 생태학자는 아니야. 난 날씨를 연구하고 예측하는 기상학 분야에서 일하고 싶어.

go into meteorology, you know, studying and predicting weather.

M That sounds like a pretty clear goal to me.

W Well, yes and no. As a meteorologist I would have a very specific job description, but that doesn't help me decide where I would actually work. Many different industries have positions for people who can predict the weather: shipping, oil drilling, transportation—

M The evening news!

W Yes, that too. So, I don't really know where I want to apply my knowledge when I join the labor force.

M So, is this class a required course for you?

W Yes, it is. I have to take a wide variety of classes, ranging from computer science to physics. Meteorology is actually a pretty difficult field to study. It incorporates so many different sciences. I have to take a full class load every semester.

M 4 That sounds intense. What made you so interested in studying the weather?

W 4 My hometown did. I'm from Casper, Wyoming, and we get all kinds of extreme weather there—blizzards in the winter, tornadoes in the summer, and it is always windy. So, the weather has always had a significant influence on my life. After I learned about the meteorology major that they offer here, I knew what I was going to study.

M 5 Does your major require an internship? That could help you decide what to do after you graduate.

W 5 Yes, it does. I guess I should start searching for some good options.

남 꽤나 명확한 목표인 것 같은데.

여 음, 그럴 수도 있고 아닐 수도 있고. 기상학자로서 나는 굉장히 구체적인 직무 기술서가 있지만 그게 내가 실제로 어디에서 일하게 될 것인지 결정하는 데 도움이 되진 못해. 많은 다른 산업군에도 날씨를 예측할 수 있는 사람들을 위한 자리가 있거든. 해운, 석유 채굴, 수송 등 말이야.

남 저녁 뉴스도!

여 맞아, 거기도. 그래서 내가 직업을 얻게 되었을 때, 내 지식을 어디에 적용시키고 싶은지 아직 잘 모르겠어.

남 그래서 이 수업이 너한테 필수 과목인 거야?

여 응. 난 컴퓨터 공학에서부터 물리학에 이르기까지 다양한 과목들을 들어야 해. 기상학은 사실 공부하기 꽤나 어려운 분야지. 아주 많은 다른 과학 분야를 포함하고 있거든. 난 매 학기 과목들을 꽉 채워서 들어야 해.

남 4 힘들겠구나. 근데 뭐 때문에 날씨 연구에 그렇게 관심을 가지게 된 거야?

여 4 내 고향 때문에. 난 와이오밍주의 캐스퍼 출신인데, 그곳 사람들은 모든 종류의 기상이변을 겪어. 겨울에는 눈보라, 여름에는 토네이도, 그리고 항상 바람이 많이 불지. 그래서 날씨는 항상 내 삶에 큰 영향을 끼쳤어. 여기에서 제공되는 기상학 전공에 대해 배우고 나서, 난 내가 무엇을 공부하게 될지 알게 됐어.

남 5 너희 전공도 인턴십이 필수니? 그게 졸업한 후에 네가 뭘 할지 결정하는 데 도움이 될 수도 있는데.

여 5 응, 필요해. 좋은 데가 있나 좀 찾아봐야겠어.

1. What are the speakers mainly talking about?

(A) 300 level courses that are good for taking as an elective
(B) Required classes for a meteorology major
(C) What they have planned for their future and career goals
(D) Various career options for meteorology majors

2. Why does the woman say this:

W Wait, aren't you a business major? What are you doing in an ecology course?

(A) She knows the man is doing something suspicious in the class.
(B) She thinks that the man does not have to take an ecology course.
(C) She believes that the class would be too hard for the man.

1. 화자들은 주로 무엇에 관해 이야기하는가?

(A) 선택 과목으로 수강하기 좋은 300레벨 과목들
(B) 기상학 전공자를 위한 필수 과목들
(C) 자신들의 미래 계획과 직업 목표
(D) 기상학 전공자들을 위한 다양한 직업 선택권

2. 여자는 왜 이렇게 말하는가:

여 "잠깐, 너 경영 전공 아니었어? 생태학 수업엔 웬일이니?"

(A) 남자가 그 수업에서 수상한 무언가를 하고 있다는 것을 알았기 때문에
(B) 남자가 생태학 과목을 들을 필요가 없다고 생각하기 때문에
(C) 수업이 남자에게는 너무 어려울 것이라고 생각하기 때문에

Diagnostic Test

Ⓓ She feels glad to see the man in the class that she is taking.

Ⓓ 자신이 듣고 있는 과목에서 남자를 만났다는 사실이 기뻐서

3. Why is the man taking this course?

Ⓐ It is an elective course for a meteorology major.
Ⓑ It is a required course for an ecology minor.
Ⓒ It is important to him because he needs more credits.
Ⓓ It is enjoyable since he cares about the environment.

3. 남자는 왜 이 과목을 수강하는가?

Ⓐ 기상학 전공자에게 선택 과목이기 때문에
Ⓑ 생태학 부전공자에게 필수 과목이기 때문에
Ⓒ 학점이 더 필요해서 그에게 중요하기 때문에
Ⓓ 환경에 관심이 많기에 수강하기 즐거운 과목이라서

4. Why did the woman decide to major in meteorology?

Ⓐ She was inspired by a relative to become a weather forecaster.
Ⓑ She was heavily influenced by extreme weather conditions.
Ⓒ She wants to share information about it with other people.
Ⓓ She wanted a major that could provide her various job options.

4. 여자는 왜 기상학을 전공하기로 했는가?

Ⓐ 기상 캐스터가 된 친척에게 영감을 받아서
Ⓑ 자신이 기상이변에 엄청난 영향을 받아서
Ⓒ 기상학에 대한 정보를 다른 사람들과 공유하고 싶어서
Ⓓ 다양한 직업 선택권을 제공해 줄 수 있는 전공을 원해서

5. What will the woman do next?

Ⓐ Consider what kind of field she wants to work in
Ⓑ Search for any kind of available jobs online
Ⓒ Go and see an advisor to talk about changing her major
Ⓓ Try to find an internship position that is related to her major

5. 여자는 다음에 무엇을 할 것인가?

Ⓐ 어떤 분야에서 일하고 싶은지 생각해본다
Ⓑ 가능한 온라인 채용 공고를 검색해본다
Ⓒ 자신의 전공을 바꾸는 것에 대해 이야기할 조언자를 만난다
Ⓓ 전공과 관련된 인턴 자리를 알아본다

어휘 business n 경영학 | major n 전공 | ecology n 생태학 | administration n 행정 | forbid v 금지하다 | introductory adj 입문의 | minor n 부전공 | requirement n 필수 조건, 요소 | green adj 환경 보호의, 환경친화적인 | pollute v 오염시키다 | contribute to 기여하다 | global warming 지구 온난화 | ecologist n 생태학자 | meteorology n 기상학 | predict v 예측하다 | meteorologist n 기상학자 | specific adj 구체적인, 명확한 | job description 직무 기술서 | oil drilling 석유 채굴 | transportation n 수송 | labor force 노동력, 노동 인구 | incorporate v 포함하다 | intense adj 강렬한, 극심한 | blizzard n 눈보라 | tornado n 회오리바람 | significant adj 중대한

Lecture 1

본서 | P. 24

Man: Student | Woman: Professor

[6-11] Listen to part of a discussion in an art class.

W [6] The images you can see on this stone are called petroglyphs, and such drawings have been found worldwide. In this sample, which is called Newspaper Rock due to the dense collection of images on it, you can see the typical motifs for petroglyphs. These include people's hands, human figures, and animals. [7] More sophisticated ones actually depict entire scenes of hunting expeditions or tell other stories like creation myths and historical conflicts. Many also include geometric shapes, which can also be quite intricate, and some are even mazes. [8] They are

남자: 학생 | 여자: 교수

미술 수업 중 토론의 일부를 들으시오.

여 [6] 이 돌에서 볼 수 있는 그림은 암각화라고 불리는데, 이러한 그림들은 전 세계적으로 발견되어 왔습니다. 그림들이 빽빽하게 모여 있어서 신문 바위라고 불리는 이 샘플에서는 암각화의 일반적인 주제들을 볼 수 있죠. 이는 사람의 손, 인간의 형상, 그리고 동물들을 포함합니다. [7] 좀 더 세련된 것들은 실제로 전체적인 사냥 원정 장면을 묘사하거나 창조 신화와 역사적 갈등과 같은 다른 이야기들을 전하기도 합니다. 많은 암각화들이 또한 기하학적 모양을 포함하는데, 그것은 꽤나 복잡하며 심지어 몇

typically prehistoric, although there are more recent samples created by cultures that remained relatively primitive until fairly recently.

M 8 Professor, is it fair to call them primitive? I mean, some of these cultures had pretty well-organized societies, didn't they?

W You are quite correct, but you mistake my intention. I meant technologically less advanced, not inferior.

M Um, professor, I have a different question. Are the paintings found in caves like Lascaux, France, considered petroglyphs?

W No, although they are very similar in many aspects. Cave paintings are called "petrographs", which just means "rock image", whereas petroglyph means "rock carving". In essence, they are distinguished by technique, or medium if you will. 9 Petroglyphs are created by removing surface material from a stone by carving, picking, or abrading the stone with other tougher material. The outer surface has been weathered, so it has a different color from the interior stone called a patina. Removing this patina creates a color contrast that is used to draw the image. 9 Petrographs are painted onto the surface with natural pigments like charcoal and ocher, and they are more delicate. Just breathing on them damages them.

10 But, that doesn't mean that petroglyphs cannot be damaged easily. In fact, scientists often damage them when they try to record them. Over time, the revealed stone will weather too, making it difficult to see the images with untrained eyes. In the past, scientists would try to reproduce them by placing paper over them and rubbing it with chalk. This caused minor damage, but others would attempt to restore the images by removing more stone or applying paint to the stone as the original artists sometimes did. Such efforts are misguided as they do not restore the image—they destroy the original. In worse cases, people will add their own images. At best, this makes the originals difficult to study, and at worst, it destroys the older images. Worse still, some people remove entire images from the stone as souvenirs, which causes two serious problems. It disrupts the continuity of the images and destroys their context, and it often obliterates other images around them. For these reasons, scientists also no longer try to remove these images to preserve them in museums. There is special legislation to protect these valuable images in some countries, and those who are caught face serious fines and incarceration.

11 For many cultures, these are the only record of their existence we can find. Of course, we may be able to unearth bones nearby, but graves can only provide limited

개는 미로이기도 해요. 8 꽤 최근까지 비교적 원시적으로 남아 있었던 문명들에서 만든 더 최근의 샘플들도 있지만, 암각화는 일반적으로 선사 시대의 것들입니다.

남 8 교수님, 그들을 원시적이라고 부르는 것이 타당한가요? 제 말은, 이들 문명 중 몇몇은 상당히 잘 조직된 사회를 갖추고 있었잖아요, 그렇지 않나요?

여 학생의 말이 맞지만, 저의 의도를 오해했네요. 제 말은, 이들이 질적으로 낮은 문명이 아니라 기술적으로 덜 발전했다는 말이었어요.

남 음, 교수님, 다른 질문이 있습니다. 프랑스의 라스코에서 발견된 벽화들도 암각화로 볼 수 있나요?

여 아니요, 그들이 많은 면에서 매우 비슷하긴 하지만 아닙니다. 동굴 벽화들은 그저 '바위 그림'이라는 뜻의 '암화'라고 불리는 반면, 암각화는 '바위 조각'을 의미합니다. 본질적으로 이 둘은 기술 혹은 수단에 의해 구별되죠. 9 암각화는 다른 더 단단한 재료로 돌을 조각하고, 파내기하고, 혹은 연마하는 방법으로 돌의 표면을 제거하여 만들어집니다. 겉 표면은 풍화 작용으로 인해 돌 내부의 색과 다른, 녹청이라 불리는 것을 갖고 있죠. 그림을 그리는 데 사용되는 색의 대비는 이 녹청을 제거함으로써 만들어집니다. 9 암화는 숯이나 황토 같은 자연 색소로 돌의 표면에 그린 것이며, 훨씬 더 연약합니다. 이들에게 그저 숨만 내쉬어도 손상을 입어요.

10 그러나 이는 암각화가 쉽게 손상을 입을 수 없다는 뜻은 아닙니다. 실제로, 과학자들은 이들을 기록하려고 할 때 종종 손상을 입히죠. 시간이 지나면서, 드러난 돌들도 풍화 작용을 거쳐서 미숙련된 눈으로 보면 알아보기 어려울 겁니다. 과거에는 과학자들이 암각화들 위에 종이를 놓고 분필로 문지르는 방법으로 이들을 복제하려고 했었죠. 이 방법은 작은 손상을 일으켰지만, 다른 이들은 원작가가 때때로 그랬듯이 돌을 더 제거하거나 페인트를 칠함으로써 그림을 다시 복원하려 했어요. 이러한 노력들은 원본을 복원하는 것이 아니라 파괴하는 것이기 때문에 잘못된 판단입니다. 더 심한 경우에는 사람들이 그들만의 그림을 더하려고 했어요. 이 방법은 잘해 봤자 원본 연구를 더 어렵게 만들 뿐이며, 최악의 경우 예전 그림을 파괴합니다. 안 좋은 경우는 또 있는데, 어떤 이들은 기념물로 삼겠다며 돌에서 그림 전체를 떼어내는데, 이는 두 가지 심각한 문제를 초래합니다. 그림의 연속성을 방해하며 내용을 파괴하고, 종종 주변의 다른 그림들을 지워버리죠. 이러한 이유들로 인해 과학자들은 더 이상 이들을 박물관에 보존하기 위해 떼어내려고 하지 않습니다. 몇몇 나라에는 이 귀중한 그림들을 보호하기 위한 특별법이 있으며, 파괴하려다 잡힌 사람들은 엄청난 벌금을 물거나 투옥되기도 해요.

information. Rock art provides us a window into the minds of these ancient people.

11 What did they think about, what did they value, and how did they see their world? These are all important questions that rock art can help us answer.

They are also important because they are the genesis of writing. In some cultures, we can trace the evolution from simple images of the actual things they represent, logograms, to images that symbolized concepts, ideograms. The next step, which many of these cultures never had the opportunity to take, was to develop a written language. The images would have come to represent individual syllables, and then simplified in form until they were not images at all, just symbols. After further simplification, they would become individual letters and constitute an alphabet.

11 많은 문명에 있어, 이 벽화들은 우리가 그들의 존재를 찾을 수 있는 유일한 기록입니다. 물론 근처에서 뼈들을 발굴할 수도 있겠지만 무덤에서 얻을 수 있는 정보에는 한계가 있죠. 암석 벽화는 고대 사람들의 마음을 볼 수 있는 창을 우리에게 제공해 줍니다.

11 그들은 무슨 생각을 했고, 무엇을 가치 있게 여겼으며, 그리고 세상을 어떻게 보았을까요? 이들은 우리가 답하는 데 암석 벽화가 도움이 될 수 있는 모두 중요한 질문들입니다.

암석 벽화가 중요한 또 다른 점은 이들이 글쓰기의 시초이기 때문입니다. 우리는 몇몇 문명에서 실제 사물들의 단순한 이미지를 나타내는 어표에서부터 개념을 상징화한 표의 문자까지의 진화를 추적할 수 있어요. 이들 많은 문명이 기회를 갖지 못했던 다음 단계는 문자 언어를 발전시키는 것이었죠. 그림들은 각 음절들을 나타냈고, 그 뒤 그림이 아닌 기호가 될 때까지 형상으로 단순화되었습니다. 단순화 과정을 더 거쳐 각각의 글자가 되고 문자를 구성하게 되는 것이죠.

6. What is the discussion mainly about?

Ⓐ The origin of written languages in some regions
Ⓑ The characteristics and importance of petroglyphs
Ⓒ The study of petroglyphs and petrographs
Ⓓ The methods used for creating petroglyphs

7. According to the discussion, what is one of the common motifs for petroglyphs?

Ⓐ People who are planting and harvesting
Ⓑ Methods for gathering fruits and vegetables
Ⓒ Different stories regarding myths and history
Ⓓ Various tools that were used for hunting

8. Listen again to part of the discussion. Then answer the question.

W They are typically prehistoric, although there are more recent samples created by cultures that remained relatively primitive until fairly recently.
M Professor, is it fair to call them primitive?

Why does the student say this:

M Professor, is it fair to call them primitive?

Ⓐ He thinks the professor is underestimating the societies of well-developed cultures.

6. 토론은 주로 무엇에 대한 것인가?

Ⓐ 몇몇 지역의 문자 언어의 기원
Ⓑ 암각화의 특징과 중요성
Ⓒ 암각화와 암화의 연구
Ⓓ 암각화를 만드는 데 사용된 기법들

7. 토론에 의하면, 암각화의 흔한 주제들 중 하나는 무엇인가?

Ⓐ 씨를 심고 추수하는 사람들
Ⓑ 과일과 채소를 모으는 방법들
Ⓒ 신화와 역사에 대한 다양한 이야기들
Ⓓ 사냥에 사용된 여러 가지 도구들

8. 토론의 일부를 듣고 질문에 답하시오.

여 꽤 최근까지 비교적 원시적으로 남아 있었던 문명들에서 만든 더 최근의 샘플들도 있지만, 암각화는 일반적으로 선사 시대의 것들입니다.
남 교수님, 그들을 원시적이라고 부르는 것이 타당한가요?

학생은 왜 이렇게 말하는가:

남 교수님, 그들을 원시적이라고 부르는 것이 타당한가요?

Ⓐ 잘 발달된 문명의 사회를 교수가 저평가한다고 생각한다.

Ⓑ He is not sure whether he is allowed to call their cultures primitive or not.

Ⓒ He is emphasizing that calling other cultures primitive could be insulting to them.

Ⓓ He wants to distinguish some prehistoric societies and cultures as primitive ones.

9. According to the discussion, what is the difference between petroglyphs and petrographs? Choose 2 answers.

Ⓐ Harder material was used for petroglyphs.

Ⓑ Petroglyphs were more colorful than petrographs.

Ⓒ Petrographs are destroyed more easily.

Ⓓ Petroglyphs were more common than petrographs.

10. Why does the professor mention chalk?

Ⓐ To give an example of a common tool that ancient people used

Ⓑ To illustrate that it was helpful for adding finer details to images

Ⓒ To introduce a medium the people used for creating petroglyphs

Ⓓ To explain one of the older methods for recording petroglyphs

11. According to the professor, what can be inferred about rock art?

Ⓐ It represents people's highly developed skills in stone masonry.

Ⓑ It was found mostly in caves, which were located in remote regions.

Ⓒ It was usually very long, extending more than 2 meters.

Ⓓ It provides more information than bones do when studying prehistoric people.

Ⓑ 그들의 문명을 원시적이라고 부르는 것이 허락되었는지 확실하지 않다.

Ⓒ 다른 문명을 원시적이라고 부르는 것이 그들에게 모욕적일 수 있다고 강조하고 있다.

Ⓓ 몇몇 선사 시대 사회와 문화를 원시적인 것으로 구별하고 싶어 한다.

9. 토론에 의하면, 암각화와 암화의 차이는 무엇인가? 두 개를 고르시오.

Ⓐ 암각화에는 더 단단한 재료가 사용되었다.

Ⓑ 암각화는 암화보다 더 색채가 풍부했다.

Ⓒ 암화는 더 쉽게 파괴된다.

Ⓓ 암각화는 암화보다 더 흔했다.

10. 교수는 왜 분필을 언급하는가?

Ⓐ 고대 사람들이 사용했던 일반적인 도구의 예시를 들려고

Ⓑ 분필이 그림에 더 섬세한 세부 사항들을 추가하는 데 도움이 되었다는 것을 보여주려고

Ⓒ 암각화를 만드는 데 사람들이 사용했던 수단을 소개하려고

Ⓓ 암각화를 기록하는 좀 더 오래된 기법들 중 하나를 설명하려고

11. 교수에 의하면, 암석 벽화에 대해 무엇을 추론할 수 있는가?

Ⓐ 사람들의 뛰어나게 발달된 석공술을 나타낸다.

Ⓑ 대부분 외진 지역에 위치해 있는 동굴들에서 발견되었다.

Ⓒ 보통 매우 길이가 길었으며 2미터가 넘게 뻗어 있었다.

Ⓓ 선사 시대 사람들에 대해 연구할 때 뼈보다 더 많은 정보를 제공한다.

어휘 petroglyph n 암각화, 암면 조각 I worldwide adj 전 세계적인 I dense adj 빽빽한 I typical adj 일반적인 I motif n 주제, 모티프 I sophisticated adj 세련된, 교양 있는 I depict v 그리다, 묘사하다 I expedition n 탐험, 원정 I myth n 신화 I historical adj 역사적인 I conflict n 갈등 I geometric adj 기하학의 I intricate adj 복잡한 I maze n 미로 I typically adv 보통, 일반적으로 I prehistoric adj 선사 시대의 I recent adj 최근의 I relatively adv 비교적 I primitive adj 원시 사회의, 원시적인 I intention n 의도, 목적 I technologically adv 기술적으로 I advanced adj 선진의, 고급의 I inferior adj 열등한, 질 낮은 I aspect n 측면, 양상 I carve v 조각하다, 깎아서 만들다 I distinguish v 구별하다 I abrade v 마멸시키다 I patina n (돌이나 금속의 표면에 생기는) 녹청 I contrast n 차이, 대비 I pigment n 색소 I charcoal n 숯 I ocher n 황토 I delicate adj 연약한, 섬세한 I damage v 손상을 입히다 I record v 기록하다, 적어 놓다 I reveal v 드러내다, 밝히다 I untrained adj 훈련을 받지 않은, 미숙련의 I reproduce v 복제하다, 복사하다 I chalk n 분필, 백악 I restore v 회복시키다, 되찾다 I souvenir n 기념품 I disrupt v 방해하다, 지장을 주다 I continuity n 지속성, 연속성 I context n 맥락, 전후 사정 I obliterate v 없애다, 지우다 I preserve v 보존하다, 보호하다 I legislation n 제정법 I valuable adj 귀중한 I fine n 벌금 I incarceration n 투옥, 감금 I existence n 존재 I unearth v 발굴하다, 파내다 I ancient adj 고대의 I genesis n 기원, 발생 I evolution n 진화 I represent v 나타내다 I logogram n 어표 I symbolize v 상징하다 I ideogram n 표의 문자, 기호 I syllable n 음절 I simplify v 단순화하다, 간소화하다 I simplification n 단순화, 간소화 I constitute v ~를 구성하다

Man: Professor | Woman: Student

[12-17] Listen to part of a discussion in a biology class.

M 12 Traditionally, we humans have viewed ourselves as the most intelligent species on the planet, and we have created a hierarchy among members of the animal kingdom based upon our perception of their intelligence relative to our own. 13 Which animals do you think typically fall within the top five?

W 13 Well, chimpanzees obviously, since they are our closest genetic cousins and they use tools. Dolphins are very intelligent as well. They use sophisticated language and are very social.

M 13 Yes, both are good choices. Are there any others?

W 13 Dogs are very smart. We use them to perform a variety of tasks and they understand commands. Horses seem pretty smart, too. Oh, and elephants! They show emotions similar to empathy and grief!

M Again, those are all very good choices. 12, 14 However, did you notice that for each species, you named a specific type of intelligence or ability that shows how clever they are? All of those are traits that we naturally look for since we also possess them. And, therein lies the flaw with human evaluation of animal intelligence: our system of evaluation is human-centric. We perceive them as having limited abilities, but our view is biased.
Because of this, many experiments regarding animal intelligence are being re-examined, and new evidence is being discovered. 15 This evidence was always present, but because scientists did not notice it, they assumed it to be entirely absent. Unfortunately, it has influenced much of our research. For example, imagine that you are walking through a forest. As you walk, you hear and see many animals; however, you do not hear or see any woodpeckers. Does the fact that you are not experiencing any evidence of woodpeckers mean that they do not exist in that forest?

W No, not really. They could just be sleeping or something.

M Exactly! But, researchers have often taken that view when studying nonhuman animal intelligence. Now, let's analyze two species: dogs; which are traditionally thought of as intelligent, and sheep; which are considered to lack intelligence. Interestingly, these are believed to be the two oldest domesticated species, although for different purposes. Dogs were domesticated to be companion animals to help us hunt, herd livestock, and provide protection. Sheep were tamed to be livestock used for food and sometimes as beasts of burden. That is where our biased view begins.

남자: 교수 | 여자: 학생

생물학 수업 중 토론의 일부를 들으시오.

남 12 전통적으로, 우리 인간들은 스스로를 지구상에서 가장 지능이 높은 종으로 여겨 왔습니다. 그리고 우리는 동물계에 속한 동물들을 우리에게 상대적인 지능에 기반하여 계급을 매겼습니다. 13 일반적으로 상위 5위 안에 드는 동물이 무엇일 거라고 생각하나요?

여 13 음, 당연히 침팬지예요. 우리와 유전적으로 가장 닮았고, 도구를 사용하니까요. 돌고래들 역시 매우 지능이 높아요. 정교한 언어를 사용하고 매우 사회적인 동물들이죠.

남 13 네, 둘 다 좋은 답변들이네요. 다른 동물들이 또 있을까요?

여 13 개들도 매우 똑똑해요. 우리는 개들로 하여금 여러 가지 일들을 하도록 하고, 개들은 명령을 알아들어요. 말들 역시 꽤 똑똑해 보이죠. 아, 그리고 코끼리요! 코끼리들은 공감이나 슬픔과 비슷한 감정을 보여요.

남 또다시 좋은 답변들을 해줬네요. 12, 14 그러나 알아차렸나요? 이들이 얼마나 똑똑한지를 보여주는 특정한 종류의 지능이나 능력을 학생이 언급했다는 것을요. 이 모든 특징들은 우리가 이미 가지고 있기에 자연스럽게 다른 동물들에게서도 찾게 되는 특성들입니다. 그리고 여기에 인간이 평가하는 동물 지능의 결함이 있어요. 우리의 평가 체계가 인간 중심적이라는 거죠. 우리는 동물들이 제한적인 능력을 가지고 있다고 인식하지만, 이러한 시각은 편향된 것입니다.
이 때문에 동물 지능에 대한 많은 실험들이 다시 관찰되고 있으며 새로운 증거가 발견되고 있어요. 15 이 증거는 항상 있었지만 과학자들이 알아차리지 못했기에 아예 존재하지 않는 것으로 가정했던 것입니다. 불행히도, 이는 우리의 연구에 많은 영향을 끼쳤어요. 예를 들어, 여러분이 숲속을 걷고 있다고 상상해 보세요. 걸으면서 여러분은 많은 동물들을 보고 듣습니다. 그러나 딱따구리를 보거나 듣지는 못해요. 딱따구리의 흔적을 여러분이 경험하지 못한다는 사실이 그들이 그 숲에 존재하지 않는다는 걸 의미할까요?

여 아니요, 그런 건 아닙니다. 그냥 잠을 지고 있거나 그런 걸 수도 있어요.

남 바로 그거예요! 그러나 연구원들은 인간이 아닌 동물들을 연구할 때 종종 이러한 인식을 가졌어요. 그럼 이제, 전통적으로 지능이 높다고 여겨졌던 개와 지능이 떨어진다고 여겨졌던 양, 이 두 동물들을 분석해봅시다. 흥미롭게도, 개와 양은 인간에 의해 가

We noticed particular traits in dogs that we considered valuable, but that the sheep lacked. So, over thousands of years, we trained and selectively bred dogs to fulfill our own needs. In addition, most of the modern breeds only came into existence in the last few centuries, and intelligence varies a lot between breeds, so it is reasonable to say that we have made dogs into what we want them to be. **16** Are they actually intelligent? Well, if we examine their wild cousins—wolves, foxes, coyotes, etc.—then I doubt anyone would call them intelligent.

17 Yet, we consider sheep to be among the least intelligent species. The traits that made them useful as livestock and pack animals are the very reasons that we consider them unintelligent. They tend to flock together and move in a disorganized fashion, and they spend all day docilely eating grass. However, recent research has revealed that when given initial learning tests, they rate as well or higher than rats and monkeys on certain tasks. Not only that, but they seem to have good facial recognition, can mentally map out their surroundings, and may even be able to plan ahead. Sheep have been able to perform tasks that other large mammals except for primates appear to lack the executive cognitive ability to successfully complete. This clearly shows that we need to reevaluate our standards.

장 오래 전부터 사육된 두 종의 동물들로 알려져 있습니다. 비록 이들을 사육한 목적은 서로 다르지만요. 개는 인간의 사냥 돕기, 가축 몰기, 보호 제공을 위한 반려 동물로 사육되었습니다. 양은 먹거리로 사용되기 위해 가축으로 길들여졌으며 때로는 짐을 나르는 데도 쓰였어요. 여기에서 우리의 편향된 시각이 시작된 겁니다.

우리는 양이 가지고 있지 않은, 우리가 생각했을 때 가치 있는 특별한 특성들을 개에게서 발견했습니다. 그래서 수천 년의 시간에 걸쳐 우리는 우리의 필요를 만족시키기 위해 개를 훈련시켰고 선택적으로 번식시켜 왔어요. 그리고 대부분의 현대 교배종들은 지난 몇 세기 안에 생겨난 종들이며 이들의 지능은 교배종에 따라 매우 다릅니다. 그러므로 우리가 개들을 우리가 원하는 모습으로 만들어왔다고 말하는 게 타당한 거겠죠. **16** 개들은 실제로 지능이 높을까요? 음, 개들의 야생 사촌들인 늑대, 여우, 코요테 등을 살펴보면 이들이 지능이 높다고 말할 사람은 별로 없을 것 같군요.

17 그런데도 우리는 양들을 가장 지능이 낮은 동물들 중 하나로 여기고 있습니다. 가축으로, 그리고 짐 나르는 동물로 쓸모 있다는 특성이 바로 이들을 지능이 낮다고 여기게 된 이유인 것이죠. 양들은 떼를 짓는 경향이 있으며 무질서하게 이동하고, 온순하게 풀을 뜯으며 하루를 보냅니다. 그러나 초기 학습 테스트를 했을 때 양들이 특정 과제에서 쥐와 원숭이와 비슷하거나 더 높은 점수를 받았다고 최근의 연구에서 밝혀졌습니다. 그뿐만이 아니라, 이들은 얼굴 인식을 잘하며 주변 환경을 마음속으로 그려볼 수 있으며, 그리고 심지어 미리 계획을 세울 수도 있다는 것이 밝혀졌어요. 영장류를 제외한 다른 대형 포유류들은 고급 인식 능력이 부족하여 성공적으로 해낼 수 없는 것처럼 보이는 과제들을 양들은 성공적으로 해낼 수 있었습니다. 이는 우리의 기준을 다시 평가할 필요가 있다는 것을 분명히 보여주죠.

12. What is the main topic of the discussion?

Ⓐ How complex the theories regarding intelligent animals are
Ⓑ How humanity's perspective on intelligent species can have flaws
Ⓒ How five intelligent species are smarter than sheep
Ⓓ How scientists proved the intelligence of different animals

13. Why does the professor mention the top five intelligent animals?

12. 토론의 주제는 무엇인가?

Ⓐ 지능이 높은 동물들에 대한 이론들이 얼마나 복잡한가
Ⓑ 지능이 높은 종들에 대한 인간의 인식에 어떻게 오류가 있을 수 있는가
Ⓒ 지능 높은 다섯 종의 동물들이 어떻게 양보다 더 똑똑한가
Ⓓ 과학자들이 서로 다른 동물들의 지능을 어떻게 증명했는가

13. 교수는 왜 지능이 상위 5위인 동물들을 언급하는가?

Ⓐ To explain how they are related to the topic of the lecture
Ⓑ To continue the discussion regarding them from the last class
Ⓒ To check if the students finished their reading assignment
Ⓓ To describe how the lecture topic is influenced by them

Ⓐ 이들이 강의의 주제에 어떻게 관련되어 있는지 설명하려고
Ⓑ 지난 시간에 이어 이들에 대한 토론을 계속하려고
Ⓒ 학생들이 읽기 과제를 끝냈는지 확인하려고
Ⓓ 강의의 주제가 이들에 의해 어떠한 영향을 받았는지 서술하려고

14. According to the professor, what is the problem with human evaluation of animal intelligence?

Ⓐ Not enough animals were evaluated by scientists.
Ⓑ There are some traits that both humans and animals share.
Ⓒ The technology that mankind possess right now still needs improvement.
Ⓓ Humans have not evaluated animal behavior objectively.

14. 교수에 의하면, 동물의 지능에 대한 인간의 평가는 어떠한 문제점을 가지고 있는가?

Ⓐ 충분히 많은 동물들이 과학자들에 의해 평가되지 않았다.
Ⓑ 인간과 동물 둘 다 공유하고 있는 몇몇 특성이 있다.
Ⓒ 인간이 현재 보유하고 있는 기술은 여전히 발전이 필요하다.
Ⓓ 인간은 객관적으로 동물의 행동을 평가하지 않았다.

15. What does the professor try to convey through the example of woodpeckers?

Ⓐ Observing animals in the wild can bring unexpected discoveries.
Ⓑ Holding on to one's belief regarding animal behavior can be difficult.
Ⓒ Trusting one's instinct is vital when it comes to examining animal intelligence.
Ⓓ Just because something is not visible, that doesn't mean it is not there.

15. 교수는 딱따구리의 예시를 통해 무엇을 전달하려고 하는가?

Ⓐ 야생에서 동물들을 관찰하는 것은 예기치 못한 발견을 가져올 수 있다.
Ⓑ 동물의 행동에 대해 믿음을 가지는 것은 어려울 수 있다.
Ⓒ 동물의 지능을 관찰함에 있어 스스로의 본능을 믿는 것은 중요하다.
Ⓓ 무언가가 눈에 보이지 않는다고 해서 그곳에 없다는 것은 아니다.

16. Why does the professor say this:

> M Are they actually intelligent? Well, if we examine their wild cousins—wolves, foxes, coyotes, etc.—then I doubt anyone would call them intelligent.

Ⓐ He thinks people should reevaluate their own beliefs regarding dogs.
Ⓑ He feels sorry that dogs' wild cousins are not very intelligent.
Ⓒ He wants to know if the students really view any of these animals as smart.
Ⓓ He believes that dogs often show some resemblance to their cousins.

16. 교수는 왜 이렇게 말하는가:

> 남 개들은 실제로 지능이 높을까요? 음, 개들의 야생 사촌들인 늑대, 여우, 코요테 등을 살펴보면 이들이 지능이 높다고 말할 사람은 별로 없을 것 같군요.

Ⓐ 사람들이 스스로 개에 대한 믿음을 재평가해야 한다고 생각한다.
Ⓑ 개들의 야생 사촌들이 그다지 지능이 높지 않다는 것에 유감을 느낀다.
Ⓒ 학생들이 이 동물들 중 어떤 것을 정말로 똑똑하다고 보는지 알고 싶어한다.
Ⓓ 개들이 그들의 사촌들과 닮은 점을 종종 보인다고 믿는다.

17. What can be inferred about sheep?

Ⓐ Their learning ability is far superior to that of dogs.
Ⓑ They showed startling behavior when exposed to unfamiliar surroundings.

17. 양에 대해 무엇을 추론할 수 있는가?

Ⓐ 이들의 학습 능력은 개들보다 훨씬 뛰어나다.
Ⓑ 낯선 환경에 노출되면 매우 놀라운 행동을 보였다.

Ⓒ Their evaluation as not-intelligent animals should be reconsidered.

Ⓓ They graze and move together in a disorganized fashion on purpose.

Ⓒ 이들이 지능적이지 않다는 평가는 재고되어야 한다.

Ⓓ 이들은 일부러 무질서하게 함께 풀을 뜯고 이동한다.

어휘 traditionally adv 전통적으로 | intelligent adj 똑똑한, 지능이 있는 | hierarchy n 계급, 계층 | perception n 지각, 자각 | intelligence n 지능 | relative adj 상대적인 | typically adv 일반적으로 | obviously adv 당연히 | genetic adj 유전의 | sophisticated adj 정교한, 세련된 | social adj 사회적인 | command n 명령 | empathy n 공감 | grief n 슬픔 | notice v 알아차리다 | species n 종 | specific adj 특정한 | trait n 특성 | naturally adv 자연스럽게 | possess v 소유하다 | flaw n 결함, 흠 | evaluation n 평가 | human-centric adj 인간 중심의 | perceive v 인지하다 | biased adj 선입견이 있는 | entirely adv 완전히 | absent adj 없는, 부재한 | woodpecker n 딱따구리 | nonhuman adj 인간이 아닌 | analyze v 분석하다 | domesticated adj 길들여진, 사육된 | companion n 동반자 | herd v (짐승을) 몰다 | livestock n 가축 | protection n 보호 | tame v 길들이다 | beast of burden 짐을 나르는 짐승 | particular adj 특별한 | valuable adj 귀중한 | selectively adv 선택적으로 | breed v 번식시키다, 사육하다 | fulfill v 만족시키다 | existence n 존재 | flock v 떼를 짓다, 무리를 짓다 | disorganized adj 무질서한, 체계적이지 않은 | docilely adv 온순하게 | initial adj 처음의, 초기의 | facial adj 얼굴의 | recognition n 인식 | mentally adv 정신적으로 | mammal n 포유류 | primate n 영장류 | executive adj 고급의 | cognitive adj 인식의 | complete v 완료하다 | reevaluate v 재평가하다 | standard n 기준

Conversation 2

본서 | P. 30

Man: Student | Woman: Professor

[1-5] Listen to part of a conversation between a student and a professor.

W Hey, Perry! You're looking well rested.

M Hi, Dr. Park! Yes, fall break was great. Spending a nice week at home was just the thing that I needed.

W I hope you were able to get some reading done too.

M I'm afraid not, although I regret it now.

W Well, it wasn't mandatory reading, so that's alright. But I do think you would have enjoyed the material.

M Yes, based on the title, I think so too. It seems to be just the kind of information I am interested in these days.

W **2** Well, I hope you get the chance to read it. Depending on what you decide to write on, you might find it really helpful.

M Right, I had that feeling. As a matter of fact, I think I want to write about something on the topic of language development.

W Really? I'm so glad you're so interested in it. Do you have any ideas in particular?

M Well, I was wondering if I could write about my nephew. He's just 18 months old, and it's been fascinating to see his language capacities change and grow.

W There's usually a lot happening at that age. What changes are you starting to see?

M Up until a few weeks ago, he only spoke in single words, mostly things like "dada" and "mama." But recently, he's started to understand things that his parents say. Of course, it's just simple stuff, basic commands like "stop that" or "come here."

남자: 학생 | 여자: 교수

학생과 교수의 대화를 들으시오.

여 안녕하세요, 페리! 푹 쉬신 것 같네요.

남 안녕하세요, 박 박사님! 네, 가을 방학은 좋았어요. 집에서 한 주를 잘 보내는 것이 저에게 딱 필요한 일이었죠.

여 독서도 좀 하셨길 바라요.

남 아쉽게도 못했는데, 이제 후회되네요.

여 뭐, 의무적으로 읽어야 하는 책은 아니었으니, 괜찮아요. 하지만 재미있게 보실 거라고 생각해요.

남 네, 제목만 보면 저도 그렇게 생각해요. 요즘 제가 딱 관심을 갖는 정보인 것 같아요.

여 **2** 그럼, 꼭 읽어보셨으면 좋겠네요. 어떤 내용을 쓰느냐에 따라, 정말 도움이 될 수도 있을 것 같아요.

남 네, 저도 그런 느낌이 들었어요. 사실, 언어 발달에 관한 글을 쓰고 싶다는 생각이 들어요.

여 정말요? 관심이 있다니 정말 다행이네요. 특별히 생각나는 게 있나요?

남 글쎄요, 제 조카에 대해 글을 써도 될까 생각 중이에요. 이제 막 18개월인데, 조카의 언어 능력이 변화하고 성장하는 것을 보는 것은 정말 흥미롭습니다.

여 그 나이에는 보통 많은 일이 일어나죠. 어떤 변화가 보이기 시작했나요?

남 몇 주 전까지만 해도 아들은 주로 "다다", "마마" 같은 한 단어로만 말을 했어요. 하지만 최근에는 부모님이 하는 말을 알아듣기 시작했어요. 물론 "그만해"나 "이리 와"와 같은 간단한 기본 명령입니다.

W That's great! It sounds like his language skills are developing on cue. A psychologist would say he's just starting the second stage of language skill development, where he's starting to understand things that people he's familiar with say.

M Yes! That's it! **3(D)** He can understand things that his parents say, but he can't understand me so well. And he definitely doesn't seem to understand sentences that his parents' friends say to him. He's also starting to make a few two-word sentences. He says things like "Hi, puppy!" or "Big dog."

W Once again, everything he's doing is exactly as described in language development textbooks. His parents will have to start getting used to that. **3(D)** He'll mostly be speaking in two-word sentences until the third stage, when he'll start using three-to-four-word sentences. That usually comes around the age of three, but if he's early, it could come while he's still two.

M Interesting. So that brings us to the question that I wanted to ask you: **1** could I write my paper on my nephew? I've been spending a lot of time observing him, even before I started taking your class. **4** Believe it or not, I've even taken notes because I find the whole thing so interesting.

W **4** That's not going to cut it. I commend your diligence and interest, but this particular assignment is another matter. The instructions make it pretty clear that it has to be based on literary research and not observational research.

M Is there some way to make it work? I am confident I can write a good paper on this. What if I promise to dedicate a certain portion of my research to secondary data? Say, 40 percent?

W Well the thing is, field research like what you want to do would require watching and observing more than just one kid. Plus, fieldwork is something that you'll be doing in your senior seminar, not in our class. I'm not necessarily against you mentioning your nephew in the paper, but you would need to devote a much larger portion of it to literary research. I would expect more than 95 percent to be focused on that. The remaining 5 percent might be used for discussion of other topics such as your nephew, as long as these topics serve as good examples to further demonstrate what you have found in your literary research.

M Alright. **5** I guess I need to give this a bit more thought!

여 잘됐네요! 아이의 언어 능력이 제때 발달하고 있는 것 같네요. 심리학자들은 이제 막 언어 능력 발달의 두 번째 단계에 진입했다고 표현하는데, 이 단계는 친숙한 사람들이 하는 말을 이해하기 시작하는 단계죠.

남 네! 그거예요! **3(C)** 부모님이 하는 말은 알아듣는데 제 말은 잘 못 알아듣는 것 같아요. 그리고 부모님 친구들이 말하는 문장은 확실히 이해하지 못하는 것 같아요. 두 단어로 된 문장들도 몇 개 만들기 시작했습니다. "안녕, 강아지!"나 "큰 개"와 같은 말을 하죠.

여 다시 한번 말하지만, 조카가 하는 모든 행동은 언어 발달 교과서에 설명된 것과 똑같아요. 부모님은 이제 익숙해지기 시작해야 할 거예요. **3(D)** 3~4단어 문장을 사용하기 시작하는 3단계의 이전까지는 대부분 두 단어 문장으로 말하게 될 것입니다. 보통 3세 무렵에 시작되지만, 빠르면 2세 때 시작될 수도 있습니다.

남 흥미롭네요. 그게 제가 물어보고 싶었던 질문과 이어지는데요. **1** 제 조카에 대한 논문을 써도 될까요? 저는 교수님 수업을 듣기 전부터 조카를 관찰하는 데 많은 시간을 보냈어요. **4** 믿기 어려우시겠지만, 저는 모든 것이 너무 흥미로워서 메모까지 했어요.

여 **4** 그것만으로는 부족해요. 학생의 성실함과 관심은 칭찬하지만 이 과제는 다른 문제입니다. 지시 사항에 따르면 관찰 연구가 아닌 학술 연구를 기반으로 해야 합니다.

남 어떻게 안 될까요? 저는 이 문제에 대해 좋은 논문을 쓸 수 있다고 확신합니다. 연구의 일정 부분을 2차 데이터에 할애하겠다고 약속하면 어떨까요? 예를 들어 40% 정도?

여 사실 학생이 하고자 하는 것과 같은 현장 연구는 한 명 이상의 어린이를 지켜보고 관찰해야 한다는 것이 문제입니다. 게다가, 현장 조사는 우리 수업이 아니라 졸업반 세미나에서 하게 될 일이에요. 논문에서 조카를 언급하는 것에 반대하는 것은 아니지만, 문헌 연구에 훨씬 더 많은 부분을 할애해야 할 것입니다. 저는 95% 이상이 문헌 연구에 집중되는 것을 기대해요. 나머지 5%는 조카와 같은 다른 주제에 대한 논의에 사용할 수 있으며, 이러한 주제가 문헌 연구에서 발견한 내용을 더 잘 보여줄 수 있는 좋은 예가 된다면 사용할 수 있습니다.

남 알겠습니다. **5** 좀 더 생각해 봐야겠어요!

1. Why does the student go to see the professor?

- (A) To analyze the language development of his nephew
- (B) To propose a topic for a class paper
- (C) To share information about his fall break
- (D) To talk about a supplementary reading

1. 학생이 교수를 만나러 간 이유는 무엇인가?

- (A) 조카의 언어 발달을 분석하기 위해
- (B) 수업 논문의 주제를 제안하기 위해
- (C) 가을 방학에 대한 정보를 공유하기 위해
- (D) 보충 독서에 대해 이야기하기 위해

2. Why is the professor disappointed that the student couldn't read the reading?

Ⓐ It was a required reading for the class.
Ⓑ It would have been greatly helpful to the student's paper topic.
Ⓒ It would have been useful for the student.
Ⓓ There will be no time to read it during the semester.

3. Which of the following is true about the student's nephew? Choose 2 answers.

Ⓐ He is currently towards the end of the second stage of language development.
Ⓑ He is mostly speaking in single-word utterances.
Ⓒ He understands his parents better than other speakers.
Ⓓ He will speak in very simple sentences for the next few months.

4. Listen again to part of the lecture. Then answer the question.

M Believe it or not, I've even taken notes because I find the whole thing so interesting.
W That's not going to cut it.

Why does the professor say this:

W That's not going to cut it.

Ⓐ She cannot reduce the student's workload.
Ⓑ The student's interest and diligence is misplaced.
Ⓒ She expects the student's notes are not going to be very detailed.
Ⓓ She does not find his research proposal sufficient.

5. What will the student most likely do next?

Ⓐ He will look for secondary data to use in his paper.
Ⓑ He will go over his notes on his nephew.
Ⓒ He will reconsider his choice of topic.
Ⓓ He will make an outline for his paper that meets his professor's demands.

2. 교수가 학생이 강의 자료를 읽지 못한 것에 실망한 이유는 무엇인가?

Ⓐ 수업에 필요한 필독 자료였기 때문이다.
Ⓑ 학생의 논문 주제에 큰 도움이 되었을 것이다.
Ⓒ 학생에게 유용했을 것이다.
Ⓓ 학기 중에 읽을 시간이 없을 것이다.

3. 다음 중 학생의 조카에 대해 사실인 것은 어느 것인가? 두 개를 고르시오.

Ⓐ 그는 현재 언어 발달의 두 번째 단계가 끝날 무렵이다.
Ⓑ 그는 보통 단일 단어로 말하고 있다.
Ⓒ 그는 다른 사람들보다 부모님의 말을 더 잘 이해한다.
Ⓓ 앞으로 몇 달 동안은 매우 간단한 문장으로 말할 것이다.

4. 강의의 일부를 다시 듣고 질문에 답하시오.

남 믿기 어려우시겠지만, 저는 모든 것이 너무 흥미로워서 메모까지 했어요.
여 그것만으로는 부족해요.

교수가 왜 이렇게 말하는가:

여 그것만으로는 부족해요.

Ⓐ 교수는 학생의 작업량을 줄일 수 없다.
Ⓑ 학생의 관심과 부지런함이 잘못되었다.
Ⓒ 교수는 학생의 노트가 매우 상세하지 않을 것으로 예상한다.
Ⓓ 교수는 학생의 연구 제안서가 충분하지 않다고 생각한다.

5. 이 학생은 다음으로 어떤 일을 할 가능성이 가장 높은가?

Ⓐ 자신의 논문에 사용할 보조 데이터를 찾을 것이다.
Ⓑ 그의 조카에 대한 자신의 메모를 검토할 것이다.
Ⓒ 자신이 선택한 주제를 재고할 것이다.
Ⓓ 교수의 요구 사항을 충족하는 논문 개요를 작성할 것이다.

어휘 rested adj 휴식을 충분히 취한 | fall break 가을 방학 | home n 집 | mandatory adj 의무적인 | material n 자료 | topic n 주제 | language development 언어 발달 | nephew n 조카 | capacity n 능력 | change v 변하다 | grow v 성장하다 | single adj 단일한 | understand v 이해하다 | command n 명령어 | stage n 단계 | familiar adj 익숙한 | sentence n 문장 | textbook n 교과서 | observe v 관찰하다 | class n 수업 | note n 노트, 기록 | diligence n 근면 | assignment n 과제 | instruction n 지시 사항 | literary research 문헌 연구 | observational adj 관찰의 | field research 현장 연구 | senior seminar 졸업 세미나 | discussion n 토론 | example n 예 | demonstrate v 보여주다

Man: Student | Woman: Professor

[6-11] Listen to part of a lecture in a film class.

W 6 I want to continue on our film genre series today and pick up where we left off. We last discussed the concept of genres, the different genres we encounter, and how filming technology and techniques change with each genre. Today, I want to dive into our first genre. Who here enjoys a good romantic comedy? I see. I'm glad to see that the genre isn't a dying artform. 7 The genre isn't at the top of my list personally, nor is it, from what I can tell, for most of the people around me. But that said, I have to acknowledge that the genre has great merit. 8 After all, if it didn't, surely William Shakespeare would never have dwelled on the comedic aspects of love so deeply. For instance, let's look at *Much Ado About Nothing*. Throughout the story of Claudio and Hero, audience members would laugh out loud at the physical humor, wordplay, and witty banter, among other comic devices. Shakespeare clearly understood that the tension that comes from the human experience of love pairs extremely well with humor. Funny moments would catch people off guard, and the release of tension would cause such an intensely strange feeling. He also understood that love was inherently funny. People do, say, and feel absurd things when they are in love.

M 8 I had no idea the idea of combining romance and humor to create a genre went back so far.

W Yes, it's really surprising how far back the roots of genres go. Now of course, Shakespeare, for all his expertise in creating drama, knew nothing about film. Still, he did arguably lay out the romantic comedy formula for us: two people meet and somehow become involved in a conflict, but then end up living happily ever after together. In the world of film, there were two movies that we might label as among the first romantic comedies: *Sherlock Jr.* and *Girl Shy*. But these were silent films, so many film historians skip these. It was quite difficult to create a genre centered around love and humor without dialogue. Perhaps we'll talk about those another day. Among the first rom coms we see among the so-called "talkies," *It Happened One Night* from 1934 stands out. 9 This is the perfect example of what we call "comedies of manners." It's a pretty familiar setup. A rich person falls in love with a poorer person, and all types of conflict and humor arise from this class disparity. In *It Happened One Night*, a wealthy woman falls in love with a dashing newspaper reporter who has just lost his job. Released right in the middle of the American Depression, the love and humor that arose between these

남자: 학생 | 여자: 교수

영화 강의의 일부를 들으시오.

여 6 오늘은 영화 장르 시리즈를 계속 이어가면서 지난번 이야기한 부분부터 다시 시작하겠습니다. 지난 시간에는 장르의 개념과 우리가 접하는 다양한 장르, 그리고 각 장르에 따라 촬영 기술과 기법이 어떻게 달라지는지에 대해 논의했습니다. 오늘은 첫 번째 장르를 살펴보고자 합니다. 로맨틱 코미디를 좋아하시는 분 계시나요? 그렇군요. 이 장르가 죽어가는 예술 장르가 아니어서 다행이네요. 7 개인적으로도 그렇고 제 주변 사람들도 대부분 로맨틱 코미디를 그다지 좋아하지 않아요. 하지만 이 장르에 큰 장점이 있다는 것은 인정해야 합니다. 8 그렇지 않았다면 윌리엄 셰익스피어가 사랑의 희극적 측면을 그렇게 깊이 있게 곱씹어 생각하지 않았을 것이 분명하니까요. 예를 들어, 〈헛소동〉을 살펴봅시다. 클라우디오와 히어로의 이야기가 진행되는 동안 관객들은 몸 개그, 말장난, 재치 있는 농담 등 다양한 희극적 장치에 큰 소리로 웃곤 했습니다. 셰익스피어는 사랑이라는 인간의 경험에서 오는 긴장감이 유머와 매우 잘 어울린다는 것을 분명히 이해했습니다. 유머러스한 순간은 사람들을 방심하게 만들고, 긴장이 풀리면 강렬하고 묘한 감정을 불러일으킵니다. 그는 또한 사랑이 본질적으로 재미있다는 것을 이해했습니다. 사람들은 사랑에 빠지면 터무니없는 일을 하고, 말하고, 느끼죠.

남 8 로맨스와 유머를 결합해 장르를 만들겠다는 생각이 이렇게까지 거슬러 올라갈 줄은 몰랐어요.

여 네, 장르의 뿌리가 얼마나 오래전으로 거슬러 올라가는지 정말 놀랍습니다. 물론 셰익스피어는 드라마 창작에 대한 전문 지식이 있었지만 영화에 대해서는 전혀 몰랐습니다. 하지만 그는 두 사람이 만나 갈등을 겪다가 결국에는 함께 행복하게 산다는 로맨틱 코미디의 공식을 제시했습니다. 영화계에서는 최초의 로맨틱 코미디로 분류할 수 있는 두 편의 영화 〈셜록 2세〉와 〈걸 샤이〉가 있습니다. 하지만 이 영화들은 무성 영화였기 때문에 많은 영화 역사학자들은 이 영화들을 제외하곤 합니다. 대화 없이 사랑과 유머가 중심이 되는 장르를 만드는 것은 꽤 어려운 일이었습니다. 이 이야기는 다음에 다시 하도록 하죠. 소위 '토키'라고 불리는 영화 중 최초의 로맨틱 코미디 1934년 작 〈어느 날 밤에 생긴 일〉이 눈에 띕니다. 9 이것은 우리가 '풍속희극'이라고 부르는 것의 완벽한 예입니다. 꽤 익숙한 설정입니다. 부자가 가난한 사람과 사랑에 빠지고, 이 계급적 격차에서 온갖 종류의 갈등과 유머가 생겨납니다. 영화 〈어느 날 밤에 생긴 일〉에서는 부유한 여성이 실

two characters spoke volumes. It told people that money really didn't buy you everything you wanted, but money and perhaps even love did give people hope.

10 We also see romantic comedies take the form of so-called "screwball comedies." Does anybody here play baseball? If so, you might have heard of screwballs in that context. When a pitcher throws a screwball, it means the ball flies in an unexpected path. Screwball comedies are similar to this. They take unexpected twists and turns using witty dialogue, slapstick comedy, and fast-paced plots. Audiences are taken on a ride throughout the story. Arguably the poster child of the screwball rom com is Katharine Hepburn. In her 1938 film *Bringing Up Baby*, Hepburn plays a wealthy heiress who comes across a handsome paleontologist who is trying to secure a million dollars for his museum. The film's arsenal of humor includes masquerade, farce, absurdism, slapstick, situational humor, and more. That list itself takes you on quite a roller coaster ride! And this diversity in humor styles reflects the twists and turns in the movie's plot as well.

What comes next is an openness to more mature themes. In the 1960s and 1970s, people began speaking more freely about these issues due to societal changes. What's more, film regulators introduced an age rating system, which meant that films could explore more adult-oriented themes as long as they were only shown to older audiences. **11** Films like *Desk Set* and *Lover Come Back* are excellent examples of this era's romantic comedy. There's one scene from the latter that I wanted to show you. Let's get the lights.

직한 멋진 신문 기자와 사랑에 빠집니다. 미국 대공황의 한가운데에 개봉한 이 영화는 두 인물 사이에서 벌어지는 사랑과 유머를 통해 많은 것을 말해줍니다. 이 영화는 돈으로 원하는 모든 것을 살 수는 없지만, 돈과 사랑은 사람들에게 희망을 줄 수 있다는 메시지를 전했습니다.

10 로맨틱 코미디는 소위 '스크루볼 코미디'의 형태를 띠기도 합니다. 여기 야구를 하는 분이 있나요? 그렇다면 그런 맥락에서 스크루볼에 대해 들어보셨을 겁니다. 투수가 스크루볼을 던질 때 공이 예상치 못한 경로로 날아간다는 뜻입니다. 스크루볼 코미디도 이와 비슷합니다. 재치 있는 대화, 슬랩스틱 코미디, 빠르게 진행되는 플롯을 통해 예상치 못한 반전을 선사합니다. 관객은 이야기 내내 스릴을 만끽합니다. 스크루볼 로맨틱 코미디의 대명사는 단연 캐서린 헵번입니다. 1938년 영화 〈베이비 길들이기〉에서 헵번은 박물관을 위해 백만 달러를 확보하려는 잘생긴 고생물학자를 만나게 되는 부유한 상속녀 역을 맡았습니다. 이 영화에는 거짓 행세, 희극, 부조리극, 슬랩스틱, 상황 유머 등 다양한 유머가 등장합니다. 이 목록만 봐도 롤러코스터를 타는 기분이 듭니다! 그리고 이러한 다양한 유머 스타일은 영화 줄거리의 우여곡절도 반영하고 있습니다.

다음으로는 보다 성숙한 주제에 대한 개방성입니다. 1960년대와 1970년대에 사람들은 사회적 변화로 인해 이러한 문제에 대해 더 자유롭게 이야기하기 시작했습니다. 또한 영화 감사 기관은 연령 등급 시스템을 도입하여 영화가 연령대가 높은 관객에게만 상영되는 한 성인용 주제를 더 많이 다룰 수 있게 되었습니다. **11** 〈사랑의 전주곡〉이나 〈연인이여 돌아오라〉과 같은 영화는 이 시대의 로맨틱 코미디를 보여주는 훌륭한 예입니다. 후자의 한 장면을 보여드리고 싶었습니다. 불을 끄죠.

6. What does the professor mainly talk about?

Ⓐ Some of romantic comedy's landmark feature films
Ⓑ Characteristics and types of romantic comedy
Ⓒ The roots and history of romantic comedy as a genre
Ⓓ The influence of various rom com sub genres on subsequent movements

7. What is the professor's opinion on romantic comedies?

Ⓐ She is relieved to see a few people enjoy the genre.
Ⓑ She believes that romantic comedies have been on the decline in recent years.
Ⓒ The genre doesn't suit her taste as much as other genres.
Ⓓ The genre receives more attention than it deserves.

6. 교수는 주로 무엇에 대해 이야기하는가?

Ⓐ 로맨틱 코미디의 획기적인 장편 영화 몇 편
Ⓑ 로맨틱 코미디의 특징 및 유형
Ⓒ 장르로서의 로맨틱 코미디의 뿌리와 역사
Ⓓ 다양한 로맨틱 코미디 하위 장르가 이후의 경향에 미친 영향

7. 로맨틱 코미디에 대한 교수의 의견은 무엇인가?

Ⓐ 그녀는 몇몇 사람들이 이 장르를 즐기는 것을 보고 안도한다.
Ⓑ 그녀는 최근 몇 년 동안 로맨틱 코미디가 쇠퇴하고 있다고 생각한다.
Ⓒ 이 장르는 다른 장르만큼 그녀의 취향에 맞지 않는다.
Ⓓ 이 장르가 과분한 관심을 받는다.

8. According to the lecture, how does romantic comedy find its roots in Shakespeare?
Ⓐ Shakespeare worked with the interplay of romance and comedy in some of his plays.
Ⓑ *Much Ado About Nothing* provided the formula for modern romantic comedy films.
Ⓒ Shakespeare used comedy to make love stories less boring.
Ⓓ Shakespeare added physical humor, wordplay, and witty banter to some of his plays' tense moments.

9. According to the lecture, which of the following is true of comedies of manners? Choose 2 answers.
Ⓐ Films from this genre lacked dialogue.
Ⓑ The films often dealt with issues of economic disparity.
Ⓒ They were among the first so-called "talkies" of the film industry.
Ⓓ The genre became popular around the time of the American Depression.

10. According to the lecture, why were films such as *Bringing Up Baby* labeled as screwball comedies?
Ⓐ The plots of these films can be compared to a certain type of baseball pitch.
Ⓑ Their films often featured an absurd blend of many comedy types.
Ⓒ Katharine Hepburn used the term in one of her most iconic films.
Ⓓ The characters in these films were often very unusual.

11. What will the class most likely do next?
Ⓐ The teacher will turn on a few more lights for the class.
Ⓑ They will learn about the neoclassical romantic comedies of the 90s.
Ⓒ They will read part of the script of *Lover Come Back*.
Ⓓ They will watch a clip from a romantic comedy the professor just mentioned.

8. 강의에 따르면, 로맨틱 코미디는 셰익스피어에게서 어떻게 그 뿌리를 찾을 수 있나?
Ⓐ 셰익스피어는 그의 몇몇 희곡에서 로맨스와 코미디의 상호작용을 다루었다.
Ⓑ 〈헛소동〉이 현대 로맨틱 코미디 영화의 형식을 제공했다.
Ⓒ 셰익스피어는 사랑 이야기를 덜 지루하게 만들기 위해 코미디를 사용했다.
Ⓓ 셰익스피어는 연극의 긴장감 넘치는 순간에 몸 개그, 말장난, 재치 있는 농담을 추가했다.

9. 강의에 따르면, 다음 중 풍속희극에 해당하는 것은 다음 중 어느 것인가? 두 개를 고르시오.
Ⓐ 이 장르의 영화들은 대사가 부족했다.
Ⓑ 이 영화들은 종종 경제적 격차 문제를 다루었다.
Ⓒ 이 영화들은 영화 산업의 첫 번째 소위 "토키" 영화 중 하나였다.
Ⓓ 이 장르는 미국 대공황 시기에 인기를 끌었다.

10. 강의에 따르면, 〈베이비 길들이기〉와 같은 영화들이 스크루볼 코미디로 분류된 이유는 무엇인가?
Ⓐ 이 영화들의 플롯은 특정 유형의 야구 투구 구종에 비유할 수 있다.
Ⓑ 이 영화들은 종종 여러 가지 코미디 유형을 터무니없이 혼합한 것이 특징이다.
Ⓒ 캐서린 헵번이 자신의 가장 상징적인 영화 중 하나에서 이 용어를 사용했다.
Ⓓ 이 영화에 등장하는 캐릭터들은 종종 매우 특이했다.

11. 학급이 다음에 할 일로 가능성이 가장 높은 것은 무엇인가?
Ⓐ 교사는 수업을 위해 조명을 몇 개 더 켤 것이다.
Ⓑ 학생들은 90년대의 신고전주의 로맨틱 코미디에 대해 배울 것이다.
Ⓒ 〈연인이여 돌아오라〉의 대본 일부를 읽을 것이다.
Ⓓ 교수가 방금 언급한 로맨틱 코미디의 클립을 시청한다.

어휘 continue v 계속하다 | film genre 영화 장르 | concept n 개념 | encounter v 마주치다 | filming technology 촬영 기술 | technique n 기법 | dive into 살펴보다 | romantic comedy 로맨틱 코미디 | dying artform 죽어가는 예술 형태 | merit n 장점 | dwell on 곱씹어 생각하다 | comedic adj 코미디의 | aspect n 측면 | audience n 관객 | physical humor 몸 개그 | wordplay 언어유희 | witty banter 재치 있는 농담 | comic device 희극적 장치 | tension n 긴장감 | human experience 인간 경험 | pair v 짝을 이루다 | catch off guard 무방비 상태로 만들다 | release n 해방 | intensely adv 강렬하게 | absurd adj 불합리한 | root n 뿌리 | drama n 드라마 | formula n 공식 | conflict n 갈등 | ever after 그 후로 계속 | silent film 무성 영화 | dialogue n 대화 | comedy of manners 풍속희극 | class disparity 계

급 격차 | dashing adj 멋진, 늠름한 | newspaper reporter 신문 기자 | American Depression 미국 대공황 | screwball comedy 스크루볼 코미디 | baseball n 야구 | pitcher n 투수 | unexpected adj 예상치 못한 | witty dialogue 재치 있는 대화 | slapstick comedy 슬랩스틱 코미디 | fast-paced adj 빠른 속도의 | poster child 대표적 인물 | heiress n 상속녀 | paleontologist n 고생물학자 | museum n 박물관 | masquerade n 거짓 행세 | farce n 풍자극 | absurdism n 부조리주의 | situational humor 상황 유머 | roller coaster 롤러코스터 | mature adj 성숙한 | societal change 사회적 변화 | age rating system 연령 등급 시스템 | adult-oriented adj 성인용

Lesson 01 Main Idea

본서 | P. 40

Practice

Passage 1	B	Passage 2	B	Passage 3	D
Passage 4	B	Passage 5	C	Passage 6	B
Passage 7	C	Passage 8	D	Passage 9	C

Test

Passage 1	1. A	2. C	3. D	4. C	5. A
Passage 2	1. D	2. A, C	3. D	4. C	5. B

Practice

본서 | P. 44

Passage 1 Man: Professor | Woman: Student

Listen to part of a conversation between a student and a professor.

W Good afternoon, Professor Norton. Are you busy at the moment?

M Not at all, Bethany, how can I help you?

W I wasn't able to get a copy of the material you gave out in class today. They ran out before they reached my desk.

M I see. Of course you can. I'll get my assistant to make you a copy immediately. Oh, while you are here, I'd like to discuss your paper proposal. Could you spare a few minutes?

W My proposal? Certainly, Professor Norton.

남자: 교수 | 여자: 학생

학생과 교수의 대화를 들으시오.

여 안녕하세요, 노턴 교수님. 지금 바쁘신가요?

남 괜찮아요, 베타니, 무엇을 도와드릴까요?

여 오늘 수업 때 나눠주셨던 자료 복사본을 받지 못했어요. 제 책상에 오기 전에 다 떨어졌거든요.

남 전혀요. 물론 복사본 받을 수 있죠. 지금 내 조교에게 바로 한 부 복사해주라고 할게요. 아, 학생이 여기 왔으니 말인데, 학생의 리포트 제안서에 관해 논의하고 싶네요. 잠깐 시간 좀 낼 수 있나요?

여 제 제안서요? 그럼요, 노턴 교수님.

Q. Why did the student come to see the professor?

(A) To provide the reason why the student missed a class
(B) To ask for a handout that the student did not receive
(C) To discuss ideas for the student's next writing assignment
(D) To talk about an assignment that the student failed to complete

Q. 학생은 왜 교수를 만나러 왔는가?

(A) 학생이 수업에 참석하지 못한 이유를 제시하기 위해
(B) 학생이 받지 못한 프린트물을 요청하기 위해
(C) 학생의 다음 글쓰기 과제를 위한 아이디어를 논의하기 위해
(D) 학생이 완성하지 못한 과제에 대해 이야기하기 위해

어휘 copy n 복사본 | run out 떨어지다, 고갈되다 | assistant n 조교 | immediately adv 즉시, 바로 | discuss v 논의하다 | proposal n 제안서

Passage 2

Man: Professor | Woman: Student

Listen to part of a conversation between a student and a professor.

W Excuse me, professor. Can I speak to you about the school newspaper for a minute?

M Go ahead. What's on your mind?

W Well, I'm having some problems with a student reporter for the sports section. His stories are well written and he is really good at reporting, but he never meets the deadlines. I've spoken to him many times, but he doesn't seem to respond.

M There're some people who just cannot manage their time well enough to submit reports on time. It's difficult to motivate people to make deadlines, but that's your job as an editor.

W What can I do, then?

남자: 교수 | 여자: 학생

학생과 교수의 대화를 들으시오.

여 실례합니다, 교수님. 학교 신문에 대해 잠시 이야기 좀 할 수 있을까요?

남 말해보세요. 무슨 일이죠?

여 저, 스포츠 섹션의 학생 기자와 문제가 좀 있어서요. 그 기자는 기사도 잘 쓰고 보도에도 정말 능숙해요. 하지만 마감일을 지킨 적이 없어요. 제가 여러 번 이야기했지만, 반응이 없어요.

남 제때 보고서를 제출할 만큼 충분히 시간을 잘 관리할 수 없는 사람들이 좀 있죠. 마감일을 맞추도록 동기 부여를 하는 건 어려워요. 하지만 그것이 편집자로서 학생의 역할이죠.

여 그렇다면 제가 뭘 할 수 있을까요?

Q. Why did the student want to speak to the professor?

(A) She needs a new sports reporter for the school newspaper.

(B) She has a problem with the school newspaper's sports reporter.

(C) She wants to become a sports reporter for the school newspaper.

(D) She wants to create a sports section in the school newspaper.

Q. 학생은 왜 교수와 이야기하기를 원했는가?

(A) 학교 신문에 새로운 스포츠 기자가 필요해서

(B) 학교 신문 스포츠 기자와 문제가 있어서

(C) 학교 신문 스포츠 기자가 되고 싶어서

(D) 학교 신문에 스포츠 섹션을 만들고 싶어서

어휘 reporter n 기자 | report v 보도하다 | deadline n 마감 기한 | respond v 반응하다 | manage v 관리하다, ~를 해내다 | submit v 제출하다 | motivate v 동기 부여를 하다 | editor n 편집자

Passage 3

Man: Student | Woman: Housing officer

Listen to part of a conversation between a student and a housing officer.

W Good afternoon. How may I help you?

M I applied for my room to be repainted ages ago, but nothing's been done. I've had all my stuff packed away and boxed up to keep it out of the way of the workmen.

W That's strange. We usually repaint rooms very quickly to avoid inconveniencing people. Let me check the system to see what's happened. Ahh? Ahh... The painter's been around twice, but nobody was home. You didn't check the box on the form to allow access to your room when you were out, so he couldn't get inside.

M Oh, I didn't notice that when I filled out the form. What should I do now?

남자: 학생 | 여자: 기숙사 담당자

학생과 기숙사 담당자의 대화를 들으시오.

여 안녕하세요. 무엇을 도와드릴까요?

남 오래 전에 제 방을 새로 칠해달라고 신청했는데, 아무것도 안 해줘서요. 일하시는 분들에게 방해가 안 되도록 제 짐들을 다 싸서 보관하려고 박스에 담아 치워 놓았어요.

여 이상하군요. 저희는 대개 사람들을 불편하게 만드는 걸 피하기 위해서 페인트칠을 아주 빨리 다시 하거든요. 어떻게 된 일인지 시스템을 확인해 볼게요. 아? 아... 페인트 칠하는 사람이 두 번 갔는데 아무도 없었군요. 학생은 양식상에서 부재중일 때 방에 들어가는 것을 허락하는 빈칸에 표시를 하지 않았어요. 그래서 그가 들어갈 수 없었네요.

남 오, 양식을 작성할 때 그건 알아차리지 못했어요. 그럼 이제 어떻게 해야 하죠?

Q. What are the speakers discussing?

Ⓐ Hiring workmen to repaint the school dormitories
Ⓑ Problems with a painting in a dormitory room
Ⓒ Applying to have a dormitory room repainted
Ⓓ Organizing access to a student's room in order to paint it

Q. 화자들은 무엇에 관해 이야기하고 있는가?

Ⓐ 학교 기숙사 페인트칠을 다시 하기 위해 인부들을 고용하는 것
Ⓑ 기숙사 방에 있는 그림과 관련된 문제
Ⓒ 기숙사 방을 다시 페인트칠하도록 신청하는 것
Ⓓ 학생의 방을 칠하러 들어갈 수 있도록 조정하는 것

어휘 apply v 신청하다, 지원하다 I repaint v 다시 페인트칠하다 I stuff n 물건 I workman n 일꾼, 일하는 사람 I strange adj 이상한 I avoid v 피하다 I inconvenience v 불편하게 하다 I access n 접근, 허용 I notice v 알아차리다

Passage 4

Man: Student | Woman: Registrar

Listen to part of a conversation between a student and a registrar.

M Can I sign up for swimming classes here? I've been looking forward to the opening of the new pool because I've always wanted to learn how to swim. When I heard the pool was opening on Friday, I came straight over here to sign up.

W You can sign up here, but you know that swimming classes are not free. The pool is free for recreational use, but students who want to take classes have to pay 100 dollars a semester because we have to pay the instructors.

M That's OK. I didn't expect free classes.

남자: 학생 | 여자: 학적부 직원

학생과 학적부 직원의 대화를 들으시오.

남 여기서 수영 강습을 등록할 수 있나요? 저는 항상 수영을 배우고 싶었기 때문에 새로운 수영장 개장을 고대하고 있었어요. 금요일에 수영장이 개장했다는 소식을 듣고 등록하러 곧장 여기로 온 거예요.

여 여기서 등록하실 수 있어요. 하지만 수영 강습은 무료가 아닌 것 아시죠. 수영장을 일반적으로 사용하는 것은 무료지만, 우리도 강사료를 지급해야 하기 때문에 강습을 원하는 학생들은 학기당 100달러를 내야 해요.

남 좋아요. 무료 강습을 기대하지는 않았어요.

Q. What is the conversation mainly about?

Ⓐ Plans to open a new swimming pool on the campus
Ⓑ Registration for swimming classes at the new campus pool
Ⓒ The opening ceremony for an on-campus swimming pool
Ⓓ Hiring swimming instructors for the new campus swimming pool

Q. 대화는 주로 무엇에 관한 것인가?

Ⓐ 캠퍼스에 새로운 수영장을 열기 위한 계획
Ⓑ 새로운 교내 수영장에서 수영 강습 등록
Ⓒ 교내 수영장 개장 기념식
Ⓓ 새로운 교내 수영장에 수영 강사를 고용하는 것

어휘 sign up 신청하다 I recreational adj 오락의, 여가의 I instructor n 강사 I expect v 예상하다

Passage 5

Man: Professor | Woman: Student

Listen to part of a conversation between a student and a professor.

W Good morning, professor. Do you have a minute? I need your help with my grant application.

M How can I help you, Sarah?

W I have to submit this request form for a grant to fund my dissertation research. I'd like you to look over what I've written and give me feedback.

M Okay. Well, I have just one suggestion. The grant committee will be interested in why you need the funding and how you'll use it. So, put the points that answer those two

남자: 교수 | 여자: 학생

학생과 교수의 대화를 들으시오.

여 안녕하세요, 교수님. 시간 좀 있으세요? 제 연구비 신청과 관련해서 교수님의 도움이 필요해서요.

남 어떻게 도와줄까요, 사라?

여 논문 연구에 필요한 기금을 충당할 보조금을 받으려면 이 요청서를 제출해야 해요. 제가 쓴 것을 검토해보시고 피드백을 해주셨으면 해요.

남 좋아요. 음, 한 가지 제안이 있어요. 보조금 위원회는 학생이 자금 지원을 필요로 하는 이유와 자금을 어떻게 사용할지에 관심이 있을 거예요. 그러니까 앞부분에 그 두 질문에 대한 답을 요점으로 적어

questions in the beginning. Things like your methodology and your cost estimates.

W What about explaining the need for the research?

M You need to state your topic and hypothesis and then move straight into how the money will be used. That's what's important here.

W Thank you for your help. I'll make the change before I submit the application.

넣도록 해요. 학생의 연구 방법론과 비용 견적 같은 것 말이죠.

여 연구의 필요성을 설명하는 건 어떨까요?

남 학생의 주제와 가설을 진술하고 나서 바로 그 돈이 어떻게 사용될지 설명하세요. 그것이 여기서 중요한 거예요.

여 도와주셔서 감사합니다. 신청서 제출 전에 수정할게요.

Q. What aspect of the grant application does the professor mainly discuss?

Ⓐ How to submit a request form for a grant application
Ⓑ How to improve the organization of her dissertation
Ⓒ How to arrange the information in her grant application
Ⓓ How to apply for a grant for dissertation research

Q. 교수는 보조금 신청의 어떤 면을 주로 이야기하는가?

Ⓐ 보조금 신청을 위한 요청서 제출 방법
Ⓑ 학생의 논문 구성을 개선하는 방법
Ⓒ 보조금 신청서에 정보를 배열하는 방법
Ⓓ 논문 연구를 위한 보조금 신청 방법

어휘 grant n 보조금, 지원금 | application n 신청, 지원 | submit v 제출하다 | dissertation n 학위 논문 | suggestion n 제안 | committee n 위원회 | methodology n 방법론 | cost estimate 비용 견적 | explain v 설명하다 | state v 진술하다, 말하다 | hypothesis n 가설

Passage 6

Man: Cafeteria manager | Woman: Student

Listen to part of a conversation between a student and a cafeteria manager.

W Excuse me. I was told to look for Bob, the cafeteria manager, to ask about working part-time here. Do you know where he is?

M I'm Bob. We have a few different vacancies at the moment. What kind of work do you want to do?

W Well, my friend told me you were looking for cashiers and assistants, and I would like to work as a cashier.

M Oh, I'm sorry. All the cashier posts have been filled. Oh, before we go any further, how long can you work here? I don't want people working here for just a few weeks and then moving on.

W I'd like to work here for at least a semester. I want to save up for a trip this summer and to pay for next semester's tuition.

M Hmm... A semester... Well, I have one opening as a serving assistant from 10 a.m. to 2 p.m. on weekdays. Would that be...

W Well, actually, I have class during that time on Tuesdays and Thursdays, but I can work the other three days.

M I'm afraid that's not possible. I could put your name down as a potential temporary worker for... when the regular part-timers are sick. You could also look for other jobs at the Student Union. I'm sure that you'll find another job there.

W I will try the Student Union, thanks for your time.

남자: 구내 식당 매니저 | 여자: 학생

학생과 구내식당 매니저의 대화를 들으시오.

여 실례합니다. 여기서 하는 파트타임 일에 관해 문의하려면 구내 식당 매니저 밥을 찾으라고 해서요. 그 분이 어디 계신지 아세요?

남 제가 밥이에요. 지금 몇 가지 다른 일자리가 있어요. 어떤 일을 하길 원하죠?

여 음, 제 친구가 여기서 계산원과 보조원을 찾고 있다고 말하던데 저는 계산원으로 일하고 싶어요.

남 아, 미안해요. 계산원 자리는 모두 마감됐어요. 아, 다른 걸 묻기 전에, 여기서 얼마나 일할 수 있죠? 단지 몇 주 일하고 나서 그만둘 사람은 원하지 않아요.

여 저는 적어도 한 학기는 여기서 일하고 싶어요. 이번 여름 여행 비용을 모으고 다음 학기 등록금을 내고 싶거든요.

남 흠... 한 학기라... 음, 주중에 오전 10시에서 오후 2시까지 서빙 보조 자리가 하나 있어요. 그 자리를...

여 음, 사실, 화요일과 목요일 그 시간에 수업이 있지만 다른 3일은 일할 수 있어요.

남 그건 안 되겠네요. 고정 파트타임 직원이 아플 때 일할 수 있는 임시 직원으로 이름을 올려줄 수는 있어요. 학생회에서 다른 일자리를 알아볼 수도 있고요. 거기서 다른 일자리를 찾을 수 있을 거라고 생각해요.

여 학생회에 알아봐야겠군요. 시간 내주셔서 감사합니다.

Q. Why was the student looking for the cafeteria manager?
Ⓐ To complain about the cafeteria's menu
Ⓑ To apply for a part-time job
Ⓒ To receive training as a cashier
Ⓓ To get advice on part-time jobs

Q. 학생은 왜 구내 식당 매니저를 찾았는가?
Ⓐ 식당 메뉴에 대해 불평하려고
Ⓑ 파트타임 일자리에 지원하려고
Ⓒ 계산원으로서 교육을 받으려고
Ⓓ 파트타임 일에 관해 조언을 구하려고

어휘 vacancy n 공석, 비어 있음 I cashier n 계산원 I assistant n 보조, 조교 I tuition n 등록금 I potential adj 잠재적인 I temporary adj 일시적인, 임시의 I regular adj 정규의

Passage 7

Man: Student | Woman: University employee

Listen to part of a conversation between a student and a university employee.

M Can you help me? I have a problem with my grade report.
W What seems to be the problem?
M Well, I haven't received my report from last quarter yet, but all my friends have already got theirs.
W All the reports were sent out two weeks ago. It should have reached you by now. Um... Did you move during the last quarter? It might have gone to an old address.
M No, I haven't moved. I've been in the same apartment since my freshman year, and I received other university mail there a few days ago, so the address on file should be correct.
W I see. Um, did you do all of your final exams? Reports for students who missed their final exams were only mailed out a few days ago, so one of those might still be in the mail.
M No, I took all of my exams. Actually, I really need the report today, so I can register for an extra class. Is it possible to get a copy of it here?
W Give me a moment, please. I will look up your details on the computer. I can print out a provisional copy for you, so you can register for your new course.
M Thank you.

남자: 학생 | 여자: 대학교 직원

학생과 대학교 직원의 대화를 들으시오.

남 저 좀 도와주실 수 있으세요? 제 성적표에 문제가 있어서요.
여 무슨 문제인가요?
남 음, 지난 학기 성적표를 아직 받지 못했는데, 친구들은 전부 벌써 받았어요.
여 모든 성적표는 2주 전에 발송됐어요. 지금쯤이면 학생에게 도착했어야 하는데요. 음... 지난 학기 동안 이사했나요? 아마도 예전 주소로 갔을 수도 있겠군요.
남 아니요, 이사하지 않았어요. 전 1학년 때 이후로 줄곧 같은 아파트에 살고 있어요. 그리고 며칠 전에 거기서 학교에서 보낸 다른 우편물을 받았어요. 그러니까 서류에 있는 주소는 틀림없이 맞을 거예요.
여 알겠어요. 음, 모든 과목의 기말고사를 다 봤나요? 기말고사를 놓친 학생들의 성적표는 며칠 전에 발송되었는데, 거기에 속한다면 아직 발송 중일 거예요.
남 아니에요. 저는 전 과목 시험을 다 봤어요. 사실, 오늘 그 성적표가 정말 필요해요. 그래야 추가 수업에 등록할 수 있거든요. 여기서 복사본을 받을 수 있을까요?
여 잠시 기다려보세요. 컴퓨터로 학생의 세부 정보를 찾아보죠. 임시 복사본을 출력할 수 있어요. 그럼 학생은 새로운 강좌를 등록할 수 있을 거예요.
남 감사합니다.

Q. Why does the man visit the university center?
Ⓐ To ask about the process of mailing grade reports
Ⓑ To discuss the inaccuracies on a student's report
Ⓒ To discuss the student's not receiving his report
Ⓓ To ask about the delay in sending out grade reports

Q. 남자는 왜 대학교 센터를 방문하는가?
Ⓐ 성적표를 발송하는 절차에 대해 물어보기 위해
Ⓑ 학생 성적표의 오류에 대해 논의하기 위해
Ⓒ 학생이 성적표를 받지 못한 것에 대해 논의하기 위해
Ⓓ 성적표 발송 지연에 대해 물어보기 위해

어휘 grade report 성적표 I register v 등록하다 I detail n 세부 사항 I provisional adj 임시의, 잠정적인

Passage 8

Man: Student | Woman: Professor

Listen to part of a conversation between a student and a professor.

W Ah, Peter, congratulations! You've been nominated for a full scholarship for next year.

M Wow! That's great! That will solve a lot of problems for me. I was worried about saving enough for my tuition, but now I can relax about it.

W Before you get too excited, this is just the first stage of the selection process for scholarships. You have to prepare some documentation and submit it to the Dean's Office for the scholarship committee to look at when making the final decision.

M What paperwork do they need? How long do I have to get it all together?

W First, you need a letter of recommendation from your academic department office, but don't worry about that, we'll take care of it.

M Can I ask who will write it? I'm not sure I'm that popular with all my professors.

W Don't worry. It was at the department's suggestion that you were nominated in the first place. It will be a very strong letter of recommendation. It will be sent to the Dean's Office for you today.

M Oh, OK. What do I have to do then?

W You need to get a transcript of last semester's grades. You did well in all your classes, right?

M I was in the top 2 percent in all of my classes.

W Good. Then all you have to worry about is writing an SOP.

M What is that?

W It is a Statement of Purpose. Basically, an essay in which you introduce yourself, your professional and academic goals, and how you intend to utilize your intended study plans after graduation.

M That sounds complicated. I have never written one before, so I'm not sure if I can write a good one. Is there someone who can help me, or give me feedback on my SOP before I submit it?

W I'm sure you will do fine. One of the department secretaries can help you with the proofreading if you need it. Remember you have to submit it before the end of this month. That gives you two weeks to prepare everything.

남자: 학생 | 여자: 교수

학생과 교수의 대화를 들으시오.

여 피터, 축하해요! 학생은 내년도 전액 장학금 지급 대상자로 추천되었어요.

남 와! 잘됐군요! 그럼 많은 문제가 해결되겠네요. 등록금을 어떻게 모을까 걱정했거든요. 하지만 이제 그 문제는 마음 놓아도 되겠어요.

여 너무 흥분하기 전에, 이건 장학금을 받기 위한 선발 과정의 첫 번째 단계일 뿐이에요. 학생은 서류를 몇 가지 준비하고 장학금 위원회가 최종 결정을 할 때 볼 수 있도록 학과장실에 그 서류를 제출해야 해요.

남 어떤 서류가 필요한가요? 모두 준비하려면 시간이 얼마나 걸릴까요?

여 우선, 학과 사무실의 추천서가 필요해요. 하지만 그건 걱정 말아요. 우리가 해결할 수 있으니까요.

남 어느 분이 추천서를 쓸 건지 여쭤봐도 될까요? 제가 모든 교수님들에게 그리 인기가 있는 것 같진 않아서요.

여 걱정 말아요. 학생이 우선적으로 추천된 건 학과의 제안 때문이었어요. 그건 아주 강력한 추천서일 거고, 오늘 학생을 위해 학과장실로 전해질 거예요.

남 아, 알겠습니다. 그럼 저는 무엇을 해야 하나요?

여 지난 학기 성적표 사본이 필요해요. 학생은 모든 과목 성적이 다 좋죠?

남 모든 과목에서 상위 2%에 속했어요.

여 잘했어요. 그렇다면 학생이 염려할 것은 SOP를 쓰는 것밖에 없군요.

남 그게 뭔가요?

여 학업계획서예요. 기본적으로, 학생 자신과 학생의 전문적, 학문적 목표를 소개하고 졸업 후 학업 계획을 어떻게 활용할 것인지 보여주는 에세이예요.

남 복잡하게 들리네요. 전에 그런 걸 써 본 적이 없어서 잘 쓸 수 있을지 확신이 안 서요. 저를 도와주거나 학업계획서를 제출하기 전 피드백을 줄 누군가가 있을까요?

여 학생은 잘할 수 있을 거라 믿어요. 필요하다면 학과 비서 중 한 명이 교정하는 걸 도와줄 수 있을 거예요. 이달 말까지 제출해야 한다는 걸 잊지 말아요. 모든 걸 준비할 시간이 2주 있군요.

Q. What is the conversation mainly about?

Ⓐ How to be nominated for a scholarship

Ⓑ How to apply for a full grant

Ⓒ The selection process for scholarship students

Ⓓ What paperwork to prepare when nominated for a scholarship

Q. 화자들은 주로 무엇에 관해 이야기하는가?

Ⓐ 장학금 후보에 추천되는 방법

Ⓑ 전액 보조금을 신청하는 방법

Ⓒ 장학생 선발 과정

Ⓓ 장학금 후보에 추천되었을 때 준비해야 할 서류

어휘 nominate v 후보를 지명하다, 추천하다 | scholarship n 장학금 | tuition n 등록금 | relax v 안심하다, 긴장을 풀다 | selection process 선발 과정 | documentation n 서류 | submit v 제출하다 | dean n 학과장 | paperwork n 서류 작업 | letter of recommendation 추천서 | transcript n 성적 증명서 | grade n 성적 | statement of purpose 학업계획서 | basically adv 기본적으로 | professional adj 전문적인 | academic adj 학문적인 | intend v 의도하다 | utilize v 이용하다, 사용하다 | graduation n 졸업 | complicated adj 복잡한 | secretary n 비서 | proofreading n 교정

Passage 9

Man: Bookstore clerk / Woman: Student

Listen to part of a conversation between a student and a bookstore clerk.

W Hi. I'd like to submit my application for the customer service assistant job.

M Do you have any experience working in a bookstore?

W Well, I've been a customer at this store for four years, as long as I've been a student. I'm a master's student now, so I know this place like the back of my hand.

M So, you're familiar with the on-line search system?

W I bet I could find anything in less than 5 minutes! I know the in-store system as well as the campus link database for inter-store transfers.

M That sounds good. What other skills do you have to offer?

W Well, I'm a library science major, so I'm familiar with manual indexing procedures as well as computer databases. I volunteered at the main library last year to get practical experience. I was at the front desk as a customer service rep. I also ran some orientation seminars for first year students.

M Do you know what the hours are for this job? If you're a master's student, you must be quite busy.

W How many hours per week are required?

M It's 20 hours a week, mostly evenings. Can you manage that kind of schedule?

W Actually, it's perfect for me. My classes are in the morning, and that gives me the afternoons to work on my thesis.

M Are you available to meet the manager for an interview later this afternoon?

W Sure. What time?

M Let's go with 5 p.m. He has an opening in his schedule then, and I think he'll want to meet you.

W Great. I'll see you at 5.

Q. What are the speakers mainly discussing?

Ⓐ The topic of the student's master's thesis
Ⓑ The student's volunteer activities at the library
Ⓒ The student's qualifications for the job
Ⓓ The student's status as a long-time customer

남자: 서점 직원 / 여자: 학생

학생과 서점 직원의 대화를 들으시오.

여 안녕하세요. 고객 서비스 센터 보조원 자리에 지원서를 제출하고 싶은데요.

남 서점에서 일한 경험이 있나요?

여 음, 제가 학생이었을 때, 4년 동안 이 서점 고객이었어요. 지금은 석사 과정 중이고요. 그래서 저는 이 곳을 제 손바닥 보듯이 잘 알아요.

남 그렇다면, 온라인 검색 시스템에 익숙한가요?

여 저는 제가 5분 이내에 그 어떤 것도 찾아낼 수 있다고 장담해요. 서점 간 이동을 위한 캠퍼스 링크 데이터베이스뿐만 아니라 서점 내 시스템도 알아요.

남 좋아요. 다른 기술도 가지고 있나요?

여 음, 저는 도서관학 전공자예요. 그래서 컴퓨터 데이터베이스뿐만 아니라 수동 색인 작업 절차도 잘 알아요. 실전 경험을 하기 위해 지난해에는 중앙도서관에서 자원봉사를 했어요. 고객 서비스 센터 대표로 안내 데스크에 있었고, 1학년생들을 위해서 몇몇 오리엔테이션 세미나를 진행하기도 했어요.

남 이 일자리가 몇 시간 일해야 하는 자리인지 알고 있나요? 석사 과정이라면 꽤 바쁠 텐데.

여 일주일에 몇 시간이나 일해야 하죠?

남 일주일에 20시간이에요. 대부분 저녁이고요. 이런 스케줄을 감당할 수 있겠어요?

여 사실, 저한테는 너무 좋아요. 제 수업들은 오전에 있어서 오후에는 논문과 관련된 작업을 할 수 있어요.

남 오늘 오후 늦게 매니저를 만나서 면접 볼 수 있겠어요?

여 물론이죠. 몇 시에요?

남 오후 5시로 하죠. 그때 매니저가 시간이 되는데, 학생을 만나고 싶어할 것 같네요.

여 좋아요. 5시에 뵙겠습니다.

Q. 화자들은 주로 무엇에 관해 이야기하고 있는가?

Ⓐ 학생의 석사 논문 주제
Ⓑ 학생의 도서관 자원봉사 활동
Ⓒ 일자리에 대한 학생의 자격
Ⓓ 장기 고객으로서 학생의 상태

어휘 submit v 제출하다 | application n 지원서 | familiar with ~에 익숙한 | inter-store 가게[매장] 간의 | transfer n 이동 | manual index 수동 색인 | procedure n 절차 | volunteer v 자원봉사를 하다 | practical adj 실제적인, 현실적인 | thesis n 논문

Passage 1

Man: Student | Woman: Registrar

[1-5] Listen to part of a conversation between a student and a registrar.

W Good morning, how may I help you?

M Good morning. 1 I'm looking for some information on your summer program. Is it possible for a student to attend classes here when they are registered at another university?

W It shouldn't be a problem. New Jersey University has a policy of open admittance for summer programs, but it does depend on which classes you want to attend.

M Well, 2 I'm majoring in International Marketing at Boston University, but I'll be staying with my parents in New Jersey during the summer, so I thought I could take some courses here then. I've already set up a part-time job at the bakery just outside the school during the summer school.

W Well, 4 we have close ties to Boston Uni, so I am sure there will be no problems attending the courses and being given credit for them.

M There is one other thing. Can I get financial aid for the summer program? I'll be working but my wages will not be enough to cover my tuition fees.

W That can be arranged. Do you want a grant or a scholarship? We have a merit scholarship program for students over a certain grade point average. There are also two private grants for marketing students.

M Well, I get pretty good grades. I try to keep my GPA between 3.6 and 4.0. I'm on a full scholarship at Boston. Can I apply for the merit scholarship? How much of the tuition does it cover?

W For summer school, the scholarship for someone with a GPA of 3.6 and higher covers the full tuition fee but not books and other materials. 3 You need to fill out this form and bring in your transcripts from Boston. You can also get your student ID for the summer when you bring those documents in.

M What subjects can I take here?

W I would need to see your transcripts to give you accurate information on your class choices. Some subjects have certain prerequisite courses and grades.

M 4 I would like to take an economics course and maybe international relations or something like that as well as a marketing course.

W 5 Some of those classes fill up pretty quickly, so you shouldn't wait too long. When could you bring in the documentation?

M I can probably get it all together tomorrow. I have my transcripts at my parents' house.

남자: 학생 | 여자: 학적부 직원

학생과 학적부 직원의 대화를 들으시오.

여 안녕하세요. 무엇을 도와드릴까요?

남 안녕하세요. 1 여름 계절 학기에 대한 정보를 좀 찾고 있는데요. 다른 대학의 재학생도 이 대학에서 수업을 들을 수 있나요?

여 그건 문제가 되지 않아요. 뉴저지주 대학은 여름 계절 학기에 누구나 참석할 수 있는 규정이 있어요. 단, 학생이 어떤 강좌를 듣고 싶어하는지에 달렸죠.

남 음, 2 저는 보스턴 대학에서 국제 마케팅을 전공하고 있어요. 하지만 여름에 뉴저지주에 있는 부모님 댁에 머무를 예정이거든요. 그래서 여기서 몇 가지 강좌를 들을 수 있을 거라고 생각했어요. 여름 계절 학기 동안 학교 밖에 있는 제과점에 아르바이트 자리도 벌써 구했어요.

여 음, 4 우리는 보스턴 대학과 가까운 관계니까 강좌를 수강하고 학점을 받는 것에 문제가 없을 거라고 확신해요.

남 한 가지 더 있어요. 여름 계절 학기를 위해 재정 보조를 받을 수 있을까요? 제가 일은 하겠지만 급여가 제 등록금을 해결할 만큼 충분하지 않을 것 같아서요.

여 그것도 해결될 수 있어요. 보조금을 원하나요, 아니면 장학금을 원하나요? 일정 학점 이상의 학생을 위한 성적 우수 장학금 제도가 있어요. 물론 마케팅 전공 학생들을 위한 개인 보조금도 두 종류 있어요.

남 전 학점이 꽤 좋아요. 평균 학점을 3.6에서 4.0으로 유지하려고 노력하죠. 저는 보스턴 대학에서 전액 장학금을 받아요. 제가 성적 우수 장학금을 신청할 수 있을까요? 그 장학금으로 얼마만큼의 학비를 지원 받을 수 있나요?

여 여름 계절 학기의 경우, 평균 학점 3.6이거나 그 이상인 학생을 위한 장학금은 책값과 기타 자료비를 제외한 학비 전부를 지원해줘요. 3 이 양식을 작성하고 보스턴 대학의 성적 증명서를 가져와야 해요. 그 서류들을 제출하면 여름 동안 사용할 학생증도 받을 수 있어요.

남 제가 여기서 무슨 과목을 들을 수 있죠?

여 수업 선택에 관해 정확한 정보를 주려면 학생의 성적 증명서를 봐야 해요. 몇몇 과목은 필수 강의와 학점이 있어요.

남 4 저는 경제학 강의를 듣고 싶어요. 그리고 마케팅 과정뿐 아니라 국제 관계학이나 그와 유사한 과정도 듣고 싶어요.

여 5 그런 수업의 일부는 무척 빨리 마감되니까 학생은 시간이 별로 없어요. 언제 서류를 가져올 수 있죠?

남 아마도 내일 모두 가져올 수 있을 거예요. 성적 증

W Okay. I won't be here tomorrow, but I'll tell the staff on duty tomorrow to deal with your paperwork and advise you on the subjects to take.

M OK, thanks.

명서가 부모님 댁에 있거든요.

여 좋아요. 저는 내일 안 나오지만, 내일 근무하는 직원에게 학생의 서류를 처리하고 학생이 들을 수 있는 과목을 알려주라고 말해둘게요.

남 네, 감사합니다.

1. What is the conversation mainly about?

Ⓐ Applying to attend summer school
Ⓑ Applying to change universities
Ⓒ Applying for financial aid
Ⓓ Applying to extra classes

2. What made the student apply to a different university?

Ⓐ It offers more varied classes.
Ⓑ It has better professors.
Ⓒ It is near his parents' house.
Ⓓ It has classes his school doesn't offer.

3. What documents will the student submit the next day?

Ⓐ A letter of reference and a transcript
Ⓑ An application form and an SOP
Ⓒ A transcript and the tuition fees
Ⓓ An application form and a transcript

4. What is the student's attitude toward his studies?

Ⓐ He enjoys studying and wants to stay in school for as long as possible.
Ⓑ He hates school but studies to please his parents.
Ⓒ He is a motivated student who wants to take classes in advance.
Ⓓ He is a lazy student and tries to avoid studying.

5. Why does the registrar say this:

> W Some of those classes fill up pretty quickly, so you shouldn't wait too long. When could you bring in the documentation?

Ⓐ To warn the student his desired classes are popular
Ⓑ To warn the student he might not be accepted
Ⓒ To warn the student the classes might be cancelled
Ⓓ To warn the student the classes will be big

1. 대화는 주로 무엇에 관한 것인가?

Ⓐ 여름 계절 학기 수강 신청
Ⓑ 대학 변경 신청
Ⓒ 재정 지원 신청
Ⓓ 추가 수업 신청

2. 왜 학생은 다른 대학에 신청을 하려고 했는가?

Ⓐ 더 다양한 수업을 제공해서
Ⓑ 더 나은 교수진을 보유하고 있어서
Ⓒ 부모님 댁에서 가깝기 때문에
Ⓓ 그의 대학에서는 제공하지 않는 수업이 있어서

3. 학생은 다음 날 어떤 서류를 제출할 것인가?

Ⓐ 추천서와 성적 증명서
Ⓑ 지원서와 학업계획서
Ⓒ 성적 증명서와 등록금
Ⓓ 지원서와 성적 증명서

4. 공부에 대한 학생의 태도는 어떠한가?

Ⓐ 공부를 즐기고 가능한 한 오랫동안 학교에 머물기를 원한다.
Ⓑ 학교를 싫어하지만 부모님을 기쁘게 해드리기 위해 공부한다.
Ⓒ 미리 수업을 듣고 싶어 하는 의욕적인 학생이다.
Ⓓ 게으르고 공부를 피하려 한다.

5. 학적부 직원은 왜 이렇게 말하는가:

> 여 그런 수업의 일부는 무척 빨리 마감되니까 학생은 시간이 별로 없어요. 언제 서류를 가져올 수 있죠?

Ⓐ 학생에게 그가 원하는 수업들이 인기가 있다는 것을 경고하려고
Ⓑ 학생에게 그의 수강 신청이 받아들여지지 않을 수도 있다는 것을 경고하려고
Ⓒ 학생에게 그 수업들이 취소될 수도 있다는 것을 경고하려고
Ⓓ 학생에게 그 수업들은 규모가 클 거라고 경고하려고

어휘 attend v 참석하다, 참여하다 I register v 등록하다 I policy n 규정 I admittance n 입장 허가 I major v 전공하다 I tie n 유대, 연계 I credit n 학점 I graduation n 졸업 I financial aid 재정 지원 I tuition n 등록금, 수업료 I arrange v 처리하다 I grant n 보조금 I scholarship n 장학금 I private adj 사적인 I apply v 지원하다 I transcript n 성적 증명서 I accurate adj 정확한 I prerequisite n 필수 요건 I documentation n 서류 I paperwork n 문서 작업

Passage 2

Man: Student | Woman: Housing officer

[1-5] Listen to part of a conversation between a student and a housing officer.

W Good afternoon, how can I help you today?

M Hi, I have an issue with my housing situation.

W Then you have come to the right place. What is troubling you?

M 1 I am going to live off of campus in an apartment beginning next month, so I need to get my deposit back. How long will that take?

W Well, we have to inspect the room to assess any damage that may have occurred while you were an occupant. 2(C) If there is anything that requires repair work, that amount will be deducted from your deposit before it is returned to you.

M Yes, I understand that, but how long will it take for that inspection to occur?

W 2(A) We normally do them after final exams, so they are issued about two weeks later.

M 1 But, I am going to move out of the dormitory next month, not at the end of the semester. Would it be possible for me to receive it earlier?

W That would be somewhat problematic. First, how many roommates do you currently have in your dorm room?

M Uh, three. There are four people total including me.

W Alright, then all three of your roommates must accept responsibility for any repairs that may become necessary.

M I guess that makes sense, since they would be staying. We all get along pretty well, so I don't think that will present a problem.

W If you get along well with your roommates, then why do you want to leave mid-semester? Most people who want to do so have problems with their roommates.

M Well, that isn't the case for me. 3 My friend has been renting an apartment since the beginning of the school year, but one of his roommates has to relocate for his work. So, they need another person to take his place. But, I need to provide three months' rent in order to move in.

W I see. Is that the reason that you cannot wait until the end of the semester?

M Yes, I need the deposit money in order to pay that much to the landlord.

W 4 Alright, there is some red tape to cut through, but we should be able to help you. 5 First, you need to get your roommates to sign a form saying that they will pay for any

남자: 학생 | 여자: 기숙사 직원

학생과 기숙사 직원의 대화를 들으시오.

여 안녕하세요. 어떻게 도와 드릴까요?

남 안녕하세요. 기숙사 거주에 문제가 있어서요.

여 그럼 맞는 장소에 오셨네요. 무엇이 문제인가요?

남 1 다음 달 초부터 캠퍼스 밖의 아파트에서 살 계획인데, 그래서 기숙사 보증금을 돌려받아야 해요. 돈을 돌려받는 데 얼마나 걸릴까요?

여 음, 학생이 기숙사에 사는 동안 어떠한 손상이라도 생겼는지 평가하기 위해 방을 점검해야 해요. 2(C) 수리가 필요한 부분이 있다면, 보증금을 학생에게 돌려주기 전에 그 보증금에서 수리 비용을 제할 거예요.

남 네, 그건 이해합니다. 하지만 그 점검을 할 때까지는 얼마나 걸리죠?

여 2(A) 보통 기말시험이 끝난 뒤에 해요. 그러니까 약 2주 뒤에 하는 거죠.

남 1 하지만 저는 학기 말이 아니라 다음 달에 기숙사에서 나올 예정이에요. 좀 더 일찍 보증금을 받을 수 있을까요?

여 그건 좀 문제가 될 수 있겠네요. 먼저, 현재 학생은 기숙사에서 몇 명의 룸메이트들과 살고 있나요?

남 음, 세 명이요. 저를 포함해서 총 네 명이죠.

여 좋아요. 그럼 룸메이트 세 명 모두 만약 어떤 경우라도 수리가 필요하면 그에 대한 책임을 져야 해요.

남 제 룸메이트들은 계속 남아 있을 테니 그게 맞는 말 같네요. 저희 모두 꽤 잘 어울렸으니 그게 문제가 될 것 같진 않아요.

여 만약 룸메이트들과 잘 지냈다면, 왜 학기 중간에 기숙사를 나가려는 건가요? 학기 중간에 나가려는 학생들 대부분이 룸메이트들과 문제가 있거든요.

남 음, 저의 경우는 아니에요. 3 제 친구가 이번 학년 초부터 아파트를 빌렸었는데, 룸메이트들 중 하나가 일 때문에 이사를 가야 해요. 그래서 그 사람의 자리를 대신할 다른 사람이 필요한 거죠. 그렇지만 이사하기 위해서는 월세 3달치를 미리 내야만 해요.

여 그렇군요. 그게 학생이 학기 말까지 기다릴 수 없는 이유인가요?

남 네, 집주인에게 그 정도의 돈을 지불하기 위해서는 보증금이 필요해요.

여 4 좋아요. 형식적인 절차를 밟아야 하긴 하지만, 학생을 도와줄 수 있을 거예요. 5 먼저 학생이 기숙사에 사는 동안 생겼을지 모르는 손상에 대한 어떠

repair costs for damage to the dorm room that may have occurred while you were living there.

M Alright, where do I get those forms?

W Actually, I can print one out for you. Hang on a moment… OK, here you are. And you should only need one form. As you can see, there are spaces for four signatures.

M Um, what about this part here at the bottom? There is a space for the signature of a witness.

W Oh, yes. 5 You need a university employee to witness the signing process to ensure that all of the parties are willing and understand what the result of signing this document will be.

M 5 So, should I bring them all here to sign it?

W 5 What? Oh, no, there is no need for that. Your residence assistant's signature will be sufficient, since he is an employee.

M Great. Then I should be back here tomorrow. How long will it take to receive my deposit?

W Once you fill out the official request form, it should take about three business days to reach your bank account.

한 수리 비용도 지불하겠다는 룸메이트들의 서명을 양식에 받아야 해요.

남 알겠습니다. 그 양식은 어디서 받을 수 있죠?

여 사실, 학생에게 프린트해줄 수 있어요. 잠시만요... 자, 여기 있어요. 그리고 한 장만 있으면 돼요. 여기 보면 알겠지만, 네 개의 서명을 위한 공간이 있거든요.

남 음, 여기 밑에 있는 부분은 뭔가요? 증인의 서명을 위한 공간이 있는데요.

여 아, 맞아요. 5 당사자들 모두가 동의했고, 이 서류에 서명하는 것의 결과가 어떤 것인지 이해했다는 것을 확인하는 서명 절차를 증명해 줄 학교 직원이 있어야 해요.

남 5 그럼, 이 양식에 서명하기 위해 제 룸메이트들을 모두 데려와야 하나요?

여 5 네? 아, 아니에요. 그럴 필요 없어요. 학생의 기숙사 조교의 서명이면 충분해요. 기숙사 조교도 직원이니까요.

남 잘됐네요. 그럼 내일 다시 오겠습니다. 보증금을 받는 데는 얼마나 걸릴까요?

여 공식 요청서를 작성하면, 보증금이 학생의 계좌에 입금되기까지 약 3일의 영업일이 걸릴 거예요.

1. Why did the student come to see the housing officer?

Ⓐ To inquire if there are any empty rooms available in other dormitories

Ⓑ To get her advice on dealing with roommates who are always very noisy

Ⓒ To see if he could convince the officer to remove a fine from his account

Ⓓ To find a way to get his housing deposit back earlier than the original date

2. What is true about the room inspection? Choose 2 answers.

Ⓐ It usually takes place after the final exam period.

Ⓑ Students can schedule the date at the beginning of a new term.

Ⓒ If repair work is required, residents have to pay for it.

Ⓓ All residents should be present during the room inspection.

3. Why is the student moving out of the dormitory?

Ⓐ If he lives with his friend, he doesn't have to pay rent for three months.

Ⓑ He was having some trouble with his current roommates.

Ⓒ Living off-campus is cheaper than living in the dormitory.

1. 학생은 왜 기숙사 직원을 찾아왔는가?

Ⓐ 다른 기숙사에 빈 방이 있는지 알아보기 위해

Ⓑ 언제나 시끄러운 룸메이트들을 어떻게 상대해야 하는지 조언을 듣기 위해

Ⓒ 그의 명의로 매겨진 벌금을 없애달라고 직원을 설득할 수 있는지 보기 위해

Ⓓ 원래 날짜보다 더 빨리 보증금을 돌려받을 수 있는 방법이 있는지 알아보기 위해

2. 기숙사 방 점검에 대해 옳은 것은 무엇인가? 두 개를 고르시오.

Ⓐ 기말시험 기간 뒤에 이루어진다.

Ⓑ 학생들은 새 학기 초에 날짜를 지정할 수 있다.

Ⓒ 만약 수리가 필요하다면 거주자들이 그 비용을 지불해야 한다.

Ⓓ 방 점검을 하는 동안 거주자들이 모두 있어야 한다.

3. 학생은 왜 기숙사에서 나가려고 하는가?

Ⓐ 친구와 함께 살게 된다면 3달간 집세를 내지 않아도 되기 때문에

Ⓑ 현재 룸메이트들과 문제를 겪고 있었기 때문에

Ⓒ 캠퍼스 밖에서 사는 것이 기숙사에서 사는 것보다 돈이 더 적게 들기 때문에

Ⓓ His friend, who is living off-campus, needs a new roommate.

Ⓓ 캠퍼스 밖에서 사는 그의 친구가 새 룸메이트를 필요로 하기 때문에

4. Why does the woman say this:

W Alright, there is some red tape to cut through, but we should be able to help you.

Ⓐ To ask the student to clean his room thoroughly and make necessary repairs
Ⓑ To emphasize that moving out of a dormitory in the middle of the term is usually forbidden
Ⓒ To tell the student that there are some official guidelines for this process
Ⓓ To point out the fact that she is doing something that she is not allowed to do

4. 여자는 왜 이렇게 말하는가:

여 좋아요, 형식적인 절차를 밟아야 하긴 하지만, 학생을 도와줄 수 있을 거예요.

Ⓐ 방을 깨끗이 청소하고 필요한 수리를 받으라고 요청하기 위해
Ⓑ 학기 중간에 기숙사에서 나가는 것은 보통 금지되어 있다고 강조하기 위해
Ⓒ 이 과정에 대한 몇 가지 공식적인 지침이 있다는 것을 학생에게 말해주기 위해
Ⓓ 자신이 하도록 허락받지 않은 무언가를 하고 있다는 것을 강조하기 위해

5. What will the student most likely do?

Ⓐ Fill out the required paperwork and give them to his residence assistant
Ⓑ Visit his residence assistant with his current roommates
Ⓒ Go and find another housing officer to make a repair appointment
Ⓓ Discuss with his roommates who is going to pay for repair work

5. 학생이 다음에 할 가능성이 가장 높은 것은 무엇인가?

Ⓐ 필요한 서류 작업을 하고 기숙사 조교에게 제출한다.
Ⓑ 현재의 룸메이트들과 함께 기숙사 조교를 찾아간다.
Ⓒ 수리 작업 시간을 예약하기 위해 다른 기숙사 직원을 찾아간다.
Ⓓ 누가 수리 작업의 비용을 낼 것인지 룸메이트들과 이야기한다.

어휘 deposit n 보증금 I inspect v 점검하다, 검사하다 I assess v 평가하다, 가늠하다 I damage n 손상 I occur v 일어나다, 발생하다 I occupant n 입주자, 사용자 I repair n 수리 I deduct v 공제하다, 제하다 I inspection n 점검, 검사 I normally adv 보통 I dormitory n 기숙사 I problematic adj 문제가 있는 I currently adv 현재 I responsibility n 책임 I relocate v 이동하다, 이전하다 I landlord n 주인, 임대주 I red tape 형식적인 절차 I form n 서류, 양식 I signature n 서명 I witness n 증인 I ensure v 보증하다, 확실하게 하다 I party n 당사자 I official adj 공식적인 I bank account 은행 계좌

Lesson 02 Details

본서 I P. 50

Practice

Passage 1	D	Passage 2	A	Passage 3	B
Passage 4	C	Passage 5	C	Passage 6	B, D
Passage 7	A	Passage 8	A	Passage 9	B
Passage 10	A	Passage 11	1. D 2. A 3. C	Passage 12	1. D 2. A 3. C, D

Test

Passage 1	1. D	2. B	3. A, B	4. B	5. C, D
Passage 2	1. C	2. B	3. C, D	4. A	5. B

Passage 1

Man: Professor | Woman: Student

Listen to part of a conversation between a student and a professor.

M Hello, Cassie, I'm glad you could make it.

W Hello, professor, you said you wanted to discuss my presentation?

M Yes, I think that the topic you have now is just too broad. The causes of the American Civil War are a huge topic, especially for a speech of this length. You should narrow it down a bit more. Instead of all the reasons, maybe you could focus on something like why the poor Southerners supported the conflict.

W Actually, I would really like to focus on the formation of African American units. Why they wanted to fight and the difficulties that they faced.

M That... would also work quite well.

남자: 교수 | 여자: 학생

학생과 교수의 대화를 들으시오.

남 안녕하세요, 캐시, 올 수 있어서 다행이에요.

여 안녕하세요, 교수님. 제 발표에 관해 논의하고 싶다고 하셨죠?

남 그래요. 지금 학생의 주제는 너무 범위가 넓은 것 같아요. 남북 전쟁의 원인들은 엄청나게 큰 주제이고, 이 길이의 발표에는 특히 더 그렇죠. 조금 더 범위를 좁혀야 해요. 모든 이유들에 관해 발표하는 대신, 왜 가난한 남부인들이 갈등을 지지했는지 같은 것에 집중할 수 있죠.

여 사실, 저는 아프리카계 미국인 부대들의 형성에 집중하고 싶어요. 왜 그들이 싸우고 싶어 했는지, 그리고 그들이 마주했던 어려움에 관해서요.

남 그것도... 상당히 괜찮겠네요

Q. What will the woman do a presentation on?

Ⓐ Reasons that the war was fought
Ⓑ The beginning of the American Civil War
Ⓒ Why poor Southerners opposed the war
Ⓓ The experiences of African American soldiers

Q. 여자는 무엇에 관해 발표할 것인가?

Ⓐ 전쟁이 일어난 이유들
Ⓑ 남북 전쟁의 시작
Ⓒ 가난한 남부인들이 전쟁을 반대한 이유
Ⓓ 아프리카계 미국인 군인들의 경험

어휘 discuss v 논의하다 | broad adj 넓은 | American Civil War (미국의) 남북 전쟁 | narrow down ~를 좁히다 | conflict n 갈등 | formation n 형성 | unit n 부대 | difficulty n 어려움 | face v 맞닥뜨리다

Passage 2

Man: Student | Woman: Professor

Listen to part of a conversation between a student and a professor.

M Excuse me, professor. Could I ask you some questions?

W Sure, what do you need to know?

M As you know, I am applying for an overseas internship in France. There are many documents that I need. I have provided a letter of recommendation from my language professor, a certification of my French language skills, and an essay about why I want the position written in French.

W Great, then you just need to submit copies of your transcript and résumé and a completed application form.

M Fantastic, I have all but one of those, and the registrar's office can give me that.

남자: 학생 | 여자: 교수

학생과 교수의 대화를 들으시오.

남 실례합니다, 교수님. 뭔가 여쭤봐도 괜찮을까요?

여 그럼요, 무엇이 알고 싶나요?

남 교수님도 아시겠지만 제가 프랑스의 외국 인턴십에 지원하려고 하는데요. 필요한 서류들이 많아요. 언어 교수님의 추천서, 프랑스어 구사 능력 인증서, 그리고 왜 그 일자리를 원하는지 프랑스어로 쓴 에세이를 보냈어요.

여 훌륭해요. 그러면 이제 학생의 성적 증명서 사본과 이력서, 그리고 작성한 지원서를 제출하기만 하면 돼요.

남 잘됐네요. 그것들 중 하나만 빼고 다 있거든요. 그리고 그건 교무처에서 받을 수 있어요.

Q. What document does the man need to get?

Ⓐ A copy of his transcript
Ⓑ A letter of recommendation

Q. 남자는 어떤 서류를 받아야 하는가?

Ⓐ 성적 증명서 사본
Ⓑ 추천서

Ⓒ A certificate of his language ability
Ⓓ An essay written in French

Ⓒ 언어 능력 인증서
Ⓓ 프랑스어로 쓴 에세이

어휘 apply v 지원하다 I overseas adj 해외의, 외국의 I provide v 제공하다 I letter of recommendation 추천서 I certification n 인증서 I submit v 제출하다 I transcript n 성적 증명서 I résumé n 이력서 I completed adj 작성한, 완성된 I application form 지원서 I fantastic adj 환상적인

Passage 3

Man: University employee | Woman: Student

Listen to part of a conversation between a student and a university employee.

W Excuse me, I need some information about withdrawing from a course.

M Well, then you got here just in time. Today is the deadline for withdrawing from classes. Oh, you do realize that it's too late to get a refund…

W Yeah, I know that. Now I am just worried about protecting my grade point average. This physics course is way more difficult than I thought. I am just not prepared for it.

M That is understandable. Can you give me your student ID number?

W Sure, here is my ID card.

M Great, now let's call up your schedule for this semester.

남자: 대학교 직원 | 여자: 학생

학생과 대학교 직원의 대화를 들으시오.

여 실례합니다. 수강을 취소하는 것에 관한 정보가 필요해서요.

남 음, 그렇다면 학생은 딱 시간에 맞춰 왔네요. 오늘이 수업 취소 마감일이거든요. 아, 그리고 환불을 받기엔 너무 늦었다는 걸 아시죠...

여 네, 알고 있어요. 저는 지금 그저 제 GPA(평점)를 지키는 게 걱정될 뿐이에요. 이 물리학 수업은 제가 생각했던 것보다 훨씬 더 어려워요. 제가 그냥 준비가 안 됐어요.

남 이해해요. 학생증 번호를 주시겠어요?

여 네, 여기 제 학생증이요.

남 좋아요. 그럼 이제 이번 학기 학생의 스케줄을 봅시다.

Q. What does the woman want to do?
Ⓐ Get a refund for a course
Ⓑ Drop a class she cannot handle
Ⓒ Add a class to her schedule
Ⓓ Look up her grade point average

Q. 여자는 무엇을 하고 싶어 하는가?
Ⓐ 수업을 환불받는다
Ⓑ 감당할 수 없는 수업을 취소한다
Ⓒ 일정에 수업을 추가한다
Ⓓ 평점을 알아본다

어휘 withdraw v 철회하다, 취소하다 I deadline n 마감 기한 I realize v 깨닫다 I refund n 환불 I protect v 보호하다 I grade point average (GPA) 평점 I physics n 물리학 I understandable adj 이해할 수 있는

Passage 4

Man: Student | Woman: Professor

Listen to part of a conversation between a student and a professor.

M Sorry I missed class this morning. I had a doctor's appointment. Here is my excuse form.

W Thank you for getting one—many students forget they need to do that. During class today, students chose field trips from the list of art exhibits I provided.

M I was really looking forward to that assignment. What should I do?

W You were not the only student absent, and there are some choices remaining. First, you need to pair up with someone. Then you can choose from what is left.

M OK, then what?

남자: 학생 | 여자: 교수

학생과 교수의 대화를 들으시오.

남 오늘 아침에 수업에 참석하지 못해서 죄송합니다. 검진이 있었어요. 여기 사유서입니다.

여 가져와줘서 고마워요. 많은 학생들이 사유서를 제출해야 한다는 걸 잊어버리죠. 오늘 수업에서 학생들이 내가 제공한 미술 전시회 목록에서 현장 학습을 선택했어요.

남 그 과제를 정말 기대하고 있었어요. 저는 뭘 해야 하죠?

여 결석한 사람은 학생뿐만이 아니고, 남은 선택지들이 몇 개 있어요. 먼저, 누군가와 짝을 지어야 해요. 그 다음에 남은 선택지에서 고를 수 있어요.

남 알겠습니다. 그 다음에는요?

W Then you need to decide how you will divide up the work for your report about the exhibit.

여 그 후에는 그 전시회에 관한 보고서 작업을 어떻게 나눌지 결정해야 해요.

Q. What does the man need to do first?

Ⓐ Visit an art exhibition
Ⓑ Write a report
Ⓒ Locate a partner to work with
Ⓓ Select a destination

Q. 남자는 먼저 무엇을 해야 하는가?

Ⓐ 전시회를 방문한다
Ⓑ 보고서를 작성한다
Ⓒ 함께 작업할 파트너를 찾는다
Ⓓ 목적지를 선택한다

어휘 doctor's appointment 검진, 진료 | excuse form 사유서 | field trip 현장 학습 | assignment n 과제 | absent adj 결석한, 부재의 | pair up 짝을 이루다 | divide v 나누다

Passage 5 Man: Student | Woman: Professor

Listen to part of a conversation between a student and a professor.

M Hello, Professor Bennet, can I talk to you for a minute?
W Hello, David. Sure, I don't have any more appointments today. How can I help you?
M I need some advice.
W Hopefully I can give you some. What is your situation?
M In class the other day, you mentioned a photography magazine that your colleague edits, and you said that he is open to submissions from students.
W Yes, I did. Do you have some photos that you would like to have published?
M No, I don't... at least not yet. I was thinking about submitting an essay.
W Okay, he publishes essays as well if they are about photography. What did you write about?
M Well, I'm not done yet, but I am writing about Polaroid photography.
W Hmm, he gets a lot of essays like that.
M You don't think he would be interested?
W I suppose that would depend upon how well you write. What about the medium were you going to focus on?
M Well, I am analyzing how the constraints of the medium can actually create brilliant artworks.
W That sounds interesting. Do you have any artists whose work you were planning to discuss?
M Uh, yes, actually. One photographer uses Polaroid photographs to recreate classic artworks, while the other does spontaneous portraits.
W Well, they do sound interesting. How about you let me look over your essay when it is completed, and I will help you shape it into a publishable form?
M That sounds great, professor, thank you.

남자: 학생 | 여자: 교수

학생과 교수의 대화를 들으시오.

남 안녕하세요, 베넷 교수님, 잠시 이야기를 해도 될까요?
여 안녕하세요, 데이비드. 그럼요, 오늘은 더 이상 약속이 없어요. 어떻게 도와줄까요?
남 교수님의 조언이 필요해요.
여 제가 조언해줄 수 있길 바라요. 어떤 상황인가요?
남 저번 수업 시간에 교수님의 동료분이 편집을 하신다는 사진 잡지를 언급하셨고, 그분이 학생들의 제출도 받는다고 하셨는데요.
여 그래요, 그랬죠. 출판되길 원하는 사진들이 있나요?
남 아니요, 없어요... 적어도 아직은 그래요. 저는 에세이 제출을 생각하고 있었어요.
여 그렇군요, 그 동료는 사진에 관한 거라면 에세이도 출판해요. 무엇에 관해 썼나요?
남 음, 아직 완성하진 않았지만 폴라로이드 사진에 관해 쓰고 있어요.
여 흠, 그런 에세이는 매우 많이 받아요.
남 그분이 관심을 갖지 않을 거라고 생각하세요?
여 학생이 얼마나 잘 쓰냐에 달려 있는 것 같네요. 폴라로이드라는 수단의 어떤 점에 집중하려고 하죠?
남 음, 저는 수단의 제약이 어떻게 실제로는 멋진 작품을 만들어내는지 분석하고 있어요.
여 그건 흥미롭네요. 논의하려고 계획 중인 작품의 예술가가 있나요?
남 어, 네, 그렇습니다. 어떤 사진작가는 고전 예술 작품을 재창조하기 위해, 다른 사진작가는 즉흥적인 인물 사진을 찍기 위해 폴라로이드 사진을 이용하더군요.
여 음, 확실히 흥미롭네요. 완성되면 그 에세이를 나에게 보여주고, 그걸 출판할 만한 형태로 다듬는 걸 내가 도와주면 어떨까요?
남 정말 좋네요, 교수님, 감사합니다.

Q. What is the student's essay about?

Ⓐ The evolution of a type of photography
Ⓑ Constraints that a medium places on artists
Ⓒ How limitations can create great artworks
Ⓓ Why artists replicate the work of others

Q. 학생의 에세이는 무엇에 관한 것인가?

Ⓐ 어떤 사진술 종류의 진화
Ⓑ 수단이 예술가에게 주는 제약
Ⓒ 제한이 훌륭한 작품을 만들어내는 방법
Ⓓ 예술가가 다른 예술가의 작품을 복제하는 이유

어휘 appointment n 약속, 예약 | situation n 상황 | colleague n 동료 | edit v 편집하다 | submission n 제출 | publish v 출간하다 | analyze v 분석하다 | constraint n 제약, 제한 | brilliant adj 훌륭한 | discuss v 논의하다 | spontaneous adj 즉흥적인 | portrait n 인물 사진 | complete v 완성하다 | shape into ~로 다듬다, 만들다

Passage 6

Man: Student | Woman: Housing officer

Listen to part of a conversation between a student and a housing officer.

M Hello, is this the housing office?

W Yes, it is. Do you have an issue I can help you with?

M Uh, yes, I hope so. I am an exchange student, and I will be studying here this semester. I was told I can move into my room this weekend, so I came to get a look at it.

W Really? Welcome to New York!

M Thank you, but I believe that a mistake has been made. **(D)** I requested a private apartment, but I was not assigned one. The email I received says that I have room 129 in Lancaster Hall, but that building is a dormitory. **(B)** And the room is also already fully occupied.

W Do you have a copy of that email? That is the room it indicates, and Lancaster Hall is a dormitory rather than apartments. How did you register for your housing?

M I registered online. There was a menu of housing options, and I chose an apartment. Then I received an email which said that I could move in this weekend.

W Okay, let me check your student record. Since you are an exchange student, you should already have a file. What is your full name?

M My name is on the paper you are holding in your hand.

W Oh, right, sorry... Marcus Fitzhugh. Hmm, your file says that you have been assigned an apartment for this semester, but that is clearly not the case. Let me get my supervisor. I am sure we can sort this out.

M Thank you.

남자: 학생 | 여자: 기숙사 직원

학생과 기숙사 직원의 대화를 들으시오.

남 안녕하세요. 여기가 기숙사 사무실인가요?

여 네, 맞아요. 제가 도와드릴 문제가 있으신가요?

남 어, 네. 도와줄 수 있으시길 바라요. 저는 교환 학생인데 여기서 이번 학기에 공부하게 됐거든요. 이번 주말에 제 방으로 이사할 수 있다는 말을 들어서 한 번 보러 왔어요.

여 그래요? 뉴욕에 온 걸 환영해요!

남 감사합니다. 하지만 실수가 있었던 것 같네요. **(D)** 저는 개인 아파트를 신청했지만 배정받지 못했어요. 제가 받은 이메일에는 랭커스터홀의 129호실을 받게 됐다고 쓰여 있었는데, 그 건물은 기숙사거든요. **(B)** 그리고 그 방은 이미 사람이 다 차 있어요.

여 그 이메일 사본이 있나요? 저 방이 이메일에 나온 호실이고, 랭커스터홀은 아파트가 아니라 기숙사가 맞아요. 주거 신청을 할 때 어떻게 했나요?

남 온라인으로 신청했어요. 주거 옵션에 관한 메뉴가 있어서 아파트를 선택했죠. 그 뒤 이번 주말에 이사할 수 있다는 이메일을 받았고요.

여 알겠어요. 학생의 기록을 확인해 볼게요. 교환 학생이라 이미 파일이 있을 거예요. 학생의 이름이 뭐죠?

남 제 이름은 지금 들고 계신 사본에 적혀 있어요.

여 아, 그렇죠, 미안해요... 마커스 피츠휴. 흠, 학생의 파일에는 이번 학기에 아파트가 배정되었다고 나와 있는데 실제로는 그렇지 않은 것 같네요. 제 상사를 불러올게요. 이 문제를 해결할 수 있을 거예요.

남 감사합니다.

Q. According to the student, what are the problems with the room he was assigned? Choose 2 answers.

Ⓐ It is not in the building he wanted.
Ⓑ It has no remaining openings.
Ⓒ It requires him to have many roommates.
Ⓓ It is the wrong kind of room.

Q. 학생의 말에 따르면, 그가 배정받은 방의 문제는 무엇인가? 두 개를 고르시오.

Ⓐ 그가 원했던 건물이 아니다.
Ⓑ 남는 자리가 없다.
Ⓒ 많은 룸메이트와 살도록 요구한다.
Ⓓ 다른 종류의 방이다.

어휘 housing office 기숙사 사무실 I exchange student 교환 학생 I private adj 개인의, 사적의 I assign v 배정하다 I occupy v 점령하다, 차지하다 I indicate v 가리키다 I register v 등록하다 I record n 기록 I supervisor n 관리자, 감독관 I sort out 문제를 해결하다, 정리하다

Passage 7

Man: Bookstore clerk | Woman: Student

Listen to part of a conversation between a student and a bookstore clerk.

W Excuse me. Do you have *Advanced Particle Theory* by Matthew Stevens? I can't seem to find it on the shelves.

M Umm... Let me check our computer system. Is that Matthew with one "t" or two?

W Two, I think.

M Ah, I'm afraid all our copies of that textbook are sold out. It's already a month into the semester, and most students come in during the first week of classes.

W Oh, no. I really need that book. Is there anything I can do to get a copy, could I order an extra copy?

M I'm sorry, but only a professor can order extra textbooks. You could try the academic bookstores off-campus. There is one on Patterson's Square that usually has a good selection. Otherwise, you could ask your professor and ask if he has an extra copy.

W I've tried all the other stores. I'm afraid to ask my professor. I've been going to class without the book for a whole month, and he's pretty angry about it. I'll be in big trouble if I can't get a copy before my next class. I'm really worried I'll be thrown out of the course or something.

M Well, umm... then there is only one possible solution. Put a message on the student bulletin boards explaining your situation and ask if someone has an old copy they can sell to you.

W I've never used the bulletin boards. Do I need to ask for some kind of permission?

M Well, if you use the corkboards on campus, you need to get a campus notice form from the Student Union. There is a popular on-line board, UniTalk.com. It just takes a minute to register and create an on-line identity, and you can put your message in the used books forum. I would suggest you use both.

W Oh, thanks. I'll go over to the Student Union right now.

Q. What is the problem that the student has with asking her professor for the book?

Ⓐ She is afraid of her professor's reaction.
Ⓑ She knows her professor does not have it.
Ⓒ She has already tried that and failed.
Ⓓ She is not doing a good job in her class.

남자: 서점 직원 | 여자: 학생

학생과 서점 직원의 대화를 들으시오.

여 실례합니다. 매튜 스티븐스의 〈고급 입자론〉 있나요? 책장에서 찾을 수가 없는 것 같아서요.

남 음... 저희 컴퓨터 시스템에서 확인해드릴게요. '매튜'에 t가 하나예요? 둘이에요?

여 둘이에요, 제 생각엔.

남 아, 안타깝게도 저희가 가지고 있는 그 교재는 모두 판매됐어요. 학기가 시작된 지 벌써 한 달이나 지난 데다 대부분의 학생들이 수업 첫째 주에 왔었거든요.

여 오, 안 돼요. 전 정말 그 책이 필요해요. 그 책을 구할 수 있는 방법이 없나요? 추가본을 주문할 수 있을까요?

남 미안하지만 교수님만 교재를 추가로 주문하실 수 있어요. 캠퍼스 밖에 있는 학교 서점에 가보세요. 패터슨 광장에 하나 있는데 보통 좋은 책들이 있더군요. 아니면 교수님께 부탁드리거나 여분의 책이 있는지 여쭤보세요.

여 다른 서점에는 모두 가봤어요. 교수님께 청하기는 좀 곤란해요. 한 달 내내 교재 없이 수업에 들어가서 교수님이 그 때문에 매우 화를 내셨거든요. 다음 수업 전까지 책을 구하지 못하면 크게 혼날 거예요. 그 과목에서 쫓겨나지는 않을까 정말 걱정이에요.

남 글쎄, 음... 한 가지 가능한 해결 방법이 있긴 해요. 학생 게시판에 본인의 사정을 설명하는 메시지를 올리고, 헌 책을 가지고 있는 사람이 있는지, 그 책을 학생에게 팔 수 있는지 물어보세요.

여 게시판을 한 번도 이용해 본 적이 없어요. 허가 같은 것을 받아야 하나요?

남 글쎄요, 캠퍼스에 있는 코르크 게시판을 사용하는 경우라면 학생회에서 캠퍼스 게시물 신청서를 받아야 해요. UniTalk.com이라는 인기 있는 온라인 게시판이 있어요. 등록하고 온라인 ID를 만드는 데 1분밖에 안 걸리고, 중고 서적 포럼에 메시지를 올릴 수 있어요. 두 가지 방법 모두 사용해보라고 권하고 싶네요.

여 오, 감사합니다. 지금 당장 학생회에 가봐야겠어요.

Q. 학생이 교수에게 책에 관해 요청하는 것에 어떤 문제가 있는가?

Ⓐ 교수의 반응을 두려워한다.
Ⓑ 교수가 그 책을 가지고 있지 않다는 것을 안다.
Ⓒ 이미 시도해 보았지만 실패했다.
Ⓓ 수업 성적이 좋지 않다.

어휘 textbook n 교재, 교과서 | be sold out 매진되다 | academic adj 학교의, 학문적인 | selection n 선택, 선택 가능한 것들 | solution n 해결책 | bulletin board 게시판 | explain v 설명하다 | permission n 허가 | notice n 알림, 공지 | popular adj 인기 있는 | register v 등록하다 | identity n 신원, 정체 | forum n 포럼, 광장

Passage 8

Man: Student | Woman: Professor

Listen to part of a conversation between a student and a professor.

M Excuse me, professor. Do you have a minute?

W Yes, what is it?

M Well, I'm having some trouble finding good reference material for my assignment on bird migration, and I was wondering if you could recommend some sources.

W You can't find information on bird migration? There are probably millions of books and articles on the topic. It seems like a new article on migration is published every six months or so.

M Well, it's not that I can't find sources so much as that I don't really know how to approach the subject. Every resource I look at has a totally different approach, so I am confused. Would a summary of the source material be okay?

W At university you should take information and process it. Read many sources to develop an opinion on migration, then develop that opinion based on a chosen source, and find other sources to support your ideas.

M Ah, I got it now. This is great! I know exactly what to do in my assignment. Oh, one more question, can I draw a comparison between migratory birds and those that hibernate?

W You are aware that you only have a 1,500-word limit. You cannot really afford to go off on tangents. I'm looking for a concise, well-researched, well-supported piece of writing on bird migration. Hibernation has nothing to do with that.

남자: 학생 | 여자: 교수

학생과 교수의 대화를 들으시오.

남 실례합니다, 교수님. 잠시 시간 있으세요?

여 네, 무슨 일이죠?

남 저, 조류의 이동에 관한 과제를 위해 좋은 참고 자료를 찾는 데 약간 문제가 있어요. 교수님께서 자료를 좀 추천해주실 수 있는지 궁금해서요.

여 조류 이동에 관한 정보를 찾을 수 없다고요? 그 주제에 관한 책과 논문이 수백만 개가 있어요. 이동에 대한 새로운 논문이 거의 6개월마다 발간되는 것 같은데요.

남 음, 제가 자료를 찾을 수 없는 것이 아니라 주제에 접근하는 방법을 모르겠어요. 제가 보는 자료가 전부 전혀 다른 접근법을 가지고 있어서 헷갈려요. 자료를 요약하는 것도 괜찮나요?

여 대학에서는 정보를 취해 그 정보를 가공해야 해요. 많은 자료를 읽어서 이동에 대한 의견을 발전시키고, 선택한 자료를 토대로 그 의견을 발전시켜서 본인의 생각을 뒷받침할 수 있는 다른 자료를 찾으세요.

남 아, 이제 알겠어요. 좋네요! 과제에서 무엇을 해야 할지 이제 정확히 알겠어요. 아, 한 가지 질문이 더 있는데 철새와 동면하는 새를 비교해도 될까요?

여 1,500단어로 제한되어 있다는 걸 알고 있겠죠. 다른 방향으로 나갈 여유가 없을 거예요. 나는 조류의 이동에 관한 간결하면서도 충분한 조사를 토대로 명확한 근거가 뒷받침된 글을 기대하고 있어요. 동면은 그것과 아무 관계가 없어요.

Q. Why didn't the professor believe that the student couldn't find resources?

(A) She knew there were many books and articles on the subject.
(B) She has published an article on the subject every six months.
(C) She had made sure the library had relevant resources.
(D) She had created a reading list on the subject for the students.

Q. 교수는 왜 학생이 자료를 찾지 못했다는 것을 믿지 않았는가?

(A) 그 주제에 관한 책과 논문이 많다는 것을 알기 때문에
(B) 자신이 6개월마다 그 주제에 관한 논문을 발간했기 때문에
(C) 도서관에 관련 자료가 있도록 확실히 했기 때문에
(D) 학생들을 위해 자료에 관한 도서 목록을 만들었기 때문에

어휘 reference n 참고 자료, 인용 자료 | migration n 이주 | recommend v 추천하다 | article n 기사, 글 | approach v 접근하다 | totally adv 전혀, 완전히 | confused adj 혼란스러운 | summary n 요약 | process v 가공하다 | develop v 발전시키다, 개발하다 | exactly adv 정확히 | comparison n 비교 | hibernate v 동면하다 | go off on a tangent 주제에서 벗어나다, 옆길로 새다 | concise adj 간결한

Passage 9

Man: Student | Woman: Store employee

Listen to part of a conversation between a student and a store employee.

W Good morning, how may I help you?

M Yes, I came to check if my computer has been repaired yet. I brought it in on Saturday.

W Hmm... Saturday... Oh! I remember! Actually, we have had a bit of a problem finding a new power switch button, so it's not ready yet. Because your computer is not one of the major brands, it's difficult to find replacement parts for it.

M How much longer do you think it'll take to find a suitable power switch button?

W Well, I had a hard time finding someone who made a power switch button that would fit, but I finally found a place yesterday and placed an order. It should get here in a few days, so you could probably pick it up this... Friday or Saturday at the latest.

M Friday or Saturday? I have to do homework on my computer that's due for Thursday. What am I going to do?

W I'm really sorry. If I had the right components, I could fix your computer immediately. I could even name all the places I have looked for.

M Well... I have a cousin who has the same computer as I do, and as far as I know, he doesn't really use it anymore. I might be able to get the power button from my cousin's computer.

W That will definitely speed things up. When can you ask your cousin? You see, if you can get the power switch button from your cousin, I'll have to cancel the one I've ordered today before they ship it out.

M He's in a class right now, but I can call him in about 30 minutes to check.

W OK, but you have to let me know by this afternoon if you can get the button from your cousin or not; otherwise, I'll still have to charge you for the ordered part.

남자: 학생 | 여자: 매장 직원

학생과 매장 직원의 대화를 들으시오.

여 안녕하세요. 어떻게 도와드릴까요?

남 네. 제 컴퓨터가 수리되었는지 확인하러 왔어요. 토요일에 가지고 왔었는데요.

여 음... 토요일이라... 오! 기억해요! 실은, 새 전원 스위치 버튼을 찾는 데 다소 어려움이 있어서 아직 준비가 되지 않았어요. 학생의 컴퓨터가 유명 상표가 아니라서 교체 부품을 구하기가 힘들어요.

남 적합한 전원 스위치 버튼을 찾는 데 얼마나 더 걸릴 것 같으세요?

여 음, 그것에 적합한 전원 스위치 버튼을 만드는 사람을 찾는 데 어려움을 겪었지만 결국 어제 한 곳을 찾아서 주문했어요. 며칠 후면 여기로 올 예정이고, 학생이 아마 늦어도 금요일이나 토요일에는 ... 컴퓨터를 찾으러 오면 될 거예요.

남 금요일이나 토요일이요? 목요일이 마감인 과제를 컴퓨터로 해야 해요. 어쩌면 좋죠?

여 정말 미안해요. 맞는 부품이 있었으면 컴퓨터를 바로 고칠 수 있었을 텐데요. 심지어 내가 알아봤던 곳의 이름을 모두 알려줄 수도 있어요.

남 그럼... 제 사촌이 제가 가진 것과 같은 컴퓨터를 가지고 있고, 더 이상 그 컴퓨터를 사용하지 않고 있는 걸로 알고 있어요. 제 사촌 컴퓨터에서 전원 버튼을 구할 수 있을지도 모르겠어요.

여 그러면 확실히 일이 빨라질 거예요. 사촌에게 언제 물어볼 수 있나요? 알다시피 학생 사촌에게서 전원 스위치 버튼을 가져올 수 있다면 업체에서 배송하기 전에 오늘 주문했던 것을 취소해야 해요.

남 사촌은 지금 수업 중이지만, 30분 후쯤 전화해서 확인할 수 있어요.

여 좋아요. 하지만 사촌에게서 버튼을 구할 수 있는지 없는지 오늘 오후까지는 제게 알려줘야 해요. 그렇지 않으면 주문한 부품에 대해서 학생에게 비용을 청구해야 할 테니까요.

Q. What is the problem with fixing the computer?

Ⓐ It is a discontinued model, so they can't find parts for it.
Ⓑ It is an obscure brand, so parts are hard to find.
Ⓒ It is a limited edition model, so parts need to be made for it.
Ⓓ The suppliers are sold out of parts for that particular model.

Q. 컴퓨터를 수리하는 데 어떤 문제가 있는가?

Ⓐ 판매가 중단된 모델이어서 부품을 찾을 수 없다.
Ⓑ 잘 알려지지 않은 상표여서 부품을 찾기 어렵다.
Ⓒ 한정판 모델이어서 부품을 따로 제작해야 한다.
Ⓓ 그 해당 모델의 부품이 품절되었다.

어휘 repair v 수리하다 | replacement n 교체, 대체 | suitable adj 적합한 | component n 부품, 요소 | immediately adv 즉시, 바로 | ship v 배송하다 | charge v 요금을 부과하다

Passage 10

Man: Professor | Woman: Student

Listen to part of a conversation between a student and a professor.

W Good morning, Professor Donald. How are you doing today?

M Oh... Well, Sarah, thanks for asking. How can I help you?

W Umm... Well, I'm having trouble deciding on a major and wanted your advice. I've really been enjoying your class, you know, and um, I'm considering choosing English literature as a result, but I'm not sure what to do.

M Hmm... That's great. I'm always happy to hear when a student is enjoying my class and is inspired to choose English lit as their course of study. What's your question?

W Well... I've always been good at the sciences. I took advanced classes in biology and physics in high school. Honestly, English was never my strong point. But, really, like your class, it's interesting, I had no idea literature could be so moving. It really makes me want to read and study more.

M Hmm, I see your dilemma. Way back when I was a university student, I had the same problem deciding my major. I had this uncle who was a veterinarian. He was great—funny, smart, and everyone loved him... me too. Uh, so admiring him and always loving animals myself, I dreamt of being a vet.

W Really? I thought about being a vet, too!

M However, in the opposite position of yourself, I had no talent in the natural sciences and struggled with biology and chemistry in high school, but did well in the humanities. In the end, as you can see, I decided to follow my talents and study literature. I still love animals and have several pets, but figured the difficulties of studying a subject for which I had no natural talent would, uh, eventually take the fun and interest out of it.

W Hmm... That makes sense. I would hate to stress myself out struggling in my major.

M But that's not to say that you shouldn't continue to study literature and take classes. Unlike me, you may be talented in both arenas. You may choose to minor in English lit or even do a double major like biology and literature.

W Can I do that? Does it take a long time to graduate that way?

M Sure you can. I have one student who is an aeronautical engineering-creative writing double major. With planning, it only takes one additional year, and you have so many possible roads to choose in the end. Just talk to your academic counselor about the requirements.

남자: 교수 | 여자: 학생

학생과 교수의 대화를 들으시오.

여 안녕하세요, 도널드 교수님. 잘 지내시죠?

남 오... 그래요, 사라, 물어봐줘서 고마워요. 무엇을 도와줄까요?

여 음... 저기, 전공을 결정하는 데 어려움이 있어서 교수님의 조언을 듣고 싶어서요. 아시다시피 저는 교수님의 수업을 듣는 것이 정말 재미있고, 또, 음, 그 때문에 영문학을 선택할까 고민하고 있지만 무엇을 해야 할지 확신이 없어요.

남 음... 좋군요. 난 학생들이 내 수업을 재미있게 듣고, 그래서 자신들의 학과 과정으로 영문학을 선택하고 싶어진다는 말을 들으면 언제나 행복해요. 학생의 질문은 뭔가요?

여 그런데... 저는 늘 과학을 잘했어요. 고등학교 때 고급 생물학과 물리학 수업을 들었습니다. 솔직히 영어는 제가 잘하는 과목이 전혀 아니었어요. 하지만, 교수님 수업은 정말 재미있어요. 문학이 그렇게 감동을 줄 수 있는지 몰랐어요. 교수님의 수업을 통해서 저는 정말 더 많이 읽고 공부하고 싶어졌어요.

남 음, 학생의 딜레마를 알겠어요. 내가 대학생이었을 때로 돌아가보면 나 역시 전공을 선택하는 데 같은 문제를 겪었어요. 나에겐 수의사 삼촌이 계셨어요. 그분은 멋졌어요. 재미있고 똑똑해서 모든 사람들이 그분을 좋아했죠... 나 역시도요. 그래서 그분을 존경하고, 또 늘 동물들을 사랑했기 때문에 수의사가 되는 꿈을 꾸었어요.

여 정말이세요? 저도 수의사가 되려고 생각했어요!

남 하지만 학생과는 반대로, 나는 자연 과학에 재능이 없었고, 고등학교 때는 생물이나 화학과 씨름을 했지만 인문학은 잘했어요. 결국 보다시피 나는 내 재능을 따라 문학을 공부하기로 결심했어요. 여전히 동물을 좋아해서 애완동물을 몇 마리 기르고 있지만, 선천적으로 재능이 없는 학과를 공부하는 어려움이 결국은 공부의 재미와 흥미를 잃게 만든다는 걸 알게 됐죠.

여 음... 그건 이해가 돼요. 제 전공과 씨름하면서 스트레스 받는 건 싫을 거예요.

남 하지만 그렇다고 문학 공부와 수강을 그만두어야 한다는 말은 아니에요. 나와 달리, 학생은 두 가지 분야에 모두 재능이 있을지도 몰라요. 영문학을 부전공으로 선택하거나 생물학과 문학을 복수 전공으로 할 수도 있잖아요.

여 그럴 수도 있나요? 그 방법으로 졸업하려면 시간이 오래 걸리나요?

남 물론 그럴 수 있어요. 항공 공학과 문예 창작을 복수 전공하는 학생도 있어요. 계획을 가지고 실행한다면 1년밖에 더 걸리지 않고, 마지막에는 선택할 수 있는 길이 많아지겠죠. 지도 교수님과 필요조건에 대해 이야기해 보세요.

W Thanks, Professor Donald. I'll go make an appointment with her now!

여 감사해요. 도널드 교수님. 지금 바로 지도 교수님과 약속을 잡으러 가야겠어요.

Q. How was the professor's experience in choosing a major similar to the student's?

Ⓐ He wanted to major in something that he was interested in but lacked talent to do so.
Ⓑ He also wanted to be an English literature major but was good at science.
Ⓒ He studied science before doing graduate study in literature.
Ⓓ He decided to major in science and humanities at the same time.

Q. 전공을 결정할 때 교수의 경험은 학생과 어떻게 비슷했는가?

Ⓐ 흥미는 있었지만 재능이 없는 과목을 전공하기를 원했다.
Ⓑ 그 역시 영문학 전공을 원했었지만 과학을 잘했다.
Ⓒ 문학 대학원에서 공부하기 전에 과학을 공부했었다.
Ⓓ 동시에 과학과 인문학을 전공하기로 결정했다.

Lesson 02 Conversations

어휘 advice n 조언 | consider v 생각하다, 고려하다 | English literature 영문학 | inspired adj 영감을 받은 | advanced adj 상급의 | biology n 생물 | physics n 물리학 | veterinarian n 수의사 | admire v 존경하다, 동경하다 | natural science 자연 과학 | struggle v 힘겹게 나아가다, 싸우다 | humanities n 인문학 | arena n 활동 무대, ~계 | minor v 부전공을 하다 | double major 복수 전공 | graduate v 졸업하다 | aeronautical engineering 항공 공학 | additional adj 추가의, 부가의 | academic adj 학문의, 학술의 | requirement n 필요 조건 | appointment n 약속, 예약

Passage 11

Man: Student | Woman: Librarian

Listen to part of a conversation between a student and a librarian.

M Hi, 1 I just wanted to check these books out.
W 1 Sure. Do you have a student ID card?
M 1 Oh, right. Well, I am a student, but I haven't received my ID card yet.
W Hmm, I see. Well, anyone is welcome to use the library, but only students can check books out. You can understand that we need to see an ID to make sure you're a student.
M Yes, but isn't there any way I can check out these books now?
W I'm afraid not. Sorry. 2 But you can use the books as long as you're in the library, um, and you can make copies if you need to. We have machines on every floor, and copies cost ten cents each. Just leave the books by the machine when you're done, and the library staff will reshelve them.
M Oh, that's good. Hey, um, can I get a friend to check out books for me?
W Sure, as long as they know they're responsible if you damage or lose the books. Some people aren't willing to take that responsibility.
M Great! I'm sure one of my friends will. I kind of need these books right away.
W 3 You know, you should check with Student Support Center and make sure they issued your card. Most students have theirs already. Do you know where the office is?

남자: 학생 | 여자: 도서관 사서

학생과 도서관 사서의 대화를 들으시오.

남 안녕하세요. 1 이 책들을 대출하고 싶은데요.
여 1 네. 학생증이 있나요?
남 1 아, 맞다. 음, 학생이기는 한데 아직 학생증을 받지 못했어요.
여 흠, 그렇군요. 음, 누구든 도서관을 이용할 수는 있지만 책 대출은 학생들만 할 수 있어요. 학생이라는 걸 확인하려면 저희가 학생증을 봐야 한다는 점을 이해해주세요.
남 네, 하지만 제가 지금 이 책들을 대출할 수 있는 다른 방법은 없나요?
여 안타깝지만 없어요. 미안해요. 2 하지만 도서관에 있는 동안에는 그 책들을 이용할 수 있어요. 음, 그리고 필요하면 복사를 할 수도 있어요. 층마다 복사기가 있고 복사비는 한 장에 10센트예요. 복사가 끝나면 책을 복사기 옆에 두면 도서관 직원들이 다시 책장에 놓을 거예요.
남 오, 괜찮네요. 저기, 친구가 대신 책을 대출해줘도 되나요?
여 물론이에요. 그 친구분이 학생이 책을 훼손하거나 분실하는 경우에 책임을 져야 한다는 사실을 알고 있다면요. 그런 책임을 지고 싶어하지 않는 사람들도 있거든요.
남 잘됐네요! 제 친구 중에 해줄 친구가 있을 거예요. 이 책들이 지금 당장 좀 필요하거든요.
여 3 저, 학생 지원 센터에 알아봐서 학생증이 발급되었는지 확인해 보세요. 대부분의 학생이 이미 학생

M Um, it's in the University Center, isn't it?

W Yes, on the second floor.

M Super, I'll check with them and come back when I get my ID. But, um, could you hold these behind the desk for me, so no one else takes them?

W Sure can, but only for twenty-four hours. After that, we have to put them back on the shelf.

M Hopefully, I'll have my card by then. I'll head over to Student Support Center right now. Thanks for your help.

증을 가지고 있거든요. 사무실이 어디에 있는지 아세요?

남 음, 대학 센터에 있잖아요, 아닌가요?

여 네, 2층이에요.

남 잘됐네요. 알아보고 학생증이 나오면 다시 올게요. 하지만, 음, 다른 사람들이 가져가지 않도록 이 책들을 책상 뒤에 보관해 주시겠어요?

여 물론 보관해 줄 수 있지만 24시간 동안만이에요. 그 이후에는 책들을 책장에 다시 갖다 놓아야 해요.

남 그때까지는 제 학생증이 나왔으면 좋겠네요. 지금 바로 학생 지원 센터에 가봐야겠어요. 도와주셔서 감사합니다.

1. With what is the conversation mainly concerned?

(A) Finding the University Center
(B) Getting a student ID card
(C) Learning about Student Support Center
(D) Checking out books without a student ID card

2. Which of the following is an option according to the librarian?

(A) Use the books in the library and make photocopies
(B) Complain to the head librarian about the policy
(C) Check out the books using a temporary library card
(D) Borrow a friend's ID card and check out the books

3. Where should the student check to get his ID card?

(A) In the library
(B) At the 1st floor of the University Center
(C) At Student Services
(D) At the Student Center

1. 대화는 주로 무엇에 관한 것인가?

(A) 대학 센터를 찾는 것
(B) 학생증 발급을 받는 것
(C) 학생 지원 센터에 관해 알아보는 것
(D) 학생증 없이 책을 대출하는 것

2. 도서관 사서가 제시한 선택 사항은 다음 중 어느 것인가?

(A) 도서관에서 책을 이용하고 복사를 한다
(B) 수석 사서에게 규정에 관해 불만을 제기한다
(C) 임시 도서관 카드를 사용해 책을 대출한다
(D) 친구의 학생증을 빌려서 책을 대출한다

3. 학생증이 나왔는지 확인하려면 어디로 가야 하는가?

(A) 도서관에
(B) 대학 센터 1층에
(C) 학생 서비스에
(D) 학생 회관에

어휘 reshelve v (책 등을) 제자리에 갖다 놓다 I responsible adj 책임이 있는 I damage v 훼손하다, 손상을 입히다 I issue v 발급하다

Passage 12

Man: Professor | Woman: Student

Listen to part of a conversation between a student and a professor.

W Excuse me. Do you have a moment to chat, Professor Evans? I'm Marilyn Sinclair from your Monday morning class.

M Sure, Marilyn. Come in and have a seat.

W Thank you. 3 I missed the class earlier this week and wondered if I could get the handouts from you.

M Okay. Why were you absent?

W 1 Oh, my car wouldn't start. I decided to catch a bus, but it was so slow that I didn't arrive on campus until after your class had finished.

남자: 교수 | 여자: 학생

학생과 교수의 대화를 들으시오.

여 실례합니다. 에번스 교수님, 잠시 이야기 나누실 시간 있으세요? 저는 교수님의 월요일 아침 수업을 듣고 있는 마릴린 싱클레어라고 합니다.

남 물론이죠, 마릴린. 들어와서 앉아요.

여 감사합니다. 3 이번 주 초 수업에 출석하지 못해서 교수님께서 나눠주신 수업 자료를 받을 수 있을지 여쭤보러 왔습니다.

남 좋아요. 왜 결석했죠?

여 1 오, 제 차가 시동이 걸리지 않았어요. 버스를 탔지만, 너무 늦게 가는 바람에 교수님의 수업이 끝난 후에야 캠퍼스에 도착할 수 있었습니다.

M Hmm... Is this the first time you've missed the class?

W Yes, it is.

M Oh, OK. 2 You remember that attendance and class participation count for 10% of your mark, right? So, you'd better make sure you can attend all the classes from now on. I'll make a note of this to remind myself to take your problem into consideration when I'm calculating your grade at the end of the semester.

W I'll be sure to be here for every class. I appreciate your understanding this time. 3(D) Did I miss any material that may be on the exam next week?

M 3(D) Yes, of course there will be some information from Monday's class on the exam. Did you read the section on long-term investments?

W 3(D) Yes, and I completed the review and comprehension questions with no problems.

M That's great! Well, it sounds like you won't have any trouble with the test questions then. 3(C) Here's the handout you missed. It covers the points from Monday's class. Let me know if you have any questions once you've had time to go over it. Feel free to email me or drop by the office again on Thursday. Office hours are 3 to 5 in the afternoon.

W Thank you, Professor Evans!

M You're welcome. See you in class on Monday.

남 흠... 수업을 빠진 것은 이번이 처음인가요?

여 네, 그렇습니다.

남 오, 그래요. 2 출석과 수업 참여도가 성적의 10%를 차지한다는 것을 기억하죠? 그러니까 지금부터 모든 수업에 출석할 수 있도록 확실히 해두는 것이 좋을 거예요. 학기말에 학생의 성적을 계산할 때 이 문제를 참고할 수 있도록 이 사실을 적어둘게요.

여 모든 수업에 반드시 출석하겠습니다. 이번 결석을 이해해주셔서 감사해요. 3(D) 제가 다음 주 시험에 나올 수 있는 내용을 놓친 것이 있나요?

남 3(D) 그럼요. 당연히 월요일 수업에 나왔던 내용 중 일부가 시험에 출제될 거예요. 장기 투자에 관한 부분은 읽었나요?

여 3(D) 네, 그리고 복습 및 이해력 문제들도 문제없이 마쳤습니다.

남 훌륭하군요! 그럼, 시험 문제에 별 문제가 없다는 말 같군요. 3(C) 학생이 받지 못한 수업 자료가 여기 있어요. 여기에는 월요일 수업의 요점이 들어 있어요. 일단 읽어보고 질문이 있으면 알려줘요. 편하게 이메일을 보내거나, 아니면 목요일에 다시 사무실에 들러도 괜찮아요. 집무 시간은 오후 3시부터 5시까지예요.

여 감사합니다, 에번스 교수님!

남 천만에요. 월요일 수업에서 봐요.

1. Why did the student miss class on Monday?

Ⓐ She overslept.
Ⓑ She missed the bus.
Ⓒ She misunderstood when the class was scheduled.
Ⓓ She had car trouble.

2. What does the professor tell the student?

Ⓐ The student must attend every remaining class.
Ⓑ The student must write a make-up essay.
Ⓒ The student will have points deducted from her final grade due to her absence.
Ⓓ The student should read the section on long-term investments again.

3. What did the student do with the help of the professor?

Choose 2 answers.

Ⓐ She got a copy of the test from last semester.
Ⓑ She got her car fixed.
Ⓒ She got the materials that she requested.
Ⓓ She found out what would be covered on the test

1. 학생은 왜 월요일에 수업을 놓쳤는가?

Ⓐ 늦잠을 잤다.
Ⓑ 버스를 놓쳤다.
Ⓒ 수업 예정일을 잘못 알고 있었다.
Ⓓ 차에 문제가 생겼다.

2. 교수는 학생에게 무엇을 말하고 있는가?

Ⓐ 학생은 남은 모든 수업에 출석해야 한다.
Ⓑ 학생은 보충 에세이를 써야 한다.
Ⓒ 학생은 결석으로 인해 학기말 성적에서 감점된 점수를 받을 것이다.
Ⓓ 학생은 장기 투자에 관한 부분을 다시 읽어야 한다.

3. 학생은 교수의 도움으로 무엇을 했는가?

두 개를 고르시오.

Ⓐ 지난 학기 시험의 복사본을 받았다.
Ⓑ 차를 수리했다.
Ⓒ 요청한 자료를 받았다.
Ⓓ 시험에서 어떤 내용이 나올지 알았다.

어휘 handout n 인쇄물, 수업 자료 | absent adj 결석한, 부재한 | attendance n 출석 | participation n 참여 | mark n 성적 | consideration n 고려 | calculate v 계산하다 | appreciate v 감사하다 | investment n 투자 | complete v 완성하다, 끝내다 | comprehension n 이해력, 이해 | drop by 들르다

Passage 1

Man: Student | Woman: University housing officer

[1-5] Listen to part of a conversation between a student and a university housing officer.

W **1, 3(A)** I realize that you requested a private room in the dormitory, but usually only senior students get private rooms.

M Well, I just heard from my friend, who is a senior, that **2** there are some private rooms available. He said that all the seniors have been given private rooms, and there are still some rooms left.

W That's not technically correct. **3(B)** We have assigned rooms to most of the seniors, but there are still some seniors on a waiting list.

M **3(B)** A waiting list?

W **3(B)** Yes. We just sent them emails yesterday, asking them to contact us. We haven't heard back from all of them yet.

M When is the deadline for them to contact you?

W We probably won't know how many private rooms are available to junior students until next week.

M But school starts in 3 days! I need to arrange a room before next week!

W Why don't you reserve another type of room for now and move later if a private room becomes available?

M What other type of room can I get now?

W It looks like we have several quad rooms on the fifth floor and a few double rooms on the ground floor. We also have apartments, co-ops, and homestays available to every student.

M A quad room is for four people, right?

W That's right.

M I don't want three roommates, so a quad is not a good option for me. **4** And I'm not crazy about a room on the ground floor. It will probably be very noisy. However, if it means having just one roommate, **5(C)** I guess I'll reserve one of the double rooms on the ground floor.

W OK. **5(C)** I've booked room 103 for you and made a note in your file that you would like to move to a private room if possible.

M Thanks. The ground floor is a non-smoking floor, isn't it?

W Actually, the whole building is designated non-smoking now. It is a smoke-free residence.

M That's good news!

W **5(D)** We'll be in touch if a private room becomes available.

M Thanks again. You've been a great help.

남자: 학생 | 여자: 대학 기숙사 직원

학생과 대학 기숙사 직원의 대화를 들으시오.

여 **1, 3(A)** 학생이 기숙사에 1인실을 요청했던데, 보통 상급생만 1인실을 받을 수 있어요.

남 음, 상급생인 친구에게 들었는데 **2** 남아 있는 1인실이 몇 개 있다고 하던데요. 상급생들 모두에게 1인실이 배정되었고, 아직 방이 몇 개 남아 있다고 해서요.

여 그건 원칙적으로 맞는 말이 아니에요. **3(B)** 상급생들 대부분에게 방을 배정했지만 아직도 대기자 명단에 남아 있는 상급생들이 있어요.

남 **3(B)** 대기자 명단이요?

여 **3(B)** 네, 바로 어제 대기자들에게 우리에게 연락하라고 이메일을 보냈어요. 아직 그 학생들 모두에게서 답장을 받지 못했어요.

남 연락 기한이 언제까지인가요?

여 다음 주까지는 하급생에게 1인실이 몇 개나 가능할지 알 수 없어요.

남 하지만 3일 후면 수업이 시작되는데요! 다음 주 전에 방을 마련해야 해요!

여 우선 다른 종류의 방을 예약하고 이후에 1인실이 나오면 옮기는 건 어때요?

남 지금 제가 받을 수 있는 방은 어떤 게 있죠?

여 5층에 4인실이 몇 개 있고 1층에 2인실이 몇 개 있는 것 같아요. 또 모든 학생들을 대상으로 한 아파트, 공동 주택, 그리고 홈스테이가 있어요.

남 4인실은 4명이 쓰는 방이죠, 그렇죠?

여 맞아요.

남 전 룸메이트가 3명인 건 싫으니까 4인실은 저한테 맞지 않네요. **4** 그리고 방이 1층에 있는 것도 별로 좋아하지 않아요. 아마 아주 시끄러울 거예요. 하지만 룸메이트가 단 한 명이라는 의미라면 **5(C)** 1층의 2인실 중 하나를 예약하는 게 좋겠네요.

여 좋아요. **5(C)** 103호실을 예약해드렸고, 학생의 파일에 가능하면 1인실로 옮기고 싶어 한다고 적어놨어요.

남 감사합니다. 1층은 금연층이죠, 아닌가요?

여 사실, 현재 건물 전체가 금연 구역으로 지정되어 있어요. 비흡연 거주지라는 말이죠.

남 그거 잘됐네요!

여 **5(D)** 1인실이 나오면 연락 드릴게요.

남 다시 한번 감사드려요. 많은 도움이 됐어요.

1. **What are the speakers mainly discussing?**
   Ⓐ How to apply for off-campus housing
   Ⓑ The difficulties of living with roommates
   Ⓒ Housing options for senior students
   Ⓓ Getting assigned to a dormitory room

2. **What problem does the student discuss with the housing officer?**
   Ⓐ He wanted to apply for a double room.
   Ⓑ He didn't want to have any roommates.
   Ⓒ He wanted to live in a dormitory where smoking was allowed.
   Ⓓ He had an argument with his roommate and wanted to move.

3. **Why is it difficult for the student to get the type of room that he wants?** Choose 2 answers.
   Ⓐ He is not a senior, and private rooms are usually reserved for seniors.
   Ⓑ Some senior students haven't yet been assigned to private rooms.
   Ⓒ There is a housing shortage on campus.
   Ⓓ All private rooms were booked on a first-come, first-served basis.

4. **What is the student's concern with the double room?**
   Ⓐ He may not like his roommate.
   Ⓑ It will probably be quite distracting.
   Ⓒ It is a room where smoking is allowed.
   Ⓓ There is no private bathroom.

5. **How does the housing officer solve the student's problem?** Choose 2 answers.
   Ⓐ She gives him a private room as per his request.
   Ⓑ She offers him an off-campus apartment on a temporary basis.
   Ⓒ She reserves a double occupancy room for him.
   Ⓓ She will contact him if there is a single room available.

1. **화자들은 주로 무엇에 관해 이야기를 나누고 있는가?**
   Ⓐ 캠퍼스 밖에 있는 숙소를 신청하는 방법
   Ⓑ 룸메이트와 함께 사는 것의 어려움
   Ⓒ 상급생을 위한 숙소 선택지
   Ⓓ 기숙사 방 배정 받는 것

2. **학생은 기숙사 직원과 어떤 문제에 관해 이야기를 나누는가?**
   Ⓐ 학생은 2인실을 신청하고 싶어 했다.
   Ⓑ 학생은 룸메이트를 원하지 않았다.
   Ⓒ 학생은 흡연이 가능한 기숙사에서 지내고 싶었다.
   Ⓓ 학생은 룸메이트와 다퉜고 방을 옮기기를 원했다.

3. **왜 학생이 원하는 종류의 방을 구하기 힘든가?** 두 개를 고르시오.
   Ⓐ 학생은 상급생이 아니고, 1인실은 보통 상급생에게 배정된다.
   Ⓑ 상급생 중 일부가 아직 1인실을 배정받지 못했다.
   Ⓒ 캠퍼스에 주거 시설이 부족하다.
   Ⓓ 모든 1인실은 선착순으로 예약되었다.

4. **2인실에 관한 학생의 걱정은 어떤 것인가?**
   Ⓐ 룸메이트를 좋아하지 않을 수도 있다.
   Ⓑ 아마 상당히 산만할 것이다.
   Ⓒ 흡연이 가능한 방이다.
   Ⓓ 개인 화장실이 없다.

5. **기숙사 직원은 학생의 문제를 어떻게 해결하는가?** 두 개를 고르시오.
   Ⓐ 학생의 요청대로 학생에게 1인실을 준다.
   Ⓑ 임시로 캠퍼스 밖의 아파트를 제공한다.
   Ⓒ 학생에게 2인실을 예약해준다.
   Ⓓ 1인실이 나오면 학생에게 연락할 것이다.

어휘 technically adv 엄밀히 말하면 | assign v 배정하다 | waiting list 대기자 명단 | arrange v 마련하다 | reserve v 예약하다 | quad n 4인실, 4개짜리 물건 | ground floor 1층 | co-op(=cooperative) adj 협동조합식의, 협력하는 | make a note in ~에 써 놓다, 필기하다 | designated adj 지정된 | residence n 거주지

Passage 2

Man: Student advisor | Woman: Student

[1-5] Listen to part of a conversation between a student and a student advisor.

M Good morning, Tanith, how was your spring break?

남자: 학생 지도 교수 | 여자: 학생

학생과 학생 지도 교수의 대화를 들으시오.

남 안녕하세요, 타니스, 봄 방학은 어떻게 보냈나요?

W Oh, it was fantastic. I was able to visit my family in Lebanon for the whole week.

M That sounds wonderful. 1 May I ask why you wanted to see me this morning?

W 1 Yes, I was wondering about the process for changing my major.

M Oh, you've decided that you no longer wish to study mathematics?

W Well, yes and no.... You know that I have also been taking many science classes in addition to my core classes and math major courses, right?

M Yes, I noticed that your class load has been very science heavy. I was actually considering whether I should suggest that you add a science minor to your course plan.

W Yes, I have been thinking about that, too. I also considered declaring a second major.

M That is also an option, but that would be an extremely heavy workload. You might have to graduate a little later than you planned if you do that.

W Unfortunately, that isn't really an option. I want to get a master's degree as well. So, I think it would be in my best interest to switch my major to science, and biology specifically.

M Is there any particular reason why you want to do this?

W Yes. I have always loved science, and I am pretty good at math. It was a difficult decision when I first declared my major. Over my vacation, I spent a lot of time hiking through the mountains, and I realized what I really want to do with my life. 2 I want a career in conservation. The forests there are so beautiful, but the animals need our help to survive. That's why I want to major in biology, and then get a master's degree in ecology.

M I see. It sounds like you have given this a lot of thought. Fortunately, you are in your second year, so you should be able to graduate on time. However, it will not be easy. Science courses are notoriously difficult to register for, so you have to keep your schedule as open as possible.

W Yes, I have heard that.

M With that in mind, 3(C) I think that you should take some of the lower level required courses over the summer. Equivalent classes for many subjects are offered at Dayton Community College during their summer session.

W I suppose I could do that.

M 3(D) Not only that, but there are a certain number of laboratory and research project hours required for science majors. Since laboratory courses are not available in the summer, I think that you should look into joining research projects for the summer. You can do valuable field work that will also look good on your résumé later in life.

여 아, 너무 좋았어요. 레바논에 있는 저희 가족들을 일주일간 방문할 수 있었거든요.

남 정말 좋네요. 1 오늘 아침 학생이 나를 보고자 했던 이유를 물어도 될까요?

여 1 네, 제 전공을 바꾸는 과정에 대해 궁금한 게 있어서요.

남 아, 더 이상 수학을 공부하지 않기로 결정한 건가요?

여 음, 그렇기도 하고 아니기도 해요.... 제가 다른 중요한 수업들과 수학 전공 과목들뿐만 아니라 다수의 과학 수업들도 듣고 있었다는 것을 아시죠?

남 그래요, 학생이 듣는 과목들이 과학 중심이라는 걸 알아차렸어요. 사실 학생의 공부 계획에 과학 부전공을 제안해야 하나 생각하고 있었죠.

여 네, 그것도 생각하고 있었어요. 복수 전공을 하는 것도 고려해 봤고요.

남 그것도 한 방법이긴 하지만 정말로 수업 양이 많아질 거예요. 만약 그렇게 한다면 학생이 계획한 것보다 좀 더 늦게 졸업해야 할 수도 있어요.

여 안타깝게도 그건 가능한 방법이 아니에요. 저는 석사 과정도 하고 싶거든요. 그래서 전공을 과학, 구체적으로 말해 생물로 바꾸는 게 가장 좋을 것 같다고 생각했어요.

남 학생이 이렇게 하고 싶어하는 특별한 이유라도 있나요?

여 네, 저는 항상 과학을 좋아했고 수학을 꽤 잘 해요. 전공을 처음 선택했을 때는 결정을 내리기가 어려웠죠. 이번 방학 때 산에서 하이킹을 하며 많은 시간을 보냈는데 그러다 제가 제 인생에서 무슨 일을 정말 하고 싶은지 깨달았어요. 2 저는 환경 보호 관련 일을 하고 싶어요. 숲은 정말로 아름답지만 동물들이 생존하기 위해서는 우리의 도움을 필요로 하거든요. 그게 제가 생물을 전공한 뒤 생태학으로 석사 과정을 하고 싶어 하는 이유예요.

남 그렇군요. 이 문제에 대해 깊이 생각해본 것 같네요. 다행히도 학생은 2학년이니 시간에 맞춰 졸업할 수 있을 거예요. 하지만 쉽진 않을 겁니다. 과학 과목들은 등록이 어렵기로 악명이 높기 때문에 할 수 있는 한 최대로 스케줄을 비워놔야 해요.

여 네, 그렇게 들었어요.

남 그것을 염두에 두고, 3(C) 학생이 여름에 필수 입문 수업들 몇 개를 들어야 한다고 생각해요. 많은 과목에서 동일한 수업들이 데이튼 지역 대학에서 여름 학기에 제공되거든요.

여 그렇게 할 수 있을 것 같네요.

남 3(D) 그뿐 아니라, 과학 전공 학생들은 실험과 연구 프로젝트 시간을 채워야 해요. 실험 수업들은 여름 학기에는 없으니 여름에 있는 연구 프로젝트에 참여하는 걸 알아봐야 할 것 같군요. 나중에 이력서에도 도움이 될 귀중한 현장 일을 할 수 있어요.

W Wow, that is going to make the next two summers pretty busy. I really should have made this decision sooner, huh?

M Don't be too hard on yourself. 4 Many people decide to change their majors. At least you realized this before you finished your bachelor's degree. Many only realize they should have studied something else after they enter the job market. It's never too late to learn something new, but…

W But, deciding to do that sooner rather than later helps?

M Yes, exactly.

W Alright, so what exactly do I need to do to make these changes happen?

M First, you need to file some very important paperwork. 5 Then, I'm afraid that we will need to find you a new advisor.

여 와, 앞으로 2년간 여름이 매우 분주해지겠네요. 제가 이 결정을 좀 더 빨리 내렸어야 했어요, 그렇죠?

남 너무 자신을 탓하지는 말아요. 4 많은 사람들이 전공을 바꾸기로 결정하니까요. 적어도 학생은 학사 과정을 마치기 전에 이 사실을 깨달았잖아요. 많은 사람들이 취업 시장에 뛰어든 뒤에야 다른 것을 공부했어야 했다고 깨달아요. 새로운 것을 배우기에 너무 늦은 때란 없지만...

여 하지만, 나중에 하는 것보다 미리 하기로 결정하는 게 더 도움이 된다는 말씀이시죠?

남 맞아요, 바로 그거예요.

여 알겠습니다. 그럼 이렇게 바꾸기 위해서는 제가 정확히 무엇을 해야 하죠?

남 먼저, 매우 중요한 서류들을 작성해야 해요. 5 그런 뒤에는 안타깝지만 학생에게 새로운 지도 교수를 찾아줘야 해요.

1. What is the purpose of the student's visit to the advisor?
   - (A) Submitting some paperwork related to a trip to Lebanon
   - (B) Asking questions regarding declaring a double major
   - (C) Getting help to change her major to a different subject
   - (D) Explaining the unavoidable situation of changing universities

2. Why does the student want to change her major?
   - (A) She thinks that majoring in biology will lead to better job options.
   - (B) She realized that she wanted to work with nature and animals.
   - (C) She does not find math interesting anymore and prefers science courses.
   - (D) She wants to have a lighter class load than she currently does.

3. What will the student have to do to graduate on time?
   Choose 2 answers.
   - (A) She needs to transfer to Dayton Community College.
   - (B) She should start looking for some internship positions.
   - (C) She should register for some introductory level courses during the summer.
   - (D) She needs to gain some experience by participating in research projects.

4. What is the advisor's opinion about changing one's major?
   - (A) He thinks it is not unusual since people often change their mind.

1. 학생이 지도 교수를 찾아온 목적은 무엇인가?
   - (A) 레바논 여행과 관련된 서류 제출하는 것
   - (B) 복수 전공을 하는 것과 관련하여 질문하는 것
   - (C) 다른 과목으로 전공을 바꾸는 것에 대해 도움 받는 것
   - (D) 다른 학교로 가야만 하는 피치 못할 상황 설명하는 것

2. 학생은 왜 전공을 바꾸고 싶어하는가?
   - (A) 생물을 전공하는 것이 더 좋은 구직 기회를 열어줄 것이라고 생각한다.
   - (B) 자연과 동물들과 함께 일하고 싶어한다는 것을 깨달았다.
   - (C) 수학을 더 이상 흥미롭게 여기지 않으며 과학 수업들을 더 선호한다.
   - (D) 지금 듣는 수업 양보다 좀 덜 부담스러운 수업 양을 원한다.

3. 예정에 맞춰 졸업하기 위해 학생은 무엇을 해야 하는가? 두 개를 고르시오.
   - (A) 데이튼 지역 대학으로 전학해야만 한다.
   - (B) 인턴십 자리를 찾아보기 시작해야 한다.
   - (C) 여름에 들을 입문 단계 수업들을 등록해야 한다.
   - (D) 연구 프로젝트에 참여하여 경험을 쌓아야 한다.

4. 전공을 바꾸는 것에 대한 지도 교수의 의견은 무엇인가?
   - (A) 사람들이 종종 마음을 바꾸기에 특이한 일이 아니다.

Ⓑ He doubts it is wise to change it during a person's junior or senior year.
Ⓒ He believes that many people do not know what they want to do.
Ⓓ He finds it interesting that so many people are confused about their career.

Ⓑ 3학년 혹은 4학년 때 바꾸는 것이 현명한 것인지를 의심한다.
Ⓒ 많은 사람들이 자신이 무엇을 하고 싶어하는지를 모른다고 믿는다.
Ⓓ 이렇게 많은 사람들이 자신의 진로에 대해 혼란스러워한다는 것을 흥미롭게 여긴다.

5. Why does the advisor say this:

> M Then, I'm afraid that we need to find you a new advisor.

Ⓐ He is not interested in helping students who are changing their majors.
Ⓑ He cannot help the student since he is not in the same department.
Ⓒ He is convinced that the student is making a serious mistake.
Ⓓ He does not know how to help the student with the necessary paperwork.

5. 지도 교수는 왜 이렇게 말하는가:

> 남 그런 뒤에는 안타깝지만 학생에게 새로운 지도 교수를 찾아줘야 해요.

Ⓐ 전공을 바꾸는 학생들에게 도움을 주는 데에 관심이 없다.
Ⓑ 같은 학과에 있는 것이 아니기에 학생을 도와줄 수 없다.
Ⓒ 학생이 심각한 실수를 하고 있다고 믿는다.
Ⓓ 필요한 서류와 관련해서 학생을 어떻게 도와줘야 할지 모른다.

어휘 fantastic adj 환상적인 | core adj 핵심의 | minor n 부전공 | second major 복수 전공 | option n 선택 사항, 선택권 | workload n 업무량, 작업량 | specifically adv 구체적으로, 특별히, 분명히 | declare v 선언하다 | conservation n 보호, 보존 | survive v 생존하다 | ecology n 생태학 | fortunately adv 다행히도, 운이 좋게도 | notoriously adv 악명 높게 | register v 등록하다 | required course 필수 과목 | equivalent adj 동등한 | laboratory n 실험실 | field work 현장 작업 | résumé n 이력서 | decision n 결정 | job market 인력 시장 | paperwork n 서류, 서류 작업

Lesson 03 Function & Attitude

본서 | P. 58

Practice

Passage 1	C	Passage 2	A	Passage 3	C
Passage 4	B	Passage 5	D	Passage 6	B
Passage 7	C	Passage 8	D	Passage 9	A
Passage 10	A	Passage 11	D	Passage 12	C
Passage 13	1. C 2. A	Passage 14	1. C 2. B		

Test

Passage 1	1. C	2. D	3. C	4. B	5. D
Passage 2	1. C	2. A	3. C, D	4. D	5. B

Practice

본서 | P. 69

Passage 1 Man: Librarian | Woman: Student

Listen to part of a conversation between a student and a librarian.

M Excuse me, are you aware that the library is closing soon?

남자: 도서관 사서 | 여자: 학생

학생과 도서관 사서의 대화를 들으시오.

남 실례합니다. 도서관이 곧 닫는다는 걸 알고 있나요?

W Um, yes. I'm sorry, but these are reference books.
M Oh, I see. You do know that you can photocopy pages from books that you cannot check out. The copy machine is even on this floor.
W Yes, but I will be done soon.
M OK, keep an eye on the time. I have many books to put away before my shift ends.
W Yes, I will do that. Thank you.

여 음, 네. 죄송해요, 하지만 이건 참고 도서들이에요.
남 아, 그렇군요. 대출할 수 없는 책들은 프린트할 수 있다는 걸 알고 있겠죠. 복사기도 이 층에 있고요.
여 네, 하지만 곧 끝나요.
남 알겠어요. 시간을 엄수하도록 하세요. 일이 끝나기 전에 정리해야 할 책이 많거든요.
여 네, 그럴게요. 감사합니다.

Q. What does the woman mean when she says this:

W I'm sorry, but these are reference books.

Ⓐ The librarian should not bother the student.
Ⓑ The student still has much information to find.
Ⓒ Certain materials cannot be removed from the library.
Ⓓ The copier may damage the books if she uses it.

Q. 여자는 다음과 같이 말하며 무엇을 의미하는가:

여 죄송해요, 하지만 이건 참고 도서들이에요.

Ⓐ 도서관 사서는 학생을 방해해서는 안 된다.
Ⓑ 학생은 아직 찾아야 할 정보가 많다.
Ⓒ 특정 자료들은 도서관에서 대출할 수 없다.
Ⓓ 복사기를 사용하면 복사기가 책을 훼손할 수도 있다.

어휘 aware adj ~을 알고 있는, 인지하는 I reference book 참고 도서 I photocopy v 복사하다

Passage 2

Man: Student | Woman: Professor

Listen to part of a conversation between a student and a professor.

M Hello, professor. I heard that the final exam will be cumulative. Didn't you say earlier that it would be only on material covered after the midterm?
W Yes, I did say that. But the professor who makes the exams for this entry level course decided to make it all inclusive.
M Huh, then I guess I better get to work.
W I don't think you have any reason to worry, Kevin. Your midterm score was very high.
M Do you really think so?

남자: 학생 | 여자: 교수

학생과 교수의 대화를 들으시오.

남 안녕하세요, 교수님. 기말고사가 누적 시험이 될 거라고 들었어요. 전에는 중간고사 뒤에 다룬 내용에 관해서만 나온다고 하지 않으셨나요?
여 맞아요, 그렇게 말했죠. 하지만 이 입문 수업의 시험을 출제하는 교수님께서 시험에 전부 포함하는 걸로 결정하셨거든요.
남 흠, 그렇다면 빨리 공부해야겠네요.
여 걱정할 이유는 없을 것 같아요, 케빈. 학생의 중간고사 점수는 매우 높았으니까요.
남 정말 그렇게 생각하세요?

Q. What is the woman's opinion of the exam?

Ⓐ She thinks the student is already well prepared.
Ⓑ She believes that it will be very difficult.
Ⓒ She wishes that she was allowed to write it.
Ⓓ She feels that the student is wasting time.

Q. 시험에 관한 여자의 의견은 무엇인가?

Ⓐ 학생이 이미 잘 준비되었다고 생각한다.
Ⓑ 매우 어려울 거라고 믿는다.
Ⓒ 자신이 출제했으면 하고 바란다.
Ⓓ 학생이 시간 낭비를 한다고 본다.

어휘 cumulative adj 누적의 I cover v 다루다 I inclusive adj 포괄적인, 포함하는

Passage 3

Man: Professor | Woman: Student

Listen to part of a conversation between a student and a professor.

W Professor, you wanted to see me?
M Yes, please have a seat. Were you in class when I assigned your report?

남자: 교수 | 여자: 학생

학생과 교수의 대화를 들으시오.

여 교수님, 저를 보길 원하셨다고요?
남 그래요, 앉아요. 내가 리포트 과제를 내줬을 때 학생은 수업에 있었나요?

W Me? Of course I was, Professor. I haven't missed any of your lectures. Actually, I was kind of confused by some of the guidelines. They don't correspond with what I learned in my composition class.

M Ah, I see. That is because you are writing a history report. Some of the rules for composing history papers are unique to the subject.

W I'm sorry. If you can explain what I need to change, I would be happy to do so.

여 저요? 물론이죠, 교수님. 저는 교수님의 강의를 한 번도 빼먹은 적이 없어요. 사실, 가이드라인 일부가 좀 혼란스럽긴 했어요. 제가 작문 수업에서 배웠던 내용과 일치하지 않거든요.

남 아, 그렇군요. 그것은 학생이 역사 리포트를 쓰고 있기 때문이에요. 역사 리포트 작성에 관한 규칙들 중 일부는 이 과목 특유의 것이죠.

여 죄송합니다. 제가 고쳐야 하는 점을 설명해주실 수 있다면 기꺼이 그렇게 할게요.

Q. Why does the professor say this:

M Were you in class when I assigned your report?

Ⓐ To indicate that the student should change her topic
Ⓑ To emphasize the importance of regular attendance
Ⓒ To suggest that the student wrote her paper incorrectly
Ⓓ To express concern about the student's performance

Q. 교수는 왜 이렇게 말하는가:

남 내가 리포트 과제를 내줬을 때 학생은 수업에 있었나요?

Ⓐ 학생이 주제를 바꿔야 한다고 말하기 위해
Ⓑ 정기적으로 수업에 참석하는 것의 중요성을 강조하기 위해
Ⓒ 학생이 리포트를 잘못 썼다는 점을 시사하기 위해
Ⓓ 학생의 성적에 관해 우려를 표현하기 위해

어휘 assign v 과제를 내주다, 배정하다 I confused adj 혼란스러운, 혼동되는 I correspond v 부합하다, 일치하다 I composition n 작문 I compose v 작성하다, 구성하다 I unique to ~특유의

Passage 4

Man: Student | Woman: University employee

Listen to part of a conversation between a student and a university employee.

M Hello, I would like to register for these classes.

W Then you have come to the right place. Alright, these look like pretty standard courses with no prerequisites. But, I cannot help you yet.

M What? Why not?

W Because your advisor has not signed it yet. You see this part right here?

M Oh, no, I didn't know that I needed an advisor's signature.

W Have you been assigned an advisor?

M Yes, but I haven't met with her.

W I cannot register you for any courses without your advisor's approval—even if they are standard courses.

M I'm sorry. This is my first semester of university.

남자: 학생 | 여자: 대학교 직원

학생과 대학교 직원의 대화를 들으시오.

남 안녕하세요, 이 수업들을 등록하고 싶어요.

여 그럼 맞는 장소에 오셨네요. 좋아요, 전제 조건이 없는 꽤 일반적인 수업들 같네요. 하지만 아직 도와줄 수는 없어요.

남 네? 왜죠?

여 학생의 지도 교수님이 아직 서명하지 않았기 때문이에요. 여기 이 부분 보이죠?

남 아, 이런. 지도 교수님의 서명이 필요하다는 건 몰랐어요.

여 지도 교수님을 배정 받았나요?

남 네, 하지만 아직 만나진 않았어요.

여 지도 교수님의 승인 없이는 어떤 수업도 등록할 수 없어요. 일반적인 수업들이라고 해도요.

남 죄송합니다. 이번이 대학교 첫 학기라서요.

Q. Why does the student say this:

M This is my first semester of university.

Ⓐ He has not had time to meet his advisor.
Ⓑ He does not know about university procedures.
Ⓒ He forgot that he needed to have permission.
Ⓓ He thinks that he should be allowed to register anyway.

Q. 학생은 왜 이렇게 말하는가:

남 이번이 대학교 첫 학기라서요.

Ⓐ 아직 지도 교수를 만날 시간이 없었다.
Ⓑ 대학교 절차에 대해 모른다.
Ⓒ 허락을 받아야 한다는 것을 잊어버렸다.
Ⓓ 그래도 등록할 수 있어야 한다고 생각한다.

어휘 register v 등록하다 | standard adj 일반적인 | prerequisite n 전제 조건, 필수 요건 | advisor(=academic advisor) n 지도 교수, 상담사 | signature n 서명 | assign v 배정하다 | approval n 승인

Passage 5

Man: Professor | Woman: Student

Listen to part of a conversation between a student and a professor.

W Hi Professor Lee, are you busy?

M Not really. What's on your mind?

W I am having some trouble with writing my paper. I think I may have chosen too large of a topic. I have found so many related topics that I am not sure which ones I should include.

M That often happens when writing about psychology. How about you make an outline of the main topic, and list the subtopics at the end? I will look it over and help you decide which ones are worth including.

W That sounds like a good idea. When should I give it to you?

M How about tomorrow morning?

W Did you say tomorrow morning? I, uh, I'll see what I can do...

남자: 교수 | 여자: 학생

학생과 교수의 대화를 들으시오.

여 안녕하세요, 이 교수님. 바쁘신가요?

남 별로 바쁘지 않아요. 무슨 용건인가요?

여 제 리포트를 쓰는 데 좀 어려움이 있어서요. 너무 광범위한 주제를 선택한 것 같아요. 관련된 주제들을 너무 많이 찾아서 무엇을 포함해야 할지 모르겠어요.

남 심리학에 관해 쓸 때 자주 일어나는 일이죠. 대주제의 개요를 만든 다음, 마지막에 소주제들을 나열해 보면 어떨까요? 내가 살펴보고 어떤 것들을 포함하는 것이 좋은지 정하는 걸 도와줄게요.

여 좋은 생각이세요. 언제 드릴까요?

남 내일 아침은 어때요?

여 내일 아침이라고 하셨나요? 어, 뭘 할 수 있는지 볼게요...

Q. What is the woman's attitude toward the professor's suggestion?

(A) She is not satisfied with the advice that he gave her.

(B) She believes that it will be simple to do what he said.

(C) She feels that he doesn't understand her situation.

(D) She thinks that the deadline is too soon.

Q. 교수의 제안에 대한 여자의 태도는 어떠한가?

(A) 교수가 준 조언에 만족하지 않는다.

(B) 교수가 이야기한 것을 하는 게 간단할 거라고 믿는다.

(C) 교수가 자신의 상황을 이해하지 못한다고 느낀다.

(D) 마감 기한이 너무 짧다고 생각한다.

어휘 related adj 관련된 | psychology n 심리학 | subtopic n 소주제

Passage 6

Man: Student | Woman: Professor

Listen to part of a conversation between a student and a professor.

M Hi professor. My name is John Watson. I was wondering if you had a moment to talk.

W John Watson? I must say that the name doesn't ring a bell.

M That's part of the reason I wanted to talk to you. I'm in your movie history class.

W Movie history? Oh! That's a very large class. I usually don't remember many students unless they are very active in class.

M Yeah, you probably won't remember me, then. I've only been there two days since the beginning of the semester.

W I see. And what did you want to talk to me about?

M Well, I'm really enjoying the class, but I have a situation, and I would really like to change my status in that class. You see, I'm taking four other courses and they turned out to be more than I bargained for.

남자: 학생 | 여자: 교수

학생과 교수의 대화를 들으시오.

남 안녕하세요 교수님. 제 이름은 존 왓슨입니다. 잠시 이야기할 시간이 있으신가 해서요.

여 존 왓슨이요? 낯익은 이름은 아닌 것 같네요.

남 그것도 제가 교수님과 이야기를 하고 싶어했던 이유 중 하나입니다. 저는 교수님의 영화사 수업을 듣고 있습니다.

여 영화사 수업? 아! 그건 정말 규모가 큰 수업이죠. 학생들이 수업에서 매우 적극적이지 않은 이상 많은 학생들을 기억하지 못해요.

남 네, 그럼 아마 저를 기억하지 못하실 거예요. 이번 학기가 시작되고 이틀만 갔거든요.

여 그렇군요. 학생은 무엇에 관해 이야기하고 싶었던 거죠?

남 음, 수업은 정말 재미있지만 일이 생겨서 저의 수업 상태를 바꾸고 싶어요. 저, 제가 다른 수업을 네 개 듣는데 제가 예상했던 것보다 더 버겁게 돼서요.

W That's only five classes. That's pretty standard. I don't see what the problem is.

여 그러면 전부 다섯 개잖아요. 그건 상당히 일반적이에요. 무엇이 문제인지 모르겠네요.

Q. What does the professor mean when she says this:

W That's pretty standard.

Ⓐ The student comes to class fairly regularly.
Ⓑ The student's course load is not unusual.
Ⓒ The course normally has many students.
Ⓓ The class is not a high-level course.

Q. 교수는 다음과 같이 말하며 무엇을 의미하는가:

여 그건 상당히 일반적이에요.

Ⓐ 학생은 수업에 상당히 정기적으로 온다.
Ⓑ 학생의 수업 양은 특이한 것이 아니다.
Ⓒ 이 수업에는 보통 학생들이 많다.
Ⓓ 이 수업은 높은 단계의 수업이 아니다.

어휘 ring a bell 낯이 익다 I active adj 활동적인, 적극적인 I situation n 상황, 문제 I status n 상태 I bargain for ~을 예상하다 I standard adj 일반적인

Passage 7

Man: Student I Woman: Housing officer

Listen to part of a conversation between a student and a housing officer.

M Hello, are you in charge here?

W Yes, I'm the on-duty housing officer today. What seems to be the problem?

M Well, I got this report from your office saying that my room was inspected, which I didn't know about, and I've been cited for some sort of safety violation. Is it okay for them to enter people's rooms like that?

W Yes, we were having housing inspections all this week. You really need to check the student bulletin board more often.

M OK, the form I received has a check in the box indicating "electrical equipment," but that's all it says. I have no idea what they are talking about.

W What's your name and student ID?

M I'm Brent Weir. Student ID 185-353.

W All right, Mr. Weir. The inspector noted that you have a halogen desk lamp and that is strictly against the university fire code.

M Seriously? Huh, well, I don't have the money right now. Would it be alright if I paid you at the end of the month?

W I think we can work something out.

남자: 학생 I 여자: 기숙사 담당자

학생과 기숙사 담당자의 대화를 들으시오.

남 안녕하세요. 담당자이신가요?

여 네, 제가 오늘 근무하는 담당 직원입니다. 어떤 문제가 있으신가요?

남 음, 제 방이 제가 알지 못했던 점검을 받았고 안전 규정 위반으로 소환되었다는 이 보고서를 받았어요. 그렇게 사람들의 방에 들어가도 되는 건가요?

여 네, 이번 주 내내 주거지 점검을 하고 있었거든요. 학생은 학생 게시판을 더 자주 확인해야겠네요.

남 알겠습니다. 제가 받은 양식에는 '전자 장비'라고 쓰인 박스에 표시가 되어 있어요. 하지만 그게 다예요. 무슨 말을 하는 건지 전혀 모르겠어요.

여 학생의 이름과 학생 번호가 무엇인가요?

남 브렌트 웨어입니다. 학생 번호는 185-353이에요.

여 그래요, 웨어 학생. 검사관은 학생이 할로겐 책상 램프를 갖고 있다고 했고, 이건 학교 소방법에 크게 위반됩니다.

남 정말인가요? 흠, 지금은 돈이 없는데요. 이번 달 말에 지불해도 괜찮나요?

여 어떻게 해볼 수 있을 거예요.

Q. What does the woman mean when she says this:

W You really need to check the student bulletin board more often.

Ⓐ The student should have known the university code.
Ⓑ The student should have arranged to be at his room.
Ⓒ The student should have known about the inspections.
Ⓓ The student should have posted a notice on the board.

Q. 여자는 다음과 같이 말하며 무엇을 의미하는가:

여 학생은 학생 게시판을 더 자주 확인해야겠네요.

Ⓐ 학생은 대학 규정을 알았어야 했다.
Ⓑ 학생은 방에 있었어야 했다.
Ⓒ 학생은 점검에 관해 알았어야 했다.
Ⓓ 학생은 게시판에 공지를 게시했어야 했다.

어휘 in charge ~를 맡은, 담당인 | on-duty 근무 중인 | inspect v 점검하다, 조사하다 | cite v 소환하다 | safety n 안전 | violation n 위반 | bulletin board 게시판 | electrical equipment 전자 장비 | inspector n 검사관 | strictly adv 엄격하게 | fire code 소방법

Passage 8 Man: Student | Woman: Librarian

Listen to part of a conversation between a student and a librarian.

M Can you help me? I need some assistance in learning how to use the library.

W Well, I'm happy to help you, but didn't you learn the procedures at freshman orientation?

M I got into town late, so I wasn't able to attend the orientation.

W That's too bad. We cover a lot of important information then. You really should have come to orientation. Anyway, how can I help you today?

M I need to borrow a book, but I don't know where to find it.

W If you know the author's name, then you can look on the shelves directly using the first three letters of the author's last name. For example, books by Ernest Hemingway can be found on the shelf under "HEM".

M I see, but I don't know the name of the author. I need a book that's a general reference about Latin American literature.

W Okay. That's a little harder and will require the use of the computer.

남자: 학생 | 여자: 도서관 사서

학생과 도서관 사서의 대화를 들으시오.

남 저를 도와주실 수 있나요? 도서관을 이용하는 법을 배우는 데 도움이 필요해요.

여 음, 기꺼이 돕겠지만, 그 절차는 신입생 오리엔테이션에서 배우지 않았나요?

남 이 도시에 늦게 도착해서 오리엔테이션에 참석하지 못했어요.

여 안타깝네요. 그때 중요한 정보를 많이 다루거든요. 오리엔테이션에 왔어야 했어요. 어쨌든, 오늘 어떻게 도와줄까요?

남 책을 빌려야 하는데 그 책을 어디서 찾아야 할지 모르겠어요.

여 저자의 이름을 안다면 저자의 성에서 첫 세 글자를 가지고 직접 책장들을 찾아볼 수 있어요. 예를 들어, 어니스트 헤밍웨이의 작품들은 'HEM'이라고 표시된 책꽂이 칸에서 찾을 수 있죠.

남 그렇군요. 하지만 저자의 이름을 몰라요. 라틴 아메리카 문학에 관해 일반적으로 참조할 수 있는 책이 필요해요.

여 알겠어요. 그건 좀 더 어렵고 컴퓨터 사용을 필요로 하죠.

Q. What is the attitude of the librarian toward orientation?

(A) She thinks orientation should be made mandatory for all new students.

(B) She thinks orientation information can be learned in other ways.

(C) She thinks orientation provides no important information and is unnecessary.

(D) She thinks orientation is important for new students to attend.

Q. 오리엔테이션에 관한 사서의 태도는 어떠한가?

(A) 오리엔테이션이 모든 신입생에게 필수가 되어야 한다고 생각한다.

(B) 오리엔테이션 정보는 다른 방법으로 배울 수 있다고 생각한다.

(C) 오리엔테이션이 중요한 정보를 제공하지 않고 불필요하다고 생각한다.

(D) 오리엔테이션이 신입생이 참석해야 하는 중요한 것이라고 생각한다.

어휘 assistance n 도움 | procedure n 절차 | attend v 참석하다 | directly adv 직접, 바로 | general adj 일반적인 | reference n 참조, 인용 | literature n 문학

Passage 9 Man: Student | Woman: University employee

Listen to part of a conversation between a student and a university employee.

M Are you in charge of the field trips for the Art Department?

W I sure am. I'm Marge Lecter, the Art Department Coordinator. How can I help you?

M I'm writing a paper on post-modernist sculptors, and I need to go to the Museum of Modern Art. But, I don't know how to get access.

남자: 학생 | 여자: 대학교 직원

학생과 대학교 직원의 대화를 들으시오.

남 미술학부 현장 학습 담당자이신가요?

여 맞아요. 저는 마지 렉터이고 미술학부 코디네이터입니다. 어떻게 도와드릴까요?

남 제가 포스트모더니스트 조각가들에 관한 리포트를 쓰는데 현대 미술관에 가야 하거든요. 하지만 어떻게 가는 건지 모르겠어요.

W Okay, just let me see your student ID. Mark Wilson... hmm... There's a little problem here. It seems that you signed up to go on the 15th of this month. I'm assuming that since you're here....

M That's right. I was scheduled to go, but I had to work at the last minute, so I decided to put it off.

W Well, that creates a bit of a problem. If a student doesn't fill out a cancellation form, then the student is recorded as having attended the trip.

M Why is that a problem? I paid my activities fee!

W You see, your fees only pay for one student trip.

여 알겠어요, 학생증을 보여주세요. 마크 윌슨... 흠... 여기 작은 문제가 있네요. 학생이 이번 달 15일에 미술관에 가는 걸 신청했던 것 같군요. 학생이 여기 왔으니 그 말은....

남 맞습니다. 가기로 일정이 잡혀 있었는데 갑자기 일을 해야 했어요. 그래서 가는 것을 미루기로 결정했어요.

여 음, 그렇다면 문제가 생기네요. 만약 취소 양식을 작성하지 않는 경우에는 그 학생이 현장 학습에 참여한 걸로 기록되거든요.

남 그게 왜 문제죠? 저는 활동 비용을 지불했는데요!

여 저, 학생이 낸 요금은 1회 학생 현장 학습에 대해서만 지불한 거니까요.

Q. What does the woman mean when she says this:

W I'm assuming that since you're here....

(A) The student must have missed his appointment.
(B) The student should go to a different department.
(C) The student needs to pay an additional fee.
(D) The student has to make a new reservation.

Q. 여자는 다음과 같이 말하며 무엇을 의미하는가:

여 학생이 여기 왔으니 그 말은....

(A) 학생이 예약을 놓친 게 분명하다.
(B) 학생은 다른 부서로 가야 한다.
(C) 학생은 추가 요금을 지불해야 한다.
(D) 학생은 새로운 예약을 해야 한다.

어휘 in charge of ~를 맡은, 담당인 | sculptor n 조각가 | modern art 현대 미술 | access n 접근, 이용 | sign up 신청하다, 등록하다 | assume v 가정하다 | cancellation n 취소 | record v 기록하다 | attend v 참석하다

Passage 10

Man: Radio director | Woman: Student DJ

Listen to part of a conversation between a student DJ and a radio director.

M Sally! Have you heard the news? Your radio show got the highest ratings last semester!

W Oh, really? But how did you find out?

M Well, the station sent out surveys to 500 student listeners, and your show came in number 1 in most categories.

W Fantastic! I never knew I had so many listeners!

M It's good that you're having so much success, but there is one downside.

W What's that?

M They complained that you don't always mention the names of the songs when you play them.

W I know, but it just gets so repetitive.

M That's true, but this is one of our responsibilities. After all, we are in the radio business.

W What should I do?

M I think you need to do two additional things: one, when you come on the air, list the artists and songs you're going to play. Second, put your playlist on the station's website after the show is over.

W That's not too hard. I can do that.

남자: 라디오 감독 | 여자: 학생 DJ

학생 디제이와 라디오 감독의 대화를 들으시오.

남 샐리! 소식 들었어요? 학생의 라디오 쇼가 저번 학기에 가장 높은 평가를 받았어요!

여 오, 정말인가요? 하지만 어떻게 아셨나요?

남 음, 방송국에서 500명의 학생 청취자들에게 설문지를 보냈고 학생의 쇼가 대부분의 카테고리에서 1위를 차지했어요.

여 정말 좋네요! 그렇게 청취자들이 많은 줄 몰랐어요!

남 학생이 이렇게 성공을 거두니 좋지만, 한 가지 부정적인 평가가 있어요.

여 그게 뭔가요?

남 학생이 음악을 틀 때 곡의 이름을 항상 언급하지 않는다고 사람들이 불만을 제기했어요.

여 알아요, 하지만 그건 너무 반복적인 일이 되는 걸요.

남 그건 그래요, 하지만 그게 우리의 책임 중 하나예요. 어쨌든 우린 라디오 업계에서 활동하고 있으니까요.

여 어떻게 해야 할까요?

남 학생이 두 가지를 추가로 해야 한다고 생각해요. 첫째, 라디오 방송을 하게 되면 학생이 틀 곡과 가수들의 목록을 작성하는 거죠. 두 번째로는, 방송이 끝난 뒤 학생의 선곡표를 라디오 방송국의 웹사이트에 올리는 거예요.

여 어렵지 않네요. 할 수 있어요.

Q. What is the woman's attitude about her responsibilities?

Ⓐ She thinks that some tasks are tedious.
Ⓑ She wants the rules to be made clearer.
Ⓒ She is ignoring the man's suggestions.
Ⓓ She feels the changes are unnecessary.

Q. 자신의 책임에 관한 여자의 태도는 어떠한가?

Ⓐ 일부 일이 지루하다고 생각한다.
Ⓑ 규정이 더 명확해지길 원한다.
Ⓒ 남자의 제안을 무시하고 있다.
Ⓓ 변화가 불필요하다고 느낀다.

어휘 rating n 점수, 평가 I survey n 설문지, 설문 조사 I fantastic adj 환상적인 I success n 성공 I downside n 부정적인 면 I complain v 불평하다 I mention v 언급하다 I repetitive adj 반복적인, 반복되는 I responsibility n 책무, 책임 I additional adj 추가의

Passage 11

Man: Professor | Woman: Student

Listen to part of a conversation between a student and a professor.

W Professor Kuchar, I'm glad I caught you. Did you have a chance to look over the first draft of my term paper?
M As a matter of fact, I did, and I have a couple of comments.
W Alright, what should I work on?
M First of all, your topic is really good. Since your major is international politics, it makes sense that you chose to discuss trade barriers and tariffs.
W Where did I go wrong, then? I also thought the topic was very relevant. Also, it's a subject I know a lot about.
M That may be part of your problem. You see, your outline contains some strong main ideas, but you lack any concrete support. It's almost like you're just using your own knowledge without consulting the experts.
W Trade is an expertise of mine.
M Oh, I'm not questioning your knowledge, but that doesn't excuse you from doing the work properly. I want you to take your main points and go back to the library or get online and find specific support from renowned experts. Then, you should have fixed the major holes in your paper.

남자: 교수 | 여자: 학생

학생과 교수의 대화를 들으시오.

여 쿠차 교수님, 뵙게 돼서 다행이에요. 제 학기 리포트의 초안을 살펴볼 기회가 있으셨나요?
남 사실 봤어요. 그리고 말할 부분이 좀 있어요.
여 알겠습니다. 제가 무엇을 작업해야 하나요?
남 먼저, 학생의 주제는 아주 좋아요. 학생의 전공이 국제 정치학이니 무역 장벽과 관세를 논의하기로 결정한 건 말이 되죠.
여 그렇다면 어디서 잘못된 거죠? 저 또한 주제가 아주 적절하다고 생각했어요. 그리고 제가 많이 알고 있는 주제예요.
남 아마 그게 학생의 문제일 수 있어요. 보면 학생의 개요에는 몇 가지 좋은 주요 개념들이 있지만 구체적인 근거는 부족해요. 마치 전문가의 견해를 참고하지 않고 스스로의 지식만 이용하는 것 같아요.
여 무역은 제 전문인걸요.
남 아, 학생의 지식을 의심하는 건 아니지만 그 점이 제대로 리포트를 쓰지 않아도 된다는 건 아니죠. 주요 개념은 갖고 도서관에 가거나 온라인에서 명성 있는 전문가들로부터 구체적인 근거를 찾으세요. 그렇게 한 뒤에는 리포트에 있는 주된 허점들을 고치게 될 거예요.

Q. What does the man mean when he says this:

M That may be part of your problem.

Ⓐ The student is trying to impress him.
Ⓑ The student needs to edit her work carefully.
Ⓒ The student should listen to criticism.
Ⓓ The student seems overconfident.

Q. 남자는 다음과 같이 말하며 무엇을 의미하는가:

남 아마 그게 학생의 문제일 수 있어요.

Ⓐ 학생이 교수에게 좋은 인상을 주려고 한다.
Ⓑ 학생이 과제를 주의 깊게 수정해야 한다.
Ⓒ 학생은 비판에 귀를 기울여야 한다.
Ⓓ 학생이 지나치게 자신만만해 보인다.

어휘 first draft 초안 I international politics 국제 정치학 I discuss v 논의하다 I trade barrier 무역 장벽 I tariff n 관세 I relevant adj 적절한, 관련 있는 I concrete adj 구체적인, 명확한 I knowledge n 지식 I consult v 참고하다 I expert n 전문가 I trade n 무역, 교역 I expertise n 전문, 전문 분야 I question v 의심하다, 의문을 가지다 I excuse v (무례·작은 실수 등을) 봐 주다, 면제해 주다 I properly adv 제대로 I renowned adj 명성 있는, 유명한 I fix v 고치다

Passage 12

Man: Student | Woman: Manager

Listen to part of a conversation between a student and a manager.

M Excuse me, are you busy right now? I need to talk to you about the snack bar.

W The snack bar? Is there some sort of problem?

M I wanted to talk to you about the possibility of extending the snack bar hours during midterm exams next week.

W Extending the hours? What exactly did you have in mind?

M Normally, the snack bar closes at 10 o'clock, which is fine during regular weeks, but while midterms are going on, students stay up late and therefore need snacks to keep them going.

W I can certainly understand that. I remember those days! How late were you thinking of extending?

M Could you extend the hours until 1 a.m. during that week? Would that be a problem?

W It definitely will be. You have to remember that the workers at the snack bar are also students like you, and not only do they have to study for their own exams, but they also have to get a good night's sleep before taking their exams.

M I understand that and I can sympathize. But I have this petition that is signed by 100 students who said that they will utilize the snack bar during exam week.

W Hmmm. 100 names, you say? That number may just make it affordable for the snack bar to stay open a couple of hours.

남자: 학생 | 여자: 관리자

학생과 관리자의 대화를 들으시오.

남 실례합니다. 지금 바쁘세요? 매점에 관해 이야기하고 싶은 게 있어서요.

여 매점이요? 뭔가 문제가 있나요?

남 다음 주 중간고사 기간 동안 매점 운영 시간을 연장하는 가능성에 관해 이야기하고 싶었어요.

여 운영 연장이요? 정확히 어떤 생각을 갖고 있는 거죠?

남 보통 매점은 밤 10시에 문을 닫는데, 이건 평상시의 주에는 상관없지만, 중간고사가 치러지는 동안에는 학생들이 늦게까지 깨어 있기 때문에 계속 버티려면 간식이 필요하거든요.

여 그건 확실히 이해할 수 있어요. 그 시절이 기억나네요! 얼마나 늦게까지 연장을 생각하고 있었죠?

남 그 주에는 새벽 1시로 연장해주실 수 있나요? 그게 문제가 될까요?

여 확실히 문제가 되죠. 매점에서 일하는 직원들도 학생과 같은 학생들이라는 것을 기억해야 하고, 그 사람들도 자기 시험을 위해 공부해야 하는 건 물론 시험을 보기 전 잠을 잘 자야 하니까요.

남 이해하고, 공감할 수 있습니다. 하지만 시험 주에 매점을 이용하겠다고 한 학생들 100명이 서명해준 탄원서를 여기 가져왔어요.

여 흠. 100명이라고 했죠? 그 숫자라면 매점이 몇 시간 더 운영될 수 있는 비용이 가능해지겠군요.

Q. What is the woman's opinion of the man's request?

(A) She thinks that it is completely unreasonable.
(B) She wants to help him, but the rules do not allow it.
(C) She believes that she may be able to accommodate him.
(D) She feels that he should be more considerate of other students.

Q. 남자의 요청에 대한 여자의 의견은 무엇인가?

(A) 완전히 말도 안 된다고 생각한다.
(B) 남자를 돕고 싶지만 규정이 허락하지 않는다.
(C) 아마 남자의 요구를 수용할 수 있을 거라고 본다.
(D) 남자가 다른 학생들을 더 배려해야 한다고 느낀다.

어휘 possibility n 가능성 | extend v 연장하다 | exactly adv 정확히 | normally adv 보통 | certainly adv 확실히 | definitely adv 확실히 | sympathize v 공감하다 | petition n 탄원서 | utilize v 이용하다 | affordable adj 감당할 수 있는, 가격이 알맞은

Passage 13

Man: Registrar | Woman: Student

Listen to part of a conversation between a student and a registrar.

W Hello. I have a problem with the scheduling of some of my classes. Is it still possible to change my schedule?

M You just beat the clock! Tomorrow is the final day, so let's see if we can fix your problem.

W That's good! I signed up for Principles of Management, BUS 320, with Dr. Pearl, and originally that class was scheduled to take place in the afternoon, but when I accessed my

남자: 학적부 직원 | 여자: 학생

학생과 학적부 직원의 대화를 들으시오.

여 안녕하세요. 수강 계획을 세우는 데 문제가 좀 있어서요. 아직도 스케줄 변경이 가능한가요?

남 제때 찾아왔어요! 내일이 마지막 날이니 학생의 문제를 해결할 수 있는지 보죠.

여 잘됐네요! 펄 교수님의 비즈니스 320 수업 '경영 원리'에 등록했어요. 원래는 그 수업이 오후에 있을 예정이었는데 제가 어젯밤 온라인으로 일정에 접속했더니 아침 9시로 재조정되었더군요.

schedule on-line last night, I noticed that it was rescheduled to 9 o'clock in the morning.

M Hmm... 1 It wouldn't surprise me if he did. Yeah, you're right. BUS 320 has been moved from the afternoon to the morning. Is that going to be a problem for you?

W I was afraid of that. Unfortunately, I work mornings, so I schedule all of my classes for the afternoon.

M Hmm... So, what are you thinking? Can you afford to drop it?

W Well, I don't have much of a choice. But I'm definitely going to need to take a class to make up for that one. I have to take a standard schedule in order to graduate in the spring.

M I got it. So, you'll be looking for a business elective that counts the same as BUS 320, and it has to be in the afternoon or evening. Is that right?

W That's correct. Also, if it's at all possible, I would still like to take one of Dr. Pearl's classes. I heard his lecture is really good.

M 2 Yeah, everybody does. I took a class with him when I was a graduate student. He's the top in his field.

W Is that a fact?

M You better believe it. 2 He has written most of the definitive texts on management and accounting. Alright! This class might work for you. Dr. Pearl teaches Business Law 380 from 6 to 9 on Thursday nights. It's a long class, but that might serve your purpose. How about that?

W That would be perfect! Is the class still open?

M Well, it's an honors class, so enrollment is limited to 15 students, and there are already 12 in there. Do you want me to sign you up?

W Absolutely! That should work out nicely.

M Okay. Let me repeat this back to you. You want to drop BUS 320 at 9 a.m. on Mondays and Fridays and pick up BUS 380 on Thursdays from 6 to 9 p.m. Is that right?

W That's it. Just in the nick of time!

1. Why does the man say this:

M It wouldn't surprise me if he did.

Ⓐ He is wondering why the student has come to see him.

Ⓑ He wants to know why the professor ignores his students.

Ⓒ He thinks it is common for that professor to change his schedule.

Ⓓ He is implying that the student should have expected what happened.

남 흠... 1 그분이 그러셨다고 해도 놀랍지 않을 거예요. 그래요, 학생 말이 맞네요. 비즈니스 320 수업이 오후에서 오전으로 바뀌었어요. 그게 학생에게 문제가 되나요?

여 그걸 걱정했어요. 유감스럽게도 제가 아침에 일을 해서 모든 수업을 오후로 정했거든요.

남 흠... 그럼, 어떻게 할 생각인가요? 수강을 포기할 수 있어요?

여 글쎄요, 선택의 폭이 넓지 않네요. 하지만 그 수업을 대체할 수업을 꼭 들어야 해요. 봄에 졸업하려면 정규 스케줄에 따라야 하거든요.

남 알겠어요. 그럼 학생은 비즈니스 320과 같은 학점의 비즈니스 선택 과목 가운데 오후나 저녁 수업을 찾아야겠군요. 맞죠?

여 맞아요. 그리고 만약 가능하다면 펄 교수님 수업 중 하나를 꼭 듣고 싶어요. 그분 수업이 정말 좋다고 들었거든요.

남 2 네, 다들 좋아해요. 제가 대학원을 다닐 때 그분 수업을 들었죠. 그분은 이 분야에서 최고예요.

여 정말이에요?

남 그럼요, 믿으세요. 2 그분은 경영과 회계 분야에서 권위 있는 교과서 대부분을 집필했어요. 좋아요! 이 수업이 학생에게 괜찮겠어요. 펄 교수님께서 목요일 저녁 6시부터 9시까지 비즈니스 법률 380 수업을 가르치세요. 긴 수업이지만 학생의 목적에 맞을 것 같은데요. 어때요?

여 완벽해요! 그 수업 아직도 등록할 수 있나요?

남 음, 이건 고급반 수업으로 15명 정원인데 벌써 12명 등록했네요. 등록해 줄까요?

여 물론이죠! 그게 잘 맞겠어요.

남 좋아요. 확인할게요. 월요일과 금요일 오전 9시 수업인 비즈니스 320 수업의 수강 신청을 취소하고, 목요일 저녁 6시부터 9시까지인 비즈니스 380 수업을 선택했어요. 맞죠?

여 맞아요. 아슬아슬하게 때를 맞췄네요!

1. 남자는 왜 이렇게 말하는가:

남 그분이 그러셨다고 해도 놀랍지 않을 거예요.

Ⓐ 학생이 왜 자신을 보러 왔는지 궁금해한다.

Ⓑ 왜 교수가 학생들을 무시하는지 알고 싶어 한다.

Ⓒ 그 교수가 일정을 바꾸는 것은 흔한 일이라고 생각한다.

Ⓓ 학생이 그 일을 예상했어야 한다고 암시한다.

2. What is the man's opinion of the professor?
Ⓐ He thinks that he is an unrivaled expert on his subject.
Ⓑ He was not impressed by him when he was a student.
Ⓒ He believes students give the professor too much credit.
Ⓓ He feels that he should teach more classes than he does.

2. 교수에 관한 남자의 의견은 무엇인가?
Ⓐ 자신의 분야에서 독보적인 전문가라고 생각한다.
Ⓑ 학생이었을 때 그 교수에게서 깊은 인상을 받지 못했다.
Ⓒ 학생들이 교수를 과대평가한다고 생각한다.
Ⓓ 교수가 지금보다 더 많은 수업을 가르쳐야 한다고 생각한다.

어휘 beat the clock 시간 전에 끝내다, 마치다 | principle n 원리, 원칙 | originally adv 원래 | access v 접속하다, 이용하다 | unfortunately adv 안타깝게도, 공교롭게도 | afford v 감당하다, 해내다 | definitely adv 틀림없이, 분명히 | standard adj 표준의, 정규의 | graduate v 졸업하다 | elective n 선택 과목 | count v 간주하다, 세다 | field n 분야 | definitive adj 권위 있는, 최고의 | purpose n 목적 | enrollment n 등록 | absolutely adv 절대적으로 | in the nick of time 아슬아슬하게 때를 맞추어

Passage 14

Man: Postal worker | Woman: Student

Listen to part of a conversation between a student and a postal worker.

W Hi. I was hoping you could help me. I'm leaving town for a few months and I need to know some options about what I can do with my mail.

M Okay. Why don't you explain exactly what's going on, and I'll give you the best options based on your current situation.

W Alright. I'm going to Spain for three months on a student exchange program.

M Spain! How wonderful!

W Yes, I'm really excited. But, what exactly can I do? I'm worried that either I won't be able to receive my letters or something important is going to get lost.

M You don't have to worry about anything like that. 1 We don't make those kinds of mistakes anymore.

W I see.

M Hmm... Well, it sounds like you need either a "temporary change of address" or "hold mail" service.

W Alright, what exactly are those two?

M 2 Well, a "temporary change of address" means that all of your mail will be forwarded to your new address in Spain.

W 2 Well... hmm... I'm not sure about that. It sounds like there's a good chance that some things will get lost. What's the second option?

M The second option is that we hold all of your mail here at this branch. That way nothing will get lost.

W But then how do I deal with all of my bills? If they go unpaid, there will be a mess when I get back!

M What you need to do is set up electronic payment for all of those important payments. Most companies do that these days. That way you can access the bills on the Internet and you won't have any problems when you get back.

남자: 우체국 직원 | 여자: 학생

학생과 우체국 직원의 대화를 들으시오.

여 안녕하세요. 저를 좀 도와주셨으면 해요. 저는 몇 달 동안 도시를 떠나 있을 거예요. 그래서 제 우편물을 어떻게 할 수 있는지에 대해 몇 가지 선택사항을 알고 싶어요.

남 좋아요. 무슨 일인지 정확히 설명해주시면 제가 학생의 현재 상황에 따라 최선의 방법을 알려줄게요.

여 네. 저는 교환 학생 프로그램으로 세 달 동안 스페인에 갈 예정이에요.

남 스페인! 멋지네요!

여 네, 정말 기대돼요. 하지만 제가 정확히 어떻게 할 수 있나요? 편지를 받을 수 없거나 중요한 걸 분실할까 봐 걱정돼요.

남 그런 건 걱정할 필요 없어요. 1 우리는 그런 실수는 더 이상 하지 않아요.

여 알겠습니다.

남 흠... 음, 학생은 '임시 주소 변경'이나 '편지 보관' 서비스가 필요한 것 같네요.

여 네, 그 두 가지는 정확히 뭐죠?

남 2 음, '임시 주소 변경'은 학생의 모든 우편물이 스페인의 새 주소로 보내지는 것을 의미하죠.

여 2 음... 글쎄요. ... 확신이 안 드네요. 뭔가 분실될 가능성이 클 것 같아요. 두 번째 방법은요?

남 두 번째 방법은 우리가 이 지점에서 학생의 우편물을 모두 보관하는 거예요. 그러면 아무것도 잃어버리지 않겠죠.

여 하지만 그렇다면 청구서를 전부 어떻게 처리하죠? 지불하지 않으면 제가 돌아왔을 때 곤란해질 거예요.

남 학생은 모든 중요한 결제에 전자 결제를 설정해 둬야겠네요. 대부분의 회사들이 요즘 그렇게 하고 있어요. 그렇게 하면 인터넷에서 청구서를 볼 수 있고, 돌아왔을 때 아무 문제가 없을 거예요.

W That sounds good. I have a lot of magazine and newspaper subscriptions, too. Will it be a problem with them taking up space in the post office?
M Yes, it can be. You need to call the newspapers and magazines and have them put a hold on delivery as well.
W Okay. I'll put a hold on all of my mail until I return from Spain.
M Right. So, hmm... when exactly are you getting back?
W I don't know really. I'm studying for three months, but I'm hoping to travel around Europe a little before I get back. Is that going to be a problem?
M Not at all. Just come back here with proper ID when you want your mail to start being delivered again.

여 좋네요. 저는 잡지와 신문도 많이 구독하고 있어요. 우체국에서 공간을 차지할 텐데 문제가 있을까요?
남 네, 문제가 될 수 있어요. 신문사와 잡지사에 전화를 해서 배달도 중지해야겠네요.
여 알겠습니다. 스페인에서 돌아올 때까지 모든 우편물 수신을 멈춰둘게요.
남 좋아요. 그러니까 음... 정확히 언제 돌아오나요?
여 저도 잘 몰라요. 세 달 동안 공부를 할 예정이지만 돌아오기 전에 유럽을 좀 여행하고 싶어서요. 문제가 될까요?
남 전혀요. 학생의 우편물이 다시 배달되기를 원할 때 적절한 신분증을 가지고 여기 다시 오면 돼요.

1. What does the man mean when he says this:

M We don't make those kinds of mistakes anymore.

(A) His employer has changed its official policies.
(B) His employer has replaced problematic employees.
(C) His employer has lost items it should have delivered.
(D) His employer does not work with students anymore.

2. What is the student's attitude toward a temporary change of address?

(A) She thinks forwarding the mail is a good idea.
(B) She does not think that it sounds very reliable.
(C) She is surprised that few people choose that option.
(D) She would prefer that only some of the mail be forwarded.

1. 남자는 다음과 같이 말하며 무엇을 의미하는가:

남 우리는 그런 실수는 더 이상 하지 않아요.

(A) 회사에서 공식 규정을 바꿨다.
(B) 회사가 문제를 일으키는 직원을 바꿨다.
(C) 회사가 배달했어야 했던 물건을 잃어버린 적이 있다.
(D) 회사는 더 이상 학생들과 일하지 않는다.

2. 임시 주소 변경에 관한 학생의 태도는 어떠한가?

(A) 우편을 전달하는 것이 좋은 생각이라고 본다.
(B) 그다지 신뢰할 만하지 않다고 본다.
(C) 아주 적은 수의 사람들이 이 옵션을 선택한다는 것이 놀랍다.
(D) 우편의 일부만 전달받는 것을 선호한다.

어휘 exactly adv 정확히 | current adj 현재의 | situation n 상황 | temporary adj 임시의 | foward v (물건·정보를) 보내다, 전달하다 | branch n 지점 | bill n 공과금 청구서 | mess n 엉망, 난장판 | electronic adj 전자의 | access v 접근하다, 이용하다 | subscription n 구독 | proper adj 적절한

Test

본서 | P. 72

Passage 1

Man: Student | Woman: Lab proctor

[1-5] Listen to part of a conversation between a student and a lab proctor.

W Welcome to the chemistry lab. Can I help you?
M 1 Yes, I need to use the lab today. It's very urgent.
W Certainly, we should be able to help you today. What's your name?
M Martin Steinberg.
W Okay. What class are you registered in, Mr. Steinberg?
M I will be attending CHEM 202 this semester.

남자: 학생 | 여자: 실험실 감독관

학생과 실험실 감독관의 대화를 들으시오.

여 화학 실험실에 어서 오세요. 어떻게 도와드릴까요?
남 1 네, 저는 오늘 실험실을 사용해야 해요. 아주 급해요.
여 물론, 우리는 오늘 학생을 도울 수 있을 거예요. 이름이 뭐죠?
남 마틴 스타인버그요.
여 좋아요. 무슨 수업에 등록되었죠, 스타인버그 학생?
남 이번 학기에 화학 202를 들을 예정이에요.

W Just one moment. Hmm. According to the computer, you're not registered in that class.

M I'm aware of that.

W Well, until it does, I'm afraid I can't give you a key to the lab.

M Let me explain. Unfortunately, I waited until the week before classes started to try to register, so when I tried to register for that class, all the spaces were filled up. The registrar told me to get permission from the lecturer. So, I went to the professor. And he said that usually some students drop out a week or two into the semester, so he normally allows a few extra registrations. He gave me an override to get into the class, but the office was closed, so I plan to register tomorrow.

W If you haven't even registered, how do you know what the assignments are? What I mean is, what do you plan to use the lab for?

M Well, **2** I have friends in the class, so I've seen a copy of the syllabus. I know there's an assignment due next week, and I'd like to get a head start on it.

W Well, that's very conscientious of you, but I really think your time would be better spent getting registered first, and then coming back here to do your lab work.

M Look, I promise that I'll register first thing tomorrow, but I really need to use the lab today. If I don't get started on the assignment, I'm really going to get behind the rest of the class.

W I'm sorry, but there's a strict school policy about using the lab. Students must be registered in a chemistry class. Otherwise, they are not allowed in the lab.

M But I really want to impress my professor. Besides, next week I'll have a lot of work in all my other classes.

W **3** I understand your dilemma. Sorry that there's nothing I can do here.

M But... there's got to be some way I can get in to do my assignment. I'm not a thief of any kind.

W **4** I'll tell you what you can do. If you have a friend who is in that class, you can go into the lab with that person. Just make sure that your friend is with you at all times.

M Really? That's great! I'll get my friend Chris to come with me.

W Just a minute! I'm going to have to ask you to keep this a secret. **5** It's strictly against school policy.

M Okay, I won't tell anyone.

W I could lose my job if anyone found out that I've told you this. So, please don't tell anyone about it.

M Don't worry. You're doing me a big favor, and I really appreciate it.

여 잠시만요. 흠, 컴퓨터를 보니 학생은 그 수업에 등록되어 있지 않아요.

남 저도 알아요.

여 그럼 등록할 때까지는 학생에게 실험실 열쇠를 줄 수 없을 것 같네요.

남 제가 설명할게요. 불행히도 제가 개강 전주까지 수강 신청을 안 했어요. 그래서 제가 그 수업에 등록하려 했을 때 모든 자리가 다 차버렸죠. 학적부 직원은 교수님께 허락을 받으라고 했어요. 그래서 교수님에게 갔는데 교수님은 보통 몇 명의 학생들이 학기 첫 주나 둘째 주에 그만둔다고 말씀하셨어요. 그래서 추가 등록을 일부 허락하곤 하신대요. 교수님은 수업에 들어갈 수 있게 추가 등록하도록 해주셨지만 사무실이 닫혀 있어서 내일 등록할 계획이에요.

여 만약 등록도 하지 않은 상태라면 숙제가 무엇인지 어떻게 알죠? 내 말은, 왜 실험실을 사용하려고 하는 거죠?

남 음, **2** 그 수업에 친구들이 있어요. 그래서 강의 계획서를 봤어요. 다음 주까지 과제물이 있는데 미리 시작하고 싶어서요.

여 음, 매우 성실하군요. 하지만 나는 우선 등록하는 데 시간을 할애하는 것이 나을 거라고 생각해요. 그러고 나서 실험실 과제를 하기 위해 여기로 다시 오세요.

남 저기, 내일 아침 제일 먼저 등록부터 하기로 약속할게요. 하지만 저는 정말 오늘 실험실을 사용해야 해요. 숙제를 시작하지 않으면 수업에서 진짜 뒤쳐질 거예요.

여 미안하지만 실험실 사용에 관한 학교 방침이 엄격해요. 학생들은 반드시 화학 수업에 등록되어야만 해요. 그렇지 않으면 실험실에 들어갈 수 없어요.

남 하지만 저는 정말 교수님께 좋은 인상을 남기고 싶어요. 게다가, 다음 주에 다른 수업 과제물도 많이 있어요.

여 **3** 나도 학생의 처지를 이해해요. 제가 여기서 할 수 있는 일이 없어서 유감이네요.

남 하지만... 제가 숙제를 하기 위해 들어갈 수 있는 다른 방법이 있을 거예요. 저는 도둑이 아니잖아요.

여 **4** 학생이 할 수 있는 것들을 말해줄게요. 만약 그 수업을 듣는 친구가 있다면 같이 실험실에 들어가도 돼요. 친구와 항상 같이 있도록 하세요.

남 정말이요? 멋져요! 제 친구 크리스와 함께 오도록 할게요.

여 잠깐만요! 이건 비밀로 해달라고 부탁해야겠군요. **5** 이건 학교에서 엄격히 금하고 있거든요.

남 네. 아무에게도 말하지 않을게요.

여 만약 내가 학생에게 이렇게 말했다는 걸 누군가 알게 되면 저는 실직할 수도 있어요. 그러니 이 얘기는 아무한테도 하지 마세요.

남 걱정 마세요. 저에게 큰 호의를 베푸셨어요. 정말 감사합니다.

1. **What topic are the speakers discussing?**
   - (A) The proper way to do a lab assignment
   - (B) How to register for the chemistry class
   - (C) How the student can gain access to the lab
   - (D) Bringing guests into the labs on campus

2. **What made the student come to the lab?**
   - (A) The student registered late and needs to catch up on work.
   - (B) The professor ordered the student to begin lab work.
   - (C) The student is meeting a friend at the lab.
   - (D) The student wants to start his coursework early.

3. **What is the lab proctor's attitude toward the student?**
   - (A) She is irritated by the student's stubbornness.
   - (B) She seems indifferent toward the student.
   - (C) She feels sympathy toward the student.
   - (D) She has a firm attitude toward the student.

4. **What does the lab proctor do for the student?**
   - (A) She gives the student access to the lab on another day.
   - (B) She tells the student another way to get into the lab.
   - (C) She provides the student keys to another lab on campus.
   - (D) She opens the door of the chemistry lab for the student.

5. **Why does the lab proctor say this:**

   W It's strictly against school policy.

   - (A) She is directing the student to read the rules.
   - (B) She is emphasizing the severity of the policy.
   - (C) She is encouraging the student to register for class.
   - (D) She is indicating that she is taking a risk for him.

1. 화자들은 무슨 주제에 관해 이야기하고 있는가?
   - (A) 실험실 과제를 하는 적절한 방법
   - (B) 화학 수업에 등록하는 법
   - (C) 학생이 실험실 출입 권한을 얻을 수 있는 방법
   - (D) 캠퍼스 내 실험실들에 손님을 데려오기

2. 학생이 실험실에 온 이유는 무엇인가?
   - (A) 늦게 등록했기에 과제를 따라잡아야 한다.
   - (B) 교수가 실험실 일을 시작하라고 지시했다.
   - (C) 친구를 실험실에서 만나려고 한다.
   - (D) 학습 과제를 미리 시작하고 싶어 한다.

3. 학생에 대한 실험실 감독관의 태도는 어떠한가?
   - (A) 학생의 고집에 짜증이 났다.
   - (B) 학생에게 무관심한 것 같다.
   - (C) 학생에게 동정심을 느낀다.
   - (D) 학생에게 확고한 태도를 갖고 있다.

4. 실험실 감독관은 학생에게 무엇을 해주는가?
   - (A) 다른 날 실험실 출입을 하게 해준다.
   - (B) 실험실에 들어올 수 있는 다른 방법을 말해 준다.
   - (C) 캠퍼스 내의 다른 실험실 열쇠를 준다.
   - (D) 화학 실험실 문을 열어준다.

5. 실험실 감독관은 왜 이렇게 말하는가:

   여 이건 학교에서 엄격히 금하고 있거든요.

   - (A) 학생에게 규칙을 읽으라고 안내하고 있다.
   - (B) 규정의 엄격함을 강조하고 있다.
   - (C) 수업에 등록하라고 학생을 장려하고 있다.
   - (D) 학생을 위해 위험을 무릅쓰고 있다는 것을 밝히고 있다.

어휘 urgent adj 급한, 긴급의 | register v 등록하다, 신청하다 | explain v 설명하다 | unfortunately adv 안타깝게도, 불행하게도 | registrar n 학적부 직원 | permission n 허가 | give an override 이미 정원이 다 찬 강의에 (별도의 요청을 통해) 추가 등록하게 해주다 | assignment n 과제 | syllabus n 강의 계획서, 교수 요목 | conscientious adj 성실한 | strict adj 엄격한 | policy n 규정 | impress v 깊은 인상을 주다 | dilemma n 딜레마 | thief n 도둑 | appreciate v 감사하다

Passage 2

Man: Student | Woman: Student advisor

[1-5] Listen to part of a conversation between a student and a student advisor.

M Excuse me. Is this Professor Brody's office?

W No, well, it was. Now it's my office. I am Professor Perkins.

M Did he move to another office?

남자: 학생 | 여자: 지도 교수

학생과 지도 교수의 대화를 들으시오.

남 실례합니다. 브로디 교수님 사무실 맞나요?

여 아니요, 음, 그분의 사무실이었죠. 이제는 제 사무실이에요. 전 퍼킨스 교수고요.

남 그분은 다른 사무실로 옮기셨나요?

W 1 You might say that. He is no longer with us—

M 1 Did something happen to him? Is he alright?

W 1 What? Oh, sorry. That was a poor choice of words on my part. Professor Brody accepted a position at a different university. He doesn't teach here anymore. I was an associate professor last year, and I have taken over his position on the staff here.

M Oh, I see.

W Since I am his replacement, perhaps I can help you?

M I hope so. I took his opera course last semester.

W Which opera course are you referring to?

M Oh, I'm sorry. It was Music Appreciation 204, the one where you get to go to an opera after the midterm exam.

W Ah, yes. That is one of the most popular courses. Did you enjoy the class?

M Yes, I did. My friend is taking the course this term—probably with you. She said that you would be going to see a performance of one of Richard Wagner's operas.

W Yes, we are going to see *Der Ring Des Nibelungen* this year.

M 2 That is what she told me. Wagner is my favorite composer, but I have yet to see a live performance of that opera. Not only that, but I was unable to attend the opera when I took the class. That was a different opera, but I was hoping to attend this year's performance. Would that be possible?

W I would like to say yes. But I am afraid not. 3(C) There are a few reasons why that would be impossible. Firstly, you would have to be auditing the course, but it is too late to register to do that. 3(D) Secondly, we have already reserved our tickets. As you know, the *Ring Cycle* is an epic that is essentially four operas in a series. As such, it is extremely difficult to produce them all, much less consecutively. We will be seeing them one per week for four weeks. So the tickets are in high demand, and we purchased ours accordingly. If you had come during the second week of class, maybe we could have accommodated you, but now…

M I understand. As you said, such productions are rare, so they are difficult to attend. Do I have any other options that you know of?

W Obviously, I cannot guarantee anything, but you have a few options. Firstly, you can try to purchase your own ticket. It is unlikely, but there may be a few seats still open.

M Should I go to the opera house in person to do so?

여 1 그렇게 말해도 되겠죠. 더 이상 우리와 함께 안 계세요.

남 1 무슨 일이 일어났나요? 그분은 괜찮으신가요?

여 1 네? 아, 미안해요. 내가 말을 잘못했네요. 브로디 교수님은 다른 대학의 직책을 맡으셨거든요. 더 이상 여기서 가르치지 않으시죠. 저는 작년에 부교수였고, 여기서 그분의 자리를 맡게 된 거죠.

남 아, 그렇군요.

여 제가 그분을 대신해 들어왔으니 학생을 도와줄 수 있을지도 모르겠네요.

남 그러실 수 있길 바라요. 저는 저번 학기에 브로디 교수님의 오페라 수업을 들었었어요.

여 어떤 오페라 수업을 말하는 거죠?

남 아, 죄송합니다. 음악 감상 204 수업이었어요. 중간고사 뒤에 오페라를 감상하러 가는 수업이었죠.

여 아, 네. 가장 인기 있는 수업들 중 하나죠. 그 수업이 마음에 들었나요?

남 네, 전 그 수업을 좋아했어요. 이번 학기에 제 친구가 그 수업을 들어요. 아마 교수님의 수업일 거예요. 리처드 바그너의 오페라 공연들 중 하나를 보러 갈 거라고 말하더군요.

여 네, 올해 우리는 〈니벨룽의 반지〉를 관람할 거예요.

남 2 제 친구가 저에게 그렇게 말했어요. 바그너는 제가 가장 좋아하는 작곡가지만, 아직 라이브로 그 오페라를 본 적은 없어요. 그뿐만이 아니라, 제가 이 수업을 들었을 때 저는 오페라를 보러 갈 수 없었어요. 그건 다른 오페라였지만, 올해의 공연에 제가 참석할 수 있을까 해서요. 가능할까요?

여 가능하다고 말하고 싶어요. 하지만 안 되겠네요. 3(C) 왜 안 되는지에 대한 이유가 몇 개 있어요. 먼저, 그러기 위해서는 수업을 청강해야 하는데 등록을 하기에는 이미 늦었죠. 3(D) 두 번째로, 우리는 이미 표를 예약했어요. 학생도 알겠지만 〈니벨룽의 반지〉는 사실 네 개의 오페라가 한 개의 시리즈로 된 서사극이에요. 그래서 이 작품을 전부 제작하는 건 물론이고 연속으로 상영하는 것도 극히 어렵죠. 우리는 4주에 걸쳐 한 주에 하나씩 관람할 겁니다. 그래서 표에 대한 수요가 높고, 우리는 그에 맞춰 표를 구매했어요. 만약 수업 2주차에 학생이 왔었다면 받아줄 수도 있었겠지만, 지금은…

남 이해합니다. 교수님이 말씀하신 대로 이런 오페라 제작은 흔한 것이 아니라 참석하기도 힘들죠. 혹시 이 오페라를 볼 수 있는 다른 방법은 없을까요?

여 물론 어떤 것도 보장할 수는 없지만, 방법은 몇 가지 있어요. 먼저, 직접 표를 사는 방법이 있죠. 가능성은 별로 없지만 아직 자리가 몇 개 남아 있을 수도 있으니까요.

남 구매하기 위해서는 오페라 극장에 직접 가야 하나요?

W 4 You could purchase them online, but I would recommend doing so face-to-face. The manager of the Variant Opera House is a friend and alumnus of this university. If you ask to speak to him in person and present your school ID, it might increase your chances of getting tickets.

M Ok, that sounds like a good idea. I should get over there immediately.

W Hold on a second. 5 That is a possibility, but it is a slim one. Another option would be to volunteer to become an usher. For such a large production, they always need extra personnel. You would have to carry out an usher's duties, distributing programs, assisting patrons, escorting people to their seats, etc. You would not be paid as a volunteer, but you would be able to see quite a bit of the performance for free. Not only that, but you might also get a chance to meet some of the cast and crew. I cannot make you any promises, but they are both options worth considering.

M I understand. Thank you for your time, Professor Perkins.

여 4 온라인에서도 살 수 있지만 직접 가서 구매하는 걸 추천해요. 베리언트 오페라 극장의 매니저는 내 친구고, 이 학교의 졸업생이기도 하죠. 그분을 직접 만나서 말하겠다고 요청하고 학생증을 보여주면 표를 살 확률이 높아질 수 있어요.

남 좋은 생각이에요. 지금 당장 가봐야겠어요.

여 잠시만 기다려요. 5 가능성이 있긴 하지만 희박한 거잖아요. 또 다른 방법은, 공연 안내인 자원 봉사를 하는 거예요. 이렇게 큰 오페라 제작은 항상 더 많은 인력을 필요로 하니까요. 프로그램을 나눠주고, 후원자들을 보조하고, 그리고 사람들을 좌석으로 안내하는 등의 안내인 업무를 해야겠죠. 자원 봉사이기에 보수를 받지는 못하겠지만 공연의 꽤나 많은 부분을 공짜로 볼 수 있을 거예요. 그뿐만이 아니라 공연의 출연진과 스태프들을 만날 기회가 있을 수도 있죠. 아무것도 약속할 수는 없지만 생각해볼 만한 방법들이에요.

남 알겠습니다. 시간 내주셔서 감사합니다. 퍼킨스 교수님.

1. Listen again to part of the conversation. Then answer the question.

W You might say that. He is no longer with us—
M Did something happen to him? Is he alright?
W What? Oh, sorry. That was a poor choice of words on my part.

Why does the professor say this:

W That was a poor choice of words on my part.

(A) She doubts if the student knows what she is saying.
(B) She wants to apologize to the student for being offensive.
(C) She noticed that what she said could have been misleading.
(D) She feels bad for telling such sad news to the student.

2. Why did the student come to see the professor?

(A) To get some advice about watching an opera he is interested in
(B) To ask her how the former professor is doing at his new school
(C) To pay for his tickets for the opera the class is going to watch
(D) To get her permission to volunteer as an usher for the opera

1. 대화의 일부를 듣고 질문에 답하시오.

여 그렇게 말해도 되겠죠. 더 이상 우리와 함께 안 계세요.
남 무슨 일이 일어났나요? 그분은 괜찮으신가요?
여 네? 아, 미안해요. 내가 말을 잘못했네요.

교수는 왜 이렇게 말하는가:

여 내가 말을 잘못했네요.

(A) 그녀가 말하는 것을 학생이 알고 있는지 의심한다.
(B) 불쾌하게 행동한 것에 대해 학생에게 사과하고 싶어 한다.
(C) 그녀가 말한 것이 오해의 소지가 있다는 것을 알아차렸다.
(D) 학생에게 이렇게 슬픈 소식을 전하게 되어 유감으로 생각한다.

2. 학생은 왜 교수를 찾아왔는가?

(A) 관심 있는 오페라 관람에 대한 조언을 얻기 위해
(B) 전 교수님이 새 학교에서 어떻게 지내시는지 여쭤보기 위해
(C) 수업에서 관람하려는 오페라 표 가격을 지불하기 위해
(D) 공연 안내원으로 자원 봉사를 하는 데 교수의 허락을 받기 위해

3. What are the reasons that the professor cannot let the student attend this year's opera performance?
Choose 2 answers.
Ⓐ The student already took the same course last semester.
Ⓑ The tickets are sold out since the opera is so popular.
Ⓒ The student came too late to register for the class.
Ⓓ All students in the class already purchased their tickets.

4. Why does the professor mention the Variant Opera House?
Ⓐ To inform the student about a part-time position they offer
Ⓑ To explain the capacity of the opera house to the student
Ⓒ To tell the student that the opera house has a long history
Ⓓ To suggest the student go there to meet the manager

5. What is the professor's opinion of the options she suggests to the student?
Ⓐ She thinks that purchasing one's own ticket is best.
Ⓑ She believes they cannot ensure that the student will see the performance.
Ⓒ She feels working as an usher is good because the student can earn some money.
Ⓓ She knows they require the permission of the manager of the opera house.

3. 교수가 올해의 오페라 공연에 학생을 참석시키지 못하는 이유는 무엇인가? 두 개를 고르시오.
Ⓐ 지난 학기에 이미 똑같은 수업을 들었기 때문에
Ⓑ 오페라의 인기가 너무 많아서 표가 전부 매진되었기 때문에
Ⓒ 수업 등록을 하러 너무 늦게 왔기 때문에
Ⓓ 수업을 듣는 모든 학생들이 이미 표를 구매했기 때문에

4. 교수는 왜 베리언트 오페라 극장을 언급하는가?
Ⓐ 그 극장에서 제공하는 파트타임 일을 학생에게 알려주려고
Ⓑ 그 극장이 수용할 수 있는 인원을 학생에게 설명해주려고
Ⓒ 그 극장이 매우 긴 역사를 지니고 있다는 것을 학생에게 말하려고
Ⓓ 그 극장에 가서 매니저를 만나볼 것을 학생에게 제안하려고

5. 교수가 학생에게 제안하는 방법들에 대한 교수의 의견은 어떠한가?
Ⓐ 본인이 직접 표를 구매하는 것이 가장 좋다고 생각한다.
Ⓑ 두 가지 방법들이 학생이 공연을 볼 수 있다는 보장은 해줄 수 없다고 생각한다.
Ⓒ 학생이 돈을 벌 수 있으므로 안내인으로 자원봉사하는 것이 좋다고 느낀다.
Ⓓ 두 가지 방법들은 오페라 극장 매니저의 허가를 필요로 한다는 것을 알고 있다.

어휘 accept v 받아들이다, 수락하다 I associate professor 부교수 I replacement n 대체 I refer to 언급하다, 가리키다 I appreciation n 감상, 감사 I midterm exam 중간고사 I popular adj 인기가 많은 I performance n 공연 I composer n 작곡가 I attend v 참석하다 I audit v 청강하다 I register v 등록하다 I reserve v 예약하다 I epic n 서사시 I essentially adv 근본적으로, 기본적으로 I consecutively adv 연속하여 I demand n 수요 I accordingly adv 부응하여, 그에 맞춰 I accommodate v 수용하다, 공간을 제공하다 I production n (영화·연극의) 제작 I guarantee v 보장하다 I purchase v 구매하다 I recommend v 추천하다 I face-to-face adj 마주보는, 대면하는 I alumnus n 졸업생 I immediately adv 즉시 I slim adj 빈약한, 보잘것없는 I personnel n 인원, 직원 I usher n 좌석 안내원, 안내 담당자 I duty n 직무, 의무 I distribute v 나눠주다, 분배하다 I assist v 보조하다, 돕다 I patron n 후원자 I escort v 에스코트하다, 안내하다

Lesson 04 Connecting Contents

본서 I P. 76

Practice

Passage 1 Yes – A, C / No – B, D, E
Passage 2 Internship 1 – A, D / Internship 2 – B, C
Passage 3 1. Yes – A, B, D / No – C 2. B
Passage 4 1. Yes – A, C / No – B, D, E 2. D

Test

Passage 1 1. C 2. B 3. Yes – A, E / No – B, C, D 4. A 5. D
Passage 2 1. A 2. A 3. D 4. C 5. B

Passage 1

Man: Librarian | Woman: Student

Listen to part of a conversation between a student and a librarian.

M You look lost. Can I help you?

W You sure can. I'm supposed to watch some videos for a Spanish class I'm taking. My professor has put a series of videos on reserve for us to watch and then write an assignment.

M Okay. (B) Just give me your library card or student ID and you can sign up for the multi-media equipment and room.

W Pardon? I'm not sure I understand. I've never used the library before, and I was hoping to check out these videos to watch them in my dorm room.

M Another new freshman! I'm afraid that won't be possible. (E) The videos are to be used in house only, so if you want to watch them you have to sign up for one of the video rooms.

W A video room? What's that?

M Well, the video rooms are lab facilities where students can watch videos or listen to tapes for research. (D) Students can sign up for either a small room for one to three people or a larger room that can sit between four and six.

W Won't that create a logjam? I mean, there're 30 students in that class and there're only a limited number of tapes, right? Isn't that pushing it?

M Don't worry. Your professor ordered enough tapes for everyone. (A) However, you need to be aware that the maximum time to reserve a video room is two hours and the duration of each tape is 30 minutes. I say this because most students find it helpful to watch foreign language tapes more than once. (C), (D) Additionally, you can only sign up on the day or the day before you wish to use the room.

W That's good to know. (E) Since I can't check out tapes, I'm going to need to know about lab availability. I have class until six o'clock, so I'm only available to come after that.

M Now that could be a problem. (D) Evenings are our busiest times and the labs fill up quickly. So I'm definitely going to advise you to book a day in advance if you're coming at night.

W Right. Thanks. Let me go ahead and sign up for a small room tomorrow night at seven.

남자: 도서관 사서 | 여자: 학생

학생과 도서관 사서의 대화를 들으시오.

남 뭔가 잘 찾지 못하고 계시는 것 같은데요. 제가 도와드릴까요?

여 네. 지금 듣고 있는 스페인어 수업에 필요한 비디오를 봐야 하는데요. 교수님께서 우리가 시청하고 과제를 하도록 비디오 시리즈를 예약해 놓으셨어요.

남 알겠습니다. (B) 도서관 카드나 학생증을 주시면 멀티미디어 장비와 시청각실을 신청할 수 있어요.

여 다시 한번 말씀해 주시겠어요? 제가 제대로 이해했는지 잘 모르겠네요. 전에 도서관을 한 번도 이용해 본 적이 없어서요. 전 비디오를 대여해서 제 기숙사 방에서 보고 싶었는데요.

남 또 다른 신입생이로군요! 그렇게는 할 수 없어요. (E) 비디오는 도서관 안에서만 볼 수 있어요. 그러니까 비디오를 보고 싶다면 시청각실 중 한 곳을 신청한 후 볼 수 있어요.

여 시청각실이요? 그게 뭐예요?

남 음, 시청각실이란 학생들이 연구를 하는 데 필요한 비디오를 보거나 테이프를 들을 수 있는 연구 시설이에요. (D) 학생들은 1명에서 3명까지 앉을 수 있는 작은 시청각실이나 4명에서 6명이 같이 들어갈 수 있는 더 큰 시청각실을 신청할 수 있어요.

여 순서가 밀리지는 않을까요? 그 수업은 30명의 학생이 듣는데 테이프는 한정된 수량만 있는 거죠, 맞죠? 너무 무리 아닌가요?

남 걱정하지 말아요. 교수님께서 모든 학생들이 볼 수 있도록 여유 있게 주문하셨어요. (A) 그렇지만 학생이 알아둬야 할 것은 시청각실을 최장 2시간 동안 예약할 수 있고, 각 테이프의 상영시간은 30분이에요. 내가 이렇게 말하는 이유는 대부분의 학생들이 외국어 테이프를 한 번 이상 보는 것이 도움이 된다고 생각하기 때문이에요. (C), (D) 그리고 시청각실을 사용하고 싶은 날 당일이나 하루 전에만 신청할 수 있어요.

여 좋은 정보네요. (E) 테이프를 대여할 수 없으니까 시청각실을 사용할 수 있을지 알아둬야겠군요. 6시까지 수업이 있어서 그 이후에나 올 수 있어요.

남 그렇다면 문제가 될 수 있어요. (D) 저녁이 가장 붐비기 때문에 시청각실이 빨리 차요. 그러니까 만약 밤에 오게 된다면 하루 전에 미리 예약하라고 꼭 조언을 해주고 싶군요.

여 알겠어요. 감사합니다. 그럼 먼저 가서 내일 저녁 7시에 쓸 작은 시청각실 하나를 예약할게요.

Q. In the conversation, the speakers discuss the requirements for watching foreign language videos. Indicate in the table below whether each of the following is one of those requirements. Click in the correct box for each sentence.

	Yes	No
Ⓐ Video rooms can be reserved in two-hour blocks.	✓	
Ⓑ Students must present their student ID card.		✓
Ⓒ Rooms must be reserved on the day or the day before they will be used.	✓	
Ⓓ Students must reserve rooms at least a few days in advance to watch videos.		✓
Ⓔ Students may check out the videos for up to one week.		✓

Q. 대화에서 화자들은 외국어 영상을 보기 위해 필요한 조건을 논의한다. 다음 각 사항이 그 필수 조건들 중의 하나인지 아닌지 표시하시오. 각 문장에 대해 맞는 칸에 표시하시오.

	예	아니오
Ⓐ 시청각실은 두 시간 단위로 예약할 수 있다.	✓	
Ⓑ 학생들은 반드시 학생증을 제시해야만 한다.		✓
Ⓒ 방은 사용 당일이나 그 전날 예약되어야만 한다.	✓	
Ⓓ 학생들은 비디오를 보기 위해 적어도 며칠 전에는 예약을 해야 한다.		✓
Ⓔ 학생들은 최대 일주일까지 비디오를 빌릴 수 있다.		✓

어휘 reserve n 예약 | assignment n 과제 | freshman n 1학년생 | sign up 신청하다 | facility n 시설 | logjam n 정체 | limited adj 제한된 | aware adj ~을 알고 있는, 인지하는 | maximum adj 최대의 | duration n 지속, 기간 | helpful adj 도움이 되는, 유용한 | additionally adv 추가로 | availability n 이용 가능성 | fill up (자리가) 차다 | definitely adv 분명히, 확실히 | in advance 미리

Passage 2 Man: Academic counselor | Woman: Student

Listen to part of a conversation between a student and an academic counselor.

W Are you busy, Dr. Gibson?

M Not at all, Denise. Come on in and have a seat. What can I do for you?

W With the end of the semester coming up, I was interested in getting a summer internship to gain some experience and make a little extra money. Just one thing though. I know my major is biology, but I was hoping to get a position somewhere in the business field.

M Interesting. I'll try to help you, but you're a sophomore and normally summer internships are reserved for juniors and seniors.

W Really? That doesn't seem very fair!

M Also, with your majoring in biology, you're going to have a hard time convincing a business that you would be an asset. Do you have any other skills that they might find useful?

W Yes, I'm fluent in French.

M French? Okay. That's a good start. Let me see what's available. I've got a couple of openings. **(D)** The first one is in the marketing department of a shoe company. It doesn't pay very much, but it looks like you would get a lot of experience, and **(A)** the competition is probably pretty scarce. **(C)** The second one is very interesting; it's at an international insurance company. **(B)** The money is higher and you'll certainly learn a lot, but the downside is going to be that the competition to get in is going to be pretty harsh.

남자: 학업진로 상담교수 | 여자: 학생

학생과 학업진로 상담교수의 대화를 들으시오.

여 바쁘세요, 깁슨 교수님?

남 아뇨, 데니스. 들어와서 앉아요. 무엇을 도와줄까요?

여 학기말이 다가오면서 경험도 좀 쌓고 돈도 벌어보려고 여름 인턴십에 관심을 갖게 되었어요. 그런데 한 가지 문제가 있어서요. 제 전공이 생물학인데 비즈니스 분야의 일자리를 얻고 싶어요.

남 흥미롭군요. 제가 돕도록 해보죠. 그런데 학생은 2학년이고 인턴십은 보통 3, 4학년 학생들을 위한 거예요.

여 정말이요? 그건 아주 공평하진 않은 것 같아요!

남 게다가 전공이 생물학이라 학생이 회사 업무에 도움이 될 거라는 걸 납득시키기 힘들 거예요. 도움이 될 만한 기술이 있나요?

여 네, 불어를 잘해요.

남 불어요? 좋아요. 시작이 좋네요. 어떤 자리가 있나 한번 봅시다. 자리가 두 개 있네요. **(D)** 첫 번째는 신발 회사의 마케팅 부서 자리예요. 급여를 그리 많이 주지는 않지만 많은 경험을 쌓을 수 있을 것 같아요. **(A)** 아마 경쟁이 거의 없을 거예요. **(C)** 두 번째 자리는 아주 재미있겠네요. 국제 보험 회사예요. **(B)** 급여가 더 높고 분명 배울 게 많을 거예요. 하지만 단점은 들어가려면 경쟁이 꽤 치열할 거란 거죠.

W Still, it sounds really good, so I'd like to give the second one a shot.

M All right. I'm going to need a copy of your résumé and a letter of recommendation within two weeks.

W Hmm... I've got the letter, but I'm sorry to say my résumé could use some sprucing up.

M I'll tell you what. There's a résumé-writing seminar the day after tomorrow at the conference center. Why don't you go there and get them to help you with it?

W That's perfect! Thanks so much for your help.

여 그래도 정말 괜찮은 자리 같은데요. 두 번째 자리를 시도해 보고 싶어요.

남 좋아요. 2주 내로 학생의 이력서와 추천서가 한 부씩 필요해요.

여 음... 추천서는 받았는데 이력서는 손을 좀 봐야 해요.

남 실은, 모레 컨퍼런스 센터에서 이력서 작성 세미나가 있어요. 거기 가서 도움을 받는 게 어때요?

여 그거 좋겠네요! 도와주셔서 정말 감사해요.

Q. In the conversation, the speakers discuss the advantages of two internships. Indicate in the table below which internship has each advantage. Click in the correct box for each phrase.

	Internship 1	Internship 2
Ⓐ Not much competition for the position	✓	
Ⓑ The pay is fairly high for an internship		✓
Ⓒ The position is at an international company		✓
Ⓓ Offers experience in marketing	✓	

Q. 대화에서 화자들은 두 인턴십의 장점을 논의하고 있다. 어떤 인턴십이 각 장점을 가졌는지 아래 표에 표시하시오. 각 구절에 대해 맞는 칸에 표시하시오.

	인턴십 1	인턴십 2
Ⓐ 일자리를 놓고 경쟁이 심하지 않다	✓	
Ⓑ 인턴십 치고 급여가 꽤 높다		✓
Ⓒ 국제적인 회사의 일자리다		✓
Ⓓ 마케팅 경험을 제공한다	✓	

어휘 biology n 생물학 | position n 직책, 일자리 | business n 사업, 상업 | field n 분야 | sophomore n 2학년생 | normally adv 보통 | reserve v 따로 남겨두다, 예약하다 | convince v 납득시키다, 설득하다 | asset n 자산 | fluent adj 유창한 | competition n 경쟁 | scarce adj 부족한, 드문 | international adj 국제의 | insurance n 보험 | certainly adv 확실히, 분명히 | downside n 단점 | harsh adj 가혹한 | résumé n 이력서 | letter of recommendation 추천서 | spruce up 단장하다, 맵시 있게 가꾸다 | (I'll) tell you what (제안을 할 때) 있잖아, 저 말이야

Passage 3

Man: Professor | Woman: Student

Listen to part of a conversation between a student and a professor.

W Professor Howell, Do you have a minute?

M Maggie! This is an unexpected surprise! Can I help you with something or did you just want to talk?

W I know, I know. I've had a couple of crucial absences. Still, I would like to talk to you about this research paper.

M Certainly. What would you like to know? Do you have questions about content or procedure?

W Content. I'm a little confused about the nature of the assignment. Do we only have to observe the test children and then record how they react during the experiment?

M Uh, that's just the tip of the iceberg, I'm afraid. **1(A)** First, you need to go to the library and do as much research as possible on Childhood Behavioral Development. **1(B)** After that, you need to predict certain behavioral patterns based on this research. After that...

남자: 교수 | 여자: 학생

학생과 교수의 대화를 들으시오.

여 하웰 교수님, 잠깐 시간 있으세요?

남 매기! 생각지도 못했는데 놀랍군요! 뭐 도와줄 게 있어요, 아니면 그냥 이야기를 하고 싶은 건가요?

여 알아요, 알아요. 제가 중요한 날에 몇 번 결석을 했죠. 그래도 이 학기말 리포트에 관해 이야기를 하고 싶어서요.

남 그럼요. 뭘 알고 싶은가요? 내용에 관한 질문인가요, 아니면 과정에 관한 질문인가요?

여 내용이요. 과제물의 본래 취지가 조금 헷갈려서요. 실험 대상 아이들을 관찰하고 실험 기간 동안 아이들이 어떻게 반응하는지를 기록하기만 하면 되나요?

남 미안하지만 그건 단지 빙산의 일각이에요. **1(A)** 우선, 도서관에 가서 아동 행동 발달에 관해 가능한 한 많이 조사하세요. **1(B)** 그 후에, 이 조사를 기반으로 특정 행동 패턴을 예측해야 돼요. 그리고 나서...

W Then, where does the observation come in?
M Oh-oh, you didn't let me finish. 1(D) I was going to say that after you make your predictions, then you should go and observe the test subjects and see if any of the behavior you observe backs up your research.
W Where on Earth am I supposed to find that many children in such a wide array of ages!
M I'll remind you I went over the procedure on the first day in class in which we discussed this project.
W I'm sorry, but I missed that day because I overslept.
M Oh, I don't have time to go over this with you again, but 2 go see the assistant in the psychology department, and she will go over it in detail.
W I'm sorry again. I'll go and do that immediately.
M That's alright. You just need to pick up the slack for the rest of the term. Anyway, the assistant can provide you with the names and contact information of the parents who have agreed to do the project. You should be able to contact them independently and set up an appointment.
W Thanks again. Sorry for keeping you.
M No problem. See you in class.

여 그렇다면 어디에서 관찰이 이루어지죠?
남 어어, 내 말이 아직 끝나지 않았어요. 1(D) 학생이 예측을 한 후에 실험 대상에게 가서 관찰하고 학생이 한 조사를 뒷받침하는 어떤 행동들이 있는지 보라는 얘기를 하려고 했어요.
여 도대체 어디에서 이렇게 방대한 연령대의 아이들을 많이 찾을 수 있나요?
남 이 프로젝트에 관해 이야기했던 수업 첫날에 실험 과정에 대해 살펴봤던 것을 기억하나요?
여 아, 죄송해요. 제가 늦잠을 자서 그 수업을 못 들었어요.
남 오, 지금 학생한테 이걸 다시 이야기해줄 시간은 없지만, 2 심리학과 조교에게 가면 이걸 자세히 다시 설명해줄 거예요.
여 다시 한번 죄송해요. 지금 바로 가서 그렇게 할게요.
남 괜찮아요. 뒤처진 부분을 학기 나머지 기간 동안 따라잡을 필요가 있어요. 어쨌든, 그 조교가 이 프로젝트에 참여하기로 한 학부모들의 이름과 연락처를 줄 거예요. 학생은 그들과 개별적으로 연락을 한 후 약속을 잡아야 해요.
여 다시 한번 감사합니다. 시간 뺏어서 죄송해요.
남 괜찮아요. 수업 때 봐요.

1. In the conversation, the speakers discuss the requirements of a research paper. Indicate in the table below which of the requirements apply to the student's assignment. Click in the correct box for each phrase.

	Yes	No
(A) Conduct research at the library on Childhood Behavioral Development	✓	
(B) Make predictions about behavioral patterns that may arise	✓	
(C) Locate children to participate in the behavioral study		✓
(D) Observe the test subjects to see if their behavior corresponds with research	✓	

2. Why does the professor mention the assistant in the psychology department?
(A) To express how annoyed he is by the student's attitude
(B) To direct the student to someone else who can provide help
(C) To show the student the first step for starting her assignment
(D) To tell the student that he needs to help someone else right now

1. 대화에서 화자들은 학기말 리포트의 필수 조건에 관해 논의한다. 어떤 필수 조건이 학생의 과제에 적용되는지 아래의 표에 표시하시오. 각 구절에 대해 맞는 칸에 표시하시오.

	예	아니오
(A) 도서관에서 아동 행동 발달에 관해 조사하기	✓	
(B) 발생할 수 있는 행동 패턴에 관해 예측하기	✓	
(C) 행동 연구에 참여할 아이들 찾기		✓
(D) 실험 대상의 행동이 조사와 부합하는지 관찰하기	✓	

2. 교수는 왜 심리학과 조교를 언급하는가?
(A) 학생의 태도에 자신이 얼마나 짜증이 났는지 표현하려고
(B) 도움을 줄 수 있는 다른 누군가에게 학생을 보내려고
(C) 학생에게 과제를 시작하는 첫 단계를 보여주려고
(D) 지금 다른 사람을 도와야 한다고 말하려고

어휘 unexpected adj 예상하지 못한 I crucial adj 중요한 I absence n 결석, 부재 I content n 내용 I procedure n 과정, 절차 I confused adj 혼란스러운, 헷갈리는 I assignment n 과제 I observe v 관찰하다 I record v 기록하다 I react v 반응하다 I experiment n 실험 I iceberg n 빙산 I childhood n 아동기 I behavioral development 행동 발달 I predict v 예측하다 I certain adj 특정한 I subject n (연구·실험) 대상 I back up 뒷받침하다, 지지하다 I array n 집합체, 모음 I discuss v 논의하다 I oversleep v 늦잠 자다 I assistant n 조교 I immediately adv 즉시, 즉각 I pick up the slack (밀린/뒤처진) 일을 처리하다 I contact information 연락처 I independently adv 따로, 개별적으로 I appointment n 약속, 예약

Passage 4

Man: Student | Woman: University employee

Listen to part of a conversation between a student and a university employee.

W Good morning. Do you need help with something?

M Yeah. I think I'm a little lost. Is this the registrar's office?

W Yes, it is.

M Uhhh... I'm not sure if you can, but I do have a question, and I hope you can direct me to someone who can help me.

W I'll do the best I can.

M Well, I was a graduate student and I went here in the early 90's. I graduated from the medical school in 2001. **1(A),(E)** I need my transcripts and a letter of recommendation that are supposed to be here. I heard I could get them online, but when I accessed your website, it said I had to come down here.

W **1(C)** Yes, unfortunately a new federal law prevents us from giving out any private information without checking an ID in person.

M **2** Are you sure? I'm positive that a fellow alumnus was able to upload her transcripts directly to a prospective employer.

W I would seriously doubt that. The law was enacted in 2001 to prevent any sort of identity theft.

M Wow! Is that a fact?

W Let's see if I can help you while you're here. What's your name?

M Scott. Adam Scott.

W And the year of graduation?

M 2001.

W One second please while I access your information. Okay, here you are, Doctor Scott. I have your records.

M Great! Can you give me four copies of the transcripts and three copies of the letter of recommendation?

W **1(D)** I'm sorry. It takes one working day to process. However, if you show me your ID now, I can mail out your documents tomorrow, and you will get them in 2 to 3 working days.

M Okay. That should be fine. My address is 2456 East Sawgrass Avenue, Kingstree, South Carolina, 29556. Is there any charge for this service?

W None at all, Doctor Scott. **1(B)** We mail all of the documents to our alumni free of charge provided the delivery doesn't exceed 10 copies per year.

남자: 학생 | 여자: 대학교 직원

학생과 대학교 직원의 대화를 들으시오.

여 안녕하세요. 도움이 필요하신가요?

남 네, 제가 약간 헤매고 있는 것 같네요. 여기가 학적부 사무실인가요?

여 네, 그래요.

남 어... 도와주실 수 있을지 모르겠는데요, 질문이 있는데 도와줄 수 있는 사람에게 좀 안내해 주셨으면 해요.

여 최선을 다해 보죠.

남 음, 전 대학원 학생이었고 90년대 초에 여길 다녔어요. 2001년에 의과대학을 졸업했고요. **1(A),(E)** 여기 성적증명서와 추천서가 필요해요. 온라인으로 받을 수 있다고 들었는데, 웹사이트에 접속하니 여기로 와야 한다고 되어 있더라고요.

여 **1(C)** 네, 아쉽게도 새로운 연방법 때문에 직접 신분증을 확인하지 않고는 개인 정보를 내주지 못하게 되어 있어요.

남 **2** 확실하신가요? 제 동문 중 한 명이 성적 증명서를 장래의 고용주에게 직접 전송할 수 있었던 걸로 알고 있는데요.

여 그럴 리가요. 모든 종류의 신원 도용을 금하도록 2001년에 법이 제정되었는 걸요.

남 와! 그게 사실이에요?

여 여기 계신 동안 도와드릴 수 있는지 보죠. 성함이 어떻게 되시죠?

남 스캇이요. 아담 스캇이에요.

여 졸업 연도는요?

남 2001년이요.

여 정보를 검색하는 동안 잠시 기다려주세요. 네, 여기 있네요, 스캇 박사님. 기록을 찾았어요.

남 잘됐네요! 성적 증명서 네 장과 추천서 세 장을 주실 수 있나요?

여 **1(D)** 죄송하지만 처리하는 데 하루가 걸려요. 하지만 지금 신분증을 보여주시면 서류를 내일 우편으로 보내드릴 수 있어요. 그럼 2~3일 내에 받으실 거예요.

남 네, 좋아요. 제 주소는 2456 동부 서그래스가, 킹스트리, 사우스캐롤라이나주, 29556이에요. 요금을 내야 하나요?

여 전혀 없어요, 스캇 박사님. **1(B)** 배송량이 1년에 10부를 넘지 않으면 졸업생에게 모든 서류를 무료로 우편으로 보내고 있어요.

M Boy! I'm glad I found you!
W Will that be all today?
M It certainly will. Thank you so much for your help.

남 와! 제가 담당자를 제대로 만났군요.
여 다른 사항은 없으신가요?
남 네. 도와주셔서 정말 감사합니다.

1. In the conversation, the speakers discuss the process by which documents may be obtained. Indicate in the table below whether each of the following is indicated about that process.

Click in the correct box for each sentence.

	Yes	No
Ⓐ The person must come to the university in person.	✓	
Ⓑ There is a limit to the number of documents that can be obtained.		✓
Ⓒ The person must present a valid identification card.	✓	
Ⓓ The transcripts take a week to process.		✓
Ⓔ The person may access the documents on the university website.		✓

2. Why does the man mention a fellow alumnus?

Ⓐ To tell the woman that she misunderstood him
Ⓑ To show the woman has wrong information
Ⓒ To ask the woman to make an exception
Ⓓ To persuade the woman that she could be wrong

1. 대화에서 화자들은 서류를 받을 수 있는 절차를 논의한다. 다음 각 사항이 그 절차에 나타나 있는 것인지 아래 표에 표시하시오.

각 구절에 대해 맞는 칸에 표시하시오.

	예	아니오
Ⓐ 신청자가 직접 대학에 와야 한다.	✓	
Ⓑ 받을 수 있는 서류의 수량에는 한계가 있다.		✓
Ⓒ 신청자는 유효한 신분증을 제시해야 한다.	✓	
Ⓓ 성적 증명서는 처리하는 데 일주일이 걸린다.		✓
Ⓔ 신청자는 대학교 웹사이트에서 서류에 접근할 수도 있다.		✓

2. 남자는 왜 동문 한 명을 언급하는가?

Ⓐ 여자가 자신의 말을 오해했다고 말하려고
Ⓑ 여자가 잘못된 정보를 갖고 있다는 것을 보이려고
Ⓒ 여자에게 예외를 만들어달라고 부탁하려고
Ⓓ 여자가 틀렸을 수도 있다고 설득하려고

어휘 registrar n 학적부 | direct v 안내하다 | graduate student 대학원생 | transcript n 성적 증명서 | letter of recommendation 추천서 | unfortunately adv 아쉽게도 | prevent v 금지하다, 막다 | private adj 개인의 | alumnus n 졸업생 (pl. alumni) | directly adv 직접, 바로 | prospective adj 장래의, 유망한 | doubt v 의심하다 | enact v 제정하다 | identity theft 신원 도용 | record n 기록 | process v 처리하다 | working day 근무 시간대, 업무일 | exceed v 넘다, 초과하다

Test

본서 | P. 84

Passage 1

Man: Professor | Woman: Student

[1-5] Listen to part of a conversation between a student and a professor. In the conversation, the professor and his student are discussing a well-made play, which is a genre of play and not an opinion of quality.

M Hello, Patricia. Please come in and have a seat.
W Hello, Professor. Your teaching assistant said that you wanted to see me?
M Yes, but don't worry. It's nothing serious. **1** I just wanted to check to see how you are doing with your term paper. Have you selected a play from the list to write about?

남자: 교수 | 여자: 학생

학생과 교수의 대화를 들으시오. 대화에서 교수와 그의 학생은 연극의 질에 대한 의견이 아닌 연극의 한 장르인 웰메이드 극에 대해 토론하고 있다.

남 안녕하세요, 패트리샤. 들어와서 앉아요.
여 안녕하세요, 교수님. 교수님께서 절 보자고 하셨다고 조교님에게 들었는데요?
남 맞아요. 하지만 걱정 마요. 심각한 일은 아니니까요. **1** 학생이 학기말 과제를 어떻게 하고 있는지 알고 싶었을 뿐이에요. 과제에서 쓸 연극 하나를 목록에서 골랐나요?

W Yes—I chose Henrik Ibsen's *A Doll's House*. I am going to write about how his play turned the conventions of the well-made play on their heads. So I figured I should start the essay by explaining how the term "well-made play" came to be. As you know, it was Eugene Scribe who coined the term to describe the genre that he perfected...

M Yes, I do know that. **2** But, do your readers need a lot of background information? It probably isn't necessary to go into a lot of historical detail. As you said, Ibsen took the genre and drastically altered it.

W But I should give a definition of that genre of play in order to explain how it was changed, shouldn't I?

M Yes, you should do that. I meant that you shouldn't focus too much on Scribe or his and other authors' works. The genre became well established, and many authors like Alexandre Dumas wrote in it and put their own unique spin on the style. There is quite a bit of history that you need not include. Focus more on the genre itself, and what Ibsen did with it.

W Okay, I see your point.

M So, what are the defining characteristics of a well-made play?

W **3(E)** Uh, the audience knows more than some of the characters do. Um, I mean, the story depends on an important piece of information that some characters do not know, but the other characters and the audience do know.

M Good, what else?

W **3(A)** Most of the actual story has occurred before the curtain rises. **3(B)** Also, the play usually takes place in one place like a living room. There is a mystery that needs to be resolved. **3(C)** And the main character wins in the end.

M Okay, you covered all of the main points. How well does Ibsen's play fit this definition?

W His play has all of the necessary components. In fact, it is practically a textbook example of a well-made play. That is, except for the ending. The ending is far from happy. No one wins, and it is very open. There are many unanswered questions. Nora, the wife character, just leaves the house. It's like she abandons the play along with her family. She just ceases to be a character.

M Actually, that is a very good way of putting it. Have you looked up what critics at the time said about the play?

여 네, 저는 헨릭 입센의 〈인형의 집〉을 골랐어요. 그의 연극이 어떻게 웰메이드 극의 전통을 뒤집어 놓았는지 쓸 거예요. 그래서 제 에세이를 '웰메이드 극'이라는 단어가 어떻게 생겨났는지에 대해 설명하는 걸로 시작해야 한다고 봤어요. 교수님도 아시겠지만 자신이 완성한 이 장르를 묘사하기 위해 그 이름을 붙인 건 유진 스크리브였죠...

남 맞습니다, 알고 있어요. **2** 하지만 학생의 독자들이 많은 배경 정보를 필요로 할까요? 너무 많은 역사적 세부 사항으로 들어갈 필요는 없을 것 같아요. 학생이 말했듯 입센이 이 장르를 받아들여 철저하게 바꿔놨으니까요.

여 하지만, 어떻게 변화했는지 설명하기 위해서는 이 장르의 연극에 대한 정의를 해야 하잖아요, 그렇지 않나요?

남 네, 물론 그래야죠. 내 말은, 학생이 스크리브나 그와 다른 작가들의 작품에 너무 많이 초점을 맞춰서는 안 된다는 거였어요. 이 장르는 확실히 자리를 잡았고, 알렉산더 뒤마와 같은 많은 작가들이 작품을 썼고 이 양식에 독특한 파생점을 더했어요. 학생이 포함하지 않아도 되는 역사가 꽤 많죠. 장르 그 자체와 입센이 그 장르에 무엇을 했는지에 더 집중하도록 하세요.

여 네, 무슨 말씀이신지 알겠어요.

남 그래서 웰메이드 극을 정의하는 특징들에는 무엇이 있나요?

여 **3(E)** 어, 관객들은 연극 속의 몇몇 인물들보다 더 많은 것을 알고 있어요. 음, 제 말은, 연극의 이야기가 몇몇 인물들이 알지 못하는 중요한 정보에 의존하고 있지만 다른 인물들과 관객은 알고 있죠.

남 좋아요, 또 뭐가 있죠?

여 **3(A)** 실제 이야기의 대부분은 막이 오르기 전에 이미 일어났어요. **3(B)** 또한, 연극은 거실과 같은 한 장소에서 이루어지죠. 풀어야 하는 미스터리가 있어요. **3(C)** 그리고 주인공은 마지막에 승리를 거둬요.

남 좋아요, 모든 요점들을 다 다뤘군요. 입센의 연극은 이 정의에 얼마나 잘 들어맞나요?

여 그의 연극은 모든 필요한 요소를 다 갖추고 있어요. 사실, 웰메이드 극의 교과서적 예시와 다름없죠. 다만 결말을 제외하고요. 결말은 행복과 거리가 멀어요. 누구도 승리를 쟁취하지 않고, 매우 열린 결말이죠. 답하지 않은 질문들이 매우 많아요. 아내 역의 노라는 그냥 집을 떠나요. 가족과 함께 연극 자체를 버리는 느낌이죠. 극 속의 인물이 되는 것을 그만둬요.

남 사실, 학생이 말한 게 아주 좋은 표현이군요. 당시의 평론가들이 이 연극에 대해 뭐라고 했는지 찾아봤나요?

W Oh, yes, I have. Most of them were very harsh with their reviews. Many of them seemed to genuinely hate the play! They acted like it was a crime against drama.

M Again, very well put. That is exactly what they thought it was. **4** The theater in those days avoided controversial subject matter. European theater was expected to embody strict moral standards related to family life and proper behavior.

W Right, but Ibsen was a realist—one of the first dramatic realists. **4, 5** He examined the realities that actually lay under the surface of "proper" society. He revealed things that people did not want to acknowledge, especially about how women were treated by society. **5** The broken marriage he depicted in *A Doll's House* was very upsetting to them.

M Yes, indeed it was. He ended up having to write alternate endings for the play to be performed in other countries where that topic was considered to be too scandalous.

여 아, 네, 찾아봤어요. 대부분이 논평에서 매우 냉혹한 평가를 했더군요. 다수가 진심으로 이 연극을 싫어한 것처럼 보였어요! 이 연극이 극에 대한 범죄라도 되는 것처럼 행동했죠.

남 다시 한번 매우 잘 말해줬어요. 그게 바로 평론가들이 생각한 것이었어요. **4** 그 당시의 연극은 논란의 요소가 있는 주제를 피했어요. 유럽의 연극은 가정생활에 관련된 엄격한 도덕 기준과 바른 행동을 그리도록 기대되었죠.

여 맞아요. 하지만 입센은 현실주의자였어요—최초의 현실주의 극작가들 중 하나였죠. **4, 5** '올바른' 사회 표면 아래에 실제로 자리하는 현실을 관찰했어요. 그는 사람들이 인정하고 싶어하지 않았던 것들을 드러냈어요, 특히 여성이 사회에 의해 어떻게 다루어지는지를요. **5** 〈인형의 집〉에서 그가 그려낸 결혼의 파국은 사람들에게 매우 불쾌한 것이었어요.

남 맞아요. 정말로 그랬죠. 이 주제가 너무 논란이 된다고 여겨지는 다른 나라들에서 공연을 하기 위해 입센은 다른 결말을 써야만 했습니다.

1. Why did the professor want to see the student?

Ⓐ To explain the concept of a well-made play to the student
Ⓑ To clarify the information the student included in her paper
Ⓒ To see if the student was doing okay with her assignment
Ⓓ To discuss certain characteristics of *A Doll's House*

2. What is the professor's opinion of the information that the student provided?

Ⓐ He considers historical background not necessary for the student's paper.
Ⓑ He finds some of it to be excessive for the readers.
Ⓒ He thinks the student should revise some controversial issues.
Ⓓ He believes that the information supports the student's view well.

3. In the conversation, the speakers discuss the characteristics of a well-made play. Indicate in the table below whether each of the following is one of those characteristics. Click in the correct box for each sentence.

	Yes	No
Ⓐ Most of the action has already taken place before the play begins.	✓	

1. 교수는 왜 학생을 보고자 했는가?

Ⓐ 웰메이드 극의 개념을 학생에게 설명하기 위해
Ⓑ 학생이 과제에 포함한 정보를 명확히 하기 위해
Ⓒ 학생이 과제를 잘하고 있는지 보기 위해
Ⓓ 〈인형의 집〉의 어떤 특징들을 논의하기 위해

2. 학생이 제시한 정보에 대한 교수의 의견은 어떠한가?

Ⓐ 역사적 배경이 학생의 과제에 불필요하다고 본다.
Ⓑ 어떤 정보는 독자에게 과하다고 본다.
Ⓒ 논란이 될 만한 몇몇 주제는 수정해야 한다고 생각한다.
Ⓓ 정보가 학생의 관점을 잘 뒷받침한다고 믿는다.

3. 대화에서 화자들은 웰메이드 극의 특징을 논의한다. 다음 각 사항이 그 특징인지 아래 표에 표시하시오. 각 구절에 대해 맞는 칸에 표시하시오.

	예	아니오
Ⓐ 사건의 대부분은 극이 시작되기 전에 이미 일어났다.	✓	

Ⓑ The play is set in a public space with many people watching.		✓
Ⓒ The protagonist meets a sudden and surprising end.		✓
Ⓓ Its story develops as the characters leave the play one by one.		✓
Ⓔ There is a pivotal piece of information that some characters lack.	✓	

4. What can be inferred about *A Doll's House*?

Ⓐ It introduced ideas that were not dealt with at that time.
Ⓑ It was controversial due to its influence on society.
Ⓒ It ended up emphasizing the immoral nature of man.
Ⓓ It received both positive and negative reviews from critics.

5. How was *A Doll's House* different from traditional well-made plays?

Ⓐ It introduced more than one ending for each theater.
Ⓑ It embraced the theme of marriage and concentrated heavily on it.
Ⓒ It developed its story around a woman's life, which was not popular at the time.
Ⓓ It focused on themes that people viewed as uncomfortable and taboo.

Ⓑ 연극은 많은 사람들이 보는 공공 장소를 배경으로 설정된다.		✓
Ⓒ 주인공이 갑작스럽고 놀라운 결말을 맞는다.		✓
Ⓓ 인물들이 한 명씩 극을 떠나면서 이야기가 전개된다.		✓
Ⓔ 일부 인물들이 가지고 있지 않은 중심 정보가 있다.	✓	

4. 〈인형의 집〉에 대해 무엇을 추론할 수 있는가?

Ⓐ 당시 다뤄지지 않던 생각들을 접하게 했다.
Ⓑ 사회에 끼친 이 작품의 영향으로 인해 논란이 많았다.
Ⓒ 인간의 부도덕한 본성을 강조했다.
Ⓓ 평론가들로부터 긍정적, 부정적 평가 둘 다를 받았다.

5. 〈인형의 집〉은 전통적인 웰메이드 극과 어떻게 달랐는가?

Ⓐ 각 극장에 하나 이상의 결말을 도입했다.
Ⓑ 결혼이라는 주제를 아우르고 그것에 많이 집중했다.
Ⓒ 여자의 삶을 중심으로 이야기를 발전시켜나갔는데, 이는 당시 인기 있는 주제가 아니었다.
Ⓓ 사람들이 불편해하고 금기시하는 주제들에 집중했다.

어휘 teaching assistant 조교 I select v 고르다, 선별하다 I play n 연극 I convention n 전통 I well-made play 웰메이드 극 I turn ~ on one's head 큰 변화를 겪다 I coin v 새로운 낱말/어구를 만들다 I genre n 장르 I perfect v 완벽하게 하다 I background information 배경 정보 I historical adj 역사적인 I drastically adv 철저하게, 급격하게 I alter v 바꾸다 I spin n 회전, 파생 I defining adj 정의하는 I audience n 관객 I resolve v 해결하다 I cover v 다루다 I definition n 정의 I component n 요소 I practically adv 사실상 I unanswered adj 답변하지 않은, 해답이 나오지 않은 I abandon v 버리다, 떠나다 I cease v 그치다, 멈추다 I critic n 비평가, 평론가 I harsh adj 가혹한, 냉혹한 I genuinely adv 진정으로 I crime n 범죄 I controversial adj 논란이 많은 I embody v 포함하다, 담다 I strict adj 엄격한 I moral adj 도덕상의, 도의적인 I proper adj 적절한 I realist n 현실주의자, 사실주의자 I dramatic adj 연극의 I reality n 현실 I treat v 대하다, 다루다 I depict v 그리다, 묘사하다 I upsetting adj ~에게 불편한, 속상하게 하는 I alternate adj 대안이 되는, 대체의 I scandalous adj 추문의, 물의를 빚는

Passage 2 Man: Student | Woman: Professor

[1-5] Listen to part of a conversation between a student and a professor.

M Hello, Professor Hahn, here are the evaluations from my class.
W Thank you. Do you have a few minutes to spare?
M Sure, how can I help you?

남자: 학생 | 여자: 교수

학생과 교수의 대화를 들으시오.

남 안녕하세요, 한 교수님. 여기 저희 수업에서 작성한 평가입니다.
여 고마워요. 잠깐 시간 좀 낼 수 있나요?
남 네, 어떻게 도와드릴까요?

W Well, as you know, I have to screen applicants for the opening in our department.

M Yes, that is why we had to fill out these evaluations. They took a little bit longer to fill out than I had expected them to. I guess you wanted to get as much information from us as possible.

W Exactly, so, 1 can I ask your opinion of the professors who taught your course this week?

M They were both pretty good.

W Yes, they were, but could you be more specific?

M Well, the woman's presentation was quite impressive and very entertaining. You could tell that she is a film expert. She really knows her subject well.

W That is true. She is considered to be at the top of her field. But, the man seemed quite knowledgeable as well.

M 2 Yes, but I found his presentation harder to understand. He used too much jargon.

W Oh, really? I hadn't noticed.

M 2 Yes, he used a lot of terms that didn't really seem necessary. I had to ask the woman sitting next to me what some of them meant.

W I see. Did you feel that he was trying to show off his vocabulary?

M No, not really. It just seemed overly technical. But, the woman was very easy to understand. I think that is why I liked her presentation more.

W So, you didn't have any problem understanding her accent? It was rather strong.

M No, she is Scottish, right?

W Yes, she is originally from Glasgow.

M 3 Where is the man from? He sounded like he's American.

W 3 Oh, yes, he's from Baltimore, which isn't far from here. So, if you had to choose one of them to have as your professor, which one would you choose?

M I would definitely choose the woman. As you said, she is at the top of her field.

W Yes, I did say that. 4 However, just because someone knows a lot about their subject, doesn't necessarily make them the best instructor.

M She is a good instructor, though. She was more engaging.

W She was very entertaining. But, did you feel like you learned a lot from her?

M Um, I hadn't really thought about that. I guess I learned some. Yeah. Her interpretation of some movies that I had already seen was rather different than I would have expected. But, she supported her points well.

여 음, 학생도 알겠지만 우리 학부의 비어 있는 교수직에 지원한 지원자들을 가려내야 해요.

남 네, 그래서 저희가 이 평가서를 작성했죠. 예상했던 것보다 작성하는 데 시간이 좀 더 걸렸어요. 저희로부터 가능한 한 많은 정보를 얻으려고 하셨던 것 같네요.

여 바로 그거예요. 그래서 1 이번 주에 수업을 가르쳤던 교수님들에 대한 학생의 생각이 어떤지 물어봐도 될까요?

남 두 분 다 잘 가르치셨어요.

여 네, 그랬겠죠. 하지만 더 구체적으로 말해줄 수 있나요?

남 음, 여자 교수님의 발표가 꽤 인상적이었고 매우 재미있었어요. 영화 전문가라는 걸 알 수 있었죠. 자기가 얘기하고자 하는 주제를 매우 잘 알고 계세요.

여 맞아요. 그 분야에서 최고로 여겨지는 분이죠. 하지만 남자 교수도 꽤 지식이 많은 것처럼 보였어요.

남 2 네, 하지만 그분의 발표가 이해하기 더 어려웠어요. 전문 용어들을 너무 많이 쓰셨거든요.

여 아, 그래요? 알아차리지 못했네요.

남 2 네, 그다지 필요하지 않아 보이는 단어들을 많이 사용했어요. 제 옆에 앉아 있는 여자분에게 단어 몇 개가 무슨 뜻인지를 물어봐야 했죠.

여 그랬군요. 자신의 어휘를 자랑하기 위한 것처럼 느껴졌나요?

남 아니요, 그건 아닙니다. 그저 너무 전문적으로 보였어요. 하지만 여자 교수님은 이해하기 매우 쉬웠죠. 그래서 제가 그분의 발표를 더 좋아한 것 같아요.

여 그래서 그녀의 억양을 이해하는 데는 문제가 없었나요? 억양이 꽤 강했는데요.

남 문제없었습니다. 스코틀랜드 분이죠, 그렇죠?

여 네, 글래스고 출신이에요.

남 3 남자 교수님은 어디 출신이신가요? 미국 분처럼 들렸어요.

여 3 아, 맞아요. 여기서 그다지 멀지 않은 볼티모어에서 오셨죠. 그래서, 만약 학생이 두 분 중 한 명을 교수님으로 선택해야 한다면 어떤 분을 선택할 건가요?

남 저는 틀림없이 여자 교수님을 선택할 거예요. 교수님이 말하셨듯이, 자기 분야에서 최고잖아요.

여 네, 그렇게 말했죠. 4 하지만 자신의 분야에 대해 많이 알고 있다고 해서 그 사람이 가장 훌륭한 교수가 되는 건 아니에요.

남 그래도 그분은 좋은 강사였어요. 더 호감이 가는 쪽이었어요.

여 매우 즐거운 강의를 했죠. 하지만 학생이 그 교수로부터 많이 배웠다고 생각하나요?

남 음, 그 생각은 해보지 못했어요. 좀 배운 것 같긴 해요. 제가 이미 봤던 영화들에 대한 그분의 해석은 제가 예상했던 것과 꽤 달랐어요. 하지만 자신의 요점을 잘 뒷받침했어요.

W How about from the man? Did you learn anything from him?

M Well, I did learn some new vocabulary from him, and a few facts, too.

W 5 But, you prefer the woman.

M 5 Yes, I do. It sounds like you already prefer the man, though.

W 5 I guess I do. I just think he brings more to the table. He is well educated on both film and theater. He could teach Shakespeare just as well as he could do cinematic history.

M I was not aware that he was a drama expert. That could make him a more attractive choice.

W It could. But, ultimately, the choice is not mine to make. That is up to the dean of the department. I am just making recommendations. She will be the one to make the final decision.

여 남자 교수님은 어떤가요? 그분에게서 뭔가 배웠나요?

남 음, 새로운 단어들과 사실들에 대해 좀 배우긴 했어요.

여 5 하지만 학생은 여자 교수를 더 선호하는군요.

남 5 네, 그렇습니다. 하지만 교수님은 이미 남자 교수님을 더 선호하시는 것 같네요.

여 5 그런 것 같아요. 그분이 기여를 더 많이 한다고 생각해요. 영화와 연극 둘 다 매우 훌륭한 교육을 받은 분이거든요. 세익스피어를 영화의 역사만큼이나 잘 가르칠 수 있어요.

남 희곡 전문가라는 건 몰랐어요. 이러한 점이 그분을 더 매력적인 선택으로 보이게 할 수 있겠네요.

여 그럴 수도 있죠. 하지만 결국, 결정을 내리는 건 내가 아니에요. 우리 학과의 학과장님이 결정을 내리시니까요. 저는 그저 추천을 할 뿐이죠. 최종 결정을 내리는 건 그분이에요.

1. What are the speakers mainly discussing?

Ⓐ The differences between the two candidates who applied for a teaching position

Ⓑ The teaching styles of two teaching assistants during a film studies class

Ⓒ The evaluation of two people who applied to become teaching assistants

Ⓓ The topics of the sample lessons that two different professors taught

2. Why does the student prefer the female professor to the male professor?

Ⓐ He did not like the male professor's usage of technical terms.

Ⓑ He thinks the female professor's explanation was more direct.

Ⓒ He likes the female professor since she is an expert in Shakespeare.

Ⓓ He felt bored during the male professor's lecture and did not learn anything.

3. Why does the professor mention Baltimore?

Ⓐ To explain why the male professor is a better candidate

Ⓑ To provide more background information of the male professor

Ⓒ To show another difference between the two professors

Ⓓ To confirm that the student's assumption is correct

1. 화자들은 주로 무엇을 논의하고 있는가?

Ⓐ 교수직에 지원한 두 후보자의 차이점

Ⓑ 영화 연구 수업에서 두 조교의 가르치는 스타일

Ⓒ 조교가 되기 위해 지원한 두 사람에 대한 평가

Ⓓ 두 명의 교수들이 가르친 샘플 수업의 주제들

2. 학생은 왜 남자 교수보다 여자 교수를 선호하는가?

Ⓐ 남자 교수가 전문 용어를 사용한 점을 좋아하지 않았다.

Ⓑ 여자 교수의 설명이 더 직접적이었다고 생각한다.

Ⓒ 여자 교수가 세익스피어 전문가라서 좋아한다.

Ⓓ 남자 교수의 강의가 지루했고 아무것도 배우지 못했다.

3. 교수는 왜 볼티모어를 언급하는가?

Ⓐ 왜 남자 교수가 더 나은 후보자인지 설명하려고

Ⓑ 남자 교수의 배경 정보를 더 제공하려고

Ⓒ 두 교수들 사이의 또 다른 차이점을 보이려고

Ⓓ 학생의 가정이 옳다는 것을 확인해 주려고

4. What is the professor's opinion of the female professor?
Ⓐ Her ability to explain complex concepts will be very helpful in the future.
Ⓑ She showed excellent skill for making students participate in a class discussion.
Ⓒ She is good at what she does, but she might not be the best candidate.
Ⓓ Her accent would be somewhat problematic when she teaches students.

5. Listen again to part of the conversation. Then answer the question.

W But, you prefer the woman.
M Yes, I do. It sounds like you already prefer the man, though.
W I guess I do. I just think he brings more to the table.

Why does the woman say this:

W I just think he brings more to the table.

Ⓐ To illustrate the importance of Shakespeare and cinematic history in the class
Ⓑ To emphasize the contribution the male professor makes to the lecture's overall quality
Ⓒ To convince the student that the male professor is a better teacher than the woman
Ⓓ To express her opinion regarding the competition between the two professors

4. 여자 교수에 대한 교수의 의견은 어떠한가?
Ⓐ 복잡한 개념을 설명하는 그녀의 능력이 미래에 아주 도움이 될 것이다.
Ⓑ 학생들이 수업 토의에 참여하게 하는 훌륭한 능력을 보였다.
Ⓒ 자기 일을 잘하지만 최고의 후보는 아닐 수 있다.
Ⓓ 학생들을 가르칠 때 억양이 좀 문제가 될 수도 있다.

5. 대화의 일부를 다시 듣고 질문에 답하시오.

여 하지만 학생은 여자 교수를 더 선호하는군요.
남 네, 그렇습니다. 하지만 교수님은 이미 남자 교수님을 더 선호하시는 것 같네요.
여 그런 것 같아요. 그분이 기여를 더 많이 한다고 생각해요.

여자는 왜 이렇게 말하는가:

여 그분이 기여를 더 많이 한다고 생각해요.

Ⓐ 수업에서 세익스피어와 영화 역사의 중요성을 보이려고
Ⓑ 강의의 전반적인 질에 남자 교수가 하는 기여를 강조하려고
Ⓒ 남자 교수가 여자 교수보다 더 나은 교사라고 학생에게 납득시키려고
Ⓓ 두 교수들 사이의 경쟁에 관한 자신의 의견을 표현하려고

어휘 evaluation n 평가 | spare v (시간·돈 등을) 내다, 할애하다 | screen v 확인하다, 가려내다 | applicant n 지원자 | opening n 공석, 결원 | department n 학과, 부서 | specific adj 구체적인 | presentation n 발표 | impressive adj 인상적인 | entertaining adj 즐거움을 주는 | expert n 전문가 | knowledgeable adj 아는 것이 많은 | jargon n (특정 분야의 전문) 용어 | overly adv 너무, 몹시 | technical adj 전문적인, 기술적인 | accent n 억양 | originally adv 원래, 본래 | definitely adv 틀림없이, 분명히 | not necessarily 반드시 ~은 아닌 | instructor n 강사, 교사 | engaging adj 호감이 가는 | prefer v 선호하다 | bring to the table 그룹에 기여하다, 이익을 제공하다 | cinematic adj 영화의 | attractive adj 매력적인 | ultimately adv 결국, 궁극적으로 | dean n (대학의) 학과장 | recommendation n 추천

Lesson 05 Inference

본서 | P. 88

Practice

Passage 1	B	Passage 2	A	Passage 3	C
Passage 4	C	Passage 5	D	Passage 6	A
Passage 7	D	Passage 8	1. D 2. B 3. C	Passage 9	1. C 2. A 3. C

Test

Passage 1	1. C	2. C	3. B, C	4. D	5. B
Passage 2	1. B	2. D	3. B	4. D	5. C

Practice

본서 | P. 94

Passage 1

Man: University employee | Woman: Student

Listen to part of a conversation between a student and a university employee.

W Hello, can you help me?

M Hi. Maybe, what do you need?

W I just had a meeting with the student loan office, and they told me that I need to get a campus job to continue to receive my financial aid.

M Well, you came to the right place. What kinds of work are you interested in doing? There are still a few open positions.

W That is good to hear. Um, I am majoring in education so...

M Well, all the teaching assistant positions have been filled. There are a few tutoring jobs still open, though. What subject do you plan to teach?

W Uh, my focus is on secondary mathematics.

M Great, do you think you can handle tutoring students on higher math?

W Oh, yes. I am proficient at all levels—even calculus.

M Then you should be a pretty popular tutor! I may even come see you sometime. You will need to get in touch with Professor Dunkirk. She is in charge of the math tutoring office. Once she approves you, I can process your employment paperwork.

W That sounds excellent. Do you happen to know if she is in her office?

M No, but I can find that out for you. Hold on a moment.

남자: 대학교 직원 | 여자: 학생

학생과 대학교 직원의 대화를 들으시오.

여 안녕하세요. 저를 좀 도와주실 수 있으세요?

남 안녕하세요. 가능하다면요. 무슨 일이시죠?

여 방금 학자금 대출 사무실 담당자와 만났는데 재정 지원을 계속 받기 위해서는 제가 캠퍼스 일자리를 구해야 한대요.

남 음, 제대로 잘 찾아오셨어요. 어떤 일을 하는 데 관심이 있으세요? 아직 신청할 수 있는 자리들이 몇 군데 있어요.

여 다행이네요. 음, 저는 교육 전공이라...

남 음, 조교 자리는 모두 다 찼어요. 하지만 개인 교습은 여전히 자리가 있어요. 어떤 과목을 가르치려고 하시죠?

여 음, 중등 수학에 주력하고 있어요.

남 잘됐네요. 더 높은 수준의 수학을 학생들에게 가르치는 일을 하실 수 있나요?

여 아, 네. 저는 모든 수준에 다 능통해요. 미적분까지도요.

남 그렇다면 상당히 인기 많은 개인 지도 교사가 되겠군요! 저도 언제 들르게 될지도 모르겠어요. 덩케르크 교수님과 연락하셔야 할 거예요. 그분이 수학 개인 지도 사무실을 책임지고 있거든요. 교수님께서 허락하시면 제가 고용을 위한 서류 작업을 처리할 수 있어요.

여 정말 잘됐네요. 혹시 교수님이 사무실에 계시는지 아시나요?

남 아니요. 하지만 알아봐드릴 수 있어요. 잠시만요.

Q. What can be inferred about the man?

(A) He has experience as a tutor.
(B) He is not very good at math.
(C) He does not think the woman is qualified.
(D) He is not interested in hiring the woman.

Q. 남자에 관해 무엇을 추론할 수 있는가?

(A) 개인 지도 교사 경험이 있다.
(B) 수학을 아주 잘하지는 못한다.
(C) 여자가 자격이 있다고 생각하지 않는다.
(D) 여자를 고용하는 데 관심이 없다.

어휘 student loan 학자금 대출 | continue v 계속하다 | financial aid 재정 지원 | secondary mathematics 중등 수학 | handle v ~를 해내다, 다루다 | proficient adj 능숙한, 능통한 | calculus n 미적분 | popular adj 인기가 많은 | approve v 승인하다 | process v 처리하다 | employment n 고용

Passage 2

Man: Professor | Woman: Student

Listen to part of a conversation between a student and a professor.

M Hello, Jessica.

W Hello Professor Reyes, you wanted to speak to me?

M Yes, I read your latest story. You are a very talented writer.

남자: 교수 | 여자: 학생

학생과 교수의 대화를 들으시오.

남 안녕하세요, 제시카.

여 안녕하세요, 레예스 교수님. 저에게 하실 말씀이 있으시다고요?

남 그래요. 학생의 최근 소설을 읽었어요. 학생은 매우 소질이 뛰어난 작가네요.

W Thank you, I was pretty proud of that one.

M As well you should be. Have you considered getting it published?

W I would love to get some of my writing published, but I wouldn't know where to start.

M I take it you are unaware of our campus literary magazine.

W No, but I thought it was a poetry magazine.

M Oh, we often publish poetry, but we also accept fiction and essays.

W How do I go about submitting my work?

M If you go on the school website and go to the literature department's page, there is a link to the magazine site. There is an email address that you can send your work to. Just write an email and attach the story to it before you send it.

W What should I say in the email?

M Not much. Just say who you are and give a brief summary of the story. If the editor in chief is interested, she will read the full story. If she wants to publish it, she will contact you.

W OK, that sounds pretty straightforward.

M Oh, but I should warn you. The magazine doesn't pay authors for their work. It doesn't have much funding.

W Oh, that's fine. I would just like to see my work in print.

여 감사합니다. 저도 그 작품이 상당히 자랑스러워요.

남 자랑스러워해야죠. 혹시 그 소설을 출판하는 걸 생각해 본 적 있나요?

여 제 글의 일부를 정말 출판하고 싶지만, 어디서부터 시작해야 할지 모르겠어요.

남 학생이 우리 학교의 캠퍼스 문학 잡지를 모르는 것 같군요.

여 아닙니다, 하지만 전 그게 시 잡지인 줄 알았어요.

남 오, 우리는 시를 자주 출판하지만 소설과 에세이도 받아요.

여 제 작품을 제출하려면 어떻게 해야 하나요?

남 학교 웹사이트에 들어가서 문학과 페이지로 가면 잡지 사이트 링크가 있어요. 거기에 학생의 작품을 보낼 수 있는 이메일 주소가 있죠. 이메일을 쓰고 보내기 전 작품을 첨부하기만 하면 돼요.

여 이메일에는 뭐라고 써야 하죠?

남 딱히 쓸 건 없어요. 학생이 누구인지 말하고 이야기를 간단히 요약하세요. 만약 편집자가 흥미를 가지면 소설 전체를 다 읽을 거예요. 편집자가 출판하고 싶으면 학생에게 연락할 거고요.

여 알겠습니다. 상당히 간단하네요.

남 아, 하지만 알려줄 게 있네요. 잡지가 작가들에게 돈을 주지는 않아요. 자금이 별로 없거든요.

여 아, 그건 괜찮습니다. 그냥 출판되어 나온 제 작품을 보고 싶어요.

Q. What can be inferred about the professor?

Ⓐ He works on the campus literary magazine.
Ⓑ He often submits stories to the magazine.
Ⓒ He does not think the woman is qualified.
Ⓓ He is a well-known and popular author.

Q. 교수에 관해 무엇을 추론할 수 있는가?

Ⓐ 캠퍼스 문학 잡지 일을 한다.
Ⓑ 잡지에 이야기를 자주 제출한다.
Ⓒ 여자가 자격이 된다고 생각하지 않는다.
Ⓓ 유명하고 인기 많은 작가이다.

어휘 talented adj 재능이 많은 I proud adj 자랑스러워하는, 자랑스러운 I poetry n 시 I straightforward adj 간단한, 쉬운

Passage 3 Man: Student | Woman: Registrar

Listen to part of a conversation between a student and a registrar.

M Hello, can you help me?

W Hopefully, what seems to be your problem?

M I've been trying to register for this class, but it's already full, so I was wondering if you could get me an override, so I can enter the class. If I can't get in, I won't be able to graduate until next spring.

W Well, only professors can give overrides. What was the name of the class?

M Hmm... Reading Strategies 101.

남자: 학생 | 여자: 학적부 직원

학생과 학적부 직원의 대화를 들으시오.

남 안녕하세요. 저를 도와주실 수 있으신가요?

여 그럴 수 있길 바라요. 어떤 문제가 있으신가요?

남 이 강의에 등록하려고 했지만 벌써 인원이 다 차서, 강의에 들어갈 수 있게 추가 등록을 해주실 수 있나 해서요. 수강하지 못하면 내년 봄까지 졸업할 수가 없어요.

여 음, 교수님들만 추가 등록을 해주실 수 있어요. 강의 이름이 뭐였나요?

남 음... 독해 전략 101이에요.

W Reading Strategies? 101? That's a required class for freshmen! Why on Earth did you wait until your senior year to take it?

M I know. I know. It was really foolish of me to wait this long. I wasn't sure if I had to take it or not.

W It's a core class for everyone! The whole student body has to take it! Didn't your academic advisor tell you that?

M He might have. I really don't remember. Is there any way you can help me?

W Your best plan of action is to contact the professor of this class directly.

M I already tried to email Dr. Rickenbacker, but I haven't heard back yet.

W Hmmm... Dr. Rickenbacker is famous for not checking his emails very often.

M What am I going to do then?

W What I would do is tape a note explaining your situation on his office door and leave your phone number so he can get in touch with you.

M Thanks. I'll try that.

W You're welcome. Good luck!

여 독해 전략이요? 101? 그 강의는 신입생 필수 과목이잖아요! 대체 왜 수강하는 걸 4학년이 될 때까지 기다린 거죠?

남 네. 알아요. 이렇게 오래 기다리다니 정말 바보 같은 짓이죠. 그 강의를 들어야 하는지 아닌지 잘 몰랐거든요.

여 그 강의는 모든 학생들의 필수 과목이에요! 학생들 전부 그 과목을 들어야 한다고요. 지도 교수님이 말씀해주시지 않았나요?

남 아마 말씀하셨을 텐데, 생각이 안 나요. 뭐라도 도움을 받을 수 있는 방법이 있을까요?

여 학생이 할 수 있는 제일 좋은 방법은 이 강의를 담당하는 교수님께 직접 연락하는 거예요.

남 벌써 리켄배커 교수님께 이메일을 보냈지만 아직 답을 듣지 못했어요.

여 음... 리켄배커 교수님은 이메일을 그리 자주 확인하지 않는 걸로 유명한데요.

남 그럼 어떻게 해야 하죠?

여 저라면 교수님 연구실 문에 학생의 상황을 설명하는 메모를 붙여놓고 교수님이 연락하실 수 있도록 전화번호를 남기겠어요.

남 감사합니다. 그렇게 해볼게요.

여 천만에요. 행운을 빌어요!

Q. What can be inferred about the student's situation?

Ⓐ His academic advisor didn't tell him he should take the course.
Ⓑ The class always fills up very quickly every semester.
Ⓒ He was not sure if the class was required to graduate.
Ⓓ He already had a full schedule in his freshman year.

Q. 학생의 상황에 대해 무엇을 추론할 수 있는가?

Ⓐ 지도 교수가 이 수업을 들어야 한다고 말해주지 않았다.
Ⓑ 이 수업은 매 학기마다 무척 빨리 마감된다.
Ⓒ 이 수업이 졸업에 필요한지 확신하지 못했다.
Ⓓ 이미 1학년 때 일정이 빡빡했다.

어휘 register v 등록하다 | wonder v 궁금해하다 | get an override 이미 정원이 다 찬 강의에 별도의 요청을 통해 추가 등록하다 | graduate v 졸업하다 | strategy n 전략 | required adj 필수의, 요구되는 | freshman n 1학년생 | senior n 4학년생 | foolish adj 바보 같은 | core adj 중심의, 핵심의 | contact v 연락하다 | directly adv 직접

Passage 4

Man: Housing officer | Woman: Student

Listen to part of a conversation between a student and a housing officer.

W You got a minute, Mr. Franklin?

M Sure, come on in. What can I do for you?

W My name is Kelly Dumas, and I got a letter from your office, saying that I need to vacate my dorm room as soon as possible. The problem is that I'm leaving for Canada in three months, and I have no other place to go until then. So I was wondering if it would be possible to get an extension for three months.

M What was your name again?

W Kelly Dumas.

남자: 기숙사 담당자 | 여자: 학생

학생과 기숙사 담당자의 대화를 들으시오.

여 시간 좀 있으세요, 프랭클린씨?

남 네, 들어오세요. 무슨 일인가요?

여 전 켈리 뒤마라고 하는데, 여기 사무실로부터 가능한 한 빨리 기숙사 방을 비워달라는 편지를 받았어요. 문제는 제가 석 달 후에 캐나다에 가는데 그때까지 머물 곳이 없거든요. 그래서 석 달간 연장이 가능한지 알아보려고요.

남 이름이 뭐라고 했죠?

여 켈리 뒤마요.

M Let's see. Oh, here you are. I see that you've been living in the dorms for three years already. I'm afraid the reason you got the letter in the first place is that the school has a strict policy regarding the maximum length of stay for on-campus housing. I'm sorry, but your time has expired, and you will need to make other arrangements.

W Is there any way you can make an exception this time?

M I'm afraid it's a school housing policy. We need the space for incoming freshmen who apply for dorm rooms, and they usually want as much time as possible to get acquainted with their surroundings.

W It's just that it's so difficult to find a landlord who will give me a three-month lease.

M I can relate to your situation and I sympathize, but try to put yourself in the freshmen's shoes; it's their first time away from home, they're probably a little nervous, so it just wouldn't be fair to make them wait for a dorm room.

W Guess you're right. Do you have any suggestions?

M Well, you're not the first one who has been in this position. You can check with the Student Services Office; they usually have a list of contacts that provide temporary housing.

W Great! That sounds perfect! I'll run over there right now.

M Have a great time on your trip.

남 어디 봅시다. 여기 있네요. 기숙사에서 이미 3년이나 생활했군요. 애당초 편지를 받은 이유는 학교가 기숙사 최대 거주 기간에 엄격한 방침을 가지고 있기 때문이에요. 죄송하지만 기간이 만료됐으니 다른 준비를 해야 해요.

여 이번만 예외로 해주시면 안 될까요?

남 유감스럽지만 학교 기숙사 방침이라서요. 기숙사를 신청하는 신입생들을 위해 방이 필요하고, 신입생들은 대개 주변 환경에 적응하기 위해 가능한 한 많은 시간이 필요하죠.

여 석 달간 집을 빌려줄 집주인을 찾기가 너무 어려워서 그래요.

남 학생의 상황은 이해하고 공감은 되지만 신입생들의 입장에서 생각해보세요. 처음 집을 떠나 다소 불안하기도 할 텐데 기숙사 방을 기다리게 하는 건 합당하지 않잖아요.

여 맞는 말씀이에요. 혹시 뭐 제안할만한 거 있으세요?

남 음, 이런 처지에 있는 사람이 학생이 처음은 아니에요. 학생처에 확인해 보세요. 보통 임시 숙소를 제공해주는 연락처 목록을 갖고 있거든요.

여 좋아요! 그거 좋은 생각이네요! 지금 당장 가봐야겠어요.

남 여행에서 즐거운 시간 보내세요.

Q. What is implied about the school housing policy?

Ⓐ The school housing policy allows some exceptions.
Ⓑ All the freshmen must live in the dormitories.
Ⓒ The school housing policy does not allow any exceptions.
Ⓓ Seniors must leave the dorm immediately after school finishes.

Q. 학교 기숙사 방침에 관해 무엇을 유추할 수 있는가?

Ⓐ 학교 기숙사 방침에서 일부 예외가 허용된다.
Ⓑ 모든 신입생들은 기숙사에서 생활해야 한다.
Ⓒ 학교 기숙사 방침은 예외를 허용하지 않는다.
Ⓓ 4학년들은 학교를 마치는 즉시 기숙사를 나가야 한다.

어휘 vacate v 비우다 | wonder v 궁금해하다 | extension n 연장 | strict adj 엄격한 | policy n 규정 | maximum adj 최대의 | length n 기간, 길이 | expire v 만료되다 | arrangements n 준비, 채비 | exception n 예외 | incoming adj 도착하는, 들어오는 | freshman n 1학년생 | apply v 신청하다, 지원하다 | acquainted with ~에 익숙한, 아는 | surroundings n 환경, 주변 | landlord n 집주인, 임대주 | lease n 임대차 계약 | relate to ~를 이해하다 | situation n 상황 | sympathize v 공감하다, 동정하다 | nervous adj 긴장한 | suggestion n 제안 | temporary adj 임시의

Passage 5

Man: Technician | Woman: Student

Listen to part of a conversation between a student and a technician.

W Hi, could you help me? I need a hand with my notebook.

M Well, you've come to the right place. What seems to be the problem?

W I just bought this yesterday at the Campus Computer Store and it won't boot up. I push the ON/OFF button and nothing happens!

M Hmm... Let me have a look at it. Well... have you taken any computer courses here in the computer center?

남자: 기술자 | 여자: 학생

학생과 기술자의 대화를 들으시오.

여 안녕하세요. 도와주실 수 있나요? 제 노트북에 도움이 필요해요.

남 제대로 잘 찾아왔네요. 무슨 문제인가요?

여 제가 이것을 바로 어제 캠퍼스 컴퓨터 매장에서 샀는데 부팅이 안 돼요. 전원 버튼을 눌러도 아무 일이 일어나지 않아요!

남 음... 한번 보죠. 저... 컴퓨터 센터에서 컴퓨터 수업을 들은 적 있어요?

W Nope. I am the last one to ask about the computer. See? I don't even know how to turn on the computer.
M Well... do you know that I offer a class here on Monday and Wednesday evenings on basic computer use? You can take that if you're interested.
W Really? I might be... what do you teach?
M Some basics about the hardware—the notebook itself, in your case—and the operating system.
W That sounds great! I'll definitely go!
M Great! A-hah! Here's the problem. There's a plastic strip, which is used to protect the ON/OFF button during shipping, see? Take that off. Okay, now try to turn on your notebook.
W Oh, boy... Do I ever feel stupid now!
M You're not the first person I've helped with this—and you won't be the last! Well, anyway, I will see you in class next Monday.
W Right! And, thank you so much.

여 아니요. 전 컴퓨터에 대해서 정말 아는 게 없어요. 아시겠죠? 어떻게 켜는지조차 모르잖아요.
남 음... 월요일과 수요일 저녁에 내가 컴퓨터 사용법에 관한 기초 수업을 진행하는 것 알고 있어요? 관심 있으면 그 수업을 들어도 돼요.
여 정말로요? 관심이 있을지도요... 무엇을 가르치세요?
남 하드웨어에 대한 기본 사항들, 학생의 경우에는 노트북 자체가 되겠고 운영 시스템도 가르쳐요.
여 좋아요! 꼭 들을게요!
남 좋아요! 아하! 여기 문제가 있었군요. 노트북을 배송할 때 전원 버튼을 보호하기 위해 사용되는 플라스틱 끈이 문제였네요. 보이죠? 그걸 뜯어내세요. 됐어요. 이제 노트북을 켜보세요.
여 오, 맙소사... 정말 바보 같네요!
남 이런 문제로 도와준 사람이 학생이 처음은 아니에요. 그리고 마지막도 아닐 거고요! 어쨌든, 그럼 다음 주 월요일 수업 때 봐요.
여 네! 정말 감사합니다.

Q. What can be inferred about the woman?

(A) She has decided to major in computer science.
(B) She will probably want to get a refund on her purchase.
(C) She has never owned a notebook computer before.
(D) She will attend a class about computers on Monday.

Q. 여자에 관해 무엇을 추론할 수 있는가?

(A) 컴퓨터 공학을 전공하기로 결심했다.
(B) 구매한 것을 환불받고 싶어 할 것이다.
(C) 한 번도 노트북 컴퓨터를 소유해 본 적이 없다.
(D) 월요일에 컴퓨터 관련 수업에 참석할 것이다.

어휘 boot up 부팅하다 | operating system 운영 시스템 | definitely adv 꼭, 분명히 | strip n 끈 | protect v 보호하다 | shipping n 배송

Passage 6

Man: Student | Woman: Administrator

Listen to part of a conversation between a student and an administrator.

W Hi, there! How can I help you?
M Well, I just got my registration form and it says I'm only registered for three classes, but I need to take five courses this semester.
W Hmm. OK, let me check this for you on the computer. Oh, here's your file. According to the computer, you lost your place in those two courses because you didn't pay your tuition on time.
M That's because I was away on vacation until Monday. I paid my tuition as soon as I got back.
W Well, the deadline was last Friday. At that point, since you hadn't paid, you were removed from the class list to allow other students on the waiting list to enroll in the course.
M I thought I would just be charged a late fee, not kicked out of courses! Is it possible to get back into those courses again?

남자: 학생 | 여자: 행정 직원

학생과 행정 직원의 대화를 들으시오.

여 안녕하세요! 뭘 도와드릴까요?
남 네, 방금 수강신청서를 받았는데 강의가 3개만 등록되어 있다고 나와 있어요. 하지만 전 이번 학기에 5개를 들어야 하거든요.
여 음, 알겠어요. 컴퓨터에서 확인해 볼게요. 아, 여기 학생의 파일이 있네요. 컴퓨터를 보니 학생이 수업료를 제때 내지 않아서 그 두 개의 강의에서 빠진 걸로 나오네요.
남 그건 제가 휴가를 갔다가 월요일에 왔기 때문이에요. 돌아오자마자 수업료를 냈는데요.
여 음, 마감일이 지난주 금요일이었어요. 그 당시에 학생이 수업료를 내지 않았기 때문에 수강 신청 대기자 명단에 있는 다른 학생들이 강의에 등록할 수 있도록 학생을 강의에서 뺀 거예요.
남 저는 강의에서 쫓겨나는 게 아니라 그냥 연체료를 물게 될 거라 생각했어요! 그 수업들을 다시 등록할 수 있을까요?

W Let me check. Some spots in the English class have opened up, but the Asian Studies class is full and has eight students on the waiting list. What would you like to do?

M Please enroll me in the English class and put me on the waiting list for the other course.

W There is also a Chinese History class available. Would you be interested in that class instead of Asian Studies?

M When is the Chinese History class?

W It's on Monday and Wednesday evenings, 7 to 10. What do you think?

M That would work into my timetable well, actually. Sure. Put me in that class, please.

W You're all set. You're back in the English class and also enrolled in Chinese History instead of Asian Studies.

M Thanks for your help!

여 확인해 볼게요. 영어 강의는 몇 자리가 비어 있지만, 아시아학 강의는 인원이 다 찼고 대기자 명단에 8명의 학생이 있네요. 어떻게 하시겠어요?

남 영어 강의는 등록해 주시고, 다른 강의는 대기자 명단에 올려주세요.

여 중국사 강의도 수강이 가능해요. 아시아학 대신 그 강의에 관심 있어요?

남 중국사 강의는 언제 있나요?

여 월요일과 수요일 저녁 7시에서 10시까지네요. 어때요?

남 제 시간표에 맞겠네요. 네, 그 강의에 넣어주세요.

여 다 됐어요. 영어 강의에 다시 등록이 됐고 아시아학 대신 중국사 강의에 등록됐어요.

남 도와주셔서 감사합니다!

Q. What does the administrator imply about the Asian Studies class?

Ⓐ It is not likely that the student will get into the class.

Ⓑ The class is not very useful to students with his major.

Ⓒ There are not many people interested in taking it.

Ⓓ The class is usually held in the evening.

Q. 행정 직원은 아시아학 수업에 관해 무엇을 암시하는가?

Ⓐ 학생이 이 수업에 들어갈 것 같지 않다.

Ⓑ 이 수업은 학생과 같은 전공의 학생들에게는 그다지 유용하지 않다.

Ⓒ 이 수업을 듣는 데 관심이 있는 사람들은 많이 없다.

Ⓓ 이 수업은 보통 밤에 진행된다.

어휘 registration **n** 등록 | tuition **n** 수업료, 등록금 | deadline **n** 마감 기한 | enroll **v** 등록하다 | charge **v** 요금을 부과하다 | waiting list 대기자 명단 | be all set 준비가 되어있는

Passage 7

Man: Student | Woman: University employee

Listen to part of a conversation between a student and a university employee.

M Hello, I've got a serious problem that needs immediate attention!

W Okay. I sure hope I can help. What seems to be the problem?

M I haven't been paid for my work-study program! It's been two weeks already and I haven't seen a penny!

W I understand that you're upset. Let me see if I can help. So, what's your name?

M Johnson. Jack Johnson.

W Just a minute, Mr. Johnson. Let me see... Well, there doesn't seem to be any information at all. Your name doesn't come up on any of the systems. There must have been some problem with the system, and unfortunately everything is done automatically, so I'm not sure what I can do.

M What on Earth am I supposed to do now? My rent is a week overdue!

남자: 학생 | 여자: 대학교 직원

학생과 대학교 직원의 대화를 들으시오.

남 안녕하세요. 즉시 처리해야 할 심각한 문제가 있어요!

여 네. 도와드릴 수 있었으면 좋겠네요. 무슨 문제인가요?

남 학생 근로 프로그램의 급여를 받지 못했어요! 벌써 2주나 한 푼도 받지 못했다고요!

여 화가 나실 만하군요. 도와드릴 수 있을지 알아볼게요. 이름이 무엇인가요?

남 존슨이요. 잭 존슨이에요.

여 잠시만요, 존슨 학생. 어디 보자... 음, 정보가 전혀 없는 것 같은데요. 학생 이름이 시스템 어디에도 나오질 않아요. 시스템에 문제가 있는 것 같은데, 안타깝게도 모든 업무가 자동으로 처리되기 때문에 저도 어떻게 해야 할지 모르겠네요.

남 그럼 도대체 어떻게 하란 말인가요? 집세가 일주일이나 밀렸다고요!

W You know, now that I think about it, the Technology Department sent out a memo saying some of the information from the payroll files had been wiped out because of a virus.

M I really wish that somebody had let me know!

W I'm so sorry. Hmm... Somebody from our office should have let the teacher's assistants know! I know what we can do. Fill out this form and return it to me by tomorrow. I will contact all the appropriate departments and we'll get this straightened out right away!

M But I need the money today!

W I know you do, but I'm afraid that's just not going to be possible. I'll do whatever I can to expedite the process, but I think tomorrow is going to be the soonest we can get your money.

M Okay. I guess tomorrow will be fine.

여 아, 생각해보니 기술 부서에서 바이러스 때문에 급여 파일의 일부 정보가 지워졌다는 메모를 보냈었어요.

남 그럼 누군가 제게 알려줬더라면 좋았을 텐데요!

여 죄송합니다. 음... 저희 사무실에서 조교들에게 알렸어야 했는데! 이렇게 하세요. 이 양식을 작성해서 내일까지 저에게 주세요. 모든 해당 부서에 문의해서 이 문제를 바로 해결해 드릴게요.

남 하지만 전 오늘 돈이 필요하다고요!

여 알겠습니다만, 그건 불가능할 것 같네요. 신속히 처리하도록 최선을 다하겠지만 빨라야 내일 돈을 드릴 수 있을 거예요.

남 알겠어요. 내일이라면 괜찮을 것 같네요.

Q. What is implied about the payroll office?

Ⓐ Its computer system was taken down by a virus.
Ⓑ It has recently updated its operating software.
Ⓒ Its computers operate without human assistance.
Ⓓ It does not communicate well with other departments.

Q. 급여 사무실에 관해 무엇이 암시되었는가?

Ⓐ 이곳의 컴퓨터 시스템이 바이러스 때문에 먹통이 되었다.
Ⓑ 운영 소프트웨어를 최근 업데이트했다.
Ⓒ 이곳의 컴퓨터는 인간의 도움 없이 작동한다.
Ⓓ 다른 부서와 소통이 원활하게 이뤄지지 않는다.

어휘 immediate adj 즉각적인 | attention n 처리, 주의, 집중 | upset adj 언짢은, 기분이 나쁜 | unfortunately adv 안타깝게도 | automatically adv 자동으로 | overdue adj 기한이 지난 | wipe out 지우다 | appropriate adj 적절한 | straighten out 해결하다, 바로잡다 | expedite v 더 신속히 처리하다

Passage 8

Man: Student | Woman: Professor

Listen to part of a conversation between a student and a professor.

W Well, good morning, Craig.

M Good morning, Professor Jullian. Can I talk with you about re-scheduling my final exam?

W Sure, I have a few minutes. Take a seat.

M Thanks. I'm pretty excited, actually. I got a call yesterday from a big law firm in New York. As you know, I'm graduating this semester, and I've been applying for jobs. This law firm is interested in hiring me as a legal assistant. They told me to come to the Big Apple for an interview!

W That's great news! I'm sure you'll get the job.

M Actually, of all the jobs I applied for, this is the one most appealing to me. I'd like to go to law school eventually, and I know I'll learn a lot working in a company like this one.

W I'm sure you will. Sounds like a wonderful opportunity. What's the scheduling problem?

남자: 학생 | 여자: 교수

학생과 교수의 대화를 들으시오.

여 안녕하세요, 크레이그.

남 안녕하세요, 줄리안 교수님. 기말시험 일정 조정에 대해 말씀 좀 나눌 수 있을까요?

여 네, 시간이 좀 있군요. 앉아요.

남 감사합니다. 사실 기분이 굉장히 좋아요. 어제 뉴욕에 있는 큰 법률 회사에서 전화를 받았어요. 아시다시피 제가 이번 학기에 졸업을 해서 일자리를 구하고 있었어요. 이 법률 회사에서 저를 법률 사무소 직원으로 고용하고 싶다고 면접을 보러 뉴욕으로 오라네요.

여 그거 정말 좋은 소식이네요. 꼭 합격할 거예요.

남 사실, 제가 지원한 일자리 중 이게 제일 마음에 들어요. 전 나중에 로스쿨에 가고 싶은데 이런 회사에서 일하면 배우는 게 많을 거예요.

여 정말 그럴 거예요. 굉장히 좋은 기회 같네요. 일정 문제는 뭔가요?

M Wouldn't you know it. The day that they want to interview me is the day of the final exam. If I don't go to the interview that day, they won't hire me. Is there any way that I can take the exam on a different day?

W Let me think for a minute. Well, school policy doesn't allow anyone to take an exam later than the scheduled time. But I don't think there is a rule against taking the exam early. That could work.

M So, there's a chance I could take the exam before I leave for New York?

W 1 Usually, I wouldn't allow it. But you've been a good student, and I think you'll learn a lot in a job like this that you'll never learn in school. Can you be ready to take the exam a few days early?

M Yes, I can. I've kept up to date on the class assignments, and I've got good marks going into the final. So, sure, I'll be okay.

W Alright then. I'll make arrangements to have you take it a few days early. I'll need to prepare a different exam than the other students will be taking. It would be better if you took a completely different test. It may be more difficult than the regular exam. Can you handle that?

M Yes, I'm sure I'll do fine. 2 By the way, could I possibly take the exam on Tuesday morning? I'm supposed to go for the interview the next day.

W Looks like that would fit into my schedule, too. So, I'll meet you here in my office at 10 a.m. Tuesday morning, and you'll have 2 hours to finish. 3 Okay, now, tell me more about this job!

남 뭐겠어요. 하필이면 면접일이 기말 시험일이에요. 그날 면접보러 가지 않으면 절 고용하지 않을 거예요. 혹시 기말시험을 다른 날 볼 수 있는 방법이 있을까요?

여 생각을 좀 해봅시다. 음, 학교 정책상 그 누구도 정해진 시간 이후에 시험을 볼 수는 없어요. 하지만 시험을 일찍 보면 안 된다는 규칙은 없는 것 같군요. 그렇게 하면 되겠네요.

남 그럼 제가 뉴욕에 가기 전에 시험을 볼 수 있는 건가요?

여 1 보통은 허락하지 않지만, 학생이 착실한 데다 학교에서 절대 배울 수 없는 것들을 그런 일에서 많이 배우게 될 거라고 생각하니까요. 기말시험을 며칠 앞당겨서 볼 수 있겠어요?

남 네, 볼 수 있어요. 수업 과제물을 꼬박꼬박했고 좋은 성적을 받았으니 괜찮을 거예요.

여 그럼 알겠어요. 며칠 일찍 시험을 볼 수 있도록 준비할게요. 다른 학생들이 볼 시험과 다른 시험을 준비해야 해요. 완전히 다른 시험을 보는 게 좋을 거예요. 아마 정규 시험보다 더 어려울지도 몰라요. 괜찮겠어요?

남 네, 잘 해낼 수 있을 겁니다. 2 그런데 가능하면 화요일 아침에 시험을 봐도 될까요? 그 다음날 면접을 보게 되어 있거든요.

여 내 일정에도 맞을 것 같네요. 그럼 화요일 아침 10시에 여기 내 사무실에서 보죠. 시험 시간은 2시간을 줄게요. 3 자, 그럼 이제 그 일자리에 대해 좀 더 말해봐요!

1. What does the professor imply about the student?

Ⓐ He should not be asking the professor for favors.
Ⓑ He has no chance of passing the interview.
Ⓒ He cannot afford to miss the final examination.
Ⓓ He deserves to receive special treatment.

2. What will the student most likely do on Wednesday?

Ⓐ He will take his final exam.
Ⓑ He will fly to New York.
Ⓒ He will refuse the job offer.
Ⓓ He will visit the professor's office.

3. What will the professor most likely do next?

Ⓐ Write a new test for the student to take
Ⓑ Help the student study for his exam
Ⓒ Discuss the company the student may work at
Ⓓ Make travel arrangements for the student

1. 교수는 학생에 관해 무엇을 암시하는가?

Ⓐ 학생은 편의를 봐달라고 교수에게 부탁해서는 안 된다.
Ⓑ 학생은 면접에 통과할 확률이 없다.
Ⓒ 학생은 기말시험을 놓쳐서는 안 된다.
Ⓓ 특별 대우를 받을 자격이 있다.

2. 학생은 수요일에 무엇을 할 것 같은가?

Ⓐ 기말시험을 볼 것이다.
Ⓑ 뉴욕으로 비행기를 타고 갈 것이다.
Ⓒ 일자리 제안을 거절할 것이다.
Ⓓ 교수의 사무실에 방문할 것이다.

3. 교수는 다음에 무엇을 할 것 같은가?

Ⓐ 학생이 볼 새로운 시험을 집필한다
Ⓑ 학생이 시험 공부를 하는 것을 돕는다
Ⓒ 학생이 일하게 될지도 모르는 회사에 대해 논의한다
Ⓓ 학생을 위해 여행 준비를 해준다

어휘 graduate v 졸업하다 I apply v 지원하다 I hire v 고용하다 I legal assistant 법률 사무소 직원 I Big Apple (=New York) 뉴욕시 I appeal v 관심을 끌다, 매력적이다 I eventually adv 결국 I Wouldn't you know it (예기치 못한 상황 등에 대한 당혹감을 표시) 에이, 저런 I policy n 규정 I assignment n 과제 I arrangement n 준비, 마련, 주선 I prepare v 준비하다 I completely adv 완전히 I regular adj 정규의 I handle v 해내다

Passage 9

Man: Professor | Woman: Student

Listen to part of a conversation between a student and a professor.

M Hello, Kristen, where were you this morning?

W Hello, professor. I lost one of my contacts, so I had to go to the store to pick up a new pair. That meant I was unable to come to class, which prevented me from giving you my homework. I didn't want to lose points for turning it in late.

M Yes, thank you for being so responsible. **1** I know from experience that it is difficult to do most things when you cannot see things properly. But I may have accepted your excuse.

W Well, I'm here now, so here is my homework.

M Hmmm, Kristen, this is on notebook paper, which is fine. But, you have turned in all of your assignments this way. Do you not have a workbook?

W Um, no.

M You bought the textbook, right? They usually come together.

W Actually, no, I did not. The bookstore was sold out when I tried to buy one. I had to borrow one from my classmate to do my homework. And I'm not the only one.

M **2** I don't understand how this could happen. I always make sure to have the bookstore order extra copies of every textbook I use—especially for this class, since it is a required course for all history majors.

W Are you the only professor that teaches this course?

M Most of the time, yes. **2** But, since it is a required course, the university may have opened another class and assigned a different instructor. Hmm... I am teaching three periods this semester, but there are four total! Who is teaching the other session? Oh, it's head of the history department! I wish he had told me.

W Is there anything you can do about it?

M **3** I will call the campus bookstore. Then, I will tell the head about the situation.

남자: 교수 | 여자: 학생

학생과 교수의 대화를 들으시오.

남 안녕하세요, 크리스틴. 오늘 아침에 어디 있었나요?

여 안녕하세요, 교수님. 제가 콘택트렌즈 하나를 잃어버려서 새것을 사기 위해 판매점에 가야만 했어요. 그래서 수업에 참석할 수 없었고, 제 과제를 제출할 수 없었다는 거죠. 늦게 제출해서 점수가 깎이는 건 원하지 않았어요.

남 그래요, 책임감 있게 행동해줘서 고마워요. **1** 제대로 무언가를 볼 수 없다면 뭔가를 하기가 어렵다는 걸 나도 경험을 통해 알고 있어요. 하지만 내가 학생이 말한 이유를 들어주었을 수도 있었을 텐데요.

여 음, 아무튼 제가 여기 왔으니까요, 여기 과제물입니다.

남 흠, 크리스틴. 이건 종이에 한 과제이고 그것도 상관은 없어요. 하지만 학생은 모든 과제물을 이렇게 제출했죠. 워크북은 없나요?

여 음, 없어요.

남 교과서를 샀잖아요, 그렇죠? 보통 두 개가 같이 나오는데요.

여 사실, 아니에요, 사지 않았어요. 제가 사려고 했을 때 서점에서 책이 다 팔렸거든요. 과제를 하기 위해 같이 수업을 듣는 친구에게서 빌려야만 했어요. 그리고 그렇게 하는 건 저 혼자만이 아니에요.

남 **2** 어떻게 이런 일이 일어났는지 모르겠군요. 내가 사용하는 모든 교과서는 여분으로 몇 부 주문하도록 서점에 항상 확인하는데요. 특히 모든 역사 전공 학생에게 필수인 이 과목은 말이죠.

여 이 과목을 가르치는 분은 교수님뿐인가요?

남 대부분 그래요. **2** 하지만 이게 필수 과목이라 대학에서 또 다른 수업을 개강해서 다른 교수를 배정했을지도 모르죠. 흠... 나는 이번 학기에 세 개의 수업을 가르치는데 네 개가 있네요! 이 다른 수업은 누가 가르치는 걸까요? 아, 역사 학과장님이시군요! 그분이 나에게 말해줬다면 좋았을 텐데요.

여 교수님이 해주실 수 있는 일이 있나요?

남 **3** 학교 서점에 전화할게요. 그리고 학과장님에게 이 상황에 관해 말할게요.

1. What can be inferred about the professor?

Ⓐ He would not have allowed the student to turn in her assignment late.

Ⓑ He does not think that the student had a good reason to miss class.

1. 교수에 관해 무엇을 추론할 수 있는가?

Ⓐ 학생이 과제를 늦게 제출하는 것을 허락하지 않았을 것이다.

Ⓑ 학생이 수업에 빠질 충분한 이유가 있었다고 생각하지 않는다.

Ⓒ He has also had to replace his corrective lenses unexpectedly.
Ⓓ He does not accept homework that is not done in the workbook.

2. What is implied about the other instructor?
Ⓐ He did not order enough books for the extra students.
Ⓑ He normally does not teach this level of classes.
Ⓒ He has to inform other teachers about his schedule.
Ⓓ He will not be able to help the student with her problem.

3. What will the professor most likely do next?
Ⓐ He will find out who is teaching the extra class.
Ⓑ He will give the student a copy of the book.
Ⓒ He will contact the campus bookstore.
Ⓓ He will call the head of his department.

Ⓒ 자신도 예기치 못하게 교정 렌즈를 교체해야 했었다.
Ⓓ 워크북에 하지 않은 숙제는 받지 않는다.

2. 다른 교수에 관해 무엇이 암시되었는가?
Ⓐ 추가 학생들을 위해 충분한 책을 주문하지 않았다.
Ⓑ 보통 이 수준의 수업은 가르치지 않는다.
Ⓒ 다른 교수들에게 자신의 일정을 알려야 한다.
Ⓓ 학생의 문제를 도와줄 수 없을 것이다.

3. 교수는 다음에 무엇을 할 것 같은가?
Ⓐ 추가 수업을 누가 가르치는지 알아낼 것이다.
Ⓑ 학생에게 책 복사본을 줄 것이다.
Ⓒ 학교 서점에 연락할 것이다.
Ⓓ 자기 학과의 학과장에게 전화할 것이다.

어휘 contacts n 콘택트렌즈 I prevent v 막다, 방해하다 I responsible adj 책임감 있는 I properly adv 제대로 I accept v 받아들이다 I excuse n 이유, 변명 I assignment n 과제 I required adj 필수의 I situation n 상황

Test

본서 I P. 98

Passage 1

Man: Student | Woman: Professor

[1-5] Listen to part of a conversation between a student and a professor.

M Professor Pepper? Do you have a moment? **1** I want to talk to you about switching to the Honors Program.

W I've got a second. Sit down. Okay. What did you want to know?

M I... I guess I'm not sure. I've thought about maybe continuing on to do graduate studies, but....

W You're currently enrolled in the B.A. philosophy program, is that right?

M Yes. I'm in my third year, but I've decided that I want to study for my Ph.D., eventually.

W Well, **2** if you're considering going on to do graduate studies of any kind, you'll definitely want to switch to the B.A. Honors Program. It's a prerequisite for an M.A. or Ph.D., as you're probably aware. It is possible to enter graduate studies without an Honors degree, but it's certainly not the best way to go about it.

M Yes, well... so... I was wondering what is involved in the Honors Program.

W There are details about it in the undergraduate calendar, but I can give you a general idea. **3(B)** I guess the main thing is the senior thesis. You'd have to write about 50 to 65 pages representing original research and study. That's a major undertaking and takes a great deal of time and effort.

남자: 학생 | 여자: 교수

학생과 교수의 대화를 들으시오.

남 페퍼 교수님? 시간 있으세요? **1** 심화 과정으로 전환하는 것에 대해 좀 여쭤보고 싶은데요.

여 시간이 좀 있네요. 앉으세요. 자, 뭘 알고 싶은가요?

남 음... 잘 모르겠어요. 대학원 과정을 계속 공부하고 싶은데....

여 현재 철학 학사 과정에 등록되어 있군요, 그렇죠?

남 네. 3학년이에요. 하지만 최종적으로 박사 과정을 목표로 공부하기로 결심했어요.

여 음, **2** 어떤 전공이든 대학원 공부를 할 생각이 있다면 틀림없이 학사 심화 과정으로 바꾸는 게 좋을거예요. 아마 알고 있겠지만 그게 석사나 박사 과정을 위한 필수 조건이거든요. 우등 학사 학위 없이 대학원 과정에 들어가는 것도 가능하긴 하지만 분명 최상의 방법은 아니죠.

남 네, 그래서... 심화 과정과 연관된 것을 알고 싶어요.

여 학부 학사 일정에 자세한 내용이 나와 있지만 대강의 내용을 설명해 줄게요. **3(B)** 중요한 것은 4학년 논문이에요. 독자적인 연구 조사에 대한 50에서 65페이지 정도의 논문을 써야 하죠. 그게 주된 내용이고 시간과 노력이 굉장히 많이 들어요.

M Wow, you make it sound pretty tough.

W Well, it is. It isn't like the essays you're used to writing. First of all, it is longer and there are higher expectations for the content. You can't just quote writers who agree with your position. You've got to comment on other positions and really discuss the arguments and why you agree or disagree with them. And of course, you'd need to take your own clear position and defend it. **3(C)** Also, you'd have to defend your work in an oral exam in front of two faculty readers as well as the advisor. So your final degree is awarded on the basis of the thesis, the oral examination, and your course grades.

M Hmm, I see. It really is hard to decide which plan I should go for.

W I don't want to discourage you, but I think you should go into this with your eyes open. Lots of students decide that they'd benefit more from further coursework than from writing a thesis. On the other hand, many students find that writing a thesis is an exciting challenge and consider it the peak of their philosophy education. I think one reason you'd choose to write a thesis is if there is something you are interested in looking into and writing about.

M There are lots of things I'd like to write about, like some of the issues from your Continental Philosophy course. But, I guess I'm having a hard time understanding what a thesis would be like.

W Well, **4** why don't you go and take a look at some senior theses that have been awarded prizes. They're available in the library.

M **4** Well, I'll definitely do that. Thank you.

W Oh, and by the way, Joel, **5** if you do decide to write a thesis on something from the Continental Philosophy course, I'd be happy to be your advisor.

M Thanks a lot, Professor Pepper. You've given me a lot to think about.

남 와, 굉장히 힘들게 들리네요.

여 네, 그래요. 평소에 쓰던 에세이와는 달라요. 우선, 더 길고 내용에 대한 기대 수준이 더 높죠. 학생의 의견과 일치하는 저자들의 말을 그냥 인용할 수는 없어요. 다른 의견에 대해 견해를 밝혀야 하고 논점과 그 논점들에 동의하거나 동의하지 않는 이유를 실제로 논의해야 하죠. 물론, 자신의 분명한 입장을 취하고 거기에 대해 설명해야 해요. **3(C)** 또한, 두 명의 학부 교수와 지도 교수 앞에서 구두로 논문에 대해 입증해야 하죠. 이렇게 논문, 구두 시험, 그리고 학과 점수를 기반으로 최종 학점이 수여돼요.

남 네, 그렇군요. 어떤 계획을 택해야 할지 결정하기가 정말 어렵네요.

여 의욕을 꺾고 싶진 않지만 상황을 제대로 파악하고 이걸 시작해야 할 것 같아요. 많은 학생들이 논문을 쓰는 것보다 교과 학습을 더 하는 게 더 이익이라고 결정하는 반면, 다른 많은 학생들은 논문을 쓰는 것이 흥미진진한 도전이며 철학 교육의 절정이라고 생각하죠. 조사하고 글을 쓰는 것에 흥미가 있다면 논문을 쓰는 걸 선택하는 것도 좋을 거라고 생각해요.

남 교수님의 대륙 철학 강좌의 몇 가지 주제를 비롯해서 써보고 싶은 것들이 많아요. 하지만 논문이 어떤 건지 이해하기가 힘들어요.

여 음, **4** 상을 받은 몇몇 선배들의 논문을 찾아보는 게 어때요? 도서관에서 볼 수 있을 거예요.

남 **4** 정말 그래야겠어요. 감사합니다!

여 아, 그나저나 조엘, **5** 대륙 철학 강좌의 내용에 대해 논문을 쓰기로 결정한다면 내가 기꺼이 지도 교수가 되어줄게요.

남 정말 감사합니다, 페퍼 교수님. 많은 것을 생각하게 해주셨어요.

1. What is the main topic of the conversation?

Ⓐ The student wants a higher grade.
Ⓑ The student is debating changing majors.
Ⓒ The student is considering the Honors Program.
Ⓓ The student is failing the professor's class.

2. What does the professor imply about the Honors Program?

Ⓐ The Honors Program is only for Continental Philosophy.
Ⓑ The student is not eligible for the Honors Program.
Ⓒ The Honors Program is worth the extra work.
Ⓓ There are a limited number of spaces in the Honors Program.

1. 대화의 주제는 무엇인가?

Ⓐ 학생은 더 높은 점수를 원한다.
Ⓑ 학생은 전공을 바꾸는 것을 놓고 논의하고 있다.
Ⓒ 학생은 심화 과정을 고려하고 있다.
Ⓓ 학생은 교수의 수업에서 거의 낙제하고 있다.

2. 교수는 심화 과정에 관해 무엇을 암시하는가?

Ⓐ 심화 과정은 대륙 철학만을 위한 것이다.
Ⓑ 학생은 심화 과정을 들을 자격이 되지 않는다.
Ⓒ 심화 과정은 추가적인 일을 할 만한 가치가 있다.
Ⓓ 심화 과정에는 자리가 제한되어 있다.

3. What are two key features of the Honors Program?

Choose 2 answers.

(A) Doing lots of presentations
(B) Writing a thesis
(C) Taking an oral exam
(D) Taking a long written exam

4. What is the student most likely to do next?

(A) He will meet the professor to develop his thesis.
(B) He will apply to the university for funding.
(C) He will apply to enter the Honors Program.
(D) He will read some work by previous graduates.

5. What does the professor offer to do for the student?

(A) To write a letter of recommendation
(B) To become the student's advisor
(C) To get the student into the program
(D) To help the student with the thesis

3. 심화 과정의 두 가지 주요 특징은 무엇인가?

두 개를 고르시오.

(A) 다수의 발표
(B) 논문 쓰기
(C) 구두 시험 보기
(D) 긴 필기 시험 보기

4. 학생은 다음에 무엇을 할 것 같은가?

(A) 논문을 발전시키기 위해 교수를 만날 것이다.
(B) 대학에 재정 지원을 신청할 것이다.
(C) 심화 과정에 들어가기 위해 지원할 것이다.
(D) 이전 졸업생들의 작업물을 읽어볼 것이다.

5. 교수는 학생을 위해 무엇을 하겠다고 제안하는가?

(A) 추천서 쓰기
(B) 학생의 지도 교수 되기
(C) 학생을 그 과정에 넣기
(D) 학생의 논문 작업 돕기

어휘 graduate study 대학원 공부 I currently adv 현재 I enroll v 등록하다 I B. A. (Bachelor of Arts) 학사 (학위) I philosophy n 철학 I decide v 결심하다, 결정하다 I Ph. D. (Doctor of Philosophy) 박사 (학위) I eventually adv 결국 I consider v 고려하다 I definitely adv 틀림없이, 분명히 I prerequisite n 필수 조건 I aware adj 알고 있는, 인지하는 I certainly adv 확실히 I undergraduate adj 학부의 I general adj 일반적인 I thesis n 논문 I represent v 보여주다, 나타내다 I original adj 원래의, 독창적인 I undertaking n 일, 프로젝트 I effort n 노력 I expectation n 기대 I content n 내용 I quote v 인용하다 I comment v 견해를 밝히다 I discuss v 논의하다 I argument n 논거, 주장 I defend v 방어하다, 변호하다 I oral exam 구술 시험 I award v 수여하다 I discourage v 사기를 떨어뜨리다, 막다 I benefit v 이익을 얻다 I challenge n 도전, 모험 I peak n 절정, 정점 I Continental Philosophy 대륙 철학 I prize n 상

Passage 2

Man: Student | Woman: Academic advisor

[1-5] Listen to part of a conversation between a student and an academic advisor.

W Good afternoon, Ian, what brings you to my office today?

M Hello, Professor Yansen, I need your advice about my classes next semester.

W You haven't registered for next semester yet? The deadline is this Friday!

M No, I have registered. **1** But, I was unable to get into a required class that I need to take.

W **1** Hmm, what class might that be?

M **1** I need to take a biology class with a laboratory credit, but the class is already full.

W You need to take one specific class? Which one?

M Biology 302: Applied Anatomy.

W Let me check on my computer. Ah, there are still openings for the course on Tuesday and Thursday from 3 to 5 p.m. Why don't you take it then?

M **2** I would, but I already registered for another course on Tuesday and Thursday from 2 to 4 p.m.

남자: 학생 | 여자: 지도 교수

학생과 지도 교수의 대화를 들으시오.

여 안녕하세요, 이안. 오늘 무슨 일로 제 연구실에 온 건가요?

남 안녕하세요, 얀센 교수님. 다음 학기에 제가 들을 수업에 대해 조언이 필요해서요.

여 다음 학기 수강 신청을 아직 하지 않은 건가요? 이번 주 금요일이 마감인데요!

남 아니요, 등록했어요. **1** 그렇지만 제가 들어야 하는 수업 하나를 등록할 수가 없어서요.

여 **1** 흠, 그게 무슨 수업인가요?

남 **1** 실험실 학점이 포함된 생물학 수업을 하나 들어야 하는데 수업이 이미 꽉 찼더군요.

여 특정한 강의 하나를 들어야 하는 건가요? 그게 무슨 수업이죠?

남 생물 302, 응용 해부학이에요.

여 컴퓨터에서 잠시 확인해 볼게요. 아, 화요일과 목요일 오후 3시부터 5시까지 아직 빈 자리가 있네요. 이걸 들으면 되지 않아요?

남 **2** 그러고 싶지만 이미 다른 수업이 화요일과 목요일 오후 2시부터 4시에 있어서요.

W I see. What class is that? Is it also a required course?

M Yes, it is. It's Chemistry 105.

W OK, I am quite familiar with that course. It does not have a laboratory credit, which is somewhat unusual for a chemistry course. It is about chemical processes in nature.

M Yes, and since I am majoring in biochemical engineering, I need both classes.

W 3 Have you considered taking one of them as an online course?

M 3 No, I didn't know that was possible for science classes.

W 3 Well, it often isn't, especially if they have a lab requirement. But, according to the course summary, the chemistry class can be taken as an online course. The lectures are available through the department website, and you would only need to show up in person for the midterm and final exams.

M Would I be able to attend study sessions or visit the professor if I need help with understanding the material?

W Generally, yes, that is possible. When you take a class through the Internet, you are actually required to meet with the professor at least twice during the semester regarding your term paper.

M This actually sounds like a pretty convenient way to take a class. 4 Are there any drawbacks that you haven't mentioned?

W 4 Yes, there are a few. The main one is that you cannot take the pop quizzes that the professor gives during the lectures. Those count for 5% of your overall grade.

M That is enough to change your total grade for the class. How can you make them up? Do I have to write an extra paper or something?

W That depends upon the class and the professor. Professors usually increase the percentage of your grade that comes from the midterm exam, since that also assesses whether or not you are keeping up with the class much like a pop quiz would.

M That sounds reasonable. So, what do I need to do?

W First, you need to register for that chemistry class as soon as possible. 5 To register for the online class, you need a form signed by your advisor and the class professor. Since I am your advisor, you're halfway there. I know this professor, so I will call her on your behalf. Then you need to go to her office to get her signature. Her name is Professor Diana Stepanov, and her office is room 023 in Margrave Hall.

M Thank you for your help!

1. Why did the student come to see the academic advisor?

Ⓐ To enquire about the requirements for the class he wants to take

여 그렇군요. 그게 무슨 수업인가요? 이 수업 역시 필수 과목인가요?

남 네, 그렇습니다. 화학 105예요.

여 아, 그 수업을 좀 알아요. 실험실 학점이 없는 강의인데, 화학 강의치고 흔한 일은 아니죠. 자연에서 일어나는 화학 작용에 대한 수업이에요.

남 네, 그리고 제가 생화학 공학을 전공하고 있기 때문에 전 두 수업을 다 들어야 해요.

여 3 이들 중 하나를 온라인 강의로 듣는 건 생각해 봤나요?

남 3 아니요, 과학 수업들을 온라인 강의로 들을 수 있다는 건 몰랐어요.

여 3 음, 보통 듣기 힘들죠. 특히 실험이 필수인 강의라면요. 하지만 강의 요약에 따르면 이 화학 수업은 온라인 강의로 듣는 것이 가능해요. 학과 홈페이지에서 강의를 들을 수 있고, 중간고사와 기말고사 시험 때만 직접 가서 시험을 보면 돼요.

남 수업 내용을 이해하는 데 도움을 받기 위해 스터디 시간에 참여하거나 교수님을 방문할 수 있나요?

여 일반적으로, 네, 가능해요. 인터넷으로 강의를 들으면 학기말 리포트 관련으로 한 학기에 교수님을 적어도 두 번 이상 만나는 게 필수거든요.

남 강의를 듣기에 꽤나 편리한 방법 같네요. 4 아직 말씀하지 않은 단점이 혹시 있나요?

여 4 네, 몇 개 있어요. 중요한 문제는 교수님이 강의 시간에 내는 쪽지시험을 학생이 볼 수 없다는 거죠. 이 쪽지시험은 전체 성적의 5%를 차지해요.

남 최종 성적을 바꾸기에는 충분한 비율이네요. 어떻게 이걸 대신할 수 있죠? 리포트를 하나 더 쓰거나 다른 방법이 있나요?

여 수업과 교수님에 따라 달라요. 교수님들은 보통 중간고사 성적이 차지하는 비율을 올릴 거예요. 쪽지시험처럼 중간고사도 학생이 이 수업을 잘 따라오고 있는지 아닌지를 평가하니까요.

남 합리적이네요. 그래서 제가 무엇을 하면 되나요?

여 먼저, 가능한 한 빨리 그 화학 수업에 등록하세요. 5 온라인 강의에 등록하기 위해서는 지도 교수와 수업을 가르치는 교수님의 서명이 있는 양식이 필요해요. 내가 학생의 지도 교수이니 절반은 된 거죠. 이 교수님을 아니까 학생 대신 전화해 줄게요. 그럼 그분의 서명을 받으러 연구실로 가야 해요. 다이애나 스테파노프 교수님이고, 연구실은 마그레이브홀의 023호예요.

남 도와주셔서 감사합니다!

1. 학생은 왜 지도 교수를 찾아왔는가?

Ⓐ 들으려고 하는 강의의 필수 요건을 묻기 위해

Lesson 05 Conversations

Ⓑ To get help regarding a class that he could not register for
Ⓒ To ask some questions about his chemistry assignment
Ⓓ To decide what classes he should take for his career

2. Why is the student unable to take the class that is on Tuesday and Thursday?
Ⓐ He wants to reserve some time for doing his assignments.
Ⓑ He usually has laboratory sessions during that time.
Ⓒ He has a part-time job on Tuesdays and Thursdays.
Ⓓ He already has another class that coincides with the class.

3. Why does the advisor mention an online course?
Ⓐ To point out the fact that the university offers many online lectures
Ⓑ To explain that the student can still take the class he wants
Ⓒ To persuade the student to start taking more of them in the future
Ⓓ To emphasize that some chemistry classes are only offered online

4. According to the advisor, what is the disadvantage of taking an online course?
Ⓐ The student is going to miss laboratory sessions.
Ⓑ The student will lose 10% of his final grade.
Ⓒ The student is not allowed to attend study sessions.
Ⓓ The student will not be able to take pop quizzes.

5. What will the student most likely do next?
Ⓐ Go back to his room and find another available biology course
Ⓑ Visit another building to pay for his class tuition
Ⓒ Go to see Professor Stepanov to get her signature
Ⓓ Call Professor Stepanov to ask for further instructions

Ⓑ 수강 신청을 할 수 없었던 강의에 대해 도움을 받기 위해
Ⓒ 화학 과제와 관련해 몇 가지 질문을 하기 위해
Ⓓ 커리어를 위해 어떤 수업을 들어야 할지 결정하기 위해

2. 학생은 왜 화요일과 목요일에 있는 강의를 들을 수 없는가?
Ⓐ 과제를 하기 위해 시간을 좀 아껴두고 싶어 한다.
Ⓑ 보통 그 시간에 실험이 있다.
Ⓒ 화요일과 목요일에 파트타임 일을 한다.
Ⓓ 이 수업과 겹치는 다른 수업이 이미 있다.

3. 지도 교수는 왜 온라인 강의를 언급하는가?
Ⓐ 대학에서 많은 온라인 강의를 제공한다는 사실을 알려주기 위해
Ⓑ 학생이 원하는 수업을 여전히 들을 수 있다고 설명하기 위해
Ⓒ 미래에는 더 많은 온라인 강의를 수강하라고 학생을 설득하기 위해
Ⓓ 몇몇 화학 수업들은 온라인에서만 수강 가능하다는 것을 강조하기 위해

4. 지도 교수에 의하면, 온라인 강의를 듣는 것의 단점은 무엇인가?
Ⓐ 실험 시간을 놓치게 될 것이다.
Ⓑ 최종 성적의 10%를 잃게 될 것이다.
Ⓒ 스터디 시간에 참여할 수 없다.
Ⓓ 쪽지시험을 볼 수 없을 것이다.

5. 학생은 다음에 무엇을 할 것 같은가?
Ⓐ 방으로 돌아가서 다른 가능한 생물학 수업을 찾는다
Ⓑ 수업 등록금을 납부하기 위해 다른 건물에 간다
Ⓒ 스테파노프 교수의 서명을 받기 위해 그녀를 찾아간다
Ⓓ 스테파노프 교수에게 전화하여 다음에 무엇을 해야 하는지 물어본다

어휘 deadline n 마감일, 기한 I required adj 필수의 I laboratory n 실험실 I specific adj 특정한, 구체적인 I applied anatomy 응용 해부학 I opening n 빈 자리, 공석 I familiar with ~에 익숙한 I chemical adj 화학의 I biochemical engineering 생화학 공학 I summary n 요약 I department n 학과, 부서 I attend v 참석하다 I session n (특정 활동을 위한) 시간 I material n 내용, 소재, 자료 I convenient adj 편리한 I drawback n 단점, 결점, 문제점 I pop quiz 깜짝/쪽지 시험 I assess v 평가하다, 가늠하다 I reasonable adj 타당한, 합리적인 I on someone's behalf ~를 대신하여 I signature n 서명

Lesson 01 Office Hours

본서 | P. 104

Test

Passage 1	1. C	2. A	3. D	4. C	5. D
Passage 2	1. A	2. D	3. B, D	4. D	5. C
Passage 3	1. C	2. A	3. A, D	4. B	5. C
Passage 4	1. B	2. B	3. D	4. A	5. A
Passage 5	1. B	2. A	3. A	4. C	5. C
Passage 6	1. B, C	2. A	3. A, D	4. B	5. D

Test

본서 | P. 106

Passage 1 Man: Student | Woman: Professor

[1-5] Listen to part of a conversation between a student and a professor.

W Kevin, may I talk to you for a moment?

M Of course, Professor Taylor. Is something wrong?

W I'm not sure. You are aware that your presentation proposal was due on Monday, aren't you?

M Was it? I thought it was due next Monday… does that mean I missed some points?

W 1 No, the proposal is not included as a part of your overall grade, but it is very important. It lets me know where you are at with your research. Since you didn't hand yours in, I am concerned about your progress. Should I be?

M 1 Oh, then allow me to put your mind at ease. I have been spending many hours on my research, and I believe I have found a very good topic to use.

W This topic has to do with genetic traits?

M Indeed it does. Um, first, let me ask you a question.

W Go ahead.

M 2 Do you like broccoli, kale, or asparagus?

W 2 Uh, not particularly, no. Why?

M 2 Neither do I. I don't like anything bitter. Be it vegetables, beverages, or medication. From what I've been able to learn so far, this is not a new phenomenon. Serious scientific study of it goes back to the 1930s.

W 2 Is that so? And it's tied to genetics?

M Yes, but the researchers at the time didn't know that. DNA was not isolated as the genetic material that biological traits are inherited through until the following decade.

남자: 학생 | 여자: 교수

학생과 교수의 대화를 들으시오.

여 케빈, 잠깐 이야기 좀 해도 될까요?

남 물론이에요, 테일러 교수님. 뭔가 문제라도 있나요?

여 잘 모르겠네요. 발표 제안서 기한이 월요일이었던 걸 알고 있죠, 그렇죠?

남 그랬나요? 저는 그게 다음 주 월요일이라고 생각했어요... 그 말은, 제가 몇 점을 놓쳤다는 말씀이신가요?

여 1 아니에요, 제안서는 학생의 전체 성적에 포함되지 않거든요. 그렇지만 매우 중요해요. 학생이 조사를 어느 정도 하고 있는지 알게 해주니까요. 제안서를 제출하지 않아서 학생의 진행 상황이 걱정이 됐어요. 내가 걱정해야 할까요?

남 1 아, 제가 교수님을 안심시켜드릴 수 있어요. 저는 조사에 많은 시간을 들였고, 발표에 쓸 아주 좋은 주제를 찾아냈다고 믿어요.

여 이 주제가 유전적 특징에 관한 것인가요?

남 물론 그렇습니다. 하지만 먼저, 질문 하나 드려도 될까요?

여 네, 하세요.

남 2 브로콜리, 케일 혹은 아스파라거스 좋아하세요?

여 2 음, 아니요, 그다지 좋아하지 않아요. 왜죠?

남 2 저도 마찬가지예요. 전 쓴 것을 싫어해요. 야채, 음료, 약이든 뭐든요. 제가 지금까지 배운 것에 의하면 이건 새로운 현상이 아니에요. 이에 대한 진지한 과학적 연구는 1930년까지 거슬러 올라가요.

여 2 그래요? 그리고 이게 유전학과 관련 있다는 거죠?

남 네, 하지만 그 당시의 연구원들은 그 사실을 몰랐어요. DNA는 생물학적 특징이 유전되어 내려오는 유전적 물질로서 분류되지 않았고, 그 분류가 이루어진 건 10년 뒤였죠.

W Correct, however, the concept is much older.

M Right, that goes back to Gregor Mendel, the father of genetics.

W Good to see that you pay attention in class.

M 3 In 1931, a scientist working for Dupont named Arthur L. Fox noticed that some people found a chemical called... um, hold on a moment... ah, actually, I'm not sure how to pronounce that... a chemical abbreviated as PTC. Um, some people thought it tasted bitter, while others tasted nothing from it. So, at a scientific meeting, he and a colleague conducted an experiment on the attendees. The majority of them, about 65 percent, thought it was bitter, 28 percent tasted nothing, and the remainder reported differing taste sensations.

W Was his colleague Albert F. Blakeslee?

M Yes, it was. As you know, he was a botanist, and more importantly, a geneticist.

W Interesting. 3 So, these two scientists decided that tasting bitter compounds might be a genetic trait?

M 3 Yes, and in the 1960s, a scientist named Roland Fischer established that the ability to taste PTC and a compound called PROP was related to a genetic predisposition regarding food preference and body type. In the 1990s, Linda Bartoshuk coined a term for such people: Supertasters.

W Supertasters? I suppose that makes sense.

M Yes, and her research revealed that about 25% of the population are nontasters and another 25% are supertasters, with the remaining 50% percent falling somewhere in between. That means that most people find some bitter tastes offensive while others don't bother them much or at all.

W Then you and I would be supertasters?

M Possibly. Not all picky eaters are supertasters, nor is the opposite true.

W Have they identified which gene is responsible?

M They believe it is a gene called TAS2R38. This gene has two types. People who express both of either extreme are supertasters or nontasters. Those who express both types are more moderate tasters.

W 4 OK, I'm convinced about your research topic. You don't need to turn in a proposal. Just turn all of this into a coherent presentation. Do you have any ideas in that regard?

M Yes, I do. I was thinking of conducting my own taste test. 5 I don't know if I can obtain PTC or PROP, but the grocery store should provide me with plenty of options.

여 맞아요. 하지만 그 개념은 훨씬 더 오래된 것이죠.

남 네, 유전학의 아버지인 그레고어 멘델까지 거슬러 올라갑니다.

여 수업 시간에 집중하는 걸 보니 좋네요.

남 3 1931년에 듀폰 사를 위해 일하던 아서 L. 폭스라는 이름의 한 과학자가 몇몇 사람들이 음... 어떻게 발음해야 하는지를 모르겠네요... PTC라고 축약해서 쓰는 화학 물질을 발견했다는 것을 알아차렸어요. 몇몇 사람들은 그 물질이 쓴 맛이 난다고 생각한 반면 다른 이들은 아무 맛도 느끼지 못했죠. 그래서 한 과학 회의에서 그와 그의 동료는 참석자들에게 실험을 하나 했어요. 그들 중 다수, 약 65%는 쓴 맛이 난다고 생각했고 28%는 아무 맛도 느끼지 못했고, 남은 사람들은 다른 맛들이 난다고 보고했죠.

여 그의 동료가 앨버트 F. 블레이크슬리였나요?

남 네, 맞아요. 아시겠지만 그는 식물학자였고, 더 중요한 것은 유전학자였어요.

여 흥미롭네요. 3 그래서 이 두 과학자들이 쓴 맛의 화합물을 느끼는 것이 유전적 특징일 수 있다고 결정한 건가요?

남 3 네. 그리고 1960년대에는 롤랜드 피셔라는 과학자가 PTC와 PROP라는 화합물을 맛볼 수 있는 능력은 음식의 선호와 체형에 관한 유전적 성향과 관련되어 있다는 것을 밝혔어요. 1990년대에는 린다 바토슉이 그런 사람들을 위한 새로운 단어를 만들었죠. 초미각자요.

여 초미각자요? 말이 되는 것 같긴 하네요.

남 네, 그리고 그녀의 연구는 인구의 약 25%가 비미각자이며, 다른 25%가 초미각자라고 밝혔어요. 나머지 50%는 그 사이 어딘가에 속하죠. 그 말은, 대부분의 사람들이 몇몇 쓴 맛을 기분 나쁘게 여기는 한편 다른 사람들은 그다지 혹은 전혀 신경 쓰지 않는다는 의미예요.

여 그럼 학생과 나는 초미각자인가요?

남 가능성이 있죠. 음식에 까다로운 사람이 모두 초미각자는 아니고, 까다롭지 않은 사람도 초미각자는 아니에요.

여 어떤 유전자가 원인이 되는지는 밝혀냈나요?

남 과학자들은 TAS2R38이라고 불리는 유전자 때문이라고 믿습니다. 이 유전자에는 두 종류가 있어요. 양 극단을 표현하는 사람들은 초미각자나 비미각자예요. 두 종류를 다 표현하는 사람들은 좀 더 중간의 미각자입니다.

여 4 좋아요, 학생의 연구 주제에 설득됐어요. 제안서는 제출하지 않아도 됩니다. 그저 이 모든 것들을 논리 정연한 발표로 만들기만 하세요. 그에 대해 어떤 생각이라도 있나요?

남 네, 있습니다. 제 자신의 미각 테스트를 하는 걸 생각했어요. 5 제가 PTC나 PROP 물질을 구할 수 있을지는 모르겠지만, 식품점에는 많은 옵션이 있겠죠.

W Excellent. I look forward to your presentation.

여 훌륭해요. 학생의 발표가 기대되네요.

1. What are the speakers mainly discussing?

Ⓐ The effects of eating various bitter vegetables
Ⓑ The reason why some people do not like vegetables
Ⓒ The student's research for a class presentation
Ⓓ The reasons for not being able to do a presentation on time

2. Why does the student ask the professor whether or not she likes broccoli?

Ⓐ To introduce the topic of the research he has been working on
Ⓑ To find out if she dislikes vegetables like he does
Ⓒ To ask why she does not like bitter vegetables
Ⓓ To make a point about the bitter-tasting foods

3. According to the student's research, why are some people not affected by the bitterness of vegetables?

Ⓐ They have become used to the taste.
Ⓑ They suffered a childhood trauma.
Ⓒ They only eat them with sauces.
Ⓓ They have a genetic predisposition.

4. What can be inferred about the student?

Ⓐ He would do anything to avoid eating bitter things.
Ⓑ He is not sure if his topic would be good for the presentation.
Ⓒ He has prepared a lot for his class presentation.
Ⓓ He has a mutation in his DNA related to taste.

5. What does the man mean when he says this:

> M I don't know if I can obtain PTC or PROP, but the grocery store should provide me with plenty of options.

Ⓐ He doesn't know if the chemicals are legal to purchase.
Ⓑ He is hoping to get inspiration by going shopping.
Ⓒ He thinks that the grocery pharmacy may have the chemicals he needs.
Ⓓ He believes he will be able to find certain ingredients from the store.

1. 화자들은 주로 무엇에 대해 논의하고 있는가?

Ⓐ 다양한 쓴 채소를 섭취하는 것의 효과
Ⓑ 몇몇 사람들이 채소를 싫어하는 이유
Ⓒ 수업 발표를 위한 학생의 연구
Ⓓ 제시간에 발표를 하지 못하는 이유

2. 학생은 왜 교수에게 브로콜리를 좋아하는지 혹은 싫어하는지를 묻는가?

Ⓐ 그가 해 왔던 연구의 주제를 소개하기 위해
Ⓑ 교수도 그와 마찬가지로 채소를 싫어하는지 알아보기 위해
Ⓒ 왜 쓴 채소를 싫어하는지를 묻기 위해
Ⓓ 쓴 맛 나는 음식에 대한 주장을 하기 위해

3. 학생의 연구에 따르면, 왜 어떤 사람들은 채소의 쓴맛에 영향을 받지 않는가?

Ⓐ 그 맛에 익숙해졌다.
Ⓑ 어린 시절에 트라우마를 겪었다.
Ⓒ 소스만 곁들여 먹는다.
Ⓓ 유전적 성향을 가지고 있다.

4. 학생에 대해 무엇을 추론할 수 있는가?

Ⓐ 쓴 것을 먹지 않기 위해서라면 무엇이든 할 것이다.
Ⓑ 자신의 주제가 발표에 적합한지 확신하지 못한다.
Ⓒ 수업 발표를 위해 많은 준비를 했다.
Ⓓ 미각과 관련한 그의 DNA에 변형이 있다.

5. 남자는 다음과 같이 말하며 무엇을 의미하는가:

> 남 제가 PTC나 PROP 물질을 구할 수 있을지는 모르겠지만, 식품점에는 많은 옵션이 있겠죠.

Ⓐ 화학 물질을 구매하는 것이 합법적인지 모른다.
Ⓑ 쇼핑을 감으로써 영감을 얻기를 기대하고 있다.
Ⓒ 식료품점의 약국에 그가 필요로 하는 화학 물질이 있을 수도 있다고 생각한다.
Ⓓ 가게에서 특정 재료를 찾을 수 있을 것이라고 믿는다.

어휘 proposal n 제안서 | overall adj 전체의, 종합적인 | hand in 제출하다 | progress n 진행, 진척 | genetic trait 유전적 특징 | particularly adv 특히, 특별히 | medication n 약(약물) | phenomenon n 현상 | tied to ~와 관련 있는 | genetics n 유전학 | isolated adj 고립된, 외떨어진 | biological adj 생물학의 | inherit v 물려받다, 상속받다 | decade n 10년 | abbreviate v 축약하다, 줄여 쓰다 | conduct v (특정한 활동을) 하다, 지휘하다 | attendee n 참석자 | remainder n 나머지 | sensation n 감각 | botanist n 식물학자 | geneticist n 유전학자 | compound n 화합물, 혼합물 | establish v 밝히다, 수립하다 | predisposition n 성향, 경향 | preference n 선호 | population n 인구 | offensive adj 불쾌한 | picky adj 까다로운 | identify v 발견하다, 확인하다 | moderate adj 중간의, 보통의 | convince v 설득하다 | coherent adj 논리 정연한, 일관성 있는

Lesson 01 Conversations

Passage 2

Man: Professor | Woman: Student

[1-5] Listen to part of a conversation between a student and a professor.

M Lauren, I am glad that you could come see me on such short notice. Please have a seat.

W Hello, professor. It's no trouble. I am free for the rest of the day, actually.

M That's good to hear.

W Uh, am I in trouble?

M No, not really. I was looking over your paper last night, and I noticed a few potential problems in your bibliography.

W Oh, really? Did I make some incorrect entries?

M No, **1, 2** your bibliography is correctly written. A few of your sources are questionable, though. Your paper is about renewable energy sources, but this website is for a company that manufactures solar panels. That presents somewhat of a conflict of interest. I am not saying that they are providing false information, but they are not the most reliable source since they stand to profit from people having a positive idea about their product. That is why it is better to gather information from the websites of universities, institutes that conduct independent research, and scientific journals.

W **2** I understand. Since they are motivated by profit, they might… exaggerate?

M Exactly. I am not saying that they cannot be a useful source of information, but you should not quote them as an authority in your paper. By looking at your other sources, I am sure you can find a different source to cite for this information.

W OK, I will make those changes. Ah! While I am here, can I ask you a few questions?

M Of course. What would you like to know?

W I read that some countries have begun building tidal turbines. Do those operate in the same way as wind turbines?

M Essentially, yes. They both use the energy from natural phenomena to create electricity. **3(D)** They have the potential to create energy more reliably than either wind turbines or solar panels. Wind is very unpredictable, and solar energy cannot be used on cloudy days. The tide, however, is consistent and very predictable. That means that we cannot only ensure that they will produce electricity every day, but we also know what time of day it will happen.

W **4** Do they have any negative effect on the environment?

남자: 교수 | 여자: 학생

학생과 교수의 대화를 들으시오.

남 로렌, 너무 갑자기 보자고 했는데도 와줘서 다행이네요. 여기 앉아요.

여 안녕하세요, 교수님. 어려운 일도 아닌데요. 사실, 이제 오늘 수업은 다 끝났거든요.

남 잘됐네요.

여 음, 제가 뭔가 잘못했나요?

남 아니, 아니에요. 어젯밤 학생의 리포트를 보고 있었는데, 학생의 참고 문헌에서 문제가 생길 가능성이 있는 부분들을 몇 군데 알아차렸어요.

여 아, 정말이세요? 제가 뭔가를 잘못 입력했나요?

남 아니요, **1, 2** 학생의 참고 문헌 자체는 올바르게 쓰였어요. 그렇지만 학생이 참고 문헌으로 쓴 자료들 몇 개에 의구심이 드는군요. 리포트는 재생 가능한 에너지원에 대한 것이었지만, 이 웹사이트는 태양 전지판을 제조하는 회사의 웹사이트잖아요. 이는 이해의 충돌을 일으키는 거예요. 이 회사에서 거짓 정보를 제공하고 있다고 말하는 건 아니지만, 사람들이 자신들의 제품에 긍정적인 생각을 가지도록 만들어야 회사가 이익을 보기 때문에 가장 믿을 만한 자료가 아니라는 거죠. 그래서 대학교나 독립적인 연구를 진행하는 기관들, 그리고 과학 잡지에서 정보를 얻는 게 더 나아요.

여 **2** 알겠어요. 이 회사는 이윤에 동기 부여를 받기 때문에... 과장할 수 있다는 말씀이시죠?

남 바로 그거예요. 쓸모 있는 자료가 될 수 없다고 말하는 건 아니지만, 학생의 리포트에 권위 있는 자료로써 이 웹사이트를 인용해서는 안 돼요. 학생의 다른 자료들을 보니 이 정보를 위해 인용할 다른 자료를 찾을 수 있을 거라고 확신해요.

여 네, 수정하도록 하겠습니다. 아! 여기 왔으니 말인데, 몇 개만 여쭤봐도 될까요?

남 물론이죠. 무엇이 알고 싶은가요?

여 일부 국가들이 조수 작용 터빈을 건설하기 시작했다고 읽었어요. 이 터빈들은 풍력 발전용 터빈과 같은 방식으로 작동하는 건가요?

남 근본적으로는 그래요. 둘 다 전기를 생산하기 위해 자연 현상으로부터 나오는 에너지를 사용하죠. **3(D)** 조수 작용 터빈은 풍력 발전용 터빈이나 태양 전지판보다 더 믿을 만하게 에너지를 생산할 가능성을 갖고 있어요. 바람은 예측하기가 매우 힘들고 태양 전지판은 흐린 날에는 사용할 수가 없죠. 그러나 조수는 변함이 없고 매우 예측이 쉬워요. 그 말은 조수 작용 터빈이 매일 전기를 생산할 것이라고 보장할 수 있을 뿐만 아니라, 하루의 어느 시간대에 그 일이 일어날지 알 수 있다는 것 또한 의미하죠.

여 **4** 환경에 부정적인 영향은 없나요?

M That is a good question. Many people have the impression that renewable energy sources have no negative effects on the environment. Of course, this is not true. Solar panels and turbines are both made of plastic, which is made from oil, and metal, which is mined. What makes them desirable is that they do not produce pollution when they operate. So, they can offset the cost of building them by producing clean energy.

W And wind turbines can kill birds, right?

M Uh, yes, that can happen, but it isn't common. Tidal turbines could have serious side effects, too. They could kill marine life, and they can alter erosion patterns. They also have to deal with threats that other alternative energy sources do not. **3(B)** For example, saltwater is extremely corrosive, particularly for metal parts. So, they have to use special alloys to make parts that will be continuously submerged. **5** If you are really interested in them, I recommend you look into the tidal turbine arrays that have been built near New York City, Norway, and England.

W OK, thank you for your time, professor.

남 좋은 질문이에요. 많은 사람들이 재생 가능 에너지원이 환경에 전혀 부정적인 영향을 주지 않을 것이라는 인상을 갖고 있죠. 물론 이것은 사실이 아니에요. 태양 전지판과 터빈들 둘 다 석유로 만든 플라스틱과 채굴된 금속으로 만들어지니까요. 이들 재생 가능 에너지가 매력적인 이유는 이들이 작동할 때 환경 오염을 일으키지 않는다는 점이에요. 그래서 깨끗한 에너지를 생산함으로써 건설에 들어가는 비용을 상쇄할 수 있죠.

여 그리고 풍력 발전용 터빈은 새들을 죽일 수 있어요, 그렇죠?

남 아, 맞아요. 일어날 수 있는 일이지만, 흔한 건 아니에요. 조수 작용 터빈도 심각한 부작용을 일으킬 수는 있어요. 바다 생물들을 죽일 수도 있고, 침식 유형을 바꿔놓을 수도 있거든요. 그리고 다른 대체 에너지원들에는 없는 위협에도 대처해야 합니다. **3(B)** 예를 들어, 바닷물은 매우 부식성이 강해요. 특히 금속 부품에 말이죠. 그래서 계속 물에 잠겨 있는 부품들을 만들기 위해 특별한 합금을 사용해야 합니다. **5** 학생이 이것들에 정말 관심이 있으면, 뉴욕, 노르웨이, 그리고 영국 가까이 지어진 조수 작용 터빈들을 찾아보는 걸 추천해요.

여 알겠습니다. 시간 내 주셔서 감사합니다, 교수님.

Lesson 01 Conversations

1. Why did the professor want to see the student?

Ⓐ To question the credibility of the references the student used

Ⓑ To cast doubt on the student's ability to cite references

Ⓒ To ask the student to add information regarding wind turbines

Ⓓ To explain the difference between tidal and wind turbines

2. What is the biggest problem of using company websites as resources?

Ⓐ It creates conflict between the student's ideas and reality.

Ⓑ It cannot provide enough information for the paper.

Ⓒ It might lead the writer to use wrong information and data.

Ⓓ It can provide the writer with information from a biased perspective.

3. According to the professor, what is true about tidal turbines? Choose 2 answers.

Ⓐ Utilizing them eventually brings negative effects on the environment.

1. 교수는 왜 학생을 보고자 했는가?

Ⓐ 학생이 사용한 참고 문헌의 신뢰성에 의문을 제기하기 위하여

Ⓑ 참고 문헌을 인용하는 학생의 능력을 의심하기 위하여

Ⓒ 풍력 발전용 터빈에 대해 정보를 추가하라고 말하기 위해

Ⓓ 조수 작용 터빈과 풍력 발전용 터빈 사이의 차이점을 설명하려고

2. 회사 웹사이트를 참고 자료로 사용하는 것의 가장 큰 문제점은 무엇인가?

Ⓐ 학생의 관점과 현실 사이에 갈등을 만들어낸다.

Ⓑ 리포트에 충분한 양의 정보를 제공해 주지 못한다.

Ⓒ 작성자가 잘못된 정보와 자료를 사용하도록 이끌 수 있다.

Ⓓ 작성자에게 편향된 시각에서 나온 정보를 줄 수 있다.

3. 교수에 따르면, 조수 작용 터빈에 대해 옳은 것은 무엇인가? 두 개를 고르시오.

Ⓐ 이들을 사용하는 것은 결국 환경에 부정적인 영향을 가져온다.

Ⓑ They cannot be made of common metals since they are vulnerable to seawater.

Ⓒ They depend on weather conditions too much, thus limiting their usage.

Ⓓ Using tidal turbines is more dependable than utilizing solar panels.

4. Listen again to part of the conversation. Then answer the question.

W Do they have any negative effect on the environment?
M That is a good question.

Why does the professor say this:

M That is a good question.

Ⓐ He is surprised by the student's insight into environmental problems.

Ⓑ He thought the student would ask other questions related to tidal turbines.

Ⓒ He thinks the student already knows much about her research topic.

Ⓓ He wants to tell the student that there are indeed some drawbacks.

5. Why does the professor mention New York City, Norway, and England?

Ⓐ To give examples of the places that have constructed tidal turbines

Ⓑ To show how these places affected the development of tidal turbines

Ⓒ To provide more references that could be useful for the student's paper

Ⓓ To tell the student to do more research regarding these important locations

Ⓑ 바닷물에 취약하기 때문에 흔한 금속으로는 만들 수 없다.

Ⓒ 날씨 조건에 너무 영향을 많이 받기에 사용에 제한을 받는다.

Ⓓ 조수 작용 터빈을 사용하는 것이 태양 전지판을 사용하는 것보다 더 신뢰성이 있다.

4. 대화의 일부를 다시 듣고 질문에 답하시오.

여 환경에 부정적인 영향은 없나요?
남 좋은 질문이에요.

교수는 왜 이렇게 말하는가:

남 좋은 질문이에요.

Ⓐ 환경 문제에 대한 학생의 통찰력을 보고 놀랐다.

Ⓑ 학생이 조수 작용 터빈에 관련된 다른 질문을 할 것이라고 생각했다.

Ⓒ 학생이 그녀의 연구 주제에 대해 이미 많은 것을 알고 있다고 생각한다.

Ⓓ 실제로 단점이 몇 가지 있다고 학생에게 말하고 싶어한다.

5. 교수는 왜 뉴욕, 노르웨이, 그리고 영국을 언급하는가?

Ⓐ 조수 작용 터빈을 건설한 장소들의 예를 들기 위해

Ⓑ 이 장소들이 조수 작용 터빈의 발달에 어떤 영향을 미쳤는지 보여주려고

Ⓒ 학생의 리포트에 도움이 될 만한 더 많은 참고 자료들을 제공하려고

Ⓓ 이 중요한 장소들에 대해 더 많이 조사하라고 학생에게 말하려고

어휘 short notice 촉박한 통보 | potential adj 가능성 있는, 잠재적인 | bibliography n 참고 문헌 | incorrect adj 부정확한 | entry n 수록, 입력 | questionable adj 의심스러운, 미심쩍은 | renewable adj 재생 가능한 | energy source 에너지원 | manufacture v 제조하다 | solar panel 태양 전지판 | conflict n 갈등 | false adj 거짓의, 틀린, 사실이 아닌 | reliable adj 믿을 수 있는 | profit v 이익을 내다, 수익을 내다 | positive adj 긍정적인 | institute n 기관 | conduct v (특정한 활동을) 하다 | independent adj 독립적인 | scientific journal 과학 잡지 | motivate v 이유가 되다, 동기를 부여하다 | exaggerate v 과장하다 | quote v 인용하다 | authority n 권위 | cite v 인용하다 | tidal turbine 조수 작용에 의한 터빈 | operate v 작동하다 | wind turbine 풍력 발전용 터빈 | phenomenon n 현상 (pl. phenomena) | electricity n 전기 | reliably adv 믿을 수 있게, 확실히 | unpredictable adj 예측할 수 없는 | consistent adj 변함이 없는, 한결같은, 일관된 | ensure v 반드시 ~하게 하다 | negative adj 부정적인 | impression n 인상, 느낌 | mine v 캐다, 채굴하다 | desirable adj 바람직한, 호감 가는 | common adj 흔한 | erosion n 침식, 부식 | alternative energy source 대체 에너지원 | corrosive adj 부식성의 | particularly adv 특히 | alloy n 합금 | continuously adv 계속해서, 연속적으로 | submerge v 물 속에 잠기다 | array n 집합체, 무리

Passage 3

Man: Professor | Woman: Student

[1-5] Listen to part of a conversation between a student and a professor.

M Good afternoon, Kristin, how can I help you?

W Hello, professor. **1** I have a question about today's lecture.

M **1** I thought I saw your hand go up at the end of class. This must be an important question if it cannot wait until our next class on Wednesday.

W I'm sorry. I know you usually say to bring up questions that there wasn't time for during the next session. If you are too busy, I can do that.

M No, I'm not busy at the moment. The reason I invite students to ask questions during the next session is so that the other students can benefit from the answers as well. That being said, this question seems important to you, so ask away.

W Thank you. In the lecture, you were talking about how animals sleep similarly to humans. Their brains go through sleeping states like ours do, including REM sleep. I know that most of human dreaming takes place during REM sleep, so does that mean that other animals dream as well?

M There is much debate about that question, but **2** some scientists think that they have found conclusive evidence that proves that animals do indeed dream. Tell me, do you have any pets?

W **2** I have a dog. He's a mini Pinscher.

M **2** Have you ever noticed your dog moving in his sleep?

W **2, 3(A)** Yes, his legs sometimes twitch, and his breathing becomes more labored. It seems like he might be dreaming about running. He yips and even barks sometimes, too.

M **2, 3(A)** Those are exactly the kind of signs that made researchers think that animals dream. Recently, they have monitored the brain activity in rats as they learn to find their way through a maze. When the animals are sleeping, they monitor the same cell groups that were activated when they were in the maze, and they show the same pattern of activity.

W That is fascinating. So, the theory about humans also applies to animals. They use dreaming as a way to process memories.

M That is how they have interpreted their data.

W But, that raises another question... how realistic is their data? I mean, isn't it always better to observe animals in their natural habitat? Wouldn't being in a laboratory affect their sleeping patterns? I know I sleep differently in an unfamiliar environment.

남자: 교수 | 여자: 학생

학생과 교수의 대화를 들으시오.

남 안녕하세요, 크리스틴. 어떻게 도와줄까요?

여 안녕하세요, 교수님. **1** 오늘 수업에 대해 질문이 있어서요.

남 **1** 학생이 수업 끝날 때쯤 손을 든 걸 본 것 같았어요. 다음 수업이 있는 수요일까지 기다릴 수 없다면 분명히 중요한 질문이겠군요.

여 죄송합니다. 시간이 없을 때에는 보통 다음 수업 시간에 질문하라고 말씀하시는 걸 알고 있어요. 너무 바쁘시다면 다음 시간에 여쭤볼게요.

남 아니요, 지금은 바쁘지 않아요. 내가 학생들에게 다음 시간에 질문하라고 요청하는 이유는, 다른 학생들도 그 답을 듣고 도움을 얻을 수 있도록 하기 위해서예요. 그렇긴 해도, 이 질문이 학생에게 중요해 보이니 질문하세요.

여 감사합니다. 강의 시간에 교수님께서 어떻게 동물들이 인간과 비슷하게 잠을 자는지에 대해 말씀하셨어요. 우리의 뇌처럼 동물들의 뇌도 REM 수면을 포함하는 수면 상태를 지닌다고요. 사람이 꾸는 꿈의 대부분이 REM 수면 동안 일어난다는 걸 알고 있는데, 그 말은 동물들 역시 꿈을 꾼다는 의미인가요?

남 그 질문에 대해서는 논쟁이 많지만, **2** 몇몇 과학자들은 동물들이 실제로 꿈을 꾼다는 것을 증명하는 결정적인 증거를 발견했다고 생각합니다. 학생은 반려동물을 기르고 있나요?

여 **2** 네, 개를 길러요. 미니어처 핀셔예요.

남 **2** 학생의 개가 자는 동안 움직이는 걸 알아차린 적이 있나요?

여 **2, 3(A)** 네, 때때로 다리가 움찔거리고, 호흡이 가빠질 때가 있어요. 달리고 있는 꿈을 꾸는 걸지도 모르겠어요. 가끔 낑낑거리기도 하고, 심지어 짖기도 해요.

남 **2, 3(A)** 그런 것들이 과학자들로 하여금 동물들도 꿈을 꾼다고 생각하게 한 바로 그 징후들이에요. 최근 과학자들은 쥐들이 미로를 빠져나가는 법을 배우는 동안의 뇌 활동을 관찰했어요. 이 쥐들이 잠들었을 때 과학자들은 이들이 미로에 있었을 때 활성화되었던 동일한 세포 그룹을 관찰했는데, 같은 활동 패턴을 보였어요.

여 정말 흥미롭네요. 그래서 사람에 대한 이론이 동물에게도 적용되는군요. 동물들도 기억을 처리하기 위한 한 방법으로 꿈을 사용하는 거요.

남 과학자들은 그들의 자료를 그렇게 해석하죠.

여 하지만, 다른 질문이 생겼어요... 이들의 자료가 얼마나 현실적인 건가요? 제 말은, 자연 서식지에서 동물들을 관찰하는 것이 항상 더 낫지 않나요? 실험실에 있다는 사실이 동물들의 수면 패턴에 영향을 주진 않을까요? 저는 제가 낯선 장소에 있으면 잠을 좀 다르게 잔다는 걸 알거든요.

M That is a legitimate concern, but these rats were most likely raised in captivity. **3(D)** There are scientists working on technology that would allow us to monitor animal's brain activity in the wild. Tracking devices have been used for decades, but it is difficult making something sensitive enough to monitor brain activity that is both durable and light enough that the animals will not try to remove it.

W **4** Oh, yes, I can see how that would be a problem. I would love to take part in research like that. Maybe someday…

M **4** Why wait? You might be able to do that now. There are many research projects taking place at this university. They do not advertise their activities on campus, but they usually need qualified undergraduate students to be research assistants. Doctor Kandaris is currently working on developing such transmitters. She plans on testing them on rodents in the Sonoran Desert in Arizona next summer.

W **5** Really? That sounds fantastic! Do you know if she still needs any help?

M She might. Here is her email address. Send her an email stating your interest and any relevant experience you may have.

W OK, I will. Thank you, professor!

남 일리 있는 걱정이지만, 이 쥐들은 포획되어 길러졌을 가능성이 높아요. **3(D)** 야생에서 동물들의 뇌 활동을 관찰할 수 있도록 하는 기술을 연구하는 과학자들이 있어요. 추적 장치가 수십 년간 사용되어 왔지만, 동물들이 이를 제거하려고 시도하지 않을 정도로 지속력이 오래 가면서 가벼운, 뇌 활동을 관찰하기 충분할 정도로 민감한 장치를 만들기는 쉽지 않죠.

여 **4** 아, 네, 왜 문제가 있는지 알 것 같아요. 그런 연구에 정말 참여해보고 싶네요. 언젠가는 할 수 있겠죠...

남 **4** 기다릴 필요 있나요? 지금 할 수도 있죠. 지금 우리 대학에서도 많은 연구 프로젝트들이 진행되고 있어요. 캠퍼스에서 그들의 연구 활동을 광고하지는 않지만 연구 조교가 될 만한 자격을 갖춘 학부생을 보통 필요로 하고 있죠. 칸다리스 박사가 현재 이런 발신기를 제작하는 연구를 하고 있어요. 내년 여름에 애리조나주의 소노란 사막에서 설치류들에게 이 기계를 시험해볼 계획이죠.

여 **5** 진짜요? 정말 멋지네요! 그분이 아직도 도움을 필요로 하는지 혹시 아시나요?

남 그럴지도 모르죠. 여기 그분의 이메일 주소가 있어요. 학생의 흥미 분야와 학생이 가지고 있는 관련 경험을 적어서 이메일을 보내보세요.

여 네, 그럴게요. 감사합니다, 교수님!

1. Why did the student come to see her professor?

(A) To get his opinion regarding the theme of her final paper
(B) To get the email address of Doctor Kandaris from him
(C) To ask a question that she was not able to ask during the class
(D) To explain why she was not able to understand the class material

2. What can be inferred about animals' sleep?

(A) There is a high chance that they dream like humans do.
(B) They often exhibit different sleeping patterns from humans'.
(C) The evidence of animal dreaming was found about 10 years ago.
(D) Their dreaming does not take place during REM sleep.

3. What do the student and the professor say about observing animals in their sleep? Choose 2 answers.

(A) They show some possible signs of dreaming like twitching or barking.
(B) The brain activity of animals in sleep is dramatically different from humans'.

1. 학생은 왜 교수를 찾아왔는가?

(A) 기말 논문의 주제에 대해 교수의 의견을 듣기 위해
(B) 칸다리스 박사의 이메일 주소를 얻기 위해
(C) 수업 시간에 물어보지 못했던 질문을 하기 위해
(D) 왜 수업 자료를 이해할 수 없었는지 설명하기 위해

2. 동물들의 잠에 대해 무엇을 추론할 수 있는가?

(A) 인간이 꿈을 꾸는 것처럼 동물들도 꿈을 꿀 가능성이 높다.
(B) 종종 인간의 수면 패턴과 다른 수면 패턴을 보인다.
(C) 동물들이 꿈을 꾼다는 증거는 약 10년 전에 발견되었다.
(D) 동물들의 꿈은 REM 수면 동안 나타나지 않는다.

3. 학생과 교수는 잠을 자는 동물들을 관찰하는 것에 대해 무엇이라고 말하는가? 두 개를 고르시오.

(A) 움찔거리거나 짖는 등 꿈을 꾸고 있다는 가능성을 나타내는 징후를 보인다.
(B) 잠을 자는 동물들의 뇌 활동은 인간들의 뇌 활동과 상당히 다르다.

Ⓒ Tracking devices were used when animals were observed in a laboratory setting.
Ⓓ Observing them in the wild is difficult and needs further technical development.

4. Listen again to part of the conversation. Then answer the question.

> W Oh, yes, I can see how that would be a problem. I would love to take part in research like that. Maybe someday....
> M Why wait?

Why does the professor say this:

> M Why wait?

Ⓐ He does not want the student to waste her time.
Ⓑ He is encouraging the student to take an opportunity now.
Ⓒ He is telling the student to be patient because there will be other opportunities.
Ⓓ He does not understand why the student is reluctant to participate.

5. What is the student's attitude toward Doctor Kandaris' research project?

Ⓐ She enjoyed being part of the project and wants to participate again.
Ⓑ She is unable to make a decision because she feels confused.
Ⓒ She sees it as a great opportunity and she is interested in it.
Ⓓ She wants to join the project but is too busy with her class schedule.

Ⓒ 추적 장치는 동물들이 실험실 환경에서 관찰되었을 때 사용되었다.
Ⓓ 야생에서 동물들을 관찰하는 것은 어렵고 추가 기술의 발전이 필요하다.

4. 다음 대화의 일부를 다시 듣고 질문에 답하시오.

> 여 아, 네, 왜 문제가 있는지 알 것 같아요. 그런 연구에 정말 참여해보고 싶네요. 언젠가는 할 수 있겠죠...
> 남 기다릴 필요 있나요?

교수는 왜 이렇게 말하는가:

> 남 기다릴 필요 있나요?

Ⓐ 학생이 시간 낭비하기를 원하지 않는다.
Ⓑ 지금 기회를 잡으라고 학생을 격려하고 있다.
Ⓒ 다른 기회가 있을 테니 인내심을 가지라고 말하고 있다.
Ⓓ 학생이 왜 참여를 망설이는지 이해하지 못한다.

5. 칸다리스 박사의 연구 프로젝트에 대한 학생의 태도는 어떠한가?

Ⓐ 그 프로젝트의 일원으로 일하는 것을 즐겼고 다시 참여하고 싶어한다.
Ⓑ 혼란스러워서 결정을 내릴 수 없다.
Ⓒ 매우 좋은 기회라고 여기고 흥미를 느낀다.
Ⓓ 프로젝트에 참여하고 싶지만 수업 일정 때문에 너무 바쁘다.

Lesson 01 Conversations

어휘 session n (특정 활동을 위한) 시간 | benefit v 도움을 얻다, 덕을 보다 | similarly adv 비슷하게, 유사하게 | sleeping states 수면 상태 | REM sleep 렘 수면 | debate n 논쟁 | conclusive adj 결정적인, 확실한 | prove v 증명하다 | indeed adv 정말, 확실히 | notice v 알아차리다 | twitch v 움찔하다 | labored adj 애쓰는 | yip v 깽깽 울다 | bark v 짖다 | monitor v 관찰하다 | brain activity 뇌 활동 | maze n 미로 | activate v 활성화시키다 | fascinating adj 흥미로운 | apply v 적용하다 | process v 처리하다 | memory n 기억 | interpret v 해석하다 | realistic adj 현실적인 | observe v 관찰하다 | natural habitat 자연 서식지 | laboratory n 실험실 | affect v 영향을 미치다 | unfamiliar adj 낯선 | legitimate adj 타당한, 정당한 | concern n 걱정 | captivity n 포획, 감금 | tracking device 추적 장치 | decade n 10년 | sensitive adj 민감한 | durable adj 내구성이 있는 | remove v 제거하다 | advertise v 광고하다 | qualified adj 자격이 있는 | undergraduate adj 학부의 | currently adv 현재 | transmitter n 발신기 | test v 시험하다 | rodent n 설치류 | relevant adj 관련 있는

Passage 4

Man: Professor | Woman: Student

[1-5] Listen to part of a conversation between a student and a professor.

M Good afternoon, Tamara. How are you this afternoon?
W Fine, I'm glad you had time to see me.

남자: 교수 | 여자: 학생

학생과 교수의 대화를 들으시오.

남 안녕하세요, 타마라. 오늘 잘 지내고 있나요?
여 네, 저를 볼 시간이 있으셔서 다행이에요.

M Have a seat. How is your term paper coming along? You chose to write about Margaret Cavendish, correct?

W Yes, I think my research is pretty much complete, and I have gotten started on my rough draft.

M Excellent. What are your thoughts about Lady Cavendish?

W She was a remarkable woman, and quite controversial in her time. She was a natural philosopher and the first woman to be invited to attend a meeting of the Royal Society of London in 1667. She watched a series of experiments performed by Robert Boyle and Robert Hooke. Then the Royal Society banned women!

M Yes, and that ban lasted until 1945, so she must have made an impression, but apparently not a very good one.

W **2** Well, she was a woman of extremes. She was cripplingly shy, so she dressed flamboyantly in an effort to seem outgoing. She also refuted Aristotle's teachings and mechanical philosophy in favor of a vitalist model. She believed that atoms were active, and this and many of her other ideas have proven to be fairly accurate.

M All true... I can see that you have made a good start. **1, 3** What did you want to see me about?

W **1, 3** I heard that there is an opening for a teaching assistant in the Philosophy Department. I was hoping to apply for that position.

M **3** Ah, yes, there is such an opening, but aren't you a sophomore?

W Yes, I am. Is that a problem? Many of my friends are teaching assistants for other departments.

M Yes, but all of the TAs in our department are graduate students who are required to teach actual classes. So, I'm afraid you're just not eligible.

W Oh, I see. Now that you mention it, my lower level course instructors did seem pretty young.

M Yes, as we are a small department, we need them to do that.

W Okay, then I guess I should get back to writing my paper.

M Hold on a second, Tamara. You cannot be a TA for us, but you could be a tutor. You clearly have an advanced knowledge of philosophy since you are taking such high-level courses as a sophomore. Many students struggle with our intro courses, though. **4** Would you be interested in helping them one-to-one?

W **4** Sure! Who are you currently discussing in class?

남 앉으세요. 학기말 리포트는 어떻게 진행되고 있나요? 학생은 마가렛 캐번디시에 대해 쓰기로 했었죠, 맞나요?

여 네, 일단 조사는 거의 끝난 것 같아요. 그리고 초고를 쓰기 시작했어요.

남 훌륭해요. 캐번디시 부인에 대한 학생의 생각은 어떤가요?

여 그녀는 놀라운 여성이었고, 그녀가 살던 시대에 꽤나 논란의 여지가 많았던 사람이었어요. 자연 철학자였고, 1667년에 런던 왕립학회 모임에 참석하도록 초대 받은 최초의 여성이었죠. 그녀는 로버트 보일과 로버트 훅이 진행하던 몇 가지 실험들을 봤었어요. 그 후 왕립학회가 여성의 참석을 금지했어요!

남 맞아요, 그리고 이 금지령이 1945년까지 지속되었으니, 그녀가 뭔가 인상을 남기긴 했지만 별로 좋은 인상은 아니었던 게 분명해요.

여 **2** 음, 그녀는 극단적인 면을 가진 여성이었어요. 그녀는 심하게 수줍음을 많이 타서 외향적으로 보이려고 화려한 옷차림을 했죠. 또한 활력론자 모델을 지지하여 아리스토텔레스의 가르침과 기계론에 반박하기도 했어요. 원자들이 활동적이라고 믿었고, 이 믿음과 다른 많은 생각들이 꽤나 정확한 것으로 밝혀졌죠.

남 모두 맞아요... 출발이 순조롭다는 걸 알겠네요. **1, 3** 무슨 용건으로 저를 보러 온 거죠?

여 **1, 3** 철학과에 조교 자리가 하나 있다고 들었어요. 그 자리에 지원하고 싶어서요.

남 **3** 아, 네, 그런 자리가 있긴 한데, 학생은 2학년 아닌가요?

여 네, 맞아요. 그게 문제가 되나요? 다른 학과에 있는 제 친구들 다수가 조교인데요.

남 네, 그렇지만 우리 학과의 모든 조교들은 실제 수업을 가르칠 의무를 가진 대학원생들이에요. 그래서 유감이지만 학생은 자격이 안 될 것 같아요.

여 아, 그렇군요. 교수님이 말하셨으니 말인데, 더 쉬운 단계 수업의 강사들이 실제로 꽤 어려 보이긴 했어요.

남 그래요, 우리 학과는 작기 때문에 그들이 그렇게 해줘야 해요.

여 알겠습니다. 그럼 저는 이제 다시 리포트를 쓰러 돌아가야겠네요.

남 잠깐만 기다려요, 타마라. 우리 학과의 조교가 될 수는 없지만, 개인 지도 교사가 될 수는 있어요. 학생은 2학년임에도 불구하고 높은 단계의 수업들을 듣고 있으니 확실히 철학에 대해 뛰어난 지식을 가지고 있어요. 하지만 많은 학생들이 철학과의 입문 수업에서 어려움을 겪죠. **4** 일대일로 그 학생들을 도와주는 일에 흥미가 있나요?

여 **4** 그럼요! 지금 수업에서 누구에 대해 가르치고 계신가요?

M 4 Jeremy Bentham.

W Oh, so you are working on moral philosophy and utilitarianism. He was a radical. He had strong opinions on individual rights, equality, and the separation of church and state. He called for the abolition of slavery, the death penalty, and physical punishment. He believed that the greatest happiness for the greatest number of people was the true measure of right and wrong.

M Yes, indeed he did. I can see that you will be a good tutor.

W 5 When do you need me to start?

M 5 Tonight, if you are available. You need to come to the classroom next to this office at 7 p.m. on Tuesday, Wednesday, and Thursday. Would that be possible?

W 5 Yes, my schedule should be open on those nights. I am not taking any evening courses this semester. Am I allowed to study for other classes when no one needs help?

M Yes, that would be fine.

남 4 제레미 벤담이에요.

여 아, 그럼 윤리학과 공리주의에 대해 가르치고 계신 거군요. 벤담은 급진주의자였어요. 그는 개인의 권리, 평등, 그리고 교회와 국가의 분리에 대해 강한 의견을 가지고 있었죠. 노예 제도, 사형, 그리고 체벌의 폐지를 주장하기도 했습니다. 최대 다수의 최대 행복이 옳고 그름의 진정한 척도라고 믿었죠.

남 네, 정말 그랬죠. 학생은 좋은 개인 지도 교사가 될 수 있을 것 같네요.

여 5 제가 언제 시작하면 되나요?

남 5 만약 가능하다면 오늘 밤에요. 이 사무실 옆에 있는 교실로 화요일, 수요일, 목요일 저녁 7시에 와야 해요. 가능한가요?

여 5 네, 이 날들에는 가능해요. 이번 학기에는 저녁 수업을 하나도 듣고 있지 않거든요. 도움을 필요로 하는 사람이 없으면 다른 수업 공부를 해도 되나요?

남 네, 괜찮아요.

1. Why did the student come to see her professor?

Ⓐ To see if she is doing well with her class presentation
Ⓑ To ask questions about a teacher's assistant position
Ⓒ To discuss the topic of her thesis paper with the professor
Ⓓ To reschedule her working shift as a teacher's assistant

2. What was mentioned about Margaret Cavendish?

Ⓐ She dressed outrageously since she liked showing off.
Ⓑ She was a philosopher who expressed some radical ideas.
Ⓒ She tried to convince other philosophers with her theories.
Ⓓ She shared her ideas with the public and gained support.

3. Listen again to part of a conversation. Then answer the question.

> W I heard that there is an opening for a teaching assistant in the Philosophy Department. I was hoping to apply for that position.
> M Ah, yes, there is such an opening, but aren't you a sophomore?

Why does the professor say this:

> M Ah, yes, there is such an opening, but aren't you a sophomore?

Ⓐ To suggest the student apply for the position quickly

1. 학생은 왜 교수를 찾아왔는가?

Ⓐ 수업 발표와 관련해서 잘하고 있는지를 확인하기 위해
Ⓑ 조교 일자리에 대해 질문을 하기 위해
Ⓒ 논문의 주제에 대해 교수와 논의하기 위해
Ⓓ 조교 일의 스케줄을 다시 조정하기 위해

2. 마가렛 캐번디시에 대해 언급된 것은 무엇인가?

Ⓐ 자랑하는 것을 좋아했기 때문에 충격적인 옷차림을 했다.
Ⓑ 몇몇 극단적인 생각을 표현했던 철학자였다.
Ⓒ 자신의 이론으로 다른 철학자들을 설득하려고 했다.
Ⓓ 자신의 생각을 대중과 공유하였고 지지를 얻었다.

3. 대화의 일부를 다시 듣고 질문에 답하시오.

> 여 철학과에 조교 자리가 하나 있다고 들었어요. 그 자리에 지원하고 싶어서요.
> 남 아, 네, 그런 자리가 있긴 한데, 학생은 2학년 아닌가요?

교수는 왜 이렇게 말하는가:

> 남 아, 네, 그런 자리가 있긴 한데, 학생은 2학년 아닌가요?

Ⓐ 이 일자리에 빨리 지원하라고 학생에게 제안하려고

Ⓑ To make sure that the information he has is up-do-date
Ⓒ To tell the student that she is too advanced for the position
Ⓓ To imply that she may be ineligible for the position

4. Why does the professor mention Jeremy Bentham?
Ⓐ To tell the student who she needs to know about for a tutoring session
Ⓑ To introduce the topic of the next discussion in her class
Ⓒ To ask the student to study more about him for her term paper
Ⓓ To emphasize the influence he had on Lady Cavendish

5. What can be inferred about the student?
Ⓐ She will start working as a philosophy tutor soon.
Ⓑ She is going to change her schedule to work as a tutor.
Ⓒ She is taking small-credit classes this semester.
Ⓓ She will teach only on Tuesdays and Wednesdays.

Ⓑ 그가 가지고 있는 정보가 최신의 것인지 확인하려고
Ⓒ 이 일자리에는 학생의 실력이 너무 뛰어나서 맞지 않다는 것을 말해주려고
Ⓓ 이 일자리에 자격이 안 될 수도 있다는 것을 암시하려고

4. 교수는 왜 제레미 벤담을 언급하는가?
Ⓐ 개인 교습 시간을 위해 학생이 누구를 알아야 하는지 말하기 위해
Ⓑ 학생의 다음 수업 토론의 주제를 소개하기 위해
Ⓒ 학생의 학기말 리포트를 위해 그에 대해 더 공부하라고 하기 위해
Ⓓ 그가 캐번디시 부인에게 끼친 영향을 강조하기 위해

5. 학생에 관해 무엇을 추론할 수 있는가?
Ⓐ 곧 철학 개인 지도 교사로 일을 시작할 것이다.
Ⓑ 개인 지도 교사로 일하기 위해 일정을 바꿀 것이다.
Ⓒ 이번 학기에 적은 학점의 수업들을 듣고 있다.
Ⓓ 화요일과 수요일에만 가르칠 것이다.

어휘 term paper 학기말 리포트 I complete adj 완료된 I rough draft 초고 I remarkable adj 놀라운, 놀랄 만한 I controversial adj 논란이 많은 I natural philosopher 자연 철학자 I ban v 금지하다 n 금지(법) I impression n 인상 I apparently adv 분명히 I extreme n 극단, 극도 I cripplingly adv 심하게, 주체할 수 없이 I flamboyantly adv 현란하게, 대담하게 I outgoing adj 외향적인, 사교적인 I refute v 논박하다, 반박하다 I mechanical philosophy 기계론 I vitalist n 활력론자 I atom n 원자 I accurate adj 정확한 I position n (일)자리, 지위 I sophomore n (고등학교, 대학교) 2학년 I eligible adj (자격·조건이 되어서) ~를 할 수 있는 I instructor n 강사, 교사 I currently adv 현재, 지금 I moral philosophy 윤리학 I utilitarianism n 공리주의 I radical n 급진주의자 I right n 권리 I equality n 평등 I separation n 분리 I abolition n 폐지 I slavery n 노예 제도 I death penalty 사형 I physical punishment 체벌

Passage 5

Man: Student | Woman: Professor

[1-5] Listen to part of a conversation between a student and a professor.

W Good afternoon, Dan. How may I help you?

M Hello Professor Diaz, 1 I wanted to speak to you about using more environmentally friendly art supplies in the classroom. I've been looking into some companies that make them, and I really think we should consider using them. I was told that you are responsible for deciding what to purchase?

W I see. No one person has that responsibility. We usually discuss such things as a group. I and the other art professors, I mean. However, I am the person who usually places the order. 2 If you have been researching this topic, then I assume that you have noticed that green art supplies are not cheap. Actually, all art supplies tend to be expensive to get any decent quality.

남자: 학생 | 여자: 교수

학생과 교수의 대화를 들으시오.

여 안녕하세요, 댄. 무슨 일로 도움이 필요한가요?

남 안녕하세요, 디아즈 교수님. 1 좀 더 환경친화적인 미술 용품들을 수업 시간에 사용하는 것에 대해 교수님과 이야기하고 싶었어요. 환경친화적 미술 용품들을 만드는 회사들을 좀 찾아봤는데, 우리 학교에서도 정말 이것들을 사용해야 한다고 생각해서요. 어떤 미술 용품을 구매할지 교수님께서 결정하신다고 들었어요.

여 그렇군요. 한 사람이 그 권한을 가지고 있는 것은 아니에요. 그런 일들은 그룹으로 모여서 논의하거든요. 내 말은, 나와 다른 미대 교수님들이 함께요. 하지만 보통 주문을 하는 사람이 나예요. 2 학생이 이 주제에 대해 조사를 했다면, 환경친화적 미술 용품들이 그다지 값이 싸지 않다는 걸 알아차렸을 거예요. 사실, 모든 미술 용품들에 있어서 질이 괜찮은 것들은 비싼 경향이 있죠.

M Yes, I have, and no, they aren't. Sometimes they cost twice as much. It's just, well, you know that a lot of the more inexpensive paints and chemicals come from manufacturers whose governments allow them to pollute much more than they should.

W Yes, and the wood used for tools and easels is often harvested from trees in rain forests. There are many hidden costs to these items. 2 I would like to use them more than we do, but I'm afraid we just don't have the money for it. We have already gone over budget this semester—

M Oh? We have? I didn't realize. I'm sorry if I wasted your time.

W Now, hold on a minute. I wasn't finished. 3 If you would like, you can write an official proposal. I would be willing to submit it for you at our next meeting.

M When is your next meeting?

W It will be in the beginning of November. In about three weeks. We will be discussing next semester's budget then. We have to turn in our budget request before final exams.

M Really? I would be glad to!

W Great. If enough of you and your classmates bring this kind of matter to their attention, the board members might make changes. That being said, I would like you to know that we already purchased some environmentally friendly supplies that you may already be using. What is your major?

M It's fine arts, with a focus on oil painting.

W That's what I figured based upon which supplies you mentioned. 4 The new easels and the canvas you've been using are both made from recycled materials. Thankfully, those were relatively cheap.

M 4 Oh, I didn't realize that.

W 4 Are you satisfied with the quality of those materials?

M Hmm? Yes, I am very satisfied. I had no idea that they were recycled. They seemed new.

W Excellent, 5 then I have a request to make of you. Could you put together a petition and get your fellow art majors to sign it for me, stating that you would support the university making a contract with that company? If we make that kind of business arrangement, we can get your green supplies at a discount. The board of directors likes to have partnerships like that. That allows us to get funding from the government more easily.

M Of course, I'll get on that immediately. I guess I have some work to do now.

W Yes, you do. If you need any help or advice with the paperwork, let me know. You have to go to the university center to get the documents you will need to fill out. Go to the student activities center.

남 네, 알아차렸어요. 그리고 맞아요. 값이 싸진 않아요. 때로는 가격이 거의 두 배일 때도 있어요. 음, 그저, 교수님도 아시잖아요. 값이 더 싼 물감과 화학 물질들은 이들이 환경을 더 과도하게 오염시키는 것을 방관하는 정부 아래 있는 제조사들로부터 나온다는 걸요.

여 맞아요. 그리고 도구와 이젤에 사용되는 목재는 종종 열대 우림의 나무들로부터 얻어지죠. 이 물품들에는 숨겨진 비용들이 많아요. 2 나도 우리가 현재 사용하는 것보다 더 많은 환경친화적 물품들을 사용하고 싶지만, 유감스럽게도 우리는 그럴 돈이 없어요. 이번 학기에는 이미 예산을 초과했기 때문에—

남 아, 그런가요? 몰랐습니다. 교수님의 시간을 빼앗았다면 죄송합니다.

여 잠깐만 기다려요. 아직 말을 다 한 게 아니에요. 3 학생이 괜찮다면, 공식 제안서를 쓸 수도 있어요. 교수진들의 다음 회의에서 내가 제출해줄 생각이 있어요.

남 다음 회의는 언제인가요?

여 11월 초에 할 거예요. 약 3주 후에요. 그때 다음 학기의 예산에 대해 논의할 거예요. 기말고사 기간 전에 예산 신청을 제출해야 해요.

남 정말인가요? 물론 하겠습니다!

여 잘됐네요! 학생과 학우들이 더 많이 이러한 문제를 학교에 제기해서 그들의 주의를 끌면 이사회에서 변경할지도 몰라요. 말 나온 김에 우리가 이미 환경친화적인 미술 용품들을 몇 개 구입했다는 걸 학생에게 말하고 싶네요. 학생이 이미 사용하고 있을 수도 있어요. 전공이 무엇인가요?

남 미술이고, 유화에 중점을 두고 있어요.

여 학생이 언급했던 미술 용품들을 들었을 때 그럴 거라고 생각했어요. 4 학생이 사용하고 있는 새 이젤과 캔버스는 재활용된 재료로 만들어진 것들이에요. 다행히도, 이것들은 상대적으로 가격이 쌌죠.

남 4 아, 알아차리지 못했네요.

여 4 이 물품들의 품질에는 만족하나요?

남 흠? 네, 매우 만족합니다. 재활용된 재료로 만들어진 줄은 전혀 몰랐어요. 완전히 새것 같았거든요.

여 좋아요. 5 그럼 학생에게 부탁할 것이 있어요. 탄원서를 작성해서 다른 미술 전공자 학생들도 거기 서명할 수 있도록 해줄래요? 학교가 그 회사와 계약하는 것을 여러분이 지지한다는 것을 밝히는 탄원서 말이에요. 이러한 사업 협정을 맺으면 환경친화적 용품들을 더 싼 가격에 구매할 수 있어요. 이사회는 이러한 협업 관계를 맺는 걸 좋아하고요. 그렇게 된다면 정부로부터 지원을 더 쉽게 받을 수 있어요.

남 물론입니다. 바로 작성할게요. 이제 할 일이 생겼네요.

여 그렇네요. 문서 작성에 대해 도움이나 조언이 필요하다면 알려주세요. 학교 사무실에 가서 작성해야 하는 서류들을 받아야 해요. 학생 활동 사무실로 가세요.

M Okay, I will. Thank you for meeting with me, professor.
W No problem.

1. What are the speakers mainly discussing?

Ⓐ The benefits of buying art supplies that cause no harm to the environment
Ⓑ Using and purchasing green art supplies in the art department
Ⓒ Finding a green art supply company to be the university's partner
Ⓓ Getting advice regarding how to write an official petition

2. What makes using environmentally friendly art supplies difficult?

Ⓐ They are usually too expensive to fit in the art department budget.
Ⓑ The school only accepts items manufactured by the university's partners.
Ⓒ The university would not purchase them because they are made overseas.
Ⓓ The green art supply companies are not certified by the government.

3. What does the professor suggest the student do?

Ⓐ Submit a proposal to the university regarding the use of green art supplies
Ⓑ Collect art major students' signatures to increase the department budget
Ⓒ Purchase and use environmentally friendly art supplies himself
Ⓓ Continue his research on the advantages of using green art supplies

4. Listen to part of the conversation. Then answer the question:

W The new easels and the canvas you've been using are both made from recycled materials. Thankfully, those were relatively cheap.
M Oh, I didn't realize that.
W Are you satisfied with the quality of those materials?

Why does the professor say this:

W Are you satisfied with the quality of those materials?

Ⓐ To compare the quality and price of those two types of art supplies

남 네, 알겠습니다. 만나주셔서 감사합니다, 교수님.
여 천만에요.

1. 화자들은 무엇에 대해 주로 이야기하고 있는가?

Ⓐ 환경에 전혀 해를 끼치지 않는 미술 용품들을 사는 것의 이점
Ⓑ 미술학부에서 환경친화적 미술 용품을 구입하고 사용하는 것
Ⓒ 대학교의 파트너로 환경친화적 미술 용품 회사를 찾는 일
Ⓓ 공식 탄원서를 쓰는 것에 대해 조언 얻기

2. 환경친화적인 미술 용품을 사용하는 것에 있어서 어려운 점은 무엇인가?

Ⓐ 물품들이 보통 너무 비싸서 미술학부의 예산에 맞지 않는다.
Ⓑ 대학교는 대학교와 파트너십을 맺은 생산자들의 물품들만 허용한다.
Ⓒ 이 물품들이 외국에서 만들어졌기 때문에 대학 측에서는 구매를 하지 않을 것이다.
Ⓓ 환경친화적 미술 용품들을 제조하는 회사들은 정부의 인가를 받지 않았다.

3. 교수는 학생에게 무엇을 하라고 제안하는가?

Ⓐ 환경친화적 미술 용품의 사용에 대해 학교에 제안서를 제출한다
Ⓑ 미술학부의 예산을 증대시키기 위해 미술 전공 학생들의 서명을 받는다
Ⓒ 학생이 직접 환경 친화적 미술 용품을 구매하고 사용한다
Ⓓ 환경친화적 미술 용품을 쓰는 것의 이점에 대한 조사를 계속한다

4. 대화의 일부를 듣고 질문에 답하시오.

여 학생이 사용하고 있는 새 이젤과 캔버스는 재활용된 재료로 만들어진 것들이에요. 다행히도, 이것들은 상대적으로 가격이 쌌죠.
남 아, 알아차리지 못했네요.
여 이 물품들의 품질에는 만족하나요?

교수는 왜 이렇게 말하는가:

여 이 물품들의 품질에는 만족하나요?

Ⓐ 그 두 가지 미술 용품의 가격과 질을 서로 비교하려고

Ⓑ To ask him about the benefits of using supplies made of recycled materials
Ⓒ To inquire about the student's opinion of some green art supplies
Ⓓ To decide whether or not to write a customer review about them

Ⓑ 재활용된 재료로 만들어진 물품들을 사용하는 것의 이점에 대해 물어보려고
Ⓒ 몇몇 환경친화적 미술 용품에 대한 학생의 의견을 물어보려고
Ⓓ 이 물품들에 대해 고객 후기를 쓸지 말지를 결정하려고

5. Why does the professor mention a business arrangement?
Ⓐ To explain that the board of directors prefer having business partners
Ⓑ To tell the student about the process of writing an official petition
Ⓒ To illustrate a way of buying green art supplies at reduced prices
Ⓓ To show the necessity of one when it comes to big department budgets

5. 교수는 왜 사업 협정을 언급하는가?
Ⓐ 이사회가 사업 파트너를 갖는 것을 선호한다고 설명하기 위해
Ⓑ 공식 탄원서를 작성하는 과정에 대해 학생에게 말해주기 위해
Ⓒ 환경친화적 미술 용품을 할인된 가격으로 사는 방법을 보여주기 위해
Ⓓ 규모가 큰 부서 예산의 경우 사업 협정의 필요성을 보여주기 위해

어휘 environmentally adv 환경적으로 | friendly adv 친화적인 | supply n 용품, 물품 | responsible adj 책임지고 있는, 책임이 있는 | purchase v 구입하다 | place an order 주문하다 | assume v 가정하다 | notice v 알아차리다 | green adj 환경친화적인 | decent adj 괜찮은 | chemical n 화학 물질 | manufacturer n 생산 회사 | pollute v 오염시키다 | harvest v 거둬들이다, 추수하다 | rain forest 열대 우림 | budget n 예산 | official adj 공식적인 | proposal n 제안서 | submit v 제출하다 | request n 신청, 요청 | fine arts 미술 | oil painting 유화 | recycle v 재활용하다 | petition n 탄원서 | fellow adj 동료의 | state v 주장하다 | contract n 계약 | discount n 할인 | board of directors 이사회 | paperwork n 서류 작업

Passage 6

Man: Professor | Woman: Student

[1-5] Listen to part of a conversation between a student and a professor.

M Good afternoon, Keira, what can I do for you?
W Hello Professor Neville, I was hoping to discuss something with you if you aren't busy right now.
M I am free for a while. What's on your mind?
W **1(B)** I am planning to apply for an internship and I need your advice.
M Okay, tell me about the internship.
W It's an internship at a music company, in their marketing department.
M That sounds good. That would be a valuable experience for you.
W Yes, I think so too. **2** But my concern is that I am not very good at business writing. I mean, I passed the course, but not with a very good grade. I don't understand why, since I am quite good at other kinds of writing like essays and research papers.
M Ah, well, business writing is a unique type of writing. **3(A)** In essay writing and research papers, you often introduce the topic at the beginning, but you don't really get to the point until the end. That is one of the biggest mistakes people make. When you are communicating for business, you

남자: 교수 | 여자: 학생

학생과 교수의 대화를 들으시오.
남 안녕, 키이라, 뭘 도와줄까요?
여 안녕하세요, 네빌 교수님, 지금 바쁘지 않으시면 잠시 교수님과 이야기했으면 하는데요.
남 잠깐 동안은 괜찮아요. 무슨 일인가요?
여 **1(B)** 인턴십에 지원하려고 하는 데 교수님의 조언이 필요해서요.
남 좋아요, 인턴십에 대해 말해 봐요.
여 음악 회사의 마케팅 부서 인턴십이에요.
남 그거 괜찮겠네요. 학생에게 귀중한 경험이 되겠어요.
여 네, 저도 그렇게 생각해요. **2** 하지만 비즈니스 작문을 잘 못해서 걱정이에요. 제 말은, 수업은 통과했지만 아주 좋은 성적을 받진 못했어요. 저는 에세이나 연구 과제와 같은 다른 작문은 꽤나 잘해서 이해가 가질 않아요.
남 아, 흠, 비즈니스 작문은 특수한 종류의 글쓰기죠. **3(A)** 에세이나 연구 과제에서는 주제를 처음에 소개하지만, 요점은 거의 마지막에 밝히죠. 그게 사람들이 하는 가장 큰 실수 중 하나예요. 업무 때문에 소통을 할 때는 직접적이어야만 해요. 학생이 무슨 말을 하는지 글을 읽는 쪽에서 이해할 수 있도록 배경 지식을 줘야만 한다면 그건 괜찮지만, 그걸로 글

need to be direct. If there is background information that you need to give the reader for them to understand what you are saying, that is fine, but don't start with that. So, you should think about what you have to say, and get to that immediately.

W Oh—that is pretty different from academic writing.

M **3(D)** Yes; and there are other differences too. You should cut out unnecessary things. In essays in particular, people get very creative with their vocabulary, so they make sentences that are unnecessarily long. For business writing, you should not use three words when one is enough. You should also avoid using passive voice and other kinds of indirect language. **4** And, you should be careful with jargon and using 20-dollar words.

W **4** Okay, I can understand not using jargon and slang, but what are 20-dollar words?

M **4** Well, many people think that using big words makes them seem intelligent. But most of the time, it just makes it look like you are trying to impress people. For example, I could say that I am *providing assistance* to you, but it would be much easier to just say that I am *helping* you.

W Oh, I see. I guess we do that a lot with other styles of writing.

M Yes, but with practice, you should be able to write for business well. Do you have any other questions?

W Could you look at the essay I wrote to apply for the internship? I now have the feeling that it would not be a good sample of business writing, though.

M Certainly. Oh, but before I start, did you include any anecdotes in your essay? For acceptance essays, even for a business internship, it is important to include a story about your own experiences that shows why you would be the best candidate.

W Yes, I did. **5** I wrote about how I helped to organize the music performance competition that we held on campus during spring break last year. I was the committee treasurer, and it was not an easy task. We had funding issues and production costs went over budget, but in the end, we made it happen.

M **5** That sounds perfect for an internship in music marketing.

W **1(C)** Oh, there is one more thing. Do you think you could write me a letter of recommendation?

M Of course. I would be happy to.

을 시작하면 안 돼요. 그래서 무슨 말을 해야만 하는지 생각을 해봐야 하고, 즉시 요점으로 들어가야 하는 거죠.

여 아, 학술적인 글쓰기와는 많이 다르네요.

남 **3(D)** 맞아요. 그리고 다른 차이점들도 있어요. 불필요한 것들은 잘라내야 해요. 특히 에세이의 경우, 사람들은 자신들이 사용하는 단어에 있어 매우 창의적이 되는 경우가 있어요. 그래서 불필요하게 긴 문장을 써요. 비즈니스 작문의 경우, 한 단어만으로도 충분한데 세 단어를 써서는 안 됩니다. 또한 수동태나 다른 종류의 간접적인 언어를 쓰는 것을 피해야 해요. **4** 그리고 전문 용어나 20달러짜리 단어와 같은 것들도 주의해야 하죠.

여 **4** 네, 전문 용어나 속어를 쓰지 않는 것은 이해할 수 있지만, 20달러짜리 단어가 무엇인가요?

남 **4** 음, 많은 사람들이 뭔가 있어 보이는 단어를 사용하는 것이 자신을 똑똑하게 보이도록 만들어줄 거라고 생각하죠. 하지만 대부분의 경우 그저 다른 이들에게 인상을 심어주려고 하는 것처럼 보일 뿐이에요. 예를 들어, 나는 *학생에게 조력을 제공하고 있다*고 말할 수 있지만, 그냥 학생을 *도와주고 있다*고 말하는 게 더 쉽겠죠.

여 아, 알겠어요. 다른 종류의 글쓰기에서는 이런 식으로 많이 쓰는 것 같네요.

남 그래요. 하지만 연습을 하면 비즈니스 작문도 잘 할 수 있게 될 거예요. 다른 질문은 없나요?

여 인턴십에 지원하기 위해 쓴 제 에세이를 봐주실 수 있나요? 지금 생각하니 좋은 비즈니스 작문의 예가 될 것 같지는 않아서요.

남 물론이죠. 아, 시작하기 전에, 학생은 에세이에 자신의 일화를 포함했나요? 지원을 위한 에세이의 경우, 심지어 비즈니스 인턴십의 경우라도 왜 학생이 가장 적합한 후보인지를 보여주는 학생 자신의 경험들에 대한 이야기를 포함시키는 게 중요해요.

여 네, 썼어요. **5** 작년 봄 방학 때 캠퍼스에서 열렸던 음악 퍼포먼스 대회를 조직하는 것을 도왔던 것에 대해 썼어요. 저는 운영회의 회계였는데, 쉬운 일이 아니었어요. 자금 문제가 있었고 제작 비용은 예산을 넘어섰지만 결국에는 대회가 개최될 수 있도록 했죠.

남 **5** 음악 마케팅 인턴십에 완벽한 것처럼 보이네요.

여 **1(C)** 아, 하나 더 있어요. 저에게 추천서를 써주실 수 있으신가요?

남 물론이죠, 기꺼이요.

1. What is the purpose of the student's visit? Choose 2 answers.

Ⓐ To get the professor's help with writing effective essays

1. 학생이 찾아온 목적은 무엇인가? 두 개를 고르시오.

Ⓐ 효과적인 에세이를 쓰는 데 교수의 도움을 받기 위해

Ⓑ To ask for the professor's advice regarding her internship opportunity.
Ⓒ To see if the professor would be willing to provide a reference letter
Ⓓ To acquire information on using personal anecdotes in an essay

2. What is the student's opinion about business writing?
Ⓐ She does not feel confident doing it since she did not do well in the class.
Ⓑ She thinks it is confusing since it is quite similar to academic writing.
Ⓒ She believes she can manage since she is good at writing research papers.
Ⓓ She sees it as quite challenging since she does not have much business experience.

3. What are the differences between business and essay writing? Choose 2 answers.
Ⓐ Business writing usually starts with the purpose of writing.
Ⓑ Business writing tends to use much more indirect language.
Ⓒ People tend to make more mistakes in business writing.
Ⓓ Essay writing is often more creative than business writing.

4. Why does the professor mention 20-dollar words?
Ⓐ To show an example of why people make mistakes with their word choices
Ⓑ To name one of the mistakes that people often make when they do business writing
Ⓒ To emphasize that business writing should not be longer than research papers
Ⓓ To give another example of things that make business writing less restrictive

5. What makes the professor think the student's anecdote is perfect for the intern position?
Ⓐ It shows that the student is aware of how to organize a team to win a competition.
Ⓑ It shows that the student knows how to manage production costs and deal with a small budget.
Ⓒ It shows that the student was able to overcome difficult situations even though she was new.
Ⓓ It shows that the student already has some experience in coordinating music-related events.

Ⓑ 자신의 인턴십 기회에 관해 교수의 조언을 요청하기 위해
Ⓒ 교수가 학생을 위해 추천서를 써줄 생각이 있는지 알아보기 위해
Ⓓ 에세이에 개인의 일화를 사용하는 것에 대한 정보를 얻기 위해

2. 비즈니스 작문에 대한 학생의 의견은 어떠한가?
Ⓐ 수업에서 잘 해내지 못했기 때문에 자신이 없다.
Ⓑ 학술적 글쓰기와 꽤 비슷하기 때문에 혼란스럽다고 생각한다.
Ⓒ 연구 과제 글쓰기를 잘하기 때문에 해낼 수 있을 것이라고 믿는다.
Ⓓ 업무 경험이 많이 없기 때문에 꽤 어렵게 느낀다.

3. 비즈니스 작문과 에세이 작문의 차이점은 무엇인가? 두 개를 고르시오.
Ⓐ 비즈니스 작문은 글을 쓰는 목적으로 시작된다.
Ⓑ 비즈니스 작문은 보통 훨씬 더 간접적인 언어를 쓰는 경향이 있다.
Ⓒ 사람들은 비즈니스 작문에서 더 많은 실수를 하는 경향이 있다.
Ⓓ 에세이 작문은 비즈니스 작문보다 보통 더 창의적이다.

4. 교수는 왜 20달러짜리 단어를 언급하는가?
Ⓐ 왜 사람들이 단어 선택에 실수를 하는 지에 대한 예를 보여주기 위해
Ⓑ 사람들이 비즈니스 작문을 할 때 종종 저지르는 실수들 중 하나를 예시로 들기 위해
Ⓒ 비즈니스 작문은 연구 과제 작문보다 길어서는 안 된다는 점을 강조하기 위해
Ⓓ 비즈니스 작문을 덜 제한적으로 만드는 또 다른 예시를 들기 위해

5. 교수는 왜 학생의 일화가 인턴직에 완벽하다고 생각하는가?
Ⓐ 대회에서 우승하기 위해 팀을 어떻게 조직해야 하는지 학생이 알고 있다는 것을 보여주기 때문에
Ⓑ 학생이 제작 비용을 관리하는 법과 적은 예산에 대처하는 방법을 알고 있다는 것을 보여주기 때문에
Ⓒ 학생이 이런 경험이 처음이었음에도 어려운 상황을 극복할 수 있었다는 것을 보여주기 때문에
Ⓓ 학생이 음악 관련 행사를 조직하는 데 이미 약간의 경험이 있다는 것을 보여주기 때문에

어휘 marketing n 마케팅 I department n 부서 I direct adj 직접적인 I background information 배경 정보 I immediately adv 즉시 I unnecessarily adv 불필요하게 I passive voice 수동태 I indirect adj 간접적인 I jargon n 전문/특수 용어, 은어 I big words 거창한 말 I impress v 깊은 인상을 주다 I assistance n 도움, 지원 I anecdote n 일화 I acceptance n 받아들임, 수락 I competition n 대회 I committee n 위원회 I treasurer n 회계 담당자 I production cost 제작 비용 I budget n 예산 I letter of recommendation 추천서

Lesson 02 Service-Related

본서 I P. 118

Test

Passage 1	1. C	2. C	3. D	4. B	5. C
Passage 2	1. D	2. A	3. B	4. C	5. B
Passage 3	1. A	2. C	3. C	4. Yes – C, D / No – A, B	5. B
Passage 4	1. B	2. A	3. C	4. D	5. Yes – B, C / No – A, D, E
Passage 5	1. B	2. C	3. C	4. A	5. D
Passage 6	1. B	2. D	3. C, D	4. C	5. A

Test

본서 I P. 120

Passage 1 Man: University employee | Woman: Student

[1-5] Listen to part of a conversation between a student and a university employee.

W Excuse me, but can you help me?

M That's why I am here. What do you need?

W 1 I need to make 500 copies of this flyer, but that copier doesn't seem to be working. 2 We are trying to raise funds for a program to buy sandboxes for local preschools.

M Sandboxes for preschools, eh? May I see your flyer?

W Sure, we are going to have a meeting next week at Miller Hall.

M My son is going to start preschool soon, so I am currently interested in them. What exactly is it that you are doing?

W 2 Well, I am a graduate student in psychology. I have been observing toddlers and how they play together. A few of my classmates and I are organizing a project to analyze preschool age children and how they play together in a creative environment. That is why we have selected sandboxes as our project's basis. In a sandbox, the children must use their imaginations to play games. There is no structure like with board games.

M Interesting. What are you going to be doing at this meeting?

W We are going to explain our project and how it will work. We hope to raise enough funds to start our research. If we can demonstrate it in action, then we will have a better chance of receiving funding from the state government.

남자: 대학교 직원 | 여자: 학생

학생과 대학교 직원의 대화를 들으시오.

여 실례합니다. 좀 도와주실 수 있나요?

남 그래서 제가 여기 있는 거예요. 무슨 도움이 필요하시죠?

여 1 이 전단지를 500장 복사해야 하는데 저 복사기가 작동하는 것 같지 않네요. 2 저희는 지역의 유치원들을 위한 모래 놀이통을 구입하는 프로그램을 위해 기금을 모으려고 하거든요.

남 유치원을 위한 모래 놀이통이라고요? 전단지를 봐도 될까요?

여 네, 다음 주에 밀러홀에서 모임을 가질 거예요.

남 제 아들이 곧 유치원에 가기 시작할 거라서 저도 현재 관심이 있어요. 학생이 하는 게 정확히 무엇인가요?

여 2 음, 저는 심리학을 전공하는 대학원생이에요. 저는 유아들과 이들이 어떻게 함께 노는지를 관찰했어요. 같이 수업을 듣는 몇몇 친구들과 저는 유치원 나이의 아이들과 창조적인 환경에서 이들이 어떻게 노는가를 분석하려는 프로젝트를 준비하고 있어요. 그래서 모래 놀이통을 저희 프로젝트의 기반으로 선택했어요. 모래 놀이통에서 아이들은 놀이를 하기 위해 상상력을 활용해야 하거든요. 보드 게임과 같은 구조가 있는 게 아니니까요.

남 흥미롭네요. 이 모임에서는 무엇을 할 예정인가요?

여 저희의 프로젝트에 대해, 그리고 어떤 방식으로 운영될 것인지에 대해 설명할 거예요. 연구를 시작하기에 충분할 정도의 기금을 모으길 바라고 있어요. 저희가 행동으로 보여줄 수 있다면 주 정부에서 지원금을 받을 가능성이 더 커지니까요.

M So, you will be asking people who attend to make donations? For how much?

W Yes, that is the plan. We will be asking for 15 dollars per donation.

M That's a bit expensive. 3 Will they receive anything in return?

W 3 Yes, we will be handing out copies of this book on educating young children. Hold on a moment. I have a copy here in my backpack...

M 3 Ah! My wife wanted to buy this book. How can you just give them away?

W 3 Well, we aren't just giving them away. Guests will be giving us donations. The author is my thesis advisor, Professor Marat. Do you know him?

M Yes! Well, I sort of know him. He comes in here all the time. I have helped him locate journals, books, and other material.

W 4 Right, well, he's my advisor. So, he is letting us use his books as promotional material. He becomes more famous, and we get more support.

M 4 That sounds like a good give-and-take relationship.

W Yes, we hope so.

M 5 But, I am afraid I have to disappoint you. That copier is out of order. I've been waiting for the maintenance technician to show up all morning to repair it. You'll have to use one of the copiers on the third floor. But, they only make black and white copies.

W That is fine since these flyers don't have any other colors on them.

M Yes, but you will be feeding it coins for an hour. If you would like, I can override the coin operation machine and make the copies for you. Then you can pay the library for the copies directly at the counter.

W That would be very nice, thank you.

M Like I said, I am here to help. Could you give me a copy of the flyer before you leave?

W Of course, take a couple if you would like. Give them to your friends who also have little children.

M I would be happy to.

남 그래서 모임에 참석하는 사람들에게 기부를 요청할 건가요? 얼마나 요청할 생각인가요?

여 네, 그게 계획이에요. 15달러씩 기부를 요청하려고 해요.

남 좀 비싸네요. 3 참석자들이 대신 뭔가를 받게 되나요?

여 3 네, 어린이들의 교육에 관한 이 책을 선물할 거예요. 잠시만요. 제 가방에 책이 있어요....

남 3 아! 제 아내가 이 책을 사고 싶어했어요. 어떻게 이 책들을 그냥 줄 수 있는 거죠?

여 3 음, 그냥 주는 건 아니에요. 참석자들은 기부금을 낼 테니까요. 이 책의 저자는 제 논문 지도 교수님인 마라 교수님이에요. 그분을 아세요?

남 알아요! 음, 안다고 볼 수 있죠. 여기 항상 오시거든요. 그분이 학술지, 도서, 그리고 다른 것들을 찾는 걸 도와드렸어요.

여 4 맞아요. 음, 그분이 제 지도 교수님이세요. 그래서 저희가 홍보용 자료로 이 책을 쓰도록 허락해 주셨어요. 교수님은 더 많이 알려지시고, 저희는 더 많은 지원을 받을 수 있으니까요.

남 4 서로 주고받는 좋은 관계 같네요.

여 네, 그렇게 되길 바라요.

남 5 하지만 학생에게 실망스러운 소식을 들려줘야겠네요. 저 복사기는 현재 고장 난 상태예요. 유지 보수 기술자가 와서 저 복사기를 고치기를 아침 내내 기다리고 있어요. 3층에 있는 복사기들 중 하나를 써야 할 거예요. 하지만 그 복사기들은 흑백 복사만 가능해요.

여 이 전단지들은 다른 색이 없으니 흑백 복사도 괜찮아요.

남 네, 하지만 한 시간 동안 복사기에 동전을 넣고 있어야 할 거예요. 학생이 좋다면 동전 작동 기계를 변경해서 복사를 하게 해줄 수 있어요. 그러면 카운터에서 바로 도서관에 비용을 지불할 수 있죠.

여 그럼 정말 좋겠네요. 감사합니다.

남 말씀드렸듯이, 전 도움을 주기 위해 여기 있으니까요. 가기 전에 전단지 한 장 줄 수 있나요?

여 그럼요. 원하시면 몇 장 더 가져가세요. 어린 아이가 있는 다른 친구분들에게 나눠주셔도 돼요.

남 그러면 좋죠.

1. What is the student's problem?

Ⓐ She has too many papers to make copies of.
Ⓑ She noticed that the copy machine is not taking coins.
Ⓒ She cannot get the copy machine to print her flyers.
Ⓓ She needs change to run the copy machine.

1. 학생의 문제는 무엇인가?

Ⓐ 복사해야 할 종이의 분량이 너무 많다.
Ⓑ 복사기가 동전을 받아들이지 않는다는 것을 알아차렸다.
Ⓒ 복사기로 전단지를 복사하지 못하고 있다.
Ⓓ 복사기를 작동시키기 위해 잔돈을 필요로 한다.

2. What is the purpose of the fundraising event the student is organizing?

Ⓐ Paying for her graduate school tuition to continue her research
Ⓑ Providing playthings for little children who need help
Ⓒ Purchasing sandboxes for some preschools to do research
Ⓓ Making sandboxes and board games for child participants

3. What can be inferred about the fundraising event?

Ⓐ The student will give out a book that is worth 15 dollars.
Ⓑ Professor Marat is in charge of organizing the event.
Ⓒ The state government is also supporting the event.
Ⓓ The attendees will be receiving Professor Marat's book.

4. What is the employee's opinion about the fundraising event?

Ⓐ He thinks many people would be willing to pay 15 dollars.
Ⓑ He thinks the students did an excellent job of planning it.
Ⓒ He believes that the event will be a huge success.
Ⓓ He feels that the event needs more promotion in the school.

5. What does the employee suggest the student do?

Ⓐ Get some help from the technician to fix the copy machine
Ⓑ Get enough coins to print 500 flyers in the library
Ⓒ Use another copy machine on another floor
Ⓓ Find someone to help her making copies of the flyers

2. 학생이 조직하고 있는 모금 행사의 목적은 무엇인가?

Ⓐ 연구를 계속하기 위해 대학원 학비를 지불하는 것
Ⓑ 도움을 필요로 하는 어린 아이들에게 장난감을 제공하는 것
Ⓒ 연구를 위해 몇몇 유치원들을 위한 모래 놀이통을 구입하는 것
Ⓓ 어린이 참가자들을 위해 모래 놀이통과 보드 게임을 만드는 것

3. 모금 행사에 대해 무엇을 추론할 수 있는가?

Ⓐ 학생은 15달러 상당의 도서를 나눠줄 것이다.
Ⓑ 마라 교수는 이 행사를 준비하는 책임자이다.
Ⓒ 주 정부에서도 이 행사를 후원하고 있다.
Ⓓ 참석자들은 마라 교수의 책을 받게 될 것이다.

4. 모금 행사에 대한 직원의 의견은 어떠한가?

Ⓐ 많은 사람들이 15달러를 기꺼이 내려 할 것이라고 생각한다.
Ⓑ 학생이 이 행사를 매우 잘 계획했다고 생각한다.
Ⓒ 이 행사가 엄청난 성공을 거둘 것이라고 믿는다.
Ⓓ 이 행사가 학교 내에서 더 홍보되어야 한다고 생각한다.

5. 직원은 학생에게 무엇을 하라고 제안하는가?

Ⓐ 복사기를 고치기 위해 기술자의 도움을 받는다
Ⓑ 도서관에서 500장의 전단지를 복사하기 위해 충분한 동전을 갖고 있는다
Ⓒ 다른 층에 있는 다른 복사기를 사용한다
Ⓓ 전단지를 복사하는 것을 도와줄 누군가를 찾는다

어휘 flyer n 전단지, 광고지 | copier n 복사기 | raise v 모으다 | fund n 기금 | sandbox n 모래 놀이통 | preschool n 유치원 | currently adv 현재 | exactly adv 정확히 | toddler n 유아, 걸음마를 배우는 아이 | organize v 조직하다 | analyze v 분석하다 | basis n 근거, 기준 | imagination n 상상력 | structure n 구조, 뼈대 | demonstrate v (증거를 들어가며) 보이다 | attend v 참석하다 | donation n 기부, 기부금 | thesis n 논문 | locate v ~의 정확한 위치를 알아내다 | promotional adj 홍보의 | maintenance n 유지, 보수 | technician n 기술자 | repair v 수리하다 | feed v (기계에) 넣다 | override v 변경하다 | directly adv 곧장, 바로

Passage 2

Man: Student | Woman: Dining services director

[1-5] Listen to part of a conversation between a student and a dining services director.

M Excuse me, is this the dining services office?
W Yes, it is. How may I help you today?
M **1** Well, I think that my parents bought me the wrong meal plan. It has far too many meals on it. I don't think I can use all of these within one semester.

남자: 학생 | 여자: 식당 서비스 관리자

학생과 식당 서비스 관리자의 대화를 들으시오.

남 실례합니다. 여기가 식당 서비스 사무실인가요?
여 네, 맞아요. 어떻게 도와드릴까요?
남 **1** 음, 저희 부모님이 제게 잘못된 식권을 사주셨어요. 끼니가 너무 많이 있거든요. 한 학기에 이걸 다 사용할 수 있을 것 같지 않아서요.

W 2 Hmm, how many meals do you have left?

M 2 This says I have 70 meals left, but there are only two weeks of school remaining.

W Oh, yeah. You're going to have some left over for sure.

M 1 Can I use them next semester? I mean, do they carry over to the next semester?

W No, I am afraid that they don't. You must use them within the semester for which they are purchased.

M Oh, I see. 1 In that case, can I get a refund for the meals that I don't use?

W That is also impossible. We do not provide refunds for meal plans. It's against school policy.

M I understand. Are these meal plans transferrable?

W I'm not sure I understand what you mean.

M Could I give them to a friend who has run out of meals on his plan?

W No, you cannot transfer them to his account, but you could pay for his meals when you go to the dining hall together.

M Well, that is something at least. Alright then, I think I need to buy a smaller meal plan for next semester.

W Which plan are you on now? Can I see your student ID card?

M Yes, here's my student ID card.

W Okay, just let me pull up your file... You had the 240-meal plan. Are you a freshman?

M Yes. I will be a sophomore next year.

W Okay, parents often buy that plan for freshman students so they can focus on their studies without having to worry about where their meals will come from.

M Yes, but it turned out to be far too many for me.

W Unfortunately, that often happens. However, you can choose a different plan for next semester. 3 There is one with 195 meals. Do you think that would be better for you?

M 3 Hmm, I'm not sure. How about this option? Could I have the plan that has 150 meals?

W That plan is normally for junior and senior students. You will be in your second year, not your third or fourth. Since upperclassmen that live in dormitories have many outside activities and meetings, they typically need fewer meals.

M 4 So... I can't use that meal plan?

W 4 Oh, yes, you can. You just need to talk to your parents and tell them which meal plan they should select when they pay for next semester's tuition. The year guidelines are just that: guidelines. So, yes, you can have the 150 meal plan. Just remember that if you run out of meals on your plan, you will need to pay for your additional meals as you eat them, so they will be more expensive.

여 2 흠, 얼마나 남았는데요?

남 2 여기 보면 70번 남았다고 쓰여 있는데, 이제 학기가 2주밖에 남지 않았거든요.

여 아, 맞아요. 학생은 분명히 끼니가 좀 남겠네요.

남 1 다음 학기에 써도 되나요? 제 말은, 다음 학기까지 이월 가능한가요?

여 아니요, 안타깝게도 안 돼요. 구매한 학기 내에 모두 사용해야만 하거든요.

남 아, 그렇군요. 1 그렇다면 아직 사용하지 않은 끼니들에 대해 환불 받을 수는 있나요?

여 그것도 안 돼요. 식권 환불은 제공하지 않아요. 학교 규정에 어긋나는 것이라서요.

남 물론 그렇겠죠. 이 식권은 양도 가능한가요?

여 학생이 무슨 말을 하는 건지 잘 모르겠어요.

남 자기 식권을 다 사용한 친구에게 제가 가진 식권을 줄 수 있나요?

여 아니요, 친구의 계정으로 식권을 옮기는 것은 불가능하지만, 함께 식당에 가서 그를 위해 식사를 사줄 수는 있겠죠.

남 음, 적어도 그런 방법은 있군요. 그렇다면 저는 다음 학기에는 더 적은 양의 식권을 구매해야겠어요.

여 지금 어떤 식권을 사용하고 있나요? 학생증을 봐도 될까요?

남 네, 여기 제 학생증입니다.

여 알겠어요, 학생의 파일을 찾아볼게요... 학생은 240끼니의 식권을 구매했었군요. 1학년인가요?

남 네, 내년에 2학년이 됩니다.

여 그렇군요. 부모님들이 종종 1학년생들이 식사 걱정을 할 필요 없이 공부에 집중할 수 있도록 이 식권을 구매하시죠.

남 네, 하지만 저에겐 너무 많았어요.

여 안타깝게도 자주 일어나는 일이에요. 하지만 다음 학기엔 다른 식권을 선택할 수 있어요. 3 195끼니 식권이 있네요. 이게 학생에게 더 나을 것 같나요?

남 3 흠, 잘 모르겠어요. 이건 어떤가요? 150끼니 식권을 구매해도 되나요?

여 그 식권은 보통 3학년이나 4학년생들을 위한 거예요. 학생은 3학년이나 4학년이 아닌 2학년이 될 거잖아요. 기숙사에 사는 상급생들은 많은 외부 활동과 모임을 갖다 보니 일반적으로 식사를 적게 필요로 하거든요.

남 4 그럼... 제가 그 식권을 사용할 수 없다는 말씀이세요?

여 4 아, 사용 가능해요. 그저 학생의 부모님께 다음 학기에 학생의 등록금을 지불하실 때 어떤 식권을 선택해야 할지 말씀드리면 돼요. 지침은 그저 지침일 뿐이니까요. 그래서 네, 학생은 150끼니 식권을 선택할 수 있어요. 다만 학생이 식권을 다 사용하게 된다면 추가로 하는 식사는 따로 결제해야만 해요. 그래서 더 비쌀 거라는 거죠.

M Yes, I realize that. But, I would rather risk that than have left over meals that I cannot use.

W 5 You know, maybe you should start a petition. If you can gather enough signatures, maybe you can get the university to change its policies about refunding student meal plans.

M 5 That's a pretty good idea. Where would I get the form for that?

W 5 You can get a general petition form at the counter across the room.

남 네, 알고 있습니다. 하지만 사용할 수 없는 끼니를 남기는 것보다는 그게 더 나은 것 같아요.

여 5 음, 학생이 탄원을 시작해봐도 좋을 것 같아요. 만약 충분히 많은 사람들의 서명을 받는다면 학교 측에서 학생들의 식권 환불에 대한 규정을 수정할 수도 있겠죠.

남 5 좋은 생각이네요. 탄원을 위한 서류는 어디에서 받을 수 있나요?

여 5 방 건너편에 있는 카운터에서 일반 탄원서를 받을 수 있어요.

1. What is the purpose of the student's visit to the dining service director?

Ⓐ Persuading the director to give him a refund for his left-over meals
Ⓑ Explaining the reason why he could not use the whole meal plan
Ⓒ Obtaining information to fill out a petition form about meal plans
Ⓓ Asking questions regarding his meal plan since he has some left over

2. What is the reason why the student thinks he will be unable to spend the rest of his meal plan?

Ⓐ The current semester will end in just a few weeks.
Ⓑ He skips meals often as he is busy with school activities.
Ⓒ He is unable to share his meal plan with a friend.
Ⓓ Students cannot spend more than three meals per day.

3. What can be inferred about the student's opinion about the meal plan with 195 meals?

Ⓐ He thinks it is more cost-effective than the 150-meal plan.
Ⓑ He still doubts if he will be able to use the entire plan.
Ⓒ He wonders if he could purchase that option next semester.
Ⓓ He feels that 195 meals would not be enough for him.

4. Listen again to part of the conversation. Then answer the question.

M So...I can't use that meal plan?
W Oh, yes, you can. You just need to talk to your parents and tell them which meal plan they should select when they pay for next semester's tuition. The year guidelines are just that: guidelines.

1. 학생이 식당 서비스 관리자를 찾아온 목적은 무엇인가?

Ⓐ 남은 끼니를 환불해 달라고 관리자를 설득하기 위해
Ⓑ 왜 식권 전부를 사용할 수 없었는지에 대한 이유를 설명하기 위해
Ⓒ 식권 관련 탄원서를 작성하는 것에 관한 정보를 얻기 위해
Ⓓ 끼니가 남았으므로 자신의 식권에 관해 질문하기 위해

2. 학생이 식권의 나머지를 쓰지 못할 것 같다고 생각하는 이유는 무엇인가?

Ⓐ 지금 학기가 몇 주 안에 끝날 것이다.
Ⓑ 학교 활동들로 바쁘기 때문에 자주 끼니를 거른다.
Ⓒ 친구와 자기 식권을 함께 사용할 수 없다.
Ⓓ 학생들은 하루에 세 끼니 이상 쓸 수 없다.

3. 195끼니 식권에 대한 학생의 의견에 대해 무엇을 추론할 수 있는가?

Ⓐ 이것이 150끼니 식권보다 좀 더 비용 효율적이라고 생각한다.
Ⓑ 자신이 끼니의 전부를 사용할 수 있을지 여전히 의문을 갖는다.
Ⓒ 이 옵션을 다음 학기에 구매할 수 있는지 궁금해한다.
Ⓓ 195 끼니는 그에게 충분하지 않을 거라고 느낀다.

4. 대화의 일부를 다시 듣고 질문에 답하시오.

남 그럼... 제가 그 식권을 사용할 수 없다는 말씀이세요?
여 아, 사용 가능해요. 그저 학생의 부모님께 다음 학기에 학생의 등록금을 지불하실 때 어떤 식권을 선택해야 할지 말씀드리면 돼요. 지침은 그저 지침일 뿐이니까요.

Why does the woman say this:

W The year guidelines are just that: guidelines.

Ⓐ To show that they are strict rules that were established by the university
Ⓑ To clarify that his parents should pay attention when purchasing meal plans
Ⓒ To explain that they do not limit the decisions of students and parents
Ⓓ To emphasize the importance of purchasing a meal plan in advance

5. What will the student do next?
Ⓐ Fill out the registration form for the next semester's meal plan
Ⓑ Pick up a form to file a petition regarding meal plans
Ⓒ Visit the Student Hall in the next building to obtain a document
Ⓓ Look for people who would be willing to support his idea

여자는 왜 이렇게 말하는가:

여 지침은 그저 지침일 뿐이니까요.

Ⓐ 지침이 학교에 의해 확립된 엄격한 규칙들이라는 것을 보여주기 위해
Ⓑ 식권을 구매할 때 학생의 부모님이 주의를 기울여야 한다는 것을 명확히 하기 위해
Ⓒ 지침이 학생과 학부모의 결정을 제한하지 않는다는 것을 설명하기 위해
Ⓓ 미리 식권을 구매하는 것의 중요성을 강조하기 위해

5. 학생은 다음에 무엇을 할 것인가?
Ⓐ 다음 학기 식권 신청서를 작성한다
Ⓑ 식권 관련 탄원서를 작성하기 위해 양식을 가져간다
Ⓒ 서류를 받기 위해 옆 건물에 있는 학생 회관을 찾아간다
Ⓓ 기꺼이 그의 생각을 지지해줄 사람들을 찾는다

어휘 meal plan 식권(학생식당 등에서 일정 금액이나 몇 회차분의 식사 비용을 미리 결제한 뒤, 그 금액 또는 횟수 안에서 식사를 이용하는 서비스) | carry over 이월되다 | refund n 환불 | policy n 규정 | transferrable adj 양도 가능한 | upperclassman n 상급생 | dormitory n 기숙사 | typically adv 일반적으로 | tuition n 등록금 | guideline n 지침 | additional adj 추가의, 부가적인 | petition n 탄원 | signature n 서명

Passage 3

Man: Student | Woman: Housing officer

[1-5] Listen to part of a conversation between a student and a housing officer.

W Good afternoon, how may I help you?

M Hello, you weren't here this morning. I talked to someone different.

W **2** That would probably have been Sean. Did you come back to ask the same question? Because if you think I will give you a different answer, you will probably be disappointed. I will most likely give you the same answer that he did.

M Oh, yes, I understand that. But could I still ask you anyway?

W Sure, I'll hear you out. What seems to be the problem?

M **1** It's about my dorm room. You know, of course, how dorm rooms are selected.

W **3, 4(C)** Yes, by a lottery system. The person who drew the number one gets to select his or her room first, and the highest number chooses last.

M Yeah, and I am pretty sure I got one of the highest numbers.

W Really? **3** What number did you get?

M **3** One thousand forty-seven…

W Oh, wow, yeah, that is pretty high.

남자: 학생 | 여자: 기숙사 직원

학생과 기숙사 직원의 대화를 들으시오.

여 안녕하세요, 어떻게 도와드릴까요?

남 안녕하세요. 오늘 아침에는 여기 안 계셨는데요. 다른 분에게 이야기를 했었어요.

여 **2** 아마 션이었을 거예요. 같은 질문을 하려고 다시 찾아오신 건가요? 제가 션과 다른 답변을 할 거라고 생각하셨다면 실망하실 거예요. 션이 한 대답과 같은 대답을 할 확률이 높거든요.

남 아, 네. 그건 이해해요. 하지만 그래도 여쭤봐도 될까요?

여 네, 말씀하세요. 문제가 무엇인가요?

남 **1** 기숙사 방 문제예요. 물론 아시겠죠, 어떻게 방 배정이 되는지를요.

여 **3, 4(C)** 네, 추첨 시스템으로 결정되죠. 1번을 뽑은 사람이 첫 번째로 자기 방을 선택하게 되고, 가장 큰 번호를 뽑은 사람이 마지막에 방을 선택해요.

남 맞아요. 그리고 전 제가 가장 큰 번호들 중 하나를 뽑았을 거라고 꽤나 확신해요.

여 그래요? **3** 몇 번을 뽑으셨는데요?

남 **3** 1047번이요….

여 오, 이런. 네, 꽤나 큰 숫자네요.

M 3 So, as you can surely understand, I am not too happy about that fact. I am a second year student, but the only rooms that will be left when my number comes up will be small and uncomfortable, and they will probably be in Harris Hall.

W Ah, yes, those rooms are often the only ones remaining for the last few people, although, if you are a second year student, you probably won't be forced to live in Harris Hall. **4(B), 4(C)** But we use the lottery system to make things fair. We used to go in alphabetical order for each class starting with the upperclassmen.

M I know, and that was really unfair. So I am glad that the lottery system is being used now. **1** The thing is, my current roommate got a really good number, but he is going to move off campus into an apartment. **1, 4(D)** So, what I want to know is if he could give me his number.

W **4(D)** Uh, no. That isn't possible.

M Are you sure? He already offered to do any paperwork that would be necessary to allow that to happen.

W **4(D)** No, I am afraid that you still cannot do that. That kind of thing was specifically forbidden when the new room selection system was set up. And I am sure that is what Sean told you as well.

M Yes, it is. So, there is nothing I can do?

W Well, that depends. There's probably no way for you to get a single room. **5** But if you have other friends with low numbers, you could ask to room with them. Once a person has selected a room, they have the option of choosing their roommate. If they decline, then they will receive one at random. But most people already have someone in mind by the time they are a second year student.

M So, does that only apply to doubles?

W No, no, it doesn't. A person can choose a triple or a quad if they want to. Then they can choose one, two, or all three of their roommates.

M Oh, I see. Sean didn't tell me that.

W He didn't? Well, then I guess your persistence paid off.

M Yes, it did. I'd better go talk to my other friends.

W Good luck with getting a room.

M Thank you. And, thank you for your help.

W No problem. I should probably have a talk with Sean.

남 3 그래서, 이해하시겠지만 이 사실이 그다지 기쁘지가 않아요. 전 2학년인데, 제 번호 차례가 돌아왔을 때 남아 있는 방들은 작고 불편한 방들일 거고, 아마 해리스홀에 있는 방들일 거예요.

여 아, 네. 그 방들이 종종 마지막에 남은 몇 명에게 돌아가는 방들이죠. 그래도 학생이 2학년이라면 해리스홀에 살도록 강요받지는 않을 거예요. **4(B), 4(C)** 하지만 우리는 공평하게 하기 위해 추첨 시스템을 이용하는 거예요. 예전에는 상급생들부터 시작해서 각 학년에서 알파벳 순으로 방 배정을 했었거든요.

남 알아요, 정말 불공평했죠. 그래서 지금 추첨 시스템이 사용되는 게 다행이라고 생각해요. **1** 문제는, 제 현재 룸메이트가 매우 좋은 번호를 뽑았는데 이제 기숙사를 나가서 아파트에서 살 예정이라는 거죠. **1, 4(D)** 그래서 제 룸메이트가 자기 번호를 저에게 줘도 되는지를 여쭤보러 왔어요.

여 **4(D)** 어, 그건 불가능해요.

남 확실한가요? 이 일을 위해 필요한 그 어떤 서류 작업이라도 하겠다고 제 룸메이트가 말했는데요.

여 **4(D)** 아니요, 그래도 여전히 안 된다고 말씀드려야겠네요. 그런 일이야말로 새로운 방 배정 시스템이 만들어졌을 때 특별히 금지한 거거든요. 그리고 학생에게 션도 이 말을 했을 거라고 봐요.

남 네, 맞습니다. 그래서, 제가 할 수 있는 건 아무것도 없나요?

여 음, 그건 상황에 달렸어요. 아마 학생이 1인실을 쓰게 될 확률은 없을 거예요. **5** 그렇지만 낮은 번호를 뽑은 친구들이 있다면, 그들과 함께 방을 쓰는 것을 요청할 수는 있어요. 일단 누군가 방을 선택하고 난 뒤에는 룸메이트를 선택하는 옵션이 있거든요. 만약 룸메이트 선택을 하지 않으면 임의로 룸메이트를 배정받게 돼요. 하지만 대부분의 학생들은 2학년쯤 되면 이미 누군가를 염두에 두고 있죠.

남 그래서, 이 경우는 2인실에만 해당되는 건가요?

여 아니에요, 그렇지 않아요. 원한다면 3인실이나 4인실도 룸메이트를 정할 수 있어요. 그 경우에는 한 명, 두 명, 혹은 세 명 전부를 정할 수가 있죠.

남 아, 그렇군요. 션이 저에게 그 말은 해주지 않았거든요.

여 그랬나요? 그럼 학생의 끈기가 빛을 봤나 보네요.

남 네, 그래요. 그럼 가서 다른 친구들과 이야기를 해봐야겠어요.

여 방 배정에 행운을 바라요.

남 감사합니다. 그리고 도와주셔서 감사합니다.

여 아니에요. 션과 이야기를 좀 해야겠네요.

1. What is the purpose of the student's return to the university office?

Ⓐ To see if he can make a change to his current situation
Ⓑ To ask for details about the process of the room selection system
Ⓒ To inquire whether it is possible to swap rooms with one of his friends
Ⓓ To obtain some information regarding choosing his roommates

2. What is the employee's concern at the beginning of the conversation?

Ⓐ She feels bad for the student since she did not grant him permission.
Ⓑ She finds the student's situation to be easy since he should already know the answer.
Ⓒ She thinks the student will be dissatisfied since she will not be of much help.
Ⓓ She believes the student has a complicated problem since he has returned.

3. What can be inferred about the student's situation based on the lottery number he drew?

Ⓐ He needs to find someone to change numbers with as soon as possible.
Ⓑ His new room might be very similar to the one that he has now.
Ⓒ He has a very low chance of getting the room that he wants to have.
Ⓓ Students who drew numbers above 1,000 are placed in Harris Hall.

4. In the conversation, the speakers discuss the regulations regarding room selection. Indicate in the table below whether each of the following is one of those regulations.

Click in the correct box for each sentence.

	Yes	No
Ⓐ Rooms are selected in alphabetical order for each class.		✓
Ⓑ Upperclassmen are given the first choice of accommodations.		✓
Ⓒ Rooms are selected using a lottery system to make it fairer.	✓	
Ⓓ Students are not allowed to exchange their lottery numbers.	✓	

1. 학생이 대학교 사무실을 다시 찾아온 이유는 무엇인가?

Ⓐ 자신의 현재 상황에 어떠한 변화라도 가져올 수 있을지 알아보기 위해
Ⓑ 방 배정 시스템 절차의 세부 사항들에 대해 묻기 위해
Ⓒ 자신의 친구들 중 하나와 방을 바꾸는 것이 가능한지 물어보기 위해
Ⓓ 룸메이트를 선택하는 것에 대한 정보를 얻기 위해

2. 대화의 초반부에 직원은 무엇을 염려하는가?

Ⓐ 자신이 승인을 해주지 않아서 학생에게 미안함을 느낀다.
Ⓑ 학생이 이미 답을 알고 있으므로 학생의 상황이 쉽다고 생각한다.
Ⓒ 자신이 그다지 도움이 되지 못할 것이므로 학생이 불만족스러워 할 것이라고 생각한다.
Ⓓ 학생이 재방문했으므로 그의 문제가 복잡하다고 믿는다.

3. 학생이 뽑은 추첨 번호에 근거하여 학생의 상황에 대해 무엇을 추론할 수 있는가?

Ⓐ 가능한 한 빨리 그와 번호를 바꿔줄 누군가를 찾아야만 한다.
Ⓑ 그의 새로운 방은 아마 지금 그가 쓰는 방과 매우 비슷할 것이다.
Ⓒ 그가 받고 싶어하는 방을 배정받을 확률은 매우 낮다.
Ⓓ 1,000번 이상의 번호를 뽑은 학생들은 해리스 홀로 방을 배정받는다.

4. 대화에서 화자들은 방 선별 규정을 논의한다. 다음 각 사항이 그 규정의 하나인지 아래의 표에 표시하시오. 각 문장에 대해 맞는 칸에 표시하시오.

	예	아니오
Ⓐ 방은 각 학년에서 알파벳 순서로 선택된다.		✓
Ⓑ 상급생들은 숙소를 첫 번째로 선택할 수 있다.		✓
Ⓒ 방은 더 공평하게 하기 위해 추첨 시스템으로 선택된다.	✓	
Ⓓ 학생들은 추첨 번호를 서로 바꾸지 못하게 되어 있다.	✓	

5. What suggestion does the employee make?

Ⓐ To look for some of his friends who were already assigned their room

Ⓑ To find people who have a good room number but do not have roommates yet

Ⓒ To search for a smaller single room that was declined by other students

Ⓓ To become a roommate of a second year student who has a higher chance

5. 직원은 어떠한 제안을 하는가?

Ⓐ 이미 방을 배정받은 친구들을 찾아보라고

Ⓑ 좋은 방 번호를 가졌지만 아직 룸메이트가 없는 사람들을 찾아보라고

Ⓒ 다른 학생들이 배정받기 거절한 좀 더 작은 1인실을 찾아보라고

Ⓓ 2학년생들이 더 나은 기회를 가지므로 2학년생과 룸메이트를 하라고

어휘 lottery n 추첨, 복권 | draw v 뽑다 | uncomfortable adj 불편한 | alphabetical adj 알파벳의 | upperclassman n 상급생 | unfair adj 불공평한 | offer v 제시하다 | paperwork n 서류 작업 | forbid v 금지하다 | decline v 거절하다, 거부하다 | random adj 임의의, 무작위의 | double n 2인실 | triple n 3인실 | quad n 4인실 | persistence n 끈기, 고집

Passage 4

Man: Library employee | Woman: Student

[1-5] Listen to part of a conversation between a student and a library employee.

M Hello, how can I help you today?

W 1 Hi, um, why is the third floor inaccessible?

M 1 It is currently being renovated.

W 2 Really? Why was I not notified that this would be happening?

M That depends. Who are you?

W 1 I am a graduate student working on my master's degree in psychology. The university's psychology department keeps its records on the third floor of this library, and I need to access them for my research.

M I see. Well, the renovations began this Monday, and they will continue until the end of the month. 3 The decision was made rather abruptly. We had been petitioning the university to replace the microfiche storage system on the third floor for years, but there was never enough money in the budget. Then, last week, they suddenly approved our plan. 2 We sent out an email to all of the professors. Your thesis advisor didn't mention the email to you?

W 2 No, she didn't. She actually isn't in the country right now. She is in Austria doing research for the book she is writing.

M 2 Oh, so I guess she was unable to tell you. Surely, you have noticed how poorly organized the filing system for those documents was.

W Yes, it seemed pretty inefficient, but the psychology records were actually very well organized. Why did they have to close the entire floor?

M Because, they are going to install new shelves and file cabinets and install new viewing stations. This means that they will also have to lay down new carpeting. So, the whole floor will be improved in various ways.

남자: 도서관 직원 | 여자: 학생

학생과 도서관 직원의 대화를 들으시오.

남 안녕하세요. 어떻게 도와 드릴까요?

여 1 안녕하세요. 음, 왜 3층에 들어갈 수 없는 거죠?

남 1 현재 보수 공사 중이에요.

여 2 정말인가요? 왜 저는 보수 공사가 있을 거라는 공지를 받지 못한 거죠?

남 사람에 따라 다르죠. 학생은 누구인가요?

여 1 심리학 석사 과정 중인 대학원생이에요. 대학교 심리학부에서 자료들을 이 도서관의 3층에 보관하는데, 저는 연구를 위해 이 자료들을 봐야 해요.

남 그렇군요. 음, 보수 공사는 이번 주 월요일에 시작되었고, 이번 달 말까지 계속될 거예요. 3 이 결정은 꽤나 갑자기 내려졌어요. 3층에 있는 마이크로피시 보관 시스템을 교체해 달라고 수년 동안 학교에 청원해 왔었지만 항상 예산이 부족했죠. 그러다 지난주에 갑자기 학교에서 도서관의 계획을 승인했어요. 2 교수님들 모두에게 이메일을 보냈죠. 학생의 논문 지도 교수님께서 학생에게 이 이메일을 언급하시지 않던가요?

여 2 아니오, 하지 않으셨어요. 사실 지금 여기 안 계세요. 집필 중인 책의 연구를 위해 오스트리아에 계시거든요.

남 2 아, 그래서 그분이 학생에게 말을 해줄 수가 없었던 것 같네요. 물론 학생도 문서 정리 시스템이 얼마나 형편없이 정리되어 있었는지 알고 있을 거예요.

여 네, 꽤나 비효율적으로 보였지만 심리학 자료들은 사실 꽤 잘 정리되어 있었어요. 왜 3층 전체를 닫아야만 하는 거죠?

남 왜냐하면 새 책장과 파일 캐비닛을 설치할 예정이고, 새 열람실 역시 설치할 거예요. 이 말은, 새 카펫을 깔아야 한다는 거죠. 그래서 3층 전체가 여러 방면으로 개선될 거예요.

W **4** Alright, but what about those of us who need to access the records that are kept there? We cannot put our theses on hold, and we have deadlines to meet.

M **4** Of course you do. That is why the materials have been relocated to the basement of Ratchet Hall.

W They have? Why didn't you say so earlier? I can just go there to do my research.

M Well, yes and no. **5(C)** Students are only allowed to enter the basement between 9 a.m. and 5 p.m.

W During class hours? How are students supposed to have an opportunity to go there during class time?

M I know it's inconvenient, but no one takes classes for the whole day every day.

W Some students do....

M True, but not graduate students, right?

W Yeah, they usually only have a few courses per semester. **5(B)** Are we still allowed to check out files?

M **5(B)** Ah, no, you cannot remove any of the files from the basement.

W Are you serious? This is really inconvenient. We can only go into the basement during class hours, and we cannot check out any files? It seems like they are actively trying to prevent us from doing our work!

M I apologize, but it is unavoidable. The basement does not have our catalog network, so we cannot keep track of the materials that are being stored there. You can look them up here and go to the basement to read them, but you cannot remove them from there.

W Couldn't you just install a computer there to do that?

M We thought of that, but our computers need to access the library server. The computers cannot hold the entire catalog on their hard drives, it is far too large.

W Oh, okay... that makes sense. Then I guess I should hurry over to Ratchet Hall.

여 **4** 좋아요. 하지만 그곳에 있는 자료를 이용해야만 하는 저희는 어떻게 해야 하죠? 논문 작업을 멈출 수도 없고, 맞춰야 할 마감 기한이 있어요.

남 **4** 물론 그렇죠. 그래서 자료들이 래칫홀의 지하로 옮겨진 거예요.

여 그랬나요? 왜 더 일찍 말해주시지 않았어요? 그곳에 가서 연구를 하면 되겠네요.

남 음, 맞기도 하고 아니기도 해요. **5(C)** 학생들은 지하에 오전 9시부터 오후 5시까지만 들어갈 수 있거든요.

여 수업이 있는 시간에요? 어떻게 학생들이 수업 시간에 그곳에 갈 수 있는 기회를 갖겠어요?

남 불편하다는 걸 알지만, 매일 하루 종일 수업을 듣는 학생들은 없잖아요.

여 몇몇 학생들은 그래요....

남 맞는 말이지만, 대학원생들은 아니잖아요. 그렇죠?

여 맞아요. 대학원생들은 한 학기에 몇 개의 과목만을 듣죠. **5(B)** 자료를 대여하는 건 여전히 가능한가요?

남 **5(B)** 아, 불가능해요. 그 지하에서 어떤 자료도 가지고 나갈 수 없어요.

여 정말로요? 이건 너무 불편하네요. 수업이 있는 시간에만 그곳에 들어갈 수 있고, 자료 대여도 할 수 없다니요? 학교 측에서 우리가 작업을 하지 못하도록 적극적으로 방해하는 것처럼 보여요!

남 미안해요. 하지만 어쩔 수가 없네요. 그 지하에는 우리 도서관의 일람표 네트워크가 없어서 그곳에 보관된 자료들을 제대로 확인할 수가 없어요. 이곳에서 그 자료들을 찾은 뒤 지하로 가서 읽을 수는 있지만, 그곳에서 자료를 가져갈 수는 없어요.

여 자료들을 확인하기 위해 거기에 컴퓨터를 설치할 수는 없나요?

남 그것도 생각해 봤지만, 우리 컴퓨터들은 도서관 서버에 접근해야만 해요. 컴퓨터들이 일람표 전체를 하드 드라이브에 저장할 수가 없어요. 너무 양이 방대하거든요.

여 아, 알겠습니다... 이해가 되네요. 그럼 래칫홀로 빨리 가봐야겠어요.

1. Why did the student come to see the library employee?

Ⓐ To receive recently updated information from the library
Ⓑ To inquire how to gain access to a certain floor of the library
Ⓒ To get his advice on finding online articles in the library
Ⓓ To find out if she can check out books at a late hour

1. 학생은 왜 도서관 직원을 만나러 왔는가?

Ⓐ 도서관으로부터 최근 업데이트된 정보를 받기 위해
Ⓑ 도서관의 특정 층에 들어가는 방법을 물어보기 위해
Ⓒ 도서관에서 온라인 기사를 찾는 것에 대해 조언을 듣기 위해
Ⓓ 늦은 시간에 도서 대여가 가능한지 알아보기 위해

2. Why was the student not notified about the renovation of the third floor?

Ⓐ Her thesis advisor was away in another country for research.
Ⓑ She was so busy that she forgot to check her email.
Ⓒ She was unable to visit the library for quite a while.
Ⓓ The university only sent notification to the library staff.

3. Listen again to part of the conversation. Then answer the question.

> M The decision was made rather abruptly. We had been petitioning the university to replace the microfiche storage system on the third floor for years, but there was never enough money in the budget. Then, last week, they suddenly approved our plan.

Why does the man say this:

> M The decision was made rather abruptly.

Ⓐ To explain that the school often does unexpected things
Ⓑ To apologize for the fact that the student has to wait for a week
Ⓒ To say that the library was not prepared for the renovation either
Ⓓ To show how surprised he is that the renovation is occurring

4. What does the library employee suggest the student do?

Ⓐ Sign her name on the waiting list to read the books at Ratchet Hall
Ⓑ Go and check out the necessary books from the library basement
Ⓒ Wait until next Monday when the renovation will be completed
Ⓓ Visit another building to find the materials needed for her thesis paper

5. In the conversation, the student states reasons that keeping documents in the basement of Ratchet Hall is inconvenient. Indicate in the table below whether each of the following is one of those reasons.

Click in the correct box for each sentence.

	Yes	No
Ⓐ Ratchet Hall is too far away from the student's dormitory.		✓

2. 학생은 왜 도서관 3층의 보수 공사에 대한 공지를 받지 못했는가?

Ⓐ 논문 지도 교수가 연구를 위해 다른 나라에 가 있었다.
Ⓑ 너무 바빠서 이메일을 확인하는 것을 잊어버렸다.
Ⓒ 한동안 도서관에 올 수 없었다.
Ⓓ 대학 측에서 도서관 직원에게만 공지를 보냈다.

3. 대화의 일부를 다시 듣고 질문에 답하시오.

> 남 이 결정은 꽤나 갑자기 내려졌어요. 수년 동안 학교에 3층에 있는 마이크로피시 보관 시스템을 교체해 달라고 청원해 왔었지만 항상 예산이 부족했죠. 그러다 저번 주에 갑자기 학교에서 도서관의 계획을 승인했어요.

남자는 왜 이렇게 말하는가:

> 남 이 결정은 꽤나 갑자기 내려졌어요.

Ⓐ 학교 측에서 종종 예상치 못한 일을 한다고 설명하기 위해
Ⓑ 학생이 일주일 동안 기다려야 한다는 사실에 대해 사과하기 위해
Ⓒ 도서관 역시 보수 공사에 준비가 되어 있지 않았다고 말하기 위해
Ⓓ 보수 공사가 이뤄지고 있다는 점에 그가 얼마나 놀랐는지 보여주기 위해

4. 도서관 직원은 학생에게 무엇을 하라고 제안하는가?

Ⓐ 래칫홀에 있는 책들을 열람하기 위해 대기자 명단에 이름을 적는다
Ⓑ 도서관 지하에 가서 필요한 도서들을 대여한다
Ⓒ 보수 공사가 끝나는 다음 주 월요일까지 기다린다
Ⓓ 논문 작업에 필요한 자료를 찾기 위해 다른 건물로 간다

5. 대화에서 학생은 래칫홀의 지하에 문서를 보관하는 것이 불편한 이유를 말하고 있다. 아래의 각 사항이 그 이유인지 표에 표시하시오.

각 문장에 대해 맞는 칸에 표시하시오.

	예	아니오
Ⓐ 래칫홀은 학생의 기숙사에서 너무 멀리 있다.		✓

Ⓑ It is prohibited to check out any of the books that are there.	✓	
Ⓒ Students cannot have access there after 5 p.m.	✓	
Ⓓ The place is too small to keep such a large amount of books.		✓
Ⓔ Ratchet Hall is currently being renovated to update its collection.		✓

Ⓑ 그곳에 있는 어떤 책도 대출하는 것이 금지되었다.	✓	
Ⓒ 학생들은 오후 5시 이후에는 그곳을 이용할 수 없다.	✓	
Ⓓ 그 장소는 그렇게 방대한 양의 책을 보관하기에는 너무 작다.		✓
Ⓔ 래칫홀은 소장 자료를 업데이트하기 위해 보수 공사 중이다.		✓

어휘 inaccessible adj 접근할 수 없는 I currently adv 현재 I renovate v 보수하다, 개조하다 I notify v 알리다, 통보하다 I master's degree 석사 학위 I psychology n 심리학 I record n 자료, 기록 I renovation n 보수, 수리 I abruptly adv 갑자기 I petition v 청원하다, 탄원하다 I replace v 대체하다 I microfiche n 마이크로피시 (책의 각 페이지를 축소 촬영한 시트 필름) I budget n 예산, 비용 I approve v 승인하다, 찬성하다 I thesis n 학위 논문 I notice v 알아차리다 I organize v 정리하다 I filing system 문서 정리 시스템 I inefficient adj 비효율적인 I entire adj 전체의 I install v 설치하다 I improve v 개선하다 I deadline n 마감 기한 I relocate v 이동시키다 I basement n 지하실 I inconvenient adj 불편한 I actively adv 적극적으로 I prevent v 막다, 방지하다 I apologize v 사과하다 I unavoidable adj 불가피한, 어쩔 수 없는 I catalog n 일람표

Passage 5

Man: Student | Woman: Employee

[1-5] Listen to part of a conversation between a student and an employee of the campus management department.

W Hello, how may I help you?

M 1 I just came here to make sure if everything is okay. There have been computer problems for the last few days, particularly in the room reservation system.

W Ah, yes, that is correct. But, you didn't have to come all the way over here to ask us that. You could have just emailed us or called.

M I guess so, but... 1 You see, I had reserved a lecture hall for a guest speaker, but I had to cancel that reservation to make a new one for a larger room. 1, 2 More people are interested in attending the event than we had anticipated. However, I have not received a confirmation email about that change.

W Yes, that isn't surprising. We have been so busy trying to fix the system that we are behind on sending out confirmation emails. I can check it for you now, though. May I have your student ID number?

M Here is my ID card.

W Thank you. We do have a reservation for you! It is for an auditorium in Blake Hall. The reservation was made about a month ago, so I guess that this is your old one?

M Yes. 3 Is there no record of the new one?

W 3 No, there isn't. You see, that is the root of our problem. We installed a new program that was supposed to make this whole system automated, but it doesn't work! So, we have had to continue doing things by hand. Your new request

남자: 학생 | 여자: 직원

학생과 대학교 운영 부서 직원의 대화를 들으시오.

여 안녕하세요. 어떻게 도와드릴까요?

남 1 저는 모든 게 괜찮은지 확인하려고 왔어요. 지난 며칠간 컴퓨터 문제들이 있었는데 특히 장소 예약 시스템이 문제였죠.

여 아, 맞아요. 하지만 그걸 물어보려고 학생이 여기까지 올 필요는 없어요. 우리에게 그냥 이메일이나 전화를 했으면 되는데요.

남 그래도 되겠지만... 1 저는 초청 연사님을 위해 강의실을 예약했었어요. 하지만 더 큰 강의실을 예약하기 위해 기존의 예약을 취소해야만 했죠. 1, 2 저희가 예상했던 것보다 더 많은 사람들이 행사 참여에 관심을 보였거든요. 하지만 그렇게 변경한 것에 대한 확인 메일을 받지 못해서요.

여 네, 놀라운 일은 아니에요. 시스템을 고치기 위해 노력하다 보니 너무 바빠서 확인 메일을 보내는 게 늦어졌거든요. 그래도 지금 학생의 용건을 확인해 줄 수 있어요. 학생 ID 번호가 무엇인가요?

남 여기 제 학생증이 있습니다.

여 고마워요. 여기 학생이 예약한 게 있네요! 블레이크 홀에 있는 강당이죠. 약 한 달 전에 한 예약이니 이것이 학생이 예전에 했던 예약인가 보네요.

남 네. 3 새 예약에 대한 기록은 없나요?

여 3 없네요. 학생도 알겠지만 이것이 우리가 가진 문제의 근원이에요. 이 모든 시스템을 자동화하는 새로운 프로그램을 설치했는데, 그게 작동이 되지 않는 거죠! 그래서 계속해서 모든 것들을 수동으로 해야만 해요. 학생의 새로운 예약 신청은 아마 다른

may have been misplaced, or one of my coworkers may have thought it was a duplicate reservation. In any case, what room did you want to change to?

M I tried to reserve room 1245 because it's much larger than the old one.

W Yes, it is. It seats about twice as many people as room 1025. Unfortunately, it is already reserved on that date at that time. Could you move your event to the afternoon, or to another date?

M No, that would be impossible. The guest speaker has to leave for Chicago in the evening that day. He cannot delay his departure, let alone stay for another day.

W Alright, then how about having it in a different building? There are two auditoriums the same size as that room in Carter Hall that are available on the morning of the 10th.

M That should work. 4 I can send out an email to everyone who has reserved a seat to attend and change the advertisement to show the new location. ...Huh? Did your computer screen just go blank?

W What?! Oh, no. Not now... ah! It's back! I'll make your new reservation quickly, before something else goes wrong. There. Room 1304 in Carter Hall is reserved for your event at 10 a.m. Is there anything else I can help you with?

M Thank you very much. No, I don't think so. Well... 5 You know, I may be able to help you out. I am majoring in computer programming. Maybe I could take a look at your program after class today. I may be able to figure out why it isn't working properly.

W 5 That would be great. Thank you! Um, when should we expect you?

M My last class ends at 4 o'clock, so around 4:30?

W That sounds good. I will let my manager know you will be coming.

M Alright, I'll see you then.

W Goodbye.

곳에 가 있을지도 모르고, 제 동료들 중 하나가 이것이 중복된 예약이라고 생각했을지도 몰라요. 어찌 됐든, 학생이 원한 새 강당은 어디였나요?

남 1245호 강당을 예약하려고 했었어요. 기존의 것보다 훨씬 더 크니까요.

여 네, 맞아요. 1025호 강당보다 거의 두 배 더 많은 사람들을 수용할 수 있죠. 안타깝게도 바로 그날 그 시간에 이 장소는 예약이 되어 있네요. 행사를 그날 오후나 다른 날로 바꾸는 것이 가능한가요?

남 아니요, 불가능해요. 초청 연사님이 그날 저녁에 시카고로 가셔야 하거든요. 하루 더 계시는 것은 말할 필요도 없고 출발을 미루실 수도 없어요.

여 알겠어요. 그렇다면 다른 장소에서 행사를 하는 것은 어때요? 10일 아침에 카터홀에 있는 이 강당과 같은 크기의 다른 강당들이 두 곳 예약 가능하거든요.

남 그러면 되겠네요. 4 행사에 참석하기 위해 좌석을 예매한 사람들에게 이메일을 보내고 새로운 장소를 보여주도록 광고를 바꿀 수 있어요. ...방금 이 컴퓨터 화면이 빈 화면으로 표시되지 않았나요?

여 네?! 아, 지금 이러면 안 되는데... 아! 다시 돌아왔네요. 다른 뭔가가 잘못되기 전에 학생의 새 예약을 빨리 해야겠어요. 자, 됐어요. 카터홀의 1304호 강당이 학생의 행사를 위해 오전 10시에 예약됐어요. 제가 도와줄 또 다른 일이 있나요?

남 정말 감사합니다. 없는 것 같아요. 음... 5 어쩌면 제가 그쪽을 도와드릴 수 있을지도 모르겠네요. 저는 컴퓨터 프로그래밍을 전공하고 있거든요. 사용하시는 프로그램을 오늘 수업이 끝난 뒤에 한 번 볼 수 있을 것 같아요. 왜 제대로 작동하지 않는 건지 알아낼 수 있을지 모르죠.

여 5 그래 준다면 정말 좋겠네요. 고마워요! 음, 몇 시쯤 올 생각인가요?

남 제 마지막 수업이 4시에 끝나니까 약 4시 30분쯤 될 거예요.

여 좋아요. 매니저에게 학생이 온다고 얘기해 놓을게요.

남 알겠습니다. 다시 뵐게요.

여 안녕히 가세요.

1. What is the purpose of the student's visit?

Ⓐ To ask questions about two lecture halls in different buildings
Ⓑ To inquire about the confirmation of his reservation
Ⓒ To repair a program for the campus management
Ⓓ To reserve another lecture hall for a guest speaker

2. What is the reason why the student wanted to change the lecture hall?

Ⓐ He always preferred room 1025 to room 1245

1. 학생이 찾아온 목적은 무엇인가?

Ⓐ 서로 다른 건물에 있는 두 강당에 대해 질문하려고
Ⓑ 그가 한 예약 확인에 대해 물어보려고
Ⓒ 대학교 운영 부서를 위해 프로그램을 고치려고
Ⓓ 초청 연사를 위해 또 다른 강당을 빌리려고

2. 학생이 강당을 바꾸고자 한 이유는 무엇인가?

Ⓐ 항상 1025호 강당을 1245호 강당보다 더 선호했다.

Ⓑ He was confused about what would be the best location.
Ⓒ He failed to predict that the audience would be so large.
Ⓓ He was not able to book a room due to a system failure.

3. What is the biggest problem with the department's new program?
Ⓐ It will not show students the changes they have made.
Ⓑ It continues to stop and freeze, canceling reservations.
Ⓒ It stopped updating the requests that were submitted.
Ⓓ It only allows automated changes to show up on the program.

4. What can be inferred about the student's new reservation?
Ⓐ The student has to notify attendees about the change of location.
Ⓑ The student has to book the lecture hall in Carter Hall himself.
Ⓒ Students cannot make new reservations currently.
Ⓓ The student has to come back again to make a new reservation.

5. What is the woman's attitude toward the student's suggestion?
Ⓐ She is interested to see how he is going to repair the computer program.
Ⓑ She feels sorry because she has to get the manager's permission first.
Ⓒ She is somewhat hesitant about the student's ability to fix the program.
Ⓓ She gladly accepts his offer since the department needs assistance.

Ⓑ 어디가 가장 좋은 장소일지 헷갈렸다.
Ⓒ 관객들이 그렇게 많을 거라고 예측하지 못했다.
Ⓓ 시스템 고장으로 인해 강당을 예약할 수 없었다.

3. 운영 부서의 새 프로그램이 가진 가장 큰 문제는 무엇인가?
Ⓐ 학생들이 무언가를 변경했을 때 그것을 보여주지 않는다.
Ⓑ 계속해서 멈추면서 예약들을 취소한다.
Ⓒ 제출된 신청들을 업데이트하는 것을 멈추었다.
Ⓓ 자동화된 변경 사항들만 프로그램에 보이도록 만든다.

4. 학생의 신규 예약에 대해 무엇을 추론할 수 있는가?
Ⓐ 학생은 장소의 변경에 대해 참석자들에게 공지해야 한다.
Ⓑ 학생은 카터홀의 강당을 자신이 직접 예약해야 한다.
Ⓒ 학생들은 현재 새로운 예약을 할 수 없다.
Ⓓ 학생은 새 예약을 하기 위해 다시 찾아와야 한다.

5. 학생의 제안에 대한 여자의 태도는 어떠한가?
Ⓐ 학생이 어떻게 컴퓨터 프로그램을 고칠지에 대해 흥미로워한다.
Ⓑ 매니저의 허락을 먼저 받아야 하기 때문에 유감스러워한다.
Ⓒ 프로그램을 고치는 학생의 능력에 대해 약간 망설이고 있다.
Ⓓ 자신의 부서에는 도움이 필요하므로 기쁘게 학생의 제안을 받아들인다.

어휘 particularly adv 특히 | reservation n 예약 | guest speaker 초청 연사 | attend v 참석하다 | anticipate v 예상하다, 예측하다 | confirmation n 확인 | auditorium n 강당 | record n 기록 | install v 설치하다 | automated adj 자동화된 | request n 신청, 요청 | misplace v 제자리에 두지 않다 | coworker n 직장 동료 | duplicate adj 이중의, 복제의 | unfortunately adv 불행히도 | delay v 미루다, 연기하다 | advertisement n 광고 | expect v 예상하다

Passage 6

Man: Student | Woman: Scholarship administrator

[1-5] Listen to part of a conversation between a student and a scholarship administrator.

M Hello, is this the office of the museum's human resources administrator?
W Yes, that's me. Do you have an appointment?
M Uh, no, I don't.

남자: 학생 | 여자: 장학금 행정 직원

학생과 장학금 행정 직원의 대화를 들으시오.

남 안녕하세요. 여기가 박물관의 인사과 행정 직원 사무실 맞나요?
여 네, 그게 저예요. 예약을 하고 왔나요?
남 어, 아니요.

W No matter, 2 do you have a copy of your résumé with you? Have you done any internships, or do you have any other related professional experience?

M Oh, I uh, I am not here for a job interview. 1 I came here to inquire about the scholarship that your museum is offering. I found this flyer about it on campus today.

W 2 I'm sorry. I just had an interview with a job applicant, so I assumed you were here for the same reason.

M 2 Are you hiring now as well?

W 2 Yes, we need a new assistant curator. So, you are interested in our scholarship. Do you have your portfolio with you?

M Not exactly, but I do have many pictures of my artworks on my smartphone.

W 4 May I see them?

M 4 Sure. Here they are.

W 4 These are some very nice sculptures. Have you ever held an exhibition?

M No, not individually. A few of my pieces have been in exhibitions staged by the university's fine arts program, though. I am working on an installation project right now. Here is a shot of it in its current state. I am transforming an old classroom into the interior of an Egyptian tomb, but the geometry of the space is deceptive. It makes the other sculptures I have placed in there stand out in unusual ways.

W Yes, it does. That is quite impressive. Unfortunately, the scholarship application process has not been finalized yet. The flyer was meant to announce its existence, not to invite applicants. At least, not yet, you see.

M Oh, alright. What can you tell me about the procedure as it stands?

W 3(C) Well, you would have to submit a formal portfolio. Since you work primarily in sculpture and three-dimensional art, we will probably accept a digital one. 3(D) There will also be an official application form that you will have to fill out. That's about all I can tell you now, though.

M Fair enough. I was also curious about the flyer. It never mentions the scholarship amount.

W Oh, well, that is for a reason. We will be asking for a complete proposal from each applicant—much like a building contractor bidding for a project. There will be an upper limit to the dollar amount that a student can receive, but that has not been decided yet.

M That's interesting. I've never heard of a scholarship like that before!

여 괜찮아요. 2 이력서 사본을 가져왔나요? 인턴십 경험이 있거나 아니면 관련된 전문 경험이 있나요?

남 아, 저는 면접을 보러 여기 온 게 아니에요. 1 이 박물관에서 주는 장학금과 관련해서 여쭤볼 게 있어서 왔어요. 오늘 캠퍼스에서 장학금에 관련된 이 전단지를 봤거든요.

여 2 미안해요. 방금 지원자 한 명의 면접을 봤거든요. 그래서 학생도 같은 이유로 여기 찾아왔으리라 생각했어요.

남 2 지금 채용도 진행 중이신가요?

여 2 네, 보조 큐레이터가 필요해요. 그럼, 학생은 우리 박물관의 장학금에 흥미가 있는 거군요. 포트폴리오를 가져왔나요?

남 그건 아니지만, 제 스마트폰에 제가 작업한 작품들의 사진을 많이 가지고 있어요.

여 4 봐도 괜찮을까요?

남 4 그럼요. 여기 있어요.

여 4 매우 멋진 조각들이네요. 전시회를 연 적은 있나요?

남 아니요, 개별적으로 해 본 적은 없어요. 대학의 미술 프로그램을 통해 개최된 전시회에 제 작품들이 몇 점 올라간 적은 있지만요. 저는 지금 설치 프로젝트 작업을 하고 있어요. 현재 상태의 사진을 찍은 게 여기 있어요. 오래된 교실을 이집트 무덤의 내부로 변형시키고 있지만, 공간의 기하학적인 면이 겉모습과는 달라요. 그래서 제가 거기에 배치한 다른 조각들을 특이한 방식으로 돋보이게 해요.

여 네, 그러네요. 꽤 인상적이에요. 불행히도 장학금 지원 절차는 아직 마무리되지 않았어요. 이 전단지는 장학금의 존재를 알리기 위한 의미였지, 지원자들을 불러 모으려던 건 아니었어요. 알겠지만, 적어도 아직까지는요.

남 아, 그렇군요. 현재 상태에서 절차에 대해 뭔가 말씀해주실 수 있나요?

여 3(C) 음, 학생은 공식 포트폴리오를 제출해야 해요. 조각과 입체 미술을 주로 작업하니까 아마 우리 쪽에서 디지털 포트폴리오를 받을 거예요. 3(D) 그리고 학생이 작성해야 하는 공식 지원서도 있을 겁니다. 하지만 이게 지금 제가 학생에게 말해줄 수 있는 전부네요.

남 괜찮아요. 전단지에 대해서도 궁금한 게 있었어요. 장학금 액수에 대해서 아무 것도 언급하지 않아서요.

여 아, 거기엔 이유가 있어요. 우린 각 지원자에게 완전한 제안서를 요구할 거예요. 프로젝트를 입찰할 때 계약자가 하는 것처럼요. 한 학생이 받을 수 있는 액수의 상한선이 있을 예정이지만, 아직 결정되지 않았어요.

남 흥미롭네요. 이런 장학금은 처음 들었어요!

W Yes, it is a pretty unusual idea. But, we want the artists to be motivated by producing their art as opposed to how much they can earn from us.

M That makes sense. I think it's a very good way to approach the issue. Can you tell me when you will begin accepting applications for the scholarship?

W Again, that date has not been set yet. If you give me your email address, I can notify you as soon as everything has been decided.

M **4, 5** Thank you. Do you think I have a chance of winning the scholarship?

W **4, 5** Well, I won't be on the panel of judges, but your work is very good. So, I would recommend applying. You'll never win if you don't.

여 네, 꽤나 흔치 않은 발상이죠. 하지만 우리는 예술가들이 우리에게서 얼마나 벌 수 있는지보다 스스로의 예술을 생산해내는 데서 동기 부여를 받기를 원해요.

남 말이 되네요. 이 문제에 매우 좋은 접근인 것 같아요. 장학금 지원자들을 언제부터 받을 예정인지 말해주실 수 있나요?

여 다시 말하지만, 날짜는 아직 정해지지 않았어요. 학생의 이메일 주소를 주면, 모든 것이 결정되는 대로 바로 알려줄게요.

남 **4, 5** 감사합니다. 제가 장학금을 받을 가능성이 있을 거라고 생각하세요?

여 **4, 5** 음, 저는 심사위원이 아니지만, 학생의 작품은 매우 훌륭해요. 그래서 전 지원하는 걸 추천해요. 지원하지 않으면 받을 수도 없을 테니까요.

1. Why did the student come to see the administrator?

Ⓐ He came to check the result of applying for a curator position.
Ⓑ He wanted to ask some questions about the museum's scholarship.
Ⓒ He was trying to find someone who can help him with his job search.
Ⓓ He does not know where to go to see the museum's art exhibition.

2. Why does the woman mention the student's résumé?

Ⓐ It shows how good of a candidate the student is for the position.
Ⓑ It is necessary for all students who want to work at the museum.
Ⓒ She wants to see if he has sufficient experience to hire him.
Ⓓ She thought he came to apply to become a curator.

3. What is true about the scholarship? Choose 2 answers.

Ⓐ The scholarship amount was included on the flyer.
Ⓑ The due date for applications is coming soon.
Ⓒ It requires students to turn in their portfolios.
Ⓓ All applicants need to submit the appropriate form.

4. What is the woman's attitude toward the student's work?

Ⓐ She feels that the man needs to work more on his skills in interior design.
Ⓑ She doubts if the man could get the scholarship, but she wants to be polite.

1. 학생은 왜 행정 직원을 찾아왔는가?

Ⓐ 큐레이터 자리에 지원한 결과를 확인하러 왔다.
Ⓑ 박물관 장학금에 대해 몇 가지 질문을 하고 싶었다.
Ⓒ 구직과 관련하여 자신을 도와줄 누군가를 찾으려 하고 있었다.
Ⓓ 박물관의 미술 전시를 보려면 어디로 가야 하는지 모른다.

2. 여자는 왜 학생의 이력서를 언급하는가?

Ⓐ 그 일자리에 학생이 얼마나 적합한 후보자인지를 보여준다.
Ⓑ 박물관에서 일하고 싶어하는 모든 학생들에게 필수적인 것이다.
Ⓒ 학생을 채용하기에 충분한 경험이 있는지를 보고 싶어한다.
Ⓓ 학생이 큐레이터가 되려고 지원하기 위해 왔다고 생각했다.

3. 장학금에 대해 옳은 것은 무엇인가?
두 개를 고르시오.

Ⓐ 장학금의 액수는 전단지에 명시되어 있었다.
Ⓑ 지원서 제출일이 다가오고 있다.
Ⓒ 학생들의 포트폴리오 제출을 필수로 한다.
Ⓓ 모든 지원자들은 적합한 지원서를 제출해야 한다.

4. 학생의 작품에 대한 여자의 태도는 어떠한가?

Ⓐ 남자가 실내 디자인에 대한 실력을 더 향상시켜야 한다고 생각한다.
Ⓑ 남자가 장학금을 받을 수 있을지 의심스럽지만 예의를 지키려고 한다.

Ⓒ She thinks it is good since she encourages him to apply for the scholarship.
Ⓓ She does not really know what to say since she is not an expert on sculpture.

5. Listen again to part of the conversation. Then answer the question.

M Thank you. Do you think I have a chance of winning the scholarship?
W Well, I won't be on the panel of judges, but your work is very good. So, I would recommend applying. You'll never win if you don't.

Why does the woman say this:

W You'll never win if you don't.

Ⓐ She is telling the student not to miss this good opportunity.
Ⓑ She is urging him to apply as soon as possible for the scholarship.
Ⓒ She is being indirect about telling the student his evaluation result.
Ⓓ She is worried about the fact that the student does not seem eager.

Ⓒ 남자에게 장학금 지원을 격려하고 있으므로 남자의 작품이 좋다고 생각한다.
Ⓓ 조각에 대해 전문가가 아니기 때문에 뭐라고 말해야 할지 모른다.

5. 대화의 일부를 다시 듣고 질문에 답하시오.

남 감사합니다. 제가 장학금을 받을 가능성이 있을 거라고 생각하세요?
여 음, 저는 심사위원이 아니지만, 학생의 작품은 매우 훌륭해요. 그래서 전 지원하는 걸 추천해요. 지원하지 않으면 받을 수도 없을 테니까요.

여자는 왜 이렇게 말하는가:

여 지원하지 않으면 받을 수도 없을 테니까요.

Ⓐ 이 좋은 기회를 놓치지 말라고 학생에게 말하고 있다.
Ⓑ 장학금에 되도록 빨리 지원하라고 재촉하고 있다.
Ⓒ 학생에게 평가 결과를 간접적으로 말해주고 있다.
Ⓓ 학생이 그다지 열정적으로 보이지 않는다는 사실에 대해 걱정하고 있다.

어휘 human resources 인사부 I appointment n 약속, 예약 I résumé n 이력서 I related adj 관련된 I professional adj 전문적인 I inquire v 묻다, 알아보다 I flyer n 전단지 I assume v 가정하다 I assistant curator 보조 큐레이터 I portfolio n 포트폴리오 I exhibition n 전시회 I individually adv 개별적으로 I installation n 설치 I current adj 현재의 I transform v 변형시키다, 바꾸다 I interior n 내부 I tomb n 무덤 I geometry n 기하학 I deceptive adj 현혹하는, 속이는 I unusual adj 특이한, 흔치 않은 I impressive adj 인상적인 I finalize v 마무리 짓다, 완결하다 I existence n 존재 I applicant n 지원자 I procedure n 절차, 방법 I submit v 제출하다 I primarily adv 주로 I complete adj 완전한 I proposal n 제안서 I contractor n 계약자 I bid v 입찰하다 I motivate v 동기 부여를 하다 I approach v 접근하다, 다가가다 I recommend v 추천하다

II. Lectures | Part 1. Lecture Question Types

Lesson 01 Main Idea

본서 I P. 138

Practice

Passage 1	A	Passage 2	B	Passage 3	A
Passage 4	C	Passage 5	A	Passage 6	A
Passage 7	C	Passage 8	C	Passage 9	C

Test

1. C **2.** D, E **3.** D **4.** A **5.** C **6.** C

Practice

본서 P. 142

Passage 1

Woman: Professor

Listen to part of a lecture in a science class.

W Right now, I want to take a look at alternative fuels and how they can possibly help us in the future. Alternative fuels are sources of energy that do not involve the use of oil, coal, natural gas, or propane. They are also usually fuels that are fairly safe for the environment. The primary reason alternative fuels are necessary is that we are quickly using up our oil and coal resources. There just isn't an endless supply of these fuels, and once our supply is depleted, we really need to have an alternative source of energy to power everything. If we do not have this, many of the things that make modern society so convenient, such as cars and other machinery, will be lost. So, let's take a closer look at the different types of alternative fuels that are out there.

여자: 교수

과학 강의의 일부를 들으시오.

여 이제, 대체 연료와 그것이 미래에 우리를 어떻게 도울 수 있는지를 살펴보려 합니다. 대체 연료는 석유, 석탄, 천연 가스와 프로판의 사용을 필요로 하지 않는 에너지원입니다. 그것들은 보통 환경에 상당히 안전한 연료들이기도 합니다. 대체 연료가 필요한 주된 이유는 우리가 석유와 석탄 자원을 빠르게 써 버리고 있다는 것입니다. 이런 연료들은 끝없이 공급되지 않습니다. 그리고 일단 공급량이 고갈되어 버리면, 동력을 공급할 대체 에너지원이 정말로 있어야 합니다. 만약 그런 것이 없다면 자동차와 기타 기계류 같이 현대 사회를 매우 편리하게 해주던 많은 것들이 사라질 것입니다. 그러면, 지금 나와 있는 여러 형태의 대체 연료들을 더 자세히 살펴봅시다.

Q. What is the lecture mainly about?

Ⓐ The importance of alternative fuels
Ⓑ The difficulty of finding an energy source to replace oil
Ⓒ The different types of alternative fuels
Ⓓ Environmental safety

Q. 강의는 주로 무엇에 관한 것인가?

Ⓐ 대체 연료의 중요성
Ⓑ 석유를 대체할 에너지원을 찾는 데 있어서의 어려움
Ⓒ 여러 종류의 대체 연료들
Ⓓ 환경 안전성

어휘 alternative adj 대체의, 대안의 | fuel n 연료 | involve v (필연적으로) 포함하다 | oil n 석유 | coal n 석탄 | natural gas 천연 가스 | propane n 프로판 | primary adj 주된 | resource n 자원 | endless adj 끊임없는 | supply n 공급량 | deplete v 고갈시키다 | convenient adj 편리한

Passage 2

Man: Professor

Listen to part of a lecture in a psychology class.

M Okay, now that we've completed our discussion of how animals learn through trial and error, let's move on to our next topic—Pavlov's dogs. There was a scientist named Ivan Pavlov who did some interesting experiments with dogs around the end of the 19th century. These experiments studied the response dogs would have if a bell sounded whenever they were given food. Pavlov found that the dogs began to associate the bells with the food. And, consequently, they started to salivate at the sound of a bell as if they were being fed, even though there wasn't any food around. From this, we see that certain behaviors can become associated with an exterior condition, and this is one of the foundations of conditioned response learning.

남자: 교수

심리학 강의의 일부를 들으시오.

남 자, 동물들이 시행착오를 통해 어떻게 학습하는가에 관한 논의를 끝냈으므로, 다음 주제인 파블로프의 개로 넘어가겠습니다. 19세기 말쯤 개를 데리고 몇 가지 흥미로운 실험을 했던 이반 파블로프라는 과학자가 있었습니다. 그는 실험을 통해 먹이를 받을 때마다 종소리가 울리면 개들이 보이게 될 반응을 연구했습니다. 파블로프는 개들이 종소리와 음식을 연관 지어 생각하기 시작하는 것을 알게 되었습니다. 그리고 그 결과, 음식이 주위에 없을 때조차도 마치 먹이가 주어지고 있는 것처럼 개들은 종소리를 들으면 침을 흘리기 시작했습니다. 이 실험을 통해 우리는 어떤 행동들은 외부 조건과 연관될 수 있고, 이것은 조건 반응 학습의 토대 중 하나라는 것을 알 수 있습니다.

Q. What is the lecture mainly about?

Ⓐ The eating habits of dogs
Ⓑ Pavlov's experiments on animal learning
Ⓒ Trial-and-error learning
Ⓓ Animal abuse in the 19th century

Q. 강의는 주로 무엇에 관한 것인가?

Ⓐ 개의 먹는 습관
Ⓑ 동물의 학습에 관한 파블로프의 실험
Ⓒ 시행 착오 학습
Ⓓ 19세기의 동물 학대

어휘 complete v 끝내다, 마치다 | discussion n 논의, 토의 | trial and error 시행착오 | experiment n 실험 | response n 반응 | associate v 연관지어 생각하다, 관련시키다 | consequently adv 그 결과 | salivate v 침을 흘리다 | behavior n 행동 | exterior adj 외부의 | condition n 조건 | foundation n 토대, 기초 | conditioned adj 조건이 있는

Passage 3

Man: Professor

Listen to part of a lecture in an engineering class.

M Great, now, I want to take a look at automation. As you may already know, automation is the use of automated machines to perform certain tasks and services. It appears everywhere in our lives, so many places, in fact, that it would be impossible to list all of the ways that these machines have changed our lives. For one thing, they have helped increase production. We can produce more things more quickly, and often of better quality. But as the quality of products increases along with the ease of attaining them, people are beginning to only expect more without appreciating what they already have. They are also becoming more and more reliant on machines... uh, to such an extent that society might have a great deal of trouble functioning if anything ever happened to its machines. I mean, just imagine if all the computers in the world stopped working. Many people would not be able to do their jobs and might even have trouble surviving.

남자: 교수

공학 강의의 일부를 들으시오.

남 좋습니다. 이제 자동화에 대해 살펴보고자 합니다. 여러분이 이미 알고 있듯이, 자동화란 어떤 작업이나 서비스를 수행하기 위해 자동화된 기계들을 사용하는 것입니다. 이는 우리 생활 모든 곳에서 볼 수 있으며, 사실 너무 많아서 이 기계들이 우리 생활을 바꿔놓은 방식들을 모두 나열하기란 불가능할 겁니다. 한 가지를 들자면, 이 자동화 기계들은 생산 증가를 도왔습니다. 우리는 더 많은 것을 더 빨리, 그리고 더 나은 품질로 생산할 수 있습니다. 하지만 제품을 손에 넣기가 쉬워짐과 더불어 제품 품질이 좋아짐에 따라 사람들은 이미 가진 것을 감사히 여기지 않고 더 많은 것을 기대하기 시작합니다. 사람들은 또한 기계에 점점 더 많이 의지하고 있습니다... 음, 만약 기계에 무슨 일이라도 생기면 사회가 기능을 하는 데 아주 큰 어려움을 겪을 정도로 말입니다. 그러니까, 세상의 모든 컴퓨터가 작동을 멈추었다고 상상해 보세요. 많은 사람들이 일을 할 수 없을 것이고, 심지어 생존에 어려움을 겪을지도 모릅니다.

Q. What is the lecture mainly about?

Ⓐ The pros and cons of automation
Ⓑ The ways that automation has helped society
Ⓒ The importance of computers to our lives
Ⓓ The increase of product quality throughout the world

Q. 강의는 주로 무엇에 관한 것인가?

Ⓐ 자동화의 장점과 단점
Ⓑ 자동화가 사회에 기여한 방식들
Ⓒ 우리 생활에 있어서 컴퓨터의 중요성
Ⓓ 전 세계에 걸친 제품 품질의 향상

어휘 automation n 자동화 | perform v 수행하다 | certain adj 어떤, 특정한 | appear v 나타나다 | production n 생산 | quality n 품질 | attain v 손에 넣다 | expect v 기대하다 | appreciate v 감사하다 | reliant adj 의존하는 | extent n 정도, 규모 | function v 기능하다 | survive v 생존하다

Passage 4

Woman: Professor

Listen to part of a lecture in a history class.

W Hello, everyone. As I'm sure you know, the reason why I'm here today is to talk to you about cliff dwellings. Many of

여자: 교수

역사 강의의 일부를 들으시오.

여 안녕하세요, 여러분. 여러분이 알고 있듯이, 오늘 저는 암굴 주거지에 대해서 말하기 위해 이 자리에 있

you may be asking yourselves at this point, "What exactly is a cliff dwelling?" Well, a cliff dwelling is a type of housing built by the Pueblo people in the western United States in Utah, Arizona, Colorado, and New Mexico. To be more specific, cliff dwellings are like apartment complexes made of clay and built into the sides of cliffs. Now, why build a house in the side of a cliff? Well, by doing this, the Pueblo people use the cliffs' overhangs to protect their houses from rain. They need to do this because their houses are made of clay and, as you can imagine, rain can cause quite a bit of damage to a clay structure. In the past, they were also able to use the cliff face to shield themselves from attack. So, let's move on to an examination of the Utah cliff dwellings and why they are especially important to modern anthropologists.

습니다. 여러분 중 다수는 이 시점에서 "암굴 주거가 정확히 뭐지?"라고 질문할 수도 있을 겁니다. 음, 암굴 주거는 미국 서부 지역의 유타주, 애리조나주, 콜로라도주, 뉴멕시코주 등에서 푸에블로족들에 의해 지어진 주거의 한 형태입니다. 더 구체적으로 말하면, 암굴 주거지는 진흙으로 만들어지고 절벽의 측면에 지어진 아파트 단지 같은 것입니다. 자, 왜 절벽의 측면에 집을 지을까요? 이렇게 함으로써, 푸에블로족들은 비로부터 집을 보호하기 위해서 절벽의 돌출 부분을 사용하는 것이죠. 집이 진흙으로 만들어졌기 때문에 이렇게 해야 합니다. 그리고 여러분이 상상할 수 있듯이, 비는 진흙으로 된 건물에 상당한 훼손을 야기할 수 있습니다. 과거에 그들은 또한 공격으로부터 자신들을 지키는 데에 절벽 표면을 이용할 수 있었습니다. 그럼, 이제 유타주 암굴 주거지에 관한 고찰과 그것들이 현대 인류학자들에게 특히 중요한 이유로 넘어가 봅시다.

Q. What is the main idea of the lecture?

Ⓐ How aggression forced the Pueblo to move to a new type of housing
Ⓑ The interest of modern scholars in the Utah cliff dwellings
Ⓒ What cliff dwellings are and why they were helpful to the Pueblo people
Ⓓ Rain and its impact on the Pueblo people's cliff dwellings

Q. 강의의 요지는 무엇인가?

Ⓐ 침략이 어떻게 푸에블로족들로 하여금 새로운 형태의 주거지로 옮겨가도록 했는가
Ⓑ 유타주 암굴 주거지에 대한 현대 학자들의 관심
Ⓒ 암굴 주거지가 무엇이고 왜 그것들이 푸에블로족들에게 도움이 되었는가
Ⓓ 비와 푸에블로족들의 암굴 주거지에 끼친 비의 영향

어휘 cliff n 암굴, 절벽 | dwelling n 주거지, 주거 | exactly adv 정확히 | specific adj 구체적인 | clay n 진흙, 점토 | overhang n 돌출부 | protect v 보호하다 | damage n 훼손, 손상, 피해 | structure n 구조물 | attack n 공격 | examination n 고찰, 조사 | anthropologist n 인류학자

Passage 5 Man: Professor

Listen to part of a lecture in a sociology class.

M At this time, I'd like to talk about impression management, which has lately become the topic of much sociological discussion. Impression management basically refers to the way... well, the way that people try to manage the image that they present to others, usually in order to hide their negative qualities. A very good example of this would, um, be the typical job interview in which a prospective employee wears his best clothes and tries to appear to be a certain person to the people interviewing him. He may try to change his vocabulary, tone of voice, opinions, and posture to make himself appear to be a more attractive candidate for the job. Of course, impression management is not always intentional and appears in many places outside of the interview room. Companies, politicians, movie stars, and everyday people

남자: 교수

사회학 강의의 일부를 들으시오.

남 이번 시간에는, 최근에 사회학 토론에서 주로 다뤄지고 있는 인상 관리에 대해서 이야기하고자 합니다. 인상 관리는 기본적으로... 음, 사람들이 다른 사람들에게 보여지는 이미지를 관리하려고 노력하는 방법을 말하는 거죠. 대개는 부정적인 자질들을 감추려고 말입니다. 아주 좋은 예로는 취업 지망생들이 좋은 옷을 입고, 자신을 면접하는 사람들에게 어떤 사람으로 보이고자 애쓰는 일반적인 취업 면접을 들 수 있습니다. 그 사람은 그 직업에 더 어울리는 후보로 보이기 위해서, 사용하는 어휘, 목소리 톤, 의견이나 자세 등을 바꿀지 모릅니다. 물론, 인상 관리가 항상 의도적인 것은 아니며, 면접실 밖 많은 장소에서 나타납니다. 회사, 정치인, 영화 배우, 그리고 일반인들은 개개인의 사람들에게, 그리

constantly struggle with how they present themselves to individual people and to the public as a whole. All of these, um, entities carefully make decisions and perform actions based on how they want to change or maintain their image.

고 대중에게 그들 자신을 어떻게 나타낼 것인가로 끊임없이 고민합니다. 이들 모두는 음, 자신의 이미지를 어떻게 바꾸거나 유지하기를 원하는가에 따라서 조심스럽게 결정을 하고 행동을 합니다.

Q. What is the lecture mostly about?

Ⓐ Good impressions that people try to make
Ⓑ The pressure people feel during job interviews
Ⓒ How society forces people to conform to its ideals
Ⓓ Public figures and their struggles with identity

Q. 강의는 주로 무엇에 관한 것인가?

Ⓐ 사람들이 만들려고 애쓰는 좋은 인상
Ⓑ 취업 면접 동안 사람들이 느끼는 압박감
Ⓒ 사회가 사람들로 하여금 이상을 따르게 하는 방법
Ⓓ 유명 인사와 정체성에 대한 그들의 노력

어휘 impression n 인상 | management n 관리 | sociological adj 사회학적인 | discussion n 토의, 논의 | refer v 가리키다, 일컫다 | present v 보이다 | hide v 숨기다 | negative adj 부정적인 | quality n 특성, 특징 | typical adj 전형적인, 일반적인 | prospective adj 장래의, 유망한 | vocabulary n 어휘 | posture n 자세 | attractive adj 매력적인 | candidate n 후보 | intentional adj 의도적인 | politician n 정치인 | constantly adv 끊임없이, 계속 | individual adj 개인의 | public n 대중 | entity n 독립체 | carefully adv 주의 깊게 | decision n 결정 | maintain v 유지하다

Passage 6

Man: Student | Woman: Professor

Listen to part of a discussion in a literature class.

W Today we will be discussing F. Scott Fitzgerald, one of the most famous American writers of the 1920s. This period was referred to as the "Lost Generation", but Fitzgerald called it the "Jazz Age". Most writers of that time expressed disillusionment with post-World War I American society. Fitzgerald's 1924 classic, *The Great Gatsby*, captures their sense of isolation and disenchantment. OK, you should have read the book. What can you tell me about Fitzgerald's feelings towards American culture?

M Well, he focused on materialism in society, and... uh, seemed quite critical of it.

W Quite so. Although Fitzgerald was known for throwing lavish parties, he did not approve of wealth being the only measure of a person's success or value in society. Did any of you notice examples or indications of this attitude in the book?

M I can't think of any specific examples, but I sensed an emptiness when reading the book. There wasn't much depth to the characters' lives.

W I think that was Fitzgerald's intention. The "Lost Generation", including Fitzgerald, felt that America lacked cultural accomplishments, compared to Europe anyway.

M Is that why he went to Europe?

W Absolutely! Fitzgerald, like other Jazz Age artists, visited Europe, especially Paris, looking for cultural inspiration. Ironically, the post-World War I period was a kind of golden age for American art and literature. Some say it was influenced by European culture, but others attribute it to the emergence of Jazz, a uniquely American music form.

남자: 학생 | 여자: 교수

문학 수업 중 토론의 일부를 들으시오.

여 오늘은 1920년대 가장 유명한 미국 작가 중 한 명인 F. 스콧 피츠제랄드에 대해서 이야기하려고 합니다. 이 시기는 '잃어버린 세대'로 일컬어집니다. 하지만 피츠제랄드는 그 시기를 '재즈 시대'라고 불렀습니다. 그 시대 대부분의 작가들은 제1차 세계 대전 후 미국 사회에 대한 환멸을 표현했죠. 피츠제랄드가 1924년에 발표한 고전인 〈위대한 개츠비〉는 그들의 고독과 각성을 포착해낸 것입니다. 자, 여러분이 그 책을 읽었어야 할 텐데요. 미국 문화에 대한 피츠제랄드의 느낌에 대해 여러분은 어떻게 말할 수 있나요?

남 음, 그는 사회의 물질주의에 초점을 맞췄어요. 그리고... 그에 대해 꽤 비판적인 듯해요.

여 그렇습니다. 비록 피츠제랄드가 사치스러운 파티를 열었다고 알려졌지만, 그는 사회에서 사람의 성공이나 가치의 유일한 척도가 부(富)라는 것에 찬성하지는 않았습니다. 여러분들 가운데 이 책에서 이런 태도의 예시나 암시를 발견한 사람 혹시 있나요?

남 구체적인 예가 생각나지는 않지만, 그 책을 읽을 때 공허함을 느꼈어요. 인물들의 삶에 깊이가 없었어요.

여 나는 그것이 피츠제랄드의 의도였다고 생각합니다. 피츠제랄드를 포함한 '잃어버린 세대'는 미국이 유럽과 비교했을 때 문화적 성과가 결여되었다고 느꼈죠.

남 그것이 그가 유럽으로 간 이유인가요?

여 그렇죠! 다른 재즈 시대 예술가들처럼, 피츠제랄드는 문화적 영감을 찾아서 유럽을, 특히 파리를 찾았습니다. 아이러니하게도, 제1차 세계 대전 후의 기간은 미국의 예술과 문학의 황금 시대였습니다. 어떤 사람들은 그것이 유럽 문화의 영향을 받았다고 하지만, 다른 사람들은 그것을 독특한 미국 음악 형태인 재즈의 출현 덕분이라고 생각합니다.

Q. What is the discussion mainly about?

Ⓐ An American author's discontent with his society in the 1920s
Ⓑ The American Jazz Age
Ⓒ The theme and main characters in *The Great Gatsby*
Ⓓ The life of F. Scott Fitzgerald

Q. 토론은 주로 무엇에 대한 것인가?

Ⓐ 한 미국 저자의 1920년 미국 사회에 관한 불만
Ⓑ 미국의 재즈 시대
Ⓒ 〈위대한 개츠비〉의 주제와 주인공들
Ⓓ F. 스콧 피츠제랄드의 생애

어휘 discuss ⓥ 논의하다 | refer ⓥ 일컫다, 가리키다 | generation ⓝ 세대 | express ⓥ 표현하다 | disillusionment ⓝ 환멸 | post ~후의 | classic ⓝ 고전 | capture ⓥ 포착하다 | isolation ⓝ 고독, 고립 | disenchantment ⓝ 각성 | materialism ⓝ 물질주의 | critical adj 비판적인 | lavish adj 호화로운, 풍성한 | approve of ~에 찬성하다 | wealth ⓝ 부 | measure ⓝ 척도 | notice ⓥ 알아차리다 | indication ⓝ 암시, 조짐 | attitude ⓝ 태도 | specific adj 구체적인 | emptiness ⓝ 공허함, 허무함 | depth ⓝ 깊이 | intention ⓝ 의도 | lack ⓥ 부족하다 | cultural adj 문화의, 문화적인 | accomplishment ⓝ 성과, 업적 | compare ⓥ 비교하다 | absolutely adv 틀림없이 | inspiration ⓝ 영감 | ironically adv 얄궂게도, 모순적이게도 | literature ⓝ 문학 | influence ⓥ 영향을 주다 | attribute to ~의 덕분으로 돌리다 | emergence ⓝ 출현, 발생 | uniquely adv 독특하게, 유일하게

Passage 7

Man: Professor

Listen to part of a lecture in a biology class.

M Good morning. I'd like to start off today by talking about a very unusual type of flower called Rafflesia. The thing that makes it so unusual is that it... well, for one thing, it smells really bad... and, for another, it's really big. If you take a look at this slide, you'll see that the Rafflesia is one huge flower. It can grow to be around a meter in diameter and can weigh as much as 10kg. But from the standpoint of a botanist, the intriguing thing about the Rafflesia is that it doesn't have chlorophyll and it doesn't photosynthesize, and this has caused a lot of debate among botanists about what exactly a plant is. We traditionally thought that plants had to photosynthesize—that it was, um, a defining characteristic of a plant. The Rafflesia, however, defies that theory, and really has very few of the traditional characteristics of a flower. So, if it doesn't photosynthesize, how exactly does the Rafflesia survive?

Well, if you'll take a look at the slide, you'll see that the Rafflesia doesn't have any roots, leaves, stems, or much else for that matter. On the surface, it's just a flower. What's hidden here, however, is that this flower is feeding off of the vine it's attached to. This makes it a parasite, and its host is always the same plant, the Tetrastigma. Basically, what the Rafflesia does is it starts as these tiny, uh, filaments inside the Tetrastigma vine. These filaments absorb nutrients and then they grow until they're ready to reproduce, which is when it actually starts to appear outside of the vine as a growth that eventually blooms into the flower that we have been looking at.

남자: 교수

생물학 강의의 일부를 들으시오.

남 안녕하세요. 오늘은 매우 독특한 종류의 꽃인 라플레시아에 관해 이야기하며 시작하고자 합니다. 그 꽃이 매우 독특한 이유는... 음, 한 가지는, 정말 나쁜 냄새가 난다는 것입니다... 그리고 또 다른 이유는 정말 거대하다는 것이죠. 이 슬라이드를 보면, 여러분은 라플레시아가 하나의 거대한 꽃이라는 것을 알 수 있을 겁니다. 이것은 지름이 약 1미터 정도까지 자랄 수 있고 무게가 10kg 정도 나갈 수 있습니다. 하지만 식물학자의 관점에서 보면 라플레시아에 관해 흥미로운 점은 엽록소가 없고 광합성을 하지 않는다는 사실이며, 이는 식물학자들 사이에서 식물이란 정확히 무엇인가에 관해 많은 논쟁을 야기했습니다. 우리는 전통적으로 식물은 광합성을 해야 한다고 생각했습니다. 그것은, 음, 식물을 정의하는 특징이었죠. 하지만 라플레시아는 그 이론을 무시하며 꽃의 전형적인 특징을 거의 가지고 있지 않습니다. 그럼 만약 광합성을 하지 않는다면 라플레시아는 정확히 어떻게 생존할까요?

음, 슬라이드를 보면, 라플레시아는 뿌리, 잎, 줄기 같은 부분을 전혀 갖고 있지 않다는 것을 알 수 있을 겁니다. 겉보기에는 그것은 단지 꽃입니다. 하지만 여기 감춰져 있는 사실은 이 꽃이 자기가 달라붙어 있는 덩굴들을 먹고 산다는 것입니다. 이것이 그 꽃을 기생 식물로 만드는 것이죠. 그리고 그것의 숙주는 항상 똑같은 식물, 테트라스티그마입니다. 기본적으로 라플레시아가 하는 것은 테트라스티그마 덩굴 안에서 작은 꽃실로부터 시작하는 것입니다. 이 꽃실들은 영양분을 흡수하며 번식할 준비가 될 때까지 성장하는데, 이때부터 실제로 라플레시아의 성장체가 덩굴 밖으로 나와서 보이기 시작하고 이것이 결국 지금 우리가 보는 꽃으로 피어나게 됩니다.

What's frustrating about this, though, is that it makes the Rafflesia incredibly difficult to study. We can't really dissect filaments because the Rafflesia's already uncommon and, well, we don't want to risk killing it. But this also means that we can't know as much as we would like about its inner workings. Basically, they're only found in remote parts of Southeast Asia, and even in those places, there aren't a lot of Rafflesias around. They aren't well-protected, and their habitats are being destroyed, which is actually one of the reasons why it's so important for us to study them now—so that we can learn how to sustain them in other, possibly artificial, habitats. The most frustrating thing of all, however, is that even if we're happy just studying the flowers and not the filaments inside the Tetrastigma vine, these flowers start to die after a few days, and that is just not enough time to work with them.

하지만 좌절감을 주는 것은 이것이 라플레시아를 연구하는 것을 엄청나게 어렵게 만든다는 것입니다. 라플레시아는 이미 드물고, 음, 우리는 그것을 죽이는 위험을 감수하고 싶지 않기 때문에 꽃실들을 해부할 수가 없습니다. 하지만 이는 또한 우리가 그것의 내부 활동에 대해서 알아내고 싶은 만큼 알 수 없다는 것을 의미합니다. 기본적으로 그것들은 동남아시아 오지에서만 발견되는데, 그 지역에서조차 라플레시아는 별로 많지 않습니다. 그것들은 잘 보호되지 않고 있으며, 서식지도 파괴되고 있습니다. 그것이 사실은 우리가 그것들을 지금 연구해야 하는 중요한 이유 중 하나입니다. 그래야 우리는 그것들을 다른 곳에서, 가능하다면 인공적인 서식지에서 기르는 방법을 알아낼 수 있습니다. 하지만 그 중에서도 가장 절망적인 것은 비록 우리가 테트라스티그마 덩굴 안의 꽃실 말고 그 꽃만을 연구하는 데 만족한다 하더라도, 이 꽃은 며칠 지나면 죽기 시작하는데 이는 꽃을 연구하기에 충분한 시간이 아니라는 겁니다.

Q. What is the main idea of the lecture?

Ⓐ Tetrastigma and how it sustains the Rafflesia
Ⓑ Photosynthesis and how plants rely on it to survive
Ⓒ Rafflesia and how it differs from most plants
Ⓓ Rafflesia's strong odor and unusual size

Q. 강의의 주제는 무엇인가?

Ⓐ 테트라스티그마와 그것이 라플레시아를 살게 하는 방식
Ⓑ 광합성과, 식물이 생존하기 위해서 광합성에 의존하는 방식
Ⓒ 라플레시아와 그것의 특징이 대부분의 식물들과 어떻게 다른가
Ⓓ 라플레시아의 강한 냄새와 별난 크기

어휘 unusual adj 독특한 | huge adj 거대한 | diameter n 지름 | weigh v 무게가 나가다 | standpoint n 관점 | botanist n 식물학자 | intriguing adj 흥미로운 | chlorophyll n 엽록소 | photosynthesize v 광합성을 하다 | debate n 논쟁 | traditionally adv 전통적으로 | defining adj 정의하는 | survive v 생존하다 | root n 뿌리 | stem n 줄기 | surface n 표면, 외면 | vine n 덩굴, 덩굴 식물 | parasite n 기생 식물 | host n 숙주 | tiny adj 아주 작은 | filament n 꽃실(꽃의 수술을 지지하는 대 부분), 가느다란 실 | absorb v 흡수하다 | nutrient n 영양분 | reproduce v 번식하다 | bloom v 피어나다 | frustrating adj 좌절감을 주는, 짜증 나는 | incredibly adv 엄청나게 | dissect v 해부하다 | risk v 위험을 무릅쓰다 | inner adj 내부의 | habitat n 서식지 | destroy v 파괴하다 | sustain v (생명을) 유지하다 | artificial adj 인공적인

Passage 8

Man: Professor | Woman: Student

Listen to part of a discussion in a geology class.

M I'd like to focus on a very important geological theory: plate tectonics. The basis for the theory is the idea that the Earth's crust, or outer shell, is not one continuous sphere, but is actually broken up into sections, called plates. The mantle, the section of the Earth directly below the crust, is a fluid layer of molten rocks. So it acts as a lubricant enabling the crust plates to slide around and bump into each other. This constant movement results in grinding, compression, and separation at the points where these plates meet, and this causes visible natural phenomena like earthquakes and

남자: 교수 | 여자: 학생

지질학 수업 중 토론의 일부를 들으시오.

남 저는 판구조론이라는 아주 중요한 지리학적 이론에 초점을 두고 싶습니다. 그 이론의 기초는 지구의 지각 즉, 외부 껍질이 계속 이어지는 하나의 구가 아니라 실제로는 판이라고 불리는 부분들로 분할되어 있다는 생각입니다. 지구 지각의 바로 아래 부분인 맨틀은 녹은 바위로 이루어진 유동층입니다. 그래서 그것은 지각판이 미끄러져서 서로 부딪치도록 해주는 윤활제 같은 역할을 하죠. 이 지속적인 움직임은 판들이 만나는 지점에서 마찰, 압축, 그리고 분리됩니다. 그리고 이것은 지진과 화산 분출과 같

volcanic eruptions. The crust plates are not all the same. They are divided into two types. Can anyone tell me what those are?

W Oceanic and continental crust plates?

M That's right. We have oceanic plates beneath the oceans and continental plates under the continents. The reason that the distinction between the two is important is that each has very different characteristics. The continental crust, for example, makes up about 40 percent of the earth's solid surface and is usually between 15 and 70 kilometers thick. The oceanic crust, on the other hand, is generally between 5 and 10 kilometers thick, but it is quite a bit denser than the continental crust.

W Does the thickness of a crust plate make such a big difference to the way it behaves that the two types of crusts have to be classified differently?

M Well, it is an important difference, but there is also another, possibly more important difference between the two types of plates. Continental crust is generally older and more stable than oceanic crust. This means that it doesn't move around a great deal. Oceanic plates, on the other hand, are constantly changing and shifting. This often involves the subduction of two plates, but I'm wondering if any of you know what subduction is?

W Well, I wanna say that subduction is when two plates push into each other and one ends up being on top.

M OK, great. That's a very good explanation. Subduction occurs when two tectonic plates begin to push into each other and then one gets pushed under the other. When this happens, rock from the plates is being sent back into the mantle of the Earth, where it is melted down. But if rock is being added to the mantle, where is the excess mass going?

W Umm... Maybe it's coming out through volcanic eruptions?

M That's exactly what happens. The material generated by the oceanic volcanoes is literally being recycled. One plate is pushed below another, and as the lower plate's material sinks toward the Earth's core, it heats up and simply melts to become the same as the rest of the material in the mantle. Then, after this happens, material returns to the surface of the Earth in a volcanic eruption, which completes the perpetual geological cycle of plate tectonics.

은 눈에 보이는 자연 현상들을 야기하기도 합니다. 지각판들이 모두 똑같지는 않습니다. 그것들은 두 가지 형태로 나뉩니다. 그것이 무엇인지 말해볼 사람 있나요?

여 대양과 대륙의 지각판들인가요?

남 맞아요. 대양 아래에는 대양판이, 그리고 대륙 아래에는 대륙판이 있어요. 그 둘을 구별하는 것이 중요한 이유는 각각이 매우 다른 특징을 가지고 있어서입니다. 예를 들면, 대륙판은 지구의 단단한 표면의 약 40%를 구성하고 있고 대개 두께가 15에서 70km죠. 반면에, 대양판은 일반적으로 두께가 5에서 10km이지만 대륙판보다 훨씬 더 밀도가 높아요.

여 지각판의 두께가 두 가지 형태의 판이 다르게 분류되어야 할 만큼 지각판이 움직이는 방식에 그렇게 큰 차이를 가져오나요?

남 음, 중요한 차이죠, 그렇지만 그 두 가지 형태의 판 사이에는 또 다른, 아마도 더 중요한 차이가 있습니다. 대륙판은 대양판보다 대개 더 오래되고 더 안정적입니다. 이는 대륙판이 많이 움직이지 않는다는 것을 의미합니다. 반면에, 대양판은 끊임없이 변화하고 바뀌고 있습니다. 이것은 종종 두 판의 섭입을 수반하는데, 혹시 여러분 중에 섭입이 무엇인지 알고 있는 사람이 있나요?

여 음, 섭입은 두 판이 서로에게 돌진해서 결국은 하나가 위에 놓이게 되는 때가 아닌가 하는데요.

남 네, 맞아요. 아주 좋은 설명입니다. 두 개의 지각 판이 서로에게 돌진하기 시작해서 하나가 다른 하나의 아래로 밀릴 때 섭입이 발생합니다. 섭입이 발생할 때 판에 있던 바위는 지구의 맨틀로 돌려보내지고 거기서 바위는 녹게 됩니다. 그런데 만약 바위가 맨틀에 더해진다면, 그 초과된 분량은 어디로 가게 될까요?

여 음... 아마도 화산 분출을 통해서 나오지 않을까요?

남 정확히 그렇게 되죠. 대양의 화산에 의해 생성된 물질은 말 그대로 재순환되고 있어요. 하나의 판은 다른 하나의 아래로 밀리고, 아래쪽 판의 물질이 지구의 핵으로 가라앉으면서 점점 뜨거워지고 녹아서 맨틀의 나머지 물질들과 똑같아지죠. 그러고 나서 물질은 화산 분출을 통해 지구의 표면으로 돌아옵니다. 이렇게 해서 판구조론의 영구적인 지질학적 순환이 완성되는 것입니다.

Q. What aspect of plate tectonics does the professor mainly discuss?

(A) The formation of tectonic plates
(B) How tectonic plates move
(C) The different types of tectonic plates
(D) How plates are destroyed

Q. 교수는 판구조론의 어떤 측면을 주로 논하는가?

(A) 지각판의 형성
(B) 지각판이 어떻게 움직이는가
(C) 지각판의 다른 형태
(D) 판이 어떻게 파괴되는가

어휘 geological adj 지질학적 | theory n 이론 | plate tectonics 판구조론 | crust n (지구의) 지각, 딱딱한 표면 | continuous adj 이어지는 | sphere n 구, 영역, 층 | mantle n 맨틀 | directly adv 바로 | fluid adj 유동체의 | molten adj 녹은 | lubricant n 윤활유 | enable v ~를 가능하게 하다 | bump into 부딪히다 | constant adj 지속적인 | grinding n 마찰, 연마 | compression n 압축, 압박 | separation n 분리 | visible adj 눈에 띄는 | phenomenon n 현상(pl. phenomena) | earthquake n 지진 | volcanic eruption 화산 분출 | divide v 나누다 | oceanic adj 대양의 | continental adj 대륙의 | distinction n 차이 | solid adj 단단한, 고체의 | surface n 표면 | dense adj 빽빽한, 밀도가 높은 | thickness n 두께 | behave v 움직이다 | classify v 분류하다 | generally adv 일반적으로 | stable adj 안정적인 | shift v 이동하다 | subduction n 섭입대 | explanation n 설명 | occur v 발생하다 | excess adj 초과한 | exactly adv 정확히 | material n 물질, 소재 | literally adv 말 그대로 | recycle v 재순환하다 | core n (지구의) 중심핵, 중심부 | complete v 완성하다 | perpetual adj 영구적인, 영속적인 | cycle n 순환, 주기

Passage 9

Woman: Professor

Listen to part of a lecture in an American history class.

W Alright, let's get started. Today's class is going to focus on the Wright Brothers. I'm sure you all learned a little bit about them when you were in grade school, but today we're going to try to get into a fair amount of detail about what they did, and, um, how they did it.

Let's begin with wing warping. Now, I don't expect you to understand all of the physics involved, but it is important for you to have a basic idea of what wing warping is and how it helped make controlled flight possible. Basically, wing warping involves changing the shape of a plane's or glider's wings so that the pilot can make it roll to the left or the right. The Wright Brothers used a kind of twisting motion with the wings of their glider so that one side would angle up and the other side would angle down. They did this by attaching wires to the ends of the wings, and then the pilot could pull the wires to make the glider go one way or the other. Now, this was a really new idea. Up until this point—we're talking about around 1899 here—glider wings had been mostly flat and the gliders themselves were difficult to control. Of course, this was dangerous for the pilot as he couldn't do anything about where he was going. To solve this problem, the Wright Brothers started studying how birds fly—the angles that their bodies took, the curvature of their wings, etc. They saw that the birds would move and re-shape their wings to change the flow of air and the direction of their flight.

OK, so they had this great new idea for a glider. They played with its design, did some research, built a model, and then they had to test the actual glider to see if it works. Now this was the hard part. They tried to choose the best location for their test flight, and, after doing some research, settled on Kitty Hawk, North Carolina.

여자: 교수

미국 역사 강의의 일부를 들으시오.

여 자, 시작할까요. 오늘의 수업은 라이트 형제에 초점을 두고자 합니다. 여러분 모두가 초등학생일 때 그들에 대해서 조금씩은 다 배웠을 거라고 생각해요. 하지만 오늘은 그들이 무엇을 했고 음, 그들이 그것을 어떻게 했는지에 대해서 꽤 세부적으로 들어가려고 해요.

날개 굴곡부터 시작하죠. 자, 나는 여러분이 이와 관련된 물리학 전부를 다 이해하기를 기대하지는 않지만, 날개 굴곡이 무엇인가, 그리고 그것이 어떻게 관제비행이 가능하도록 도와주는가에 대해 기본적으로 알고 있는 것은 중요합니다. 근본적으로 날개 굴곡은 비행기의, 또는 글라이더의 날개의 모양을 바꾸는 것인데 조종사는 날개를 왼쪽이나 오른쪽으로 돌리게 할 수 있어요. 라이트 형제는 그들의 글라이더 날개에 일종의 비틀기 동작을 이용해서 한 면이 위로 움직이고 다른 한 면은 아래로 기울도록 했어요. 날개의 끝부분에 철사를 부착함으로써 이렇게 했고, 조종사는 글라이더가 한 방향이나 다른 방향으로 가도록 철사를 당길 수 있었습니다. 이것은 정말 새로운 아이디어였어요. 이 시점까지, 그러니까 1899년경까지 글라이더의 날개는 대개 평평했고 글라이더 그 자체는 제어하기 어려웠어요. 물론 조종사가 글라이더가 가고 있는 방향에 대해 아무것도 할 수 없었으므로 이는 조종사들에게 위험했습니다. 이 문제를 해결하기 위해 라이트 형제는 새들이 나는 방법, 새의 몸이 취하는 각도, 날개의 굴곡 등을 연구하기 시작했죠. 형제는 새들이 공기 흐름과 비행의 방향을 바꾸기 위해 날개를 움직이고 모양을 바꾸는 것을 알게 되었습니다.

좋아요. 그래서 그들은 글라이더를 위한 이 멋지고 새로운 아이디어를 갖게 되었습니다. 그들은 설계를 해보고, 조사하고, 모형도 만들었습니다. 그리고 나서 작동하는지 알아보기 위해 실제 글라이더를 시험해야 했죠. 자, 여기가 힘든 부분입니다. 그들은 시험비행을 하기에 가장 좋은 장소를 고르려고 했습니다. 그리고 알아본 후 노스캐롤라이나주의 키티호크로 결정했습니다.

Now, why, of all places, would they choose a remote fishing town like Kitty Hawk? Well, they had several reasons. First, Kitty Hawk is by the sea, and that meant that it had a fair amount of wind to help the glider fly. There also weren't many trees around... so the Wright Brothers didn't have to worry about flying into anything. And Kitty Hawk was sandy. Now, why would the Wright Brothers want to go somewhere sandy? Well, basically, landing was far from perfected at this point. So it was important to have a soft surface to land on to keep the pilot and the plane in one piece.
As for taking off, the Wrights were sending their gliders down Kitty Hawk's hills to help them pick up speed. But they still just weren't getting enough lift. They were getting off the ground, but they weren't getting very high and, at times, they were just bumping up and down on the sand. All right, so how did they fix this problem? They tried to give their glider more momentum. So, around the beginning of 1903, they started experimenting with motors and propellers. And, by December, they had attached a motor and two propellers to a plane and were taking it back to Kitty Hawk to test it out. Orville Wright ended up flying this plane for twelve seconds, which was the first successful airplane flight.

왜, 모든 장소들 중에서 키티호크 같은 외딴 어촌을 골랐을까요? 음, 몇 가지 이유가 있었습니다. 첫째, 키티호크는 바닷가인데 이건 글라이더가 나는 데 도움이 되는 바람이 꽤 많이 분다는 것을 의미했죠. 또 주위에 나무가 별로 없어서... 라이트 형제는 무언가에 부딪칠 걱정을 할 필요가 없었습니다. 그리고 키티호크는 모래땅이었습니다. 자, 왜 라이트 형제는 모래가 있는 곳으로 가기를 원했을까요? 음, 근본적으로, 이 무렵에 착륙은 완벽과는 거리가 멀었습니다. 그래서 조종사와 비행기가 무사하려면 착륙할 때 표면이 부드러운 것이 중요했습니다.
이륙에 관해서 이야기하자면, 라이트 형제는 글라이더가 속력을 내는 것을 돕기 위해 키티호크의 언덕 위에서 글라이더를 내려보냈습니다. 그러나 여전히 충분히 떠오르지 못했습니다. 땅에서 떠오르긴 했지만 별로 높이 날지는 못했고, 가끔은 그냥 모래에 덜컹거리며 부딪힐 뿐이었습니다. 자, 그럼 그들은 어떻게 이 문제를 해결했을까요? 그들은 글라이더에 더 많은 운동량을 주려고 노력했습니다. 그래서 1903년 초에 그들은 모터와 프로펠러를 가지고 실험을 시작했습니다. 그리고 12월에 그들은 비행기에 모터 하나와 프로펠러 두 개를 부착했고 시험을 하기 위해 키티호크로 가져갔습니다. 결국 오빌 라이트가 12초 동안 이 비행기로 날았는데, 이것이 최초의 성공적인 비행이었죠.

Q. What is the lecture mainly about?

Ⓐ The family history of Wright Brothers
Ⓑ The importance of Kitty Hawk to the history of the airplane
Ⓒ The technique and efforts that Wright Brothers used to make gliders fly
Ⓓ The Wright Brothers' motivation for building gliders and airplanes

Q. 강의는 주로 무엇에 관한 것인가?

Ⓐ 라이트 형제의 가족사
Ⓑ 비행기의 역사에서 키티호크의 중요성
Ⓒ 글라이더가 날도록 하기 위해 라이트 형제가 사용한 기술과 노력
Ⓓ 글라이더와 비행기를 만들게 된 라이트 형제의 동기

어휘 grade school 초등학교 I detail n 세부 사항 I warping n 굴곡 I expect v 기대하다 I physics n 물리 I control v 제어하다, 통제하다 I flight n 비행 I roll v 돌리다 I twisting adj 비트는, 회전하는 I attach v 부착하다 I flat adj 평평한 I dangerous adj 위험한 I solve v 해결하다 I curvature n 굴곡 I flow n 흐름 I direction n 방향 I location n 장소 I test flight 시험비행 I remote adj 외딴 I sandy adj 모래가 많은 I perfect v 완벽하게 하다 I surface n 표면, 지표 I take off 이륙하다 I lift n 떠오름 I fix v 고치다 I momentum n 운동량 I experiment v 실험하다 I successful adj 성공적인

Test

본서 P. 144

Man: Professor | Woman: Student

[1-6] Listen to part of a discussion in an astronomy class.

M Technology has advanced quite a bit since the lunar landings in the 1960s and 70s. So much so, in fact, that the prospect of building a colony on the Moon is being seriously

남자: 교수 | 여자: 학생

천문학 수업 중 토론의 일부를 들으시오.

남 1960년대와 70년대의 달 착륙 이래 기술은 상당히 발전했습니다. 너무 발전한 나머지, 나사에서는 달에 식민지를 건설하는 것의 가능성을 진지하게 고

considered by NASA. It is not currently possible to do so, but with further advances, it could soon become a reality. **1** In order for humans to colonize the Moon, one technology in particular needs to be created: a way to supply people with oxygen. **2(D)** The Moon has a thin atmosphere, but it contains very little oxygen, so it is not feasible to extract oxygen from the air. **2(E)** The Moon's soil, on the other hand, is composed of approximately 45 percent oxygen. The regolith on the Moon is made up of various metal oxides including silicon oxide, iron oxide, and aluminum oxide. The iron oxide is contained mostly in a mineral called ilmenite, which is a mixture of iron, titanium, and oxygen. **3** In order to remove the oxygen from that mineral, it merely needs to be heated to the proper temperature. Through a process called pyrolysis—which literally means "to separate with fire"—the elements that ilmenite contains can be isolated and collected. As one scientist involved in this type of research commented, "Any material crumbles into atoms if made hot enough." This method is attractive for many reasons. It does not require raw materials to be brought from Earth, and we wouldn't need to search for a specific mineral. **4** The Moon is covered in ilmenite, so we would only need to scoop up the soil from the ground and apply heat.

W **4** But Professor, the reality is not that simple, is it?

M **4** Of course not. I am oversimplifying the situation. The regolith would have to be heated to about 2,500 degrees Centigrade for this process to work. That is very difficult and dangerous to do in a laboratory, but it becomes easier when done in a vacuum. The main problem with developing this technology is the simple fact that it would have to be done on Earth. There are samples of Moon rock and soil that were collected during the lunar landings, but they are too valuable to be used to develop the machinery that is required. There was never a lot of Moon material to begin with, but decades of research and handling by people have reduced that amount even more.

W If that's the case, can't we just simulate the regolith on Earth? Is it impossible?

M Good question. We know its exact chemical composition, so finding material on Earth that is similar is possible. Ilmenite is also common here, and basalt from Lake Superior that is mixed with glass makes a decent substitute as well. But this is not really the same as Moon regolith because that is also constantly exposed to radiation from the Sun, and this can alter its composition, which is very difficult to simulate on Earth with our dense atmosphere.

려하고 있습니다. 현재는 가능한 일이 아니지만 기술이 더 발전하게 되면 곧 현실이 될 수 있습니다. **1** 인간이 달을 식민지화하기 위해서는 특히 한 가지 기술이 개발되어야 합니다. 바로 인간에게 산소를 공급하는 방법 말이죠. **2(D)** 달의 대기는 희박하지만, 매우 적은 산소를 함유하고 있으므로 공기 중에서 산소를 추출하는 것은 실현 가능성이 없습니다. **2(E)** 반면 달의 토양은 약 45퍼센트가 산소로 구성되어 있죠. 달의 표토는 실리콘 산화물, 산화철, 그리고 산화알루미늄을 포함한 다양한 금속 산화물로 이루어져 있습니다. 산화철은 일메나이트라는 광물에 대부분 함유되어 있는데, 이것은 철, 티타늄, 그리고 산소와의 혼합물입니다. **3** 이 광물로부터 산소를 제거하기 위해서는 그냥 적절한 온도로 열을 가하면 됩니다. 문자 그대로 '불로 분리하다'라는 뜻을 가진 열분해라는 과정을 통해 일메나이트가 함유한 원소들이 서로 분리되고 채집될 수 있죠. 이러한 종류의 연구에 참여한 한 과학자가 말하길, "충분한 열을 가하기만 하면 어떠한 물질도 원소로 쪼개어진다"고 했습니다. 이 방법은 많은 점에서 매력적입니다. 지구에서 원료를 가져와야 할 필요도 없고, 특정한 광물을 찾아야 할 필요도 없습니다. **4** 달은 일메나이트로 덮여 있기 때문에 우리는 그저 땅에서 흙을 퍼서 열을 가하기만 하면 되는 거죠.

여 **4** 하지만 교수님, 현실은 그렇게 간단하지 않잖아요, 그렇죠?

남 **4** 물론 아니죠. 저는 상황을 굉장히 단순화하고 있습니다. 열분해가 일어나기 위해서는 표토가 섭씨 약 2,500도로 가열되어야 합니다. 이는 실험실에서 하기에는 매우 어렵고 위험하지만 진공에서 하면 더 쉬워집니다. 이 기술을 개발하는 데 있어 가장 큰 문제는 이를 지구에서 해야만 한다는 단순한 사실입니다. 달 착륙을 했을 때 채집한 달의 암석과 토양 샘플들이 있긴 하지만 필요한 기계를 개발하는 데 사용하기에는 너무 귀중한 것들이죠. 달에서 온 재료가 애초부터 많았던 것도 아니었지만, 사람들이 수십 년간 이것들을 연구하고 다루다 보니 그 양이 더욱 더 줄어들었습니다.

여 만약 그렇다면, 달의 표토를 지구에서 비슷하게 만들 수는 없나요? 불가능한가요?

남 좋은 질문이에요. 표토의 정확한 화학적 조성을 알고 있기 때문에 비슷한 재료를 지구에서 찾는 것이 가능합니다. 일메나이트는 지구에도 흔하며, 슈피리어 호수의 현무암을 유리와 혼합한 물질 또한 꽤나 괜찮은 대체재가 될 수 있습니다. 그러나 이것이 달의 표토와 같을 수는 없어요. 달의 표토는 화학적 조성을 바꿀 수 있는 태양 복사에 항상 노출되어 있고, 이는 지구의 밀도 높은 대기에서는 모방해 내기가 매우 어렵습니다.

Making a machine capable of heating Moon regolith to 2,500 degrees Centigrade would be difficult, and transporting it to the Moon would be even harder. **5** And once it was there, the Moon dust would be difficult to deal with. As the astronauts who went to the Moon learned, that dust gets into everything, and it is extremely abrasive, so it easily damages machines and spacesuits.

Thankfully, one method to separate regolith has been devised that uses few moving parts. **6** Using a large lens to focus sunlight onto a sample in a vacuum, scientists have been able to convert 20 percent of the simulated soil into free oxygen. After the oxygen removal process is complete, the remaining material is called slag. This heavy, metallic substance could be used to make structures and radiation shielding. So basically, nothing would be wasted. Other methods using chemical reactions and electricity have been developed, but none are currently as viable as pyrolysis. Once this process has been scaled up to produce usable amounts of oxygen, the colonization of the Moon could proceed. On the Moon, many pyrolysis machines could be built and the colony could ultimately be able to refuel spacecraft in space. This is extremely important, as 85 percent of a typical rocket's weight is its liquid oxygen fuel.

달의 표토를 섭씨 2,500도까지 가열할 수 있는 기계를 만드는 것도 어렵고, 이를 달로 운반하는 것은 더더욱 어려울 겁니다. **5** 그리고 일단 거기로 운반하고 나면, 달의 먼지가 대처하기 힘든 문제가 될 겁니다. 달에 갔던 우주 비행사들은 달의 먼지가 모든 것에 파고들며, 엄청나게 거칠어서 기계와 우주복을 쉽게 손상시킨다는 것을 알아차렸거든요.

다행히도, 적은 숫자의 작동 부품을 사용하여 달의 표토를 분리할 수 있는 방법이 고안되었습니다. **6** 진공 상태의 표본에 태양 광선을 집중시키는 거대한 렌즈를 사용해서, 과학자들은 복제 제작한 토양의 20퍼센트를 유리 산소로 전환할 수 있었습니다. 산소를 제거하는 과정이 끝난 뒤 남는 물질은 슬래그라고 불립니다. 이 무거운 금속 물질은 구조물과 방사선 차폐물을 만드는 데 사용될 수 있습니다. 그래서 사실상, 낭비되는 물질은 아무것도 없는 거죠. 화학 반응과 전기를 이용하는 다른 방법들도 개발되긴 했지만 현재 그 무엇도 열분해보다 더 실행 가능성이 있지는 않습니다. 이 과정이 사용 가능한 양의 산소를 생산하기까지 발전하면 달의 식민지화는 진행될 수 있습니다. 달에서 많은 열분해 기계들이 건설될 수 있고, 식민지는 궁극적으로 우주에 있는 우주선에 연료를 재급유해 줄 겁니다. 일반적인 로켓 무게의 85퍼센트를 차지하는 것이 액체 산소 연료이므로 이는 매우 중요합니다.

1. What is the main idea of the discussion?

Ⓐ Possible methods of isolating and collecting oxygen molecules
Ⓑ Setting up a colony in space, specifically on the Moon
Ⓒ A way to generate oxygen to sustain a colony on the Moon
Ⓓ Using pyrolysis to separate oxygen from metallic compounds

2. According to the discussion, what characteristics does the Moon have? Choose 2 answers.

Ⓐ Its soil contains a very low amount of oxygen and hydrogen.
Ⓑ It is composed of iron, hydrogen oxide, and other metals.
Ⓒ It has a thin atmosphere, which makes extracting oxygen easier.
Ⓓ Its atmosphere has a lower amount of oxygen than the Earth's.
Ⓔ It has an abundance of ilmenite, which contains oxygen.

1. 토론의 주제는 무엇인가?

Ⓐ 산소 분자를 분해하고 채집할 수 있는 가능한 방법들
Ⓑ 우주, 구체적으로 달에 식민지 설립하기
Ⓒ 달에서 식민지를 존재하게 하기 위해 산소를 생산하는 방법
Ⓓ 금속 화합물에서 산소를 분리하기 위해 열분해 사용하기

2. 토론에 따르면, 달은 어떠한 특성들을 가지고 있는가? 두 개를 고르시오.

Ⓐ 달의 토양은 매우 낮은 양의 산소와 수소를 함유하고 있다.
Ⓑ 달은 철, 산화수소, 그리고 다른 금속들로 이루어져 있다.
Ⓒ 달은 희박한 대기를 갖고 있는데, 이것이 산소 추출을 더 쉽게 만든다.
Ⓓ 달의 대기는 지구보다 더 적은 양의 산소를 갖고 있다.
Ⓔ 달은 산소를 함유하고 있는 일메나이트를 풍부하게 갖고 있다.

3. How is pyrolysis helpful in building a colony on the Moon?
   (A) It requires less ilmenite, which is necessary to supply oxygen.
   (B) Any material on the Moon can be reduced to atoms to generate oxygen.
   (C) It reduces the amount of material that needs to be brought to the Moon.
   (D) The raw resources on the Moon can be directly used to extract oxygen.

4. What is the professor's opinion about pyrolysis?
   (A) It is theoretically perfect, but the actual situation is much more challenging.
   (B) It is too dangerous and difficult to be fully utilized on the Moon.
   (C) It is as simple as it sounds if there is enough ilmenite.
   (D) It takes too much time to implement a practical solution on Earth.

5. Why does the professor mention Moon dust?
   (A) It got into machines currently operating on the Moon.
   (B) It requires a high temperature to separate compounds into atoms, making pyrolysis difficult.
   (C) It causes one of the problems that interferes with building pyrolysis machines on the Moon.
   (D) It is abrasive and can even damage spacecraft in orbit around the Moon.

6. What can be inferred about the method of pyrolysis mentioned using a lens?
   (A) It generates some metallic materials that are exposed to radiation.
   (B) It provides other leftover oxygen products that can be used for other purposes.
   (C) It does not require a man-made energy source to carry out the process.
   (D) It made it possible to establish more pyrolysis machines on the Moon.

3. 달에 식민지를 건설하는 데 있어 열분해가 어떻게 도움이 되는가?
   (A) 산소를 생산하는 데 필요한 일메나이트를 더 적게 필요로 한다.
   (B) 달에 있는 어떠한 재료도 산소를 만들어 내기 위해 원소로 분해될 수 있다.
   (C) 달로 운반해야만 하는 재료의 양을 줄여준다.
   (D) 달에 있는 원자재가 산소를 추출하는 데 직접적으로 사용될 수 있다.

4. 열분해에 대한 교수의 의견은 무엇인가?
   (A) 이론상으로는 완벽하지만 실제 상황은 훨씬 더 힘들다.
   (B) 달에서 완전히 사용되기에는 너무 위험하고 어렵다.
   (C) 일메나이트만 충분하다면 이야기하는 것만큼 간단하다.
   (D) 지구에서 실질적인 해결책을 시행하기에는 시간이 너무 오래 걸린다.

5. 교수는 왜 달의 먼지를 언급하는가?
   (A) 현재 달에서 작동 중인 기계들에 들어갔다.
   (B) 화합물을 원소로 분해하기 위해서는 높은 온도가 필요한데, 이것이 열분해를 어렵게 만든다.
   (C) 달에 열분해 기계를 건설하는 것을 방해하는 문제점들 중 하나를 야기한다.
   (D) 거친 성질을 가졌으며, 달 주변의 궤도를 도는 우주선들까지 손상을 입힐 수 있다.

6. 렌즈를 이용하는 열분해 방법에 관해 무엇을 추론할 수 있는가?
   (A) 태양 복사에 노출된 몇몇 금속 재료들을 만들어낸다.
   (B) 다른 목적을 위해 사용될 수 있는 남은 산소 산물들을 만들어낸다.
   (C) 과정을 실행하기 위해 인간이 만든 에너지원을 필요로 하지 않는다.
   (D) 더 많은 수의 열분해 기계를 달에 건설하는 것을 가능하게 만들었다.

어휘 lunar adj 달의 | landing n 착륙 | prospect n 가능성 | colony n 식민지, 거주지 | currently adv 현재, 지금 | advance n 발전, 진보 | reality n 현실 | colonize v 식민지로 만들다 | atmosphere n 대기 | feasible adj 실현 가능한 | extract v 뽑다, 얻다, 추출하다 | soil n 토양 | composed of ~로 구성된 | approximately adv 거의, ~가까이 | regolith n 표토 | metal oxide 금속 산화물 | silicon oxide 실리콘 산화물 | iron oxide 산화철 | aluminum oxide 산화알루미늄 | mineral n 광물 | ilmenite n 일메나이트, 티탄 철광 | titanium n 티타늄 | pyrolysis n 열분해 | isolate v 분리하다, 격리하다 | crumble v 바스러지다 | attractive adj 매력적인, 멋진 | scoop v 파내다, 뜨다 | oversimplify v 지나치게 단순화하다 | laboratory n 실험실 | vacuum n 진공 | valuable adj 귀중한 | machinery n 기계 | decade n 10년 | reduce v 감소시키다 | simulate v ~를 모방해서 만들다 | chemical composition 화학 조성 | common adj 흔한 | basalt n 현무암 | decent adj 괜찮은 | substitute n 대체재 | constantly adv 계속해서 | expose v 노출시키다 | radiation n 복사, 방사선 | dense adj 밀도 높은 I transport v 수송하다, 운반하다 I Moon dust 달의 먼지 I astronaut n 우주 비행사 I abrasive adj 거친 I spacesuit n 우주복 I devise v 고안하다 I convert v 변환하다 I removal n 제거 I slag n 광재, 화산암재 I metallic adj 금속의 I substance n 물질 I structure n 구조 I basically adv 기본적으로 I electricity n 전기 I viable adj 실행 가능한 I scale v (높은 곳을) 오르다 I ultimately adv 궁극적으로 I refuel v 연료를 재급유하다 I typical adj 일반적인 I weight n 무게 I liquid oxygen 액체 산소 I fuel n 연료

Lesson 02 Details

본서 I P. 146

Practice

Passage 1 C
Passage 2 D
Passage 3 B
Passage 4 C
Passage 5 D
Passage 6 A, D
Passage 7 1. A, C 2. C 3. D
Passage 8 1. B 2. C 3. A, C

Test

1. C 2. D 3. C 4. A 5. B 6. B

Practice

본서 I P. 151

Passage 1

Woman: Professor

Listen to part of a lecture in an architecture class.

W Okay, let's start off today by talking about adobe clay as it was used by the Native Americans. To begin with, however, we need to distinguish between the Native Americans' use of adobe before and after they were influenced by the Spanish. At first, Native Americans used adobe clay in its, um, pure form—it was just clay and wasn't mixed with anything else. They shaped this clay into balls and then stuck them together to make adobe houses, which worked fairly well for them. However, after the Spanish showed up, they introduced some ideas that worked even better. The first and probably most important of these ideas was for Native Americans to mix the adobe mud with straw, which made the clay stronger. They also learned how to use bricks instead of balls when building their homes. The bricks were made so that they were less susceptible to rain; they were slanted so that the rain would flow off instead of sitting on top of the bricks. They also made it easier to erect strong structures in general because of their square shape.

여자: 교수

건축학 강의의 일부를 들으시오.

여 좋아요, 오늘은 미국 원주민들이 사용했던 어도비 점토에 대해 이야기하는 것으로 시작합시다. 그러나 우선 우리는 미국 원주민들의 어도비 사용에 대해 스페인 사람들의 영향을 받기 이전과 이후를 구분할 필요가 있습니다. 처음에 미국 원주민들은 어도비 점토를, 음, 천연의 형태로 사용했습니다. 즉, 단지 점토일 뿐 다른 어떤 것도 섞이지 않은 상태였죠. 그들은 이 점토를 공 모양으로 만든 다음 서로 접착시켜 자신들에게 아주 잘 맞는 어도비 집을 만들었습니다. 하지만 스페인 사람들이 등장한 후, 그들은 훨씬 효율적인 아이디어들을 도입했습니다. 미국 원주민들에게 이런 아이디어 중 첫 번째이자 아마 가장 중요한 것은 어도비 진흙과 짚을 섞는 것이었는데, 이는 점토를 더욱 단단하게 만들었습니다. 또 그들은 집을 지을 때 공 모양 대신 벽돌을 사용하는 법을 배웠습니다. 벽돌은 비의 영향을 덜 받도록 만들어졌는데 비스듬하게 기울어져 있어서 빗물이 벽돌 위에 고이지 않고 흘러내릴 수 있었죠. 또한 벽돌의 네모난 모양 덕분에 견고한 구조를 좀 더 쉽게 세울 수 있게 되었습니다.

Q. According to the professor, what advantage did adobe bricks have over adobe balls in the rain?

(A) They could let rain sit on top of the bricks.
(B) They were flat, which kept the water from soaking in.
(C) They were slanted, which allowed the rain to run off.
(D) They wouldn't roll as much as the adobe balls did.

Q. 교수에 따르면, 비가 올 때 어도비 공에 비해 어도비 벽돌이 가진 장점은 무엇이었는가?

(A) 빗물이 벽돌 위에 고이게 해주었다.
(B) 평평해서 물이 스며들지 않게 해주었다.
(C) 경사가 있어서 빗물이 흘러내리도록 해주었다.
(D) 어도비 공이 굴러갔던 것만큼 굴러가지 않았다.

어휘 adobe clay 어도비 점토 | Native American 미국 원주민 | distinguish v 구분하다 | influence v 영향을 주다 | pure adj 순수한 | shape v 모양을 빚다 | introduce v 도입하다 | straw n 짚 | brick n 벽돌 | susceptible adj 영향을 받기 쉬운, 예민한 | slanted adj 기울어진, 비스듬한 | erect v (똑바로) 세우다

Passage 2

Man: Student | Woman: Professor

Listen to part of a discussion in a psychology class.

W Okay, everyone. Let's start today's class by talking about rewarding children in order to encourage their enjoyment of some activity. This is a topic that has caused a fair amount of debate in recent years. Now, before we start, do you think that rewarding children for participating in an activity such as drawing would be a good idea, even if they already like to draw?

M I think it'd be a good idea. It would keep the kid interested in drawing and make him want to do a good job.

W That's a good answer, and many scientists today agree with it. They say that, if a parent rewards a child for doing a good job or being creative in an activity, it can have a positive effect. At the same time, however, many say that a child shouldn't be rewarded just for doing an activity—he should be rewarded for how well he does the activity. This is how we can keep his interest.

M But... uh... what do you mean by rewarding how well he does? How would a parent determine that?

W Hmm... Well, I think the best thing I can do is to give you a personal example. My daughter likes to read, but she likes to listen to music much more. So I use music to reward her for reading. But your question is about how I do this. Well, I don't just reward her for reading in general. We set goals about which books she should read and how well she should understand them. When she reaches one of these goals, she gets a new album or a pair of concert tickets, which encourages her to read more and also improves her reading ability.

남자: 학생 | 여자: 교수

심리학 강의의 토론 일부를 들으시오.

여 자, 여러분. 오늘은 활동의 재미를 북돋우기 위해 아이들에게 보상을 주는 것에 대한 얘기로 수업을 시작하겠습니다. 최근 들어 상당한 논쟁을 불러일으키고 있는 주제 중 하나이죠. 그럼 시작하기 전에, 여러분은 그림 그리기와 같은 활동에 참여하는 것에 대해 어린이에게 상을 주는 것이 좋은 아이디어라고 생각하나요? 그림 그리는 것을 이미 좋아하는데도 말이에요.

남 저는 좋은 생각이라고 봅니다. 아이들이 그림 그리기에 계속 흥미를 가질 수 있게 해주고, 잘하고 싶게 만들 거예요.

여 좋은 대답이군요. 오늘날 많은 과학자들이 이 의견에 동의하고 있습니다. 그들은 부모들이 아이가 활동 중에 잘한 일이나 독창적인 일에 대해 상을 주면 긍정적인 효과를 나타낼 수 있다고 말합니다. 하지만, 이와 동시에 많은 이들이 아이가 단지 활동을 한 것에 대해서만 보상을 받아서는 안 된다고 말하고 있습니다. 즉, 아이가 그 활동을 얼마나 잘하고 있는가에 대해 보상을 받아야 한다는 겁니다. 이것은 어떻게 하면 아이의 흥미를 유지시킬 수 있는가의 문제이죠.

남 하지만... 음... 아이가 얼마나 잘하느냐에 대해 상을 준다는 것은 어떤 의미인가요? 부모는 어떻게 그것을 결정할 수 있을까요?

여 음... 글쎄, 그것을 설명하기에 가장 좋은 방법은 학생에게 나의 개인적인 예를 하나 들려주는 것일 듯하네요. 내 딸은 독서를 좋아하지만 음악 듣는 것을 훨씬 더 좋아해요. 그래서 나는 독서에 대한 상으로 음악을 사용합니다. 하지만 학생의 질문은 내가 어떻게 이것을 하느냐인데요. 글쎄, 나는 보통 책을 읽는 것 자체에 대해 상을 주지는 않아요. 우리는 딸아이가 어떤 책을 읽어야 하는지, 그리고 얼마나 그 책들을 잘 이해해야 하는지 목표를 정해요. 이런 목표 중 하나에 도달하면 아이는 새로운 앨범이나 콘서트 티켓 두 장을 얻게 되고, 이로써 아이가 독서를 더 많이 하도록 독려하고 아이의 독서 능력을 향상시키게 되죠.

Q. How does the professor reward her daughter for reading?

(A) By giving her extra free time
(B) By buying her more books
(C) By giving her drawing supplies
(D) By buying her music

Q. 교수는 딸이 책을 읽으면 어떻게 상을 주는가?

(A) 추가 자유 시간을 줌으로써
(B) 책을 더 사줌으로써
(C) 그림 용품을 줌으로써
(D) 음악을 사줌으로써

어휘 reward v 보상하다 | encourage v 장려하다 | recent adj 최근의 | participate v 참여하다 | creative adj 창조적인, 독창적인 | positive adj 긍정적인 | determine v 결정하다 | improve v 향상시키다

Passage 3

Man: Professor

Listen to part of a lecture in a biology class.

M Today, I would like to turn our attention to the hydrological cycle, more commonly known as the water cycle, which is the way that water continually circulates on Earth. For the most part, this process is powered by the Sun and requires a great deal of energy. However, there are many entities other than the Sun involved in the process. Just as a way of summarizing the complexity involved here, it's important to note that plants, rivers, oceans, rocks, animals, and even soil particles contribute to water's ability to move about in the hydrological cycle. The primary process of this cycle, however, involves evaporation combined with precipitation. Basically, water tends to always go back to the ocean, which results in the presence of a very large body of water that then rises into the atmosphere through evaporation. The resulting water vapor loses heat as it rises into the air, forms clouds, and returns to the Earth in the form of rain and snow. This completes the cycle, and it is in this way that around 500,000 cubic kilometers of water a year move through the water cycle.

남자: 교수

생물학 강의의 일부를 들으시오.

남 오늘 저는 지구상에서 물이 계속해서 순환하는 방식인 수문 순환, 좀 더 흔히 물의 순환이라고 알려진 과정에 관심을 돌려보려 합니다. 대부분 이 과정은 태양열에 의해 이뤄지며 많은 양의 에너지를 필요로 합니다. 그러나 이 과정에는 태양 외에도 많은 것들이 관련되어 있습니다. 이와 관련된 복잡한 사항들을 요약하자면 한 가지 방법으로 식물, 강, 바다, 바위, 동물, 그리고 토양 입자까지도 수문 순환 내에서 물을 이동하는 데 도움을 준다는 사실에 주목할 필요가 있다는 것입니다. 하지만 이 순환에서 가장 중요한 과정에는 강수와 결합된 증발이 포함됩니다. 기본적으로 물은 항상 바다로 되돌아가려는 경향이 있는데, 그 결과 매우 거대한 수역이 존재하게 되고, 이는 증발을 통해 대기 중으로 올라가게 됩니다. 이 결과로 생긴 수증기는 공기 중으로 올라감에 따라 열을 잃게 되고, 구름을 형성한 다음 비와 눈의 형태로 다시 땅으로 돌아옵니다. 이로써 순환이 완성되고, 이런 방식으로 물의 순환을 통해 1년에 약 5십만 입방 킬로미터의 물이 이동합니다.

Q. According to the professor, what provides most of the energy needed in the water cycle?

(A) Wind
(B) The Sun
(C) Heat from the Earth's core
(D) Energy released when water evaporates

Q. 교수에 따르면, 물의 순환에 필요한 에너지의 대부분을 공급하는 것은 무엇인가?

(A) 바람
(B) 태양
(C) 지구의 중심핵에서 나오는 열
(D) 물이 증발할 때 방출되는 에너지

어휘 attention n 주의, 관심 | hydrological cycle 수문 순환, 물 순환 | commonly adv 흔히, 보통 | continually adv 계속, 지속적으로 | circulate v 순환하다 | require v 필요로 하다 | entity n 독립체 | summarize v 요약하다 | complexity n 복잡함 | soil particle 토양 입자 | contribute v 기여하다 | primary adj 주된 | evaporation n 증발 | combine v 결합하다, 합치다 | precipitation n 강수 | presence n 존재 | atmosphere n 대기 | vapor n 증기 | complete v 끝내다, 완성하다

Passage 4

Man: Professor

Listen to part of a lecture in an astronomy class.

M Actually, today I'm here to talk about the lunar and solar calendars. Most people think that we have only one calendar—the Gregorian solar calendar—but there are really many different calendars out there. For us, the most important one of these "other" calendars is the lunar calendar, which is a calendar based on the phases and movements of the moon. There have been many lunar calendars, but the typical lunar calendar starts each month with a new phase of the moon.

남자: 교수

천문학 강의의 일부를 들으시오.

남 사실, 오늘 저는 태음력과 태양력에 대해 이야기하려 합니다. 대부분의 사람들은 우리가 그레고리력이라는 단 하나의 역법을 가지고 있다고 생각하지만, 역법의 종류는 정말 많습니다. 이러한 '다른' 역법들 중 우리에게 가장 중요한 것은 달의 형상과 운행을 기초로 한 태음력입니다. 많은 태음력이 있었지만, 대표적인 태음력은 매달 삭월 단계에서 시작됩니다.

What this means is that a new lunar month starts whenever a new moon, the phase when the moon appears the darkest, occurs.
Okay, so why do we use the Gregorian solar calendar instead of the lunar calendar? Well, a lunar month averages about 29.5 days, and, uh, this is just too short in a way because 12 lunar months will never equal one Earth year. The opposite problem does exist with the Gregorian solar calendar, which is longer than it should be... but we're talking about 26 seconds a year here, and that doesn't really amount to much.

즉, 새로운 음력 달은 달이 가장 어둡게 보이는 단계인 삭월 때마다 시작된다는 것을 의미합니다.
자, 그렇다면 왜 우리는 태음력 대신 그레고리력을 사용할까요? 음, 태음력의 한 달은 평균 29.5일인데, 어, 이러한 방식으로는 12개의 음력 달이 하나의 지구 관측년과 같아지기에는 너무 짧습니다. 이와 반대의 문제가 그레고리력에도 존재하는데, 그레고리력은 지구 관측년보다 더 깁니다... 하지만 이 경우에는 1년에 약 26초가 더 긴 것뿐이고, 이것은 그리 긴 시간이 아니죠.

Q. When does a new lunar month start?
Ⓐ When the Moon reaches its fullest point
Ⓑ On the 15th of each month of the Gregorian solar calendar
Ⓒ When the Moon is in its new phase
Ⓓ Approximately half a day before the start of each solar month

Q. 새로운 음력 달은 언제 시작되는가?
Ⓐ 보름달이 나타날 때
Ⓑ 그레고리력의 매달 15일
Ⓒ 달이 삭월일 때
Ⓓ 매 양력 달이 시작되기 약 반나절 전

어휘 lunar calendar 태음력 I solar calendar 태양력 I Gregorian solar calendar 그레고리력 I phase n (주기적으로 형태가 변하는 달의) 상 I typical adj 대표적인, 일반적인 I occur v 발생하다 I average v 평균 ~이 되다 I opposite adj 반대의 I exist v 존재하다

Passage 5

Woman: Professor

Listen to part of a lecture in an art history class.

W Okay, class, today we're going to talk about some exciting painters and how they helped to change the way that people look at art. These painters are known as the Impressionists, and they formed a movement that tried to revolutionize the art of the 19th century. At the time, paintings tended to be quite solemn treatments of mythological or historical subjects. Artists would sometimes depict scenes of nature, but these were usually quite gloomy and sad. There was also a great deal of attention paid to detail and the hiding of brush strokes. The Impressionists, however, wanted to change all of this by showing the world the brighter side of things. They filled their works with light and pleasant images, while indulging in the use of some progressive techniques. These techniques included focusing on the overall visual effect of a work as opposed to trying to give it a refined or finished look. Some Impressionists held onto the belief that colors should be mixed on the canvas instead of the palette, but this was a belief that many artists disregarded. In general, however, Impressionist works do tend to appear, um, choppy and unclear.

여자: 교수

미술사 강의의 일부를 들으시오.

여 여러분, 오늘 우리는 흥미로운 화가 몇 명과 그들이 어떻게 사람들이 미술을 보는 방법을 변화시켰는가에 대해 이야기할 겁니다. 이 화가들은 인상파 화가로 알려져 있고, 19세기 미술에 혁신을 일으키고자 했던 (미술) 운동을 형성했습니다. 그 당시 그림은 신화적이거나 역사적인 주제를 매우 엄숙하게 다루려는 경향이 있었습니다. 미술가들은 간혹 자연의 경치를 묘사하기도 했지만 보통 아주 우울하고 어두웠습니다. 많은 세부적인 부분에 집중하고 붓놀림을 감추는 데 주의를 기울였죠. 하지만 인상파 화가들은 세상을 향해 사물의 좀 더 밝은 부분을 보여줌으로써 이런 모든 것들을 바꾸길 원했습니다. 그들은 다소 진보적인 기법을 마음껏 사용하며 자신들의 작품을 밝고 즐거운 이미지로 채웠죠. 이러한 기법들은 세련되거나 완성된 모습을 보여주려는 노력과는 반대로 작품의 전체적인 시각적 효과에 초점이 맞춰져 있었습니다. 몇몇 인상파 화가들은 팔레트 대신 캔버스 위에서 색을 섞어야 한다는 생각을 고수했지만, 많은 화가들이 이러한 생각을 무시했습니다. 하지만 대체로 인상파 화가들의 작품은, 음, 고르지 않고 불분명하게 보이는 경향이 있죠.

This may not sound attractive, and a lot of critics in the 19th century had very harsh things to say about Impressionism because it differed so much from the traditional style. In fact, Manet himself received an especially insulting letter of rejection from the Salon in Paris, and it sparked some heated conflict between artists. Today, however, there is not so much controversy surrounding the Impressionists, and most critics agree that works by artists like Cezanne, Degas, Renoir, Manet, and Monet are some of the most beautiful around.

이것은 매력적으로 들리지 않을 수도 있습니다. 또 19세기의 많은 평론가들은 인상주의에 대해 매우 신랄한 비평을 했습니다. 그 이유는 전통적인 형식과 너무 많이 달랐기 때문이죠. 실제로 마네는 파리의 미술 전람회에서 특히 모욕적인 거절의 편지를 받았고, 그 사건은 화가들 사이에서의 다소 격한 갈등에 불을 붙였습니다. 그러나 오늘날에는 인상파 화가들을 둘러싼 논쟁이 그리 많지 않고, 대부분의 평론가들은 세잔, 드가, 르누아르, 마네, 그리고 모네와 같은 화가들의 작품이 가장 아름다운 작품에 속한다는 것을 인정하고 있습니다.

Q. What is the key characteristic of Impressionism?

Ⓐ Refined brush strokes
Ⓑ Colors mixed on the canvas
Ⓒ Heavy use of dark colors
Ⓓ A rough quality focusing on overall look

Q. 인상주의의 중요한 특징은 무엇인가?

Ⓐ 세련된 붓놀림
Ⓑ 캔버스에서 섞인 색
Ⓒ 어두운 색의 잦은 사용
Ⓓ 전체적인 모습에 초점을 두는 거친 질감

어휘 Impressionist n 인상파 화가 I movement n 운동 I revolutionize v 혁신을 일으키다 I solemn adj 근엄한, 엄숙한 I treatment n 다룸, 처리 I mythological adj 신화의, 신화적으로 I historical adj 역사적인 I depict v 묘사하다 I gloomy adj 우울한 I detail n 세부 사항 I brush stroke 붓질 I brighter adj 더 밝은 I indulge v 마음껏 하다, 충족시키다 I progressive adj 진보적인, 핵심적인 I overall adj 전반적인 I refined adj 정제된, 세련된 I belief n 믿음 I disregard v 무시하다, 묵살하다 I choppy adj 고르지 못한 I attractive adj 매력적인, 끌리는 I critic n 비평가 I harsh adj 가혹한, 냉혹한 I differ v 다르다 I traditional adj 전통적인 I insulting adj 모욕적인 I rejection n 거부, 거절 I conflict n 갈등 I controversy n 논란 I surround v 둘러싸다

Lesson 02 Lectures

Passage 6

Man: Professor | Woman: Student

Listen to part of a discussion in a biology class.

M OK, let's get started. Today, I'd like to talk about winter dormancy and how it is commonly confused with true hibernation. Now, winter dormancy refers to a state of relative inactivity shown by certain animals such as the bear, which, you are probably surprised to learn, is not a true hibernator. Anyways, certain animals enter this state of dormancy during the colder months of the year, and most people think that it is the same thing as true hibernation. But, well, it's not.

True hibernation only takes place in a limited number of animals. Hibernating animals don't just sleep more—their respiratory and metabolic systems also slow down and their core body temperatures lower significantly. In addition to all of this, true hibernators often lose awareness and fail to respond to external stimuli while they are hibernating.

W But how is that different from, um, winter dormancy? Isn't what you just described exactly the same thing that bears do?

남자: 교수 | 여자: 학생

생물학 수업 중 토론의 일부를 들으시오.

남 좋아요, 시작합시다. 오늘은 겨울 휴면에 대해서, 그리고 어떤 점에서 휴면이 동면과 흔히 혼동이 되는지 이야기하려 합니다. 자, 겨울 휴면은 곰과 같은 특정 동물에게서 나타나는 상대적인 비활동 상태를 가리키는데, 곰이 진정한 동면 동물이 아니라는 사실을 알게 되면 여러분은 놀랄지도 모릅니다. 어쨌든, 특정 동물들은 한 해 중 추운 달 동안 이런 휴면 상태에 들어가게 되고, 대부분의 사람들은 이것을 동면과 같은 것이라 생각합니다. 하지만, 글쎄, 그건 아닙니다.

진정한 동면은 제한된 수의 동물에게만 일어나는 것입니다. 동면하는 동물은 단지 잠만 더 자는 것이 아닙니다. 그들의 호흡과 신진대사 체계 역시 느려지고 심부 체온이 상당히 낮아지게 됩니다. 이 뿐만 아니라 진정한 동면 동물은 동면하는 동안 종종 의식을 잃고 외부 자극에 반응하지 못합니다.

여 하지만 겨울 휴면과, 음, 어떻게 다르죠? 방금 설명하신 것은 곰의 행동과 정확히 똑같지 않나요?

M Well, not quite. Many people think that bears sleep straight through the winter regardless of what's going on around them, but this is a myth. **(D)** Dormant bears are actually relatively easy to awaken and don't become as disoriented and inactive as true hibernators do. **(A)** Also, bears don't experience the big drop in body temperature that is associated with true hibernation.

W So why are bears so famous for hibernating then? And, um, if they don't hibernate then what kinds of animals do?

M Well, I don't know that I have an answer to your first question, other than it's just a popular myth. As for your second question, there are many animals that are true hibernators, but they are mostly rodents. The arctic ground squirrel, for example, buries itself in a hole for the winter and drops its body temperature to below freezing temperatures. Many of its internal organs, such as its heart and lungs, slow down as well. All of these changes, in combination with the very limited amount of physical movement that it shows during the winter months, make the ground squirrel a good example of a true hibernator.

남 음, 완전히 같지는 않습니다. 많은 사람들이 곰이 주변 상황과 상관없이 겨울 내내 계속해서 잠을 잔다고 생각하지만, 이것은 근거 없는 믿음입니다. **(D)** 휴면 중인 곰은 실제로 깨기가 비교적 쉽고, 진짜 동면 동물들이 하는 것처럼 방향 감각을 잃고 움직이지 못하게 되지는 않습니다. **(A)** 또한 곰들은 진정한 동면과 연관된 급격한 체온 저하도 겪지 않습니다.

여 그러면 어째서 곰이 동면을 하는 것으로 알려져 있는 건가요? 그리고, 음, 곰이 동면을 하지 않는다면 어떤 동물들이 동면을 하나요?

남 글쎄, 학생의 첫 번째 질문에 대해서는 단지 대중적인 근거 없는 믿음이라고 밖에는 답을 해줄 수가 없을 것 같네요. 학생의 두 번째 질문에 대해서 말하자면, 진정한 동면을 취하는 동물들은 많이 있지만 대부분은 설치류입니다. 예를 들어, 북극의 얼룩다람쥐는 겨울 동안 자기 몸을 구멍에 묻어서 체온을 빙점 이하로 떨어뜨립니다. 심장과 폐 같은 많은 내부 기관의 움직임 역시 늦춰집니다. 겨울 동안 나타나는 매우 제한된 양의 신체적 움직임과 더불어 이러한 모든 변화를 보면, 얼룩다람쥐가 동면 동물의 좋은 예가 될 수 있겠네요.

Q. According to the discussion, which of the following are reasons that bears aren't true hibernators? Choose 2 answers.

Ⓐ Their body temperatures do not drop enough in the winter.
Ⓑ They don't show enough activity in the winter.
Ⓒ Their heart rates are too fast in the winter.
Ⓓ They are easily awoken in the winter.

Q. 토론에 따르면, 다음 중 곰이 진정한 동면 동물이 아닌 이유는 무엇인가? 두 개를 고르시오.

Ⓐ 체온이 겨울에 충분히 떨어지지 않는다.
Ⓑ 겨울에 충분한 활동을 보이지 않는다.
Ⓒ 심장 박동수가 겨울에 너무 빠르다.
Ⓓ 겨울에 쉽게 깨어난다.

어휘 dormancy n 휴면, 비활동 상태 | commonly adv 흔히 | hibernation n 동면 | relative adj 상대적인 | inactivity n 비활동, 휴지 | limited adj 제한된 | respiratory adj 호흡의 | metabolic system 신진대사 체계 | significantly adv 상당히, 많이 | awareness n 의식 | respond v 반응하다 | external adj 외부의 | stimulus n 자극 (pl. stimuli) | describe v 묘사하다 | exactly adv 정확히 | myth n 근거 없는 믿음 | disoriented adj 방향 감각을 잃은, 혼란에 빠진 | experience v 경험하다 | associated with ~와 관련된 | popular adj 대중적인 | rodent n 설치류 | arctic adj 북극의 | bury v 묻다 | internal adj 내부의 | organ n 장기 | in combination with ~와 결합하여, 짝지어

Passage 7

Woman: Professor

Listen to part of a lecture in a geology class.

W As you all know from your reading, mountains are formed through three primary processes: uplift caused by the collision of tectonic plates, the rapid erosion of some kinds of rock, and the eruption of volcanoes. The United States has examples of all three. Although some processes formed larger mountain ranges than others, plate collision, erosion, and volcanism are more or less equally responsible for most of the mountains in the U.S. The Appalachian Mountains, stretching from Newfoundland to Alabama, were created by tectonic collision. Ah, yes, geologists theorize that long ago

여자: 교수

지질학 강의의 일부를 들으시오.

여 여러분 모두 책을 읽어서 알고 있겠지만, 산맥은 지각판의 충돌에 의해 발생되는 융기, 특정 종류의 암석의 빠른 침식, 그리고 화산 분출이라는 세 가지 주요 과정을 통해 형성됩니다. 미국에는 이 세 가지 모두에 대한 예가 있습니다. 다른 과정에 비해 더 광대한 산맥을 형성한 과정도 있지만, 미국 내 대부분의 산맥들은 대체로 동일하게 판의 충돌, 침식 작용, 그리고 화산 활동이 그 발생 원인이 되고 있습니다. 뉴펀들랜드에서 앨라배마주까지 펼쳐져 있는 애팔래치아산맥은 지각판 충돌에 의해 형성되었습

the Earth's continents were actually one large land mass. **1(C)** Over a long period of time, massive layers of solid rock drifted over the molten rock beneath, eventually breaking up the continents into the positions we see today. **1(A), 3(B)** When these solid layers, or plates, collide, they crumple into waves of solid rock. This uplift results in mountain ranges. The Appalachian Mountains probably formed as the result of several plate collisions when the North American plate ran into the African and European plates about 680 million years ago.

2 OK, the second thing that causes the development of mountains is erosion. You know that different kinds of rock wear down at different speeds. **2, 3(A)** When softer rock erodes quickly, leaving harder rock standing, well, you have a mountain. The Ozark Mountains in Arkansas and Missouri were formed through this process. Instead of being pushed up by plate collision, existing rock masses actually eroded at different rates, and the mountains we see are simply the hard rocks left over after softer rocks just eroded away.

Now, the third main process of mountain formation is volcanism. **3(C)** Everyone here knows that a volcano is molten rock that either rises to the surface because it's less dense than the surrounding rock or is pushed up due to underground pressure. This molten rock sets on the surface, cools, and can remain as great towering masses way above sea level. Mount Rainier and Mount St. Helens were both formed by volcanic eruptions. In the case of Mount St. Helens, which hasn't even been around 40,000 years now, continuing volcanic activity in 1980 literally blasted the top of the mountain clean off, actually decreasing, instead of adding to, its size.

As these three examples show, the mountains of the United States are very diverse formations. They are made of different materials, and the date and cause of each one's initial formation differs greatly from those of the others. By recognizing this, we can learn a great deal about mountains in general and understand why they can be such an interesting subject for our studies.

니다. 아, 네, 지질학자들은 오래 전에 지구의 대륙들은 사실상 하나의 커다란 땅 덩어리였다는 이론을 세웠죠. **1(C)** 오랜 기간에 걸쳐 경암의 거대한 층이 지하의 용해된 암석 위로 서서히 이동했고, 결국 대륙을 우리가 오늘날 알고 있는 위치로 나뉘게 된 것입니다. **1(A), 3(B)** 이러한 고형층 또는 판이 충돌하면 이들은 경암으로 이루어진 물결 모양으로 구겨집니다. 이러한 융기의 결과로 산맥이 만들어집니다. 애팔래치아산맥은 아마도 약 6억8천만 년 전에 북아메리카판이 아프리카 및 유럽판과 충돌했을 때 몇 번의 판의 충돌의 결과로 형성되었을 겁니다.

2 좋아요. 산맥을 형성하는 두 번째 과정은 침식 작용입니다. 여러분은 종류가 다른 암석은 다른 속도로 침식된다는 사실을 알고 있을 겁니다. **2, 3(A)** 좀 더 무른 암석이 빠른 속도로 침식되고, 좀 더 단단한 암석은 그대로 있게 되면서 산이 만들어지는 것이죠. 아칸소주와 미주리주의 오자크산맥은 이러한 과정을 통해 형성되었습니다. 판 충돌에 의해 밀려 올라가는 대신, 기존의 암석 덩어리들이 실제 각각 다른 속도로 침식되었고, 우리가 지금 보고 있는 산맥들은 무른 암석이 침식된 후 남은 단단한 암석일 뿐인 겁니다.

자, 산맥 형성의 세 번째 주요 과정은 화산 활동입니다. **3(C)** 여러분 모두 화산이 주위의 암석에 비해 밀도가 낮아 표면 위로 올라오거나 지하의 압력 때문에 밀려 올라간 용해된 암석이라는 사실을 알고 있을 겁니다. 이렇게 용해된 암석이 지표 위에 자리를 잡고 식어서 해수면보다 훨씬 위로 거대하게 우뚝 솟은 덩어리로 남을 수 있게 되죠. 레이니어산과 세인트헬렌스산 모두 화산 폭발로 형성되었습니다. 현재 약 4만 년도 되지 않은 세인트헬렌스산의 경우, 1980년의 연속적인 화산 활동으로 산 정상이 말 그대로 폭발해 없어지는 바람에 크기가 커지기보다는 사실 줄어들었죠.

이 세 가지 예들이 보여주듯이 미국의 산맥은 매우 다양한 구성체입니다. 서로 다른 물질로 만들어졌고, 각각의 초기 형성 시기와 원인이 다른 산맥들과 매우 다르죠. 이러한 사실을 인식함으로써 우리는 산맥에 대해 전반적으로 많은 것을 배울 수 있고, 산맥이 연구하기 무척 흥미로운 주제가 될 수 있는 이유를 이해할 수 있을 겁니다.

1. What features below are true of tectonic plate movement? Choose 2 answers.

Ⓐ Collisions can create mountain formations by pushing land upwards.

Ⓑ Over many years, it has caused the decomposition of soft rock.

1. 다음 특징들 중 지각 운동으로 옳은 것은 무엇인가? 두 개를 고르시오.

Ⓐ 충돌은 땅을 위로 밀어 올려서 산의 형성을 야기할 수 있다.

Ⓑ 오랜 세월이 흐르면서 지각 운동은 연암이 분해되게 했다.

Ⓒ It helped separate the Earth's landmasses into continents.
Ⓓ The plates' lack of density caused molten rock to protrude through the Earth's surface.

Ⓒ 지구의 땅덩어리를 대륙들로 분리하는 데 일조했다.
Ⓓ 판의 낮은 밀도는 지구의 표면을 통해 용해된 암석이 돌출되게 했다.

2. Which mountain or group of mountains was formed by erosion?
Ⓐ The Appalachian Mountains
Ⓑ Mt. Rainier
Ⓒ The Ozark Mountains
Ⓓ Mt. St. Helens

2. 침식 작용으로 형성된 산 또는 산맥은 어떤 것인가?
Ⓐ 애팔래치아산맥
Ⓑ 레이니어산
Ⓒ 오자크산맥
Ⓓ 세인트헬렌스산

3. Which of the following was NOT mentioned as a process of mountain formation?
Ⓐ Hard rock remains standing after soft rock gradually wears away.
Ⓑ Crust plates run into each other and form waves of solid rock.
Ⓒ Molten rock is pushed to the Earth's surface due to density and pressure.
Ⓓ Ice sheets remove softer layers of rock leaving behind low, broad mountains.

3. 다음 중 산 형성 과정으로 언급되지 않은 것은 무엇인가?
Ⓐ 무른 암석이 서서히 닳아 없어진 후 단단한 암석은 그대로 남는다.
Ⓑ 지각판들이 서로 충돌하여 단단한 바위의 산맥을 형성한다.
Ⓒ 용해된 암석은 밀도와 압력 때문에 지구의 표면으로 밀려 올라간다.
Ⓓ 대륙 빙하가 암석의 부드러운 층을 제거해 낮고 넓은 산맥을 남긴다.

어휘 primary adj 주요한, 주된 | process n 과정 | uplift n 융기, 올리기 | collision n 충돌 | tectonic plate 지질 구조판, 지각판 | rapid adj 빠른 | erosion n 침식 | eruption n 분출 | volcano n 화산 | equally adv 동일하게 | responsible for ~의 원인이 되는 | stretch v 뻗다 | geologist n 지질학자 | theorize v 이론을 제시하다 | continent n 대륙 | massive adj 거대한 | drift v 표류하다, 떠가다 | molten adj 녹은 | eventually adv 결국 | crumple v 구겨지다, 쓰러지다 | mountain range 산맥 | result n 결과 | cause v 야기하다 | development n 발달, 개발 | erode v 침식되다, 풍화되다 | exist v 존재하다 | mass n 덩어리 | rate n 속도 | surface n 표면 | dense adj 밀도가 높은 | surrounding adj 인근의, 주위의 | underground adj 지하의 | pressure n 압박, 압력 | tower v 위로 높이 솟다 | sea level 해수면 | literally adv 말 그대로 | blast v 폭발하다 | decrease v 줄어들다 | diverse adj 다양한 | material n 재료, 물질 | initial adj 초기의 | differ v 다르다 | recognize v 알아보다, 인식하다

Passage 8

Man: Professor

Listen to part of a lecture in a sociology class.

M Good afternoon. I hope everyone did the assigned homework for today. 1 I had asked you all to read about Solomon Asch's experiments on conformity because they provide an interesting example for one of the three key aspects of our discussions on social influence, an unavoidable result of living in a social group together. First of all, social influence refers to the effect people have on one another's behavior. Because we have learned over time that we have a better chance of survival and prosperity if we live and work together, there is a fundamental human need to belong to social groups.
However, to live together, we must agree on certain common beliefs, values, attitudes, and behaviors to reduce conflicts between group members and promote the common

남자: 교수

사회학 강의의 일부를 들으시오.

남 안녕하세요. 여러분 모두가 오늘 과제를 해왔기를 바랍니다. 1 여러분 모두에게 순응에 관한 솔로몬 애쉬의 실험에 대해 읽어오라고 했었는데요, 왜냐하면 그 실험들은 사회 집단으로 함께 살아가면서 피할 수 없는 결과인 사회적 영향에 관한 우리 토론에 있어서 중요한 세 가지 관점들 중 하나에 대한 흥미로운 예를 제공하기 때문입니다. 우선, 사회적 영향은 사람들이 서로의 행동에 끼치는 영향을 말합니다. 우리는 함께 살아가고 함께 일을 하면 생존하고 번영할 가능성이 더 높다는 것을 세월이 흐름에 따라 배웠기 때문에, 인간은 근본적으로 사회 집단에 속해야 할 필요가 있습니다.
하지만 함께 살기 위해서는 집단 구성원 사이에 갈등을 줄이고 공익을 증진하기 위해 어떠한 공통된

good. For example, um, you are all familiar with the concept of peer pressure. 2 Peer pressure occurs within a group of individuals, whether they're classmates, work colleagues, team members, or whatever… when a majority in that group puts social pressure on other members to change their attitude or behavior in order to conform with the rest of the group. Participation in a social group requires members, in a more or less obvious way, to follow the same social norms say, a shared fashion style, or taste in music, or general outlook on life.

Peer pressure, therefore, is an example of conformity. Solomon Asch proved this idea. 3(C) He showed a group of people a card with a line on it and asked them to find a matching line from a group of three lines on another card, with the correct choice being obvious. However, all except one person in the group were assisting Dr. Asch and chose the wrong line. Eh-hum, so when it came to the one individual who didn't know this was an experiment to choose, 76% of the participants chose the wrong line! 3(A) The presence of just one supporter reduced this to 18%! I know this is hard to believe, as we like to think of ourselves as strong and independent thinkers. But, in truth, we are socialized to conform for the benefit of society as a whole.

신념, 가치, 태도, 그리고 행동에 동의해야 하죠. 예를 들자면, 여러분 모두는 동조 압력이라는 개념에 익숙할 겁니다. 2 동조 압력은 개인들이 모인 집단 안에서 발생하죠. 그들이 급우든, 직장 동료든, 팀 구성원이든 누구든지… 그 집단의 다수가 집단의 나머지를 동화시키기 위해 태도나 행동을 바꾸도록 다른 구성원들에게 사회적 압력을 가할 때 발생합니다. 사회 집단 참여는 구성원들에게 다소 뻔한 방법으로, 똑같은 사회 규범, 말하자면 공유되는 패션 스타일이나 음악적 취향, 또는 삶에 대한 일반적 견해 등을 따를 것을 요구하죠.

따라서 동조 압력은 순응의 한 예입니다. 솔로몬 애쉬는 이 생각을 증명했어요. 3(C) 그는 한 집단의 사람들에게 선 하나가 그려진 카드를 보여준 다음 다른 카드에 그려진 세 개의 선들 가운데 일치하는 선을 찾아보라고 했습니다. 올바른 답이 명확한 상황이었죠. 하지만 그 집단에서 한 사람만 제외하고 모두 애쉬 박사의 실험을 도와주는 사람이었고, 그들은 틀린 선을 선택했습니다. 흐음, 그리고 이것이 실험인 줄 모르는 한 사람에게 선택하라고 했을 때, 참가자의 76%가 틀린 선을 골랐습니다! 3(A) 하지만 한 명의 지지자가 있을 경우에는 틀린 선을 고른 비율이 18%로 떨어졌죠. 우리는 우리 자신을 강하고 독립적인 사고자라고 여기고 싶어하기 때문에 이 결과를 믿기 어려울 겁니다. 그러나 사실 우리는 사회 전체의 이익을 위해 순응하도록 사회화되는 것입니다.

1. What does the professor indicate about social influence?

Ⓐ Conforming to a group is detrimental to society.
Ⓑ It is an inevitable part of living in social groups.
Ⓒ Peer pressure can cause people to change their beliefs.
Ⓓ It can make people do things that they would not normally do.

2. What does the professor say about peer pressure?

Ⓐ It usually has negative effects on society.
Ⓑ It seems more influential in certain countries.
Ⓒ It occurs when the majority makes others conform.
Ⓓ It proves why the majority opinion is dominant in society.

3. What did Solomon Asch's experiment on conformity show? Choose 2 answers.

Ⓐ The rate of conformity was drastically reduced by a single supporter.
Ⓑ The cards could result in many different answers.

1. 교수는 사회적 영향에 관해 무엇이라고 하는가?

Ⓐ 집단에 순응하는 것은 사회에 해롭다.
Ⓑ 사회적 집단으로 사는 것의 필연적인 부분이다.
Ⓒ 동조 압력은 사람들이 신념을 바꾸도록 할 수 있다.
Ⓓ 사람들이 평소에는 하지 않을 일을 하게 만들 수 있다.

2. 교수는 동조 압력에 관해 무엇이라고 하는가?

Ⓐ 보통 사회에 부정적 영향을 끼친다.
Ⓑ 특정 국가에서 더 영향력이 있어 보인다.
Ⓒ 다수가 다른 이들을 순응하도록 만들 때 일어난다.
Ⓓ 사회에서 왜 다수의 의견이 지배적인지 증명한다.

3. 순응에 관한 솔로몬 애쉬의 실험은 무엇을 보여주었는가? 두 개를 고르시오.

Ⓐ 순응도는 한 명의 지지자에 의해 급격히 감소했다.
Ⓑ 카드는 여러 개의 다른 정답이 나올 수 있다.

Ⓒ Only one of the test participants didn't know what was going on.

Ⓓ About a third of subjects conformed to the majority.

Ⓒ 오직 한 명의 참가자만 무슨 일이 일어나는지 모르고 있었다.

Ⓓ 약 3분의 1의 실험자가 다수에 순응했다.

어휘 conformity n 순응, 따름 | aspect n 관점, 측면 | social influence 사회적 영향 | unavoidable adj 불가피한, 어쩔 수 없는, 부득이한 | refer to ~을 나타내다, ~와 관련 있다 | behavior n 행동, 품행, 태도 | prosperity n 번영, 번성 | fundamental adj 근본적인, 필수적인 | value n 가치, 중요성 | attitude n 태도, 사고방식 | conflict n 갈등, 충돌 | promote v 고취하다, 촉진하다 | common good 공익 | concept n 개념 | peer pressure 동조 압력(집단에서 받는 사회적 압박) | individual n 개인 | colleague n 동료 | majority n (특정 집단 내에서) 가장 많은 수, 다수 | conform v 순응하다, 따르다 | obvious adj 분명한, 명백한 | social norm 사회적 규범 | outlook n 견해, 관점, 세계관 | participant n 참가자 | presence n 존재, 참석 | socialize v 사회화시키다, (사람들과) 어울리다

Test

본서 | P. 155

Man: Student | Woman: Professor

[1-6] Listen to part of a discussion in an art history class.

W OK, let me ask you some questions first. In general, why do artists do what they do, and how are artworks typically sold?

M Artists get inspired, and then they paint what they want to. They use their art to express their thoughts and beliefs. They sell their paintings through their agents, art galleries, and even online.

W 1 Yes, but how long have things been that way? The art world was very different in the past. For a specific example, let's take a look at Florence during the High Renaissance. 2 Florence was arguably at the heart of artistic development at that time, but our concept of an artist would have seemed very foreign to the people then. Most artworks from that period were done on commission, and the buyer had a lot of creative control. Artists were more like tailors than innovators. The buyer had an active role in deciding nearly every aspect of a painting. He would decide the subject matter, how much the painting would cost, even what colors would be used.

M That does sound pretty different. I mean, artists still do commissions today, but that isn't the norm. How do we know all of this?

W Well, because they wrote it all down. 3, 6 Many of the contracts that artists and their customers wrote have survived along with the paintings. Those contracts are often very detailed, and they clearly show how business was done. They explicitly describe what was to be painted in the foreground and background and what colors of paint were to be used. Two words that often appear in these documents are gold and ultramarine. And that means real gold, not just gold-colored pigment.

남자: 학생 | 여자: 교수

미술사 수업 중 토론의 일부를 들으시오.

여 좋아요, 여러분에게 먼저 질문을 몇 개 할게요. 일반적으로 화가들은 왜 예술 활동을 하고, 작품들은 보통 어떻게 팔리나요?

남 화가들은 영감을 받고 그 뒤 자신이 원하는 것을 그려요. 자신의 생각과 신념을 표현하기 위해 자신의 예술을 이용하죠. 그림들은 중개인이나 화랑을 통해서, 그리고 심지어 온라인으로 판매하기도 합니다.

여 1 맞아요. 하지만 이런 방식이 자리잡은 지 얼마나 되었을까요? 예술계는 과거에는 매우 달랐습니다. 구체적인 예를 들자면, 전성기 르네상스 시대의 플로렌스를 봅시다. 2 플로렌스는 그 당시 분명 미술 발전의 심장부라고 할 수 있을 정도였지만, 그 때의 사람들에게 우리가 가진 화가의 개념은 매우 낯설었을 겁니다. 그 시기 대부분의 작품들은 의뢰를 받아 제작되었고 구매자가 창조적인 영역을 많이 통제했죠. 화가들은 혁신자가 아니라 재단사에 더 가까웠습니다. 구매자는 그림의 거의 모든 부분을 결정하는 데 있어 적극적인 역할을 했습니다. 그림의 주제, 그림의 비용이 얼마나 들지, 그리고 어떤 색들을 사용할지를 정했죠.

남 정말 다르게 들리네요. 제 말은, 오늘날에도 화가들이 의뢰를 받긴 하지만 그게 일반적인 일은 아니잖아요. 우리가 이 모든 사실을 어떻게 아는 거죠?

여 음, 그들이 모든 것을 기록해 두었기 때문이죠. 3, 6 화가들과 고객들이 쓴 계약서 다수가 그림들과 함께 남아있습니다. 이 계약서들은 종종 매우 세부적이었고 거래가 어떻게 이루어졌는지를 명확히 보여줘요. 그림의 전경과 배경에 무엇이 그려져야 하는지, 그리고 어떤 색의 물감이 사용되어야 하는지를 분명하게 서술하고 있습니다. 이 문서들에 자주 보이는 두 단어는 금색과 군청색이에요. 그리고 여기서 말하는 금색은 그저 금색의 안료를 말하는 것

However, ultramarine was even more expensive than gold. There were other blue pigments and dyes that they could have used, but ultramarine is an intense blue that does not fade over time. **4** Ultramarine is made from a stone called lapis lazuli, most of which was imported from Asia. The stone was ground into powder and mixed into paint.

4 Since it was so expensive, it was often used for the clothing worn by the central figure of the painting, particularly when that figure was the Virgin Mary. Ultramarine was also pretty new to Europe at the time, having first been imported in the 14th century. It remained extremely expensive until a synthetic version was created in 1826. The expense of using this paint was justified because commissions not only promoted the ruler that commissioned them, but also the prestige of his city. The commissioned works were often intended for display in churches, which explains why their subjects were mostly religious. **5** But this all began to change towards the end of the 15th century.

5 At the beginning of the Renaissance, people flaunted their wealth through expensive clothing, lavish parties, et cetera. But such open displays of wealth were later seen as boorish, and people stopped showing off in this way. This change can also be seen in the art that was produced. It didn't really affect the pigments that were used. Instead, people began to focus more on the quality of the paintings that were painted. Instead of using expensive pigments, the artistic ability of the painter became important. Gold was seen on fewer canvases and more on the frames. The artists were seen less as paid servants and more as geniuses whose creativity was valued as unique. These artists were master painters that had assistants working for them. Again, these changes can be traced through the contracts they made with their customers. These documents actually specified how many hours the artist would devote to the painting and how much of the work would be done by his assistants. **6** The prestige that these artists enjoyed placed them in a superior position to their patrons. The artists chose what to paint and what story to tell. The buyers just wanted to be able to say that they owned work by that artist. The position that artists hold today can be traced to this reversal in status.

이 아니라 진짜 금을 말하는 겁니다. 그러나 군청색은 금보다 훨씬 더 값이 비쌌어요. 그 당시 사용할 수 있는 다른 푸른색의 안료와 염료가 있었지만 군청색은 시간이 지나도 바래지 않는 강렬한 파란색이었죠. **4** 군청색은 라피스 라줄리라는 광석으로부터 만들어지는데, 이 광석의 대부분이 아시아에서 수입되었습니다. 가루로 곱게 갈린 뒤 물감에 섞는 것이죠.

4 너무나 값이 비쌌기에 그림의 중심 인물의 옷을 그리는 데 자주 사용되었는데, 특히 성모 마리아를 그릴 때 사용되었습니다. 또한 군청색은 14세기에 처음 수입되어 당시 유럽에서는 꽤나 새로운 것이었어요. 1826년 합성 안료가 만들어지기까지 계속해서 엄청난 고가를 유지했습니다. 이 안료를 사용하는 데 드는 비용은 정당화되었습니다. 주문 작품들이 그림을 주문한 통치자를 홍보하는 것은 물론 그의 도시의 명성을 높였기 때문이었죠. 주문된 작품들은 종종 교회에 전시하는 목적으로 만들어졌는데, 이것이 왜 그림들의 주제가 대부분 종교적이었는지를 설명해주죠. **5** 그러나 이 모든 것이 15세기 말에 가서 변하기 시작했습니다.

5 르네상스 초반에 사람들은 비싼 의복과 화려한 파티 등으로 자신의 부를 뽐냈습니다. 그러나 이렇게 노골적인 부의 과시는 후에 천박한 것으로 보여졌기 때문에 사람들은 이런 방식으로 자랑하는 것을 그만두었죠. 이러한 변화는 당시 만들어졌던 미술 작품들에서도 볼 수 있었습니다. 사용되는 안료에 그다지 영향을 주진 않았어요. 그 대신, 사람들은 그려지는 그림 자체의 품질에 더 초점을 맞추기 시작했습니다. 값비싼 안료를 사용하는 대신 화가의 예술적 능력이 더 중요해졌죠. 금은 캔버스에서 점점 사라지기 시작했고 액자에서 더 자주 보였습니다. 화가들은 돈을 받고 일하는 하인이 아닌, 독창성이 특별하다고 인정 받는 천재로 여겨지기 시작했습니다. 이 화가들은 그들을 위해 일하는 조수들을 둔 거장 화가들이었습니다. 다시 말하지만, 이러한 변화들은 이들이 고객과 주고 받은 계약서를 통해 추적할 수 있습니다. 이 문서들은 실제로 화가가 몇 시간을 그림에 쓸 것인지, 그리고 얼마만큼의 일을 조수들이 할 것인지에 대해 명시했습니다.

6 이 화가들이 누렸던 명망이 이들을 후원자들보다 더 높은 위치에 두었습니다. 화가들은 무엇을 그릴지, 그리고 무슨 이야기를 할지 결정했어요. 구매자들은 그저 그 특정 화가의 작품을 자신들이 소유하고 있다고 말하고 싶어했습니다. 오늘날의 화가들이 점하고 있는 위치는 이 지위의 전환에 의해 일어난 것이라고 볼 수 있습니다.

1. **What is the main idea of the discussion?**
   Ⓐ The significance of some valuable pigments and their use
   Ⓑ The transition of painting styles during the Renaissance
   Ⓒ The change that occurred in the way people view artists
   Ⓓ The shift in the relationship between patrons and artists

2. **According to the discussion, how was the concept of an artist in the past different from that of today?**
   Ⓐ Artists decided the painting styles and subject matter for all of their works.
   Ⓑ Patrons financially supported artists in order to receive high-quality paintings.
   Ⓒ Artists continuously tried to resist their patrons' control over their works.
   Ⓓ Artists often had less control over their artworks because of their patrons.

3. **What can be inferred from the artwork contracts that were discovered?**
   Ⓐ Gold and ultramarine were the most popular and widely used colors at that time.
   Ⓑ Patrons provided expensive art supplies such as gold pigments to their artists.
   Ⓒ There were strict guidelines that artists needed to follow when they painted.
   Ⓓ Ultramarine pigment was used more frequently in Europe than it was in Asia.

4. **Why does the professor mention the Virgin Mary?**
   Ⓐ To explain that ultramarine was used for the most important subject of the painting
   Ⓑ To suggest that she was the most popular painting subject of the Renaissance era
   Ⓒ To describe how nobles used her image to boast about their wealth and reputation
   Ⓓ To emphasize that she and ultramarine were inseparable in the eyes of the rich

5. **What changed the concept of an artist at the end of the 15th century?**
   Ⓐ The price of expensive art supplies was significantly reduced.
   Ⓑ People came to regard boasting of wealth as vulgar.

1. **토론의 주제는 무엇인가?**
   Ⓐ 몇몇 귀중한 안료들의 중요성과 사용
   Ⓑ 르네상스 시대의 화풍 변화
   Ⓒ 사람들이 화가를 보는 관점에 일어난 변화
   Ⓓ 후원자와 화가 사이의 관계 변화

2. **토론에 따르면, 과거 화가의 개념은 오늘날 화가의 개념과 어떻게 다른가?**
   Ⓐ 화가들은 자신들의 모든 작품의 화풍과 주제를 결정했다.
   Ⓑ 후원자들은 수준 높은 그림을 받기 위해 화가들을 경제적으로 지원했다.
   Ⓒ 화가들은 계속해서 그들의 작품에 대한 후원자들의 통제에 저항했다.
   Ⓓ 화가들은 후원자들 때문에 자신들의 작품에 더 적은 통제권을 가졌다.

3. **발견된 예술 작품 계약서로부터 무엇을 추론할 수 있는가?**
   Ⓐ 금색과 군청색은 그 당시 가장 인기 있고 널리 사용된 색이었다.
   Ⓑ 후원자들은 금 안료와 같은 값비싼 미술 재료들을 화가들에게 제공했다.
   Ⓒ 화가들이 그림을 그릴 때 따라야만 했던 엄격한 가이드라인이 있었다.
   Ⓓ 군청색 안료는 아시아에서보다 유럽에서 더 자주 쓰였다.

4. **교수는 왜 성모 마리아를 언급하는가?**
   Ⓐ 군청색이 그림의 가장 중요한 주제에 쓰였음을 설명하기 위해
   Ⓑ 성모 마리아가 르네상스 시대에 가장 인기 있는 그림 주제였음을 시사하기 위해
   Ⓒ 귀족들이 부와 명성을 자랑하기 위해 어떻게 그녀의 이미지를 이용했는지 묘사하기 위해
   Ⓓ 부자들의 눈에 성모 마리아와 군청색은 뗄 수 없는 관계였음을 강조하기 위해

5. **15세기 말에 화가의 개념을 바꾼 것은 무엇인가?**
   Ⓐ 값비싼 미술 용품의 가격이 확연히 낮아졌다.
   Ⓑ 사람들이 부의 자랑을 천박한 것으로 여기게 되었다.

Ⓒ The way of displaying wealth changed from fashion to art.
Ⓓ The number of talented artists had increased from the past.

Ⓒ 부를 드러내는 방식이 패션에서 예술로 변화했다.
Ⓓ 재능 있는 화가들의 수가 과거보다 증가했다.

6. What does the phrase "reversal in status" mean at the end of the discussion?
Ⓐ People focused more on the quality of a painting than the material that was used.
Ⓑ People began to view artists as being in a higher position than the patrons who bought their art.
Ⓒ People stopped revealing their wealth to others to show that they were humble.
Ⓓ People eagerly tried to find high-quality art due to the influence of the Renaissance.

6. 토론 마지막의 '지위의 전환'은 무엇을 의미하는가?
Ⓐ 사람들은 그림에 사용된 재료보다 그림의 품질에 더 집중했다.
Ⓑ 사람들은 화가들의 그림을 사는 후원자들보다 화가들을 더 높게 여기기 시작했다.
Ⓒ 사람들은 자신들이 겸손하다는 것을 보이기 위해 타인에게 부를 드러내는 것을 그만두었다.
Ⓓ 사람들은 르네상스의 영향으로 수준 높은 미술품을 찾으려고 열심히 노력했다.

어휘 artwork n 미술품 | typically adv 일반적으로 | inspire v 영감을 주다 | agent n 중개상 | gallery n 화랑, 미술관 | arguably adv 거의 틀림없이 | artistic adj 미술의, 예술의 | concept n 개념 | foreign adj 낯선 | commission n 주문, 의뢰 | tailor n 재단사 | innovator n 혁신자, 도입자 | aspect n 측면, 양상 | norm n 일반적인 것, 표준 | contract n 계약, 계약서 | explicitly adv 분명하게, 명쾌하게 | foreground n 전경 | background n 배경 | ultramarine n 군청색 | pigment n 안료, 색소 | dye n 염료 | intense adj 강렬한 | fade v 바래다, 희미해지다 | import v 수입하다 | grind v 갈다, 빻다 | powder n 가루 | central adj 중심의 | Virgin Mary 성모 마리아 | synthetic adj 합성한, 인조의 | justify v 정당화하다 | promote v 홍보하다, 고취하다 | prestige n 명성, 위신 | intend v 의도하다 | display n 전시, 진열 | subject n 주제 | religious adj 종교적인 | flaunt v 과시하다 | lavish adj 호화로운 | boorish adj 천박한 | canvas n 캔버스 | frame n 액자 | servant n 하인, 종 | creativity n 창조성, 독창성 | trace v 자취를 추적하다 | specify v 명시하다 | devote v 바치다, 쏟다 | superior adj 우수한, 우월한 | patron n 후원자 | reversal n 전환, 반전

Lesson 03 Function & Attitude

본서 | P. 158

Practice

Passage 1 A	Passage 2 C	Passage 3 A
Passage 4 C	Passage 5 A	Passage 6 A
Passage 7 B	Passage 8 C	Passage 9 C
Passage 10 A	Passage 11 C	Passage 12 D
Passage 13 A	Passage 14 D	
Passage 15 1. B 2. B 3. C	Passage 16 1. A 2. B 3. C	

Test

1. B 2. D 3. D 4. A 5. C 6. D

Practice

본서 | P. 163

Passage 1 Woman: Professor

Listen to part of a lecture in a genetics class.

W Today we will be looking at a new organism in the Eastern United States. Many are referring to this new organism as

여자: 교수

유전학 강의의 일부를 들으시오.

여 오늘 우리는 미국 동부의 새로운 생물체를 살펴볼 겁니다. 많은 사람들이 이 새로운 생물체를 '코이늑

a "coywolf" because they believe it is a hybrid between coyotes and wolves. But things are often not as simple as they seem. DNA tests have shown that the animals are a mixture of coyotes, wolves, and dogs. These organisms cannot be considered as a fully-formed species because the actual mixture of genes varies depending upon which tests are used and where the samples were taken. In the Northeast, the animals are 60-80 percent coyote, in the central area they are 85 percent dog, and in the Southeast they are over 90 percent coyote. So, no matter the region, the animals have less than 25 percent wolf DNA. It is a well-established fact that domesticated dogs and wolves can interbreed, as people have been making wolf-dog hybrids for decades, and they probably share a common ancestor. Apparently, all three species can interbreed in the wild, although they generally prefer not to, and researchers have been unable to find evidence that these organisms are still actively mating with dogs or wolves. Therefore, some experts have decided that these organisms should be regarded as an emerging species of coyote.

대'라고 부르는데 그 이유는 이 종이 코요테와 늑대의 이종 교배 동물이라고 믿기 때문입니다. 하지만 종종 보이는 것처럼 단순하지 않을 때가 있죠. DNA 테스트는 이 동물이 코요테, 늑대와 개의 이종 교배 동물이라는 것을 보여주었습니다. 어떤 시험이 사용되었고, 어디에서 샘플이 채취되었는지에 따라 유전자의 실제 혼합이 달라지기 때문에 이 종을 완전한 형태의 종이라고 여길 수는 없어요. 동북 지역에서는 60-80퍼센트 코요테이고, 중부에서는 85퍼센트 개, 동남부에서는 90퍼센트 넘게 코요테입니다. 그래서 지역에 관계없이 이 동물은 25퍼센트 이하의 늑대 DNA를 갖고 있어요. 가축화된 개와 늑대가 이종 교배될 수 있다는 것은 확고부동한 사실이며, 사람들은 수십 년이 넘게 늑대와 개의 이종 교배를 해 왔고 이 두 동물은 아마 같은 조상을 공유하고 있을 겁니다. 명백하게, 세 종 모두 일반적으로 그러길 선호하진 않겠지만 야생에서 이종 교배가 가능하며 연구원들은 이 생물체들이 여전히 활동적으로 개나 늑대와 짝짓기를 하고 있다는 것을 보여주는 증거를 찾을 수 없었습니다. 그래서 일부 전문가들은 이 생물체가 최근 나타나기 시작한 코요테의 한 종으로 여겨져야 한다고 결정했습니다.

Q. Listen again to part of the lecture. Then answer the question.

W Many are referring to this new organism as a "coywolf" because they believe it is a hybrid between coyotes and wolves. But things are often not as simple as they seem.

Why does the professor say this:

W But things are often not as simple as they seem.

(A) To imply that people's ideas about the animals may be incorrect
(B) To show that people are mistaking a dog breed for a hybrid
(C) To indicate that coywolf is an inaccurate name for the species
(D) To state that she does not think that it is a new organism at all

Q. 강의를 다시 듣고 질문에 답하시오.

여 많은 사람들이 이 새로운 생물체를 '코이늑대'라고 부르는데 그 이유는 이 종이 코요테와 늑대의 이종 교배 동물이라고 믿기 때문입니다. 하지만 종종 보이는 것처럼 단순하지 않을 때가 있죠.

교수는 왜 이렇게 말하는가:

여 하지만 종종 보이는 것처럼 단순하지 않을 때가 있죠.

(A) 동물에 관한 사람들의 생각이 틀릴 수도 있다는 것을 드러내려고
(B) 사람들이 개를 이종 교배를 위한 동물로 잘못 생각하고 있다는 것을 보여주려고
(C) 코이늑대가 이 종에게 맞지 않는 이름이라는 것을 나타내려고
(D) 이것이 새로운 생물체라고 전혀 생각하지 않는다는 점을 주장하려고

어휘 organism n 생물 I refer to ~라고 부르다, 가리키다 I coywolf 코이늑대 I coyote n 코요테 I wolf n 늑대 I mixture n 혼합물, 혼합체 I consider v 여기다, 고려하다 I gene n 유전자 I vary v 다르다, 달라지다 I domesticated adj 길들여진, 사육된 I interbreed v 이종 교배하다 I decade n 10년 I share v 공유하다 I common adj 공통의 I ancestor n 조상 I apparently adv 명백하게, 분명히 I generally adv 일반적으로 I evidence n 증거 I actively adv 활발하게, 활동적으로 I mate v 짝짓기를 하다 I emerging adj 최근 생겨난, 만들어진

Passage 2

Man: Professor

Listen to part of a lecture in a biology class.

M Today we will continue with our discussion on life in the ocean. People began to survey the ocean floor in the 19th century, but they found only a few microscopic organisms. Of course, their survey methods left much to be desired. Dredging the ocean floor and then raising an unsealed container back to the surface is far from efficient. But they felt that this confirmed their suspicions that the deep ocean was a barren desert almost entirely devoid of life. This belief persisted until the late 1970s when scientists were studying the seafloor near the Galapagos Islands. After plate tectonics theory achieved wide acceptance in the scientific community in the 1950s, geologists predicted that there would be deep-sea vents—places where cold seawater seeps into cracks on the ocean floor, is heated by magma, and rises back through the oceanic crust to create deep-sea hot springs. They weren't entirely sure what they would look like, but they were pretty certain that they must exist.
The survey team at the Galapagos Rift was using a remotely operated still-camera attached to an unmanned submersible to take photographs. They couldn't see the images it recorded until they brought it back up, but they could receive data from its sensors. They noticed a temperature spike in the freezing waters, but they disregarded it as an anomaly. Later that day, as they were reviewing the hundreds of images that the camera took, they were shocked by the ones that corresponded to the temperature spike. They showed a dense bed of clams and mussels in the otherwise empty volcanic plain. A few days later, three people squeezed into a submarine and went down 2,500 meters to the same location. The water was a balmy eight degrees Centigrade and it was filled with minerals that had precipitated out of the vents. They found the same shellfish as well as blind crabs and mouthless tubeworms. Since then some 300 species have been found around deep-sea vents, but their discovery prompted another mystery. With no access to sunlight, how could these animals survive? Where could they be getting their energy from?

Q. Listen again to part of the lecture. Then answer the question.

M People began to survey the ocean floor in the 19th century, but they found only a few microscopic organisms. Of course, their survey methods left much to be desired.

남자: 교수

생물학 강의의 일부를 들으시오.

남 오늘 우리는 바다에 사는 생명체에 관한 논의를 계속할 겁니다. 사람들은 19세기에 해저를 탐사하기 시작했지만 미세 생물체 몇 개만을 찾아냈을 뿐이었습니다. 물론 탐사 방법들에는 아쉬운 점이 많았습니다. 해저를 훑은 뒤 밀봉되지 않은 컨테이너를 표면으로 다시 끌어 올리는 것은 효율적인 것과 거리가 멀었죠. 하지만 사람들은 이것이 심해가 생명체가 거의 전혀 존재하지 않는 황량한 사막 같을 거라는 의심을 확인해준다고 생각했습니다. 이러한 믿음은 과학자들이 갈라파고스 제도 근처의 해저를 연구하던 1970년대 말까지 지속되었습니다. 1950년대에 판구조론이 과학계에서 널리 인정 받은 뒤 지질학자들은 차가운 해수가 해저에 있는 갈라진 틈으로 들어가 마그마에 의해 데워진 뒤 심해의 온천처럼 해양 지각을 통과해 다시 올라오는 심해 열수구가 있을 것이라고 예측했습니다. 어떻게 생겼을지 완전히 확신할 수는 없었지만 존재하는 건 분명하다고 확신했죠.
갈라파고스 단층에 있던 탐사팀은 사진을 찍기 위해 무인 잠수정에 부착된, 원격으로 작동되는 스틸 카메라를 사용하고 있었습니다. 다시 위로 카메라를 가져오기 전까지는 기록된 이미지를 볼 수 없었지만 센서에서 자료를 받을 수는 있었어요. 엄청나게 차가운 물 가운데서 기온이 급증한 것을 알아차렸지만 이례적인 현상이라 보고 무시했습니다. 그날 늦게, 카메라가 찍은 수백 장의 이미지를 검토하던 중 과학자들은 온도 급증에 부합하는 사진들을 보고 충격을 받았습니다. 그 사진들은 비어 있는 화산 평원에 조개와 홍합이 빽빽히 들어찬 지점을 보여주었습니다. 며칠 뒤 세 명의 사람들이 잠수함 안에 비집고 들어가 2,500미터 아래의 같은 지점으로 내려갔습니다. 수온은 따뜻한 섭씨 8도였고 열수구에서 나온 미네랄로 가득했습니다. 과학자들은 동일한 조개류는 물론 장님 게와 입이 없는 서관충도 발견했죠. 그 이후 약 300개 종들이 심해 열수구 근처에서 발견되었지만 이들의 발견은 또 다른 수수께끼를 불러왔습니다. 햇빛이 없는데 이 동물들은 어떻게 생존할 수 있는 걸까요? 이들은 에너지를 어디에서 얻는 것일까요?

Q. 강의의 일부를 다시 듣고 질문에 답하시오.

남 사람들은 19세기에 해저를 탐사하기 시작했지만 미세 생물체 몇 개만을 찾아냈을 뿐이었습니다. 물론 탐사 방법들에는 아쉬운 점이 많았습니다.

Lesson 03 Lectures

What does the professor imply by saying this:

M Of course, their survey methods left much to be desired.

(A) The expedition found the only organisms that existed.
(B) The surveyors were not well educated about marine biology.
(C) The techniques that the scientists were using were primitive.
(D) The scientists were using the best technology available to them.

교수는 다음과 같이 말하며 무엇을 의미하는가?

남 물론 탐사 방법들에는 아쉬운 점이 많았습니다.

(A) 탐사는 존재하던 유일한 생물체를 찾아냈다.
(B) 탐사자들은 해양 생물학에 관해 잘 배우지 못한 사람들이었다.
(C) 과학자들이 사용한 기법들은 원시적인 것이었다.
(D) 과학자들은 당시 가능했던 최고의 기술을 사용하고 있었다.

어휘 continue v 계속하다 | discussion n 토론, 논의 | survey v 조사하다, 살피다 | microscopic adj 미세한 | organism n 생물체 | dredge v 훑다, 건져 올리다 | unsealed adj 밀폐되지 않은 | container n 상자, 통 | surface n 표면 | efficient adj 효율적인 | confirm v 확인해 주다, 확정하다 | suspicion n 의혹, 의심 | barren adj 척박한, 황량한 | desert n 사막 | entirely adv 완전히 | devoid of ~이 없는 | belief n 믿음 | persist v 집요하게 계속하다 | seafloor n 해저 | plate tectonics 판 구조론 | achieve v 달성하다, 성취하다 | acceptance n 받아들임, 수락, 동의 | geologist n 지질학자 | predict v 예측하다 | deep-sea vent 심해 열수구 | crack n 갈라진 곳, 틈 | magma n 마그마 | crust n 지각, 딱딱한 층 | hot springs 온천 | exist v 존재하다 | remotely adv 원격으로, 멀리서 | attach v 부착하다 | unmanned adj 무인의 | submersible n 잠수정 | notice v 알아차리다 | spike n 급등, 급증 | disregard v 무시하다, 묵살하다 | anomaly n 변칙, 이례 | correspond v 일치하다, 부합하다 | dense adj 밀도가 높은 | clam n 조개 | mussel n 홍합 | volcanic plain 화산 평원 | squeeze into 비집고 들어가다 | submarine n 잠수함 | balmy adj 아늑한, 훈훈한 | precipitate v 촉발하다, 치닫게 하다 | shellfish n 조개류, 갑각류 | blind crab 장님 게 | mouthless adj 입이 없는 | tubeworm n 서관충 | discovery n 발견 | prompt v 촉발하다, 유도하다 | mystery n 미스터리, 수수께끼 | access n 접근, 이용 | survive v 생존하다

Passage 3

Man: Professor

Listen to part of a lecture in an environmentology class.

M Let us return to a topic that was brought up yesterday, that being PCB pollution. Researchers in Canada and Scandinavia are finding polar bears with reproductive system abnormalities and weakened immune systems. The problem has been traced to high levels of an entirely man-made substance, polychlorinated biphenyls, or PCBs. PCBs, made commercially available in liquid and more viscous forms, were used in heavy industry, in paints and plastics, and as nearly fire-proof insulators and coolants for electric hardware. In the U.S., their use was discontinued in the late 70s, but that's of little consolation since PCBs need decades to break down and become non-toxic. What's worse, the U.S. Environmental Protection Agency estimates that 150 million pounds of PCBs are circulating freely in the environment, and 290 million pounds are lying in unsealed dumps.
Then, how do PCBs find their way into polar bears in the arctic regions? No one's feeding them PCB sandwiches, but PCBs can travel by air, by ocean currents, and along the food chain. Although PCBs don't mix well with water, they are volatile. A little evaporation can lift them into the air, where they can be inhaled, or rained down to be inhaled later. And ocean currents can also bring them to the poles,

남자: 교수

환경학 강의의 일부를 들으시오.

남 어제 나왔던 주제인 PCB 오염으로 돌아갑시다. 캐나다와 스칸디나비아의 연구원들이 생식계 이상과 손상된 면역 체계를 갖고 있는 북극곰을 발견하고 있습니다. 문제의 원인은 전적으로 인간이 만들어 낸 물질인 폴리염화비페닐, 즉 PCB로부터 비롯된 것으로 밝혀졌습니다. 액체 또는 더 농후한 점성액 상태로 상업용으로 쓸 수 있게 만들어진 PCB는 중공업과 페인트 및 플라스틱에서 사용되었으며, 전자 제품의 불연성 단열제와 냉각제로 사용되었습니다. 미국에서는 70년대 후반에 PCB의 사용이 중지되었지만, 이 오염 물질이 전부 분해되어 무독성이 되기까지는 십여 년의 시간이 필요하므로 그다지 큰 위로가 되지는 않습니다. 설상가상으로 미국 환경 보호국은 1억 5천 파운드에 해당하는 PCB 물질이 우리 주변에서 막힘없이 순환하고 있고, 2억 9천 파운드의 PCB 물질이 밀폐되지 않은 공간에 그대로 버려지고 있다고 추정합니다.
그럼 PCB 물질은 북극 지역에서 어떻게 북극곰에게 전해지는 걸까요? 그 누구도 북극곰에게 PCB 샌드위치를 먹이거나 하진 않지만 PCB는 공기나 해류, 먹이 사슬을 통해서 전해질 수 있습니다. PCB 물질은 물에 잘 섞이지 않지만 휘발성입니다. 약간만 증발해도 이 오염 물질은 대기 중으로 올라

where they're ingested by animals and plants and passed up the food chain. In this situation, PCBs enter fish when they eat polluted plankton, seals eat the fish, and bears get even more PCBs because they eat the seals. Basically, since toxic concentration levels increase towards the top of the food chain, and polar bears are at the top of arctic food chain, they get the most poison.

Ahhh, so the results aren't pretty. Scientists in Norway discovered that seven of 200 female polar bears bore cubs with both female and male genitals. Such bears are called hermaphrodites. They are still able to reproduce, but this figure is certainly worrisome. Other studies have linked high PCB levels in bears to reproduction failures in males and weakened immune systems in both sexes. Does this have any bearing on our lives? Sure, we don't live around the poles, but we live much nearer the original sources of PCBs. Paints, plastics, railway ties, contaminated landfills, and telephone poles can continue to release PCBs for decades, slowly ruining human health, so slowly, the effects are being absorbed into the, quote and unquote, normal health problems of entire countries.

가 흡입되거나 나중에 비로 내려 흡입될 수 있어요. 그리고 해류 또한 PCB 물질을 극지방으로 옮기는데, 이때 동물과 식물이 이를 섭취하게 되고 먹이 사슬로 이동하게 됩니다. 이 상황에서 물고기가 오염된 플랑크톤을 섭취할 때 PCB가 물고기에게 들어가고, 물고기를 바다표범이 먹고, 곰은 바다표범을 먹기 때문에 훨씬 더 많은 PCB 물질을 지니게 되는 겁니다. 기본적으로 독성의 농축 수준은 먹이 사슬 꼭대기로 올라갈수록 높아지고, 북극곰은 북극의 먹이 사슬 맨 위에 있기 때문에 가장 많은 독성을 섭취하게 되는 거죠.

아아, 그래서 결과는 좋지 않아요. 노르웨이의 과학자들은 200마리의 암컷 북극곰들 중 7마리가 암컷과 수컷의 생식기 모두를 가진 아기 곰을 낳았다는 것을 발견했습니다. 이런 곰들은 자웅동체라고 불립니다. 이들은 여전히 번식할 수 있지만 이러한 수치는 확실히 걱정스러워요. 다른 연구는 곰들에게 있는 높은 PCB 수치를 수컷의 번식 실패 및 양쪽 성별 모두에서 나타나는 약화된 면역 시스템과 연관 지었습니다. 우리 삶에도 관련이 있을까요? 물론이죠, 우리는 극지방 근처에 살지는 않지만 PCB 물질의 원래 출처와 훨씬 더 가까이 살고 있습니다. 페인트, 플라스틱, 철도의 침목, 오염된 매립지와 전신주는 수십 년 동안 PCB 물질을 계속 방출하여 인간의 건강을 천천히 해치고 있습니다. 정말 천천히 진행되어서 PCB의 영향이 소위 '전 세계의 일반적인 건강 문제'로 잘못 치부될 정도로요.

Q. Listen again to part of the lecture. Then answer the question.

> M Other studies have linked high PCB levels in bears to reproduction failures in males and weakened immune systems in both sexes. Does this have any bearing on our lives?

Why does the professor say this:

> M Does this have any bearing on our lives?

Ⓐ To imply that humans may be ignoring a serious health threat

Ⓑ To express his skepticism that humans need to be concerned

Ⓒ To point out that only people who often eat seafood are affected

Ⓓ To indicate that only people living near the poles need to worry

Q. 강의의 일부를 다시 듣고 질문에 답하시오.

> 남 다른 연구는 곰들에게 있는 높은 PCB 수치를 수컷의 번식 실패 및 양쪽 성별 모두에서 나타나는 약화된 면역 시스템과 연관 지었습니다. 우리 삶에도 관련이 있을까요?

교수는 왜 이렇게 말하는가:

> 남 우리 삶에도 관련이 있을까요?

Ⓐ 인간이 심각한 건강 위협 요소를 무시하고 있을 수도 있다는 점을 암시하려고

Ⓑ 인간이 염려해야 한다는 점에 관해 의심을 표현하려고

Ⓒ 해산물을 자주 먹는 사람들만 영향을 받는다는 점을 언급하려고

Ⓓ 극지방 근처에 사는 사람들만 걱정해야 한다는 점을 가리키려고

어휘 PCB (polychlorinated biphenyl) n 폴리염화비페닐(비페닐의 염소화체로 불연성 및 전기절연성이 좋으나 쉽게 분해되지 않아 환경 오염 문제를 일으킴) | pollution n 오염 | polar bear 북극곰 | reproductive adj 생식의, 번식의 | abnormality n 이상, 기형 | weaken v 약하게 하다 | immune system 면역 체계 | trace v 추적하다, 추적해서 찾아내다 | entirely adv 완전히 | man-made adj 인간이 만든 | substance n 물질 | commercially adv 상업적으로 | viscous adj 끈적거리는, 점성이 있는 | heavy industry 중공업 | nearly adv 거의 | insulator n 단열재, 절연체 | coolant n 냉각제 | electric hardware 전기 하드웨어 | discontinue v 중단하다 | consolation n 위로 | decade n 10년 | non-toxic adj 무독성의 | estimate v 추정하다, 추산하다 | circulate v 순환하다 | unsealed adj 밀폐되지 않은 | dump n 폐기장 | arctic adj 극지방의 | ocean current 해류 | food chain 먹이 사슬 | volatile adj 휘발성의, 불안한 | evaporation n 증발 | inhale v 들이마시다 | ingest v 삼키다, 먹다 | plankton n 플랑크톤 | seal n 바다표범 | concentration n 농도 | discover v 발견하다 | cub n (곰, 사자, 여우 등의) 새끼 | genital n 생식기 | hermaphrodite n 자웅동체 | figure n 수치 | worrisome adj 걱정스러운, 우려되는 | link v 연관짓다 | failure n 실패 | railway tie (철도) 침목 | contaminated adj 오염된 | landfill n 쓰레기 매립지 | telephone pole 전신주 | release v 방출하다 | ruin v 망가뜨리다 | effect n 결과, 영향 | absorb v 흡수하다 | quote and unquote 따옴표 열고 닫고(무언가를 인용할 때 쓰는 표현)

Passage 4

Man: Professor | Woman: Student

Listen to part of a discussion in a nutritional science class.

M Good afternoon, class. Our topic today is the health food trend that is sweeping the world's markets. These days, organic food sales are growing by about 40% a year, a figure that asserts the significance of this trend. It all started with a focus on whole grains, dried beans, fresh fruit and vegetables, oils without trans-fat acids and other health-related foods. But, nowadays, it's no longer enough to buy fresh food, since such food can still contain a lot of chemicals. You have to do some research to find out what you are actually eating these days.

W Then, does the label "organic food" suggest that other foods are inorganic? It just seems like a cheap marketing move.

M Well, of course, all foods are organic to some extent, but organic means a food produced without artificial fertilizers and chemicals. People are scared of those things, so they are choosing organic foods. Are they doing the right thing? Harmful viruses and bacteria can be found on non-organic or organic food, but you can remove them by properly cooking meat and vegetables. But chemicals are another matter. Cows that eat corn and hay grown with chemical pesticides and herbicides will produce beef laced with chemicals, and unlike viruses, you can't kill chemicals with boiling water or a microwave. So, legislation has been passed to protect consumers. Still, I recently read that the National Organic Standards have been seriously weakened. Unfortunately, a few pesticides had already been permitted on organic farms, but now—and this is hard to accept—even more of them are receiving the green light. And to make matters worse, hormones and antibiotics have been legally administered to dairy cows for quite some time. So, it's becoming quite a disturbing trend that might make the "organic" label meaningless.

남자: 교수 | 여자: 학생

영양학 강의의 토론 일부를 들으시오.

남 안녕하세요, 여러분. 오늘 주제는 세계 시장을 휩쓸고 있는 건강 식품 트렌드입니다. 오늘날 유기농 식품의 판매는 일년에 약 40%씩 늘어나고 있고, 이 수치는 이러한 트렌드의 중요성을 확인시켜준다고 할 수 있습니다. 이것은 모두 정맥하지 않은 곡물, 말린 콩, 신선한 과일과 채소, 트랜스 지방산이 들어 있지 않은 기름과 다른 건강 관련 식품들에 대한 관심으로부터 시작되었습니다. 하지만 요즘에는 그런 식품들까지도 많은 화학 물질을 포함하고 있기 때문에 더 이상 신선한 식품을 사는 것만으로는 충분하지 않죠. 오늘날에는 여러분이 실제로 무엇을 먹고 있는지 알아보기 위해 조사를 좀 해야 할 겁니다.

여 그럼 '유기농 식품'이라는 라벨은 다른 식품들은 무기물이라고 말하는 건가요? 그건 그저 저열한 판촉 수단 같은데요.

남 음, 물론 모든 식품은 어느 정도는 유기물이지만, 유기농이란 의미는 인공 비료나 화학 물질 없이 생산된 식품을 말합니다. 사람들은 이것들을 무서워하기에 유기농 식품을 선택하죠. 올바른 행동을 하고 있는 것일까요? 해로운 바이러스나 세균은 유기농이 아닌 식품에서든 유기농 식품에서든 발견될 수 있지만 이들은 고기와 야채를 제대로 조리하여 제거할 수 있습니다. 하지만 화학 물질은 또 다른 문제예요. 화학 살충제와 제초제를 뿌려서 수확한 옥수수와 건초를 먹은 소는 화학 물질이 첨가된 소고기를 생산할 것이고 바이러스와 달리 그런 화학 물질은 끓는 물이나 전자레인지로도 죽일 수 없습니다. 그래서 소비자를 보호하기 위한 법안이 제정되었죠. 하지만 나는 최근에 국내 유기농 식품 기준이 심각하게 약화되었다는 내용을 읽었습니다. 안타까운 사실은, 이미 유기농 농장에 약간의 살충제 사용이 허용되고 있었는데, 이제는, 받아들이기 힘들지만, 그것보다 훨씬 더 많은 살충제가 허용되고 있습니다. 설상가상으로 꽤 오랫동안 젖소에게 호르몬과 항생제를 사용하는 것이 법적으로 허용되어 왔습니다. 그래서 이건 '유기농'이라는 라벨을 무의미하게 만들 수 있는 지극히 불안한 트렌드가 되어 가고 있어요.

Q. What is the professor's attitude about the organic food industry?

Ⓐ It protects its consumers.
Ⓑ It is full of corruption.
Ⓒ It is not very reliable.
Ⓓ It is not very profitable.

Q. 유기농 음식 산업에 관한 교수의 태도는 어떠한가?

Ⓐ 소비자를 보호한다.
Ⓑ 부정 부패로 가득하다.
Ⓒ 그다지 믿을만하지 않다.
Ⓓ 수익성이 별로 없다.

어휘 sweep v 휩쓸다 | figure n 수치, 액수 | assert v 주장하다 | significance n 중요성 | whole grain 통알곡 | trans-fat 트랜스 지방 | contain v 함유하다 | chemical n 화학 물질 | inorganic adj 무기물의 | to some extent 어느 정도는 | artificial adj 인공의 | fertilizer n 비료 | harmful adj 유해한 | remove v 제거하다 | pesticide n 살충제 | herbicide n 제초제 | laced with ~가 가미된 | legislation n 법률 제정, 입법 | consumer n 소비자 | recently adv 최근 | standard n 기준 | seriously adv 심각하게 | weaken v 약하게 하다 | permit v 허용하다 | accept v 받아들이다, 용인하다 | green light (사업 등에 대한) 허가, 승인 | antibiotic n 항생제 | legally adv 법적으로 | administer v 관리하다, 운영하다 | disturbing adj 불안함을 주는 | meaningless adj 의미가 없는

Passage 5

Woman: Professor

Listen to part of a lecture in a marketing class.

W This week, we are going to look at the market and its role in driving sales. Before we start talking about market-driven companies, though, I will briefly talk about product-driven companies. So, product-driven companies are those which look internally to determine how to boost sales. They may do this by, for example, determining what their customers think of the company's product. This means product-driven companies aren't as concerned with potential customers as they are with keeping their current customers happy.

The thing is, just because one customer wants your product doesn't mean everyone will. If you want your company to grow, you will need to do research. External research is what differentiates a product-driven company from a market-driven company. Market-driven companies pay very close attention to consumer spending habits and work on developing a relationship with new consumers. A market-driven company maintains its competitive edge by converting this market knowledge into innovative products and services.

Alright? So, let's say you are a market-driven company and you want to know what will get people to buy what you are selling. Basically, the answer is packaging and advertising—both are pretty important. Think about it... packaging is essential because, well, it is a part of our daily lives and we see it all around us. So, it must be eye-catching and appealing, or it won't sell. Advertising, like packaging, must get people's attention, right? Advertising must enable people to make positive associations with a product.

여자: 교수

마케팅 강의의 일부를 들으시오.

여 이번 주에는 시장과 판매 촉진에 있어 시장의 역할에 대해 살펴볼 겁니다. 하지만 시장 중심 회사들에 대한 이야기를 시작하기 전에, 상품 중심 회사에 관해 간단히 이야기하도록 하겠습니다. 상품 중심 회사는 판매를 촉진하는 방법을 결정하기 위해 내부로 시선을 돌리는 회사들입니다. 예를 들면 고객이 그 회사의 상품을 어떻게 생각하는지 판단함으로써 말이죠. 이는 상품 중심 회사가 현재의 고객을 행복하게 하는 만큼 잠재 고객에게 관심을 두지는 않는다는 의미입니다.

문제는 한 명의 고객이 회사의 상품을 원한다고 해서 모든 사람이 그러지는 않을 거라는 얘기죠. 만약 당신의 회사가 성장하기를 원한다면 조사를 해야만 합니다. 외부 조사가 바로 상품 중심 회사와 시장 중심 회사를 다르게 만드는 부분입니다. 시장 중심 회사들은 소비자의 소비 습관에 매우 깊은 관심을 기울이고 새로운 고객과 관계를 발전시키려고 하죠. 시장 중심 회사는 이 시장 지식을 혁신적인 상품과 서비스로 전환하여 경쟁적 우위를 유지합니다.

알겠죠? 자, 여러분이 시장 중심 회사이고, 무엇이 여러분이 판매하는 물건을 사람들로 하여금 구매하게 하는지 알고 싶어 한다고 합시다. 기본적으로, 답은 포장과 광고이고 둘 다 매우 중요하죠. 생각해 보세요... 포장은 우리 일상 생활의 일부이고 우리 주변 모든 곳에서 보기 때문에 필수적입니다. 그래서 포장은 시선을 끌고 마음을 움직일 수 있어야 하고, 안 그러면 팔리지 않을 겁니다. 포장과 마찬가지로 광고도 사람들의 관심을 끌어야 합니다, 그렇

Lesson 03 Lectures

This can be done by using celebrities, attractive models, beautiful beaches, or cute babies, you know, depending on the target market. Advertisers may also use more abstract concepts in their ads such as "speed," "freedom," or "longevity."

죠? 광고는 사람들이 상품에 관해 긍정적인 연상을 하도록 만들 수 있어야 합니다. 이는 목표 시장에 따라 유명인, 매력적인 모델과 아름다운 해변, 또는 귀여운 아기들을 이용해서 이루어질 수 있죠. 광고주들은 또한 광고에서 '속도', '자유', 또는 '지속성'과 같은 더 추상적인 개념을 사용할 수도 있습니다.

Q. What is the professor's attitude toward product-driven companies?

Ⓐ She feels that their focus is too limited.
Ⓑ She thinks that they should do more internal research.
Ⓒ She believes that they are more successful.
Ⓓ She advises against working for them.

Q. 상품 중심 회사에 관한 교수의 태도는 어떠한가?

Ⓐ 집중 분야가 너무 제한되었다고 본다.
Ⓑ 더 많은 내부 연구를 해야 한다고 생각한다.
Ⓒ 이 회사들이 더 성공적이라고 믿는다.
Ⓓ 이 회사들을 위해 일하는 것을 반대한다.

어휘 role n 역할 | drive v 추진하다, 만들다, 몰아가다 | sales n 판매 | briefly adv 간단히 | product n 제품 | internally adv 내부적으로 | determine v 결정하다 | boost v 신장시키다 | customer n 고객 | potential adj 잠재적인 | current adj 현재의 | grow v 성장하다 | external adj 외부의 | differentiate v 다르게 하다 | attention n 주의, 관심 | spending habit 소비 습관 | develop v 개발하다 | relationship n 관계 | maintain v 유지하다 | competitive adj 경쟁적인 | convert *A* into *B* A를 B로 바꾸다 | knowledge n 지식 | innovative adj 혁신적인 | packaging n 포장 | advertising n 광고 | eye-catching 시선을 잡아 끄는 | appealing adj 매력적인 | positive adj 긍정적인 | association n 연상, 연관 | celebrity n 유명인 | attractive adj 매력적인 | advertiser n 광고주 | abstract adj 추상적인 | concept n 개념 | longevity n 수명, 오래 지속됨

Passage 6

Woman: Professor

Listen to part of a lecture in a psychology class.

W Good afternoon. Today's focus is on an aspect of psychology that is less concerned with pathologies and psychological illness and more on, well, happiness! First of all, we will discuss some common misconceptions about happiness. Dr. Myers, one of the leading psychologists in the field of positive psychology, has studied thousands of people from various social classes in order to determine if, in fact, affluence affects happiness. He's concluded that excessive poverty does have negative effects on happiness. I mean, if you are so poor that you are struggling for your survival on a daily basis, then you may not experience much happiness. However, more moderate wealth does not produce greater happiness than a middle class income. So those with more money are not necessarily happier than those with less money.

So, what makes some people happier than others? First of all, self-esteem plays a pretty important role. It seems that people who like themselves, who don't want to be taller or thinner or whatever, are happier than people who do want to change. This makes sense, right? But look at me. My few extra pounds affect my blood pressure, so I need to lose weight. But how can I change if I like myself just as I am?

여자: 교수

심리학 강의의 일부를 들으시오.

여 안녕하세요. 오늘은 병리학과 심리학적 질병보다는 행복과 더 관련이 많은 심리학의 한 면에 초점을 두도록 하죠. 먼저, 행복에 관한 몇 가지 흔한 오해에 대해 논의해 보겠습니다. 긍정 심리학 분야의 유명한 심리학자 중 한 명인 마이어스 박사는 실제로 풍요가 행복에 영향을 끼치는지 판단하기 위해 다양한 사회 계층 출신의 사람을 수천 명 연구했습니다. 그는 극심한 가난이 행복에 부정적 영향을 줄 수 있다는 결론을 내렸습니다. 내 말은, 만약 여러분이 너무 가난해서 하루하루 생존을 위해 분투한다면 행복을 그다지 경험하지 못할 수도 있다는 거예요. 하지만 중산층의 수입보다 좀 더 부유한 것이 더 큰 행복을 주지는 않습니다. 그래서 돈을 더 많이 가진 사람이 돈을 더 적게 가진 사람보다 반드시 더 행복하지는 않아요.

그럼, 무엇이 일부 사람들을 다른 사람들보다 더 행복하게 만들까요? 먼저, 자존감이 꽤 중요한 역할을 합니다. 자기 자신을 좋아하는, 즉 키가 더 커지거나 더 날씬해지거나 하기를 바라지 않는 사람들은 변화를 원하는 사람들보다 행복합니다. 말이 되죠? 하지만 저를 보세요. 불필요한 몇 파운드의 살이 혈압에 영향을 미치고 있어서 저는 살을 뺄 필요가 있습니다. 하지만 제가 있는 그대로의 저 자신을 좋아하는데 어떻게 바뀔 수 있을까요?

Positive psychology encourages me to be happy with the way I am now, but my doctor is telling me to change. See the problem?

Now, sociability, like self-esteem, is also pretty important. Those who socialize a lot, go to church, marry, join clubs, and so on are happier than those who don't. So, loners tend not to be as happy as sociable people. According to the positive psychologists, one should always focus on positive things. That is not to say that we should disregard anything negative. In fact, these psychologists simply stress that it's important to think positively about these bad things. For example, if you find out that a family member is sick, be optimistic about their recovery rather than letting it affect your life in a negative way.

긍정 심리학은 지금 제 모습 그대로에 만족하라고 격려합니다. 그러나 저의 주치의는 변하라고 말하죠. 문제점이 보이나요?

자, 자존감과 마찬가지로 사교성 역시 꽤 중요합니다. 사회 활동을 많이 하고, 교회에 다니고, 결혼하고, 동아리에 참여하거나 하는 사람들은 그러지 않는 사람들보다 더 행복합니다. 그래서 고독한 사람들은 사교적인 사람들만큼 행복하지 못한 경향이 있습니다. 긍정 심리학자들에 따르면 사람들은 항상 긍정적인 것에 초점을 두어야만 합니다. 부정적인 것은 다 무시해야 한다고 말하는 것은 아니에요. 사실, 이 심리학자들은 나쁜 일들에 관해 긍정적으로 생각하는 것이 중요하다고 강조할 뿐입니다. 예를 들면, 만약 당신이 가족 중 누가 아픈 것을 알았다면 그 사실이 당신의 삶에 부정적인 영향을 끼치게 두기보다는 가족의 건강이 회복될 거라고 낙관적으로 생각하라는 거죠.

Q. Listen again to part of the lecture. Then answer the question.

W Positive psychology encourages me to be happy with the way I am now, but my doctor is telling me to change. See the problem?

Why does the professor say this:

W See the problem?

Ⓐ To point out a contradiction in approaches to happiness
Ⓑ To express her dissatisfaction with positive psychology
Ⓒ To illustrate the difficulty she has had with losing weight
Ⓓ To explain why money does not really make people happy

Q. 강의의 일부를 다시 듣고 질문에 답하시오.

여 긍정 심리학은 지금 제 모습 그대로에 만족하라고 격려합니다. 그러나 저의 주치의는 변하라고 말하죠. 문제점이 보이나요?

교수는 왜 이렇게 말하는가:

여 문제점이 보이나요?

Ⓐ 행복에 접근하는 방법들의 모순점을 지적하려고
Ⓑ 긍정 심리학에 대한 불만을 표현하려고
Ⓒ 몸무게 감량에 관해 겪은 어려움을 설명하려고
Ⓓ 왜 돈이 사람들을 행복하게 하지 못하는지 설명하려고

Lesson 03 Lectures

어휘 concerned with ~와 관련된 I pathology n 병리학 I psychological illness 심리학적 질병 I common adj 흔한 I misconception n 오해 I positive adj 긍정적인 I various adj 다양한 I determine v 결정하다 I affluence n 풍족, 부유함 I conclude v 결론을 내리다 I excessive adj 과도한, 지나친 I poverty n 가난 I negative adj 부정적인 I struggle v 분투하다, 힘겨워하다 I survival n 생존 I experience v 경험하다 I income n 수입 I not necessarily 반드시 ~은 아닌 I self-esteem n 자존감 I blood pressure 혈압 I lose weight 체중을 감량하다 I encourage v 장려하다, 격려하다 I sociability n 사교성 I socialize v 사람을 사귀다 I optimistic adj 낙관적인 I recovery n 회복

Passage 7 Man: Professor

Listen to part of a lecture in a biology class.

M Now we're going to look at food chains and the paradox connected to them. The paradox concerns the fragility of food chains and how important they are. So, let's start with the basics. Food chains describe the feeding relationships among species in an ecological community. This relationship can also be described as the movement of energy. This flow of energy goes from producers, or plant life, to herbivores, to carnivores, and to decomposers. Let's take a standard example. Elephants consume leaves and

남자: 교수

생물학 강의의 일부를 들으시오.

남 이제 먹이 사슬과 그 사슬에 관련된 모순점을 살펴볼 겁니다. 이 모순점은 먹이 사슬이 깨지기 쉽다는 점과 먹이 사슬이 얼마나 중요한지에 관한 겁니다. 그럼 기본부터 시작하죠. 먹이 사슬은 생태계에서 종들 사이의 먹이 관계를 말해줍니다. 이 관계는 또한 에너지의 이동으로 묘사될 수도 있어요. 이 에너지의 흐름은 생산자 또는 식물에서 초식동물, 육식동물, 그리고 분해자까지 이어지는 것이죠. 전형적인 예를 봅시다. 코끼리는 나뭇잎을 소비하고 나무

destroy trees, right? Consequently, the missing trees allow grasses to flourish, the grasses provide food for herds of herbivores, which in turn provide food for large predators.
So, although elephants usually have no direct relationship to lions, the food chain connects them quite closely. Got it? Without elephants, there's no grass, no grazing herds, therefore no lions. This is what makes elephants a 'keystone species'. Species like elephants are likened to the keystone in an arch—without that one stone, the arch collapses. That is a lot of pressure on elephants, eh? I mean, without them, the food chain breaks and a number of species will die. Pretty fragile, right?
Another example of fragility is Guillemots, who are very specialized consumers. They're beautiful birds living between Scotland and Scandinavia. They're almost entirely dependent on a sand eel diet. But the local sand eel populations have pretty much all died, or migrated north... uh, why north? Because cold-water plankton, the energy source of the sand eel, is moving north, to cooler waters. Yep, that's global warming again. So, without the sand eel, guillemots don't really stand a chance. You see how much more fragile food chains are because of specialization?

를 파괴합니다. 그렇죠? 결과적으로 사라진 나무들은 풀이 무성하게 자라게 하고, 그 풀은 초식동물에게 먹이를 공급하고 초식동물은 더 큰 육식동물에게 먹이를 공급합니다.
그래서 비록 코끼리가 사자와 직접적인 관계가 없다고 해도 먹이 사슬은 그들을 꽤 가깝게 연결합니다. 이해가 되나요? 코끼리가 없으면 풀도, 풀을 뜯는 동물 무리도 없고 따라서 사자도 없어요. 이것이 코끼리를 '핵심종'으로 만듭니다. 코끼리 같은 종은 아치의 쐐기돌과 같아서 그 한 돌이 없으면 아치가 무너집니다. 이건 코끼리에게 엄청난 부담이겠죠, 그렇죠? 내 말은 코끼리가 없다면 먹이 사슬은 깨지고 다수의 종이 죽을 겁니다. 상당히 연약하죠, 그렇죠?
연약함의 또 다른 예시는 매우 분화된 소비자들인 바다오리입니다. 이 동물들은 스코틀랜드와 스칸디나비아 사이에 사는 아름다운 새들이에요. 거의 전적으로 까나리만 먹고 살죠. 그러나 그 지역의 까나리는 거의 다 죽었거나 북쪽으로 이주했어요... 어, 왜 북쪽일까요? 까나리의 에너지 원천인 한류 플랑크톤이 북쪽의 더 차가운 물로 이동하고 있기 때문입니다. 네, 또 지구 온난화가 원인이죠. 그래서 까나리가 없다면 바다오리는 사실 생존 가망이 없는 겁니다. 자, 분화 때문에 먹이 사슬이 얼마나 더 깨지기 쉬운지 알겠죠?

Q. Listen again to part of the lecture. Then answer the question.

M But the local sand eel populations have pretty much all died, or migrated north... uh, why north? Because cold-water plankton, the energy source of the sand eel, is moving north, to cooler waters. Yep, that's global warming again.

Why does the professor say this:

M Yep, that's global warming again.

(A) To indicate that climate change threatens keystone species
(B) To imply that global warming should be a familiar explanation
(C) To show how tired he is of discussing that particular concept
(D) To state that he has already talked about it in the lecture

Q. 강의의 일부를 다시 듣고 질문에 답하시오.

남 그러나 그 지역의 까나리는 거의 다 죽었거나 북쪽으로 이주했어요... 어, 왜 북쪽일까요? 까나리의 에너지 원천인 한류 플랑크톤이 북쪽의 더 차가운 물로 이동하고 있기 때문입니다. 네, 또 지구 온난화가 원인이죠.

교수는 왜 이렇게 말하는가:

남 네, 또 지구 온난화가 원인이죠.

(A) 기후 변화가 핵심종들을 위협한다는 것을 가리키려고
(B) 지구 온난화가 익숙한 설명일 것임을 암시하려고
(C) 이 특정 개념을 논의하는 것이 얼마나 지겨운지 보이려고
(D) 강의에서 이것에 대해 이미 이야기했다고 말하려고

어휘 food chain 먹이 사슬 | paradox n 모순, 역설 | connect v 연결하다 | concern v ~와 관련되다 | fragility n 연약함, 부서지기 쉬움 | relationship n 관계 | ecological adj 생태계의 | producer n 생산자 | herbivore n 초식 동물 | carnivore n 육식 동물 | decomposer n 분해자 | standard adj 기준의 | consume v 소비하다 | destroy v 파괴하다 | consequently adv 결과적으로 | flourish v 번성하다, 잘 자라다 | predator n 포식자 | direct adj 직접적인 | graze v 풀을 뜯다 | herd n (동물 등의) 떼, 무리 | keystone species 핵심종 | collapse v 무너지다 | pressure n 압박 | specialized adj 전문화된 | entirely adv 완전히 | dependent adj 의존하는 | sand eel 까나리, 양미리 | population n 개체수 | migrate v 이주하다 | global warming 지구 온난화 | specialization n 분화, 특수화

Passage 8

Woman: Professor

Listen to part of a lecture in a geography class.

W Prior to the establishment of the prime meridian, navigation was a pretty chaotic affair. For a ship to navigate effectively, it needs to know where it is on the surface of the planet. This requires creating a grid pattern on maps. Since the Earth is more or less spherical, creating lines of latitude is fairly simple. The zero line, or equator, must go around the center of the planet from north to south. Determining where the lines that measure distance from east to west should begin wasn't so easy. Most countries that were maritime powers had chosen their own meridians, usually passing through a part of their own country. These meridians served their purpose, but if a vessel went into waters that its country had not charted, the crew had to rely on local maps which did not correspond to their own measurements.

The lack of agreement on such measurements also affected other areas. People agreed upon the lengths of seconds, minutes, and hours, but they didn't necessarily agree on what time it was at any given moment. This was a major hassle for the railroads that were constructed in the mid nineteenth century. Of course it could not be the same time at two locations that were far apart, but how much difference was there? The lines of longitude were also necessary to create time zones to regulate this. So, in 1884, a conference was held in Washington D.C. that was attended by 41 delegates from 25 nations. They ultimately decided to use the prime meridian of the British Empire, which was based at the Royal Observatory, Greenwich in London, England. It was established in 1851, and many countries had already decided to use it. So it was the obvious choice.

Q. Listen again to part of the lecture. Then answer the question.

W It was established in 1851, and many countries had already decided to use it. So it was the obvious choice.

What does the professor imply by saying this:

W So it was the obvious choice.

Ⓐ The decision had essentially been made before the meeting.
Ⓑ The British Empire was the most powerful nation so it won.
Ⓒ The Greenwich meridian was chosen because it was already popular.
Ⓓ The Royal Observatory was ideally situated, so it was selected.

여자: 교수

지리학 강의의 일부를 들으시오.

여 본초 자오선이 수립되기 전 항해는 상당히 혼란스러운 일이었습니다. 배가 효율적으로 항해하려면 자기가 지구 표면 어디에 있는지를 알아야 하죠. 이는 지도에 그리드 패턴을 만드는 일을 요구합니다. 지구는 다소 구 모양이어서 위도 선을 만드는 것은 상당히 간단합니다. 기준선 영점 즉, 적도는 북쪽에서 남쪽으로 지구의 중심을 지나야 했습니다. 동쪽에서 서쪽 사이의 거리를 측정하는 선들이 어디서 시작되어야 하는지 결정하는 것이 쉽지 않았죠. 제해권을 가졌던 대부분의 나라들은 자신들의 자오선을 선택했고 이 자오선들은 보통 자기들 나라 일부를 지났습니다. 이 자오선들은 도움이 되었지만 만약 배가 자국에서 지도로 만들지 않은 바다에 들어갈 경우 선원들은 자신들의 단위에 부합하지 않는 지역 지도에 의존해야 했죠.

이러한 측정에 관해 합의가 이루어지지 않았다는 점은 다른 영역에도 영향을 주었습니다. 사람들은 초와 분, 시간의 길이에는 동의했지만 어떤 순간에 몇 시여야 한다는 데는 딱히 동의하지 않았습니다. 이 점은 19세기 중반 건설된 철도에 있어 중요한 문제였습니다. 당연히 서로 멀리 떨어져 있는 두 지점이 같은 시간일 수는 없지만, 얼마만큼의 시차가 있는 걸까요? 이를 규제하기 위한 시간대를 만들기 위해서는 경도 선들 또한 필요했습니다. 그래서 1884년 한 회담이 워싱턴 D.C에서 열렸고 25개국에서 온 41명의 대표들이 참석했습니다. 이 사람들은 결국 영국 런던의 그리니치에 있는 왕립 천문대에 기반한 대영 제국의 본초 자오선을 사용하기로 결정했습니다. 이것은 1851년 수립되었고 많은 나라들이 이미 사용하기로 결정한 상태였죠. 그래서 명백한 선택지였습니다.

Q. 강의의 일부를 다시 듣고 질문에 답하시오.

여 이것은 1851년 수립되었고 많은 나라들이 이미 사용하기로 결정한 상태였죠. 그래서 명백한 선택지였습니다.

교수는 이렇게 말하며 무엇을 암시하는가?

여 그래서 명백한 선택지였습니다.

Ⓐ 결정은 사실상 회의 전에 이뤄졌다.
Ⓑ 대영 제국이 가장 강력한 나라였기에 이겼다.
Ⓒ 그리니치 자오선은 이미 널리 쓰이고 있었기에 선택되었다.
Ⓓ 왕립 천문대가 이상적인 곳에 있었기에 선택되었다.

어휘 prime meridian 본초 자오선 | navigation n 항해, 운항 | chaotic adj 혼란스러운, 혼돈 상태인 | affair n 일, 문제 | effectively adv 효과적으로 | surface n 표면 | require v 요구하다 | grid pattern 그리드 패턴 | spherical adj 구 모양의, 구체의 | latitude n 위도 | equator n 적도 | determine v 결정하다 | distance n 거리 | maritime power 제해권 | serve a purpose 도움이 되다 | vessel n 선박, 배 | chart v 지도를 만들다, 기록하다 | rely on ~에 의존하다 | correspond v 부합하다, 일치하다 | measurement n 측정 | agreement n 동의, 합의 | affect v 영향을 주다 | hassle n 귀찮은 상황 | railroad n 철도 | construct v 건설하다 | difference n 차이 | longitude n 경도 | regulate v 규제하다 | attend v 참석하다 | delegate n 대표 | ultimately adv 결국, 궁극적으로 | Royal Observatory 왕립 천문대 | establish v 설립하다, 세우다 | obvious adj 명백한

Passage 9

Man: Professor

Listen to part of a lecture in a biology class.

M Cells are the smallest independent metabolic units of life. All organisms are composed of these tiny building blocks of life capable of absorbing and using energy. Though they seem so vital to understanding the basic composition of all organisms, they weren't discovered until the Age of Enlightenment in the Netherlands. It was then that Antonie van Leeuwenhoek improved microscope lens technology and developed microscopes able to make things look 270 times larger.

Well, microscope technology has improved a lot since then, so you'd think we'd know everything by now. But that definitely isn't the case. So far, we've learned that cells contain chromosomes, which means they contain all the genetic information necessary for regulating their functions and for creating new cells. Cells are generally composed of 5 or more of a total of 12 distinct parts, with no type of cell having all 12. But all cells have plasma membranes and ribosomes. They reproduce and produce protein by means of the ribosomes. And cells can respond to changes in their surroundings and to internal changes. Well, we know all this and more, but it seems as though the more we learn the less we know. You see, as we discover the parts of one thing and learn how they function and interact we learn that those parts have still smaller parts, and those parts have even smaller parts. Every year we learn of new parts like porosomes, which are organelle parts that are invisible without electron microscopes.

남자: 교수

생물학 강의의 일부를 들으시오.

남 세포는 생명체에서 가장 작은 독립적인 신진대사 단위입니다. 모든 유기체는 에너지를 흡수하고 사용할 수 있는 이 생명의 작은 기초 단위들로 이루어져 있습니다. 세포는 모든 유기체의 기본 구성을 이해하는 데 필수적인 것으로 보이지만 계몽주의 시대가 되어서야 네덜란드에서 발견되었습니다. 그때 안톤 판 레이우엔훅이 현미경 렌즈 기술을 발달시켰고 270배로 확대해서 보여주는 현미경을 개발했죠.

자, 현미경 기술은 그 뒤로 많이 발전했으므로 여러분은 우리가 이제 모든 것을 안다고 생각할 겁니다. 하지만 결코 그렇지 않아요. 지금까지 우리는 세포가 염색체를 가지고 있다는 것을 배웠고 이는 세포가 기능을 조절하고 새로운 세포를 형성하는 데 필요한 모든 유전자 정보를 가지고 있다는 뜻입니다. 세포는 일반적으로 뚜렷하게 다른 12개 요소 중 5개 혹은 그 이상으로 구성되어 있고, 12개 전부를 가진 세포는 없습니다. 하지만 모든 세포는 혈장 세포막과 리보솜을 가지고 있어요. 이들은 리보솜의 도움으로 번식하고 단백질을 생산합니다. 그리고 세포는 주변 환경 변화와 내부 변화에 대응할 수 있습니다. 음, 우리는 이 모든 것과 그 이상을 알고 있지만 더 많이 알수록 더 적게 알게 되는 것 같습니다. 무언가의 일부분을 발견하고 그것들이 어떻게 기능하고 상호 작용하는지 알게 되면서 우리는 그 부분들이 여전히 더 작은 부분을 가지고 있고, 그 부분들이 훨씬 더 작은 부분을 갖고 있다는 것을 알게 됩니다. 전자 현미경 없이는 보이지 않는 세포 기관의 일부인 포로솜 같은 새로운 부분들을 매년 알게 되죠.

Q. What is the professor's opinion about Antonie van Leeuwenhoek?

Ⓐ He feels that he brought the Age of Enlightenment in the Netherlands.
Ⓑ He believes that he is given too much credit in the scientific community.
Ⓒ He thinks that his innovations were integral to the discovery of cells.
Ⓓ He regards him as the first scientist to ever view organic cells.

Q. 안톤 판 레이우엔훅에 관한 교수의 의견은 무엇인가?

Ⓐ 그가 네덜란드에 계몽주의 시대를 불러왔다고 본다.
Ⓑ 과학계에서 너무 과대평가되었다고 믿는다.
Ⓒ 그의 혁신이 세포의 발견에 필수적이었다고 생각한다.
Ⓓ 유기 세포를 본 최초의 과학자로 생각한다.

어휘 independent adj 독립적인 | metabolic adj 신진대사의 | organism n 생물 | composed of ~로 구성된 | absorb v 흡수하다 | vital adj 필수적인 | composition n 구성 | discover v 발견하다 | Age of Enlightenment 계몽주의 시대 | improve v 나아지다, 향상시키다 | microscope n 현미경 | definitely adv 분명히 | chromosome n 염색체 | genetic adj 유전적인 | function n 기능 | plasma membrane 혈장 세포막, 원형질 막 | ribosome n 리보솜 | respond v 대응하다, 반응하다 | surroundings n 주변 환경 | internal adj 내부의 | porosome n 포로솜, 세포 미세공 | organelle n 세포 기관 | invisible adj 보이지 않는, 투명한

Passage 10

Woman: Professor

Listen to part of a lecture in a psychology class.

W Inhibition—if you've forgotten what you read—is the ability to ignore or forget negative consequences and what we consider irrelevant information. I said "ignore or forget" because we're not certain that some animals have memories to forget. Consider houseflies. A housefly can bump into a window repeatedly, repeating this action without inhibition because its instincts are way too strong. If you try to kill it, it doesn't keep a greater distance from you because it doesn't remember you.

Well, then how about animals with more developed brains? They are a bit different. When a dog is abused once by someone, it won't soon forget it. But it may repeat the mistake of coming near that person when it needs that person. Say, hmm... when the person is feeding the dog. However, when a dog makes the mistake of crossing a busy street, and survives, it's sure to do it again because whenever there's no real negative consequence there's no sense of a mistake. Sure, there are some factors that can change this rule, since there are some things animals fear instinctively, like their natural enemies, with which they're not likely to make any mistakes.

With humans, the ability to both remember and inhibit memories is highly developed, and this ability has positive, but not permanent, consequences. For example, when you're trying to remember yesterday's readings about evolution, your brain intentionally inhibits memories of everything else you've experienced, allowing you to focus more effectively on evolution. This is clearly beneficial as you concentrate on what's most important at that moment. On the other hand, once practice stops, or the brain gets tired, there's a rebound effect in which inhibited memories return.

여자: 교수

심리학 강의의 일부를 들으시오.

여 만약 여러분이 읽은 내용을 잊어버렸다면, 억제는 부정적인 결과나 우리가 생각하기에 상관없는 정보를 무시하거나 잊어버리는 능력입니다. '무시하거나 잊어버린다'라고 말한 이유는 일부 동물이 잊어버릴 기억을 가지고 있다는 것조차 확실하지 않기 때문입니다. 집파리를 생각해 보세요. 집파리는 본능이 너무 강하기 때문에 계속 창문에 부딪치면서 억제 없이 이 행동을 되풀이합니다. 여러분이 죽이려고 하면 여러분을 기억하지 못하기 때문에 전보다 더 멀리 도망가지 않아요.

그럼, 더 발달된 뇌를 가진 동물들은 어떨까요? 이들은 약간 다릅니다. 개는 한번 누군가에게 학대를 당하면 쉽게 잊지 않습니다. 하지만 그 사람이 필요할 때는 가까이 가는 실수를 반복할 수도 있죠. 말하자면, 흠... 그 사람이 개한테 먹이를 준다든가 할 때요. 하지만 개가 붐비는 거리를 건너가는 실수를 했다가 살아남는다면 분명히 다시 할 겁니다. 왜냐하면 실제로 부정적인 결과가 초래되지 않으면 실수라고 생각하지 못하기 때문입니다. 물론 이 법칙을 바꿀 수 있는 요소가 있긴 합니다. 동물들이 본능적으로 두려워하여 그 어떤 실수도 하지 않을 천적 같은 것들이 있으니까요.

인간의 경우에는 기억하는 능력과 기억을 억제하는 두 가지 능력이 모두 매우 발달되어 있으며 이 능력은 영구적이지는 않지만 긍정적인 결과를 가져옵니다. 예를 들어, 여러분이 어제 읽은 진화에 대한 내용을 기억하려고 하면 여러분의 뇌는 진화에 관해 더욱 효율적으로 집중하도록 여러분이 경험한 다른 모든 기억을 의도적으로 억제합니다. 이는 여러분이 그 순간 가장 중요한 것에 집중할 때 분명히 도움이 됩니다. 반면 이러한 활동이 멈추거나 뇌가 피곤해지면 억제된 기억이 다시 돌아오는 반동 효과가 있습니다.

Q. Listen again to part of the lecture. Then answer the question.

W I said "ignore or forget" because we're not certain that some animals have memories to forget. Consider houseflies.

Why does the professor say this:

W Consider houseflies.

Q. 강의의 일부를 다시 듣고 질문에 답하시오.

여 '무시하거나 잊어버린다'라고 말한 이유는 일부 동물이 잊어버릴 기억을 가지고 있다는 것조차 확실하지 않기 때문입니다. 집파리를 생각해 보세요.

교수는 왜 이렇게 말하는가?

여 집파리를 생각해 보세요.

Lesson 03 Lectures

Ⓐ To introduce an example of a species with little mental capacity
Ⓑ To show how houseflies display a basic level of inhibition
Ⓒ To indicate that houseflies are well known for their inhibition
Ⓓ To state people underestimate the insect's cognitive abilities

Ⓐ 지능이 거의 없는 종의 예를 소개하려고
Ⓑ 집파리가 기본적인 수준의 억제를 어떻게 보여주는지 보이려고
Ⓒ 집파리가 억제로 잘 알려져 있다는 점을 지적하려고
Ⓓ 사람들이 이 곤충의 인지 능력을 저평가한다고 말하려고

어휘 inhibition n 억제 | negative adj 부정적인 | consequence n 결과 | consider v 여기다, 생각하다 | irrelevant adj 상관 없는, 불필요한 | memory n 기억 | housefly n 집파리 | instinct n 본능 | distance n 거리 | remember v 기억하다 | develop v 발달하다 | abuse v 학대하다 | repeat v 반복하다 | survive v 생존하다 | positive adj 긍정적인 | permanent adj 영구적인 | evolution n 진화 | intentionally adv 의도적으로 | inhibit v 억제하다, 저해하다 | experience v 경험하다 | effectively adv 효율적으로 | beneficial adj 이득이 되는 | concentrate v 집중하다 | rebound v 되돌아오다

Passage 11

Man: Student | Woman: Professor

Listen to part of a discussion in an astronomy class.

W Uh, okay, have any of you ever seen a shooting star? Have you ever wondered what a shooting star really is? A shooting star can be anything from an asteroid to a meteorite, and even a comet, which is today's topic. Not so long ago, many people actually believed that comets were bad omens—you know, signs that bad things were about to happen.

M Excuse me, professor. I know some historical accounts and works of art that link comets to terrible things like wars and plagues. So, is it possible that some comets cause, uh, bad luck?

W Well, there's little modern scientific proof of such links. And here's why: science tells us that comets are just small bodies in space. They are just chunks of ice and dust that sometimes approach the center of the solar system before disappearing back to the distant edges. They have a solid nucleus, a cloudy atmosphere, and a tail. It is in fact the tail of the comet that is the most easily noticed when it is seen with the naked eye from space. Did any of you see the tail of Halley's Comet in 1986? Halley's Comet is the most famous comet of our times.

M Professor, um, I think most of us were too young to have seen it.

W Right, good point. Then stay fit and healthy so that you can catch it the next time around. Halley's Comet will make another appearance in 2061. It comes quite close to the Earth on a regular basis—if you can call every 75 years 'regular'! Ahem... but more on that in a moment.
As I was saying, uh, every comet, including Halley's Comet, has a nucleus that is made of ice surrounding bits of rock and dust. When comets get close enough to the Sun, heat makes some of the ice start to evaporate, and then jets of

남자: 학생 | 여자: 교수

천문학 강의의 토론 일부를 들으시오.

여 어, 좋아요. 여러분 중 유성을 본 사람이 있나요? 여러분은 유성이 정말 무엇을 의미하는지 궁금하게 생각해 본 적 있나요? 유성은 소행성부터 운석, 심지어 오늘의 주제인 혜성에 이르기까지 그 어떤 것도 될 수가 있습니다. 그렇게 오래 전도 아닌 시기에, 많은 사람들은 혜성이 나쁜 징조라고 실제로 믿었어요. 말하자면, 나쁜 일이 곧 일어날 거라는 신호라고 믿었죠.

남 죄송한데요, 교수님. 저는 전쟁이나 전염병과 같은 끔찍한 일과 혜성을 연관 지은 몇 가지 역사적인 일이나 미술작품들을 알고 있는데요. 그럼, 혜성들이 불운을 야기할 가능성도 있는 건가요?

여 음, 그런 연관성에 대한 현대 과학적 증거는 거의 없습니다. 이유는 이렇죠. 과학은 혜성이 단지 우주의 작은 물체일 뿐이라고 말합니다. 그것들은 멀리 떨어진 외곽으로 다시 사라지기 전에 가끔씩 태양계의 중심에 접근하는 얼음과 먼지 덩어리들일 뿐입니다. 단단한 핵, 탁한 대기, 그리고 꼬리를 가지고 있죠. 실제로 혜성의 꼬리는 대기권 밖에서 육안으로 봤을 때 가장 쉽게 눈에 띕니다. 여러분 중 1986년에 핼리 혜성의 꼬리를 본 사람 있나요? 핼리 혜성은 이 시대에 가장 유명한 혜성입니다.

남 교수님, 음, 저희 대부분은 너무 어려서 보지 못했을 거라고 생각해요.

여 맞아요. 잘 지적했어요. 그렇다면 다음에 그 기회를 잡으려면 건강을 유지하세요. 핼리 혜성은 2061년에 다시 모습을 드러낼 거니까요. 그것은 규칙적으로 지구에 아주 가까이 옵니다. 만약 매 75년을 '규칙적'이라고 부를 수 있다면 말이죠! 에헴... 그 내용에 대해서는 잠시 뒤에 더 설명할게요.
말했듯이 핼리 혜성을 포함한 모든 혜성은 바위 조각과 먼지를 둘러싼 얼음으로 만들어진 핵을 가지

gas and dust particles are released from the ice. That's, uh, how we get those spectacular long tails on comets that we see from the Earth. Comet tails can sometimes be millions of kilometers long. Now, how do we classify comets? Well, we recognize two types: short-term and long-term. Short-term comets orbit the Sun rather quickly; they take less than 200 years to make that trip. Long-term comets, on the other hand, take longer than 200 years. Most scientists believe that short-term comets come from the area of space near Pluto. And, um, as far as we can tell, long term comets travel in from far beyond Pluto. Um, Halley's Comet is a short-term one, and it's special because it makes return trips! In 1986, a NASA spacecraft actually studied Halley's comet as it flew into the inner solar system and past the Earth.

M Is it true that comets crash into planets?

W Naturally. Comets that do crash into a planet's surface cause craters, such as those seen on Mars. Craters on our own moon were caused by such collisions, and although craters are hard to locate on a planet like ours, there's a growing body of evidence that the Earth is covered in them. And we'll probably get plenty more.

고 있습니다. 혜성이 태양에 충분히 가까이 다가가면 열이 얼음의 일부를 증발시키고, 가스 분출물과 먼지 입자가 얼음에서 떨어집니다. 그렇게 해서 우리가 지구에서 혜성의 멋진 긴 꼬리를 볼 수 있게 되는 거죠. 혜성의 꼬리는 때로 수백만 킬로미터의 길이가 되기도 합니다. 자, 혜성을 어떻게 분류할까요? 음, 단기와 장기 두 가지 유형으로 분류합니다. 단기 혜성은 태양 궤도를 다소 빠르게 돌아요. 태양 궤도를 도는 데 200년이 채 안 걸립니다. 반면 장기 혜성은 200년 이상 걸립니다. 대부분의 과학자들은 단기 혜성이 명왕성 근처 지역으로부터 온다고 믿습니다. 그리고 우리가 알기로 장기 혜성은 명왕성 너머 먼 곳에서 옵니다. 음, 핼리 혜성은 단기 혜성이며 왕복 여행을 하기 때문에 특별하죠! 1986년에 나사의 우주선이 핼리 혜성이 태양계 안쪽으로 날아들어서 지구를 지나갈 때 실제로 그것을 관측하고 연구했습니다.

남 혜성이 행성에 충돌한다는 것이 사실인가요?

여 맞아요. 행성의 표면에 충돌하는 혜성들은 화성에서 볼 수 있는 것과 같은 분화구를 만듭니다. 달에 있는 분화구들도 그런 충돌에 의해 생겼고, 비록 그런 분화구들을 우리 지구와 같은 행성에서 발견하기는 힘들지만 지구가 사실 그것들로 덮여 있으며 앞으로 더 많은 분화구가 생길 거라는 증거가 늘어나고 있어요.

Q. What is the professor's opinion about Halley's comet?

Ⓐ She feels that scientists spend too much time studying it.
Ⓑ She believes that the comet will not pass the Earth again.
Ⓒ She thinks that the comet is unique because it returns so often.
Ⓓ She does not understand why the students do not know about it.

Q. 핼리 혜성에 관한 교수의 의견은 무엇인가?

Ⓐ 과학자들이 이 혜성의 연구에 너무 많은 시간을 보낸다고 본다.
Ⓑ 혜성이 다시 지구를 지나가지 않을 것이라고 믿는다.
Ⓒ 자주 돌아오기 때문에 독특하다고 생각한다.
Ⓓ 왜 학생들이 이 혜성을 모르는지 이해하지 못한다.

어휘 shooting star 유성 | wonder v 궁금해 하다 | asteroid n 소행성 | meteorite n 운석 | comet n 혜성 | omen n 징조, 조짐 | historical adj 역사적인 | account n 설명, 기술 | terrible adj 끔찍한 | plague n 전염병 | approach v 접근하다 | disappear v 사라지다 | distant adj 먼 | nucleus n 핵, 세포핵 | atmosphere n 대기 | notice v 알아차리다 | naked eye 육안, 맨눈 | fit adj (몸이) 건강한, 탄탄한 | appearance n 출현, 나타남 | regular adj 규칙적인, 정기적인 | surround v 둘러싸다 | dust n 먼지 | evaporate v 증발하다 | jet n 분출 | particle n 입자 | release v 방출하다 | spectacular adj 장관을 이루는, 극적인 | classify v 분류하다, 구분하다 | recognize v 인정하다 | Pluto n 명왕성 | spacecraft n 우주선 | crash into 충돌하다 | naturally adv 물론, 당연히 | crater n 분화구 | collision n 충돌 | evidence n 증거

Passage 12 Man: Professor

Listen to part of a lecture in an art class.

M OK, let's get started. Today's lecture is on the American sculptor Gutzon Borglum's Mount Rushmore and its predecessors. As we've seen, with the arrival of civilizations, most notably Ancient Egypt and Babylon,

남자: 교수

미술 강의의 일부를 들으시오.

남 자, 시작합시다. 오늘 수업은 미국인 조각가인 거촌 보글럼이 러시모어산에 남긴 조각과 그 전에 존재했던 조각들에 관한 것입니다. 우리가 보았듯, 문명의 출현, 특히 고대 이집트와 바빌론 같은 문명의

came the development of colossal stone sculptures. These ranged anywhere from religious monuments to towering, 1,000-ton obelisks. However, the subjects of these works have generally been the political leaders of the day. Indeed, they functioned as tributes to the leaders directing these civilizations. Arguably, the most colossal and definitive sculpture of the ancient world is the Great Sphinx of Giza, which represents a lion with a man's face. Its meaning has been highly debated, but most Egyptologists agree that it records the likeness of King Khafre, the Fourth-dynasty pharaoh and builder of the Sphinx.

On the other side of the world in modern times, this tradition of paying tribute to political leaders was carried on here in the United States. Mount Rushmore depicts four prominent historical American leaders. It took 14 years to carve out of a granite-faced hillside in the Black Hills of South Dakota. Different from ancient colossal sculptures, which were made using hand tools of hammered and sharpened copper, Mount Rushmore was made using explosives and air-powered power tools. Surprisingly, even with this kind of power, it still took over six and a half years of actual working time to complete this monumental feat. This brings to light how big an undertaking a colossal sculpture is. I mean... just look at how amazing and industrious the Ancient Egyptians were with their original "elbow grease" techniques. Compared to their modern counterparts, they were no less effective, just slower and probably a lot more tired! I say this not trying to take anything away from the workers at Mount Rushmore. Indeed, as a testament to Borglum's methods, not one worker was ever killed in all of those years of explosions and extreme weather. Although not as immense as the task of forming this young nation, both the construction of Mount Rushmore and the final product serve as metaphors of U.S. history.

출현으로 거대한 바위 조각의 발전이 시작됐습니다. 이런 조각들은 종교적 기념물에서부터 우뚝 솟은 1,000톤의 방첨탑까지 이릅니다. 하지만 이 작품들의 주제는 대부분 그 시대의 정치적 지도자였어요. 실제로 그것들은 문명을 이끄는 지도자들에 대해 찬사를 표하는 기능을 했습니다. 주장하건대 아마 가장 거대하고 결정적인 고대 시대의 조각은 인간의 얼굴을 한 사자를 표현한 기자의 스핑크스입니다. 그 의미는 대단히 논쟁거리가 되었지만 이집트를 연구하는 대부분의 학자들은 4대 왕조의 파라오이자 스핑크스의 건설자인 카프레 왕과의 유사점을 기록하고 있다는 점에 동의합니다.

정치 지도자에게 감사 표시를 하는 이러한 전통은 현대에 와서 지구 반대편에 있는 미국으로 이어졌습니다. 러시모어산은 역사적으로 중요한 미국인 지도자 네 명을 묘사하죠. 사우스타코다주의 블랙힐스 산지에 있는 화강암 표면 언덕 비탈에 조각을 새기는 데에 14년이 걸렸습니다. 망치로 두들겨 펴고 날카롭게 만든 구리로 된 수공구를 사용해서 만든 고대의 거대한 조각과 달리, 러시모어산은 폭발물과 공압식 공구를 사용해서 만들어졌습니다. 놀랍게도 이런 힘으로도 이 기념비적인 공적을 완성하는 데는 실제로 6년 반이나 걸렸어요. 이는 거대한 조각을 새기는 일이 얼마나 큰 일인지 보여줍니다. 제 말은... 고대 이집트 사람들이 그들이 고안해낸 '힘든 노동' 기술을 얼마나 잘 해냈고 부지런했는지를 보세요. 현대의 조각가들과 비교하면 단지 더 느리고 아마 훨씬 더 피곤했겠지만 효율성 면에서는 오늘날과 뒤지지 않습니다! 러시모어산을 만든 일꾼들의 공을 깎아 내리려고 이런 말을 하는 것은 아닙니다. 실제로 보글럼의 방법에 관한 증언으로, 몇 해 동안의 폭발과 극심한 날씨에도 한 명의 일꾼도 죽지 않았다고 합니다. 이 신흥 국가를 만드는 일만큼 거대하지는 않지만, 러시모어산의 건설 공사와 그 최종 결과물은 둘 다 모두 미국 역사를 상징하는 역할을 하고 있습니다.

Q. What is the professor's attitude toward the creation of Mount Rushmore?

Ⓐ He thinks that the location of the monument was poorly chosen.
Ⓑ He believes that it is inferior to the sculptures of ancient Egypt.
Ⓒ He feels that they should have been able to finish more quickly.
Ⓓ He is impressed by how safe the workers were using such techniques.

Q. 러시모어산의 창조에 관한 교수의 태도는 어떠한가?

Ⓐ 기념물의 장소가 잘못 선택되었다고 본다.
Ⓑ 고대 이집트의 조각들보다 열등하다고 믿는다.
Ⓒ 더 빨리 끝낼 수 있었어야 한다고 느낀다.
Ⓓ 이러한 기술을 일꾼들이 안전하게 사용해서 깊은 인상을 받았다.

어휘 sculptor n 조각가 | predecessor n 이전 것, 전임자 | arrival n 도래, 도착 | civilization n 문명 | notably adv 특히, 뚜렷이 | development n 발달, 개발 | colossal adj 거대한, 엄청난 | sculpture n 조각품, 조각 | religious adj 종교의 | obelisk n 오벨리스크, 방첨탑 | generally adv 일반적으로 | political adj 정치적인 | function v 기능하다 | tribute n 헌사, 찬사 | arguably adv 주장하건대, 거의 틀림없이 | definitive adj 결정적인 | debate v 논쟁하다 | tradition n 전통 | depict v 묘사하다 | prominent adj 중요한, 유명한 | historical adj 역사적인 | carve out 새기다 | granite n 화강암 | hammer v (망치로) 두드려 펴다 | sharpen v 날카롭게 만들다 | copper n 구리 | explosive n 폭발물 | complete v 완성하다 | monumental adj 기념비적인 | feat n 업적 | undertaking n 일, 프로젝트 | industrious adj 근면한, 부지런한 | elbow grease 힘든 노동 | compare v 비교하다 | counterpart n 상대, 대응 관계에 있는 것 | testament n 증거 | explosion n 폭발 | extreme adj 극단적인 | immense adj 거대한 | construction n 건설 | metaphor n 은유, 비유, 상징(하는 것)

Passage 13

Woman: Professor

Listen to part of a lecture in a health science class.

W Good morning, everyone. I hope you had a good night's sleep, and if you didn't... well, perhaps today's topic will be especially interesting to you, as it might be to the 60 million who sometimes suffer from "it". Well, today's topic is insomnia. Maybe you think you know an insomniac, but to qualify as a true insomniac isn't easy. During my own university days, my roommate used to study quite late, then later and later until she gave up on sleeping. She just lay in bed, awake, for a couple of hours before showering and starting again. Now that's an example of a true insomniac. Fortunately, most insomniacs just suffer from transient insomnia, not long-term or chronic insomnia. But whatever kind of insomnia you suffer from, it just means you can't sleep—some people just can't fall asleep and others can't stay asleep—usually it's both.

Most insomnia cases are transient or acute insomnia, both of which are very short-term insomnia. It's caused by temporary problems, for example, jet-lag, which belongs to the "circadian rhythm sleep disorders" category. Shift workers, obviously night-shift workers, tend to have the same problem. Because they've broken their regular 24-hour sleep schedule, or must sleep when the sun is up, they start to suffer from insomnia. Transient insomnia can also have bio-chemical causes. Certain kinds of prescriptions or overindulgence in late-night coffee or alcohol... the results can be eye-opening, right? And, digestive system disorders, asthma, any kind of chronic pain like arthritis, or even a broken heart—any source of stress can cause insomnia.

Chronic insomnia is long term and less common. This often has the same causes as transient insomnia. Students like to complain about my surprise-quiz policy, but this policy prevents late-night cramming, which isn't good for you.

여자: 교수

보건학 강의의 일부를 들으시오.

여 안녕하세요, 여러분. 여러분이 지난밤 잘 잤기를 바랍니다. 만약 그러지 못했다면... 음, 아마도 오늘의 주제는 여러분에게 특히 더 흥미로울 겁니다. 가끔씩 '이것' 때문에 고통 받는 6천만 명의 사람들에게도 그러하듯이 말이죠. 음, 오늘의 주제는 불면증입니다. 아마도 여러분은 불면증 환자를 알고 있다고 생각하겠지만, 진정한 불면증 환자로 간주되는 것은 쉽지 않습니다. 대학 시절에 제 룸메이트는 꽤 늦게까지 공부하곤 했는데, 점점 더 늦어지고 늦어져서 마침내 잠자는 것을 포기하는 데까지 이르렀죠. 두어 시간 동안 침대에 그냥 깬 채로 누워 있다가 샤워를 하고 다시 공부를 시작하곤 했습니다. 자, 이것이 진정한 불면증 환자의 예입니다. 다행히도, 대부분의 불면증 환자들은 장기나 만성의 불면증이 아닌 일시적인 불면증으로 고통받습니다. 그러나 여러분이 겪는 것이 어떤 종류의 불면증이든 간에, 그것은 여러분이 잠을 잘 수 없다는 것을 의미합니다. 어떤 사람들은 아예 잠들지를 못하고, 어떤 사람들은 수면 상태를 유지할 수 없죠. 대개는 둘 다고요.

대부분의 불면증은 일시적 또는 급성 불면증, 즉, 아주 단기간의 불면증입니다. 둘 다 일시적인 문제, 예를 들면 '24시간 주기 수면 리듬 장애'의 범주에 속하는, 시차로 인한 피로와 같은 것에 의해서 야기됩니다. 교대 근무자들, 명확히 말하자면 밤 교대 근무자들이 이와 같은 문제점을 가지고 있는 경향이 있어요. 왜냐하면 그들은 규칙적인 24시간 수면 스케줄이 깨졌거나 해가 떠 있을 때 잠을 자야 하기 때문에 불면증을 겪기 시작하죠. 일시 불면증은 또한 생화학적 원인 때문일 수도 있습니다. 특정 종류의 약 처방이나 늦은 밤의 커피나 술 탐닉... 그 결과는 눈이 번쩍 뜨일 수 있어요, 그렇죠? 그리고 소화계 장애, 천식, 관절염과 같은 만성 통증, 그리고 심지어 실연까지, 어떠한 원인의 스트레스도 불면증을 야기할 수 있습니다.

만성 불면증은 장기적이고 흔하지 않습니다. 이것은 흔히 일시적인 불면증과 원인이 같아요. 학생들은 제 예고 없는 쪽지시험에 대해서 불평하곤 하지만, 이런 방침은 늦은 밤의 벼락치기를 막아주죠.

If you're not careful, or just unlucky, a long-term pattern can develop. Add a little depression and you could be a full-fledged, tossing and turning insomniac. What are some popular remedies for insomnia? Well, my father suffered from insomnia since his early twenties and my grandmother painted his room blue like a calm sea and used to have him sniff lavender before going to bed. Sounds funny, right? But herbal remedies used to be very common. Sleeping pills are over-prescribed and lots of people are taking them because they want that extra hour or two of sleep. Generally speaking, I'm a big fan of non-medicinal intervention, and insomnia is particularly suited to non-medicinal solutions. This means living a healthy lifestyle, keeping a regular bedtime, and having a calming sleeping environment. The bed should be a kind of sacred place free of distractions like books, televisions, radios, telephones, and laptops, and—did I forget something? Get some exercise during the day, keep the room cool, and if you're kept up by loud neighbors, buy a white noise machine or just run a fan next to your bed.

밤샘 벼락치기는 여러분에게 좋지 않아요. 주의하지 않는다면, 또는 단지 운이 없어도 장기적인 불면증으로 발전할 수 있습니다. 약간의 우울함이 보태진다면 완전히 발전된, 잠 못 이루고 뒤척이는 불면증 환자가 될 수 있어요. 불면증에 대한 가장 인기 있는 치료법은 뭘까요? 음, 제 아버지는 20대 초반부터 불면증으로 고생하셨죠. 그래서 우리 할머니는 아버지의 방을 고요한 바다처럼 파란색으로 칠하셨고 잠자리에 들기 전에 라벤더 향을 맡도록 하곤 하셨어요. 우습게 들리죠? 하지만 허브 치료법은 매우 흔하게 쓰이곤 했습니다. 수면제는 과처방되고 있으며 많은 사람들이 한두 시간 더 자기 위해 수면제를 복용하죠. 대체로 저는 약을 먹지 않는 방법에 전적으로 찬성하는 사람입니다. 그리고 불면증은 특히 약을 복용하지 않는 해결책이 적합합니다. 즉, 건강한 생활 습관, 규칙적인 취침 시간 그리고 조용한 수면 환경을 지키며 생활하는 것입니다. 침대는 책, 텔레비전, 라디오, 전화기, 그리고 노트북 같이 주의를 산만하게 하는 것이 없는 신성한 장소여야 해요. 음, 빠뜨린 게 있나요? 낮에 운동을 하고, 방을 시원하게 유지하세요. 그리고 만약 시끄러운 이웃 때문에 밤잠을 못 잔다면, 백색 소음 기계를 구입하거나 침대 옆에 선풍기를 틀어놓으세요.

Q. Listen again to part of the lecture. Then answer the question.

> W Transient insomnia can also have bio-chemical causes. Certain kinds of prescriptions or overindulgence in late-night coffee or alcohol... the results can be eye-opening, right?

Why does the professor say this:

> W the results can be eye-opening, right?

Ⓐ To illustrate the effects of certain drugs in an amusing way
Ⓑ To show how surprising the effects of some chemicals are
Ⓒ To indicate how some chemical causes operate in the body
Ⓓ To state that many people are unaware of the causes of insomnia

Q. 강의의 일부를 다시 듣고 질문에 답하시오.

> 여 일시 불면증은 또한 생화학적 원인 때문일 수도 있어요. 특정 종류의 약 처방이나 늦은 밤의 커피나 술 탐닉… 그 결과는 눈이 번쩍 뜨일 수 있어요, 그렇죠?

교수는 왜 이렇게 말하는가:

> 여 그 결과는 눈이 번쩍 뜨일 수 있어요, 그렇죠?

Ⓐ 특정 약물의 효과를 재미있는 방식으로 묘사하려고
Ⓑ 어떤 화학 물질들의 효과가 얼마나 놀라울 수 있는지 보이려고
Ⓒ 일부 화학 물질의 원인들이 몸에서 어떻게 작용하는지 나타내려고
Ⓓ 많은 사람들이 불면증의 원인을 인지하지 못한다고 말하려고

어휘 suffer v 고통받다 | insomnia n 불면증 | insomniac n 불면증 환자 | fortunately adv 다행히도 | transient adj 일시적인, 순간의 | chronic adj 만성의 | acute adj 급성의 | temporary adj 일시적인 | jet-lag n 시차로 인한 피로 | circadian rhythm 24시간 주기 리듬 | sleep disorder 수면 장애 | bio-chemical adj 생화학의 | prescription n 처방 | overindulgence n 탐닉, 방임 | digestive system 소화계 | asthma n 천식 | arthritis n 관절염 | complain v 불평하다 | prevent v 막다 | cramming n 벼락치기 | depression n 우울증 | full-fledged adj 본격적인 | toss and turn 뒤척이다 | remedy n 해결책, 처리 방안 | sleeping pill 수면제 | generally adv 일반적으로 | intervention n 개입, 중재 | particularly adv 특히 | regular adj 정기적인 | sacred adj 신성한, 성스러운 | distraction n 집중을 방해하는 것

Passage 14

Man: Professor

Listen to part of a lecture in an economics class.

M "The Great Depression" was a prolonged economic crisis that originated in the U.S. but was powerful enough to affect the global economy. The devastation of the Great Depression lasted from 1929 to 1941, leaving about a third of Americans unemployed. Banks went bankrupt and factories were shut down. Many people were left hungry and homeless, resulting in large-scale suffering. I think calling this period "the Great Depression" ... that is a bit of an understatement.

What caused the Great Depression? Well, the debate is over whether it was a free market failure or a succession of bank failures that resulted in panic and reduced money supply. Either way, the stock market crashed on October 29th, 1929, setting off the Depression. But such a major crash doesn't just suddenly happen. The crash was preceded by over a decade of falling production and increasing unemployment. Consequently, wealth became concentrated in a few hands. As unemployment began to skyrocket, stock values became inflated—all of this was well before the Great Depression. In other words, the stock market crash was just a symptom of a much larger problem.

Now, as you can imagine, coping with the Depression was not an easy feat. The New Deal, instigated by President Roosevelt in 1933, was a step toward dealing with this economic crisis. The New Deal was a system of restructuring the economy in order to stimulate demand. This would create jobs and relief for the needy. It also included reforming the financial system in order to regulate the securities industry, control competition, and set minimum wages. Furthermore, the New Deal encouraged the creation of unions that would then raise wages and increase worker spending power.

But was it the New Deal alone that helped pull the U.S. out of the Depression? Though the New Deal helped, many believe that it was the industrial build-up of World War II that helped pull the U.S. out of adversity. During the war, thousands of people were employed in the once closed factories and shipyards building airplanes, jeeps, ships, and so on, that were used in the war. The U.S. benefited financially, politically and militarily after the Great Depression... rather, after the Second World War. The U.S. gained a foothold on Europe and subsequently became the most powerful nation in the world. With such a massive gain in power, the U.S. naturally acquired its fair share of enemies, resulting in the Cold War. So, now let's focus on the impact of the Cold War on the U.S. economy.

남자: 교수

경제학 강의의 일부를 들으시오.

남 '대공황'은 미국에서 시작되었지만 세계 경제에 영향을 미칠 만큼 강력했던 장기적인 경제 위기였습니다. 대공황의 참상은 1929년에서 1941년까지 지속되었고 미국인의 약 3분의 1을 실업 상태로 만들었습니다. 은행들은 파산했고 공장들은 문을 닫았죠. 많은 사람들이 굶주리고 노숙자가 되었으며 대규모의 고통이 초래되었어요. 이 시기를 '대공황'이라고 부르는 것은... 약간 절제된 표현 같다고 생각합니다.

무엇이 대공황을 야기했을까요? 음, 그것이 자유 시장의 실패였는지 아니면 연쇄적인 은행 파산이 공황을 야기하고 자금 공급을 감소시킨 것인지에 대해서는 논쟁이 있습니다. 어느 쪽이든, 1929년 10월 29일에 증권 시장이 붕괴하면서 불황의 시작을 알렸습니다. 그러나 그런 대규모 붕괴는 그냥 갑자기 시작되지는 않습니다. 붕괴 이전에 이미 10년 넘게 생산 감소와 실업 증가라는 문제가 존재했죠. 결과적으로, 부는 소수의 손에 집중되었습니다. 실업이 급속도로 증가하기 시작하면서, 주식의 가치가 폭등했습니다. 이 모두는 대공황 훨씬 전에 일어났어요. 다시 말해서, 주식 시장 붕괴는 단지 훨씬 더 큰 문제의 징후일 뿐이었죠.

자, 여러분이 상상할 수 있듯 불황에 대처하는 것은 쉬운 일이 아니었습니다. 1933년에 루즈벨트 대통령에 의해 실시된 뉴딜정책은 이러한 경제 위기를 극복하기 위한 조치였습니다. 뉴딜정책은 수요를 자극하기 위해서 경제 구조를 개혁하는 체계였죠. 이것은 일자리를 창출하고 빈곤을 완화하기 위한 것이었습니다. 그것은 또한 증권 산업을 규제하고, 경쟁을 통제하며, 최저 임금을 설정하기 위해 재정 체계를 개혁하는 것을 포함했습니다. 더 나아가 뉴딜정책은 임금을 올리고 노동자들의 소비력을 증가시킬 수 있는 노동조합의 설립을 촉진했습니다.

그러나 불황에서 미국을 끌어내도록 도운 것이 뉴딜정책뿐이었을까요? 비록 뉴딜정책이 도움이 되긴 했지만 많은 사람들은 미국을 역경에서 끌어낸 것은 제2차 세계대전이 가져온 산업 재건이라고 믿고 있습니다. 전쟁 기간 동안 수천 명의 사람들이 한때 문을 닫았던 공장과 조선소에 고용되었는데 이는 전쟁에서 사용되는 비행기, 지프차, 배 등을 만들기 위해서였죠. 미국은 대공황 이후 재정적, 정치적, 그리고 군사적으로 이득을 봤습니다... 오히려, 제2차 세계대전 이후라고 해야겠죠. 미국은 유럽에 발판을 마련했고 그 결과 세계에서 가장 힘있는 국가가 되었습니다. 이처럼 막강한 힘을 얻게 되면서 미국은 그에 합당한 적을 갖게 되었고, 결국 냉전 시대를 가져왔죠. 그럼 이제 냉전이 미국 경제에 끼친 영향에 초점을 맞춰봅시다.

Lesson 03 Lectures

Q. Listen again to part of the lecture. Then answer the question.

M I think calling this period "the Great Depression" ... that is a bit of an understatement.

Why does the professor say this:

M that is a bit of an understatement.

Ⓐ To show that the effects of the economic downturn are often exaggerated
Ⓑ To illustrate the importance of the stock market crash on a global scale
Ⓒ To indicate that people do not understand how important the event was
Ⓓ To state that the common name for a period in history is poorly chosen

Q. 강의의 일부를 다시 듣고 질문에 답하시오.

남 이 시기를 '대공황'이라고 부르는 것은... 약간 절제된 표현 같다고 생각합니다.

교수는 왜 이렇게 말하는가:

남 약간 절제된 표현 같다고 생각합니다.

Ⓐ 경기 침체의 영향은 종종 과장된다는 것을 보여주려고
Ⓑ 주식 시장 폭락의 중요성을 국제적 규모로 설명하려고
Ⓒ 사람들이 이 사건이 얼마나 중요한지 이해하지 못한다고 밝히려고
Ⓓ 역사의 한 시기에 대한 통칭이 잘못 선택되었다고 말하려고

어휘 The Great Depression 대공황 I prolonged adj 오래 계속되는, 장기적인 I economic crisis 경제 공황 I originate v 시작하다, 유래하다 I powerful adj 강력한 I affect v 영향을 미치다 I devastation n 대대적인 파괴, 손상 I last v 지속되다 I unemployed adj 실직한, 실업자인 I bankrupt v 파산하다 I homeless adj 노숙자의 I suffering n 고통 I understatement n 절제된 표현 I debate n 논쟁 I free market 자유 시장 I failure n 실패 I succession n 연속, 연쇄 I reduce v 줄이다, 감소하다 I stock market 주식 시장 I crash v 폭락하다 I precede v ~에 앞서다, 선행하다 I decade n 10년 I production n 생산 I increase v 증가하다 I unemployment n 실업, 실업률 I consequently adv 그 결과, 따라서 I concentrated adj 집중된 I skyrocket v 폭등하다 I stock value 주가 I inflate v 부풀다, 폭등하다 I symptom n 증상 I cope with 대응하다, 대처하다 I feat n 위업 I The New Deal 뉴딜정책 I instigate v 실시하다, 착수하다 I restructure v 개혁하다, 구조를 조정하다 I stimulate v 자극하다, 격려하다 I demand n 수요 I relief n 완화, 경감 I needy n 어려운 사람들 I reform v 개혁하다 I financial system 금융 제도 I regulate v 규제하다, 단속하다 I securities industry 증권업 I competition n 경쟁 I minimum wage 최저 임금 I encourage v 장려하다 I union n 노동 조합 I spending power 구매력 I industrial adj 산업의 I adversity n 역경 I factory n 공장 I shipyard n 조선소 I jeep n 지프차 I benefit v 이득을 보다 I politically adv 정치적으로 I militarily adv 군사적으로 I foothold n 발판, 기반 I subsequently adv 그 뒤에, 나중에 I massive adj 거대한 I naturally adv 자연스럽게 I acquire v 얻다, 습득하다 I impact n 영향

Passage 15

Woman: Professor

Listen to part of a lecture in a botany class.

W Last week, we were talking about some of the ways that plants have adapted to different regions of the world, and the main example was the vines that climb up trees to get sunlight from higher in the canopy. But the rain forest, where a lot of these vines grow, is a very comfortable place for plants with abundant rainfall. Well, today let's look at another group of plants that have managed to adapt to life in the desert, which is one of the most difficult environments on the planet. I'm talking, of course, about cacti. Or, as we botanists call them, succulents. Now, succulent isn't a common word, but it means "water-storing" and was consequently chosen as the name for various types of cacti, which of course store water. But, um, an important thing is how exactly they do that. 1 So, thinking like a plant... if we

여자: 교수

식물학 강의의 일부를 들으시오.

여 지난주에 우리는 식물이 세계의 다른 지역에 적응하는 방법들 중 몇 가지에 대해서 이야기했습니다. 그리고 그 주된 예는 차양보다 더 높은 곳으로부터 태양빛을 받기 위해 나무 위로 올라가는 덩굴식물들이었습니다. 그러나 이러한 덩굴식물이 많이 자라는 열대 우림은 풍부한 강우량으로 식물들에게 매우 편안한 장소입니다. 자, 오늘은 지구상에서 가장 척박한 환경들 중 하나인 사막에서의 삶에 적응해낸 다른 무리의 식물들을 살펴볼 겁니다. 물론 선인장에 대해 말하고 있는 거예요. 우리 식물학자들은 이걸 다육 식물이라고도 부르죠. 다육 식물은 흔한 단어는 아니지만 '물을 저장하고 있는'이라는 뜻이고 그 결과 물론 물을 저장하는 다양한 종류의 선인장을 가리키는 이름으로 선택되었습니다. 하지만, 음, 중요한 것은 그것들이 대체 어떻게 물을 저장하느냐예요. 1 그래서 식물의 입장에서 생각해 보면...

were in this very hot, dry place, we would want to hold onto whatever water we could get to survive. But this is easier said than done.

Basically, most plants have very thin stems and little thin leaves, so they'd just dry right out in the desert because there's not much place for water to be stored. Cacti, on the other hand, are pretty thick, right? I mean, you look at a cactus and it looks rather sturdy with its thicker exterior and its spikes... allowing it to hold more water and definitely setting it apart from other plants. In fact, the first thing you notice when you look at a succulent is that its structure is so different from other plants. I mean, the basic structure's the same; it has a stem and branches, but they are much thicker than in other plants and there are no leaves. This means that the little water that they can get from dew, mist, or fog can be stored deep inside the structure of the plant, reducing the chance that the Sun will evaporate it. Actually, the, uh, core of the stem is spongy and hollow so that the succulents can hold that water. But succulents also have this thick, waxy outer layer that prevents water from evaporating or escaping the plant.

One thing we don't notice—not usually anyway, is the root structure. 2 Desert succulents can have root systems that cover far more area than their height would suggest. A young saguaro might be only 12cm high, yet its root system can fill an area of about 2 meters in diameter never more than 10cm deep. Other types of succulents have root systems that can shrink so much that the entire plant disappears under the ground. It's an amazing way to protect oneself from drought. 3 The most well-known feature of cacti is its spikes. This is an adaptation, and it serves an obvious purpose: defense. I mean, think about it. Being out in the desert and having all these marvelous survival adaptations means that you're more vulnerable, actually. You aren't surrounded by other plants in the desert like you would be in the forest. For herbivores in the desert you're probably the only available source of water and food. That makes you an easy target for being eaten. So, those spines function to discourage animals from eating the cactus or from trying to remove water from it. All of these things... the spikes, the waxy skin, unique structure, and the ability to hold water... they are all important adaptations. Actually, it's really interesting to see how adaptable nature is.

만약 우리가 매우 뜨겁고 건조한 지역에 있다면 생존하기 위해 구할 수 있는 어떠한 물이든 붙들려고 할 겁니다. 그러나 말은 쉽죠.

기본적으로 대부분의 식물은 매우 가는 줄기와 아주 얇은 잎을 갖고 있어서 물이 저장될 충분한 공간이 없어 사막에서 바로 말라버립니다. 반면 선인장은 매우 두꺼워요, 그렇죠? 제 말은, 선인장을 보면 두꺼운 외피와 가시 때문에 다소 억세 보입니다... 이는 더 많은 물을 저장하게 하고 다른 식물들과 명백히 구분되게 하죠. 실제로 다육 식물을 볼 때 처음으로 알아차리게 되는 것은 구조가 다른 식물들과 매우 다르다는 점입니다. 제 말은, 기본적인 구조는 같습니다. 줄기와 가지는 가지고 있지만, 그게 다른 식물들에 비해 더 두껍고 잎이 없죠. 이는 선인장이 이슬, 안개비나 안개 등에서 얻을 수 있는 소량의 물을 구조 내부에 깊이 저장할 수 있어서 태양이 물을 증발시켜버릴 가능성을 줄인다는 뜻입니다. 사실, 어, 줄기의 핵은 다육 식물이 물을 저장할 수 있도록 스펀지 같고 속이 비어 있습니다. 그러나 다육 식물은 또한 물이 증발하거나 없어지는 것을 막는 두껍고 밀랍 같은 외피층을 가지고 있죠.

우리가 보통 알아차리지 못하는 한 가지는 뿌리 구조입니다. 2 사막 다육 식물은 키를 봤을 때 느껴지는 것보다 훨씬 더 넓은 지역을 덮는 뿌리 체계를 가질 수 있어요. 어린 사와로 선인장은 키가 12센티미터밖에 되지 않을지는 모르지만 뿌리는 깊이가 10센티미터를 넘지 않으면서 지름이 약 2미터 되는 지역을 채울 수 있습니다. 다른 종류의 다육 식물은 엄청나게 오그라들어서 식물 전체가 땅 아래로 사라질 수도 있는 뿌리 체계를 가지고 있어요. 가뭄으로부터 자신을 지키는 놀라운 방법이죠. 3 선인장의 가장 잘 알려진 특징은 가시입니다. 이것은 적응 형태이며 명백한 목적이 있어요. 방어죠. 제 말은, 생각해 보세요. 사막에 있는데 이 모든 놀라운 생존 적응 형태를 가지고 있다는 점은 사실 더 약하다는 뜻입니다. 사막에서는 숲과 같이 다른 식물들에게 둘러싸여 있지 않습니다. 사막에 있는 초식 동물들에게는 이것들이 아마 물과 먹이로 이용 가능한 유일한 자원일 겁니다. 그 점이 다육 식물을 잡아 먹기 쉬운 목표물로 만들죠. 그래서 이 가시들은 동물들로 하여금 선인장을 먹거나 물을 빼앗으려는 시도를 단념하게 하는 기능을 합니다. 이 모든 것들... 뾰족한 가시, 매끄러운 표면, 독특한 구조와 물을 저장하는 능력... 모두 중요한 적응 형태입니다. 사실 자연이 얼마나 적응력이 강한지를 보는 것은 정말 흥미롭습니다.

1. **Listen again to part of the lecture. Then answer the question.**

W So, thinking like a plant... if we were in this very hot, dry place, we would want to hold onto whatever water we could get to survive. But this is easier said than done.

Why does the professor say this:

W But this is easier said than done.

Ⓐ To state that the rain forest is not as easy to live in as people think
Ⓑ To indicate that any organism would have difficulty finding enough water
Ⓒ To question how well cacti actually are adapted to their environment
Ⓓ To illustrate how impressive the adaptations of cacti are

2. **What is the professor's opinion of the saguaro cactus?**
Ⓐ She thinks its ability to retract itself underground is amazing.
Ⓑ She is impressed by the large diameter of its root system.
Ⓒ She is surprised at how quickly the cactus is able to grow.
Ⓓ She believes that it holds the most water of any cactus species.

3. **Listen again to part of the lecture. Then answer the question.**

W The most well-known feature of cacti is its spikes. This is an adaptation, and it serves an obvious purpose: defense. I mean, think about it. Being out in the desert and having all these marvelous survival adaptations means that you're more vulnerable, actually.

Why does the professor say this:

W I mean, think about it.

Ⓐ To point out that cacti adaptations could have negative results as well
Ⓑ To illustrate the effectiveness of cacti's defensive adaptations
Ⓒ To encourage the students to imagine what caused adaptations

1. 강의의 일부를 다시 듣고 질문에 답하시오.

여 그래서 식물의 입장에서 생각해 보면... 만약 우리가 매우 뜨겁고 건조한 지역에 있다면 생존하기 위해 구할 수 있는 어떠한 물이든 붙들려고 할 겁니다. 그러나 말은 쉽죠.

교수는 왜 이렇게 말하는가:

여 그러나 말은 쉽죠.

Ⓐ 열대우림은 사람들이 생각하는 것처럼 살기 쉽지 않다고 말하려고
Ⓑ 어떤 생물이라도 충분한 물을 찾는 데 어려움을 겪을 것이라고 설명하려고
Ⓒ 선인장이 사실 그들의 환경에 얼마나 잘 적응했는지 의문을 던지려고
Ⓓ 선인장의 적응이 얼마나 대단한 것인지 묘사하려고

2. 사와로 선인장에 관한 교수의 의견은 무엇인가?
Ⓐ 지하에서 움츠러드는 능력이 굉장하다고 생각한다.
Ⓑ 뿌리 체계의 커다란 지름에 깊은 인상을 받았다.
Ⓒ 이 선인장이 얼마나 빨리 자라는지에 대해 놀랐다.
Ⓓ 어떤 선인장 종보다 가장 많은 물을 저장한다고 믿는다.

3. 강의의 일부를 다시 듣고 질문에 답하시오.

여 선인장의 가장 잘 알려진 특징은 가시입니다. 이것은 적응 형태이며 명백한 목적이 있어요. 방어죠. 제 말은, 생각해 보세요. 사막에 있는데 이 모든 놀라운 생존 적응 형태를 가지고 있다는 점은 사실 더 약하다는 뜻입니다.

교수는 왜 이렇게 말하는가:

여 제 말은, 생각해 보세요.

Ⓐ 선인장의 적응이 부정적 결과 또한 가질 수 있다는 점을 지적하려고
Ⓑ 선인장의 방어적 적응이 가진 효율성을 설명하려고
Ⓒ 무엇이 적응을 야기했을지 상상해 보도록 학생들을 장려하려고

Ⓓ To indicate that the students should know what she is discussing	Ⓓ 자신이 논의하고 있는 것에 대해 학생들이 알아야 한다고 말하려고

어휘 adapt v 적응하다 | vine n 덩굴 식물 | canopy n 캐노피(숲의 나뭇가지들이 지붕 모양으로 우거짐) | rain forest 열대우림 | comfortable adj 편안한 | abundant adj 풍부한 | rainfall n 강우(량) | cactus n 선인장 (pl. cacti) | botanist n 식물학자 | succulent n 다육 식물 | store v 저장하다 | consequently adv 그 결과, 따라서 | various adj 다양한 | survive v 생존하다 | sturdy adj 튼튼한, 견고한 | exterior n 외부 | spike n 가시 | definitely adv 분명히, 확실히 | notice v 눈치채다, 알아차리다 | structure n 구조 | stem n 줄기 | branch n 가지 | dew n 이슬 | mist n 엷은 안개 | fog n 안개 | reduce v 감소하다, 줄이다 | evaporate v 증발하다 | spongy adj 스펀지 같은, 흡수성이 좋은 | hollow adj 비어 있는 | waxy adj 밀랍 같은; 매끈한 | prevent v 막다, 방지하다 | escape v 탈출하다 | root n 뿌리 | height n 높이 | saguaro n 사와로 선인장 | shrink v 줄어들다 | entire adj 전체의 | drought n 가뭄 | obvious adj 분명한, 뻔한 | purpose n 목적 | defense n 방어 | marvelous adj 놀라운, 믿기 어려운 | vulnerable adj 연약한 | surround v 둘러싸다 | herbivore n 초식 동물 | function v 기능하다 | discourage v 그만두게 하다 | remove v 제거하다

Passage 16

Man: Professor

Listen to part of a lecture in a biology class.

M **1** Would you hang a mollusk around your neck? The reason I'm asking is because today we are going to be looking at pearls, which actually develop from secretions within mollusks. This doesn't paint a very attractive picture of a pearl's beginnings. But pearls are still synonymous with romance and attraction in most people's minds. Although considered beautiful, pearls have a not-so appealing origin, being formed in the slimy interior of mollusks when a tiny particle accidentally slips inside the protective shell of a mollusk. Reacting to this, the creature prevents irritation by covering the particle with a substance called nacre, which can best be compared with umm... human mucous. You know, the stuff your nose secretes to protect the lungs from dust, bacteria, and viruses. In any case, nacre is secreted by the mantle, the outer layer of living mollusk tissue. This nacre forms the shell that protects the animal from predators. However, when a particle enters the shell, nacre forms little balls called pearls around the particle. This process is, of course, very slow, taking years for the nacre to build up, solidify, and form a pearl.

Okay, as you know, pearls aren't cheap. Prices reflect size, roundness and luster, which is the reflective quality of a pearl. The thinner the layers of nacre, the greater the luster. However, most pearls lack luster, size, or roundness, or a combination of these qualities. So they aren't cut out for the ballroom or the dinner theater. And because most pearls are not round and flawless, but are misshapen, poorly colored and badly blemished, a good quality pearl is scarce and relatively expensive. It is this quality that is driving a whole

남자: 교수

생물학 강의의 일부를 들으시오.

남 **1** 연체동물을 목에 걸겠습니까? 이런 질문을 하는 이유는 오늘 수업에서 연체동물 속에서 분비물로 만들어지는 진주에 대해 살펴볼 것이기 때문입니다. 이 사실은 진주의 탄생을 멋지게 그려 보이지는 못합니다. 하지만 진주는 여전히 대부분 사람들의 마음속에서 로맨스, 매력과 같은 의미를 가집니다. 진주는 아름답다고 여겨지지만 그 탄생 과정은 별로 매력적이지 않은데요, 연체동물의 끈적끈적한 조직 내부에서 생겨나는 것으로 연체동물의 보호막 안에 작은 입자가 우연히 들어갔을 때 형성됩니다. 이에 대한 반응으로 이 생물은 진주층이라고 불리는 물질로 내부에 침투한 입자를 덮어 자극을 방지하는데, 이는 음... 인간의 점액, 즉 먼지, 박테리아, 바이러스로부터 폐를 보호하려고 코에서 나오는 분비물과 가장 잘 비교될 수 있습니다. 어떤 경우든 진주층은 살아 있는 연체동물 조직의 외부층인 외피에서 분비됩니다. 이 진주층은 포식자에게서 동물을 보호하는 껍질을 형성합니다. 하지만 입자가 껍질 속으로 들어오면 진주층은 그 입자 주위에 진주라고 불리는 작은 공들을 형성합니다. 물론 이 진행은 매우 느려서 진주층이 축적되어 굳고 진주가 되는 데 수년이 걸리죠.

좋아요, 여러분이 알다시피 진주는 값이 싸지 않습니다. 가격은 크기, 둥글기, 진주의 반사적인 특징을 가리키는 광택을 반영합니다. 진주층의 표면이 얇을수록 광택이 뛰어나죠. 그러나 대부분의 진주들은 광택, 크기, 둥글기 또는 이러한 특징들의 결합면에서 부족함이 있습니다. 그래서 무도회장이나 저녁 공연에 하고 가기에는 적합하지 않습니다. 그리고 대부분의 진주들은 둥글지 않고 흠이 있으며, 흉하고, 색이 예쁘지 않고 심하게 손상되었기 때문에 품질이 좋은 진주는 부족하고 상대적으로 비쌉니다. 전체 업계로 하여금 진주를 취급하도록 이끄

industry to provide pearls. 2 Since only one in thousands of mollusks contain a pearl, and most pearls are useless, our appetite for pearls is being satisfied by pearl farming enterprises. These businesses began in Japan in the early 20th century and have spread to America, China, and the South Pacific, which is famous for its big black pearls. 3 Pearl farmers embed a grain of sand or a spherical piece of shell into a mollusk, so every mollusk produces a pearl. Because humans are helping, pearl values have crashed.

는 것이 바로 이 품질입니다. 2 연체동물 수천 마리 중에 한 마리 정도만이 진주를 가지고 있고 대부분의 진주는 쓸모가 없기 때문에 진주를 향한 우리의 욕구는 진주 양식 산업을 통해 충족됩니다. 이 사업은 20세기 초에 일본에서 시작되었고, 미국, 중국, 그리고 커다란 흑진주로 유명한 남태평양으로 퍼졌습니다. 3 진주 양식업자들은 모래 낟알이나 구 모양의 조개 조각을 연체동물 안에 삽입해 모든 연체동물이 진주를 생산하게 하죠. 사람들의 도움 덕분에 진주의 가치는 크게 하락했습니다.

1. Listen again to part of the lecture. Then answer the question.

M Would you hang a mollusk around your neck? The reason I'm asking is because today we are going to be looking at pearls, which actually develop from secretions within mollusks.

Why does the professor say this:

M Would you hang a mollusk around your neck?

Ⓐ To introduce the topic of the lecture he is going to give
Ⓑ To question whether people know where jewelry comes from
Ⓒ To indicate that some organisms create beautiful shells
Ⓓ To illustrate how different cultures value different things

2. What is the professor's attitude toward pearl farming?

Ⓐ He thinks it requires the lives of too many mollusks.
Ⓑ He believes that it is much more efficient than catching them.
Ⓒ He feels that is driven purely by human greed and fashion.
Ⓓ He questions whether it actually helps wild mollusks.

3. Listen again to part of the lecture. Then answer the question.

M Pearl farmers embed a grain of sand or a spherical piece of shell into a mollusk, so every mollusk produces a pearl. Because humans are helping, pearl values have crashed.

Why does the professor say this:

M Because humans are helping, pearl values have crashed.

1. 강의의 일부를 다시 듣고 질문에 답하시오.

남 연체동물을 목에 걸겠습니까? 이런 질문을 하는 이유는 오늘 수업에서 연체동물 속에서 분비물로 만들어지는 진주에 대해 살펴볼 것이기 때문입니다.

교수는 왜 이렇게 말하는가:

남 연체동물을 목에 걸겠습니까?

Ⓐ 자기가 설명할 강의 주제를 소개하려고
Ⓑ 보석이 어디에서 오는지를 사람들이 아는지 질문하려고
Ⓒ 일부 생물은 아름다운 껍질을 만들어낸다는 점을 보이려고
Ⓓ 서로 다른 문화에서는 다른 것들을 가치 있게 여긴다는 점을 설명하려고

2. 진주 양식에 대한 교수의 태도는 어떠한가?

Ⓐ 너무 많은 연체동물의 생명을 필요로 한다고 생각한다.
Ⓑ 이들을 잡는 것보다 훨씬 더 효율적이라고 믿는다.
Ⓒ 오직 인간의 욕심과 패션 때문에 주도된다고 본다.
Ⓓ 야생 연체동물을 실제로 돕는지 의심한다.

3. 강의의 일부를 다시 듣고 질문에 답하시오.

남 진주 양식업자들은 모래 낟알이나 구 모양의 조개 조각을 연체동물 안에 삽입해 모든 연체동물이 진주를 생산하게 하죠. 사람들의 도움 덕분에 진주의 가치는 크게 하락했습니다.

교수는 왜 이렇게 말하는가:

남 사람들의 도움 덕분에 진주의 가치는 크게 하락했습니다.

Ⓐ To state that farmed pearls are not genuine pearls
Ⓑ To indicate that human-made copies are worthless
Ⓒ To explain how farmed pearls affected sales of real pearls
Ⓓ To illustrate how humans have learned to farm pearls

Ⓐ 양식 진주는 진짜 진주가 아니라고 말하려고
Ⓑ 인간이 만든 복제품은 가치가 없다고 말하려고
Ⓒ 양식 진주가 진짜 진주의 판매에 어떤 영향을 주었는지 설명하려고
Ⓓ 인간이 어떻게 진주를 양식하는지를 배웠는지 설명하려고

어휘 mollusk n 연체동물 I pearl n 진주 I develop v 성장하다, 변하다 I secretion n 분비물 I attractive adj 매력적인 I synonymous adj 비슷한 뜻을 갖는 I romance n 연애, 로맨스 I attraction n 끌림, 매력 I consider v 여기다, 생각하다 I appealing adj 매력적인, 호감의 I slimy adj 끈적끈적한 I interior n 내부 I tiny adj 아주 작은 I particle n 입자 I accidentally adv 우연히, 실수로 I protective adj 보호하는 I react v 반응하다 I prevent v 막다, 방지하다 I irritation n 자극 I cover v 덮다 I substance n 물질 I nacre n 진주층 I compare v 비교하다 I mucous n 점액 I secrete v 분비하다 I dust n 먼지 I mantle n 꺼풀, 맨틀 I tissue n 조직 I predator n 포식자 I enter v 들어가다 I form v 형성하다 I solidify v 굳어지다, 굳다 I reflect v 반영하다 I luster n 광택 I combination n 결합, 혼합 I ballroom n 무도회장 I flawless adj 흠이 없는 I misshapen adj 모양이 일그러진 I blemish v 흠집을 내다 I scarce adj 흔치 않은 I relatively adv 상대적으로 I industry n 업계 I contain v 함유하다 I useless adj 쓸모 없는 I appetite n 욕구 I satisfy v 만족시키다 I farming n (어류) 양식 I enterprise n 기업, 회사 I spread v 퍼지다 I embed v 끼워 넣다 I spherical adj 구 모양의, 구체의 I produce v 생산하다 I crash v 폭락하다, 추락하다

Test

본서 I P. 170

Man: Professor

[1-6] Listen to part of a lecture in a health science class.

M Let's get started. Umm, 1 today, we are going to begin looking into language disorders and their causes. Of course, we will look at the brain and its processes in addition to the disorders that affect a patient's ability to use language, whether it's speaking, listening, reading, or writing. The disorders of the brain that reduce or eliminate language production and comprehension are known as aphasia, and there are several different types, which, of course, reveal themselves with different symptoms. Aphasia is usually caused by damage to the language centers of the brain. 2 But before we take a closer look at aphasia and its causes, we should review the major regions of the brain and their responsibilities. And I'll do my best to keep it brief.
The entire brain works with the same data, but certain parts of it tend to work differently. The right hemisphere of the brain, which processes information as it happens, has generally been thought of as the center for creativity and emotional perception. It doesn't attach meaning to information. It only gathers perceptual information, data sensed through the eyes, ears, and body. 3 Really, it relies on the left hemisphere to link information, which is accomplished through interpreting the meaning of something by reasoning, obviously important for using language. So, the right hemisphere is not really crucial to our understanding of aphasia. What matters in our studies of language disorders is the left hemisphere of the brain.

남자: 교수

보건학 강의의 일부를 들으시오.

남 시작하죠. 음, 1 오늘은 언어 장애와 그 원인에 대해서 살펴보려고 합니다. 물론, 말하기든 듣기든 읽기든 쓰기든 환자가 언어를 사용하는 능력에 영향을 미치는 장애뿐만 아니라 뇌와 그 과정들을 살펴볼 겁니다. 언어 생성과 이해 능력을 감소시키거나 없애는 뇌 장애는 실어증이라고 알려져 있으며 이는 여러 다양한 형태가 있고, 물론 서로 다른 증상으로 나타납니다. 실어증은 보통 뇌의 언어 중추부에 손상을 입기 때문에 일어나죠. 2 그러나 실어증과 그 원인을 자세히 살펴보기 전에 뇌의 주요 부분과 그 기능을 다시 살펴봐야 합니다. 최대한 짧게 설명하도록 할게요.
뇌의 전체는 똑같은 정보를 가지고 기능하지만 특정 부분은 다르게 기능하는 경향이 있습니다. 정보가 발생하는 대로 이를 처리하는 뇌의 우반구는 전체적으로 창의력과 감정 지각의 중추로 여겨져 왔습니다. 이곳은 정보에 의미를 부여하지 않아요. 눈과 귀, 신체를 통해 감지되어 지각된 정보와 데이터를 수집할 뿐입니다. 3 사실, 우반구는 정보를 연결하기 위해 좌반구에 의존하는데, 이는 언어 사용에 당연히 중요한 추론으로 의미를 해석하는 일을 통해 행해집니다. 그래서 우반구는 실어증을 이해하는 데 엄청나게 중요하지는 않아요. 언어 장애에 대한 우리의 연구에 있어 중요한 부분은 뇌의 좌반구입니다.

The left hemisphere processes information linearly, meaning it places data in sequence, one bit of information after the other. Accordingly, the ability to use speech, a linear system of expression, is centered in this region. Broca's and Wernicke's areas are the two most prominent language areas of the brain, and they are both located in the left hemisphere. They function as the language centers of the brain by producing and comprehending speech and processing language. As you can assume, any damage inflicted on either one of these areas, whether it is in the form of a disease or physical injury, is going to have a profound effect on an individual's ability to use language.

Broca's area is located in the frontal lobe of the language dominant area of the brain's left hemisphere. And there is an often-devastating disorder known as Broca's aphasia, resulting from damage to this region. **4** The effects of this damage can make a person mute or inhibit their language to the point that they can only use single words or short, basic phrases like "good morning" or "in the room." It is sometimes possible for a Broca's aphasic to create sentences, but it's extremely difficult for them to put a sentence together. In addition to these devastating consequences, their reading ability is significantly affected. However, and this might not make sense, Broca's aphasics usually find their listening skills relatively unaffected. They are able to follow conversations and commands, yet when they try to participate in these same interactions verbally, they find they can't. As you can guess from the symptoms of Broca's aphasia, it must be very frustrating for Broca's aphasics in their day-to-day lives, fully understanding what is being said to and around them, but not being able to express themselves in the way they want. So it may come as no surprise to you that a large number of Broca's aphasics also develop depression later on. Now what exactly leads to a disease that is so serious it damages someone's ability to use language? The leading cause of Broca's aphasia is stroke, although other causes of brain damage, such as head injuries, brain tumors, and infection can also result in not just Broca's aphasia, but all other types of aphasia as well.

Wernicke's aphasia is similar to Broca's aphasia in that it has profound effect on an individual's language abilities. However, its effects contrast Broca's aphasia in that the individual still retains their speaking ability. In fact, they are often able to still speak fluently. **5** But a Wernicke's aphasic is likely to use incorrect words, jargon, and even made-up words that have no meaning. And their problems don't end here.

좌반구는 정보를 연속적으로 처리하는데, 그 말은 자료를 차례대로, 하나의 정보 뒤에 또 다른 정보를 놓는 식으로 둔다는 의미입니다. 따라서 말을 하는 능력, 즉 표현의 선형 체계는 이 구역에 중점을 두고 있습니다. 브로카 영역과 베르니케 영역은 뇌의 언어 관장 부분에서 가장 두드러진 두 부분이며 둘 다 좌반구에 있습니다. 이들은 말을 만들어내고 이해하도록 하며 언어를 처리함으로써 뇌의 언어 중추로서 기능합니다. 여러분이 짐작할 수 있듯 이 두 부분 중 어느 하나라도 손상을 입게 된다면 그것이 질병이든 신체적 외상이든 개인의 언어 사용 능력에 심각한 영향을 미치게 됩니다.

브로카 영역은 뇌 좌반구의 언어를 관장하는 부위 중 전두엽에 위치해 있습니다. 그리고 때때로 매우 심각한 장애인 '브로카 실어증'이라고 알려진 질환이 있는데 이 구역에 손상을 입어 발생하는 것입니다. **4** 이 손상에 따른 결과는 사람을 벙어리로 만들거나 그저 한 단어 또는 '안녕하세요'나 '방에서'와 같은 짧고 기본적인 구만 쓸 수 있는 정도에 머물게 합니다. 브로카 실어증에 걸린 환자들은 때로는 문장을 만드는 것도 가능하지만 하나의 문장을 조합하는 것은 매우 힘듭니다. 이런 치명적인 결과에 더해, 환자들의 읽기 능력도 크게 영향을 받습니다. 그러나 잘 이해되지 않을지도 모르지만, 브로카 실어증 환자는 듣기 능력에는 비교적 영향을 받지 않습니다. 대화와 명령을 이해할 수는 있지만 이러한 상호작용에 말로 참여하려고 하면 할 수가 없죠. 브로카 실어증의 증상에서 짐작할 수 있듯 이 브로카 실어증 환자들은 자신에게 하는 말, 그리고 주변에서 말하는 것을 다 이해하지만 원하는 대로 자신을 표현할 수 없기 때문에 일상생활에서 상당한 좌절감을 느낄 겁니다. 그래서 상당히 많은 브로카 실어증 환자들에게 후에 우울증이 나타난다는 것은 별로 놀라운 일이 아닐지도 모릅니다. 그렇다면 언어를 사용하는 능력에 손상을 줄 정도로 심각한 질병을 야기하는 것이 무엇일까요? 브로카 실어증의 주된 원인은 뇌졸중이며, 비록 머리 부상이나 뇌종양, 감염 등의 다른 뇌 손상 원인들도 있지만 이들은 브로카 실어증뿐만 아니라 다른 모든 종류의 실어증도 야기할 수 있습니다.

베르니케 실어증은 개인의 언어 능력에 심각한 영향을 끼친다는 점에서 브로카 실어증과 비슷합니다. 하지만 그 영향 면에서는 개인이 여전히 말할 수 있는 능력을 유지한다는 점에서 브로카 실어증과 다릅니다. 사실, 종종 그들은 여전히 유창하게 말할 수 있습니다. **5** 하지만 베르니케 실어증 환자는 부정확한 단어와 특수 용어, 또는 아무 의미 없이 새로 만들어낸 단어를 쓰는 경향이 있습니다. 그리고 그들의 문제는 여기서 끝이 아니에요. 안타깝

Sadly, they also have a serious problem understanding the auditory qualities of another's speech. For example, they can't sense rhythm, tone, and even the emotion of a person talking to them. **6** Well, we are running out of time, so we are going to have a look at some other types of aphasia in our next class.

게도 다른 사람들의 말이 가진 청각적 특성을 이해하는 데 심각한 문제를 겪습니다. 예를 들면, 리듬과 말투, 심지어 사람이 말할 때의 감정도 인지하지 못합니다. **6** 음, 시간이 모자라니 다음 수업에서 실어증의 다른 유형들에 대해서 살펴보도록 합시다.

1. What is the speaker mainly discussing?

Ⓐ Wernicke's aphasics and the challenges they face in life
Ⓑ The brain and two common language disorders
Ⓒ Why Broca's aphasics can understand spoken language
Ⓓ How people suffer from language disorders

2. Listen again to part of the lecture. Then answer the question.

M But before we take a closer look at aphasia and its causes, we should review the major regions of the brain and their responsibilities. And I'll do my best to keep it brief.

What does the professor imply by stating this:

M And I'll do my best to keep it brief.

Ⓐ He thinks that the students should already know what he is going to explain.
Ⓑ He understands that the students want to move on to more interesting topics.
Ⓒ He knows that there is a wealth of information on the subject that needs to be covered.
Ⓓ He wants to provide a basic background before the main topic of the class.

3. What does the professor say about the brain?

Ⓐ It is very difficult for the brain to organize information sequentially.
Ⓑ The right hemisphere is central to the production of language.
Ⓒ Language disorders can sometimes result in disease.
Ⓓ The left hemisphere is the center of using language.

4. What is the result of Broca's aphasia?

Ⓐ There is a decrease in speaking and reading ability with few effects on listening ability.
Ⓑ Listening skills decrease with moderately-affected speaking ability.
Ⓒ Listening skills decrease with speech remaining fluent but nonsensical.

1. 화자는 주로 무엇을 논의하고 있는가?

Ⓐ 베르니케 실어증 환자들과 그들이 삶에서 마주하는 어려움
Ⓑ 뇌와 두 종류의 흔한 언어 장애
Ⓒ 브로카 실어증 환자들이 말로 하는 언어를 알아들을 수 있는 이유
Ⓓ 사람들이 언어 장애로 겪는 고통

2. 강의의 일부를 다시 듣고 질문에 답하시오.

남 그러나 실어증과 그 원인을 자세히 살펴보기 전에 뇌의 주요 부분과 그 기능을 다시 살펴봐야 합니다. 최대한 짧게 설명하도록 할게요.

교수는 이렇게 말하며 무엇을 암시하는가:

남 최대한 짧게 설명하도록 할게요.

Ⓐ 자신이 설명할 것을 학생들이 이미 안다고 생각한다.
Ⓑ 학생들이 더 흥미로운 주제로 넘어가고 싶어 한다는 것을 이해한다.
Ⓒ 다뤄야 하는 주제에 관해 정보가 풍부하다는 것을 안다.
Ⓓ 수업의 주제로 들어가기 전에 기본적인 배경을 제공하고 싶어한다.

3. 교수는 뇌에 관해 뭐라고 말하는가?

Ⓐ 뇌가 정보를 순차적으로 정리하는 것은 무척 어렵다.
Ⓑ 우반구는 언어 생산의 중추이다.
Ⓒ 언어 장애는 때때로 질병을 야기할 수 있다.
Ⓓ 좌반구는 언어 사용의 중추이다.

4. 브로카 실어증의 결과는 무엇인가?

Ⓐ 말하기와 읽기 능력이 저하되며 듣기 능력에는 거의 영향이 없다.
Ⓑ 듣기 능력이 저하되고 말하기 능력은 보통 정도로 영향을 받는다.
Ⓒ 듣기 능력은 저하되며 말하기는 유창하지만 무의미한 말들이다.

Ⓓ There is a significant decrease in only speaking ability.

5. What is the professor's attitude toward people with Wernicke's aphasia?

Ⓐ He thinks it's impressive that Wernicke's aphasics can even survive.
Ⓑ He understands the difficulties that come from having a listening disorder.
Ⓒ He feels pity for Wernicke's aphasics as they suffer from several problems.
Ⓓ He wants people to speak more clearly when interacting with stroke victims.

6. What will the professor most likely discuss in the next lecture?

Ⓐ He will discuss Wernicke's aphasia in more detail.
Ⓑ He will explore how the language centers function.
Ⓒ He will address a question raised during the class.
Ⓓ He will introduce some other language disorders.

Ⓓ 말하기 능력만 심각하게 저하된다.

5. 베르니케 실어증을 가진 사람들에 대한 교수의 태도는 어떠한가?

Ⓐ 베르니케 실어증 환자들이 생존할 수 있다는 점이 대단하다고 생각한다.
Ⓑ 듣기 장애를 가졌을 때 오는 어려움을 이해한다.
Ⓒ 다수의 문제 때문에 고통 받는 베르니케 실어증 환자들을 안쓰럽게 생각한다.
Ⓓ 뇌졸중 피해자들과 교류할 때 사람들이 더 명확히 말했으면 한다.

6. 교수는 다음 강의에서 무엇을 논의할 것 같은가?

Ⓐ 베르니케 실어증에 대해 더 상세하게 논의할 것이다.
Ⓑ 언어 중심부가 어떻게 기능하는지 살펴볼 것이다.
Ⓒ 수업 도중에 제시된 질문을 다룰 것이다.
Ⓓ 다른 언어 장애를 소개할 것이다.

어휘 disorder n 장애, 이상 | cause n 원인 | process n 절차, 과정 | affect v 영향을 주다 | reduce v 줄이다 | eliminate v 제거하다 | production n 생산 | comprehension n 이해 | aphasia n 실어증 | reveal v 드러내다 | symptom n 증상 | responsibility n 책임, 역할 | hemisphere n 반구 | process v 처리하다 | creativity n 창의성 | emotional adj 감정적인 | perception n 인식, 자각 | attach v 붙이다, 부여하다 | perceptual adj 지각의 | rely v 의존하다 | accomplish v 완수하다, 성취하다 | interpret v 해석하다 | reasoning n 추론 | obviously adv 명백히 | crucial adj 필수적인 | linearly adv 연속적으로 | sequence n 연속적인 사건, 순서 | accordingly adv 부응해서, 그에 맞춰 | expression n 표현 | region n 지역 | prominent adj 중요한, 두드러진 | function v 기능하다 | comprehend v 이해하다 | assume v 가정하다 | inflict v (괴로움 등을) 가하다, 안겨주다 | injury n 부상 | profound adj 엄청난, 깊은 | frontal lobe 전두엽 | dominant adj 주된, 우세한 | devastating adj 파괴적인 | mute adj 벙어리의, 무언의 | inhibit v 억제하다, 저해하다 | aphasics n 실어증 환자 | consequence n 결과 | significantly adv 심각하게, 크게 | relatively adv 상대적으로, 비교적 | conversation n 대화 | command n 명령 | participate v 참여하다 | interaction n 상호 작용 | verbally adv 말로, 구두로 | frustrating adj 불만스러운, 좌절감을 주는 | develop v 발전시키다, 개발하다 | depression n 우울증 | exactly adv 정확히 | damage v 손상을 입히다 | stroke n 뇌졸중 | tumor n 종양 | infection n 감염 | contrast v 대조하다, 대비시키다 | retain v 보유하다 | fluently adv 유창하게 | incorrect adj 틀린 | jargon n 특수 용어 | auditory adj 청각의

Lesson 04 Connecting Contents

본서 | P. 172

Practice

Passage 1	A	**Passage 2**	C	**Passage 3**	A
Passage 4	B	**Passage 5**	D	**Passage 6**	A
Passage 7	E - C - B - A	**Passage 8**	Yes – A, C, D / No – B, E	**Passage 9**	E - A - D - C
Passage 10	C - A - E - B	**Passage 11**	Yes – A, B, D / No – C, E		

Passage 12 1. C - D - A - B 2. B
Passage 13 1. C 2. Yes – A, B, C / No – D, E
Passage 14 1. B - C - A - D 2. A

Test

1. C **2.** A **3.** B **4.** C **5.** B, C **6.** B - D - E - C

Passage 1

Woman: Professor

Listen to part of a lecture in an art history class.

W Surrealism is one of the many art movements that began between the world wars. Like Dadaism, it was a reaction to the horrors of a war led by an incompetent elite class of society. Many of the empires and monarchies that had governed the world prior to the Great War were deposed or relegated to minor roles in the aftermath. This was in line with the anarchist ideals of the Dadaists, but the surrealists craved order. Their movement emerged during a decade of peace and prosperity, and they were trying to move beyond the wounds from the war. Surrealism was very much a retreat from reality by survivors who did not want to dwell on the past. They focused on exploring the relationship between the conscious and unconscious mind as it was delineated by Sigmund Freud. The great artists of the movement painted in a very traditional style, but they rejected the stark reality of previous art styles in favor of painting dreams as if they were real. They tried to find the meaning in life by exploring the mysteries of the mind and imagination.

여자: 교수

미술사 강의의 일부를 들으시오.

여 초현실주의는 두 차례의 세계 대전 사이에 시작된 많은 미술 운동 중 하나입니다. 다다이즘처럼 사회의 무능한 엘리트 집단이 주도한 전쟁의 참상에 대한 반응이었죠. 세계 대전 전에 세계를 다스렸던 많은 제국과 군주들이 그 여파로 작은 역할로 물러나거나 좌천되었습니다. 이는 다다이스트들의 무정부주의자 이상과 일치하지만 초현실주의자들은 질서를 갈망했어요. 이들의 운동은 평화와 부흥의 10년 사이 부상했으며 전쟁의 상처를 딛고 나아가려 했습니다. 초현실주의는 과거에 머물고 싶어 하지 않았던 생존자들이 현실에서 도피한 거라고 볼 수 있습니다. 이들은 지그문트 프로이트가 기술한 의식과 무의식 사이의 관계를 탐험하는 데 중점을 두었습니다. 이 운동의 유명한 화가들은 아주 전통적인 양식으로 그림을 그렸지만, 기존 미술 양식이 보여준 냉혹한 현실을 거부하고 꿈을 마치 현실처럼 그리는 것을 선호했습니다. 이들은 정신세계의 신비와 상상을 탐구하는 것을 통해 삶의 의미를 찾으려 노력했습니다.

Q. Why does the professor mention Dadaism in the lecture?

Ⓐ To contrast it with Surrealism as an art form
Ⓑ To illustrate why one movement was more popular
Ⓒ To explain what influenced the creation of surrealism
Ⓓ To compare the techniques that the artists used

Q. 교수는 왜 강의에서 다다이즘을 언급하는가?

Ⓐ 미술 형태로서의 초현실주의와 대조하려고
Ⓑ 왜 한 운동이 더 인기있었는지 설명하려고
Ⓒ 초현실주의의 발현에 영향을 준 것을 설명하려고
Ⓓ 화가들이 사용했던 기법을 비교하려고

어휘 surrealism n 초현실주의 | movement n 운동 | Dadaism n 다다이즘 | reaction n 반응 | horror n 공포, 경악 | incompetent adj 무능한 | empire n 제국 | monarchy n 군주 | govern v 다스리다 | depose v 물러나게 하다, 퇴위시키다 | relegate v 좌천시키다, 강등시키다 | aftermath n 여파, 후유증 | anarchist n 무정부주의자 | ideal n 이상 | crave v 갈망하다, 열망하다 | order n 질서 | emerge v 부상하다, 나타나다 | decade n 10년 | prosperity n 부흥 | wound n 상처 | retreat n 후퇴 | survivor n 생존자 | dwell v 머물다 | explore v 탐사하다, 탐구하다, 살피다 | conscious adj 의식의 | unconscious adj 무의식의 | delineate v 기술하다 | traditional adj 전통적인 | reject v 거부하다 | stark adj 냉혹한 | previous adj 이전의 | mystery n 수수께끼, 신비, 미스터리 | imagination n 상상

Passage 2

Man: Professor

Listen to part of a lecture in an ecology class.

M OK, class. What I'd like to talk about today is something that is important to all of our lives—the greenhouse effect. Now, this term gets tossed around quite a bit, but I'm not sure that all of you will fully understand what it really means. So, I'd like to take a minute to explain how the greenhouse effect works and why it is becoming more and more important.
OK, the greenhouse effect revolves around carbon dioxide

남자: 교수

생태학 강의의 일부를 들으시오.

남 좋아요, 여러분. 오늘 이야기하고 싶은 것은 우리 모두의 삶에 중요한 것입니다. 바로 온실 효과죠. 자, 이 용어는 자주 논의되지만 여러분 모두가 이것이 진짜로 무엇을 의미하는지 이해하고 있는지는 잘 모르겠습니다. 그래서 온실 효과가 어떻게 작용하고 왜 그것이 점점 더 중요해지는지 잠시 설명하도록 하겠습니다.
자, 온실 효과는 이산화탄소와 그 특성을 중심으로

and its properties. The Earth's atmosphere contains a good deal of carbon dioxide and this stops heat from escaping into outer space. Now, people have started to think that this is a bad thing, but it's not entirely. Without the greenhouse effect, the Earth would be significantly colder and much of it would become uninhabitable. With that said, however, humans have been adding a lot of carbon dioxide to the atmosphere in the form of pollution, which is raising the temperature to such a degree that people are beginning to worry about melting ice caps and serious weather changes. If the rate of heating continues to increase it could become a runaway greenhouse effect, which is how Venus became so inhospitable to life. Therefore, we really should appreciate the greenhouse effect but also be conscious of how it could change our lives.

합니다. 지구의 대기는 상당한 양의 이산화탄소를 함유하고 있으며 이것은 열기가 우주 공간으로 빠져나가는 것을 막죠. 지금 사람들은 이것이 나쁜 것이라고 생각하기 시작했지만 전부 그렇지는 않습니다. 온실 효과가 없다면 지구는 훨씬 더 추워질 것이고 지구의 대부분이 거주할 수 없어질 겁니다. 하지만 그 말이 나왔으니 말인데, 인류는 오염의 형태로 대기에 이산화탄소를 엄청나게 더하기 시작했고, 이는 온도를 높여 사람들이 만년설이 녹는 것과 심각한 기후 변화를 걱정해야 할 정도가 되었습니다. 만약 더워지는 속도가 계속해서 증가한다면 걷잡을 수 없는 온실 효과가 될 수 있고, 금성이 이런 식으로 사람이 살 수 없는 곳이 되었죠. 그래서 우리는 온실 효과에 감사해야 하지만 이것이 우리의 삶을 어떻게 바꿀 수 있는지를 의식해야만 합니다.

Q. Why does the professor mention Venus in the lecture?

Ⓐ To introduce the concept of the greenhouse effect
Ⓑ To tell the students how the greenhouse effect can be positive
Ⓒ To explain what could possibly happen to the Earth
Ⓓ To indicate how the planet is similar to our own

Q. 교수는 강의에서 왜 금성을 언급하는가?

Ⓐ 온실 효과의 개념을 소개하려고
Ⓑ 온실 효과가 어떻게 긍정적일 수 있는지 학생들에게 말하려고
Ⓒ 지구에 어떤 일이 일어날 수 있는지 설명하려고
Ⓓ 그 행성이 우리가 사는 행성과 어떻게 비슷한지 보여 주려고

어휘 greenhouse effect 온실 효과 | toss around 논의하다 | revolve v ~을 중심으로 하다, 돌다, 회전하다 | carbon dioxide 이산화탄소 | property n 특성 | atmosphere n 대기 | contain v 포함하다, 함유하다 | escape v 빠져나가다 | outer space 우주 공간 | entirely adv 완전히 | significantly adv 크게, 심각하게 | uninhabitable adj 거주할 수 없는 | with that said 말이 나온 김에 | pollution n 오염 | raise v 올리다, 높이다 | degree n 정도 | ice cap 만년설 | runaway adj 걷잡을 수 없는, 급속한 | inhospitable adj 사람이 살기 힘든 | appreciate v 인정하다, 고마워하다 | conscious adj 의식하는

Passage 3

Woman: Professor

Listen to part of a lecture in a biology class.

W This afternoon's class is going to be about a truly amazing bird, the hummingbird. Now I'm not sure if you've ever seen live hummingbirds before, but if you have, you know just how beautiful and interesting they can be. There are hummingbirds that fly around sometimes in my backyard, and I always feel intrigued watching them hover and fly. And this is probably the most spectacular thing about the hummingbird—the way that it flies, I mean. It can hover in the air in a unique way while also being capable of high-speed dives of up to 63 miles per hour. In addition to this, the hummingbird can flap its wings as fast as 75 wing beats per second. Not surprisingly, the hummingbird has developed muscles that are very strong for its relatively small size.

In fact, the breast muscles of a hummingbird can comprise about 30% of its total body weight. Of course, those

여자: 교수

생물학 강의의 일부를 들으시오.

여 오늘 오후 수업은 정말 놀라운 새인 벌새에 관한 것입니다. 여러분이 전에 살아 있는 벌새를 본 적이 있는지 모르겠지만 만약 본 적이 있다면 이 새가 얼마나 아름답고 흥미로운지 알 거예요. 우리 집 뒤뜰에 가끔 벌새들이 날아다니는데 공중을 맴돌며 날아다니는 것을 볼 때면 늘 호기심을 갖게 되죠. 그리고 이 점이 아마 벌새의 가장 멋진 점일 겁니다. 그러니까, 날아다니는 방식 말이에요. 벌새는 아주 특이한 방식으로 공중을 맴돌고 시속 63마일이라는 매우 빠른 속도로 급강하할 수도 있습니다. 이뿐 아니라, 벌새는 초당 75번의 날갯짓을 하며 매우 빠르게 날개를 퍼덕일 수 있습니다. 놀랄 것도 없이, 벌새는 상대적으로 작은 크기에 비해 근육이 무척 강하게 발달했죠.

사실 벌새의 가슴 근육은 전체 몸무게에서 대략 30퍼센트 정도를 차지할 수 있습니다. 물론 이 가슴

muscles are still very small, as the total body weight of a hummingbird is usually between, um, two and, uh, twenty grams. Overall, the hummingbird is an amazing bird that packs a huge number of interesting characteristics into a very small body. However, there are some mysteries surrounding the hummingbird, and I'd like to take a look at those together.

근육은 여전히 매우 적다고 말할 수 있지만요. 벌새의 총 무게가 대개, 음, 2그램에서, 어, 20그램 정도밖에 되지 않기 때문이죠. 전반적으로 벌새는 매우 작은 몸 안에 아주 많은 흥미로운 특징을 지닌 놀라운 새입니다. 하지만 벌새를 둘러싼 의문점이 몇 가지 있는데, 이것을 함께 살펴보고자 합니다.

Q. Why does the professor mention the hummingbirds in her backyard?

Ⓐ To introduce the interesting way that hummingbirds fly
Ⓑ To inform the students about the hummingbird's habitat
Ⓒ To tell the students where they can go to study hummingbirds
Ⓓ To describe some of the reasons why the hummingbird is important

Q. 교수는 왜 자신의 집 뒤뜰의 벌새를 언급하는가?

Ⓐ 벌새가 날아다니는 흥미로운 방식을 소개하려고
Ⓑ 벌새의 서식지에 관해 학생들에게 알려주려고
Ⓒ 학생들이 벌새를 연구하기 위해 어디로 가면 되는지 말하려고
Ⓓ 벌새가 중요한 이유 몇 가지를 설명하려고

어휘 truly adv 진정으로 I amazing adj 놀라운 I hummingbird n 벌새 I intrigued adj 아주 흥미로워 하는 I hover v 맴돌다 I spectacular adj 극적인, 장관의 I flap v 퍼덕이다 I muscle n 근육 I relatively adv 상대적으로, 비교적 I breast n 가슴 I comprise v ~으로 구성되다, 이뤄지다 I pack v ~을 가지다 I surround v 둘러싸다

Passage 4

Man: Professor

Listen to part of a lecture in a paleontology class.

M I'd like to move to the subject of how paleontologists are now using X-rays to study fossils without damaging them. In the past, there was a great deal of difficulty involved in cleaning away the rock from a fossil using chisels and power tools so that it could be studied properly, and sometimes the fossils themselves were damaged in the process.

With the help of X-rays, however, we can now examine fossils without painstakingly cleaning away the rock and risking harm to the fossil. Instead, we can just look at X-ray pictures that show the fossil through the rock. X-ray photography also allows us to study more aspects of fossils than we could in the past. With x-rays, we can clearly see the microscopic parts of fossils that we might never have detected before. Tiny embryonic cells that we didn't even know about before can now be analyzed with great precision thanks to this technology.

Special computers are also helping us create three dimensional models of fossils which, in turn, allows us to explore egg and bone structures in quite extraordinary ways. All of this seemed impossible to paleontologists in the past, but today they are a very real part of the study of fossils.

남자: 교수

고생물학 강의의 일부를 들으시오.

남 고생물학자들이 아무런 손상 없이 화석을 연구하기 위해 어떻게 엑스레이를 사용하는지 그 주제로 넘어가도록 하겠습니다. 과거에는 화석을 정확히 연구하기 위해 끌이나 전동 공구를 이용해 화석에서 암석을 제거하는 데 많은 어려움이 있었고 때때로 이 과정에서 화석 자체가 손상되기도 했습니다.

하지만 엑스레이의 도움으로 이제는 힘들여 암석을 제거하거나 화석을 손상시킬 위험 없이 화석을 관찰할 수 있습니다. 대신 암석을 꿰뚫어 화석을 보여주는 엑스레이 사진을 보면 되죠. 엑스레이 사진은 과거에 비해 화석의 좀 더 많은 면을 연구할 수 있도록 해줍니다. 엑스레이 덕분에 전에는 감지하지 못했던 화석의 매우 미세한 부분을 분명하게 관찰할 수 있습니다. 전에는 알지도 못했던 미세한 배아세포도 이러한 기술 덕분에 이제 매우 정확히 분석할 수 있습니다.

또한 특수 컴퓨터가 화석의 3차원 모델을 만들어낼 수 있게 돕고 매우 특별한 방식으로 알이나 뼈의 구조를 분석하게 해줍니다. 이 모든 게 과거 고생물학자들에게는 불가능해 보였지만 오늘날에는 화석 연구의 매우 현실적인 한 부분이 되었죠.

Q. Why does the professor mention chisels and power tools in the lecture?

Ⓐ To explain how fossils are often damaged
Ⓑ To illustrate how fossils were studied in the past
Ⓒ To show how fossil skeletons are reconstructed
Ⓓ To give an example of tools used by archaeologists

Q. 교수는 왜 강의에서 끌과 전동 공구를 언급하는가?

Ⓐ 어떻게 화석이 종종 손상을 입는지 설명하려고
Ⓑ 과거에 화석이 어떻게 연구되었는지 설명하려고
Ⓒ 화석 뼈대가 어떻게 재구성되는지 보이려고
Ⓓ 고고학자들이 사용하는 도구의 예시를 들려고

어휘 subject n 주제 I paleontologist n 고생물학자 I fossil n 화석 I damage v 손상을 입히다 I chisel n 끌 I power tool 전동 공구 I properly adv 정확히, 제대로 I examine v 관찰하다 I painstakingly adv 힘들여, 공들여 I risk v 위험을 각오하다 I harm v 손상을 입히다, 해를 끼치다 I aspect n 측면, 양상 I microscopic adj 미세한 I detect v 감지하다 I embryonic adj 배아의 I cell n 세포 I analyze v 분석하다 I precision n 정확함, 정확(성) I explore v 분석하다, 탐구하다 I extraordinary adj 특별한, 놀라운

Passage 5

Man: Professor

Listen to part of a lecture in an ecology class.

M How many of you remember the Exxon Valdez disaster? Hmm... No one? Well, perhaps you're just a little bit too young, eh? Anyway, today, we'll discuss this sad historical event and its impact on, well, the world, really. In the late 1960s and early 1970s, the United States hoped to decrease the country's dependence on foreign oil by using oil from Alaska. Experts believed that Alaska had the largest oil reserves ever found on the North American continent, so the Trans-Alaskan Pipeline was built in 1977. The Trans-Alaskan Pipeline brought crude oil to the Alaskan coast, and oil tankers brought it south. Well, you know, environmentalists had always protested the pipeline, and in March of 1989 disaster struck when the Exxon Valdez tanker sank near the Alaskan coast. Almost 11 million gallons of oil spilled into Alaska's fragile coastal ecosystem. That was the largest oil spill in U.S. history, and was, obviously, a source of great concern to outraged environmentalists.

Let me tell you about the cleanup process. First and foremost, it wasn't easy. Among several problems was a setback caused by a storm that spread the oil slick far and wide, onto the long stretch of shoreline and out into the sea. This changed the problem from a large but relatively isolated oil spill to one that overwhelmed the cleanup project. Actually, the storm combined the oil with salt water, creating a mixture that does not burn easily. This prevented the project from using the crude but cost-efficient solution of burning surface oil to remove it from the ocean's surface.

Both traditional and non-traditional methods were used to clean up the spill. Since oil is lighter than water, affected beaches were blasted with hot water in order to force the oil back into the water, where it could be skimmed more efficiently. Other efforts included burning oil on the water's surface, using dispersants to scatter it farther into the ocean, and manually cleaning any rocks and animals that

남자: 교수

생태학 강의의 일부를 들으시오.

남 여러분 중 엑슨발데스호 참사를 기억하는 사람이 몇 명이나 되죠? 흠... 아무도 없나요? 음, 아마도 여러분 나이가 너무 어리기 때문인가 보군요, 그렇죠? 어쨌든 오늘은 이 안타까운 역사적 사건과 그것이 전 세계에 미친 영향에 대해 논의할 것입니다. 1960년대 후반과 1970년대 초, 미국은 알래스카에서 나는 석유를 사용함으로써 외국산 석유에 대한 국가 의존도를 줄이고자 했습니다. 전문가들은 알래스카가 북미 대륙에서 발견된 것 가운데 가장 큰 원유 매장량을 갖고 있다고 믿었기 때문에 1977년 알래스카 횡단 송유관을 건설하게 됩니다. 알래스카 횡단 송유관은 알래스카 해변으로 원유를 운반했고 유조선이 그 원유를 남쪽으로 운반했습니다. 음, 환경론자들은 줄곧 송유관 사용에 반대했는데, 1989년 3월 엑슨발데스 유조선이 알래스카 해변 가까이에서 침몰하면서 끔찍한 참사가 일어났습니다. 거의 천백만 갤런의 석유가 알래스카의 손상되기 쉬운 해안 생태계로 흘러 들어갔습니다. 이는 미국 역사상 가장 규모가 컸던 석유 유출이었고 격분한 환경론자들에게는 분명 아주 큰 걱정거리였습니다.

그 정화 과정에 대해 이야기할게요. 무엇보다도 그 과정은 쉽지 않았습니다. 여러 가지 문제 가운데 석유 기름막을 해변 전체와 바다 속으로 널리 퍼지게 한 폭풍 문제가 있었어요. 양은 많지만 상대적으로 범위가 좁았던 석유 유출을 폭풍은 정화 프로젝트를 압도하는 심각한 문제로 바꾸어 놓게 됩니다. 실제로 폭풍이 석유와 바닷물을 섞이게 해서 쉽게 타지 않는 혼합물이 만들어졌습니다. 이는 정화 프로젝트에서 바다 표면의 석유를 태워 없애는 거칠지만 비용 면에서 효율적인 해결책을 사용할 수 없게 만들었죠.

기존의 방법과 새로운 방법 모두 정화를 위해 사용되었습니다. 기름은 물보다 더 가볍기 때문에 오염된 해변에서는 고온의 물 폭탄을 터뜨려 기름을 다

were coated with oil. One of the newer and more advanced treatments used was bioremediation. Bioremediation uses a fertilizer that encourages the growth of microbes that actually eat oil. Despite these and other methods, only about 15% of the oil was actually recovered, while umm, a large percentage was burned off, cleaned up, evaporated or dispersed. Still, the ecological impact was devastating. Along about roughly 1,000 miles of shoreline, sea mammal, fish, and bird populations were severely affected. Some affected species are still struggling, and their future remains uncertain even today. And yet, despite the lengthy and disappointing cleanup, things could have been even worse.

시 바다로 내보냈는데, 이는 더 효과적으로 찌꺼기를 걷어내기 위해서였습니다. 다른 시도는 물 표면의 기름을 태우는 것과 분산제를 사용하여 바다 표면의 기름을 멀리 흩어지게 하는 것, 기름으로 뒤덮인 돌과 동물을 수작업으로 깨끗하게 만드는 것이 있었습니다. 사용된 좀더 새롭고 진보한 방법 중 하나는 생물적 환경 정화였어요. 생물적 환경 정화는 실제로 기름을 먹는 미생물의 성장을 촉진하기 위해 비료를 사용합니다. 이러한 여러 다른 방법에도 불구하고 단지 15퍼센트 정도의 기름만이 회수된 반면, 음, 많은 양의 기름이 연소되고, 정화되고, 증발되고, 또는 흩어졌습니다. 그렇지만 생태학적 여파는 참담했습니다. 대략 천 마일에 달하는 해안에 걸쳐 바다 포유류, 물고기, 새의 개체수가 심각하게 영향을 받았습니다. 일부 오염된 종은 아직까지도 고통을 받고 있으며 그들의 미래는 오늘날까지도 불확실합니다. 하지만 장기화되고 실망스러웠던 정화 과정이었긴 하지만 상황은 더 나빴을 수도 있었습니다.

Q. Why does the professor talk about the different oil clean-up methods?

Ⓐ To classify them into traditional and non-traditional methods

Ⓑ To indicate the scale of the environmental catastrophe

Ⓒ To examine why some were more effective than others

Ⓓ To emphasize the difficulty of cleaning up the Exxon Valdez oil spill

Q. 교수는 왜 각기 다른 기름 정화 방법들에 관해 이야기하는가?

Ⓐ 이들을 전통적 방법과 비전통적 방법으로 분류하기 위해

Ⓑ 이 환경적 재앙의 규모를 나타내기 위해

Ⓒ 왜 어떤 방법은 다른 방법보다 더 효율적이었는지 알아보기 위해

Ⓓ 엑슨발데스호 석유 유출 정화의 어려움을 강조하기 위해

어휘 disaster n 참사, 재앙 | discuss v 논의하다 | historical adj 역사적인 | impact n 영향 | decrease v 줄이다, 감소하다 | dependence n 의존 | foreign adj 외국의 | reserve n 매장량 | continent n 대륙 | Trans-Alaskan Pipeline 알래스카 횡단 송유관 | crude oil 원유 | environmentalist n 환경 운동가 | protest v 항의하다, 반대하다 | fragile adj 손상되기 쉬운, 취약한 | coastal adj 해안의 | ecosystem n 생태계 | concern n 걱정, 우려 | outraged adj 격분한 | cleanup n 정화 | foremost adj 가장 중요한 | setback n 차질 | oil slick 유막 | stretch n 길게 뻗은 지역, 구간 | shoreline n 해안가, 물가 | relatively adv 상대적으로 | isolated adj 고립된, 동떨어진 | overwhelm v 압도하다 | combine v 합치다 | prevent v 막다 | crude adj 거친, 있는 그대로의 | efficient adj 효율적인 | solution n 해결책 | surface adj 표면의 | traditional adj 전통적인 | blast v 폭발시키다, 폭파하다 | skim v 걷어 내다 | dispersant n 분산제 | scatter v 흩다 | manually adv 손으로, 수공으로 | coat v 덮다 | advanced adj 진보한 | treatment n 처리, 치료 | bioremediation n 생물적 환경 정화 | fertilizer n 비료 | encourage v 장려하다 | growth n 성장 | microbe n 미생물 | recover v 되찾다, 회수하다 | evaporate v 증발하다 | disperse v 흩다, 흩어지게 하다 | ecological adj 생태학적 | devastating adj 대단히 파괴적인 | population n 개체수 | struggle v 힘겨워하다 | uncertain adj 불확실한 | lengthy adj 너무 긴, 오랜 | disappointing adj 실망스러운

Passage 6

Man: Student | Woman: Professor

Listen to part of a discussion in an art class.

W Okay, last time we talked a little bit about what art is and how we determine whether or not something is art, and we found that there were many different answers to this question. As we talk today, I'd like for you to think about

남자: 학생 | 여자: 교수

미술 수업 중 토론의 일부를 들으시오.

여 좋아요. 지난 시간에 우리는 예술이 무엇인지, 어떻게 예술인지 아닌지 결정하는 방법에 대해 이야기했고, 이 질문에 대해 아주 많은 다양한 답변들이 있었어요. 오늘은 여러분에게 이러한 질문들이 환

how these questions apply to environment art. To begin with, however, has anyone heard of environment art before or know what it is?

M Is it art that deals with a lot of natural things? Or, um, maybe tries to say something about environmental problems?

W Well, neither really, but good try. Environment art doesn't have to deal with natural things, but it often uses natural materials or can exist in an outdoor environment. To be more specific, environment art is really art that is meant to be placed in a certain location, meaning that the artist designs the work so that it will work well in a specific place with specific surroundings. And, well, for example, think of a sculpture or another kind of art object that must be integrated into its environment, which is how we get the name environment art.

M I guess you're saying environment art is art that works well in specific places... so, with certain lighting or certain types of buildings or...?

W Right, but maybe an example will help you understand. Maya Lin is a fairly famous artist who has done a lot of environment art. Her Vietnam Veterans' Memorial was intended to go in a certain place and uses certain features of that place to convey its message. If we moved it to a different place, much of that message would be lost or changed. Because of this, the memorial is an environment work.

M So, Maya Lin isn't an environment artist because she has concerns about the environment? She's an environment artist because, um, she designs things that only go in one place?

W Well, you know, that is true. However, she has also done a lot of work that shows her concern for the environment. She's often used natural recycled materials, such as windshield glass from old cars, and incorporated nature into her art with the hope that it will help people appreciate Earth more. The best example I can give you is "The Wave Field" at the University of Michigan. It's a group of grass waves... around fifty of them, I believe... built into one of the university's lawns. In a way, it looks like an ocean of grass in the middle of the campus. And a lot of the students often sit and relax on those grassy waves, which really illustrates one of the most important things about Maya Lin. That is, she uses natural shapes and materials to make something beautiful... but she's also creating something that people can interact with and that helps people feel relaxed in nature.

경 예술에 어떻게 적용되는지 생각해 보라고 말하고 싶군요. 하지만 우선 환경 예술에 관해 전에 들어본 사람이나 그것이 무엇인지 아는 사람 있나요?

남 많은 자연적인 것들을 다루는 예술인가요? 아니면, 음, 환경 문제에 관해 이야기하려는 예술인가요?

여 음, 사실 둘 다 아니지만 시도는 좋았어요. 환경 예술은 자연 속의 대상을 다룰 필요는 없지만 자연적인 재료를 자주 사용하고 야외 환경에 설치될 수 있죠. 좀 더 구체적으로 이야기하면, 환경 예술은 어떤 특정한 위치에 설치되는 예술을 말합니다. 특정한 환경을 가진 특정한 장소와 작품이 잘 어울리도록 예술가가 디자인하는 것을 의미해요. 예를 들자면, 환경과 조화를 이루어야 하는 조각이나 기타 다른 종류의 예술품을 생각해 보세요. 그래서 환경 예술이라는 이름을 갖게 된 거죠.

남 환경 예술은 특정한 장소와 잘 어울리는 예술이라는 말씀이시군요... 그래서 특정 조명이나 특정 형태의 건물 등과 함께 가는...?

여 맞아요. 하지만 예를 들면 이해가 쉬울 거예요. 마야 린은 수많은 환경 예술 작업을 했던 상당히 유명한 예술가입니다. 그녀의 작품 중 베트남 참전 용사 기념상은 특정한 위치에 놓이고 작품의 메시지를 전달하기 위해 그 장소의 특수한 특징을 이용합니다. 만일 그 작품을 다른 장소로 옮긴다면, 그 메시지의 대부분은 상실되거나 또는 변질될 거예요. 이 때문에 그 기념상은 환경 예술 작품인 거죠.

남 그럼, 마야 린이 환경에 관심을 가졌기 때문에 환경 예술가인 게 아니라는 말씀이시죠? 그녀가 환경 예술가인 이유는 음, 그녀가 어떤 한 장소에 잘 어울리는 작품을 디자인했기 때문인 거죠?

여 음, 맞아요. 하지만 그녀는 환경에 대한 관심을 보여주는 많은 작품을 만들기도 했어요. 낡은 차의 바람막이 창유리 같은 천연 재활용 재료를 자주 사용했고, 사람들이 지구를 더 소중히 여기는 데 도움이 되고자 하는 소망으로 예술작품을 자연과 결합했어요. 제가 들 수 있는 최고의 예는 미시간 대학에 있는 〈웨이브 필드〉입니다. 이 작품은 잔디 물결이 여럿 모여 있는 것인데 제가 알기로는... 대략 50여 개의 잔디 물결이 대학 잔디밭 한 곳에 설치되어 있어요. 어떻게 보면, 교정 한가운데 있는 잔디 바다처럼 보이죠. 그리고 많은 학생들이 그 잔디 물결에 앉아 휴식을 취하곤 합니다. 이것이 마야 린에 관한 가장 중요한 점을 보여주고 있지요. 말하자면 그녀는 자연 그대로의 모습과 재료로 아름다운 작품을 만들 뿐 아니라 사람들이 그것과 상호작용할 수 있고 사람들이 자연 안에서 휴식을 취하는 데 도움이 되는 작품을 만듭니다.

Q. How does the professor proceed with her discussion of environment art?

Ⓐ She explains a concept and then provides examples of it.
Ⓑ She describes an artwork then explains the concepts behind it.
Ⓒ She gives the history of an artistic movement and talks about its important artists.
Ⓓ She examines an artist's works then discusses her personal history.

Q. 교수는 환경 예술 논의를 어떻게 진행해 나가는가?

Ⓐ 개념을 설명한 뒤 그 개념의 예시를 제공한다.
Ⓑ 예술 작품을 묘사한 뒤 그 뒤에 숨겨진 개념을 설명한다.
Ⓒ 한 예술 운동의 역사를 말한 뒤 중요 예술가들에 대해 이야기한다.
Ⓓ 예술가의 작품을 관찰한 뒤 그 사람의 개인사에 대해 논의한다.

어휘 determine v 결정하다 I exist v 존재하다 I outdoor adj 야외의 I specific adj 구체적인 I certain adj 특정한 I surroundings n 주변 환경 I sculpture n 조각 I integrate v 통합하다 I convey v 전달하다 I concern n 우려, 걱정 I recycled adj 재활용된 I windshield glass 바람막이 창유리 I incorporate v 포함하다 I appreciate v 고마워하다 I lawn n 잔디밭 I interact v 상호작용하다 I relaxed adj 느긋한, 여유 있는

Passage 7

Man: Professor

Listen to part of a lecture in an American history class.

M Today, I'd like to start off by talking about Tecumseh, a famous Native American who showed a great deal of leadership ability in his life. He was born around 1768 and, consequently, lived during a time of warfare during which the European Americans were trying to take possession of Native American land. Uh, if you don't know what I mean here, you might want to look at the Indian Removal Act of 1830 and its plan to move Native Americans west of the Mississippi. In any case, **(E)** Tecumseh became the chief of the Shawnee tribe in 1789, and he greatly resented the encroachments on Native American land. The movement of American settlers westward increased rapidly **(C)** after the Louisiana Purchase, and **(B)** he tried to bring all of the Native American tribes together in order to form a unified front against the United States. **(A)** He also joined the British in the War of 1812, and, he displayed a great deal of strategic ability before his death in 1813.

남자: 교수

미국 역사 강의의 일부를 들으시오.

남 오늘은 일평생 위대한 지도력을 몸소 보여준 미국 원주민인 티컴세에 대해 이야기해 보도록 합시다. 티컴세는 1768년경 태어나서 유럽계 미국인들이 아메리카 원주민의 땅을 빼앗고자 했던 전쟁 시기에 살았습니다. 음, 제 말을 이해하지 못하겠으면, 아메리카 원주민들을 미시시피주 서부로 이주시키려던 1830년의 인디언 이주법과 그 계획을 보면 좋을 거예요. 어쨌든 **(E)** 티컴세는 1789년 쇼니 부족의 족장이 되었으며 아메리카 원주민의 땅이 침략당하는 것에 분노했습니다. **(C)** 루이지애나주 매입 이후 서쪽으로 향하는 미국 정착민들의 움직임은 급격히 빨라졌고, 그는 미국에 대항하여 **(B)** 통합된 전선을 구축하기 위해 모든 아메리카 원주민 부족을 하나로 모으려고 노력했습니다. **(A)** 그는 또한 1812년 전쟁에서 영국과 손을 잡았고 1813년 세상을 떠나기 전까지 뛰어난 전략적 역량을 보여주었습니다.

Q. The professor described some of the events that occurred during the life of Chief Tecumseh in the lecture. Put those events in the correct order. Drag each answer choice to the space where it belongs. One of the answer choices will not be used.

Ⓐ The Shawnee and other tribes sided with the British in the War of 1812.
Ⓑ Tecumseh tried to rally other Native American Tribes to form a confederacy.
Ⓒ The United States purchased the Louisiana Territory from France.
Ⓓ The Indian Removal Act was passed by the United States government.
Ⓔ Tecumseh became the chief of his tribe, the Shawnee.

Q. 교수는 강의에서 티컴세 족장의 삶에서 일어난 사건 일부를 서술했다. 이 사건들을 올바른 순서로 놓으시오. 각 보기를 알맞은 곳에 끌어다 넣으시오. 보기 중 하나는 사용되지 않는다.

Ⓐ 쇼니와 다른 부족들이 1812년 전쟁 때 영국의 편에 섰다.
Ⓑ 티컴세가 연맹을 형성하기 위해 다른 미국 원주민 부족들을 결집시키려고 했다.
Ⓒ 미국이 프랑스로부터 루이지애나주 영토를 구입했다.
Ⓓ 인디언 이주법이 미국 정부에서 통과되었다.
Ⓔ 티컴세가 자신의 부족인 쇼니의 지도자가 되었다.

1	(E) Tecumseh became the chief of his tribe, the Shawnee.
2	(C) The United States purchased the Louisiana Territory from France
3	(B) Tecumseh tried to rally other Native American Tribes to form a confederacy.
4	(A) The Shawnee and other tribes sided with the British in the War of 1812.

1	(E) 티컴세가 자신의 부족인 쇼니의 족장이 되었다.
2	(C) 미국이 프랑스로부터 루이지애나주 영토를 구입했다.
3	(B) 티컴세가 연맹을 형성하기 위해 다른 미국 원주민 부족들을 결집시키려고 했다.
4	(A) 쇼니족과 다른 부족들이 1812년 전쟁 때 영국의 편에 섰다.

어휘 Native American 미국 원주민 | consequently adv 그 결과, 따라서 | warfare n 전투, 전쟁 | possession n 소유, 차지 | removal n 이동, 이전 | chief n 족장 | tribe n 부족 | resent v 분개하다, 억울해 하다 | encroachment n 침략, 침해 | settler n 정착민 | rapidly adv 급격히 | unify v 통합하다, 통일하다

Passage 8

Woman: Professor

Listen to part of a lecture in an astronomy class.

W Now let's move on to Uranus. It is the seventh planet from the Sun, so **(B)** its orbit lies between Saturn and Neptune. Although it is closer to the Sun than Neptune, its surface temperature is actually colder. In fact, **(C)** it is the coldest planet in our solar system at negative 224 degrees Centigrade. **(E)** Its atmosphere is mostly comprised of hydrogen and helium, but it also contains water, methane, and ammonia. Its high methane content means that the atmosphere reflects blue wavelengths of light, **(D)** giving the planet its smooth blue appearance. Like its neighboring planets, Uranus has a magnetosphere, a ring system, and many moons. What differentiates Uranus from all other planets, however, is its axial tilt. **(A)** Most planets rotate on an axis that is nearly vertical. By comparison, Uranus is lying on its side with its axis pointing toward and away from the Sun.

여자: 교수

천문학 강의의 일부를 들으시오.

여 이제 천왕성으로 넘어갑시다. 천왕성은 태양에서 7번째로 떨어져 있는 행성이기에 **(B)** 궤도가 토성과 해왕성 사이에 놓여 있습니다. 해왕성보다 태양에 가깝지만, 표면 온도는 사실 더 춥죠. 실제로, 천왕성은 섭씨 −224도로 **(C)** 우리 태양계에서 가장 추운 행성입니다. **(E)** 대기는 대부분 수소와 헬륨으로 이루어져 있지만 물과 메탄, 암모니아도 함유하고 있습니다. 높은 메탄 함유량은 대기가 빛의 푸른 파장을 반사하여 **(D)** 행성이 매끄러운 푸른 외형을 가진다는 것을 의미합니다. 이웃에 있는 행성들처럼 천왕성도 자기권과 고리계, 많은 위성을 갖고 있습니다. 그러나 천왕성과 다른 모든 행성들을 구분 짓는 것은 바로 자전축 기울기입니다. **(A)** 대부분의 행성은 거의 수직으로 놓인 축을 중심으로 돕니다. 이에 비해 천왕성은 축이 태양 쪽에서 태양 반대편 쪽으로 향하고 있어 옆으로 누워 있죠.

Q. In the lecture, the professor listed many features of the planet Uranus. Indicate which of the following features are mentioned in the lecture. Click in the correct box for each sentence.

	Yes	No
(A) The planet rotates on a horizontal axis.	✓	
(B) Its orbit lies between Jupiter and Saturn.		✓
(C) Its temperature is the lowest in the solar system.	✓	
(D) The planet looks blue because of its atmosphere.	✓	
(E) Its atmosphere is composed mostly of methane.		✓

Q. 강의에서 교수는 천왕성의 다양한 특징을 열거한다. 다음 중 어느 특징이 강의에서 언급되었는지 표시하시오. 각 문장에 대해 맞는 칸에 표시하시오.

	예	아니오
(A) 이 행성은 수평축을 중심으로 회전한다.	✓	
(B) 이 행성의 궤도는 목성과 토성 사이에 놓여 있다.		✓
(C) 이 행성의 기온은 태양계에서 가장 낮다.	✓	
(D) 이 행성은 대기 때문에 푸른색으로 보인다.	✓	
(E) 행성의 대기는 대부분 메탄으로 구성되어 있다.		✓

어휘 orbit ⓝ 궤도 | surface temperature 표면 온도 | solar system 태양계 | atmosphere ⓝ 대기 | comprised of ~으로 구성된 | hydrogen ⓝ 수소 | helium ⓝ 헬륨 | methane ⓝ 메탄 | ammonia ⓝ 암모니아 | content ⓝ 함유량 | reflect ⓥ 반사하다 | wavelength ⓝ 파장 | appearance ⓝ 외형, 생김새 | magnetosphere ⓝ 자기권 | moon ⓝ 위성 | differentiate ⓥ 구분 짓다, 다르게 하다 | axial tilt 자전축 기울기 | rotate ⓥ 회전하다 | vertical adj 수직의 | by comparison 그에 비해 | lie ⓥ 눕다

Passage 9

Man: Professor

Listen to part of a lecture in a zoology class.

M Most filter-feeding animals live in bodies of water. This is also true for the largest filter feeder, which is also the largest animal in the world today, the blue whale. Blue whales are a type of baleen whale, which means that they do not have teeth in their massive mouths. Instead, they have large keratin plates that hang from their upper jaw that they use as a filter. **(E)** When a blue whale wants to feed, it will locate a large school of plankton and swim through it. As it passes through the whale opens its mouth and **(A)** takes a giant mouthful of water full of small fish, krill, and other tiny organisms. Then it closes its mouth and forces the water out through its lips. **(D)** The small organisms are trapped by the baleen plates, and the **(C)** whale swallows them after most of the water is gone.

남자: 교수

동물학 강의의 일부를 들으시오.

남 대부분의 여과 섭식 동물은 물에서 삽니다. 가장 거대한 여과 섭식 동물이자 오늘날 세계에서 가장 큰 동물이기도 한 흰긴수염고래도 마찬가지입니다. 흰긴수염고래는 수염고래의 일종이며, 그 말은 이 동물의 거대한 입 안에 이빨이 없다는 뜻입니다. 대신 위턱에서 내려온 커다란 케라틴 판이 있어 필터로 사용하죠. **(E)** 흰긴수염고래가 먹이를 먹고 싶을 때는 큰 플랑크톤 떼를 찾아내 헤엄쳐 지나갑니다. 지나가면서 고래는 입을 열어 작은 물고기와 크릴새우, 그 외의 다른 생물로 가득한 **(A)** 거대한 양의 물을 빨아들이죠. 그 뒤 입을 닫고 입술을 통해 물을 밀어냅니다. **(D)** 작은 생물들은 고래 수염판에 갇히게 되고 **(C)** 고래는 물이 대부분 빠지면 이것들을 삼킵니다.

Q. In the lecture, the professor described how a blue whale feeds. Put the steps in the correct order. Drag each answer choice to the space where it belongs. One of the answer choices will not be used.

Ⓐ It takes a huge mouthful of sea water.
Ⓑ It forces the water out through its blow hole.
Ⓒ The whale swallows its prey after expelling the water.
Ⓓ The baleen plates trap small organisms in its mouth.
Ⓔ The whale locates a large group of its preferred prey.

1	Ⓔ The whale locates a large group of its preferred prey.
2	Ⓐ It takes a huge mouthful of sea water.
3	Ⓓ The baleen plates trap small organisms in its mouth.
4	Ⓒ The whale swallows its prey after expelling the water.

Q. 강의에서 교수는 흰긴수염고래가 먹이를 먹는 방식을 묘사한다. 이 단계들을 올바른 순서로 놓으시오. 각 보기를 알맞은 곳에 끌어다 넣으시오. 보기 중 하나는 사용되지 않는다.

Ⓐ 고래가 거대한 양의 해수를 들이킨다.
Ⓑ 고래가 분수공을 통해 물을 밀어낸다.
Ⓒ 고래가 물을 뱉어낸 뒤 먹이를 삼킨다.
Ⓓ 수염판이 고래의 입 속에 작은 생물을 가둔다.
Ⓔ 고래가 선호하는 먹이 떼를 찾는다.

1	Ⓔ 고래가 선호하는 먹이 떼를 찾는다.
2	Ⓐ 고래가 거대한 양의 해수를 들이킨다.
3	Ⓓ 수염판이 고래의 입 속에 작은 생물을 가둔다.
4	Ⓒ 고래가 물을 뱉어낸 뒤 먹이를 삼킨다.

어휘 filter-feeding adj 여과 섭식의 | blue whale 흰긴수염고래 | baleen whale 수염 고래 | massive adj 거대한 | keratin plate 케라틴 판 | jaw ⓝ 턱 | school ⓝ (물고기·해양 동물의) 떼, 무리 | krill ⓝ 크릴새우 | organism ⓝ 생물 | force ⓥ 억지로 ~하다 | trap ⓥ 가두다 | swallow ⓥ 삼키다

Passage 10

Woman: Professor

Listen to part of a lecture in an ecology class.

W Many ancient stone tools were produced through a process

여자: 교수

생태학 강의의 일부를 들으시오.

여 많은 고대 석기가 '두들겨 깨기'라는 과정을 통해

called knapping. **(C)** When a crafter wanted to make a knife, he would find a large stone of the kind best suited to that purpose—often obsidian—and **(A)** break it into smaller pieces. Then he chose the piece that was closest in shape to the desired final product. Using a harder stone, he would then carefully **(E)** chip off small pieces to get the rough form of a blade. Then he took smaller tools and chipped off even smaller flakes of stone until he had a sharp edge. The blade would be fairly difficult to use in that state, though, so **(B)** he would make a handle out of wood or bone and attach it to the blade with animal sinew.

생산되었습니다. **(C)** 도구를 만드는 사람이 칼을 만들고 싶었을 경우 그 목적에 가장 잘 맞는 큰 돌을 찾을 겁니다. 보통 흑요석이죠. 그 뒤 **(A)** 더 작은 조각으로 부숩니다. 그런 다음 원하는 최종 형태의 결과물과 가장 비슷한 모양의 조각을 택합니다. 그런 다음 그는 더 단단한 돌을 이용해 조심스럽게 칼날의 대략적인 형태를 만들기 위해 **(E)** 작은 조각을 떼어냅니다. 그리고 나서 더 작은 도구들을 갖고 날카로운 날이 나올 때까지 돌의 더 작은 조각을 떼어내죠. 하지만 칼은 그 상태로는 사용하기가 상당히 힘들기 때문에, **(B)** 나무나 뼈로 손잡이를 만든 뒤 동물의 힘줄을 이용해 칼에 부착했습니다.

Q. In the lecture, the professor describes how a knife is made. Put the steps in the correct order. Drag each answer choice to the space where it belongs. One of the answer choices will not be used.

Ⓐ The crafter shatters the stone to reduce its size.
Ⓑ The crafter fashions a handle and tie it with a blade.
Ⓒ The crafter locates a big piece of rock to work on.
Ⓓ The crafter uses sinew to sharpen the edge.
Ⓔ The crafter shapes the stone by slowly removing its flakes.

1	Ⓒ The crafter locates a big piece of rock to work on.
2	Ⓐ The crafter shatters the stone to reduce its size.
3	Ⓔ The crafter shapes the stone by slowly removing its flakes.
4	Ⓑ The crafter fashions a handle and tie it with a blade.

Q. 강의에서 교수는 칼이 만들어지는 과정을 묘사한다. 이 단계들을 올바른 순서로 놓으시오. 각 보기를 알맞은 곳에 끌어다 넣으시오. 보기 중 하나는 사용되지 않는다.

Ⓐ 도구를 만드는 사람이 크기를 줄이기 위해 돌을 부순다.
Ⓑ 도구를 만드는 사람이 손잡이를 만들어 칼에 부착한다.
Ⓒ 도구를 만드는 사람이 작업할 큰 조각의 돌을 찾는다.
Ⓓ 도구를 만드는 사람이 날을 날카롭게 만들기 위해 힘줄을 사용한다.
Ⓔ 도구를 만드는 사람이 조각을 천천히 제거하며 모양을 만든다.

1	Ⓒ 도구를 만드는 사람이 작업할 큰 조각의 돌을 찾는다.
2	Ⓐ 도구를 만드는 사람이 크기를 줄이기 위해 돌을 부순다.
3	Ⓔ 도구를 만드는 사람이 조각을 천천히 제거하며 모양을 만든다.
4	Ⓑ 도구를 만드는 사람이 손잡이를 만들어 칼에 부착한다.

어휘 ancient adj 고대의 | stone tool 석기 | produce v 생산하다 | process n 과정 | knapping n 내핑(세게 쳐서 깨기) | crafter n 무언가를 만드는 사람 | purpose n 목적 | obsidian n 흑요석 | desired adj 원하는 | product n 생산물, 제품 | carefully adv 주의 깊게 | chip off 떨어져 나가게 하다 | rough form 대강의 형태 | flake n 조각 | blade n 날 | fairly adv 상당히 | handle n 손잡이 | attach v 부착하다 | sinew n 힘줄

Passage 11

Man: Professor

Listen to part of a lecture in a history class.

M Hello everyone and welcome to today's lecture on a little bit of American history—the Harlem Renaissance. Well, there's an economic renaissance happening there now, but today we'll speak of a cultural renaissance, which happened mostly in the 1920s, just between World War I and the Great

남자: 교수

역사 강의의 일부를 들으시오.

남 모두들 안녕하세요. 오늘 강의에 온 것을 환영하고 오늘은 미국 역사에 대해서 조금 다루게 될 겁니다. 바로 할렘 르네상스죠. 음, 지금은 경제 르네상스가 일어나고 있지만, 오늘 우리는 제1차 세계 대전과 대공황 사이, 즉 대부분 1920년대에 일어난 문화적

Depression. Although, perhaps renaissance is the wrong word, since it means "rebirth" and African-American culture wasn't reborn in Harlem as a copy of some older, original form.

(B) The Harlem Renaissance included the birth of jazz music, **(D)** the birth of serious black theater, **(A)** the rise of black-authored socio-critical literature, and the rise of African subjects like the so-called "primitivism" in the visual arts. We could talk all day about what makes these four developments unique in the history of African-American culture, but let's focus a little on just two, the literary and the visual arts. In literature, authors Nella Larsen and Zora Neale Hurston spoke out and brought sophistication never before seen in published African-American literature. Intense irony and symbolism also mark Larsen's masterpieces *Quicksand* and *Passing*. In the visual arts, the direct representation of masks, dancing figures and other African images by artists, and real African-American people in paintings were shocking to some people.

How did so much change in the 1920s? Did genius and courage suddenly appear in Harlem? Or, did social, economic and cultural factors finally allow for this to happen? Well, probably a bit of both. A number of factors stimulated a creative surge resulting in the Harlem Renaissance. Racial pride was perhaps the single-most important factor fueling it. This concept began with the writings of W. E. B. Du Bois, considered one of the leaders of the 20th century black movement, and continued with the writer Alain Locke, who unlike Du Bois, mentored young artists, most notably the predominant author Langston Hughes. Hughes, perhaps more than any other figure, spread the ideas of cultural pride and racial consciousness while also encouraging the black aesthetic. Also, boosting these developments were Pablo Picasso's interest in African themes and the fledgling jazz music genre. These helped bring black art and culture into the American mainstream, creating a processional effect that inspired even more African-American artists to have a hand in the Harlem Renaissance.

르네상스에 관해 이야기할 겁니다. 다만 르네상스라는 말은 잘못된 표현일 것도 같네요. 왜냐하면 르네상스는 '재탄생'을 의미하는데 아프리카계 미국인 문화는 더 오래된 어떤 원형의 복제품으로서 할렘에서 재탄생한 것이 아니니 말입니다.

(B) 할렘 르네상스는 재즈 음악의 탄생, **(D)** 진지한 흑인 연극의 탄생, **(A)** 흑인 작가의 사회 비판적 문학의 등장, 시각 예술에서 소위 '원시주의'라고 불리는 아프리카 주제들의 등장을 포함합니다. 아프리카계 미국인 문화의 역사에서 왜 이 네 가지 발달이 특별한지에 대해서 하루 종일이라도 이야기할 수 있지만, 문학과 시각 예술 두 가지에 대해서만 중점을 두겠습니다. 문학에서 작가 넬라 라슨과 조라 닐 허스턴은 공개적으로 목소리를 높였고 출간된 아프리카계 미국인 문학에서 지금까지 본 적 없던 세련됨을 가져왔습니다. 극도의 반어법과 상징적 표현 또한 라슨의 대작 〈퀵샌드〉와 〈패싱〉의 특징입니다. 시각 예술에서는 예술가들에 의한 가면과 춤추는 인물 및 기타 아프리카의 이미지에 대한 직접적인 묘사와 그림에 표현된 실제 아프리카계 미국인의 모습은 일부 사람들에게는 충격적이었습니다.

1920년대에 어떻게 이렇게 많은 변화가 일어났을까요? 천재성과 용기가 갑자기 할렘에 등장했을까요? 아니면 사회, 경제, 문화적 요소가 마침내 이것이 발생하도록 만든 것일까요? 음, 아마도 둘 다 조금씩 맞을 것입니다. 많은 요소가 창의적인 변화의 물결을 자극했고 할렘 르네상스라는 결과를 초래했습니다. 인종적 자부심이 아마 이를 자극한 가장 중요한 단일 요소일 겁니다. 이 개념은 20세기 흑인 운동 지도자 중 한 명으로 간주되는 윌리엄 에드워드 부르크하르트 뒤 보이스의 작품으로 시작되었고 작가인 알레인 로크가 뒤를 이었는데, 로크는 뒤 보이스와 다르게 젊은 작가들을 이끌어 주었고 그 중에서도 가장 주목할 만한 인물로 (할렘 르네상스의) 중심적 작가인 랭스턴 휴즈가 있습니다. 휴즈는 흑인 미학을 독려하는 동시에 아마도 다른 어떤 인물보다도 더 많이 문화적 자부심과 인종적 의식을 퍼뜨렸습니다. 또한 이런 발전을 북돋운 것은 아프리카 주제에 관한 파블로 피카소의 관심과 신생 재즈 음악 장르였습니다. 이는 흑인 예술과 문화를 미국의 주류로 끌어들이는 데 도움을 주었고 훨씬 더 많은 아프리카계 미국인 예술가들이 할렘 르네상스에 참여하도록 영향을 주는 연속적인 결과를 이끌어냈습니다.

Q. In the lecture, the professor listed many developments that contributed to the Harlem Renaissance. Indicate which of the following developments are mentioned in the lecture.

Click in the correct box for each sentence.

Q. 강의에서 교수는 할렘 르네상스에 기여한 다양한 발전을 언급한다. 다음 중 어떤 발전이 강의에서 언급되었는지 표시하시오. 각 문장에 대해 맞는 칸에 표시하시오.

	Yes	No
Ⓐ The creation of black-authored literature that was critical of society	✓	
Ⓑ The birth of jazz music	✓	
Ⓒ An increase in immigration from African countries		✓
Ⓓ The beginnings of black theater	✓	
Ⓔ African Americans served in the military in World War I		✓

	예	아니오
Ⓐ 사회 비판적인 흑인 저자의 문학 창조	✓	
Ⓑ 재즈 음악의 탄생	✓	
Ⓒ 아프리카 국가들로부터의 이민의 증가		✓
Ⓓ 흑인 연극의 시작	✓	
Ⓔ 제1차 세계 대전에서 군인으로 복무한 미국 흑인들		✓

어휘 economic adj 경제의 I renaissance n 르네상스 I cultural adj 문화의 I rebirth n 재탄생 I original adj 원래의, 독창적인 I socio-critical adj 사회 비판적인 I literature n 문학 I primitivism n 원시주의 I visual art 시각 예술 I sophistication n 교양, 세련 I publish v 출판하다, 발행하다 I intense adj 극심한, 강렬한 I irony n 아이러니, 역설 I symbolism n 상징주의 I masterpiece n 걸작 I representation n 묘사, 나타냄 I genius n 천재성 I courage n 용기 I appear v 나타나다 I stimulate v 자극하다, 활발하게 하다 I creative adj 창의적인 I surge n 급등, 급증 I racial adj 인종의 I pride n 자부심, 긍지 I fuel v 자극하다, 부채질하다 I concept n 개념 I notably adv 특히 I predominant adj 두드러진, 뚜렷한 I consciousness n 의식, 자각 I aesthetic n 미학 I boost v 북돋우다, 신장하다 I fledgling adj 신생의, 새내기의 I mainstream n 주류 I processional adj 연속적인, 행렬의 I have a hand in ~에 관여하다

Passage 12

Man: Professor | Woman: Student

Listen to part of a discussion in a meteorology class.

M Okay, are you ready for a whirlwind on tornadoes? Good! So, what is a tornado? Technically, it's a funnel or column of spinning air. They're spawned by supercells, which are large storms that can create one or even dozens of tornadoes. In 1974, one extremely large supercell generated over 150 tornadoes in a two-day period. **1(C)** Supercells form when moist, warm air meets cool, dry air, creating an intense storm. **1(D)** Because it is less dense, the warm air rises higher in the atmosphere. **1(A)** Add a little wind and you get the extreme spinning of air that can touch down as a tornado.

OK. Now, tornadoes can spin at a speed of hundreds of miles per hour and travel at rates of over 60 miles per hour. They're difficult to measure, but there is one system used to rate tornadoes—the Fujita or F-Scale. This ranking system is based on levels of property damage. The F-Scale ranks tornadoes from the calm F0 to the extremely hazardous and destructive F5. In the U.S., the country where tornadoes occur most often, about 75% of tornadoes are F0 or F1 storms, which cause little damage. Less than 1% of tornadoes qualify as F4's or F5's. That being said, these fierce tornadoes actually account for well over half of all

남자: 교수 | 여자: 학생

기상학 수업 중 토론의 일부를 들으시오.

남 토네이도의 회오리 바람에 대해 이야기할 준비 됐나요? 좋습니다! 자, 토네이도는 무엇일까요? 엄밀히 말하면 회전하는 공기의 깔때기 또는 기둥을 말합니다. 토네이도는 슈퍼셀에 의해 만들어지는데 슈퍼셀은 하나 혹은 심지어 수십 개의 토네이도까지도 만들어낼 수 있는 거대한 폭풍우입니다. 1974년에 초대형 슈퍼셀 하나가 이틀 만에 150개 이상의 토네이도를 발생시켰죠. **1(C)** 슈퍼셀은 축축하고 따뜻한 공기가 차갑고 건조한 공기를 만나 형성되고, 강한 폭풍을 만듭니다. **1(D)** 따뜻한 공기는 밀도가 더 낮기 때문에 대기 중의 더 높은 곳으로 올라가죠. **1(A)** 약간의 바람만 더해지면 토네이도로 지상에 내려올 수 있는 극심한 공기의 회전이 생성되는 것입니다.

좋아요. 자, 토네이도는 시속 수백 마일 속도로 회전할 수 있고, 시간당 60마일 이상의 속도로 이동할 수 있습니다. 토네이도를 측정하기는 어렵지만 등급을 매기는 데 사용되는 시스템이 하나 있어요. 후지타 등급 또는 F 등급이라고 하는 것입니다. 이 등급 시스템은 재산 피해 수준에 기반합니다. F-Scale은 토네이도를 잔잔한 F0부터 극도로 위험하고 파괴적인 F5까지의 순위로 나열합니다. 토네이도가 가장 자주 발생하는 미국의 경우, 약 75퍼센트의 토네이도가 거의 피해를 주지 않는 F0 또는 F1 수준의 토네이도입니다. 전체 토네이도의 1퍼센트 이하만 F4 또는 F5로 간주되죠. 그렇다고는 해도, 이 맹렬한 토네이도들이 토네이도로 인한 사망

tornado deaths and most of the tornado-related property damage.

W You said the U.S. has more tornadoes than any other country, but I never really hear much about tornadoes. Does the media just not tell us about them or are there really not that many?

M Oh, there are plenty of tornadoes here in the U.S. In fact, there are between 800 and 1,000 in the United States each year. And the National Weather Service issues emergency broadcasts to warn people about them. They issue two types of alerts: "tornado watches" and "tornado warnings." **1(B)** A tornado watch means that meteorologists fear that weather conditions favor the formation of a tornado. Tornado warnings, on the other hand, are issued when a tornado has already formed or is just about to form. At that point, you'd better be seeking shelter from the storm! **2** As some of you may know, I did my Master's at Kansas University, and one afternoon during my last semester, a tornado warning was issued. Everyone was evacuated from the classrooms and moved into shelters located on campus. We were all scared to death, even though it turned out to be a false alarm.

W But isn't Kansas supposed to get a lot of tornadoes? I mean, I know a lot of states in the Midwest experience tornadoes, but is Kansas one of those states?

M Yes, it is. The majority of tornadoes in the U.S. occur in a line of states running north to south through the middle of the country appropriately called "Tornado Alley". Tornado Alley begins in Texas and extends north through Oklahoma, Kansas, Nebraska and South Dakota.

W Um, professor, what about the biggest tornado in history? Where did it occur?

M Well, since official record-keeping of tornadoes began in 1950, the largest, uh, recorded tornado was in Nebraska—an F4 tornado nearly two and a half miles wide. The costliest tornado—in terms of dollars, that was a tornado in Georgia, in March of... um, 1973. That storm caused over a billion dollars of damage even then, which would be roughly five billion dollars by today's standards. Terrible and awesome, any way you look at it, really.

자의 절반 이상, 토네이도 관련 재산 피해 대부분의 원인입니다.

여 다른 나라보다 미국에서 더 많은 토네이도가 발생한다고 말씀하셨는데 전 실제로 토네이도 이야기를 많이 들어본 적이 없어요. 매체가 우리에게 알려주지 않는 건가요, 아니면 실제로 그렇게 많이 발생하지 않는 건가요?

남 아, 미국에서는 수많은 토네이도가 발생합니다. 사실 매년 미국에서 800에서 1,000건 사이의 토네이도가 발생하죠. 그리고 국립 기상청에서는 사람들에게 이 위험을 경고하기 위해 긴급 방송을 합니다. 두 가지 종류의 주의를 발령하는데 '토네이도 주의보'와 '토네이도 경계 경보'가 있습니다. **1(B)** 토네이도 주의보는 기상 조건이 토네이도의 발생에 적합하다고 기상학자들이 우려하고 있음을 의미합니다. 반면, 토네이도 경계 경보는 토네이도가 이미 형성되었거나 막 형성되려고 할 때 발령됩니다. 그 시점이 되면 폭풍우로부터 안전한 장소를 찾아야 합니다! **2** 여러분 중 일부는 알고 있겠지만 나는 석사 과정을 캔자스 대학교에서 했는데, 마지막 학기의 어느 날 오후 토네이도 경계 경보가 발령됐어요. 모든 사람들이 교실에서 나와 캠퍼스에 위치한 비상 대피소로 이동했죠. 결국에는 잘못된 경보로 판명되었지만, 우린 모두 무서워서 죽는 줄 알았어요.

여 하지만 캔자스주는 토네이도가 많이 발생하는 곳이지 않나요? 중서부에 있는 많은 주(州)들이 토네이도를 경험한다는 것은 알지만, 캔자스주도 그 중 하나인가요?

남 맞습니다. 미국 내 대다수의 토네이도가 미국 한가운데를 관통해 북쪽에서 남쪽으로 한 줄로 늘어선 주들에서 발생하고, 이들은 딱 적당하게도 '토네이도 길'이라고 불립니다. 토네이도 길은 텍사스에서 시작되어 오클라호마, 캔자스, 네브래스카, 그리고 사우스다코타주를 통과하며 북쪽으로 뻗어나가죠.

여 음, 교수님, 역사상 가장 큰 토네이도는요? 어디서 발생했나요?

남 음, 토네이도의 공식 기록 작성은 1950년에 시작되었기 때문에 기록된 가장 큰 토네이도는 네브래스카주에서 있었어요. 폭이 거의 2.5마일에 달하는 F4 등급의 토네이도였습니다. 달러로 계산할 경우 가장 비용이 많이 든 토네이도는 어... 1973년 3월에 조지아주에서 발생한 토네이도입니다. 그 폭풍우는 그 당시 돈으로도 십억 달러 이상의 피해를 가져왔고, 오늘날의 기준으로 하면 대략 오십억 달러에 해당합니다. 어느 쪽으로 보든 정말 끔찍하고 어마어마한 토네이도였어요.

1. In the discussion, the professor described the series of events that take place when a tornado forms. Put those events in the correct order. Drag each answer choice to the space where it belongs. One of the answer choices will not be used.

Ⓐ Strong winds cause the rising air to rotate.
Ⓑ A tornado watch is declared by the National Weather Service.
Ⓒ Warm moist air meets cool dry air forming a supercell.
Ⓓ Warm air rises up through the storm clouds.
Ⓔ The storm extends down to the ground.

1	Ⓒ Warm moist air meets cool dry air forming a supercell.
2	Ⓓ Warm air rises up through the storm clouds.
3	Ⓐ Strong winds cause the rising air to rotate.
4	Ⓑ A tornado watch is declared by the National Weather Service.

2. Why does the professor mention Kansas during the discussion?

Ⓐ To explain the area covered by the region called Tornado Alley
Ⓑ To provide a story about his own experience with a tornado warning
Ⓒ To state a statistic about the occurrence of tornadoes
Ⓓ To illustrate the amount of damage that a single tornado can cause

1. 토론에서 교수는 토네이도가 형성될 때 일어나는 일들을 묘사한다. 이 일들을 올바른 순서로 배열하시오. 각 보기를 알맞은 곳에 끌어다 넣으시오. 보기 중 하나는 사용되지 않는다.

Ⓐ 강한 바람이 상승하는 공기를 회전하게 만든다.
Ⓑ 기상청에서 토네이도 주의보를 발령한다.
Ⓒ 따뜻하고 축축한 공기가 차갑고 건조한 공기를 만나 슈퍼셀을 형성한다.
Ⓓ 따뜻한 공기가 폭풍우 구름을 통해 상승한다.
Ⓔ 폭풍우가 땅으로 뻗어 내려온다.

1	Ⓒ 따뜻하고 축축한 공기가 차갑고 건조한 공기를 만나 슈퍼셀을 형성한다.
2	Ⓓ 따뜻한 공기가 폭풍우 구름을 통해 상승한다.
3	Ⓐ 강한 바람이 상승하는 공기를 회전하게 만든다.
4	Ⓑ 기상청에서 토네이도 주의보를 발령한다.

2. 교수는 왜 토론에서 캔자스주를 언급하는가?

Ⓐ 토네이도 길이라고 불리는 지역을 설명하기 위해
Ⓑ 토네이도 경계 경보에 관련한 자신의 경험 이야기를 하기 위해
Ⓒ 토네이도 발생에 관한 통계를 말하기 위해
Ⓓ 한 토네이도가 야기할 수 있는 피해의 양을 설명하기 위해

어휘 whirlwind n 회오리 바람 | tornado n 토네이도 | technically adv 엄밀히 말하면 | funnel n 깔때기 | column n 기둥 | spin v 회전하다, 돌다 | spawn v (결과·상황을) 낳다 | supercell n 슈퍼셀(강한 회전 상승기류를 동반하는 뇌우) | extremely adv 극히 | generate v 발생시키다, 만들어내다 | intense adj 극심한, 강렬한 | dense adj 밀도가 높은 | measure v 측정하다 | rate v 등급을 매기다 | property n 재산, 소유물 | damage n 손상, 피해 | rank v (등급·순위를) 매기다, 평가하다 | hazardous adj 위험한 | destructive adj 파괴적인 | fierce adj 사나운, 험악한 | related adj 연관된 | emergency broadcast 긴급 방송 | warn v 경고하다 | issue v 발표하다, 공표하다 | alert n 경보 | meteorologist n 기상학자 | formation n 형성 | shelter n 대피소, 피신처 | evacuate v 대피하다 | majority n 다수 | appropriately adv 알맞게, 어울리게 | alley n 골목, 좁은 길 | extend v 연장하다, 확대하다 | costly adj 대가가 큰, 많은 돈이 드는 | roughly adv 대략 | standard n 기준

Passage 13

Woman: Professor

Listen to part of a lecture in a physics class.

W Alright, today I'd like to discuss color and our perception of color. Now, we can't do that without talking about light and about the internal structure of our eyes and our optic nerves. 1 In fact, our perception of color is based mostly on the eyes' response to light. In terms of this response to light, there are three main factors that determine the colors that we see: hue, brightness, and saturation. There is another component: intensity. But it is actually part of brightness so we'll get around to it in a moment.

여자: 교수

물리학 강의의 일부를 들으시오.

여 좋아요. 오늘은 색과 색의 인지에 관해 이야기하려고 합니다. 자, 빛과 우리 눈의 내부 구조, 시신경에 대해 언급하지 않고는 오늘의 주제를 이야기할 수 없죠. 1 사실, 색 인지는 빛에 대한 우리 눈의 반응에 대부분 기반합니다. 이 빛에 대한 반응이라는 면에서, 우리가 보는 색을 결정하는 주된 요소가 3개 있습니다. 색조와 광도, 채도입니다. 또 다른 요소로는 강도가 있죠. 하지만 강도는 광도에 포함되므로 이 부분에 대한 이야기는 잠시 후에 하겠습니다.

1 First, however, we're going to talk about hue. Hue is usually what we mean when we say "color". Before we consider how bright or dark, rich or dispersed a color is, we ask ourselves questions such as "Is it red or orange, green or blue, or something in between?" Light actually reaches the eye in waves, and **2(A)** the distance between the crests of these waves determines which hues we see. Light waves at the violet end of the spectrum have a short distance between crests while light waves at the red end of the spectrum have a longer distance between crests. So, we see the color purple when the wavelengths reaching our eyes have peaks occurring relatively close together. We see blue when the peaks are a little farther apart. We see green when the wavelengths are even farther apart, and so on through yellow, orange and red.

1 OK, let's move onto the second factor, brightness. **2(B)** Brightness is determined by the amount of light present, which is also known as intensity. We all know that some shades of blue are brighter than others. This is due to greater or lesser degrees of light entering the eye. If the light is weak, the color won't be very bright. If, however, the light is strong or intense, the color will appear far brighter to the eye.

1 Saturation, on the other hand, is a little more difficult to understand. It's the third factor in the perception of color and refers to the intensity of the hue, which is determined by how complex the light is. Now, you might be asking yourself, "How does the intensity of the hue differ from the hue itself?" Well... **2(C)** the intensity of the hue refers to how evenly light is distributed across different wavelengths. To help you understand the difference, think of a color that you might describe as "rich plum," which would approach a single, narrow wavelength. Think of that plum color versus a color you might describe as a faded violet. The violet color would have more and wider wavelengths and therefore a less intense color.

OK, I hope that all makes sense. We'll do a short review at the end of class to go over the three factors again. Before we can do that, we need to know more about some of the formulas associated with light and color. Knowing these will help us understand how colors really work.

1 하지만 먼저, 우리는 색조에 관해 이야기할 겁니다. 색조는 주로 우리가 '색'이라고 말할 때 의미하는 것입니다. 색이 얼마나 밝고 어두운가, 진하거나 흐린가를 고려하기 전 우리는 "이게 빨간색인가 주황색인가, 초록색인가 파란색인가, 아니면 그 중간인가?"와 같은 질문을 스스로에게 합니다. 빛은 사실 파장으로 눈에 도달하는데, **2(A)** 이 파장의 정점들 사이의 거리가 우리가 보는 색조를 결정합니다. 스펙트럼의 자주색 끝에 있는 빛 파장은 정점 사이의 거리가 짧은 반면 스펙트럼의 빨간색 끝의 빛 파장은 정점들 간의 거리가 더 깁니다. 따라서 우리의 눈에 도달하는 파장이 상대적으로 정점이 서로 가깝게 발생할 때 우리는 보라색을 보게 됩니다. 정점들이 조금 더 멀리 떨어져 있으면 파란색을 보게 되죠. 파장들이 그보다 더 떨어져 있으면 초록색을 보게 되고, 그런 식으로 계속해서 노란색과 주황색, 그리고 빨간색을 보게 됩니다.

1 좋아요, 두 번째 요소인 광도로 넘어가죠. **2(B)** 광도는 존재하는 빛의 양에 따라 결정되며 이는 강도라고도 합니다. 우리 모두 어떤 파란 색조는 다른 파란색보다 더 밝다는 것을 알고 있습니다. 이는 눈에 들어오는 빛의 많고 적음의 정도 때문입니다. 만약 빛이 약하면 색은 그렇게 밝지 않을 것입니다. 그러나 만약 빛이 강하거나 세면 색은 훨씬 더 밝게 보일 것입니다.

1 반면 채도는 이해하기가 좀 더 어렵습니다. 이는 색의 인지에서 세 번째 요소이며, 빛이 얼마나 복잡한지로 결정되는 색조의 강도를 가리킵니다. 이제 여러분은 '색조의 강도와 색조가 어떻게 다르지?'라는 질문을 하고 있을지 모릅니다. 음... **2(C)** 색조의 강도는 빛이 여러 다른 파장들에 걸쳐 얼마나 고르게 분포돼 있는지를 가리킵니다. 그 차이점을 이해하는 데 도움을 주자면, '진한 자주색'이라고 묘사할 수 있는 색을 떠올려보면 이는 단일의 좁은 파장에 가까울 것입니다. 그 자주색을 색이 바랜 보라색이라고 묘사할 수 있는 색과 비교해 보세요. 그 보라색은 더 많고 넓은 파장을 가지고 있어서 덜 강렬한 색을 띱니다.

좋아요, 다 이해했기를 바랍니다. 수업 마지막에 이 세 가지 요소를 다시 한 번 간단히 복습해볼 겁니다. 그러기 위해서는 빛과 색에 관련된 몇 가지 공식에 대해 더 알아야 할 필요가 있습니다. 이 공식들을 알면 색이 진짜로 어떻게 기능하는지를 이해하는 데 도움이 될 것입니다.

1. How does the professor proceed with her explanation of color?

Ⓐ She identifies the steps in a process and explains how they are connected.

1. 교수는 색에 관한 설명을 어떻게 진행하는가?

Ⓐ 진행 과정의 단계를 구분하고 이것들이 어떻게 연결되는지 설명한다.

Ⓑ She describes and explains the reasons for a change.
Ⓒ She identifies and explains parts of a phenomenon.
Ⓓ She defines and analyzes mathematical formulas.

Ⓑ 묘사를 한 뒤 변화의 이유를 설명한다.
Ⓒ 한 현상의 부분들을 구분하고 설명한다.
Ⓓ 수학 공식을 정의하고 분석한다.

2. In the lecture, the professor lists the factors that influence how we perceive color. Indicate which of the following factors are mentioned in the lecture.

Click in the correct box for each phrase.

	Yes	No
Ⓐ The distance between the crests of waves	✓	
Ⓑ The amount of light that is present	✓	
Ⓒ The distribution of light across wavelengths	✓	
Ⓓ The angle at which the light is being reflected		✓
Ⓔ The movement of the object being observed		✓

2. 강의에서 교수는 우리가 색을 인지하는 데 영향을 미치는 요인들을 나열한다. 다음 중 어떤 요인들이 강의에서 언급되었는지 표시하시오.

각 문장에 대해 맞는 칸에 표시하시오.

	예	아니오
Ⓐ 파장 정점들 사이의 거리	✓	
Ⓑ 존재하는 빛의 양	✓	
Ⓒ 여러 파장들에 걸친 빛의 분포	✓	
Ⓓ 빛이 반사되는 각도		✓
Ⓔ 관찰되는 사물의 움직임		✓

어휘 discuss v 논의하다 | perception n 인지, 지각 | internal adj 내부의 | structure n 구조 | optic nerve 시신경 | response n 반응 | determine v 결정하다 | hue n 색조 | brightness n 광도 | saturation n 채도 | component n 요소 | intensity n (빛 등의) 강도 | disperse v 흩어지다 | wave n 파장 | distance n 거리 | crest n 정점, 최고조 | spectrum n 스펙트럼 | wavelength n 파장 | peak n 정점, 꼭대기 | relatively adv 상대적으로, 비교적 | shade n 색조, 음영 | refer to ~를 가리키다 | complex adj 복잡한 | evenly adv 고르게, 균등하게 | distribute v 분포하다, 퍼뜨리다 | describe v 묘사하다 | plum adj 자주색의 | approach v 접근하다 | faded adj 색이 바랜 | formula n 공식 | associated with ~와 관련된

Passage 14

Man: Professor | Woman: Student

Listen to part of a discussion in an American history class.

M Alright, class, I'd like to start today by picking up from where we left off last week. Does anyone remember what we were discussing before time ran out?

W Uh... We were talking about the time leading up to the Revolutionary War... and, uh, you started to mention some protest that took place in, uh, 1772?

M Yes, that's right, but it was 1773. And the trouble started much earlier. **1(B)** Way back in 1767, Charles Townshend imposed the British Townshend Acts. These acts imposed taxes on things American colonists could only get through their British ruler—stuff like lead, paint, paper, glass, and tea. What's worse, the money from these taxes went to the British in charge of the colony. The colonists saw this as a threat to their smaller, elected local government, and they responded by importing their own goods and with a short-lived riot. Uh, the riot somewhat predictably led the British

남자: 교수 | 여자: 학생

미국사 수업 중 토론의 일부를 들으시오.

남 좋아요, 여러분. 지난주에 중단했던 부분에서 다시 시작해 보도록 하죠. 수업을 마치기 전에 우리가 논의하던 내용을 기억하는 사람 있나요?

여 어... 미국 독립 전쟁으로 이어지는 시기에 대해 논의했는데... 교수님께서 어, 1772년인가에 일어난 어떤 시위에 관해 언급하기 시작하셨던 것 같아요.

남 네, 맞아요. 그런데 그건 1773년입니다. 그리고 문제는 훨씬 전부터 시작되었습니다. **1(B)** 1767년으로 돌아가서, 찰스 톤젠드가 영국의 톤젠드 조례를 도입했습니다. 이 조례들은 미국 식민지 사람들이 영국 통치자를 통해서만 얻을 수 있는 물건에 세금을 부과했습니다. 납, 페인트, 종이, 유리와 차 같은 물건들이었죠. 더 심한 문제는 이 세금으로 거둬들인 돈이 식민지를 감독하는 영국으로 갔다는 것이었습니다. 식민지 주민들은 이를 자신들이 선출한 소규모 지방 정부에 대한 위협이라고 보았고, 직접 상품을 수입하고 일시적인 폭동을 일으키며 대응했습니다. 어, 그리고 어느 정도 예상했듯이 폭동은 영국

to close their colonial assemblies. Of course, this didn't fix anything, and as you can imagine, it only further increased tensions. One of the protests called the Boston Tea Party occurred on the night of December 16, 1773. **1(D)** On that night, American colonists dressed up like Native Americans and protested British rule by dumping tons of imported British tea into the Boston Harbor. Well, this might seem like a strange beginning for any struggle for independence, but in fact the Boston Tea Party set the stage for the American Revolution.

W But didn't the British end up getting rid of the Townshend Acts? Why were the colonists so upset if they were getting their way?

M Well, I guess that's true. Most of the laws in the Townshend Acts were withdrawn, but in 1773, the Tea Act continued to tax tea imported to the colonies. This act prohibited colonists from importing tea from countries other than Britain, and maintained the tax on British tea so that they could continue supporting British rule of the colonies. Well, you can guess what happened next. **1** Once again, colonists viewed the Act as an injustice, at least as an aggressive assertion of British control. **1(C)** So, in November of 1773, colonists in Boston rebelled, refusing to allow ships carrying British tea to unload their cargo. **1(A)** This measure was countered by Thomas Hutchinson, the British governor of the Massachusetts colony. He just refused to allow ships to depart without unloading.

W So there was pretty much a standoff over the tea, and the British weren't backing down.... Is that why the Boston Tea Party happened?

M Yes. Exactly. It was a standoff that ended on December 16. **1(D)** On that day the colonists, led by Samuel Adams, decided to unload all that tea by dumping it right into Boston Harbor. The British demanded payment, which the colonists refused, and so the British closed the harbor, cutting off goods and supplies to Boston. But, ah, that wasn't all. **2** The following year, in 1774, out of revenge for the Boston Tea Party, the British passed the Intolerable Acts laws, which virtually eliminated colonial independence. The Intolerable Acts statutes may have been the final straw for American colonists. Indeed, the U.S. Constitution forbids many of the Intolerable Acts statutes. For example, American citizens cannot be forced to let military troops live in their homes.

인들로 하여금 식민지 의회의 문을 닫게 만들었습니다. 물론 이것은 아무것도 해결하지 못했고 여러분이 상상할 수 있듯 긴장감만 고조시켰죠. 시위 중 하나로 보스턴 차 사건이라 불리는 일이 1773년 12월 16일 밤에 발생했습니다. **1(D)** 그날 밤, 미국의 식민지 주민들이 미국 원주민 차림을 하고 엄청난 양의 수입 영국차를 보스턴 항구에 버리며 영국의 지배에 대항했습니다. 음, 이건 독립을 위한 노력으로선 자칫 이상한 시작으로 보일 수도 있지만, 실제로 보스턴 차 사건은 미국 독립 전쟁의 기초를 마련해 주었습니다.

여 하지만 영국이 결국 톤젠드 조례를 철회하지 않았나요? 자신들의 뜻대로 되었다면 식민지 주민들은 왜 그렇게 분개한 건가요?

남 음, 맞아요. 톤젠드 조례에 있던 대부분의 법 조항이 철회되었지만 1773년에 차 조례가 식민지로 수입되는 차에 계속해서 세금을 부과했습니다. 이 조례는 식민지 주민들이 영국 외의 다른 나라에서 차를 수입하는 것을 막았고 영국 차에 대한 세금은 계속 유지하여 결국 영국의 식민지 통치를 계속 지원하게 했습니다. 음, 다음에 어떤 일이 발생했을지 추측할 수 있을 거예요. **1** 또 다시 식민지 주민들은 이 조례를 부당한 것으로, 적어도 영국의 공격적인 지배력 행사로 여겼습니다. **1(C)** 그래서 1773년 11월, 보스턴의 식민지 주민들이 영국 차를 운반하는 배가 화물을 내리는 것을 막으면서 반란을 일으켰죠. **1(A)** 매사추세츠주 식민지의 영국 총독이었던 토마스 허친슨은 이런 조치에 반발했습니다. 그는 배가 짐을 내리지 않고 떠나는 것을 허락하지 않았어요.

여 차를 두고 거의 교착 상태가 되었는데 영국도 뒤로 물러나지 않았고.... 그래서 보스턴 차 사건이 일어난 건가요?

남 네. 정확해요. 교착 상태는 12월 16일에 끝났습니다. **1(D)** 그날 새뮤엘 애덤스가 이끄는 식민지 주민들은 보스턴 항구에 차를 전부 던져 넣기로 결정했어요. 영국은 보상을 요구했지만 식민지 주민들은 이를 거부했고 영국은 항구를 폐쇄하여 보스턴으로 들어오는 상품과 물자를 차단했죠. 하지만, 어, 그게 전부는 아니었습니다. **2** 다음 해인 1774년, 보스턴 차 사건에 대한 보복으로 영국은 사실상 식민지의 독립성을 없앤 '참을 수 없는 법'을 통과시켰습니다. 이 참을 수 없는 법의 법령은 미국의 식민지 주민들에게 마지막 한계였을 거예요. 실제로 미국 헌법이 참을 수 없는 법 중 다수의 법령을 금지하고 있습니다. 예를 들어 미국 시민은 집에 군대를 주둔시키도록 강요당할 수 없습니다.

Lesson 04 Lectures

1. **In the discussion, the professor described the series of events that led up to the Boston Tea Party. Put those events in the correct order. Drag each answer choice to the space where it belongs. One of the answer choices will not be used.**

Ⓐ The governor forbade ships from departing without unloading their cargo.
Ⓑ The British Empire imposed the Townshend Acts.
Ⓒ The colonists refused to allow ships to unload their cargo.
Ⓓ Colonists in disguise boarded the ship and threw the tea overboard.
Ⓔ The parliament passed the laws known as the Intolerable Acts.

1	Ⓑ The British Empire imposed the Townshend Acts.
2	Ⓒ The colonists refused to allow ships to unload their cargo.
3	Ⓐ The governor forbade ships from departing without unloading their cargo.
4	Ⓓ Colonists in disguise boarded the ship and threw the tea overboard.

2. **Why does the professor talk about the Intolerable Acts?**

Ⓐ To give an example of why the colonists were outraged and motivated to strive for independence
Ⓑ To give the students more background about why the colonists rebelled in 1773
Ⓒ To explain why the U.S. Constitution took the form that it did
Ⓓ To explain how the Townshend Acts were related to future acts by Britain

1. **토론에서 교수는 보스턴 차 사건으로 이어진 일련의 사건들을 묘사한다. 이 사건들을 올바른 순서로 배열하시오. 각 보기를 알맞은 곳에 끌어다 넣으시오. 보기 중 하나는 사용되지 않는다.**

Ⓐ 총독이 화물을 내리지 않고는 배가 떠나지 못하게 했다.
Ⓑ 대영 제국이 톤젠드 조례를 도입했다.
Ⓒ 식민지 주민들이 배가 화물을 내리는 것을 거부했다.
Ⓓ 변장한 식민지 주민들이 배에 올라 차를 배 밖으로 던져버렸다.
Ⓔ 의회가 '참을 수 없는 법'으로 알려진 법을 통과시켰다.

1	Ⓑ 대영 제국이 톤젠드 조례를 도입했다.
2	Ⓒ 식민지 주민들이 배가 화물을 내리는 것을 거부했다.
3	Ⓐ 총독이 화물을 내리지 않고는 배가 떠나지 못하게 했다.
4	Ⓓ 변장한 식민지 주민들이 배에 올라 차를 배 밖으로 던져버렸다.

2. **교수는 왜 '참을 수 없는 법'에 관해 이야기하는가?**

Ⓐ 왜 식민지 주민들이 분노했고 독립을 위해 노력하게 되었는지 예를 들으려고
Ⓑ 왜 식민지 주민들이 1773년에 반란을 일으켰는지에 관한 배경을 학생들에게 더 제공하려고
Ⓒ 왜 미국 헌법이 이런 형식을 갖게 되었는지 설명하려고
Ⓓ 톤젠드 조례가 영국의 향후 조례들과 어떻게 관련되었는지 설명하려고

어휘 Revolutionary War 독립 전쟁 | protest n 시위 | impose v 도입하다, 시행하다, 부과하다 | tax n 세금 | colonist n 식민지 주민 | threat n 위협 | elected adj 선거로 뽑은 | respond v 반응하다 | import v 수입하다 | riot n 폭동 | predictably adv 예상대로 | assembly n 의회, 집회 | increase v 증가하게 하다, 높이다 | tension n 긴장 | occur v 발생하다 | dump v 버리다 | strange adj 이상한 | struggle n 분투 | independence n 독립 | upset adj 화가 난, 언짢은 | withdraw v 철회하다 | prohibit v 금지하다 | maintain v 유지하다 | injustice n 불평등, 부당함 | aggressive adj 공격적인 | assertion n (권리 등의) 행사, 주장 | rebel v 반란을 일으키다, 저항하다 | refuse v 거부하다 | unload v (짐을) 내리다 | cargo n 화물 | measure n 조치 | counter v 대응하다 | governor n 총독, 주지사 | standoff n 교착 상태 | demand v 요구하다 | supply n 불품 | revenge n 복수 | intolerable adj 참을 수 없는 | virtually adv 사실상 | eliminate v 제거하다 | statute n 법규, 법령 | final straw 최후의 결정타, 마지막 한계 | constitution n 헌법 | forbid v 금지하다 | citizen n 시민 | military troop 군 병력, 군대

Man 1, 2: Student | Woman: Professor

[1-6] Listen to part of a discussion in an architecture class.

W **2** Alright, I'm sure many of you have traveled to Las Vegas... and I'm sure some of you made the trip by car. What I'm wondering, however, is how many of you visited the Hoover Dam on your way to Las Vegas?

M1 I went to the dam once with my family. It was pretty fun actually, but, um, I don't know if it can compare with Vegas.

W **1,3** Now, I know the Hoover Dam doesn't have all of the excitement that the casinos have, but it does have an important place in America's development and it also has a very interesting history behind it. It was built during the Great Depression, and it really provided a lot of inspiration to a population that was going through a period of hopelessness and dejection.

M2 Professor, I'm sorry to interrupt, but I'm a little lost. Maybe I'm the only one here who doesn't know, but what exactly is the Hoover Dam? And, um, where is it located?

W Ah, I'm sorry. The Hoover Dam is a huge dam in a stretch of the Colorado River that flows between Arizona and Nevada. It provides a lot of electricity to states out in the western U.S. The main thing that you need to know, however, is that the Hoover Dam is just big. At the time, the process involved in making the dam would've seemed almost unimaginable. Many historians also believe that the money spent on building the dam did a lot to stimulate the U.S. economy. **4** I'm not sure that the effect was as great as many believe. But there is some evidence to support the idea that the dam helped. I mean, it cost a lot to build—we're talking around $49 million— and many jobs were created because of its construction.

M1 But how does high cost equate to, uh, economic improvement? Shouldn't the government have been trying to save money?

W Well, you have to think about it this way. The money the government spent on construction didn't just disappear. It helped construction workers feed their families, and it also funded construction companies and parts suppliers. In other words, it helped a stagnant economy become more active.

But... that isn't to say that the Hoover Dam didn't have its opponents. **5(B), (C)** Some people were worried that the dam's construction would possibly cause earthquakes or flooding. There were also those who thought the project was just too big to be undertaken... Arizona and Nevada were still remote places back then, so a major initial problem was how to get construction equipment and supplies out there.

남자 1, 2: 학생 | 여자: 교수

건축학 수업 중 토론의 일부를 들으시오.

여 **2** 좋아요. 여러분 중 많은 수가 라스베가스로 여행을 가봤을 겁니다. 그 중에는 차로 간 사람도 있을 거예요. 하지만 라스베가스로 가는 도중 후버 댐을 방문한 사람은 몇 명이나 되나요?

남1 가족들이랑 후버 댐에 한 번 갔어요. 꽤 재미있긴 했지만, 음, 라스베가스와 비교할 정도인지는 모르겠네요.

여 **1, 3** 자, 후버 댐이 카지노만큼 재미있지는 않겠지만 미국 발전에 중요한 역할을 하고 있고, 그 뒤에는 흥미로운 역사가 있습니다. 후버 댐은 대공황 때 지어졌는데, 절망과 실의에 빠진 시기를 겪고 있던 사람들에게 정말 큰 영감을 줬죠.

남2 교수님, 방해해서 죄송한데 잘 이해가 안 돼요. 저만 모르는 것일 수도 있는데, 후버 댐이 정확히 뭐죠? 그리고 어디에 있나요?

여 아, 미안해요. 후버 댐은 아리조나주와 네바다주 사이에 넓게 흐르는 콜로라도강 지역에 있는 큰 댐입니다. 이 댐은 미국 서부의 주에 다량의 전기를 공급합니다. 하지만 여러분이 알아야 할 중요한 점은 후버 댐이 무척 크다는 것입니다. 당시에는 그 댐을 만드는 과정이 거의 상상조차 할 수 없는 것처럼 보였을 겁니다. 많은 역사가들은 또한 그 댐을 짓는 데 쓰였던 돈이 미국 경제를 활성화하는 데 많은 역할을 했다고 믿고 있죠. **4** 많은 사람들이 생각하는 것만큼 효과가 대단했는지는 모르겠습니다. 하지만 그 댐이 도움이 됐다는 주장을 뒷받침하는 증거는 좀 있습니다. 제 말은, 짓는 데 돈이 엄청나게 들었거든요. 약 4천9백만 달러나요. 그리고 이 건설로 일자리도 많이 생겨났습니다.

남1 하지만 돈이 많이 든 것이 어떻게, 음, 경제 개선과 같은가요? 정부는 돈을 아끼려고 했어야 하지 않나요?

여 음, 이렇게 생각해 보세요. 정부가 건설에 쓴 돈은 그냥 사라진 게 아닙니다. 건설 노동자들이 가족을 부양하는 데 도움을 주었고, 건설 업계와 건축 자재 공급업자들에게도 자금을 제공했죠. 다른 말로 하자면 침체된 경제가 더 활기 있도록 하는 데 도움을 준 겁니다.

하지만... 후버 댐에 반대하는 사람이 없었다는 말은 아닙니다. **5(B), (C)** 어떤 사람들은 댐 건설이 지진이나 홍수를 일으킬 수도 있다고 걱정했습니다. 프로젝트가 너무 커서 착수하기 어렵다고 생각한 사람들도 있었죠.... 그 시절 아리조나주와 네바다주는 여전히 외진 지역이었고 초기의 주요 문제는 건설 장비와 자재를 거기까지 어떻게 운반하는가 하는

6(B) The only thing to do was to spend a lot of money on roads and other kinds of transportation. Housing and supplies for the workers also had to be built before construction could take place.

In addition to all of this, the project had to deal with the Colorado River. 6(D) If the Hoover Dam was going to be built on the floor of that large river, that river had to be diverted. Concrete tunnels and a cofferdam were built to direct the river around the dam construction site. Only then did construction begin. Even after these problems were taken care of, the process was not simple. Concrete heats up as it cures due to chemical reactions in the ingredients. The amount of concrete to be used was so large that experts thought that it would get so hot that it would crack when it cooled. 6(E) To prevent this, concrete was poured in interlocking rows and columns that were cooled by piping installed inside of the concrete blocks. 6(C) Cold water was poured into the pipes to cool the concrete and prevent it from heating up, and afterwards the pipes were filled with concrete to make a solid concrete structure.

것이었습니다. 6(B) 할 일은 도로 및 다른 종류의 운송 수단에 많은 돈을 쓰는 것 뿐이었습니다. 건설이 시작되기 전에 일꾼들을 위한 집과 부대 시설도 지어야 했습니다.

이 모든 것 외에도, 이 프로젝트는 콜로라도강 문제를 해결해야 했죠. 6(D) 후버 댐이 그 큰 강의 바닥 위에 지어지려면 강물의 방향을 전환해야 했습니다. 강물의 방향을 댐 건설 지점의 주변으로 향하게 하기 위해 콘크리트 터널과 임시 물막이 댐을 지었습니다. 그런 다음에야 댐 건설을 시작할 수 있었죠. 이러한 문제들을 처리하고 난 뒤에도 진행은 간단하지 않았습니다. 콘크리트는 재료들의 화학 반응 때문에 양생할 때 열기가 올라옵니다. 사용될 콘크리트의 양이 너무 많았기에 전문가들은 콘크리트가 너무 뜨거워지는 바람에 식을 때 금이 갈 거라고 생각했습니다. 6(E) 이를 방지하기 위해 서로 맞물리는 줄과 기둥에 콘크리트를 부었는데, 그것들은 콘크리트 블록 안에 설치된 관으로 수송되면서 냉각됩니다. 6(C) 콘크리트를 식히고 그것이 뜨거워지는 것을 막기 위해 차가운 물을 파이프 안에 부었고, 그런 다음 단단한 콘크리트 구조물을 만들기 위해 콘크리트로 파이프를 채웠습니다.

1. What is the discussion mainly about?

Ⓐ The development of construction processes in the western U.S.
Ⓑ The Great Depression and the attempts to counteract its effects
Ⓒ The Hoover Dam's importance and how it was built
Ⓓ The Colorado River's impact on American construction projects

2. Why does the professor mention the students' taking trips to Las Vegas?

Ⓐ To use their personal experiences as an introduction to the lecture's topic
Ⓑ To begin talking about how the Hoover Dam has helped improve Las Vegas
Ⓒ To give an example of how the Hoover Dam has increased tourism in Nevada
Ⓓ To compare the two places and how they are both interesting tourist attractions

3. According to the professor, how did the construction of the Hoover Dam affect the American public?

Ⓐ It resulted in increased spending that pushed Americans even further into debt.

1. 토론은 주로 무엇에 관한 것인가?

Ⓐ 미국 서부의 건설 과정 전개
Ⓑ 대공황과 그 영향에 대응하기 위한 시도
Ⓒ 후버 댐의 중요성과 댐이 지어진 경위
Ⓓ 콜로라도강이 미국 건설 프로젝트에 미친 영향

2. 교수는 왜 학생들의 라스베가스 여행을 언급하는가?

Ⓐ 학생들의 개인적 경험을 강의 주제의 도입부로 사용하려고
Ⓑ 후버 댐이 라스베가스를 개선하는 데 어떻게 도움이 되었는지 이야기하기 시작하려고
Ⓒ 후버 댐이 네바다주의 관광을 어떻게 증대했는지 예시를 들려고
Ⓓ 이 두 장소를 비교하고 둘 다 어떻게 흥미로운 관광 명소인지 비교하려고

3. 교수에 따르면, 후버 댐의 건설은 미국 대중에게 어떤 영향을 끼쳤는가?

Ⓐ 소비를 증가시켜 미국인들을 더 큰 빚으로 밀어 넣었다.

Ⓑ It gave Americans hope that they could overcome the difficulties facing them.
Ⓒ It caused Americans to move to the western states in search of economic opportunities.
Ⓓ It diverted Americans' water supply and forced them to find alternative sources of water.

4. Listen again to part of the discussion. Then answer the question.

> W I'm not sure that the effect was as great as many believe. But there is some evidence to support the idea that the dam helped.

What does the professor imply when she says:

> W I'm not sure that the effect was as great as many believe.

Ⓐ The dam actually had an overall negative effect on the economy.
Ⓑ The dam was unable to generate as much electricity as planned.
Ⓒ The dam was beneficial for some people but not the entire country.
Ⓓ The dam discouraged people from moving to the Las Vegas area.

5. According to the professor, which of the following are reasons that people opposed the building of the dam? Choose 2 answers.

Ⓐ Water pollution
Ⓑ Earthquakes
Ⓒ Flooding
Ⓓ Landslides
Ⓔ Air pollution

6. In the discussion, the professor described the process of constructing the Hoover Dam. Put the steps in the correct order. Drag each answer choice to the space where it belongs. One of the answer choices will not be used.

Ⓐ The pipes were removed and concrete was poured into the holes.
Ⓑ The government had roads and housing constructed for the workers.
Ⓒ Water was run through pipes to keep the concrete from heating up.

Ⓑ 미국인들에게 그들이 직면한 어려움을 극복할 수 있다는 희망을 주었다.
Ⓒ 미국인들이 경제적 기회를 찾아 서부 주로 이동하게 만들었다.
Ⓓ 미국인들의 상수도원의 방향을 바꾸고 대체 수자원을 찾도록 강요했다.

4. 토론의 일부를 다시 듣고 질문에 답하시오.

> 여 많은 사람들이 생각하는 것만큼 효과가 대단했는지는 모르겠습니다. 하지만 그 댐이 도움이 됐다는 주장을 뒷받침하는 증거는 좀 있습니다.

교수는 이렇게 말할 때 무엇을 암시하는가:

> 여 많은 사람들이 생각하는 것만큼 효과가 대단했는지는 모르겠습니다.

Ⓐ 댐은 사실 전반적으로 경제에 부정적 영향을 끼쳤다.
Ⓑ 댐은 계획했던 것만큼 많은 전력을 생산할 수 없었다.
Ⓒ 댐은 일부 사람들에게 이익이 되었지만 나라 전체까지는 아니었다.
Ⓓ 댐은 사람들이 라스베가스 지역으로 이주하는 것을 좌절시켰다.

5. 교수에 따르면, 다음 중 어떤 것이 사람들이 댐 건설에 반대한 이유인가? 두 개를 고르시오.

Ⓐ 물 오염
Ⓑ 지진
Ⓒ 홍수
Ⓓ 산사태
Ⓔ 공기 오염

6. 토론에서 교수는 후버 댐 건설 과정을 묘사했다. 이 단계들을 올바른 순서로 배열하시오. 각 보기를 알맞은 곳에 끌어다 넣으시오. 보기 중 하나는 사용되지 않는다.

Ⓐ 파이프를 제거한 뒤 콘크리트를 그 구멍에 부었다.
Ⓑ 정부에서 노동자들을 위해 도로와 주거 시설을 건설했다.
Ⓒ 콘크리트가 뜨거워지는 것을 막기 위해 물이 파이프를 통해 흐르게 했다.

Ⓓ The Colorado River was diverted from its usual course.
Ⓔ Pipes were set in the framework before concrete was poured.

1	Ⓑ The government had roads and housing constructed for the workers.
2	Ⓓ The Colorado River was diverted from its usual course.
3	Ⓔ Pipes were set in the framework before concrete was poured.
4	Ⓒ Water was run through pipes to keep the concrete from heating up.

Ⓓ 콜로라도강이 평소의 물길에서 방향이 전환되었다.
Ⓔ 콘크리트를 붓기 전 파이프를 틀 안에 설치했다.

1	Ⓑ 정부에서 노동자들을 위해 도로와 주거 시설을 건설했다.
2	Ⓓ 콜로라도강이 평소의 물길에서 방향이 전환되었다.
3	Ⓔ 콘크리트를 붓기 전 파이프를 틀 안에 설치했다.
4	Ⓒ 콘크리트가 뜨거워지는 것을 막기 위해 물이 파이프를 통해 흐르게 했다.

어휘 wonder v 궁금해 하다 | compare v 비교하다 | excitement n 신나는 일, 흥분 | development n 발전, 개발 | Great Depression 대공황 | inspiration n 영감 | population n 사람들, 인구 | hopelessness n 절망 | dejection n 실의 | interrupt v 방해하다, 가로막다 | exactly adv 정확히 | stretch n 쭉 뻗은 지역 | flow v 흐르다 | electricity n 전기 | unimaginable adj 상상할 수 없는 | historian n 역사가 | stimulate v 활성화시키다, 부양시키다 | economy n 경제 | evidence n 증거 | construction n 건설, 공사 | equate v 동등시하다 | improvement n 향상, 개선 | fund v 자금을 대다 | supplier n 공급 회사 | stagnant adj 침체된 | active adj 활기 있는 | opponent n 반대자 | earthquake n 지진 | flooding n 홍수 | undertake v 착수하다 | remote adj 외진 | initial adj 초기의, 처음의 | equipment n 장비 | transportation n 수송, 운송 | divert v 방향을 바꾸다, 전환하다 | cofferdam n 임시 물막이 | direct v ~로 향하다 | cure v (콘크리트를) 양생하다 | chemical reaction 화학 반응 | ingredient n 재료 | expert n 전문가 | crack v 갈라지다 | prevent v 막다, 방지하다 | pour v 붓다 | interlock v 서로 맞물리다 | install v 설치하다 | solid adj 고체의, 단단한

Lesson 05 Inference

본서 | P. 184

Practice

Passage 1 C
Passage 2 B
Passage 3 B
Passage 4 B
Passage 5 D
Passage 6 C
Passage 7 B
Passage 8 D
Passage 9 1. B 2. C 3. D
Passage 10 1. C 2. D 3. A

Test

Passage 1 1. B 2. B 3. C 4. D 5. A, C 6. C
Passage 2 1. B 2. A 3. A 4. C 5. B 6. A

Practice

본서 | P. 188

Passage 1 Man: Professor

Listen to part of a lecture in an American history class.

M In today's class, I'd like to talk about the history of America's relationship with oil. When I say oil, however, I do not just mean petroleum. I am also talking about whale oil, which was a major source of energy for Americans in the 1700s and 1800s. In these years, it was used to fuel lamps

남자: 교수

미국 역사 강의의 일부를 들으시오.

남 오늘 수업에서는 미국 역사와 기름의 관계에 대해 이야기하겠습니다. 하지만 제가 말하는 기름이란 단지 석유만을 의미하는 것이 아닙니다. 1700년대와 1800년대 미국인들에게 주요 에너지원이었던 고래 기름도 말하는 겁니다. 이 시기에 고래 기름

and was very lucrative for businessmen who invested in hunting whales for oil. In fact, by the mid-1800s, America's whaling industry was a huge industry involving over 600 ships and millions of liters of whale oil each year. In spite of this size, however, the whaling industry could not keep up with the United States' growing demands for fuel. America's industrialization and its economic growth were requiring larger amounts of fuel, and, with the advent of petroleum oil, which was less expensive and more easily produced, whale oil started to become obsolete. By the 1900s, petroleum oil had taken over America's fuel market. Americans relied on it for the vast majority of their energy needs, and by the middle of the century, many Americans would have found it hard to live without oil. As we've been learning, however, the possibility of having to live without petroleum is becoming more and more likely. The world's oil supplies are not infinite, and countries are now starting to look to other energy sources to fuel their societies.

은 램프에 연료를 공급했고, 기름을 위해 고래 사냥에 투자하는 사업가들은 돈을 굉장히 많이 벌었죠. 사실, 1800년대 중반 미국의 고래 산업은 600개가 넘는 선박을 가진 대규모 사업이었고 매년 수백만 리터의 고래 기름을 생산했습니다. 하지만 이러한 규모에도 불구하고, 고래 산업은 미국의 증가하는 연료 수요를 따라잡을 수가 없었습니다. 미국의 산업화와 경제적 성장은 더 많은 양의 연료를 필요로 하게 되었고, 덜 비싸고 더 쉽게 생산할 수 있는 석유의 출현으로 고래 기름은 쓸모가 없어지기 시작했습니다. 1900년대가 되자 석유는 미국의 연료 시장을 장악하게 되었습니다. 미국인들은 대부분의 에너지 수요를 석유에 의존했고, 20세기 중반이 되자 많은 미국인들이 석유 없이는 생활하기 어렵다는 걸 알게 되었죠. 그러나 우리가 배웠듯이 석유 없이 생활해야 할 가능성이 점점 더 높아지고 있습니다. 세계의 석유 자원은 무한하지 않기 때문에, 여러 나라가 이제 사회에 연료를 공급하기 위한 다른 에너지원을 찾기 시작했습니다.

Q. What can be inferred about the whaling industry in the United States?

Ⓐ It exported oil products around the world.
Ⓑ It was the largest contributor to the nation's export.
Ⓒ It contributed greatly to the country's economy.
Ⓓ It supported the industrialization of the nation.

Q. 미국의 고래 산업에 관해 무엇을 추론할 수 있는가?

Ⓐ 세계 전역에 기름 제품을 수출했다.
Ⓑ 국가 수출에서 가장 큰 기여자였다.
Ⓒ 나라의 경제에 크게 기여했다.
Ⓓ 국가 산업화를 뒷받침했다.

어휘 relationship n 관계 | petroleum n 석유 | whale oil 고래 기름 | fuel v 연료를 공급하다 | lucrative adj 수익성이 좋은 | invest v 투자하다 | industry n 산업 | demand n 수요 | industrialization n 산업화 | economic growth 경제 성장 | require v 필요로 하다, 요구하다 | advent n 출현, 도래 | obsolete adj 쓸모 없는, 구식의 | rely v 의존하다 | vast adj 막대한 | infinite adj 무한한

Passage 2

Woman: Professor

Listen to part of a lecture in a biology class.

W Good morning, everyone. Today I'd like to talk about something that is important to each and every one of you—blood. Blood has so many different aspects. I mean, I could teach a whole semester of classes on blood alone. For example, isn't it interesting that women have 4 to 5 liters of blood while men have 5 to 6 liters in their bodies? And most people carry around a huge number of blood cells every day; we're talking about 25 trillion red blood cells and 50 billion white blood cells! Let's start by talking about the red blood cells, which cause blood to have its red color. They take oxygen from the lungs and circulate it throughout the body. Then they return to the lungs with carbon dioxide that is subsequently pushed out of the body. Next, we have the

여자: 교수

생물학 강의의 일부를 들으시오.

여 안녕하세요, 여러분. 오늘은 여러분 모두에게 중요한 것, '혈액'에 대해 이야기해 보도록 하겠습니다. 혈액은 매우 다양한 측면을 지니고 있습니다. 한 학기 강의 전체를 혈액에 대해서만 가르칠 수도 있을 정도죠. 예를 들어, 남자는 몸에 5~6리터의 혈액을 지니고 있는 한편, 여성은 4~5리터를 지니고 있다는 점이 흥미롭지 않습니까? 그리고 대부분의 사람들이 매일 굉장히 많은 수의 혈구를 몸에 지니고 다닙니다. 25조 개의 적혈구와 500억 개의 백혈구를 말하는 거예요! 먼저 혈액이 붉은색을 띠게 하는 적혈구에 대해 이야기합시다. 적혈구는 폐에서 산소를 운반해 몸 전체에 순환시킵니다. 그런 다음 적혈구가 이산화탄소를 가지고 폐로 돌아가면 이산화탄소가 몸 밖으로 배출됩니다. 다음으로는 혈액의 노

Lesson 05 Lectures

plasma, which is the watery yellow part of blood. It helps to make blood clot, which helps our wounds stop bleeding and is a very important bodily function. Without this, minor injuries could be much more serious. Then there are the white blood cells. These come from our bone marrow, and they help defend the body against infections and illnesses. If this component of our blood were not present, we would be susceptible to all kinds of things and much more fragile creatures overall.

란색 액체 부분인 혈장이 있습니다. 혈장은 혈액이 응고하도록 해주어 상처가 났을 때 출혈을 멎게 해 주는 것으로 몸에서 매우 중요한 기능을 합니다. 혈장이 없으면 조그만 상처도 굉장히 심각해질 수 있어요. 그 다음으로는 백혈구가 있습니다. 백혈구는 우리 골수에서 나오며 감염과 질병으로부터 몸을 방어합니다. 혈액에 이 요소가 없으면 우리는 모든 다양한 것들에 감염되기 쉬워질 것이고 전반적으로 훨씬 더 연약한 생명체가 될 거예요.

Q. What is implied about blood plasma?

Ⓐ It is the main component in blood.
Ⓑ It allows wounds to heal more quickly.
Ⓒ It defends the body against illnesses.
Ⓓ It is a watery yellow fluid produced by the body.

Q. 혈장에 관해 무엇이 암시되었는가?

Ⓐ 피의 주된 요소이다.
Ⓑ 상처가 더 빨리 낫게 해준다.
Ⓒ 질병으로부터 몸을 방어한다.
Ⓓ 몸에서 만들어지는 물 같은 노란 액체이다.

어휘 trillion n 1조 | red blood cell 적혈구 | white blood cell 백혈구 | oxygen n 산소 | lung n 폐 | circulate v 순환하다 | carbon dioxide 이산화탄소 | subsequently adv 그 뒤에, 나중에 | plasma n 혈장 | clot v 응고하다 | wound n 상처 | function n 기능 | injury n 상처 | bone marrow 골수 | defend v 방어하다 | infection n 감염 | illness n 질병 | component n 요소 | susceptible adj 감염되기 쉬운 | fragile adj 연약한

Passage 3

Man: Professor

Listen to part of a lecture in a linguistics class.

M Today we're going to talk about an ongoing debate among linguists. This debate is over how language is first acquired by young children, and there are two main positions. There are those who believe that children are born with knowledge of universal grammar—the basic structure that is behind all languages—in their brains. Then there are those who believe that linguistic ability is not innate but acquired through exposure to a language. Well, in general, members of the first group of people—known as nativists—cite the rapid rate at which young children gain proficiency in language use as evidence of a pre-existing knowledge of grammatical structure. They argue that if children did not possess this knowledge, they would not be able to determine the structural basis of language based on a few years of exposure to its use because it is far too complicated. Proponents of the second theory, however, point out that parents and other adults talk to children in simplified, grammatically correct speech that is conducive to language learning. Adults speak slowly when dealing with children, and they often repeat things as a way of teaching the child how to use a language. Because of this, the second theory says that children start with no prior knowledge of grammatical structures and simply accumulate knowledge of these structures by observing and learning from the adults around them.

남자: 교수

언어학 강의의 일부를 들으시오.

남 오늘은 언어학자들 사이에서 계속 논쟁 중인 주제에 관해 이야기할 겁니다. 이 논쟁은 어린 아이들이 처음에 언어를 어떻게 습득하는지에 관한 것으로, 두 가지 주요 입장이 있습니다. 어린 아이들이 모든 언어의 뒤에 있는 기본 구조인 보편 문법에 대한 지식을 뇌 속에 보유한 채로 태어난다는 학자들이 있어요. 한편 언어 능력은 타고나는 것이 아니며 단지 언어에 노출되어 습득되는 것이라고 생각하는 학자들이 있습니다. 음, 일반적으로 '생득론자'라고 알려진 첫 번째 그룹의 학자들은 어린 아이들이 언어 사용에 빠르게 능숙해지는 것을 문법 구조에 대한 지식이 이미 존재한다는 증거로 들고 있습니다. 이들은 언어의 구조적 기본이 굉장히 복잡하기 때문에 만일 어린 아이들이 이런 지식을 갖고 있지 않다면 몇 년의 언어 노출만으로 언어의 구조적 기본을 알아낼 수 없을 거라고 주장합니다. 그러나 두 번째 이론을 지지하는 사람들은 부모와 다른 어른들이 간단하면서도 문법적으로 정확한 말로 어린 아이들에게 얘기하는 것이 언어 학습에 도움이 된다고 지적합니다. 어른들은 아이들을 다룰 때 천천히 얘기하며, 아이들에게 언어 사용법을 가르치는 방법으로 반복해서 말하곤 합니다. 이런 이유로, 두 번째 이론은 아이들이 문법 구조에 대한 사전 지식 없이 단지 주변의 어른들을 관찰하고 배움으로써 문법 구조에 대한 지식을 쌓는다고 말합니다.

Q. In the lecture, what is implied about a pre-existing knowledge of grammatical structures?

Ⓐ It would cause a child to do better than others in school.
Ⓑ It would cause children to learn language quickly.
Ⓒ It would cause simplified learning to be unnecessary.
Ⓓ It would cause children to repeat things to adults.

Q. 강의에서 문법적 구조에 관해 이미 존재하는 지식에 대해 무엇이 암시되었는가?

Ⓐ 학교에서 아이가 다른 아이들보다 더 잘하게 해준다.
Ⓑ 아이들이 언어를 빠르게 배우도록 한다.
Ⓒ 단순화된 학습을 불필요하게 만든다.
Ⓓ 아이들이 어른에게 말을 반복하게 한다.

어휘 debate n 논쟁 I linguist n 언어학자 I acquire v 습득하다 I knowledge n 지식 I universal adj 보편적인 I grammar n 문법 I innate adj 선천적인, 타고난 I exposure n 노출 I nativist n 선천성 지지자 I cite v 언급하다, 인용하다 I rapid adj 급격한 I proficiency n 숙달, 능숙 I evidence n 증거 I pre-existing adj 이미 존재하는 I argue v 주장하다 I possess v 소유하다 I determine v 알아내다, 밝히다 I complicated adj 복잡한 I proponent n 지지자 I simplified adj 단순화된 I conducive adj ~에 좋은 I repeat v 반복하다 I prior adj 이전의, 사전의 I accumulate v 축적하다 I observe v 관찰하다

Passage 4

Woman: Professor

Listen to part of a lecture in an architecture class.

W Today, we're going to talk about a very interesting structure: the igloo. The igloo is sometimes built by Inuit hunters during the winter and can provide a very comfortable shelter. In fact, the igloo is surprisingly warm. The body heat of its inhabitants is trapped inside the structure, keeping the inside of the igloo warm. In this way, the ice walls act in much the same way that modern aluminum insulation does. Contrary to what you may believe, however, igloos are not used as permanent shelters and only act as temporary housing for Inuit on hunting trips. With that said, our main focus today is going to be how igloos are actually built. It is an amazing process that is both complex and simple at the same time. To begin, a circular outline is made in the snow that the igloo will be built on, and ice blocks are carved out of dry, hard snow. The builder begins to place these blocks on top of each other in a circle around him. When he runs out of blocks, he cuts blocks out of the walls he has already built up. By doing this, the blocks become increasingly smaller as the walls grow taller. They also lean in more and more so that eventually the space left in the roof becomes too small for more blocks. When this happens, a small piece of snow is packed into the remaining hole and a small slit is cut out to make a chimney. The final step occurs when a door is cut under the blocks, completing the igloo.

여자: 교수

건축학 강의의 일부를 들으시오.

여 오늘은 매우 흥미로운 구조물인 이글루에 관해 이야기할 겁니다. 이글루는 때때로 겨울 동안 이누이트족 사냥꾼들에 의해 지어지며 매우 안락한 쉼터를 제공할 수 있습니다. 사실, 이글루는 놀랄 만큼 따뜻해요. 거주자의 체열이 구조물 내부에 갇혀서 이글루의 내부를 따뜻하게 유지해주죠. 이런 식으로 얼음벽은 현대의 알루미늄 단열 재료와 매우 유사한 방식으로 작용합니다. 하지만 아마도 여러분이 믿고 있는 것과는 달리, 이글루는 영구적인 쉼터로 사용되는 것이 아니라 사냥 여행을 위해 이누이트족이 쓰는 임시 숙소에 불과합니다. 그 말이 나왔으니 말인데, 오늘 우리가 중점을 둘 부분은 이글루가 실제로 어떻게 지어지는가 하는 것입니다. 복잡한 동시에 간단한 놀라운 과정이죠. 먼저 이글루가 지어질 눈밭 위에 원형 윤곽을 그린 뒤 건조하고 단단한 눈에서 얼음 덩어리를 깎아냅니다. 집을 짓는 이는 자신의 주위에 원형으로 이 얼음 덩어리를 차곡차곡 위로 쌓아 올립니다. 덩어리를 다 쓰면 이미 쌓아 올린 벽에서 덩어리를 잘라냅니다. 이렇게 하면 벽이 높아질수록 얼음 덩어리가 점점 작아지죠. 또 점점 더 안쪽으로 기울게 되면서 마지막에는 지붕에 남아 있는 공간이 얼음 블록을 넣기에는 너무 작아지게 됩니다. 이렇게 되면 작은 눈 덩어리로 남아 있는 구멍을 메우고, 굴뚝을 만들기 위해 조그만 틈을 냅니다. 마지막 단계로 덩어리들 아래 문을 잘라내면 이글루가 완성됩니다.

Q. What can be inferred about Inuit people from the professor's comments?

Ⓐ Inuit people stay in their igloos until the structures melt.
Ⓑ Inuit people generally live in structures other than igloos.

Q. 교수의 말에서 이누이트족에 관해 무엇을 추론할 수 있는가?

Ⓐ 이누이트족은 구조물이 녹을 때까지 이글루에 머무른다.
Ⓑ 이누이트족은 일반적으로 이글루가 아닌 구조물에서 산다.

Lesson 05 Lectures

Ⓒ Inuit people have small families that do not require much space.
Ⓓ Inuit people think that the interiors of igloos are too cold.

Ⓒ 이누이트족은 많은 공간을 필요로 하지 않는 작은 가족을 갖고 있다.
Ⓓ 이누이트족은 이글루 내부가 너무 춥다고 생각한다.

어휘 structure n 구조물 I igloo n 이글루 I comfortable adj 편안한 I shelter n 쉼터, 대피소 I surprisingly adv 놀라울 만큼 I inhabitant n 거주자, 주민 I trap v 가두다 I aluminum n 알루미늄 I insulation n 단열재 I contrary to ~와 반대로 I permanent adj 영구적인 I temporary adj 임시의 I complex adj 복잡한 I circular adj 원형의, 둥근 I carve v 조각하다, 깎아 만들다 I increasingly adv 점차 I eventually adv 결국 I roof n 지붕 I slit n 틈 I chimney n 굴뚝 I occur v 발생하다 I complete v 완성하다

Passage 5

Man: Professor

Listen to part of a lecture in a psychology class.

M Alright, class. It's time to talk about how the mind best learns things. We're going to be dealing with three general principles that scientists have come up with over the past century or so. The first rule is that, if you want to remember something, it is generally better to study it longer. For example, a student who studies for a geography test for an hour will usually do better than a student who only studies for five minutes—assuming, of course, that both students are of the same ability. Now, this may seem very simple and obvious, but it is still an important rule that provides the foundation for our second and third rules.
The second rule states that, given the same amount of total study time, it is better to study for a short period of time at regular intervals than it is to study for a long period of time only once. So, to use the example of students studying for a geography test again, a student who studies for a test for one hour a day, each day for six days will typically do better than a student who studies for six hours on a single day. This idea has a strong relation to the idea behind the third rule, which tells us that, if we have only a limited amount of time to learn something, it is still better to study something and then wait a little while before reviewing it. Take the previous example again. A geography student who studies the capitals of countries on a flashcard and then waits five or ten minutes before reviewing the information on that flashcard will be able to memorize the capitals better than a student who looks at the names of capitals for a long time without waiting and then just moves onto the next subject without reviewing.

남자: 교수

심리학 강의의 일부를 들으시오.

남 자, 여러분. 이제 사물을 가장 잘 배우는 방법에 관해 이야기할 시간입니다. 대략 지난 한 세기 동안 과학자들이 알아낸 세 가지 일반적인 원리에 관해 다룰 거예요. 첫 번째 법칙은 만일 여러분이 무언가를 기억하고 싶다면 보통 더 오래 공부하는 것이 더 좋다는 겁니다. 예를 들어, 지리학 시험을 위해 1시간 동안 공부하는 학생은 보통 5분 동안만 공부하는 학생보다 더 잘할 겁니다. 물론 두 학생의 능력이 동일하다는 가정 하에서요. 자, 이 규칙은 매우 단순하고 명백해 보일 수 있지만 두 번째와 세 번째 규칙의 토대를 제공하는 중요한 규칙입니다.
두 번째 규칙은 총 학습 시간이 동일하다면, 규칙적인 간격으로 짧은 시간 동안 공부하는 것이 긴 시간 동안 한 번 공부하는 것보다 낫다는 거예요. 따라서 지리학 시험 공부를 하는 학생의 예를 다시 들자면, 매일 한 시간 동안 6일간 시험 공부를 한 학생이 하루에 6시간 공부한 학생보다 일반적으로 더 잘할거라는 겁니다. 이 개념은 세 번째 규칙의 이면에 있는 생각과 깊은 관계가 있는데 이 세 번째 규칙은 무언가를 배울 시간이 제한되어 있다면 공부를 한 다음 잠시 기다렸다 복습하는 것이 더 낫다는 것입니다. 앞의 예를 다시 들죠. 플래시 카드로 여러 나라의 수도에 대해 학습한 다음 5~10분간 기다린 뒤 플래시 카드의 내용을 복습한 학생은 기다리는 시간 없이 연속해서 오랜 시간 동안 수도들의 이름을 쳐다보고 나서 복습 없이 그냥 다른 과목으로 넘어가는 학생보다 수도들을 더 잘 외울 겁니다.

Q. What generalization can be made from the professor's lecture?
Ⓐ Students should never study the same information for over five minutes.
Ⓑ Students who perform well often study a lot the day before a test.

Q. 교수의 강의를 통해 어떤 일반화를 할 수 있는가?
Ⓐ 학생들은 같은 정보를 5분 넘게 공부해서는 안 된다.
Ⓑ 좋은 성적을 내는 학생들은 종종 시험 전날 많이 공부한다.

Ⓒ Flashcards are the best way for students to learn geographical facts.
Ⓓ Learning something over time is better than learning it quickly.

Ⓒ 학생들이 지리학적 사실을 배우는 데 플래시 카드가 가장 좋은 방법이다.
Ⓓ 시간을 들여 무언가를 익히는 것이 빠르게 익히는 것보다 더 낫다.

어휘 deal with 다루다 I general adj 일반적인 I principle n 원리, 원칙 I geography n 지리학 I assume v 가정하다 I obvious adj 명백한 I foundation n 기초 I regular adj 규칙적인 I interval n 간격, 사이 I typically adv 일반적으로 I relation n 관계 I limited adj 제한된 I review v 복습하다, 검토하다 I previous adj 이전의 I capital n 수도 I flashcard n 플래시 카드(그림, 글자 등이 적힌 학습용 카드) I memorize v 외우다

Passage 6 Woman: Professor

Listen to part of a lecture in an environmentology class.

W OK, I'm sure all of you have heard of El Ninõ, which means "little boy" in Spanish by the way, but I don't know how many of you know what El Ninõ really is. It is a change in weather patterns that occurs in the Pacific Ocean around South America between every two and seven years. This change occurs when water in the Pacific becomes significantly warmer as winds fail to push warm water currents to the west. Now, you may be asking yourself, "What's so bad about warm water?" The answer to this question, however, is complex. One practical problem with it is that it leads to economic problems for many South American fishermen who cannot catch enough fish. On a larger scale, the world's entire weather system changes when El Ninõ occurs. The amount of rainfall in North and South America increases, which can lead to flooding and other problems associated with thunderstorms. In areas of the western Pacific, on the other hand, there is less rainfall, which can lead to droughts and other problems. So, can you see how El Ninõ might affect the lives of millions of people? This has prompted scientists to study weather patterns in greater detail. It has also helped everyday people to realize how small changes in wind and water currents can lead to big problems in the world's weather systems. Now, if you look at the overhead screen, you'll be able to get an even more detailed idea of how air and water currents move throughout the world.

여자: 교수

환경학 강의의 일부를 들으시오.

여 좋아요, 여러분 모두 스페인어로 '어린 소년'을 의미하는 엘니뇨에 대해 들어봤겠지만, 여러분 중에 실제로 엘니뇨가 무엇인지 아는 사람이 몇 명이나 될지 모르겠군요. 엘니뇨는 매 2년에서 7년마다 남미 부근 태평양에서 발생하는 기후 패턴의 변화입니다. 이 변화는 바람이 난류를 서쪽으로 밀어 보내지 못하게 되면서 태평양의 물이 상당히 더 따뜻해질 때 발생합니다. 자, 여러분은 스스로에게 "물이 따뜻한 게 뭐가 문제지?"라고 물을 수 있을 거예요. 그런데 이 질문에 대한 답은 복잡합니다. 한 가지 실질적인 문제는 많은 남미 어부들이 물고기를 충분히 잡을 수 없게 되는 경제적 문제를 야기한다는 것입니다. 좀 더 넓은 규모로 보면, 엘니뇨가 발생할 경우 세계의 전체 기후 체계가 변화합니다. 북미와 남미의 강우량이 증가하고, 그것은 홍수 및 뇌우와 연관된 기타 문제를 초래할 수 있죠. 한편, 서태평양 지역에서는 강우량이 적어져 가뭄과 다른 문제를 야기할 수 있습니다. 이제 엘니뇨가 어떻게 수백만 명의 삶에 영향을 줄 수 있는지 이해하겠죠? 엘니뇨는 과학자들이 기후 패턴을 더욱 상세히 연구하게 했습니다. 또한 일반 사람들이 바람과 물의 흐름의 작은 변화가 어떻게 세계 기후 체계에 큰 문제를 초래할 수 있는지 깨닫게 해주었습니다. 이제 이 오버헤드 프로젝트 화면을 보면 전 세계적으로 공기와 물의 흐름이 어떻게 이동하는지 훨씬 더 자세히 알 수 있을 거예요.

Q. What can be deduced about El Ninõ from the lecture?
Ⓐ It results in increased rainfall throughout the world.
Ⓑ It contributes to a sharp increase in boating accidents.
Ⓒ It causes natural disasters around the world.
Ⓓ It brings about problems on the Atlantic side of South America.

Q. 강의에서 엘니뇨에 관해 무엇을 추론할 수 있는가?
Ⓐ 전 세계에 강우량 증가를 야기한다.
Ⓑ 보트 사고의 급격한 증가에 일조한다.
Ⓒ 전 세계에 자연 재해를 일으킨다.
Ⓓ 남아메리카의 대서양 쪽에 문제를 일으킨다.

어휘 occur v 발생하다 | significantly adv 상당히 | water current 해류 | complex adj 복잡한 | practical adj 현실적인, 실제의 | economic adj 경제의 | fisherman n 어부 | entire adj 전체의 | rainfall n 강우량 | flooding n 홍수 | associated with ~와 관련된 | thunderstorm n 뇌우 | drought n 가뭄 | affect v 영향을 끼치다 | prompt v 촉발하다 | realize v 깨닫다

Passage 7

Man: Professor | Woman: Student

Listen to part of a discussion in a biology class.

M Today, we're going to talk about sharks. First things first. Sharks are among the oldest living animals on the Earth and have been around for over 400 million years. They are truly remarkable creatures. The shark is a fish, so of course it's cold-blooded and breathes through gills. But it differs from other types of fish because its skeleton is composed of flexible cartilage rather than solid, inflexible bone. So, sharks have unusual flexibility, a real asset in the waters where it makes its home. Actually, this is the reason why sharks were able to survive for such a long time. Sharks also have remarkable sensory abilities. They have reasonably good eyesight, and their eyes are well adapted to hunting for food in dim light. However, their sense of smell is much stronger, and the ability to detect smells takes up an astounding 30% of the shark's entire brain. With that said, what are we told not to do when we are in the water and there are sharks around?

W Not to bleed...

M Okay, true enough. We shouldn't bleed when we are in the water with sharks. But you really should try your best not to move. This is because sharks are equipped with a column of cells called the "lateral line" that enables them to perceive vibrations in the water. So, they are very sensitive to movement. But their most unique and unusual sensory feature is the ability to sense the small electrical pulses generated by the nervous systems of other animals.

W So sharks are like the perfect hunters? I knew they were dangerous, but I didn't know they had so many adaptations to help them kill other animals... and humans...

M Of course, sharks are infamous hunters. You've probably all seen the film *Jaws* right? But actually very few sharks are large enough to do any serious damage to large mammals, and most species eat only small fish and plankton. Although movies and books like to make them out to be dangerous predators and man-eaters, fewer than 10% of the 350 species identified by scientists are dangerous to humans.

W But I thought all sharks had teeth? So wouldn't even the little ones be, uh, dangerous... even to humans?

M Well, most sharks have teeth. So, technically, those are all capable of biting humans, but only three kinds of sharks—

남자: 교수 | 여자: 학생

생물학 수업 중 토론의 일부를 들으시오.

남 오늘은 상어에 대해 이야기하겠습니다. 먼저 살펴볼 점을 봅시다. 상어는 지구상에서 가장 오래 살아온 동물 중 하나이며 4억 년이 넘는 시간 동안 존재했습니다. 정말로 놀라운 피조물이죠. 상어는 어류이므로 물론 냉혈동물이며 아가미를 통해 호흡합니다. 하지만 다른 종류의 물고기와 다른 점은 골격이 딱딱하고 견고한 뼈가 아닌 유연한 연골로 구성됐다는 겁니다. 그래서 상어는 서식지인 물속에서 정말 큰 자산이 되는 보기 드문 유연성을 갖고 있습니다. 사실상 그것은 상어가 그렇게 오랜 시간 살아남을 수 있었던 이유죠. 상어는 또한 놀라운 감지 능력을 갖고 있습니다. 상당히 좋은 시력을 갖고 있으며 눈은 희미한 불빛에서 먹이를 사냥하는 데 잘 적응되어 있습니다. 그러나 후각은 훨씬 더 강력하며, 냄새를 탐지하는 기능이 상어 뇌 전체의 30%나 차지하고 있습니다. 그 말이 나왔으니 말인데, 상어가 있는 물속에서 하지 말아야 할 일은 무엇일까요?

여 피를 흘리지 않는 거요....

남 네, 그렇죠. 상어와 함께 물속에 있을 때 피를 흘려선 안 됩니다. 하지만 정말로 움직이지 않도록 최선을 다할 필요가 있습니다. 상어에게는 물속의 진동을 감지할 수 있게 해주는 '측선'이라는 일렬로 된 세포가 있기 때문입니다. 그래서 움직임에 매우 민감해요. 하지만 상어의 가장 희귀하고 비범한 감각 기능은 다른 동물들의 신경계에서 발생되는 작은 전기 펄스를 감지하는 능력입니다.

여 그럼 상어가 완벽한 사냥꾼이란 말인가요? 상어가 위험한 줄은 알았지만 다른 동물들과... 사람들을.... 잡아 먹는 데 도움이 되는 적응 구조가 그렇게 많은 줄은 몰랐어요.

남 물론 상어는 악명 높은 사냥꾼입니다. 아마 다들 영화 〈죠스〉를 봤을 거예요, 그렇죠? 하지만 실제로 아주 소수의 상어들만 큰 포유류에게 심각한 해를 입힐 수 있을 정도로 크고, 대부분의 종은 작은 물고기와 플랑크톤만 먹습니다. 영화와 책이 상어를 위험한 포식자나 식인 상어로 만들긴 하지만 과학자들이 알아낸 350종 중 10% 미만의 상어만 인간에게 위협이 됩니다.

여 하지만 모든 상어들이 이빨을 가지고 있잖아요? 그러니까 작은 상어라 하더라도 인간에게... 어, 위험하지 않을까요?

남 음, 대부분의 상어가 이빨을 갖고 있습니다. 그래서 엄밀히 따지자면, 모든 상어가 인간을 물 수 있지만

the Great White, the Tiger, and the Bull shark—pose any real threat to humans. The largest shark—the Whale Shark—is approximately 50 feet long. While it looks pretty scary, it only eats plankton and small sea animals. The smallest shark is called the Spined Pygmy Shark and it is less than 8 inches long.

대백상어, 뱀상어, 황소상어 세 종류만 사람들에게 진짜 위협이 되죠. 가장 큰 상어인 고래상어는 길이가 약 50피트입니다. 상당히 무서워 보이지만 플랑크톤과 작은 바다 동물들만 먹죠. 가장 작은 상어는 가시 피그미 상어라고 하는데 길이가 8인치 미만입니다.

Q. What does the professor imply about the lateral line?

Ⓐ It allows the shark to perceive its prey in the dark.
Ⓑ It allows the shark to sense a human being moving in the water.
Ⓒ It allows the shark to breathe through its gills.
Ⓓ It allows a shark to swim in a circular pattern all day.

Q. 교수는 측선에 관해 무엇을 암시하는가?

Ⓐ 상어가 어둠 속에서 먹이를 감지하게 해준다.
Ⓑ 상어로 하여금 인간이 물 속에서 움직이는 것을 감지하게 해준다.
Ⓒ 상어가 아가미를 통해 숨을 쉬게 해준다.
Ⓓ 상어가 하루 종일 원을 그리며 헤엄치도록 해준다.

어휘 remarkable adj 놀라운 I cold-blooded adj 냉혈의 I gill n 아가미 I differ v 다르다 I skeleton n 뼈 I composed of ~로 구성된 I flexible adj 유연한 I cartilage n 연골 I solid adj 단단한 I inflexible adj 경직된, 유연하지 않은 I unusual adj 특이한, 흔치 않은 I flexibility n 유연함 I asset n 자산, 재산 I survive v 생존하다 I sensory adj 감각의 I reasonably adv 상당히, 꽤 I eyesight n 시력 I adapt v 적응하다 I dim adj 희미한 I detect v 감지하다 I astounding adj 믿기 어려운, 경악스러운 I entire adj 전체의 I bleed v 피를 흘리다 I lateral line 측선 I perceive v 인지하다 I vibration n 진동 I sensitive adj 민감한 I movement n 움직임 I sense v 감지하다 I electrical pulse 전기 펄스 I generate v 발생시키다 I nervous system 신경계 I infamous adj 악명 높은 I serious adj 심각한 I mammal n 포유류 I predator n 포식자 I technically adv 엄밀히 따지면 I bite v 물다 I Great White Shark 대백상어 I Tiger Shark 뱀상어 I Bull Shark 황소상어 I threat n 위협 I Whale Shark 고래상어 I approximately adv 대략 I scary adj 무서운 I Spined Pygmy Shark 가시 피그미 상어

Passage 8

Woman: Professor

Listen to part of a lecture in an ecology class.

W Okay, now I would like to move on to a problem that doesn't get much attention in the media but which is still a serious problem. What's going on is that the world's fertile topsoil is slowly disappearing. This is called topsoil-erosion, and it's affecting the entire world right now and making crops more difficult to grow. The consequences of this are obvious, so I'd rather focus on the causes. Most of them involve humans and how they are infringing upon nature, but it is important to remember that erosion occurred long before humans even existed. That is what has produced sea cliffs, certain lakes, and even the Grand Canyon.
With that said, humans are speeding up the process of erosion and also hurting themselves through overproduction and overpopulation. They're farming more animals than ever before and doing so in smaller and smaller areas. With more animals present in these spaces, it then becomes possible for the animals to eat up all of the vegetation on a plot of land. After this happens, the soil is left exposed and can be washed or blown away easily. At the same time, high concentrations of animals can compact the soil, which prevents more vegetation from growing in the area.

여자: 교수

생태학 강의의 일부를 들으시오.

여 자, 이제 미디어에서는 많은 관심을 받지 못하지만 여전히 심각한 문제에 관해 이야기하려고 합니다. 바로 세계의 비옥한 표토가 서서히 사라지고 있다는 것입니다. 이것을 표토 침식이라고 하며 현재 전 세계에 영향을 미치고 있고, 농작물의 성장을 더욱 어렵게 만들고 있습니다. 이에 대한 결과는 명백하기 때문에 원인에 집중하겠습니다. 원인의 대부분이 인간과 인간이 자연을 어떻게 침해하고 있는지와 관련되어 있지만 침식은 인간이 존재하기 오래 전부터 발생했다는 점을 기억하는 것이 중요합니다. 그것은 해식 절벽과 특정 호수들, 심지어 그랜드 캐니언까지 만들었어요.
그 말이 나왔으니 말인데, 인간은 침식 과정을 가속화할 뿐 아니라 과잉 생산과 과잉 인구를 통해 스스로에게 해를 입히고 있습니다. 그 어느 때보다 많은 동물을 사육하고 있으며 점점 더 좁은 공간에서 하고 있죠. 이런 좁은 공간에 동물이 더 많아지면서 그 구역에 있는 초목을 모두 먹어버리는 일이 가능해집니다. 그렇게 되고 나면 토양은 노출된 채 남겨지고 쉽게 씻겨 나가거나 소실될 수 있죠. 동시에 동물들이 밀집해 있으면 토양이 단단하게 다져지고, 이는 그 지역에서 더 이상의 초목이 자라지 못하게 합니다.

Humans are also cutting down way too many trees. When they do this and don't try to plant more trees, the soil once again has nothing to protect it or hold it down. It is vulnerable to erosion and can be blown away more easily. We're also farming improperly, which is leading to the same type of problem where plants can't grow on land anymore and then it erodes. But what do I mean by improper farming here? Well, um, certain irrigation methods leave too much salt in the ground, which hinders plant growth. Farmers are also failing to give the soil the time it needs to replenish itself before they plant new crops and overusing fertilizers. To cut to the chase, farmers are just abusing the land and trying to make it produce more than it should. Humans just aren't looking toward the future. They're trying to get everything now, but they aren't thinking about the consequences of demanding so much from the land they live on. Eventually, this is going to lead to some serious problems in terms of soil erosion and soil infertility.

또한 인간들은 너무 많은 나무를 베고 있어요. 나무를 베고 더 많은 나무를 심지 않으면 다시 토양을 보호하거나 지탱할 것이 없어지게 됩니다. 침식에 취약해지고 더 쉽게 소실될 수 있죠. 그리고 우리는 부적절하게 경작을 해서 식물이 땅에서 더 이상 자랄 수 없게 하는 동일한 문제를 초래하고 그로 인해 토양은 침식됩니다. 하지만 여기서 부적절한 경작이란 무엇일까요? 음, 어떤 관개 방법은 땅에 너무 많은 염분을 남겨 식물의 성장을 방해합니다. 또한 농부들은 새로운 농작물을 경작하기 전에 땅이 스스로 회복할 수 있는 시간을 주지 않으며, 비료를 남용합니다.
단도직입적으로 말하자면, 농부들은 토지를 남용하고 있으며 적정량 이상으로 더 많이 생산하게 하려 합니다. 인간은 미래를 내다보지 않고 있어요. 지금 당장 모든 것을 얻으려 하지만 자신들이 사는 땅에 많은 것을 요구하고 난 뒤의 결과에 대해서는 생각하지 않죠. 결국 이는 토양 침식과 토양 불모라는 심각한 문제로 이어질 겁니다.

Q. What does the professor imply about current agricultural practices?

Ⓐ Raising large herds of animals compacts the soil.
Ⓑ Too much salt is building up in the soil.
Ⓒ Fertilizers accumulate in the ground water.
Ⓓ Farmers are using up the land that can be farmed.

Q. 교수는 현재의 농업 관행에 관해 무엇을 암시하는가?

Ⓐ 큰 무리의 동물들을 기르는 것은 토양을 다져지게 만든다.
Ⓑ 너무 많은 염분이 토양에 쌓이고 있다.
Ⓒ 비료가 지하수에 축적된다.
Ⓓ 농부들이 경작할 수 있는 땅을 다 고갈시키고 있다.

어휘 attention n 주의, 주목 | fertile adj 비옥한 | topsoil n 표토 | erosion n 침식 | affect v 영향을 주다 | entire adj 전체의 | crop n 작물 | consequence n 결과 | obvious adj 명백한 | cause n 원인 | infringe v 침해하다 | occur v 발생하다 | exist v 존재하다 | sea cliff 해식 절벽 | hurt v 다치게 하다 | overproduction n 과잉 생산 | overpopulation n 인구 과잉 | vegetation n 초목, 식물 | exposed adj 노출된 | blow away 날려버리다 | concentration n 집중 | compact v (단단히) 다지다 | prevent v 막다, 방해하다 | vulnerable adj 취약한 | improperly adv 그릇되게, 틀리게 | erode v 침식되다 | improper adj 부적절한 | irrigation n 관개 | hinder v 저해하다 | growth n 성장 | replenish v 다시 채우다, 보충하다 | overuse v 남용하다 | fertilizer n 비료 | to cut to the chase 본론으로 들어가다 | abuse v 남용하다, 학대하다 | demand v 요구하다 | infertility n 불모

Passage 9

Man: Professor

Listen to part of a lecture in a history class.

M I know some of you have probably heard the name Sumer before, but do any of you know what Sumer was? Not really? Well, Sumer was an amazing civilization that began taking shape around 3000 B.C. in Mesopotamia—the region between the Tigris and Euphrates Rivers. It was a class-based society that had people who performed all of the functions of a major civilization: leaders, merchants, field workers, and everything else. It was very advanced. **1** In fact, it is the society that invented the wheel and began

남자: 교수

역사 강의의 일부를 들으시오.

남 여러분 중 일부는 아마 수메르라는 이름을 전에 들어 봤을 거란 걸 알지만, 여러분 중에 수메르가 무엇인지 아는 사람 있나요? 잘 모른다고요? 음, 수메르는 티그리스와 유프라테스강들 사이에 있는 지역인 메소포타미아에서 기원전 3000년경 모습을 갖추기 시작한 놀라운 문명이었습니다. 이 문명은 계급 기반 사회였으며 주요 문명의 모든 기능을 수행하는 사람들이 있었죠. 지도자와 상인, 일꾼, 그리고 그 밖의 모든 것들이요. 매우 진보한 문명이었습니다. **1** 이는 또한 실제로 바퀴를 발명해 운송에 쓰

using it in transportation. Yes, I know that you thought that the cavemen did this, but it was actually the Sumerians. They came up with the wheel while creating artwork and then began applying the concept to carts and other things. Quite innovative to say the least. Sumerian writing is also the oldest known form of writing, which probably helped Sumer develop intricate governmental and judicial systems. Organized schools were even developed for students to learn writing and other disciplines. All in all, Sumerian society was quite sophisticated. But that sophistication didn't stop Sumer from collapsing due to over-farming. That's right... due to over-farming.

To begin with, the Sumerians had to deal with flooding. The major rivers in Sumer were above the farmers' fields, which meant that it was easy for water to overflow and destroy the crops. The Sumerians handled this pretty well, however, and began building embankments to hold back the water. But then they had to deal with how to get water to their crops now that the rivers were prevented from reaching them. They ended up building an interesting irrigation system with canals leading from the river. Once again, Sumer was doing quite well and handling situations in a sophisticated manner. **2** But the water from the canals ended up just sitting in the fields where it then evaporated, leaving a lot of salt on the surface of the land. This meant that the farmers had to stop using the land for a while before planting again. I mean, without doing this, there would be no way for the salt to disappear because the farmers would have to water the crops to make them grow, and that would mean that more salt would build up and it wouldn't be able to move back into the ground. **3** And the amazing thing is that the farmers knew this... They knew that, if they kept irrigating, the salt problem would just become worse and worse. Unfortunately, the Sumerian leaders did not know this—or rather did not want to listen to what the farmers were saying. Consequently, they told the farmers that they must continue farming the land to meet the civilization's food demands. So, the farmers kept farming, and the land became worse.

Eventually, Sumerians became impoverished and desperate. As a result, they began fighting with each other and with the government and the leadership lost control. Their very organized society pretty much became a chaotic free-for-all. As you can imagine, Sumer was weakened, and the Akkadians took advantage of this fact around 2300 B.C. They took over the kingdom, but this did not stop the decline in land quality that plagued the region.

기 시작한 사회이기도 했습니다. 네, 여러분이 원시인들이 이 일을 했다고 생각한다는 걸 알지만 실제로는 수메르인들이었습니다. 이들은 그림을 그리면서 바퀴를 생각해냈고 이 개념을 수레와 다른 물건들에 적용하기 시작했습니다. 과장이 아니라 정말 혁신적이었죠. 수메르인의 문자 또한 가장 오래된 것으로 알려진 문자이며 이 문자가 아마 수메르인들이 정교한 정부와 사법 체계를 발전시키는 데 도움을 줬을 겁니다. 학생들이 글쓰기와 다른 학문 분야를 배울 수 있는 조직화된 학교도 생겨났습니다. 전반적으로 수메르 사회는 매우 세련된 사회였습니다. 하지만 그러한 세련됨도 수메르인들이 과잉 경작으로 붕괴하는 것을 막지는 못했습니다. 그래요... 과잉 경작 때문이었습니다.

먼저, 수메르인들은 홍수에 대처해야만 했습니다. 수메르의 주요 강들은 농지의 위쪽에 있었는데, 이것은 물이 범람하여 농작물을 망치기가 쉬웠다는 의미입니다. 하지만 수메르인들은 이에 상당히 잘 대처하여 물을 막을 수 있는 제방을 만들기 시작했어요. 그러나 이제 강이 농지에 닿지 못하게 되었기 때문에 농작물에 물을 댈 방법을 찾아야 했습니다. 결국 강에서 이어지는 수로가 있는 흥미로운 관개 시스템을 만들어냈죠. 또 다시 수메르인들은 매우 잘 해내고 있었고 세련된 방식으로 상황에 대처했습니다. **2** 하지만 수로에서 온 물은 그냥 들판에 고여 있다 증발하며 지표면에 많은 염분을 남겼습니다. 이는 농부들이 다시 경작을 하려면 잠시 토지의 사용을 중단해야 했다는 의미였습니다. 제 말은, 그렇게 하지 않으면 농부들이 작물을 기르기 위해 물을 줘야만 하는데, 그러면 더 많은 염분이 쌓이게 되고 땅 속으로 돌아가지 못하게 되므로 염분이 사라질 방법이 없었습니다. **3** 그리고 놀라운 점은 농부들이 이 사실을 알고 있었다는 것이었습니다.... 계속 물을 끌어오면 염분 문제가 점점 더 악화될 거라는 걸 알았죠. 안타깝게도 수메르 지도자들은 그걸 몰랐거나, 또는 농부들이 하는 말에 귀를 기울이려 하지 않았습니다. 그 결과, 지도자들은 식량 수요를 충족할 수 있도록 농부들에게 계속 땅을 경작하라고 지시했죠. 그래서 농부들은 경작을 계속했고 땅은 점점 악화되었습니다.

결국 수메르인들은 매우 궁핍해지고 절박해졌어요. 그 결과 서로, 그리고 정부와도 싸우기 시작했고 지도층은 통제력을 잃었습니다. 바로 그 조직화되었던 사회는 혼돈스러운 무질서 상태가 되었습니다. 여러분의 상상대로, 수메르는 약화되었고 기원전 2300년경 아카드인들이 이 기회를 이용했죠. 이들이 왕국을 점령했지만, 이것도 이 지역을 괴롭힌 토질의 하락을 멈추지는 못했습니다.

1. What can be inferred about the Sumerian culture?
   Ⓐ Their writing system is the basis for Western languages.
   Ⓑ They were responsible for many innovations.
   Ⓒ They had very early legal and judicial systems.
   Ⓓ They practiced an organized form of religion.

2. What can be concluded about salt from the lecture?
   Ⓐ Salt from the soil was seeping into rivers that Sumerians drank from.
   Ⓑ When vegetables absorb too much salt, it can be harmful to humans.
   Ⓒ An abundance of salt in the ground prevents crop growth.
   Ⓓ Salt encourages the growth of certain plants but not others.

3. What does the professor imply about Sumerian leaders?
   Ⓐ They supported the farmers' recommendations.
   Ⓑ They were not effective at governing their people.
   Ⓒ They organized the projects that tamed the rivers.
   Ⓓ They were not knowledgeable about agriculture.

1. 수메르 문명에 관해 무엇을 추론할 수 있는가?
   Ⓐ 이들의 문자 체계는 서양 언어의 기반이다.
   Ⓑ 그들은 많은 혁신을 해냈다.
   Ⓒ 매우 초기의 법과 재판 체계를 갖고 있었다.
   Ⓓ 조직화된 형태의 종교를 믿었다.

2. 강의에서 염분에 관해 어떤 결론을 내릴 수 있는가?
   Ⓐ 수메르인들이 마시는 강으로 토양에서 온 염분이 흘러 들어가고 있었다.
   Ⓑ 야채가 너무 많은 염분을 흡수하면 인간에게 해가 될 수 있다.
   Ⓒ 땅 속의 너무 많은 염분은 작물 성장을 방해한다.
   Ⓓ 염분은 특정 식물의 성장을 촉진하지만 다른 식물은 아니다.

3. 교수는 수메르 지도자들에 관해 무엇을 암시하는가?
   Ⓐ 농부들의 권고사항을 지지했다.
   Ⓑ 사람들을 다스리는 데 효율적이지 못했다.
   Ⓒ 강을 길들이는 프로젝트를 조직했다.
   Ⓓ 농업에 관해 잘 알지 못했다.

어휘 amazing adj 놀라운, 멋진 | civilization n 문명 | class-based 계급을 기반으로 하는 | society n 사회 | perform v 수행하다 | function n 기능 | merchant n 상인 | advanced adj 진보한 | invent v 발명하다 | wheel n 바퀴 | transportation n 운송, 교통 | caveman n 원시인 | artwork n 예술 작품 | apply v 적용하다 | concept n 개념 | innovative adj 혁신적인 | develop v 개발하다, 발전시키다 | intricate adj 복잡한 | judicial adj 사법의 | organized adj 조직화된 | discipline n 지식 분야 | sophisticated adj 세련된, 정교한 | collapse v 붕괴하다 | over farm 지나치게 경작하다 | flooding n 홍수 | overflow v 넘치다, 넘쳐 흐르다 | destroy v 파괴하다 | crop n 농작물 | handle v 다루다 | embankment n 제방 | prevent v 막다, 방해하다 | irrigation n 관개 | canal n 수로, 관 | situation n 상황 | evaporate v 증발하다 | surface n 표면 | unfortunately adv 안타깝게도 | consequently adv 그 결과, 따라서 | demand n 수요 | eventually adv 결국 | impoverished adj 빈곤한 | desperate adj 절박한, 자포자기한 | chaotic adj 혼돈 상태인 | free-for-all 무질서 상태 | weaken v 약화시키다 | take advantage of ~를 이용하다 | kingdom n 왕국 | decline n 하락, 감소 | plague v 괴롭히다, 성가시게 하다 | region n 지역

Passage 10

Man: Student | Woman: Professor

Listen to part of a discussion in a sociology class.

W Yesterday, we were talking about the changes in society over the last several decades. Of course, population plays a key role in the development of any society. Today, we'll look at the effects of overpopulation. In 1798, British economist Thomas Malthus published his *An Essay on the Principle of Population*. It set off a debate that continues to this day. **1** Malthus revealed in his studies of population growth that the number of people would soon outpace the planet's ability to produce food.

M I'm sorry, but I don't understand. Uh, what do you mean by "outpace the planet's ability to supply food" here?

W **1** Well, to put it in other words, famine or starvation is

남자: 학생 | 여자: 교수

사회학 수업 중 토론의 일부를 들으시오.

여 어제 우리는 지난 몇 십 년에 걸친 사회의 변화에 관해 이야기했습니다. 물론 인구는 모든 사회의 발전에 중요한 역할을 합니다. 오늘은 인구 과잉의 영향을 살펴보도록 하겠습니다. 1798년 영국 경제학자 토마스 맬서스가 〈인구론〉을 출판했습니다. 이 책은 오늘날까지 계속되는 논쟁을 제기했죠. **1** 맬서스는 인구 증가에 관한 그의 연구에서 사람들의 수가 지구의 식량 생산 능력을 곧 앞지를 거라고 밝혔습니다.

남 죄송하지만 이해가 안 가요. 음, '지구의 식량 제공 능력을 앞지른다'는 게 무슨 뜻인가요?

여 **1** 다른 말로 하자면, 미래에는 기아와 굶주림을 피

inevitable in the future. Although Malthus' predictions haven't come true—yet, the possibility of overpopulation continues to be debated in many branches of the social sciences. So in Malthus' view, overpopulation means "humans in numbers requiring more resources than are available." As we all know, the world's population is growing fast! At the beginning of the 17th century, global population was estimated to be around 600 million. By the beginning of the twentieth century, that number was a little over 1.5 billion. Advances in medicine and agriculture during the last few hundred years are credited for helping more people live on Earth and live longer, too. The downside of that is that by 1960, the population had doubled to 3 billion. By the beginning of 2000, the number had doubled again to the figure of 6 billion. Now there are over 7.7 billion. Anyone feeling crowded yet?

M So are scientists concerned about what will happen if this growth continues? I mean, there's no way we can support ourselves if, um, our population keeps doubling like that, right?

W Yes, that's true... 2 but experts don't believe that this rate of growth will continue. Although technology will continue to save lives and extend life spans, researchers believe that people are choosing to have fewer children. That will have a significant impact on population growth. In fact, China had a one child policy for some time. The Earth's population won't decrease, probably, nor will it double again.

M Oh, well, how fast do they think population will grow then if it's not going to double? Do they think that the growth will be fairly slow?

W Yes, current estimates suggest that we will add only a couple more billion people every twenty-five years. We are constantly developing better ways to grow and harvest food, making the Earth better able to accommodate population increases. 3 So, while some social scientists, including me, remain concerned about overpopulation, the vast majority of experts believe that the Earth's resources are sufficient to cope with the demands of a huge population. Although Thomas Malthus is given credit for having pioneered the study of population, few scientists today share his concerns that the Earth is in imminent danger of overpopulation.

할 수 없다는 겁니다. 비록 맬서스의 예측이 아직까지는 실현되지 않았지만 인구 과잉의 가능성은 사회 과학의 많은 분야에서 계속되는 논쟁거리입니다. 그러니까 맬서스의 관점에서 인구 과잉은 '인간의 수가 사용할 수 있는 것보다 더 많은 자원을 필요로 하는 것'을 의미합니다. 우리 모두 알다시피 세계의 인구는 빠르게 증가하고 있습니다! 17세기 초에는 세계 인구가 6억 명 정도로 추정되었습니다. 20세기 초에는 15억이 조금 넘었죠. 지난 수백 년 동안의 의학과 농업의 발전 또한 지구상에 더 많은 사람들이 더 오래 살 수 있게 해주었습니다. 이것의 부정적인 면은 1960년에 이르자 인구가 두 배로 불어나 30억 명이 되었다는 것이죠. 2000년 초반에는 수가 다시 두 배가 되어 60억이 되었습니다. 이제는 77억이 넘죠. 누구 혼잡하다고 느끼는 사람 없나요?

남 그래서 과학자들은 이런 증가가 계속될 경우 발생할 일을 염려하는 건가요? 만약 인구가 그렇게 계속해서 두 배로 증가한다면 우리 스스로를 지탱할 수 있는 방법이 없잖아요, 그렇죠?

여 네, 맞아요... 2 하지만 전문가들은 이런 증가율이 계속될 거라고 생각하지 않습니다. 기술이 계속 인간의 생명을 구하고 수명을 연장하겠지만 연구원들은 사람들이 자식을 더 적게 낳기를 선택하고 있다고 믿습니다. 이는 인구 증가에 상당한 영향을 미칠 겁니다. 실제로 중국에서는 꽤 오랫동안 한 자녀 정책을 시행해 왔죠. 지구의 인구가 줄지는 않겠지만 다시 두 배가 되지도 않을 겁니다.

남 아, 전문가들은 인구가 두 배가 안 된다면 얼마나 빨리 증가할 거라고 생각하나요? 서서히 증가할 거라고 생각하나요?

여 네, 현재 추정으로는 매 25년마다 약 20억 명 정도만 늘어날 거라고 합니다. 인간은 계속해서 식량을 재배하고 수확하는 더 좋은 방법을 개발하여 지구가 인구 증가를 더 잘 수용하도록 하고 있습니다. 3 그래서 저를 비롯한 일부 사회 과학자들이 인구 과잉을 계속 염려하고 있지만 대다수의 전문가들은 지구의 자원이 거대한 인구의 수요에 대처할 만큼 충분하다고 믿습니다. 비록 토마스 맬서스는 인구에 대한 연구를 개척한 공로로 인정 받고 있지만, 오늘날 소수의 과학자만 지구가 임박한 인구 과잉 위험에 처해 있다는 그의 염려에 공감합니다.

1. What is implied about Malthus' overpopulation theory?

Ⓐ It was proven to be an interesting but groundless theory.

Ⓑ It was based on a small study with an insufficient sample size.

1. 맬서스의 인구 과잉 이론에 관해 무엇을 추론할 수 있는가?

Ⓐ 흥미롭지만 근거 없는 이론으로 밝혀졌다.

Ⓑ 불충분한 샘플 크기의 작은 연구에 기반한 것이다.

Lesson 05 Lectures

Ⓒ It was very controversial among social scientists.
Ⓓ It was the basis for economics in the Western world today.

2. What can be inferred about China's one child policy?
Ⓐ It had little to no practical effect on population growth.
Ⓑ It was a poorly conceived policy that did more harm than good.
Ⓒ It was designed by people who believed Malthus' predictions.
Ⓓ It may have helped to slow down overall population growth.

3. What does the professor imply about Malthus' predictions?
Ⓐ They may still prove correct.
Ⓑ They were a product of his time.
Ⓒ They should be disregarded.
Ⓓ They were partially accurate.

Ⓒ 사회 과학자들 사이에서 아주 논란이 많았다.
Ⓓ 오늘날 서양 세계 경제의 기반이다.

2. 중국의 한 자녀 정책에 관해 무엇을 추론할 수 있는가?
Ⓐ 인구 증가에 아예 영향이 없거나 아주 적은 영향만 미쳤다.
Ⓑ 장점보다 단점이 더 많았던 형편없이 실행된 정책이었다.
Ⓒ 맬서스의 예측을 믿은 사람들이 계획했다.
Ⓓ 전반적인 인구 증가를 늦추는 데 도움을 줬을 수도 있다.

3. 교수는 맬서스의 예측에 관해 무엇을 암시하는가?
Ⓐ 여전히 옳다고 밝혀질 수도 있다.
Ⓑ 그가 살던 시기의 산물이다.
Ⓒ 무시해야 한다.
Ⓓ 부분적으로 옳았다.

어휘 society n 사회 | decade n 10년 | population n 인구 | development n 발달, 개발 | overpopulation n 인구 과잉 | economist n 경제학자 | publish v 출간하다 | principle n 원리 | debate n 논쟁 | reveal v 드러내다 | growth n 성장, 증가 | outpace v 앞지르다, 앞서다 | produce v 생산하다 | supply v 제공하다 | famine n 기근 | starvation n 굶주림 | inevitable adj 불가피한, 필연적인 | prediction n 예측 | possibility n 가능성 | branch n 분야 | require v 요구하다, 필요로 하다 | resource n 자원 | estimate v 추산하다 | medicine n 의학 | agriculture n 농업 | downside n 부정적인 면 | be credited for 인정받다 | billion n 10억 | crowded adj 붐비는, 빽빽한 | concerned adj 염려하는, 우려하는 | expert n 전문가 | extend v 연장하다 | life span 수명 | significant adj 큰, 중요한 | impact n 영향 | decrease v 감소하다 | constantly adv 지속적으로 | harvest v 수확하다 | accommodate v 공간을 제공하다, 수용하다 | vast adj 어마어마한, 방대한 | majority n 다수 | sufficient adj 충분한 | cope with 대처하다 | demand n 수요 | pioneer v 개척하다 | imminent adj 임박한 | danger n 위험

Test

본서 | P. 192

Passage 1

Man: Professor

[1-6] Listen to part of a lecture in an English literature class.

M **1** Today we will be examining one of the most famous authors in English history, Daniel Defoe, and the main reason for that fame: his novel *Robinson Crusoe*. Originally published in 1719, his book is considered by many to be the first English novel. Of course, that designation depends upon how one defines the term novel. How would you define a novel? To give you a broad definition, **2(D)** a novel is a long narrative of fictional events, usually sequential events, **2(B)** written in prose. And, *Robinson Crusoe* fits within it nicely. **3** Defoe originally embarked upon a career as a general merchant, and enjoyed some business success, but most of his ventures ended in failure and he was constantly

남자: 교수

영문학 강의의 일부를 들으시오.

남 **1** 오늘 우리는 영국 역사에 있어 가장 유명한 작가들 중 한 명인 대니얼 디포를 살펴볼 것이고, 그가 유명한 가장 주된 이유인 그의 소설 〈로빈슨 크루소〉에 대해서도 알아볼 겁니다. 1719년에 처음으로 출판된 그의 소설은 많은 이들에 의해 최초의 영문 소설로 간주되죠. 물론 이렇게 지명되는 것은 소설이라는 단어를 어떻게 정의하느냐에 달려 있습니다. 소설을 어떻게 정의해야 할까요? 넓은 범위의 정의를 내리자면, **2(D)** 소설은 허구의 사건들에 대한 긴 서술인데, 이 사건들은 대개 순차적으로 일어나며 **2(B)** 산문으로 쓰여 있습니다. 그리고, 〈로빈슨 크루소〉는 이 정의에 잘 들어맞죠. **3** 디포는 원래 종합 상사로 일을 시작했고 사업적으로 약간의 성공을 맛보기도 했지만 대부분의 모험이 실패로 끝났

in debt. As an author, he had much more success, but most of his early work was poems and essays of a very political nature. These were often published as anonymous pamphlets, and they stirred up much controversy that sometimes threatened his life and even landed him in prison. However, not all of his pamphlets were like this, and one titled *A True Relation of the Apparition of One Mrs. Veal the Next Day after her Death to One Mrs. Bargrave at Canterbury the 8th of September, 1705* was a precursor of his career in fiction.

4 I know that it is a really long title, but such titles were common at the time. In fact, the full title of *Robinson Crusoe* was originally *The Life and Strange Surprising Adventures of Robinson Crusoe, Of York, Mariner: Who lived Eight and Twenty Years, all alone in an uninhabited Island on the Coast of America, near the Mouth of the Great River Oroonoque; Having been cast on Shore by Shipwreck, wherein all the Men perished but himself. With An Account of how he was at last as strangely deliver'd by Pyrates.* Books didn't have dust jackets with pictures and plot synopses, so the titles often informed the reader exactly what they would be reading about.

5(A) In that edition, the fictional protagonist was credited as the author of the text, allowing Defoe to pass it off as a travelogue of actual events. Such books were immensely popular at that time, and he used that to his advantage, publishing four editions in its first year of publication. In the novel, Crusoe had many fantastic adventures including encounters with cannibals, captives, and mutineers until he is eventually rescued. **5(C)** The story of the novel is believed to have been inspired by the experiences of Alexander Selkirk, who was an actual castaway for four years on an island west of Chile. Due to the novel's popularity, the island was actually later renamed from Mas a Tierra to Robinson Crusoe Island. **5(C)** However, recent research has revealed that many other stories, both fictional and not, may have contributed to Defoe's tale. He may have been inspired by a translation of a novel by Ibn Tufail that also took place on a desert island, or Robert Knox's retelling of his abduction in Sri Lanka, then known as Ceylon. Another strong candidate is Henry Pitman's account of his escape from a prison colony in the Caribbean, where he was imprisoned for political reasons, after which he too was shipwrecked and had many adventures on a desert island. Whether or not Defoe read the book cannot be confirmed, but he most likely knew about it since his publisher was the son of the

고 항상 빚을 지고 있는 상태였습니다. 작가로서의 그는 훨씬 더 큰 성공을 거두었지만 그의 초기 작품들은 매우 정치적인 성격을 가진 시와 에세이들이었죠. 이 작품들은 종종 익명의 팜플렛으로 출판되었고, 많은 논란을 불러일으켜서 때로는 그의 생명을 위협하기도 했으며 그가 투옥되도록 만들기도 했습니다. 그러나 모든 팜플렛들이 그러했던 건 아니었고, 〈죽은 다음날인 1705년 9월 8일에 캔터베리에서 바그레이브양에게 나타난 빌양의 유령에 대한 진짜 관계〉라는 제목의 팜플렛이 소설가로서의 전조가 되었습니다.

4 매우 긴 제목이라는 걸 알지만, 이러한 제목들은 그 당시 흔했어요. 사실 〈로빈슨 크루소〉의 원래 제목은 이것이었습니다. 〈조난을 당해 자신을 제외한 모든 선원이 사망하고, 아메리카 대륙 오루노크강 가까운 무인도 해변에서 28년 동안 홀로 살다가 마침내 기적적으로 해적선에 구출된 요크 출신 뱃사람 로빈슨 크루소가 그려낸 자신의 생애와 기이하고도 놀라운 모험 이야기〉. 그 당시의 책들은 그림이나 책의 줄거리가 실린 표지를 가지고 있지 않았기에 제목이 독자들에게 그들이 정확히 어떠한 이야기를 읽게 될 것인지 종종 알려주는 역할을 했죠.

5(A) 해당 판에서 허구의 주인공은 이 책의 작가로 공인되며 디포로 하여금 이 소설이 실제 사건들을 실은 여행기로 보일 수 있도록 했습니다. 이런 책들은 그 당시 엄청나게 인기가 있었으며 그는 이것을 장점으로 이용했는데, 출판한 지 1년 만에 4판까지 책을 인쇄했어요. 소설에서 크루소는 마침내 구조될 때까지 식인종, 포로, 그리고 폭도들과의 만남을 포함한 환상적인 모험을 합니다. **5(C)** 이 소설의 이야기는 알렉산더 셀커크라는 인물의 경험에서 영감을 받은 것으로 알려져 있는데, 이 인물은 칠레의 서쪽에 있는 섬에서 4년간 실제로 조난 생활을 했던 사람입니다. 책의 인기 덕에 이 섬은 실제로 후에 마스아티에라라는 이름에서 로빈슨 크루소섬으로 이름이 바뀌게 되죠. **5(C)** 그러나 최근의 연구는 허구이든지 허구가 아니든지 다수의 많은 이야기들이 모두 디포의 이야기에 기여했을 수 있다는 것을 밝혀냈습니다. 이븐 투파일이라는 사람이 쓴, 외딴 섬에 무대를 둔 소설의 번역본을 보고 영감을 받았을 수도 있고, 혹은 그 당시 실론이라고 알려졌던 스리랑카에서 로버트 녹스라는 인물이 겪은 납치 이야기에 영감을 받았을 수도 있습니다. 또 다른 강력한 후보자는 헨리 피트먼의 이야기입니다. 그는 카리브해에 위치한 유배 식민지에서 탈출했는데, 정치적인 이유로 그곳에 투옥되어 있었습니다. 그 뒤에 이 인물 역시 난파당해 외딴 섬에서 많은 모험을 겪죠. 디포가 이 책을 읽었는지 아닌지는 밝혀지지 않았지만 아마 알고 있었을 가능성이 큰데,

man who published Pitman's story.

6 Unlike most other literature of the time, *Robinson Crusoe* was a first person narrative, which initially brought it harsh criticism. The standard was to use the third person omniscient point of view, which allows the reader to know everything that happens and all of the characters' thoughts. The limited scope of Crusoe's narrative, of course, is more fitting of the travelogue it was initially published as being. Since then, fictional stories told from the limited perspective of the protagonist's mind have become quite common. 1 Therefore, the first person narrative is seen as one of Defoe's greatest contributions to English literature.

그 이유는 그의 소설을 출판한 사람이 피트먼의 이야기를 출판한 사람의 아들이었기 때문입니다.

6 당시 대부분의 문학들과 달리 〈로빈슨 크루소〉는 1인칭 시점으로 쓰여진 소설이며, 그로 인해 처음에는 가혹한 평가를 받았습니다. 당시의 기준은 3인칭 전지적 작가 시점으로 글을 쓰는 것이었는데, 이 시점은 독자로 하여금 일어나는 모든 사건들과 모든 인물들의 생각을 알 수 있도록 해줍니다. 물론 크루소의 제한된 범위에서의 사건 서술은 원래 여행기라고 출판된 것에 더 적절히 들어맞죠. 그 이후로 주인공의 마음에서 나오는 제한된 시점의 허구적인 이야기들이 매우 흔해지게 되었습니다. 1 그렇기에 1인칭 시점은 디포가 영문학에 한 가장 큰 기여 중 하나로 여겨지고 있습니다.

1. What is the lecture mainly about?

Ⓐ The difference between Defoe's work and his contemporaries
Ⓑ The characteristics and the influence of a famous novel
Ⓒ The development of first person narrative novels
Ⓓ The history of the travelogue and its development over time

2. According to the lecture, what is true about a novel?

Choose 2 answers.

Ⓐ It is often short or medium in length.
Ⓑ It takes the form of prose.
Ⓒ It describes events that happen simultaneously.
Ⓓ It talks about fictional events.

3. Why does the professor mention a general merchant?

Ⓐ To illustrate how Defoe was financially unstable during his lifetime
Ⓑ To compare the salary of a merchant to that of an author
Ⓒ To explain that Defoe did not begin his career as a writer
Ⓓ To show how being a merchant influenced *Robinson Crusoe*

4. What is the professor's attitude toward novels with long titles?

Ⓐ He doubts whether having a long title for novels was really necessary.
Ⓑ He thinks that popularity of a novel did not depend on its title.

1. 강의는 주로 무엇에 대한 것인가?

Ⓐ 디포의 작품과 동시대 작가들 작품 사이의 차이점
Ⓑ 한 유명한 소설의 특징과 그 영향
Ⓒ 1인칭 시점 소설의 발달
Ⓓ 여행기의 역사와 시간의 흐름에 따른 발전

2. 강의에 따르면, 소설에 관해 옳은 것은 무엇인가?

두 개를 고르시오.

Ⓐ 짧거나 중간 길이이다.
Ⓑ 산문의 형태를 취한다.
Ⓒ 동시에 일어나는 사건들을 기술한다.
Ⓓ 허구의 사건들에 대한 것이다.

3. 교수는 왜 종합 상사를 언급하는가?

Ⓐ 디포가 삶 전반에 걸쳐 얼마나 경제적으로 불안정했는지를 보여주려고
Ⓑ 상인 급여를 작가의 급여와 비교하려고
Ⓒ 디포가 직업을 소설가로 시작하지 않았다는 것을 설명하려고
Ⓓ 상인으로 일했던 것이 〈로빈슨 크루소〉에 어떤 영향을 미쳤는지 보여주려고

4. 긴 제목을 가진 소설들에 대한 교수의 의견은 무엇인가?

Ⓐ 소설에 긴 제목을 붙이는 것이 정말 필요한 것이었는지 의심한다.
Ⓑ 소설의 인기가 제목에 달린 것이 아니었다고 생각한다.

Ⓒ He knows that novels that had long titles tended to become more popular.

Ⓓ He believes that it was not an unusual thing during Defoe's time.

5. What is indicated about *Robinson Crusoe*?

Choose 2 answers.

Ⓐ Defoe pretended that the protagonist of the novel was the writer of the story.

Ⓑ It instantly became popular because people were interested in the life of a castaway.

Ⓒ Defoe wrote the novel based on the experiences of some other travelers.

Ⓓ Robinson Crusoe, the protagonist of the novel, was a castaway for four years.

6. What can be inferred from the professor's explanation about *Robinson Crusoe*?

Ⓐ Its unusual narrative style is what made Defoe receive a positive critical response.

Ⓑ It influenced the general style of travelogues in many European countries.

Ⓒ The readers could not see through everything that was happening in the novel.

Ⓓ The novel switches back and forth from a first person narrative to a third person one.

Ⓒ 긴 제목을 가진 소설들이 더 인기를 끄는 경향이 있었다는 것을 알고 있다.

Ⓓ 디포가 살던 시대에는 특이한 일이 아니었다고 믿는다.

5. 〈로빈슨 크루소〉에 대해 시사된 것은 무엇인가?

두 개를 고르시오.

Ⓐ 디포는 소설의 주인공이 이야기의 작가인 것으로 꾸몄다.

Ⓑ 사람들이 조난자의 삶에 관심이 있었기 때문에 즉시 유명해졌다.

Ⓒ 디포는 몇몇 다른 여행가들의 경험에 기반하여 이 소설을 썼다.

Ⓓ 소설의 주인공인 로빈슨 크루소는 4년간 조난 생활을 했다.

6. 〈로빈슨 크루소〉에 대한 교수의 설명에서 무엇을 유추할 수 있는가?

Ⓐ 이 소설의 특이한 서술 스타일은 디포가 평단의 긍정적인 반응을 받도록 만들었다.

Ⓑ 많은 유럽 국가들에서 여행기의 일반적 양식에 영향을 끼쳤다.

Ⓒ 독자들은 소설에서 일어나는 모든 일들을 꿰뚫어볼 수 없었다.

Ⓓ 소설은 1인칭 시점에서 3인칭 시점으로 왔다 갔다한다.

어휘 examine v 살펴보다 | author n 작가 | originally adv 원래, 본래 | publish v 출판하다 | designation n 지정, 지명 | define v 정의하다, 규정하다 | broad adj 넓은 | definition n 정의, 의미 | narrative n 서술, 묘사 | fictional adj 소설의, 허구적인 | sequential adj 순차적인 | prose n 산문 | embark v 시작하다 | venture n 모험 | constantly adv 끊임없이, 거듭 | debt n 빚 | political adj 정치의, 정치적인 | anonymous adj 익명인 | pamphlet n 팜플렛 | stir up ~를 고무하다, 각성시키다 | controversy n 논란 | threaten v 협박하다 | relation n 관계, 관련 | apparition n 유령, 허깨비 | precursor n 전조, 선도자 | uninhabited adj 사람이 살지 않는 | cast v 던지다 | shipwreck n 조난 사고, 난파 | perish v 죽다, 소멸하다 | deliver v 구조하다 | dust jacket 책의 표지, 커버 | synopsis(pl. synopses) n 줄거리, 개요 | inform v 알리다, 통지하다 | protagonist n 주인공 | travelogue n 여행기, 기행문 | immensely adv 엄청나게, 대단히 | publication n 출판, 발행 | encounter n 맞닥뜨리다, 부딪치다 | cannibal n 식인종 | captive n 포로 | mutineer n 폭도 | rescue v 구하다, 구조하다 | castaway n 조난자 | popularity n 인기 | contribute v 기여하다, 일조하다 | inspire v 영감을 주다, 고무하다 | translation n 해석 | retell v 다시 바꾸어 말하다 | abduction n 납치 | candidate n 후보 | prison colony 유배지 | imprisoned adj 수감된 | literature n 문학 | first person narrative 1인칭 시점 | initially adv 처음에 | harsh adj 가혹한, 냉혹한 | criticism n 비평, 평론 | standard n 규범, 기준 | third person 3인칭 | omniscient adj 전지적인 | point of view 시점, 관점 | scope n 범위 | perspective n 관점 | contribution n 기여

Passage 2

Woman: Professor

[1-6] Listen to part of a lecture in a biology class.

W **2** Have any of you seen huge groups of birds flying over the campus lately? I know I have... and, let me tell you, it's quite amazing and a little scary at the same time—at least if you've seen Alfred Hitchcock's *The Birds*. But—and this may be an obvious question—**1, 2** why are birds appearing in such large groups right now? The answer is that winter

여자: 교수

생물학 강의의 일부를 들으시오.

여 **2** 최근 거대한 새 무리가 캠퍼스 위를 날아가는 것을 본 사람 있나요? 저는 봤습니다... 그리고 그건 아주 놀라운 동시에 좀 무섭기도 합니다. 적어도 여러분이 알프레드 히치콕의 〈새〉를 봤다면 말이죠. 너무 뻔한 질문이겠지만, **1, 2** 왜 새들은 지금 그렇게 큰 무리로 나타나는 걸까요? 답은 겨울이 오고

is coming and they are flying south for the winter. This is called bird migration, and it is going to be the subject of my lecture today.

First, I want to tackle the idea of why exactly birds migrate. Of course, we have the obvious reason that they want to escape the cold weather, but there's more. First of all, there's the fact that cold weather equals less food for birds. Many birds like to eat bugs, right? Well, as I'm sure you've noticed, there tend to be fewer bugs in the winter than in the summer, which means that the birds will have trouble locating enough of them for vital nutrients. **3** But we also have birds that live in or near water and eat other things. For them, the big problem is that water begins to freeze as the weather grows colder. When this happens, ducks, for example, don't have a place to live and swim. They also have trouble finding food when the water forms layers of ice on its surface.

Do birds actually know this though? I mean, do they say to themselves, "Oh, I'm getting cold, and I can't find as much food as I could a couple of weeks ago. I should go somewhere better." The answer is "not really". It's an instinctual thing, and there are several biological processes going on inside birds that cause them to migrate. **4** Hormones are produced as winter approaches, and this leads to a build-up of fat in the birds' bodies, which prepares them for the flight south. It also changes birds' behavioral patterns, and even birds that are living in climate-controlled observatories begin acting differently as their bodies change.

The other question we need to ask is, "How in the world do birds know where to go?" **5** Some scientists have noted that birds follow land structures like coastlines and mountains to know where to go, but I have some strong objections to some of the evidence they cite. Other scientists have studied the effect that the Sun has on birds. They have found that birds tend to orient themselves by looking at the position of the Sun and constantly reconfiguring their direction throughout the day to help them head the right way. Amazingly enough, birds are also believed to be able to detect magnetic fields with their noses—yes, their noses. They can detect which directions the Earth's magnetic fields are coming from and use that to help them determine which way is south.

So, a bird in North America will try to fly away from the magnetic energy coming from the north and the North Pole. Although amazing, that isn't the only thing that birds do with their noses. A bird can also smell out a good source of food or listen for certain sounds to know where it wants to stay. Obviously, this is used when the birds are very close to their

있어서 겨울을 나려고 남쪽으로 날아간다는 겁니다. 이것을 조류 이주라고 하며 오늘 강의의 주제입니다.

먼저, 새들이 이주하는 정확한 이유를 따져보고 싶군요. 물론 새들이 추운 날씨에서 벗어나려 한다는 분명한 이유를 알고 있지만 그뿐만이 아닙니다. 먼저 새들에게 추운 날씨는 더 적은 먹이를 의미하는 것과 같다는 사실입니다. 많은 새들이 곤충을 먹는 것을 좋아하잖아요, 그렇죠? 네, 눈치 챘겠지만 겨울에는 여름보다 벌레가 적어서 새들이 필수 영양분을 섭취하기 위한 충분한 양의 벌레를 찾기가 힘듭니다. **3** 하지만 물 또는 물 근처에 살면서 다른 것들을 먹는 새도 있죠. 이 새들의 경우 큰 문제는 날씨가 더 추워지면서 물이 얼기 시작한다는 것입니다. 이렇게 되면, 예를 들어 오리 같은 경우, 살 곳과 헤엄칠 곳이 없어지게 되는 겁니다. 또한 물 표면에 얼음층이 형성되면 먹이를 찾기도 어려워지죠.

하지만 새들이 실제로 이걸 알까요? 제 말은, 새들이 "아, 추우니까 몇 주 전만큼 먹이를 많이 찾을 수가 없어. 더 나은 곳으로 가는 게 좋겠다." 이렇게 스스로에게 이야기할까요? 정답은 "그렇지 않다"입니다. 이건 본능적인 것이며 새들 몸 안에는 새들을 이동하게 하는 몇 가지 생물학적 과정이 진행되고 있습니다. **4** 겨울이 다가오면 호르몬이 생성되고 이것이 새의 몸에 지방이 쌓이도록 하여 남쪽 비행에 대비하게 해줍니다. 이는 또한 새들의 행동 패턴을 바꾸는데, 기후가 통제되는 관측소에서 사는 새들까지도 몸이 변화하면서 다르게 행동하기 시작합니다.

여기서 해야 하는 또 다른 질문은 "대체 새들은 어떻게 어디로 가야 하는지 알까?"입니다. **5** 일부 과학자들은 새들이 어디로 갈지를 알기 위해 해안선과 산 등 땅의 구조를 따라간다고 했지만 저는 이들이 인용한 일부 근거에 강한 반대 의견을 갖고 있습니다. 다른 과학자들은 태양이 새에게 미치는 영향을 연구했습니다. 새가 태양의 위치를 보고 방향을 잡은 후 올바른 길로 가기 위해 하루 종일 방향을 계속해서 재조정한다는 점을 밝혀냈죠. 놀랍게도 새들은 코로 자기장을 탐지할 수 있는 것으로도 알려져 있습니다. 네, 코로 말이죠. 지구의 자기장이 어디서 오는지 방향을 탐지할 수 있고 그것을 이용하여 어느 쪽이 남쪽인지 알아내는 데 도움을 받습니다.

그래서 북아메리카에 있는 새는 북쪽과 북극에서 오는 자기력으로부터 멀리 날아가려고 할 겁니다. 놀랍지만 새들은 코를 사용해서 이것만 할 수 있는 게 아닙니다. 새는 좋은 먹이 출처를 냄새로 감지할 수 있고 특정 소리를 듣고 어디에 머무를지 알 수도 있습니다. 당연히 이는 새들이 최종 목적지에 아주 가까워졌을 때 사용하는 것이겠지만, 길을 찾는 데

final destinations, but it is still an important way for them to find their way. 6 As you can see, bird migration is much more complicated than it looks. It's not just simply birds deciding to fly south. There are magnetic fields, hormones, and all sorts of other things involved. And, while some people might feel that looking at it from a scientific perspective takes away from the beauty of actually watching the birds fly in formation way up in the sky, I personally think that the beauty is enhanced by knowing how complex and how effective the process I am watching is.

여전히 중요한 방법이죠. 6 여러분도 알겠지만 조류 이주는 보기보다 훨씬 더 복잡합니다. 새들이 그냥 남쪽으로 날아가기로 하는 게 아니에요. 자기장과 호르몬, 그리고 다른 모든 종류의 것들이 연관되어 있죠. 그리고 일부 사람들은 과학적 관점에서 이주를 보는 것이 새들이 하늘에서 대형을 이루며 날아가는 것을 실제로 보는 아름다움을 빼앗아간다고 느낄 수도 있겠지만, 개인적으로는 제가 지금 보고 있는 과정이 얼마나 복잡하고 효율적인지를 앎으로써 그 아름다움이 더 커진다고 생각합니다.

1. What is the lecture mainly about?

Ⓐ How bird species behave differently during the winter
Ⓑ How birds migrate and find their way as winter approaches
Ⓒ How birds' bodies are deeply sensitive to outside changes
Ⓓ How birds use their instincts to determine how they should act

2. Why does the professor mention birds on the university campus?

Ⓐ To use something familiar to introduce the lecture's topic
Ⓑ To give the students an example of how birds know to migrate
Ⓒ To clarify a previous point about bird flight patterns during winter
Ⓓ To explain why the topic of the lecture is important to everyone

3. What can be inferred about ducks from the lecture?

Ⓐ They eat things that are found in or under water.
Ⓑ They do not have thick plumage to protect them from snow.
Ⓒ They do not migrate in the same direction as other birds.
Ⓓ They do not fly very well when the air is cold.

4. According to the lecture, what do hormones do to birds' bodies as winter approaches?

Ⓐ Muscle is built up in their wings and chests.
Ⓑ Their brains signal them to store food.
Ⓒ Their bodies develop more fat under their feathers.
Ⓓ Their noses become more sensitive to change.

1. 강의는 주로 무엇에 관한 것인가?

Ⓐ 새 종들이 겨울에 어떻게 다르게 행동하는가
Ⓑ 겨울이 다가옴에 따라 새들이 어떻게 이동하고 길을 찾는가
Ⓒ 새들의 몸이 어떻게 외부 변화에 매우 민감한가
Ⓓ 새들이 어떤 방식으로 본능을 이용해 어떻게 행동해야 하는지 알아내는가

2. 교수는 왜 대학교 캠퍼스의 새들을 언급하는가?

Ⓐ 무언가 익숙한 것을 이용해 강의의 주제를 소개하려고
Ⓑ 새들이 이주하는 방법을 어떻게 아는지에 대한 예시를 학생들에게 주려고
Ⓒ 겨울 동안의 새들의 비행 유형에 관한 이전의 요점을 명확히 하려고
Ⓓ 왜 강의의 주제가 모두에게 중요한지 설명하려고

3. 강의에서 오리에 관해 무엇을 추론할 수 있는가?

Ⓐ 물속이나 그 아래서 발견되는 것들을 먹는다.
Ⓑ 눈으로부터 그들을 지켜줄 두터운 깃털이 없다.
Ⓒ 다른 새들과 같은 방향으로 이주하지 않는다.
Ⓓ 공기가 차가우면 잘 날지 못한다.

4. 강의에 따르면, 겨울이 다가오면서 호르몬은 새들의 신체에 어떤 작용을 하는가?

Ⓐ 날개와 가슴에 근육이 붙는다.
Ⓑ 뇌가 먹이를 저장하라는 신호를 보낸다.
Ⓒ 몸이 깃털 아래에 지방을 더 만들어낸다.
Ⓓ 코가 변화에 더 민감해진다.

5. What is the professor's attitude toward the idea the birds use land structures to navigate?
Ⓐ She believes that it is probably the best-supported theory.
Ⓑ She believes that some of the evidence supporting it is not reliable.
Ⓒ She believes that birds rely more heavily on other forms of navigation.
Ⓓ She believes that the scientists studying the phenomenon are mistaken.

6. What is implied about bird migration?
Ⓐ Temperature is not the only factor birds depend on when migrating.
Ⓑ Birds are able to find their groups using the Earth's magnetic field.
Ⓒ Some bird species do not migrate so they store food for the winter.
Ⓓ All species of birds fly south when they migrate for the winter.

5. 새가 땅의 구조를 사용해 길을 찾는다는 생각에 관한 교수의 태도는 어떠한가?
Ⓐ 이게 가장 잘 입증된 이론이라고 본다.
Ⓑ 이 이론을 뒷받침하는 증거의 일부는 믿을 만한 것이 아니라고 본다.
Ⓒ 새가 다른 형태의 길 찾기에 더 크게 의존한다고 본다.
Ⓓ 이 현상을 연구하는 과학자들이 실수한 거라고 본다.

6. 새 이주에 관해 무엇이 암시되었는가?
Ⓐ 온도는 새들이 이주할 때 의지하는 유일한 요인은 아니다.
Ⓑ 새들은 지구 자기장을 이용하여 무리를 찾을 수 있다.
Ⓒ 일부 새 종들은 이주하지 않기에 겨울을 위해 먹이를 저장한다.
Ⓓ 모든 종의 새들이 겨울을 위해 이주할 때 남쪽으로 날아간다.

어휘 huge adj 거대한, 큰 | amazing adj 놀라운, 멋진 | scary adj 무서운 | obvious adj 명백한, 뻔한 | appear v 나타나다 | migration n 이주 | tackle v 솔직하게 말하다, 따지다 | exactly adv 정확히 | migrate v 이주하다 | escape v 탈출하다 | equal v ~와 같다 | notice v 알아차리다 | locate v 찾다 | vital adj 필수적인 | nutrient n 영양분 | freeze v 얼어붙다 | surface n 표면 | instinctual adj 본능적인 | biological adj 생물학의, 생물체의 | process n 과정, 절차 | hormone n 호르몬 | approach v 접근하다 | build-up n 쌓임, 강화 | prepare v 준비하다 | flight n 비행 | behavioral adj 행동의 | observatory n 관측소 | differently adv 다르게 | note v 주목하다 | structure n 구조 | coastline n 해안 지대 | objection n 반대 | evidence n 증거 | cite v 인용하다 | orient v 자기 위치를 알다 | constantly adv 지속적으로, 계속 | reconfigure v 변경하다 | direction n 방향 | detect v 감지하다 | magnetic field 자기장 | determine v 알아내다 | destination n 목적지 | complicated adj 복잡한 | perspective n 관점 | formation n 대형, 편대 | personally adv 개인적으로 | enhance v 높이다, 향상시키다 | complex adj 복잡한 | effective adj 효율적인

II. Lectures　Part 2. Lecture Topics

Lesson 01 Anthropology

본서 | P. 198

Test

1. B　2. C　3. A, C　4. D　5. A　6. D

Test

본서 | P. 199

Man: Professor | Woman: Student

[1-6] Listen to part of a discussion in an anthropology class.

M The native tribes of North America were both quite numerous and varied. Of course, many tribes can be

남자: 교수 | 여자: 학생

인류학 수업 중 토론의 일부를 들으시오.

남 북미의 원주민 부족들은 상당히 수가 많았을 뿐만 아니라 다양했습니다. 물론 많은 부족들이 언어, 생

grouped together by language, lifestyle, region, and common cultural practices. But, one must be careful when referring to specific tribes by the terms Europeans used for them. These were often catch-all terms and sometimes entirely inaccurate or learned from other tribes who were antagonistic towards the tribe in question. For example, the Inuit people of the arctic regions of the U.S., Canada, and Greenland were referred to collectively as Eskimo, a term that the French actually borrowed from their neighboring cultural group, the Algonquian. The name translates roughly to "eaters of raw meat," which was a fairly accurate description of their diet, but they consider it to be a pejorative term. Today we will be looking at a custom that was shared by many tribes in the Northern Pacific coastal region and a few tribes in particular. Just keep in mind that I am not using blanket terms, but naming examples from the area.

1, 2 The custom we are going to focus on is potlatch. A potlatch is a gift-giving ceremony that was hosted by aristocrats on important days like weddings, funerals, birthdays, etc. **3(A), 4** These ceremonies appear to be public displays of wealth that could become quite extreme in some tribes. It was not unheard of Kwakiutl hosts to bankrupt themselves in order to outdo a previous potlatch host, but such reckless excess would have been frowned upon among the Salish. At the ceremonies, gifts were given to guests and other items would be destroyed, usually by burning. However, potlatches were actually a complex social ritual that both conferred and confirmed people's status in their communities. When they were held by high-ranking members of the population, they would also include guests from other tribes. **3(C)** These large potlatches were sometimes used to moderate conflicts between the tribes. The status of a particular family was not established by the amount of material goods that they possessed, but by the amount of material goods that they distributed through their potlatch.

W Professor, what kinds of gifts would they give? I mean, what were typical potlatch gifts?

M **5** Well, that varied somewhat, but blankets, clothing, carved wood items like kitchen utensils and decorations, storable food items, canoes, and slaves. They also exchanged coppers, which were beaten copper plates. Just about any kind of property, really. Except they did not distribute property like local resources—good fishing grounds or

활 방식, 지역, 그리고 공통의 문화적 관행으로 함께 묶일 수는 있지만요. 그러나 유럽인들이 이 부족들을 언급할 때 사용한 단어로 특정한 부족을 언급할 때는 주의해야만 합니다. 이들은 종종 두리뭉실한 단어들이며 때때로 완전히 틀리거나 언급하는 부족에 대해 적대적인 부족들로부터 배운 단어일 수 있습니다. 예를 들어, 미국과 캐나다, 그린란드의 극지방에 거주하는 이누이트 부족들은 전체적으로 에스키모인이라고 언급되는데, 이 단어는 프랑스인들이 사실 이들의 이웃 문화 집단인 알곤킨족들이 사용하는 단어를 빌린 것입니다. 이 이름은 대략 '날고기를 먹는 사람들'이라는 뜻으로 해석되는데, 이 부족의 식습관을 꽤나 정확히 설명하지만 이 부족은 에스키모라는 단어를 경멸적인 의미로 생각합니다. 오늘 우리는 북태평양 연안 지역의 많은 부족들이 공유하는 관습과 특히 몇몇 부족들에 대해 이야기할 겁니다. 제가 포괄적인 용어를 사용하는 것이 아니라 그 지역의 예시를 언급하고 있다는 걸 기억하세요.

1, 2 우리가 집중해서 볼 관습은 포틀래치입니다. 포틀래치는 결혼, 장례식, 생일 등의 중요한 날에 귀족들에 의해 열렸던 선물 증정식입니다. **3(A), 4** 이 행사는 부를 다른 이들에게 과시하기 위한 것으로 보이는데, 몇몇 부족들의 경우 매우 극단적으로 변하기도 했습니다. 콰키우틀 부족의 경우 행사 주최자가 이번의 포틀래치 주최자를 넘어서기 위해 파산까지 하는 경우가 아예 없지는 않았으나 이런 도를 넘는 무모한 행위는 살리시 부족에서는 얼굴을 찡그릴 만한 것이었습니다. 행사에서는 손님들에게 선물이 주어졌고 다른 것들은 파괴되었는데, 보통 불에 태워 파괴했습니다. 그러나 포틀래치는 사실 공동체 안에서 지위를 부여하고 또한 확인하는 복잡한 사회적 의식이었습니다. 포틀래치가 부족들 가운데서 높은 지위에 있는 이들에 의해 열리면, 그들은 다른 부족의 손님들 역시 초대했습니다. **3(C)** 이 큰 포틀래치는 때때로 부족들 간의 갈등을 완화하기 위해 사용되기도 했습니다. 특정 가문의 지위는 그들이 소유한 물질적 재화의 양으로 정립되는 것이 아니라 그들이 포틀래치를 통해 나눠준 물질적 재화의 양으로 정립되는 것이었습니다.

여 교수님, 어떤 종류의 선물을 나눠주었나요? 제 말은, 전형적인 포틀래치 선물은 어떤 것들이었나요?

남 **5** 음, 다양한 것들이 있었지만 담요, 옷, 조각한 나무로 된 주방용품이나 장식용품과 같은 물건들, 저장 가능한 음식, 카누, 그리고 노예 등이었습니다. 이들은 또한 구리를 교환했는데, 두들겨서 만들어진 구리 접시였습니다. 사실 어떤 종류의 재산이라도 상관없었죠. 지역 자원과 같은 물질의 분배를 제외하면요. 낚시하기 좋은 장소나 열매가 풍부한 숲

Lesson 01 Lectures

parts of the forest where berries were abundant. They had a much broader concept of property than Europeans, kind of like intellectual property today, but resources were for the community and did not belong to any one family. But, the potlatch was not just for giving gifts. The host family would also provide entertainment through singing and dancing that told stories, and there would be a feast. **6** But, things changed after Europeans arrived.

6 Like the rest of the Americas, the Pacific Northwest also suffered during the Great Dying. The Spanish explorers introduced new diseases to the Native American world, and as much as ninety percent of their population perished. Afterward, common people began to host potlatches as well. Then in the 19th century, the Canadian and U.S. governments banned the custom. In their opinion, it was "a worse than useless custom" that they viewed as wasteful, unproductive, and contrary their own civilized values. This may be partly due to the fact that some tribes, like the Tlingit, included their slaves in the property that was gifted and sometimes in that which was destroyed. These bans lasted until the mid-20th century. Today, the custom has returned to some tribes, but not on the scale it once had.

의 일부 등 말입니다. 그들은 유럽인들보다 훨씬 더 넓은 재산 개념을 가지고 있었는데, 오늘날의 지적 재산과 비슷했어요. 그러나 자원은 공동체를 위한 것이었으며 어느 한 가족에 속한 것이 아니었습니다. 그러나 포틀래치는 그저 선물 증정만을 위한 것이 아니었죠. 행사 주최자 가족은 이야기가 있는 노래와 춤을 통해 여흥 또한 제공했고, 연회도 열었습니다. **6** 그러나 유럽인들이 도착한 뒤에는 상황이 바뀌었습니다.

6 아메리카 대륙의 다른 지역들과 마찬가지로 북태평양 역시 대몰살(유럽인들이 북미에 옮겨온 질병으로 인해 수많은 원주민들이 사망한 현상)로 인해 고통을 겪었습니다. 스페인 탐험가들은 미 원주민들의 세계에 새로운 질병을 가져왔고 약 90%의 원주민 인구가 목숨을 잃었죠. 그 뒤 일반인들도 포틀래치를 열기 시작했습니다. 그리고 19세기에는 캐나다와 미국 정부가 이 관습을 금지했습니다. 그들은 포틀래치를 자신들의 관점에서 낭비적이고, 비생산적이고, 그들의 문명화된 가치에 반하는 것으로 보았으며, '없느니만 못한 관습'으로 여겼습니다. 이는 틀링기트 부족을 포함한 몇몇 부족들이 선물로 주거나 때때로 파괴하기도 하는 재산에 노예를 포함했다는 사실이 부분적으로 원인이 된 것으로 보입니다. 이 금지령은 20세기 중반까지 계속되었습니다. 오늘날 이 관습은 몇몇 부족에게 다시 돌아왔지만 지난날과 같은 규모는 아닙니다.

1. What is the discussion mainly about?

Ⓐ The life of North American tribes, especially the way they obtained their food
Ⓑ A distinctive custom that was once widely shared by some North American tribes
Ⓒ The social structure of Native American tribes and its development
Ⓓ The different food distributing ceremonies of Native American tribes

2. According to the discussion, what is a potlatch?

Ⓐ A celebration of a new season
Ⓑ A gathering for sharing food
Ⓒ A ritual for gift distribution
Ⓓ An annual social gathering

3. What was the purpose of the potlatch ceremony?

Choose 2 answers.

Ⓐ Showing others how wealthy the host is
Ⓑ Sharing the hunting methods of each tribe
Ⓒ Resolving conflicts between the tribes
Ⓓ Collecting a communal food supply

1. 토론은 주로 무엇에 대한 것인가?

Ⓐ 북미 원주민들의 생활, 특히 그들이 음식을 구하는 방법
Ⓑ 일부 북미 부족들이 한 때 널리 공유한 독특한 관습
Ⓒ 북미 부족들의 사회 구조와 그 발달
Ⓓ 북미 부족들의 서로 다른 음식 분배 행사들

2. 토론에 의하면, 포틀래치는 무엇인가?

Ⓐ 새로운 계절을 축하하는 행사
Ⓑ 음식 나눔을 위한 모임
Ⓒ 선물 분배를 위한 의식
Ⓓ 매년 열리는 사회 모임

3. 포틀래치 행사의 목적은 무엇인가?

두 개를 고르시오.

Ⓐ 주최자가 얼마나 부유한지 다른 이들에게 보이는 것
Ⓑ 각 부족의 사냥 방법을 공유하는 것
Ⓒ 부족들 간의 갈등을 해소하는 것
Ⓓ 공동의 식량 공급원을 모으는 것

4. **What can be inferred about a potlatch?**
Ⓐ Ordinary people were not allowed to receive gifts.
Ⓑ It was heavily influenced by English explorers.
Ⓒ It is still celebrated these days by a wide variety of tribes.
Ⓓ Poor people were simply not able to afford one.

4. **포틀래치에 대해 무엇을 추론할 수 있는가?**
Ⓐ 일반인들은 선물을 받는 것이 허용되지 않았다.
Ⓑ 영국의 탐험가들에 의해 크게 영향을 받았다.
Ⓒ 많은 다양한 부족들에 의해 여전히 열리고 있다.
Ⓓ 가난한 이들은 그냥 포틀래치를 할 수 없었다.

5. **According to the professor, what are some gifts that were usually given in a potlatch?**
Ⓐ Kitchen supplies made of wood
Ⓑ Various animals for farming
Ⓒ Weapons that were made of copper
Ⓓ Carpets and fabrics that were woven

5. **교수에 의하면, 포틀래치에서 보통 주어지는 선물은 무엇인가?**
Ⓐ 나무로 만들어진 주방 용품
Ⓑ 농사를 위한 다양한 동물들
Ⓒ 구리로 만들어진 무기들
Ⓓ 짜서 만든 카펫과 직물

6. **Why does the professor mention the Great Dying?**
Ⓐ To explain the influence of the Spanish explorers on the English settlers
Ⓑ To give an example of a religious ritual that was widely spread during the time
Ⓒ To illustrate the harsh living conditions of the Native Americans in the U.S.
Ⓓ To introduce an event that brought changes to a traditional custom

6. **교수는 왜 대몰살을 언급하는가?**
Ⓐ 영국 정착민들에게 스페인 탐험가들이 끼친 영향을 설명하기 위해
Ⓑ 그 당시 널리 퍼졌던 종교 의식의 한 예를 들기 위해
Ⓒ 미국의 원주민들의 가혹한 생활 환경을 묘사하기 위해
Ⓓ 전통적 관습에 변화를 가져온 한 사건을 소개하기 위해

어휘 native adj 원주민의, 토박이의 | tribe n 부족 | numerous adj 많은 | cultural practice 문화적 관행 | catch-all adj 두리뭉실한 | inaccurate adj 부정확한, 오류가 있는 | antagonistic adj 적대적인 | arctic adj 북극의 | collectively adv 전체적으로 | translate v 해석하다 | roughly adv 대략, 거의 | raw adj 날것의 | pejorative adj 경멸적인 | custom n 관습, 풍습 | coastal adj 해안의 | blanket term 포괄적 용어 | potlatch n 포틀래치(북미 북서지역 인디언 사이의 선물 분배 행사) | host v 주최하다, 열다 | aristocrat n 귀족 | funeral n 장례식 | public display 공개 과시 | bankrupt v 파산하다 | outdo v 능가하다 | reckless adj 무모한, 신중하지 못한 | excess n 지나침 | frown v 얼굴을 찌푸리다 | destroy v 파괴하다 | complex adj 복잡한 | social ritual 사회적 의식 | confer v 부여하다, 수여하다 | confirm v 확인하다 | population n 인구, 주민 | moderate v 완화하다, 조정하다 | conflict n 갈등 | establish v 설립하다, 수립하다 | possess v 소유하다 | distribute v 분배하다 | typical adj 전형적인 | carve v 조각하다 | utensil n 기구, 도구 | decoration n 장식품, 장식 | storable adj 저장할 수 있는 | canoe n 카누 | copper n 구리 | property n 재산 | local resource 현지 자원 | abundant adj 풍부한 | broad adj 넓은 | intellectual property 지적 재산 | entertainment n 여흥, 오락 | feast n 연회, 잔치 | explorer n 탐험가 | introduce v 소개하다 | disease n 질병 | perish v 죽다, 소멸하다 | ban v 금지하다 | useless adj 쓸모 없는 | wasteful adj 낭비적인 | unproductive adj 비생산적인 | contrary v 반대의 | civilized adj 문명화된, 개화된 | last v 지속되다, 계속되다 | scale n 규모, 범위

Lesson 02
Lectures

Lesson 02 Archaeology

본서 | P. 201

Test

1. A 2. C 3. B, C 4. C 5. D 6. D

Test

본서 | P. 202

Man: Professor | Woman: Student

[1-6] Listen to part of a discussion in an archaeology class.

W 1 When humans first reached Great Britain has long been

남자: 교수 | 여자: 학생

고고학 수업 중 토론의 일부를 들으시오.

여 1 인류가 영국에 처음으로 도착한 시기는 오랫동안

debated. Certainly, we know that anatomically modern humans, a segment of Homo sapiens often called Cro-Magnons, reached England by around 33,000 years ago. We can be sure of this because the skeletal remains of a young man from the Aurignacian culture were found in Wales. However, these people were forced to leave when the Last Glacial Maximum made the land uninhabitable. Humans did not return until around 14,000 BCE as the ice sheets retreated.

M 2 Professor, you called them anatomically modern humans. What about other types of humans, or at least human ancestors? Did any of them reach England?

W 2 Thank you, Eric, for providing that segue. When discussing early human migration, it is important that we agree upon what we are defining as human. **3(B), 3(C)** When we trace back the lineage of modern humans, the earliest example we can find is Homo erectus, who first left Africa around 1.8 million years ago. These ancestors expanded around the Eastern Mediterranean into Eurasia, but made little progress beyond that. Our next predecessor, Homo heidelbergensis, emerged around 600,000 years ago, and is believed to be the ancestor of both Neanderthals and Homo sapiens. The earliest humans with Neanderthal traits already inhabited Europe and Asia between 600,000 to 350,000 years ago, and so-called true Neanderthals appeared around 250,000 to 200,000 years ago. Homo sapiens developed in Africa around 200,000 years ago, but they did not expand into Europe until around 40,000 years ago, a few thousand years before the Neanderthals disappeared.

There is evidence of Neanderthals reaching the Island of Jersey by around 250,000 BCE, and they are believed to have reached the rest of Britain by 130,000 BCE, where they remained dominant until around 30,000 BCE. Earlier still, evidence in the form of a shinbone found in a quarry in Sussex points to Homo heidelbergensis as reaching here by 480,000 BCE. **4** No older remains have been found, but human-worked flints were found in Suffolk that date back to 700,000 BCE. Since their discovery in 2003, that was assumed to be the earliest human presence in Britain. However, that changed in 2010.

Scientists digging on the beach in Norfolk discovered 78 flint artifacts, many of which showed evidence of being shaped by humans. Along with animal fossils found at the site and

논쟁거리가 되어 왔습니다. 우리는 확실히 해부학적 현대 인류, 종종 크로마뇽인이라고 불리는 호모 사피엔스의 한 분류가 약 33,000년 전 영국에 도착했다는 것을 알고 있습니다. 웨일즈에서 오리냐크 문화의 젊은 남자 유골이 발견되었기에 이는 확실합니다. 그러나 이 사람들은 마지막 최대 빙하기로 인해 이 대륙에서 거주할 수 없게 되자 떠나야만 했습니다. 빙하가 물러난 기원전 약 14,000년까지 인류는 돌아오지 않았어요.

남 2 교수님, 그들을 해부학적 현대 인류라고 부르셨는데요, 다른 종류의 인류는 어떤가요, 아니면 적어도 인류의 조상은요? 그들 중 누구라도 영국에 도착했나요?

여 2 다음 주제로 넘어가게 해줘서 고마워요, 에릭. 초기 인류의 이동에 대해 이야기할 때 우리가 무엇을 인류라고 정의하는지 동의하는 것이 중요합니다. **3(B), 3(C)** 현대 인류의 혈통을 거슬러 올라가 보면, 우리가 찾을 수 있는 가장 초기의 예는 약 180만 년 전에 처음 아프리카를 떠난 호모 에렉투스입니다. 이 조상들은 지중해 동부에서 유라시아 지역으로 확장해 나갔지만 그 너머로는 진전을 보이지 못했습니다. 우리가 볼 다음의 조상은 호모 하이델베르겐시스인데, 이들은 60만 년 전에 나타났으며 네안데르탈인과 호모 사피엔스의 조상으로 여겨지고 있습니다. 네안데르탈인의 특징을 가진 최초의 인류는 이미 60만년 전부터 35만년 전 사이에 유럽과 아시아에 거주했으며, 소위 진짜 네안데르탈인이라 불리는 이들도 25만년 전부터 20만년 전 사이에 나타났습니다. 호모 사피엔스는 아프리카에서 약 20만년 전에 나타났지만 4만년 전까지는 유럽으로 영역을 확장하지 않았는데, 이 시기는 네안데르탈인이 사라지기 약 수천 년 전입니다.

기원전 약 25만년 경에 네안데르탈인들이 저지섬에 도착했다는 증거가 있는데, 이들은 기원전 13만년 경까지 영국의 나머지 지역에 도달한 것으로 보이며, 기원전 3만년까지 이곳에서 우세하게 살았습니다. 그보다 더 이전에는, 서식스주의 한 채석장에서 정강이뼈의 형태로 발견된 증거가 호모 헤이델베르겐시스가 기원전 48만년에 이곳에 도착했다는 것을 가리키고 있습니다 **4** 이보다 더 이전의 유해는 발견되지 않았지만 기원전 70만년으로 거슬러 올라가는, 인간이 만든 부싯돌이 서퍽에서 발견되었어요. 2003년에 발견된 이래 이것이 영국에 있었던 가장 최초 인류의 흔적이라고 추정되었습니다. 그러나 2010년에 이 추정은 바뀌었죠.

노퍽의 해변에서 발굴을 하던 과학자들이 78개의 부싯돌 유물을 찾아냈는데, 그것들 중 다수가 인간에 의해 만들어진 모양을 보이고 있었습니다. 그

known climatic changes, they have dated this settlement to between 850,000 to 950,000 years ago. 5 This means that the people who made these tools must have been members of the group known as Homo antecessor, who are not regarded as part of the lineage of modern humans. Indeed, many see them as an evolutionary dead end. However, their presence in England at that time indicates that they were able to tolerate fairly harsh conditions. Winters would have been about 3 degrees Centigrade cooler than in England today. Therefore, scientists theorize that these people must have already evolved enough to make and wear basic clothing, construct shelters, and use fire.

M 6 How do they know that they could make shelters?

W 6 They do not, but they think that they must have. You see, the area they were living in was the ancient delta of the Thames River's old course. The river has changed course considerably since then. There was little natural shelter available in a region of salt marshes and grasslands, but there was forest nearby. They must have used the trees to build some kind of shelters to survive the winter. There were many animals to hunt, so they settled there, despite the weather.

현장에서 발견된 동물의 화석과 이미 알려진 기후 변화를 놓고 보았을 때, 이 정착지는 약 85만년에서 95만년 전 사이에 있었던 것으로 보입니다. 5 이 말은, 이 부싯돌들을 만든 인류가 호모 안테세소르라고 알려진 그룹의 일원이었다는 것인데, 이들은 현대 인류의 혈통에 속한 것으로 여겨지지 않습니다. 실제로 많은 이들이 호모 안테세소르를 진화의 막다른 길로 보고 있죠. 그러나 그 시기에 영국에 있었던 그들의 존재는 이들이 꽤나 혹독한 환경을 견뎌낼 수 있었다는 것을 보여줍니다. 그때의 겨울은 오늘날의 영국 기후보다 섭씨 3도가 더 낮았어요. 그래서 과학자들은 이들이 기본적인 옷가지를 만들어 입고, 피난처를 만들고, 불을 사용할 정도로 이미 진화했을 것이라는 이론을 세우고 있습니다.

남 6 이들이 피난처를 만들 수 있었다는 것을 어떻게 알죠?

여 6 알지 못하지만, 분명히 그랬을 것이라고 생각하고 있습니다. 학생도 알겠지만 이들이 살던 지역은 템스강의 옛 물길의 고대 삼각주였습니다. 강의 흐름은 그 이후 상당히 바뀌었죠. 해수 소택지와 풀밭으로 이루어진 지역에서 자연적 피난처는 찾기 어려웠지만, 근처에는 숲이 있었습니다. 이들은 분명히 겨울을 살아남기 위해 나무들을 이용해서 어떤 종류의 피난처를 만들었을 겁니다. 그곳에는 사냥할 동물이 많았으므로 그들은 날씨에도 불구하고 그곳에 정착한 것이죠.

1. What is the discussion mainly about?

Ⓐ Tracing back the history of human inhabitance of England
Ⓑ Observing different theories regarding the existence of modern humans
Ⓒ Discussing the startling discovery made at Norfolk in 2010
Ⓓ Finding various patterns of early human migration in Europe

2. Listen again to part of the discussion. Then answer the question.

M Professor, you called them anatomically modern humans. What about other types of humans, or at least human ancestors? Did any of them reach England?
W Thank you, Eric, for providing that segue.

Why does the professor say this:

W Thank you, Eric, for providing that segue.

1. 토론은 주로 무엇에 대한 것인가?

Ⓐ 영국의 인류 거주 역사 거슬러 올라가는 것
Ⓑ 현대 인류의 존재에 대한 여러 다른 이론들을 관찰하는 것
Ⓒ 2010년에 노퍽에서 있었던 놀라운 발견에 대해 논의하는 것
Ⓓ 유럽에서 있었던 초기 인류 이동의 다양한 유형을 알아보는 것

2. 토론의 일부를 다시 듣고 질문에 답하시오.

남 교수님, 그들을 해부학적 현대 인류라고 부르셨는데요. 다른 종류의 인류는 어떤가요, 아니면 적어도 인류의 조상은요? 그들 중 누구라도 영국에 도착했나요?
여 다음 주제로 넘어가게 해줘서 고마워요, 에릭.

교수는 왜 이렇게 말하는가:

여 다음 주제로 넘어가게 해줘서 고마워요, 에릭.

Lesson 02 Lectures

Ⓐ She wants the student to realize that he made a keen observation.
Ⓑ She is aware of the fact that she must introduce today's topic.
Ⓒ She wants to thank the student for providing a transition.
Ⓓ She appreciates the man participating so eagerly in the discussion.

3. What is true about the earliest modern humans?
Choose 2 answers.
Ⓐ There is still debate regarding whether they are really the earliest ones.
Ⓑ Homo erectus, who did not make it to England, was the earliest modern humans.
Ⓒ They used to reside on the African continent before they started migrating.
Ⓓ They appeared in England around 14,000 BCE, when the ice sheets withdrew.

4. What can be inferred about the earliest human presence in Britain?
Ⓐ Many shinbones of Neanderthals prove that they were moving from place to place.
Ⓑ Homo sapiens dominated the region until the climate suddenly became harsh.
Ⓒ The estimated period was established with evidence of their impact, not their remains.
Ⓓ The discovery of Homo heidelbergensis revealed that they were the first inhabitants.

5. What does the professor explain about Homo antecessor?
Ⓐ Their presence eventually decreased the animal population in the forest.
Ⓑ They are considered to be the earliest ancestor of modern humans.
Ⓒ To prepare for natural disasters, they built shelters underground.
Ⓓ They had the ability to cope with tough, cold weather conditions.

6. Why does the professor mention the Thames River?
Ⓐ To describe how it influenced the weather conditions of the region
Ⓑ To point out the main water source of Homo antecessors to students
Ⓒ To show the environmental obstructions the Homo antecessors faced

Ⓐ 학생이 날카로운 관찰을 했다는 것을 깨닫기를 바란다.
Ⓑ 오늘 강의의 주제를 소개해야 한다는 것을 알고 있다.
Ⓒ 전환을 하게 해준 학생에게 고마움을 표하고 싶어한다.
Ⓓ 학생이 토론에 매우 열정적으로 참여하는 것이 고맙다.

3. 최초의 현대 인류에 대해 옳은 것은 무엇인가?
두 개를 고르시오.
Ⓐ 이들이 정말로 최초의 인류인지에 대한 논쟁이 계속되고 있다.
Ⓑ 영국까지 도달하지 못한 호모 에렉투스가 최초의 현대 인류였다.
Ⓒ 이주를 시작하기 전에 아프리카 대륙에서 거주했었다.
Ⓓ 빙하가 물러났을 때 기원전 약 14,000년에 영국에 나타났다.

4. 영국에서의 최초의 인류 존재에 대해 무엇을 추론할 수 있는가?
Ⓐ 많은 수의 네안데르탈인 정강이뼈들은 이들이 한 곳에서 다른 곳으로 옮겨 다녔다는 것을 입증한다.
Ⓑ 호모 사피엔스는 기후가 갑자기 혹독해지기 전까지 이 지역을 지배했다.
Ⓒ 가정된 시기는 이들이 끼친 영향에 대한 증거를 통해 확립된 것이지, 유해를 통해 확립된 것이 아니다.
Ⓓ 호모 하이델베르겐시스의 발견은 이들이 최초의 거주자였다는 것을 드러냈다.

5. 호모 안테세소르에 대해 교수는 무엇이라고 설명하는가?
Ⓐ 이들의 존재는 결국 숲의 동물 개체 수를 감소시켰다.
Ⓑ 현대 인류의 가장 오래된 조상으로 간주된다.
Ⓒ 자연 재해에 대비하기 위해 지하에 피난처를 만들었다.
Ⓓ 힘들고 추운 기후 환경에 대처할 수 있는 능력이 있었다.

6. 교수는 왜 템스강을 언급하는가?
Ⓐ 이 강이 지역의 기후 조건에 어떻게 영향을 주었는지 묘사하려고
Ⓑ 호모 안테세소르의 주요 수원을 학생들에게 가르쳐주려고
Ⓒ 호모 안테세소르가 맞닥뜨린 환경적 장애물을 보여주려고

Ⓓ To support the evolutionary theory that was provided by scientists.	Ⓓ 과학자들이 제시한 진화 이론을 지지하려고

어휘 Great Britain 대영제국(England, Wales, Scotland를 합쳐 부르는 명칭) | debate v 논쟁하다 | certainly adv 분명히, 틀림없이 | anatomically adv 해부학적으로 | modern adj 현대의 | segment n 분류, 부분 | Homo sapiens 호모 사피엔스 | Cro-Magnon n 크로마뇽인 | skeletal adj 뼈대의, 해골의 | remains n 남은 것, 유적 | force v 강요하다 | Last Glacial Maximum 마지막 최대 빙하기 | uninhabitable adj 사람이 살 수 없는 | ice sheet 대륙 빙하 | retreat v 물러가다, 빠져나가다 | ancestor n 조상 | segue n (한 주제에서 다른 주제로) 넘어감 | migration n 이주 | define v 정의하다 | trace back 거슬러 올라가다 | lineage n 혈통, 가계 | Homo erectus 호모 에렉투스, 직립 원인 | expand v 확장하다 | progress n 진전, 진척 | predecessor n 이전 것, 전임자 | Homo heidelbergensis 호모 하이델베르겐시스 | emerge v 출현하다, 나타나다 | Neanderthals n 네안데르탈인 | trait n 특징 | inhabit v 거주하다 | disappear v 사라지다 | evidence n 증거 | dominant adj 우세한 | shinbone n 정강이뼈 | quarry n 채석장 | flint n 부싯돌 | discovery n 발견 | presence n 있음, 존재 | artifact n 유물 | fossil n 화석 | site n 현장 | climatic adj 기후의 | settlement n 정착지 | homo antecessor 호모 안테세소르 | evolutionary adj 진화의 | dead end 막다른 길 | indicate v 나타내다 | tolerate v 참다, 견디다 | harsh adj 혹독한, 냉혹한 | theorize v 이론을 세우다 | construct v 건설하다 | shelter n 피난처 | ancient adj 고대의 | delta n 삼각주 | considerably adv 상당히, 많이 | salt marsh 해수 소택지 | grassland n 풀밭

Lesson 03 Architecture

본서 | P. 204

Test

1. A　2. C　3. B　4. C　5. C　6. D

Test

본서 | P. 205

Man: Student | Woman: Professor

[1-6] Listen to part of a discussion in an architecture class.

W Completed in 2560 BCE, the Great Pyramid of Giza is one of the most iconic structures ever erected by mankind. There is much about the pyramid that we know from historical records. It was built to be the final resting place of the Pharaoh Khufu, and its construction was overseen by his nephew Hemiunu. When completed, it stood 146.5 meters tall, but over the passage of time, this has been reduced by the removal of stones and weathering to about 139 meters. At completion, it is estimated to have contained over two million blocks that would have weighed 5.9 million metric tons. The outermost layer was made of slanted stones that created a smooth surface. It was completed in only 20 years, and it was the tallest building in the world until the Lincoln Cathedral's spire was topped out in 1300 CE. The majority of the stones were limestone, although the burial chamber is granite. 2 Amazingly, the limestone was cut using copper chisels and moved using manpower. These stones literally weighed a few tons each, but they still managed to transport them many kilometers. This was most

남자: 학생 | 여자: 교수

건축학 수업 중 토론의 일부를 들으시오.

여 기원전 2560년에 완성된 기자의 대 피라미드는 인류가 세운 가장 상징적인 건축물 중 하나입니다. 역사적인 기록으로 인해 우리가 이 피라미드에 대해 알고 있는 것이 많죠. 파라오 쿠푸의 마지막 안식처가 되기 위해 지어졌으며 건설은 그의 조카인 헤미우누에 의해 감독되었습니다. 완성되었을 당시 146.5미터의 높이였으나 시간이 흐르면서 돌들이 없어진다거나 풍화 작용으로 인해 139미터로 줄어들었습니다. 완성되었을 당시 200만 개 이상, 약 590만 톤에 달하는 돌덩이들로 이루어졌을 것이라고 추정됩니다. 가장 바깥쪽의 층은 비스듬한 돌들로 이루어져 있었는데 이 돌들이 피라미드의 매끄러운 표면을 만들어냈습니다. 완공되는 데는 20년밖에 걸리지 않았으며, 서기 1300년 링컨 대성당 첨탑이 지어지기 전까지 세계에서 가장 높은 건축물이었습니다. 돌들의 대부분은 석회암이었지만, 묘실은 화강암으로 되어 있었습니다. 2 놀랍게도 석회암은 구리로 만들어진 끌로 잘려졌으며 인력을 사용하여 옮겨졌습니다. 이 돌들은 말 그대로 각각 몇 톤씩 되는 돌들이었음에도 불구하고 그들은 수 킬로미터에 걸쳐 돌들을 운반해냈죠. 이 작업은 나

likely accomplished by using wood sleds that were pulled and pushed across sand that was wetted down with water. We know this because of paintings that show them doing just that, and modern scientists have replicated the process with much success. The water makes the sand form a hard, smooth surface that the sleds move across without the sand piling up in front of them. 1 But, despite how much we do know, there is still something important that we cannot be certain about: just how exactly did they build it? Over the years, many theories have been proposed, but since they didn't leave us any pictures of the process, we really don't know.

M Didn't they use Hebrew slaves?

W Actually, no, they didn't. Evidence has been found that indicates they were paid laborers, many of whom were professional stonecutters. We actually owe that story to the Greek historian Herodotus who visited the pyramid in 400 BC, over 2,000 years after it was built. He also provided us with the oldest known theory regarding the method of construction. 3 He claims to have seen people moving large stones using a wooden crane, and we know that they did indeed have such machines available. However, cranes need a flat surface to sit upon, and the larger the crane, the larger the base would have to be. In order to move the stones up the side of the pyramid, the cranes would have to rest upon the pyramid itself, and there would have to have been many of them to pass the stones up. But, there would not have been large enough spaces for the cranes to rest on, nor did they have the vast amounts of wood they would have needed.

Most subsequent explanations involve some kind of ramp. 4 The first was a single straight ramp with an 8 degree grade to it. Any steeper and the men would not have been able to move the blocks up it. However, a straight ramp with that incline would have been nearly two kilometers long. Not only has no evidence of such a ramp been found, but it also would have required about the same amount of material as the pyramid, which would have made it a much more difficult undertaking. Others have suggested that the ramp may have climbed one side of the pyramid by making switchbacks, or by spiraling around the outside of the pyramid. The switchbacks would still have required too much material, and the spiral would have obscured the base of the structure. If it were concealed in this way, the builders would have been unable to see the corners of the base,

무 썰매를 이용해 물로 젖게 한 모래 위로 밀고 당겨가며 해냈을 가능성이 큽니다. 우리는 이 과정을 그대로 보여주는 그림이 있기에 알 수 있고, 현대의 과학자들이 이 과정을 성공적으로 모방해냈습니다. 물이 모래를 단단하고 매끄러운 표면으로 만들어 썰매를 끌 때 썰매 앞에 모래가 쌓이지 않으면서 썰매가 움직일 수 있도록 해주었죠. 1 그러나 우리가 얼마나 알든지 상관없이 확신할 수 없는 중요한 문제가 있습니다. 이들은 피라미드를 정확히 어떤 방식으로 지은 걸까요? 수년 동안 많은 이론들이 제시되었지만, 그들이 이 과정에 대해 어떤 그림도 남기지 않았기에 확실히 알지 못합니다.

남 히브리인 노예들을 쓰지 않았나요?

여 사실, 아니에요. 그들이 돈을 받고 일하는 노동자들이었고, 다수가 전문적인 석공들이었다는 걸 보여주는 증거가 발견되었습니다. 이 이야기는 사실 그리스의 역사학자였으며, 이 피라미드가 지어진 지 2,000년도 넘어서 기원전 400년에 이곳을 방문한 헤로도토스에게서 온 것입니다. 그는 또한 피라미드 건축 방법에 대해 알려진 것들 중 가장 오래된 가설을 제시하기도 했죠. 3 그는 사람들이 나무 기중기를 사용하여 커다란 돌들을 옮기는 것을 봤다고 주장하는데, 실제로 그들이 이러한 기계를 가지고 있었다는 것을 우리는 알고 있습니다. 그러나 기중기는 평평한 표면에 놓여져야 하며 크면 클수록 바닥의 면적 또한 넓어져야 하죠. 피라미드 측면으로 돌들을 올려 보내기 위해 기중기들은 피라미드 자체에 놓여져야 했을 것이며, 돌들을 위쪽으로 옮기기 위해서는 많은 수가 있어야 했을 겁니다. 그러나 이 기중기들이 모두 놓일 만큼 충분한 공간이 없었을 뿐 아니라, 필요한 만큼의 엄청난 양의 나무 역시 없었을 것으로 보입니다.

이어지는 대부분의 설명들은 일종의 경사로와 관련된 것들입니다. 4 첫 번째는 경사가 8도인 한 개의 직선 경사로입니다. 기울기가 이보다 조금이라도 더 가파르다면 사람들은 돌을 위로 옮기지 못했을 겁니다. 그러나 이러한 기울기의 직선 경사로라면 길이가 거의 2킬로미터나 되었을 겁니다. 이런 경사로가 있었다는 증거가 발견되지 않았을 뿐 아니라 이 경사로를 만들기 위해서는 피라미드와 거의 같은 양의 재료가 필요했을 텐데, 이는 이 일을 훨씬 더 어렵게 만드는 것이었습니다. 다른 이들은 지그재그로 만들어진 경사로가 피라미드의 한쪽 면을 올라갔을 것이라고 제안하거나, 피라미드의 바깥쪽을 감는 나선형으로 올라왔을 것이라고 제안했습니다. 지그재그 경사로는 여전히 너무나 많은 재료를 필요로 했을 것이고, 나선형은 구조물의 기반을 가렸을 겁니다. 이런 방식으로 피라미드가 가려졌다면 건축자들은 기반의 모서리를 볼 수 없었을 것이

which would have made accurate measurement nearly impossible. Still, the spiral ramp used in conjunction with cranes and lever lifting seems the most likely explanation. Or, it did.

Architect Jeanne-Pierre Houdin has devised what he thinks is the most likely method based upon an idea from his father. Houdin created a computer-aided drafting model of the pyramid to test his hypothesis. Working alone for 4 years, he was later joined by 3-D software company Dassault Systemes. He announced his hypothesis to the world through a book in 2006. He believes that the bottom 30% of the pyramid was built using the external spiraling ramp model. 5 However, for the remainder of the building, he thinks that they used an internal ramp. This would have consisted of tunnels spiraling up the inside of the pyramid, but they would have opened at the corners to allow the stones to be rotated with cranes. The upper portion would have been constructed using the stones from the external part of the ramp, neatly explaining why there is no evidence of the ramp. 5 His theory is supported by measurement of stone density in the structure using microgravimetry, which appears to show the presence of the internal ramp. 6 This hypothesis has many critics, though. They do not think the Egyptians would have been capable of such an intricate feat.

고, 정확한 측정이 거의 불가능했을 겁니다. 어쨌든, 기중기와 함께 사용된 나선형의 경사로와 지렛대가 가장 그럴 듯한 설명이죠. 혹은, 그랬었습니다.

장-피에르 우댕이라는 건축가가 그의 아버지의 생각으로부터 착안하여 가장 그럴 듯한 방법을 고안했습니다. 우댕은 그의 가설을 시험해 보기 위해 컴퓨터의 도움을 받은 피라미드 모형을 만들었죠. 홀로 4년간 연구하다 그는 후에 3-D 소프트웨어 회사인 다쏘 시스템과 함께하게 되었습니다. 그는 저서를 통해 2006년에 그의 가설을 세상에 발표했죠. 그는 피라미드 아랫부분의 30%는 외부 나선형 경사로 모델을 사용하여 지어졌다고 믿습니다. 5 그러나 건축물의 나머지는 내부 경사로를 사용하여 지어졌다고 생각하죠. 이는 피라미드 내부에서 터널이 나선을 그리며 올라가는 구조인데, 피라미드의 모서리 부분은 열려 있어 기중기로 돌들을 회전시킬 수 있었을 겁니다. 피라미드의 윗부분은 외부 경사로의 석재를 이용해 지어졌을 것이며, 이는 왜 경사로에 대한 증거가 없는지를 설명해 줍니다. 5 그의 가설은 건축물 내부의 돌 밀도를 미세중량측정 기술로 측정한 결과에 의해 뒷받침되었는데, 측정 결과는 내부 경사로의 존재를 보여주는 것처럼 보였습니다. 6 그러나 이 가설을 비판하는 사람들도 많습니다. 그들은 이집트인들이 이렇게 복잡한 뛰어난 일을 할 수 있는 능력이 없었다고 생각하죠.

1. What is the discussion mainly about?

- (A) The possible explanations about the construction of the Pyramid of Giza
- (B) The mystery behind the actual purpose of the Pyramid of Giza
- (C) The information regarding the working conditions of Hebrew slaves
- (D) The French architect who proposed the accurate construction method

2. Why does the professor mention a copper chisel?

- (A) To illustrate one of the most famous Egyptian inventions
- (B) To explain another method for moving the stones upward
- (C) To give an example of a simple tool that was used for cutting limestone
- (D) To show that the Egyptians derived their idea from little objects

1. 토론은 주로 무엇에 대한 것인가?

- (A) 기자의 피라미드 건설에 관해 가능한 설명들
- (B) 기자의 피라미드의 실제 용도에 관한 수수께끼
- (C) 히브리인 노예들의 근무 환경에 대한 정보
- (D) 정확한 건설 방법을 제안한 프랑스 건축가

2. 교수는 왜 구리로 만든 끌을 언급하는가?

- (A) 이집트인들의 가장 유명한 발명품들 중 하나를 묘사하려고
- (B) 돌들을 위로 옮기는 또 다른 방법을 설명하려고
- (C) 석회암을 자르는 데 사용된 간단한 도구의 예시를 들려고
- (D) 이집트인들은 작은 사물로부터 아이디어를 얻었다는 것을 보여주려고

3. **What was the main problem with the first theory mentioned in the discussion?**
   Ⓐ Using cranes for construction was still in development.
   Ⓑ There would have been no room to place the cranes.
   Ⓒ It was unable to explain how the stones were transported.
   Ⓓ It is difficult to use wood crane since it is too weak for stones.

4. **According to the professor, what happens if a single straight ramp has an 8 degree grade?**
   Ⓐ It brings the fastest results for transporting limestone.
   Ⓑ The empty space inside the pyramid could collapse.
   Ⓒ The ramp becomes far too long to be used.
   Ⓓ It won't be able to support itself and will break apart soon.

5. **According to the professor, how did the microgravimetry device give possible evidence to support Houdin's theory?**
   Ⓐ It revealed traces of the wooden cranes used in construction.
   Ⓑ It found that there was empty space inside the pyramid.
   Ⓒ It discovered a spiral figure resembling an internal ramp.
   Ⓓ It made calculations about where the ramps had been placed.

6. **What can be inferred about the three methods presented by the professor?**
   Ⓐ The wooden crane theory can explain how Egyptians transported the limestone.
   Ⓑ Evidence shows that all of three were used to build the Great Pyramid of Giza.
   Ⓒ The existence of a spiral ramp made the construction rather more time-consuming.
   Ⓓ Houdin's method still needs more supporting evidence to be proven accurate.

3. **토론에서 처음으로 언급된 이론의 가장 큰 문제점은 무엇인가?**
   Ⓐ 건축에 기중기를 사용하는 것은 아직 개발 중에 있었다.
   Ⓑ 기중기들을 놓을 공간이 없었을 것이다.
   Ⓒ 돌들이 어떻게 운송되었는지를 설명하지 못한다.
   Ⓓ 나무 기중기는 돌을 운반하기에는 너무 약해서 사용하기 어렵다.

4. **교수에 따르면, 하나의 직선 경사로의 기울기가 8도가 되면 어떤 일이 일어나는가?**
   Ⓐ 가장 빠르게 석회암을 운반하게 된다.
   Ⓑ 피라미드 내부의 빈 공간이 무너질 수 있다.
   Ⓒ 경사로가 사용하기에 너무 길어진다.
   Ⓓ 스스로를 지탱하지 못해 금세 부서질 것이다.

5. **교수에 따르면, 미세중량측정 방식은 어떻게 우댕의 이론에 가능성 있는 증거를 제공했는가?**
   Ⓐ 건설에 사용된 나무 기중기의 흔적을 드러냈다.
   Ⓑ 피라미드 내부에 비어 있는 공간이 있다는 것을 밝혀냈다.
   Ⓒ 내부 경사로와 유사한 나선형의 물체를 발견했다.
   Ⓓ 경사로가 어디에 놓였을지 계산했다.

6. **교수가 제시한 세 가지 방법들에 대해 무엇을 추론할 수 있는가?**
   Ⓐ 나무 기중기 이론은 이집트인들이 어떻게 석회암을 운반했는지 설명해 준다.
   Ⓑ 세 방법 모두 기자의 대 피라미드를 건설하는 데 사용되었음을 증거가 보여준다.
   Ⓒ 나선형 경사로의 존재는 건설에 시간이 더 걸리게 만들었다.
   Ⓓ 우댕의 방법은 정확하다고 입증되려면 여전히 뒷받침하는 증거가 더 필요하다.

어휘 iconic adj 상징적인, 우상의 | erect adj 똑바로 선 | historical adj 역사적인 | record n 기록 | oversee v 감독하다 | reduce v 축소하다, 감소시키다 | removal n 제거 | weathering n 풍화 | estimate v 추정하다, 추산하다 | contain v 포함하다 | weigh v 무게가 ~이다, 무게를 달다 | outermost adj 가장 바깥쪽의 | slanted adj 비스듬한, 기울어진 | smooth adj 매끈한, 매끄러운 | spire n (교회의) 첨탑 | limestone n 석회암 | burial chamber 묘실 | granite n 화강암 | copper n 구리 | chisel n 끌 | manpower n 인력 | literally adv 말 그대로, 문자 그대로 | transport v 운송하다 | accomplish v 완수하다, 성취하다 | sled n 썰매 | replicate v 복제하다 | pile up 쌓이다 | theory n 이론, 학설 | Hebrew n 히브리인 | indicate v 나타내다, 보여주다 | laborer n 노동자, 인부 | professional adj 전문적인 | stonecutter n 석공 | crane n 기중기 | vast adj 어마어마한, 방대한 | subsequent adj 다음의, 차후의 | explanation n 설명 | ramp n 경사로, 램프(화물 적재 등을 위한 경사면, 경사 계단) | steep adj 가파른, 비탈진 | incline n ~쪽으로 기울다 | undertaking n 일, 프로젝트 | switchback n 지그재그식 도로 | spiral v 나선, 소용돌이 | obscure v 보기 어렵게 하다, 모호하게 하다 | conceal v 감추다, 숨기다 | accurate adj 정확한, 정밀한 | measurement n 측량, 측정 | conjunction n 결합, 연결 | aid v 지원하다, 돕다 | drafting n 기초, 기안 | hypothesis n 가설, 추측 | external adj 외부의, 밖의 | remainder n 나머지 | internal adj 내부의, 안의 | consist of ~로 구성되다 | rotate v 회전하다 | presence n (특정한 곳에) 있음, 존재 | critic n 비평가 | intricate adj 복잡한 | feat n 위업, 재주

Test

1. D 2. A 3. B, D 4. A 5. C 6. C

Test

본서 | P. 208

Woman: Professor

[1-6] Listen to part of a lecture in an art history class.

W **1** Today, we will be looking at the works of one of the greatest painters in history, Rembrandt van Rijn. He was a prolific painter and printmaker who was well versed in the techniques of his predecessors and added his own discoveries to the artistic knowledge of his time. **1** His paintings were unique in many ways, and we are still learning about how he created his influential works.

2 One of the most obvious of his techniques is his masterful use of chiaroscuro, an Italian term that describes the use of starkly contrasted light and shadow to both create depth and focus the painting on a center of interest. In Rembrandt's case, that was typically the face, particularly the eyes, and the hands of the people in his portraits. The clothing and the jewelry that a person wore are detailed near those focal points, but they fade into the nebulous dark of the background.

3(D) Another obvious aspect of his painting style is how heavily Rembrandt applied his paint. **3(B)** He used a relatively small palette of colors that only rarely included blue or green. His unfinished paintings show that he usually began with his image painted in transparent shades of brown, and not a blank white canvas, which added a golden glow often remarked upon in his paintings. This would be followed by a layer of grays that defined the areas of light and shadow. Afterward, he would methodically paint one area at a time and alter his palette as the areas demanded. **3(D)** This resulted in a thick layering of paint that appeared to give the subject an actual physical presence, and prompted a contemporary of his to comment that any portrait by Rembrandt was "so heavily loaded that you could lift it from the floor by its nose".

1, 4 Since these techniques define his paintings, they are typically used to determine whether a painting attributed to the artist was really painted by him, by one of his many

여자: 교수

미술사 강의의 일부를 들으시오.

여 **1** 오늘은 역사상 가장 위대한 화가들 중 한 명인 렘브란트 반 라인의 작품들을 살펴볼 겁니다. 그는 이전 사람들의 기법을 훌륭하게 익혔고 그가 살았던 시대의 예술적 지식에 자신의 발견들을 더한, 다작을 한 화가이자 판화 제작자였습니다. **1** 그의 그림들은 많은 점에서 독특하며 우리는 여전히 어떻게 그가 그의 영향력 있는 작품들을 창조한 것인지를 배우고 있는 중입니다.

2 그의 기법들 중 가장 뚜렷한 것은 원숙한 명암법의 사용입니다. 이것은 이탈리아어에서 온 단어인데, 빛과 그림자의 극명한 대비를 사용하여 깊이를 만들어내는 동시에 그림의 초점을 관심의 중심에 맞추게 해주는 것을 말합니다. 렘브란트의 경우 이는 주로 그의 초상화 속 인물들의 얼굴, 특히 눈과 손이었어요. 인물이 걸치고 있는 의복과 보석은 이러한 초점 가까이에서는 매우 섬세하게 그려져 있지만, 배경의 흐릿한 어둠 속으로 사라집니다.

3(D) 렘브란트의 화풍 중 또 하나 뚜렷한 것은 그가 물감을 매우 두텁게 사용했다는 점입니다. **3(B)** 그는 상대적으로 적은 수의 색깔들을 사용했으며 파란색이나 초록색은 거의 사용하지 않았어요. 미완성인 그의 작품들은 그가 보통 비어 있는 하얀색의 캔버스에 그림을 그린 것이 아니라 엷은 갈색으로 칠한 캔버스에 그림을 그리기 시작했다는 것을 보여주는데, 이는 렘브란트의 그림에서 자주 언급되는 금색의 빛을 더해주는 것이죠. 이 뒤에는 빛과 그림자의 영역을 결정하는 회색의 층들을 입혔습니다. 그 다음에는 한 번에 한 구역만을 체계적으로 그렸고, 구역에 필요한 대로 팔레트의 구성을 바꾸었죠. **3(D)** 이로 인해 그림의 대상에 실제적인 물리적 존재감을 더해주는 두터운 물감 층이 생겨났고, 그의 동시대 인물 중 한 명은 렘브란트가 작업한 모든 초상화들은 '너무 두텁게 물감이 칠해져서 그림 속 인물의 코를 잡고 그림을 바닥에서 들어올릴 수 있을 정도'라고 말하기도 했습니다.

1, 4 이러한 기법들이 렘브란트의 그림을 정의하므로 이러한 점들은 렘브란트가 그렸다고 여겨지는 그림이 정말로 그의 그림인지, 그의 많은 제자들 중

students, or is a forgery. This process is particularly difficult with his students since he had them copy his paintings as a learning tool. Of course, we cannot remove such paintings from the museums where they are kept and analyze their layers physically. That would result in destroying potentially priceless works of art.

However, advanced technology has proven very valuable in identifying the origins of paintings; specifically, a technique called autoradiography. With a conventional X-radiography scanner, the device generates a beam of X-rays that is directed at an object. If the interior of an object is made up of materials with different densities, they block more or less of the X-rays. With a painting, this can be used to separate and analyze the layers of paint that were applied. **5** An autoradiograph, on the other hand, receives radiation emitted from the object itself to create an image. This is achieved by bathing the painting with neutrons. Since different elements will behave in different ways when the neutrons hit their atoms, this tells the researchers what elements the paints contain. The data can be used to map out where the pigment was applied. For example, the white that Rembrandt used contained lead, and the red contained mercury. This allows them to map out each brushstroke that went into making a painting.

These scanning techniques were used to determine whether a painting called *Old Man with Beard* was a genuine Rembrandt. X-ray images of the painting showed that there might be another image hidden underneath that of the old man. Using autoradiography, researchers learned that the bottom layers of paint contained a large amount of copper. By combining the two technologies, they were able to reveal the lower layers of paint and what they depicted. Firstly, they could tell that the first painting on the canvas was unfinished because it lacked most of the pigments that are in the finished painting above it. Second, they were able to discern the outline of the original image, which appeared to be a young man wearing a beret. **6** This was significant because it resembled self-portraits that Rembrandt had done as a young man. Taken along with the composition of the paints and the types of brushstrokes, the researchers felt safe in declaring the painting to be a legitimate Rembrandt.

하나가 그린 그림인지, 아니면 위조인지를 밝혀내는 데 일반적으로 사용됩니다. 이 방법은 렘브란트의 제자들에게 특히 어렵습니다. 렘브란트가 그림을 배우게 하기 위해 제자들에게 자기 그림을 베끼도록 시켰기 때문입니다. 물론, 이 그림들이 보관된 박물관에서 이 그림들을 가져다가 물리적으로 이 그림 층들을 분석할 수는 없죠. 값을 매길 수 없는 엄청난 가치를 가진 미술품을 파괴하게 될 테니까요.

하지만 기술의 발전이 그림의 기원을 밝혀내는 데 있어 매우 중요하다는 것이 판명되었습니다. 특히 방사능 사진 촬영이라는 기술이 그렇습니다. 기존의 X선 투과 시험에서는 장치가 사물을 향해 X선 빔을 쐈습니다. 물체의 내부가 서로 다른 밀도의 물질들로 만들어져 있으면 X선을 더 막거나 덜 막았죠. 그림의 경우 이것은 그림에 쓰여진 물감의 층을 나누고 분석하는 데 사용될 수 있습니다. **5** 반면 방사능 사진 촬영 기술은 사물로부터 직접 방출되는 방사선을 받아들여 이미지를 만들어냅니다. 이것은 그림을 중성자에 완전히 노출시킴으로써 가능해지죠. 중성자가 서로 다른 원소의 원자와 부딪치게 되면 이 원소들은 각기 다른 방식으로 반응을 하고, 이러한 반응이 연구원들에게 그림이 어떤 원소를 포함하고 있는지를 말해주는 겁니다. 이 자료는 안료가 어느 부분에 칠해졌는지를 알아내는 데 쓸 수 있습니다. 예를 들어, 렘브란트가 사용했던 흰색은 납을 함유하고 있었고, 적색은 수은을 함유하고 있었습니다. 이는 연구원들로 하여금 그림을 그리는 데 있어 적용된 각 붓놀림을 식별할 수 있도록 도와줍니다.

이러한 촬영 기술들은 렘브란트의 〈수염을 기른 노인의 초상〉이라 불리는 그림이 진짜로 렘브란트 작품인지를 밝혀내기 위해 사용되었습니다. 그림의 X선 이미지가 노인의 그림 아래에 또 다른 숨겨진 그림이 있을 수 있다는 가능성을 찾아냈습니다. 방사능 사진 촬영 기술을 이용해서 연구원들은 그림의 아래 층이 많은 양의 구리 성분을 함유하고 있다는 것을 밝혀냈습니다. 두 기법을 결합하여 그들은 아래 층과 거기에 무엇이 그려져 있었는지를 밝혀낼 수 있었습니다. 첫째, 연구원들은 캔버스에 처음으로 그려졌던 그림이 미완성이라는 것을 알 수 있었는데, 그 그림에는 그 위에 덧그려진 완성작에 포함된 대부분의 안료가 없었기 때문이었습니다. 두 번째로, 그들은 원래 그림의 윤곽을 식별할 수 있었는데, 베레모를 쓴 젊은 남자로 보였습니다. **6** 이는 렘브란트가 젊은 시절 그렸던 자화상들과 유사했기에 매우 중요했습니다. 물감들의 구성과 붓놀림의 종류를 함께 살펴봤을 때, 연구원들은 안심하고 이 그림이 진짜로 렘브란트가 그린 것이 맞다는 결론을 내릴 수 있었습니다.

1. **What is the main idea of the lecture?**
   Ⓐ The influence of Rembrandt on his students and the chiaroscuro techniques they shared
   Ⓑ Some advanced tools that were used recently to prove a painter's works authentic
   Ⓒ A painter's most well-known artwork and the reasons why it became so popular
   Ⓓ The art techniques of a certain painter and the method used for proving his works genuine

2. **Why did Rembrandt use chiaroscuro technique in his works?**
   Ⓐ To emphasize particular parts of the object or person in the painting
   Ⓑ To show the importance of background and foreground when it comes to portraits
   Ⓒ To guide the viewers' perspectives to the center of the artwork effectively
   Ⓓ To highlight his heavy focus on detail, especially a person's jewelry and clothing

3. **What are the characteristics of Rembrandt's painting style?** Choose 2 answers.
   Ⓐ He painted the whole canvas in transparent shades of gray first.
   Ⓑ He avoided using a wide spectrum of colors for his works.
   Ⓒ He enjoyed applying an excessive amount of paint.
   Ⓓ He often used many layers to make the subject more real.

4. **Why does the professor mention forgery?**
   Ⓐ To introduce another problem authenticating a genuine Rembrandt painting
   Ⓑ To explain the process of making a forgery of the works of a famous painter
   Ⓒ To emphasize the fact that Rembrandt's paintings were often forged
   Ⓓ To illustrate that Rembrandt's painting style was hard to reproduce

5. **What can be inferred about autoradiography?**
   Ⓐ It has a function similar to the conventional X-radiography scanner.
   Ⓑ It can only detect red and white colors, which contain lead and mercury.
   Ⓒ It shows where pigments were used by determining the elements in them.

1. **강의의 주제는 무엇인가?**
   Ⓐ 렘브란트가 그의 학생들에게 끼친 영향과 그들이 공유한 명암 기법들
   Ⓑ 한 화가의 작품을 진품이라고 밝혀내기 위해 최근 사용된 몇 가지 발전된 도구들
   Ⓒ 한 화가의 가장 잘 알려진 작품과 그 작품이 왜 그렇게 유명해졌는지에 대한 이유들
   Ⓓ 특정 화가의 그림 기법들과 그의 작품들을 진품이라고 밝혀내기 위해 사용된 방법

2. **렘브란트는 왜 그의 작품들에서 명암법을 사용했는가?**
   Ⓐ 그림 속 사물이나 사람의 특정한 부분들을 강조하려고
   Ⓑ 초상화에 있어 배경과 전경의 중요성을 보여주려고
   Ⓒ 그림을 보는 이의 관점을 효과적으로 그림의 중앙으로 인도하려고
   Ⓓ 세부 묘사, 특히 인물의 보석이나 옷에 대한 그의 강한 관심을 강조하려고

3. **렘브란트의 화풍의 특징은 무엇인가?**
   두 개를 고르시오.
   Ⓐ 캔버스 전체를 먼저 옅은 회색으로 칠했다.
   Ⓑ 작품들에 다양한 범위의 색깔을 사용하는 것을 피했다.
   Ⓒ 과다한 양의 물감을 사용하는 것을 즐겼다.
   Ⓓ 대상을 더 실감나도록 만들기 위해 많은 층을 사용했다.

4. **교수는 왜 위조를 언급하는가?**
   Ⓐ 진품 렘브란트 그림임을 증명하는 데 있어서의 또 다른 문제를 소개하기 위해
   Ⓑ 유명한 화가의 작품을 위조하는 과정을 설명하기 위해
   Ⓒ 렘브란트의 그림들이 종종 위조되었다는 사실을 강조하기 위해
   Ⓓ 렘브란트의 화풍이 복제하기 어려웠다는 것을 보여주기 위해

5. **방사능 사진 촬영 기술에 대해 무엇을 추론할 수 있는가?**
   Ⓐ 기존의 X선 촬영과 비슷한 기능을 가지고 있다.
   Ⓑ 납과 수은을 함유한 적색과 흰색만을 감지할 수 있다.
   Ⓒ 안료에 들어 있는 성분을 밝혀냄으로써 안료가 어디에 쓰였는지 보여준다.

Ⓓ It is able to distinguish between the brushstroke styles of different painters.

6. Which of the following is true about *Old Man with Beard*?
Ⓐ Rembrandt ran out of some paint colors before he finished the second layer.
Ⓑ Its second layer was eventually left unfinished by Rembrandt.
Ⓒ The use of autoradiography revealed that it was a genuine Rembrandt.
Ⓓ The top layer and the bottom layer both used a large amount of copper.

Ⓓ 서로 다른 화가들의 붓놀림 방식을 구분할 수 있다.

6. 〈수염을 기른 노인의 초상〉에 대해 옳은 것은 무엇인가?
Ⓐ 렘브란트는 두 번째 층 작업을 완성하기 전에 몇몇 물감들을 다 써버렸다.
Ⓑ 이 그림의 두 번째 층은 렘브란트에 의해 결국 미완성인 채로 남았다.
Ⓒ 방사능 사진 촬영 기술의 사용은 이 그림이 렘브란트의 진품이라는 것을 드러냈다.
Ⓓ 그림의 위층과 아래층 모두 많은 양의 구리를 사용했다.

어휘 prolific adj 다작하는 | printmaker n 판화 제작자 | verse v ~에 정통하다, 숙달하다 | predecessor n 이전의 사람 | influential adj 영향력 있는 | masterful adj 능수능란한 | chiaroscuro n 명암법 | term n 용어, 단어 | describe v 묘사하다, 서술하다 | starkly adv 완전히 | contrasted adj 대조되는, 대비되는 | depth n 깊이 | focus v 집중하다, 초점을 맞추다 | typically adv 보통, 일반적으로 | particularly adv 특히, 특별히 | portrait n 초상화 | focal point 초점, 중심 | fade v 바래다, 희미해지다 | nebulous adj 흐릿한, 모호한 | background n 배경 | obvious adj 분명한, 명백한 | relatively adv 상대적으로, 비교적 | palette n (특정 화가가 쓰는) 색깔들, 팔레트 | rarely adv 드물게 | transparent adj 투명한 | glow n 빛 | remark v 언급하다 | define v 정의하다, 규정하다 | methodically adv 체계적으로, 조직적으로 | alter v 바꾸다 | demand v 요구하다 | physical adj 물질의, 육체의 | prompt v 촉발하다 | contemporary n 동시대의 | attribute v ~의 것이라고 보다 | forgery n 위조 | analyze v 분석하다 | destroy v 파괴하다 | potentially adv 잠재적으로 | priceless adj 값을 매길 수 없는 | valuable adj 가치 있는 | identify v 확인하다, 알아보다 | origin n 기원 | specifically adv 분명히, 명확하게 | autoradiography n 방사능 사진 촬영 | conventional adj 관습적인, 관례적인 | generate v 발생시키다, 만들어 내다 | direct v 향하다 | interior n 내부 | density n 밀도 | radiation n 방사선 | emit v 방출하다, 내뿜다 | neutron n 중성자 | element n 성분, 요소 | behave v 행동하다 | atom n 원자 | pigment n 안료, 색소 | lead n 납 | mercury n 수은 | brushstroke n 붓놀림 | beard n 수염 | genuine adj 진품의, 진짜의 | combine v 결합하다, 갖추다 | depict v 그리다, 묘사하다 | discern v 파악하다, 알아차리다 | outline n 윤곽 | beret n 베레모 | self-portrait n 자화상 | composition n 구성 | declare v 선언하다 | legitimate adj 진짜의, 합법의, 정당한

Lesson 05 Astronomy

본서 | P. 210

Test
1. A **2.** B **3.** C **4.** A, C **5.** B, D **6.** D

Test

본서 | P. 211

Man: Student | Woman: Professor

[1-6] Listen to part of a discussion in an astronomy class.

W In general terms, a constellation is a grouping of stars that form a pattern and have a name. Of course, anyone can look at the sky and create shapes from the stars and other celestial objects they see. **2** However, there is an official list of constellations that was compiled in 1930 by the International Astronomical Union, or IAU. These 88 constellations cover the entire night sky. Since that list was made, all other star patterns are referred to as asterisms.

남자: 학생 | 여자: 교수

천문학 수업 중 토론의 일부를 들으시오.

여 일반적인 용어로 말하자면, 별자리는 패턴을 형성하고 이름을 가지는 별들의 한 무리입니다. 물론 누구든지 하늘을 보고 별과 다른 천체를 보며 모양을 만들어낼 수 있죠. **2** 하지만 1930년에 국제천문연맹(IAU)에서 종합해 만든 공식적인 별자리 목록이 있습니다. 이 88개의 별자리가 밤하늘 전체를 덮고 있죠. 이 목록이 만들어진 뒤로 다른 모든 별들의 패턴은 성군으로 불립니다. 이 목록에 있는 많

Many of the constellations on that list correspond to those created by the ancient Greeks, but they were not the first to compile such lists.

3 It is impossible to say who first gazed up at the night sky and decided that a particular set of stars looked like an animal, person, or object. However, we do know that we have been doing so for a very long time. The earliest evidence of this practice comes from cave paintings. In some of these early artworks, there are patterns of dots that initially didn't make any sense to scientists. Then, people realized that some of them were arranged like the stars in modern constellations. Many different cultures created their own sets of constellations, and some of those are very similar. However, as I said earlier, those that are not on the list are called asterisms by the IAU. **1** One asterism that shows up in many cultures is the Big Dipper. This group of seven stars forms a shape that is recognized as a long-handled ladle, a plow, and a bear. **4(A), 5(D)** According to the IAU list, it is an asterism contained within the constellation Ursa Major, which is also a bear.

M Professor, why did they think that it looks like a bear? I mean, it is vaguely animal-shaped, but why a bear?

W **4(C)** Actually, Mark, I agree with you. As you can see in this illustration where someone has drawn a bear over the stars, it has a long tail. No bear that I have ever seen has a tail like that. But, then again, many of the constellations don't look much like what they are named for. As you said, at least it looks kind of like an animal. Look at its neighbor, Ursa Minor. What does that look like to you?

M Um, it looks a lot like the Big Dipper, but smaller. And, it's at a different angle.

W Yes, indeed it does. Which is why it is often called the Little Dipper. But, there is a long tradition of seeing that asterism as a bear as well. Many cultures that are geographically distinct have their own stories about Ursa Major involving a bear. This similarity may come from a common oral tradition that extends back to around 13,000 years ago. Bears have been significant to many cultures, and for good reason. They are the largest land predators, and they display traits and abilities that we see as similar to our own. **5(B)** But, other cultures see it as very different things. In Burmese, it is referred to with the general term for crustaceans. And in

은 수의 별자리들이 고대 그리스인들이 만든 것과 일치하지만, 고대 그리스인들이 이러한 목록을 만든 최초의 사람들은 아니었어요.

3 누가 먼저 밤하늘을 올려다보고 특정한 무리의 별들이 동물, 사람, 혹은 물체처럼 보인다고 정한 건지 말하기는 불가능합니다. 그러나 매우 오래 전부터 이렇게 해 왔다는 것은 알고 있죠. 이러한 관행을 보여주는 가장 초기의 증거는 동굴 벽화에서 나옵니다. 이 초기 미술 작품들 중 일부에는 과학자들이 처음에는 이해하지 못했던 점으로 된 패턴들이 있었습니다. 그 뒤에 사람들은 이 점들의 일부가 현대의 별자리에 있는 별들처럼 배열되어 있다는 것을 깨달았습니다. 다양한 문화권에서 각자의 별자리들을 만들어냈고 그 중 몇몇은 매우 비슷하기도 합니다. 그러나 앞서 말했듯, 목록에 없는 별무리들은 IAU에 의해 성군이라고 불립니다. **1** 많은 문화권에서 나타나는 성군 하나는 바로 북두칠성입니다. 일곱 개의 별로 이루어진 이 별무리는 긴 손잡이가 달린 국자, 쟁기, 그리고 곰의 형태로 보여집니다. **4(A), 5(D)** IAU 목록에 따르면, 이 성군은 큰곰자리라는 또 다른 곰의 형태를 가진 별자리에 포함되어 있습니다.

남 교수님, 왜 사람들은 이것이 곰을 닮았다고 생각한 건가요? 제 말은, 이 별무리가 애매하게 동물의 모양을 하고 있긴 하지만, 왜 곰인가요?

여 **4(C)** 사실, 마크, 나도 학생의 말에 동의해요. 누군가가 별들 위에 곰을 그려놓은 이 삽화를 보면 알겠지만, 이 곰은 긴 꼬리를 가지고 있어요. 제가 지금까지 본 곰들 중 어떤 곰도 이런 꼬리를 가지고 있진 않았죠. 하지만 많은 수의 별자리들이 그들에게 붙여진 이름과 같은 모양을 가지고 있진 않습니다. 학생이 말했듯, 적어도 동물처럼 보이기는 해요. 옆에 자리한 작은곰자리를 보세요. 학생에겐 무엇처럼 보이나요?

남 음, 북두칠성이랑 상당히 비슷하지만 조금 더 작아 보이네요. 그리고 각도가 달라요.

여 네, 바로 그렇습니다. 이것이 소북두칠성이라고 종종 불리는 이유죠. 하지만 이 성군 역시 곰으로 봤던 오랜 전통이 있습니다. 지리학적으로 분명하게 구분되는 곳에 자리했던 많은 문화권은 큰곰자리에 대해 곰과 관련된 고유의 이야기들을 가지고 있습니다. 이 유사점은 약 13,000년 전까지 거슬러 올라가는 공통된 구전에서 온 것일 수도 있습니다. 곰들은 많은 문화권에서 중요하게 여겨졌고, 거기에는 이유가 있었죠. 이들은 가장 덩치가 큰 육지 포식자이며, 우리 인간과 유사한 특성과 능력을 보입니다. **5(B)** 그러나 이것은 다른 문화권에서는 아주 다른 것으로 보기도 합니다. 버마에서는 일반적으로 갑각류를 지칭하는 용어로 이 성군을 불렀습니다. 그

Finnish, it is a salmon weir, which is a type of wooden frame used to catch fish.
So, the decision to go with the larger Greek constellation seems somewhat arbitrary to me. Especially when the brightest stars are all contained within the portion that makes the Big Dipper. However, other factors may come into play here. The reason that the IAU made its list in the first place was to aid in the naming of objects called variable stars. These stars fade and brighten instead of steadily shining. So, they are named for the constellation they appear in. Ursa Major is much larger than the Big Dipper. As I said, the 88 constellations encompass the entire night sky, so a larger asterism made defining that space easier.
6 I mentioned arbitrariness... and that is actually quite important to remember. All of the constellations are arbitrary. Our view of the stars is unique to our planet. From any other point in space, the arrangement of the stars would look different. This is particularly true since the objects that make up constellations are often quite distant from each other in space. But, that makes another point in favor of the Big Dipper. Five of its seven stars are not only close to each other, but they also move together through space. They are a cluster of stars that most likely formed together and are slowly spreading apart.

리고 핀란드에서는 연어 둑으로 불렸는데, 이건 물고기를 잡는 데 사용된 나무 틀의 일종입니다.
그래서 좀 더 큰 그리스의 별자리를 따라 가기로 결정한 것은 제게 다소 임의적으로 보입니다. 특히나 가장 밝은 별들이 모두 북두칠성을 이루는 부분 안에 포함되어 있기에 말이죠. 그러나 여기에는 다른 요인들이 있을 수 있습니다. IAU에서 애초에 이 목록을 만든 이유는 변광성이라 불리는 물체들의 이름을 붙이는 데 도움을 주기 위해서였습니다. 이 별들은 지속적으로 빛나는 대신 희미해졌다가 다시 빛납니다. 그래서 이들이 모습을 드러내는 별자리에 맞춰 이름이 붙여졌죠. 큰곰자리는 북두칠성보다 훨씬 더 크기가 큽니다. 이미 말했지만, 88개의 별자리들은 밤하늘 전체를 아우르기 때문에, 크기가 더 큰 성군은 그 공간을 확정하는 것을 더 쉽게 해주죠.
6 앞에서 임의라는 말을 했었는데... 이건 사실 상당히 중요하게 기억해둬야 할 부분입니다. 모든 별자리들은 임의적입니다. 별들을 보는 우리의 관점은 우리 지구에서만 있는 것입니다. 우주의 다른 어떤 공간에서든 이 별들의 배열은 다르게 보일 겁니다. 별자리를 만드는 천체들이 종종 우주에서 서로 꽤 멀리 떨어져 있기에 특히 그렇습니다. 하지만 이는 북두칠성의 손을 들어주는 다른 요인입니다. 일곱 개의 별들 중 다섯 개가 서로와 가까울 뿐만 아니라 우주 공간에서 서로 함께 움직입니다. 이들은 아마도 함께 형성되었다가 천천히 흩어지고 있는 별무리일 겁니다.

1. What is the discussion mainly about?
Ⓐ One of the most well-known examples of an asterism and its characteristics
Ⓑ The characteristics of the relationship between Ursa Major and Ursa Minor
Ⓒ Interesting features of ancient Greek astronomy and its influence
Ⓓ The difference between past and modern ways of naming the stars

2. According to the discussion, what are asterisms?
Ⓐ Clusters of stars that are physically close to each other
Ⓑ Groupings of stars that are not considered constellations
Ⓒ The classification of stars that have many different names
Ⓓ The stars that are visible in the night sky from Earth

1. 토론은 주로 무엇에 대한 것인가?
Ⓐ 성군의 가장 잘 알려진 예시들 중 하나와 그 특징들
Ⓑ 큰곰자리와 작은곰자리 관계의 특징
Ⓒ 고대 그리스 천문학의 흥미로운 특징과 그 영향
Ⓓ 별자리를 명명하는 과거 방식과 현대 방식의 차이점

2. 토론에 따르면, 성군은 무엇인가?
Ⓐ 물리적으로 서로 가까운 별무리들
Ⓑ 별자리로 간주되지 않는 별무리들
Ⓒ 다양하고 많은 이름을 가진 별들의 분류
Ⓓ 지구의 밤하늘에서 보이는 별들

3. **Why does the professor mention cave paintings?**

Ⓐ To show how astronomy has changed throughout history

Ⓑ To indicate their influence on naming constellations and asterisms

Ⓒ To point out that grouping and naming stars have been done for a long time

Ⓓ To tell the students that ancient astronomy still remains a mystery

4. **According to the discussion, which of the following are true about asterisms?** Choose 2 answers.

Ⓐ They can be located inside a constellation.

Ⓑ Most of them were named by the ancient Greeks.

Ⓒ Their shapes do not always follow their names.

Ⓓ The official list of asterisms was compiled by the IAU.

5. **According to the discussion, which of the following are true about the Big Dipper?** Choose 2 answers.

Ⓐ Its relationship with the Little Dipper has yet to be discovered.

Ⓑ Many cultures have referred to it with different names.

Ⓒ Its resemblance to a bear has been internationally agreed upon.

Ⓓ It can be found inside of a constellation named Ursa Major.

6. **What can be inferred from the professor's explanation regarding arbitrariness?**

Ⓐ When stars move away from each other, they are no longer part of an asterism.

Ⓑ Constellations are bound to change someday since all stars fade eventually.

Ⓒ Stars that shine constantly were called variable stars by astronomers.

Ⓓ The arrangement of stars changes depending on one's location in the universe.

3. **교수는 왜 동굴 벽화를 언급하는가?**

Ⓐ 역사를 통틀어 천문학이 어떻게 바뀌었는지 보여주려고

Ⓑ 별자리와 성군의 이름을 붙이는 데 대한 동굴 벽화의 영향을 시사하려고

Ⓒ 별들을 무리 짓고 이름을 붙이는 일이 매우 오래 전부터 이루어져 왔다는 것을 지적하려고

Ⓓ 고대의 천문학이 여전히 수수께끼로 남아 있다고 학생들에게 말하려고

4. **토론에 따르면, 다음 중 성군에 관해 옳은 것은 무엇인가?** 두 개를 고르시오.

Ⓐ 별자리 안에 위치할 수 있다.

Ⓑ 대부분이 고대 그리스인들에 의해 이름 지어졌다.

Ⓒ 모양이 항상 이름을 따라가는 것은 아니다.

Ⓓ 성군의 공식적인 목록은 IAU에 의해 만들어졌다.

5. **토론에 따르면, 다음 중 북두칠성에 관해 옳은 것은 무엇인가?** 두 개를 고르시오.

Ⓐ 소북두칠성과의 관계는 아직 발견된 바가 없다.

Ⓑ 많은 문화권에서 북두칠성을 다른 이름으로 불렀다.

Ⓒ 곰과 닮았다는 것은 국제적으로 동의가 이루어졌다.

Ⓓ 큰곰자리라는 별자리 안에서 발견될 수 있다.

6. **임의성에 대한 교수의 설명에서 무엇을 추론할 수 있는가?**

Ⓐ 별들이 서로에게서 멀어지면 그들은 더 이상 성군의 일부가 아니다.

Ⓑ 모든 별들이 결국 희미해지기 때문에 별자리들도 언젠가는 변하게 되어 있다.

Ⓒ 지속적으로 빛나는 별들은 천문학자들에 의해 변광성이라고 불렸다.

Ⓓ 별들의 배열은 관찰자가 우주의 어느 위치에 있느냐에 따라 달라진다.

어휘 general adj 일반적인 | constellation n 별자리, 성좌 | celestial adj 천체의, 천상의 | official adj 공식적인 | compile v 하나로 종합하다, 엮다, 편집하다 | asterism n 성군 | correspond v 일치하다, 부합하다 | gaze v 응시하다, 바라보다 | particular adj 특정한, 특별한 | evidence n 증거 | practice n 관행 | cave painting 동굴 벽화 | artwork n 미술 작품 | initially adv 처음에 | arrange v 배열하다 | Big Dipper 북두칠성 | ladle n 국자 | plow n 쟁기 | vaguely adv 애매하게, 희미하게 | illustration n 삽화 | Little Dipper 소북두칠성 | tradition n 전통 | geographically adv 지리적으로 | distinct adj 뚜렷한, 분명한 | oral tradition 구전 | extend v 확장하다 | predator n 포식자 | display v 보이다, 진열하다 | trait n 특성 | crustacean n 갑각류 | weir n 둑 | arbitrary adj 임의적인, 제멋대로인 | variable star 변광성 | fade v 희미해지다 | steadily adv 꾸준히 | encompass v 아우르다, 망라하다 | define v 한정하다, 명백히 보여주다 | arrangement n 배열 | cluster n 무리, 군 | spread apart 뿔뿔이 흩어지다

Test

1. A **2.** B **3.** C **4.** D **5.** A, C **6.** B

Test

본서 | P. 215

Man: Student | Woman: Professor

[1-6] Listen to part of a discussion in a biology class.

W As we have discussed in class already, every species within an ecosystem plays an important role in the food chain. In one way or another, they all rely upon one another directly or indirectly. **1, 2** Some species, however, play a role that is disproportionate to the size of their population in terms of how unique and crucial it is to the continued functioning of their ecosystem. These animals are referred to as keystone species because, like the keystone of a stone arch, if they are removed, the structure may collapse entirely. The organisms that are keystone species are often predators, but they aren't always. A small population of predators can quite efficiently control the population and distribution of a very large number of prey species. **3** In fact, a single large predator like a mountain lion can have a huge territorial range. The big and small game including deer, rabbits, and birds are all influenced by the mountain lion's presence. Where the smaller species select to make their homes and their feeding habits are affected by the single large predator's behavior. Even scavengers are affected since they feed upon the carrion the lion leaves behind.

M I understand how the mountain lion affects the animals by preying on them, but how does its disappearance affect them?

W Well, if you remove the predator, the prey species' populations can grow unchecked. They will quickly overtax their food and water resources, which will cause their population to collapse. One species disappears, then another, and another—it's like a row of dominoes. Once the first one falls, it's nearly impossible to stop the chain reaction.
4 The term keystone species was created by zoologist Robert T. Paine, who proved his theory in a rather unusual way. In fact, he probably would not be allowed to repeat such an experiment today.

남자: 학생 | 여자: 교수

생물학 수업 중 토론의 일부를 들으시오.

여 이미 수업에서 이야기했듯이 생태계 안의 모든 종들은 먹이 사슬에서 중요한 역할을 합니다. 어떤 방식으로든 모두 서로에게 직접적으로 혹은 간접적으로 의지하고 있죠. **1, 2** 그러나 몇몇 종들은 그들 생태계의 지속적인 기능에 있어 독특함이나 중대함 면에서 개체 수의 크기에 비해 어울리지 않는 역할을 하고 있습니다. 이 동물들은 핵심종이라고 불리는데 그 이유는 돌로 만든 아치형 구조물이 쐐기돌이 제거되면 무너지는 것과 같이, 핵심종들이 없어지면 그들 서식지의 생태계 구조가 완전히 무너질 수 있기 때문입니다. 핵심종인 생물들은 많은 경우 포식자이지만, 항상 그런 것은 아닙니다. 적은 수의 포식자들은 아주 큰 규모의 피식자 종들의 개체 수와 분포를 효율적으로 통제할 수 있습니다. **3** 실제로, 퓨마와 같은 덩치가 큰 포식자 하나가 매우 넓은 활동 영역을 가질 수 있습니다. 사슴, 토끼, 그리고 새들을 포함하여 크고 작은 사냥감들이 모두 퓨마의 존재에 의해 영향을 받죠. 더 작은 종들이 어디에 보금자리를 만들고 먹이 습관을 형성하는지가 한 커다란 포식자의 행동에 의해 영향을 받습니다. 심지어 죽은 동물을 먹는 동물들조차 영향을 받는데, 이것은 이 동물들이 퓨마가 남긴 썩은 고기를 먹기 때문이에요.

남 퓨마가 이들을 사냥함으로써 동물들에게 영향을 주는 건 알겠는데, 퓨마가 사라지는 게 이들에게 어떤 영향을 미치는 거죠?

여 음, 포식자를 제거하면 피식자 종들의 개체 수가 걷잡을 수 없이 불어날 수 있어요. 피식자 종들은 먹이와 수원을 금세 지나치게 많이 쓸 것이고, 이는 이들 개체의 붕괴를 가져오는 원인이 되죠. 한 종이 없어지면 그 뒤로 다른 하나, 그리고 또 다른 하나가 무너지는 게 도미노와 똑같습니다. 일단 맨 처음 하나가 넘어지면 그 뒤로 이어지는 연쇄 반응을 멈추기는 거의 불가능하죠.
4 핵심종이라는 용어는 동물학자인 로버트 T. 페인에 의해 만들어졌는데, 그는 상당히 독특한 방법으로 그의 이론을 증명했습니다. 사실상 오늘날 그런 실험을 다시 하는 것은 아마 허락되지 않을 겁니다.

In 1969, there was less oversight of scientists in the field. Normally, scientists would observe the habitat of a species and record changes, but he experimented by deliberately changing the habitat by removing what he believed to be an important species. Paine and his students went to Tatoosh Island, Washington, over a period of 25 years and removed all of the Pisaster ochraceus sea stars they could find in a tidal area in order to see what effect it had when they were gone. It had a profound one. In their absence, the mussel population exploded, and they outcompeted other species. Clearly, the sea stars were a keystone species.

Another example of an aquatic keystone species is the sea otters of the Pacific Northwest. **5(A)** Sea otters feed mainly upon marine invertebrates, and they are particularly fond of sea urchins. Sea urchins feed upon the roots of kelp plants, which support a wide variety of species by providing both food and shelter in the dense kelp forests. When the urchins eat the kelp roots, the giant seaweeds drift away and die, crippling the ecosystem. The main predators of sea otters are orcas and sharks, who account for over ten percent of sea otter deaths. This has prevented them from expanding their range further north. The main threat to otters for over 100 years, however, was men. Hunters exploited them up until 1911 for their highly valuable fur and almost entirely eradicated them. **5(C)** When hunting the animals was banned, only 1,000 to 2,000 remained in the wild. Since then, captive breeding programs and conservation have allowed them to rebound, recovering nearly two-thirds of their former range. This has led to kelp also re-inhabiting vast areas, restoring the ecosystem. Areas that the sea otters have not reclaimed are often called urchin barrens due to their destruction of the habitat.

6 Two herbivores that act as keystone species are prairie dogs and elephants. Prairie dogs dig tunnels underground and feed on grasses, thus retaining water in the soil and providing new plant growth for large grazing animals. Elephants have a taste for acacia trees, which spread very quickly. The elephants uproot the trees and feed upon them, preventing them from turning the savannah into forest. This preserves the wide variety of animals that rely upon the grasses for food or prey upon those that do.

1969년에는 현장에서의 과학자들에 대한 감독이 좀 덜했습니다. 보통 과학자들은 한 종의 서식지를 관찰하고 변화를 기록하는데, 페인은 그가 중요하다고 믿은 종을 제거함으로써 서식지를 의도적으로 변화시키는 실험을 했습니다. 페인과 그의 학생들은 워싱턴주의 타투시섬으로 가서 25년에 걸쳐 감조 구역에 사는 피사스테르 오크라케우스 불가사리 종을 모두 제거했는데 이는 이들이 없어지면 어떤 영향이 있는지 보기 위해서였습니다. 엄청난 영향이 있었죠. 이 불가사리들이 사라지자 홍합 개체 수가 폭발적으로 늘어났고, 홍합이 다른 종들을 생존 경쟁에서 앞서 버렸습니다. 확실히 이 불가사리들이 핵심종이었던 거죠.

수생 핵심종의 또 다른 예는 태평양 연안 북서부에 사는 해달입니다. **5(A)** 해달은 주로 바다의 무척추동물들을 먹고 살아가는데 특히 성게를 좋아합니다. 성게들은 켈프 해초의 뿌리를 먹으며 살아가는데, 이 켈프 해초들은 빽빽하게 숲을 이뤄 다양한 종들에게 먹이와 피난처 둘 다를 제공합니다. 성게가 켈프 뿌리를 먹으면 이 커다란 해초들이 떠내려가 죽게 되면서 생태계가 손상됩니다. 해달의 주된 포식자는 범고래와 상어인데 이들이 해달 사망 원인의 10퍼센트를 차지합니다. 이것이 해달들이 더 북쪽으로 지역을 넓히지 못하게 막았습니다. 그러나 지난 100년간 해달에게 있어 주된 위협은 인간이었어요. 사냥꾼들은 해달의 매우 귀한 털 때문에 1911년까지 그들을 남획했고 거의 멸종 위기에 다다르게 했습니다. **5(C)** 해달 사냥이 금지되었을 무렵에는 단 1,000마리에서 2,000마리만이 야생에 남아 있었죠. 그 이후로 포획 사육과 보존은 해달들을 다시 살아나게 만들었고, 이전 개체 수의 3분의 2까지 수를 회복시켰습니다. 이는 켈프 해초가 광대한 지역에 다시 자라나도록 이끌었고 생태계를 회복시켰습니다. 해달이 아직 되찾지 않은 지역들은 종종 성게 불모지라고 불렸는데, 이는 성게들이 서식지를 파괴했기 때문입니다.

6 핵심종의 역할을 하는 두 가지 초식 동물들로는 프레리도그와 코끼리가 있습니다. 프레리도그는 땅속에 굴을 파고 풀을 뜯어먹는데, 토양이 물을 유지할 수 있도록 하고 더 큰 풀을 뜯는 동물들을 위해 새로운 식물이 성장하게 합니다. 코끼리들은 아카시아 나무를 좋아하는데, 이 나무들은 매우 빨리 번식하죠. 코끼리들은 이 나무를 뿌리째 뽑아 먹어서 사바나가 숲이 되는 것을 막습니다. 이는 풀을 뜯어 먹는 다양한 동물들과 이 동물들을 잡아먹는 동물들을 보호합니다.

Lesson 06
Lectures

1. **What is the discussion mainly about?**
   Ⓐ Some species' roles and their ecological impact
   Ⓑ The importance of keystone species in the ocean
   Ⓒ The relationship between sea otters and sea urchins
   Ⓓ Robert T. Paine's radical experiment in the 1960s

2. **According to the discussion, what are keystone species?**
   Ⓐ Predators that prevent the overgrowth of trees in the savannah
   Ⓑ Species that are irreplaceable since they play vital roles in their ecosystems
   Ⓒ Plant eaters who influence the growth of grass and other plant species
   Ⓓ A few species that are near extinction and in need of conservation

3. **What can be inferred about a mountain lion?**
   Ⓐ It revealed that predators can survive without prey for quite a long time.
   Ⓑ It can deplete its resources faster than any other predators in the region.
   Ⓒ Even though it is a solitary predator, it can have a huge effect on its surroundings.
   Ⓓ Because of its wide territorial range, its influence is often overestimated.

4. **Listen again to part of the discussion. Then answer the question.**

   W The term keystone species was created by zoologist Robert T. Paine, who proved his theory in a rather unusual way. In fact, he probably would not be allowed to repeat such an experiment today.

   Why does the professor say this:

   W He probably would not be allowed to repeat such an experiment today.

   Ⓐ To talk about Paine's innovative nature and the consequences it brought
   Ⓑ To show how much scientists have to worry about keeping their financers happy
   Ⓒ To emphasize the scale and the difficulty of Paine's experiment
   Ⓓ To tell her students that Paine's experiment was a controversial one

1. **토론은 주로 무엇에 대한 것인가?**
   Ⓐ 일부 종들의 역할과 그 생태학적 영향
   Ⓑ 바다에서의 핵심종의 중요성
   Ⓒ 해달과 성게의 관계
   Ⓓ 1960년대 로버트 T. 페인의 과격한 실험

2. **토론에 의하면, 핵심종은 무엇인가?**
   Ⓐ 사바나에서 나무가 너무 많이 자라는 것을 막는 포식자들
   Ⓑ 생태계에서 중요한 역할을 하기 때문에 대체 불가능한 종들
   Ⓒ 풀과 다른 식물 종들의 성장에 영향을 미치는 초식 동물들
   Ⓓ 멸종 위기에 놓여 보존이 필요한 몇몇 종들

3. **퓨마에 대해 무엇을 추론할 수 있는가?**
   Ⓐ 포식자가 먹이 없이도 꽤 오랫동안 생존할 수 있다는 것을 보여주었다.
   Ⓑ 그 지역의 다른 어떤 포식자들보다도 더 빨리 자원을 고갈시킬 수 있다.
   Ⓒ 독자적으로 행동하는 포식자이지만 주변 환경에 큰 영향을 미칠 수 있다.
   Ⓓ 넓은 활동 영역으로 인해 그 영향이 종종 과대평가된다.

4. **토론의 일부를 다시 듣고 질문에 답하시오.**

   여 핵심종이라는 용어는 동물학자인 로버트 T. 페인에 의해 만들어졌는데, 그는 상당히 독특한 방법으로 그의 이론을 증명했습니다. 사실상 오늘날 그런 실험을 다시 하는 것은 아마 허락되지 않을 겁니다.

   교수는 왜 이렇게 말하는가:

   여 사실상 오늘날 그런 실험을 다시 하는 것은 아마 허락되지 않을 겁니다.

   Ⓐ 페인의 혁신적인 천성과 그것이 불러온 결과에 대해 이야기하기 위해
   Ⓑ 자금 지원자들을 기쁘게 하는 것에 관해 과학자들이 얼마나 걱정해야 하는지를 보이기 위해
   Ⓒ 페인의 실험의 규모와 어려움을 강조하기 위해
   Ⓓ 학생들에게 페인의 실험이 논란의 여지가 있는 것이었다고 말하기 위해

5. **What is true about the sea otters of the Pacific Northwest?** Choose 2 answers.
Ⓐ They are responsible for maintaining the population size of kelp plants.
Ⓑ It was reported that about 2,000 of them are living in the region in these days.
Ⓒ Their population increased after hunting was banned by the government.
Ⓓ They maintain symbiotic relationships with sea urchins and kelp plants.

6. **Why does the professor mention prairie dogs and elephants?**
Ⓐ To name some animals that influence keystone species
Ⓑ To give some herbivore examples of keystone species
Ⓒ To compare their roles as keystone species in their ecosystems
Ⓓ To introduce the topics of the next lecture to the students

5. **태평양 연안 북서부의 해달에 대해 옳은 것은 무엇인가?** 두 개를 고르시오.
Ⓐ 켈프 해초의 개체 수 유지를 맡고 있다.
Ⓑ 근래 약 2,000마리가 그 지역에 서식한다고 알려져 있다.
Ⓒ 정부에 의해 사냥이 금지된 뒤로 개체 수가 증가했다.
Ⓓ 성게 및 켈프 해초와 공생 관계를 유지하고 있다.

6. **교수는 왜 프레리도그와 코끼리를 언급하는가?**
Ⓐ 핵심종에 영향을 주는 몇몇 동물들을 언급하려고
Ⓑ 초식 동물 핵심종의 예시를 들려고
Ⓒ 그들의 생태계에서의 핵심종으로서의 역할을 비교하려고
Ⓓ 학생들에게 다음 강의의 주제를 소개하려고

어휘 species n 종 | ecosystem n 생태계 | food chain 먹이 사슬 | rely v 의지하다 | directly adv 직접적으로 | indirectly adv 간접적으로 | disproportionate adj 어울리지 않는, 불균형의 | population n 인구, 개체 수 | crucial adj 중대한, 결정적인 | functioning n 기능, 작용 | keystone species 핵심종 | collapse v 붕괴하다 | entirely adv 완전히 | predator n 포식자 | efficiently adv 효율적으로 | distribution n 분포 | prey n 먹이, 사냥감 | mountain lion 퓨마 | territorial adj 영토의, 세력의 | range n 범위 | game n 사냥감 | presence n 존재, (특정한 곳에) 있음 | scavenger n 죽은 동물을 먹는 동물 | carrion n 썩어 가는 고기 | disappearance n 사라짐, 소실 | unchecked adj 걷잡을 수 없이, (손을 쓰지 않고) 놔둔 | overtax v 무리하다, 혹사하다 | water resource 수원 | domino n 도미노 | chain reaction 연쇄 반응 | zoologist n 동물학자 | prove v 증명하다 | repeat v 반복하다 | oversight n 감독, 관리 | observe v 관찰하다 | habitat n 서식지 | record v 기록하다 | deliberately adv 의도적으로 | sea star 불가사리 | tidal area 감조 구역 | profound adj 엄청난, 깊은 | absence n 부재 | mussel n 홍합 | explode v 폭발적으로 증가하다 | outcompete v 경쟁에서 이기다 | clearly adv 명확하게 | aquatic adj 수중의, 물 속의 | otter n 해달 | invertebrate n 무척추동물 | particularly adv 특히 | sea urchin 성게 | kelp plant 켈프(다시마목의 대형 해조류) | shelter n 피신처 | dense adj 빽빽한, 우거진 | seaweed n 해초 | drift away 떠내려가 버리다 | cripple v 심각한 손상을 주다 | orca n 범고래 | expand v 확장하다 | exploit v 착취하다, 이용하다 | eradicate v 박멸하다 | captive breeding 포획 사육 | conservation n 보호, 보존, 관리 | rebound v 다시 되돌아오다, 반등하다 | vast adj 어마어마한 | restore v 회복시키다, 되찾다 | reclaim v 되찾다 | barren n 불모지 | destruction n 파괴 | herbivore n 초식 동물 | prairie dog 프레리도그 | tunnel n 터널, 굴 | retain v 유지하다, 보유하다 | graze v (가축이) 풀을 뜯어먹다 | uproot v 뿌리째 뽑다 | preserve v 지키다, 보존하다

Lesson 07 Lectures

Lesson 07 Chemistry

본서 | P. 217

Test
1. D **2.** B, D **3.** A **4.** B **5.** C **6.** A

Test

본서 | P. 218

Man: Professor

[1-6] Listen to part of a lecture in a chemistry class.

M Isotopes are variants of a chemical element that possess

남자: 교수

화학 강의의 일부를 들으시오.

남 동위 원소는 화학 원소의 변종인데, 그들의 일반적

a different number of neutrons than the normal version of their atomic element. They have the same number of protons and electrons, though. So, they occupy the same position on the periodic table, hence their name: 'isos' means equal, and 'topos' means place. The atomic number refers to the number of protons it contains, so **2(B)** isotopes have the same atomic number as a normal atom, but their differing number of neutrons means that they have a different mass number. Separating isotopes from normal atomic elements can be extremely difficult, and molecules of elements often contain a mixture of isotopes and normal atoms. **2(D)** Some isotopes are unstable, so they shed their extra neutrons, which is the basis for the emission of radiation. **1, 3, 4** However, other isotopes are stable and do not decay, so they can increase in concentration over time. Their enduring concentration in an organism can be used to establish a variety of data about an organism's experiences. This property of stable isotopes has proven to be particularly valuable to law enforcement.

4 For example, let us take a look at hydrogen. Hydrogen is the most common element in the universe, and it forms three different isotopes. The first contains only a proton and an electron, and it makes up 99.98% of the hydrogen in existence. The other forms are called deuterium, containing one neutron, and tritium, containing two neutrons. While tritium is radioactive and unstable, deuterium is stable, and not subject to change. In fact, it is so immutable that scientists believe that all of the deuterium in the universe was created during the Big Bang. **4, 5** Deuterium is commonly found in water, and its concentration varies depending upon the source of the water, which is particularly useful to forensic scientists.

The other component of water, oxygen, also occurs in common isotopes, including oxygen-18. The water that people drink usually comes from surface water sources like lakes and rivers, which are replenished by rainwater. That rainwater begins as evaporation from the oceans, where deuterium and oxygen-18 are in their highest concentrations. The average global concentration of these isotopes in the water supply is referred to as the Global Meteoric Water Line. The word average is of particular importance, because the ratio of these isotopes actually varies widely as determined by localized variations in temperature, climate, altitude, and most importantly, distance from the ocean where they entered the water cycle. These many factors make the isotopic signatures of different areas quite distinguishable. Approximately 30% of the hydrogen found in human hair comes from the water we consume, and human hair grows at an average of 5 millimeters every two weeks. So, the concentration of

인 형태의 원소와 다른 숫자의 중성자를 가지고 있습니다. 하지만 같은 수의 양성자와 전자를 가지고 있어요. 그래서 원소 주기율표에서는 같은 위치를 차지하고 있기에 이들의 이름이 생겨난 겁니다. 'isos'는 같다는 의미이며 'topos'는 위치를 의미하죠. 원자 번호는 그 원자가 가지고 있는 양성자의 숫자를 가리키는데, 그렇기에 **2(B)** 동위 원소는 보통의 원자와 같은 원자 번호를 가지고 있지만 다른 수의 중성자를 가졌으므로 질량수는 다릅니다. 보통 원소에서 동위 원소를 분리하는 것은 극히 어려우며, 원소의 분자들은 종종 동위 원소와 보통 원소의 혼합물을 가지고 있습니다. **2(D)** 몇몇 동위 원소들은 불안정해서 남는 중성자를 떨어내는데, 이는 방사선 방출의 이유가 되죠. **1, 3, 4** 그러나 다른 동위 원소들은 안정적이며 붕괴되지 않아서, 시간이 흐름에 따라 농도가 증가할 수 있습니다. 생물에게서 오래도록 지속되는 이들의 농도는 한 생물의 경험에 대해 다양한 정보를 밝혀내는 데 사용될 수 있습니다. 안정적인 동위 원소들의 이러한 속성은 법률 집행에 특히 중요한 것으로 증명되었습니다.

4 예를 들어, 수소를 살펴보도록 합시다. 수소는 우주에서 가장 흔한 원소이며 세 개의 다른 동위 원소를 형성합니다. 첫 번째는 양성자와 전자만을 가지고 있으며, 존재하는 수소의 99.98%를 차지합니다. 다른 두 동위 원소들은 한 개의 중성자를 가진 듀테륨과 두 개의 중성자를 가진 트리튬이라 불리는 것들입니다. 트리튬은 방사성이며 불안정한 반면, 듀테륨은 안정적이고 변하지 않죠. 실제로 너무나도 변함이 없기에 과학자들은 우주에 존재하는 모든 듀테륨이 빅뱅 때 만들어졌다고 믿습니다. **4, 5** 듀테륨은 흔히 물에서 발견되며 물의 원천에 따라 농도 역시 달라지는데 이러한 점은 특히 법의학자들에게 유용합니다.

물의 다른 요소인 산소 또한 산소-18을 포함해 흔한 동위 원소들이 존재합니다. 사람들이 마시는 물은 보통 강수에 의해 다시 채워지는 호수나 강과 같은 표층수원에서 오죠. 이 강수는 듀테륨과 산소-18이 가장 높은 농도로 존재하는 바다에서 증발하기 시작합니다. 수원 내의 이 동위 원소들의 세계 평균 농도는 지구 천수선으로 불리죠. 평균이라는 단어가 특히 중요한데, 왜냐하면 이 동위 원소들의 비율이 현지에 따른 변화, 즉 온도, 기후, 고도, 그리고 가장 중요하게는 이들이 물의 순환을 시작하는 바다로부터의 거리에 따라 아주 다양해질 수 있기 때문입니다. 이 많은 요인들이 서로 다른 지역들의 동위 원소 특징을 매우 구별하기 쉽게 만듭니다. 인간의 머리카락에서 볼 수 있는 거의 30%의 수소가 우리가 마시는 물에서 오는데, 인간의 머리카락은 2주마다 평균 5밀리미터씩 자랍니다. 그래서, 인간의

these isotopes in human hair samples can tell scientists where a person has been spending their time. This can aid criminal investigations by providing the recent whereabouts of an unknown victim or a suspect. These heavier isotopes typically fall out of the rain sooner, meaning that concentrations are heaviest in coastal areas.

1,6 There are other uses of stable isotopes in law enforcement. The same isotopes can also be effective in the fight against counterfeited items including money and consumables. U.S. dollar bills are made from rag-paper containing cotton, which bears the isotopic signature of the water the cotton plants were given while growing. So, if the signature is different from the bills that the government has been printing, they can not only be identified as fake, but also traced to the source of the materials used to make them. **6** Wines and spirits can also be very valuable, so counterfeit versions are available in the market. Since beverages like champagne and Scotch whisky must originate in Champagne, France and Scotland to be considered authentic, their signature can easily determine if they are real or not.

머리카락 내의 이 동위 원소들의 농도는 이 사람이 어디서 지냈는지를 과학자들에게 말해줄 수 있어요. 이는 알려지지 않은 피해자나 용의자의 최근 행적을 제공함으로써 범죄 수사에 도움을 줄 수 있습니다. 이 더 무거운 동위 원소들은 일반적으로 빗물에서 일찍 떨어져 나오는데, 이 말은 해안 지역에서 그 농도가 가장 높다는 의미입니다.

1, 6 안정적인 동위 원소들을 법률 집행에 사용하는 다른 방법도 있습니다. 위에서 언급한 동위 원소들은 돈이나 소모품을 포함하는 위조 물품 퇴치에도 효율적일 수 있어요. 미국의 달러 지폐는 면을 포함하고 있는 넝마로 만든 종이로 만들어지는데, 이 넝마 종이는 목화가 자라는 동안 주어진 물의 동위 원소적 특징을 가지고 있습니다. 그래서 만약 어떠한 특징이 정부에서 인쇄한 지폐의 특징들과 다르면 위조라고 확인할 수 있을 뿐만 아니라, 이 위조 지폐들을 만드는 데 사용된 재료의 근원까지 추적할 수 있어요. **6** 와인과 술 역시 매우 높은 가치를 지니고 있을 수 있어서 시장에서 위조품들을 찾아볼 수 있습니다. 샴페인이나 스카치 위스키와 같은 주류들은 진품으로 인정되려면 프랑스의 샹파뉴 지역과 스코틀랜드에서 만들어져야만 하기 때문에, 동위 원소의 특징은 이 주류들이 진짜인지 모조품인지 쉽게 알아낼 수 있죠.

1. What is the main topic of the lecture?

Ⓐ Hydrogen concentration in rainwater in recent years
Ⓑ Radioactive decay and the half-lives of certain isotopes
Ⓒ Different properties of stable and unstable isotopes
Ⓓ Various uses of stable isotopes in law enforcement

2. According to the lecture, what are the characteristics of isotopes? Choose 2 answers.

Ⓐ They have the same number of neutrons as their normal atomic element.
Ⓑ They have a different mass number than their normal atomic element.
Ⓒ When they are separated, they produce radioactive waste.
Ⓓ When they are unstable, they discard extra neutrons.

3. What is the professor's opinion about stable isotopes?

Ⓐ He thinks they are important, especially in the field of law enforcement.
Ⓑ He knows that their use should be developed further in the future.

1. 강의의 주제는 무엇인가?

Ⓐ 최근 수년간 강수에서의 수소 농도
Ⓑ 특정 동위 원소들의 방사성 붕괴와 반감기
Ⓒ 안정적 동위 원소와 불안정한 동위 원소의 다른 속성들
Ⓓ 법률 집행에서의 안정적 동위 원소의 다양한 쓰임

2. 강의에 따르면, 동위 원소의 특징은 무엇인가?
두 개를 고르시오.

Ⓐ 보통 원소와 똑같은 수의 중성자를 가지고 있다.
Ⓑ 보통 원소와 다른 질량수를 가지고 있다.
Ⓒ 분리되면 방사성 폐기물을 만들어낸다.
Ⓓ 불안정한 상태에서는 남는 중성자를 버린다.

3. 안정적인 동위 원소에 대한 교수의 의견은 무엇인가?

Ⓐ 법률 집행 분야에서 특히 중요하다고 생각한다.
Ⓑ 이들의 사용이 미래에 더욱 발전되어야 한다는 것을 알고 있다.

Ⓒ He believes that they should be treated carefully because of their nature.
Ⓓ He feels that their use is limited to just a few applications.

4. Why does the professor mention hydrogen?
Ⓐ To illustrate the difference between hydrogen and deuterium
Ⓑ To introduce a widely used type of isotope and its applications
Ⓒ To explain how it is the most easily found element on the Earth
Ⓓ To describe the role it plays in predicting criminal acts

5. Why is deuterium important in the area of forensic science?
Ⓐ It is most commonly found in lakes, rivers, and oceans.
Ⓑ It can provide a person's current whereabouts.
Ⓒ Its concentration differs depending on the location of the water source.
Ⓓ Its abundance in rainwater can provide environmental information.

6. What can be inferred about counterfeited items?
Ⓐ Stable isotopes can identify if they are real or fake.
Ⓑ Stable isotopes are used to produce counterfeited money.
Ⓒ Most of them contain stable isotopes in their signature.
Ⓓ Their location can make stable isotopes unstable.

Ⓒ 이들의 특성 때문에 조심스럽게 다루어져야 한다고 믿는다.
Ⓓ 이들의 사용이 몇 가지 응용법에만 국한되어 있다고 느낀다.

4. 교수는 왜 수소를 언급하는가?
Ⓐ 수소와 듀테륨의 차이에 대해 묘사하려고
Ⓑ 널리 사용되는 종류의 동위 원소와 그 응용법을 소개하려고
Ⓒ 수소가 어떻게 지구에서 가장 쉽게 발견되는 원소인지 설명하려고
Ⓓ 범죄 행위 예측에서 수소가 맡고 있는 역할을 묘사하려고

5. 법의학에 있어 듀테륨은 왜 중요한가?
Ⓐ 호수, 강, 그리고 바다에서 가장 흔히 발견된다.
Ⓑ 어떤 인물의 현재 행방을 알려줄 수 있다.
Ⓒ 수원의 위치에 따라 농도가 달라진다.
Ⓓ 강수에 풍부하게 들어 있어서 환경적 정보를 제공해 준다.

6. 위조 물품에 대해 무엇을 추론할 수 있는가?
Ⓐ 안정적 동위 원소가 이들이 진짜인지 가짜인지를 알아낼 수 있다.
Ⓑ 안정적 동위 원소는 위조 지폐 생산에 사용된다.
Ⓒ 대부분이 특징으로 안정적 동위 원소를 가지고 있다.
Ⓓ 이들의 위치가 안정적 동위 원소를 불안정하게 만들 수 있다.

어휘 isotope n 동위 원소 | variant n 변종 | possess v 소유하다 | neutron n 중성자 | proton n 양성자 | electron n 전자 | occupy v 차지하다, 사용하다 | periodic table 주기율표 | hence adv 이런 이유로 | contain v 함유하다 | differ v 다르다 | mass number 질량수 | separate v 분리하다 | molecule n 분자 | unstable adj 불안정한 | shed v 떨어뜨리다, 흘려버리다 | basis n 이유, 근거, 기초 | emission n 방출 | radiation n 방사선 | stable adj 안정된 | decay v 붕괴하다 | concentration n 농도 | endure v 견디다, 인내하다 | establish v 설립하다, 수립하다 | property n 속성 | valuable adj 귀중한 | law enforcement 법률 집행 | hydrogen n 수소 | existence n 존재 | deuterium n 듀테륨, 중수소 | tritium n 트리튬, 삼중수소 | radioactive adj 방사능의 | immutable adj 불변의 | forensic scientist 법의학자 | component n 요소 | oxygen n 산소 | surface water 표층수 | replenish v 다시 채우다, 보충하다 | evaporation n 증발 | ratio n 비율 | localize v 현지화하다 | variation n 변화 | altitude n 고도 | water cycle 물 순환 | signature n 특징 | distinguishable adj 구별할 수 있는 | approximately adv 거의, 대략 | consume v 소모하나 | aid v 돕나 | criminal investigation 범죄 수사 | victim n 피해자 | suspect n 용의자 | typically adv 보통, 일반적으로 | coastal adj 해안의 | counterfeit v 위조하다 | consumable n 소모품 | rag-paper n 넝마로 만든 종이 | bear v 가지다, 지니다 | identify v 확인하다 | fake adj 가짜의 | trace v 추적하다, 밝혀내다 | authentic adj 진품의, 진짜의

Lesson 08 Communications

본서 | P. 220

Test

1. B **2.** B **3.** C **4.** D **5.** A **6.** A, D

Test 본서 | P. 221

Man: Professor

[1-6] Listen to part of a lecture in a communications class.

M Since large-scale transmission of electricity was achieved in the 19th century, there have been countless inventions that have made our lives more convenient. One of the first appliances that made its way into homes was electric lights, and these were quickly followed by other inventions like refrigerators and vacuum cleaners. 1 However, the invention that had the most significant effect was the radio.

For a radio to work, an electromagnetic signal is sent out by a transmitter and received by an antenna, which transfers the signal to a receiver that can turn the signal back into sound. Radio broadcasting began in the early 20th century with messages sent in Morse code, much like a telegraph. 2 The important difference between the two was that a telegraph had to be linked to its message source by a wire. Radio is wireless, which makes it far more useful.

It is unknown who achieved the first wireless signal with enough power to carry voice and music. However, many amateur radio stations existed by 1910, and the U.S. government began regulating their transmissions in 1912 to pave the way for commercial broadcasters. However, there was a great deal of doubt about this. Newspaper publishers realized that radio broadcasting had great potential, but they were unsure if it would take off. So, many of them had their own transmission equipment installed secretly. Then, the election results of the 1920 election were broadcast by radio, and they knew it would become significant. The first commercial radio broadcasters received their licenses, and by 1928 there were three national radio networks. Two were owned by the National Broadcasting Company and one by the Columbia Broadcasting System.

3 What made radio in the U.S. unique was that it was commercialized. Unlike in the U.K., where radio stations were funded with funds from taxes, American radio stations were funded by the companies that they played advertisements for. Ownership of radio receivers

남자: 교수

커뮤니케이션 강의의 일부를 들으시오.

남 대규모의 송전이 19세기에 이루어지면서, 우리의 삶을 더욱 편안하게 만들어준 수많은 발명품들이 있었습니다. 가정에 처음으로 도입된 기기들 중 하나는 전등이었고, 전구의 뒤를 이어 냉장고와 청소기 등 다른 발명품들이 빠르게 등장했어요. 1그러나 가장 중요한 영향을 끼친 발명품은 바로 라디오였습니다.

라디오가 작동하기 위해서는 전자기 신호가 송전기에 의해 보내지고 안테나에 의해 이 신호를 전달받게 되는데, 이 안테나는 신호를 수신기로 전달하고 수신기가 이 신호를 소리로 바꾸게 됩니다. 라디오 방송은 20세기 초기에 시작되었는데, 전신과 흡사하게 모스 부호로 메시지를 전달했어요. 2 전신과 라디오의 중요한 차이점은, 전신은 메시지의 근원에 선으로 연결되어 있어야 했다는 겁니다. 라디오는 무선이기에 훨씬 더 유용하죠.

목소리와 음악을 전송하기에 충분한 힘을 가진 최초의 무선 신호를 성공적으로 만들어낸 사람이 누구인지는 알려져 있지 않습니다. 하지만 1910년 무렵에는 다수의 아마추어 라디오 방송국들이 존재했고, 미국 정부는 1912년에 민간 방송을 위한 길을 닦기 위해 이들 방송국들의 전파를 통제하기 시작했습니다. 그러나 이에 대해서는 많은 의심이 있었습니다. 신문사들은 라디오 방송이 엄청난 가능성을 가지고 있다는 것을 깨달았지만 성공할지는 확신하지 못했습니다. 그래서 다수가 비밀리에 자기들만의 전파 장치를 설치했습니다. 그 뒤 1920년의 선거 결과가 라디오로 방송되었고, 이들은 라디오가 중요해질 것이라는 걸 알았습니다. 최초의 민간 라디오 방송사들이 허가를 받았고, 1928년까지 세 개의 국영 라디오 네트워크가 생겼습니다. 그들 중 둘은 전미방송회사의 소유였고, 나머지 하나는 컬럼비아 방송사의 소유였습니다.

3 미국 라디오의 특별한 점은 바로 상업화되었다는 것입니다. 세금으로 라디오 방송국들의 자금이 지원되었던 영국과 달리 미국의 라디오 방송국들은 이 방송국들에서 광고를 내보내는 회사들에 의해 지원을 받았죠. 라디오 수신기 소유는 30년대에 급

Lesson 08 Lectures

skyrocketed in the thirties, and radio became an integral part of people's lives. Stations broadcast a variety of programming, including music programs. This was particularly important to the popularity of Jazz music, as the youth of the nation were exposed to this new form of music by radio. Sports programming was also extremely popular as it allowed fans to listen to their favorite teams' play instead of going to the stadium.

4 Although radio was mainly used for entertainment, the live reports of dramatic events that it offered also boosted its popularity. President Franklin D. Roosevelt was the first president to exploit this new medium. During the Great Depression and the Second World War, he made 30 broadcasts called "fireside chats." During these talks, he dispelled rumors and explained the reasoning behind new policies. This new type of direct and intimate communication between the president and his people made him extremely popular.

After the war, portable radio receivers became more affordable, and car manufacturers began installing them. This allowed people to listen to the radio during their commute or while traveling. However, the development of television eroded radio's position as the main source of entertainment and news, so the stations adapted. **5** They shifted the balance in favor of music programs, and news and other features were spread out between them. The first of these was the top 40 format wherein the most recently released songs were played, giving birth to pop music. These music programs became dominant as network control lessened. Local stations were told to devote a certain amount of their broadcast time to particular programs and to play certain songs, but their program hosts were given a lot of freedom. These people came to be referred to as disc jockeys, and they became famous in their communities.

Then FM radio was introduced, which allowed for high fidelity stereo sound to be broadcast by using frequency modulation. This format allowed for very high-quality sound, and it was quickly adopted by another youth music movement: rock-and-roll. Rock stations became common, and other genres also switched over from AM to FM. **6** Little else changed until the 70s and 80s, when talk radio took off. DJs gave way to talk show hosts who used their programs to interview celebrities and discuss current events and politics. Eventually, they began airing calls to

증했고, 라디오는 사람들의 삶에 필수적인 부분이 되었습니다. 방송국들은 다양한 프로그램들을 방송했는데, 여기에는 음악 프로그램들도 포함되었습니다. 이는 재즈 음악의 인기에 특히 중요했는데, 미국의 젊은 세대들이 라디오에 의해 이 새로운 형태의 음악에 노출되었기 때문입니다. 스포츠 프로그램 역시 사람들이 경기장에 가는 대신 좋아하는 팀의 경기를 들을 수 있도록 해주었기 때문에 엄청나게 많은 인기를 얻었습니다.

4 라디오는 주로 오락을 위해 사용되었지만, 극적인 사건을 전해주는 생방송 보도 역시 라디오의 인기를 크게 높였습니다. 프랭클린 D. 루즈벨트 대통령은 이 새로운 매체를 이용한 최초의 대통령이었어요. 대공황과 제2차 세계 대전 동안 그는 '노변 담화'라 불리는 30번의 방송을 했습니다. 이 담화 동안 그는 소문을 일축했고 새 정책들이 만들어진 이유를 설명하기도 했습니다. 대통령과 국민들 사이의 이러한 직접적이고 친밀한 새로운 형식의 소통은 대통령을 매우 인기 있는 인물로 만들었습니다.

전쟁이 끝난 뒤, 휴대용 라디오 수신기들은 비용이 더 저렴해졌으며 자동차 제조 업체에서 이들을 차에 설치하기 시작했습니다. 이는 사람들이 통근을 하거나 여행을 하는 동안 라디오를 들을 수 있게 했죠. 그러나 TV의 발전이 뉴스와 오락의 주된 원천이었던 라디오의 위치를 약화시켰고 라디오 방송국들은 이에 적응해 변했습니다. **5** 이들은 음악 프로그램에 비중을 더 두었고 뉴스와 다른 특징의 방송들은 음악 프로그램 사이로 분산시켰습니다. 그 첫 번째는 가장 최신 발매된 음악들을 상위 40위 형식으로 방송하는 것이었는데, 이것이 팝 음악을 탄생시켰습니다. 이 음악 프로그램들은 네트워크 통제가 느슨해지면서 주된 프로그램이 되었습니다. 지역의 라디오 방송국들은 일정한 양의 방송 시간을 특정한 프로그램과 특정한 음악에 할애하도록 되어 있었지만 프로그램 진행자들에게는 많은 자유가 주어졌습니다. 이 사람들은 디스크 자키라고 불리게 되었고 그들의 공동체에서 유명해졌죠.

그 뒤 FM 라디오가 도입되었는데, 이는 주파수 변조를 이용하여 고성능 스테레오 사운드가 방송될 수 있도록 했습니다. 이 형식은 매우 질이 좋은 소리를 들려줄 수 있었는데, 또 다른 젊은이들의 음악 운동인 로큰롤에 빠르게 적용되었습니다. 록 음악 방송국이 흔해졌고, 다른 장르들 역시 AM에서 FM으로 바뀌었어요. **6** 70년대와 80년대에는 전화 토론 프로그램이 시작된 것 외에는 많이 바뀐 것이 없었습니다. DJ들은 토크쇼 진행자들에게 자리를 내주었는데 그들은 유명인들을 인터뷰하고 시사와 정치를 논의하는 데 프로그램을 이용했어요. 결국, 이들은 전화 통화를 방송에 내보내기 시작해서 대중

the station, allowing the public to achieve momentary fame. **6(A)** Today, digital music recordings and the Internet have erased much of radio's power, but the industry continues to attract listeners.

이 순간적인 유명세를 얻을 수 있도록 했습니다. **6(A)** 오늘날 디지털 음악 녹음과 인터넷이 라디오의 영향력을 대부분을 지워버렸지만 라디오 업계는 계속해서 청취자들을 끌어들이고 있습니다.

1. What is the lecture mainly about?

Ⓐ The changes in people's perception of radio
Ⓑ The development of radio as a medium
Ⓒ The influence of radio on forms of communication
Ⓓ The relationship between radio and politics

2. According to the lecture, why was radio more useful than the telegraph?

Ⓐ Its operation was much simpler than that of the telegraph.
Ⓑ It did not have to be linked to the message source by wire.
Ⓒ It was able to receive and send messages through wire.
Ⓓ It used hardware that was much more inexpensive.

3. What made radio in the U.S. different from that of other countries?

Ⓐ It charged companies higher costs for advertising their products.
Ⓑ Most U.S. radio stations were owned by private companies.
Ⓒ Companies that were promoted on air financed U.S. radio.
Ⓓ It was supported mostly by taxes and was owned by the government.

4. Why does the professor mention "fireside chats"?

Ⓐ To illustrate the relationship between radio and wars
Ⓑ To show the strong influence of radio on U.S. history
Ⓒ To examine the first time radio was used for politics
Ⓓ To provide an example of what boosted radio's popularity

5. What can be inferred about the change in radio after the development of television?

Ⓐ It put more emphasis on music and eventually influenced the music industry.
Ⓑ It started to prefer news programs over other programs.
Ⓒ It moved from having a few channels to more than a hundred of them.
Ⓓ It gave birth to disc jockeys, who played live music on radio shows.

1. 강의는 주로 무엇에 대한 것인가?

Ⓐ 라디오에 대한 사람들의 인식 변화
Ⓑ 매체로써의 라디오의 변화
Ⓒ 커뮤니케이션의 형태에 라디오가 미친 영향
Ⓓ 라디오와 정치의 관계

2. 강의에 따르면, 라디오는 왜 전신보다 더 유용했는가?

Ⓐ 작동이 전신보다 훨씬 더 쉬웠다.
Ⓑ 선에 의해 메시지의 근원에 연결될 필요가 없었다.
Ⓒ 선을 통해 메시지를 주고받을 수 있었다.
Ⓓ 훨씬 값이 덜 나가는 하드웨어를 사용했다.

3. 미국의 라디오를 다른 나라의 라디오와 다르게 만든 것은 무엇인가?

Ⓐ 회사들의 상품 광고에 더 높은 비용을 청구했다.
Ⓑ 대부분의 미국 라디오 방송국들은 사기업들에 의해 소유되었다.
Ⓒ 방송에서 광고된 회사들이 미국의 라디오를 경제적으로 지원했다.
Ⓓ 대부분 세금으로 지원되었으며 정부의 소유였다.

4. 교수는 왜 '노변담화'를 언급하는가?

Ⓐ 라디오와 전쟁의 관계를 묘사하기 위해
Ⓑ 라디오가 미국 역사에 끼친 강한 영향력을 보이기 위해
Ⓒ 라디오가 정치에 이용된 최초의 사례를 들기 위해
Ⓓ 라디오의 인기를 높인 것에 관한 예시를 제공하기 위해

5. TV의 발전 이후 라디오에 일어난 변화에 대해 무엇을 추론할 수 있는가?

Ⓐ 음악에 더 중점을 두었고 결국 음악 산업에 영향을 끼쳤다.
Ⓑ 다른 프로그램들보다 뉴스 프로그램을 더 선호하기 시작했다.
Ⓒ 소수의 채널만 있던 것에서 수백 개의 채널이 넘도록 변화되었다.
Ⓓ 라디오 쇼에서 라이브 음악을 연주하는 디스크 자키를 탄생시켰다.

6. **According to the lecture, what is true about radio today?**
Ⓐ There are fewer disc jockeys compared to the past.
Ⓑ Most people prefer watching television to listening to radio.
Ⓒ Its accessibility and use have improved from before.
Ⓓ Radio programs expanded beyond the area of music.

6. **강의에 따르면, 오늘날의 라디오에 대해 옳은 것은 무엇인가?**
Ⓐ 과거에 비해 소수의 디스크 자키들이 있다.
Ⓑ 대부분의 사람들이 TV 시청을 라디오 듣기보다 더 선호한다.
Ⓒ 그 접근성과 사용성이 전보다 더 향상되었다.
Ⓓ 라디오 프로그램들이 음악의 영역을 넘어 확장되었다.

어휘 large-scale adj 대규모의 | transmission n 전송, 송신 | electricity n 전기 | countless adj 무수한 | invention n 발명품, 발명 | convenient adj 편리한 | appliance n 기기 | electric light 전등 | refrigerator n 냉장고 | vacuum cleaner 청소기 | significant adj 중요한 | electromagnetic signal 전자기 신호 | transmitter n 송신기 | antenna n 안테나 | transfer v 전송하다 | receiver n 수신기 | broadcasting n 방송 | telegraph n 전신 | wire n 전선 | wireless adj 무선의 | amateur n 아마추어 | regulate v 규제하다 | commercial adj 상업의 | doubt n 의심 | publisher n 발행인, 출판사 | potential n 가능성 | equipment n 장비 | install v 설치하다 | secretly adv 비밀리에 | election n 선거 | license n 허가 | commercialize v 상업화하다 | fund v 자금을 대다 n 자금 | advertisement n 광고 | ownership n 소유 | skyrocket v 급등하다 | integral adj 필수적인 | popularity n 인기 | expose v 노출시키다 | mainly adv 주로 | entertainment n 즐거움, 오락 | dramatic adj 극적인 | boost v 북돋우다 | exploit v 이용하다, 활용하다 | medium n 수단, 매체 | Great Depression 대공황 | fireside n 난롯가 | dispel v 떨쳐 버리다, 없애다 | direct adj 직접적인 | intimate adj 친밀한 | portable adj 휴대용의, 휴대가 쉬운 | affordable adj (비용을) 감당할 수 있는 | manufacturer n 제조자, 생산자 | commute n 통근 | erode v 약화시키다 | adapt v 적응하다 | shift v 움직이다 | dominant adj 주된 | devote v 바치다, 기울이다 | introduce v 소개하다 | high fidelity (라디오, 전축이 원음을 재생하는) 고충실도, 하이파이 | frequency modulation 주파수 변조 | celebrity n 유명인 | air v 방송하다 | momentary adj 순간적인, 찰나의 | erase v 지우다 | industry n 산업, 업계 | attract v 끌어들이다, 마음을 끌다

Lesson 09 Economics

본서 | P. 223

Test

1. B 2. B 3. C 4. A, B 5. D 6. C

Test

본서 | P. 224

Man: Student | Woman: Professor

[1-6] Listen to part of a discussion in an economics class.

W **1** Nearly all companies or corporate organizations will face a crisis during their existence, and how they handle that situation could very well determine their entire future. In a broad sense, like we discussed earlier, a crisis is a significant threat to the operations of a company that can have negative repercussions on the organization, its stockholders, or the entire industry if not dealt with effectively. A crisis typically consists of a threat to an organization that is unexpected and requires a rapid response. Any crisis carries with it three interconnected threats. Can someone tell me what they are?

M They are public safety, financial loss, and loss of reputation.

W Thank you, Chris. Yes, crises like product harm and industrial accidents can directly threaten people with injury

남자: 학생 | 여자: 교수

경제학 수업 중 토론의 일부를 들으시오.

여 **1** 거의 모든 회사나 법인 조직들은 존재하는 동안 위기를 마주하게 되는데, 이들이 그 상황을 어떻게 처리하느냐가 기업의 미래 전체를 결정할 수 있습니다. 우리가 저번에 이야기했듯이 좀 더 넓게 보자면, 위기는 기업 경영에 커다란 위협입니다. 효과적으로 처리하지 않는 경우에는 기업과 주주, 나아가서는 산업 전반에 부정적 영향을 줄 수 있습니다. 일반적으로 위기는 예측하지 못했으며 빠른 대처를 필요로 하는, 회사에 위험이 되는 요소로 구성되어 있습니다. 모든 위기가 서로 연결된 세 종류의 위험을 불러오죠. 이것들이 뭔지 누가 말해줄 수 있나요?

남 공공의 안전, 재정적 손실, 그리고 평판의 손실입니다.

여 고마워요, 크리스. 네, 제품의 위험성, 산업 재해와 같은 위기들은 부상 혹은 인명 손실로 사람들을 직

and loss of life. They can also inflict financial losses by disrupting normal operations, decreasing market share and stock purchase rates, or by incurring lawsuits by victims and fines. 1 So, we need to learn the ways to deal with a crisis effectively to avoid those three interconnected threats. 2 First, the worse a crisis is, the more important it becomes to make a quick, concise, and accurate statement to the public regarding the event. If the crisis presents a direct and immediate threat to the public, then they must be informed as rapidly as possible. For example, in the case of a chemical spill, people in the vicinity must be told how dangerous the chemical is and whether or not they should evacuate. Failure to do so could result in avoidable casualties, which will severely damage the organization's reputation when their preventable nature becomes public knowledge. As you would expect, it can also result in massive financial losses due to litigation. 3 In less dangerous situations, the failure to quickly address the public can result in misinformation. If an organization does not release a statement quickly, people begin to speculate, which often results in inaccurate rumors spreading. People want to be informed, so they will listen to anyone who seems confident about what they are saying.

And, that brings up another important point. Organizations should carefully select their spokespeople and train them accordingly. The statement "no comment" sounds like an admission of guilt, but a poorly delivered announcement can be equally damaging. 4(A) A statement should be clear and use layman's terms, 4(B) and the speaker should maintain eye contact and avoid dissembling language like "uh..." and "er..." and making nervous gestures. They must also be provided with the most accurate and current information about the situation. If false or incomplete information is given, retractions and corrections can be made, but credibility will already be lost. And, this also has a chance of bringing big financial losses to the organization.

5 On the subject of credibility, it is extremely important that the organization admit responsibility for the crisis. The initial press release must acknowledge their guilt and express their apologies while at the same time showing determination to resolve the situation and take care of those who have been affected. If an organization is only partly at fault, then discovery of their limited responsibility will improve their reputation once the crisis has been resolved. 5 However, if they try to shift the blame onto other parties involved, it can have disastrous results for public sentiment. This type

접적으로 위협할 수 있어요. 또한 기업의 정상적인 운영을 방해해서 시장 점유율과 주식 매입률을 감소시키거나 피해자들의 소송과 벌금을 초래하여 재정적 손실을 가져옵니다. 1 그래서 우리는 이 세 개의 상호 연결된 위험들을 피하기 위해 위기에 효율적으로 대처하는 방법들을 배워야 합니다.

2 먼저, 위기가 심각하면 할수록 위기에 대해 대중에게 빠르고, 간결하고, 정확한 진술을 하는 것이 더욱 더 중요해집니다. 위기가 대중에게 직접적이고 즉각적인 위험이 될 경우, 가능한 한 빨리 대중에게 이에 대해 알려야만 해요. 예를 들어, 화학 물질 유출이 일어났을 경우 인근의 사람들은 이 물질이 얼마나 위험한지 그리고 대피를 해야 하는지 아닌지에 대해 알아야 합니다. 이에 실패하면 막을 수 있었던 사상자가 발생할 수 있고, 그걸 막는 것이 가능했다는 것을 대중이 알게 되면 기업의 평판을 심각하게 훼손할 수 있습니다. 예상할 수 있듯 소송으로 인한 막대한 재정적 손실로 이어질 수 있습니다. 3 조금 덜 위험한 상황의 경우, 대중에게 빠르게 상황 전달을 하지 않으면 잘못된 정보가 생겨날 수 있어요. 기업에서 성명서를 빨리 발표하지 않으면 사람들은 추측을 하기 시작할 것이고, 이는 부정확한 소문이 퍼지게 만듭니다. 사람들은 정보를 얻고 싶어하기 때문에 자신이 말하는 것에 확신이 있어 보이는 사람들의 말을 듣게 되죠.

그리고 이것은 또 다른 중요한 점을 보여줍니다. 기업에서는 대변인을 신중하게 선택하고 그에 따라 이들을 교육시켜야 합니다. "드릴 말씀이 없습니다"라는 말은 책임을 인정하는 것처럼 들리지만, 좋지 않게 전달된 발표 역시 마찬가지로 기업에 손해를 입힐 수 있습니다. 4(A) 발표는 명확하고 일반인들이 쓰는 용어를 사용해야 하며, 4(B) 발표자는 사람들과 눈을 계속 맞추면서 "어..."나 "음..." 같은 숨기는 듯한 말이나 긴장한 제스처를 하는 걸 피해야 합니다. 또한 상황에 대해 가장 정확한 최신 정보를 가지고 있어야 합니다. 잘못되었거나 불완전한 정보가 주어지면 철회와 수정을 하는 것은 가능하지만 신뢰는 이미 잃은 것입니다. 그리고 이 역시 기업에 커다란 재정적 손실을 초래할 가능성이 있습니다.

5 신뢰도에 대해서 말인데, 기업이 위기에 대한 책임을 인정하는 것이 정말로 중요합니다. 초기 보도에서는 그들의 책임을 인정하고 사의를 표하는 한편, 상황을 해결하고 피해를 입은 사람들을 책임지려는 결심 역시 보여야 합니다. 만약 기업이 부분적으로만 잘못이 있다면, 그들이 제한적으로만 책임이 있었다는 걸 알게 되면 위기가 해결될 때 기업의 평판이 다시 개선될 것입니다. 5 그러나 만약 위기에 관련된 다른 이들의 탓을 하려 한다면 대중의 정서에 처참한 결과를 가져올 수 있죠. 이런 종류의

of situation often affects manufacturing companies that have to outsource parts. 5, 6 For example, carmakers often purchase components from other manufacturers, so fixing blame can be difficult. In one case, tires on SUVs began having catastrophic failures, but the tire company and the SUV maker blamed each other after first blaming the vehicle owners! In addition, they failed to make it clear what steps they intended to take to remedy the situation, until they were forced to testify at a government hearing. Needless to say, the reputations of both companies suffered.

상황은 외부 업체에 위탁하는 일이 많은 제조회사들에 종종 영향을 미칩니다. 5, 6 예를 들어, 자동차 제조 업체에서는 종종 다른 생산업체들로부터 부품을 구입하므로 한 사람의 탓만을 하긴 어렵죠. 한 사례에서는, SUV 차량들의 타이어에서 정말로 심각한 결함이 일어나기 시작했지만 타이어 회사와 SUV 제조 업체가 먼저 자동차 주인들을 탓한 뒤 서로를 탓하기 시작했어요! 그리고 그들은 정부 공판에서 증언하도록 요구되기 전까지 이 상황을 해결하기 위한 절차를 분명히 하는 데 실패했습니다. 말할 필요도 없이, 두 기업 다 평판에 심각한 영향을 입었죠.

1. What is the discussion mainly about?

Ⓐ Varying types of crises and how they influence people's lives
Ⓑ Different ways to deal with a crisis that a company encountered
Ⓒ People's opinion on a company's credibility in times of crisis
Ⓓ Examples of some companies that dealt with crises wisely

2. When there is a crisis, why is it important to make a quick statement to the public?

Ⓐ The public wants to know every detail about the crisis since they are curious.
Ⓑ If the crisis is a serious one, it is directly related to saving people's lives.
Ⓒ Failure to do so could result in even bigger threats to the entire nation.
Ⓓ It is required by the United States Constitution since the beginning of the 20th century.

3. What can be inferred about misinformation?

Ⓐ It will get out of control and governmental interference would be required.
Ⓑ It has a high chance of preventing the damage done to a company.
Ⓒ It often results from a company's delayed response regarding a crisis.
Ⓓ It can teach people the significance of dealing with different crises.

4. According to the discussion, what is required of a company's carefully selected spokesperson? Choose 2 answers.

Ⓐ Conveying information to people by using words that are easy to understand

1. 토론은 주로 무엇에 대한 것인가?

Ⓐ 위기의 다양한 종류들과 이들이 사람들의 삶에 어떻게 영향을 미치는지
Ⓑ 기업이 위기에 부딪혔을 때 이에 대처하는 다양한 방법들
Ⓒ 위기의 순간에 기업의 신뢰도에 대한 사람들의 의견
Ⓓ 위기에 현명하게 대처한 몇몇 기업들의 예시

2. 위기가 생겼을 경우, 왜 대중에게 빠른 성명을 발표하는 것이 중요한가?

Ⓐ 대중은 궁금해하기 때문에 사건의 모든 세부 사항에 대해 알고 싶어한다.
Ⓑ 위기가 심각할 경우 이는 사람들의 생명을 구하는 것과 직접적으로 연관이 있다.
Ⓒ 그렇게 하지 않을 경우 나라 전체에 더 큰 위험이 야기될 수 있다.
Ⓓ 20세기 초 이래 미국 헌법에 의해 요구되는 것이다.

3. 잘못된 정보에 대해 무엇을 추론할 수 있는가?

Ⓐ 통제를 벗어날 것이고 국가의 개입이 필요하게 될 것이다.
Ⓑ 기업에 손해가 일어나는 것을 막을 가능성이 높다.
Ⓒ 위기에 대한 기업의 늑장 대응으로 인해 종종 발생한다.
Ⓓ 여러 종류의 위기에 대처하는 것의 중요성을 사람들에게 가르쳐줄 수 있다.

4. 토론에 따르면, 기업에서 신중하게 선택한 대변인에게는 무엇이 요구되는가? 두 개를 고르시오.

Ⓐ 이해하기 쉬운 단어를 사용하여 사람들에게 정보를 전달하는 것

Ⓑ Acting confidently by making eye contact and not making distracting gestures
Ⓒ Providing detailed information to the press, Internet, and broadcasters
Ⓓ Cooperating with government authorities regardless of the size of the crisis

Ⓑ 시선을 맞추며 자신 있게 행동하는 것과 방해되는 제스처를 하지 않는 것
Ⓒ 언론, 인터넷, 방송국에 자세한 정보를 제공하는 것
Ⓓ 위기의 크기에 관계 없이 정부당국자들과 협력하는 것

5. Why does the professor mention carmakers?
Ⓐ To tell the students that carmakers have dealt with some crises recently
Ⓑ To give an example of a good way to take responsibility in times of crisis
Ⓒ To describe the hardships and results they face when a crisis occurs
Ⓓ To point out the significance of a company taking responsibility for a crisis

5. 교수는 왜 자동차 제조 업체를 언급하는가?
Ⓐ 자동차 제조 업체들이 최근 몇몇 위기에 대처해왔다는 것을 학생들에게 말해주려고
Ⓑ 위기의 순간에 책임을 지는 좋은 방법의 예시를 들려고
Ⓒ 위기가 발생했을 경우 자동차 제조 업체들이 부딪히는 어려움과 결과를 서술하려고
Ⓓ 기업이 위기에 대한 책임을 지는 것의 중요성을 강조하려고

6. Listen again to part of the discussion. Then answer the question.

W For example, carmakers often purchase components from other manufacturers, so fixing blame can be difficult.

Why does the professor say this:

W so fixing blame can be difficult.

Ⓐ She is explaining why companies try to blame the customers for the problem.
Ⓑ She is saying that many companies often fail to acknowledge their mistakes.
Ⓒ She is showing why companies should accept responsibility even if they are unsure.
Ⓓ She is emphasizing that customers want to know who the guilty party is.

6. 토론의 일부를 다시 듣고 질문에 답하시오.

여 예를 들어, 자동차 제조 업체에서는 종종 다른 생산업체들로부터 부품을 구입하므로 한 사람의 탓만을 하긴 어렵죠.

교수는 왜 이렇게 말하는가:

여 한 사람의 탓만을 하긴 어렵죠.

Ⓐ 왜 회사들이 문제에 관해 고객 탓을 하려고 하는지 설명하고 있다.
Ⓑ 많은 회사들이 실수를 인정하는 데 실패한다고 말하고 있다.
Ⓒ 회사가 확실하지 않더라도 왜 책임을 받아들여야 하는지 보여주고 있다.
Ⓓ 고객들은 잘못한 쪽이 누구인지 알고 싶어 한다고 강조하고 있다.

어휘 corporate organization 법인 조직 | face v 마주보다, 대면하다 | crisis n 위기, 고비 | existence n 존재, 현존 | handle v 다루다, 처리하다 | entire adj 전체의 | broad adj 넓은 | significant adj 중요한 | threat n 위협 | operation n 사업, 영업 | negative adj 부정적인 | repercussion n 영향 | stockholder n 주주 | industry n 산업, 업계 | effectively adv 효과적으로 | typically adv 일반적으로 | consist of ~로 구성되다 | unexpected adj 예상치 못한 | rapid adj 빠른 | interconnected adj 상호 연결된 | public safety 공공의 안전 | reputation n 평판, 명성 | industrial accident 산업 재해 | directly adv 직접적으로 | injury n 부상 | inflict v (해를) 가하다, 입히다 | disrupt v 방해하다, 지장을 주다 | decrease v 감소시키다 | market share 시장 점유율 | stock purchase rate 주식 매입률 | incur v 초래하다 | lawsuit n 소송, 고소 | victim n 피해자 | fine n 벌금 | avoid v 피하다 | concise adj 간결한, 축약된 | accurate adj 정확한 | statement n 성명, 진술 | present v 보여주다, 나타내다 | immediate adj 즉각적인 | inform v 알리다, 통지하다 | chemical spill 화학 물질 유출 | vicinity n 인근, 부근 | evacuate v 대피하다 | failure n 실패 | casualty n 피해자, 사상자 | severely adv 심하게 | damage v 손상시키다 | preventable adj 막을 수 있는 | massive adj 거대한, 엄청난 | litigation n 소송, 고소 | address v 연설하다 | misinformation n 오보 | speculate v 추측하다 | rumor n 소문, 유언비어 | spread v 퍼지다 | confident adj 자신감 있는 | carefully adv 주의하여, 조심스럽게 | spokesperson n 대변인 | accordingly adv 그에 따라, 부응하여 | admission n 시인, 인정 | guilt n 죄책감, 책임 | poorly adv 형편없이, 저조하게 | deliver v 연설, 강연 등을 하다 | announcement n 발표 | layman's term 쉬운 단어, 일반적인 단어 | maintain v 유지하다, 지키다 | dissembling adj 꾸미는, 숨기는 | incomplete adj 불완전한, 미완성의 | retraction n 철회, 취소 | correction n 정정, 수정 | credibility n 신뢰성 | admit v 인정하다 | responsibility n 책임 | initial adj 처음의, 초기의 | press release 보도 자료 | apology n 사과 | resolve v 해결하다 | blame v ~를 탓하다 I disastrous adj 처참한 I sentiment n 정서, 감정 I manufacturing n 제조업 I outsource v 외주를 주다, 외부에 위탁하다 I component n 요소, 부품 I catastrophic adj 큰 재앙의 I intend v 의도하다 I remedy v 개선하다, 바로잡다 I testify v 증언하다, 진술하다 I needless adj 불필요한 I suffer v 시달리다, 고통 받다

Lesson 10 Engineering

본서 I P. 226

Test

1. B 2. D 3. A 4. A, B 5. C 6. C

Test

본서 I P. 227

Man: Student | Woman: Professor

[1-6] Listen to part of a discussion in an engineering class.

W The majority of electrical wiring uses copper wire because it has the highest level of conductivity of any non-precious metal. Electrical conductivity measures how efficiently a material is able to transport an electrical charge. Aluminum also conducts electricity fairly well, possessing about 61% of the conductivity of copper. This means that aluminum wire must have a much bigger diameter to carry the same amount of charge as copper wire. 2 Silver, on the other hand, has higher conductivity than copper, rating at about 106% higher than copper. Unfortunately, silver is expensive and very soft, severely limiting its usefulness. Therefore, copper has been the industry standard for power transmission since the 19th century. 1 However, there are other elements and alloys that can reach a state of almost perfect electrical conductivity if they are subjected to the proper conditions. These materials are called superconductors.

3 When they are cooled to below a temperature that is specific to each substance, these materials achieve precisely zero electrical resistance. This phenomenon is called superconductivity, and it was originally discovered by a Dutch physicist named Heike Kamerlingh Onnes in 1911. It is a quantum mechanical phenomenon that is characterized by the total ejection of magnetic field lines from the interior of a material as it enters into its superconducting state.

In any conductive material, its electrical resistance will gradually decrease as its temperature is lowered, but normal conductors still show some amount of resistance even at zero degrees Kelvin, or absolute zero. This is often due to impurities contained in the metal and other defects, but 4(A) superconducting materials behave in a dramatically different way. When they reach their specific critical temperature, the resistance plummets to zero. Unfortunately,

남자: 학생 | 여자: 교수

공학 수업 중 토론의 일부를 들으시오.

여 대다수의 전기 배선은 구리선을 사용하는데, 이는 구리가 비귀금속 중 가장 높은 전도성을 가지고 있기 때문입니다. 전기 전도성은 어떠한 물질이 얼마나 효율적으로 전하를 수송할 수 있는지를 측정합니다. 알루미늄 역시 전도성이 꽤나 높으며 구리의 약 61%의 전도성을 가졌습니다. 이는 같은 양의 전하를 운반하는 데 알루미늄 전선의 지름이 구리 전선보다 더 넓어야 한다는 것을 의미합니다. 2 한편, 은은 구리보다 약 106% 더 높은 전도성을 가지고 있습니다. 불행히도 은은 비쌀 뿐만 아니라 매우 부드러워서 사용에 심각한 제한이 있죠. 그래서 구리가 19세기 이후 송전을 위한 산업 표준이 되어 왔습니다. 1 그러나, 알맞은 환경에 놓이기만 한다면 거의 완벽한 상태의 전기 전도성에 달할 수 있는 다른 원소와 합금이 있습니다. 이 물질들은 초전도체라고 불리죠.

3 각 물질에 특정되어 있는 온도 이하로 물질이 식혀지게 되면, 이 물질들은 정확히 전기 저항이 0인 상태에 이릅니다. 이 현상은 초전도성이라고 불리며 네덜란드의 물리학자인 헤이커 카메를링 오너스에 의해 1911년 발견되었어요. 이 현상은 물질이 초전도 상태에 들어가면 내부에서 자기장선을 완전히 밀쳐 내는 것으로 특징지어진 양자 역학적 현상입니다.

어떠한 전도성을 가진 물질이든 그것의 전기 저항은 온도가 낮아지면 서서히 감소하지만, 보통의 전체들은 켈빈 온도 0도, 즉 절대 영도에서도 여전히 약간의 저항을 보입니다. 이는 종종 금속에 함유된 불순물이나 다른 결함으로 인해 발생하는 것이지만, 4(A) 초전도성 물질들은 극적으로 다르게 반응합니다. 특정 임계 온도에 다다르면 저항값이 0으로 급격히 감소하죠. 불행히도 실험해 본 모든 물

the highest such critical temperature of any tested substance was at around 23 degrees Kelvin, which is an extremely difficult temperature to maintain. **4(B)** One method that was used to do this was to bathe the material in liquid helium, which is quite hard to produce and is therefore far too expensive to use outside of experiments. **4(B), 5** Then, in 1986, other materials were discovered that could achieve critical temperature around 120 K, which can be reached by using liquid nitrogen, a much easier substance to obtain and use.

M Professor, even if liquid nitrogen is much less expensive than helium, doesn't it limit the kinds of applications that superconductors can be used for? I mean, it still seems impractical.

W Well, most of the current uses involve superconducting magnets, which are electromagnets made with coils of superconducting wire. When properly cooled with liquid nitrogen, they generate intense magnetic fields more powerful than almost any conventional electromagnet. Surprisingly, they can actually be cheaper to operate because the coils of superconductive wire do not lose any of the energy put into as heat like the regular ones do. But, you are correct; **6** they are only used for some very specific purposes where the risk of exposure to the coolant is low. They are used in devices where strong magnetic fields are required for them to function like particle accelerators, magnetic separation processes, and mass spectrometers, but most people encounter them in hospitals where they form the essential components of magnetic resonance imaging machines. MRI machines are used widely in hospitals to aid in medical diagnoses without having to resort to technologies that utilize potentially harmful ionizing radiation such as X-ray imaging.

M So, MRIs are not dangerous to patients? They pose no risk to the health of patients?

W No, of course they can be dangerous to particular patients. The powerful magnetic fields that they generate can interfere with electronic implants like pacemakers. They can also affect metal implants like surgical steel pins in bones by causing them to heat up. And, they can cause some physiological effects like nausea and dizziness. Concerns regarding biological iron like the iron in red blood cells have been raised, but no evidence of damage has been recorded.

질의 이러한 임계 온도 중 가장 높은 값은 켈빈 온도로 23도였는데, 이는 극히 유지하기 어려운 온도입니다. **4(B)** 이를 유지하기 위해 사용된 한 가지 방법은 그 물질을 액체 헬륨으로 감싸는 방법이었는데, 액체 헬륨은 상당히 만들기 어렵기 때문에 실험실 밖에서 사용하기에는 매우 비용이 많이 드는 물질입니다. **4(B), 5** 그러던 중 1986년에 약 120 켈빈 온도에서 임계 온도에 도달할 수 있는 물질이 발견되었는데, 이는 구하고 사용하기 훨씬 더 쉬운 액체 질소를 이용해 도달할 수 있는 온도였습니다.

남 교수님, 액체 질소가 헬륨보다 훨씬 더 가격이 낮다고는 해도 초전도체들이 사용될 수 있는 적용처의 종류를 제한하지 않나요? 제 말은, 여전히 비실용적으로 보여요.

여 음, 현재 사용되는 경우의 대부분은 초전도 전선으로 만들어진 전자석인 초전도 자석과 관련된 것입니다. 액체 질소를 이용해 적절히 온도가 내려가면 이들은 종래의 거의 어떠한 전자석이 만들어내는 것보다 더 강력한 엄청난 자기장을 만들어냅니다. 놀랍게도 이들은 가동에 돈이 덜 드는데, 초전도성 전선이 투입한 에너지를 보통의 전선들처럼 열로 잃지 않아서 가능한 것입니다. 하지만 학생의 말이 맞아요. **6** 냉각수 노출의 위험이 적은, 매우 특정한 목적을 위한 곳에만 쓰이고 있죠. 입자 가속기, 자력 분리 과정, 그리고 질량 분석계와 같이 강한 자기장 기능이 요구되는 장치들에 사용되는데, 대부분의 사람들은 초전도성 물질을 병원에서 자기 공명 영상 장치의 필수적인 부품으로 마주하게 됩니다. MRI 기계들은 X선 촬영처럼 잠재적으로 위험성이 있는 전리 방사선을 사용하는 기술을 쓰지 않고 의학적 진단을 도울 수 있도록 병원들에서 널리 사용되고 있습니다.

남 그럼, MRI는 환자들에게 위험하지 않은 건가요? 환자들의 건강에 위험을 전혀 야기하지 않나요?

여 아뇨, 물론 특정 환자들에게는 위험할 수 있겠죠. 이 장치가 만들어내는 강력한 자기장은 심박 조율기 등의 전자 임플란트를 방해할 수 있습니다. 또한 뼈에 박은 철심과 같은 금속 임플란트들에 영향을 줘서 뜨거워지게 만들 수 있습니다. 그리고 메스꺼움이나 어지러움과 같은 생리학적 영향 역시 일으킬 수 있습니다. 적혈구 내의 철과 같은 생물학적 철 성분에 대한 우려 역시 제기되었지만, 그 피해에 대한 증거는 아직 발견되지 않았어요.

1. **What is the discussion mainly about?**
   (A) Some drawbacks that occur when using superconductors
   (B) The characteristics of materials named superconductors

1. 토론은 주로 무엇에 대한 것인가?
   (A) 초전도체를 사용할 때 발생하는 몇 가지 문제점들
   (B) 초전도체라고 불리는 물질들의 특징

Lesson 10 Lectures

Ⓒ The frequent use of superconductors in the medical field

Ⓓ Comparing the properties of copper and other metals

2. Listen again to part of the discussion. Then answer the question.

> W Silver, on the other hand, has higher conductivity than copper, rating at about 106% higher than copper. Unfortunately, silver is expensive and very soft, severely limiting its usefulness.

Why does the professor say this:

> W Unfortunately, silver is expensive and very soft, severely limiting its usefulness.

Ⓐ To show why silver is only used in electricity experiments

Ⓑ To state that silver is actually the best metal for wiring

Ⓒ To question why copper is generally used to transmit electricity

Ⓓ To indicate why silver is not suitable for electrical wiring

3. According to the discussion, what are superconductors?

Ⓐ Materials that have zero electrical resistance when put into a proper state

Ⓑ Materials that are resistant to extreme temperatures as low as zero degrees Kelvin

Ⓒ Materials that can maintain heat longer than other non-precious metals

Ⓓ Materials that change their electromagnetic nature as they lose energy

4. What is true of superconductors? Choose 2 answers.

Ⓐ They need to be at their critical temperature to achieve superconductivity.

Ⓑ Liquid helium and liquid nitrogen can be used for temperature control.

Ⓒ Their superconductivity gradually increases when the temperature is high.

Ⓓ Heike K. Onnes discovered the ideal temperatures for all superconductors.

5. Why does the professor mention liquid nitrogen?

Ⓐ To show how it can possibly turn copper and silver into superconductors

Ⓑ To give an example of another superconductor that is used in the industry

Ⓒ 의학계에서의 빈번한 초전도체 사용

Ⓓ 구리와 다른 금속들의 성질 비교

2. 토론의 일부를 다시 듣고 질문에 답하시오.

> 여 한편, 은은 구리보다 약 106% 더 높은 전도성을 가지고 있습니다. 불행히도 은은 비쌀 뿐만 아니라 매우 부드러워서 사용에 심각한 제한이 있죠.

교수는 왜 이렇게 말하는가:

> 여 불행히도 은은 비쌀 뿐만 아니라 매우 부드러워서 사용에 심각한 제한이 있죠.

Ⓐ 왜 은이 전기 실험에만 사용되는지를 보이려고

Ⓑ 사실 은은 배선에 가장 좋은 금속이라고 말하려고

Ⓒ 왜 구리가 전기를 전도하는 데 일반적으로 쓰이는지 질문하려고

Ⓓ 왜 은이 전기 배선에 적합하지 않은지 알려주려고

3. 토론에 따르면, 초전도체는 무엇인가?

Ⓐ 적절한 상태에 놓였을 때 전기 저항이 0이 되는 물질들

Ⓑ 켈빈 0도만큼 낮은 극단적인 온도를 버틸 수 있는 물질들

Ⓒ 다른 비귀금속들보다 열을 더 오래 유지할 수 있는 물질들

Ⓓ 에너지를 잃으면서 전자기적 특성을 변화시키는 물질들

4. 초전도체들에 대해 옳은 것은 무엇인가? 두 개를 고르시오.

Ⓐ 초전도성을 띠려면 그 임계 온도에 다다른 상태여야 한다.

Ⓑ 액체 헬륨과 액체 질소가 온도 통제에 사용될 수 있다.

Ⓒ 이들의 초전도성은 온도가 높을 때 서서히 증가한다.

Ⓓ 헤이커 카메를링 오너스는 모든 초전도체들의 이상적 온도를 발견했다.

5. 교수는 왜 액체 질소를 언급하는가?

Ⓐ 액체 질소가 어떻게 구리와 은을 초전도체로 바꾸는지 보여주려고

Ⓑ 산업에서 사용되는 또 다른 초전도체의 예시를 들려고

Ⓒ To name a substance that can be used to reach critical temperatures

Ⓓ To illustrate the process of cooling superconductors to 23 degrees Kelvin

Ⓒ 임계 온도에 도달하기 위해 사용할 수 있는 물질을 말해주려고

Ⓓ 켈빈 23도로 초전도체들을 식히는 과정을 묘사하려고

6. What can be inferred about the use of superconductors?

Ⓐ They are rarely useful for X-ray imaging and MRI systems in hospitals.

Ⓑ Scientists are trying to replace liquid nitrogen with other materials for better performance.

Ⓒ For now, their use is limited to certain settings because of their cooling system.

Ⓓ It is potentially dangerous to people's health because of their radioactive nature.

6. 초전도체 사용에 관해 무엇을 추론할 수 있는가?

Ⓐ 병원의 X선과 MRI 시스템에 유용하게 쓰이는 경우가 거의 드물다.

Ⓑ 과학자들은 더 나은 성과를 위해 액체 질소를 다른 물질로 대체하려 하고 있다.

Ⓒ 현재로서는 냉각 시스템 때문에 이것의 사용은 특정 환경으로 제한되어 있다.

Ⓓ 방사능 특성 때문에 사람들의 건강에 위험할 수 있다.

어휘 majority n 대다수 | electrical wiring 전기 배선 | copper n 구리 | conductivity n 전도성 | non-precious metal 비귀금속 | measure v 측정하다 | efficiently adv 효율적으로 | transport v 운반하다, 수송하다 | electrical charge 전하 | aluminum n 알루미늄 | conduct v (열, 전기를) 전도하다 | electricity n 전기, 전력 | possess v 소유하다 | diameter n 지름 | unfortunately adv 불행히도 | severely adv 심하게 | limit v 제한하다 | usefulness n 유용성 | industry standard 산업 표준 | power transmission 송전 | alloy n 합금 | be subjected to ~을 받다[겪다] | proper adj 제대로 된, 적절한 | superconductor n 초전도체 | specific adj 특정한 | substance n 물질 | achieve v 도달하다, 달성하다 | precisely adv 정확히 | resistance n 저항 | phenomenon n 현상 | superconductivity n 초전도성 | discover v 발견하다 | physicist n 물리학자 | quantum mechanical 양자 역학적인 | characterized adj 특징 지어진 | ejection n 방출, 배출 | magnetic field line 자기장선 | interior n 내부 | enter v 들어가다 | gradually adv 서서히, 점차 | absolute zero 절대 영도 | impurity n 불순물 | defect n 결함 | dramatically adv 극적으로 | critical temperature 임계 온도 | plummet v 곤두박질치다 | maintain v 유지하다 | liquid n 액체 | helium n 헬륨 | produce v 생산하다 | nitrogen n 질소 | obtain v 구하다, 얻다 | application n 적용 | impractical adj 비현실적인, 터무니없는 | electromagnet n 전자석 | coil n 코일, (둥글게 꼬아 놓은) 전선 | generate v 발생시키다 | intense adj 극심한, 강렬한 | conventional adj 종래의, 전통적인 | operate v 작동하다 | risk n 위험 요소 | coolant n 냉각수 | device n 장치 | particle accelerator 입자가속기 | magnetic separation 자력 분리 | mass spectrometer 질량 분석계 | encounter v 맞닥뜨리다 | essential adj 필수적인 | component n 부품, 요소 | magnetic resonance imaging 자기 공명 영상법(MRI) | diagnosis n 진단(pl. diagnoses) | resort to 기대다, 의지하다 | utilize v 활용하다, 이용하다 | ionizing radiation 전리 방사선 | patient n 환자 | pose v 제기하다 | particular adj 특정한 | interfere v 방해하다, 간섭하다 | implant n 임플란트(수술을 통해 인체에 주입 또는 심는 물질) | pacemaker n 심박 조율기 | physiological adj 생리학의 | nausea n 메스꺼움 | dizziness n 어지러움 | biological adj 생물학적

Lesson 11 Environmental Science

본서 | P. 229

Test

1. D **2.** B, C **3.** D – A – C – B **4.** B **5.** B **6.** A

Test

본서 | P. 231

Man: Professor | Woman: Student

[1-6] Listen to part of a discussion in an environmental science class.

M Unlike other materials, plastic is notoriously difficult to recycle. Glass, paper, and metals like steel and aluminum can be converted back into a liquid state and reformed into

남자: 교수 | 여자: 학생

환경 과학 수업 중 토론의 일부를 들으시오.

남 다른 물질들과 달리 플라스틱은 재활용이 어렵기로 악명이 높습니다. 유리, 종이, 그리고 강철이나 알루미늄과 같은 금속은 액체 상태로 전환되어서 우리

any product that we desire. 2(B) However, plastic tends to burn when heated, releasing toxic chemicals, and 2(C) different types cannot be mixed. But, what if they could be? 1 Recent research has provided means by which plastics can be converted back into petroleum products.

The key to this process is to remove oxygen from the environment so that the carbon molecules in the plastic cannot combust. This is achieved by using superheated water and extreme pressure, which essentially replicates the geologic conditions under which the original petroleum was formed. This process is called thermal depolymerization, but despite its name, the process is not particularly complicated. 3(D) The plastic waste is shredded and mixed with water, 3(A) and then it is placed into a pressurized chamber where it is heated to about 350 degrees Centigrade. 3(C) When the water converts into steam, its natural conversion increases the pressure in the chamber to 40 times standard air pressure. This is maintained for 15 minutes and then the chamber is opened, instantly boiling off the water through a reaction called flash evaporation. 3(B) What remains is a mixture of mineral solids and crude hydrocarbons that are sent to a second reactor that heats them to 500 degrees, breaking them down further. The procedure takes plastics, which are basically long-chain carbon molecules, and breaks them down into smaller and simpler molecules. This results in light petroleum oil and gases like methane and propane. When the feed material is plastic bottles, the byproducts of this process are about 70 percent oils, 16 percent gases, 6 percent solids, and 8 percent steam. The oils and gases can then be used to create new plastics, or as various types of fuel.

W 4 Does this process only work with plastics? There are many other carbon-based waste materials.

M 4 Indeed there are, and many of them can also be used. These include crops and plant matter, medical waste, sewage sludge, animal waste, and even vehicle tires. Of course, the outputs for these materials vary widely depending on their water content and density. The process is remarkably effective, and it can even break down dangerous materials like poisons and pathogens by destroying their carbon chains. So, thermal depolymerization can be used to not only dispose of biohazard materials, but also to convert them into usable oil.

W Does thermal depolymerization have any negative effects on the environment?

M 5 Well, the process does require energy to work, but the

가 원하는 어떠한 물질로도 다시 만들어지는 것이 가능합니다. 2(B) 하지만 플라스틱은 가열했을 때 타는 성질이 있으며, 타면서 유독성 화학 물질을 방출하고, 2(C) 서로 다른 종류가 섞일 수도 없습니다. 그런데 만약 이것이 가능하다면 어떨까요? 1 최근의 연구는 플라스틱을 석유 물질로 다시 되돌리는 수단을 찾았습니다.

이 과정에 있어 가장 중요한 점은 플라스틱 내부의 탄소 분자들이 연소되지 못하도록 환경에서 산소를 제거하는 것입니다. 이는 과열된 물과 극단적으로 높은 압력을 사용해서 얻을 수 있는데, 본질적으로는 원래의 석유가 형성된 지질학적 조건을 재현한 겁니다. 이 과정은 열분해라고 불리는데 이런 이름에도 불구하고 과정은 특별히 복잡하지 않습니다. 3(D) 플라스틱 쓰레기를 잘게 갈아서 물과 섞고, 3(A) 압력실 안에 넣어 섭씨 350도까지 가열합니다. 3(C) 물이 증기로 변화될 때 이 자연적인 변환이 압력실의 압력을 표준 기압의 40배가 넘도록 증가시켜요. 이 과정은 15분간 지속된 뒤 압력실을 개방하여 급속 증발이라 불리는 반응을 통해 물을 즉시 증발시킵니다. 3(B) 이 과정을 통해 남는 것은 고체 형태의 광물과 가공되지 않은 상태의 탄화수소 합성물인데, 이 합성물은 두 번째 반응 장치로 보내져서 섭씨 500도까지 가열되어 더더욱 잘게 쪼개지죠. 이 과정은 원래 긴 사슬형의 탄소 분자인 플라스틱을 더 작고 간단한 구조의 분자로 분해하는 것입니다. 이 결과로 경석유와 메탄과 프로판과 같은 가스가 만들어지죠. 재활용한 물질이 플라스틱 병일 경우, 이 과정으로 얻어지는 부산물은 70퍼센트가 석유, 16퍼센트가 가스, 6퍼센트가 고체, 그리고 8퍼센트가 증기입니다. 석유와 가스는 새로운 플라스틱을 만드는 데 쓰여질 수도 있고, 혹은 다양한 종류의 연료를 만드는 데 쓰일 수도 있어요.

여 4 이 열분해 과정은 플라스틱에만 적용되나요? 탄소를 기본으로 만들어진 다양한 폐기물이 많잖아요.

남 4 확실히 그렇죠, 그리고 그들 중 다수에도 적용할 수 있어요. 여기에는 작물과 식물성 물질, 의료 폐기물, 하수 침전물, 가축 배설물, 그리고 심지어 차량 타이어까지 포함됩니다. 물론 이러한 물질들을 처리함으로써 얻어지는 결과는 이들의 수분 함유량과 밀도에 의해 크게 달라집니다. 이 처리 과정은 놀라울 정도로 효율적이며 독성 물질이나 병원균과 같은 위험 물질들까지도 이들의 탄소 사슬을 파괴하는 방법으로 분해할 수 있습니다. 그래서 열분해는 생물학적 위험이 있는 물질을 처리하는 데 사용될 수 있을 뿐만 아니라 이들을 쓸모 있는 석유로 전환시키는 데 사용될 수도 있습니다.

여 열분해가 환경에 부정적인 영향을 주지는 않나요?

남 5 흠, 이 과정이 작동하기 위해서는 분명히 에너지

resulting oil and gas offset the fuel needed to do so. Not only that, but the processing plants also often use a portion of this gaseous fuel to supply the energy needed to heat the materials in a subsequent batch, which makes this process very energy efficient.

W Does that mean that thermal depolymerization does not create pollution? What about the solid matter that is left over?

M **5** Well, those solids are mostly carbon-based as well, and they can also be reused in many ways. They can be used to make filters, fertilizers, and even fuel, too. **But, the process does have its limitations. Since the process operates by breaking down long carbon-chains into smaller ones, molecules that are already small, like methane and carbon dioxide, cannot be transformed into oil through this process. So, thermal polymerization cannot be used to eliminate greenhouse gases that are produced by burning fossil fuels.** **5, 6** That being said, the oil produced through this process has many advantages over fossil fuels. A great deal of energy is used to remove oil, coal, and natural gas from the ground and to transport them to the people that will use them. We already have an abundance of plastic garbage, food waste, and plant matter that is buried in landfills where it cannot decompose. Using thermal polymerization, landfills can become mines for fuel materials, and the huge amount of garbage that is dumped into the ocean every year can be reused instead.

를 필요로 하지만 나중에 얻어지는 석유와 가스가 이 과정에 필요한 연료를 상쇄합니다. 그것뿐만 아니라 열분해 처리 시설들은 종종 이 가스 형태의 연료 일부를 사용하여 다음에 처리하는 물질들을 가열하는 데 필요한 에너지를 제공하는데, 이는 열분해 과정을 매우 에너지 효율적으로 만들죠.

여 **그 말은 열분해 처리가 오염물질을 만들어내지 않는다는 말씀이신가요? 처리 과정에서 남는 고체들은요?**

남 **5** 음, 이 고체 물질들도 대부분 탄소에 기반한 것들이며 여러 가지 방법으로 재사용이 가능합니다. 필터, 비료, 그리고 심지어 연료를 만드는 데도 사용될 수 있어요. **그러나 열분해 과정도 분명 한계가 있습니다. 이 과정이 긴 탄소 사슬 분자를 더 작은 분자로 분해하는 방식으로 진행되기 때문에 이미 크기가 작은 분자를 가진 메탄이나 이산화탄소 등은 이 과정을 통해 석유로 변환될 수 없어요. 그래서 열분해는 화석 연료를 태움으로써 생산되는 온실 가스를 제거하는 데는 사용이 불가능합니다.** **5, 6** 화석 연료 얘기가 나왔으니 말인데, 열분해를 통해 생산되는 석유는 화석 연료에 비해 많은 이점을 가지고 있어요. 땅으로부터 석유, 석탄, 천연 가스를 파내고 이들을 사용할 사람들에게 운송하는 데 엄청난 에너지가 들어갑니다. 우리는 이미 엄청난 양의 분해되지 않는 플라스틱 쓰레기, 음식물 쓰레기, 그리고 식물성 물질을 매립지에 쌓아두고 있어요. 열분해를 사용하면 매립지가 연료 물질 광산이 될 수 있고, 매년 바다로 버려지는 엄청난 양의 쓰레기가 재사용될 수 있습니다.

1. What is the main idea of the discussion?

Ⓐ Ways to develop thermal depolymerization to use it for other recycled products
Ⓑ The process of breaking down carbon chains with thermal depolymerization
Ⓒ Various methods of utilizing thermal depolymerization in a safer environment
Ⓓ The advantages of using thermal depolymerization for recycling various products

2. According to the discussion, what are the downsides of traditional plastic recycling? Choose 2 answers.

Ⓐ It only depends on combustion.
Ⓑ Harmful chemicals are often generated by it.
Ⓒ Other kinds of products cannot be recycled together.
Ⓓ It changes most products into solid matter.

1. 토론의 주제는 무엇인가?

Ⓐ 다른 재활용 제품들에도 사용하기 위해 열분해를 발전시키는 방법들
Ⓑ 열분해로 탄소 사슬을 분해하는 과정
Ⓒ 열분해를 더 안전한 환경에서 사용하는 다양한 방법들
Ⓓ 다양한 제품들을 재활용하는 일에 열분해를 이용하는 것의 이점

2. 토론에 따르면, 전통적인 플라스틱 재활용의 단점은 무엇인가? 두 개를 고르시오.

Ⓐ 연소에만 의존한다.
Ⓑ 그 과정에서 유해한 화학 물질들이 종종 만들어진다.
Ⓒ 다른 종류의 제품들이 함께 재활용될 수 없다.
Ⓓ 대부분의 제품을 고체로 바꾼다.

3. The professor describes the process of recycling plastics by thermal depolymerization. Put the steps below in order.

Ⓐ The mixture is heated to an extremely high temperature.
Ⓑ The matter is subjected to about 500 degrees Celsius.
Ⓒ The mixture is exposed to high pressure for 15 minutes.
Ⓓ The plastic is reduced to small pieces and is put into water.

Step	
Step 1	Ⓓ The plastic is reduced to small pieces and is put into water.
Step 2	Ⓐ The mixture is heated to an extremely high temperature.
Step 3	Ⓒ The mixture is exposed to high pressure for 15 minutes.
Step 4	Ⓑ The matter is subjected to about 500 degrees Celsius.

4. What is true about thermal depolymerization?

Ⓐ Its effect on the environment is questionable because it produces methane.
Ⓑ It can help recycle many different kinds of products that are carbon-based.
Ⓒ Its performance heavily depends on the content of the material it recycles.
Ⓓ It breaks down carbon molecules and creates new chemicals.

5. What is the professor's opinion of thermal depolymerization?

Ⓐ He thinks it requires too much energy input compared to the output.
Ⓑ He considers it to be efficient and quite safe for the environment.
Ⓒ He sees it as the perfect solution for recycling plastics.
Ⓓ He believes it actually has a negative impact on the environment.

6. What can be inferred about the future of thermal depolymerization?

Ⓐ It has great potential since it can help reduce a massive amount of waste and garbage.
Ⓑ It will be developed further to solve the problem of removing greenhouse gases.
Ⓒ It can be used in a variety of ways, though it still has some limitations regarding transportation.
Ⓓ It will get support from the public since it can reduce gas prices in the long run.

3. 교수는 열분해를 통해 플라스틱을 재활용하는 과정을 설명한다. 아래의 과정을 순서대로 나열하시오.

Ⓐ 혼합물을 극도로 높은 온도로 가열한다.
Ⓑ 물질을 섭씨 500도에 놓는다.
Ⓒ 혼합물을 높은 압력에 15분간 노출한다.
Ⓓ 플라스틱을 작은 조각으로 분해해서 물에 넣는다.

단계	
1 단계	Ⓓ 플라스틱을 작은 조각으로 분해해서 물에 넣는다.
2 단계	Ⓐ 혼합물을 극도로 높은 온도로 가열한다.
3 단계	Ⓒ 혼합물을 높은 압력에 15분간 노출한다.
4 단계	Ⓑ 물질을 섭씨 500도에 놓는다.

4. 열분해에 대해 옳은 것은 무엇인가?

Ⓐ 메탄을 생성해내기 때문에 환경에 끼치는 영향은 문제가 있어 보인다.
Ⓑ 탄소로 만들어진 많은 다양한 종류의 제품들을 재활용하는 데 도움을 줄 수 있다.
Ⓒ 재활용하는 물질에 함유된 것에 따라 성능이 크게 좌우된다.
Ⓓ 탄소 분자들을 분해해서 새로운 화학 물질을 만든다.

5. 열분해에 대한 교수의 의견은 무엇인가?

Ⓐ 에너지 산출량에 비해 투입량이 너무 많이 요구된다고 생각한다.
Ⓑ 효율적이고 환경에 꽤나 안전하다고 본다.
Ⓒ 플라스틱을 재활용하는 데 있어 완벽한 해결책이라고 본다.
Ⓓ 사실 환경에 부정적인 영향을 끼친다고 믿는다.

6. 열분해의 미래에 대해 무엇을 추론할 수 있는가?

Ⓐ 엄청난 양의 폐기물과 쓰레기를 줄이는 데 도움을 줄 수 있으므로 큰 가능성을 지니고 있다.
Ⓑ 온실 가스를 제거하는 문제를 해결하려면 더 개발되어야 한다.
Ⓒ 운송과 관련해 여전히 몇 가지 제약이 있으나 다양한 방법으로 사용될 수 있다.
Ⓓ 장기적으로 봤을 때 연료비를 감소시킬 수 있으므로 대중으로부터 지지를 얻을 것이다.

어휘 plastic n 플라스틱 | notoriously adv 악명 높게 | recycle v 재활용하다 | metal n 금속 | steel n 강철 | aluminum n 알루미늄 | convert v 전환시키다, 개조하다 | liquid n 액체 | reform v 다시(고쳐) 만들다 | release v 방출하다 | toxic adj 유독성의 | chemical n 화학 물질 | petroleum n 석유 | carbon n 탄소 | molecule n 분자 | combust v 연소시키다 | achieve v 달성하다 | superheat v 과열하다 | essentially adv 근본적으로, 본질적으로 | replicate v 복제하다 | geologic adj 지질학의, 지질의 | condition n 조건 | form v 형성하다 | thermal depolymerization 열분해 | particularly adv 특별히 | complicated adj 복잡한 | shred v 분쇄하다, 잘게 자르다 | pressurize v 압력을 가하다 | chamber n (특정 목적을 위한) -실(室) | centigrade n 섭씨 | conversion n 전환, 개조 | standard air pressure 표준 기압 | maintain v 유지하다 | instantly adv 즉시 | boil off 증발시키다 | reaction n 반응 | flash evaporation 순간 증발 | mixture n 혼합물 | mineral n 광물, 무기물 | solid n 고체 | crude adj 원래 그대로의, 미가공의 | hydrocarbon n 탄화수소 | reactor n 반응 장치, 원자로 | basically adv 원래, 기본적으로 | methane n 메탄 | propane n 프로판 | byproduct n 부산물 | steam n 증기 | crop n 작물 | sewage sludge 하수 침전물 | vehicle n 차량, 탈것 | tire n 타이어, 바퀴 | output n 생산량, 산출량 | widely adv 널리 | content n 내용물 | density n 밀도, 농도 | remarkably adv 두드러지게, 현저하게 | effective adj 효과적인 | poison n 독 | pathogen n 병원균 | destroy v 파괴하다 | dispose v 처리하다, 없애다 | biohazard adj 생물학적으로 위험한 | offset v 상쇄하다 | plant n 시설, 공장 | portion n 부분 | supply v 공급하다 | subsequent adj 다음의, 차후의 | batch n 한 회분, 묶음 | filter n 필터, 여과 장치 | fertilizer n 비료 | fuel n 연료 | limitation n 제한, 제약 | operate v 작동하다 | carbon dioxide 이산화탄소 | transform v 변형시키다 | eliminate v 제거하다 | greenhouse gas 온실가스 | fossil fuel 화석 연료 | coal n 석탄 | transport v 운송하다, 운반하다 | abundance n 풍부 | landfill n 매립지 | decompose v 분해하다, 부패하다 | mine n 광산 | dump into 버리다

Lesson 12 Film Studies

본서 | P. 233

Test

1. C **2.** A, C, D **3.** A **4.** D **5.** B **6.** C

Test

본서 | P. 234

Man: Professor

[1-6] Listen to part of a lecture in a film studies class.

M 1 The distinctions between classical acting and method acting can be difficult to define. Before the development of the motion camera, all acting was done upon the stage, and such performances demanded particular abilities from the actors. Since they were separated from the audience, they had little need to express their emotions through their facial expressions. Of course, they could still use their body language, but 2(A) the gestures had to be exaggerated to allow the audience to see them. 2(C), (D) Since the entire story of the play was told through the actor's lines and the narrator's retelling of events, an actor's main tool was their voice.

An actor had to train their voice in many ways. They needed to be able to be loud—not to yell, but to project their voice so that the whole audience could hear them. 3 They needed to train their lungs and vocal chords to withstand long monologues and long overall performances. Shakespeare's plays would often take many hours to perform, and they still do today. They also needed to have good pronunciation and an easily understood accent. So, an actor really needed to train and take good care of their voice.

When films began, the voice suddenly was no longer

남자: 교수

영화학 수업의 일부를 들으시오.

남 1 전통적 연기와 메소드 연기의 차이는 정의하기 어려울 수도 있습니다. 영화 카메라가 개발되기 전에는 모든 연기가 무대 위에서 이루어졌고, 그러한 연기는 배우들에게 특정한 능력을 요구했습니다. 관객과 떨어져 있기 때문에 얼굴 표정을 통해 감정을 표현할 필요가 그다지 없었죠. 물론 바디랭귀지는 여전히 사용했지만 2(A) 관객이 볼 수 있도록 몸짓을 과장해야만 했습니다. 2(C), (D) 배우의 대사와 내레이터가 사건을 다시 이야기해주는 방식으로 극의 줄거리 전체가 전달되었기 때문에 배우의 주된 도구는 목소리였습니다.

배우는 여러 가지 방법으로 자신의 목소리를 훈련시켜야 했어요. 소리를 지르지 않고도 모든 관객이 들을 수 있도록 큰 소리를 낼 수 있어야 했습니다. 3 긴 독백과 긴 공연 전반을 견딜 수 있도록 폐와 성대를 훈련해야 했습니다. 셰익스피어의 연극은 때때로 공연하는 데 많은 시간이 걸리며, 오늘날에도 그러합니다. 배우는 또한 발음이 좋아야 하며, 쉽게 알아들을 수 있는 억양을 가져야 합니다. 그래서 배우는 자신의 목소리를 훈련하고 잘 챙겨야 했죠.

영화가 시작되면서 갑자기 목소리는 더 이상 요인이 아니게 되었는데, 영화에는 소리가 없었기 때문

a factor, because the films did not have sound. The overstated body language of the stage was still useful, though, and more importantly, the camera could do close-ups. This made the nuances of normal facial expressions suddenly clearly visible to the audience, and they became a vital part of acting. When sound was introduced through the first talkies, speaking came back to the forefront. This is when we can begin to talk about classical acting in respect to film. Constantin Stanislavski created the classical acting system and he published his theories in English in the 1936 edition of his book *An Actor Prepares*. His training method includes many techniques.

First, there was an emphasis on physical acting, such as body language and other physical actions. Next, Stanislavski focused on the script itself, finding the "through line of actions" that unifies the plot of the story. He also stressed exploring the subtext, the underlying elements of the story that are not overtly stated. And finally, he strongly advocated using one's imagination as a way to find the soul of the character and to relate to the other actors. Specifically, Stanislavski encouraged actors to personalize the role through affective memory—to take one's own real-life experiences that are similar to those of the character and use them as a way to identify more closely with that character. When one did not have any useful experiences, he advised imagining the experiences in great detail to understand the character's motivation. As Stanislavski was a trained actor and director of theater, he also focused on the classical theater techniques for developing one's acting voice.

Later, Lee Strasberg, who was trained in classical acting, developed his own system, which is now called method acting. Method acting training involves many of the same basic techniques as classical acting, but it approaches the performance from a different angle. **4** In classical acting, actors try to understand their characters and to put themselves inside those characters. The actors ask themselves how their characters would react to a situation and act accordingly. In method acting, actors put the characters into themselves—they internalize the characters. They become the characters so completely that they do not ask how they should react; the actors simply react in the way that feels natural to them. This creates an emotional rawness and sensitivity that earlier acting often seemed to be lacking.

5 Many method actors become their characters so completely that they "stay in character" even when they are not filming, or even on set. To do so, some actors go to extreme lengths of transformation. They will lose or gain

이었습니다. 하지만 무대에서 쓰였던 과장된 바디 랭귀지는 여전히 유용했고, 더 중요한 점은 카메라가 클로즈업을 할 수 있었다는 것입니다. 이로 인해 보통의 얼굴 표정이 지닌 뉘앙스가 갑자기 관중에게 뚜렷하게 보이게 되었고 연기에서 가장 중요한 부분이 되었습니다. 최초의 발성 영화를 통해 소리가 도입되자, 말하기가 다시금 중요해졌습니다. 이 시점에서 바로 우리는 영화에서의 전통적 연기 방식에 대해 이야기할 수 있게 됩니다. 콘스탄틴 스타니슬랍스키는 전통적 연기 체계를 만들었고 그의 저서인 1936년판 〈배우 수업〉에서 자신의 이론을 영어로 출간했습니다. 그의 훈련 방법에는 많은 기법이 있죠.

먼저, 바디 랭귀지나 다른 신체적 행동과 같은 신체적 연기에 중점을 두었습니다. 다음으로 슬랍스키는 극본 자체에 집중하고, 이야기의 내용을 통일하는 '행동의 관통선'을 찾아냈습니다. 그는 또한 명백하게 드러나지 않은, 이야기의 숨겨진 요소인 서브텍스트 분석을 강조했습니다. 그리고 마지막으로 인물의 영혼을 찾고 다른 배우들과 관계를 쌓기 위한 방법으로 상상력을 이용하는 것을 강하게 주장했습니다. 구체적으로 말해, 슬랍스키는 정서적 기억을 통해 역할을 자신의 것으로 만들라고 배우들을 장려했어요. 극중 인물의 경험과 비슷한, 배우가 실제로 겪은 경험을 이용해 그 인물과 더 비슷해질 수 있도록 하는 것이죠. 쓸 만한 경험이 없을 때는 인물의 동기 부여를 이해하기 위해 그 경험을 아주 세부적인 요소까지 상상해 보라고 조언했습니다. 슬랍스키는 훈련을 받은 배우이자 극단 감독이었기에 연기할 때의 목소리 개발을 위해 전통적인 연극 기법에 집중했습니다.

이후, 전통적 연기 훈련을 받은 리 스트라스버그가 오늘날 메소드 연기라고 불리는 자신만의 체계를 발전시켰습니다. 메소드 연기 훈련은 전통적 연기의 기본적인 기법과 많은 점에서 같지만 연기에 다른 관점으로 접근합니다. **4** 전통적 연기에서 배우는 인물을 이해하려고 노력하고, 그 인물에 자신을 집어넣으려고 노력하죠. 그 인물이 어떤 상황에 어떻게 반응할지를 자신에게 묻고 그에 따라 연기합니다. 메소드 연기에서는 배우가 자신에게 인물을 대입합니다. 인물을 내면화하는 것이죠. 자기 자신이 완전히 그 인물이 되어 그가 어떻게 반응할지 묻지 않아도 될 정도입니다. 그저 자신에게 자연스러운 방식으로 반응하죠. 이는 기존의 연기에 부족해 보였던 있는 그대로의 감정과 감성을 만들어냅니다.

5 많은 메소드 연기자들이 너무 완전히 자신이 맡은 인물이 되다 보니 촬영을 하고 있지 않을 때나 세트에서도 '그 인물로 머물러' 있습니다. 이렇게 하기 위해 어떤 배우들은 엄청난 변신을 거칩니다. 몸

large amounts of weight, learn foreign languages, study other jobs, and even give themselves physical disabilities. 6 There is a famous story about two actors that were working on a movie together that shows this distinction. The younger actor was a method actor who did not bathe or sleep for days to get into the proper mindset to play his character. The other was an older, classical actor. When he saw his younger costar's condition he asked him, "Why don't you just act?" For the classical actor, a character is something he creates for the camera. For the method actor, a character is something that he becomes.

무게를 엄청나게 감량하거나 늘리기도 하고, 외국어를 배우고, 다른 일자리들에 대해 연구하고, 스스로에게 신체적으로 장애를 주기도 합니다. 6 이러한 차이점을 보여주는, 한 영화를 같이 촬영하게 된 두 배우에 대한 유명한 이야기가 있습니다. 더 젊은 배우는 자신의 인물을 연기하기 위해 그에 적절한 사고방식을 갖추려고 며칠 동안 씻지도 잠을 자지도 않는 메소드 연기자였습니다. 다른 배우는 나이가 더 많은 전통적 연기를 하는 배우였죠. 젊은 배우의 상태를 본 이 배우는 "그냥 연기하면 되잖아요?"라고 물었다고 합니다. 전통적 연기자에게 인물은 카메라를 위해 자신이 만드는 것입니다. 메소드 배우에게 인물은 자신이 무엇이 되는 것이죠.

1. What is the main topic of the lecture?

- (A) The requirements of stage acting
- (B) The development of method acting
- (C) The comparison of classical and method acting
- (D) The changes that film brought to acting

2. According to the professor, what are some characteristics of stage performances? Choose 3 answers.

- (A) The use of exaggerated body language
- (B) Expressing emotion through facial expressions
- (C) Heavy reliance upon the lines of the play
- (D) Narration to explain what is happening
- (E) Sudden changes in an actor's voice

3. According to the professor, what made performing Shakespeare's plays so difficult?

- (A) They take hours to perform.
- (B) They required the actors to use accents.
- (C) The actors had to speak loudly.
- (D) The lines were difficult to pronounce.

4. What defines the difference between classical and method acting most clearly?

- (A) The kind of vocal training the actor goes through
- (B) The way in which the performance is filmed
- (C) The director's treatment of the film cast
- (D) The actor's relationship with the character

5. What can be inferred about method acting?

- (A) Actors must take drastic measures to become the characters they play.
- (B) Staying in character can affect an actor's personal life.
- (C) Preparing for roles can require actors to study intensely.

1. 강의의 주제는 무엇인가?

- (A) 무대 연기에 필요한 조건들
- (B) 메소드 연기의 발달
- (C) 전통적 연기와 메소드 연기의 비교
- (D) 영화가 연기에 가져온 변화

2. 교수에 따르면, 무대 연기의 특징은 무엇인가? 세 개를 고르시오.

- (A) 과장된 바디 랭귀지 사용
- (B) 얼굴 표정을 통한 감정 표현
- (C) 연극 대사에 대한 많은 의존
- (D) 무슨 일이 일어나고 있는지 설명해주는 내레이션
- (E) 배우의 목소리에 일어나는 갑작스러운 변화들

3. 교수에 따르면, 셰익스피어 연극을 연기하기 어렵게 만드는 것은 무엇인가?

- (A) 공연하는 데 몇 시간이 걸린다.
- (B) 배우들이 억양을 사용하도록 했다.
- (C) 배우들이 크게 말해야만 했다.
- (D) 대사를 발음하기 어려웠다.

4. 전통적 연기와 메소드 연기의 차이점을 가장 뚜렷하게 드러내는 것은?

- (A) 연기자가 받는 발성 훈련의 종류
- (B) 연기가 촬영되는 방식
- (C) 영화 출연진에 대한 감독의 대우
- (D) 인물과 배우와의 관계

5. 메소드 연기에 대해 무엇을 추론할 수 있는가?

- (A) 배우들은 자신이 연기하는 인물이 되기 위해 극단적인 방법을 취해야만 한다.
- (B) 극중 인물로 지내는 것은 배우의 개인적 삶에 영향을 줄 수도 있다.
- (C) 배역 준비는 배우들이 엄청난 연구를 하도록 한다.

Ⓓ Actors may never fully return to their normal selves.

Ⓓ 배우들은 보통의 모습으로 완전히 돌아오지 못할 수도 있다.

6. How does the professor conclude the lecture?

Ⓐ By giving the listeners an assignment for the next session
Ⓑ By inviting his audience to provide him with examples
Ⓒ By telling an anecdote that illustrates his point
Ⓓ By providing a summary of the lecture as a whole

6. 교수는 강의를 어떻게 끝맺는가?

Ⓐ 다음 시간을 위한 과제를 내주면서
Ⓑ 청중들에게 예시를 달라고 유도하면서
Ⓒ 자신의 요점을 설명해주는 일화를 말하면서
Ⓓ 강의 전체를 요약하면서

어휘 distinction n 차이 I classical acting 전통적 연기 I method acting 메소드 연기 I define v 정의하다 I development n 개발, 발달 I motion camera 영화 촬영기 I stage n 무대 I performance n 연기 I particular adj 특정한 I separate v 분리하다 I audience n 관중 I express v 표현하다 I gesture n 몸짓, 제스처 I exaggerate v 과장하다 I entire adj 전체의 I actor n 배우 I narrator n 서술자, 내레이터 I retell v 다시 말하다 I train v 훈련하다 I loud adj (소리가) 큰 I yell v 소리지르다 I project v 보여 주다, 나타내다 I lung n 폐 I vocal chord 성대 I withstand v 견뎌내다, 이겨내다 I monologue n 독백 I overall adj 종합적인, 전체의 I pronunciation n 발음 I accent n 억양 I factor n 요인 I overstate v 과장하다 I close-up 근접 촬영 I nuance n 뉘앙스, 미묘한 차이 I facial expression 얼굴 표정 I clearly adv 확실히, 명확히 I visible adj 보이는 I vital adj 필수적인 I introduce v 도입하다 I talkie n 발성 영화 I forefront n 선두, 중심 I in respect to ~에 관하여 I publish v 출판하다 I theory n 이론 I emphasis n 강조 I physical adj 신체적인, 물리적인 I script n 대본, 극본 I unify v 통합하다, 통일하다 I plot n 줄거리 I stress v 강조하다 I explore v 탐험하다 I subtext n 서브텍스트, 언외의 의미, 숨은 이유 I underlying adj 근본적인, 근원적인 I element n 요소 I overtly adv 공공연하게 I advocate v 주장하다, 옹호하다 I imagination n 상상력 I specifically adv 구체적으로 I personalize v 개인의 필요에 맞추다 I affective adj 정서적인 I identify with ~와 동일시하다 I useful adj 유용한 I experience n 경험 I advise v 조언하다 I motivation n 동기부여 I approach v 접근하다 I situation n 상황 I accordingly adv 부응해서, ~에 맞춰 I internalize v 내면화하다 I completely adv 완전히 I react v 반응하다 I natural adj 자연스러운 I emotional adj 정서의, 감정의 I rawness n (감정적인) 원초성 I sensitivity n 세심함, 감성 I lack v 부족하다, 결여되다 I transformation n 변신 I disability n 장애 I proper adj 적절한, 제대로 된 I mindset n 사고방식 I costar n 함께 주연을 맡은 배우

Lesson 13 Geology

본서 I P. 236

Test

1. A **2.** A **3.** D **4.** C, D **5.** C **6.** B

Test

본서 I P. 237

Man: Professor I Woman: Student

[1-6] Listen to part of a discussion in a geology class.

M As we discussed in our last session, the brilliant shades of colors that are visible in some arid and desert areas are the results of sediment deposition and subsequent erosion. **2** Layers of sediment form into sandstone, limestone, volcanic tuff, and other sedimentary rocks over time due to the pressure exerted by the layers above them. This typically occurs in seas and lakes over millions of years. Later, the environment changes, and the water disappears, leaving behind a flat and mostly featureless plain. What happens next varies somewhat by area, but geological forces often push the layers of rocks upward, and then they begin to erode. The action of wind and water strips away layers

남자: 교수 I 여자: 학생

지질학 수업 중 토론의 일부를 들으시오.

남 지난 시간에 이야기했듯이, 몇몇 건조한 사막 지역에서 볼 수 있는 밝은 색조들은 침전물의 퇴적과 뒤이은 부식의 결과입니다. **2** 침전물의 층은 시간이 흐르면서 위에 쌓이는 층들로 인해 가해지는 압력 때문에 사암, 석회암, 응회암, 그리고 다른 퇴적암으로 형성됩니다. 이는 흔히 바다나 호수에서 수백만 년에 걸쳐 일어납니다. 후에 환경이 바뀌고 물이 사라지며 평평하고 특색 없는 평원이 남죠. 그 뒤 일어나는 일은 지역에 따라 약간씩 다르지만 지질학적 힘이 종종 암석층을 위로 밀어 올리고 이 층들이 침식되기 시작합니다. 바람과 물의 작용이 층들을

unevenly, revealing different layers of sedimentary rock with different colors caused by the minerals contained within them. This can create a beautiful spectacle like the Painted Desert of Arizona, where the hills show a veritable rainbow of colors.

1 In addition, this process also can create some very interesting rock formations like the ones in this picture. Pretty amazing, aren't they? These images were taken in Bryce Canyon, Utah, where they exist in abundance. However, such formations can be found in many other locations around the world. Actually, all that is required to make them is sedimentary rock and a fairly arid climate. These structures are called hoodoos in North America, and as you can see, they consist of a pillar of softer sedimentary layers, which is capped with a stone that is much larger in diameter. They also often have an irregular pattern of bulges in the pillar because of the different types of rock in it, and that shape has been compared to totem poles.

W Excuse me, professor. But, why are they called hoodoos?

M **3** Ah, well, that is because they look so bizarre. You see, we didn't always have the level of understanding of geology that we have today. Plus, the native peoples often associated them with their gods or other mystical forces. Since they were a mystery to scientists as well, they said it seemed like the natives were right, maybe some magical force was responsible. And, a popular term for such beliefs was hoodoo, based on a mystical religion in the Americas called Voodoo. However, today we know exactly how they are made.

Let's take a closer look at hoodoos. They are usually formed in valleys, and canyons in particular, and there are two weathering processes at work. A canyon is created by a river or stream carving its way downward through layers of rock, and its tributary streams leave plateaus jutting out into the valley. This exposes the layers of rock to the elements from many directions. Then frost-wedging begins to affect the rock. Arid regions often suffer from extreme differences in temperature between day and night. **4(C)** In the winter, melting snow will seep into cracks in the rock and then freeze again at night. Water expands as it freezes, which gradually pushes off chunks of rock. Since the layers of rock are different, some lose much more mass than others in this fashion. **4(D), 5** In the summer, the little rain that is received also shapes the stone. Even in areas with little pollution, the

고르지 않게 벗겨내서 퇴적암의 서로 다른 층들과 이들 내부에 함유된 광물로 인해 나타나는 다양한 색을 드러냅니다. 이는 애리조나주에 있는 페인티드 사막과 같은 아름다운 장관을 만들어낼 수 있는데, 이곳의 언덕은 진정한 무지갯빛 색을 보여주죠.

1 게다가, 이러한 과정은 여기 있는 이 사진과 같은 흥미로운 암반 성상을 만들어낼 수도 있어요. 정말 멋지죠, 그렇지 않나요? 이 사진들은 유타주의 브라이스 캐니언에서 찍힌 것인데, 이곳엔 이러한 암반 성상들이 매우 많습니다. 그러나 이러한 암반 성상은 세계 곳곳의 다른 지역들에서도 발견할 수 있어요. 사실 이들을 만들어내는 데 필요한 것은 그저 퇴적암과 상당히 건조한 기후뿐입니다. 이 구조는 북미에서는 후두라 불리는데, 여기 보이는 것처럼 이들은 좀 더 무른 퇴적암 기둥 위에 훨씬 더 지름이 큰 돌이 얹혀진 모양이에요. 이들은 또한 기둥에 서로 다른 유형의 암석이 있기 때문에 불규칙적인 패턴으로 튀어나온 모양들을 갖고 있는데, 그 모양은 토템 폴에 비교되어 왔어요.

여 실례합니다, 교수님. 그런데 왜 이것들이 후두라고 불리는 거죠?

남 **3** 아, 음, 그건 이것들이 상당히 기이하게 생겼기 때문이에요. 학생도 알겠지만, 오늘날 우리가 갖고 있는 수준의 지질학에 대한 이해를 우리가 항상 갖고 있었던 건 아니었어요. 게다가, 원주민들은 종종 후두를 그들의 신 혹은 다른 신비한 힘과 결부시키곤 했습니다. 이것들은 과학자들에게도 수수께끼였기 때문에 과학자들은 원주민들의 생각이 맞는 것처럼 보인다고, 아마 어떤 마술적인 힘이 원인일 것이라고 말했습니다. 그리고 이러한 종류의 믿음을 나타내는 유명한 단어로 후두가 있었는데, 부두라 불리는 미 대륙의 신비로운 종교에 기반한 것입니다. 그러나 오늘날 우리는 이들이 정확히 어떻게 만들어졌는지 알고 있죠.

후두들을 좀 더 자세히 들여다 봅시다. 이들은 보통 계곡에 만들어지는데 특히 협곡에 형성되며, 이를 만들어내는 풍화 과정이 두 가지 있습니다. 협곡은 강이나 물줄기가 암석층을 통해 아래로 흘러 돌을 깎아 내리면서 만들어지는데, 지류가 고원을 계곡으로 돌출되도록 만들죠. 이는 암석층을 여러 방향으로 노출시킵니다. 그 뒤 얼음의 쐐기 작용이 암석에 영향을 주기 시작합니다. 건조한 지역은 종종 낮과 밤의 극단적인 온도 차에 시달리죠. **4(C)** 겨울에는 녹은 눈이 암석의 갈라진 틈으로 스며들었다가 밤에 얼어붙습니다. 물은 얼면서 팽창하는데, 이는 돌 덩어리를 서서히 밀어냅니다. 암석층의 돌들이 서로 다르기에 이 과정에서 어떤 돌들은 다른 돌들보다 훨씬 더 많이 깎여나갑니다. **4(D), 5** 여름에는 이 지역에 내리는 적은 양의 비가 돌의 모양을

Lesson 13 Lectures

rain is slightly acidic, which affects layers that contain limestone more than those made of sandstone or mudstone. So, the rocks continue to erode at different rates as the water rounds off their outer surfaces. Over time, this separates the stones into separate pillars that continue to erode. An upper layer of harder stone will form the capstone of the hoodoo. As the erosion decreases the diameter of the pillar beneath it, the capstone becomes kind of like a protective shield, slowing the process and creating the fantastic shapes we see today. Of course, ultimately, the capstone will fall, and the pillar will erode away.
Areas that contain these features have been popular with people for millennia. 6 As I mentioned before, many believed their gods lived near them, and in many parts of the world they even dug temples into the cliff walls near them. Others found more utilitarian purposes for the formations. In the Cappadocia region of Turkey, people actually carved out homes in the softer stone of the pillars. Today, they are popular tourist destinations.

만들어냅니다. 오염이 적은 지역이더라도 비는 약간의 산성을 띠고 있는데 사암이나 이암으로 만들어진 층보다 석회암 층에 더 많은 영향을 끼칩니다. 그래서 바위들은 물이 바깥 표면을 깎아낼 때 서로 다른 속도로 계속해서 침식됩니다. 시간이 흐르면서 이 과정은 바위들을 각각의 기둥들로 분리하는데, 이것들은 계속해서 침식됩니다. 위쪽 층의 더 단단한 바위가 후두의 갓돌을 형성합니다. 침식 작용이 아래쪽 기둥의 지름을 감소시킬 때 갓돌은 보호하는 방패 역할을 해서 이 과정을 늦추고 오늘날 우리가 보는 아름다운 형상들을 만들어냈죠. 물론 궁극적으로 이 갓돌은 떨어질 것이고 기둥은 계속해서 침식될 겁니다.
이러한 특징을 지닌 지역은 수백 년에 걸쳐 사람들에게 인기를 얻어 왔습니다. 6 앞서 언급했듯이 많은 사람들이 그들의 신이 가까이 살고 있다고 믿었고, 세계 곳곳에서 심지어 이들 가까이의 절벽에 사원을 파서 만들기도 했습니다. 또 다른 이들은 이 암반 성상에서 더 실용적인 목적을 발견했습니다. 터키의 카파도키아 지역에서 사람들은 실제로 기둥의 더 무른 돌을 파내어 집을 만들었습니다. 오늘날 이곳은 매우 유명한 관광지입니다.

1. What is the discussion mainly about?
Ⓐ The formation and the characteristics of a mysterious geological structure
Ⓑ The reason behind the color variation of stones in Bryce Canyon
Ⓒ The influence that hoodoos had to the inhabitants in the region
Ⓓ The geographical advantages that hoodoos have for their formation

2. What can be inferred about hoodoos?
Ⓐ They usually require many years to form.
Ⓑ Their outer surface is flat and smooth in general.
Ⓒ They were used as material for totem poles in the past.
Ⓓ They can only be found in Utah and Arizona.

3. Listen again to part of the discussion. Then answer the question.

M Ah, well, that is because they look so bizarre. You see, we didn't always have the level of understanding of geology that we have today.

Why does the professor say this:

M You see, we didn't always have the level of understanding of geology that we have today.

1. 토론은 주로 무엇에 관한 것인가?
Ⓐ 신비로운 지질학적 구조의 형성과 특징
Ⓑ 브라이스 캐니언의 암석이 다양한 색조를 갖게 된 이유
Ⓒ 후두가 그 지역의 거주민들에게 미친 영향
Ⓓ 후두 형성에 있어서의 지리학적 이점

2. 후두에 대해 무엇을 추론할 수 있는가?
Ⓐ 형성되는 데 오랜 시간을 필요로 한다.
Ⓑ 바깥 표면이 일반적으로 평평하고 매끄럽다.
Ⓒ 과거에 토템 폴의 재료로 사용되었다.
Ⓓ 유타주와 애리조나주에서만 찾아볼 수 있다.

3. 토론의 일부를 다시 듣고 질문에 답하시오.

남 아, 음, 그건 이것들이 상당히 기이하게 생겼기 때문이에요. 학생도 알겠지만, 우리는 오늘날 우리가 갖고 있는 수준의 지질학에 대한 이해를 항상 갖고 있었던 건 아니었어요.

교수는 왜 이렇게 말하는가:

남 학생도 알겠지만, 오늘날 우리가 갖고 있는 수준의 지질학에 대한 이해를 우리가 항상 갖고 있었던 건 아니었어요.

Ⓐ He is explaining that geology is a discipline that was developed fairly recently.
Ⓑ He is telling the students that mysterious things did happen in the past.
Ⓒ He is trying to convince his students to have a better appreciation of geology.
Ⓓ He is saying that the name of hoodoos came from people's uncertainty.

4. What are the two weathering processes that form hoodoos? Choose 2 answers.
Ⓐ Windstorms in the winter
Ⓑ Solar radiation during summer
Ⓒ Expansion of water during winter
Ⓓ Acidic rainwater in the summer

5. According to the discussion, why do rocks in this area erode at different rates?
Ⓐ The weather in the area is continuously becoming hotter and more arid.
Ⓑ Since they are all located in different places, some erode more quickly than others.
Ⓒ Limestone is more affected by acidic rain than sandstone and mudstone are.
Ⓓ Some stones are less frequently exposed to rain than other stones.

6. Why does the professor mention the Cappadocia region of Turkey?
Ⓐ To recommend students another good region to study and see hoodoos
Ⓑ To give an example to students of how people in the past used these formations
Ⓒ To illustrate the well-preserved condition of the hoodoos in this area
Ⓓ To compare the hoodoos in Bryce Canyon and the ones in the Cappadocia region

Ⓐ 지질학이 꽤 최근에 발전된 학문이라는 것을 설명하고 있다.
Ⓑ 신비로운 일이 과거에 일어났었다고 학생들에게 말하고 있다.
Ⓒ 지리학의 가치를 더 느껴야 한다고 학생들을 설득하고 있다.
Ⓓ 후두의 이름이 사람들의 불확실함에서 왔다고

4. 후두를 형성하는 두 개의 풍화 과정들은 무엇인가? 두 개를 고르시오.
Ⓐ 겨울의 폭풍우
Ⓑ 여름의 태양 복사
Ⓒ 겨울의 물 팽창
Ⓓ 여름의 산성비

5. 토론에 의하면, 이 지역의 암석들은 왜 서로 다른 속도로 침식되었는가?
Ⓐ 이 지역의 기후가 계속해서 더 뜨겁고 더 건조해지고 있다.
Ⓑ 암석들이 모두 다른 장소에 위치해 있기 때문에 몇몇은 다른 것들보다 더 빨리 침식되었다.
Ⓒ 석회암이 사암이나 이암보다 산성비에 더 많은 영향을 받는다.
Ⓓ 어떤 암석들은 다른 암석들보다 비에 덜 노출되었다.

6. 교수는 왜 터키의 카파도키아 지역을 언급하는가?
Ⓐ 학생들에게 후두를 연구하고 볼 수 있는 또 다른 좋은 지역을 추천하려고
Ⓑ 학생들에게 과거의 사람들이 이 암반 성상을 어떻게 이용했는지 예시를 들려고
Ⓒ 이 지역 후두의 잘 보존된 상태를 묘사하려고
Ⓓ 브라이스 캐니언과 카파도키아 지역의 후두를 비교하려고

어휘 shade n 색조 | arid adj 매우 건조한 | sediment n 퇴적물, 침전물 | deposition n 퇴적, 퇴적물 | subsequent adj 뒤이은, 그 다음의 | erosion n 침식, 부식 | sandstone n 사암 | limestone n 석회암 | volcanic tuff 응회암 | sedimentary rock 퇴적암 | pressure n 압력 | exert v (영향력을) 가하다, 행사하다 | typically adv 보통, 일반적으로 | flat adj 평평한 | featureless adj 특색 없는 | plain n 평원, 평지 | geological adj 지질학의 | erode v 침식되다, 풍화시키다 | unevenly adv 고르지 않게 | spectacle n 장관 | veritable adj 진정한 | canyon n 협곡 | abundance n 풍부 | formation n 형성 | pillar n 기둥 | cap v (꼭대기나 끝을) 덮다 | diameter n 지름 | irregular adj 고르지 못한 | bulge n 툭 튀어나온 것 | totem pole n 토템 폴 (아메리카 원주민 사회에서 토템의 상을 그리거나 조각한 기둥) | bizarre adj 기이한, 엽기적인 | associate v 연상하다, 결부 짓다 | mystical adj 신비스러운 | valley n 계곡 | weathering n 풍화 | carve v 깎다, 조각하다 | tributary n (강의) 지류 | plateau n 고원 | jut out 돌출하다 | expose v 드러내다, 노출하다 | element n 요소, 성분 | frost-wedging n 얼음의 쐐기 작용 | seep v 스며들다, 배다 | expand v 확장하다 | gradually adv 서서히 | pollution n 오염 | acidic adj 산성의 | mudstone n 이암 | capstone n 갓돌 | decrease v 줄이다, 감소시키다 | ultimately adv 궁극적으로 | utilitarian adj 실용적인 | tourist destination 관광지

Test

1. B 2. A 3. C 4. A, C 5. D 6. C

Test

본서 | P. 240

Man: Professor | Woman: Student

[1-6] Listen to part of a discussion in a U.S. history class.

M **1, 4** As I am sure you are all aware, the capital of our nation is Washington D.C. This was not always the case, however, as the Continental Congress held its sessions in many cities, but most often in Philadelphia, Pennsylvania. In fact, both the First and Second Continental Congresses met there, as did the Congress of the Confederation after the colonies won their independence from England in 1783. Beginning in March of that year, the Congress of the Confederation began meeting there, but on June 17, 1783, the unthinkable happened.

According to the Articles of the Confederation, the congress only exercised complete control of the military in times of war, and many soldiers at that time were not happy. **2** A group of 400 soldiers stationed in Philadelphia sent a message to the Congress demanding payment for their service in the Revolutionary War and threatened to take action if their demands were not met. Congress ignored their message, and no action was taken that day. However, more soldiers arrived two days later, swelling the ranks to about 500 men. On its own, this imminent rebellion was disconcerting, what made it even worse was that the soldiers had control of the weapons and munitions stored in the city. The Congress appealed to the Pennsylvania Council to send the state militia to help them, as was customary since they didn't control the army in normal situations. The council refused. This led the Congress to flee to Princeton, New Jersey. **3** It also led to two major decisions: the federal government needed to have its own seat of power, and it needed to be able to protect itself.

3 In Article One, Section 8 of the United States Constitution, they made provisions to ensure just that. It stated that they could establish a square-shaped district no larger than ten miles on each side that should be created on land ceded from existing states. This district would be the Seat of the Government of the United States, and the legislature would have the right to build forts, warehouses, dockyards, etc. as it deemed necessary. However, there were still two major

남자: 교수 | 여자: 학생

미국 역사 수업 중 토론의 일부를 들으시오.

남 **1, 4** 여러분 모두 알고 있으리라 확신하지만, 우리 나라의 수도는 워싱턴 D.C.입니다. 그러나 항상 그래 왔었던 것은 아닙니다. 대륙 회의는 여러 도시들에서 열렸고, 대부분이 펜실베니아주의 필라델피아에서 열렸어요. 실제로 첫 번째와 두 번째 대륙 회의가 그곳에서 이루어졌으며 1783년에 식민지들이 영국으로부터 독립을 이뤄낸 뒤의 연합 회의 역시 필라델피아에서 있었습니다. 그 해 3월부터 연합 회의는 그곳에서 열리기 시작했지만, 1783년 6월 17일에 생각지도 못했던 일이 일어났습니다.

연방 규약에 의하면, 의회는 전시에만 군에 대한 완전한 군의 지휘권을 행사했는데, 그 당시의 많은 군인들이 심기가 불편한 상태였습니다. **2** 필라델피아에 주둔하고 있던 400명의 군인들이 독립 전쟁에서의 군 복무에 대한 급여 지불을 요구하는 성명을 의회에 전달했으며 요구 사항이 받아들여지지 않을 경우 조치를 취하겠다고 위협했죠. 의회는 이 성명을 무시했으며 그날에는 아무 일도 일어나지 않았습니다. 그러나 이틀 뒤 더 많은 군인들이 도착했고, 숫자는 500명으로 늘어났습니다. 이 임박한 반란 자체만으로도 당황스러웠는데, 이를 더 심각하게 만든 것은 이 군인들이 그 도시에 보관되어 있던 무기와 군수품을 통제할 수 있었다는 겁니다. 의회는 전시가 아닌 일상 상황에는 군대를 통솔하지 않았기에 관례대로 펜실베니아주 의회에 그들을 도울 주 민병대를 보내줄 것을 탄원했습니다. 주 의회는 이것을 거부했어요. 이로 인해 의회는 뉴저지주의 프린스턴으로 피신해야 했습니다. **3** 또한 이 사태는 두 가지의 중요한 결정으로 이어졌어요. 연방 정부는 그 자신만의 권력을 가져야만 하며, 스스로를 지킬 수 있어야만 한다는 것이었습니다.

3 미 헌법 제 1조 8절에서 바로 이를 보장하기 위한 조항이 만들어졌습니다. 이 조항에서는 의회가 기존의 주들로부터 양도받은 토지에 각 변의 길이가 10마일이 넘지 않는 사각형의 구역을 설립할 수 있다고 언급하고 있습니다. 이 구역이 미 정부 소재지가 되며, 입법부는 필요하다고 간주할 시 요새, 창고, 조선소 등을 건설할 수 있는 권리를 가집니다.

issues to be resolved. The first was the issue that had led the soldiers to take such extreme measures. The nation owed huge amounts of debt due to the Revolutionary War. The second was even more difficult, and became inextricably linked to the first. **4(A)** They had to decide where to build the capital.

4(C) The capital had traditionally been located in Philadelphia, and after a brief stint in Princeton, it came to rest in New York City. Naturally, northern citizens thought that the permanent seat of government should be located in one of the country's most prominent cities, all of which were in the North. Accordingly, southern citizens wanted the capital to be located in the South to protect their agrarian interests. This deadlock only became more serious when the issue of the nation's debt came into question. The government had accrued a huge amount of debt during the war, and then declared that it was only liable to repay a tiny fraction of it. To avoid bankruptcy, it then shifted the debt to the state governments. However, the southern states paid off their shares of the debt much more quickly than the northern ones.

5 Alexander Hamilton was later tasked with firmly calculating the nation's debt. His report stated that there was an astonishing $77 million still owed to foreign and domestic creditors. It was then assumed that the states should all assume a share of this debt, which was extremely unpopular with the southern states. To convince them to accept this plan, it was agreed that the capital would be located in the center of the nation between Maryland and Virginia in the South. The land selected was located along the Potomac River, with about sixty percent on the Maryland side. **6** The 100 square mile area encompassed two existing cities: Georgetown in Maryland and Alexandria in Virginia. The capital itself began as the City of Washington, which still forms the historic core of the District of Columbia.

W Professor, I've been wondering about this for a long time, and I think that now is as good a time as any to ask. Why the District of Columbia? What is Columbia?

M Ah, that is the term that people of the time used to refer to the United States. Since they attributed the European discovery of the Americas to Christopher Columbus, this became a poetic term for it. The City of Washington was constructed pretty rapidly, and the Congress held its first session there on November 17, 1800.

그러나 여전히 해결해야만 하는 문제가 두 가지 있었습니다. 첫 번째는 군인들로 하여금 그렇게 극단적인 조치를 취하도록 만든 문제였습니다. 미국은 독립 전쟁으로 인해 엄청난 금액의 빚을 지고 있었죠. 두 번째 문제는 더욱 어려운 것이었으며 첫 번째와 불가분하게 얽혀 있었습니다. **4(A)** 그들은 수도를 어디에 지을지 결정해야만 했습니다.

4(C) 수도는 전통적으로 필라델피아에 위치해 왔고, 프린스턴에서 잠시 머문 뒤 뉴욕으로 오게 되었습니다. 자연적으로 북부 주민들은 영구적인 정부 소재지가 나라의 가장 중요한 도시들 중 하나에 세워질 것이라고 생각했는데, 이 도시들은 모두 북부에 있었죠. 그런 까닭에 남부의 주민들은 그들의 농업적 이익을 보호하기 위해 수도가 남부에 세워지기를 원했습니다. 이 교착 상태는 나라의 빚이 문제로 제기되자 더욱 심각해질 뿐이었습니다. 정부는 전쟁 동안 엄청난 금액의 빚을 끌어안게 되었고 지극히 소량의 금액만을 변상한다고 선언했습니다. 파산을 피하기 위해 정부는 주 정부들에 이 빚을 넘겼죠. 그러나 남부의 주들이 북부 주들보다 훨씬 더 빠르게 그들 몫의 빚을 갚았습니다.

5 알렉산더 해밀턴은 후에 국가의 빚을 확실하게 계산하는 임무를 맡게 됩니다. 그의 보고서는 미 정부가 여전히 외국과 국내의 채권자들에게 7,700만 달러라는 믿기 힘든 액수의 빚을 지고 있다고 보고했습니다. 그 뒤에 각각의 주들 모두가 이 빚을 일부씩 갚아야 한다는 가정이 내려졌는데, 이는 남부의 주들에서 극도로 평이 좋지 않았습니다. 이 계획을 수락하도록 남부의 주들을 설득하기 위해 수도가 메릴랜드주와 남부 버지니아주 사이 국토의 가운데 위치하게 하기로 합의가 이뤄졌습니다. 선택된 토지는 포토맥강을 따라 자리잡은 곳이었는데, 약 60%가 메릴랜드주 쪽에 있었습니다. **6** 100평방마일의 구역은 두 개의 기존 도시들을 둘러싸고 있었는데, 메릴랜드주의 조지타운과 버지니아주의 알렉산드리아였죠. 수도 자체는 워싱턴시로 시작되었고, 여전히 컬럼비아 특별구의 역사적 중심부를 형성하고 있습니다.

여 교수님, 오래 전부터 궁금했었던 건데, 지금이 여쭤보기 좋을 때라는 생각이 들어요. 왜 컬럼비아 특별구인가요? 왜 컬럼비아죠?

남 아, 그건 그 당시의 사람들이 미국을 가리킬 때 쓰던 단어입니다. 유럽의 미 대륙 발견이 크리스토퍼 콜럼버스 덕분이었다고 여겼기 때문에 이 단어는 그걸 가리키는 시적 용어가 되었죠. 워싱턴시는 상당히 빠른 속도로 건설되었고, 의회는 1800년 11월 17일 그곳에서 첫 회의를 열었습니다.

Lesson 14
Lectures

1. **What is the discussion mainly about?**
   (A) The influence of Christopher Columbus on the United States
   (B) How Washington D.C. became the capital of the United States
   (C) The early structure of the U.S. government and its development
   (D) What contributed to the outbreak of the Revolutionary War

2. **According to the discussion, what was the reason behind the soldiers' rebellion?**
   (A) Despite their service during the Revolutionary War, they were not paid.
   (B) They wanted the capital to be moved to the southern region of the U.S.
   (C) After they were discharged from the army, they had nowhere else to go.
   (D) They wanted to sell the munitions and weapons to a foreign country.

3. **Why does the professor mention Article One, Section 8 of the United States Constitution?**
   (A) To provide an explanation regarding the treatment of the United States soldiers
   (B) To show the students the past process of repaying debt to other countries
   (C) To emphasize how the federal government lacked power to protect itself
   (D) To point out its importance in every aspect of U.S. society and culture

4. **According to the professor, what is true about the capital?** Choose 2 answers.
   (A) The Continental Congress had no official capital.
   (B) Finding the location for it was an easy task.
   (C) Princeton was the capital for a short period.
   (D) People had to vote to select the location of the capital.

5. **What can be inferred about the debt the U.S. had back then?**
   (A) Southern states had to pay back the full debt.
   (B) Most of it was owed to Great Britain and France.
   (C) Domestic creditors did not get their money back.
   (D) It eventually influenced the location of the capital.

1. **토론은 주로 무엇에 대한 것인가?**
   (A) 크리스토퍼 콜럼버스가 미국에 끼친 영향
   (B) 어떻게 워싱턴 D.C가 미국의 수도가 되었는가
   (C) 미 정부의 초기 구조와 그 발달
   (D) 독립 전쟁의 발발에 무엇이 기여하였는가

2. **토론에 따르면, 군인들이 반란을 일으킨 이유는 무엇인가?**
   (A) 독립 전쟁 당시 복무했음에도 불구하고 보수를 받지 못했다.
   (B) 수도가 미국 남부 지역으로 옮겨지기를 원했다.
   (C) 군 제대 후 어디에도 갈 곳이 없었다.
   (D) 외국에 군수품과 무기를 팔기 원했다.

3. **교수는 왜 미 헌법 제 1조 8절을 언급하는가?**
   (A) 미국 군인들의 대우에 대한 설명을 하기 위해
   (B) 다른 나라에 빚을 갚는 과거의 과정을 학생들에게 보여주려고
   (C) 연방 정부가 스스로를 보호할 수 있는 힘이 부족했음을 강조하려고
   (D) 미국 사회와 문화 모든 면에 있어 그것의 중요성을 지적하려고

4. **교수에 의하면, 수도에 대해 옳은 것은 무엇인가?** 두 개를 고르시오.
   (A) 대륙 회의는 공식적인 수도를 갖고 있지 않았다.
   (B) 수도의 위치를 찾는 것은 쉬운 일이었다.
   (C) 프린스턴은 잠시 동안 수도였다.
   (D) 사람들은 수도의 위치를 선정하기 위해 투표를 해야만 했다.

5. **그 당시 미국이 지고 있던 빚에 대해 무엇을 추론할 수 있는가?**
   (A) 남부의 주들이 모든 빚을 다 지불해야만 했다.
   (B) 대부분의 빚은 영국과 프랑스에 진 것이었다.
   (C) 국내 채권자들은 그들의 돈을 돌려받지 않았다.
   (D) 결국 수도의 위치에 영향을 끼쳤다.

6. Listen again to part of the discussion. Then answer the question.

M The 100 square mile area encompassed two existing cities: Georgetown in Maryland and Alexandria in Virginia. The capital itself began as the City of Washington, which still forms the historic core of the District of Columbia.

Why does the professor say this?

M The 100 square mile area encompassed two existing cities: Georgetown in Maryland and Alexandria in Virginia.

Ⓐ To explain how large the capital was compared to those of other countries
Ⓑ To show the students how the name of the capital has changed
Ⓒ To illustrate the history of the District of Columbia as the capital
Ⓓ To ask the students to focus on some other interesting points

6. 토론의 일부를 다시 듣고 질문에 답하시오.

남 100평방 마일의 구역은 두 개의 기존 도시들을 둘러싸고 있었는데, 메릴랜드주의 조지타운과 버지니아주의 컬럼비아였죠. 수도 자체는 워싱턴시로 시작되었고, 여전히 컬럼비아 특별구의 역사적 중심부를 형성하고 있습니다.

교수는 왜 이렇게 말하는가:

남 100평방 마일의 구역은 두 개의 기존 도시들을 둘러싸고 있었는데, 메릴랜드주의 조지타운과 버지니아주의 컬럼비아였죠.

Ⓐ 다른 나라의 수도들에 비해 미국의 수도가 얼마나 컸는지 설명하려고
Ⓑ 수도의 이름이 어떻게 바뀌었는지 학생들에게 보여주려고
Ⓒ 수도로서의 컬럼비아 특별구의 역사를 설명하려고
Ⓓ 다른 흥미로운 요소에 집중할 것을 학생들에게 요청하려고

어휘 Continental Congress 대륙 회의(독립 혁명 당시 13개 미국 식민지 대표자들의 회의) | session n 회의 | Congress of the Confederation 연합 회의 | colony n 식민지 | independence n 독립 | unthinkable adj 상상도 할 수 없는 | exercise v (권리·권력을) 행사하다 | station v 배치하다, 주둔시키다 | Revolutionary War 미국 독립 전쟁 | threaten v 위협하다 | swell v 증가시키다, 늘리다 | imminent adj 임박한 | rebellion n 반란, 폭동 | disconcerting adj 당황하게 하는 | munition n 군수품 | militia n 민병대 | customary adj 관례의 | refuse v 거부하다 | flee v 도망가다, 피신하다 | federal government 연방 정부 | provision n 조항, 규정 | ensure v 보장하다 | cede v 양도하다 | seat of the government 정부 소재지 | fort n 요새 | warehouse n 창고 | dockyard n 조선소 | deem v 간주하다 | resolve v 해결하다 | extreme adj 극단적인 | measure n 조치 | owe v 빚을 지다 | debt n 빚 | inextricably adv 불가분하게 | traditionally adv 전통적으로 | stint n 일정 기간 동안의 일, 활동 | permanent adj 영구적인 | prominent adj 중요한, 유명한 | accordingly adv 이러하여, 이에 부응하여 | agrarian adj 농업의 | deadlock n 교착 상태 | accrue v 누적하다, 축적하다 | liable to ~에게 변상해야 하는 | fraction n 아주 적은 부분, 일부 | bankruptcy n 파산 | firmly adv 확실하게, 단단히 | calculate v 계산하다 | astonishing adj 놀라운, 믿기 힘든 | creditor n 채권자 | convince v 설득하다 | encompass v 둘러싸다 | historic adj 역사적인 | attribute to ~의 덕분으로 돌리다 | discovery n 발견 | poetic adj 시적의 | construct v 건설하다 | rapidly adv 빠르게

Lesson 15 Lectures

Lesson 15 Linguistics

본서 | P. 242

Test

1. A　2. D　3. D　4. B　5. A　6. C

Test

본서 | P. 243

Man: Professor | Woman 1, 2: Student

[1-6] Listen to part of a discussion in a linguistics class.

M 1 Most organisms seem to have some form of communication. Even bacteria communicate via chemical

남자: 교수 | 여자 1, 2: 학생

언어학 수업 중 토론의 일부를 들으시오.

남 1 대부분의 생물은 어떤 형태의 의사 소통 방식을 갖고 있는 것처럼 보입니다. 심지어 박테리아도 화

signals... but the question is, can members of different species communicate with each other?

W1 Sure, they can. 2 Haven't chimps and gorillas shown the ability to communicate with sign language, even producing novel sentences?

M 2 Yes, they have. But, they were taught by humans. Can anyone think of an example outside of a laboratory?

W2 I think so. Don't many animals inform potential predators that eating them would be unwise by having bright markings on their bodies?

M Yes, they do. 3 That kind of warning coloration is called aposematism, and many types of insects, amphibians, and reptiles use bright colors, often red and/or yellow contrasted against black and white, to show that they have a painful bite or sting or that their flesh is poisonous. But, that is a kind of passive communication. What I am referring to is active communication between predator and prey. One example of this can be found between ground squirrels and rattlesnakes. These two species are engaged in what is referred to as antagonistic coevolution, which means that they develop behavior and physical attributes in order to gain an advantage over each other. For the rattlesnakes, such adaptations include their extremely sensitive chemical sensing, their pit organs, camouflage, highly toxic venom, and lightning-fast striking ability.

W1 4 Professor, what are pit organs?

M 4 Ah, they are organs located on a rattlesnake's head behind its nostrils that can sense infrared energy. Essentially, they allow the snake to "see" the heat signature that its prey's body gives off. They are so sensitive that even a blind snake can target vulnerable spots on its prey's body. To combat this array of weaponry, the squirrels have evolved their own arsenal of counter measures. These include extremely fast and acrobatic maneuvers to dodge strikes, partial immunity to snake venom, and a battery of physical displays and signals that appear to deter the snakes from striking at all. Taken altogether, these adaptations show that these species have profoundly influenced one another.

5 Squirrels communicate with other members of their species in various ways, including a method called tail-flagging. They also use this technique when they encounter a rattlesnake, and the researchers think it serves two purposes. The first is to signify that the squirrel is aware of the snake's presence, and therefore prepared to flee if the snake attacks. Striking and pursuit use a great deal

학 신호로 소통을 하죠... 그러나 의문점은, 다른 종의 생물들이 서로 소통을 할 수 있을까요?

여1 물론 할 수 있어요. 2 침팬지와 고릴라가 수화로 소통하는 능력을 보이지 않았나요? 심지어 새로운 문장까지 만들면서요.

남 2 맞아요. 그랬죠. 그러나 이들은 인간들에 의해 교육 받은 겁니다. 누구 실험실 밖에서의 예시를 들어줄 사람 있나요?

여2 제가 할 수 있을 것 같아요. 많은 동물들이 몸의 밝은 무늬를 통해 잠재적 포식자들에게 자신을 먹는 것이 어리석은 짓이라고 알려주지 않나요?

남 네, 그렇습니다. 3 그런 종류의 경고를 위한 천연색은 경계색이라고 불리는데, 많은 종류의 곤충, 양서류, 그리고 파충류들이 밝은 색을 사용하죠, 흑백에 대비되는, 종종 빨갛거나 노란 색들 말이죠. 이 색들을 이용해 그들에게 물리거나 쏘이면 고통스럽다거나, 그들의 살이 독성을 띄고 있다는 것을 보여줍니다. 그러나 이는 수동적인 종류의 소통이에요. 내가 말하고 있는 것은 포식자와 먹이 사이의 능동적인 소통입니다. 이것의 한 예는 얼룩다람쥐와 방울뱀에게서 찾아볼 수 있습니다. 이 두 종의 동물들은 적대적 공진화라고 불리는 관계에 있는데, 이는 서로가 서로를 제압하기 위한 이점을 갖기 위해 행동과 신체적 특징을 발전시키는 것을 뜻하죠. 방울뱀의 경우 이러한 적응은 이들의 엄청나게 민감한 화학적 감각과 열 감지 기관, 위장, 치명적인 독, 그리고 번개처럼 빠른 공격 능력 등입니다.

여1 4 교수님, 열 감지 기관이 무엇인가요?

남 4 아, 방울뱀의 코 뒤쪽 머리에 위치해 있는 기관인데 적외선 에너지를 감지할 수 있어요. 본질적으로 말해 이 기관은 먹이의 몸에서 나오는 열 신호를 뱀이 '보도록' 도와줍니다. 지극히 민감하기 때문에 눈이 먼 뱀조차 먹이의 몸에 있는 취약한 부분을 공격할 수 있습니다. 이러한 다수의 무기들과 맞서기 위해 다람쥐들은 그들 자신의 대책 무기들을 발달시켰습니다. 이는 공격을 피하기 위한 매우 빠르고 곡예 같은 움직임, 뱀의 독에 대한 부분적인 면역성, 그리고 뱀이 아예 공격을 하지 못하도록 막는 것처럼 보이는 여러 신체적 과시와 신호 등을 포함합니다. 종합해보면, 이 적응들은 얼룩다람쥐와 방울뱀이 서로에게 매우 깊은 영향을 주었다는 것을 보여주죠.

5 다람쥐들은 꼬리 세우기라 불리는 방법을 포함한 여러 방법으로 다른 다람쥐들과 소통합니다. 그들은 또한 방울뱀과 마주쳤을 때 이 방법을 사용하며, 연구원들은 이것이 두 가지의 목적을 갖고 있다고 생각합니다. 첫 번째는 다람쥐가 뱀이 있다는 것을 인식하고 있으며, 뱀이 공격할 경우 도망갈 준비가 되었다는 것을 의미하기 위한 것입니다. 공격과

of energy that will be wasted if the snake fails to capture its prey. So, the squirrels will often move very close to the snake, wagging their tail the whole time, showing the snake that they know exactly where it is, and that any attempt to strike will be wasted. Of course, this is not always true, sometimes the snake will still successfully strike, which is where the squirrels' other adaptations come into play. It will desperately leap away from the attack and flee to a safe distance.

The second purpose could be to confuse the snake. These squirrels also have the ability to heat up their tails, which would make the tail-wagging display more vivid to the snake's infrared senses. The heated, bushy tail may create the impression that the tail is a viable striking point, which of course it is not since it is mostly fur. **6** In order to test their hypothesis, the scientists created robotic squirrels that can wag and heat their tails. They have found that the snakes will strike the robots' heads like they are real animals. They have also discovered that the snakes are less likely to attack if the robot engages in tail-flagging; particularly if the tail is heated.

먹이를 쫓아가는 것은 매우 많은 에너지를 필요로 하는 일이며, 만약 뱀이 먹이 포획에 실패한다면 에너지를 헛되이 쓰게 되는 거죠. 그래서 다람쥐들은 종종 뱀에게 매우 가까이 다가가고, 그동안 계속 꼬리를 흔들고 있는데, 이는 뱀이 어디 있는지 정확히 알고 있으며, 공격하려는 어떠한 시도도 낭비가 될 것이라는 것을 보여주는 거죠. 물론 이것이 항상 맞는 건 아닙니다. 때때로 뱀이 성공적으로 공격을 할 때가 있으므로 다람쥐의 다른 적응이 필요하게 되죠. 다람쥐는 필사적으로 뛰어올라 공격에서 벗어나 안전 거리까지 도망칩니다.

두 번째 목적은 뱀을 혼란스럽게 만들기 위한 겁니다. 이 다람쥐들은 꼬리를 뜨겁게 만드는 능력 또한 가지고 있는데, 이것이 꼬리 흔드는 모습을 뱀의 적외선 감지 기능에 더욱 더 생생하게 보이도록 만들죠. 뜨거워진 숱이 많은 꼬리는 다람쥐의 꼬리가 공격 가능한 지점이라는 인상을 줄 수 있는데, 물론 다람쥐의 꼬리가 대부분 털이기에 이는 사실이 아닙니다. **6** 이 가정을 실험하기 위해 과학자들이 꼬리를 흔들고 뜨겁게 만들 수 있는 로봇 다람쥐를 만들었습니다. 이들은 뱀이 마치 진짜 동물인 것처럼 로봇 다람쥐의 머리를 공격한다는 것을 알아냈죠. 또한 로봇 다람쥐가 꼬리를 세우고, 특히 꼬리를 뜨겁게 만들 경우 뱀이 공격을 할 가능성이 적다는 것을 밝혀냈습니다.

1. What is the main topic of the discussion?

Ⓐ Active communication between different animal species

Ⓑ The advantage of tail-flagging and tail heating for squirrels

Ⓒ The effective communication of animals inside a laboratory

Ⓓ The general relationship between predator and prey in nature

2. Listen to part of the discussion and answer the question.

W Haven't chimps and gorillas shown the ability to communicate with sign language, even producing novel sentences?

M Yes, they have. But, they were taught by humans. Can anyone think of an example outside of a laboratory?

Why does the professor say this:

M Can anyone think of an example outside of a laboratory?

1. 토론의 주제는 무엇인가?

Ⓐ 서로 다른 종의 동물들 사이의 능동적 의사소통

Ⓑ 다람쥐들의 꼬리 세우기와 꼬리 뜨겁게 만들기의 이점

Ⓒ 실험실 안 동물들의 효율적인 의사소통

Ⓓ 자연 속에서 포식자와 먹이 사이의 일반적 관계

2. 토론의 일부를 듣고 질문에 답하시오.

여 침팬지와 고릴라들이 수화로 소통하는 능력을 보이지 않았나요? 심지어 새로운 문장까지 만들면서요.

남 맞아요, 그랬죠. 그러나 이들은 인간들에 의해 교육 받은 겁니다. 누구 실험실 밖에서의 예시를 들어줄 사람 있나요?

교수는 왜 이렇게 말하는가:

남 누구 실험실 밖에서의 예시를 들어줄 사람 있나요?

Ⓐ He believes that the class should go on a field trip someday.
Ⓑ He thinks that the student did not comprehend his question.
Ⓒ He feels sorry for students since their ideas are always so predictable.
Ⓓ He wants an example that was not influenced by human actions.

Ⓐ 이 수업에서 언젠가 현장 학습을 가야 한다고 믿는다.
Ⓑ 학생이 그의 질문을 이해하지 못했다고 생각한다.
Ⓒ 학생들의 생각이 항상 너무 예측 가능하기에 유감스러워한다.
Ⓓ 인간의 활동에 영향을 받지 않은 예시를 원한다.

3. According to the discussion, how do animals of different species communicate with each other?
Ⓐ They display a variety of body language to make one another nervous.
Ⓑ Predators show aggressive behavior toward their prey when they are near.
Ⓒ They use chemical signals to each other at a close distance.
Ⓓ Prey organisms utilize warning coloration to make their predators give up.

3. 토론에 따르면, 다른 종의 동물들은 서로 어떻게 의사소통하는가?
Ⓐ 서로를 긴장하게 만들기 위해 다양한 바디 랭귀지를 보여준다.
Ⓑ 포식자들은 먹이가 가까이 있을 때 그들에게 공격적인 행동을 보인다.
Ⓒ 가까운 거리에서 서로에게 화학 신호를 사용한다.
Ⓓ 먹이 생물들은 포식자들을 포기하게 만들기 위해 경고하는 천연색을 사용한다.

4. What role do the pit organs of rattlesnakes play?
Ⓐ They make the snake produce more energy.
Ⓑ They help the snake to sense prey's body heat.
Ⓒ They increase the snake's speed for a moment.
Ⓓ They allow the snake to process its food faster.

4. 방울뱀의 열 감지 기관은 어떤 역할을 하는가?
Ⓐ 뱀이 더 많은 에너지를 생산해내도록 한다.
Ⓑ 먹이의 체열을 감지하도록 돕는다.
Ⓒ 순간적으로 뱀의 속도를 높여준다.
Ⓓ 뱀이 먹이를 더 빨리 소화시키도록 한다.

5. Why does the professor mention tail-flagging?
Ⓐ To give an example of one of the ways that squirrels communicate
Ⓑ To explain the importance of how squirrels consume their food
Ⓒ To point out another advantage that squirrels have when fighting
Ⓓ To illustrate how it can help squirrels by scaring away their predators

5. 교수는 왜 꼬리 세우기를 언급하는가?
Ⓐ 다람쥐가 의사소통하는 방법들 중 하나에 대한 예시를 들기 위해
Ⓑ 다람쥐가 먹이를 섭취하는 방법의 중요성을 설명하기 위해
Ⓒ 싸울 때 다람쥐들이 가진 또 다른 이점을 강조하기 위해
Ⓓ 포식자들에게 겁을 줘 쫓아버리는 데 꼬리 세우기가 어떻게 도움을 주는지 묘사하기 위해

6. What can be inferred about the scientists' experiment with robotic squirrels?
Ⓐ Robotic squirrels failed to confuse snakes since they were made by humans.
Ⓑ Snakes were able to distinguish the robotic squirrels from real ones.
Ⓒ Squirrels' ability to flag their heated tails is quite useful for avoiding snakes.
Ⓓ Tail heating ability scared away the snakes and helped the squirrels survive.

6. 과학자들의 로봇 다람쥐 실험에서 무엇을 추론할 수 있는가?
Ⓐ 로봇 다람쥐는 인간에 의해 만들어져서 뱀을 혼란시키는 데 실패했다.
Ⓑ 뱀은 진짜 다람쥐와 로봇 다람쥐를 구별할 수 있었다.
Ⓒ 뜨거워진 꼬리를 세우는 다람쥐의 능력은 뱀을 피하는 데 꽤 유용하다.
Ⓓ 꼬리를 뜨겁게 만드는 능력은 뱀을 도망가게 만들었고 다람쥐가 생존하게 해주었다.

어휘 organism n 생물, 유기체 I communication n 의사 소통 I chemical signal 화학 신호 I chimp n 침팬지 I sign language 수화 I novel adj 새로운, 참신한 I laboratory n 실험실 I inform v 알리다, 통지하다 I potential adj 잠재적이 있는, 가능성이 있는 I predator n 포식자 I unwise adj 어리석은 I marking n 무늬, 표시 I warning n 경고 I coloration n 천연색 I aposematism n 경계색 I amphibian n 양서류 I reptile n 파충류 I contrast v 대조하다, 대비시키다 I painful adj 고통스러운 I sting n 침, 쏘는 것 I flesh n 살, 피부 I poisonous adj 유독한 I passive adj 수동적인 I refer to 언급하다 I active adj 능동적인 I prey n 먹이, 사냥감 I ground squirrel 얼룩다람쥐 I rattlesnake n 방울뱀 I engage in ~에 관련하다 I antagonistic adj 적대적인 I coevolution n 공진화 (여러 종이 서로 영향을 주며 진화해 가는 일) I physical adj 신체적인, 육체의 I attribute n 속성 I adaptation n 적응 I sensitive adj 민감한 I pit organs 뱀의 입 근처에 있는 열 감지 기관 I camouflage n 위장 I toxic adj 유독성의 I venom n 독 I strike v (갑자기) 공격하다, 덮치다 I nostril n 콧구멍 I infrared adj 적외선의 I vulnerable adj 취약한, 연약한 I combat v 싸우다, 전투를 벌이다 I array n 집합, 모음 I weaponry n 무기 I evolve v 발달시키다 I arsenal n (집합적) 무기 I counter measure 대책 I acrobatic adj 곡예의 I maneuver n 책략, 술책 I dodge v 재빨리 움직여 피하다 I partial adj 부분적인 I immunity n 면역력 I a battery of 일련의 I deter v 단념시키다, 그만두게 하다 I profoundly adv 깊이, 극심하게 I tail-flagging (동물의) 꼬리 치켜세우기 I encounter v 맞닥뜨리다 I signify v 의미하다, 뜻하다 I presence n (특정한 곳에) 있음, 존재 I flee v 달아나다, 도망하다 I pursuit n 뒤쫓음, 추구 I capture v 포획하다 I wag v 흔들다, 흔들리다 I desperately adv 필사적으로, 자포자기하여 I leap v 뛰다 I vivid adj 생생한, 선명한 I bushy adj 숱이 많은, 무성한 I viable adj 실행 가능한 I fur n 털 I hypothesis n 가설, 추측 I robotic adj 로봇의 I particularly adv 특히, 특별히

Lesson 16 Literature

본서 I P. 245

Test

1. A **2.** C, D **3.** B, D **4.** B **5.** C **6.** A

Test

본서 I P. 246

Man: Student | Woman: Professor

[1-6] Listen to part of a discussion in an English literature class.

W **1** Widely considered to be one of the best novelists in the history of English Literature, Jane Austen was virtually unknown in her own time. **2(C)** This is because, like many other female authors of the 19th century, she at first concealed her identity. When her first novel, *Sense and Sensibility*, was released, its authorship was stated as "By a Lady". **2(D)** Her subsequent novels, *Pride and Prejudice*, *Mansfield Park*, and *Emma*, gradually brought her some fame and positive critical acclaim, but she benefited little from them financially. Today, however, her books are revered by fans worldwide, and *Pride and Prejudice* was even voted the second best-loved book in the UK. Her stories are set in the world of the landed gentry—the land-owning class in England that ranged in status from middle class to minor aristocracy—and typically revolved around the realities faced by women in that society. **1, 3(D)** Her work is renowned for its realism, social commentary, often stinging irony, and **3(B)** how the experiences of her protagonists often paralleled her own life in many ways.

남자: 학생 | 여자: 교수

영문학 수업 중 토론의 일부를 들으시오.

여 **1** 영문학 역사에서 가장 뛰어난 소설가들 중 한 명으로 널리 여겨지는 제인 오스틴은 생전에는 거의 알려지지 않았습니다. **2(C)** 그 이유는 19세기의 다른 많은 여성 소설가들처럼 그녀 역시 처음에는 정체를 숨겼기 때문이었어요. 그녀의 첫 번째 소설인 〈이성과 감성〉이 발표되었을 때, 책의 저자는 '한 숙녀'라고 명시되었습니다. **2(D)** 그 뒤로 발표된 소설들인 〈오만과 편견〉, 〈맨스필드 파크〉, 그리고 〈엠마〉는 그녀에게 점차 명성과 호평을 가져다 주었지만 재정적으로는 그다지 이득을 보지 못했습니다. 그러나 오늘날 그녀의 작품들은 전 세계적으로 팬들에게 추앙 받고 있으며 〈오만과 편견〉은 심지어 영국에서 가장 사랑 받는 책 투표에서 2위를 거두기도 했습니다. 그녀의 이야기들은 토지를 소유한 지주 계층들의 세계에 배경을 두고 있어요. 중산층부터 소귀족까지의 지위를 포함한, 영국의 토지를 소유한 계급들의 이야기죠. 그리고 일반적으로 그 사회에서 여성들이 마주하는 현실을 중심으로 이야기가 전개됩니다. **1, 3(D)** 그녀의 작품은 사실성, 사회에 대한 해석, 종종 날카로운 아이러니로 잘 알려져 있고, **3(B)** 주인공들의 경험이 많은 점에서 그녀 자신의 삶과 종종 유사하다는 점 등으로도 알려져 있습니다.

4 Like Elizabeth, the protagonist of *Pride and Prejudice*, Jane was born into a family that existed around the lower edge of the landed gentry. Her parents were both from established families, but they were not rich. Her father was a clergyman for much of her life, and he supplemented that steady but small income by farming and teaching boys who boarded with the family.

M How many siblings did Jane Austen have? Elizabeth had four sisters, was Jane's family similarly large?

W Indeed it was. She had 7 siblings, although they were rather the opposite of Elizabeth's. Jane had six brothers and one sister, Cassandra. The girls were understandably very close and confided in each other. Also, unlike her characters, neither Jane nor Cassandra married. They were both single until their deaths. Of course, Jane had suitors, but none of them became solid relationships. Considering how prominent a theme marriage is in the novel, this is somewhat surprising to many readers. 5 The famous opening line of the novel does state that "It is a truth universally acknowledged that a single man in possession of a good fortune must be in want of a wife".

M 5 But, doesn't the novel actually turn that notion on its head? Instead of the man needing a wife, the woman is in need of a husband with a fortune.

W That is a very astute observation, Jack. 6 Yes, the novel does portray marriage as an activity that is more economic than social. Elizabeth, Jane, and her friend Charlotte all marry men who are financially stable, which makes them appropriate choices. Her sister Lydia eloped with George Wickham, who was a penniless soldier, making him wholly undesirable to her family. This leads into another theme of the book: the importance of wealth. Men in the novel like Colonel Fitzwilliam could marry into wealth, but for women it was vital. By law, a woman could not inherit her family's fortune, which had to go to a male heir. Elizabeth's cousin William Collins was her family's heir, but she refused his proposal, thereby losing any share of her own family's wealth. Therefore, she had to marry someone of a higher rank with a fortune of his own in order to secure her future. But, being headstrong and independent, she ignored such pragmatic reasons and married a man she had grown to respect for his character, Fitzwilliam Darcy. Although, it should be noted that he did have his own fortune.

4 〈오만과 편견〉의 주인공인 엘리자베스와 같이 제인은 토지를 소유한 지주 계급 중에서도 하위 계급에 속하는 한 가정에서 태어났습니다. 그녀의 부모님 둘 다 존경 받는 가문의 사람들이었으나 부자는 아니었어요. 그녀의 아버지는 그녀 삶의 대부분 동안 성직자였고, 안정적이지만 적은 수입을 농사 일과 그들 가족과 함께 하숙하던 소년들을 가르치는 일로 보충했습니다.

남 제인 오스틴은 형제자매가 몇 명이나 있었나요? 엘리자베스는 네 명의 자매가 있었는데, 제인의 가족들도 그와 비슷하게 많았나요?

여 실제로 그랬습니다. 그녀는 7명의 형제자매가 있었는데, 엘리자베스의 가족과는 오히려 반대였죠. 제인에게는 여섯 명의 남자 형제들과 자매인 카산드라가 있었습니다. 두 자매는 당연히 매우 친했고 서로에게 마음을 털어놓았죠. 또한 소설의 인물들과는 다르게 제인과 카산드라 둘 다 결혼을 하지 않았습니다. 죽을 때까지 미혼으로 남았죠. 물론 제인에게는 구혼자들이 있었으나 그들 중 누구도 확실한 관계로 발전하지는 않았습니다. 결혼이라는 주제가 그녀의 소설에서 얼마나 중요한지를 생각한다면 많은 독자들에게 꽤나 놀라운 일이죠. 5 이 소설의 유명한 첫 문장은 이렇게 말합니다. "재산이 많은 미혼 남자에게 아내가 필요하다는 것은 누구나 인정하는 진리이다".

남 5 하지만, 소설은 사실 그 개념을 뒤집지 않나요? 남자가 아내를 필요로 하는 대신, 여자가 재산을 가진 남편을 필요로 하니까요.

여 매우 날카로운 관찰이에요, 잭. 6 그래요, 소설은 결혼을 사회적이기보다 경제적인 활동으로 묘사하고 있죠. 엘리자베스, 제인, 그리고 친구인 샬럿은 모두 경제적으로 안정되어 적절한 선택으로 여겨지는 남자들과 결혼합니다. 여동생인 리디아는 무일푼의 군인이어서 가족들에게 달갑지 않았던 조지 위컴과 사랑의 도피를 하죠. 이는 책의 또 다른 주제로 이어집니다. 부의 중요함이죠. 소설에서 피츠윌리엄 대령과 같은 남자들은 부를 찾아 결혼할 수 있지만, 여자들에게 그것은 필수적인 것이었습니다. 법에 의해 여성은 가족의 재산을 상속받을 수 없었고, 이 재산은 남자 상속인에게 돌아갔습니다. 엘리자베스의 사촌인 윌리엄 콜린스는 그녀 가족의 상속자였지만 그녀가 그의 청혼을 거절했기에 그녀는 가족이 소유한 재산의 모든 몫을 잃게 되었습니다. 그래서 그녀는 미래를 보장받기 위해 소유한 재산이 많은, 더 높은 계급의 남자와 결혼해야만 했어요. 그러나 고집이 세고 독립적이었던 그녀는 이러한 실리적인 이유들을 무시하고 성품을 존경하게 된 피츠윌리엄 다시와 결혼합니다. 비록 그가 자기 재산을 꽤 소유한 남자였다는 사실은 짚고 넘어가야 하겠지만요.

1. What is the main topic of the discussion?

Ⓐ The life of a prominent author and what her works show
Ⓑ The successful career of an author and her legacy
Ⓒ The typical family life of the 19th century England
Ⓓ The notion of women and marriage during the 19th century

2. According to the discussion, what is true about Jane Austen? Choose 2 answers.

Ⓐ She usually wrote novels with fantasy and mythical themes.
Ⓑ She achieved international success when her second novel was published.
Ⓒ She did not publish her first novel under her real name.
Ⓓ She was not able to make a fortune with her novels.

3. What are the characteristics of Jane Austen's novels? Choose 2 answers.

Ⓐ Overcoming physical and psychological hardships
Ⓑ Reflecting the author's own life through the protagonists' lives
Ⓒ Criticizing political and cultural issues using sarcasm
Ⓓ Representing the author's views on society

4. Why does the professor mention Elizabeth, the protagonist of *Pride and Prejudice*?

Ⓐ To further explain the psychological development in the novel
Ⓑ To show some similarities between Elizabeth and Jane Austen
Ⓒ To describe how Jane Austen portrayed a typical English woman
Ⓓ To point out that Elizabeth's character was based on Austen's sister

5. Listen again to part of the discussion. Then answer the question.

W The famous opening line of the novel does state that "It is a truth universally acknowledged that a single man in possession of a good fortune must be in want of a wife."
M But, doesn't the novel actually turn that notion on its head?

Why does the student say this:

M But, doesn't the novel actually turn that notion on its head?

1. 토론의 주제는 무엇인가?

Ⓐ 저명한 작가의 삶과 그녀의 작품이 보여주는 것들
Ⓑ 한 작가의 성공적인 경력과 그녀가 남긴 유산
Ⓒ 19세기 영국의 일반적인 가족의 삶
Ⓓ 19세기의 여성과 결혼에 대한 인식

2. 토론에 따르면, 제인 오스틴에 대해 옳은 것은 무엇인가? 두 개를 고르시오.

Ⓐ 보통 판타지와 신화적 주제들을 가지고 소설을 썼다.
Ⓑ 두 번째 소설이 출판되었을 때 세계적인 성공을 거두었다.
Ⓒ 본명으로 첫 번째 소설을 출판하지 않았다.
Ⓓ 그녀의 작품들로 많은 돈을 벌지 못했다.

3. 제인 오스틴 소설의 특징은 무엇인가? 두 개를 고르시오.

Ⓐ 신체적, 정신적 어려움 극복하기
Ⓑ 주인공들의 삶을 통해 작가 자신의 삶 투영하기
Ⓒ 비꼬는 말로 정치적, 문화적 문제 비판하기
Ⓓ 사회에 대한 작가의 관점 나타내기

4. 교수는 왜 〈오만과 편견〉의 주인공인 엘리자베스를 언급하는가?

Ⓐ 소설 내에서의 심리 발달에 대해 더 설명하기 위해
Ⓑ 엘리자베스와 제인 오스틴 사이의 유사점들을 알려주기 위해
Ⓒ 제인 오스틴이 어떻게 일반적인 영국 여성을 그렸는지 묘사하기 위해
Ⓓ 엘리자베스라는 인물이 오스틴의 자매에 기반한 것이라고 지적하기 위해

5. 토론의 일부를 다시 듣고 질문에 답하시오.

여 이 소설의 유명한 첫 문장은 이렇게 말합니다. "재산이 많은 미혼 남자에게 아내가 필요하다는 것은 누구나 인정하는 진리이다".
남 하지만, 소설은 사실 그 개념을 뒤집지 않나요?

학생은 왜 이렇게 말하는가:

남 하지만, 소설은 사실 그 개념을 뒤집지 않나요?

Lesson 16 Lectures

Ⓐ Jane Austen actually thought that marriage is not a necessary thing.
Ⓑ *Pride and Prejudice* was able to point out the irony of marriage.
Ⓒ The story of *Pride and Prejudice* is the opposite of the quote.
Ⓓ In *Pride and Prejudice*, most of the male characters do not get married.

Ⓐ 제인 오스틴은 사실 결혼이 필요한 것이 아니라고 생각했다.
Ⓑ 〈오만과 편견〉은 결혼의 역설적인 점을 지적할 수 있었다.
Ⓒ 〈오만과 편견〉의 이야기는 인용구와 반대이다.
Ⓓ 〈오만과 편견〉에서 대부분의 남자 인물들은 결혼을 하지 않는다.

6. What can be inferred about *Pride and Prejudice*?
Ⓐ It emphasizes the importance of marriage as a financial benefit.
Ⓑ It tried to describe young women who are in financial trouble.
Ⓒ It shows that marrying someone of higher rank was almost impossible.
Ⓓ It displays the rise of the middle class and minor aristocracy.

6. 〈오만과 편견〉에 대해 무엇을 추론할 수 있는가?
Ⓐ 재정적 이득으로서의 결혼의 중요성을 강조한다.
Ⓑ 재정적 어려움에 처한 젊은 여성들을 묘사하려고 했다.
Ⓒ 더 높은 계급의 사람과 결혼하는 것은 거의 불가능했다는 것을 보여준다.
Ⓓ 중산층과 소귀족 계층의 상승을 보여준다.

어휘 widely adv 널리 | novelist n 소설가 | virtually adv 사실상 | conceal v 감추다, 숨기다 | identity n 정체 | sense n 이성 | sensibility n 감성 | release v 발표하다 | authorship n 저자 | subsequent adj 다음의, 차후의 | pride n 오만, 교만 | prejudice n 편견 | gradually adv 점차, 서서히 | positive adj 긍정적인 | critical adj 비평적인, 비판적인 | benefit v 득을 보다 | financially adv 재정적으로 | revere v 숭배하다 | landed adj 많은 토지를 소유한 | gentry n (영국의 경우) 지주 계급, 상류층, 신사들 | range v ~를 아우르다 | aristocracy n 귀족 | typically adv 보통, 일반적으로 | revolve v ~를 중심으로 전개하다, 회전하다 | reality n 현실 | renowned adj 명성 있는 | realism n 사실성 | commentary n 해설 | stinging adj 날카로운, 찌르는, 쏘는 | protagonist n 주인공 | parallel v ~와 유사하다 | established adj 인정 받는 | clergyman n 남자 성직자 | supplement v 보충하다 | steady adj 꾸준한, 변함 없는 | income n 소득, 수입 | board v 하숙하다 | understandably adv 당연히 | confide in 마음을 주다 | suitor n 구혼자 | solid adj 확실한, 견고한 | prominent adj 중요한, 유명한 | theme n 주제, 테마 | universally adv 일반적으로 | acknowledge v 인정하다 | possession n 소유 | fortune n 재산, 부 | notion n 개념, 관념 | astute adj 예리한, 빈틈 없는 | observation n 관찰 | portray v 그리다, 묘사하다 | economic adj 경제의 | stable adj 안정된 | appropriate adj 적절한 | elope v 눈이 맞아 함께 달아나다 | penniless adj 무일푼인 | undesirable adj 원하지 않는, 달갑지 않은 | colonel n 대령 | vital adj 필수적인 | inherit v 상속받다 | heir n 상속자 | refuse v 거부하다 | proposal n 청혼 | headstrong adj 완고한, 고집불통의 | independent adj 독립적인 | pragmatic adj 실리적인

Lesson 17 Music

본서 | P. 248

Test

1. B **2.** B, C **3.** A **4.** B **5.** D **6.** D

Test

본서 | P. 249

Man: Professor | Woman: Student

[1-6] Listen to part of a discussion in a music history class.

M **1** Originating around the mid-1890s, ragtime is a genre of music that is viewed as being distinctly American. **2(C)** Named for its irregular or "ragged" rhythm, it evolved from dance music in the nightclubs of African-American districts

남자: 교수 | 여자: 학생

음악사 수업 중 토론의 일부를 들으시오.

남 **1** 1890년대 중반에 생겨난 래그타임은 뚜렷하게 미국적이라고 여겨지는 음악 장르입니다. **2(C)** 불규칙적이고 '들쑥날쑥한' 리듬 때문에 이러한 이름을 갖게 되었는데, 세인트루이스와 뉴올리언스의 아프

in St. Louis and New Orleans. **2(B)** It was a modification of classical music, particularly the marching music popularized by John Philip Sousa, with a rhythmic influence from African music and a heavy emphasis on the piano. Although Ernest Hogan is credited as one of the chief innovators responsible for developing it, and even came up with the name of the genre, **3** composer Scott Joplin is the most famous artist of the style. Joplin's rise to fame began with his publication of the *Maple Leaf Rag*, and continued with a series of hits including *The Entertainer*. Because *Maple Leaf Rag* was printed, it was able to influence many other artists with its unique melodies, harmony, and pacing. However, his star faded along with the music as jazz took precedence.

W But, didn't jazz evolve from ragtime? Many musicians played in both styles.

M That is true, **4** many musicians did dabble in both styles, and both types of music were created by African Americans, but it can be difficult to trace the actual development of a style of music. To do so you would need to speak with the musicians who created it, which of course is impossible. The recordings of ragtime that still exist were mostly recorded by jazz musicians, though, because its height of popularity preceded the widespread availability of recorded music. At that time, it was distributed as sheet music, much like classical music was. Jazz also tends to be more improvised, so no two recordings are exactly the same, whereas ragtime was written down.

Despite its name, ragtime is not actually a time meter like many other styles of music tend to be. For example, a waltz has a 3/4 meter, and a march has a 2/4 meter. Rather, it is an effect that could theoretically be applied to any meter, so a ragtime piece with a 3/4 meter would correctly be labeled a ragtime waltz. In fact, ragtime is defined by its syncopation or disruption of the rhythm by melodic touches that the musician plays between the beats. **5** The syncopation is not meant to detract from the beat, but to accentuate it in an effort to inspire the audience to dance. As I said earlier, it originated in nightclubs.

6 Scott Joplin's contributions to the art form were largely responsible for it receiving nationwide attention and popular

리카계 미국인 구역에 있던 나이트클럽의 댄스 음악으로부터 진화했습니다. **2(B)** 클래식 음악의 한 가지 변형 종이었는데, 특히 존 필립 수자가 대중화한 행진 음악의 변형으로, 아프리카 음악의 리듬으로부터 영향을 받았고 피아노를 매우 강조했죠. 비록 어니스트 호건이 래그타임을 발전시킨 가장 중요한 혁신가들 중 하나로 인정받고 있고, 심지어 이 장르의 이름을 붙인 사람이긴 하지만 **3** 작곡가 스콧 조플린이 래그타임 스타일의 가장 유명한 음악가입니다. 그는 〈단풍잎 래그〉의 출판과 함께 명성을 얻기 시작했으며 〈엔터테이너〉를 포함한 여러 히트곡들을 계속 발표했죠. 〈단풍잎 래그〉는 종이에 프린트되어 나왔기에 그 독특한 멜로디, 하모니, 그리고 박자가 다른 많은 예술가들에게 영향을 끼칠 수 있었습니다. 그러나 재즈가 앞서나가기 시작하면서 그의 인기는 래그타임 음악과 함께 빛이 바래기 시작했습니다.

여 그렇지만 재즈는 래그타임에서 진화한 장르 아닌가요? 많은 음악가들이 이 두 스타일로 연주했는데요.

남 맞아요. **4** 많은 음악가들이 두 스타일 모두에 손을 댔고, 재즈와 래그타임 둘 다 아프리카계 미국인들에 의해 만들어진 것이지만 한 음악의 스타일이 실제로 어떻게 발전했는지 추적하기란 어려울 수 있어요. 그러기 위해서는 이 장르를 만든 음악가들과 이야기를 나눠야 하는데, 물론 이는 불가능하죠. 하지만 지금까지 존재하는 래그타임 녹음곡들은 대부분 재즈 음악가들이 녹음한 것인데, 이는 래그타임 음악 인기의 절정기가 음반이 널리 이용 가능해진 시기보다 앞섰기 때문이었습니다. 그 시기에 음악은 클래식 음악과 마찬가지로 악보로 유통되었습니다. 재즈는 또한 즉흥적인 경향이 더 컸는데, 그 때문에 두 개의 녹음곡이 완전히 똑같은 경우가 없었던 반면, 래그타임의 경우는 곡이 악보로 기록되었습니다.

그 이름에도 불구하고 래그타임은 사실 다른 많은 스타일의 음악이 그러한 것처럼 박자가 있는 것은 아닙니다. 예를 들어, 왈츠는 3/4박자를 가지고 있고, 행진곡은 2/4박자죠. 오히려 래그타임은 이론상 어떠한 박자에도 응용될 수 있는 것 같아요. 그래서 3/4박자를 가진 래그타임 곡은 정확하게 말하자면 래그타임 왈츠로 이름 붙여지죠. 실제로 래그타임은 당김음이나 박자 사이에 음악가가 연주해 넣는 멜로디에 의한 리듬의 단절로 정의됩니다. **5** 당김음은 박자를 흐트러뜨리기 위한 것이 아니라, 관객들이 춤을 추도록 고무하기 위해 박자를 강조하기 위한 것입니다. 앞서 말했듯이, 래그타임은 나이트클럽에서 시작되었어요.

6 스콧 조플린의 래그타임에 대한 기여는 래그타임이 전국적으로 주목을 받고 대중적인 인기를 얻도

Lesson 17
Lectures

appeal. He penned 44 original ragtime compositions, and he even wrote a ballet and two operas. But his first major contribution was when he played it at the Chicago World's Fair of 1893. Since over 27 million guests attended that six-month event, he secured an unbelievably large and varied audience. Joplin sought to elevate ragtime from its perceived lowly stature, and he incorporated many European aspects into his compositions.

W So, does that explain why he wrote his operas?

M Well, yes and no. His opera *Treemonisha* did contain ragtime elements, but he used them judiciously and in moderation. He did not set out to compose a ragtime opera, but it was definitely an African American opera due to its story of elevating a slave community through the virtues of education. Sadly, his operas did not receive much recognition at the time. Ragtime experienced several revivals, one of the largest of which was in the 1970s. This occurred due to three events. Firstly, pianist Joshua Rifkin published a tribute to Joplin that was a compilation of his compositions. He played them in the serious style that Joplin had intended and was nominated for a Grammy in 1971. Then, the New York Public Library released a two-volume collection of his works. Finally, the 1973 movie *The Sting* had a soundtrack of his pieces as played by Marvin Hamlisch, and his rendition of *The Entertainer* won an Academy award. The popularity of the song, and ragtime as a revived genre, was confirmed by the song's reaching number 3 in the American Top 40 on May 18, 1974.

록 만들었습니다. 그는 독창적인 44개의 래그타임 곡들을 작곡했고, 심지어 발레 하나와 오페라 두 편을 작곡했습니다. 그러나 그의 가장 중요한 첫 번째 기여는 1893년 시카고 만국 박람회에서 연주한 것이었어요. 2천 7백만 명이 넘는 방문객들이 이 6개월간의 행사에 다녀가서 그는 믿을 수 없을 만큼 규모가 크고 다양한 관객을 확보할 수 있었습니다. 조플린은 래그타임이 급이 낮다는 인식으로부터 그 위상을 높이려고 했고, 작품에 유럽적인 요소들을 많이 포함시켰죠.

여 그게 그가 오페라를 작곡한 이유인가요?

남 음, 그렇기도 하고 아니기도 합니다. 그의 오페라 〈트리모니샤〉는 래그타임 요소를 가지고 있긴 했지만 조플린은 래그타임을 신중하게 절제해서 사용했습니다. 래그타임 오페라를 작곡하려 한 것은 아니었지만, 교육의 미덕을 통해 한 노예 공동체의 위상을 끌어올린다는 내용이었기에 분명히 아프리카계 미국인들의 오페라였습니다. 슬프게도 그의 오페라는 그 당시에 많은 인정을 받지는 못했어요. 래그타임은 몇 차례의 부흥을 겪었는데, 가장 큰 부흥기는 1970년대에 있었습니다. 이는 세 가지의 사건으로 인해 발생했습니다. 먼저, 피아니스트 조슈아 리프킨이 조플린에게 헌정하는 그의 작품 모음집을 발표했습니다. 그는 조플린이 의도했던 대로 이 곡들을 진지한 스타일로 연주했고, 1971년에 그래미 상 후보에 올랐습니다. 그 뒤, 뉴욕 공립 도서관에서 조플린의 작품들을 두 권의 작품집으로 내놓았습니다. 마지막으로, 1973년에 영화 〈스팅〉에서 마빈 햄리시가 연주한 조플린의 곡을 사운드트랙으로 사용했으며, 햄리시의 〈엔터테이너〉 연주는 아카데미 상을 수상했죠. 이 곡과 되살아난 장르로서 래그타임의 인기는 1974년 5월 18일에 〈엔터테이너〉가 아메리칸 톱 40 차트에서 3위에 이르며 확인되었습니다.

1. What is the discussion mainly about?

Ⓐ A music composer who had a lasting impact on jazz
Ⓑ The important characteristics of a certain genre of music
Ⓒ Three events that led to the revival of ragtime
Ⓓ Famous musicians who experimented with various genres

2. According to the discussion, what is true about ragtime? Choose 2 answers.

Ⓐ John Philip Sousa is credited as the first innovator of ragtime.

1. 토론은 주로 무엇에 대한 것인가?

Ⓐ 재즈에 오래도록 지속될 영향을 남긴 한 작곡가
Ⓑ 한 음악 장르의 중요한 특징들
Ⓒ 래그타임의 부활을 이끈 세 가지 사건들
Ⓓ 다양한 장르를 실험한 유명한 음악가들

2. 토론에 의하면, 래그타임에 관해 옳은 것은 무엇인가? 두 개를 고르시오.

Ⓐ 존 필립 수자는 래그타임의 첫 번째 혁신가로 인정받는다.

Ⓑ It included some features of marching music and classical music.
Ⓒ The name came from its unexpected and irregular rhythm.
Ⓓ It first appeared in New York City and gained popularity there.

3. Why does the professor mention Scott Joplin?
Ⓐ To introduce a fundamental figure of ragtime music
Ⓑ To show his influence on classical musicians
Ⓒ To emphasize his achievements in marching music
Ⓓ To bring up another topic regarding the history of jazz

4. What is the relationship between ragtime and jazz?
Ⓐ Jazz actually preceded ragtime music.
Ⓑ They both evolved around the same time.
Ⓒ Ragtime music heavily influenced jazz.
Ⓓ They had a huge impact on marching music.

5. Listen again to part of the discussion. Then answer the question.

M The syncopation is not meant to detract from the beat, but to accentuate it in an effort to inspire the audience to dance. As I said earlier, it originated in nightclubs.

Why does the professor say this:

M As I said earlier, it originated in nightclubs.

Ⓐ To ask the students to do some more research
Ⓑ To show that he is not sure why ragtime originated in nightclubs
Ⓒ To explain the concept of ragtime during the 1970s
Ⓓ To emphasize that the music was intended to make people dance

6. What can be inferred about Scott Joplin?
Ⓐ He worked with Joshua Rifkin and received a Grammy Award.
Ⓑ He became famous for his opera rather than ragtime music.
Ⓒ He brought about the revival of ragtime during the 1970s.
Ⓓ He helped ragtime to gain widespread appeal with the public.

Ⓑ 행진 음악과 클래식 음악의 일부 특성들을 포함했다.
Ⓒ 예상할 수 없고 불규칙적인 리듬에서 그 이름이 유래되었다.
Ⓓ 처음에 뉴욕시에서 시작되었고 그곳에서 인기를 얻었다.

3. 교수는 왜 스콧 조플린을 언급하는가?
Ⓐ 래그타임 음악의 핵심적인 인물을 소개하기 위해
Ⓑ 클래식 음악가들에게 그가 끼친 영향을 보이기 위해
Ⓒ 행진 음악에 있어 그의 업적을 강조하기 위해
Ⓓ 재즈의 역사에 관련하여 또 다른 주제를 제시하기 위해

4. 래그타임과 재즈의 관계는 무엇인가?
Ⓐ 재즈가 사실 래그타임 음악보다 먼저 나왔다.
Ⓑ 둘 다 비슷한 시기에 발전했다.
Ⓒ 래그타임 음악이 재즈에 큰 영향을 주었다.
Ⓓ 둘 다 행진 음악에 큰 영향을 미쳤다.

5. 토론의 일부를 다시 듣고 질문에 답하시오.

남 당김음은 박자를 흐트러뜨리기 위한 것이 아니라, 관객들이 춤을 추도록 고무하기 위해 박자를 강조하기 위한 것입니다. 앞서 말했듯이, 래그타임은 나이트클럽에서 시작되었어요.

교수는 왜 이렇게 말하는가:

남 앞서 말했듯이, 래그타임은 나이트클럽에서 시작되었어요.

Ⓐ 학생들에게 더 많이 조사하라고 요청하려고
Ⓑ 왜 래그타임이 나이트클럽에서 시작되었는지 확실치 않다는 것을 보이려고
Ⓒ 1970년대의 래그타임의 개념을 설명하려고
Ⓓ 래그타임 음악이 사람들을 춤추게 하기 위한 것이었음을 강조하려고

6. 스콧 조플린에 대해 무엇을 추론할 수 있는가?
Ⓐ 조슈아 리프킨과 함께 작업하였고 그래미상을 수상했다.
Ⓑ 래그타임 음악보다는 오페라로 인해 유명해졌다.
Ⓒ 1970년대에 래그타임 음악의 부활을 가져왔다.
Ⓓ 래그타임 음악이 대중의 폭넓은 관심을 끄는 데 도움이 되었다.

어휘 genre n 장르 | distinctly adv 뚜렷하게, 명백하게 | irregular adj 불규칙적인 | ragged adj 들쑥날쑥한, 울퉁불퉁한 | evolve v 진화하다 | district n 구역, 지구 | modification n (개선을 위한) 변형 | classical music 고전 음악, 클래식 | particularly adv 특히, 특별히 | marching music 행진곡 | popularize v 많은 사람들에게 알리다 | rhythmic adj 리듬의 | emphasis n 강조 | innovator n 혁신가 | responsible adj 책임지고 있는 | composer n 작곡가 | publication n 발표, 출판 | pacing n 속도 | fade v 바래다, 희미해지다 | precedence n 우선 | dabble in ~에 손을 대다 | trace v 추적하다, 찾아내다 | height n 정점 | popularity n 인기 | precede v ~에 앞서다 | widespread adj 광범위한, 널리 퍼진 | distribute v 유통하다, 분배하다 | improvise v 즉흥적으로 하다 | theoretically adv 이론상 | correctly adv 바르게, 정확하게 | label v 표를 붙이다 | define v 정의하다, 규정하다 | syncopation n 당김음 | disruption n 중단, 두절 | detract v 주의를 다른 데로 돌리다 | accentuate v 강조하다, 두드러지게 하다 | inspire v 고무하다 | contribution n 기여 | nationwide adj 전국적인 | pen v (글 등을) 쓰다 | secure v 획득하다, 확보하다 | elevate v 승격시키다, 올리다 | perceive v 인지하다 | stature n 위상 | incorporate v 포함하다 | aspect n 측면, 양상 | composition n 작품 | judiciously adv 신중하게, 분별력 있게 | moderation n 적당함, 절제 | virtue n 선행, 미덕 | recognition n 인정 | revival n 부흥, 부활 | tribute n 헌사, 찬사 | compilation n 모음집 | nominate v 지명하다, 후보에 올리다 | release v 공개하다, 발표하다 | rendition n 연주, 공연 | confirm v 확실하게 하다, 확인하다

Lesson 18 Paleontology

본서 | P. 251

Test

1. B 2. A, C 3. D 4. B 5. D 6. A

Test

본서 | P. 252

Man: Professor | Woman: Student

[1-6] Listen to part of a lecture in a paleontology class.

M **1** Since the 19th century, scientists have been looking for what are referred to as "missing links". These are organisms that bridge the gap between an earlier animal group and other groups that are believed to have evolved from that group. Based upon the concepts of evolution, researchers have reasoned that these organisms must have existed. Unfortunately, the fossil record is far from complete, so many of these transitional species have been difficult to find. It is easy to see that fish evolved long before tetrapods, or four-legged animals, which were the animals that moved from the water onto the land. Therefore, there must have been one or more species that shared characteristics of both fish and tetrapods. The characteristics that clearly differentiate tetrapods are the way that they breathe, their ability to move their heads separately from their torsos, and how they move around. **1, 2** For example, fish breathe through gills, while land animals use lungs. The gills of fish are believed to have evolved into the structures of the inner ears of tetrapods. One species that had a mixture of these traits is Tiktaalik roseae.

Tiktaalik lived during the Devonian period about 375 million years ago. The creature was a predator with a head shaped somewhat like a crocodile's and filled with sharp teeth. It had a long, flat body that could grow up to 3 meters long, if not longer. Not enough complete specimens have been discovered to be certain about its average length. Tiktaalik

남자: 교수 | 여자: 학생

고생물학 강의의 일부를 들으시오.

남 **1** 19세기 이래 과학자들은 '잃어버린 고리'라 불리는 것들을 탐색해 왔습니다. 이 잃어버린 고리란 초기의 동물군과 이 동물군에서 진화한 것으로 보이는 다른 동물군 사이를 이어주는 생물들이죠. 진화의 개념에 기반하여 연구원들은 이 생물들이 분명히 존재했을 거라고 추론했습니다. 안타깝게도 화석 기록은 결코 완전하지 않아서 이 이행종들의 다수를 찾기가 어려웠어요. 물고기가 사지 동물보다 훨씬 더 먼저 진화했다는 사실은 알기 쉬운데, 사지 동물 즉 다리가 네 개 달린 동물들은 물에서 살다 육지로 옮겨갔기 때문입니다. 그러므로 물고기와 사지 동물 둘 다의 특성을 공유하는 종이 하나 혹은 그 이상 존재했었을 겁니다. 사지 동물을 분명히 구분하는 특성은 이들이 숨을 쉬는 방법, 몸통과 머리를 따로 움직일 수 있는 능력, 그리고 움직이는 방식 등입니다. **1, 2** 예를 들어, 물고기는 아가미로 숨을 쉬지만 육지 동물은 폐로 숨을 쉽니다. 물고기의 아가미는 사지 동물의 내이 구조로 진화한 것으로 보입니다. 이러한 특성들이 혼합된 종이 바로 틱타알릭 로제입니다.

틱타알릭은 약 3억 7천 5백만 년 전 데본기에 살았습니다. 이 생물은 악어와 비슷한 머리에 날카로운 이빨이 가득한 포식자였어요. 길고 납작한 몸은 최대 3미터까지 자랄 수 있었습니다. 평균 길이를 확신할 수 있을 정도로 충분히 많은 완전한 표본들이 발견되지는 않았어요. 틱타알릭은 다른 물고기들처

had gills, scales, and fins like other fish, but it had many other features that differentiate it from them. **2(A)** It was among the first fish ever to have an actual neck, which allowed it to move its head from side to side or up and down. If any other fish tries to move like that, it must move its entire body because of the bony plates in its gill area. Tiktaalik did not have those plates.

The animal also had large forelimbs that resemble arms in many ways. They had larger shoulders complete with shoulder blades, large muscles attached to the humerus, or upper arm bone, and very mobile wrist joints. **3** The limbs were still tipped with fins, but they also show attachment points for large muscles, which means that the fin was both strong and flexible. Taken all together, this kind of limb structure suggests that the animal could use its forelimbs like arms. It may have just used them to anchor itself to the bottom in a strong current, but it could have also used them to support its weight and move around on land.

W Why would it want to move around on land? I mean, why leave the water in the first place?

M Well, there are many possible reasons. **4** There were many plants growing on the land at the time, and they were shedding leaves into the water. This organic matter would have hosted bacteria that used oxygen as they ate it. That would deplete the oxygen in the water, so animals would need to stay near the surface, or even leave the water to get their oxygen. The plants were also increasing the oxygen content of the air, so it may have become more advantageous to use that supply than the water's. To climb out of the water, a fish would need limbs like the ones that Tiktaalik had.

5 Its gills were actually two nostril-like holes on top of its head above the eyes called spiracles. The location of the spiracles would have allowed Tiktaalik to breathe air at the surface of the water without having to climb out, much like a whale. **2(C)** Of course, gills do not work unless they are wet, so Tiktaalik must have developed some form of basic lungs to pull oxygen out of the air it breathed. This is supported by the fact that it had a strong, rounded ribcage.

6 Due to the number of traits that Tiktaalik shares with both fish and tetrapods, and the fact that it predates tetrapods by a few million years, it is a strong candidate for being a missing link. There were many other animals at this time that developed similar features, so it is difficult to say which one was the ancestor of land animals. However, there

럼 아가미, 비늘, 그리고 지느러미를 갖고 있었지만 다른 물고기와는 구별되는 특징들이 많았습니다. **2(A)** 머리를 양 옆으로 또는 위아래로 움직일 수 있게 해주는, 진짜 목이 있었던 최초의 물고기들 중 하나였습니다. 다른 물고기가 이렇게 머리를 움직이려 할 경우에는 아가미 근처의 골판들 때문에 몸 전체를 움직여야만 합니다. 틱타알릭에게는 이러한 골판들이 없었죠.

이 동물은 또한 여러 가지 면에서 팔과 비슷한 커다란 앞다리를 갖고 있었습니다. 어깨뼈를 갖춘 더 넓은 어깨가 있었고, 상완골 즉 위쪽 팔뼈에 큰 근육이 붙어 있었으며, 아주 잘 움직이는 손목 관절 또한 갖추고 있었어요. **3** 사지의 끝에는 여전히 지느러미가 달려 있었지만 큰 근육이 있었다는 것을 보여주는 부착점 또한 있는데, 이는 지느러미가 강한 동시에 유연했다는 의미입니다. 이 모든 점을 종합해 봤을 때, 이러한 사지 구조는 틱타알릭이 앞다리를 팔처럼 쓸 수 있었다는 것을 암시합니다. 강한 해류에 맞서 바닥에 붙어 있기 위해 사용했을 수도 있지만, 무게를 떠받치고 육지에서 움직이기 위해 사용했을 수도 있죠.

여 왜 육지에서 돌아다니려고 했을까요? 제 말은, 애초에 왜 물에서 나오는 걸까요?

남 음, 가능한 이유들이 많이 있습니다. **4** 당시 육지에는 많은 식물들이 자라고 있었고, 이 식물들이 물에 잎을 떨어뜨렸어요. 이 유기 물질은 잎을 먹어 치우면 산소를 소모하는 박테리아를 갖고 있었을 겁니다. 그로 인해 물 속의 산소가 고갈되면, 동물들은 수면 가까이에 머무르거나 심지어 산소를 얻기 위해 물을 떠나야만 했을 겁니다. 식물들이 공기 중의 산소 농도를 증가시켰으므로 물 속의 산소보다 공기 중에서 공급되는 산소를 이용하는 게 더 유리했을 겁니다. 물 밖으로 기어 올라오기 위해서, 물고기는 틱타알릭이 가졌던 것 같은 사지가 필요했겠죠.

5 이 생물의 아가미는 사실 기문이라고 불리는, 눈 위쪽 머리 꼭대기에 있는 두 개의 콧구멍이었습니다. 기문의 위치 덕분에 틱타알릭은 고래처럼 물 밖으로 나가지 않고도 수면에서 숨을 쉴 수 있었습니다. **2(C)** 물론 아가미는 물에 젖어 있지 않는 한 기능을 하지 못하므로 틱타알릭은 숨을 쉬는 공기에서 산소를 끌어올 만한 기본적인 폐의 형태를 발달시켰을 겁니다. 이 주장은 틱타알릭이 강하고 둥근 흉곽을 가졌다는 사실로 뒷받침됩니다.

6 물고기와 사지 동물 모두와 공유하는 다수의 특성, 그리고 사지 동물을 수백만 년 앞선다는 사실로 인해 틱타알릭은 잃어버린 고리가 될 수 있는 강력한 후보입니다. 이 시대에 비슷한 특성을 발달시킨 다른 동물들도 존재했으므로 어떤 동물이 육지 동물의 조상인지 말하기는 어렵습니다. 그러나 고리

doesn't necessarily have to be one link. There could have been many transition animals from which land animals descended.

가 하나여야 할 필요는 없죠. 육지 동물의 유래가 된 많은 종류의 이행 동물이 존재했을 수 있습니다.

1. What is the main topic of the lecture?

Ⓐ How fish evolved to become land organisms
Ⓑ The characteristics of a possible missing link organism
Ⓒ Common species from the Devonian period
Ⓓ The process by which gills developed into lungs

2. What are the characteristics of Tiktaalik that fish lack?

Choose 2 answers.

Ⓐ It could move its head separately from its body.
Ⓑ It had bony plates located on the sides of its neck.
Ⓒ It breathed air into its lungs.
Ⓓ Its body was covered with scales.

3. How were Tiktaalik's front limbs different from modern tetrapods?

Ⓐ They had mobile wrist joints.
Ⓑ They had attachment points for large muscles.
Ⓒ They had large shoulder blades.
Ⓓ They had fins at the ends of them.

4. According to the professor, why would Tiktaalik leave the water?

Ⓐ To avoid infectious bacteria
Ⓑ To be able to get more oxygen
Ⓒ To have access to a food source
Ⓓ To escape from predators

5. Why does the professor mention a whale?

Ⓐ To name an animal that made a similar transition
Ⓑ To emphasize that many aquatic species breathe air
Ⓒ To suggest what an organism may have evolved into
Ⓓ To provide an example of a similar body structure

6. What can be inferred about missing links?

Ⓐ People often assume that animals with similar traits must share the same ancestor.
Ⓑ Transitional organisms are now easy to find due to the completeness of the fossil record.
Ⓒ Many fossils of missing links were discovered during the 19th century.
Ⓓ Missing link organisms always show the transitions between different habitats.

1. 강의의 주제는 무엇인가?

Ⓐ 어떻게 물고기가 진화하여 육지 생물이 되었는지
Ⓑ 잃어버린 고리일 가능성이 있는 한 생물의 특징들
Ⓒ 데본기의 일반적인 종들
Ⓓ 아가미가 폐로 발달한 과정

2. 물고기에게 없는 틱타알릭의 특징들은 무엇인가?

두 개를 고르시오.

Ⓐ 몸과 머리를 따로 움직일 수 있었다.
Ⓑ 목의 양편에 위치한 골판들이 있었다.
Ⓒ 폐로 숨을 쉬었다.
Ⓓ 몸이 비늘로 덮여 있었다.

3. 틱타알릭의 앞다리는 오늘날 사지 동물들의 팔과 어떻게 달랐는가?

Ⓐ 쉽게 움직이는 손목 관절이 있었다.
Ⓑ 커다란 근육을 위한 부착점이 있었다.
Ⓒ 큰 어깨뼈가 있었다.
Ⓓ 끝에 지느러미가 달려 있었다.

4. 교수에 따르면, 틱타알릭은 왜 물을 떠났는가?

Ⓐ 감염을 일으키는 세균을 피하기 위해
Ⓑ 산소를 더 얻기 위해
Ⓒ 먹잇감을 얻기 위해
Ⓓ 포식자를 피하기 위해

5. 교수는 왜 고래를 언급하는가?

Ⓐ 비슷한 이행을 한 다른 동물을 말하려고
Ⓑ 많은 수중 생물이 공기로 숨을 쉰다고 강조하려고
Ⓒ 어떤 생물이 진화하여 고래가 되었는지 시사하려고
Ⓓ 비슷한 신체 구조의 예를 들려고

6. 잃어버린 고리에 대해 무엇을 추론할 수 있는가?

Ⓐ 사람들은 종종 비슷한 특징을 가진 동물들은 같은 조상을 가졌을 것이라고 가정한다.
Ⓑ 이행 생물들은 완전한 화석 기록 덕분에 이제 찾기 쉽다.
Ⓒ 잃어버린 고리의 많은 화석들이 19세기에 발견되었다.
Ⓓ 잃어버린 고리 생물들은 항상 서로 다른 서식지들 사이의 이행을 보여준다.

어휘 missing link 잃어버린 고리(진화 과정에서 사이에 존재했을 것으로 추정되지만 화석은 발견되지 않은 동물) | organism n 생물 | bridge v 다리를 놓다 | evolve v 진화하다 | concept n 개념 | evolution n 진화 | exist v 존재하다 | unfortunately adv 불행히도, 안타깝게도 | fossil n 화석 | complete adj 완전한 | transitional adj 이행의, 과도의 | tetrapod n 사지 동물 | share v 공유하다 | characteristic n 특징 | differentiate v 구별하다, 구분 짓다 | separately adv 따로따로, 별도로 | torso n 몸통 | gill n 아가미 | lung n 폐 | mixture n 혼합 | trait n 특성 | Devonian adj 데본기의 | predator n 포식자 | crocodile n 악어 | flat adj 평평한 | specimen n 표본, 샘플 | average adj 평균의 | length n 길이 | scale n 비늘 | fin n 지느러미 | neck n 목 | entire adj 전체의 | bony adj 뼈의, 뼈가 많은 | plate n 뼈판, 골판 | forelimb n 앞다리 | resemble v 닮다, 유사하다 | shoulder blade 어깨뼈, 견갑골 | muscle n 근육 | attach v 붙이다, 부착하다 | humerus n 상완골 | mobile adj 이동하는 | wrist n 손목 | joint n 관절 | limb n 팔, 다리 | tipped with ~가 달린 | flexible adj 유연한 | anchor v 고정시키다, 기반을 두다 | current n 해류 | shed v 떨어뜨리다, 흘리다 | host v (기생동식물의) 숙주 역할을 하다 | deplete v 고갈시키다 | surface n 표면 | nostril n 콧구멍 | spiracle n 공기구멍, 기문, 숨구멍 | whale n 고래 | ribcage n 흉곽 | predate v ~보다 앞서 오다 | ancestor n 조상 | not necessarily adv 반드시 ~은 아닌 | descend v 유래하다

Lesson 19 Photography

본서 | P. 254

Test

1. A **2.** B **3.** D **4.** B – A – D – C **5.** D **6.** C

Test

본서 | P. 255

Man: Student | Woman: Professor

[1-6] Listen to part of a lecture in a photography class.

W **1** Louis Daguerre was a French artist and inventor who is best known for his invention of the daguerreotype photographic process, which resulted in him being considered one of the fathers of photography. **2** However, it is important to realize that there also were rival inventors who developed their own techniques and others who developed similarly effective processes that were lost to obscurity.

Daguerre was a skilled artist trained in architecture, theater design, and panoramic painting. The first invention he is credited with incorporated all of these skills into a type of theater called diorama. Images were intricately rendered on linen and then sunlight reflected with mirrors was used to alter the image by refocusing the light on other areas or opposite sides of the fabric layers. This was used to show before and after images, to shift a scene from day to night, or to show other gradual changes. The dioramas were a popular sensation that brought Daguerre instant fame and imitators. Then, in 1829, he formed a partnership with Nicéphore Niépce, who was trying to recreate images by using chemicals that reacted to light.

M How much had Niépce achieved before Daguerre joined him? I mean, how much of the work could Daguerre genuinely claim as his?

남자: 학생 | 여자: 교수

사진학 강의의 일부를 들으시오.

여 **1** 루이 다게르는 프랑스의 예술가이자 발명가로, 다게레오타이프 사진술의 발명으로 가장 잘 알려져 있습니다. 그로 인해 그는 사진의 아버지 중 한 명으로 여겨집니다. **2** 그러나 자신만의 기술을 발전시킨 경쟁 발명가들이 있었을 뿐만 아니라, 비슷하게 효과적인 방법을 개발했지만 잊혀져 간 발명가들이 있었다는 것을 깨닫는 것도 중요합니다.

다게르는 건축, 무대 디자인, 그리고 파노라마 회화 교육을 받은 실력 있는 예술가였습니다. 그가 발명한 것으로 인정 받은 첫 번째 발명품은 이 모든 기술들을 하나로 합친 디오라마라는 이름의 일종의 극장 장치였습니다. 이미지를 정교하게 리넨에 만든 뒤 거울로 반사된 햇빛이 이 이미지를 바꾸는 데 사용되었는데, 몇 겹으로 겹친 천의 다른 부분이나 반대편에 빛을 재조명하는 방식이었죠. 이 장치는 전과 후의 이미지를 보여준다거나, 장면을 낮에서 밤으로 바꾼다거나, 다른 점진적 변화를 보여주는 데 사용되었습니다. 디오라마는 큰 인기를 얻었던 선풍적인 장치였고 다게르에게 즉각적인 명성과 모방자들을 가져다 주었습니다. 그리고 나서 1829년에, 그는 빛에 반응하는 화학 물질을 이용하여 이미지를 재창조하려는 시도를 하고 있었던 니세포르 니엡스와 동업을 하게 됩니다.

남 니엡스는 다게르가 함께하기 전까지 얼마나 많은 것들을 이룩했나요? 제 말은, 다게르는 얼마만큼의 업적을 순수하게 자신이 이룬 것이라고 주장할 수 있나요?

W 3 Well, Niépce is responsible for creating the oldest surviving image made with a photographic process. Niépce's letters to his sister reveal that he had some success duplicating images with silver salts as early as 1816, but the images were negatives—light where they should be dark and dark where they should be light—and they darkened completely when exposed to light for viewing. Therefore, he had abandoned that path of research. Using a plate of pewter covered in bitumen of Judea, he created a permanent image from a camera obscura of the view from a window. The light hardened the bitumen that was exposed to it, and the softer material was removed with a solvent. Together, they improved upon this technique, but the exposure time required was still many hours. 3 After Niépce's death in 1833, Daguerre continued their research but he returned to the silver salts with which Niépce had previously experimented.
4(B) Daguerre coated a sheet of copper with a thin layer of silver and 4(A) exposed it to iodine vapor, 4(D) which produced a thin layer of silver iodide. 4(C) This light-sensitive compound was exposed in the camera to create a distinct image, but the exposure time was still quite long... about 10 minutes. But, he learned that a much shorter exposure could create an invisible result that could be rapidly developed through exposure to mercury vapor, which also fixed the image, or made it permanent. These daguerreotypes were delicate and light friction could destroy the image, so they were framed with glass over them. He gave his invention to the French government with the understanding that he would receive a pension and the process would be made free to the public.
5 Oblivious to Niépce and Daguerre's research, William Henry Fox Talbot developed his own technique using paper coated with light-sensitive silver chloride, which darkened when exposed to light, and he fixed the image using common salt. When Daguerre's work was made public in 1839, the description of the process was vague, so Talbot thought his 1835 photographs gave him precedence. He soon discovered that their techniques differed considerably. Daguerreotypes quickly became popular, and Talbot continued to improve his technique. Eventually he created the calotype process, which also used chemicals for latent image development. This was further refined when Frederick Scott Archer replaced the paper with glass plates, creating the collodion process, which was used to produce images on iron plates called tintypes. These were fast and relatively cheap and easy to produce, so they replaced daguerreotypes.

여 3 음, 니엡스는 사진술로 만들어진 가장 오래된 이미지를 창조한 인물입니다. 니엡스가 누이에게 보낸 편지들은 그가 은염을 사용하여 이미 1816년부터 이미지를 복제하는 데 상당한 성공을 거두었다는 것을 보여줍니다. 그러나 이 이미지들은 음화였습니다. 어두워야 할 곳은 밝고, 밝아야 할 곳은 어두운 이미지였죠. 그리고 감상을 위해 빛에 노출될 경우 완전히 검게 변해버렸습니다. 그래서 그는 이 쪽으로는 연구를 그만두었습니다. 그는 유대 역청으로 덮인 백랍 판을 이용하여 카메라 옵스큐라로 창문에서 보이는 경치를 영구적인 이미지로 만들어냈습니다. 빛은 빛에 노출된 역청 부분을 단단하게 만들었고, 더 부드러운 부분은 용제로 제거되었습니다. 다게르와 니엡스는 함께 이 기법을 개선해 나갔지만 여기에 필요한 노출 시간은 여전히 몇 시간이나 되었습니다. 3 1833년 니엡스가 사망한 뒤, 다게르는 이 연구를 계속했지만 니엡스가 예전에 실험했던 은염으로 돌아갔습니다.
4(B) 다게르는 구리 판을 얇은 은층으로 코팅한 4(A) 뒤 요오드 증기에 노출시켰는데, 4(D) 이는 얇은 요오드화은 층을 만들어냈습니다. 4(C) 빛에 민감한 이 화합물은 뚜렷한 이미지를 만들기 위해 카메라 내부에서 노출되었지만 노출 시간은 여전히 길었습니다... 약 10분이었어요. 그러나 그는 훨씬 짧은 노출 시간이 보이지 않는 결과물을 만들 수 있으며 이 결과물이 수은 증기에 노출되면 빠르게 현상되고 이미지를 고정시키거나 영구적으로 만들 수 있다는 것을 알게 되었습니다. 이 다게레오타이프들은 부서지기 쉬었고 가벼운 마찰도 이미지를 파괴할 수 있었기에 위에 유리 틀을 덮어주어야 했습니다. 다게르는 연금을 받고 이 처리 과정이 대중에게 무료로 공개된다는 합의 하에 프랑스 정부에 그의 발명을 넘겨주었습니다.
5 니엡스와 다게르의 연구에 대해 알지 못한 채 윌리엄 헨리 폭스 탤벗은 빛에 민감해서 빛에 노출되면 검게 변하는 염화은으로 코팅한 종이를 사용하는 그만의 기법을 발전시켰으며, 일반 소금을 이용해서 이미지를 고정시켰습니다. 다게르의 업적이 1839년에 대중에게 공개되었을 때 과정에 대한 설명이 모호했기에 탤벗은 자신의 1835년도 사진들이 다게르를 앞섰다고 생각했습니다. 그는 곧 서로의 기법이 상당히 다르다는 것을 발견했습니다. 다게레오타이프는 빠르게 인기를 얻었고, 탤벗은 그의 기법을 계속해서 발전시켰습니다. 결국 그는 캘러타이프 사진술을 발명했는데, 이 방법 역시 잠상을 현상하기 위해 화학 약품을 사용하는 것이었습니다. 이 기법은 프레데릭 스콧 아처가 종이를 유리판으로 교체한 콜로디온 사진술을 만들어냄으로써 더욱 개선되었는데, 이 방식은 틴타이프라고 불리는

6 These men are all considered the fathers of photography, but there were others working at the same time. Hércules Florence also produced images using silver nitrate paper in Brazil starting in 1832. Unfortunately, he made little effort to publicize his success, and his name was lost to history until recently.

철판에 이미지를 만들어내는 데 사용되었습니다. 이 방법은 빨랐으며 상대적으로 가격이 저렴했고 만들기가 쉬워서 다게레오타이프를 대체했습니다.

6 이 사람들은 모두 사진의 아버지라고 여겨지는 인물들이지만, 동시대에 연구를 하던 다른 사람들도 있었습니다. 헤르쿨레스 플로렌스 역시 1832년부터 브라질에서 질산은 종이를 사용하여 이미지를 만들어냈습니다. 불행히도 그는 그의 성공을 알리는 데 노력을 거의 기울이지 않았고, 그의 이름은 최근까지도 역사 속에서 사라졌었죠.

1. **What is the lecture mainly about?**
   - (A) The inventors that led the development of photography
   - (B) The creation of the first diorama and camera obscura
   - (C) The difference between daguerreotypes and calotypes
   - (D) The influence that Niépce had on Daguerre

2. **What does the professor say about Louis Daguerre?**
   - (A) He had many rivals that influenced his invention of photographic techniques.
   - (B) He was not the only one who played a significant role in creating photography.
   - (C) He spent more than 10 years on developing his daguerreotype process.
   - (D) He did not receive credit for the invention of the diorama while he was alive.

3. **What can be inferred about Nicéphore Niépce?**
   - (A) He had a hard time importing bitumen from Judea.
   - (B) He had conflicts with Daguerre, which caused their separation.
   - (C) He was able to invent the camera obscura after a few years of research.
   - (D) He ended up not finishing his experiment with silver salts.

4. **The professor explains Daguerre's experiment with silver salts for creating images. Put the steps below in order.**
   - (A) Expose copper to iodine vapor.
   - (B) Cover copper sheet with silver.
   - (C) Expose silver iodide in the camera.
   - (D) Silver iodide is produced.

Step 1	(B) Cover copper sheet with silver.
Step 2	(A) Expose copper to iodine vapor.
Step 3	(D) Silver iodide is produced.
Step 4	(C) Expose silver iodide in the camera.

1. **강의는 주로 무엇에 대한 것인가?**
   - (A) 사진술의 발달을 이끈 발명가들
   - (B) 최초의 디오라마와 카메라 옵스큐라의 발명
   - (C) 다게레오타이프와 캘러타이프의 차이
   - (D) 니엡스가 다게르에 끼친 영향

2. **교수는 루이스 다게르에 대해 무엇이라고 말하는가?**
   - (A) 그는 그의 사진 기법 발명에 영향을 준 많은 경쟁자들이 있었다.
   - (B) 사진술을 만드는 데 중요한 역할을 한 것은 그 혼자만이 아니었다.
   - (C) 다게레오타이프 사진술을 발전시키는 데 10년 이상을 쏟았다.
   - (D) 생전에 디오라마의 발명에 대해 인정받지 못했다.

3. **니세프로 니엡스에 대해 무엇을 추론할 수 있는가?**
   - (A) 유대에서 역청을 수입하는 데 어려움을 겪었다.
   - (B) 다게르와 갈등을 겪었으며 이것이 그들의 결별을 초래했다.
   - (C) 몇 년간의 연구 후에 카메라 옵스큐라를 발명할 수 있었다.
   - (D) 은염에 대한 연구를 결국 끝마치지 못했다.

4. **교수는 은염으로 이미지를 만들어내는 다게르의 실험에 대해 설명한다. 아래의 과정을 순서대로 배열하시오.**
   - (A) 구리를 요오드 증기에 노출시킨다.
   - (B) 구리판을 은으로 덮는다.
   - (C) 요오드화은을 카메라 내부에서 노출시킨다.
   - (D) 요오드화은이 생성된다.

1 단계	(B) 구리판을 은으로 덮는다.
2 단계	(A) 구리를 요오드 증기에 노출시킨다.
3 단계	(D) 요오드화은이 생성된다.
4 단계	(C) 요오드화은을 카메라 내부에서 노출시킨다.

5. According to the lecture, which of the following is true about William Henry Fox Talbot?
Ⓐ He sold his invention to a French company.
Ⓑ He mostly experimented with negative images.
Ⓒ He was also a colleague of Daguerre, studying silver salt.
Ⓓ He did not know about the work of Daguerre.

6. Listen again to part of the lecture. Then answer the question.

W These men are all considered the fathers of photography, but there were others working at the same time.

Why does the professor say this:

W but there were others working at the same time.

Ⓐ She is trying to convince her students to do more research about photographers.
Ⓑ She forgot to mention other photographers who had influenced Louis Daguerre.
Ⓒ She wants to say that other people also contributed to the development of photography.
Ⓓ She is emphasizing the importance of photography and its history to her students.

5. 강의에 의하면, 윌리엄 폭스 탤벗에 대해 옳은 것은 무엇인가?
Ⓐ 자신의 발명품을 프랑스 회사에 팔았다.
Ⓑ 대부분 음화 이미지에 대한 실험을 했다.
Ⓒ 은염을 연구했으며 다게르의 동료이기도 했다.
Ⓓ 다게르의 연구에 대해 모르고 있었다.

6. 강의의 일부를 다시 듣고 질문에 답하시오.

여 이 사람들은 모두 사진의 아버지라고 여겨지는 인물들이지만, 동시대에 연구를 하던 다른 사람들도 있었습니다.

교수는 왜 이렇게 말하는가:

여 동시대에 연구를 하던 다른 사람들도 있었습니다.

Ⓐ 사진사들에 대해 더 연구하라고 학생들을 설득하려 하고 있다.
Ⓑ 루이스 다게르에게 영향을 미친 다른 사진사들을 언급하는 것을 잊었다.
Ⓒ 다른 사람들 또한 사진술의 발전에 기여했다고 말하고 싶어 한다.
Ⓓ 사진술의 중요성과 그 역사에 대해 학생들에게 강조하고 있다.

어휘 inventor n 발명가 | invention n 발명 | daguerreotype n 다게레오타이프(은판 사진법) | photographic adj 사진의 | rival adj 경쟁의, 경쟁적인 | similarly adv 비슷하게, 유사하게 | effective adj 효과적인 | obscurity n 잊혀짐 | skilled adj 숙련된 | architecture n 건축학 | panoramic adj 파노라마의 | incorporate v 포함하다 | diorama n 디오라마(배경을 그린 큰 막에 여러 가지 물건을 배치하고, 조명을 잘 활용해 실제 모습처럼 보이게 만든 무대 장치) | intricately adv 복잡하게 | render v (어떤 상태가 되도록) 만들다, 하다 | reflect v 반사하다 | alter v 변하게 하다 | refocus v 초점을 다시 맞추다 | fabric n 직물, 천 | shift v 옮기다, 이동하다 | gradual adj 점진적인 | sensation n 센세이션(돌풍을 일으키는 것) | instant adj 즉각적인 | fame n 명성 | imitator n 모방하는 사람 | partnership n 동업자, 파트너 | recreate v 재창조하다 | chemical n 화학 물질 | genuinely adv 진정으로, 순수하게 | claim v 주장하다 | reveal v 드러내다, 밝히다 | duplicate v 복사하다, 복제하다 | silver salt 은염 | negative n 음화 | expose v 노출하다 | abandon v 버리다 | pewter n 백랍, 땜납 | bitumen n 역청 | permanent adj 영구적인 | camera obscura 카메라 옵스큐라(암상자) | harden v 단단하게 하다 | solvent n 용제, 용액 | exposure time 노출 시간 | coat v (막과 같은 것을) 덮다, 입히다 | copper n 구리 | iodine n 요오드 | vapor n 증기 | silver iodide 요오드화은 | sensitive adj 민감한, 예민한 | compound n 화합물 | distinct adj 뚜렷한 | invisible adj 보이지 않는 | mercury n 수은 | delicate adj 부서지기 쉬운, 연약한 | pension n 연금 | silver chloride 염화은 | description n 설명, 기술, 묘사 | vague adj 모호한 | precedence n 우선(함) | considerably adv 많이, 상당히 | calotype n 캘러타이프(요오드화은을 이용한 19세기의 사진술) | latent image 잠상(사진 현상 전의 눈에 보이지 않는 상) | refine v 개선하다 | replace v 대체하다 | tintype n 틴타이프(철판사진) | relatively adv 비교적 | silver nitrate 질산은 | publicize v 알리다, 광고하다

Test

1. A 2. A 3. D 4. C 5. A 6. B

Test

본서 | P. 258

Man: Professor | Woman: Student

[1-6] Listen to part of a discussion in a physics class.

M Today we will continue our discussion of alternate fuel sources by looking at some of the more controversial options. Perhaps the most hotly contested form of alternative energy sources is nuclear energy. So, who can tell me what the two types of nuclear reactions are?

W 1 Fission and fusion are the two types. Fission is when an atom is split, and fusion is when two atoms are combined. Both reactions release huge amounts of energy, but fission is more dangerous.

M Yes, thank you, Clara. Both fission and fusion occur constantly in nature, and we are influenced by them every day. Fission occurs when an isotope of an element is involved in a nuclear reaction or experiences radioactive decay. In either case, the nucleus of an atom splits into smaller parts, lighter nuclei of different elements, and releases both electromagnetic radiation and neutrons. The kinetic energy of the neutrons causes chain reactions, and that is how fission can be used to produce power, by sustained chain reaction. 2 Unfortunately, it also releases free neutrons and gamma radiation, both of which are very harmful to living things. 3 Humans have harnessed fission in two ways: as weapons and to generate electricity. Today, there are 435 nuclear reactors operating in 30 countries, which account for about twelve percent of total electricity production, and 13 nations depend on fission reactors for at least 25 percent of their energy production. 4 So, as you can see, this form of alternative energy production already has a firm foothold. However, not only is the process dangerous, as reactors must be constantly monitored to make sure they do not fail and suffer a meltdown like the ones in Chernobyl and Fukushima, but they also produce large amounts of radioactive waste. All radioactive elements have a half-life, which means that after a set period of time, their radiation output will be cut in half. However, some of these fission byproducts will remain dangerous for thousands of years.

남자: 교수 | 여자: 학생

물리학 수업 중 토론의 일부를 들으시오.

남 오늘 우리는 좀 더 논란이 많은 옵션들을 살펴보며 대체 연료 자원에 대한 이야기를 계속할 겁니다. 아마 가장 뜨거운 쟁점이 되고 있는 형태의 대체 에너지 자원은 원자력이겠죠. 그래서, 핵반응의 두 종류를 누가 이야기해줄 수 있나요?

여 1 그 두 종류는 핵분열과 핵융합입니다. 핵분열은 원자가 분열하면서 일어나고, 핵융합은 두 개의 원자들이 결합하며 일어나죠. 두 반응 모두 거대한 양의 에너지를 방출하지만, 핵분열이 더 위험합니다.

남 맞습니다. 고마워요, 클라라. 핵분열과 핵융합 둘 다 자연에서 지속적으로 일어나며 우리는 매일 그것들의 영향을 받고 있습니다. 핵분열은 한 원소의 동위원소가 핵반응을 일으키거나 방사성 붕괴를 경험할 때 일어납니다. 어떤 경우이건 원자의 핵은 더 작은 부분으로 분열되어 다른 원소의 더 가벼운 원자핵이 되며, 전자기 방사선과 중성자를 방출합니다. 중성자들의 운동 에너지는 연쇄 반응을 일으키고, 이것은 에너지를 생산하기 위해 핵분열이 어떻게 사용되는지를 말해주죠. 바로 지속적인 연쇄 반응을 통해서입니다. 2 불행히도 핵분열은 자유 중성자들과 감마선 역시 방출하는데, 이들 둘은 생물에게 매우 해롭습니다. 3 인류는 핵분열을 두 가지 방법으로 활용했습니다. 무기와 전력 생산이죠. 오늘날 30개국에서 435개의 원자로들이 가동되고 있으며 이는 전력 생산 총량의 12%를 차지합니다. 그리고 13개국이 에너지 생산량의 적어도 25%를 핵분열 원자로에 의지하고 있죠. 4 그래서 여러분도 알겠지만 이 형태의 대체 에너지 생산은 이미 굳게 기반을 잡고 있습니다. 그러나 그 과정은 위험할 뿐만 아니라 많은 양의 방사성 폐기물이 배출됩니다. 그래서 원자들은 체르노빌이나 후쿠시마에 있는 원자로들처럼 고장이 나서 노심 용융이 일어나지 않도록 항상 감시해야만 합니다. 모든 방사성 원소는 반감기를 가지고 있는데, 이 말은 정해진 시간이 지나면 이들의 방사선 생산량이 반으로 줄어든다는 것을 의미합니다. 그러나 핵분열로 인해 생겨난 몇몇 부산물들은 수천 년 동안 위험한 상태로 남아 있을 수 있습니다.

Fusion, on the other hand, offers a much cleaner fuel source. Fusion is actually the key source of energy in our solar system as our Sun, like all stars, is essentially a super-massive fusion reactor. Fusion occurs when two or more atoms collide with each other at extremely high speed and form a new nucleus, 5 releasing energy and neutrons, but without creating new radioactive nuclei. So, unlike fission reactors, fusion reactors would not produce radioactive waste to be disposed of. The reactor and its components will become radioactive, but they would only remain so for 50 to 100 years, and the radiation would be confined to the plant itself. 5 In addition, fusion reactions produce far more energy than fission reactions and fusion reactors can simply be shut down. As I mentioned before, fission reactors must be constantly monitored to prevent the chain reaction from becoming uncontrollable and resulting in a meltdown. However, when a fusion plant is shut down, the production of free neutrons would cease within a few milliseconds.

W If that is the case, then why do we still use fission reactors instead of fusion reactors to generate electricity?

M 6 The reason that we don't use fusion reactors is that we are unable to produce them at present. We have used powerful laser arrays to successfully fuse atoms, but the process requires far more energy than it releases. That is extremely important, because even if a reactor is functioning, if its energy output does not exceed its input, then it is useless for energy production. The only manmade fusion device that has been able to break even, to have its output match its input, to date was the hydrogen bomb codenamed Ivy Mike, which was detonated in the Enewietak Atoll in 1952. That could hardly be considered a controlled reaction, and the device was ignited with a fission reaction. In addition, the fuel for such reactions is difficult to obtain. Most research at present uses deuterium, a form of hydrogen, and Helium-3, a form of helium, both of which are quite rare on Earth. So, while fusion reactors would provide an almost ideal alternative energy source, we are forced to rely on much more dangerous and environmentally harmful fission reactors for the time being.

다른 한편으로, 핵융합은 훨씬 깨끗한 연료 자원을 제공합니다. 핵융합은 사실 우리 태양계의 가장 중요한 에너지원인데, 태양이 다른 모든 별들과 마찬가지로 근본적으로는 아주 거대한 핵융합 원자로이기 때문이죠. 핵융합은 두 개 이상의 원자들이 매우 빠른 속력으로 서로 충돌하여 새로운 핵을 형성하며 일어나는데, 5 이 과정에서 에너지와 중성자가 방출되지만 새로운 방사성 핵은 만들어지지 않습니다. 그래서 핵분열 원자로와는 다르게 핵융합 원자로는 처리해야만 하는 방사능 폐기물을 만들어내지 않습니다. 원자로와 그 부품들은 방사성을 띠겠지만 단지 50-100년 동안만이며 방사선은 시설 내부에만 한정될 겁니다. 5 또한 핵융합 반응은 핵분열 반응보다 훨씬 더 많은 에너지를 생산하며, 핵융합 원자로는 간단히 가동을 멈출 수 있습니다. 앞서 언급했듯이, 핵분열 원자로는 연쇄 반응이 통제를 벗어나 노심 용융으로 이어지는 것을 막기 위해 항시 감시되어야만 하죠. 그러나 핵융합 시설을 멈추면 자유 중성자의 생산은 수 밀리초 내로 중단됩니다.

여 만약 그렇다면, 왜 핵융합 원자로로 전력을 생산하는 대신 여전히 핵분열 원자로를 사용하고 있는 건가요?

남 6 핵융합 원자로를 사용하지 않는 이유는 우리가 지금 현재로서는 그것들을 만들어낼 수 없기 때문입니다. 우리는 강력한 레이저 배열을 이용해서 원자를 성공적으로 융합했지만, 그 과정은 방출하는 에너지보다 훨씬 더 많은 에너지를 필요로 합니다. 이것은 매우 중요한데, 원자로가 작동한다 해도 에너지의 생산량이 투입량을 넘어서지 못하면 에너지 생산에 쓸모가 없기 때문입니다. 오늘날까지 만들어진 것들 중 손익 평형을 맞출 수 있었던, 즉 생산량을 투입량과 같게 만들 수 있었던 유일한 인공 핵융합 장치는 아이비 마이크라는 코드명을 가진 수소 폭탄이었는데, 그것은 1952년 에네웨타크 환초에서 폭발했죠. 이는 통제된 반응이라고 보기 어려우며 그 장치는 핵분열 반응을 이용해 점화되었습니다. 또한, 이러한 반응을 위한 연료는 얻기가 어렵습니다. 현재의 연구 대부분은 수소의 한 형태인 듀테륨을 이용하거나 헬륨의 한 형태인 헬륨-3를 이용하는데, 이 둘은 지구에서 찾아보기 꽤 힘든 것들입니다. 그래서 핵융합 원자로가 거의 이상에 가까운 대체 에너지 자원을 공급할 수 있긴 하지만, 우리는 당분간 훨씬 더 위험하고 환경적으로 해로운 핵분열 원자로에 기댈 수밖에 없습니다.

1. What is the discussion mainly about?
   (A) The advantages and disadvantages of fission and fusion reactors

1. 토론은 주로 무엇에 대한 것인가?
   (A) 핵분열 원자로와 핵융합 원자로의 장점과 단점

Ⓑ The creation of fission reactors and their effect on the environment
Ⓒ The harmful and lasting impact of radioactive waste
Ⓓ The development of fusion reactors over the last 50 years

2. What is true about nuclear reactions?

Ⓐ Fission emits substances that can be dangerous to humans.
Ⓑ Fission occurs every day while fusion occurs rarely in nature.
Ⓒ Fission can generate electricity while fusion cannot.
Ⓓ Fusion needs to be observed since it is very unstable.

3. Listen again to part of the discussion. Then answer the question.

> M Humans have harnessed fission in two ways: as weapons and to generate electricity. Today, there are 435 nuclear reactors operating in 30 countries, which account for about twelve percent of total electricity production, and 13 nations depend on fission reactors for at least 25 percent of their energy production.

Why does the professor say this:

> M Today, there are 435 nuclear reactors operating in 30 countries, which account for about twelve percent of total electricity production, and 13 nations depend on fission reactors for at least 25 percent of their energy production.

Ⓐ He doubts if these fission reactors will be able to survive a meltdown in the future.
Ⓑ He is convincing the audience that depending on nuclear energy is important.
Ⓒ He feels the need to educate people on the dangers of depending on nuclear energy.
Ⓓ He wants to point out that many countries already depend on fission energy.

4. Why does the professor mention Chernobyl and Fukushima?

Ⓐ To emphasize the importance of protecting the environment
Ⓑ To contrast them in terms of fission reaction and its process
Ⓒ To give some examples of the instability of fission reactors
Ⓓ To illustrate his point about the danger of building reactors

Ⓑ 핵분열 원자로의 생성과 그것이 환경에 미치는 영향
Ⓒ 방사성 폐기물의 해롭고 오래 지속되는 영향
Ⓓ 지난 50년간의 핵융합 원자로의 발전

2. 핵반응에 대해 옳은 것은 무엇인가?

Ⓐ 핵분열은 인간에게 해로울 수 있는 물질을 방출한다.
Ⓑ 핵분열은 매일 일어나는 반면 핵융합은 자연에서 드물게 나타난다.
Ⓒ 핵분열은 전기를 생산할 수 있으나 핵융합은 생산하지 못한다.
Ⓓ 핵융합은 매우 불안정하므로 주시해야 한다.

3. 토론의 일부를 다시 듣고 질문에 답하시오.

> 남 인류는 핵분열을 두 가지 방법으로 활용했습니다. 무기와 전력 생산이죠. 오늘날 30개국에서 435개의 원자로들이 가동되고 있으며 이는 전력 생산 총량의 12%를 차지합니다. 그리고 13개국이 에너지 생산량의 적어도 25%를 핵분열 원자로에 의지하고 있죠.

교수는 왜 이렇게 말하는가:

> 남 오늘날 30개국에서 435개의 원자로들이 가동되고 있으며 이는 전력 생산 총량의 12%를 차지합니다. 그리고 13개국이 에너지 생산량의 적어도 25%를 핵분열 원자로에 의지하고 있죠.

Ⓐ 이 핵분열 원자로들이 미래에 노심 용융을 견뎌낼 수 있을지 의심스럽다.
Ⓑ 원자력에 의지하는 것이 중요하다고 청중을 설득하고 있다.
Ⓒ 원자력에 의지하는 것의 위험성에 대해 사람들을 교육해야 할 필요성을 느낀다.
Ⓓ 많은 나라들이 이미 핵분열 에너지에 의존하고 있다는 것을 지적하고 싶어한다.

4. 교수는 왜 체르노빌과 후쿠시마를 언급하는가?

Ⓐ 환경 보호의 중요성을 강조하려고
Ⓑ 두 곳의 핵분열 반응과 그 과정을 비교하려고
Ⓒ 핵분열 원자로의 불안정성에 대한 예시를 들려고
Ⓓ 원자로 건설의 위험성에 대한 자신의 의견을 설명하려고

5. According to the discussion, what is true about a fusion reactor?
Ⓐ It does not generate radioactive nuclei after the collision.
Ⓑ It produces a smaller amount of energy than a fission one.
Ⓒ It does not require a large amount of fuel for operating.
Ⓓ It is more difficult to control than a fission reactor.

5. 토론에 의하면, 핵융합 원자로에 대해 옳은 것은 무엇인가?
Ⓐ 충돌 뒤 방사성 핵을 생성하지 않는다.
Ⓑ 핵분열보다 더 적은 양의 에너지를 생산한다.
Ⓒ 가동하는 데 많은 양의 연료를 필요로 하지 않는다.
Ⓓ 핵분열 원자로보다 통제하기가 더 어렵다.

6. Why is it difficult to operate fusion reactors at present?
Ⓐ Dangerous reactions used for making a hydrogen bomb could occur.
Ⓑ Materials used for fusion reactions are hard to obtain on Earth.
Ⓒ The amount of energy in the input and output are equal to each other.
Ⓓ Technologies such as laser arrays for fusing atoms need to be improved.

6. 현재 핵융합 원자로를 가동하는 것이 왜 어려운가?
Ⓐ 수소 폭탄을 만드는 데 사용된 위험한 반응들이 일어날 수 있다.
Ⓑ 핵융합 반응을 위해 필요한 물질들은 지구에서 구하기 어렵다.
Ⓒ 투입량과 생산량의 에너지가 서로 같다.
Ⓓ 원자들을 융합시키기 위한 레이저 배열 기술이 더 발전되어야 한다.

어휘 alternate fuel 대체 연료 | controversial adj 논란이 많은 | contested adj 경쟁의, 이론이 제기되는 | nuclear energy 핵에너지, 원자력 | nuclear reaction 핵반응 | fission n 핵분열 | fusion n 핵융합 | split v 분열하다 | combine v 결합하다 | release v 방출하다 | constantly adv 끊임없이 | isotope n 동위 원소 | element n 원소 | radioactive decay 방사성 붕괴 | nucleus n (원자)핵(pl. nuclei) | electromagnetic adj 전자기의 | radiation n 방사선 | neutron n 중성자 | kinetic energy 운동 에너지 | chain reaction 연쇄 반응 | sustained adj 지속되는, 일관된 | gamma radiation 감마선 | harness v 이용하다, 활용하다 | generate v 발생시키다, 만들어 내다 | electricity n 전기, 전력 | nuclear reactor 원자로 | operate v 가동되다, 작동하다 | firm adj 견고한, 단단한 | foothold n 발판, 기반 | monitor v 관찰하다, 감시하다 | meltdown n 원자로 노심의 용융(방사능 유출로 이어지는 심각한 사고) | radioactive waste 방사성 폐기물 | half-life n (방사성 물질의) 반감기 | output n 생산량, 산출량 | byproduct n 부산물 | essentially adv 본질적으로 | massive adj 거대한 | collide v 충돌하다, 부딪치다 | dispose of 처리하다, 없애다 | component n 요소, 부품 | confine v 국한시키다, 가두다 | millisecond n 1000분의 1초 | laser n 레이저 | array n 배열, 정렬 | fuse v 녹이다, 녹다 | function v 기능하다 | exceed v 넘다, 초과하다 | manmade adj 인공의 | hydrogen bomb 수소 폭탄 | detonate v 폭발하다 | ignite v 점화되다, 불이 붙다 | obtain v 얻다 | deuterium n 듀테륨(중수소) | helium n 헬륨 | ideal adj 이상적인

Lesson 21 Physiology

본서 | P. 260

Test
1. A **2.** B, C **3.** B, C, E **4.** B **5.** D **6.** C

Test

본서 | P. 261

Man: Professor

[1-6] Listen to part of a lecture in a physiology class.

M **1** As you know, all organisms have a limited life span, and they all age. Plants and animals undergo visible and invisible changes as they age, which are caused by cellular deterioration. But, why does this happen? The cells in our

남자: 교수

생리학 강의의 일부를 들으시오.

남 **1** 여러분 모두 알겠지만 모든 생물은 제한된 수명을 갖고 있고, 모두 노화합니다. 식물과 동물들은 노화하면서 눈에 보이거나 눈에 보이지 않는 변화를 겪게 되는데, 이는 세포의 퇴화로 인해 일어납니다. 하지만, 왜 이런 일이 일어날까요? 우리 몸 안

bodies are constantly being replaced with newly made cells, so why does the quality of those cells degrade over time?
2(B) All cells have a kind of internal clock that decides how long each cell will live. This makes sense as we know that they are replaced. However, the internal clock is actually a bit more complicated. It not only determines how long a cell will live, but **2(C)** it also determines how many times that cell can reproduce itself successfully. Once that limit has been reached, the cell will continue to replicate, but the copies will be imperfect, causing degradation.
However, this does not sufficiently explain the aging that we can observe. Clearly, some external factor must be influencing cell replication, which is where the free radical theory originates. Oxygen is a requirement for life for the majority of animal species on Earth, but it is also a very destructive element. **3(C)** Rust and combustion are both examples of oxygen breaking down molecules of chemical compounds through a process called oxidation. **3(B)** This destructive element also affects living cells through molecules called free radicals. **3(E)** Not all free radicals are harmful; in fact, many biological processes depend upon them to function. Many types of harmful free radicals are produced within the body by inflammation, injuries, and even exercise. They can also be caused by external sources like pollution, radiation, drugs, chemicals like pesticides and solvents, and ozone.
Free radicals are created when molecules break down through chemical processes that leave them with an oxygen atom that has an odd number of electrons. **4** This means that they are unbalanced, so they will readily take an electron from another molecule they encounter to become balanced. This creates a domino effect, where each subsequent molecule takes an electron from another molecule to become stable. This chain reaction can affect any molecules in an organism's body, including fats, proteins, and nucleic acids. That last one, nucleic acids, is extremely important because that means that free radicals can damage DNA. As this damage accumulates within the DNA of cells, it causes aging and diseases that are associated with aging, including cancer, heart disease, and Alzheimer's.
However, there are molecules that can counteract the effects of free radicals called antioxidants. These are molecules that can interact with free radicals and end the electron exchange chain reaction before it can damage

의 세포들은 계속해서 새로 만들어진 세포들로 대체되고 있는데도 왜 이 세포들의 질은 시간이 흐르면서 퇴화하는 걸까요?
2(B) 모든 세포들은 각 세포가 얼마나 사느냐를 결정하는 생체 시계를 가지고 있습니다. 우리는 세포들이 계속 대체된다는 걸 알고 있으므로 이는 이치에 맞습니다. 그러나 이 생체 시계는 사실 좀 더 복잡합니다. 세포가 얼마나 오래 사느냐를 결정할 뿐만 아니라 **2(C)** 몇 번이나 성공적으로 스스로를 복제할 것인지도 결정하거든요. 일단 그 한계에 도달하면, 세포의 자가복제는 계속되겠지만 복제된 세포들은 불완전할 것이고 따라서 질적 저하가 발생합니다.
그러나 이는 우리가 관찰할 수 있는 노화를 충분히 설명하지는 않습니다. 분명히 몇몇 외부적인 요인들이 세포 복제에 영향을 주고 있긴 하고, 여기서 유리기 이론이 유래되었습니다. 산소는 지구에 서식하는 대다수의 동물 종이 살아가는 데 있어 필수 요소이지만, 그와 동시에 매우 파괴적인 원소이기도 합니다. **3(C)** 녹과 연소는 둘 다 산화라는 과정을 통해 산소가 화합물 분자를 분해하는 경우의 예시들입니다. **3(B)** 또한 이 파괴적인 원소는 유리기라고 불리는 분자들을 통해 살아 있는 세포들에게도 영향을 줍니다. **3(E)** 모든 유리기들이 해로운 것은 아니에요. 사실 많은 생물학적 과정들이 기능하는 데 있어 유리기에 의존하고 있죠. 해로운 유리기들의 많은 종류가 체내에서 염증, 상처, 그리고 심지어 운동으로도 만들어집니다. 오염, 방사선, 약물, 살충제나 용제 등의 화학 약품, 오존과 같은 외부적 원인으로도 야기될 수 있습니다.
유리기는 분자가 화학적 과정을 통해 분해되어 홀수 전자를 가진 산소 원자를 남길 때 만들어집니다. **4** 이 말은 산소 원자가 불안정하다는 의미로, 산소 분자는 안정화되기 위해 다른 분자와 만날 때 그 분자에게서 전자를 하나 빼앗아오게 되죠. 이 과정은 도미노 효과를 일으켜서 각 분자들이 모두 안정화를 위해 다음 분자들로부터 전자를 하나씩 가져오게 됩니다. 이 연쇄 반응은 지방, 단백질, 핵산을 포함하여 생물의 체내에 있는 어떠한 분자에도 영향을 미칠 수 있어요. 마지막에 언급한 핵산은 정말로 중요한데, 이 말이 유리기가 DNA에 손상을 입힐 수 있다는 의미이기 때문입니다. 이러한 손상이 세포의 DNA에 축적되면 노화를 야기하며 암, 심장병, 알츠하이머병을 포함한 노화 관련 질병 역시 야기합니다.
하지만 유리기의 영향에 맞서 싸울 수 있는 분자들이 있는데 이들은 산화 방지제라고 불립니다. 이들은 유리기와 교류할 수 있는 분자들로 유리기가 중요한 분자에 손상을 입히기 전에 전자 교환 연쇄 반

important molecules. 5 Antioxidants include vitamins A and E as well as a type of enzymes called superoxide dismutases, or SODs for short. SODs are proteins whose reactive sites contain metallic elements like copper, zinc, iron, etc. These enzymes can be found both within cells and outside of them. Experiments with SODs have shown that animals that possessed many of them lived longer and were healthier. Researchers interpreted this to mean that free radicals contribute to aging, whereas SODs play a role in youth and longevity.

6 On the other hand, some experiments led to a modification of free radical theory. Scientists studying roundworms found that restricting their calorie intake seemed to make them healthier and live longer. Limiting the amount of food that the worms consumed exposed them to fewer free radicals. However, another experiment showed that the reduced caloric intake actually causes the roundworms' respiration to increase. Essentially, they breathed in more oxygen, which exposed them to more free radicals. The scientists suggested that the worms possessed a gene that responded to the free radicals in a way that promoted longevity. Others thought that this proved that free radicals may not actually play a role in DNA damage that contributes to aging, so research on the roles of free radicals and SODs continues.

응을 멈출 수 있습니다. 5 산화 방지제에는 비타민 A와 E, 그리고 초과산화물 불균등화효소 즉 줄여서 SODs라고 불리는 효소 형태가 있습니다. SODs는 반응 위치에 구리, 아연, 철 등의 금속성 원소를 포함하는 단백질입니다. 이 효소들은 세포 안과 밖 양쪽에서 발견됩니다. SODs에 대한 실험들은 SODs를 많이 보유한 동물들이 더 오래 살았고 더 건강했다는 것을 보여줬습니다. 연구원들은 유리기가 노화의 원인이 되는 반면 SODs는 젊음과 수명에 관한 역할을 하는 것으로 이를 해석했습니다.

6 반면에 몇몇 실험들은 유리기설에 대한 수정으로 이어졌습니다. 회충을 연구하던 과학자들은 이들의 칼로리 섭취를 제한하는 것이 이들을 더 건강하고 오래 살도록 만드는 것 같다고 봤습니다. 회충이 소비하는 먹이의 양을 제한하는 것이 더 적은 수의 유리기에 이들을 노출시킨 거죠. 그러나 다른 실험은 감소한 칼로리 섭취가 사실 회충의 호흡이 증가하도록 만들었다는 것을 보여주었습니다. 기본적으로, 더 많은 산소를 들이마셔서 더 많은 유리기에 노출되었다는 겁니다. 과학자들은 회충들이 유리기에 반응하여 어떤 방식으로 장수를 촉발하는 유전자를 가지고 있다는 설을 제시했습니다. 다른 이들은 이 실험들이 사실 유리기가 노화의 원인이 되는 DNA 손상에 어떤 역할을 하는 것이 아닐지도 모른다는 걸 증명했다고 봅니다. 그렇기에 유리기와 SODs의 역할에 대한 연구는 계속되고 있죠.

1. What is the lecture mainly about?
   Ⓐ Reasons behind the aging of cells and related research
   Ⓑ Observing imperfect cells and their effect on the human body
   Ⓒ Discoveries regarding free radical theory and their legacy
   Ⓓ Different theories about cell aging and how to prevent it

2. According to the professor, what are the roles of the internal clock? Choose 2 answers.
   Ⓐ It enables body cells to duplicate successfully.
   Ⓑ It decides the longevity of cells in an organism.
   Ⓒ It can regulate the amount of cell reproduction.
   Ⓓ It determines the limitation of imperfect cells.

1. 강의는 주로 무엇에 대한 것인가?
   Ⓐ 세포의 노화에 관한 이유와 그와 관련된 연구
   Ⓑ 불완전한 세포의 관찰과 그것들이 인간의 몸에 미치는 영향
   Ⓒ 유리기설에 대한 발견들과 그 유산
   Ⓓ 세포 노화와 이를 어떻게 방지하느냐에 대한 서로 다른 이론들

2. 교수에 의하면, 생체 시계의 역할들은 무엇인가? 두 개를 고르시오.
   Ⓐ 몸의 세포가 성공적으로 복제되도록 만든다.
   Ⓑ 생물의 세포 수명을 결정한다.
   Ⓒ 세포 복제의 양을 규제할 수 있다.
   Ⓓ 불완전한 세포의 제한을 결정한다.

3. **What are the characteristics of oxygen?** Choose 3 answers.

Ⓐ Most oxygen molecules have the potential of becoming free radicals.
Ⓑ Oxygen molecules that bring negative effects are called free radicals.
Ⓒ It breaks down some chemical compounds through combustion.
Ⓓ Oxygen becomes free radicals when an organism is under too much stress.
Ⓔ Some free radicals do not bring harmful results to organisms.
Ⓕ Inflammation and injuries are the main causes of harmful oxygen molecules.

4. **Why does the professor mention the domino effect?**

Ⓐ To give an example of the effects free radicals could bring
Ⓑ To illustrate how free radicals destroy DNA and cells
Ⓒ To emphasize the importance of oxygen for organisms
Ⓓ To explain the chemical processes that create free radicals

5. **What is true about superoxide dismutases(SODs)?**

Ⓐ Experiments show that they could possibly cause damage to DNA.
Ⓑ They are the result of the free radical chemical chain reaction.
Ⓒ They are a type of antioxidant that fights against oxygen molecules.
Ⓓ Some researchers believe that they contribute to healthier cells.

6. **What can be inferred about the free radical theory?**

Ⓐ It is actually the reason behind prolonged cell life in organisms.
Ⓑ It reminded scientists of the role of antioxidants in the human body.
Ⓒ It cannot yet prove that free radicals are one of the causes of cell aging.
Ⓓ It approaches the cell aging process in a very indirect way.

3. **산소의 특징들은 무엇인가?** 세 개를 고르시오.

Ⓐ 대부분의 산소 분자들은 유리기가 될 가능성을 가지고 있다.
Ⓑ 부정적인 영향을 가져오는 산소 분자들은 유리기라고 불린다.
Ⓒ 산소는 연소를 통해 몇몇 화합물을 분해된다.
Ⓓ 산소는 생물이 너무 많은 스트레스를 받을 때 유리기가 된다.
Ⓔ 몇몇 유리기는 생물에게 악영향을 가져오지 않는다.
Ⓕ 염증과 상처는 해로운 산소 분자를 만들어내는 주된 원인들이다.

4. **교수는 왜 도미노 효과를 언급하는가?**

Ⓐ 유리기가 가져올 수 있는 영향들의 예시를 들기 위해
Ⓑ 유리기가 어떻게 DNA와 세포들을 파괴하는지 설명하기 위해
Ⓒ 생물들에 있어 산소의 중요성을 강조하기 위해
Ⓓ 유리기를 만들어내는 화학적 과정들을 설명하기 위해

5. **초과산화물 불균등화효소(SODs)에 대해 옳은 것은 무엇인가?**

Ⓐ 실험들은 SODs가 DNA에 손상을 일으킬 가능성이 있다는 것을 보여준다.
Ⓑ 유리기의 화학적 연쇄 반응의 결과이다.
Ⓒ 산소 분자에 대항해 싸우는 산화 방지제의 한 종류이다.
Ⓓ 몇몇 연구원들은 이들이 더 건강한 세포에 기여한다고 믿는다.

6. **유리기설에 대해 무엇을 추론할 수 있는가?**

Ⓐ 사실 생물의 연장된 세포 수명 뒤에 숨겨진 이유이다.
Ⓑ 인간의 신체 내 산화 방지제들의 역할에 대해 과학자들에게 상기시켜 주었다.
Ⓒ 유리기가 세포 노화 원인의 하나라고 아직 증명할 수는 없다.
Ⓓ 세포 노화의 과정에 매우 간접적인 방식으로 접근했다.

어휘 organism n 생물 | limited adj 제한된 | life span 수명 | age v 노화하다, 나이를 먹다 | undergo v 겪다, 받다 | visible adj 가시적인, 눈에 보이는 | invisible adj 눈에 보이지 않는 | cellular adj 세포의 | deterioration n 퇴화, 약화 | constantly adv 끊임없이 | replace v 대체하다 | degrade v 퇴화하다 | internal adj 내부의 | complicated adj 복잡한 | determine v 결정하다 | reproduce v 복제하다, 복사하다 | successfully adv 성공적으로 | replicate v 복제하다 | copy n 복제품 | imperfect adj 불완전한 | sufficiently adv 충분히 | external adj 외부적인 | free radical theory 유리기설 | originate v 비롯되다, 유래하다 | requirement n 필수 조건 | destructive adj 파괴적인 | rust n 녹 | combustion n 연소 | molecule n 분자 | chemical compound 화합물 | oxidation n 산화 | biological adj 생물학적인 | function v 기능하다 | inflammation n 염증 | injury n 부상 | radiation n 방사선 | pesticide n 살충제 | solvent n 용해성 물질 | ozone n 오존 | odd adj 홀수의 | electron n 전자 | unbalanced adj 불균형의 | encounter v 맞닥뜨리다 | domino effect 도미노 효과 | subsequent adj 그 다음의, 차후의 | stable adj 안정된 | chain reaction 연쇄 반응 | fat n 지방 | protein n 단백질 | nucleic acid 핵산 | accumulate v 축적하다 | disease n 질병 | associated with ~와 관련된 | cancer n 암 | heart disease 심장병 | Alzheimer's n 알츠하이머 병 | counteract v 대응하다 | antioxidant n 산화 방지제 | interact v 교류하다 | enzyme n 효소 | superoxide dismutase 초과산화물 불균등화효소 | reactive adj 반응하는 | metallic adj 금속성의 | copper n 구리 | zinc n 아연 | iron n 철 | interpret v 해석하다 | contribute v ~의 원인이 되다 | longevity n 수명 | modification n 수정, 변경 | roundworm n 회충 | restrict v 억제하다 | calorie n 열량, 칼로리 | intake n 섭취 | consume v 소비하다 | expose v 노출하다 | reduced adj 감소한 | respiration n 호흡 | essentially adv 기본적으로 | possess v 소유하다 | promote v 장려하다, 촉진하다

Lesson 22 Psychology

본서 | P. 263

Test

1. B 2. C 3. A 4. B 5. C 6. D

Test

본서 | P. 264

Man: Student | Woman: Professor

[1-6] Listen to part of a discussion in a psychology class.

W Throughout the history of psychology, scientists have tried to determine what parts of the brain control different activities. 1 More recently, scientists have been trying to isolate which parts of the brain control our emotions, and one valuable tool in this type of research has been functional magnetic resonance imaging, or fMRI for short. fMRI is used to monitor brain activity based upon the amount of blood that flows to a part of the brain and the level of oxygen in that blood. This technique is, of course, based upon the standard MRI machine, which uses a powerful magnetic field to create 3-D images of the body's internal structure. The magnetic field is generated by an extremely powerful electro-magnet in the tube of the MRI machine. This field affects the nuclei of atoms in the tissue, which are usually randomly aligned. When a powerful magnetic field is applied, the hydrogen nuclei in water align with the direction of the field. The signal from the hydrogen atoms in water varies according to the type of tissue they are contained in. In the brain, gray matter, white matter, and cerebral spinal fluid respond differently, creating extremely detailed scans.

An fMRI begins with a basic MRI scan, however, it utilizes additional software and hardware to locate and monitor activity in the brain over time. 2 Instead of hydrogen, an fMRI scan detects changes in the amount of oxygen that is being supplied to the brain tissue. 3 When neurons become more active, they require more oxygen. The flow of blood through capillaries in that part of the brain increases, and

남자: 학생 | 여자: 교수

심리학 강의 중 토론의 일부를 들으시오.

여 심리학의 역사를 통틀어 과학자들은 뇌의 어떤 부분들이 서로 다른 활동들을 통제하는지 알아내려고 시도했습니다. 1 최근 들어, 과학자들은 뇌의 어떤 부분이 우리의 감정을 통제하는지를 따로 구분했고, 이러한 종류의 연구에 귀중한 도구가 바로 기능적 자기 공명 영상, 혹은 줄여서 fMRI입니다. fMRI는 뇌의 한 부분으로 흘러 들어가는 피의 양과 그 피에 함유된 산소 레벨에 근거하여 뇌의 활동을 관찰하는 데 사용되죠. 물론 이 기술은 신체 내부 구조의 3-D 이미지를 만들어내기 위해 강력한 자기장을 이용하는 일반적인 MRI 기계에 기반을 두고 있습니다. 자기장은 MRI 기계의 튜브 내에 있는 엄청나게 강력한 전자석에 의해 생성됩니다. 이 자기장은 조직 내 원자의 원자핵들에 영향을 미치는데, 이들은 보통 무작위로 배열되어 있습니다. 강력한 자기장이 적용되면 수분 내의 수소 원자핵들이 자기장의 방향을 따라 배열됩니다. 수분 내 수소 원자들로부터 나오는 신호는 이들이 포함되어 있는 조직에 따라 다릅니다. 뇌에서는 회백질, 백질, 뇌 척수액이 각각 다르게 반응하며 매우 섬세한 스캔이 이루어집니다.

fMRI는 기본적인 MRI 스캔으로 시작하지만, 시간의 흐름에 따른 뇌 안의 활동을 추적하고 관찰하기 위해 추가적인 소프트웨어와 하드웨어를 사용합니다. 2 수소 대신, fMRI 스캔은 뇌 조직으로 운반되는 산소의 양 변화를 감지합니다. 3 뉴런들이 더 활동적이 되면 더 많은 산소를 필요로 하게 되죠. 그 부분의 뇌의 모세 혈관을 통한 혈류는 증가하고, 적

the increased oxygen in the red blood cells gives off a different magnetic signal that is used to track brain activity. This type of MRI imaging is called blood oxygenation level dependent, or BOLD, imaging. In a basic fMRI experiment, a test subject will lie in the scanner with a screen in front of their face. This screen will show a series of images with blank screens between them, alternating every 30 seconds. The MRI scanner will track how their brain signals change in response to the images. **4** Some areas will see increased activity, while others will become less active. The pause is needed because the blood flow response takes time to become observable. Researchers look at the brain activity as it is represented by image pixels that change color according to the level of activity. This can result in brightly colored images that show activity through many regions of the brain or tiny clusters of color that represent very focused activity. These not only show what part of the test subjects' brain responded, but can also be used to interpret what emotions they feel when they view an image.

M If we can use fMRI scans to pinpoint activity and interpret emotions, then why do we still use questionnaires? Isn't this more reliable and efficient?

W **5** Well, there are a few reasons that we still use more traditional means. Firstly, MRI scans are fairly expensive. Secondly, the subject's brain chemistry could be altered by medication, or he may have preexisting brain conditions that alter its activity. It is important to note that we use young, healthy individuals to map out neural responses, so people with altered brains may respond differently. In addition, many people tend to misinterpret the data they gather. If a subject is shown images of angry faces, his amygdala may light up, while others didn't. The patients whose amygdalae lit up later report feeling fear. If the experiment is repeated later on, and similar results are gained, they may assume that the amygdala lights up when people are scared. So, when patients in an experiment are shown different images, and their amygdalae also light up, we may assume that they are experiencing fear. However, the amygdala can show increased activity with many different emotions. **6** The experimenters may interpret things when there isn't really anything to interpret. So, it is important to question

혈구 내 증가한 산소는 뇌 활동을 추적하는 데 사용되는 서로 다른 자기 신호를 보내게 되는 것입니다. 이러한 유형의 MRI 영상은 혈류 산소 수준 즉 BOLD 영상이라고 불립니다. 기본적인 fMRI 실험에서 실험 대상은 스캐너 안에 누워 있고, 이들의 얼굴 앞에는 화면이 하나 있어요. 이 화면이 매 30초마다 이미지들을 보여주는데, 각 이미지 사이에는 빈 화면이 뜨게 됩니다. MRI 스캐너는 영상에 반응하여 뇌의 신호가 어떻게 변화하는지를 추적하죠. **4** 몇몇 부분들은 증가된 활동을 보일 것이고, 다른 부분들은 덜 활동적이 될 것입니다. 이미지 사이의 멈춤이 필요한 데 그것은 혈류 반응을 관찰할 수 있게 되기까지 시간이 좀 걸리기 때문입니다. 연구원들은 활동의 수준에 따라 변화하는 색을 보이는, 이미지 픽셀로 표현된 뇌의 활동을 봅니다. 이는 뇌의 많은 부분들에 걸친 활동을 보여주는 밝은 색으로 표현된 이미지일수도 있고, 매우 집중된 활동을 나타내는 색의 작은 집합체일 수도 있습니다. 이들은 실험 대상들 뇌의 어떠한 부분이 반응했는지를 보여줄 뿐만 아니라, 실험 대상이 어떠한 이미지를 봤을 때 어떤 감정을 느꼈는지 이해하는 데 사용될 수도 있습니다.

남 우리가 만약 fMRI 스캔을 이용해 뇌의 활동을 정확히 집어내고 감정을 해석할 수 있다면, 왜 여전히 질문지를 사용하는 건가요? fMRI가 더 신뢰할 수 있고 효율적이지 않나요?

여 **5** 음, 우리가 아직도 더 전통적인 수단을 사용하는 이유가 몇 가지 있습니다. 첫째, MRI 스캔은 꽤 비쌉니다. 둘째, 실험 대상자의 뇌 화학 작용이 약물로 인해 변화할 수도 있고, 뇌 활동에 변화를 주는 기존의 뇌 질환을 가지고 있을 수도 있어요. 우리가 신경 반응을 살펴보기 위해 젊고 건강한 사람들을 실험 대상으로 쓴다는 사실을 기억해야 하는 게, 변화된 뇌를 가진 사람들은 좀 다르게 반응할 수가 있기 때문이죠. 또한, 많은 사람들이 자기들이 수집한 정보를 잘못 해석하는 경향이 있어요. 한 실험 대상이 화난 얼굴들의 이미지를 보고 편도체 부분의 색이 밝아졌는데 다른 사람들은 그러지 않았다고 가정합시다. 편도체가 밝아졌던 환자들이 후에 공포를 느꼈다고 보고합니다. 후에도 이 실험이 반복되고 비슷한 결과가 나온다면, 사람들이 무서움을 느낄 때 편도체가 밝아진다는 가정을 하게 될 겁니다. 그래서 실험에서 환자들에게 다른 이미지를 보여주었는데 이들의 편도체 또한 밝아진다면, 이들 역시 공포를 느끼고 있는 것이라고 가정하게 될 수 있습니다. 그러나 편도체는 서로 다른 수많은 감정들에 대해 활동 증가를 보여줄 수 있습니다. **6** 실험자들은 사실 해석할 만한 것이 아무것도 없는데도 무언가를 해석하려 할 수 있어요. 그래서 fMRI 자료를

Lesson 22 Lectures

the patients before, during, and after the experiments to accurately interpret the fMRI data. The long questionnaires help researchers to gather data without the patients giving answers based on what they think the researchers want.

정확히 해석하기 위해 실험 전, 실험 중간, 그리고 실험 후에 환자들에게 질문을 하는 것이 중요합니다. 긴 질문지는 환자들이 연구원들이 원한다고 생각하는 답변을 하게 만드는 일 없이 연구원들이 자료를 모으는 데 도움을 줍니다.

1. What is the discussion mainly about?
   Ⓐ Ways to analyze fMRI data with questionnaires
   Ⓑ Observing emotion through brain activity using fMRI
   Ⓒ Differences between fMRI and a basic MRI scanning
   Ⓓ Interpreting neuron signals to control emotion

2. What is the difference between the fMRI and MRI?
   Ⓐ The fMRI enables people to control neuron activity.
   Ⓑ MRI scanning uses a powerful magnetic field for imaging.
   Ⓒ The fMRI detects changes in the oxygen supply inside the brain.
   Ⓓ MRI does not show the full internal structure of the human body.

3. What can be inferred about neurons?
   Ⓐ They depend upon more oxygen as their activity increases.
   Ⓑ They show a decrease in their use of hydrogen over time.
   Ⓒ Their activity can be observed through black and white images.
   Ⓓ Their behavior changed when the fMRI experiment began.

4. What is true about the experiments conducted using fMRI?
   Ⓐ Participant groups consisted of people varying in age from their 20s to 50s.
   Ⓑ Researchers could observe areas with increased and decreased activity.
   Ⓒ Participants were asked to describe different images displayed in front of them.
   Ⓓ Scientists were able to distinguish participants' emotions with various colors.

5. What is the professor's opinion toward questionnaires?
   Ⓐ He thinks they will not be used when fMRIs are more developed.
   Ⓑ He believes students will be able to realize their importance someday.

1. 토론은 주로 무엇에 대한 것인가?
   Ⓐ 질문지와 함께 fMRI 자료를 분석하는 방법들
   Ⓑ fMRI를 사용하여 뇌의 활동을 통해 감정 관찰하기
   Ⓒ fMRI와 기본적인 MRI 스캐닝의 차이점들
   Ⓓ 감정을 통제하기 위해 뉴런 신호 해석하기

2. fMRI와 MRI의 차이점은 무엇인가?
   Ⓐ fMRI는 사람들로 하여금 뉴런 활동을 통제하도록 만들어준다.
   Ⓑ MRI 스캐닝은 촬영을 위해 강력한 자기장을 사용한다.
   Ⓒ fMRI는 뇌 안에서 일어나는 산소 공급 변화를 감지한다.
   Ⓓ MRI는 인체의 모든 내부 구조를 보여주지는 않는다.

3. 뉴런에 대해 무엇을 추론할 수 있는가?
   Ⓐ 활동이 증가할수록 더 많은 산소를 필요로 한다.
   Ⓑ 시간이 흐를수록 수소 사용이 감소하는 것을 보여준다.
   Ⓒ 이들의 활동은 흑백 영상을 통해 관찰될 수 있다.
   Ⓓ 이들의 활동은 fMRI 실험이 시작되자 변화했다.

4. fMRI를 사용하여 진행된 실험에 대해 옳은 것은 무엇인가?
   Ⓐ 실험자 그룹은 20대에서 50대 사이의 다양한 연령층으로 이루어졌다.
   Ⓑ 연구원들은 증가하거나 감소한 활동을 보인 부분들을 관찰할 수 있었다.
   Ⓒ 참가자들은 눈 앞에 보여진 여러 영상들을 묘사하도록 요청받았다.
   Ⓓ 과학자들은 참가자들의 감정을 다양한 색으로 구별할 수 있었다.

5. 질문지에 대한 교수의 의견은 무엇인가?
   Ⓐ fMRI가 더 발전하면 쓰이지 않을 것이라고 생각한다.
   Ⓑ 학생들이 질문지의 중요성을 언젠가는 깨달으리라고 믿는다.

Ⓒ He knows that they are helpful even though they seem old-fashioned.
Ⓓ He doubts if they are necessary in a long-term perspective.

Ⓒ 구식으로 보이더라도 도움이 된다는 것을 알고 있다.
Ⓓ 장기적인 관점으로 봤을 때 이들이 필요한지 의심스럽다.

6. What can be inferred about using questionnaires after the experiment?
Ⓐ Some participants try to manipulate the test result during questionnaires.
Ⓑ The longer the questionnaires are, the better the results of the experiment.
Ⓒ Using questionnaires eventually provides less information about the participant.
Ⓓ It is necessary to prevent any alteration of the results from occurring.

6. 실험 뒤에 질문지를 사용하는 것에 대해 무엇을 추론할 수 있는가?
Ⓐ 어떤 참가자들은 질문지 응답을 통해 실험 결과를 조종하려고 한다.
Ⓑ 질문지가 길면 길수록 실험 결과의 질도 더 향상된다.
Ⓒ 질문지를 사용하는 것은 결국 참가자에 관한 정보를 덜 제공한다.
Ⓓ 결과를 변화시킬 수 있는 것을 모두 배제하려면 이 과정이 필요하다.

어휘 isolate v 구분하다, 따로 떼어내다 | emotion n 감정 | valuable adj 가치 있는 | functional adj 기능적인 | magnetic adj 자기의, 자석의 | resonance n 공명, 울림 | imaging n 영상 | monitor v 관찰하다 | standard adj 일반적인 | magnetic field 자기장 | internal adj 내부의 | structure n 구조 | generate v 생산하다 | electro-magnet n 전자석 | tube n 튜브, 관 | tissue n 조직 | randomly adv 무작위로 | apply v 적용하다 | align v 배열하다 | direction n 방향 | vary v 서로 다르다 | contain v 포함하다, 함유하다 | cerebral spinal fluid 뇌 척수액 | utilize v 이용하다 | additional adj 추가적인, 부가적인 | detect v 감지하다, 탐지하다 | capillary n 모세 혈관 | track v 추적하다, 뒤쫓다 | oxygenation n 산화 | dependent adj 의존하는 | alternate v 번갈아 나오다 | observable adj 관찰할 수 있는 | represent v 대표하다 | cluster n 무리 | interpret v 해석하다, 이해하다 | pinpoint v 정확히 찾아내다, 보여주다 | questionnaire n 설문지 | reliable adj 믿을 수 있는, 신뢰할 수 있는 | efficient adj 효율적인 | alter v 바꾸다 | medication n 약물 | preexisting adj 기존의 | misinterpret v 잘못 이해하다 | amygdala n 편도체 | report v 알리다, 발표하다 | repeat v 반복하다 | assume v 가정하다 | accurately adv 정확히, 정밀하게

Lesson 23 Sociology

본서 | P. 266

Test

1. D **2.** C **3.** B **4.** C, D **5.** A **6.** D

Test

본서 | P. 267

Woman: Professor

[1-6] Listen to part of a lecture in a sociology class.

W What exactly is ethics? Ethics is a branch of philosophy that is devoted to defining what is right and wrong, and being able to organize, defend, and recommend actions as being morally correct or flawed. But, how do we decide what is right and wrong? **2** Many European philosophers have focused upon the consequences of a given action as the way to determine whether that action was morally correct or not. This is called consequentialist theory, and it says that the end justifies the means. This argument has been used by many people to justify taking an action that

여자: 교수

사회학 강의의 일부를 들으시오.

여 윤리학은 무엇일까요? 윤리학은 무엇이 옳고 그른지를 정의하고, 어떠한 행동이 도덕적으로 맞는지 아니면 흠이 있는지를 정리하고, 옹호하고, 추천하는 데 전념하는 철학의 한 분야입니다. 하지만 어떻게 무엇이 옳고 그른지를 정의할까요? **2** 많은 유럽의 철학자들은 어떠한 행동이 도덕적으로 옳은지 그른지를 판단하기 위해 주어진 행동의 결과에 집중했습니다. 이것은 결과주의적 이론이라고 불리며, 어떠한 행동의 결과가 수단을 정당화한다고 주장합니다. 이 주장은 보통 도덕적으로 옳지 않다고 여겨지는 행동이 긍정적인 결과를 불러왔을 때 그 행동

is generally viewed as morally wrong but it had a positive result. However, this is not the intention of the philosophy.

1, 3 A chief concept in this school of thought is called utilitarianism, which holds that the morally correct action is the one with the highest degree of utility. Utility, or usefulness, can be defined in many ways, but it usually focuses on pleasure, economic security, and lack of suffering. As Jeremy Bentham stated, "it is the greatest happiness of the greatest number that is the measure of right and wrong." So, whatever action will do the most good for the most people is the correct course of action. **4(C)** However, other utilitarianists reject the idea that utility can be measured purely by quantity. One such philosopher is John Stuart Mill, **4(D)** who believed that pleasure cannot be viewed so objectively. He wrote that "some kinds of pleasure are more desirable and more valuable than others." He considered it ridiculous to ignore the fact that quality is considered as well as quantity when any decision is made. So, questions of morality must also reflect the fact that some consequences are more desirable than others.

According to Mill, this does not necessarily mean that the more desirable choice will be made. **5** People often choose the less desirable option for the greater good of the people in their social group. For example, people need to obtain resources and goods to satisfy their physical needs. If there is a limited supply of these things, not everyone can satisfy their needs, so there will be conflict when others try to take those same goods for themselves. So, people develop rules as a society to help them maximize their happiness. Within these rules, a person does not try to get as many goods or resources as possible, but enough to be comfortable and satisfied. They have a duty to society that they must keep in order for the most people to be as happy as possible. Since society has agreed upon such a system, it can enforce the rules against those who disobey them and limit the happiness of others.

However, that sense of duty can often create situations in which people are torn between two actions. People feel a sense of duty to their society, but they also feel one to their family. Utilitarianist philosophers have tried to provide similar ethical guidelines for such situations, but they have proven impractical.

6 A good example of this moral dilemma was provided by Jean-Paul Sartre. He wrote about a student whose brother was killed when the German army invaded France in 1940.

을 정당화하기 위해 많은 사람들이 이용했죠. 그러나 이것은 이 이론의 의도가 아닙니다.

1, 3 이 학설의 주된 개념은 공리주의라고 불리는데, 도덕적으로 옳은 행동이 가장 높은 유용성을 가져온다는 개념입니다. 유용성 즉 쓸모 있음은 많은 방법으로 정의 가능하지만 보통 쾌락, 경제적 안정성, 그리고 고통의 부재에 집중합니다. 제러미 벤담은 "최대 다수의 최대 행복이 옳고 그름의 척도가 된다"라고 말했죠. 그래서 가장 많은 사람들에게 가장 좋은 것은 무슨 행동이든지 올바른 행동의 방향으로 여겨집니다. **4(C)** 그러나 다른 공리주의자들은 유용성이 순전히 양으로만 평가될 수 있다는 생각을 부정합니다. 이러한 철학자들 중 한 명이 존 스튜어트 밀이었는데, **4(D)** 그는 쾌락이 객관적으로 나타낼 수 없는 것이라고 믿었습니다. 그는 "어떤 종류의 쾌락은 다른 종류의 쾌락보다 더 바람직하고 더 가치 있다"고 썼죠. 그는 어떠한 결정에서든 양뿐만 아니라 질 또한 고려된다는 사실을 무시하는 것은 말이 되지 않는다고 여겼습니다. 그래서 도덕성에 대한 질문은 어떤 결과들은 다른 결과들보다 더 바람직하다는 사실을 반영해야만 했습니다.

밀에 따르면, 이 말은 반드시 더 바람직한 결정들이 내려질거라는 의미는 아닙니다. **5** 사람들은 그들이 속한 사회적 그룹 내 구성원들의 공익을 위해 덜 바람직한 결정을 내릴 때가 종종 있죠. 예를 들어, 사람들은 그들의 육체적 필요를 만족시키기 위해 자원과 재화를 구해야만 합니다. 만약 이러한 물질들의 공급이 제한되어 있다면, 모든 사람들이 자신의 필요를 만족시킬 수는 없을 것이므로 다른 이들이 같은 재화를 가져가려 할 때 갈등이 일어나겠죠. 그래서 사람들은 서로 최대한의 행복을 누리기 위해 한 사회로서 규정들을 발전시켰습니다. 이 규정들 안에서 한 개인은 가능한 한 많은 재화나 자원을 가지려 하지 않고, 그저 충분히 편안하고 만족스러울 만큼의 양을 가져갑니다. 가장 많은 사람들이 가능한 한 행복할 수 있도록 규칙을 지킬 사회에 대한 의무가 있죠. 이러한 체계에 사회가 동의했기에 규칙에 불복종하고 다른 이들의 행복을 제한시키는 이들에게 이 규칙들을 강요할 수 있습니다.

그러나 이러한 의무감은 사람들을 종종 두 종류의 행동 사이에서 갈등하게 만들 수도 있습니다. 사람들은 사회에 의무감을 느끼지만, 동시에 그들의 가족에게도 의무감을 느끼죠. 공리주의 철학자들은 이러한 상황을 위해 도덕적인 지침을 제시하려고 노력했지만 이 지침들은 비현실적인 것으로 밝혀졌습니다.

6 이러한 도덕적 딜레마의 좋은 예는 장폴 사르트르에 의해 제시되었습니다. 그는 1940년에 독일군이 프랑스를 침략했을 때 형제를 잃은 한 학생에 대

He feels compelled to join the military to avenge his brother and free his country from its oppressors. However, he also has to consider his mother, who he would have to leave at home alone while he fights. If he chooses to go to the front, he can provide maximum happiness to the greatest number of people, but he would disappoint his mother. But, he could die on his first day in combat. What would he have achieved? On the other hand, if he stays home, he could make his mother happy, but his people would remain conquered. Would making his mother happy for the present be a better choice if it meant that they would live under an oppressive regime for years? There is no clear moral choice to be made here as both actions can have positive and negative consequences.

해 썼습니다. 그는 형제의 원수를 갚고 나라를 압제자들로부터 구하기 위해 참전해야 할 것 같은 느낌을 받습니다. 그러나 만약 그가 전쟁에 나가게 된다면 집에 혼자 남겨지실 어머니 역시 생각해야 합니다. 만약 그가 전선에 나가게 된다면 가장 많은 수의 사람들에게 가장 많은 행복을 줄 수 있겠지만, 어머니를 실망시킬 겁니다. 그러나 전투 첫날 사망할 수도 있죠. 그는 무엇을 이룬 걸까요? 다른 한편으로는, 만약 그가 집에 남는다면 어머니를 기쁘게 해 드릴 수는 있겠지만 조국의 사람들은 여전히 정복당한 채로 남아 있을 것입니다. 현재의 상황에서 어머니를 기쁘게 하는 것이 수년 간 압제적인 정권 아래 살아가야 하는 것보다 더 나은 선택일까요? 이 두 가지 행동 모두 긍정적이고 부정적인 결과를 낳을 수 있기 때문에 여기에는 명확하게 도덕적이라고 볼 수 있는 선택이 없습니다.

1. What is the lecture mainly about?

Ⓐ The characteristics of utilitarianism and opposing perspectives
Ⓑ Different concepts of famous philosophers including Mill and Sartre
Ⓒ The influence of utilitarianism in the 21st century in Europe
Ⓓ The concept of utilitarianism and philosophers' views about it

2. What is true about the consequentialist theory?

Ⓐ It was misused by criminals who wanted to justify their actions.
Ⓑ It states that the process has the biggest influence on the result.
Ⓒ It views a positive outcome as the most important thing.
Ⓓ It is one of the many branches of the utilitarianist theory.

3. Why does the professor mention Jeremy Bentham?

Ⓐ To explain how his early view on utilitarianism influenced others
Ⓑ To express the chief concept of utilitarianism in a precise way
Ⓒ To point out the philosopher who had the greatest influence on utilitarianism
Ⓓ To illustrate the ideas regarding utilitarianism during the 1940s

1. 강의는 주로 무엇에 대한 것인가?

Ⓐ 공리주의의 특징들과 그에 대립되는 관점들
Ⓑ 밀과 사르트르를 포함한 유명한 철학자들의 서로 다른 개념들
Ⓒ 21세기 유럽에서 공리주의가 미친 영향
Ⓓ 공리주의의 개념과 그에 대한 철학자들의 견해

2. 결과주의적 이론에 대해 옳은 것은 무엇인가?

Ⓐ 자신들의 행동을 정당화하고자 했던 범죄자들에 의해 오용되었다.
Ⓑ 과정이 결과에 가장 중요한 영향을 끼친다고 주장한다.
Ⓒ 긍정적인 결과를 가장 중요한 것으로 본다.
Ⓓ 공리주의 이론의 많은 학파들 중 하나이다.

3. 교수는 왜 제러미 벤담을 언급하는가?

Ⓐ 공리주의에 대한 그의 초기 관점이 다른 이들에게 어떻게 영향을 미쳤는지 설명하려고
Ⓑ 공리주의의 가장 주요한 개념을 정확하게 표현하려고
Ⓒ 공리주의에 가장 많은 영향을 미친 철학자를 언급하려고
Ⓓ 1940년대의 공리주의에 대한 생각을 보여주려고

4. **According to the lecture, why were there conflicts among philosophers regarding utilitarianism?**

Choose 2 answers.

Ⓐ The definition of utility can easily vary from person to person.
Ⓑ Pleasure always depends on the balance of both quality and quantity.
Ⓒ Pleasure is not something that can be described by only quantity.
Ⓓ People have different views regarding what is good and profitable.

5. **What can be inferred about the professor's example of people obtaining resources and goods?**

Ⓐ People can limit their desires for the advantages of a larger group.
Ⓑ People will learn how to take advantage of others over time.
Ⓒ People sometimes choose to leave a group rather than compromise.
Ⓓ People will always try to satisfy themselves by taking as many goods as possible.

6. **In the lecture, what does Jean-Paul Sartre's moral dilemma example signify?**

Ⓐ All actions and decisions people face have positive and negative sides.
Ⓑ Providing maximum happiness to the largest number of people should be prioritized.
Ⓒ In wars, people always experience dilemmas due to life and death situations.
Ⓓ People often encounter a conflict between the duties to society and family.

4. **강의에 따르면, 공리주의에 대해 왜 철학자들 사이에 갈등이 있었는가?** 두 개를 고르시오.

Ⓐ 유용성에 대한 정의는 사람에 따라 매우 쉽게 달라질 수 있다.
Ⓑ 쾌락은 질과 양의 균형에 항상 의존한다.
Ⓒ 쾌락은 단지 양으로만 설명될 수 있는 것이 아니다.
Ⓓ 사람들은 무엇이 좋고 유익한지에 대해 서로 다른 시각을 가지고 있다.

5. **자원과 재화를 얻으려는 사람들에 대한 교수의 예시에서 무엇을 추론할 수 있는가?**

Ⓐ 사람들은 더 큰 공동체의 이익을 위해 자기 욕망을 제한할 수 있다.
Ⓑ 사람들은 시간이 흐르며 어떻게 다른 이들을 이용하는지를 배울 것이다.
Ⓒ 사람들은 때때로 타협하기보다는 공동체를 떠나는 쪽을 선택한다.
Ⓓ 사람들은 항상 가능한 한 많은 재화를 가져감으로써 자신을 만족시키려고 할 것이다.

6. **강의에서 장폴 사르트르의 도덕적 딜레마 예시는 무엇을 나타내는가?**

Ⓐ 사람들이 맞닥뜨리는 모든 행동과 결정은 긍정적이고 부정적인 면을 가지고 있다.
Ⓑ 가장 많은 수의 사람들에게 최대한의 행복을 제공하는 것이 우선 순위에 놓여야 한다.
Ⓒ 전쟁에서 사람들은 언제나 삶과 죽음의 상황으로 인해 딜레마를 경험한다.
Ⓓ 사람들은 종종 사회에 대한 의무와 가정에 대한 의무 사이에서 갈등을 겪는다.

어휘 ethics n 윤리학, 도덕 I branch n 분야, 분파 I philosophy n 철학 I devote v 바치다, 전념하다 I define v 정의하다 I organize v 정리하다 I defend v 옹호하다, 방어하다 I recommend v 추천하다 I morally adv 도덕적으로 I flawed adj 흠이 있는 I consequence n 결과 I consequentialist n 결과주의자 I theory n 이론 I justify v 정당화하다 I mean n 수단 I argument n 주장 I generally adv 일반적으로 I intention n 의도 I chief adj 주된, 주요한 I concept n 개념 I school of thought 학설, 학파 I utilitarianism n 공리주의 I utility n 유용성 I economic adj 경제적인 I security n 보장, 안심 I suffering n 고통 I reject v 거부하다 I purely adv 순전히, 오직 I quantity n 수량 I objectively adv 객관적으로 I desirable adj 바람직한, 호감 가는 I ridiculous adj 터무니없는 I ignore v 무시하다 I quality n 질 I morality n 도덕, 도덕성 I reflect v 반영하다 I obtain v 얻다, 구하다 I satisfy v 만족시키다 I physical adj 육체의, 신체의 I conflict n 갈등 I maximize v 최대화하다 I resource n 자원 I comfortable adj 편안한 I duty n 의무 I enforce v 강요하다, 집행하다, 시행하다 I disobey v 불복종하다 I ethical adj 윤리적인 I impractical adj 비현실적인 I dilemma n 딜레마 I compel v 강요하다, ~하게 만들다 I avenge v 복수하다 I oppressor n 압제자 I combat n 전투 I conquer v 정복하다 I regime n 정권

Actual Test 1

본서 | P. 272

Conversation 1	1. B	2. B	3. B	4. A	5. C	
Lecture 1	6. C	7. C	8. A	9. B, D	10. A	11. A
Conversation 2	1. C	2. A	3. B	4. C	5. B, D	
Lecture 2	6. C	7. A, C, D	8. A	9. D	10. D – B – C – A	11. C
Lecture 3	12. D	13. B	14. D	15. A	16. D	17. B

Conversation 1

본서 | P. 274

Man: Student | Woman: Librarian

[1-5] Listen to part of a conversation between a student and a librarian.

W Welcome to the library. I'm Judy Wiscot. How may I help you?

M 1 I keep getting these notices from the library telling me that I need to return a book that I checked out for one of my classes.

W Okay. Let's see if we can get to the bottom of this. What's your name and ID number?

M My name is Jim Furyk, and my ID number is 93895.

W All right. Here we are. You checked out *Paradigms and Methodologies in Transactional Behavior*. The book was due two weeks ago. That's why you've been getting return request notices. Is that right?

M Well, it's like this. 2 I'm a senior psychology major, and I was under the impression that seniors were permitted an indefinite extension providing that they needed the materials.

W 2, 3 That's true, but you're forgetting one important condition. While it is true that seniors are allowed to keep books out longer than underclassmen, the seniors must immediately return the books when another student requests the book.

M 3 I don't think I understand why the policy exists in the first place. I mean, if another student can request the book at any time, then the senior doesn't have any guarantee to keep the book! For example, the book that I've checked out is a resource that everybody needs in the psych department, but only seniors depend on it for our final projects that we need in order to graduate. Do you catch my meaning?

남자: 학생 | 여자: 도서관 사서

학생과 도서관 사서의 대화를 들으시오.

여 도서관에 온 걸 환영합니다. 전 주디 위스콧이에요. 어떻게 도와드릴까요?

남 1 제 수업을 위해 대출했던 책을 반납하라는 통지를 도서관에서 계속해서 받고 있어서요.

여 그렇군요. 어떻게 된 일인지 한번 알아보죠. 학생 이름과 학생증 번호가 뭐죠?

남 제 이름은 짐 퓨릭이고 학생증 번호는 93895예요.

여 좋아요. 찾았어요. 〈매매 행태의 범례와 방법론〉이라는 책을 대출했군요. 그 책의 대출 기한이 2주 전이었어요. 그게 바로 학생이 계속해서 반납 통지를 받았던 이유네요. 맞죠?

남 음, 그건 이렇게 된 거예요. 2 저는 심리학 전공 4학년 학생인데 4학년 학생에게는 자료가 필요하다면 무한정 대출 기간을 연장할 수 있게 해주는 줄 알았어요.

여 2, 3 맞아요. 하지만 학생은 한 가지 중요한 조건을 잊었군요. 4학년 학생들이 하급생들보다 더 오랜 기간 책을 대출할 수 있기는 하지만, 다른 학생이 그 책을 대출하기를 원한다면 즉시 해당 도서를 반납해야 해요.

남 3 그럼 애초에 왜 그런 정책이 있는 건지 이해가 안 되네요. 제 말은, 만약 다른 학생이 도서를 어느 때라도 요청할 수 있다면 4학년 학생이 그 책을 계속 볼 수 있도록 보장을 받지 못한다는 거잖아요! 예를 들어, 제가 대출한 책이 심리학과의 모든 학생들에게 필요한 것이긴 하지만 4학년생만 졸업을 위한 최종 프로젝트를 위해 그 책이 꼭 필요하다고요. 제 말 이해하세요?

W 4 Yes, I catch it, but return requests happen less frequently than you might think. Generally, we have plenty of copies of each book, so seniors can keep the books out for the whole semester without anybody missing them.

M I understand, but the number of books the library owns doesn't change my predicament. I still really need this book.

W The rule states that after the return request is satisfied, and the second student is finished with the book, then the library will call the first student to come and pick up the book for a second time.

M That's great service, but again, it doesn't help me at the moment. I have to keep this book in order to pass.

W How about this? Why don't you come back into the office and copy the vital pages on the library's machine free of charge? That way your work won't be interrupted.

M That's very kind of you! Is there any way I'll be able to get the book back soon?

W 5 It will depend on how long the new requester needs to keep the book. Underclassmen get only two weeks for a check out. However, normally, they don't keep the book for that long. If that happens, we'll get the book back to you as soon as possible.

M Great! Thanks so much for your patience. Can I make those copies now?

W Certainly, why don't you come on back, and I'll get somebody to help you.

여 4 네, 무슨 말인지 알아요. 하지만 반납 요청은 학생이 생각하는 것보다 드물게 일어나요. 일반적으로 도서마다 충분히 여러 권을 보유하고 있기 때문에, 4학년 학생들이 다른 학생들의 요구 없이 한 학기 내내 그 도서를 볼 수 있어요.

남 이해가 되긴 하지만, 도서관이 보유하고 있는 도서의 수가 제가 처한 어려운 상황을 바꿔주지는 않는다고요. 전 여전히 이 책이 정말 필요해요.

여 규정에 따르면 도서 반납 요청이 충족되어 두 번째 학생이 이 책을 다 사용하고 나면 도서관에서 첫 번째 학생에게 전화를 걸어 다시 그 책을 대출해 갈 수 있게 해줘요.

남 좋은 제도네요. 하지만 지금 당장은 저에게 도움이 되지 않아요. 수업에 낙제하지 않으려면 이 책이 꼭 필요해요.

여 이렇게 하는 건 어때요? 여기 사무실로 들어와서 중요한 페이지만 무료로 복사해 가는 건 어때요? 그렇게 하면 학생의 학업에 무리가 없을 것 같은데요.

남 정말 친절하시네요! 제가 그 책을 빨리 다시 받아볼 수 있는 방법이 있을까요?

여 5 이 책을 신청한 학생이 얼마나 오랫동안 책을 대출하느냐에 달려 있겠군요. 하급생들은 대출 기간이 2주뿐이에요. 하지만 일반적으로 그렇게 오래 빌리지는 않아요. 만약 그렇다면, 가능한 한 빨리 학생이 책을 다시 대출할 수 있게 해줄게요.

남 좋아요! 양해해 주셔서 감사합니다. 지금 바로 복사할 수 있을까요?

여 물론이에요. 뒤쪽으로 들어오세요. 학생을 도와 줄 사람을 찾아줄게요.

1. Why does the student go to the library?
   - (A) To check out some materials for a paper he is writing
   - (B) To find out why he is receiving notices from the library
   - (C) To inquire about obtaining notes for a psychology lecture
   - (D) To request a timeline for picking up reserve materials

2. What is a key feature of the library's checkout policy?
   - (A) Seniors are permitted to keep books out without a time limit.
   - (B) Seniors are permitted to keep books out longer with some restrictions.
   - (C) All underclassmen must return books as soon as seniors request them.
   - (D) Seniors and underclassmen have the same library privileges.

1. 학생은 왜 도서관에 갔는가?
   - (A) 작성 중인 리포트를 위해 몇 가지 자료를 대출하려고
   - (B) 왜 자신이 도서관으로부터 계속 통지를 받고 있는지 알아보려고
   - (C) 심리학 수업 노트를 얻는 것에 대해 문의하려고
   - (D) 예약 자료를 가져갈 일정을 요청하려고

2. 도서관 대출 정책의 주요 특징은 무엇인가?
   - (A) 4학년생들은 기간 제한 없이 책을 대출할 수 있다.
   - (B) 4학년생들은 약간의 제약과 함께 책을 좀 더 오래 대출할 수 있다.
   - (C) 4학년생이 책을 요청하는 즉시 모든 하급생들은 그 책을 반납해야 한다.
   - (D) 4학년생과 하급생들은 도서관에서 똑같은 권리를 갖는다.

3. **Listen again to part of the conversation. Then answer the question.**

> W That's true, but you're forgetting one important condition. While it is true that seniors are allowed to keep books out longer than underclassmen, the seniors must immediately return the books when another student requests the book.
> M I don't think I understand why the policy exists in the first place.

What does the student imply when he says this:

> M I don't think I understand why the policy exists in the first place.

Ⓐ He does not comprehend the rules of the book return policy.
Ⓑ He is irritated about the ineffective book return policy.
Ⓒ He thinks the policy regarding a senior extension is unfair.
Ⓓ He believes that the library should lengthen the policy time.

4. **What is true about the return request?**
Ⓐ It is something that does not happen that often.
Ⓑ It guarantees a semester-long checkout for seniors.
Ⓒ It requires students to fill out a form.
Ⓓ It has to be fulfilled within a week.

5. **What is the likely outcome of the conversation?**
Ⓐ The student will be allowed to keep the book until the completion of his project.
Ⓑ The student will no longer be able to check books out from the library.
Ⓒ The student will return the book but receive it back sooner than thought.
Ⓓ The student will not utilize the services of the library any longer.

3. 대화의 일부를 다시 듣고 질문에 답하시오.

> 여 맞아요, 하지만 학생은 한 가지 중요한 조건을 잊었군요. 4학년 학생들이 하급생들보다 더 오랜 기간 책을 대출할 수 있기는 하지만, 다른 학생이 그 책을 대출하기를 원한다면 즉시 해당 도서를 반납해야 해요.
> 남 그럼 애초에 왜 그런 정책이 있는 건지 이해가 안 되네요.

학생은 다음과 같이 말하며 무엇을 의미하는가:

> 남 그럼 애초에 왜 그런 정책이 있는 건지 이해가 안 되네요.

Ⓐ 도서 반납 정책의 규칙을 이해하지 못한다.
Ⓑ 비효율적인 도서 반납 정책에 짜증이 났다.
Ⓒ 4학년생의 대출 기간 연장과 관련한 정책이 불공평하다고 생각한다.
Ⓓ 도서관이 정한 기간을 늘려야 한다고 생각한다.

4. 도서 반납 요청에 관해 옳은 것은 무엇인가?
Ⓐ 그다지 자주 일어나지 않는 일이다.
Ⓑ 4학년생에게 한 학기 내내 대출을 보장한다.
Ⓒ 학생들이 양식을 작성하도록 요구한다.
Ⓓ 1주일 내에 이행되어야 한다.

5. 이 대화의 결과는 어떠하겠는가?
Ⓐ 학생이 프로젝트를 끝낼 때까지 책을 가지고 있는 것이 허용될 것이다.
Ⓑ 학생은 이제 더 이상 도서관에서 책을 대출할 수 없게 될 것이다.
Ⓒ 학생은 책을 반납하겠지만 생각했던 것보다 더 빨리 다시 돌려받게 될 것이다.
Ⓓ 학생은 더 이상 도서관 서비스를 이용하지 않을 것이다.

어휘 notice n 통지, 알림 | check out (책을) 대출하다 | paradigm n 전형적인 예, 양식 | methodology n 방법론 | transactional behavior 매매 행태 | psychology n 심리학 | under the impression ~라고 생각한 | permit v 허락하다 | indefinite adj 무기한의, 정해져 있지 않은 | extension n 연장 | material n 자료 | condition n 조건 | underclassman n 하급생 | immediately adv 즉시 | policy n 규정 | guarantee n 보장 | resource n 출처, 자료 | graduate v 졸업하다 | generally adv 일반적으로 | predicament n 곤경, 궁지 | satisfy v 만족하다, 충족하다 | interrupt v 방해하다 | patience n 인내

Man: Professor

[6-11] Listen to part of a lecture in an astronomy class.

M 6 Let's start today's lecture by talking about Pluto, the planet we know the least about in our solar system, but are learning more about day by day. In fact, when I say planet I'm actually wrong. In 2006, the official status of Pluto was changed from planet to dwarf planet. A dwarf planet is like a planet except for one thing, its gravity isn't strong enough to clear the area around it, so it shares its neighborhood with other objects. But, Pluto used to be considered the 9th planet, the furthest planet from the Sun, and the smallest planet in our solar system—until 2006 when it was reclassified. 7 In fact, Pluto is so remote and so small that it wasn't until 1930 that it was even discovered, quite by accident. You see, there was this mathematical model that said the gravity of an as-yet-undiscovered planet must be influencing Neptune's orbit. So, a team of astronomers got busy trying to track down this mysterious 9th planet. And they found one. But, strangely, the calculations that had started their search turned out to be wrong. So, I guess that if it hadn't been for that lucky little miscalculation, we might still not know about the existence of Pluto. And although we know that it exists, we don't have much information about it. 8 Even with today's best telescope, the Hubble, we can only get very low quality, fuzzy pictures of Pluto.

So, like I said, information about Pluto is constantly changing. But, we do know that it's composed mostly of rock and ice and its orbit around the Sun isn't like the other planets'. Their orbits are all circular, but Pluto's orbit isn't a circle; it's an oval—sort of a "squashed circle shape". That means that at some points in its orbit it gets closer to the Sun—closer than Neptune, in fact. And at other times, it is very far away from the Sun. 9(B) We also know that Pluto has a thin atmosphere of nitrogen, carbon monoxide, and methane. But there's something really strange about its atmosphere. Normally, Pluto is a chilly minus 270 degree Celsius. But when the planet is on the part of its orbit that takes it farthest away from the Sun, it gets even colder.

남자: 교수

천문학 강의의 일부를 들으시오.

남 6 명왕성에 대한 이야기로 오늘의 수업을 시작해 봅시다. 명왕성은 우리 태양계 행성 중에서 우리가 알고 있는 바가 가장 적지만 서서히 더 알아가고 있는 행성이죠. 사실, 행성이라고 말하는 것은 잘못된 것입니다. 2006년에 명왕성의 공식적인 지위는 행성에서 왜행성으로 바뀌었습니다. 왜행성은 한 가지를 빼고는 행성과 같은데, 그 한가지는 중력이 그 주변 지역에 아무것도 존재하지 못하게 할 만큼 세지 않기 때문에 다른 물체와 그 주변을 공유한다는 점입니다. 하지만 명왕성은 2006년에 새롭게 분류되기 전까지 아홉 번째 행성이자 태양으로부터 가장 먼 행성, 우리 태양계에서 가장 작은 행성으로 여겨져 왔습니다. 7 실제로, 명왕성은 너무 멀리 있고 크기도 너무 작아서 1930년이 되어서야 발견되었고, 그것도 거의 우연에 의해서였어요. 무슨 말이냐 하면, 아직 발견되지 않은 행성의 중력이 해왕성의 궤도에 영향을 주고 있다는 수학적 모델이 있었습니다. 따라서 천문학자들로 구성된 팀이 이 신비로운 아홉 번째 행성을 추적하기 위해 바삐 움직였습니다. 그리고 하나를 찾아냈죠. 그러나 이상하게도, 그들로 하여금 조사를 착수하게 했던 계산은 틀린 것으로 밝혀졌습니다. 그러니 그런 우연한 작은 계산 착오가 없었더라면 우리는 여전히 명왕성의 존재에 대해 모르고 있지 않을까 생각합니다. 그리고 비록 명왕성이 존재한다는 것은 알지만, 그에 대한 정보는 많지가 않아요. 8 오늘날 최상의 망원경인 허블 망원경으로 보아도 명왕성의 영상은 아주 질이 떨어지고 흐릿합니다.

따라서 제가 말한 것처럼, 명왕성에 대한 정보는 끊임없이 바뀌고 있습니다. 그러나 우리는 명왕성이 대부분 암석과 얼음으로 구성되어 있으며 태양을 도는 궤도가 다른 행성들의 궤도와는 다르다는 것은 알고 있습니다. 다른 행성들의 궤도는 모두 원형이지만, 명왕성의 궤도는 원형이 아니고 타원형, 일종의 '눌린 원형'입니다. 이 말은 궤도의 어떤 지점에서 명왕성은 태양과 더 가까워진다는 말이며, 실제로 해왕성보다 더 태양과 가까워집니다. 또 다른 지점에서는 태양과 매우 멀리 떨어지게 되죠. 9(B) 우리는 또한 명왕성이 질소, 일산화탄소, 그리고 메탄으로 된 얇은 대기를 갖고 있다는 것을 알고 있습니다. 그러나 그 대기와 관련해 정말 이상한 것이 있어요. 일반적으로 명왕성은 섭씨 영하 270도로 매우 춥습니다. 하지만 이 행성이 궤도상 태양으로부터 가장 먼 곳에 왔을 때는 더 차가워집니다.

9(D) During that time, most of the atmosphere freezes and falls to the surface as frost and snow. We're talking about the whole planet hidden under a thick blanket of snow! Once frozen, it doesn't thaw again for hundreds of years until Pluto swings back closer to the Sun.

It's interesting; most of what we do know about Pluto has only been learned since the late 1970s through observation from Earth alone. And we've basically done all of the research we can do from here. To find out more about the dwarf planet, we need close-up observation. **10, 11** That's why NASA sent an unmanned robot-probe, called New Horizons, to fly by Pluto and take readings and images of the surface. It was launched in January 2006, and it reached Pluto on July 14, 2015. It reached Pluto at the time when it was warmer, so its atmosphere wasn't in frozen form. You can understand why that's important, right? If the whole planet was covered in a thick layer of snow, it would obviously make the ground impossible to see. They needed to get there before the snow season started again in order to get some good pictures of the surface. For researchers like me, this is really exciting! I've been studying Pluto for almost 20 years now and have no idea what it really looks like.

9(D) 이 시기 동안, 대기의 대부분이 얼어서 서리나 눈으로 표면에 떨어지게 됩니다. 행성 전체가 두꺼운 눈의 층에 덮여 가려지는 거예요! 일단 얼면, 태양에 더 가까워지는 지점에 이르기 전까지 수백 년 동안 다시 녹지 않습니다.

흥미로운 점은 우리가 명왕성에 대해 알고 있는 대부분은 1970년대 후반에 와서야 지구에서만 이뤄진 관측을 통해 알려진 것이라는 사실입니다. 그리고 우리는 지구상에서 할 수 있는 모든 연구는 기본적으로 다 했어요. 그 왜행성에 대해 더 알기 위해서는 근접 관찰이 필요합니다. **10, 11** 이것이 NASA가 명왕성 주변을 돌며 표면의 관찰 자료와 이미지를 얻기 위해 뉴호라이즌스라는 이름의 무인 로봇 탐사선을 보낸 이유입니다. 이 탐사선은 2006년 1월에 발사되었고, 2015년 7월 14일에 명왕성에 도착했습니다. 탐사선은 명왕성이 좀 따뜻해서 대기가 얼어 있지 않았던 시기에 그곳에 도착했습니다. 왜 그것이 중요한지 알 수 있죠? 만약 행성 전체가 두꺼운 눈 층으로 덮여 있다면 땅 표면을 보는 것이 당연히 불가능할 겁니다. 표면을 잘 보여줄 사진을 찍기 위해 탐사선은 눈 내리는 계절이 시작되기 전에 그곳에 도착해야 했습니다. 저 같은 연구자들에게는 이것이 얼마나 흥미로운지 몰라요! 제가 명왕성을 지금까지 거의 20년 동안 연구했는데 실제로 어떻게 생겼는지는 알지 못하니까요.

6. What is the topic of this lecture?

Ⓐ Pluto and its constantly-changing position in the solar system
Ⓑ Pluto and the space agencies that are fighting to reach it first
Ⓒ The characteristics of Pluto and the ongoing process of learning about it
Ⓓ Pluto and the type of spacecrafts that have explored there

7. What does the professor imply about the discovery of Pluto?

Ⓐ The mistake was not very important to the discovery of Pluto.
Ⓑ Pluto exists only as a mathematical possibility.
Ⓒ Pluto was only discovered because of a mistake.
Ⓓ We know about Pluto only because of its influence on Neptune's orbit.

6. 강의의 주제는 무엇인가?

Ⓐ 명왕성과 태양계에서 계속 변하는 명왕성의 위치
Ⓑ 명왕성과 그곳에 먼저 도착하려고 다투는 항공 우주국들
Ⓒ 명왕성의 특징과 그것을 연구하려는 지속적인 과정
Ⓓ 명왕성과 명왕성을 탐사해온 우주선의 종류

7. 교수는 명왕성의 발견에 관해 무엇을 암시하는가?

Ⓐ 그 실수는 명왕성의 발견에 그다지 중요하지 않았다.
Ⓑ 명왕성은 수학적 가능성으로만 존재한다.
Ⓒ 명왕성은 실수 때문에 발견되었다.
Ⓓ 우리는 해왕성의 궤도에 미치는 명왕성의 영향 때문에 명왕성을 안다.

8. How does the professor account for the fact that so little is known about Pluto?

(A) Pluto cannot be seen clearly even with our best telescope.
(B) Pluto is large and is located very far from Earth.
(C) Pluto has only been observed from other planets.
(D) Pluto has a circular orbit, which makes it invisible for long periods.

9. What does the professor say are the characteristics of Pluto's atmosphere? Choose 2 answers.

(A) It is not affected by Pluto's orbit.
(B) It is composed of methane, carbon monoxide, and nitrogen.
(C) It is very stable.
(D) It stays frozen for hundreds of years at a time.
(E) The snow and ice covering Pluto melts spontaneously.

10. Listen again to part of the lecture. Then answer the question.

M That's why NASA sent an unmanned robot-probe, called New Horizons, to fly by Pluto and take readings and images of the surface. It was launched in January 2006, and it reached Pluto on July 14, 2015. It reached Pluto at the time when it was warmer, so its atmosphere wasn't in frozen form. You can understand why that's important, right?

Why does the professor say this:

M You can understand why that's important, right?

(A) He thinks that the students can understand based on what he has already said.
(B) He thinks that the students couldn't possibly understand why it is important.
(C) He thinks that the students already knew why the probe is important.
(D) He thinks the students will find this boring because they already know a lot about it.

11. What will the professor probably talk about next?

(A) He will go on to discuss the New Horizons mission in more detail.
(B) He will move to a discussion about Mars and the Hubble telescope.
(C) He will talk about the possibility of humans living on Pluto.
(D) He will discuss the costs and benefits of space exploration.

8. 교수는 명왕성에 대해 알려진 바가 적다는 사실을 어떻게 설명하고 있는가?

(A) 명왕성은 우리가 갖고 있는 최고 수준의 망원경을 통해서도 또렷하게 볼 수 없다.
(B) 명왕성은 거대하고 지구로부터 매우 멀리 떨어져 있다.
(C) 명왕성은 다른 행성에서만 관찰되어 왔다.
(D) 명왕성은 원형 궤도를 갖고 있어 오랜 기간 동안 눈에 띄지 않는다.

9. 교수가 말한 명왕성 대기의 특징은 무엇인가? 두 개를 고르시오.

(A) 명왕성 궤도에 영향을 받지 않는다.
(B) 메탄과 일산화탄소, 질소로 구성되어 있다.
(C) 매우 안정되어 있다.
(D) 한 번에 수백 년 동안 언 상태로 유지된다.
(E) 명왕성을 덮은 눈과 얼음은 갑자기 녹는다.

10. 강의의 일부를 다시 듣고 질문에 답하시오.

남 이것이 NASA가 명왕성 주변을 돌며 표면의 관찰 자료와 이미지를 얻기 위해 뉴호라이즌스라는 이름의 무인 로봇 탐사선을 보낸 이유입니다. 이 탐사선은 2006년 1월에 발사되었고, 2015년 7월 14일에 명왕성에 도착했습니다. 탐사선은 명왕성이 좀 따뜻해서 대기가 얼어 있지 않았던 시기에 그곳에 도착했습니다. 왜 그것이 중요한지 알 수 있죠?

교수는 왜 이렇게 말하는가:

남 왜 그것이 중요한지 알 수 있죠?

(A) 교수는 학생들이 그가 이미 이야기한 바에 근거해 이해할 수 있을 거라고 생각한다.
(B) 교수는 학생들이 그것이 왜 중요한지 아마도 이해하지 못할 거라 생각한다.
(C) 교수는 학생들이 그 탐사선이 왜 중요한지 이미 알고 있었다고 생각한다.
(D) 교수는 학생들이 그것에 대해 이미 많이 알고 있기 때문에 지루해할 것이라고 생각한다.

11. 교수는 다음에 무엇을 언급하겠는가?

(A) 뉴호라이즌스호 임무에 대해 좀 더 자세하게 논의를 계속할 것이다.
(B) 화성과 허블 망원경에 대한 논의로 넘어갈 것이다.
(C) 명왕성에서 인간이 거주할 가능성에 대해 언급할 것이다.
(D) 우주 탐사 비용과 그 이익에 관해 논의할 것이다.

어휘 solar system 태양계 | status n 지위, 상태 | dwarf planet 왜행성 | neighborhood 이웃 | reclassify v 재분류하다 | remote adj 외딴 | discover v 발견하다 | by accident 우연히, 사고로 | mathematical adj 수학의 | gravity n 중력 | influence v 영향을 주다 | astronomer n 천문학자 | track down 추적하다 | mysterious adj 신비한 | strangely adv 이상하게 | calculation n 계산 | miscalculation n 계산 착오 | existence n 존재 | telescope n 망원경 | quality n 질, 품질 | fuzzy adj 흐릿한 | constantly adv 계속, 지속적으로 | composed of ~로 구성된 | orbit n 궤도 | circular adj 원형의 | oval adj 타원형의 | squash v 짓누르다 | atmosphere n 대기 | nitrogen n 질소 | carbon monoxide 일산화탄소 | methane n 메탄 | chilly adj 쌀쌀한, 추운 | freeze v 얼어붙다 | surface n 표면 | frost n 서리 | thick adj 두꺼운 | swing v 빙 돌다, 휙 움직이다 | observation n 관찰 | unmanned adj 무인의 | obviously adv 명백히

Conversation 2

본서 | P. 280

Man: Cafeteria manager | Woman: Student

[1-5] Listen to part of a conversation between a student and a cafeteria manager.

W Hi. Can you tell me where I can find the manager?

M Yes, you've found the right person.

W Oh. Good. I need to speak to you about something. I was interested in....

M 2 Is this about the job? Because the position has been filled, we don't have any other opportunities at the moment. Why don't you come back when it's not the lunch rush?

W Whoa! I think you misunderstood me. 1 I don't know anything about a job opening; I was here to inquire about taking the baking class I read about in the student bulletin.

M Oh! That's different. I'm terribly sorry. I've been a little overwhelmed with all the traffic in here asking about the job positions lately. I've never seen it like this! What exactly are you interested in?

W Well, it's like this. 3 My friend Emily, who is on the soccer team, broke her leg playing in the regionals last week. She was in traction at the hospital for a few days, and now she's back in the dorm resting.

M Ouch! I'm very sorry to hear that.

W 3 Anyway, she's been down in the dumps because of it, so I thought I would bake her a cake to try to cheer her up. She absolutely loves cakes, but I never learned to bake one.

M That's very kind of you. You're a good friend. Is there anything we can do for her?

W Thanks. She just sits in bed all day, upset that she can't play soccer anymore. Plus it's her birthday next week. Do you think you can help me out?

M Definitely! Let me explain how this works. The cooking class goes over three days starting early next week. On Monday, there is a brief orientation followed by a simple explanation of what constitutes a cake. Then, the instructor explains all the cooking tools that are needed to make a cake.

W Hmmm. Sounds like that might be a little tedious. Can I skip that day and come on Tuesday?

남자: 구내 식당 매니저 | 여자: 학생

학생과 구내 식당 매니저의 대화를 들으시오.

여 안녕하세요. 매니저가 어디 있는지 아세요?

남 네, 전데요.

여 오. 잘됐네요. 드릴 말씀이 좀 있어서요. 제가 관심 있는 게 있는데....

남 2 일자리 때문인가요? 사람이 충원되어서 지금은 더 이상 자리가 없어요. 바쁜 점심 시간 말고 다른 때 오시겠어요?

여 와, 오해하신 것 같네요. 1 구직에 대해선 모르고요. 저는 학생 게시판에서 본 제빵 수업 수강과 관련해서 궁금한 게 있어서 왔어요.

남 아! 그거라면 상황이 다르죠. 정말 미안해요. 최근에 일자리 때문에 사람들이 너무 많이 와서 주체를 못할 정도였거든요. 이 정도로 몰려온 건 처음이어서요! 정확히 무엇에 관심이 있으신 거죠?

여 음, 그게요. 3 제 친구 에밀리가 축구 팀에서 뛰고 있는데 지난주에 지역 경기에서 뛰다가 다리가 부러졌어요. 며칠 동안 병원에서 골절 견인치료를 받다가 지금은 기숙사로 돌아와서 쉬고 있어요.

남 저런! 정말 유감이네요.

여 3 어쨌든 그것 때문에 의기소침해 있어서 그 친구를 위해 케이크를 하나 구워줄까 해서요. 친구가 케이크를 굉장히 좋아하는데, 전 케이크 굽는 것을 배운 적이 없거든요.

남 정말 사려 깊군요. 좋은 친구네요. 그 친구를 위해서 저희가 해드릴 수 있는 일이 있을까요?

여 감사합니다. 에밀리는 그냥 하루 종일 침대에 앉아 있어요. 축구를 더 이상 못한다는 사실에 괴로워하면서요. 게다가 다음 주가 생일이에요. 절 도와주실 수 있을까요?

남 그럼요! 어떻게 진행되는지 설명해 드릴게요. 요리 수업은 다음 주 초에 시작해서 3일 동안 진행돼요. 월요일에는 짧은 오리엔테이션을 한 후 케이크가 무엇으로 구성되는지에 대해 간단히 설명할 거예요. 그런 뒤 선생님이 케이크를 만드는 데 필요한 요리 도구를 전부 설명해요.

여 흠. 약간 지루할 것처럼 들리는데요. 그날은 건너뛰고 화요일에 와도 되나요?

M Bear with me. The reason we teach that part is that... so students understand the common language needed to communicate with the instructor.

W I guess that makes sense. What happens on Tuesday? Do we actually get to bake a cake in this class?

M Of course! On Tuesday, the class will choose the type of cake, learn how to mix ingredients and finally do some baking. Then, on the last day, students will learn how to use decorating tools and techniques. **4** It should be perfect for helping out your friend.

W **4** You sold me! How can I sign up? Are there any fees?

M You are a student here, right? If you're a student of this university, then all charges are covered under the student activity fee you pay every semester. Can I get your name?

W Sure. I'm Lauren Billings. Student ID number 935085. Do I need to bring anything?

M B-i-l-l-i-n-g-s. Okay. Got it. **5(B), (D)** Yes, as far as what to bring, you're going to need an apron because we just don't have enough to spare in the kitchen, and some clothes you don't mind getting dirty. But as far as all kitchen utensils like spatulas or beaters, they will be provided. Great. OK. We'll see you on Monday. The class starts right here in the kitchen at 8 o'clock sharp. Anything else?

W No, that will do it. Thanks. I'll see you on Monday.

남 제 말을 들어보세요. 우리가 그 부분을 가르치는 이유는... 학생들이 선생님과 대화할 때 주로 필요한 언어를 이해할 수 있게 하려는 거예요.

여 말이 되네요. 화요일에는 어떤 일을 해요? 수업 시간에 실제로 케이크를 굽게 되나요?

남 물론이죠! 화요일 수업 시간에 케이크의 종류를 선택하고, 어떻게 재료를 섞을지를 배우고, 마지막으로 케이크를 구워요. 그런 다음 마지막 날에 학생들은 장식 도구를 사용하는 법과 기술을 배우게 될 겁니다. **4** 친구를 돕는 데 완벽할 거예요.

여 **4** 들어야겠어요! 어떻게 등록할 수 있나요? 돈을 내야 하나요?

남 여기 학생이죠, 맞죠? 이 대학교 학생이면 모든 비용은 매 학기 내는 활동비에 포함되어 있어요. 이름을 알려주시겠어요?

여 그럼요. 로렌 빌링스입니다. 학생증 번호는 935085이에요. 제가 가져와야 하는 것이 있을까요?

남 B-i-l-l-i-i-n-g-s. 네, 됐습니다. **5(B), (D)** 네, 준비물에 대해서라면, 여기 주방에 앞치마 여분이 충분하지 않기 때문에 앞치마가 필요할 거고, 더러워져도 되는 옷을 가져오세요. 하지만 주걱이나 거품기 같은 주방용품은 전부 제공될 겁니다. 좋아요. 됐어요. 그럼 월요일에 뵙겠습니다. 수업은 정각 8시에 바로 여기 주방에서 시작합니다. 또 필요한 게 있으세요?

여 아뇨, 다 된 것 같아요. 감사합니다. 월요일에 뵐게요.

1. Why does the student go to see the cafeteria manager?

Ⓐ To make a complaint about the quality of the food
Ⓑ To apply for a vacant work position at the cafeteria
Ⓒ To ask about information involving a baking class
Ⓓ To substitute a working shift for a sick friend

2. What is the man's attitude at the beginning of the conversation?

Ⓐ He is trying to show that he is too busy to talk at the moment.
Ⓑ He is implying that the student is not qualified for the job.
Ⓒ He is stating that the cooking class has filled up.
Ⓓ He is wondering if the woman filled the lunch order.

3. What made the student want to register for the cooking class?

Ⓐ She wants to improve her cooking skills because she lives alone.
Ⓑ She wants to learn to bake a cake to cheer up her injured friend.

1. 학생은 왜 구내 식당 매니저를 보러 가는가?

Ⓐ 음식의 질에 대해서 불평하려고
Ⓑ 구내 식당의 빈 일자리에 지원하려고
Ⓒ 제빵 수업에 대한 정보를 물어보려고
Ⓓ 아픈 친구를 위해 근무를 대신하려고

2. 대화 초반에 남자의 태도는 어떠한가?

Ⓐ 지금 너무 바빠서 말할 시간이 없다는 것을 보여주려고 한다.
Ⓑ 학생이 일할 자격이 안 된다는 것을 암시하고 있다.
Ⓒ 요리 수업이 다 찼다고 이야기하고 있다.
Ⓓ 여자가 점심 식사를 주문했는지 궁금해하고 있다.

3. 학생이 요리 수업에 등록하고 싶어 하게 된 계기는 무엇인가?

Ⓐ 혼자 살기 때문에 요리 실력을 키우고 싶어 한다.
Ⓑ 다친 친구를 기쁘게 해주려고 케이크 굽는 법을 배우고 싶어 한다.

Ⓒ She is trying to impress her parents, who are coming to visit.
Ⓓ She is considering changing her major to the culinary arts.

Ⓒ 자신을 보러 오는 부모님을 감동시키려고 한다.
Ⓓ 자신의 전공을 조리로 바꾸는 것을 고려 중이다.

4. Listen again to part of the conversation. Then answer the question.

M It should be perfect for helping out your friend.
W You sold me! How can I sign up? Are there any fees?

Why does the student say this:

W You sold me! How can I sign up? Are there any fees?

Ⓐ She is excited that she got a job working at the cafeteria.
Ⓑ She is angry because she thinks the manager overcharged her.
Ⓒ She is very happy because the class will be beneficial to her.
Ⓓ She is upset at the man because he gave away her spot in the class.

4. 대화의 일부를 다시 듣고 질문에 답하시오.

남 친구를 돕는 데 완벽할 거예요.
여 들어야겠어요! 어떻게 등록할 수 있나요? 돈을 내야 하나요?

학생은 왜 이렇게 말하는가:

여 들어야겠어요! 어떻게 등록할 수 있나요? 돈을 내야 하나요?

Ⓐ 구내 식당에서 일자리를 구해서 신이 났다.
Ⓑ 매니저가 돈을 더 받았다고 생각해서 화가 나 있다.
Ⓒ 수업이 자신에게 유익할 것이라고 생각해서 매우 기뻐한다.
Ⓓ 남자가 수업의 자기 자리를 다른 사람에게 주었다고 생각해서 화가 나 있다.

5. What are two items that the student needs to bring to the cooking class? Choose 2 answers.

Ⓐ Spatula
Ⓑ Apron
Ⓒ Beater
Ⓓ Old clothes

5. 학생이 요리 수업에 가지고 와야 할 두 가지 물건은 무엇인가? 두 개를 고르시오.

Ⓐ 주걱
Ⓑ 앞치마
Ⓒ 거품기
Ⓓ 낡은 옷

어휘 position n 자리 | opportunity n 기회 | misunderstand v 오해하다 | inquire v 묻다 | bulletin n 게시판 | overwhelmed adj 압도된 | traffic n (사람들의) 혼잡함 | exactly adv 정확히 | regionals n 지역 대회 | traction n (골절 치료의) 견인 | down in the dump 우울해하는 | absolutely adv 절대적으로 | upset adj 언짢은 | definitely adv 명백히, 분명히 | explanation n 설명 | constitute v ~를 구성하다, ~이 되다 | tedious adj 지루한 | common adj 일반적인, 흔한 | communicate v 소통하다 | ingredient n 재료 | decorate v 꾸미다 | sign up 등록하다 | spare v 나누어주다, 빌려주다 | utensil n 기구, 도구 | spatula n 주걱, 뒤집개 | beater n 거품기, 먼지떨이

Lecture 2

본서 P. 282

Man: Student | Woman: Professor

[6-11] Listen to part of a discussion in a marine biology class.

W Hello everyone. 6 Let's start out today by talking about our little friends, the crustaceans. Who can tell me what a crustacean is?

M It's an underwater animal that has a hard shell and a body with three main parts, like... crabs, lobsters, and uh... shrimp.

W Right, thank you. 6 But, remember, not all crustaceans live only in the water. Some live on land too, which brings

남자: 학생 | 여자: 교수

해양 생물학 수업 중 토론의 일부를 들으시오.

여 모두 안녕하세요. 6 오늘은 먼저 우리의 작은 친구 갑각류에 대해서 이야기해 봅시다. 갑각류가 무엇인지 말해볼 사람 있나요?

남 딱딱한 껍데기와 세 부분의 몸체로 되어 있는, 일종의... 게, 가재, 어... 그리고 새우와 같은 수중 동물입니다.

여 맞습니다. 고마워요. 6 하지만 기억해야 할 것은 모든 갑각류가 물속에서만 살지는 않는다는 것입니

me to what I wanted to talk about today, our neighbor, the fiddler crab. If you go down to the harbor when the tide is out, you'll probably notice these tiny balls of mud in little piles; there are usually lots of them. Well, believe it or not, they are actually a sign that these cute little crabs, Uca Pugnax, are nearby. Let me write that up here for you. **7(A)** OK, like a lot of other small crabs, these fiddler crabs feed by scooping up mud and using their mouths to sort out the edible material, like algae, fungus, or decaying plant and animal matter, that sort of thing. So, those balls you see are actually "leftovers" from the crab, if you know what I mean. **7(C)** If you look closely, you'll see a little hole in the mud. That's where their burrow is, their home. A burrow is a tunnel that the crabs dig into the mud. They can be up to a foot deep and may connect to other tunnels. This is so they can have more than one entrance and escape from predators like fish, raccoons, water birds, and so on. Safety is one of the reasons why the crab never goes too far from its home.

Another reason they stay near their burrows is because they live in what's called the intertidal zone—an area that is covered by water at high tide. **7(D)** To keep their homes dry during high tide, they roll up a ball of mud and use it to plug the entrances before the water comes in, so that they have a tiny pocket of air to breathe until the water goes down. But when the tide is out, you'll see them out searching for food again.

OK, so here's a picture of the little guy. This one's probably about two inches or so across and fully grown, by the way. **8** The first thing you'll probably notice is that one of his front claws is huge, like a giant pair of scissors—I mean, it's huge relative to the size of the rest of the body. That tells us he's an adult male. The females' claws are smaller and the same size. **9** You might wonder what this huge claw the male has is used for. It looks too big to be useful. But, I'll give you a hint. You can see this sort of thing in other creatures, too, like goliath beetles, walruses, rhinos, bulls. Anyone?

M Well, you said they eat mud, so it's obviously not for hunting. Is it related to fighting other crabs?

W You're getting warmer. It isn't for feeding, certainly. They use it, first of all, to defend their homes from other males that might be around. Usually they just make a rattling sound to warn other crabs not to come near, but they might fight sometimes. It's not too serious though, more like arm

다. 어떤 것은 육지에서도 사는데, 오늘 이야기하고자 하는 우리의 이웃인 농게도 그러합니다. 썰물일 때 항구로 내려가면 아마도 작은 퇴적물 속에 조그만 진흙 공들이 있는 것을 볼 수 있을 겁니다. 보통 그런 것들이 굉장히 많죠. 뭐, 믿기 힘들지 몰라도, 그것들은 이 작고 귀여운 게인 습지 농게가 가까이에 있다는 뜻입니다. 여기에 이름을 써줄게요. **7(A)** 자, 다른 작은 게들처럼 이 농게는 진흙을 퍼 올려서 그 속의 조류, 균류, 부패된 식물과 동물질같이 먹을 만한 것들을 입으로 골라내면서 먹습니다. 그래서 여기 보이는 공들은, 제 말이 무슨 뜻인지 이해한다면, 사실 게들의 '먹고 남은 찌꺼기'입니다. **7(C)** 가까이서 보면 진흙 속에 작은 구멍이 보일 겁니다. 그곳이 그들의 집인 굴이 있는 곳입니다. 굴은 게들이 진흙을 파서 만든 터널입니다. 그것들은 깊이가 1피트 정도이고 다른 터널들과 연결되어 있을 수 있습니다. 이것은 입구를 한 개 이상 두어서 물고기, 너구리, 물새 등의 포식자로부터 도망칠 수 있게끔 하기 위한 것입니다. 안전은 게가 집으로부터 너무 멀리 나가지 않는 이유 중 하나예요.

굴 가까이에서 지내는 또 다른 이유는, 그것들이 만조일 때 물에 의해 덮이는 부분인 조간대라고 불리는 곳에 살기 때문입니다. **7(D)** 만조일 때 집을 마른 상태로 유지하기 위해 그들은 물이 들어오기 전에 진흙공을 만들어서 입구를 막는데, 이렇게 하면 물이 빠질 때까지 숨을 쉴 수 있는 작은 공기 주머니를 갖게 되죠. 하지만 썰물일 때 게들이 다시 밖으로 나와서 먹이를 찾는 것을 볼 수 있을 거예요.

자, 여기 이 작은 녀석의 사진을 보세요. 약 2인치 정도 될 텐데, 참고로 말하면 완전히 자란 겁니다. **8** 첫 번째로 눈에 띄는 것이 아마도 앞 집게발 하나가 마치 거대한 가위처럼 아주 크다는 점일 겁니다. 제 말은, 몸의 나머지 부분의 크기에 비해서 크다는 거죠. 이걸로 이 게가 다 큰 수컷이라는 것을 알 수 있습니다. 암컷의 집게발은 더 작고 크기가 같습니다. **9** 수컷이 지닌 커다란 집게발이 어디에 쓰이는지 아마 궁금할 겁니다. 쓸모가 있기에는 너무 커 보이죠. 하지만 힌트를 드릴게요. 이런 것은 골리앗 풍뎅이, 바다코끼리, 코뿔소, 황소와 같은 다른 동물에서도 볼 수 있습니다. 어디 한번 대답해볼 사람 있나요?

남 음, 농게들이 진흙을 먹는다고 했으니까 분명 사냥을 위한 것은 아니겠고, 다른 게들과 싸우는 것과 연관이 있는 건가요?

여 거의 근접했어요. 먹는 데 사용하는 건 아닌 게 확실하죠. 첫째로, 집게발을 사용하여 주위에 돌아다니는 다른 수컷들로부터 집을 방어합니다. 보통은 다른 게들이 다가오지 못하도록 경고하기 위해서 그냥 덜거덕거리는 소리를 내지만, 때로는 싸울 수도 있습니다. 그렇다고 굉장히 심각한 싸움은 아니

wrestling. 11 The other purpose of this over-sized claw is to attract females. During the breeding period, all of the males try to find a mate. They all stand at the edge of their burrows and as females return from foraging during low tide, they move among the males and "check them out", almost like it's a crab singles bar. Each male tries to impress the females by waving his large claw and if a female likes what she sees, she'll choose him. Now, let's take a look at the life cycle of the fiddler crab.

고, 그냥 팔씨름 같은 것이에요. 11 특대 크기 집게발의 또 다른 목적은 암컷의 관심을 끄는 것입니다. 번식 기간에 모든 수컷은 짝을 찾으려고 합니다. 그것들은 모두 굴 끝에 서 있고, 암컷들은 간조 때 먹이를 찾으러 다니다 돌아와서는, 수컷들 사이를 돌아다니면서 마치 독신 게들이 모이는 술집인 것처럼 누구를 선택할지 '훑어봅니다'. 수컷들은 모두 커다란 집게발을 흔들며 암컷의 관심을 끌려고 하고, 암컷은 만약 맘에 드는 것을 발견할 경우 그 수컷을 선택합니다. 이제 농게의 생애 주기에 대해 알아봅시다.

6. What is the discussion mainly about?

Ⓐ The life cycle of the fiddler crab
Ⓑ The role of the fiddler crab in its local ecosystem
Ⓒ The fiddler crab's features and patterns of behavior
Ⓓ The dating rituals of the fiddler crab

7. What are the main characteristics of fiddler crabs mentioned by the professor? Choose 3 answers.

Ⓐ They filter their food from mud.
Ⓑ They are most active during high tide.
Ⓒ They live in networks of small tunnels.
Ⓓ They breathe air.
Ⓔ Their main food is small birds and fish.

8. According to the professor, how can male and female crabs be differentiated?

Ⓐ Female fiddler crabs' claws are both the same size, whereas the males' aren't.
Ⓑ Female fiddler crabs remain in their burrows more than males do.
Ⓒ Female fiddler crabs look for food in the intertidal region, while males don't.
Ⓓ Both male and female fiddler crabs wave their claws during dating.

9. What does the professor infer when she talks about goliath beetles and walruses?

Ⓐ Male fiddler crabs have the same body parts as these creatures.
Ⓑ Male fiddler crabs have structures that look very similar to the structures of these organisms.
Ⓒ The behavior of male fiddler crabs is similar to these creatures.
Ⓓ The enlarged claw of male fiddler crabs has a function similar to body parts of these creatures.

6. 토론은 주로 무엇에 대한 것인가?

Ⓐ 농게의 생애 주기
Ⓑ 지역 생태계에 있어서 농게의 역할
Ⓒ 농게의 특징과 행동 패턴
Ⓓ 농게의 데이트 의식

7. 교수가 언급한 농게의 주요 특징은 무엇인가? 세 개를 고르시오.

Ⓐ 진흙으로부터 먹잇감을 걸러낸다.
Ⓑ 만조일 때 가장 활동적이다.
Ⓒ 연결되어 있는 작은 터널들 속에서 산다.
Ⓓ 공기로 숨을 쉰다.
Ⓔ 주식은 작은 새들과 물고기다.

8. 교수에 따르면, 수컷과 암컷 게들을 어떻게 구별할 수 있는가?

Ⓐ 암컷 농게의 집게발은 둘 다 같은 크기인데 수컷의 집게발은 그렇지 않다.
Ⓑ 암컷 농게는 수컷보다 굴에 더 오래 있는다.
Ⓒ 암컷 농게는 조간대에서 음식을 찾지만, 수컷은 그러지 않는다.
Ⓓ 수컷과 암컷 농게 모두 짝짓기하는 동안 집게발을 흔든다.

9. 교수는 골리앗풍뎅이와 바다코끼리에 관해 말하며 무엇을 암시하는가?

Ⓐ 수컷 농게들은 이런 동물들과 동일한 신체 부위를 가지고 있다.
Ⓑ 수컷 농게들은 이런 생물들과 무척 비슷하게 보이는 구조를 가지고 있다.
Ⓒ 수컷 농게의 행동은 이런 동물들과 유사하다.
Ⓓ 수컷 농게의 커다란 집게발은 이런 동물들의 신체 부위와 비슷한 기능을 가지고 있다.

10. Put the following words in the same order as the professor used when talking about the characteristics of the crabs.

Ⓐ Mating Behavior
Ⓑ Habitat
Ⓒ Body Structure
Ⓓ Feeding Behavior

1	Ⓓ Feeding behavior
2	Ⓑ Habitat
3	Ⓒ Body Structure
4	Ⓐ Mating behavior

11. Listen again to part of the discussion. Then answer the question.

W The other purpose of this over-sized claw is to attract females. During the breeding period, all of the males try to find a mate. They all stand at the edge of their burrows and as females return from foraging during low tide, they move among the males and "check them out", almost like it's a crab singles bar.

Why does the professor say this:

W ..., almost like it's a crab singles bar.

Ⓐ To help students understand that crabs mate very often during their lifetime
Ⓑ To demonstrate ways that females behave and ways that males try to get their attention
Ⓒ To add humor and interest and give students a vivid image that they will more easily remember
Ⓓ To help students see that crabs behave strangely during breeding season

10. 다음 단어들을 교수가 게들의 특징에 관해 이야기하며 사용한 순서대로 놓으시오.

Ⓐ 짝짓기 행동
Ⓑ 서식지
Ⓒ 신체 구조
Ⓓ 섭식 행동

1	Ⓓ 섭식 행동
2	Ⓑ 서식지
3	Ⓒ 신체 구조
4	Ⓐ 짝짓기 행동

11. 토론의 일부를 다시 듣고 질문에 답하시오.

여 특대 크기 집게발의 또 다른 목적은 암컷의 관심을 끄는 것입니다. 번식 기간에 모든 수컷은 짝을 찾으려고 합니다. 그것들은 모두 굴 끝에 서 있고, 암컷들은 간조 때 먹이를 찾으러 다니다 돌아와서는, 수컷들 사이를 돌아다니면서 마치 독신 게들이 모이는 술집인 것처럼 누구를 선택할지 '훑어봅니다'.

교수는 왜 이렇게 말하는가:

여 ... 마치 독신 게들이 모이는 술집인 것처럼

Ⓐ 게들이 일생 동안 무척 자주 짝짓기를 한다는 것을 학생들이 이해하도록 돕기 위해서
Ⓑ 암컷들이 행동하는 방식과 수컷들이 암컷들의 관심을 끌려고 하는 방식을 예를 들어가며 설명하기 위해서
Ⓒ 유머와 흥미를 더하고 학생들에게 기억하기 더 쉽도록 생생한 이미지를 주기 위해서
Ⓓ 게들이 번식 기간에 이상하게 행동하는 것을 학생들이 알도록 돕기 위해서

어휘 crustacean n 갑각류 | underwater adj 수중의, 물속의 | crab n 게 | lobster n 가재 | shrimp n 새우 | fiddler crab 농게 | harbor n 항구 | tide n 조수, 밀물과 썰물 | notice v 알아차리다 | mud n 진흙 | pile n 더미 | scoop up 뜨다, 퍼 올리다 | sort out 걸러내다 | edible adj 먹을 수 있는 | algae n 조류, 말 | fungus n 균류 | decay v 부패하다 | leftover n 찌꺼기, 남은 것 | burrow n 굴 | tunnel n 터널 | entrance n 입구 | escape v 탈출하다 | raccoon n 너구리 | safety n 안전 | intertidal zone 조간대 | plug v 막아 넣다 | claw n (게 등의) 집게발 | walrus n 바다코끼리 | rhino n 코뿔소 | bull n 황소 | defend v 방어하다 | rattle v 달가닥거리다 | warn v 경고하다 | arm wrestling 팔씨름 | attract v (주의·흥미를) 끌다 | breeding n 번식 | mate n 짝 | forage v 먹이를 찾다 | wave v 흔들다

Lecture 3

본서 P. 284

Woman: Professor

[12-17] Listen to part of a lecture in a psychology class.

W Welcome class. How many of you want to repeat everything I say, word-for-word, over and over again? Does that sound like fun? Well, this is the type of learning that is used in a teacher-centered classroom, and it is called rote learning. This is probably how your parents learned when they were children. And believe it or not, this early method of educating students survives in many classrooms even in these modern times.

So, the tradition of rote learning in schools began centuries ago. **13** In this setting, students who could memorize information, even without making any intellectual associations with the material, were considered intelligent and educated. However, this concept of intelligence had no practical basis, only proving that a student could cooperate in a passive learning environment. **12** In light of this, progressive educators began appearing in the 19th century, and an American named John Dewey would come to represent a new way of looking at how children were educated.

John Dewey is famous for not only his efforts in educational reform but also his work in philosophy and psychology. His philosophies were somewhere between Plato's society-centered thinking and Rousseau's emphasis on the individual. He felt that individuals were only meaningful if they were a fixed part of a society and that society's only importance was the existence of its individual members. Indeed, his philosophical ideas had a direct influence on his educational theories. These were based on the learning of skills and knowledge that students could apply to their lives as both individuals and members of the community. So, to make his theories a reality, he founded the University Laboratory School, now known as the Dewey School, in 1896. With curricula based on hands-on learning, the name of the school was quite appropriate. Of course, this school starkly contrasted the long-established 19th-century institutions.

Before John Dewey... umm, educational theorists, believing repetition led to skill, applied this basic concept to classroom instruction. They felt that children should be educated by learning facts memorized through repetition. Now, this method allowed students to learn information rapidly, especially data unrelated to their existing knowledge, like a vocabulary word from a foreign language. This was considered an advantage since it made the classroom an efficient learning center, with the added

여자: 교수

심리학 강의의 일부를 들으시오.

여 안녕하세요 여러분. 여러분 중 몇 명이나 제가 말하는 모든 것을, 토씨 하나 빠뜨리지 않고, 몇 번이고 반복해서 따라 말하고 싶습니까? 재미있을 것 같나요? 음, 이것은 교사 중심 수업에서 사용되는 학습 유형이고, 암기 학습이라 불립니다. 이것은 아마도 여러분의 부모님이 어렸을 때 학습한 방법일 것입니다. 그리고 믿기 힘들겠지만, 이러한 초기 교수법은 요즘과 같은 현대에도 많은 교실에서 행해지고 있습니다.

학교의 암기 학습의 전통은 몇 세기 전에 시작되었습니다. **13** 이러한 학습 환경 하에서는, 자료에 대해 아무런 지적 연상을 하지 않고서도 학습 내용을 외울 수 있었던 학생들은 똑똑하고 교육을 잘 받은 것으로 간주되었습니다. 그러나 이런 식의 지능이라는 개념은 실제적인 근거를 갖추고 있지 않았고, 오로지 학생이 수동적인 학습 환경에서도 협조적일 수 있다는 것을 증명할 뿐이었습니다. **12** 이런 관점에서 19세기에 진보적인 교육자들이 출현하기 시작했고, 존 듀이라는 미국인은 아이들이 어떻게 교육을 받는지를 바라보는 새로운 방식을 제시하게 되었습니다.

존 듀이는 교육 개혁에 있어서의 노력뿐 아니라 철학과 심리학에 있어서의 성과로도 유명합니다. 그의 철학은 플라톤의 사회 중심적인 생각과 루소의 개인에 대한 강조 사이 어딘가에 있었습니다. 그는 개인은 사회의 고정된 부분일 때만 의미가 있고 사회의 유일한 중요성은 개별 구성원들이 존재한다는 사실뿐이라고 느꼈습니다. 실제로 그의 철학 사상은 그의 교육 이론에 직접적인 영향을 미쳤습니다. 이는 학생들이 개인이자 공동체의 일원으로서 자신들의 삶에 적용할 수 있는 기술과 지식의 학습에 기반을 둔 것이었습니다. 그래서 자신의 이론을 현실화하기 위해서 그는 1896년에 지금은 듀이가 학교로 알려진 대학 실험 학교를 설립했습니다. 직접 해보는 학습에 기반을 둔 교과 과정을 볼 때 그 학교의 이름은 꽤 적절했습니다. 물론 이 학교는 설립된 지 오래된 19세기의 학원들과는 완전히 달랐습니다.

존 듀이 이전의... 음, 교육 이론가들은 반복이 기술로 이어진다고 믿고 교실 수업에 이 기본 개념을 적용했습니다. 그들은 아이들이 반복을 통해서 암기된 사실을 학습하는 방식으로 교육받아야 한다고 느꼈습니다. 자, 이 방법은 학생들이 지식을, 특히 기존의 지식과 연관이 없는 외국어 단어와 같은 지식을 빠르게 학습하도록 했습니다. 이것은 교실을 효율적인 학습 센터로 만들었고, 교사들에게는 특

Actual Test 1

bonus that it didn't require much expertise on the part of instructors. However, what Dewey felt was necessary for classrooms was opposite to the typical classroom conditions. He believed that students should use reasoning to learn and that this skill was to be acquired by experiential learning. So he would recommend a class take a field trip to learn about a location or a science experiment be carried out by students with the teacher only supervising. Also, he felt books were necessary, but they had the less important role of supplementing students' activities.

And... well... central to Dewey's classrooms was the belief that people learn by working in a social environment, seeing how their educational efforts are relevant to everyday life. Furthermore, he liked to highlight the relationship between doing an activity not considered academic, like sewing, cooking, or carpentry, and the diverse academic subjects covering these activities. So by teaching children how to cook, he believed they could learn how to add and subtract when measuring recipe quantities, how to manage time when creating a meal, and also how to cooperate and work with others. This activity would be supplemented with books and materials when necessary, but the real advantage was that students could see and enjoy the outcome of their efforts. You see... Dewey was trying to create people that had real-world knowledge, developed social skills, an advanced intellect, and professional ability.

Now in your opinion, which type of class would you prefer to take? Would you prefer to have your nose buried in a history book, learning facts, or would you prefer to be making delicious foods while covering the subjects applicable to the process? OK, if you are old like me, then maybe you would prefer to have your nose buried in a book! But seriously, most people would prefer Dewey's method. It's only natural that people prefer active learning. **15, 16** For example, my son attends a public school, but I can see that the way he learns fits Dewey's style of teaching. At home, he always plays with wooden toy blocks. He builds all kinds of structures, only to break them down and build them all over again. By doing this, he's developing his knowledge of geometry first hand and in a natural setting. And what I like is that he's having fun while learning.

For the rest of the week, we are going to be looking at some more of Dewey's methods for creating a learner-centered classroom, which, of course, should not be a quiet place.

별한 전문적 기술을 요하지 않는다는 추가적인 보너스로 인해 장점으로 간주됐습니다. 하지만 듀이가 교실에 필요하다고 느낀 것은 전통적인 교실 상황에 반대되는 것이었습니다. 그는 학생들이 학습하는 데 있어서 추론을 사용해야 하며, 이 기술은 경험적인 학습에서 습득된다고 믿었습니다. 그래서 수업 시간에 어떤 장소에 관해서 배우기 위해 현장학습을 가거나, 교사는 감독만 하는 가운데 학생들이 과학 실험을 하도록 권고했습니다. 또한 그는 책은 필요하지만, 학생들의 활동을 보완해주는 데 덜 중요한 역할을 맡고 있다고 생각했습니다.

그리고... 음... 듀이 교실의 중심이 되는 것은 사람들이 자신의 교육적 노력이 어떻게 일상 생활과 관련이 있는지를 보면서 사회적 환경 속에서 일을 함으로써 배운다는 믿음이었습니다. 더 나아가, 그는 바느질, 요리, 목공과 같은 학문적이지 않은 활동과 이러한 활동을 다루는 다양한 학문적인 주제들 사이의 관계도 강조하고 싶어했습니다. 그래서 아이들에게 요리하는 방법을 가르침으로써 아이들이 조리 시 양을 측정할 때 더하기와 빼기를 배우고, 식사를 준비하면서 시간을 관리하는 방법을 배우고, 그리고 다른 사람들과 협동해서 일하는 방법을 배울 수 있다고 믿었습니다. 이 활동은 필요할 때 책과 자료들로 보충될 수 있지만, 진짜 장점은 학생들이 자신들의 노력의 결과를 보고 즐길 수 있다는 것이었습니다. 아시겠죠... 듀이는 실제 세상의 지식, 발달된 사회적 기술, 높은 지적 능력, 그리고 전문적인 능력을 가진 사람들을 만들어내려고 노력한 것입니다.

자, 여러분 생각에는 어떤 종류의 수업을 받고 싶나요? 역사책에 코를 파묻고 사실들을 배우는 게 나을까요, 아니면 맛있는 음식을 만들면서 그 과정에 응용할 수 있는 주제들을 배우는 게 나을까요? 좋아요, 만약 여러분이 저처럼 나이가 들었다면 책에 코를 박는 것을 선호할지도 모르죠! 하지만 사실 대부분의 사람들은 듀이의 방법을 선호할 겁니다. 사람들이 활동적인 학습을 선호하는 것은 자연스러운 일입니다. **15, 16** 예를 들어, 제 아들은 공립학교를 다니지만 그 아이가 배우는 방식은 듀이 방식의 교수법입니다. 집에서 아이는 항상 나무로 된 장난감 블록을 가지고 놉니다. 온갖 종류의 구조물을 짓고, 다시 무너뜨리고, 또다시 짓습니다. 이렇게 함으로써 아이는 직접적으로, 그리고 자연스러운 환경에서 기하학 지식을 발달시킵니다. 그리고 제 마음에 드는 점은 아이가 배우는 동안 즐거워한다는 것입니다.

이번 주 남은 시간 동안 학습자 중심의 교실 환경을 형성하는 듀이의 방법들에 대해서 좀 더 알아볼 텐데, 물론 이러한 교실은 조용한 곳이 아니겠죠.

17 Students should be interacting and working toward their goals cooperatively. In accordance with this, I won't be lecturing to you. I will be giving handouts with some of Dewey's key methods along with projects you will be using to develop classroom curricula. Just remember, doing equals learning.

12. What is the lecture mainly about?

Ⓐ Using cooking to learn about other things
Ⓑ John Dewey's personal life
Ⓒ Reforms in rote-learning techniques
Ⓓ A revolutionary development in education

13. What does the professor say about memorization?

Ⓐ It's a critical part of student-centered learning.
Ⓑ It's not a useful indicator of practical intelligence.
Ⓒ It can be used in any classroom situation.
Ⓓ It cannot be influenced by repetition.

14. How is the lecture organized?

Ⓐ The spokesperson gives a biographical account of a prominent figure in 20th-century education.
Ⓑ The professor shows students feedback received from a class that used a learner-centered style.
Ⓒ The teacher introduces an alternative form of education followed by its pros and cons.
Ⓓ The instructor discusses a traditional teaching method before presenting John Dewey's alternative.

15. According to the professor, what does her son do to learn about geometry?

Ⓐ He uses toys to construct different things.
Ⓑ He breaks his toys into pieces.
Ⓒ He attends a public school taught by Dewey.
Ⓓ He practices making buildings outside in nature.

16. What is the professor's attitude toward her son's playing with wooden blocks?

Ⓐ She is disappointed that he has to use toys to learn a subject taught in schools.
Ⓑ She likes the structures he creates with the wooden toy blocks.
Ⓒ She feels that his public school should use this type of learning in its classrooms.
Ⓓ She is happy he is enjoying himself while naturally learning about geometry.

17 학생들은 서로 영향을 주고받고 목표를 향해서 협력해 나가야 합니다. 이에 따라, 저는 강의를 하지 않겠습니다. 듀이의 주요 방법들에 대한 프린트물과 함께 수업 교과 과정을 발전시켜 나가기 위해 여러분이 활용하게 될 프로젝트를 나눠주겠습니다. 이것만 기억하세요. 행하는 것이 배우는 것입니다.

12. 강의는 주로 무엇에 관한 것인가?

Ⓐ 다른 것에 대해 배우기 위해서 요리를 이용하는 것
Ⓑ 존 듀이의 사생활
Ⓒ 기계적인 학습 기법의 개혁
Ⓓ 교육에 있어 혁신적인 발달

13. 교수는 암기에 대해서 무엇이라고 말하는가?

Ⓐ 학생 중심의 학습에 있어서 중요한 부분이다.
Ⓑ 실용적 지식의 유용한 지표가 아니다.
Ⓒ 어떤 교실 상황에서도 사용될 수 있다.
Ⓓ 반복에 의해서 영향을 받을 수 없다.

14. 강의는 어떻게 구성되어 있는가?

Ⓐ 교수는 20세기 교육의 주요 인물에 대해서 전기식으로 설명을 한다.
Ⓑ 교수는 학생들에게 학습자 중심의 방식을 사용한 수업에서 얻은 피드백을 보여준다.
Ⓒ 교수는 교수법의 대안을 설명하고, 이어서 그것에 대한 찬반 양론을 개진한다.
Ⓓ 교수는 존 듀이의 대안을 설명하기 전 전통적인 교수법에 관해서 논한다.

15. 교수에 의하면, 교수의 아들은 무엇을 하면서 기하학에 대해서 배우는가?

Ⓐ 장난감을 사용해서 다양한 것들을 만든다.
Ⓑ 장난감을 산산조각 낸다.
Ⓒ 듀이가 가르치는 공립학교에 다닌다.
Ⓓ 자연 속에서 건물 짓는 것을 연습한다.

16. 아들이 나무 블록을 가지고 노는 것에 대한 교수의 태도는 어떠한가?

Ⓐ 학교에서 가르친 것을 배우는 데 장난감을 사용해야 한다는 것에 실망하고 있다.
Ⓑ 아들이 장난감 나무 블록으로 만드는 구조물을 좋아한다.
Ⓒ 아들이 다니는 공립학교에서 수업 시간에 이런 종류의 학습법을 사용해야 한다고 생각한다.
Ⓓ 기하학을 자연스럽게 배우면서 그것을 즐기고 있다는 데 기뻐한다.

17. Listen again to part of the lecture. Then answer the question.

W Students should be interacting and working toward their goals cooperatively. In accordance with this, I won't be lecturing to you.

Why does the professor say this:

W In accordance with this, I won't be lecturing to you.

(A) Since the students are already cooperating with each other, the professor doesn't want to do any lecturing in the next class.

(B) Since she lectures during the class, the students will be listening to her rather than cooperatively working toward their goals together.

(C) Since each student is already in charge of achieving his or her goals, the professor feels it is unnecessary to do any lecturing.

(D) Since listening isn't necessary in a learner-centered class, the professor feels it doesn't need to be practiced in the next class.

17. 강의의 일부를 다시 듣고 질문에 답하시오.

여 학생들은 서로 영향을 주고받고 목표를 향해서 협력해 나가야 합니다. 이에 따라, 저는 강의를 하지 않겠습니다.

교수는 왜 이렇게 말하는가:

여 이에 따라, 저는 강의를 하지 않겠습니다.

(A) 학생들이 이미 서로 협력하고 있으므로 교수는 다음 수업 시간에 더 이상 강의하고 싶지 않다.

(B) 교수가 수업 시간에 강의를 하면 학생들은 목표를 향해서 함께 협력하기보다는 교수의 말을 들을 것이다.

(C) 학생들 각자가 이미 목표 달성의 책임을 지고 있어서 교수는 강의를 할 필요가 없다고 느낀다.

(D) 학습자 중심의 수업에서 듣기는 필요하지 않기 때문에 교수는 다음 수업시간에 듣기를 연습할 필요가 없다고 느낀다.

어휘 repeat v 반복하다 | rote learning 암기 학습, 기계적 학습 | survive v 살아남다, 생존하다 | tradition n 전통 | intellectual adj 지능적인 | association n 연관, 연상 | educated adj 교육을 받은 | concept n 개념 | practical adj 실질적인 | cooperate v 협력하다 | passive adj 수동적인 | progressive adj 진보적인, 혁신적인 | represent v 보이다 | reform n 개혁, 개선 | philosophy n 철학 | psychology n 심리학 | emphasis n 강조 | individual n 개인 | meaningful adj 의미 있는 | existence n 존재 | theory n 이론 | knowledge n 지식 | apply v 적용하다 | reality n 현실 | curricula n 교육 과정 | hands-on 직접 해보는, 실천하는 | appropriate adj 적절한 | starkly adv 완전히 | contrast v 대조를 이루다 | established adj 수립된, 정립된 | institution n 기관, 관습 | repetition n 반복 | advantage n 이점 | expertise n 전문성 | opposite adj 반대의 | typical adj 전형적인, 일반적인 | reasoning n 추론, 추리 | acquire v 습득하다 | experiential adj 경험상의 | recommend v 추천하다 | experiment n 실험 | supervise v 감독하다 | supplement v 보완하다, 보충하다 | relevant adj 관련이 있는 | highlight v 강조하다 | academic adj 학문의 | sewing n 바느질 | carpentry n 목공일 | diverse adj 다양한 | subtract v 빼다 | measure v 측정하다 | quantity n 수량 | outcome n 결과 | develop v 발달시키다 | advanced adj 진보한, 발달한 | professional adj 직업적인, 전문적인 | prefer v 선호하다 | bury v 묻다 | attend v 다니다, 참석하다 | geometry n 기하학 | interact v 상호 작용하다 | in accordance with ~에 따라서 | lecture v 강의하다 | handout n 프린트물 | method n 방법 | equal v ~와 같다

Actual Test 2

본서 | P. 286

Conversation 1	1. D	2. B	3. C	4. D	5. C	
Lecture 1	6. B	7. B	8. A, C	9. A	10. D	11. A
Conversation 2	1. C	2. B	3. A, C	4. D	5. D	
Lecture 2	6. C	7. A	8. A	9. C	10. C	11. D
Lecture 3	12. C	13. B	14. B	15. C	16. A	17. C

Conversation 1

본서 P. 288

Man: Student | Woman: Resident assistant

[1-5] Listen to part of a conversation between a student and a resident assistant.

M Excuse me. Are you the head resident assistant?

W Yes, I'm Jane Kirkpatric, the head R.A. How can I be of assistance?

M Well, Ms. Kirkpatric. **1** I'm having a serious problem with my roommate. You see, I'm a morning person, that is, I wake up early and do my work and run errands first thing in the morning.

W **1** I see. Does this somehow conflict with your roommate's schedule?

M **1** You better believe it! He always stays up late, plays his music so loud we have had complaints from other students, and he even brings his friends over in the middle of the night.

W What do you have in mind? I've been working here a long time, and I've seen these situations many times before.

M Well, I think the logical solution is for one of us to move out or to exchange with another roommate, don't you think?

W **2** Well, when students go away to college, they need to learn to fend for themselves without their parents' involvement. Unfortunately, part of that experience is learning to resolve differences by yourself without having to appeal to an authority.

M You don't think I've tried? Just to give you an example of what I'm talking about. He agreed to meet me here 15 minutes ago, but he didn't bother to show up! How do you suggest I deal with that amount of irresponsibility?

W OK, I think I understand why you're upset. I'll tell you what I can do. There are a couple of options. The first is to submit your request to the Dean of Students, but to be honest, he tends to ignore these manners unless a serious violation has occurred.

M Doesn't sound very promising. You said there was a second choice?

W **3** Well, the other option is a better solution, but generally really hard to bring about. If you could find someone who is willing to switch rooms with you or your roommate, then you can move.

M Why didn't you say so before? I took the liberty of lining up someone, and I have a friend of mine who is ready to move in!

W **3, 4** Hold on just a minute. We need to get three signatures plus your own to facilitate the move. You need signatures from your current roommate, the new roommate, and the new roommate's current roommate. Do you get that?

남자: 학생 | 여자: 기숙사 조교

학생과 기숙사 조교의 대화를 들으시오.

남 실례합니다. 혹시 기숙사 수석 조교이신가요?

여 네, 기숙사 수석 조교 제인 커크패트릭입니다. 어떻게 도와드릴까요?

남 그게, 커크패트릭씨. **1** 제가 룸메이트와 심각한 문제가 있어서요. 저는 아침형 인간이라 일찍 일어나서 숙제를 하고 볼일을 아침에 먼저 처리하거든요.

여 **1** 그렇군요. 그게 룸메이트의 스케줄과 잘 맞지 않나요?

남 **1** 말도 마세요! 그 애는 항상 늦게까지 자지도 않고 음악을 너무 크게 틀어서 다른 학생들에게 불만을 사고 있어요. 그리고 심지어 한밤중에 친구들을 기숙사로 데려와요.

여 어떻게 할 생각인가요? 나는 여기서 오랫동안 일하면서 이런 경우를 전에 많이 봐왔어요.

남 제 생각으로는 우리 중 하나가 나가거나 룸메이트를 바꾸는 것이 이치에 맞는 해결책일 것 같아요, 안 그래요?

여 **2** 글쎄요, 학생들이 대학에 갈 때는 부모님의 관여 없이 자립하는 법을 배울 필요가 있어요. 안됐지만, 학교 당국에 호소하지 않고 학생 스스로 의견차를 해결하는 법을 배우는 것도 그런 경험의 일부예요.

남 제가 노력을 안 했다고 생각하세요? 제 말을 이해하실 수 있도록 한 가지 예를 들어드릴게요. 그 애는 여기서 저랑 15분 전에 만나기로 했어요. 하지만 나타나지도 않고 있잖아요! 그 정도로 무책임한 애를 제가 어떻게 더 상대해야 할까요?

여 알았어요. 왜 학생이 화가 났는지 알 것 같네요. 제가 해 드릴 수 있는 일들을 말해 볼게요. 두 가지 선택지가 있어요. 첫 번째는 학장님께 요청서를 제출하는 방법인데, 하지만 솔직히 말해 그분은 심각한 위반 행위가 아니면 이런 문제들은 무시하시는 경향이 있어요.

남 그리 잘될 것 같지 않네요. 두 번째 대안도 있다고 하셨죠?

여 **3** 음, 다른 대안은 더 좋은 해결책이긴 한데 대개 실행하기가 정말 어려워요. 학생이 만약 학생 본인이나 학생의 룸메이트와 방을 기꺼이 바꿔줄 사람을 찾는다면 그때는 방을 옮길 수 있어요.

남 왜 이제서야 그 말씀을 하세요? 제가 임의로 사람들을 좀 알아봤는데 바로 이사 올 수 있는 친구가 있어요!

여 **3, 4** 잠시만 기다려봐요. 방 이동을 가능하게 하기 위해서는 학생의 서명 외에도 세 사람의 서명이 더 필요해요. 현재 룸메이트, 새 룸메이트, 그리고 새 룸메이트의 현재 룸메이트의 서명이요. 알아들으셨나요?

M 4 I sure do. It shouldn't be a problem. All of the parties involved know each other, and in fact, we have discussed this type of scenario in the past.

W You'd better make sure you get it in writing. Just focus on getting those signatures. People have a way of making agreements without following through sometimes.

M 5 Boy, you can say that again! I'll get to work on that right away on getting the paperwork started. Is that all there is to it?

W That's the first step. After that, you need to bring the signed form back here, and I'll approve it. After that, you need to settle on a convenient time for everybody to move, which sounds like it might be a problem considering the different schedule you and your roommate are on?

M Believe me, when I get all of those signatures, I will stay up late, pack, and then move!

W Well, this looks like it will work out for everyone's best benefit. I'm glad we are able to accommodate you.

M You're glad!

남 4 그럼요. 그건 문제도 안 되죠. 관련된 모든 애들이 서로 알고 있고 또 사실상 과거에 이런 종류의 이야기를 논의한 적이 있어요.

여 학생은 서명을 서면으로 받아야 해요. 서명들을 받는 것에만 초점을 맞추세요. 사람들은 종종 동의는 해놓고 실제로 이에 따르지 않는 경향이 있어요.

남 5 정말 그래요! 지금 당장 서류작업을 시작할게요. 그게 다인가요?

여 그건 첫 번째 단계예요. 그 후에 서명한 서류를 여기로 다시 가져오면 제가 승인을 할게요. 그러고 나서, 이사하기에 모두가 편한 때를 정하면 되는데, 학생과 학생 룸메이트의 스케줄이 그렇게 다르니 문제가 되지 않겠어요?

남 염려 마세요. 서명을 다 받으면 밤늦게까지 짐을 싸서 이사할 거예요.

여 이게 모두를 위해 가장 좋은 방법인 듯 하네요. 학생을 도울 수 있어 다행이에요.

남 그렇군요!

1. What is the conversation mainly about?

(A) The speakers are discussing a problem with the dormitory lease.
(B) The speakers are debating the benefits of living in the dorm.
(C) The speakers are wondering where a late student is.
(D) The speakers are trying to resolve a roommate issue.

2. What is implied about the school's policy toward student problems in the dorms?

(A) The school has very strict regulations regarding students' behavior.
(B) The school would prefer that students solve problems on their own.
(C) The school never permits students to change rooms in mid-semester.
(D) The school allows students to change rooms at any point in the year.

3. What does the housing officer tell the student to do?

(A) She insists that the student solve the problem on his own with the roommate.
(B) She directs the student to take up the problem with the Dean of Students.
(C) She suggests that the student gather the signatures needed to change rooms.
(D) She advises the student to coordinate schedules with the roommate.

1. 대화는 주로 무엇에 관한 것인가?

(A) 화자들은 기숙사 임대 문제에 대해 논의하고 있다.
(B) 화자들은 기숙사에 사는 이점에 대해 논쟁하고 있다.
(C) 화자들은 늦은 학생이 어디 있는지 의아해하고 있다.
(D) 화자들은 룸메이트 문제를 해결하고자 애쓰고 있다.

2. 기숙사에서 학생이 겪는 문제들에 대한 학교의 정책에 관해 무엇이 암시되었는가?

(A) 학교는 학생의 행동에 관해 매우 엄격한 규정을 가지고 있다.
(B) 학교는 학생 스스로 문제를 해결하는 것을 선호한다.
(C) 학교는 학생이 학기 중에 방을 바꾸는 것을 절대로 허용하지 않는다.
(D) 학교는 학생들이 연중 어느 때라도 방을 바꾸는 것을 허용하고 있다.

3. 기숙사 직원은 학생에게 무엇을 하라고 말하는가?

(A) 혼자 힘으로 룸메이트와 문제를 해결하라고 주장한다.
(B) 학장에게 문제를 제기하라고 지도한다.
(C) 방을 바꾸는 데 필요한 서명을 모으라고 제안한다.
(D) 룸메이트와 스케줄을 조정해보라고 충고한다.

4. **What does the student say about the R.A.'s second suggestion?**
   Ⓐ He is concerned about his new roommate's current roommate.
   Ⓑ He believes it will be effective since he already got their signatures.
   Ⓒ He is worried since he needs to persuade a few people.
   Ⓓ He thinks it can work out very well since he already knows what to do.

5. **Listen again to part of the conversation. Then answer the question.**

   > M Boy, you can say that again! I'll get to work on that right away on getting the paperwork started. Is that all there is to it?

   What does the student mean when he says this:

   > M Boy, you can say that again!

   Ⓐ The student would like the R.A. to repeat the instructions.
   Ⓑ The student is upset he has to do the appropriate paperwork.
   Ⓒ The student understands the signatures are most important.
   Ⓓ The student doubts that he will be able to get all the signatures.

4. **학생은 기숙사 조교의 두 번째 제안에 관해 무엇이라고 말하는가?**
   Ⓐ 새 룸메이트의 현재 룸메이트에 관해 걱정한다.
   Ⓑ 이미 서명들을 받았기 때문에 효과적일 것이라고 믿는다.
   Ⓒ 몇 사람을 설득해야 해서 걱정하고 있다.
   Ⓓ 이미 어떻게 해야 할지 알고 있으므로 잘 될 거라고 생각한다.

5. **대화의 일부를 다시 듣고 질문에 답하시오.**

   > 남 정말 그래요! 지금 당장 서류작업을 시작할게요. 그게 다인가요?

   학생은 다음과 같이 말하며 무엇을 의미하는가:

   > 남 정말 그래요!

   Ⓐ 조교가 설명을 반복해줄 것을 원한다.
   Ⓑ 적절한 서류 업무를 해야 한다는 것에 화가 나 있다.
   Ⓒ 서명이 가장 중요하다는 것을 이해한다.
   Ⓓ 모든 서명을 받을 수 있을지 의구심이 든다.

어휘 resident assistant 기숙사 조교 | assistance n 도움 | serious adj 심각한 | errand n 할 일, 심부름 | conflict v 상충(상반) 되다, 갈등을 초래하다 | complaint n 불만 | situation n 상황 | logical adj 논리적인 | solution n 해결책 | exchange v 바꾸다 | fend for 자립하다, 혼자 힘으로 하다 | involvement n 관여, 개입 | unfortunately adv 안타깝게도 | experience n 경험 | resolve v 해결하다 | appeal v 호소하다, 간청하다 | authority n 권위, 권위자, 당국 | irresponsibility n 무책임함 | submit v 제출하다 | request n 요청 | ignore v 무시하다 | violation n 위반 | occur v 발생하다 | generally adv 일반적으로 | switch v 바꾸다 | liberty n 자유 | signature n 서명 | facilitate v 가능하게 하다 | party n 당사자 | agreement n 동의 | approve v 승인하다 | convenient adj 편리한 | accommodate v 수용하다

Lecture 1

본서 | P. 290

Man: Student | Woman: Professor

[6-11] Listen to part of a discussion in a history class.

W Yesterday, we were discussing the many Neolithic circles that have been found throughout Europe. Like Stonehenge, it is thought that many of these acted as celestial calendars that allowed people to calculate the seasons. 6 One such circle was found in Germany, and it is called the Goseck circle. It was not made with large stones like many other circles, so it lay undiscovered for a long time. Even more

남자: 학생 | 여자: 교수

역사 수업 중 토론의 일부를 들으시오.

여 어제 우리는 유럽 전역에서 발견된 많은 신석기 시대 원형 유적들에 대해 이야기했습니다. 스톤헨지처럼 이들 중 많은 수가 사람들로 하여금 계절을 계산하도록 도와주는 천체 달력의 역할을 한 것으로 보입니다. 6 이러한 원형 유적들 중 하나는 독일에서 발견되었는데, 고섹 원형 유적이라고 불리죠. 다른 많은 원형 유적들처럼 거대한 돌들로 만들어지지 않

recently, something truly remarkable was discovered not far from that site: a portable celestial calendar called the Nebra sky disk. Made of bronze inlaid with gold, the disk is about 30 centimeters across and weighs a little over two kilograms. The bronze disk has a bluish-green patina, and the gold inlay depicts the sun and or moon, and a field of stars. There are also three arcs of gold that were added later. **7** Its actual age has not been ascertained yet.

M Excuse me professor, where exactly was it found?

W In Saxony-Anhalt, Germany, about 60 kilometers west of the city of Leipzig. It was found in a prehistoric structure at the summit of a 252 meter hill in the Ziegelroda Forest. The hill is referred to as the Mittelberg, which means "central hill", and the area shows signs of human habitation dating back to the Neolithic period, including around 1,000 burial sites of the barrow type. **8(A)** From the small structure, one can view the sun set behind the tallest peak of the Harz Mountains, the Brocken, on the solstices. Since the site has such a clear astrological association, and the disk depicts celestial objects, it was quickly proposed that it was some form of calendar.

9 The disk was discovered in 1999 by treasure hunters and not archaeologists, so its authenticity was extremely questionable, and some people still think it is a forgery. The authorities heard about its existence and managed to arrange a trap to acquire it from its then owner in 2002. They eventually followed the trail back to the men who discovered it and other artifacts, who arranged to receive reduced sentences by leading the authorities to the site. They found traces that proved the items had indeed been buried there, but that did not prove their authenticity. However, microphotography has revealed marks from corrosion that could not be forged.

M What other artifacts did they find?

W **10** There were two swords, two axe heads, a chisel, and some bracelets; all bronze. These were quite important, because they allowed the scientists to determine approximately when the disk had been buried. The style of the weapons is consistent with the second millennium BCE, and they found a piece of birch bark in the site that they carbon dated to about 1600 BCE. But, that only tells us when it was buried, not when the disk was made.

았기 때문에 오랜 시간 동안 발견되지 않은 채로 남아 있었습니다. 그 지역으로부터 멀지 않은 곳에서 더 최근에 정말로 놀라운 것이 발견되었어요. 네브라 하늘 원반이라고 불리는 이동식 천체 달력이 바로 그것이죠. 청동으로 만들어져 금으로 무늬가 새겨져 있는 이 원반은 지름이 30센티미터 정도이며 무게는 2킬로그램이 약간 넘습니다. 이 청동 원반은 청록빛의 동록을 가지고 있으며 금으로 새겨진 상감은 해 혹은 달, 그리고 별무리를 묘사합니다. 나중에 추가된 세 개의 금으로 된 호도 있어요. **7** 이 원반의 실제 연도는 아직 확인되지 않았습니다.

남 실례합니다, 교수님. 이 원반은 정확히 어디에서 발견되었나요?

여 라이프치히시에서 서쪽으로 60킬로미터 떨어진 독일의 작센안할트주에서 발견되었어요. 지겔로다숲에 있는 252미터 높이의 언덕 정상에 있던 선사 시대 구조물 안에서 발견했죠. 이 언덕은 미텔베르크라고 불리는데, '중앙 언덕'이라는 뜻이며, 이 지역은 약 1,000여개의 고분 유형 매장터를 포함해 신석기 시대까지 거슬러 올라가는 인간의 거주 흔적들을 보여주고 있습니다. **8(A)** 이 작은 구조에서 하지점과 동지점에 하르츠산의 가장 높은 봉우리인 브로켄 뒤로 해가 지는 것을 볼 수 있죠. 이 부지가 명확한 점성술적 연관성을 보여주고, 원반이 천체를 묘사하고 있어서 이 원반이 달력의 한 유형이라는 가정이 금세 생겨났습니다.

9 이 원반은 고고학자들이 아닌 보물을 찾는 사람들에 의해 1999년에 발견되어서 진품인지가 극히 의심스러웠으며 어떤 이들은 여전히 이 원반이 위조품이라고 믿고 있어요. 당국에서는 이 원반의 존재에 대해 듣고 2002년에 당시 주인으로부터 이 원반을 되찾기 위한 덫을 설치하게 되었습니다. 결국 이 원반과 다른 유물들을 발견한 한 남자를 추적할 수 있었고, 이것들을 발견한 곳으로 당국을 데려간다면 감형을 해주기로 했죠. 실제로 이 물건들이 그곳에 묻혀 있었다는 것을 증명하는 흔적은 찾았지만, 그것이 이 유물들이 진품인지는 증명해주지 않았죠. 그러나 현미경 사진은 위조될 수 없는 부식 흔적을 찾아냈습니다.

남 그늘이 발견한 다른 유물들은 무엇이었나요?

여 **10** 두 개의 검, 두 개의 도끼 머리, 끌과 몇 개의 팔찌들이 있었어요. 모두 청동으로 만든 것들이었죠. 이것들은 꽤 중요한데, 그 이유는 이 유물들이 과학자들로 하여금 네브라 하늘 원반이 대략 언제쯤 묻혔는지 밝히도록 해주었기 때문입니다. 무기 양식은 기원전 2천 년경으로 일정하며, 그 현장에서 자작나무 껍질 조각 하나를 발견해 탄소 연대 측정을 했는데 기원전 1600년경의 것으로 밝혀졌습니다. 그러나 이는 원반이 언제 묻혔는지를 말해줄 뿐, 언제 만들어졌는지는 알려주지 않죠.

It was clearly added to over time, and it was a very important object, so it was probably used for many generations before it was laid in the ground.

8(C) On the disk, there is a cluster of dots that resembles the constellation of Pleiades, and other dots have been correlated to other constellations, stars, and planets. Using the gold arcs on opposite sides, the disc could be used to measure where the sun sets on the winter and summer solstices. This means it could be used as a solar calendar that they could correlate to the lunar cycle to predict when to plant and harvest crops. **11** If it is authentic, it would be the oldest discovered portable object used for this purpose. Its composition is also significant, as the copper came from Austria, and the tin and some of the gold came from Cornwall, England, which means that its makers traded extensively.

시간이 지난 뒤 매장된 것이 분명하며, 매우 중요한 물건이었기 때문에 아마 땅에 묻히기 전 수 세대에 걸쳐 사용되었을 겁니다.

8(C) 원반에는 플레이아데스 성단의 성좌를 연상하게 하는 점의 무리들이 있으며 다른 점들은 다른 성좌, 별, 그리고 행성들과 연관되어 있습니다. 서로 맞은편에 있는 금으로 새겨진 호를 이용해서 이 원반은 동지점과 하지점에 태양이 어디에서 질지 측정하는 데 사용되었을 수 있습니다. 이 말은 언제 작물을 경작하고 추수할지를 예측하기 위한 태음 주기와 연관 짓기 위해 이 원반이 양력 달력으로 사용되었을 가능성이 있다는 의미입니다. **11** 만약 이 원반이 진품이라면 이 용도를 위해 만들어진, 발견된 것들 중 가장 오래된 이동식 물체가 될 겁니다. 원반의 구성 요소 역시 중요한데, 구리가 오스트리아에서 왔으며 주석과 금 약간이 영국의 콘월에서 왔다는 점을 봤을 때 이들의 제작자들이 광범위하게 교역했다는 것을 보여주기 때문이죠.

6. What is the discussion mainly about?

Ⓐ The time-consuming process of excavating the Nebra sky disk
Ⓑ The interesting discovery that was made in Germany
Ⓒ The lives of people who lived during the Neolithic period
Ⓓ The astrological observances made with an ancient calendar

7. What is true about the Nebra sky disk?

Ⓐ It was invented for ritual purposes.
Ⓑ Its age has yet to be discovered.
Ⓒ It was made of gold, bronze, and silver.
Ⓓ Its diameter is about one meter.

8. Why did scientists assume that the Nebra sky disk was some form of calendar? Choose 2 answers.

Ⓐ The area that it was found is deeply related with astrology.
Ⓑ The numbers carved on the disk showed similarities with today's calendar.
Ⓒ There are some celestial bodies portrayed on the surface of the disk.
Ⓓ People during the Neolithic period had already been using calendars.

6. 토론은 주로 무엇에 대한 것인가?

Ⓐ 오랜 시간이 걸린 네브라 하늘 원반 발굴 과정
Ⓑ 독일에서 있었던 흥미로운 발견
Ⓒ 신석기 시대에 살았었던 사람들의 삶
Ⓓ 고대 달력으로 행해진 점성술 관찰

7. 네브라 하늘 원반에 관해 옳은 것은 무엇인가?

Ⓐ 의식을 치를 목적으로 발명되었다.
Ⓑ 그 연대가 아직 밝혀지지 않았다.
Ⓒ 금, 청동, 그리고 은으로 만들어졌다.
Ⓓ 지름이 약 1미터이다.

8. 과학자들은 왜 네브라 하늘 원반이 일종의 달력이라고 가정하였는가? 두 개를 고르시오.

Ⓐ 그것이 발견된 지역이 천문학과 깊은 관련이 있었다.
Ⓑ 원반에 새겨진 숫자들이 오늘날의 달력과 유사점들을 보여주었다.
Ⓒ 원반 표면에 몇몇 천체들이 묘사되어 있다.
Ⓓ 신석기 시대 사람들은 이미 달력을 사용하고 있었다.

9. What can be inferred about the Nebra sky disk and other artifacts?

Ⓐ Their original burial site cannot solely prove their authenticity.

Ⓑ There are various ways to prove that they were forged.

Ⓒ They were almost sold to another country by the hunters.

Ⓓ Their existence proved the widespread use of iron in the region.

10. Why does the professor mention a piece of birch bark?

Ⓐ To show the interesting use of trees during the Neolithic period

Ⓑ To emphasize the importance of small objects for a burial ritual

Ⓒ To introduce another important discovery from the Bronze Age

Ⓓ To explain how scientists discovered the burial date of the artifacts

11. Why does the professor say this:

> W If it is authentic, it would be the oldest discovered portable object used for this purpose. Its composition is also significant, as the copper came from Austria, and the tin and some of the gold came from Cornwall, England, which means that its makers traded extensively.

Ⓐ He is telling the students that many things still need to be revealed.

Ⓑ He sees the difficulty of determining whether the disk is authentic or not.

Ⓒ He finds it interesting to see the earliest trade route of mankind.

Ⓓ He is excited that the authenticity of the disk was finally made certain.

9. 네브라 하늘 원반과 다른 유물들에 관해 무엇을 추론할 수 있는가?

Ⓐ 이들이 원래 묻혀 있던 장소 자체가 이들이 진품이라는 것을 증명하지는 못한다.

Ⓑ 이들이 위조되었다는 것을 증명할 방법들이 많이 있다.

Ⓒ 사냥꾼들에 의해 다른 나라로 거의 팔릴 뻔했다.

Ⓓ 이들의 존재는 그 지역에서의 광범위한 철 사용을 증명했다.

10. 교수는 왜 자작나무 껍질 한 조각을 언급하는가?

Ⓐ 신석기 시기의 흥미로운 나무 사용을 보여주려고

Ⓑ 매장 의식에서 작은 물건들의 중요성을 강조하려고

Ⓒ 청동기 시대에 있었던 또 다른 중요한 발견을 소개하려고

Ⓓ 과학자들이 어떻게 유물들의 매장 시기를 밝혀냈는지 설명하려고

11. 교수는 왜 이렇게 말하는가:

> 여 만약 이 원반이 진품이라면 이 용도를 위해 만들어진, 발견된 것들 중 가장 오래된 이동식 물체가 될 겁니다. 원반의 구성 요소 역시 중요한데, 구리가 오스트리아에서 왔으며 주석과 금 약간이 영국의 콘월에서 왔다는 점을 봤을 때 이들의 제작자들이 광범위하게 교역했다는 것을 보여주기 때문이죠.

Ⓐ 밝혀져야 할 것들이 여전히 많이 있다고 학생들에게 말하고 있다.

Ⓑ 원반이 진품인지 아닌지를 결정하는 것의 어려움을 안다.

Ⓒ 인류 최초의 무역로를 보게 되어 흥미를 느낀다.

Ⓓ 원반이 진품이라는 것이 마침내 확인되어서 흥분했다.

어휘 Neolithic adj 신석기 시대의 | circle n 둥글게 (원을 그리며) 모여 있는 것들 | celestial adj 하늘의, 선체의 | calculate v 계산하다 | remarkable adj 놀라운 | portable adj 이동이 쉬운, 휴대 가능한 | disk n 동그랗고 납작한 판 | inlaid adj 세공을 한, 무늬를 새긴 | weigh v 무게가 ~이다 | patina n (금속의 표면에 생기는) 녹청 | inlay n 상감, 상감 세공 재료 | depict v 묘사하다 | arc n 호, 활 모양 | ascertain v 알아내다, 확인하다 | prehistoric adj 선사 시대의 | summit n 정상, 절정 | habitation n 거주, 주거 | date back to ~까지 거슬러 올라가다 | barrow n 무덤, 고분 | peak n 정상 | solstice n 지점(하지점과 동지점) | astrological adj 점성술의 | association n 연관성, 관련, 연계 | treasure hunter 보물 찾는 사람 | archaeologist n 고고학자 | authenticity n 진품, 진짜임 | questionable adj 의심스러운, 미심쩍은 | forgery n 위조된 물건 | authority n 당국 | existence n 존재 | trap n 덫, 함정 | artifact n 공예품, 인공 유물 | reduce v 감소시키다 | sentence n 형벌, 형, 선고 | microphotography n 현미경 사진 | corrosion n 부식 | axe n 도끼 | chisel n 끌 | bracelet n 팔찌 | bronze n 청동 | approximately adv 거의, 근사치의 | consistent adj 한결같은, 일관된 | millennium n 천 년 | birch bark 자작나무 껍질 | carbon date 탄소 연대를 측정하다 | generation n 세대 | cluster n 무리 | dot n 점 | constellation n 별자리, 성좌 | correlate v 연관성이 있다 | measure v 측정하다 | lunar cycle 태음 주기 | predict v 예측하다 | plant v 경작하다 | harvest v 추수하다 | composition n 구성 | tin n 주석 | trade v 교역하다, 무역하다 | extensively adv 광범위하게

Conversation 2

본서 | P. 294

Man: Registrar | Woman: Student

[1-5] Listen to part of a conversation between a student and a registrar.

M Next in line, please. Yes, how may I help you?

W 1 I need to register for a class, and I normally use the registrar's website, but I kept getting locked out of the system when I tried to book a class this morning.

M All right. Sounds like a problem we can fix. Which course were you trying to enroll in?

W 1 I was trying to get into Political Science 255. Study of North American Politics. I wanted Tuesday-Thursday afternoon class, but the system wouldn't let me get into the section I wanted.

M Ah, I can see why. All of the sections of that particular class have been filled up.

W Oh no! But that class is a prerequisite for all 300-level classes. I have to take it in order to graduate on time!

M 2 If it was so important to you, why did you wait to the last minute to register? You were allowed to register as far back as June! You're not a freshman; you should know that there are only a certain number of spaces available for each class.

W I don't understand that if these courses always fill up, why don't they open more sections?

M I couldn't really tell you that. It could have something to do with the availability of the professors. They can work only a limited number of hours per week.

W What am I going to do? If I can't take the class this semester, that will throw my timetable off for the rest of my college career!

M 3(A) Have you thought about taking summer classes? Many students make up classes that they can't take during the regular year in the summer. Plus, the class sizes are smaller and professors are usually more laid back.

W Yeah. I know that, but I normally need to work full time during the break to make tuition for the rest of the year. Are there any other options?

M Well, the best I can do is to put you on the waiting list. That means we put you on an overflow list and you wait to see if anybody drops the class you want.

W Hmm... That doesn't give me much of a chance. What are the chances that somebody or a bunch of people are going to drop?

M Well, that all depends. A lot of times people drop classes at the beginning of the semester, then we take replacements on a first come, first served basis.

W OK. Is there any way you can check and see what my position on the list is?

남자: 학적부 직원 | 여자: 학생

학생과 학적부 직원의 대화를 들으시오.

남 다음 분 오세요. 네, 무엇을 도와드릴까요?

여 1 수업에 등록하려고 하는데요. 평소에는 온라인 상으로 등록을 했는데, 오늘 아침에 등록하려고 하니까 등록 시스템에 접속이 되지 않았어요.

남 알겠어요. 우리가 해결할 수 있는 문제인 것 같군요. 어떤 수업에 등록을 하려고 했죠?

여 1 북미 정치학 수업인 정치학 255에 등록하려고 했어요. 화요일과 목요일 오후 수업을 원했는데, 시스템상으로 제가 원하는 시간대에 접근할 수 없었어요.

남 아, 왜 그런지 알겠어요. 그 수업의 모든 시간대가 이미 마감되었네요.

여 아, 이런! 그 수업은 300단계 수업을 듣기 위한 선수 과목이에요. 제때 졸업을 하려면 그 수업을 들어야만 해요!

남 2 만일 그렇게 중요한 수업이었다면, 왜 등록을 마지막 순간까지 기다렸나요? 6월부터 등록할 수 있었는데 말이죠! 신입생도 아니니 각 수업마다 등록할 수 있는 수가 정해져 있다는 것을 알았을 텐데요.

여 이해가 안 돼요. 만일 이 수업이 항상 마감된다면 좀 더 많은 시간대의 수업을 열어야 하는 것 아닌가요?

남 그렇게 말하기엔 곤란한 부분이 있어요. 그건 교수님들이 시간이 되는지 여부와 관련이 있거든요. 그분들은 매주 정해진 만큼의 시간만 일할 수 있어요.

여 그럼 전 어떻게 해야 하나요? 이번 학기에 그 수업을 들을 수 없다면, 앞으로 남은 제 학사 일정이 모두 엉망이 될 거예요!

남 3(A) 여름 계절 학기 수업을 들을 생각은 해봤어요? 많은 학생들이 정규 학기 동안 들을 수 없던 수업을 여름에 보충하거든요. 그리고 수업 정원이 더 적고 교수님들도 대개 더 여유가 있으세요.

여 네. 그건 알지만, 전 방학 동안 보통 남은 학기의 수업료를 벌기 위해 하루 종일 일해야 하거든요. 다른 방법은 없나요?

남 글쎄, 제가 할 수 있는 최선의 방법은 학생을 대기자 명단에 넣는 거예요. 다시 말해 초과 인원 명단에 이름을 넣고 다른 누군가가 학생이 원하는 수업을 취소하기를 기다리는 거죠.

여 흠... 가능성이 별로 없겠군요. 한 명이나 아니면 여러 명이 한꺼번에 수업을 취소할 가능성은 얼마나 되죠?

남 글쎄요. 상황에 따라 달라요. 많은 경우 학생들이 학기 초에 수업을 취소하는데, 그럼 저희가 선착순으로 대체 인원을 뽑아요.

여 알겠어요. 제가 명단 상에서 몇 번째에 있는지 확인해주실 수 있는 방법이 있나요?

M Sure. What was the name of that class again? Political Science 255? And, which section were you looking for?

W That's right, Polly-Sci, section C. That's a Tuesday-Thursday afternoon class, but I could be flexible with other sections if that would help the possibility of me getting into that class.

M 4 Hmmm. I'm sorry to say that it doesn't look very good. The section you're looking for actually has the fewest students on the waiting list with 27. All the other sections have far more.

W 4 That doesn't sound like much of a chance. Probably the only way to get in is right near the final withdrawal deadline. And by that time, I'll have missed most of the course!

M 3(C) Oh, have you considered auditing the class? What you can do is go to class, listen to the lectures, and that way you'll be familiar with all the class work. Then, when a regular spot opens up in the class, you can just slide in and you won't have missed anything!

W Hey! That sounds pretty good! Do I need to get special permission or something to audit a class?

M Hang on just a second! Before you get too excited, you have to consider how you're going to attend the political seminars at City Hall during the course. Usually, those meetings have limited spaces, and they are reserved for regular students only. I'll tell you what. 5 Why don't you talk this through with Professor Peterson. She's usually very helpful to students. She may have the ability to get you a spot in the seminars if you promise to always attend.

W 5 Hmm... Sounds a little complicated, with a lot of variables. But, if that's the best we can do, I'll talk with Professor Peterson. Thanks for helping me out.

남 물론이죠. 수업의 이름이 뭐라고 했죠? 정치학 255? 그리고, 어떤 시간대의 수업을 듣고 싶다고 했죠?

여 맞아요, 정치학, C섹션 수업이에요. 화요일–목요일 오후 수업이요. 그런데 만일 제가 수업에 등록할 수 있는 가능성이 높아진다면 다른 시간대도 괜찮아요.

남 4 흠, 유감이지만 상황이 좋아 보이지는 않네요. 사실 학생이 원하는 시간대의 수업에 대기자 수가 가장 적지만, 그래도 27명이에요. 다른 시간대에는 훨씬 더 많은 대기자가 있고요.

여 4 가능성이 많지 않아 보이네요. 아마 등록할 수 있는 유일한 방법은 취소 마감일이 다 되어야 나오겠네요. 그때쯤이면 전 그 수업의 대부분을 듣지 못했을 테고요!

남 3(C) 아, 수업을 청강하는 것은 생각해봤나요? 수업에 가서 강의를 들으면 돼요. 그런 방식으로 모든 수업 내용에 익숙해질 수 있어요. 그러고 나서, 정규 수업 인원에 여유가 생기면, 정식으로 수업에 들어갈 수 있고 수업 내용을 하나도 놓치지 않을 수 있죠!

여 와! 좋은 생각이에요! 수업을 청강하려면 특별히 받아야 하는 허가나 다른 어떤 것이 있나요?

남 잠깐만 기다려봐요! 너무 기뻐하기 전에, 이 수업 동안 시청에서 열리는 정치학 세미나에 참여할 수 있는 방법을 생각해봐야 해요. 대개 그 모임은 자리가 한정되어 있는데, 정규 학생들 전용이거든요. 이렇게 해보세요. 5 피터슨 교수님께 이 문제에 관해 이야기해 보세요. 그 교수님은 학생들에게 도움을 많이 주시거든요. 만일 학생이 빠지지 않고 출석한다고 약속한다면 교수님께서 세미나에 자리를 마련해주실 수 있을 거예요.

여 5 음... 변수가 많고 약간 복잡해 보이네요. 하지만 그 방법이 할 수 있는 최선이라면 피터슨 교수님께 말씀 드릴게요. 도와주셔서 감사합니다.

1. Why does the student go to the registrar's office?

(A) She wants to check an error on her tuition bill.
(B) She needs to pay a political seminar fee.
(C) She wants to sign up for a required class.
(D) She has signed up for the wrong class.

2. What is the man's attitude toward the student at the beginning of the conversation?

(A) He is annoyed by the fact that the student could not register the class herself.
(B) He is puzzled why the student took so long to register for the class.

1. 왜 학생은 학적부 사무실을 찾아가는가?

(A) 수업료 고지서의 오류에 관해 확인하길 원한다.
(B) 정치학 세미나 수업료를 지불해야 한다.
(C) 필수 과목 수업에 등록하려고 한다.
(D) 잘못된 수업에 등록했다.

2. 대화 초반에 학생에 대한 남자의 태도는 어떠한가?

(A) 학생이 스스로 수업을 등록하지 못한다는 사실에 짜증이 나 있다.
(B) 학생이 왜 수업을 등록하기까지 이렇게 오래 걸렸는지 의아해 한다.

Ⓒ He is irritated that the student is taking so long to complete the registration.
Ⓓ He is not sure if the class is really important for the student.

Ⓒ 학생이 등록을 마치는 데 너무 오래 걸려 짜증이 나 있다.
Ⓓ 이 수업이 학생에게 정말로 중요한지 확신하지 못한다.

3. What suggestions does the registrar give to the student?
Choose 2 answers.
Ⓐ He suggests that the student make up the course in the summer.
Ⓑ He suggests that the student get an override from the professor.
Ⓒ He suggests that the student try to audit the class and wait.
Ⓓ He suggests that the student take the class at a different university.

3. 학적부 직원은 학생에게 어떤 제안을 하는가?
두 개를 고르시오.
Ⓐ 학생에게 여름 학기 동안 수업을 보충하라고 제안한다.
Ⓑ 학생에게 교수님으로부터 정원 외 등록을 허락 받으라고 제안한다.
Ⓒ 학생에게 수업을 청강하며 기다리라고 제안한다.
Ⓓ 학생에게 다른 대학에서 수업을 들으라고 제안한다.

4. Listen again to part of the conversation. Then answer the question.

M Hmmm. I'm sorry to say that it doesn't look very good. The section you're looking for actually has the fewest students on the waiting list with 27. All the other sections have far more.
W That doesn't sound like much of a chance. Probably the only way to get in is right near the final withdrawal deadline. And by that time, I'll have missed most of the course!

What does the student mean when she says this:

W That doesn't sound like much of a chance.

Ⓐ She thinks the idea doesn't sound necessary.
Ⓑ She does not understand why there are so many people on the list.
Ⓒ She thinks she will get into the course soon in the semester.
Ⓓ She thinks that she will not be admitted into the class this semester.

4. 대화의 일부를 다시 듣고 질문에 답하시오.

남 흠, 유감이지만 상황이 좋아 보이지는 않네요. 사실 학생이 원하는 시간대의 수업에 대기자 수가 가장 적지만, 그래도 27명이에요. 다른 시간대에는 훨씬 더 많은 대기자가 있고요.
여 가능성이 많지 않아 보이네요. 아마 등록할 수 있는 유일한 방법은 취소 마감일이 다 되어야 나오겠네요. 그때쯤이면 전 그 수업의 대부분을 듣지 못했을 테고요!

학생은 다음과 같이 말하며 무엇을 의미하는가:

여 가능성이 많지 않아 보이네요.

Ⓐ 그 아이디어가 필요한 것 같지 않다고 생각한다.
Ⓑ 명단에 그렇게 많은 사람이 올라가 있는 이유를 이해하지 못한다.
Ⓒ 학기 중 곧 그 수업에 등록할 수 있을 것이라고 생각한다.
Ⓓ 이번 학기에 그 수업에 등록할 수 없을 것이라고 생각한다.

5. What will the student most likely do?
Ⓐ Find an open spot to audit the required course
Ⓑ Visit City Hall to sign up for the political seminar
Ⓒ Go and see Professor Peterson regarding her grade
Ⓓ Visit Professor Peterson's office to ask for help

5. 학생은 다음에 무엇을 할 것 같은가?
Ⓐ 필수 과목을 청강하기 위해 가능한 자리를 찾는다
Ⓑ 정치 세미나에 등록하기 위해 시청을 방문한다
Ⓒ 성적과 관련해 피터슨 교수를 찾아간다
Ⓓ 도움을 요청하기 위해 피터슨 교수의 사무실을 방문한다

Actual Test 2

어휘 register v 등록하다 | normally adv 보통 | get locked out (밖에 있는 채로) 잠겨서 들어가지 못하다 | fix v 바로잡다, 고치다 | enroll v 등록하다 | political science 정치학 | particular adj 특정한 | prerequisite n 필수 과목, 선행 필수 요건 | graduate v 졸업하다 | availability n (이용, 사용) 가능성 | limited adj 제한된 | timetable n 시간표 | regular adj 정규의 | laid back adj 편한, 느긋한 | tuition n 등록금 | overflow n 정원 초과, 흘러 넘침 | replacement n 대체 | flexible adj 유동적인 | possibility n 가능성 | withdrawal n 철회 | audit v 청강하다 | slide in 미끄러져 들어가다 | permission n 허락 | reserve v 따로 남겨 두다, 예약하다 | helpful adj 도움이 되는, 유용한 | attend v 참석하다 | complicated adj 복잡한 | variable n 변수

Man: Professor

[6-11] Listen to part of a lecture in a biology class.

M OK, 6 I ran out of time yesterday, so I didn't get a chance to explain how plants create new plants, which is what we call plant reproduction. So today I want to detail how seed plants actually reproduce. As you know, a seed grows into a plant, but after this, the plant must reproduce to extend its species. For this, 6 it uses its reproductive organs in a process called pollination, which can occur in two ways: through self-pollination or cross-pollination.

So what is pollination? Basically, it's the transfer of pollen from a flower's stamen to either its stigma or that of another flower. This fertilizes the plant, allowing it to develop seeds. Now, to better understand the process, it will help if we look at the structure of a plant, which has both male and female parts. 7 The stamen is the male portion of a plant, and it produces a sticky yellow powder called pollen. It's the powder that covers your car, making it yellow each spring. And there's also a female part to plants, called the pistil, the top of which has a sticky area known as the stigma.

As I said, there are a few ways plants can be pollinated, and they both have their benefits and drawbacks. Self-pollination occurs when a plant's pollen is transferred from its stamen to its own stigma, and cross-pollination occurs when a plant's pollen reaches the stigma of a different plant from its species. Therefore, pollination only occurs within a species, so an apple tree can't pollinate a cherry tree, for example. Now, the benefits of self-pollination are that only one self-pollinating plant is needed to reproduce, but with this comes some problems. Since the new plants are composed of the same genetic material, they can all be killed by the same disease. And if a plant makes a genetic adaptation, it can't pass this benefit on to others of its species. Cross-pollinating plants don't suffer from this. They can pass any helpful genetic changes on to other plants quickly. However, a pollinator, which transfers pollen from plant to plant in the form of insects, mammals, or wind, must be present for this to occur.

Pollinators' work is done by accident. What I mean is that they don't intentionally pollinate flowers. They are all at the flower to get food in the form of pollen or nectar. And

남자: 교수

생물학 강의의 일부를 들으시오.

남 좋아요. 6 어제는 시간이 부족해서 어떻게 식물이 새로운 식물을 만들어내는지, 소위 식물의 번식에 대해 설명할 기회가 없었어요. 그래서 오늘은 종자 식물들이 실제로 어떻게 번식을 하는지 자세히 설명하겠습니다. 여러분도 알다시피 종자는 성장해서 식물이 되고, 이후에는 종을 확산시키기 위해 번식을 해야 합니다. 이를 위해, 6 식물은 수분이라 불리는 과정에서 번식 기관을 이용하는데, 이러한 수분은 두 가지 방법으로 발생합니다. 자가 수분과 타화 수분이 바로 그것입니다.

그렇다면 수분이란 무엇일까요? 기본적으로 수분은 꽃 수술에서 암술머리로 또는 다른 꽃의 암술머리로 꽃가루를 이동시키는 것을 말합니다. 이것은 식물을 수정시켜 씨앗이 자라날 수 있도록 합니다. 이제 이 과정을 좀 더 잘 이해하기 위해, 수술과 암술을 모두 가진 식물의 구조를 살펴보면 도움이 될 것입니다. 7 수술은 식물의 수컷 부분으로, 꽃가루라고 불리는 끈적거리는 노란색 가루를 만들어냅니다. 매년 봄 여러분의 자동차를 뒤덮어 노랗게 만드는 가루죠. 그리고 식물에는 암술이라고 불리는 암컷 부분도 있는데, 이것의 꼭대기에는 암술머리라고 불리는 끈적거리는 부분이 있습니다.

이미 말한 대로 식물들이 수분을 할 수 있는 방법이 몇 가지 있는데, 각각 장점과 단점을 가지고 있습니다. 자가 수분은 한 식물의 꽃가루가 수술에서 자신의 암술머리로 전달될 때 일어나며, 타화 수분은 한 식물의 꽃가루가 같은 종의 다른 식물의 암술머리로 전달될 때 일어납니다. 따라서 수분은 같은 종 내에서만 일어나기 때문에, 예를 들어, 사과나무는 체리나무와 수분할 수 없는 것입니다. 자가 수분의 장점은 번식을 위해 하나의 자가 수분 식물만이 필요하다는 것인데, 여기에는 몇 가지 문제점이 따라붙습니다. 새로운 식물들이 동일한 유전 물질들로 구성되기 때문에 같은 질병으로 전부 죽을 수 있다는 것입니다. 그리고 만일 한 식물이 이에 유전적으로 적응을 한다고 해도, 이를 같은 종의 다른 식물들에게 전달할 수 없습니다. 타화 수분 식물들은 이런 문제를 겪지 않습니다. 그들은 도움이 되는 유전적 변화를 다른 식물들에게 빨리 전달할 수 있습니다. 하지만, 이를 위해서는 곤충이나 포유동물, 그리고 바람과 같이 꽃가루를 식물과 식물 사이에 전달하는 수분 매개체가 있어야만 합니다.

수분 매개체의 활동은 우연히 이루어집니다. 의도적으로 꽃들을 수분시키는 것이 아니라는 말이죠. 그들은 꽃가루나 꿀 형태로 되어 있는 먹이를 얻

since pollen is sticky, it sometimes sticks to their bodies and gets transferred when the pollinator visits another plant and accidentally drops some of the pollen on the flower's stigma. The most successful flower cross-pollinators are moths, bees, butterflies, and hummingbirds. **8** However, wind can also function as a pollinator, mainly cross-pollinating grasses like corn. In fact, it's easy to identify plants that use the wind for pollination. They don't have bright colors or flower petals because they don't need to visually attract animal pollinators. As you can assume, wind doesn't direct pollen too precisely, so it doesn't lend itself well to pollinating flowers. But for vast areas that need pollen scattered throughout, I don't know of a better pollinator.

In the last century, animal pollinator numbers have decreased, yet orchard and field sizes have steadily increased. And for the last twenty years, pollination management has become an important issue in farming. By understanding a crop's pollination needs, growers can significantly improve not only the production but also the quality of the crop. **9** For example, in the United States, blueberry producers bring in vast numbers of honeybees to act as pollinators in their fields. Although these bees are not as effective as the bees native to the area, they make up for inefficiency with sheer numbers. Of course, when the plants are out of season, there is a massive decline in the honeybee population. But the farmers are able to bring more bees to the area again in the next season while still being able to make money from their work.

10, 11 Well, that's it for pollination. But what happens after a plant is fertilized? Well, please read pages 80-110 tonight so you can get some background information on tomorrow's class. **11** And there's an important question I would like you to tell me the answer to tomorrow. Is the tomato a fruit or a vegetable?

기 위해 꽃에 접근합니다. 그리고 꽃가루는 끈적거리기 때문에 때때로 그것들의 몸에 붙게 되고, 그것들이 다른 식물에게 가서 그 꽃의 암술머리에 우연히 꽃가루를 떨어뜨리면서 꽃가루가 전해지는 것입니다. 가장 좋은 타화 수분 매개체는 나방, 벌, 나비, 그리고 벌새입니다. **8** 하지만 바람도 수분 매개체 역할을 할 수 있는데, 주로 옥수수와 같은 식물을 타화 수분시킵니다. 사실, 수분을 하는 데 바람을 이용하는 식물을 식별하는 것은 쉬운 일입니다. 이들은 수분 매개체인 동물들을 시각적으로 끌어들일 필요가 없기 때문에 밝은 색이나 꽃잎을 가지고 있지 않습니다. 여러분이 추측할 수 있는 대로 바람은 꽃가루를 정확하게 인도할 수 없기 때문에 꽃을 수분시키는 데에는 적합하지 않습니다. 그러나 사방에 꽃가루가 흩어져야 하는 방대한 지역에서는 이보다 더 나은 수분 매개체를 찾기 어렵죠.

지난 세기에 수분 매개체 역할을 하는 동물의 수는 감소해왔지만, 과수원과 밭의 규모는 꾸준히 증가해왔습니다. 그리고 지난 20년 동안 수분을 관리하는 것은 농업에 있어 중요한 문제가 되었죠. 농작물의 수분 필요성을 이해함으로써 경작자들은 생산량을 증대할 뿐만 아니라 작물의 품질도 향상시킬 수 있습니다. **9** 예를 들어, 미국에서 블루베리 농사를 짓는 사람들은 수분 매개체로 활동할 수 있도록 대량의 꿀벌을 밭으로 데려왔습니다. 비록 이 벌들은 그 지역 토종 벌들보다 효과적이지는 않지만, 많은 수만으로도 이러한 비효율성을 보완했습니다. 물론 식물을 기르는 기간이 지나고 나면 꿀벌 수가 엄청나게 줄어들겠지요. 하지만 농부들은 다음 철에 더 많은 벌들을 데려올 수 있을 것이고 여전히 작물로 수익을 거둘 수 있습니다.

10, 11 음, 이것으로 수분에 대한 이야기를 마치도록 하죠. 그런데 식물이 수분된 뒤에는 어떤 일이 일어날까요? 내일 수업에 대한 배경 지식을 좀 얻을 수 있도록 오늘 밤에 80~110페이지를 읽도록 하세요. **11** 내일 여러분이 제게 답을 해야 할 중요한 질문이 하나 있습니다. 토마토는 과일일까요, 채소일까요?

6. What is the topic of the lecture?

Ⓐ Self-pollination and how plants do it
Ⓑ The way farmers can make more money
Ⓒ The different ways plants create new plants
Ⓓ Cross-pollination and what makes it happen

7. What does the professor say about pollen?

Ⓐ It is commonly seen in the springtime.
Ⓑ It makes all flowers yellow in color.
Ⓒ It is helpful for protecting flowers.
Ⓓ It is the male portion of a plant.

6. 강의의 주제는 무엇인가?

Ⓐ 자가 수분과 식물들이 그것을 하는 방법
Ⓑ 농부들이 더 많은 돈을 벌 수 있는 방법
Ⓒ 식물이 새로운 식물을 만들어내는 다양한 방법
Ⓓ 타화 수분과 그것을 발생하게 하는 것

7. 교수는 꽃가루에 관해 뭐라고 말하는가?

Ⓐ 일반적으로 봄철에 볼 수 있다.
Ⓑ 모든 꽃들을 노랗게 만든다.
Ⓒ 꽃을 보호하는 데 도움을 준다.
Ⓓ 식물의 수컷 부분이다.

8. **What is the professor's attitude toward wind as a pollinator of large areas?**

Ⓐ He feels the wind is the best for them.
Ⓑ He thinks the wind is better for flowers.
Ⓒ He wants more information.
Ⓓ He isn't sure the wind is strong enough to be effective.

9. **How can honeybees be compared to the bees native to the area?**

Ⓐ They are less expensive than native bees.
Ⓑ They are larger than native bees.
Ⓒ They aren't as efficient at pollinating as native bees.
Ⓓ They pollinate plants faster than native bees.

10. **Listen again to part of the lecture. Then answer the question.**

> M Well, that's it for pollination. But what happens after a plant is fertilized? Well, please read pages 80-110 tonight so you can get some background information on tomorrow's class.

Why does the professor say this:

> M But what happens after a plant is fertilized?

Ⓐ To develop ideas for discussion in the next class
Ⓑ To talk about how pollination fertilizes plants
Ⓒ To inform students what they will be reading about for homework
Ⓓ To describe the process that creates new plants

11. **How does the professor conclude the lecture?**

Ⓐ By assigning homework and reviewing the lecture
Ⓑ By answering questions about pollination
Ⓒ By telling students to read about vegetables
Ⓓ By giving a homework assignment and asking a question

8. 넓은 지역의 수분 매개체로서의 바람에 관한 교수의 태도는 어떠한가?

Ⓐ 바람이 최선의 방법이라고 생각한다.
Ⓑ 바람이 꽃들에게 더 낫다고 생각한다.
Ⓒ 더 많은 정보를 필요로 한다.
Ⓓ 바람이 효과적일 만큼 강한지 확실치 않다.

9. 꿀벌은 그 지역의 토종 벌과 어떻게 비교되는가?

Ⓐ 토종 벌보다 덜 비싸다.
Ⓑ 토종 벌보다 더 크다.
Ⓒ 수분시킬 때 토종 벌만큼 효율적이지 못하다.
Ⓓ 토종 벌보다 식물들을 더 빨리 수분시킨다.

10. 강의의 일부를 다시 듣고 질문에 답하시오.

> 남 음, 이것으로 수분에 대한 이야기를 마치도록 하죠. 그런데 식물이 수분된 뒤에는 어떤 일이 일어날까요? 내일 수업에 대한 배경 지식을 좀 얻을 수 있도록 오늘 밤에 80~110 페이지를 읽도록 하세요.

교수는 왜 이렇게 말하는가:

> 남 그런데 식물이 수분된 뒤에는 어떤 일이 일어날까요?

Ⓐ 다음 수업의 토론에 관한 생각을 진전시키려고
Ⓑ 수분이 식물을 어떻게 수정시키는지 이야기하려고
Ⓒ 학생들에게 과제로 읽게 될 내용을 알려주려고
Ⓓ 새로운 식물을 만드는 과정을 설명하려고

11. 교수는 강의를 어떻게 마무리하는가?

Ⓐ 과제를 주고 강의를 복습하면서
Ⓑ 수분에 관한 질문에 답하면서
Ⓒ 학생들에게 채소에 관해 읽어보라고 말하면서
Ⓓ 과제를 주고 질문을 하면서

어휘 reproduction n 번식 | seed n 씨앗 | extend v 확장하다, 넓히다 | organ n 기관 | pollination n 수분 | occur v 발생하다 | self-pollination n 자가 수분 | cross-pollination n 타화 수분 | transfer n 이동, 전이 | pollen n 꽃가루 | stamen n 수술 | stigma n 암술머리 | fertilize v 수정하다 | structure n 구조 | sticky adj 끈적거리는 | pistil n 암술 | benefit n 장점, 이점 | drawback n 단점 | genetic adj 유전의 | disease n 질병 | adaptation n 적응 | suffer v 고통 받다 | insect n 곤충 | mammal n 포유류 | by accident 우연히, 사고로 | intentionally adv 의도적으로 | nectar n (꽃의) 꿀 | moth n 나방 | hummingbird n 벌새 | function v 기능하다 | identify v 식별하다 | visually adv 시각적으로 | attract v 끌어들이다, 유인하다 | lend v 주다, 부여하다 | vast adj 막대한 | scatter v 흩어지다, 뿌리다 | decrease v 감소하다 | orchard n 과수원 | steadily adv 꾸준히 | significantly adv 크게 | inefficiency n 비능률 | sheer adj (크기나 양을 강조하여) 순전한 | massive adj 거대한 | population n 개체수

Man: Student | Woman: Professor

[12-17] Listen to part of a discussion in a business class.

W Hello again! So, last week we were talking about marketing. 12 Today, we are going to look closer at one of the parts of marketing, advertising. Many people seem to think that "marketing" and "advertising" are the same, but they're not. Advertising is simply one of the many parts of marketing. So, what exactly is advertising then? 13 It is techniques and practices used to inform the public about something in order to get them to respond in a certain way. Confusing? Well, let me put it this way... it's a type of communication with a controlled message, for a purpose.

For over 2,000 years, advertising has been used to inform, educate, and motivate people about issues like AIDS and the environment, um... political beliefs, religious recruitment, and so on. Most commonly, though, advertisers are looking for profit... and advertising can be expensive! Believe it or not, the average cost of a single 30-second commercial spot during the Super Bowl is, like, 2.7 million dollars! If you bought a laptop for a thousand dollars, you could buy 2,700 laptops for the same price it costs to have a 30-second commercial during the Super Bowl... wow, huh?

M Excuse me, professor, you said 2.7 million dollars? Isn't that crazy? Why would a company spend millions of dollars on 30 seconds of advertising?

W Well, that's a great question, 12 and it gets us into what I really wanted to talk about, the 4 M's of advertising. Let me talk about that for a second, and I think you will find the answer, okay?

M Sure, thanks.

W So, last week we talked about the 4 P's of marketing, right? Place, product, price, and promotion. 12 Now, let's look at the 4 M's of advertising... the four most important factors companies consider when trying to plan successful advertisements: market, media, money, and message. 14 OK, first... market. Companies do research on consumers and try to figure out who their target consumer is and what the need is for the product. They think about the age and gender of who will buy their product. Knowing who to attract is very important. If a company is trying to sell diapers, its target audience would be mothers. And, to determine the need for the product, they look at results from phone surveys or mail in questionnaires, because it's usually the mothers who answer them.

남자: 학생 | 여자: 교수

경영학 수업 중 토론의 일부를 들으시오.

여 안녕하세요! 지난 시간에는 마케팅에 관해 이야기했죠. 12 오늘은 마케팅의 한 부분인 광고에 대해 자세히 살펴볼 겁니다. 많은 사람들이 '마케팅'과 '광고'를 같은 것으로 생각하는 것 같아요. 하지만 그렇지 않습니다. 광고는 마케팅의 많은 부분 중 하나일 뿐이죠. 그럼, 광고란 정확히 무엇을 말할까요? 13 대중이 특정 방식으로 반응하도록 만들기 위해서 어떤 것에 관한 정보를 주는 데 사용된 기술이나 행위를 말합니다. 복잡한가요? 음, 이렇게 이야기해 볼 수 있어요... 광고란 어떤 목적을 위해 통제된 메시지를 전달하는 소통 형식이라고 말이죠.

2천 년이 넘는 시간 동안 광고는 사람들에게 AIDS나 환경과 같은 문제들, 음... 정치 이념, 종교 집단의 모집 등에 관한 정보를 주고, 교육을 시키고, 동기를 부여하는 데 사용되어 왔습니다. 물론 일반적으로 광고주는 이윤을 추구하며... 광고에는 많은 비용이 들 수 있습니다! 믿기 힘들겠지만, 슈퍼볼 중계방송 동안 방영되는 30초짜리 상업 광고 하나에 평균 2백7십만 달러의 비용이 들어갑니다! 만일 여러분이 천 달러짜리 노트북을 산다면, 슈퍼볼을 중계할 때 방영되는 30초짜리 광고에 드는 비용으로 2천7백 대의 노트북을 살 수 있는 겁니다... 대단하죠, 정말?

남 잠시만요 교수님, 2백7십만 달러라고 하셨어요? 너무 심하지 않나요? 왜 기업은 30초짜리 광고에 수백만 달러를 소비하는 거죠?

여 음, 좋은 질문이에요. 12 그리고 제가 오늘 말하려고 하는 광고의 4M과 관련이 있어요. 조금만 이야기하면 그 답을 찾을 수 있을 거예요. 괜찮죠?

남 물론이죠. 감사합니다.

여 자, 지난주에 마케팅의 4P에 대해서 이야기했죠? 위치, 상품, 가격, 그리고 홍보. 12 이제 광고의 4M에 대해서 알아봅시다... 이건 성공적인 광고를 기획할 때 기업이 고려해야 하는 네 가지 중요한 요소로서, 시장, 매체, 비용, 그리고 메시지를 말합니다. 14 자, 우선... 시장에 대해서 얘기해 봅시다. 기업은 소비자에 대해 조사를 하고, 목표 소비자가 누구인지, 상품에 대해 어떤 수요가 있는지를 알아내려 노력합니다. 기업은 누가 물건을 구입할 것인지 그 성별과 연령에 대해 생각합니다. 누구를 끌어모아야 할지 아는 것은 매우 중요합니다. 만일 기업이 기저귀를 판매하려고 하면, 목표 대상은 어머니들일 것입니다. 그리고 상품에 대한 수요를 파악하기 위해 전화 설문이나 우편 설문의 결과를 조사할 것입니다. 왜냐하면 그 질문에 답변을 주는 사람은 대개 어머니일 테니 말이죠.

OK, the second M is media. Media is the way that the company will present the message, like, uh... commercials, magazines, internet popups, and you know, stuff like that. **15** So, they calculate which form of media will be most successful. Like... if a company is selling teaching supplies to young teachers in their 20s or in their early 30s, ads should be put into magazines for young teachers, not for old ones, right? They want to use the right media for their target consumer.

M So, in the Super Bowl, the target consumer would be uh... sports fans? And they use commercials during the Super Bowl because so many sports fans watch it?

W Exactly! Because... think of the products: beer, sports drinks and soda, chips, cars... products that average, young to middle-aged people want. **16** And, to answer the other question about why they should spend millions of dollars for those ads, let's look at the third M... money. Companies ask themselves, "Will the cost of the advertisement be a good investment?" So, advertisers have to consider the right time for ads. For instance, ads for sports items in weekend magazines aren't so good because their target consumers tend to go on weekend retreats or leaves, not read magazines. But... to put an ad on during the Super Bowl, worldwide... that's like... well, I'm sure it's over a hundred million viewers just in the U.S.! Do you think it's worth it?

M Yeah, I guess so! That's a lot of people!

W Definitely. Once the company has looked at the other three parts, they have to come up with a way to promote the product that is interesting and memorable, and think about what kind of message it sends... the fourth M, the message. Here's a funny example for you: when a soup shop owner gave out socks to customers for a sales promotion, total sales decreased instead of increased because customers associated the soup with feet. And who wants soup that reminds them of smelly feet? Bad message, right? So, they have to find the right message. **17** OK, so who can tell me again what the 4M's of advertising are?

자, 두 번째 M은 매체입니다. 매체는 상업 광고, 잡지, 인터넷 팝업 등과 같이 기업이 메시지를 전달하는 방식을 말합니다. **15** 따라서 기업은 어떤 형태의 매체가 가장 효율적일지 계산합니다. 만일 기업이 20대나 30대 초반의 젊은 선생님들에게 강의에 필요한 용품을 팔려고 한다면, 광고는 나이든 선생님이 아니라 젊은 선생님을 대상으로 하는 잡지에 게재되어야 합니다. 맞죠? 기업은 목표로 하는 소비자에 맞게 매체를 사용하기를 원합니다.

남 그럼, 슈퍼볼에서 목표로 하는 소비자는 어... 스포츠 팬들이겠네요? 그리고 기업은 많은 스포츠 팬들이 그것을 볼 테니까 슈퍼볼이 방영되는 기간 동안 상업 광고를 하고요?

여 그렇죠! 왜냐하면... 상품을 생각해 보세요. 맥주, 스포츠 음료, 탄산 음료, 감자칩, 자동차... 젊은이들부터 중년들까지 보통 사람들이 좋아하는 품목들이죠. **16** 그리고 왜 기업이 광고비로 수백만 달러를 써야 하는지에 대한 답을 얻기 위해 세 번째 M인... 비용에 대해 알아봅시다. 기업은 다음과 같이 스스로에게 묻습니다. "광고에 들이는 비용이 좋은 투자가 될까?" 그래서 광고주들은 광고를 하기에 적합한 시기를 고려해야 합니다. 예를 들어, 스포츠 용품 광고가 주말 잡지에 실리는 것은 좋지 않습니다. 왜냐하면 그 제품들의 목표 소비자들은 주말에 잡지를 읽지 않고 여행을 가거나 놀러 가는 경향이 있기 때문입니다. 하지만 슈퍼볼이 방영되는 동안 광고를 하면, 전 세계적으로... 그건 마치... 음, 미국에서만도 분명 수억 명의 시청자들이 있을 겁니다! 그럴 만한 가치가 있다는 생각이 드나요?

남 네. 그럴 것 같아요! 그건 정말 많은 수의 사람들이니까요!

여 분명 그렇죠. 일단 회사가 이러한 세 가지 부분을 고려한 뒤에는 흥미롭고 기억에 남는 상품 홍보 방법을 생각해내야 하며, 어떤 메시지를 전달할지에 대해서도 생각해야 합니다. 바로 네 번째 M인 메시지입니다. 여기 재미있는 예가 있어요. 수프 가게 주인이 판매 홍보를 위해 손님들에게 양말을 나눠 주었을 때, 총 매출은 증가하지 않고 오히려 감소했습니다. 손님들이 수프와 발을 연결해서 생각했기 때문입니다. 냄새 나는 발을 떠오르게 하는 수프를 누가 좋아할까요? 잘못된 메시지죠? 그래서 기업은 올바른 메시지를 찾아야 합니다. **17** 자, 그럼 누가 광고의 4M이 무엇인지 다시 말해볼 수 있을까요?

12. **What aspects of advertising is the professor mainly discussing?**

Ⓐ The costs and benefits of advertising

Ⓑ The types of messages that companies try to send through advertisements

12. 교수는 광고의 어떤 면을 주로 이야기하고 있는가?

Ⓐ 광고의 비용과 장점

Ⓑ 기업이 광고를 통해 전달하고자 하는 메시지의 유형

Ⓒ The main elements companies must consider when planning advertisements
Ⓓ The four types of advertising media

13. Listen again to part of the discussion. Then answer the question.

> W It is techniques and practices used to inform the public about something in order to get them to respond in a certain way. Confusing? Well, let me put it this way... it's a type of communication with a controlled message, for a purpose.

Why does the professor say this:

> W Confusing? Well, let me put it this way...

Ⓐ She does not think the students need another definition.
Ⓑ She wants to give a definition that is a little easier to understand.
Ⓒ She feels like the students should be able to understand the first definition.
Ⓓ She's trying to say that the first definition is not confusing.

14. What is the market in the 4 M's of advertising?

Ⓐ The method used to show the advertisements
Ⓑ Who will buy the product and how much they need it
Ⓒ The number of people who will see the TV commercial
Ⓓ The style the company uses to make the ad

15. According to the professor, how is market related to media?

Ⓐ Market and target consumers are more important than the media form.
Ⓑ The media that is chosen is more important than the market.
Ⓒ The target customer must be established before determining which form of media to use.
Ⓓ The media message should be chosen first, then companies can decide whom to target.

16. Why is time important in terms of the third M, 'money'?

Ⓐ It gets the most viewership and maximizes the number of potential consumers.
Ⓑ It reminds existing consumers of a certain product again to purchase.
Ⓒ It can estimate the number of people who watch the Super Bowl.

Ⓒ 광고를 기획할 때 기업이 고려해야 하는 주된 요소들
Ⓓ 광고 매체의 4가지 유형

13. 토론의 일부를 다시 듣고 질문에 답하시오.

> 여 대중이 특정 방식으로 반응하도록 만들기 위해서 어떤 것에 관한 정보를 주는 데 사용된 기술이나 행위를 말합니다. 복잡한가요? 음, 이렇게 이야기해 볼 수 있어요... 광고란 어떤 목적을 위해 통제된 메시지를 전달하는 소통 형식이라고 말이죠.

교수는 왜 이렇게 말하는가:

> 여 복잡한가요? 음, 이렇게 이야기해볼 수 있어요...

Ⓐ 학생들이 단어의 다른 정의를 필요로 한다고 생각하지 않는다.
Ⓑ 이해하기 더 쉬운 정의를 말해주려고 한다.
Ⓒ 학생들이 첫 번째 정의를 이해해야 한다고 생각한다.
Ⓓ 첫 번째 정의가 복잡하지 않다고 말하려 한다.

14. 광고의 4 M에서 시장은 무엇인가?

Ⓐ 광고를 보여주기 위해 사용되는 방법
Ⓑ 누가 상품을 구입할 것이며 그것을 얼마나 필요로 하는지
Ⓒ 텔레비전 광고를 보는 사람들의 수
Ⓓ 기업이 광고를 만드는 데 사용하는 방식

15. 교수에 따르면, 시장은 매체와 어떻게 관련되었는가?

Ⓐ 시장과 목표 소비자는 매체의 형태보다 더 중요하다.
Ⓑ 선택된 매체는 시장보다 더 중요하다.
Ⓒ 사용할 매체를 결정하기 전에 목표 소비자가 정해져야 한다.
Ⓓ 매체의 메시지가 먼저 결정되어야 하고, 기업은 그 뒤에 누구를 목표로 할지 정할 수 있다.

16. 시간은 왜 세 번째 M인 '돈'의 개념에서 중요한가?

Ⓐ 가장 많은 시청자를 모으며 잠재 고객의 수를 최대화한다.
Ⓑ 기존 고객에게 다시 구매할 특정 상품을 상기시킨다.
Ⓒ 슈퍼볼을 보는 사람들의 수를 추산할 수 있다.

Actual Test 2

Ⓓ It attracts different groups of people who can affect a company's sales.

Ⓓ 회사의 영업에 영향을 주는 다양한 무리의 사람들을 끌어들인다.

17. How does the professor conclude the discussion?
Ⓐ By repeating the main topic of the lecture
Ⓑ By giving several examples of the main topic
Ⓒ By asking the students if they can remember something
Ⓓ By reminding the students the most important example of the lecture

17. 교수는 어떻게 토론을 마무리하는가?
Ⓐ 강의의 주제를 반복하면서
Ⓑ 주제의 몇 가지 예시들을 들면서
Ⓒ 학생들에게 무언가를 기억할 수 있는지 물으면서
Ⓓ 강의에서 가장 중요한 예시를 상기시키면서

어휘 marketing n 마케팅 I advertising n 광고 I exactly adv 정확히 I technique n 기법, 기술 I practice n 행위, 관행 I inform v 알리다 I respond v 반응하다 I confusing adj 혼란스러운, 헷갈리는 I communication n 소통 I controlled adj 통제된 I purpose n 목적 I educate v 교육하다 I motivate v 동기를 부여하다 I environment n 환경 I political adj 정치적인 I belief n 신념 I religious adj 종교적인 I recruitment n 모집 I profit n 이익, 이윤 I average cost 평균 비용 I commercial n 광고 I promotion n 홍보 I factor n 요인 I consider v 고려하다 I consumer n 소비자 I attract v 끌어들이다 I diaper n 기저귀 I determine v 알아내다 I result n 결과 I questionnaire n 설문지 I calculate v 계산하다 I investment n 투자 I retreat n 휴양(여행), 은둔, 피난 I promote v 홍보하다 I memorable adj 기억할 만한 I decrease v 감소하다 I associate *A* with *B* A와 B를 연결하다, 연관 짓다 I smelly adj 냄새 나는

Actual Test 3

본서 I P. 300

Conversation 1	1. C	2. A	3. B	4. C	5. B	
Lecture 1	6. B	7. A	8. D	9. A, D	10. B	11. C
Conversation 2	1. A	2. B, C	3. C	4. C	5. D	
Lecture 2	6. D	7. A, C	8. B	9. D	10. C	11. A
Lecture 3	12. B	13. A, D	14. A	15. A	16. C	17. C

Conversation 1

본서 I P. 302

Man: Employee I Woman: Student

[1-5] Listen to part of a conversation between a student and an employee of a university art gallery.

W Hello. Um… 1 I applied to work here a few days ago. But I wasn't sure if I am really qualified for the job...

M Oh, let me find your application then. What is your name?

W Kaitlin Zhang.

M Ah, yes. Here is your application. 2 Hmm, it says here that you are applying for a volunteer position?

W 2 Yes, I am in Professor Campbell's class. He gives students who do volunteer work extra credit.

M Okay, why did you choose to do your volunteer work with us?

W Well, his course is on art history, so he wants us to volunteer with organizations or companies that are involved with that.

남자: 직원 I 여자: 학생

학생과 대학교 미술관 직원의 대화를 들으시오.

여 안녕하세요, 음... 1 며칠 전에 여기서 일하려고 지원했었어요. 그렇지만 그 일에 제가 정말 적격인지 잘 모르겠어서요...

남 아, 그럼 학생의 지원서를 찾아볼게요. 이름이 뭐죠?

여 케이틀린 장입니다.

남 아, 네. 여기 학생의 지원서가 있네요. 2 흠, 여기에는 학생이 자원 봉사 자리에 지원한다고 나와 있군요?

여 2 네, 저는 캠벨 교수님의 수업을 듣고 있어요. 그분은 자원 봉사를 하는 학생들에게 추가 점수를 주시거든요.

남 알겠어요. 학생은 왜 이곳에서 봉사 활동을 하기로 한 건가요?

여 음, 캠벨 교수님의 수업은 미술사에 대한 수업이라 그분은 저희가 그와 관련된 단체나 회사에서 자원 봉사를 하길 원하셨어요.

M I see. And, we were your first choice?

W Actually, no, you weren't. 3 I applied first at a few museums, but they didn't have any openings left. I guess the other students beat me to them.

M Fair enough… how long do you have to do your volunteer work?

W We have until the end of the semester, which is in May.

M Got off to a bit of a late start, did you?

W Yes, I suppose I did.

M How many hours of volunteer work do you need to do?

W We have to do a minimum of 20 hours.

M Okay, then you should have no problem meeting your requirement. 4 Before we can allow you to be a tour guide, you have to do some training sessions with a professional. Are you free Tuesday and Thursday afternoon?

W 4 Tuesday, yes. But, I have a midterm exams all day on Thursday.

M 4 That is unfortunate. We don't have any other guided tours scheduled for this week.

W When do you have more scheduled?

M Hmm, not until next month. Could you wait a few more weeks?

W No, I cannot. It's my own fault for waiting so long, I guess…

M Well, don't give up just yet. We have other tasks that you could perform as a volunteer. You could work in our gift shop, or you could help with our tour research.

W Tour research? What kind of research would I be doing?

M Well, we try to make our tours as informative as possible. So, our tour guides have scripts that they have to memorize. They include information about art history and artists that tourists should find interesting. But, someone has to do the initial research for those scripts. This can involve searching the Internet, interviewing people, and digging through archives of documents. It can be a very involved process.

W That sounds pretty interesting. Does it require any prior training like leading the tours?

M Not really. You just have to study our current and previous scripts. Would that fulfill your volunteering requirement?

W Yes, I believe it would. It would definitely be better than selling souvenirs in the gift shop. What do I need to do to apply for that position?

M Your online application is sufficient, but 5 you will need to have a meeting with the chief manager. He likes to interview all employees before they get to sign a contract.

W Is there a chance that I won't get the position?

남 그렇군요. 그리고 우리가 학생의 첫 번째 선택이었나요?

여 사실 아니에요. 3 먼저 몇 군데 박물관에 지원했지만 빈 자리가 없었어요. 다른 학생들이 저보다 먼저 지원한 것 같아요.

남 그렇군요… 봉사 활동을 얼마나 오래 해야 하는 거죠?

여 학기 말까지니까 5월이에요.

남 좀 늦게 시작했군요, 그렇죠?

여 네, 그런 것 같네요.

남 봉사 활동은 몇 시간이나 해야 하나요?

여 최소 20시간을 해야 해요.

남 알겠어요. 그러면 필요 조건에 부합하는 데는 문제가 없겠네요. 4 우리 미술관에서 학생을 관람 안내인으로 쓰기 전에 학생은 전문가의 연수 과정을 거쳐야 해요. 화요일과 목요일 오후에 시간이 있나요?

여 4 화요일은 되지만, 목요일은 하루 종일 중간 고사 시험이 있어요.

남 4 유감이네요. 이번 주에 따로 예정되어 있는 안내인과 함께 하는 관람 시간이 없거든요.

여 다른 관람 시간은 언제로 잡혀 있나요?

남 음, 다음 달까지는 없어요. 몇 주 더 기다릴 수 있나요?

여 아니요, 안 돼요. 너무 오래 시간을 끈 제 잘못인 것 같네요…

남 음, 아직 포기하지는 말아요. 학생이 자원 봉사자로 할 수 있는 다른 일들이 있으니까요. 기념품점에서 일할 수도 있고, 관람 조사에 도움을 줄 수도 있어요.

여 관람 조사요? 어떤 종류의 조사를 하게 되는 건가요?

남 음, 우리는 관람을 가능한 한 유익하게 만들려고 노력해요. 그래서 관람 안내인들이 암기해야 하는 대본이 있어요. 관람객들이 흥미를 느낄 만한 미술사와 미술가에 대한 정보를 포함하죠. 하지만 이런 대본을 만들기 위해서는 누군가가 먼저 조사를 해야만 해요. 이 조사에는 인터넷 검색하기, 사람들 인터뷰하기, 그리고 기록 보관소에서 문서 찾기 등이 있어요. 꽤나 복잡한 과정이 될 수 있죠.

여 상당히 흥미로운 일이네요. 이 일도 관람 안내 일처럼 사전 연수를 필요로 하나요?

남 아니에요. 그저 현재와 과거의 대본을 살펴보면 돼요. 이 일도 학생의 봉사 활동 요건을 충족시킬 수 있을까요?

여 네, 그럴 거라고 믿어요. 기념품점에서 기념품을 판매하는 것보다는 훨씬 나을 거예요. 이 자리에 지원하기 위해서는 무엇을 해야 하죠?

남 학생의 온라인 지원서로도 충분하지만, 5 우리 박물관의 책임자와 만나야만 할 거예요. 계약서에 서명을 하기 전에 모든 직원들과 인터뷰를 하고 싶어하시거든요.

여 제가 이 일을 하지 못하게 될 가능성도 있나요?

Actual Test 3

M As a volunteer, I doubt it. But, you never know.
W When could I meet him?
M Ah, he isn't here at the moment. 5 Could you come back tomorrow morning at around 10 o'clock?
W 5 Yes, I am free tomorrow.
M Great, then I will see you again tomorrow morning.
W Okay, thank you for your time.

남 자원 봉사자니까 그럴 것 같진 않아요. 하지만 알 수 없죠.
여 책임자님을 언제 만날 수 있죠?
남 아, 지금은 안 계세요. 5 내일 오전 열 시 정도에 다시 올 수 있나요?
여 5 네, 저는 내일 아무 일정도 없어요.
남 좋아요, 그러면 내일 아침에 다시 봅시다.
여 네, 시간 내주셔서 감사합니다.

1. What is the purpose of the student's visit to the university art gallery?

Ⓐ She wanted to change the date of her scheduled guided tour.
Ⓑ She was not sure if her application form was properly submitted.
Ⓒ She wanted to see if she is the right candidate for a position.
Ⓓ She was interested in working in the art gallery's souvenir shop.

2. Why does the student want to work at the university art gallery?

Ⓐ She is interested in getting the extra credit that her professor offered.
Ⓑ She is majoring in art history and volunteer activity is required for all such students.
Ⓒ She is making up for some tests she missed with volunteer activity.
Ⓓ She is trying to earn some money by working as an art tour guide.

3. Why does the student say this:

> W I applied first at a few museums, but they didn't have any openings left. I guess the other students beat me to them.

Ⓐ The other students had more experience than the student did.
Ⓑ The other students were faster at applying for those positions.
Ⓒ The other students had an advantage that the student did not have.
Ⓓ The other students were better at finding open positions.

4. Why can't the student become a tour guide?

Ⓐ She is not very good at researching art history and related reference books.

1. 학생이 대학교 미술관을 방문한 목적은 무엇인가?

Ⓐ 예정된 안내인과 함께 하는 관람 날짜를 바꾸고 싶어했다.
Ⓑ 지원서가 제대로 제출되었는지 확신할 수 없었다.
Ⓒ 일자리에 자신이 맞는 후보인지 알아보고 싶어했다.
Ⓓ 미술관의 기념품점에서 일하는 것에 흥미를 느꼈다.

2. 학생은 왜 대학교 미술관에서 일하고 싶어하는가?

Ⓐ 교수님이 주는 추가 점수를 받는 데 관심이 있다.
Ⓑ 미술사를 전공하고 있으며 봉사 활동은 모든 전공 학생들에게 있어 필수이다.
Ⓒ 놓친 시험을 봉사 활동으로 대체하려고 한다.
Ⓓ 미술 관람 안내인으로 일하면서 돈을 벌려고 한다.

3. 학생은 왜 이렇게 말하는가:

> 여 먼저 몇 군데 박물관에 지원했지만 빈 자리가 없었어요. 다른 학생들이 저보다 먼저 지원한 것 같아요.

Ⓐ 다른 학생들이 이 학생보다 더 많은 경험을 가지고 있었다.
Ⓑ 다른 학생들이 이 일자리에 지원하는 데 더 빨랐다.
Ⓒ 다른 학생들은 이 학생이 가지고 있지 않은 이점을 가지고 있었다.
Ⓓ 다른 학생들은 가능한 일자리를 찾는 데 더 뛰어났다.

4. 학생은 왜 관람 안내인이 될 수 없는가?

Ⓐ 미술사와 그와 관련된 문헌을 잘 조사하지 못한다.

Ⓑ She did not have a meeting with the chief manager to discuss the tour schedule.
Ⓒ She is unable to take two training sessions from a professional tour guide.
Ⓓ She is not majoring in art history even though she is taking Professor Campbell's class.

Ⓑ 관람 일정을 논의하기 위해 책임자와 만나지 않았다.
Ⓒ 전문 관람 안내인이 진행하는 두 번의 연수 과정에 참석할 수 없다.
Ⓓ 캠벨 교수의 수업을 듣고 있지만 미술사를 전공하고 있지는 않다.

5. What will the student most likely do next?
Ⓐ Go to see Professor Campbell tomorrow
Ⓑ Visit the gallery again tomorrow for a meeting
Ⓒ Change her appointment time to Tuesday
Ⓓ Fill out the offline application form and submit it

5. 학생이 다음에 무엇을 할 것 같은가?
Ⓐ 내일 캠벨 교수님을 만나러 간다
Ⓑ 면담을 위해 내일 미술관을 다시 방문한다
Ⓒ 예약 시간을 화요일로 바꾼다
Ⓓ 오프라인 지원서를 작성해서 제출한다

어휘 apply v 지원하다 | qualified adj 자격이 있는 | application n 지원서 | volunteer v 자원 봉사 활동을 하다 | organization n 단체 | beat (to) 앞서 ~에 당도하다 | requirement n 자격 요건 | training n 교육, 훈련 | professional n 전문가 | unfortunate adj 유감스러운 | task n 일, 과업 | perform v 행하다 | research n 조사 | informative adj 유익한, 유용한 정보를 주는 | script n 대본, 원고 | memorize v 외우다 | initial adj 처음의, 초기의 | dig v 찾아내다, 뒤지다 | archive n 기록 보관소 | document n 문서 | fulfill v 만족시키다, 채우다 | souvenir n 기념품 | sufficient adj 충분한 | contract n 계약서

Lecture 1

본서 | P. 304

Man: Professor | Woman: Student

[6-11] Listen to part of a discussion in an archaeology class.

M Today we will turn our attention to the art of the Mayan civilization—specifically their pottery. The Maya are well known for their achievements in many forms of art, including their architecture, carvings, and paintings, and these all reached a form of synthesis in their ceramic wares. The pottery of the Maya varied dramatically in style over time, so while it can be defined as being created by one culture, there were separate movements that typified its creation. 6 To analyze pottery from any culture, we must follow certain standards of classification that allow us to define to which time period it belongs. Now, who can remember from the reading what the four standards are?

W The paste, the surface treatment, and the decoration... Wait, did you say four?

M Yes, I did. You left out the shape. 7 Now, the overall shape of a vessel is quite easy to define by simply looking at it, and the shape of a vessel is typically dictated by its purpose. So, we can easily say if a piece of pottery was used for storage, drinking, etc. based on its form.
8 The first real step in identifying a type of pottery is determining its paste type. This is best achieved with a cross-section of a piece of pottery, like a shard from a broken pot, or a carefully taken sample. By looking at a cross-section, we can see what kind of clay was used to

남자: 교수 | 여자: 학생

고고학 수업 중 토론의 일부를 들으시오.

남 오늘 우리는 마야 문명의 예술, 특히 그들의 도예로 관심을 돌릴 겁니다. 마야인들은 건축, 조각, 그리고 그림을 포함한 여러 유형의 예술에 대한 업적으로 잘 알려져 있으며 이들 모두가 그들의 도자기에서 통합을 이루었어요. 마야인들의 도자기는 시간이 흐름에 따라 그 양식이 극적으로 달라졌습니다. 이 도자기들 모두가 한 문명에서 만들어졌다고 정의될 수는 있지만 이들의 창조를 특징짓는 별개의 운동들이 있었습니다. 6 어떠한 문명의 도자기를 분석할 때라도 우리는 특정 도자기가 어떤 시기에 속했는지를 정의할 수 있도록 도와주는 특정한 분류 기준들을 따라야 해요. 이제 이 네 가지 기준들이 무엇인지 읽기 과제에서 읽은 내용이 기억나는 사람 있나요?

여 반죽과 표면 처리, 그리고 장식... 잠시만요, 네 개라고 하셨나요?

남 네, 그래요. 학생은 모양을 빼놓았어요. 7 자, 어떠한 용기의 전체적인 모양은 그저 그것을 보기만 해도 쉽게 정의를 내리는 것이 가능합니다. 그리고 용기의 모양은 일반적으로 목적에 따라 달라지죠. 그래서 어떠한 도자기가 보관을 위한 것인지, 마실 때 사용하기 위한 것인지, 혹은 그 외에 사용되는지를 형태에 따라 쉽게 알 수 있어요.
8 어떠한 종류의 도자기를 확인하는 진짜 첫 번째 단계는 반죽 종류를 알아내는 것입니다. 이는 도자기의 단면을 봄으로써 알아낼 수 있습니다. 부서진

make the pot, how it was shaped, and how hot a fire it was baked in. Next, we look at how the surface was treated. Clay may be added to the surface or removed in patterns to create images. The surface may be painted or dyed, or even adorned with other objects. 9(A) The finished pot may have been glazed, and there are a variety of materials that can be used to glaze a pot. Finally, we look at the decoration itself, which is the most specific characteristic we can use to identify a type of ceramic. We look at this last because the same style of decoration can be used with different paste types and surface treatments. 9(D) Decoration can include things like colors, design themes, and images that recur that may have significant importance to the artists and their cultures. These characteristics tend to vary over time as the artists and their techniques become more refined.
Now, let's apply these standards to a few examples of Mayan pottery. The Maya made their pottery from clay that was collected from river beds and highland valleys, and they sometimes added sand and ash to strengthen it. 10 How did they make their pots? Did their technique evolve?

W 10 No, not really. They rolled clay into coils that they wound into the shape they wanted, and then they smoothed the sides. They did that throughout the history of Mayan pottery.

M Correct. 11 During the Late Preclassic Period, artists began adding limbs, heads, and other body parts to make pots that had increasingly detailed human and animal forms. For example, this pot has the head of a bird with a fish in its beak on its lid, and the bird's wings are painted on the surface around the head. It also has a reddish brown color that was typical to the period. During the Early Classic period, the shapes of the pots returned to more utilitarian shapes, but the surface treatments and decoration became more detailed. This pot is decorated with intricate carvings of serpents and people that have had some of the clay around them removed to raise them above the surface of the pot. The image is believed to show humans emerging from the underworld, an important part of the Maya creation story. It also has a shiny black glaze that was typical of its period. In the Late Classic Period, the surface treatment of pots had simplified greatly, but the images painted on them had become equally detailed. They used many different pigments to decorate pots like this one. It shows a young noble with a feathered headdress seated on his throne. There are two other figures that represent his attendants.

도자기의 조각이라던가 조심스럽게 채취된 샘플을 통해서요. 단면을 보면 도자기를 만드는 데 어떤 종류의 점토가 사용되었고, 어떤 모양이었고, 그리고 얼마나 센 불에서 구워졌는지를 알 수 있습니다. 다음으로 표면이 어떻게 처리되었는지 살펴봅니다. 그림을 만들어내기 위해 점토가 더해질 수도 있었고 패턴에 따라 점토가 제거될 수도 있었어요. 표면은 색을 칠하거나 염색을 할 수도 있었고 심지어 다른 물건들로 장식할 수도 있었습니다. 9(A) 완성된 도자기는 유약을 발라 윤기나게 했을 것이고, 도자기를 윤기나게 하는 데 사용될 수 있는 재료들은 다양해요. 마지막으로는 장식 그 자체를 살펴봅니다. 도자기 유형을 확인하는 데 사용할 수 있는 가장 구체적인 특성이죠. 우리가 장식을 마지막으로 살펴보는 이유는 같은 양식의 장식이 서로 다른 반죽이나 표면 처리에 사용될 수 있기 때문입니다. 9(D) 장식은 예술가와 그 문명에 큰 중요성을 가질 수 있는, 계속해서 나타나는 색, 디자인 주제, 그리고 그림을 포함할 수 있어요. 이 특징들은 시간이 흐르면서 예술가들과 그들이 사용하는 기법들이 더욱 세련되어지며 달라지는 경향이 있습니다.
이제 이 기준들을 마야 도자기의 몇몇 예시들에 적용해 봅시다. 마야인들은 강바닥과 산악 지대의 계곡에서 채취한 점토를 사용해서 도자기를 만들었고 이들을 강화하기 위해 모래나 재를 때때로 추가했어요. 10 이들은 도자기를 어떻게 만들었을까요? 이들의 기법이 진보했나요?

여 10 아니요, 그다지요. 마야인들은 점토를 똬리 모양으로 굴려 만든 다음 이걸 꼬아서 자신들이 원하는 모양으로 만들었고, 옆면을 매끈하게 다듬었어요. 이 방식을 마야 도자기의 역사 전반에 걸쳐 이용했죠.

남 맞아요. 11 전고전기 후반 동안 예술가들이 팔다리와 머리, 그리고 다른 신체 부분들을 더해 더욱 세부적인 인간과 동물 형상을 한 도자기를 만들기 시작했습니다. 예를 들어, 이 도자기는 뚜껑에 물고기를 부리에 물고 있는 새의 머리를 갖고 있고, 새의 날개가 머리 주변의 표면으로 그려져 있죠. 또한 이 시기의 전형적인 색이었던 적갈색을 띄고 있습니다. 고전기 초반에는 도자기들의 모양들이 좀 더 실용적인 모양으로 돌아갔지만 표면 처리와 장식은 더욱 정교해졌어요. 이 도자기는 복잡하게 조각한 뱀들과 사람들로 장식되어 있는데, 이것들을 도자기의 표면보다 더 높게 만들기 위해 이들 주변의 점토가 제거되었습니다. 이 그림은 지하 세계에서 나오는 인간들을 보여주는 것으로 알려져 있어요. 마야 창조 이야기의 중요한 부분이죠. 그리고 이 시기의 전형적인 특징인 검은색의 빛나는 유약 처리가 되어 있습니다. 고전기 후반에는 도자기들의 표면 처리가 매우 간소해졌지만 이들 위에 그려진 그림들도 마찬가지로 매우 정교해졌어요. 마야인들은

In front of him is a vessel holding a foamy drink, and the vessel looks much like the pot it is painted on. Therefore, the vessel is believed to be a funerary offering, for him to drink from in the afterlife.

여기 보이는 이러한 도자기와 같은 것들을 장식하기 위해 여러 종류의 안료를 사용했습니다. 이 도자기는 깃털이 달린 머리 장식을 쓰고 왕좌에 앉아 있는 젊은 귀족의 모습을 보여주고 있죠. 그의 수행원들을 나타내는 두 명의 다른 인물들이 있습니다.
이 귀족의 앞에는 거품이 나는 음료를 담은 그릇이 보이는데 이 그릇은 이 그림이 그려진 그릇과 매우 비슷하게 생겼어요. 그러므로 이 그릇은 이 귀족이 사후 세계에서 사용할 수 있도록 만들어진 장례용 제물인 것으로 보입니다.

6. What is the main idea of the discussion?

Ⓐ Four classifications that make Mayan pottery different from other cultures'
Ⓑ Important classifications that could help when analyzing ancient pottery
Ⓒ Some classifications that were established to study ancient and modern pottery
Ⓓ Four classifications that the Mayans organized to spread their pottery

7. What does the professor say about the shape of a vessel?

Ⓐ It plainly shows the purpose of the vessel to the viewers.
Ⓑ It is the least important factor out of the four classifications.
Ⓒ It was revealed that its shape and purpose did not always match.
Ⓓ It shows that most pottery from that period was used for drinking purposes.

8. Why does the professor mention a shard?

Ⓐ It shows the development of style in Mayan ceramics.
Ⓑ It could help archaeologists to discover the usage of the pottery.
Ⓒ It was recently discovered at an ancient Mayan settlement.
Ⓓ It can be valuable when finding out the paste type of the pottery.

9. According to the discussion, which of the following are true about the four classifications? Choose 2 answers.

Ⓐ The Mayans used varying types of materials when glazing their pottery.
Ⓑ Dry clay was used to remove any residue remaining on the surface of pottery.

6. 토론의 주제는 무엇인가?

Ⓐ 마야 도자기를 다른 문명의 도자기들과 구분되게 만드는 네 가지 분류 기준
Ⓑ 고대 도자기를 분석할 때 도움을 줄 수 있는 중요한 분류들
Ⓒ 고대와 현대의 도자기를 연구하기 위해 확립된 몇몇 분류 기준들
Ⓓ 자신들의 도자기를 전파하기 위해 마야인들이 정리한 네 가지 분류 기준들

7. 교수는 그릇의 모양에 대해 무엇이라고 말하는가?

Ⓐ 보는 이들에게 그릇의 목적을 분명하게 보여준다.
Ⓑ 네 가지 분류 기준들 중 가장 덜 중요한 요소이다.
Ⓒ 그릇의 모양과 목적이 항상 일치하는 것은 아니었음이 밝혀졌다.
Ⓓ 이 시기 대부분의 도자기들은 무언가를 마시기 위한 목적으로 사용되었다는 것을 보여준다.

8. 교수는 왜 부서진 조각을 언급하는가?

Ⓐ 마야 도자기 양식의 발전을 보여준다.
Ⓑ 고고학자들로 하여금 도자기 사용을 발견할 수 있도록 도와줄 수 있었다.
Ⓒ 최근에 고대 마야 유적지에서 발견되었다.
Ⓓ 도자기의 반죽 유형을 알아내는 데 귀중하게 쓰일 수 있다.

9. 토론에 의하면, 네 가지 분류 기준에 대해 옳은 것들은 다음 중 무엇인가? 두 개를 고르시오.

Ⓐ 마야인들은 도자기를 유약 처리할 때 다양한 종류의 재료를 사용했다.
Ⓑ 도자기에 붙은 찌꺼기를 제거하기 위해 건조한 점토가 사용되었다.

Ⓒ Types of pastes and surface work were also included in the decoration category.
Ⓓ Decorations and the theme the artist chose often depicted his culture.

10. Listen again to part of the discussion. Then answer the question.

> M How did they make their pots? Did their technique evolve?
> W No, not really. They rolled clay into coils that they wound into the shape they wanted, and then they smoothed the sides. They did that throughout the history of Mayan pottery.

Why does the student say this:

> W They did that throughout the history of Mayan pottery.

Ⓐ To highlight the importance of the technique the Mayans utilized
Ⓑ To show that the method the Mayans used did not change that much
Ⓒ To convince the professor that the Mayans' technique has a long history
Ⓓ To explain how the Mayans formed their pottery into a desired shape

11. What can be inferred about the pottery produced during the Late Preclassic period?

Ⓐ It showed serpent figures, which is the proof of their belief in the afterlife.
Ⓑ It always represented certain kinds of animals, especially birds.
Ⓒ It started to have shapes that were more complex and human-like.
Ⓓ It had carvings of significant events that occurred in history.

Ⓒ 반죽 유형과 표면 작업 또한 장식 분류에 포함되었다.
Ⓓ 예술가가 선택한 장식이나 주제는 종종 그의 문화를 묘사했다.

10. 토론의 일부를 듣고 질문에 답하시오.

> 남 이들은 도자기를 어떻게 만들었을까요? 이들의 기법이 진보했나요?
> 여 아니요, 그다지요. 마야인들은 점토를 똬리 모양으로 굴려 만든 다음 이걸 꼬아서 자신들이 원하는 모양으로 만들었고, 옆면을 매끈하게 다듬었어요. 이 방식을 마야 도자기의 역사 전반에 걸쳐 이용했죠.

학생은 왜 이렇게 말하는가:

> 여 이 방식을 마야 도자기의 역사 전반에 걸쳐 이용했죠.

Ⓐ 마야인들이 사용한 기법의 중요성을 강조하려고
Ⓑ 마야인들이 사용한 방법이 그다지 많이 변하지 않았다는 것을 보여주려고
Ⓒ 마야인들의 기술이 오랜 역사를 가지고 있다고 교수를 설득하려고
Ⓓ 마야인들이 어떻게 원하는 모양으로 도자기를 만들었는지에 대해 설명하려고

11. 전고전기 후기에 만들어진 도자기에 대해 무엇을 추론할 수 있는가?

Ⓐ 사후 세계에 대한 마야인들의 믿음의 증거인 뱀 모양을 보여주고 있다.
Ⓑ 언제나 특정 종류의 동물들, 특히 새들을 나타냈다.
Ⓒ 점점 더 복잡하고 인간과 닮은 모양들을 나타내기 시작했다.
Ⓓ 마야인들의 역사에 있었던 중요한 사건들에 대한 조각을 담고 있다.

어휘 civilization n 문명 | specifically adv 분명히, 명확하게 | pottery n 도자기, 도예 | achievement n 업적, 성취 | architecture n 건축학, 건축 양식 | carving n 조각, 새긴 무늬 | synthesis n 종합, 통합 | ceramic ware 도자기류 | vary v 서로 각기 다르다 | dramatically adv 극적으로 | define v 정의하다, 규정하다 | typify v 특징을 나타내다, 전형적이다 | analyze v 분석하다 | classification n 분류 | paste n 반죽 | surface n 표면 | treatment n 처리 | decoration n 장식 | overall adj 전체의, 종합적인 | vessel n 그릇, 통 | dictate v ~를 좌우하다, ~에 영향을 주다 | storage n 저장, 보관 | identify v 확인하다, 찾다 | cross-section n 단면 | shard n 조각, 파편 | clay n 점토 | dye v 염색하다 | adorn v 꾸미다, 장식하다 | glaze v 유약을 바르다 | recur v 반복되다 | refined adj 세련된, 고상한 | river bed 강바닥 | ash n 재 | evolve v 발달하다 | coil n (여러 겹 감아 놓은 것의 한) 고리; 소용돌이 | wind v 감다, 돌리다 | smooth v 매끈하게 하다, 반듯하게 펴다 | limb n 팔다리 | beak n 부리 | lid n 뚜껑 | typical adj 전형적인, 대표적인 | utilitarian adj 실용적인, 공리주의의 | intricate adj 복잡한 | serpent n 뱀 | emerge v 나오다 | underworld n 지하 세계 | simplify v 단순화하다 | pigment n 안료, 색소 | noble n 귀족 | feathered adj 깃털이 있는 | headdress n 머리에 쓰는 장식물 | throne n 왕좌, 옥좌 | represent v 표현하다 | attendant n 수행원 | foamy adj 거품이 나는 | funerary adj 장례의 | offering n 제물, 공물 | afterlife n 내세, 사후 세계

Conversation 2

본서 P. 308

Man: Employee | Woman: Student

[1-5] Listen to part of a conversation between a student and a university library employee.

W Excuse me, may I ask you something?

M Sure, how can I help you?

W 1 I am looking for a specific article contained in a journal. It's entitled "Film and Philosophy: Socratic Elements in 20th Century Cinema."

M Did you look it up on the computers?

W Yes I did, but I wasn't sure what it was telling me. It had a code that contained the letters FS.

M Let me check on my computer. Okay, is it featured in the Journal of Film Sciences?

W That's it.

M Well, the FS code means that it's located in the Film Studies library. I'm sure you know that our school has several libraries, and the film school has its own library as well.

W Ah, I see. I'm not a film major, so I didn't know they had their own library.

M Yes, so if you want access to this book, you're going to have to visit the film school library.

W Does it show if the book is even available?

M Well it's in the periodicals section, meaning that students aren't allowed to take it out of the library, so yes, it's available.

W Where is the library located?

M It's on our downtown campus. If you park in the parking lot under the student center, the library is located right across from it, right next to Harrison Hall.

W Unfortunately, I need it right away. My paper is due tomorrow, and I don't have a car.

M Oh. It's already pretty late, and that's pretty far to walk. Do you know anyone who has a car?

W My roommate has a car, but she's out of town today.

M I'm sorry, I don't think I can help you in this situation. I hate to say it, but you should have started on your paper earlier. 3 Putting off a research paper is one of the worst things you can do, because you never know what might go wrong at the last minute. I see it happen time and time again during finals week.

W You can say that again.

M Hey, hold on! I think you might be in luck. It says here that we have access to electronic copies of this journal. It's part of an agreement we have with the journal's publishers.

W That's great news! What do I need to do to access it?

M 4 Well, in order to read this online, you're going to have to register. Since it isn't university property, you have to

남자: 직원 | 여자: 학생

학생과 대학 도서관 직원 간의 대화를 들으시오.

여 실례합니다, 뭐 좀 물어봐도 될까요?

남 네, 무엇을 도와드릴까요?

여 1 저널에 실린 특정 기사를 찾고 있는데요. 제목이 〈영화와 철학: 20세기 영화의 소크라테스적 요소〉라는 제목이에요.

남 컴퓨터에서 찾아보셨나요?

여 네, 찾아봤지만 무슨 내용인지는 잘 몰랐어요. FS라는 글자가 포함된 코드가 있었어요.

남 제 컴퓨터에서 확인해 볼게요. 그럼, 〈영화 과학 저널〉에 실렸나요?

여 바로 그거예요.

남 FS 코드는 영화학 도서관에 있다는 뜻이죠. 우리 학교에는 여러 도서관이 있고 영화학부에도 자체 도서관이 있다는 것을 알고 계실 겁니다.

여 아, 그렇군요. 저는 영화 전공이 아니라서 도서관이 따로 있는 줄 몰랐어요.

남 네, 그래서 이 책을 보시려면 영화학교 도서관을 방문하셔야 합니다.

여 이 책이 구비되어 있는지도 표시가 되나요?

남 정기 간행물 섹션에 있기 때문에 학생들이 도서관에서 가져갈 수 없으므로 네, 이용할 수 있습니다.

여 도서관은 어디에 있나요?

남 시내 캠퍼스에 있습니다. 학생회관 아래 주차장에 주차하시면 바로 맞은편 해리슨 홀 바로 옆에 도서관이 있습니다.

여 죄송하지만 지금 당장 필요해요. 내일이 과제 마감일인데 차가 없어요.

남 오. 벌써 꽤 늦었는데 걸어가기엔 너무 멀어요. 혹시 차가 있는 사람을 알고 있나요?

여 제 룸메이트가 차가 있지만 오늘 다른 지역에 있어요.

남 미안하지만 지금 상황에서는 도와드릴 수 없을 것 같아요. 이런 말 하긴 싫지만 논문 작업을 더 일찍 시작하셨어야죠. 3 마지막 순간에 무슨 일이 생길지 모르기 때문에 연구 논문을 미루는 것은 최악의 실수 중 하나입니다. 기말고사 주간에 이런 일이 몇 번이고 반복되는 것을 봅니다.

여 그러게 말입니다.

남 이봐요, 잠깐만요! 운이 좋으신 것 같아요. 여기에는 이 저널의 전자 파일을 열람할 수 있다고 나와 있습니다. 저널 출판사와 맺은 계약의 일부입니다.

여 좋은 소식이에요! 액세스하려면 어떻게 해야 하나요?

남 4 음, 이 저널을 온라인으로 읽으려면 등록을 해야 합니다. 대학 소유가 아니기 때문에 출판사 웹사이

register on the publisher's website.

W 4 I see. Can I do that from my computer?

M 4 Unfortunately, no. Part of the agreement is for the electronic copies to be accessed only in the university libraries so that students won't print them freely. Basically, it's a way to make sure the electronic copies are used like periodicals.

W That's fine with me. I guess it's good that I'm here after all.

M Yes. Just go ahead to the computer room. Let me write down the website for you. Here you go. Just follow the instructions for registration. 5 You're going to need your student ID number and course code.

W 5 Great. I guess the journal is available only for people enrolled in film classes?

M 5 No, it's actually just for the publishers to keep track of who is reading their materials. They want to know what kinds of students are interested in film studies.

W Ah, that makes sense. Thank you so much for your help!

트에서 등록해야 합니다.

여 4 그렇군요. 제 컴퓨터에서도 할 수 있나요?

남 4 안타깝게도 불가능합니다. 계약의 일부는 학생들이 자유롭게 인쇄할 수 없도록 대학 도서관에서만 전자 사본에 액세스할 수 있도록 하는 것입니다. 기본적으로 전자 사본이 정기 간행물처럼 사용되도록 하기 위한 조치입니다.

여 전 괜찮아요. 어쨌든 제가 여기 오길 잘한 것 같아요.

남 네. 컴퓨터실로 가세요. 제가 웹사이트를 적어드릴게요. 여기 있습니다. 안내에 따라 등록하세요. 5 학생증 번호와 강좌 코드가 필요합니다.

여 5 좋아요. 저널은 영화 수업에 등록한 사람만 이용할 수 있나요?

남 5 아니요, 출판사에서 누가 자료를 읽는지 추적하기 위한 것입니다. 어떤 학생들이 영화 연구에 관심이 있는지 알고 싶어 하거든요.

여 아, 그렇군요. 도와주셔서 정말 감사합니다!

1. Why did the student meet with the employee?
   - Ⓐ To inquire about an article
   - Ⓑ To ask for directions to the satellite campus
   - Ⓒ To learn how to understand library codes
   - Ⓓ To register for a journal website

2. Why can't the student access a physical copy of the journal right away? Choose 2 answers.
   - Ⓐ It is only available as an electronic copy.
   - Ⓑ The journal is held in a different library.
   - Ⓒ The student's roommate is away.
   - Ⓓ The journal is being used by another student.

3. What can be inferred about students at the university?
   - Ⓐ Many students are unhappy about the size of the campus.
   - Ⓑ Most students have to write papers during finals week.
   - Ⓒ Many students procrastinate on their final papers.
   - Ⓓ Not many students have cars.

4. Why does the student have to register with the publisher's website?
   - Ⓐ The publisher only provides an electronic copy.
   - Ⓑ The publisher has no agreement to share material with the university.
   - Ⓒ The publisher wants to protect the material's copyrights.

1. 학생이 직원을 만난 이유는 무엇인가?
   - Ⓐ 기사에 대해 문의하기 위해
   - Ⓑ 위성 캠퍼스로 가는 길을 묻기 위해
   - Ⓒ 도서관 코드를 이해하는 방법을 배우기 위해
   - Ⓓ 저널 웹사이트에 등록하기 위해

2. 학생이 저널의 실제 사본에 바로 접근할 수 없는 이유는 무엇인가? 두 개를 고르시오.
   - Ⓐ 전자 사본으로만 제공된다.
   - Ⓑ 저널이 다른 도서관에 비치되어 있다.
   - Ⓒ 학생의 룸메이트가 다른 지역에 있다.
   - Ⓓ 다른 학생이 저널을 사용 중이다.

3. 이 대학의 학생들에 대해 유추할 수 있는 것은 무엇인가?
   - Ⓐ 많은 학생들이 캠퍼스 규모에 대해 불만을 가지고 있다.
   - Ⓑ 대부분의 학생들이 기말고사 주간에 논문을 써야 한다.
   - Ⓒ 많은 학생들이 기말 논문을 미루는 경우가 많다.
   - Ⓓ 자동차를 가지고 있는 학생이 많지 않다.

4. 학생이 출판사 웹사이트에 등록해야 하는 이유는 무엇인가?
   - Ⓐ 출판사는 전자 사본만 제공한다.
   - Ⓑ 출판사는 대학과 자료를 공유하는 데 동의한 적이 없다.
   - Ⓒ 출판사가 자료의 저작권을 보호하고자 한다.

Ⓓ The publisher wants to increase access to the material.

Ⓓ 출판사가 자료에 대한 접근성을 높이고자 한다.

5. Why does the student need to input her course code?

Ⓐ To restrict access to only film majors
Ⓑ To limit the number of times a student can access the journal
Ⓒ To ensure that the student is enrolled in the right course
Ⓓ For the sake of the publisher's record keeping

5. 학생이 강좌 코드를 입력해야 하는 이유는 무엇인가?

Ⓐ 영화 전공자로만 접근을 제한하기 위해
Ⓑ 학생이 저널에 접근할 수 있는 횟수를 제한하기 위해
Ⓒ 학생이 올바른 강좌에 등록했는지 확인하기 위해
Ⓓ 출판사의 기록 보관을 위해

어휘 article n 기사 | journal n 학술지 | entitle v 제목을 붙이다 | 20th Century 20세기 | cinema n 영화 | look up v 찾다 | letter n 글자 | check v 확인하다 | feature v 특집으로 다루다 | journal n 학술지 저널 | locate v 위치하다 | major n 전공 | access n 접근 | periodical n 정기 간행물 | available adj 이용 가능한 | downtown n 시내 | campus n 캠퍼스 | park v 주차하다 | parking lot 주차장 | right across from 바로 건너편에 | paper n 논문 | roommate n 룸메이트 | out of town 다른 지역에 있는 | research paper 연구 논문 | happen v 일어나다 | finals week 기말고사 주 | electronic adj 전자적인 | copy n 복사본 | agreement n 합의 | publisher n 출판사 | access v 접근하다 | read v 읽다 | register v 등록하다 | university n 대학 | property n 재산 | website n 웹사이트 | instruction n 안내 | student ID 학생 아이디 | course code 강좌 코드 | enroll v 등록하다 | track v 추적하다 | material n 자료 | interested adj 관심이 있는

Lecture 2

본서 | P. 310

Man: Professor | Woman: Student

[6-11] Listen to part of a lecture in a biology class.

M Good morning, everyone. I want to start our class with a reference to Charles Darwin. I'm sure all of you know that he spent considerable time on the Galapagos Islands before he came up with his theory of evolution. Upon arriving, he realized that the islands were like a little world of their own. The animals he saw were so unique, and the biodiversity was something he had never seen anywhere else. It was here that he noticed that some species inhabited neighboring islands but had varying features. He looked at finches a lot, and he saw that the finches' beaks differed on each island, adapting to the food that they ate or the habitat they lived in. He also observed iguanas quite extensively. Iguanas usually feed on animals and sometimes fish. **7(A)** But here, he saw that they even learned to dive into the water so they could feed off of green and red algae. When he studied them closely, he noticed that their noses were shaped differently from those of other iguanas. Their noses were blunter, meaning they could access and scrape off the algae growing on underwater rocks. **7(C)** Darwin also thought it was remarkable that these marine iguanas were able to somehow filter out the salt in the water.

남자: 교수 | 여자: 학생

생물학 수업에서 강의의 일부를 들으시오.

남 좋은 아침입니다, 여러분. 저는 찰스 다윈에 대한 이야기로 수업을 시작하고자 합니다. 다윈이 진화론을 내놓기 전에 갈라파고스 제도에서 상당한 시간을 보냈다는 것은 여러분 모두 알고 계실 겁니다. 도착하자마자 그는 그 섬들만의 작은 세계와 같다는 것을 깨달았습니다. 그가 본 동물들은 매우 독특했고, 그 섬의 생물 다양성은 다른 곳에서는 볼 수 없었던 것이었습니다. 그는 이곳에서 이웃 섬에 서식하지만 서로 다른 특징을 가진 종들이 있다는 것을 알아챘습니다. 그는 핀치새를 많이 관찰했는데, 섬마다 핀치새의 부리 모양이 다르고, 먹는 먹이나 사는 서식지에 따라 적응하는 모습이 다르다는 것을 알았습니다. 그는 또한 이구아나를 꽤 자세히 관찰했습니다. 이구아나는 보통 동물이나 때로는 물고기를 먹습니다. **7(A)** 하지만 그는 이구아나가 녹조류와 홍조류를 먹기 위해 물속으로 잠수하는 법까지 배운 것을 관찰했습니다. 이 이구아나를 자세히 관찰한 그는 이구아나의 코 모양이 다른 이구아나들과 다르다는 것을 발견했습니다. 섬의 이구아나의 코는 더 뭉툭해서 수중 바위에 자라는 해조류에 접근해 긁어낼 수 있었죠. **7(C)** 다윈은 이 해양 이구아나가 물속의 염분을 걸러낼 수 있다는 사실도 놀랍다고 생각했어요.

6 All this is to say that these islands helped Darwin see adaptation and evolution in its full glory. Somehow, those islands were able to show in almost hyperbolic terms the evolution that goes on with all animal and plant species on any continent. But why is it that islands are so diverse and host such unique plants and animals?

W Do islands generally have harsher weather? Many are very tropical and hot, and I'm sure a lot of extreme weather passes through these islands.

M You're kind of on the right track. You make a great observation because yes, it is true that tropical islands sometimes have hotter, more volatile weather. But that doesn't explain the biodiversity that we see on islands that are not necessarily tropical.

W 8 Then maybe it's not the weather, but just the environment itself?

M 8 You're getting warmer! Sure, some islands, like Hawaii, come seemingly out of nowhere due to underwater volcanic activity. But many other islands have broken off from larger continents through tectonic activity. What happens is that these animals that used to be part of a large continent are suddenly stuck on an island with a completely different environment. 11 Imagine if your own community suddenly ended up stuck on a remote island. The rate at which your community adapted and changed would suddenly become much faster than before. So it was with communities of non-human species as well. Evolution is much more apparent on islands, because plants and animals needed to adapt to their new environments quickly, and those that couldn't, simply disappeared.

10 When we look at the island nation of Seychelles off the coast of East Africa as an example, we see that as much as 85% of its animals are endemic to the islands. That is a staggering number. That just shows how much the animals there were forced to adapt to the unique conditions of their isolated habitat. There are examples that show how these animals are related to certain East African animals, but have evolved into completely different species. Take the Seychelles sunbird. All sunbirds have elongated beaks that curve downward, allowing them to stick them in flowers and drink nectar. But the Seychelles' beak is slightly different. The shape of the curve differs from that of their cousins in Africa. The adaptation was advantageous because of the different shapes of the hibiscus and other flowers on the islands. The end result was a new sunbird species.

So now we can understand even better how special these endemic species are. In the case of many other species on larger continents, the range of one species might cover several countries. But in the cases of many island species,

6 이 모든 것은 그 섬들이 다윈이 적응과 진화를 온전히 볼 수 있도록 도와주었다는 것을 의미합니다. 어쨌든 그 섬들은 모든 대륙의 모든 동식물종에서 일어나는 진화를 거의 과장된 방식으로 보여줄 수 있었습니다. 하지만 섬이 이렇게 다양하고 독특한 동식물이 서식하는 이유는 무엇일까요?

여 섬은 일반적으로 날씨가 더 혹독한가요? 많은 섬이 매우 열대성이고 덥고, 극한의 날씨도 많이 지나갈 것 같아요.

남 맞는 말씀입니다. 열대 섬이 때때로 더 덥고 변덕스러운 날씨를 보이는 것은 사실이기 때문에 훌륭한 관찰입니다. 하지만 그렇다고 해서 열대 섬이 아닌 섬에서 볼 수 있는 생물 다양성이 설명되지는 않아요.

여 8 그럼 날씨 때문이 아니라 환경 자체 때문일 수도 있겠네요?

남 8 점점 정답에 가까워지고 있어요! 물론 하와이 같은 일부 섬은 수중 화산 활동으로 인해 갑자기 생겨난 것처럼 보이기도 하죠. 하지만 다른 많은 섬들은 지각 활동으로 인해 더 큰 대륙에서 떨어져 나갔어요. 큰 대륙의 일부였던 동물들이 갑자기 완전히 다른 환경의 섬에 갇히게 된 것이죠. 11 여러분의 공동체가 갑자기 외딴섬에 갇히게 되었다고 상상해 보세요. 여러분의 공동체가 적응하고 변화하는 속도는 갑자기 이전보다 훨씬 빨라질 것입니다. 인간이 아닌 다른 종의 공동체도 마찬가지입니다. 식물과 동물은 새로운 환경에 빠르게 적응해야 했고, 적응하지 못한 동물은 사라졌기 때문에 섬에서는 진화가 훨씬 더 분명하게 나타납니다.

10 동아프리카 연안의 섬나라 세이셸을 예로 들면, 세이셸에 서식하는 동물의 85%가 이 섬에 서식하는 고유종이라는 사실을 알 수 있습니다. 이는 엄청난 수치입니다. 이는 그곳의 동물들이 고립된 서식지의 독특한 환경에 얼마나 적응해야 했는지를 보여줍니다. 이 동물들이 동아프리카의 특정 동물과 관련이 있지만 어떻게 완전히 다른 종으로 진화했는지 보여주는 예가 있습니다. 세이셸의 태양새를 예로 들어보죠. 모든 태양새는 아래쪽으로 구부러진 길쭉한 부리를 가지고 있어 꽃에 부리를 꽂고 꿀을 마실 수 있습니다. 하지만 세이셸 새는 부리가 약간 다릅니다. 곡선의 모양이 아프리카의 사촌들과는 다릅니다. 섬의 히비스커스와 다른 꽃의 모양이 다르기 때문에 이러한 적응이 유리했습니다. 그 결과 새로운 태양새 종이 탄생했습니다.

이제 우리는 이 고유종이 얼마나 특별한지 더 잘 이해할 수 있습니다. 더 큰 대륙에 서식하는 다른 많은 종의 경우, 한 종의 범위가 여러 국가에 걸쳐 있을 수 있습니다. 하지만 섬에 서식하는 많은 종의 경우, 한 섬이 유일한 서식지일 수 있습니다. 따라

a single island may be their sole habitat. This makes the protection of these species a very urgent matter. Let's look at the Seychelles Warbler as an example.

서 이러한 종의 보호는 매우 시급한 문제입니다. 세이셸 워블러를 예로 들어보겠습니다.

6. What is the main topic of the lecture?

Ⓐ The state of Seychellois endemic species
Ⓑ The contributions of Darwin's Galapagos Island expeditions to our understanding of evolution
Ⓒ The effects of environment on evolution
Ⓓ The evolution and adaptations of island species

7. According to the lecture, which of the following are examples of adaptation among animals on the Galapagos Islands? Choose 2 answers.

Ⓐ Iguanas feeding on algae
Ⓑ Iguanas eating fish
Ⓒ Iguanas filtering out salt from saltwater
Ⓓ Varying shapes of finches' tails

8. Listen again to part of the lecture. Then answer the question.

> W Then maybe it's not the weather, but just the environment itself?
> M You're getting warmer!

Why does the professor say this:

> M You're getting warmer!

Ⓐ The professor is making a witty reference to the hot weather of the tropics.
Ⓑ The student's second answer was more correct than the first.
Ⓒ The student's first answer was on the right track.
Ⓓ The professor is acknowledging that the student may be embarrassed.

9. According to the lecture, why do islands have more unique plant and animal species?

Ⓐ Many islands broke off from larger continents.
Ⓑ Volcanic activity altered the habitats of many island species.
Ⓒ The climate on islands is typically more inhospitable.
Ⓓ Many species were forced to adapt quickly to a new environment.

10. Why does the professor mention Seychelles?

Ⓐ To introduce a particular species that exhibits island evolution

6. 강의의 주된 주제는 무엇인가?

Ⓐ 세이셸 고유종의 상태
Ⓑ 다윈의 갈라파고스 제도 탐험이 진화에 대한 우리의 이해에 기여한 점
Ⓒ 환경이 진화에 미치는 영향
Ⓓ 섬의 종의 진화와 적응

7. 강의에 따르면, 다음 중 갈라파고스 제도에 서식하는 동물들의 적응의 예로 옳은 것은 무엇인가? 두 개를 고르시오.

Ⓐ 해조류를 먹는 이구아나들
Ⓑ 물고기를 먹는 이구아나
Ⓒ 바닷물에서 소금을 걸러내는 이구아나들
Ⓓ 핀치새의 다양한 꼬리 모양

8. 강의의 일부를 다시 듣고 질문에 답하시오.

> 여 그럼 날씨 때문이 아니라 환경 자체 때문일 수도 있겠네요?
> 남 점점 정답에 가까워지고 있어요!

교수가 왜 이렇게 말하는가:

> 남 점점 정답에 가까워지고 있어요!

Ⓐ 교수는 열대 지방의 더운 날씨를 재미있게 표현하고 있다.
Ⓑ 학생의 두 번째 답이 첫 번째 답보다 더 정확하다.
Ⓒ 학생의 첫 번째 답은 올바른 방향으로 가고 있었다.
Ⓓ 교수가 학생이 당황할 수 있음을 인정하고 있다.

9. 강의에 따르면, 섬은 왜 더 특별한 식물과 동물 종을 가지고 있는가?

Ⓐ 많은 섬들이 더 큰 대륙에서 떨어져 나갔다.
Ⓑ 화산 활동이 많은 섬의 종들의 서식지를 바꿨다.
Ⓒ 섬 기후에서는 보통 더 살기 힘들다.
Ⓓ 많은 종들이 새로운 환경에 빠르게 적응하도록 강요받았다.

10. 교수는 왜 세이셸을 언급하는가?

Ⓐ 섬에서 일어난 진화를 보여주는 특정 종을 소개하기 위해

Ⓑ To provide statistics on endemic species on islands
Ⓒ To illustrate the distinct qualities of evolution on islands
Ⓓ To discuss endemic and endangered island bird species

Ⓑ 섬의 고유종에 대한 통계를 제공하기 위해
Ⓒ 섬에서의 진화의 뚜렷한 특성을 설명하기 위해
Ⓓ 섬의 고유종과 멸종 위기에 처한 섬 조류 종에 대해 논의하기 위해

11. What will the class most likely do next?

Ⓐ They will learn about the urgency of endemic species protection through a case study.
Ⓑ They will discuss the state of several endangered species on the Seychelles islands.
Ⓒ They will discuss some of the unique adaptations of the Seychelles Warbler.
Ⓓ They will compare continental endangered species with those on islands.

11. 학생들이 다음에 할 일로 가장 가능성이 높은 것은 무엇인가?

Ⓐ 사례 연구를 통해 고유종 보호의 시급성에 대해 배울 것이다.
Ⓑ 세이셸 섬의 멸종 위기에 처한 여러 종의 상태에 대해 토론할 것이다.
Ⓒ 세이셸 워블러의 독특한 적응 방식에 대해 논의할 것이다.
Ⓓ 대륙의 멸종위기종과 섬의 멸종위기종을 비교할 것이다.

어휘 lecture n 강의 | biology n 생물학 | class n 수업 | reference n 참고 | Galapagos Islands 갈라파고스 제도 | theory n 이론 | evolution n 진화 | arrive v 도착하다 | realize v 깨닫다 | unique adj 독특한 | biodiversity n 생물 다양성 | species n 종 | inhabit v 서식하다 | neighboring adj 인접한 | feature n 특징 | beak n 부리 | adapt v 적응하다 | food n 음식 | habitat n 서식지 | observe v 관찰하다 | iguana n 이구아나 | feed v 먹이를 주다 | dive v 다이빙하다 | algae n 해조류 | blunt adj 둔한 | scrape v 긁어내다 | underwater adj 물속의 | marine adj 해양의 | filter v 여과하다 | salt n 소금 | adaptation n 적응 | continent n 대륙 | diverse adj 다양한 | host v 주최하다 | harsh adj 가혹한 | tropical adj 열대의 | weather n 날씨 | observation n 관찰 | volatile adj 변덕스러운 | environment n 환경 | volcanic adj 화산의 | tectonic adj 지각의 | remote adj 외딴 | community n 공동체 | disappear v 사라지다 | nation n 국가 | Seychelles n 세이쉘(인도양 서부의 92개 섬들로 이루어진 공화국) | endemic adj 고유의 | isolated adj 고립된 | related adj 관련된 | sunbird n 태양새 | beak n 부리 | curve n 곡선 | nectar n 꿀 | hibiscus n 무궁화 속에 속한 열대성 식물 | advantageous adj 유리한, 이로운 | protection n 보호 | urgent adj 시급한 | range n 범위 | sole adj 유일한

Lecture 3

본서 P. 312

Man: Student | Woman: Professor

[12-17] Listen to part of a lecture in an archaeology class.

W Last class, we discussed the idea of Manifest Destiny, the cultural belief that taught that "Americans" were destined to take over the rest of the continent. Now remember, at the time, the creators of this concept used the word "Americans" to mean "people from the United States." So that's how the word will be used in this lecture, even though that would not be a correct way to use the word in modern times. I want to review very quickly the three basic tenets of the concept. **13(D)** One was the exceptional nature of the American people and their institutions. The second was the mission to transform the West into the image of the agrarian East. And the third one was...?

M The sense of destiny to accomplish this mission?

W Good memory! Yes, it is often described as an inevitable destiny, so you can imagine how much of an effect this had on the emotions of these settlers. **13(A)** Today, I want

남자: 학생 | 여자: 교수

고고학 수업에서 강의의 일부를 들으시오.

여 지난 수업에서 우리는 '미국인'이 나머지 대륙을 점령할 운명이라고 가르치는 문화적 신념인 명백한 운명에 대해 논의했습니다. 당시 이 개념을 만든 사람들은 '미국인'이라는 단어를 '미국에서 온 사람들'이라는 의미로 사용했다는 것을 기억하세요. 현대에 이 단어를 사용하는 것이 올바른 방법은 아니지만 이 강의에서는 이 단어를 그렇게 사용할 것입니다. 저는 이 개념의 세 가지 기본 원칙을 매우 빠르게 짚고 넘어가고자 합니다. **13(D)** 첫 번째는 미국 국민과 기관의 예외적인 특성이었습니다. 두 번째는 서구를 농경적인 동부의 이미지로 변화시키려는 사명이었습니다. 그리고 세 번째는...?

남 이 사명을 완수해야 한다는 운명 의식?

여 기억력 좋네요! 네, 종종 피할 수 없는 운명이라고 묘사되곤 하는데요, 이것이 정착민들의 정서에 얼마나 큰 영향을 미쳤는지 짐작하실 수 있을 겁니다.

to discuss an idea that falls in line with Manifest Destiny's line of thought. It's called the Frontier Thesis and was put forward by Frederick Jackson Turner in 1893. His thesis came at a time when the frontier was officially declared closed, and America had expanded as far west as it could. Turner looked back on the 400 years of westward expansion and argued that the American ideals of liberty, equality, and democracy arose from the leaving of older societies to the East and arriving and creating newer societies in the West. At first, America's old society was Europe to the east across the ocean, while this time, it was the American Eastern Seaboard. **14** For him, the American East was a departure from the old ways of Europe, while the frontier was a departure from the old ways of the East Coast, empty space with no laws to follow and no rent to pay, where wild land was just there for the taking. **13(B), (C)** Here, they believed, America and its spirit could spread, thrive, and shape the continent into something new and purely American. For him, the frontier defined the American experience. It created the spirit and drive behind Americanism. Turner argued that this Americanization manifested itself in stages, in which land was first turned into farmland, which then ultimately led to urbanization.

The thesis received a lot of support from the US public at the time, and it's easy to imagine why. Turner attempted to provide a connected and unified account of settlers' march across the continent. However, historians have argued that his thesis didn't work in all cases. **15** Some historians have pointed out that cities like Chicago completely skipped the agrarian stage, and that when looking closely at the history of such cities, it was market forces and capitalism that brought urbanization, some unique "American nature." Pointing this out throws into question idea that the settlers had some inherent power to dominate nature. In other words, was it really an exceptional spirit that brought about urbanization? Or was it simply capitalism taking its course?

12 This idea is furthered by other historians who have pointed out other inconsistencies. For example, Turner makes no mention of the American Industrial Revolution, a potent force that many see doesn't necessarily fit cleanly into Turner's narrative. Furthermore, it's important to look at the people who contributed significantly to the development of the West in a variety of important ways, including the construction of railroads. Many of these were foreign laborers who arrived knowing nothing of life on the American frontier, and whatever attributes and attitudes they brought with them can hardly be called the

13(A) 오늘은 명백한 운명의 사상과 일맥상통하는 사상에 대해 말씀드리고자 합니다. 프런티어 사관이라고 불리는 사상은 1893년 프레더릭 잭슨 터너에 의해 제시되었습니다. 그의 논지는 공식적으로 국경이 닫혔다고 선언되고 미국이 서쪽으로 최대한 확장한 시점에 발표되었습니다. 터너는 400년간의 서부 개척을 되돌아보며 자유, 평등, 민주주의라는 미국의 이상은 오래된 사회가 동부로 떠나고 새로운 사회가 서부에 도착하여 만들어지는 과정에서 생겨났다고 주장했습니다. 처음에 미국의 구사회는 바다 건너 동쪽에 있는 유럽이었지만, 이번에는 미국 동부 해안 지역이었습니다. **14** 그에게 미국 동부는 유럽의 낡은 방식에서 벗어난 곳이었으며, 개척지는 미국 동부의 오래된 방식에서 벗어나 따라야 할 법도 없고 지대도 지불할 필요도 없는 빈 공간으로 야생의 땅을 마음대로 차지할 수 있는 곳이었죠. **13(B), (C)** 그들은 이곳에서 미국과 그 정신이 확산하고 번성하며 대륙을 새롭고 순수한 미국적인 것으로 만들 수 있다고 믿었습니다. 그에게 개척지는 미국인의 경험을 정의했습니다. 개척은 미국주의의 정신과 추진력을 생성했습니다. 터너는 이러한 미국화가 단계적으로 진행되어 토지가 먼저 농지로 바뀌고 궁극적으로 도시화로 이어졌다고 주장했습니다.

이 학설은 당시 미국 대중의 많은 지지를 받았는데, 그 이유를 쉽게 짐작할 수 있습니다. 터너는 정착민들의 대륙 횡단에 대해 연결되고 통합된 설명을 제공하려 했습니다. 그러나 역사가들은 그의 논지가 모든 경우에 적용되지는 않는다며 반론을 제기했습니다. **15** 일부 역사가들은 시카고와 같은 도시는 농업 단계를 완전히 건너뛰었으며, 이러한 도시의 역사를 자세히 살펴보면 도시화를 가져온 것은 시장의 힘과 자본주의, 즉 독특한 '미국 본성'이라고 지적했습니다. 이 점을 지적하면 정착민들이 자연을 지배할 수 있는 어떤 고유한 힘을 가지고 있다는 생각에 의문을 제기할 수 있습니다. 다시 말해, 도시화를 가져온 것이 정말 특별한 정신이었을까요? 아니면 단순히 자본주의가 그 과정을 밟아 온 것일까요?

12 이러한 생각은 다른 역사가들에 의해 다른 불일치를 지적한 다른 역사가들에 의해 더욱 힘을 얻습니다. 예를 들어, 터너는 미국 산업혁명에 대해 언급하지 않았는데, 많은 사람들이 터너의 서술에 꼭 들어맞지 않는다고 생각하는 강력한 요인입니다. 또한 철도 건설 등 여러 가지 중요한 방식으로 서구의 발전에 크게 기여한 사람들을 살펴보는 것도 중요합니다. 이들 중 상당수는 미국 개척지에서의 삶에 대해 아무것도 모르고 도착한 외국인 노동자들이었으며, 그들이 가져온 특성과 태도가 무엇이든

"American Spirit." 12, 16 Indeed, there's never been empirical evidence to show that one nationality has a monopoly on the characteristics that Turner uses to describe the so-called "American spirit." Some settlers were undoubtedly full of raw strength, curiosity, intelligence, pragmatism, and energy. But there could have been many others who were nothing like this. Show me one shy, timid American from that time period, and we're in business.

One other thing that historians have criticized is the argument that the wild, free land contributed to the frontier spirit. When looking closely at historical records, we see that a lot of the land was indeed vacant, but the truth is that it wasn't always free. In fact, it was often quite expensive. By the mid-1800s, much of the land was owned by railroad companies and speculators. But even when land was both vacant and free, the moral implications of non-Indigenous settlers moving in to claim it raise a lot of questions.

17 So, was it an American frontier spirit that drove the transformation of the continent? Or was it something else? Yes, Scott, I see your hand.

'미국 정신'이라고 부를 수는 없습니다. 12, 16 실제로 터너가 소위 '미국 정신'을 설명하는 데 사용하는 특성을 한 국적이 독점하고 있다는 것을 보여주는 경험적 증거는 한 번도 없었습니다. 일부 정착민은 의심할 여지없이 원초적인 힘, 호기심, 지성, 실용주의, 에너지로 가득 차 있었습니다. 하지만 이와는 전혀 다른 사람들도 많았을 것입니다. 그 시대의 수줍고 소심한 미국인 한 명만 보여주시면 말 다 한 거죠.

역사가들이 비판하는 또 다른 한 가지는 야생의 자유로운 땅이 개척 정신에 기여했다는 주장입니다. 역사 기록을 자세히 살펴보면 실제로 많은 땅이 비어 있었다는 것을 알 수 있지만, 사실 그 땅이 항상 공짜였던 것은 아닙니다. 사실 땅값이 상당히 비쌌던 경우가 많았습니다. 1800년대 중반까지 대부분의 토지는 철도 회사와 투기꾼이 소유하고 있었습니다. 하지만 비어 있는 땅이 공짜로 주어졌을 때도 원주민이 아닌 정착민들이 땅을 차지하기 위해 들어온다는 것은 도덕적으로 많은 의문을 불러일으킵니다.

17 그렇다면 미국 대륙의 변화를 이끈 것은 미국의 개척 정신이었을까요? 아니면 다른 무언가가 있었을까요? 네, 스콧, 손 든 게 보이네요.

12. What does the professor mainly talk about?

- (A) A summary of the Frontier Thesis
- (B) Criticisms of the Frontier Thesis
- (C) Manifest Destiny and its related theories
- (D) An analysis of American exceptionalism

13. According to the lecture, which of the following is NOT true of Manifest Destiny? Choose 2 answers.

- (A) It was the most important predecessor to the Frontier Thesis.
- (B) It taught that Americans had a mission to expand and transform.
- (C) It gave Americans meaning in their expansionary activities.
- (D) It emphasized the exceptional nature of American family and societal values.

14. According to the lecture, how is westward expansion related to the Frontier Thesis?

- (A) The East represented the old, while the West represented a departure from the old.
- (B) The American ideals of liberty, equality, and democracy were founded by societies to the West.
- (C) Westward expansion cemented once and for all the departure from the old societies of Europe.

12. 교수는 주로 무엇에 대해 이야기하는가?

- (A) 프런티어 사관에 대한 요약
- (B) 프런티어 사관에 대한 비판
- (C) 명백한 운명과 관련 이론들
- (D) 미국 예외주의에 대한 분석

13. 강의에 따르면, 다음 중 명백한 운명에 대해 사실이 아닌 것은 무엇인가? 두 개를 고르시오.

- (A) 프런티어 사관의 가장 중요한 전신이었다.
- (B) 미국인들에게 확장하고 변혁해야 할 사명이 있다고 가르쳤다.
- (C) 미국인들의 확장 활동에 의미를 부여했다.
- (D) 미국 가족 및 사회적 가치의 예외적 특성을 강조했다.

14. 강의에 따르면, 서부 영토 확상은 프런티어 사관과 어떤 관련이 있는가?

- (A) 동부는 구시대의 것을 상징하는 반면, 서부는 구시대로부터의 이탈을 상징한다.
- (B) 자유, 평등, 민주주의라는 미국의 이상은 서부로 진출한 사회들에 의해 확립되었다.
- (C) 서부로의 확장은 유럽의 구사회로부터의 이탈을 단번에 굳혔다.

Ⓓ Land in the West was free for anyone to grab, making it the perfect breeding ground for other American ideals to grow.

15. Why does the professor mention Chicago?

Ⓐ To give an example of a city that urbanized without becoming agrarian
Ⓑ To cast doubt on the idea of an exceptional American spirit
Ⓒ To point out the importance of capitalism in frontier expansion
Ⓓ To further the idea that Americanism ultimately led to urbanization

16. Listen again to part of the lecture. Then answer the question.

> W Indeed, there's never been empirical evidence to show that one nationality has a monopoly on the characteristics that Turner uses to describe the so-called "American spirit." Some settlers were undoubtedly full of raw strength, curiosity, intelligence, pragmatism, and energy. But there could have been many others who were nothing like this. Show me a shy, timid American from that time period, and we're in business.

Why does the professor say this:

> W Show me a shy, timid American from that time period, and we're in business.

Ⓐ The professor wants the students to ask themselves if any of them are shy or timid.
Ⓑ The professor is pushing for the celebration of diversity in the American entrepreneurial experience.
Ⓒ The professor is implying that it would be very easy to cast doubt on Turner's idea.
Ⓓ The professor is arguing that quieter, more thoughtful personalities contributed more to American expansion.

17. What will the class most likely do next?

Ⓐ The class will discuss further criticisms of the thesis.
Ⓑ The professor will talk about the role of Indigenous people in the frontier experience.
Ⓒ The professor will hear some of the students' opinions on the thesis.
Ⓓ The class will debate on what precisely was behind the American expansion.

Ⓓ 서부의 토지는 누구나 자유롭게 소유할 수 있었기 때문에 다른 미국적 이상이 성장할 수 있는 완벽한 발판이 되었다.

15. 교수가 시카고를 언급한 이유는 무엇인가?

Ⓐ 농업화되지 않고 도시화한 도시의 예를 들기 위해
Ⓑ 예외적인 미국 정신에 대한 관념에 의문을 제기하기 위해
Ⓒ 국경 확장에 있어서 자본주의의 중요성을 지적하기 위해
Ⓓ 미국주의가 궁극적으로 도시화로 이어졌다는 생각을 뒷받침하기 위해

16. 강의의 일부를 다시 듣고 질문에 답하시오.

> 여 실제로 터너가 소위 "미국 정신"을 설명하는 데 사용하는 특성을 한 국적이 독점하고 있다는 것을 보여주는 경험적 증거는 한 번도 없었습니다. 일부 정착민은 의심할 여지 없이 원초적인 힘, 호기심, 지성, 실용주의, 에너지로 가득 차 있었습니다. 하지만 이와는 전혀 다른 사람들도 많았을 것입니다. 그 시대의 수줍고 소심한 미국인 한 명만 보여주시면 말 다 한 거죠.

교수는 왜 이렇게 말하는가:

> 여 그 시대의 수줍고 소심한 미국인 한 명만 보여주시면 말 다 한 거죠.

Ⓐ 교수가 학생 중 수줍음이 많거나 소심한 사람이 있는지 스스로 물어보기를 원한다.
Ⓑ 교수는 미국 기업가 경험의 다양성을 축하해야 한다고 주장하고 있다.
Ⓒ 교수는 터너의 아이디어에 의문을 제기하기가 매우 쉽다는 것을 암시하고 있다.
Ⓓ 교수는 조용하고 사려 깊은 성격이 미국의 확장에 더 여러 가지 기여를 했다고 주장하고 있다.

17. 이 학생은 다음으로 어떤 일을 할 가능성이 가장 높은가?

Ⓐ 수업에서는 논문에 대한 추가 비평에 대해 토론할 것이다.
Ⓑ 교수가 프런티어 경험에서 원주민의 역할에 대해 이야기할 것이다.
Ⓒ 교수가 논문에 대한 학생의 의견을 들을 것이다.
Ⓓ 수업에서는 미국 확장의 정확한 배경이 무엇인지에 대해 토론할 것이다.

어휘 discuss v 논의하다 I Manifest Destiny 명백한 운명 I cultural adj 문화의 I belief n 신념 I American adj 미국인 I destined adj 운명이 정해진 I continent n 대륙 I creator n 창조자 I concept n 개념 I lecture n 강의 I modern times 근대사 I review v 짚고 넘어가다 I tenet n 원칙 I exceptional adj 예외적인 I nature n 본질 I institution n 기관 I mission n 임무 I transform v 변화하다 I West n 서쪽 I agrarian adj 농업의 I East n 동쪽 I destiny n 운명 I accomplish v 성취하다 I inevitable adj 불가피한 I emotion n 감정 I settler n 정착자 I Frontier Thesis 프런티어 사관 I declare v 선언하다 I expand v 확장하다 I westward adv 서쪽으로 I liberty n 자유 I equality n 평등 I democracy n 민주주의 I society n 사회 I arrive v 도착하다 I create v 창조하다 I ocean n 바다 I American Eastern Seaboard 미국 동해안 I departure n 출발 I law n 법률 I rent n 임대료 I wild adj 야생의 I spread v 퍼지다 I thrive v 번성하다 I shape v 형성하다 I spirit n 정신 I drive n 추진력 I Americanism n 미국주의 I manifest v 드러나다 I stage n 단계 I farmland n 농지 I urbanization n 도시화 I thesis n 논지 I support n 지지 I public n 대중 I account n 설명 I march n 행군; 횡단 I historian n 역사가 I case n 경우 I market forces 시장의 힘 I capitalism n 자본주의 I unique adj 독특한 I dominate v 지배하다 I exceptional adj 예외적인 I Industrial Revolution 산업혁명 I fit v 맞다 I narrative n 서술 I development n 발전 I construction n 건설 I railroad n 철도 I foreign adj 외국의 I laborer n 노동자 I attribute n 속성 I attitude n 태도 I empirical adj 경험에 근거한 I evidence n 증거 I nationality n 국적 I characteristic n 특성 I describe v 설명하다 I shy adj 수줍은 I timid adj 소심한 I period n 기간 I business n 사업 I criticize v 비판하다 I free adj 자유로운 I land n 땅 I expensive adj 비싼 I own v 소유하다 I speculator n 투기꾼 I vacant adj 빈 I moral adj 도덕적인 I implication n 함축 I non-Indigenous adj 비원주민의 I claim v 주장하다 I raise questions 의문을 제기하다 I transformation n 변형

PAGODA
TOEFL
80+ Listening | 해설서